A MAP of the COUNTY of KILDARE,

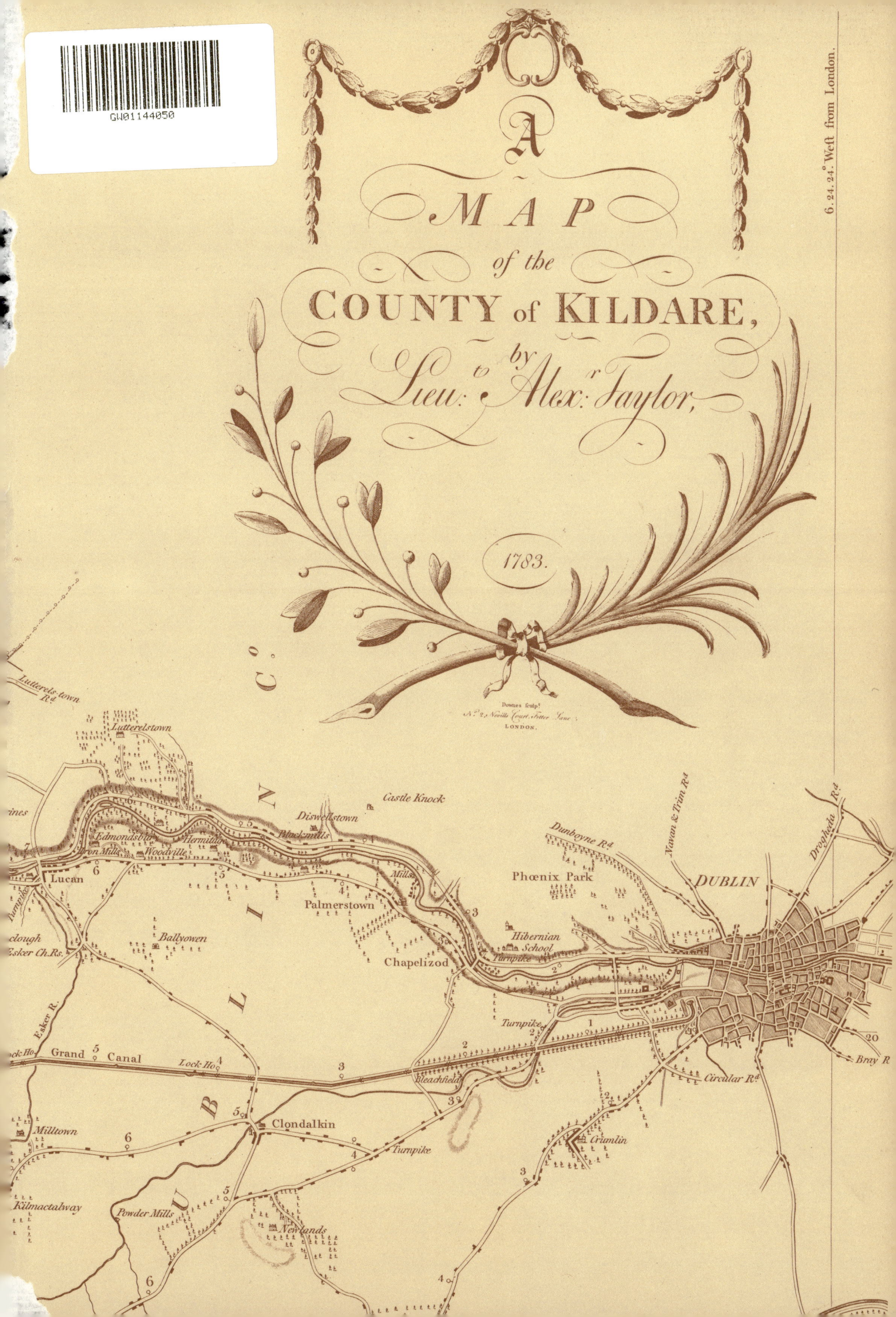

by Lieu.t Alex.r Taylor,

1783.

Dowries sculp.t
N.o 2, Neville Court, Fetter Lane,
LONDON.

6.24.24° West from London.

AA TOURING GUIDE TO IRELAND

Where glows the Irish hearth with peat
There lives a subtle spell –
The faint blue smoke, the gentle heat,
The moorland odours tell

Of white roads winding by the edge
Of bare, untamed land,
Where dry stone wall or ragged hedge
Runs wide on either hand

To cottage lights that lure you in
From rainy western skies;
And by the friendly glow within
Of simple talk and wise . . .

from Beside the Fire
by T W Rolleston

Contents

A Land of Extremes 5
Munster, a province of close horizons dominated by rolling moors and rocky peaks

Gateway to Ireland 15
The gentle landscapes of Leinster – seat of ancient High Kings and a cradle of Irish culture

Stronghold of the West 25
Wild, beautiful Connacht, a refuge of saints and the last stronghold of the pre-Norman Irish

The Face of Solitude 35
Under-populated countryside and thriving industry – the two faces of Ulster

The Sister Cities
Ireland's historic capitals, the advance guards of progress and foci of commercial wealth

Dublin 45
Belfast 58

Galleons, Gold, and Graves 65
Shipping, shipwrecks, and the epic Atlantic voyage of St Brendan

Day Drives 79
57 specially selected one-day motor tours in the Irish provinces

The Munster Wildernesses 81
Leinster of the High Kings 102
Connacht – the Last Refuge 115
Land of the Ulster Legends 125

The Gazetteer 145
More than 1,200 towns, villages, hamlets, and major geographical features with 36 town plans, all referenced to the touring atlas. Special insets describe 11 major archaeological sites

Passport to the Past 289
How history can be discovered through the early ecclesiastical architecture of the Irish people

Glossary of Terms 305
An aid to the understanding of archaeology, architecture, and placenames in Ireland

Touring Atlas of Ireland 307

Editor Russell P O Beach
Art editor Michael A Preedy MSIA

Assistant editor Michael Cady
Assistant designer Robert Johnson

Associate editor R S Rogers

A Land of Extremes researched by Peter Somerville-Large
Gateway to Ireland researched by Stephen Rynne
Stronghold of the West written and researched by Peter Owen
The Face of Solitude written and researched by Estyn Evans
The Sister Cities researched by Kitty Rogers
Galleons, Gold, and Graves adapted by Alice Clamp
Passport to the Past written and researched by Dr Peter Harbison

Day Drives compiled by the Publications Research Unit of the Automobile Association.

Gazetteer compiled by Peter Rankin, Kitty Rogers,
Mary Rogers, Brian Trainor, and Verbiage Enterprises Ltd.
Gazetteer research by the Publications Research Unit and
Dublin Branch Office of the Automobile Association.
Inset material verified by Dr M de Paor.

Feature illustrators:
Anderson Dykes Organization, Don Cordery, Bill Easter, F D Graphics,
Roy Flooks, Melton +, Outline Art Services, David Penny, Chris Woolmer.

Gazetteer illustrators:
Vic Bates, F D Graphics, Outline Art Services

Day Drive maps, Town Plans, Special Feature maps, and Atlas by the Cartographic Services Unit of the Automobile Association.

Maps in this book are based upon the Ordnance Survey by
permission of the Government of Ireland
(Permit No. 373) and with the sanction of the
Controller of HM Stationery Office.

Phototypeset by Petty and Sons Ltd, Leeds
Colour Separations by Mullis Morgan Ltd, London
Printed and bound by Graficromo, S. A.
Spain

The contents of this publication are believed correct
at the time of printing, but the current position
can be checked through the AA.

© The Automobile Association 1976   55152

ISBN 0 86145 103 1

All rights reserved. No part of this publication
may be reproduced, stored in a retrieval system,
or transmitted in any form or by any means –
electronic, mechanical, photocopying, recording,
or otherwise – unless the permission of the publisher
has been given beforehand.

Produced by the Publications Division of the Automobile Association,
Fanum House, Basingstoke, Hampshire RG21 2EA.

A Land of Extremes

St Colman's Cathedral dominates Cobh from a hilltop site on the northern curve of Cork Harbour.

Munster, where bewildering changes in scenery hide rare plants, ancient structures from the depths of prehistory, and a people who have not forgotten the depth of a Gaelic welcome.

A visitor travelling to the Munster coast on the 'Inisfallen' ferry boat may be lucky enough to catch the sea in one of its calmer moods, allowing a modicum of sleep during the crossing between Great Britain and the Republic of Ireland. On waking he will probably find himself halfway up Cork Harbour, gliding between green farming country and woodlands before reaching the picturesquely crenelated tower of Blackrock Castle and later docking within easy reach of the heart of Cork city. The ample waters that he has just passed through once sheltered great trans-Atlantic liners, which rocked at anchor within sight of Roches Point while waiting for the tender crowded with hopeful emigrants bound for the New World of America. As the liners moved out the eyes of their passengers would have devoured every last detail of the home country they were leaving behind – the tall spire of St Colman's Cathedral dominating lines of big houses that flank the northern curve of the harbour, tantalizing glimpses of Haulbowline and the former convict settlement of Spike Island, the coastline dropping away to starboard as the ships ploughed through the graveyard of the tragic 'Lusitania', and the enigmatic hump of Clear Island rising beastlike from the waves.

The air traveller in his secure cylinder of metal has a different introduction to Munster – and, of course, the Republic – as he sweeps into Shannon Airport over the surf-fringed western beaches, glimpsing the lighthouse perched at the tip of Loop Head before enjoying a privileged view of the silver Shannon winding seawards from Limerick through glistening mudflats and green fields impressed with the rings of prehistoric forts. His final view before landing synthesizes 20th-c Ireland in the tower of Bunratty Castle and the clean lines of Shannon Airport – a typical juxtaposition of ancient and modern.

The Munster boundaries
Munster covers some 9,536sqm of south-western Ireland and is a land of both scenic and geographical extremes. Its landscapes jump between bewildering, rocky confusions and soothing undulations in a madcap rush of rivers, mountains, and hills which include the country's highest peaks; the widest river-lough on the longest river, the Shannon; and the largest counties. County Cork covers a greater area than any other in the whole of Ireland, and Tipperaray – the only land-locked county in the province – is the largest inland administrative division of this nature in the country. In ancient times the province was split into five parts which were divided by the natural boundaries of rivers and mountain ranges, but historic events and migratory patterns before the coming of the Norsemen eventually combined these into two main kingdoms. The southernmost of these was known as Desmond and grew to cover lands controlled by the Fitzgerald family, while that in the north was called Thomond and included most of Clare plus parts of Tipperary and Limerick. Thomond was controlled by the O Brien family. Although the present-day borders of Munster are often vague, they still occasionally follow the old tradition of incorporating natural features. The northern border with the province of Connacht runs south east from Galway Bay and crosses the limestone hills of Clare before veering east through the Slieve Aughty Mountains and meeting Lough Derg – a wide expansion of the River Shannon. From here it runs north east along the river to a little island just north of the old Meelick Church. This island marks the point where three provinces and three counties meet – Tipperary in Munster, Galway in Connacht, and Offaly in Leinster. After Meelick the border drops sharply south through the North Riding of Tipperary, then zig-zags east to Roscrea via Riverstown, Cloughjordan, the hills around Toomyvara, and the gash of the Devil's Bit Mountain. From Roscrea it ambles south–south east to cross the Slieveardagh Hills and enter Carrick-on-Suir, where it continues east along the River Suir to meet the Barrow at the head of Waterford Harbour.

Although the provincial borders are vague, the counties of Munster are defined in a much more clear and logical manner. A winding stretch of the Shannon divides Tipperary, Limerick, and Clare, while north Kerry faces south Clare over the wide Shannon estuary. Boundary crossings on the upper stretches are provided by numerous attractive little bridges, and the estuary is spanned by a ferry boat which operates from Tarbert in Kerry, carrying both passengers and cars. Mountain ranges also play an important part in the definition of counties, just as they did for the five kingdoms in the distant past. Travellers driving from Lismore in the south-Munster county of Waterford climb the flanks of the Knockmealdown Mountains to the Gap, or Vee, where they are suddenly faced with a wonderfully scenic panorama encompassing the velvety-green fields of the fertile Golden Vale. This particular view is world famous. A winding road from Glengarriff, situated in the deep south west of Munster on the Cork side of the Beara Peninsula, crosses the boundary between Co Cork and Co Kerry via a magnificent tunnel driven through Turner's Rock in the splendid Caha Mountains. This tunnel is a fairly recent innovation, and in Victorian times travellers adventurous enough to enter these wild places had to stop in the foothills of the range so that their vehicles could be carried over the top on the shoulders of local men. This road continues through rugged scenery to

A LAND OF EXTREMES

Killarney, a town set in an arc of beautiful lakes shadowed by the Macgillycuddy's Reeks range, and forms the eastern side of a scenic route known as the Ring of Kerry. A drive from Killarney to the far-northern Munster city of Limerick, or east along the Shannon estuary from Ballylongford to Tarbert, passes through the fertile farmlands and high hills of counties Kerry and Limerick. Here the automobile invasion is by no means complete, and carts loaded with rattling milk churns drawn by ponies or donkeys are still part of the rural scene. This quality of traditionalism is enhanced by remote villages of houses splashed with soft pastel colours, and isolated gothic farmhouses with steeply-pitched roofs outlined against moving skies and the misty lines of Co Kerry's mountains. Towards the lower north and eastern parts of the province the precarious little hillside farms and settlements, each with its encircling hedge of delicate fuchsia, give way to neatly-arranged fields and whitewashed houses in landscapes somewhat gentler than the bogs and rocks of the south west.

Mountains and hills

The Munster horizons are always close because there are few areas that are not dominated by mountains. Inland are the Slieve Felims, Silvermines, and Galtees, while the coastal areas are crowded with peaks and ranges that mass together like a huge, jagged army of giants. The Galtees are shared by counties Limerick, Cork, and Tipperary and rear high above the surrounding lands to offer distant north-western views of the Shannon estuary in northern Munster – when conditions permit. Waterford is separated from Tipperary by the stern guardians of the Knockmealdown and Comeragh ranges in south-east Munster, while the giant, south-western county of Cork is crossed in the north by ranges of heights which include the Ballyhoura Hills. By far the largest concentration of ranges in the province, and the one which includes some of Ireland's highest mountains, is to be found in and around the wild peninsulas which reach into the Atlantic from south-west Munster. Here the Slieve Mish Mountains march to the tottering conclusion of Mount Brandon on the tip of the Dingle Peninsula, the mighty sickle of Macgillycuddy's Reeks culminates in lofty Carrauntuohill on the Iveragh, and the Beara Peninsula is cracked and corrugated by the wild Slieve Miskish and Caha ranges. Carrauntuohill, the name of which is said to have been derived from 'an inverted reaping hook' rises to a spectacular 3,400ft and is the highest peak in Ireland.

Most of the province's mountains are composed of sandstone or conglomerates, but northern Munster includes a limited limestone area which encompasses the countryside around Lough Gur, the strangely-eroded hills of the Burren in north-west Co Clare, and the famous Rock of Cashel rising from the Golden Vale of Tipperary in the mid-eastern part of the province. Apart from the higher mountains, the shape of the ranges as seen today is related to the inexorable movement of giant glaciers which covered much of the country during the ice age. During this period the glaciers ground the rough edges away from the sandstone, thrusting long tongues of ice down river valleys, dividing the hills, smoothing out contours, and creating corries, lakes, and passes or 'gaps' like Keimaneigh near Gougane Barra lake in west Cork. A mountain does not have to be high to be impressive, and although the Irish peaks may be small by Continental standards their locations often render them equally imposing. For instance Bantry Bay in the south west features the sharp line of the Sugarloaf above the coastal town of Glengarriff, plus the enigmatic, waterfall-washed hump of Hungry Hill. The twin peaks of The Paps rise above the Cork to Killarney road as symbols of the ancient forces of fecundity from which their Celtic name – *Da Chich Anann* – was derived. The name means 'Paps of the goddess Anu', a Celtic deity especially associated with Munster and responsible for the fertility of the province's land. In the extreme eastern part of the province is the impressive, rounded outline of Slievenamon, also strongly connected with Irish legend, while the Slieve Felim range of north Munster culminates in distinctive Keeper Hill on the Limerick and Tipperary border. Sometimes a small hill has a scale which is out of all proportion to its actual size. Ardpatrick is the highest grass-covered hill in Ireland and features fascinating relics of many pilgrimages, which it proudly carries above the relative flatness of the Limerick plain. Similarly the flat landscapes near the River Shannon are totally subdued by a little, 300ft-high mound which is known as Knockshigowna and is reputed to have been the abode of Munster's fairies.

Along the rivers

Some of the rivers and streams which rise from the spongy heather of the hills stay close to their beer-brown springs and never reach meandering maturity. An example of such is the Glengarriff, which rises in the hills above the town which bears its name and descends from one dark pool to another during its wonderfully picturesque journey through thick oakwoods, under a bridge built by Cromwell, and out into the salt expanses of Bantry Bay. In contrast is the mighty Shannon, which rises some 200m north on Ulster's Cuilcagh Mountain and flows down to Limerick city and its west-coast estuary like a great, watery highway allowing access to the vast tract of land between Lough Derg and the sea.

Limerick's Thomond Bridge spans the Shannon to link the ancient High Town – built on an island surrounded by a branch of the Shannon known as Abbey River – to the north-eastern part of the city.

A LAND OF EXTREMES

The fertility of Co Waterford's Blackwater Valley attracted great wealth and offered leisure which often encouraged eccentricity. The fanciful, Hindu-gothick gateway and lodge of Dromana Castle typify an over-relaxed existence.

The aspect of the lower Shannon remains pastoral in spite of small patches of necessary development – like the twin towers of an electricity plant that rise above the Tarbert treeline for instance – and the fields that run gently down to its banks from peaceful farms are undisturbed except by the occasional, jagged silhouette of a ruined castle. Although Shannon is the greatest river in Munster, and indeed in the whole of Ireland, it is by no means the only one. A hilly watershed that runs south-east to north-west across the top of Co Tipperary into the province of Leinster includes the Slieve Bloom range, where the Three Sisters – the Barrow, Nore, and Suir – rise to flow south and eventually combine to enter the sea at the sheltered south-coast harbour of Waterford. Of these three only the Suir belongs to the province of Munster, and for the lower part of its route forms the provincial boundary with Leinster. It issues north of the Devil's Bit Mountain in the Slieve Blooms and flows southwards between banks fringed by golden reeds and tremulous alders to reach Thurles in the heart of Co Tipperary. After passing the recently-restored Abbey of Holycross it winds through the rich countryside and prosperous towns of the Golden Vale, thence through Cahir and south until the Knockmealdown range forces it into a sudden turn east across the Co Waterford boundary. Here the Suir meets Clonmel town, capital of the South Riding of Tipperary and the place where the world's first public-transport system was put into operation during the 19thc by Charles Bianconi. George Borrow went to school here, and Laurence Sterne of *Tristram Shandy* fame was born in the town. Clonmel's old wharfs are reminders of times when ships could penetrate far up the Suir to unload their cargoes within the limits of the town. After Clonmel the brown, wooded line of the Comeragh and Knockmealdown ranges face across the broadening Suir to isolated Slievenamon, the 'mountain of the women', before the river flows into Carrick-on-Suir. This town boasts the only intact Elizabethan manor house in the whole country. Beyond Carrick the mature Suir winds its sedate way through beautiful and amazingly fertile country until a particularly long reach of the river ends at a rocky gap which reveals a sudden, striking view of Waterford town. After Waterford it meets the combined waters of the Nore and Barrow at the head of Waterford Harbour, which reluctantly provided the Danes and other invaders with a gateway into Southern Ireland.

The Rivers Blackwater and Lee rise a mere 60m from the sea in mountainous south-western Munster but, due to the tilt of the land, are forced to flow from west to east across the province before joining with the ocean. The Lee trickles from the dark waters of Gougane Barra lake, where St Finbarr's Hermitage has attracted pilgrims for some 1,500 years, and continues as a furious little mountain torrent which gradually slows and widens as it reaches more gentle countryside. Outside Cork city it loops and swings in broad meanders that carry it towards hillsides red with suburbs and its final destination at Cork Harbour. One of the Lee's tributaries, the Awbeg, has a place in Irish literature in that it was the 'gentle Mulla' so beloved of poet Edmund Spenser. The particular trout-filled, willow-banked stretch that pleased him ran past Kilcolman Castle, where he had arrived by an 'accident of fortune'; he saw the river as a distraction from bogs, solitudes, and neighbourhood quarrels.

Barren, open countryside surrounds the first part of the Blackwater's journey from the rugged heights of Kerry and Co Cork, but its later passage through north Cork and Co Waterford is marked by the more relaxed atmosphere exuded by richly-wooded demesnes and leisurely stretches of prime salmon fishing. English settlers found the Blackwater Valley a natural first choice, and many of the fine estates founded by these people managed to survive the later wars. These include the showy turrets of Lismore Castle and Hindu-gothick gateway of Dromana, both perhaps indications of leisure lapsing into eccentricity; Affane, where the Countess of Desmond was supposed to have fallen out of an apple tree at the age of 140; and the home of forgotten Valentine Greatorex, a 17th-c gentleman once celebrated as soldier, witch-finder, healer, and general worker of miracles. At Cappoquin in south-west Waterford the Blackwater shows a characteristic typical of Munster's rivers by abruptly changing course from due east to south, thence flowing through the woods of Dromana and widening to meet the sea at Youghal on the boundary between east Cork and Waterford.

Provincial towns

Most of the buildings in Munster's towns have appeared during the past 150 years or so. The courthouse and Protestant church may be of Georgian origin, but the Catholic church and substantial shop fronts – mainly three-storey and some still with their gilt lettering intact over the doors – are generally of later date. Commercial buildings of this type reflect the emergence of a Catholic middle class and were usually assembled without much attempt at town planning. Their designers obviously felt that the utilitarian purposes for which they were intended did not require beauty, but even the dour nature of these

A LAND OF EXTREMES

structures is sometimes in contrast with an unexpected piece of frivolity or elegance. Examples of such 'accidental' art can be seen at Rathkeale in Co Limerick and Listowel in Co Kerry. The former is noted for the effigy of a Chinaman painted in black, red, and gold above a shop, placed there in 1826 by grateful citizens as a mark of their esteem for a generous tea merchant; Listowel boasts a device which includes a half-naked woman flanked by a round tower and Irish wolfhound above the motto *Erin go Bragh*, also on a shopfront. Other of the province's towns are ennobled by Georgian public buildings or overshadowed by some great ruin which might date from the very foundation of the settlement. An example of the latter is Liscarroll in Co Cork, a town almost overrun by the rambling walls and outworks of its mighty castle. Roscrea in Co Tipperary is dominated by the gaunt ruins of a great abbey, while Cashel in the Golden Vale struggles to assert itself beneath the great, ruin-crowded crown of the Rock of Cashel. Many places combine both ancient and modern features within the same community limits – like Kilfinane in Co Limerick, where old shopfronts line up beside a fine, 18th-c market house to form a town backing on to a possibly pre-Norman construction comprising a trivallate mound encircled by elaborate banks and fosses.

Although many of the province's communities appear to have been blown together or strung along some road as an afterthought, others display a sense of unity that can only have resulted from careful planning. Such towns owe their growth to the activities of local landlords and include Kinsale and Fermoy in Co Cork, or places of such diverse development as Killarney in Co Kerry – one of the first of Munster's towns to reap the benefits of tourism; Tramore in Co Waterford, which owes its importance to the 18th-c fad for sea bathing; and Lisdoonvarna, centred on mineral springs at the edge of the Burren in north Clare. The patronage of wealthy landlords gave thatched, cut-limestone cottages to Adare in Co Limerick, fine terraces to Churchtown in Co Kerry, and gabled eaves to Villierstown in Co Waterford. A town as large as Youghal owes much of its design to the whim of a landlord in just the same way as does the St Andrew's-cross shape of Kenmare in Kerry, or the broad squares and sweeping streets of Mitchelstown in Cork.

Decline and rebirth

Towns which originated on the sites of fairs and boast histories that can be traced back through thousands of years of pastoral custom have had to develop their modern form while accommodating themselves around their continuing function. Housing was laid out around broad squares designed to facilitate the gathering of livestock, and on fairdays the big squares of Bantry or Bearhaven in Co Cork, Listowel or Castleisland in Co Kerry, are still jammed with milling herds and flocks of animals. However, the activity seen on such occasions is sadly deceptive, and fairs are declining as marts like the big complex in Co Cork's Bandon take over the traditional rôle. It seems that the fairs will eventually cease to exist, forcing the fair towns to find some other reason for existence if they are to continue in prosperity. Bantry has already seen the construction of an oil terminal on Whiddy and waits at the end of its namesake bay to lure in even more industrial development, while the wealth of Berehaven is supplemented by its trawler fleet. It is a general rule that places tend to decline as their fortunes change, so it is not only the fair communities that have suffered. Little settlements like Shannonvale near Clonakilty in Co Cork prospered during the hey-day of the linen industry, but after the introduction of cheap, imported cotton they fell into gradual decay around their idle scutching mills and bleaching greens, retting pits and weed-grown flax fields. All over Munster there are ghost towns which have dwindled from former importance – importance perhaps derived from the proximity of a Desmond family stronghold, a mill, or a distillery. The ancient or not-quite-so-old ruins of such an economic focal point, all different but equally as impressive, will always be found in the neighbourhood of a settlement for which progress has become an epitaph. Munster's cities owe their growth first to Viking and later to Norman settlers. Cork is the third largest city in Ireland, Waterford spans the Suir at the head of its namesake harbour, and Limerick faces Co Clare across the start of the Shannon's west-coast estuary. Although these vital communities are still expanding they remain compact, and it is said that town and country meet amongst their squares and streets. It is certainly true that a person in the centre of one of these cities is never far from open countryside.

Around the coasts

The deep rivers of Munster have allowed her main cities to be sited far enough inland to be sheltered from exposure to the wild Atlantic, but with sufficient access to the ocean to allow development of rich, sea-borne trade. The coastline itself, particularly in the west, has been hacked and torn by centuries of wind and sea in a sustained battle which has produced such features as the 700ft Cliffs of Moher in Co Clare, the jagged, ocean-moulded rocks of the south-western peninsulas, and the miles of cliff and golden sand which fringe the gentler southern shore of Co Waterford. The Cliffs of Moher form part of the province's north-western coastline, a dangerous area offering a few safe anchorages as it extends north from Loop Head at the mouth of the Shannon to Black Head and the southern side of Galway Bay. O Brien's Tower is a 19th-c folly built on the top of the Cliffs of Moher by

Dunmanus Bay, one of the five great drowned valleys that penetrate the wild, south-western coast of Ireland.

Cornelius O Brien for visitors who found the cliff edge too unnerving for comfort. It is still available for those who find the sight of giant waves reduced to fractured white lines too much, or who would rather observe the spectacular 5m of stark vertical rock from a position of comparative comfort and safety. A rock rising from the sea just a short distance from Loop Head is named after the legendary lovers Dermot and Grania and is almost as forbidding as uncompromising Moher. Love was not always sanctioned here, and tradition holds that at another moment in mythological time the super-warrior hero Cuchullain jumped from the shore to this limestone slab to escape the attentions of a lady, who subsequently fell into the intervening torrent and was drowned.

Island refuges

Beaches on the Co Kerry side of the Shannon stretch south from Beal Point to Doneen Point, where the cliffs start once more and continue to Ballybunion. After Kerry Head the Kerry and west Cork coastline is carved into five great rias or drowned valleys flanked by the rugged, south-western peninsulas whose mountains and headlands claw the moody sea like the fingers of a gnarled hand. The only features anything like these long, narrow inlets to be found in the rest of Europe are the fjords of Norway. Moving north to south from Tralee in Co Kerry the inlets are respectively known as Dingle Bay, the Kenmare River, Bantry Bay, Dunmanus Bay, and Roaring Water Bay. In the south between the bays of Dunmanus and Roaring Water is the south-westerly point of Ireland, Mizen Head, described by Edith Somerville as 'a giant spoke of headland that sticks up like a boar's tusk above the rugged lip of the Irish coast'. East of this are the prolific islands of Roaring Water Bay — big and small; pancake-flat and domed like an upturned boat; too small to provide grazing for a single cow and big enough to contain farms and roads. Clear Island is among the latter. The wilder islands off the Munster coast contrast strongly with the gentle, sloping fields of others which they have protected by absorbing the fury of devastating Atlantic storms. These rugged, isolated little places have contributed to the most beautiful of Ireland's traditions, that of the early-Christian hermit seeking perfect solitude and communion with God away from the bustle of human society. This extreme 'exile' was experienced by the little community which chose to construct its bee-hive huts and oratories near the summit of Skellig Michael, the largest of an island group which was formed by the drowning of three mountains. The group, known as the Skelligs, lies in the open Atlantic some 8m from the coast of the largest peninsula in Co Kerry. This is the Iveragh, a broad tongue of land which extends west between the Kenmare River in the south and Dingle Bay in the north. The lives of the monks who lived in this settlement were starkly simple and constantly threatened by storms and marauding Vikings for seven centuries. They may have kept a small number of animals, and it is believed that their crops were grown in earth ferried from the mainland in traditional currachs. Their diet would have been a monotonous affair occasionally supplemented by seabirds' eggs and pollack caught from the sea during calm weather.

The long age of monastic asceticism populated a great many of Munster's islands with hermits seeking the solitude of St Columcille's definition *destrum in pelago intransmeabilu*, 'a desert in a trackless sea'. It is thought that the saint associated such holy places with the environment adopted by those rigorous hermits known as The Desert Fathers of Syria. When St Brendan sallied forth from his small oratory just below the summit of Mount Brandon on the Dingle, the most northerly of these west-coast peninsulas, he and his fourteen companions may have been seeking the perfect hermitage. The ultimate anchoretic discomfort must have been their sojourn on the back of a whale. Brendan's voyage and supposed discovery of America is one of the few occasions in which an Irishman can be seen in the role of a seafarer. Although an island people, the Irish have never felt a real need for the roving restlessness of the Norsemen, and have left the majority of hard sea journeys to their saints. This may partly have been due to the limitations of Celtic boat design, which stopped after the development of the currach – a craft as unsuited to long sea voyages as the frail coracles of the Welsh. Today it is still difficult to understand how these lanky black boats manage to ride the never-ending swell of the Atlantic, and even the men of the Dingle nowadays hesitate to use them except in the calmest weather.

The 20thc has very few saints or sinners willing to contemplate the sparkle of the sea from island fortresses, and the wish to live in isolated places seems to have eroded with the coastline. In 1953 the last inhabitants of the Blasket Islands, a group situated offshore from the tip of the Dingle Peninsula, sought the relative comfort of mainland existence. This transference marked the end of a brief, brilliant period in which an eloquent community stimulated by a marvellous environment learnt to set down a record of its memories. Maurice O Sullivan, Thomas O Crohan, and Peig Sayers have produced evocative accounts which insure against their harsh, beautiful island life ever being forgotten. The population of Dursey Island, connected to the tip of the Beara Peninsula by cable car, is also becoming disenchanted with the bleak style of life and is gradually dribbling away to the mainland. Bere Island, in the sheltered waters of Bantry Bay, is not as isolated as the others but sleeps in the doldrums left when the complex demands of the British Navy died away with the echo of battleship guns that used to rattle the crockery on farmers' dressers. Of the few inhabited islands in Roaring Water Bay only Clear maintains the spirit which keeps an island community alive. Here the people have chosen to retain the Irish language.

Many of Munster's rugged little Atlantic islands support flourishing colonies of seabirds. Gannets are particularly prolific.

A LAND OF EXTREMES

Many of the islands have never been inhabited by man, and Munster is fortunate in having the Little Skellig and Bull Island – both inhabited by gannets. Birds from these rocky perches at the mouth of the Kenmare River can be seen in many places along the Munster coastline as they travel north to Ballinskelligs at the tip of the Iveragh and east along the southern coasts of Co Cork. Gannets spend their lives on the sea and only venture to dry land during nesting time. A bird observatory off the southern Cork coast on Clear records flocks of fulmars and storm petrels in migratory patterns unequalled elsewhere in Europe, and its annual sightings of rare birds are almost legendary throughout the ornithological world.

Southern shorelines

The south coast of Co Cork – and therefore the province – faces away from the full, blustery force of the ocean. The exposed rocks and peninsulas common to the west coast give way here to a series of natural harbours which begin in the west with almost land-locked Lough Hyne. Here the elements' efforts to carve away the land have resulted in a perfect miniature sea, which is less than half a mile in diameter and has a tiny entrance through which torrential tides pour twice daily. Shoals of herring and mackerel brought in with the tide find it difficult to escape through the 20ft-wide gap and dart about under oak trees that fringe the 'lagoon'. Given another million years or so the sea may erode the entrance to form a harbour like those farther to the east – the inlets of Castlehaven and Glandore, also once shrouded by oaks, and the elegant shelter of Kinsale. East from Lough Hyne the bare, rocky knuckles of headlands become fewer, the mountains retreat, and the seaboard takes on a lush aspect imparted by carefully-tended farms in areas where man has less of a struggle against the weather. Youghal town is neat and handsome like Kinsale; Dungarvan and Tramore in Co Waterford offer stretches of golden sand, and most of the coastal towns reflect the degree of prosperity evident in Cork city. Cliffs are generally associated with the western shores, so it is a surprise to find that the soft coast which runs east to Dungarvan suddenly rears itself up into a 25m range which runs a level course from here to Waterford and has a counterpart in South Wales. At the top of these cliffs, some 200ft above the sea, a weathered metal man extends a warning arm towards Brownstone Point in a gesture which has been warning ships away from the sandy reaches of Tramore since the 18thc. It was easy for vessels to mistake the treacherous waters of Tramore Bay for the safety of Waterford Harbour, at the eastern extreme of the province.

Munster is rich in the architectural debris of many ages. A cluster of relatively recent chimneys or piles of ancient, nettle-smothered stones – each preserving its own story of defeat or departure – become indistinguishable in age and purpose after only a small number of years. An ivy-covered workhouse burnt out in the 'Troubles' can appear as ancient and rather less-well preserved than a nearby castle which might be centuries old. Thus is the levelling effect of time. Ruins by the sea indicate special patterns of human behaviour which can be read in the shapes of old coastguard stations, abandoned signal towers, roofless barracks, or ruined structures of truly-ancient foundation. The cells of hermits and coastal churches recall the desire of the early-Christian for a glimpse of God through the contemplation of the sea in its many moods. Traces of very early tradition can be found among the many anchorite enclosures on Valentia Island off the Dingle Peninsula, or in the grim little tea-cosy shape of Gallarus Oratory near Smerwick Harbour in Co Kerry. This famous, corbel-roofed church is an excellent example of its type and is built to a design perfectly adapted to withstand wind and rain. It is still weather-proof after 1,000 years of exposure. The structure has given its name to a unique type of dry-masonry building and was imitated by the monks of Skellig Michael.

Ruins over the sea

Monastic and church ruins are of different origin in that the latter are usually simple Celtic shells of Romanesque character while the former, although on sites dating from the 5thc, generally feature more recent and elaborate buildings. Throughout the centuries the monasteries were in a position to attract money, and influence building design to 'the greater glory of God'. This is evident at Ardmore in Co Waterford, where St Declan's great foundation still retains its well-known round tower and preserves the special feeling of remoteness intended by the people who first grouped its buildings above the sea. This contemplative atmosphere is again found at the Abbey of Timoleague in Co Cork, and among the fine remains of the 13th-c cathedral of Ardfert, near Tralee in Co Kerry. The site of the latter has long been used and was occupied by a monastery founded by St Brendan before the cathedral. Sherkin Island lies offshore from Baltimore on the south-west coast of Co Cork and features the lichen-covered remains of a friary founded in 1460 by a member of the O Driscoll family for the Franciscans of the Strict Observance. At this time the age of the hermit and austere examples of the Desert Fathers were well in the past, but a visitor to this water-side site can still feel the ancient marine link shared by so many early-Celtic churches. Some of the most extensive monastic ruins in Munster are those of Kilcooley in a private park near Urlingford – Co Tipperary; Co Kerry's splendidly-situated Muckross Abbey near Killarney; and the recently-restored Holycross Abbey in the middle of Co Tipperary.

Ruined Timoleague Abbey is charmingly sited at the top of Courtmacsherry Bay in Co Cork, amply illustrating early monastic man's preference for coastal situations.

A LAND OF EXTREMES

Prior to the hermits the shores of the province were settled by secular men who preferred to cling to shelves of bare rock or scatter over headlands rather than face the menace of wolves among inland forests and boglands. The Irish wolf, which was not exterminated until the early 18thc, was slightly larger than other European breeds. The simple, pastoral needs of coast dwellers were supplemented by fish caught from the coastal waters. A large proportion of the tens-of-thousands of forts dotted over Ireland also occupy lonely sites on the Munster coast, ranging from ringforts to hillforts, and stone forts to promontory forts. These defended areas encompassed farms, dwellings, monastic cells, and huts which housed small early industries. A structure excavated near Garranes at Bandon in Co Cork was found to contain implements for the manufacture of glass and metal objects. Many of these forts are difficult to date because they were occupied for such a long period, some having been used as dwelling places as recently as the 17thc.

From ringforts to castles

Eighty-five per cent of the ringforts in western Cork were built on fertile, Grade-A boulder soil, indicating that the people who constructed them were less concerned with defence than in having the best available land for their cattle. However, it is difficult to believe that the carefully contrived defences of Staigue Fort on the Iveragh Peninsula in Co Kerry were erected merely to keep the weather out; a desperate and continuous fear must have motivated the construction of this and other promontory forts, and it can be assumed that they were only occupied during times of danger. Even so it must have taken stark terror to force men, women, and their livestock to take refuge in stone-built Dunbeg – poised 500ft above a wall of foam-lashed rock opposite the west coast's whale-backed Blasket Islands. Impressive strongholds meriting the name of 'castle' were first built in Ireland by Strongbow and his Norman knights, and by the end of the 16thc most of the Munster coast was guarded by these imposing piles. They were strategically placed down the west and along the south coasts from Galway Bay in the north west to Waterford in the extreme south east of the province, and were held by families whose names still ring down the centuries – de Poer, Barry, MacCarthy, O Driscoll, O Mahoney, and O Sullivan to name a few. Those built on exposed coastal rock, like Ballydevlin near Crookhaven in south-western Cork, have either been ocean-washed into history or are still undergoing the destructive process of erosion. Only recently a wall of the O Mahoney castle at Rossbrin collapsed on a calm day following a storm. It is often the precarious siting of these strongholds that makes them memorable. For example the O Driscoll tower of Dunanoir surmounts its own fragment of rock on the north side of Clear Island, off south-west Cork, facing the expanse of Roaring Water Bay with a few broken walls, part of a winding stair, mewing gulls, the soft shades of sea pink, and a tradition of buried treasure. East of Clear Island the most southerly of the great west-coast peninsulas terminates in Mizen Head, near which the castle of Dunlochy perches on Three Castles Head with 300ft cliffs dropping to the waves on one side and a quiet little lake bearded with yellow reeds on the other.

Castles which include scenes of particular terror in their history are often to be found in the finest surroundings. There can be few more beautiful situations than that of Dunboy, near Castletownbere on the Co Cork side of the Beara Peninsula, which resisted a 4,000-strong force in 1602 and was subsequently reduced to its shattered state. The O Connor stronghold of Carrigafoyle overlooks the Shannon estuary from north Kerry and has its own dock. Nowadays it is shrouded by a blanket of silence disturbed only by curlews gleaning amongst the reeds and cattle, but after a bitter siege was broken here during the Desmond wars its defenders were driven up the 80ft tower and hurled into the river below. Both Carrigafoyle and Dunboy were defeated by gunpowder. Castles that were impregnable when first built suddenly stared vulnerability in the face after guns were used during the siege of Waterford in 1492, and henceforth even the most powerful stronghold could only remain inaccessible by virtue of forest, bad roads, or bogland. Coastal castles were in a particularly bad position because attackers could ship their cannon through the inshore waters, thus avoiding inland obstacles. The art of capturing castles developed to a high degree and gave rise to such exponents as the Elizabethan soldiers Sir George Carew, Captain Flower, and Captain Roger Harvey, who helped to set a pattern of capitulation which expanded into the future. Some castles fell twice, first in the Elizabethan wars and later to Oliver Cromwell, but only a few survived to be battered during the Williamite wars. These include Carrigogunnell, the walls of which still dominate the River Shannon a few miles from Limerick city.

It should be remembered that, like the ringforts, castles were dwelling places as well as strongholds. Most are tower houses which seem to conform to a common plan in that they have four floors reached by a stair – often spiral – set into the massive thickness of the outside wall. The lowest floor was usually a vaulted storeroom, the first and second may have been used by the garrison of the castle's lord, and the top was usually where he and his family lived. In comparison to the standards of the time the lord would probably have lived in relative comfort, with furnishings which included four-poster beds and utensils fashioned of pewter and brass. The 17th-c French

Carrigogunnell Castle guards the Shannon a few miles downstream of Limerick city, and was one of the few Irish strongholds to survive until the Williamite wars.

A LAND OF EXTREMES

traveller Le Guz observed that the castles or houses of the nobility comprised four extremely high walls thatched with straw. They were, in fact, blank towers with either a complete absence of windows or a number of apertures so small that they could give little more light than would be found in a contemporary prison. The total complement of furniture was meagre, the inhabitants used rushes as floor covering and summer bedding, and they slept in straw during the winter. Although Spartan by modern standards these castles were often small islands of civilization where the Gaelic traditions of hospitality and learning were carefully fostered.

Some of the most recent remains, the survivals of gothicized palaces erected by extravagant landlords during the 19thc, are particularly impressive. Typical of these is the astonishing turreted structure of Dromore, which has a round tower sprouting from its roof and overlooks the Limerick estuary. Other impressive structures include crenellated Castlefreke near Ross Carbery in Co Cork, and the Italianate shell of Puxley Mansion standing in a forest of rhododendrons a few hundred yards from the ruins of previously-mentioned Dunboy Castle. The romantic trappings of these buildings stir the imagination falsely, and it is the deceptively simple ruins usually to be found close by that should evoke tragedy and adventure. The siege of Dunboy was ferocious even by Elizabethan standards, and the tower of Rathbarry beside Castlefreke protected Captain Arthur Freke and his family throughout a summer-long attack by 'rebels, rogues, and Papists'. Both the new Castlefreke and Puxley, the new Dunboy, saw nothing more exciting than the occasionally hilarious dinner party. This 19th-c building fad slipped back to nature in an orgy of baroque abandonment and spread with amazing gusto, producing such magnificent edifices as Brittas Castle near Thurles and Thomastown Castle near Golden, both in Co Tipperary. The walls of the former were copied from Warwick Castle in England, but the structure was never finished after the owner was killed by a piece of falling masonry. Thomastown Castle stands in an empty field and was once the home of the Earls of Llandaff. Remains include high chimneys, a gatehouse, and fake embattlements.

The crown of Munster
Munster's greatest collection of ancient ruins is undoubtedly that which crowns the 300ft Rock of Cashel in the heart of the Golden Vale. King Cormac of Munster had his royal cashel here in the 4thc, St Patrick used a shamrock to demonstrate the Trinity here in the 5thc, and the subsequent monastic ruins that still dominate the limestone crag have a grandeur that neither time nor despoilers have been able to obliterate. The sensitive modern traveller catching first sight of the rock thrusting from the green plain can feel the awe that must have been experienced by the medieval wanderer or foot soldier. Its bulk dominates the River Suir and Glen of Aherlow, and its summit offers a view which traces the rocky Galtee range to its junction with the Ballyhoura Hills and the familiar chequerboard patterns of north Cork pastures. Elizabeth Bowen, a native of the area, has described the countryside with the minute accuracy of a mapmaker – 'open, airy, not quite flat . . . fields undulating in a flowing way. Dark knolls and screens of trees; a network of hedges; abrupt stony ridges and slate glistening from roofs . . . a prevailing impression of emptiness.'

Some of the Munster grasslands, particularly those in the south-eastern parts of the province, have been undisturbed by the plough for centuries and preserve many ancient features. The winter retreat of vegetation reveals areas that fairly bubble with ringforts and early field-work systems, and it is said that no other place in Europe features the work of early man so clearly or to such a large extent. One of the most remarkable concentrations of neolithic sites can be seen in the western part of the province, gathered around the shores of Lough Gur near Hospital in Co Limerick. This beautiful horseshoe lake is wound round the green knuckle of Knockadoon Hill and lies in an area packed to overflowing with cairns, hut settlements, gallauns, stone circles, and burial places of various types. Two medieval castles and two crannogs – ancient lake dwellings – crouch at the water's edge, and close to the lakeshore are gigantic stones which rise to 9ft in height and form the largest stone circle in Ireland. Lough Gur itself is frequented by scores of wild swans and numerous other species of waterfowl. Tradition holds that the lake bottom is the home of the 'wizard' Earl of Desmond and his company of knights, who come to the surface once very seven years.

A peaceful invasion
Distance, weather, and the province's treacherous coast probably played a larger part in the protection of Munster than the coastal castles. Successful invasions by a sea-borne enemy were largely confined to the more accessible east coast of Leinster, the safe reaches of the Shannon on the west coast, or the relatively open gateway of Waterford Harbour in the south. The vast majority of seafarers came in peace to fish the plentiful waters of counties Cork and Kerry, or to trade. Somewhere near the Skelligs the Atlantic currents divide around a vast bed of plankton that spreads

The impressive Rock of Cashel has carried various strongholds since the 4thc, and the ruined state of its present ecclesiastical remains does nothing to detract from its grandeur.

along the south-west coast and once attracted the great shoals of pilchards that formed a major asset to the medieval economy. Remains of pallaces where these fish were cured can still be seen around the shores, and the excavation of one such structure at Baltimore in south-west Cork revealed thick layers of ancient fish scales. In recent times the pilchards have been replaced by mackerel and herring, which have continued to attract the fishing fleets of Europe. Traders first came to the south west in prehistoric times, when Cornishmen brought in the tin which was mixed with copper mined on the Beara Peninsula to form bronze. Ireland exported cattle, tallow, hides, and wolf skins to England and Europe during the middle ages, and although the cattle trade varied in its usual manner the export of livestock became the country's biggest source of foreign income by $c1660$. English breeders took fright, and in 1667 a law was passed to exclude Irish cattle and sheep from English markets. Soon after this another trade developed around the supply of beef and butter to the West Indies, and although Youghal entered a period of decline its south-coast neighbour Cork enjoyed increasing prosperity due to the frequency with which English and French vessels called in on their way to Jamaica or Guadaloupe and St Domingo. Growth of the city to its present status dates from this time.

Many of the smaller south-western ports and harbours have past associations with piracy and smuggling. Algerines sacked Baltimore in 1662 and abducted 110 of its inhabitants into slavery; Dutch pirates Peter Easton and Claus Campeon kept their fleets near the remote Co Cork village of Schull in readiness to pounce on homeward-bound East Indiamen; the Beara Peninsula and north shore of the Kenmare River – both conveniently out of reach of the authorities – became centres of contraband trading in the 18thc. Shipping in the 19thc is harshly dominated by the role played by the famine ships, vessels crowded with people willing to face the uncertainties of the New World rather than face starvation at home. In her book *The Great Hunger* Cecil Woodham-Smith has written how 'the Irish peasant's wild desire to escape from Ireland, combined with his utter ignorance of the sea and of geography, made him eager to risk himself in any vessel'. In the heyday of sail vast windjammers, men of war, and the East India fleet would call at isolated Crookhaven on the Beara Peninsula, the first landfall of Europe. Grain ships and tea clippers would jam the narrow harbour, their tall masts rising over the outline of the hills and their decks so close together that it was possible to walk dryshod from one side of the harbour to the other. Mackerel fleets from the Continent or the Isle of Man called at the most westerly of the province's ports, and the home fishing industry declined to such a degree that it has taken years for the vanished mackerel boats of Ireland to be replaced by trawlers. Basque and Spanish boats that now shelter in Bantry evoke memories of past Continental visitors, the clippers are replaced by oil tankers which slide round the Mizen into Bantry Bay, and Munster's ports are crowded with flotillas of private craft. The latter are more than just a frivolous substitute for the old fishing vessels; they are evidence of the important new industry, tourism. Once every two years it is possible to witness a sight almost as spectacular as the East India fleet, when yachts taking part in the Fastnet race speckle the Atlantic as they converge on the westerly splinter of rock known as Paddy's Milestone or the 'Teardrop of Ireland'. One by one they wheel round the rock and head for home.

Seasons of the south west
The association of places with seasons is very much a personal matter. A wet January evening in Macroom or a hot July afternoon spent pacing the platform at Limerick Junction will indelibly link those places with winter and summer in the individual's mind. The following glimpses of seasonal characteristics at different locations in the province should be read with this in mind. Spring comes first to the south west; in fact it can be said that the area west of a line drawn northwards from Clonakilty never experiences winter. It rains here, but even in January the weather is mild and frosts rare. Sheltered places bathed in the early sun often experience a warmth unknown in July, and the primroses which bloom before the end of February quickly spread across the fields like pale butter on warm bread. Plants known only to counties Cork and Kerry, such as Irish spurge and St Patrick's cabbage, also begin to show at this time of year and are later joined by other oddities to confound the novice botanist – including a large type of butterwort that eats flies through its leaves. Lines of dark conifers exude a resinous perfume which blankets Co Waterford's Comeragh range and the Ballyhoura Hills of Tipperary, while the woods below the River Blackwater are shot through with bluebells.

Springtime in Co Clare, a county with more affinity to the province of Connacht than to Munster, is an austere affair with none of the warm humidity of the south west. The young green foliage floats among great wedge-shaped and gallery graves that received their dead as early as 2000 BC, stone forts, early monastic sites, the

The dry, limestone rocks and pavements of the Burren area in Co Clare support a fascinating collection of rare plants.

A LAND OF EXTREMES

round tower on Scattery Island in the mouth of the Shannon, and the ruined abbey of Dysert O'Dea – perhaps the most impressive of Clare's remains. In northern Clare is the Burren, a strange limestone moonscape of terraces honeycombed with caves and vanishing rivers, miles of slabby stone without water, and the occasional farm crushed between its almost soil-less rocks. Late May carpets this strange area with flowers which are rarely seen elsewhere, and pine martens breed in the scrub undergrowth of the region. Much of the flora here is of an Alpine-Arctic type left over from the ice age, which has survived because the Burren pavement did not lend itself to the accumulation of the boglands that scatter the rest of Ireland. On the east side of the Burren, beneath the shelves of Glasgeivnagh Hill, is a string of little lakes or 'turloughs' with water levels controlled by the underground water system. On the other side of the hill the still-popular spa town of Lisdoonvarna offers its visitors a taste of the Burren's strangeness in the waters of its mineral springs. Elsewhere are interesting places like the bronze-age fortress of Ballykinvarga, guarded by extravagant *chevaux de frise* since its people thought the surrounding limestone insufficient defence against horsemen and foot soldiers; or the miniature, 12th-c cathedral at nearby Kilfenora, with a nave now used as a Protestant church and a roofless chancel which contains the effigies of bishops. Kilfenora's own particular air of mystery is enhanced by several crosses that stand near the church, and a half-ruined Georgian house sheltered in a beech grove.

The great gardens

The lakes and mountains around Killarney in Co Kerry first started to attract tourists in the 18thc, and modern visitors who go to Kate Kearney's Cottage, ride through the Gap of Dunloe, and allow themselves to be rowed down to the lower lake and Ross's Castle are following a secular pilgrimage as well-established and detailed as any holy pattern. The most dramatic way of seeing the Killarney Lakes for the first time is by way of the Kenmare road. In 1852 William Makepeace Thackeray arrived in Killarney from Glengarriff and recorded his journey in vivid little word sketches, but he made no mention of Co Kerry's famous rhododendrons as the species had only just been introduced into the country. These plants were brought from the Himalayas and thrived in the moist south west, particularly around Killarney where early June masses their smokey purple flowers against a traditional backdrop of Celtic oaks. The big gardens should also be seen in June – Garinish Island off Glengarriff, Garinish near Sneem, Derreen near Kilmakilloge – all with coral paths leading through luxuriant acres planned to look like carefully-tended jungle. Such places are natural tourist attractions, and some of the province's towns have been involved in this industry since the 18thc. The golden beaches of Tramore in Co Waterford are as popular now as they were then, and every year more people are looking to the smaller beaches at Stradbally, Ardmore, and similar places for their annual relaxation. Munster's excellent sea fishing lures anglers to try their luck in her coastal waters.

Summer to winter

Summer in the inland areas is marked by hawthorn fading in June as honeysuckle takes its place, berries ripening among the bracken, and the gradual colouring of heather on the purpling hills. Inevitably the visitor finds himself being pulled between ragwort-yellow fields to the sea, where the season brightens small towns with the bustle and trappings of regattas which, but for their picturesque appeal, might offend the silent strands and quiet rock pools with their gaiety. Towns unable to have regattas hold summer festivals instead. Some of these are ancient and based on the sale of livestock, like the Puck Fair of Killorglin in Co Kerry, which is presided over by a large Puck Goat and is possibly the best-known of its kind in Ireland. Others, like the festival at Tralee, contrast with centuries of noble history and an ancient aristocracy. Gusty winds and the smell of rain close the season, and early dusks turn the small brown hills that attend Slievenamon in Co Tipperary into cold parodies of their summer personalities. Ahenny is situated near the Co Waterford border and features two fine crosses on bases carved with an assortment of horses, Daniel, lions, and ecclesiastics. The trunks and arms of these monuments lack figurative details, but are covered with elaborate cross-hatchings, scrolls, and interweavings as rich as tapestry but as impersonal as a Mohammedan sculpture for which religious dogma had forbidden depiction of the human face and form. There was once a third cross which is said to have been more beautiful than these, but it was stolen and subsequently lost in a shipwreck off Passage East on the western shore of Waterford Harbour at the beginning of the 19thc.

In the past Co Waterford has been described like a place of eternal winter – 'the least picturesque of the counties . . . for the most part barren of trees . . . the soil, naturally poor, has had little advantage from cultivation. Its coast, moreover, is inhospitable . . .' This surprising opinion ignores the mountains that take up so much of the central and western parts of the county, the stern shoulders of the Comeraghs rising above the Dungarvan road from Carrick-on-Suir and the tiny gem of Coumshingaun Lake half-surrounded by precipitous, 1,300ft cliffs left by the mighty glaciers. In the fastnesses of the Comeraghs, which rise to some 2,597ft above sea level, are notable glacial moraines, small lakes, the oddly-termed and heather-covered 'haggy plateaux', and the remote refuge of outlaw William Crotty. Winter closes over the Munster countryside in a rush of mist and rain. It is the time when men and dogs tramp the fields in search of snipe, when huntsmen urge their horses over wet Limerick fields after the Scarteens, and when rivers overflow their banks to spread fertile silt across the floors of their valleys. The mist's particular silence is broken only by the cough of cattle, and the province is told to expect rain every two days. The warmth of the fireside comes into its own.

Early June is the best time for the visitor to see Co Kerry's beautiful Killarney Lakes – a time when the lakeshores and jaunting-car tracks are enriched by the smoky colours of rhododendron blooms.

Gateway to Ireland

The soft Leinster landscape – an antithesis to Munster's rocky violence and a cradle of ancient aristocracy, where fertile farmlands lie alongside the hidden wealth of bogland peat.

The beach at Bray in Co Wicklow, one of the best-known resorts in Leinster.

Leinster extends west from the Irish Sea to the River Shannon, and north from the south-coast counties of Waterford and Wexford to the Ulster border. 'All' roads in the Republic lead to Dublin, capital city and chief centre of the Irish Republic, but no Irishman ever talks of going east. Past history has shown the province's gentle east coast to be a weak flank unable to offer even a token geographical resistance to the aspiring invader, and Leinster's golden beaches – so beloved of the modern holidaymaker – once provided a wide-open gate through which alien cultures could sweep into the country. On fine days views of the Wicklow Hills beckoned temptingly to the Welsh across the narrow channel which separates the two countries, a fact recorded by the 13th-c historian and camp-follower Geraldus Cambrensis. He wrote: 'Ireland exercised a strong attraction on adventurous knights . . . it was very rich in booty and famed for the good temperature of the air, the fruitfulness of the soil, and the pleasant and convenient sites for dwelling, with its wide harbours open for trade, and its many landing places.' He might have added that the conquest of Ireland via Leinster was like taking sweets from a child's hand, because the country's kings and chieftains were constantly fighting amongst themselves. Nevertheless, if geography had given the east coast the rocky fangs and claws which protect the other neighbouring provinces, the Irish people may well have held together as a nation.

An aristocratic history
Those people who ignore Leinster but wax eloquent about the 'Celtic west', 'rebellious south', and 'Black North' are guilty of injustice towards this south-eastern province by forgetting the immeasurably important part which it has played in Irish history. Although the east was the way in for invasion, it was also the entrance for the most potent force in the development of the country's culture – Christianity. St Patrick landed at the mouth of the River Boyne in the year 432, and from that time until the coming of the Normans in 1169 the Celtic church flourished. Relics of this Golden Age can be found all over Leinster, and even today retain much of their pristine appeal. Surviving remains, mostly ruined but mellowed and beautified by time and weather, include monasteries, oratories, round towers, high crosses, and holy wells; the situations of such structures are always pleasant and often superb. Particularly fine examples of early-Christian architecture in the province include the graceful, $17\frac{1}{2}$ft Cross of Moone, embowered in Co Kildare's solitude; the cramped cell of St Mochta's House, near the village of Louth in the county of the same name; Timahoe's round tower and Freshford's richly-moulded doorway, both in homely surroundings. Leinster could be famous for its antiquities alone, but it is also known for the beauty of its landscapes. It has already been noted that the east coast is tame, but it undergoes a complete change of personality when it rounds the south-eastern corner of Co Wexford and finds itself face-to-face with the Atlantic Ocean. Compared with the other Irish provinces the inland regions of Leinster are highly populated, better cultivated and afforested, and have the appearance of being altogether more settled. Some areas are drier than anywhere else in Ireland, and the effects of the westerly winds that tear the country are less noticeable. The latter is especially so in the sheltered south east.

The best way of examining Leinster is by studying its individual counties, starting with Louth in the extreme north-eastern corner of the province. This is the smallest of Ireland's 32 counties and features a generally low and well-cultivated landscape which is compact rather than extensive. Northern Louth has a small upland region which faces across the provincial border and faintly echoes the mighty Mourne Mountains, which rise in Ulster's Co Down on the far shores of Carlingford Lough. All Louth's rivers are short and its woodlands unextensive – except near Ravensdale, where there is a planned forest trail. Drogheda and Dundalk are the two largest and most progressive towns in the county, and almost every other place in this area is redolent of colourful history and ancient sagas. Louth is probably the best county to link with an explanation of the old Irish epics, because the Cooley Peninsula – between Dundalk Bay and Carlingford Lough – was where many parts of these ancient, half-historical tales were enacted.

Legends alive
Long ago, certainly before Christianity in Ireland, the Cooley Peninsula was a battle area of the famous Cattle Raid of Cooley. Queen Maeve of Connacht coveted a great brown bull belonging to a Cooley chieftain, who was unwilling to let her borrow it. She set out for Ulster, the province to which this part of Louth was then attached, and advanced her armies through the thick forests and impassable bogs which protected the Gap of the North. Legend has it that the armies of the north were suffering under a magical sickness and were unable to fight, but the invaded territory was defended single-handed by heroic Cuchulain – the 'hound of Ulster'. This warrior's prowess became the subject for songs and tales, just as the heroic sagas in general have inspired W B Yeats and other well-known latter-day writers. No battlefields can be located on the peninsula, but a ford near Ardee is said to have been the place where Cuchulain fought Ferdia – his friend and the Queen's champion – for four days. A great mound on the outskirts of Dundalk is said to mark the site of

Two Olivers

During the 17thc the stage was held by two Olivers – Cromwell the villain and Plunkett the heroic Archbishop of Armagh. In August 1649 Oliver Cromwell mounted a punitive expedition to Ireland and – after his 14,000 'Ironsides' had recovered from sea sickness – marched from his Dublin landing ground to Drogheda on the southern border of Co Louth. He took the town on the third assault and put many of its people – including old men, women, and children – to death. Oliver Plunkett was made Archbishop in 1659 and immediately became a fugitive from the heavy persecution that was then the order of the day. His great contribution to the restoration of the disorganized and afflicted Catholic church was his brave perseverance in the administering of Confirmation and ordaining of priests. He has recently been canonized and now bears the title 'saint'. A tour of Louth and neighbouring Co Meath in his footsteps leads through such charming places as Ballybarrack, Ardpatrick, Louth Hall, and Glass Pistol Castle before ending at St Peter's Church in Drogheda, where the martyred Archbishop's head is enshrined. This strangely appealing death's head was snatched from a fire by the Tyburn hangman himself and still gives an impression of saintliness. Another historic milestone in Leinster's eventful 17thc was the Battle of the Boyne, which was fought upstream from Drogheda at Oldbridge in 1690. This was a victory for William and a turning point in European history. Oldbridge was the hottest part of the fray, but the battle shifted over a wide area and touched Tullyallen, Sheepwalk, Drybridge Donore, Rosnaree, Slane, and Duleek. Nowadays it is difficult to imagine the clamour of armed conflict in this peaceful countryside. Louth's many other features would take a book of their own to catalogue and describe, but no cameo of the county would be complete without at least a passing mention of the most memorable. The eastern coast road and the Cooley Mountains, in the north, both afford extensive views of particular appeal. In the far south of the county are the superb monastic remains of Mellifont and Monasterboice – both well signposted – and the Catholic Church of Collon houses an exquisite marble representation of Dorcas, wife of Percy Fitzgerald. This effigy is Victorian to the tips of its finely-worked fingers, but it belongs to no particular period of art and is more a universal expression of young womanhood than a cold memorial. Beside the main Dundalk to Knockbridge road is Cloghafarmore, the 'stone of the big man'. Legend has it that heroic Cuchulain, weakened by his many wounds, lashed his dying body to the pillar so that his wary enemies would not know whether he was dead or alive. It was not until a raven settled unmolested on the body's shoulder that his adversaries dared to approach the stone. This site still exudes an uncanny sense of presence.

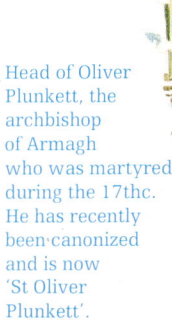

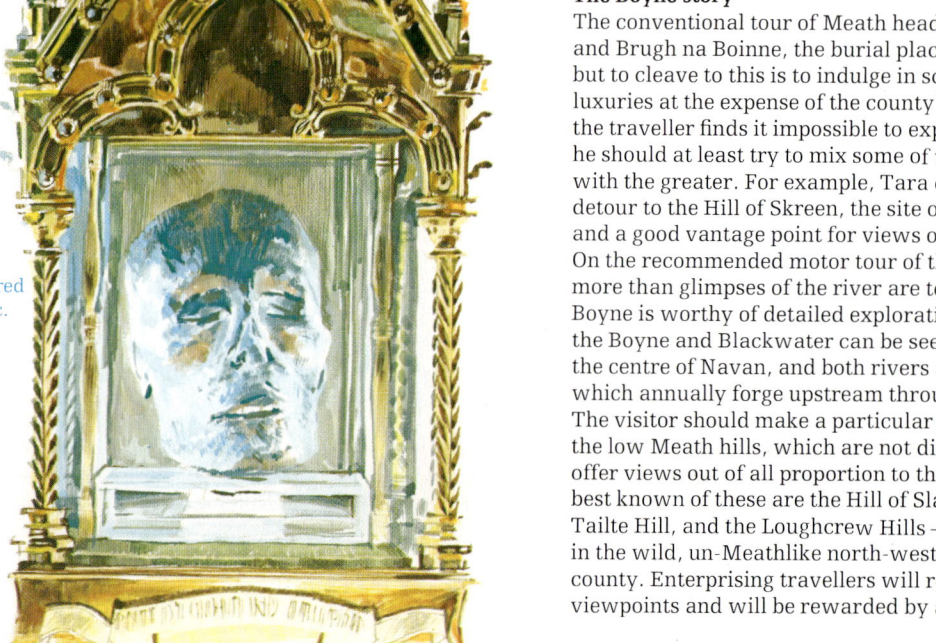

Every Irishman has an innate respect for Co Meath – the major remaining part of an ancient fifth province where the ancient High Kings of Ireland ruled from their Tara palace. This was once the most important part of the country, and the county which still bears its name has every appearance of being 'royal'. The depth and richness of the soil is unsurpassed and the traveller in the Boyne Valley, for instance, should not be unduly surprised by the opulence of the landscape. Rolling green pastures blend with rich plantations and the demesnes of great houses, while the prosperous farmsteads are scattered with prime cattle and glossy-coated horses. The fertility of Co Meath is proverbial, and the wealth of the Tara Mines (near Navan) is at last being exploited. By Irish standards the people of Co Meath are slow of speech, not readily excited, and hardly ever given to boasting. Such taciturnity is a source of wonder amongst the people of other counties, where boasting is an accepted extension to the art of story-telling. A tradition of High Kings, parliaments, national games, and feasting gives a confidence which does not need such support.

The Boyne story

The conventional tour of Meath heads straight for Tara and Brugh na Boinne, the burial place of the High Kings, but to cleave to this is to indulge in scenic and antiquarian luxuries at the expense of the county's charming detail. If the traveller finds it impossible to explore Meath in depth he should at least try to mix some of the lesser attractions with the greater. For example, Tara could be offset by a detour to the Hill of Skreen, the site of medieval remains and a good vantage point for views of the countryside. On the recommended motor tour of the Boyne Valley no more than glimpses of the river are to be had, but the Boyne is worthy of detailed exploration. The meeting of the Boyne and Blackwater can be seen from a bridge in the centre of Navan, and both rivers are alive with salmon which annually forge upstream through wooded valleys. The visitor should make a particular point of ascending the low Meath hills, which are not difficult to climb but offer views out of all proportion to their size. Perhaps the best known of these are the Hill of Slane, the Hill of Lloyd, Tailte Hill, and the Loughcrew Hills – the latter situated in the wild, un-Meathlike north-western part of the county. Enterprising travellers will readily find other viewpoints and will be rewarded by a 30m panorama to

Head of Oliver Plunkett, the archbishop of Armagh who was martyred during the 17thc. He has recently been canonized and is now 'St Oliver Plunkett'.

GATEWAY TO IRELAND

Ardbraccan House, a superb 18th-c mansion designed by James Wyatt to serve as the seat of the Bishops of Meath.

the south, the Irish Sea to the east, and mountains with Co Cavan's little hills to the west and north.

When bad weather makes driving in the countryside more of a chore than a delight, the opportunity should be taken to visit one of the county's ancient walled towns. These include Trim, Navan, Kells, and Athboy – places with origins much older than the ruined fortifications and fragments of gates for which they are so well known. St Patrick founded a monastery at Trim, and Kells (or Cenannas Mor) had a flourishing Christian settlement in the 6thc. Surviving remains of the latter include a round tower, several high crosses, and a structure known as St Colmcille's House. All four of the towns mentioned were outposts of The Pale defences and still bear witness to Anglo-Norman occupation. Trim Castle, for example, was once the largest Anglo-Norman stronghold in Ireland and is still impressive. Meath is full of fortifications of various types and ages. Some of these strongholds are ruined and some have been restored; some form the basis for beautiful Victorian romanticism and others decay peacefully next to magnificent Georgian mansions. The landlords, particularly in more recent times, had an uncanny knack for picking perfect sites which they artistically 'improved' with carefully-chosen trees from other countries. The short list of native Irish trees has thus become supplemented by limes, Spanish chestnuts, and many other exotics. Of all the great houses in Co Meath there are four which immediately come to mind in the context of arboricultural enterprise such as this. Ardbraccan House was built to a design by James Wyatt in 1766 to serve as the seat of the bishops of Meath. Traveller and historian Bishop Pocock grew the cedars that still grace its fine gardens from seeds he had acquired in Lebanon. Examples of huge sequoias introduced from California in the 1840s can be seen at Townley Hall and stand as living memorials to the Townley and Batsford families – great travellers and plant collectors. Gormanstown Castle features yew hedges and cork trees, while Headford House has a collection of conifers that may be the finest in the world.

Tara first played a significant part in Irish events over 2,000 years ago and was unquestionably the heart of the Celtic nation. Nowadays the settlement site is bald, but the area is well organized and the sense of desolation recorded by past pilgrims has been dispelled. Views from the hill are good and the situation bracing. Neolithic or early bronze-age notables lie in the cairns of Brugh na Boinne at Newgrange, Knowth, and Dowth. These sites are also interesting and well organized. It is impossible to exaggerate the importance of Newgrange as a mecca for archaeologists from all over the world, even though its past has been punctuated by Norse raids, the depredations of 19th-c amateur archaeologists, and misuse of varying degrees. It has even survived the ultimate humiliation of being forgotten for a long period.

It is impossible to consider Westmeath as a separate county because it is really an extension of Meath – a cut-off portion of the original fifth province of Ireland. There are, however, the scenic differences that should be expected in such a large area. Westmeath has the great River Shannon as its western boundary, and the scenery around its loughs is often considered some of the finest offered by inland Ireland. The 'royal' atmosphere of Meath gives way to rural homliness here. The land is a little less good and the towns, never having been forced to conform to defences like those of The Pale, are inclined to sprawl. Fishing and story-telling are more favoured than hunting and shooting; to sum up in one word, Westmeath is a little less *grand* than its aristocratic neighbour. However, the traveller leaving Meath for Westmeath is not forsaking royal circles. Here he can visit Uisneach Hill, which lies west of Mullingar and was a seat of the High Kings ages before the coming of Christianity. At the summit of the hill a stone called *Aill na Mireann* marks the junction of ancient boundaries.

Three of Westmeath's lakes are large, all are picturesque to some degree, and the county's proliferation of water is a refreshingly welcome sight to the traveller who has come from the relatively dry east and south. Their amenity value is not underrated by the county's townspeople and they all have a cherished appearance. Lough Derryvarragh, shrouded with trees and bordered by hills in north Westmeath, is particularly fine and has a curious hidden quality as if it chose to escape the crowd of lakes farther south. This quality of isolation is even more marked in Fore, a fascinating group of monastic remains sited between Loughs Lene and Bane. Of particular interest here are St Fechin's Well, his 7th-c church, a 13th-c Benedictine abbey, several ancient crosses, and fragments of walls and gates that survive from the once-fortified town. It is hard to believe that this place of profound solitude is part of the modern world. As well as the lakes Westmeath has the 18th-c Royal Canal, a disused waterway which flings a loop round Mullingar as it cuts its 90m course through the county to the Shannon.

Gateway town

Athlone stands on the River Shannon, astride the provincial border on the western side of Westmeath, and has long been valued for its strategic position in the 'centre' of Ireland. It has long been the 'gateway to Connacht', and is a bright, bustling town which has developed as a centre of inland navigation and boat building. The atmosphere is one of constant surprise and

GATEWAY TO IRELAND

optimism, the buildings are a pleasing combination of old and modern, and the urban skyline is fretted with the spires of its fine churches. Its attraction is centred on the river and further accentuated by a pleasant waterside promenade. About 9m south of Athlone in Co Offaly is Clonmacnoise, perhaps the most celebrated of all Ireland's holy places and the site where St Ciaran founded the humble basis for a great monastic city some 1,400 years ago. The Shannon acted as a highway along which students from all over Europe could travel to take advantage of the city's renowned concentration of scholarly minds. Even today it is easier to find Clonmacnoise by river than by the twisting little lanes of Offaly. The emptiness of the broad river and the repose of the landscape impressed Stephen Gwynn when he made this journey in 1914, and he recorded his experience in *The Fair Hills of Ireland*. He wrote 'A heron sluggishly flapping across the river gave a sort of key to the whole colour-scheme with its cool greys. Geese afloat ahead of us, every one mirrored and trailing a crystaline wake as it swam . . . Then suddenly across a broad, still pool we saw Clonmacnoise rising like a cloud far off: a mass of buildings, strangely suggestive in that fen country of a germinal Oxford, reduced to its essentials. The group of low walls with towers springing out of their midst was superb against the blue-grey haze.' When Gwyn actually reached the deserted place he was aghast at its ruinous state. Clonmacnoise suffered disaster heaped upon disaster – the plundering of Norsemen, raiding and burning by native Irish, and almost total destruction by the English garrison of Athlone in 1552. Restorations made in the following century were again destroyed in 1647 – this time by Cromwellian forces. It is amazing that anything exists there today, let alone some of the most beautiful remains in the country.

Harder landscapes
Leinster's overall impression of warmth and richness peters out in Co Longford, where the scenery seems to be in a frozen state of transition. The gold tints of the south are washed out and invaded by cold blue-greys and the austerity of neighbouring Connacht, a province which seems to have crept across the Shannon to claim Longford for its own. The low hills and patches of bog which make up the countryside support towns which, with the exception of Longford itself, are invariably small. The western border of the county is shared with the boundary between Leinster and Connacht and includes the shores of Lough Ree, a vast expansion in the River Shannon. This, the Shannon banks, and a number of smaller loughs are particularly beautiful, but the rest of the county is so scattered with miniature landscapes of outstanding natural attraction that it is impossible to put together a general, postcard-type view of the total area. Of all the Leinster counties Longford is the least sophisticated and perhaps the least tourist-orientated. Its people are more interesting than its topography and come from ancient roots. They are proud of their county, proud of their famous tenacity, and their septs and families still hold the lands of their ancestors in spite of medieval confiscations and 19th-c evictions. Nobody in Ireland ever refers to Longford without mentioning Annaly, the country of the O Farrell's; such is the national admiration for well-rooted families. Here the strength of tradition has fostered long, hereditary memories, so that every father's son grows up with the knowledge of the 1798 Insurrection; the Battle of Ballinamuck; the mass execution of prisoners in Ballinalee; the Famine; and the Tithe wars.

Longford families
In the mild, eastern part of the county is Edgeworthstown (or Mostrim), which was connected with the Edgeworth family of improving landlords for some 400 years. This family were well known for their sense of justice, and one member in particular – Richard, the father of Maria the novelist – was well-liked by his tenants at a time when oppression was the general rule elsewhere. In spite of this he considered it prudent to evacuate Edgeworth House in 1798, on the news that a French expedition had landed at Killala, and the village was indeed damaged by advancing insurgents and their French allies. However, so great was the esteem in which this family was held that they returned to find their personal property unmolested. The family is well documented. Maria found time to write more than just novels, and Richard was known as an inventor and experimenter but was somewhat overshadowed by his brilliant literary daughter. She is credited with having brought the novel forward as an accepted form, thus bridging the work of Fielding and Sir Walter Scott. Scott and the poet Wordsworth were visitors to Edgeworth House. Perhaps the most important Longford family was the O Fearghaill or O Farrell group, previously mentioned in the context of deep roots and ancient tradition. They were Lords of Annaly from centuries past and maintained

Monastic remains at Shannon-side Clonmacnoise. To the left in the picture is 12th-c O Rourke's Tower, and the West Cross or Cross of the Scriptures can be seen in the foreground.

their independence long after other chieftains had submitted to the English. References to them occupy more than seven columns in the ancient *Annals of the Four Masters,* and members of the family have been famous bishops and pirates, sculptors and politicians, genealogists and soldiers. Their military connections were many, and a great number of O Farrells distinguished themselves in foreign armies subsequent to the family's exile after the Treaty of Limerick in 1691. Members of the family later reached the Argentine and grew very powerful.

Leinster's wildlife
It has already been noted that aspiring invaders found the low east coast of Leinster more of an asset than a hindrance. Today these shores are unthreatened by anything more sinister than the occasional tourist, and their miles of deserted strand offer sanctuary to birds and mammals of the ocean. The five counties which share the eastern seaboard are – south to north – Wexford, Wicklow, Dublin, a tiny fragment of Meath, and Louth. Gravels and shingles form a large proportion of the seafronts in Wexford and Wicklow, and elsewhere there are long sands interrupted by the occasional headland; the entire coast forms an excellent hunting ground for the wildlife enthusiast. The chief feature of the flora here is that the majority of species are of the English type. It is necessary to go west and south west into Connacht and Munster to find Hibernian-type plants, but there are still many rarities to be found on the Leinster coast. Clovers not found anywhere else can be seen on the Murrough, a 12m spit of land north of Wicklow town, and a rare cudweed grows in profusion on shallow marine inlets at Lady's Island and Tacumshane in south Wexford. Other species include Carline thistle, sea holly, samphire, sea-stock, tree mallow, wild madder, and bloody cranesbill. Two introductions that have run amuck in Courtown Harbour, east of Gorey in north Wexford, are lily-of-the-valley and a spikey shrub known as buckthorn. Farther south near Curracloe is the great sea rush, which grows to 4ft in height, and samphire is frequent wherever there are rocks and cliffs.

The east coast has a great deal to offer the bird watcher and includes a number of sanctuaries which are maintained by the Irish Conservancy. The most important of these are Wexford Slobs and Dublin Bay's North Bull Island. The former is a 5,000-acre area of reclaimed land which operates as a headquarters of ornithological research and is equipped to receive and instruct visitors. Winter migrants, especially geese, come here in such large numbers as to make world records. Greenland white-fronted geese arrive in their thousands, as do Berwick swans, numerous wading species, and lapwings. Leinster's islands, from Lambay off the mid-east coast to the Saltees off the south coast of Wexford, provide safe nesting sites for many different types of sea birds, and the Boyne estuary in the north of the province is ideal for the watcher who prefers not to be glued to field glasses all the time. The places mentioned here are only a few of the thousands to be found along this deserted coast.

Co Dublin has a varied and beautiful coastline which has more in common with the rough, bold sea-border in south Wexford than with the east, and the county itself has been described as one of the most attractive in Ireland. Ever since 1922, the year of Irish independence, the government's policy has been one of centralization; the capital city Dublin has expanded over its rural surroundings to a greater and greater degree with each passing year since the second world war, but even the new suburbs have not unduly damaged the scenic value of its countryside. Rich farmlands still occupy the north and north east parts of the county, and the sandy land near Skerries and Rush has allowed the development of a thriving bulb and market gardening industry. South of the city, however, the countryside has retreated in the face of inevitable urban sprawl and farming is a decreasing occupation. Dublin's citizens are fortunate in having a large number of scenic and entertaining amenities within easy reach – for instance Howth, a claw of land that extends from the mainland to encompass the northern edge of Dublin Bay a mere 9m or so from the city centre. Howth may not have lakes, rivers, farms, and rustic trimmings, but it is Ireland in miniature; a tiny microcosm with a 563ft hill, precipitous cliffs, moorland, and plenty to interest the geologist, naturalist, antiquarian, and historian. It is also an excellent place for ordinary people who derive pleasure in merely staring at harbour activities and the open sea. Howth was once an island. The isthmus which connects it to the mainland is a gravel beach which was formed within the human period, although the main body of the peninsula is made up of gnarled slates and quartzite – some of the oldest rocks in the country. Fine cliff walks afford views north to the Mourne Mountains beyond the Ulster border and south to the venerable old peaks of Co Wicklow. The Bailey Lighthouse, a 19th-c edifice said to have been erected on the site of a 1st-c High King's palace, is probably the best viewpoint. Howth Castle is a battlemented structure flanked by square towers, sited near the harbour in gardens of amazing

Howth Castle, near Dublin, dates from the 16thc but has been extensively restored. Only the square towers have survived from the original structure.

GATEWAY TO IRELAND

Fishing vessels in the harbour at Skerries, a historic settlement and popular resort situated north of Dublin.

beauty. Perhaps the most well known part of the grounds is the Rhododendron Garden, where some 2,000 varieties of shrub rise in floriferous domes and cupolas which present a stunning range of red and purple hues at the appropriate time of year. Low rainfall and a climate comparable to that of the Channel Islands make Howth a very desirable place to live, and the residents are lucky to be where they are because many people consider that this promontory should be designated a nature reserve.

Dublin's resorts

Out to sea about 1m north of the harbour is Ireland's Eye, a fantastically-shaped island which features grassy swards, hillocks, cliffs, rocks, beaches, and the ever-present screaming of seabirds. Species that have been recorded as breeding here include Manx shearwaters, fulmars, kittiwakes, razorbills, black guillemots, and puffins. The scale of description for other coastal areas in the county should be reduced, but they are invariably lovely and should not be written off in the way that Victorian guide books tended to – merely as 'little fishing villages'. Loughshinney, in the northern part of the county, is still aptly described by this bald statement but is also a place of great charm and interest. Low cliffs which form the natural part of its fine harbour will fascinate geologists with their laterally compressed rock strata. Some of these layers look like shelves of leaning books, while others give the impression of crumpled pattern samples in a tailor's shop. Nearby Skerries has enough history to do honour to a university town, but it seems quite content to bask in its reputation as a highly successful seaside resort. South of Skerries and Loughshinney is popular Donabate Strand, within easy reach of the city dwellers, and even closer to Dublin is Malahide – home of the prolific landscape painter Nathanial Hone. Hone lived from 1881 to 1917 and produced an enormous number of paintings based on subjects drawn from this locality. He seldom exhibited or sold his work, and the deep pastures and sunny barley fields seen in his paintings have largely disappeared beneath a tide of buildings. Only the sand, sea, and rocks are the same as he saw them. Between Malahide and Dublin is Portmarnock, which boasts the fine Velvet Strand and wide fame in golfing circles.

The River Liffey marks the division between north and south Co Dublin and fulfils its boundary-making task with quite extraordinary decisiveness, smartly separating the bare and exposed north coast from the wooded shores of the south. A long, octopus arm of urban expansion extends along the south side of Dublin Bay to include the one-time villages of Blackrock, Monkstown, and Dun Laoghaire before terminating at Dalkey – where some of Leinster's finest scenery begins. A first appreciation of the landscape can be enjoyed from the Vico Road, which skirts the hills of Dalkey and Killiney as it forges south into an area where the climate is generally better than that of the north coast. Plants such as camellias and tree ferns thrive in Killiney gardens. Heart-lifting views of the mountains in the southern part of the county can be enjoyed from the city's streets, and prominent amongst these peaks is 1,271ft Mount Pelier, crowned by the ruins of the 18th-c Hell Fire Club. This was once a rendezvous of young Dublin bucks and bloods, and it might be said that there is still some justification for the dry comment in an American guide to Europe that this was the first and last genuine night club in Ireland.

Although the scenic attractions of counties Dublin and Kildare are of a different order, these adjacent territories have some things in common. Both have a definite north and south division between landscapes and people; north-Dublin folk regard the trans-Liffey population as soft and luxury seeking, while in Kildare the position is reversed so that it is the 'northerners' who are the grand sports and leisure men – horse mad and football crazy. It is said that the people in the top half of the county look upon the southerners as too hard-working to be wholesome, and the contrasts are even further stressed by the difference in land usage between the two parts – stock in the north and large-scale tillage in the south. It could be said that, as a county, Kildare is a doubtful success. Indigenous populations in both counties have been almost squeezed out. The old Kildare stock of Gaelic septs and Norman families has been replaced by migrants from the west and south, a changeover which has largely occurred in the 20thc due to the breaking up of landlords' estates and the re-allocation of lands by the Irish Land Commission. Dublin city is an exception because it was an English stronghold for hundreds of years and denied the Irish any share of power until the middle of the last century. Real Dubliners are scarce and the lovable Dublin Jackeen is gradually disappearing beneath waves of provincials.

The Liffey counties

One major physical feature that counties Dublin and Kildare have in common is the River Liffey, and both areas include picturesque reaches that cry out for the establishment of riverside walks. Throughout Kildare the Liffey is spanned by fine old bridges: the 14th-c New Bridge, Celbridge; Millicent, Caragh; those in Athgarvan and Harristown; and a pair named after English royalty. Part of the western Co Kildare boundary is formed by the faster River Barrow, which rushes south through the province to join the Nore and Suir before flowing into Waterford Harbour on the south coast.

GATEWAY TO IRELAND

It has been said that Kildare is a county plagued with main roads that whisk the visitor through the least attractive areas and leave the best untouched. The ideal way to savour the county's true personality is to travel by boat along the Grand Canal, which has been revitalized during the last decade by the establishment of pleasure cruising. This waterway reveals Arcadian country, while the conventional through-routes merely act as convenient corridors. Kildare's lakes are non-existent and its hills are small but prominent. Because of the relative flatness of the surrounding countryside such hills as there are – the Hill of Allen, the Chair of Kildare, and the Red Hill, Dunmurry, and Boston groups – command surprisingly far-flung views. Many are also of historical interest. The Hill of Allen is surmounted by a landlord's folly tower and has been a landmark for almost half the province since prehistoric times, when it was the winter quarters of the legendary Fianna, the Red Branch Knights. The great sprawl known as the Bog of Allen starts in northern Kildare, near the Hill of Allen, and spreads across the adjacent counties to the Shannon Valley at the western boundary of Leinster. In actual fact this is not a geographical entity because it is scattered with many patches of fertile, useable land, but its great size makes it a feature which mapmakers cannot find an excuse to leave off. For a long time it has been the pernicious habit to belittle the Irish bogs and speak scornfully of bog dwellers, but it can be considered a privilege to live near this type of country. As far as economic values are concerned Kildare is a less important bog areas than Co Offaly. However, an individual acre of this strange, flat terrain offers more biological interest than 10 acres of ordinary farmland.

Saints and horses

Any description of Kildare would be incomplete without mention of St Brigid or the county's famous horses. Some 1,500 years ago St Brigid had a nunnery under the huge oak tree which grew on the spot where Kildare Cathedral now stands, and her name echoes down the centuries in placenames, dedicated wells, churches, and modern institutions. Anybody who comes from the county will be able to show the visitor at least one memorial to this loved and holy person. Likewise, anyone who comes from Kildare is assumed to know about horses and horse racing. The owner of a car with a Kildare registration is quite likely to be asked for winning tips if he travels on race days. The justification for such an attitude is that the county and its horses are inseparable. Facilities for racing, hunting, breeding, and training exist all over the northern regions in particular, offering some of the finest and most spectacular equestrian events in the world. In the centre of the county near Kildare town is The Curragh, a great, mainly-unenclosed plain where Irish racing has its headquarters. Punchestown, situated outside Naas town, comes furiously alive for three days of racing in April; the sight of superb horses against a vast landscape and a foreground of grassy hillocks splashed with the white and gold of spring blackthorn and furze is unforgettable. The winning and losing tends to recede in importance when compared with the occasion.

The midland plains

East of Co Kildare are the mid Leinster counties of Laois and Offaly, the former dropping south to Co Kilkenny and the latter extending north to a border with Westmeath. People tend to assume a woeful expression when talking about the 'midlands' of any country, and the great central limestone plain on which these two counties are situated is no exception. This is unfortunate because limestone is an honest, geological factor which has been the making of most of Ireland, her people, and her livestock, so the especially sad attitude adopted by the Irishman discussing the 'central limestone plains' is largely undeserved. Descriptions of Irish topography should never include the word 'plain' in a 'flat' or 'level' sense, because such areas do not exist in the country. Regions so named tend to undulate.

Both counties were victims of the English 'Plantation' experiments, when English landlords and tenants were given land which had been taken from the native population. During the 16thc the O Mores of Laois and O Connors of Offaly maintained an obstinacy which was a constant source of danger to the English government, and after the failure of a rebellion led by Silken Thomas – a Fitzgerald – the English took tough measures. Forts were constructed in both territories and a few settlers were established as the start to a gradual policy of colonization. However, when the catholic Queen Mary assumed the British throne the chieftains of both counties mistakenly thought that they could gain her sympathy and proceeded to expel the newcomers. They were wrong; Mary was just as committed to the conquest of Ireland as her father Henry VIII. Acts of Parliament were passed, the territories were formed into counties named King's and Queen's County respectively, and the forts were renamed Maryborough and Philipstown in honour of the royal pair. The plantation was now on in earnest, the natives were dispossessed, and a lengthy period of ferocious warfare ensued. Raids, burnings, and massacres continued for decades until, like the Vikings and Normans before them, the settlers were absorbed by the Irish nation. Since Irish independence was established the placenames King's County, Queen's County, Maryborough, and Philipstown have been changed back to Laois, Offaly, Portlaoise, Daingean. The visitor to Laois will gain the impression of being

The world knows Co Kildare for its horses. Punchestown Racecourse, outside Naas, is the venue for several race meetings during the year. It is particularly well known for its 3-day spring meeting.

GATEWAY TO IRELAND

Offaly and Laois share the Slieve Bloom mountain range, a group of gently rounded summits which forms a conspicuous feature of central Ireland.

surrounded by a protective circle of hills, but a quick glance at the map will show the absence of such a wall. The illusion is maintained by the compactness of the landscape, and the southern barony of Cullenagh is almost a county in its own right. To travel its byways and explore its low hills, belts of trees, stream-watered fields, and innocent small towns is to know the best of the county. Four small places in Cullenagh are: Abbeyleix, with its tree-lined street and almost too self-conscious air of being a model; Ballinakill, with a very faint Dickensian atmosphere about it; Ballyroan, a typically soft-faced Leinster village; Timahoe, where ancient monastic remains include a perfect round tower and Romanesque doorway. In the eastern-central part of Laois, close to the important Stradbally to Portlaoise road, is the fascinating Rock of Dunamase. This natural limestone fortress rises 200ft above a complicated terrain of round hills and narrow defiles, and has carried a military post since earliest times. Hundreds of years ago it was a dun of native chieftains, then after the Norman occupation it was used as the site for a castle complete with fosse, gateways, bailey, courtyards, and wards. Sheer precipices protected three sides of the stronghold, and the weaker fourth side fairly bristled with man-made obstacles. Strongbow, William de Bruce, and the O Mores variously defended this ideally-situated and impregnable fortress, but there is no exact record of how many times the rock was attacked. As with many other brilliant fortifications, the rock was eventually defeated by gunpowder – a force which no early designer could ever have foreseen. Cromwellian troops set up their cannon near the rock and completely shattered the great castle; shattered it remains today, but the site is still redolent of martial power.

It seems that the Irish people detested all strangers and settlers, often with very good reason, but this was not always the case. During the Stuart period a number of Huguenot refugees established themselves around Portarlington, on the north-Laois border with Offaly, and became model colonists. They planted fruit and vegetable gardens, set up spinning and weaving industries, and generally led a peaceful, busy way of life. While the native Irish were raiding and harassing other alien settlers they left the Huguenots alone, and it is rare to hear anything but good ever spoken about these people. Portarlington includes a so-called 'French Church' plus a variety of architectural styles connected with these colonists and is well worth visiting, even though the town has been greatly remodelled.

In the same way that Co Westmeath's nest of lakes cheers and surprises the explorer travelling through inland Leinster, he is similarly refreshed by the sudden appearance of the Slieve Bloom Mountains in Laois and Offaly. This range is a conspicuous feature of central Ireland and comprises broad, rounded summits which culminate in 1,734ft Arderin. Its geological construction includes limestone giving way to old red sandstone, which is in turn replaced by silurian deposits at the summits. Several of the many roads that cross the range have been specially constructed to afford excellent views over forest and moorland, and foothill villages such as Rosenalis, Clonaslee, and Kinitty are as pleasant as their names suggest. The last mentioned of these is in Offaly and the other two lie in Laois. Almost all the valley slopes in the 18m range are planted with forest. The oldest part of an area called Mountrath Forest is situated 1,400ft above sea level and is known as Baunweigh. This was acquired by the Forestry Division in 1911 and comprises almost 2,000 acres of mature woodland, a welcome change from the knee-high conifers and saplings which mark the considerable progress made by modern Irish forestry. Given time these too will have the appeal of the older woodlands. Several thousand acres of the Slieve Blooms have been afforested with such species as Sitka spruce, firs, Japanese larch, and various others. This only a proportion of the ground thus used in Laois.

A wealth of peat
The Laois forests are a manifestation of the post-independence economy, as are also the bog developments in Offaly. Until quite recently the people of Ireland bewailed the poverty of 'Queen's County' and regarded bogland as a national liability. There was more of this so-called liability in Offaly than anywhere else in Ireland – almost as much as there was agricultural land, in fact – and the only value it seemed to have was as a source of turf for the domestic fire. Early summer used to see family teams working in the bogs to cut their winter supply of fuel, but as far as resource-usage is concerned this was like a mouse nibbling at a hay rick. That position has now changed completely, largely due to the efforts of the Bord na Mona since its foundation in 1935. Nowadays some 60,000 acres of Offaly's 100,000-acre bogland are in actual use or reserved for future exploitation. There is keen competition for the utilization of both virgin bog and ground that has been worked, because there is a world shortage of peat and the ground which is exposed after the peat has been removed – often to a depth of 12ft – is exceptionally fertile. Apart from Russia Ireland is the largest producer of this sought-after commodity in the world, so one of the moment's most urgent questions is whether it should be squandered as fuel or used as an enriching fertilizer. Machine extraction has been successful and is being developed alongside new techniques for optimum usage, including seven peat-fired power stations which supply 40 per cent of the Irish Republic's electricity. Machine 'mined' fuel is in use but

GATEWAY TO IRELAND

Leighlinbridge straddles the River Barrow in Co Carlow and features 12th-c Black Castle, which was built to command a ford. Some 2m west is the important monastic foundation of Old Leighlin.

has largely been replaced by milled peat converted into the now-famous briquettes. A characteristic sight in mid-Offaly, where the Boora Group peat-production unit is situated, is polythene-covered, mile-long heaps of milled peat awaiting transportation. This sight is somewhat hard to accept by people who remember purple heather and the Abbey Theatre cliché 'The mists that do be on the bogs'.

Moss peat is different from fuel peat and seems to have an even greater future ahead of it. It is now the standard material used for mushroom cultivation and most glasshouse crops, and whether in its natural state or impregnated with fertilizers it has great potential. Its horticultural qualities cannot be exaggerated and it is being exported in ever-increasing quantities to enrich foreign soils as far apart as the Channel Islands and Australia. Another way in which this once-despised material is used is in the production of horticultural peat pots. Over 200 million of these are manufactured each year by Erin Peat Products, and over 98 per cent are exported. Finally, the cut-away or worked areas of blanket bogs – so called to distinguish them from mountain bogs – are now in the three-fold demand: for forestry, grassland, and the cultivation of vegetables. Although the raising of high-quality vegetables on such ground is still in experimental stages the prospects are extremely bright and, to date, the results have been very gratifying. Another opening, which is yet to be fully developed, involves the cultivation of ornamental trees and shrubs. The patriots' dream of utilizing bogs has been fulfilled.

Fertile Carlow
Carlow is a small inland county which lies south of Kildare in the south-eastern part of the province. Carlow town has a cathedral, colleges, and cultural societies, but is best known for its sugar-beet factory – a state-sponsored industry founded in the mid 20's. This was a welcome sign of economic advance after the Civil War, and a rash Opposition member's description of the factory as a 'white elephant' during a heated debate has been a source of smiles for 50 years. Sugar beet and the crops grown for a food-processing industry form an agricultural focal point. Although Carlow farmers are energetic and enterprising, the landscape does not give any indication of intensive usage; all fervent activity is beautifully masked by undulating land and the profuse greenery of woods, groves, hedgerows, and bushes, meaning that the wide views offered by the county remain unchanged. One of the finest of these panoramas is afforded by the ancient stone fort of Rathgall, where four ramparts and a 1,000ft-diameter outer ring surround the visitor as he surveys tens of thousands of rich acres which spread from below his feet to the skyline. Old Leighlin, a once-imported monastic settlement in the north-west part of the county, offers views which extend across the Barrow Valley and rolling miles of land to the east-coast barrier of mountainous Co Wicklow. Places of historic interest in Carlow include St Mullin's, sited near the River Barrow in an area scattered with ancient remains; Ballymoone Castle, an early Anglo-Norman stronghold sited about 2m east of Muine Beg in western Carlow; the dolmens at Tobinstown and Brown's Hill – the latter of which boasts the largest capstone in Europe.

The mild area that includes Carlow and Co Kilkenny (to the west) is the Irish pleasance, a placid patchwork of pasture and tillage sheltered from the Atlantic weather by strategic ranges of hills. Mount Leinster and the Blackstairs Mountains stride between Carlow and Wexford in the east, the Slieveardagh and Booley hills rise along the boundary which divides the Munster county of Tipperary from Leinster's Co Kilkenny and Laois, while Mount Brandon looms above Graiguenamanagh – 'the village of monks' – in Kilkenny. The picture is completed by a group of low, bare hills which rise west of Carlow town. This Carlow–Kilkenny hinterland is split by a trio of rivers: the Slaney in the east, the Barrow in the middle, and the Nore in the west. First-time visitors to the region are invariably impressed by its atmosphere of peace and age-old settlement, and it is difficult to believe that this tranquillity is the aftermath of early, blood-sodden struggles. Co Kilkenny itself covers the south-west corner of the province and is the most typical example of the hinterland country. It is too full of interest to describe adequately in the space available here; suffice to say that the visitor must seek his own ways through its wayward lanes between compact, green landscapes. He will be delighted by his discoveries – magnificently ruined Jerpoint Abbey near Thomastown in the county's heart; Kells Priory, a few miles to the north west of this; Graiguenamanagh Abbey, overlooking the eastern border with Carlow; the ancient friary and castle of Inistioge, a town sited on a delightfully wooded stretch of the River Nore. Kilkenny city itself is saturated with history and preserves memories of a bright, hopeful period between 1642 and 1649, when the Confederation of Kilkenny met to unite the 'old English' with the Irish in defence of their faith and support of the Stuart cause.

Culture of the south east
Leinster's south-eastern corner is formed by Wexford, a county which shows a basic ethnical difference from all the other divisions in Ireland. This individuality is due to the very mixed descent of its population. Norsemen came

GATEWAY TO IRELAND

A well-known attraction of the Wicklow Mountains is Powerscourt Waterfall, a spectacular feature formed by the Dargle River as it plunges 300ft from a precipice.

here in the 9thc, and the occupying Norman armies brought Welsh and Flemish nationals with them. Intermarriage between the various invading aliens and native Gaels resulted in a blending of cultures through which two dominant racial traits survived – Norse seafaring and Norman thrift, good husbandry, respect for law, and a talent for organization. Long after this mixing process was complete came an event which still lurks at the back of every Wexfordman's mind – the 1798 Insurrection. This began when yeomen burned the Catholic chapel of Boolevogue, inciting priests and people to unite in an offensive war which was protracted, ferocious, and mainly fought on Wexford's soil. The county often claims a monopoly in this heroic stand, but it was by no means alone. Other Leinster counties played important parts, and thousands of insurgents mustered in the Ulster counties of Down and Antrim.

Links with the sea

Wexford's south and east coasts offer some of the finest sea angling in Europe, and Rosslare Harbour – south of Wexford Harbour on the eastern shore – is particularly noted by enthusiasts of the sport. South of Rosslare is Carnsore Point round which the east coast suddenly bends to run west via a confusion of bays and promontories. West of Carnsore is the perfect little fishing village of Kilmore, then the great bight of Ballyteige Bay before the ends-of-the-earth atmosphere of isolated Hook Head, which extends along the eastern side of Waterford Harbour. Countless hundreds of Wexford men have followed the Norse seafaring tradition and made their names in marine chronicles, but one of the best known of these was Commodore John Barry, founder of the American Navy. He is commemorated by a statue in Wexford town. The inland regions of the county are often considered 'models' of agricultural development, a reputation which owes little to the relatively poor ground and everything to the diligence of its farmers. At the heart of Co Wexford is Enniscorthy, considered one of the most beautifully-sited towns in Ireland. It stands on the mature River Slaney and features a massive castle containing a folk museum; an aristocratic, Pugin-designed cathedral on the steepest hill; and an old river bridge.

The Wicklow Mountains

Mountainous Wicklow guards a section of the east coast between Co Dublin in the north and Co Wexford in the south. Its massive, peat-covered granite domes create splendid mountain fastnesses and give the county a higher proportion of elevated land than any other division in the country. About 26 per cent of the land area is over the 1,000ft mark, and the magnificent Wicklow Mountains form a 40m chain which extends from the suburbs of Dublin city to the Wexford foothills. In some places the range has a breadth of 20m. Its high peaks include the hulking shapes of 2,783ft Mullaghcleevaun and 3,039ft Lugnaquilla – the highest mountain in Leinster. In contrast to these is the shapely quartzite cone of the 1,659ft Great Sugarloaf, rising above the picturesque Glen of the Downs. The latter is just one of the beautiful valleys and gorges which are a speciality of Wicklow – deep rifts in the mountains mauve with heather, gold with dwarf furze, and rusty with dried bracken in the winter months. Their wild sides are noisy with birdsong and the sound of galloping water, while their mysteries are accentuated by age-old ruins and sudden spectaculars. Feefert Church in beautiful Glendalough watches over the graves of O Toole princes and broken headstones; Powerscourt Waterfall hurls itself from 300ft near Enniskerry in the north part of the range; the solemn amphitheatre of the Glen of Imaal broods in the shadow of Lugnaquilla in the dense centre of the range. High, small lakes are cradled mirror-like between the granite folds, and the road between Woodenbridge and Aughrim traces the chattering course of the Avoca River. Near Ashford, which lies on the mid-eastern side of the range, are the exotic eucalyptus trees of Mount Usher Demesne and the Devil's Glen – a startling combination of beetling crags, hanging woods, and churning waters which charge through a defile like a rush of shock troops. In contrast are the desolate, open moorlands, green coastal farmlands, and the flat wilderness of Calary Bog. Many years ago this county was a natural fortress for rebels, the lair of bloodthirsty men who would as soon cut the throat of a settler as look at him.

Forestry started early in Wicklow, and the county has some 60,000 acres of land put over to the cultivation of trees. Hundreds of years ago Shillelagh oaks were exported to roof London's Westminster Hall, and there are still oak woods in existence around Shillelagh. Forests are associated with Wicklow in the same way that pastures are associated with Co Meath and boglands with Co Offaly. Although the link is extremely long standing its present-day strength is partly due to the efforts of Samuel Hayes, builder of 18th-c Avondale House near Rathdrum in the southern part of the county. Hayes was an arboriculturist who, in his capacity as member of parliament for Wicklow, introduced a Bill designed to encourage the cultivation and better preservation of trees. Avondale itself is now a superb forest centre.

The visitor to Leinster will find many ancient and beautiful things to occupy his attention, but if his stay is short he can gain an appreciation of the province by visiting just two places – Clonmacnoise and Avondale Forest Park. The former is a beautifully-sited distillation of all that is ancient in Leinster, while the latter offers superb sylvan surroundings and symbolizes Ireland's new appreciation of its assets.

Ancient Athlone, the 'gateway' town which has guarded a Shannon crossing for centuries.

Stronghold of the West

Wild Connacht, a rugged province which has remained aloof from invasion and preserved the ancient culture of pre-Norman Ireland.

Connacht has been described as the most Irish part of Ireland. It is a place of stones and sheep, mild rain and mountain mists that magnify the brooding qualities of an introspective landscape. It is the last unassailable bastion of Irish language and tradition, a natural stronghold bordered to the east by the River Shannon and to the west by the rolling immensity of the Atlantic Ocean. The strange, other-world aspects of its mountains and lakes, boglands and stone-scattered flats, is reflected in the pride of its people. Poets and painters have lived and died trying to capture the essence of this chameleon among provinces, but the ordinary people of the west – folk too involved with the business of living to chase the unobtainable – innocently display the spirit of their land in a way that words and paint can never emulate.

Not unnaturally, the history of the province is very closely related to its terrain. A traveller journeying west from the fat lands of Leinster will quickly understand why Connacht was allowed to go its own way for so long. Predatory invaders were not interested in struggling to occupy vast areas of stone, lakeland, and bog when there were easier, richer pickings to be had elsewhere. Most were content to leave everything west of the Shannon to the hardy tribes who lived there – tribes with the royalty of Ireland in their blood and the ruggedness of the landscape in their way of life. Athlone, an ancient town of considerable strategic importance, is referred to as the 'Gateway to Connacht'. By rights it should be known as the 'Gateway to Leinster', because it evolved from early fortifications raised to keep the men of Connacht on their own side of the river. The ford which once existed at this point was controlled by the western tribes and allowed them to drive their countless herds of cattle into the rich, inland plains of Leinster. Athlone's Anglo-Norman castle is the last of a long line built to defend a succession of bridges which were erected to replace the ford.

Even though the province was not held by an occupying force until fairly late in Irish history, there were occasions when a brave or foolhardy invader decided to try his luck in this virgin territory. It is interesting to examine these attempts in relation to the landscape, and to trace the gradual tailing off of the newcomers' enthusiasm for conquest as they penetrated farther into the inhospitable west. Among the first aliens to turn their attention to Ireland – discounting the very early peoples who became the Irish – were the Vikings, who swept through the vulnerable eastern parts of the country during the 8thc and left a trail of plundered monasteries behind them. It is easy to visualise them turning to the west as a further source of booty in the 9thc, their lean vessels prowling the coasts of Connacht and discharging bloodthirsty troops for occasional smash-and-grab raids when anything seemed worthy of attention. It is also easy to sense the growing dismay which they must have felt on facing the general desolation of the province, and the speed with which they must have dismissed it in favour of Leinster's soft eastern and southern coastlines. When the Normans arrived in the 12thc they drove many of the native Irish across the Shannon to the relatively infertile land of counties Leitrim and Roscommon – hard, unfriendly places of little interest to an occupying people. Eventually the Anglo-Norman barons in Ireland broke their king's faith and crossed the Shannon to add Connacht to their conquests, but it took them well over a century to acquire any real hold over the region. Here again they lost heart as they moved farther west. The visitor will find abundant evidence of their occupation in the fairly gentle lands that border the Shannon, but such traces become more difficult to find inside the province, and finally vanish altogether in the far west. Ireland in general has the well-attested faculty of assimilating invaders, of absorbing their culture and blending it with her own until nothing of the alien way of life remains. In Connacht this process is particularly potent. Other parts of Ireland – such as the Leinster counties of Kilkenny, Meath, and Kildare – bear the 'Norman Country' stamp in spite of assimilation, and indeed there are some parts of Connacht for which the same could be said. However, the greater part of the province has managed to stay Irish in speech, action, and thought. It is almost as if the Normans found such difficulty in gaining a toehold in the west that they became open to the subtle forces of the culture which they intended to replace. The speed with which the 'Irishness' of the province claimed would-be conquerors is almost frightening.

The unconquerable province
Armed conquest and civil occupation by English farmers and tradesmen continued to be the order of things in Ireland for many centuries after the establishment of Norman territories, but Connacht still managed to remain unmarked by foreign influences. Queen Mary adopted a policy of land confiscation and plantation which

STRONGHOLD OF THE WEST

continued through the reigns of Elizabeth and James I as an insidious form of invasion by adventurers and land speculators. Halfway through the 17thc came Cromwell and his 'Ironsides' from the New Model Army, who ruthlessly crushed any native resistance and drove many Irish landowners west 'to Hell or Connacht'. The Lord Protector was under no illusion as to the region to which he was sending them. In the last decade of the 17thc King William put a permanent end to the aspirations of the Stuart dynasty at the Battle of the Boyne in Leinster. This action, together with the oblique, centuries-long assault on Ireland as a whole, left the native populations without natural leaders and resulted in the rise of a garrison class known as the Ascendancy. In Connacht and the rest of the country the Ascendancy ruled all that was theirs – just about everything in sight – from their great houses and mansions. It seemed that Connacht had been brought to heel at last, but before long the familiar assimilative process was once more at work. The ruling class was isolated and insecure, even schizophrenic after a fashion, and completely trapped in the self-destructive economics of greed. Mistrust was rife and the Ascendancy began to crumble. At the same time it seemed to go 'Irish' and take on, for example, the easy-going way of life which abuse and subjection had encouraged in the lives of the peasantry. By the early 20thc this ruling class was in the last stages of disintegration, and the Irish people were flexing the political muscles given to them by O Connell and Parnell in the 19thc. The Irish still held Ireland and Connacht was still untamed.

The fact that the native Irish were not only still there but also politically on the move at the beginning of this century is a great tribute to their resilience, particularly when the Great Famine of the 1840's is brought into the picture. Connacht, by nature of its landscape, had always been difficult to farm at the best of times. Not surprisingly it bore the brunt of the famine; millions of people died, and the landscape was further depopulated by the emigration of entire families who preferred to chance life in the New World of America than face the spectre of starvation at home. Only recently has the scar of that experience begun to heal – a healing considerably aided by the Land Acts made at the turn of this century, and the formation of the Irish Free State after the Anglo-Irish war fought from 1919 to 1921. It would be easy to underestimate the impact of the Free State, now the Republic of Ireland, on a people possessed of an intense sense of nationality.

Peaceful invasion

Connacht today is still wild, still passively intolerant of the loud, the fickle, and the domineering. It will accept and integrate the sensitive visitor, but will repel the blustering stranger who wishes to take over rather than share in the way it has treated invaders for centuries. While the Normans, and earlier the Vikings, were breaking their backs and spirits trying to conquer Connacht by sheer force of arms, a peaceful invasion which had been going on for centuries was continuing to penetrate the wildest, most desolate corners of the province. This was the establishment of religious settlements by holy men who wished for nothing more than peace and quiet. Connacht certainly has plenty of both. There were never any monasteries of a size to compare with those in the fertile river valleys of Munster and Leinster because the land was not capable of supporting large communities, but a few interesting foundations did evolve in the more sheltered or fertile areas. One of the most famous of these is the 12th-c abbey at Cong, near the south Co Mayo border with Galway. The abbey was built by Roderick O Connor – the last Irish king – to replace a 7th-c monastery founded on the site by Fechin of Fore. Much of the abbey's fame is due to the exquisite processional Cross of Cong, which was fashioned in oak and decorated with gilt bronze and gems by a Roscommon craftsman in 1123. The cross, which is now preserved in Dublin's National Museum, includes a large central crystal which is said to have covered a fragment of the True Cross on which Christ died. Another interesting foundation, situated to the north of Cong, is the 13th-c abbey at Ballintober; this was founded by King Cathal O Connor of Connacht and remains unique in being the only church in the English-speaking world to have maintained continuity of the mass for over 750 years.

Other fascinating remains from medieval and earlier times can be found elsewhere in the province, but the religious trend for which Connacht is best known – and suited – was that of asceticism. Its numerous islands – like the Inishbofin group off the coast of Co Galway's mountainous Connemara region – offered enough isolation to suit the strictest hermit. Perhaps Inishbofin, the main island of the group, is not really a fair example. Although it features traces of monastic buildings it is altogether too picturesque and appealing to provide an idea of the severity of existence required by the ascetics. It was also used by ordinary people, as evidenced by its 17th-c castle and bright little fishing harbour. More typical is the smaller island of Inishglora, which lies off the west coast of Co Mayo's Mullet Peninsula and preserves a remarkable series of monastic remains enclosed by a wide cashel. The most fascinating building in the group is undoubtedly the tiny, 12 by 8ft St Brendan's Chapel. The 3ft-thick walls of this early cell slope inwards towards the top of the building and are breached by a doorway which features inclined jambs. Near by are *Teampaill na Naomh* – the more recent 'Church

The impressive doorway of 12th-c Cong Abbey.

Fishing vessels moored in the picturesque island harbour of Inishbofin, Co Galway.

of the Saints' – and *Teampaill na mBan*, or the 'Church of the Women'. Also inside the enclosure are three drystone beehive huts and several stone crosses. South of Inishglora are the two uninhabited islands of North and South Inishkea, both of which carry very similar remains of ancient churches. Excavations on the site of St Columba's Church, on North Inishkea, have revealed an ancient bell and a number of early-Christian grave slabs. Lough Mask, a large lake which divides the Plains of Mayo from the Partry Mountains in the south of Co Mayo, is scattered with little islands which must have seemed ideal to the hermit trying to escape wealth and comfort. Among these is Inishmaan, a tiny speck of green which rises from the middle of the lough and carries the ruins of an ancient Celtic church. This was built by St Cormac in the 6thc, was later enlarged, and was destroyed by fire in 1227. It is strange to think that this building was already an ancient monument at the time of its destruction in the 13thc.

Island people

This story of isolation and meditation in sympathy with the natural rhythms of the sea is represented time and again along the storm-fretted west coast of Connacht, sometimes by a single cell or cross on an islet scarcely big enough to graze a cow, sometimes by a sophisticated complex of a size to make the visitor wonder where on earth the inhabitants could have found their food. It is fairly easy to understand the motives which drove early holy men to seek such deprivation, but it is difficult to work out why ordinary people should choose to struggle through life in similar environments. The well-known Aran Islands, a group of three situated between counties Galway and Clare in the mouth of Galway Bay, feature numerous prehistoric remains, ecclesiastical ruins, and the settlements of a well-established lay population. According to the ancient *Annals of the Four Masters* the islands were initially populated as the result of the first great battle fought 'in the 303rd year of the world' between the Firbolgs and the invading Dedanaans. The battle site, the great plain of southern Moytura, extends north east from Cong in south Mayo and is easily recognised by its wealth of prehistoric cairns and stone circles. The victorious Dedanaans are said to have driven the Firbolgs – who had held Ireland for some 37 years – to the security and exile of Inishmore or 'Big Island', Inishman or 'Middle Island', and Inisheer, or 'Island of the East'. During the 5thc St Enda received the descendants of these refugees into the Christian church, thereby starting a monastic tradition which has left the Arans with one of the richest collections of early ecclesiastical remains in the country. The schools on the islands gained such a reputation that people from diverse origins flooded there in their hundreds during succeeding centuries, placing a great strain on the limited food supply and consequently living very frugal lives for the sake of knowledge. In the middle ages possession of the islands became the subject of a drawn-out dispute between two Irish families. After centuries of wrangling the argument was eventually settled by the English, who built and garrisoned a strong fort which later became involved in the Cromwellian and Williamite wars. This 16th-c stronghold remained fully armed for many years.

The Irish-speaking inhabitants of the Arans have long been considered unique in that they follow a life style which has largely disappeared in the rest of Ireland. This culture has made them the subjects of popular 'romantic' interest and intense academic study, with the unfortunate – if predictable – result of intrusion by mainland influences. Every year the boat operating between Galway city and Kilronan, the largest village on Inishmore, brings interested visitors from the 'outside' world of the 20thc. It is little wonder that some islanders find their rugged existence lacking when compared with the comforts which are taken for granted a mere 30 miles or so across the water. The same boat also services the other islands in this group. The struggle for food is a hard one. Scanty crops raised on pockets of earth which have been painstakingly built up from sand and seaweed are supplemented by fish caught by men who brave the ocean in their frail *currachs*, and although it can be assumed that the boat brings 'imports' of one sort or another to the islands, life there could never be called easy. The islands and their people are realistically described in Pat Mullen's book *Man of Aran*, Tom O Flahterty's *Aranmen All*, and JM Synge's play *Riders to the Sea*.

Escape to solitude

Some 4m off the coast of Co Sligo, in the waters of north-eastern Connacht, is the island of Inishmurray. This is accessible by hired boat from Grange, and preserves a very complete early-Irish monastery thought to have been founded by St Molaise during the 6thc. The enclosing cashel is of dry-stone construction and survives in an almost perfect condition. Several small chambers and passages have been created in the 7 to 15ft thickness of the wall itself, and the area surrounded contains three small churches, three beehive cells, and three altars. One of the churches, called *Teach na Teineadh* or 'The Fire House', is said to have contained a miraculous

STRONGHOLD OF THE WEST

hearth from which fires could be kindled without the usual artificial means. Translations of the Irish names given to the other two churches are 'St Molaise's House' and 'The Mens' Church', the last-mentioned having been a burial ground for men only. An island tradition held that the corpse of a woman buried in the mens' ground would be transferred overnight to 'The Womens' Church', which is sited north west of the main cashel. Presumably the same miracle would occur in reverse if a man was buried in the womens' place. Other interesting remains include grave slabs, pillar stones, and holy wells.

Connacht in miniature

Offshore from the rocky Corraun Peninsula in Co Mayo is Achill, the largest island in the country. This is separated from the mainland by narrow Achill Sound, a thin strip of water which has been little more than a token division since the construction of the swing bridge which crosses from Achill village to a point east of the island hamlet known as Achill Sound. The islands mentioned so far have been made famous by their unusual historical remains or distinctive populations, but Achill – even though it fulfills these two criteria – is best known for its magnificent scenery. Its mountainous interior and high sea cliffs place it in the same mould as the peak-scattered Corraun Peninsula, and the sound does little to disguise the union that must have existed between the two far back in geological time. Only a very small part of the island's 36,248-acre surface is suitable for cultivation. The remainder is almost a microcosm of Connacht itself, with rocky plains and boglands broken by soaring piles of rock and heather which challenge the ocean before dropping sheer to surf-fringed beaches. This wild country is occasionally relieved by the placid stillness of trout-filled lakes, or warm little communities which have existed long enough to lie naturally in the overall scheme of the landscape. Doogort is a substantial village which stands on the island's north shore and faces across good bathing sands to Blacksod Bay and the drooping tip of the Mullet Peninsula. Slievemore mountain rises to 2,204ft west of Doogort and shelters the village from the worst of the Atlantic storms – violent explosions of wind and waves that have carved the impressive Seal Caves from the mountain's seaward flank. Keel, a typical western village with 2 miles of sandy beach, lies to the west of the magnificent Menawn Cliffs, uncompromising guardians that rise sheer from the sea to 800ft and include the fascinating Cathedral Rocks – soft stone which has been eroded into a form resembling the arcades of a great religious building. A hard, dangerous climb to the top of Mennawn is rewarded by panoramic views which extend south to encompass Clare Island, at the mouth of islet-studded Clew Bay. A frequent visitor to the island, and indeed to the west coast in general, is the basking shark. Islanders used to harpoon these giant fish from their frail *currachs*, and the shark-fishing industry which operated here was serviced by a processing factory near Keel. A walk from Keel, through Dooagh, and along the cliff path to Keem Head and Achill Head opens up some of the island's finest scenery. Close to Achill Head is 2,192ft Croaghaun, a mountain which offers fine views and drops sheer to the water's edge in several places; a picturesque tarn known as the Mermaid's Looking Glass can be seen near by. Dooega is a small community which stands on the south side of the island and offers fine bathing beaches.

South of Achill is Clare Island, the most fertile and easily farmed of any off the Irish coast. During the 19thc the Congested Districts Board bought Clare and constructed a 5m wall to separate rough mountain grazing from the arable land. At the same time it abolished the unfair 'Rundale' strip-farming system and established the tenants as peasant proprietors of individual farms. Agriculture is supplemented by fishing and seaweed harvesting. Clare's coastal scenery is pleasing and often spectacular – particularly in the west, where 1,520ft Knockmore descends precipitously to the Atlantic – but the island is best known as the one-time headquarters of Grace O Malley. The O Malleys have been associated with the island at least since the 13thc, when they bowed to the custom of the times and founded an abbey at Knockmoy, but Grace was by far the most memorable member of the family. She lived in the reign of Elizabeth I and followed the life of a piratess on both land and sea, creating an eternal niche for herself in the legends of the west with exploits as subtle as they were daring. Remains of her castle, a massive square fortress of grim aspect, still stand near the harbour at the south-east corner of the island. One of her most famous coups was a 12-month probationary marriage to Sir Richard Burke, who she dismissed after placing her own men in his castles. South of Clare the ragged coastline drops towards Galway Bay and the southern limit of Connacht in a riot of rock and sea. Here the ocean's tides swirl between peninsulas and promontories which ride out from the roots of mountains; around islets as flat as green pennies or humped with spray-soaked rocks; through channels where great sailing vessels have foundered and past catches of fish invest the water with the flattery of local memory. These are places of sanctuary, where wildlife is more common than man and where rolling seascapes are constantly interrupted by the mysterious silhouettes of islands – Caher, Friar's, Inishlackan, St Macdara's, Mweenish, Gorumna, Lettermore, and many others. Some, like Mweenish and Gorumna, are linked to other islands or the mainland by bridges; some are so isolated that it is

Fishermen towing home a basking shark caught from their frail looking currach.

STRONGHOLD OF THE WEST

surprising even the gulls can find them. Each has its own air of mystery, and many preserve the precious, salt-rimed stones which mark goals won by past seekers of solitude.

A traveller journeying inland from the Connacht coast does not need to forsake water in order to explore different landscapes. In many places he would have to change his viewpoint, alter his whole perspective to accommodate the sudden vacuum left by the absence of pounding surf and rolling grey waves, but the land of Connacht reflects the sea as if it wishes to become part of it. All around the north and west coasts of the province are long, sinuous bays which probe deep into the heart of the countryside, almost as if seeking to join the innumerable lakes that spread across the lowlands and through valleys in a vast arc around the relatively dry central region – itself scored time and again by river valleys. The sight and sound of water is ever present. Sometimes it is a mild rain that drifts across the landscape like a memory, sometimes the rippling of a mountain stream or pulse of a waterfall, and sometimes a polished lake surface ring-marked by the rises of silent trout. Then there are the bogs – valleys of stone unundated by soil and water swept from the flanks of mountains, or ancient lakes suffocated by the centuries-long accumulation of vegetation and silt. Here and there people have cut turf for the hearth, leaving beer-brown pools fringed by rustling grasses and alive with wildfowl, but often the bogs are left to the devices of their own populations – as rich a collection of flora and fauna as can be found anywhere.

Along the Shannon
Any description of Connacht's inland waters should begin with its finest river – the Shannon. This, the longest and most historic river in Ireland, rises among the northern foothills of the Iron Mountains in Ulster's Co Cavan and flows south west across the provincial border into county Leitrim. Here it joins the headwaters of mountain-dominated Lough Allen, a 7 by 3-mile lake which is the first of three great expansions in the river's bed. South of the lough is the favoured angling resort of Drumshanbo, a pleasant town which stands on the last negotiable section of the river. On leaving Lough Allen the Shannon escapes the hilly country of its birth and enters the lake-scattered lowlands that accompany it for much of its journey through the province. A short distance from Allen it joins the county border between Leitrim and Roscommon, which it follows past Lough Drumharlow to Carrick-on-Shannon – the county town of Leitrim. This inland resort stands in an attractive situation and is becoming increasingly popular with exponents of aquatic sports. Its facilities for boating and angling are excellent. South of Carrick the Shannon broadens considerably and follows a looping course past Jamestown and Drumsna before entering Loughs Boderg and Bofin. As it flows through Bofin it leaves the lakelands behind and heads towards drier lowlands that begin at

The mainland of Co Galway's Connemara region, viewed from the shores of Mweenish Island.

Roosky, a village which stands at the junction of three county boundaries. From here it follows the provincial boundary between Connacht and Leinster through Lough Forbes and between distant low hills to Ballyclare, at the head of giant Lough Ree.

The waters of Lough Ree
Ree is the second largest of the three Shannon loughs and is shared by three counties – Roscommon in Connacht, and Longford and Westmeath in Leinster. It measures 15 miles long, varies from 1 to 6 miles wide, and features an irregular shore bitten by deep, tree-bordered bays and shallow inlets. Boats can be hired for trips to the lough's many attractive little islands, the more substantial of which carry remains of ancient religious foundations. Hare Island, in the south-east corner of the lake, has the ruins of a church believed to have been founded by St Cierán before he moved south to Clonmacnoise to create his famous Leinster monastery in the 6thc. Well-preserved ruins of an early monastery and church can be seen on Saint's Island, which lies in the eastern arm of the lough, while extensive castle remains survive on a rock promontory known as Rindown. The latter, which dominates the shore of Safe Harbour, has been fortified by succeeding waves of invaders – Celts, followed by the Norsemen, and finally the Normans. Other interesting ruins survive on Nun's Island and Inchmore. The northern part of the lough is named after Clothra, sister to the legendary Queen Maeve of Connacht. Tradition has it that Clothra was killed by a stone slung by an enemy while she was bathing in the lake. Much of the land along the Shannon's course between Carrick and Lough Ree can almost be included in 'Goldsmith Country', so-called because it was known and loved by the celebrated Irish poet Oliver Goldsmith. Although he was moved across the Shannon into Leinster at a tender age, the poet was born at Elphin in the heart of Roscommon and was always a devotee of central Ireland's countryside. Soon after leaving Lough Ree the Shannon passes through the ancient 'gateway' town of Athlone, then continues south with the provincial border to pass Clonmacnoise – said to be situated in the exact centre of Ireland. The monastery that St Cierán founded here, on the Leinster bank of the river, grew to become the most important ecclesiastical and learning centre in the country. Extensive remains that have been likened to a 'Shannon-side Oxford' have survived to the present day in spite of repeated attack and destruction in the past. After passing Clonmacnoise the river leaves Roscommon, still with the provincial boundary, and flows

STRONGHOLD OF THE WEST

A rare example of the Celtic La Tène period – the Turoe Stone near Loughrea in Co Galway.

along the eastern border of Co Galway to Meelick – where three counties and the provinces of Connacht, Munster, and Leinster meet on an island. From here it runs south-west, this time along the boundary between Connacht and Munster, and enters Lough Derg. Only parts of the northern and western shores of this, the largest of the Shannon's loughs, lie in Connacht's Co Galway. Most of the 25-mile lake is shared by the Munster counties of Clare and Tipperary, between which the river flows before crossing to Limerick city and entering a long estuary. Lough Derg's marvellous scenery is due partly to its irregular shores, and partly to the rugged hills and mountains which dominate its waters on three sides. Inish Cealtra, just one of its many islands, features interesting monastic remains. The waters of Derg are now harnessed to the massive Shannon Hydro-Electric Scheme, which was started in 1925 as the first project of its type in the country, but such useage does not seem to have damaged the lough's excellent fishing.

Lakes and towns

The Shannon system occupies almost the entire eastern edge of Connacht, but it would be a mistake to concentrate on this to the exclusion of all other waters. Elsewhere in the provinces are hundreds of lakes and rivers which, although not always of a size to compare with the Shannon, are just as interesting and attractive. In the centre of southern Galway is the town of Loughrea, which is famous for ancient remains preserved in the lake of the same name. These relics are mainly *crannogs*, ancient stockaded islands built by lake dwellers who looked to the water for security against attack and as a source of food. The town itself features sparse remains of a 14th-c monastry, the ruins of an ancient Norman castle, and a fine 20th-c Catholic cathedral. West of Loughrea the low ground continues to the sheltered inland shores of Galway Bay, where the eternal battle between land and water has produced strings of little islands cut from the mainland and slender arrowheads of water which probe east between promontories and mini-peninsulas. Galway city, chief town of its namesake county, occupies a site between the sea and beautiful Lough Corrib in the north-eastern corner of the bay. Corrib and the bay are connected by the Corrib River, which flows through the town to complete a great south-to-north barrier of water which separates lonely Iar Connacht and the mountains of Connemara from the low Plains of Mayo. Before the Anglo-Normans turned their attention to the west in the 13thc, the Princes of Connacht erected a strong castle to protect a strategic ford on the Corrib River. A small settlement grew up close to a Norman stronghold which replaced the original castle, and within a short time the town was walled to serve as the type of defensive outpost which had already become familiar in the rest of the country. This was the birth of Galway city. The fourteen gates which breached the old walls seem to correspond with the fourteen families of Welsh and English extraction who became entrenched there. These families managed to maintain their settlement as an island of the English way of life for many generations, but towards the middle ages the familiar assimilative process proved victorious and pushed the town back into the Irish ways of life and language. Ancient Norman names became Irish - *eg* de Burgo to Burke – and when Cromwell came to Ireland in the 17thc he had no hesitation in dubbing the families 'the fourteen tribes of Connacht'. Trade with Spain encouraged growth and prosperity, but after a Williamite siege in 1691 Galway declined and its powerful families fragmented. In spite of this – or perhaps because of the lack of progress – the town's medieval architecture survived well into the 19thc, but most examples vanished in the next hundred years or so. Only a handful of clues to the city's past remain today, including fragments of the old wall near the Corrib River, the fabric of a few medieval buildings incorporated in recent structures, and a well-preserved house known as Lynch's Castle. Galway lost its status as a borough during the 19thc and declined even farther, but nowadays it once more possesses this status and operates several thriving minor industries – not the least being tourism.

The uncharacteristically straight northern shore of Galway Bay runs west from the city and is bordered by a road which links the coastal villages of Iar Connacht. This is a large, relatively unpopulated region of low granite hills dotted with hundreds of small lakes – an untouched area of stones, twisting rivers, and the natural geometry of dry-stone walls. Visitors are generally content to be guided by the picturesque coast road and rarely penetrate the interior of Iar Connacht – difficult country used only by its few inhabitants and the occasional field-sportsman. Here the invasion of the motor car is by no means confirmed, and the easy tread of a donkey ambling home with creels stuffed full of turf for the fire is more commonplace than the roar of an internal-combustion engine. Many of the roads are better suited to the casual progress of livestock than the wheels of an automobile, and the stable is the 'garage' of the west. It is not surprising that Iar Connacht has remained aloof from outside influences, because its natural defences are equal to the contrived strength of any fortress. South are the waters of Galway Bay, west is the storm-torn Atlantic coast, and in the north are ranks of mountain sentries which rise from the intimidating fastnesses of the Connemara region. A visitor who has managed to surmount these obstacles is then faced with the passive resistance of Iar Connacht itself, the problem of finding a way though mazes of

STRONGHOLD OF THE WEST

High summits of the Connemara district rising above a lake landscape in Iar Connacht.

rivers, across water-filled hollows big enough to be called lakes, and through trackless bogs. This is angling and wildfowling country, where walking boots are of more value than the mile-eating machines of the 20thc.

A freshwater sea

The eastern extreme of Iar Connacht is protected by Lough Corrib, the vast lake which extends 27 miles from a point north of Galway city to the mountains of Joyce's Country. Its irregular shoreline penetrates deep into mountain valleys, as if seeking to join the sea and turn this part of north-western Galway into a huge Atlantic island, and surrounds 68 square miles of water which varies from shallow to 150ft deep. Corrib is the largest lake in Connacht and, after Ulster's Lough Neagh, the second largest in Ireland. It is particularly noted for its game fishing. South of the lough the ruins of castellated Menlough Castle occupy an attractive site on the banks of the Corrib River, and a little farther north are the famous marble quarries of Angliham. Annaghdown, situated near the eastern shore some 5 miles from the southern end of the lake, features the remains of a church which once served as the seat of an ancient bishopric founded by St Brendan. North west of here the lake constricts to form a $\frac{1}{2}$-mile wide straight which turns west before expanding into the deep northern section. Near here the lowland Annagkeen Castle faces across the water to high hills and the tower of Augnanure Castle, an ancient O Flaherty stronghold near Oughterard on the west bank.

North of Oughterard the lake reaches its full width and extends a long, octopus-like arm into a still valley shadowed by mountains on every side. This offshoot of the main lough is jagged with peninsulas and promontories which confuse the vision into thinking of it as a separate lake. Claggan, situated on a dumpy little peninsula which almost cuts the arm off from the west, overlooks a tiny island nearly covered by the O Flaherty's Hen Castle. Legend has it that this stronghold was built in a night and a day by a witch, who also gave the family an enchanted hen which would give them a constant supply of eggs so that they would never starve during a siege. The end of the story is reminiscent of folk tales of many other countries, and relates how the castle met its downfall when the family tired of eggs and killed the fowl for its meat. Attractive though the legend is, cold history states that the stronghold – also known as Castle Kirke – was built by the 13th-c High King of Ireland and King of Connacht, Rory O Connor. Doorus Peninsula is a slender tongue of land which penetrates 2 miles into the lough from the north shore and softens the view with its dense woodland. At the head of Doorus is the delightful hamlet of Cornamona, which stands at the western end of a natural limestone 'bridge' separating northern Lough Corrib from extensive Lough Mask. The rock which forms this isthmus is honeycombed with tunnels and caves which provide access, preferably with a guide, to the underground river which links the lakes. Clonbur stands at the centre of the isthmus, and on the shores of Lough Corrib at the eastern end of the 'bridge' is the ancient abbey at Cong, in Co Mayo. The border between Mayo and Galway cuts across the isthmus, and a dry canal which was intended as a surface link between Corrib and Lough Mask was built as a famine-relief venture. Unfortunately the porosity of the limestone had not been considered, and the water disappeared from the canal soon after it was flooded. The most notable of the many islands that speckle the surface of Corrib are Inchiquin, Inishdoorus, and Inchagoill, all of which lie in the northern section and feature interesting remains. Boats can be hired from Oughterard and Cong.

The northern continuation of the barrier created between the central plain and the western wildernesses by Lough and River Corrib is Lough Mask. Although considerably smaller than its neighbour, this 10- by 4-mile lake offers some spectacular scenery, superb fishing prospects, and many objects of antiquarian interest. The Irish-speaking community of Tourmakeady village stands on the west shore in the shadow of the Partry Mountains, while a short distance from the eastern shore is the angling resort of Ballinrobe. Of particular interest in the latter are the remains of a church which once served an ancient Augustinian monastery. Lough Mask House stands south of Ballinrobe and was once the home of Captain Boycott, whose treatment of Lord Erne's tenants and their way of dealing with him furnished the English language with a new word. It is said that even the postman refused to deliver letters which bore his name. Close to the eastern shore in south Mask is the lake's largest island, Inishcoog, which is linked to the mainland by a bridge and contains fascinating ecclesiastical remains. Close by are the ruins of a castle which is said to have stood on a separate islet before the water level fell. Deep in the mountain fastnesses west of Lough Mask is Lough Nafooey, an enchanting little lake often described as the most attractive in Ireland. Lough Carra lies north east of Mask and forms the northern end of the watery barrier started many miles south by the Corrib River's confluence with Galway Bay. Near the shore are ruins of a castle and friary which were founded by Adam de Staunton in the 13thc. A forestry plantation which now grows beside Carra covers the old estates of Moore Hall, one-time home of the novelist George Moore. He died in

STRONGHOLD OF THE WEST

The burnt-out ruin of Moore Hall, one-time home of the novelist George Moore. This illustration has been taken from an early reference, and the small pines seen in the foreground now make up a substantial plantation.

1933, and his ashes were buried beneath a cairn on the lough's Castle Island at his own request. A patient searcher can still find the ruins of the house, which was burnt after the novelist's death, amid the trees of the plantation.

Search for a fish

About 11 miles north of Carra and east of Westport, a coastal town at the head of Clew Bay, is Castlebar – the county town of Mayo. Westport lies in a wooded hollow and features the beautiful demesne of the Marquess of Sligo. It is well known for its associations with the novelist George A Birmingham (Cannon Hannay), who was Rector here and described many local features in his books. Castlebar, on the other hand, is sited in a fairly featureless region which is saved by the picturesque qualities of a few little loughs, but is itself a pleasant town full of interesting and well-made buildings. It received a charter from James I in 1613, was captured by Confederate Irish forces 28 years later, and was the place where English troops were routed by a French force in the 18th-c 'Castlebar Races'. Some miles to the north of the town are the Loughs Cullin and Conn. A narrow, rocky channel which connects these lakes can be seen at Pontoon, a favoured angling resort set in the middle of a narrow isthmus between the two waters, and fishing enthusiasts come from all over to hunt the famous Lough Conn fish. A pike caught here weighed in at an unofficial record of 53lbs. Several attractive islands dot the 8-mile long surface of Conn, and the northern part of the lake is half separated from the rest by the Errew Peninsula. A rough road along the peninsula leads to the ruins of 15th-c Errew Abbey, which was built on the site of a Celtic foundation created in the 6thc. About halfway between the northern shores of Lough Conn and attractive Killala Bay, which penetrates deep inland from Connacht's northern coast, is the town of Ballina. This is an interesting place with a 19th-c cathedral on the banks of the Moy, sparse remains of a 15th-c friary, and a well in which St Patrick is said to have baptized converts. The mountainous country west of Ballina features many attractive rivers and lakes, some of which preserve ancient bankside and island remains, but the visitor can best enjoy these by discovering them himself. Roads here are few, and the person who takes the trouble to explore this vast, sparsely populated region will be rewarded with breathtaking views which show Connacht as it really is.

East of Ballina are the lakes and rivers of the Ox or Slieve Gamph Mountains, most of which are in Co Sligo. The most interesting lake here is tiny Lough Achree, which was formed by an earthquake in 1490 and is often described as Ireland's youngest lake. Several small but attractive loughs lie east of the range between the villages of Lavagh and Ballymote. South east of the mountains, near the border between Co Sligo and Co Roscommon, is the southernmost corner of a triangle formed by three notable waters. These are Lough Gara in the south, Lough Key farther east in Roscommon, and Lough Arrow just north of Key in Co Sligo. The town of Boyle lies south of the Curlew Mountains near Lough Key and is noted for its 12th-c abbey remains. Gara is famous for its prehistoric lake dwellings, and Key lies in the luxurious depths of the forest park which cloaks its banks. One of its islands preserves early monastic remains. The largest of the three lakes is Arrow, an extensive sheet of water with several islands and an attractively irregular shoreline. Of particular interest here is the lough-side Dominican friary of Ballindoon, which was founded in the 16thc and includes an unusual tower built with superimposed rows of arcades within the church. Inishmore island rises close to the friary's shore site and also features ecclesiastical remains.

Yeats country

The last of Connacht's most important lakes is delightful Lough Gill, which lies considerably north of Lough Key and a little to the east of Sligo town in a picturesque basin lined with thick woodland on three sides. Its 5- by $1\frac{1}{2}$-mile extent is not over-large by Connacht standards, but its setting is of an almost unique beauty and is said to rival that of Munster's famous Killarney Lakes. The surrounding area offers a rich bonus of interesting historic and prehistoric remains. Gill is linked to the sea at Sligo Bay by a $2\frac{1}{2}$ mile stretch of river which passes through Sligo town and is lined by the woodlands and lawns of breathtaking demesnes. Hazlewood, on the north bank, is noted for its varied flora and is considered one of the finest country estates in Ireland. On the opposite bank of the river is Cairns Hill – so-called because it is surmounted by two cairns, a pair of cashels, and a stone circle – while near by is a simple altar at the holy well of Tobernalt. This was one of several places used for worship during the period when the Catholic faith was proscribed in Ireland, and it is still an object of pilgrimage. Lough Gill itself has well-attested connections with the celebrated poet W B Yeats, who used to spend boyhood holidays with an uncle in Sligo and wrote many of his best-known poems from the heart-felt emotions which the district inspired in him. The tiny island of Innisfree was the subject of his popular *Lake Isle of Innisfree*, and the *Fiddler of Dooney* celebrates Dooney Rock, which is situated on the south shore of Gill and offers a splendid view of the lough. Cottage Island preserves the ruins of a church, and the 42-acre Church Island features the remains of a foundation said to have been created by St Colman in the 6thc. The town of Sligo, perhaps the most important centre in the north-western part of Ireland, stands on a wooded plain near the head of Sligo Bay. In ancient

STRONGHOLD OF THE WEST

Carpets of flowers in the attractive forest park which cloaks the banks of Co Roscommon's Lough Key.

times all travellers wishing to journey north on the west-coast route had to ford the Garavogue here, so the site acquired an immense strategic importance which many people thought worth fighting over. Minimal traces of a castle which guarded the ford can still be seen. The first recorded evidence of a settlement appears in a 9th-c account of a Norse raid, but Sligo did not achieve any great importance as a town until after the construction of its castle *c* 1245 by Maurice Fitzgerald – the Earl of Kildare. During the 17thc it was taken by the forces of Sir Frederick Hamilton, and four years later it fell into the hands of Cromwellian forces. Among Sligo's most interesting features are the outstanding remains of an abbey founded by Maurice Fitzgerald around the same time as he built his stronghold. During the 15th-c the foundation was severely damaged by fire and had to be largely rebuilt, but its present ruinous condition dates from Hamilton's sack of the town some two centuries later in 1641. Considerable ruins which have survived war and weather include the domestic buildings as well as the abbey church and Chapter house, and display examples of work from both the 13th and 15thc.

Tombs and battlegrounds

South west of Sligo is Carrowmore, a low hill crowned by the most extensive group of megalithic antiquities to be found anywhere in Ireland or the British Isles. Included here are burial monuments in all stages of preservation, from unexcavated cairns to barely-recognisable circles of kerb stones. Tradition holds that the hill was the burial place of those slain in the second and final battle between the Firbolg and the De danaan – a good 200 years before the coming of the Celts. The first battle is said to have been fought near Cong in Co Mayo, but opinions on the subject vary. Farther west on the summit of 1,078ft Knocknarea is a gigantic cairn which tradition holds to be the tomb of legendary Queen Maeve, the 1st-c ruler of Connacht who managed to plunge a large part of Ireland into bloody war in her attempts to steal Ulster's fabulous Brown Bull of Cooley. Strandhill, a seaside resort dominated by Knocknarea, lies about 5 miles west of Sligo and offers two fine sandy beaches. North of the town is Drumcliff, the burial place of W B Yeats, while north and east is a great mass of mountains which covers northern Leitrim and spreads across the provincial border into Ulster. The northernmost peaks of the group form the Dartry range and include Ben Bulben, the 1,722ft 'Table Mountain' of Ireland. Its long, flattened top provides an immediate answer to any question as to the origin of this nickname. The highest peaks of the range are 2,113ft Truskmore and 2,007ft Cloghcorragh. Manorhamilton stands at the junction of four attractive valleys which quarter Leitrim's mountains, and is surrounded by the striking limestone scenery peculiar to the region. The western valley penetrates the Dartrys and contains beautiful Glencar Lough, a secluded lake fed by delicate waterfalls and set in the heart of some of Ireland's loveliest scenery. Glenade Lough lies deep in a valley which splits the mountains from south-east to north-west, and is completely dominated by the summits which tower over its shores from both sides. The other two valleys cut north-east and east on respective courses across the border into Ulster. South west of Manorhamilton, near Lough Gill, is the quiet River Bonet village of Dromahair. The O Rourke castle here is said to have been the place from which Dervorgilla – Ireland's 'Helen of Troy' – eloped with King Diarmaid MacMurrough of Leinster. MacMurrough's request for Norman aid was refused by Henry II, but was eventually used as an excuse for the Anglo-Norman invasion of Ireland which brought nearly eight centuries of strife. Whether Dromahair was associated with the factual basis of the story is a matter for conjecture, but there is no dispute over Connacht's royal connections; the High Kings who ruled Ireland from Tara in Meath came from this part of the province centuries before Norman occupation. The southern limit of the Leitrim heights is formed by the Iron Mountains, which tower above the east shore of Lough Allen and cross the boundary into Ulster. This range is balanced by a somewhat lower group on the western edge of the lough, shared by counties Sligo, Leitrim, and Roscommon.

South Leitrim is a place of plains and river valleys, with relatively open landscapes that extend south and east to cover the whole of central Connacht. Here

STRONGHOLD OF THE WEST

The strange outline of Co Sligo's Ben Bulben, which rises from the Dartry range and is known as 'The Table Mountain of Ireland'.

are the stony fields, bogs, and heaths of Ireland's central plain, a vast expanse of undulating limestone of which central Connacht forms the western extreme. This type of countryside intrudes into southern Sligo, spreads across south-east Mayo, covers the whole of Roscommon, and takes up almost all of Galway. Two of the most important 'plains' towns are Tuam and Ballinasloe, both in Co Galway. Tuam, the ecclesiastical capital of Connacht, is the seat of a Catholic archbishopric and a Protestant bishopric. St Jarlath originally founded the see in the 6th-c. The Protestant Cathedral of St Mary was built c 1152 by King Turlough O Connor of Connacht, and the sanctuary of the original building is preserved in the much altered and extended structure which stands today. The Catholic cathedral is of neo-gothick design. Tuam was once a centre of the O Connor family's power, and the town preserves many interesting buildings. Ballinasloe, a thriving market community in south-eastern Galway, was a place of great importance in ancient times and is still famous for its livestock fairs. Remains of a castle survive in the town, and a little to the south are the extensive ruins of 15th-c Clontuskert Abbey. To the east the plains are bordered by the Shannon, but in the north, west, and south they are fringed by ranges of high hills and mountains. West of Leitrim's ranges are the Slieve Gamph or Ox Mountains, which form a curving antithesis to the lowlands of central Co Sligo. The rugged little Curlew Mountains straddle the Sligo border south of Lough Arrow, and are echoed by a range of hills which runs west from Lough Gara into Co Mayo.

The holy mountain

West of Co Mayo's Lough Conn is the Nephin Beg group – over 200 square miles of the loneliest, wildest, and most awesome country in Ireland, where jagged peaks stride west to the Corraun Peninsula and face the mountains of Achill Island across the narrow division of Achill Sound. Nephin Beg mountain rises to 2,646ft from the eastern end of the range, and many of the other summits exceed the magical 2,000ft mark. South of the Nephin Begs and Clew Bay is the Murrisk country, where 2,510ft Croagh Patrick stands with all the dignity and isolation to be expected of the 'Holy Mountain' of Ireland. St Patrick is said to have climbed to the mountain's striking quartzite cone in order to spend the 40 days of Lent in lonely fast and meditation. Tradition has attached many local features to the miraculous deeds enacted by the saint during his stay here, not the least being his creation of Lough Nacorra by hurling a demon from the mountain side, and the permanent exile of all venomous creatures from Ireland. Many religious remains can be seen on the mountain, which is still the object of pilgrimage by devotees who often pursue the route with bare feet. Farther south the high Mweelrea Mountains dominate attractive Killary Harbour and merge east into the larger Partry range, which includes many peaks of over 2,000ft and shadows Lough Nafooey to the south of the border between counties Mayo and Galway. South of the county boundary are the rocky summits and inward-looking valleys of western Galway, a vast confusion of mountains and troughs forced from the land by intense volcanic activity and scoured by the irresistible progress of glaciers. Here is Joyce's Country, a rugged district which takes its name from an ancient Welsh family whose descendants still live there; the high ranges of Maamturk, Corcogemore, and the Twelve Bens of the Connemara region; the Connemara itself, famed for its fractured coastline, sturdy ponies, and ancient remains. Clifden, the 'capital' of Connemara, is a pleasant stone-built town which stands at the head of attractive Ardbear Bay and forms a good touring centre within reach of mountains to the north and the low lakelands of Iar Connacht to the south. Other good centres are Letterfrack, at the head of Ballynakill Bay; Leenane, on the south shore of fjord-like Killary Harbour; and Louisburgh, in the north-western part of the Murrisk Peninsula.

This, then, is a brief sketch of Connacht – a province which so far has managed to avoid the industrial wastelands and massive urban sprawls of modern progress. Whether or not it can continue to stand apart is a matter for concern. Tourism has already arrived and brought great benefits to depressed areas, but it is easy to visualize the trickle of visitors becoming a flood powerful enough to engulf even Connacht's well-tried individuality. Fortunately there is evidence of concern in the attitudes of those who guide tourism in Ireland, so the province may be protected from the worse aspects of 20th-c travel. Another key question concerns the exploitation of natural resources. Momentous possibilities such as the discovery of gas off the coast or mineral wealth inland could transform some of the province's finest countryside into deserts of machinery and workings. Nobody can pretend that Connacht does not need something to revitalize its economy, but whatever change is made should be encouraged to grow naturally from the intense community feeling that already exists. Perhaps in this way the spirit of Connacht can be preserved for future generations, while the wealth of the province is increased.

The Face of Solitude

... in Ulster, a province which has known great fame and greater tragedy; a place robbed of its people by famine and the promise of a new life across the Atlantic.

Newcastle, a town huddled beneath the granite domes and peaks of Co Down's venerable Mourne Mountains.

Ulster is a land of epics and folklore, a place which has inspired generations of poets and artists to translate its contrasting landscapes into tumbling chains of words or the soft beauty of water-coloured paper. It is the place where the spectacular Mourne Mountains and Giant's Causeway assert hard, geological counterpoints to the golden Donegal strands and placid Fermanagh lakes; where warm, friendly people who care little for the distinctions of class have evolved a way of life as honestly stubborn as the land from which they have grown.

The ancient province of Ulster comprises the northern part of Ireland, where the country appears to bend north-east to face Scotland over a slender strip of sea which is a mere fifteen miles wide at its narrowest. This choppy moat is known as the North Channel and divides two countries with rather similar landscapes – countries with strong cultural and historical links forged by a regular exchange of adventurous men. In 1921 six of the old province's counties – Antrim, Armagh, Down, Fermanagh, Londonderry, and Tyrone – were combined under the official title of Northern Ireland and given a large measure of self-government under the British Crown. The remaining Ulster counties of Cavan and Monaghan in the south and Donegal in the north-west became part of 'Southern Ireland' or the Irish Free State, now the Irish Republic. Thus some two-thirds of the old province comprise Northern Ireland and support nine-tenths of Ulster's $1\frac{3}{4}$-million people, a population roughly equivalent to that of an average English county or a single large conurbation.

Geography of a province
Although native Irish as a spoken tongue has all but vanished from the Northern Ireland counties it is maintained as part of an older way of life in two *Gaeltacht*, or designated Irish-speaking, areas of western Donegal. As a general rule the more traditional features of Irish culture persist amongst the rural landscapes of the far west, while innovation and the materialism of the 20thc are more evident in the east. Counties Armagh, Antrim, and Down occupy the north-eastern part of the province and encompass an area which includes Belfast and Armagh – respectively the political and commercial capital of Northern Ireland, and the historic ecclesiastical capital of all Ireland for both Roman Catholics and Episcopalians. The location of these capitals is an indication of the relative prosperity of the east and the area's proximity to Great Britain. At many periods this part of Ulster has been dominant in the affairs of the province and the country as a whole.

Ulster's landscapes show striking scenic contrasts and include a great variety of hills and lakes, boglands brown with wind-dried grasses, and a matchless coast which combines the spectacular with the peaceful. Clusters of hills linked by green lowlands scored by rivers and dotted with numerous lakes are bounded on three sides by a hungry ocean which has chewed the coastline into a confusion of peninsulas and islands. Perhaps the most individual and certainly the most isolated of the latter include Tory, off the Donegal shore, and Rathlin, off the northern coast of Antrim. An infinite variety of rocky headlands and long, sandy beaches faces the sea between penetrating tidal inlets and little fishing villages mellowed by the mild – if windy – seaboard climate. Although its proximity to the sea brings a high average rainfall to this area the springtime is relatively dry, making April and May the most glorious months of the year. Local winter temperatures are a little lower than those in the south of Ireland. In common with the rest of Ireland the Ulster uplands culminate towards the coast and greet the ocean with grassy flanks and rocky faces that are washed by the tide. In the east 2,796ft Slieve Donard rises among the striking cluster of granite domes which form the Mourne Mountains and drops suddenly into the sea at Newcastle in Co Down, while on the west coast the majestic coloured cliffs of Slieve League plummet into Donegal Bay from nearly 2,000ft.

The Ulster hill masses are a continuation of the Highlands and Uplands of Scotland, which are raggedly divided by lochs, straths, and glens partly drowned by the sea. Soft sandstones in the Belfast and Londonderry regions have eroded to form similar sea lochs. The southern edge of the Scottish Highlands dives into the sea to re-emerge as the Sperrin Mountains in south Derry and north Tyrone, naked summits which take on a Highland majesty when they bloom with late-summer heather. Similarly, the northern edge of the Scottish Southern Uplands continues in the green slopes of an escarpment that runs south west from the Co Down side of Belfast Lough.

Five of Northern Ireland's six counties meet in Lough Neagh, a vast expanse of fresh water which covers 153sqm and is fed by thirteen rivers. The Lough Neagh basin and lower Bann Valley form a small northern lowland, where the collapsed central part of a great mass of Tertiary lava has created a 50m-long by 35m-wide depression in which the waters of the lough have collected.

THE FACE OF SOLITUDE

This remarkable topographical feature represents the impingement of volcanic outpourings associated with the Inner Hebrides, the Faroes, and Iceland. On both sides, east and west, the edges of the lava are tilted up to form some of the province's most famous landmarks – the terraced sea cliffs of the Antrim coast; Ben Madigan (or Cavehill) which overlooks Belfast; the high crest of Binevenagh, a stern guard dominating the mouth of Lough Foyle – bright with cushion pink and other Alpine flowers in the spring. Other volcanic relics include Antrim's Slemish – the tough neck of a volcano left as an isolated hill by erosion – and the geometric stacks and pillars of the famous Giant's Causeway. The chalk that underlies the lava is reminiscent of England's gentle downlands, and the white cliffs of the Antrim coast are hardly less memorable than those of Dover. A unique and striking feature of these cliffs is the juxtaposition of the chalk and the overlying black basalts which have preserved it against erosion. Much of this superb coastline is visible from the famous Antrim Coast Road, a scenic route which links glen with glen and passes such charming spots as Murlough Bay, where the wooded slopes are bejewelled with late primroses and early wild hyacinths in June.

Lakes and forests

South Ulster acts as a watershed from which a profusion of lakes and rivers drain into a massive drainage system known as the Erne. Through the ages the waters which flow through this system have dissolved away the limestone to produce tortuous channels, which widen into lakes and eventually empty into the lovely, placid expanse of Lower Lough Erne. Bare limestone plateaux and hills of old red sandstone, the former famous for their caves, rise above the lakes to merge with high moorland ridges of millstone grit. However, the landforms which distinguish south Ulster more than any others are the drumlins, little streamlined hills of boulder clay left here and in the Lough Neagh basin by ice sheets grinding their way south during the last glaciation. These are strung in a broad arc which extends north east through the counties Armagh and Down, and north west into south Donegal.

The last depositions in the succession which has given the Irish landscape its physical characteristics were the turf bogs, areas where long-dead vegetation has accumulated and been prevented from decaying by its waterlogged state. These bogs cover one-sixth of the province, and in some cases are so recent in origin that man may have witnessed their beginnings. For centuries turf has been a cheap, easily-accessible fuel available to anybody with the energy to work it, and it is still cut and stacked for drying in several localities – particularly in the west. No single cause can be given for the formation of these bogs. Some are created by the infilling of lakelets among irregular deposits of glacial drift; some appear in areas subject to extensive flooding; above all, many are found in areas that were once covered by forest. Nearly all the Ulster hills are covered in blanket bog to a depth of five or six feet, and it is thought that the forests that once cloaked these naked summits disappeared during a succession of deteriorating climates between 5000 and 500 BC. From the fourth millennium BC most of the province's uplands were occupied by neolithic communities, who cleared native woodland from the better-drained sites for cultivation and grazing. Thus began the long process which was eventually to result in the almost total destruction of Ulster's forest in the 17th and 18thc, when the remaining patches of timber were felled for fuel and building. It is a fact that man has been one of the biggest single forces in the moulding of the Ulster landscape.

Nowadays man is again trying to change the landscape, but this time by re-afforesting denuded areas in a state-controlled attempt to repair past damage. Even though economic reasons have dictated the planting of exotic conifers such as the Sitka spruce, these new woodlands make a welcome contribution to the scenic variety of the hills. Several state forests were based on the parklands of great houses – known in Ulster as demesnes – where improving landlords had had the foresight to establish tree nurseries and plantations during the 18th and 19thc. Several of these are now designated forest parks and include recreational features such as nature trails and camping facilities. Tollymore, opened during 1955 as the first park of this nature in Ireland, comprises 2,000 acres of woodland in the beautiful Mourne county of Co Down. The efforts of the National Trust have ensured that several of Ulster's most scenic attractions remain unspoiled. Examples include the celebrated Giant's Causeway in Co Antrim, incomparable White Park Bay near by in Co Antrim, the wild sand dunes at Dundrum – with the Murlough nature reserve – and the Mourne coastal path in Co Down. The latter offers walkers a route carpeted with flowers and dominated by the steep Mountains of Mourne. Both the Mourne range and the Fermanagh lakelands, the latter in the western part of the province, have recently been designated areas of outstanding natural beauty.

Prehistoric landmarks

It is natural that the various activities of man through centuries past should have left their marks on the landscape. During prehistoric times the drumlin country was heavily encumbered with forests, lakelets, and bogland, and in this borderland sparse population was grouped into clans which gathered to form powerful kingdoms under the leadership of bellicose Celtic conquerors. An ancient 'travelling earthwork' known as

Even the most stout-hearted visitor hesitates to dare the Carrick-a-Rede rope bridge (NT), but local people cross quite unconcernedly.

THE FACE OF SOLITUDE

the Black Pig's Dyke runs through the area from the mouth of the Erne at west-coast Ballyshannon to south-east Armagh. Although not continuous, the earthwork is traceable in places and guards natural routes between north and south. It is thought to have been designed mainly as a defence against cattle raiding. An extension of the dyke, popularly known as The Dane's Cast, extends north along the line of the Armagh/Down boundary as far as Scarva. Many Ulster hilltops exceeding 700ft are crowned with prehistoric burial cairns which have been conspicuous landmarks since the bronze age. These were usually constructed as circular piles of boulders erected over a stone box, or cist, containing human remains and decorated clay pots which may have held foodstuffs.

While monuments of historic times are rarely of a quality to compare with those of Western Europe, some of Ulster's megalithic monuments are remarkable by any standard, even though the province does not have the great artistic displays characteristic of Leinster's Boyne Valley series. Although a few examples of such decorated hilltop graves set in round cairns can be seen here, for instance at Knockmany in Co Tyrone, the vast majority of the province's surviving megalithic tombs are gallery graves of the type known as 'court graves' because of their elaborate ceremonial entrances. These are set in long cairns placed not on hilltops but at moderate elevations in areas that had been cleared for cultivation. Portal graves, commonly called dolmens, are closely related to those of the gallery type and are architecturally very impressive when reduced to their basic elements by time and centuries of pillage. A fine example of this type is the readily-accessible Legananny Dolmen, situated near Slieve Croob in the hilly heart of Co Down. Other megalithic structures to be found in Ulster include stone circles and standing stones, a most elaborate complex of which can be seen at Beaghmore near Cookstown in Co Tyrone.

By far the most abundant of the field antiquities to be found in the province are the circular forts or raths, grass-grown ring works of earthen construction which survive amongst Ulster's cultivated fields in their thousands. These represent enclosures that surrounded farmsteads which were occupied during the first millennium of our era; those that occur in rocky areas are often built of stone and are known as *cashels*. Examples of Chieftains' headquarters, more elaborate versions of the common ring work, can be seen at Lisnagade near Scarva in Co Down, and Dunglady near Kilrea in Co Derry. A series of defensive rings on an 800ft hilltop near Londonderry encloses Grianan of Ailech, a famous royal cashel, while the hill fort of Emain Macha or Navan Fort near Armagh, another royal site, is inextricably entangled with the heroic epics and legends of ancient Ulster. Dwellings inside the raths were insubstantial and their remains are only revealed by archaeological excavation; but associated underground stone structures known as coves or souterrains are generally very well preserved. These resemble the earth houses of Scotland and the fogus of Cornwall. It is likely that they were used for the storage of perishable foodstuffs – particularly milk products, as the raths are primarily associated with communities whose economy and society were based on livestock rather than arable farming. Both legend and hard archaeological evidence associate the hill-fort and rath type of settlement with the Celtic conquerors and camp followers who came to Ireland from Great Britain and the mainland of Europe and gave the country its Gaelic language.

The Christian influence

Irish prehistory had a long, relatively undisturbed run, because the Romans never occupied the country and the full flowering of Christian art and literature did not come until the 8thc. From the 5thc onwards, however, the pagan hill-fort assembly places attracted monastic settlers intent on security, and some of these eventually developed into bishoprics. The layout of a typical monastic settlement can be seen at the excavated site of Nendrum on Mahee Island in Co Down. The most distinctive survivals from the early-Christian period are Ireland's round towers, strong pillars of masonry which performed dual service as belfries and places of refuge. Many monastic sites in the province include these structures, but none is more perfect than the fine example at Devenish, on an island in Lower Lough Erne, Co Fermanagh. The foe against which such defences were constructed was generally the Norseman, a dreaded raider who never managed to establish lasting settlements in Ulster as he did in other parts of the country. Other early-Christian monuments of interest include unusual crosses in Inishowen, Co Donegal; the High Cross and holy well at Arboe, on the Co Tyrone shore of Lough Neagh; and the ruins of several little Hiberno-Romanesque churches. An interesting example of one of the early churches can be seen on White Island in Lough Erne, where there is also a remarkable series of sculptures known as the White Island Figures, which display a strong pagan influence.

During the middle ages Gaelic-Christian culture achieved its greatest power by adapting itself to the environment and social mores of pagan Ulster. Between 1170 and 1280 the Anglo-Normans conquered and held most of Ireland, but their hold on Ulster was weak and the native pattern of life persisted everywhere except in the eastern part of the province. This had been quickly overrun by John de Courcy, who served under Henry II and whose strong castle at Carrickfergus has survived to this day. West

The fine Legananny Dolmen (NM) stands about 8m south of Ballynahinch on the slopes of Cratlieve Mountain, in Co Down.

Castlecoole in Co Fermanagh is a superb Georgian mansion by the famous architect, James Wyatt.

Ulster enlisted the aid of Norse-Gaelic mercenaries from the Western Isles of Scotland and effectively retained its independence until the chiefs of Tyrone and Tyrconnel (Donegal) were forced to surrender to English forces in 1603. Four years later the Ulster chieftains left Ireland for ever in an episode since known as the 'Flight of the Earls'. This left the province open for what is termed the Ulster Plantation, where whole families of settlers flocked to the most fertile and accessible parts of Ulster – excepting counties Antrim, Down, and Monaghan, where there had been earlier planters. The 'Plantations' were effected through 'Undertakers', who were each given up to 2,000 acres of land with the understanding that they undertook to lease small parcels of the estate to families literally 'planted' from Britain. The majority of incomers, some of whom had settled prior to 1600, were Presbyterians from south-west Scotland; many more followed after 1641, a year marked by a native rebellion which was ruthlessly quelled by Cromwell. Thirty boroughs were established in Ulster to serve as garrison points, market and fair locations, and centres of English influence. It is not surprising, therefore, to find that most Ulster towns were founded on plantation settlements. By the end of the 17thc the province had arrived at an uneasy balance between Irish and planter, Catholic and Protestant – a balance which has characterized this part of Ireland ever since.

In the year 1690 King William of Orange defeated James II in a battle fought near the River Boyne. This followed and sealed a Protestant victory at Londonderry a year earlier, when the starving inhabitants of the city were relieved from Jacobite siege by a stroke which also ensured Protestant succession to the English throne. A century later came the birth of the Protestant Orange Order; clashes between the Catholics and Protestants culminated in the Battle of the Diamond in Co Armagh in 1795 and led to the formation of an order to 'maintain the laws and peace of the country and the Protestant Constitution, and to defend the King and his heirs as long as they shall maintain the Protestant ascendancy'. Orangemen of today hold their special celebration on July 12, when processions of men wearing orange sashes and accompanied by bands parade through the towns carrying colourful banners.

Not until the second half of the 17thc did conditions in Ulster become sufficiently peaceful to allow the erection of unfortified dwellings. Domestic architecture from this period is, even so, very badly represented, although a few fortified 17th-c country houses survive in a ruined condition. Most of these were built by the 'undertakers' and take the form of a castle-type structure set in a walled enclosure or bawn. In form and name this device is peculiar to Ulster, although it does borrow some ideas on fortification from Scotland and England. All these houses date from the period between 1610 and 1625, and most are sited in counties Derry, Fermanagh, and Tyrone. Good examples elsewhere include Dalway's Bawn at Ballyhill in Co Antrim, and at Kirkistown Castle in Co Down. Among the later houses of the great landlords that have survived, either in the hands of the National Trust or the owners, are Florencecourt and Castlecoole in Fermanagh, Springhill in Derry, Castleward in Down, and the more humble Ardress House in Armagh. Their exotic Georgian elegance contrasts with the homeliness of small farmsteads and is complemented by well-planned demesnes, formal gardens, and tall park walls which assert their boundaries among the treeless fields of the countryside. Towards the end of the 18thc the linen industry created a relative prosperity which manifested itself in the comfortable houses built in vernacular Georgian style by the wealthier farmers and merchants. These buildings often displayed exteriors that were rendered and whitewashed in native fashion. Many large and distinctive merchants' houses were also built in the mid 19thc, some of which were designed by the famous Belfast architects Lanyon and Lynn.

A vanishing population
The 19thc is known for the devastating Great Famine of 1845–1847 – a grim watershed in the history and demography of Ireland and the biggest single factor contributing to the country's massive depopulation. The Irish people placed great reliance on the potato as a main food crop, and many rural communities subsisted almost entirely on this vegetable because it would ripen under the wettest conditions. This reliance resulted in total disaster when potato blight hit the country in 1845. By 1851 the population of Ireland had been reduced from $8\frac{1}{4}$- to $6\frac{1}{2}$-millions, Ulster alone losing half a million people through emigration and starvation, and the downward trend still shows itself with every census. The whole country supported a mere $4\frac{1}{2}$-million people in 1971, $1\frac{1}{2}$-million of whom lived in Northern Ireland and 200,000 in the three Irish Republic counties that make up the remainder of Ulster – Donegal, Monaghan, and Cavan. Statistics show that the number of persons living in mid and western Ulster dropped by 60 per cent between 1851 and 1971, although the population in the industrialized eastern areas has risen by 30 per cent in the same period. As a result of these demographic changes almost half of the people in Ulster are concentrated in the Belfast region.

THE FACE OF SOLITUDE

Cottages like this once made a major contribution to the Ulster landscape, but many of them have been modernized and re-roofed.

The very emptiness of Ulster's countryside exerts a powerful and somewhat ironic attraction to the discerning visitor from places where agriculture is more intensive. Compared with England and Wales the province is a deserted land. The Irish Annals record many years of famine and shortage in medieval times, and the Ulster soils – even the productive red earth derived from Antrim basalts and the brown drumlin soils of Down and Armagh – tend to be impoverished quickly by the downwash of valuable minerals if over-exposed to the weather. It is easy to understand the readiness with which 18th-c tenants and cottiers took to the cultivation of the potato, a novel and prolific food source which opened up visions of plenty. The century which followed the introduction of this new crop saw the population of Ireland leap from 5- to over 8-millions. One acre could now be made to yield sufficient food to keep a family of eight for a whole year. In many areas the wild plants and grasses which have invaded long-abandoned cultivation patches have failed to obscure the 'lazy beds', the narrow raised ridges on which potatoes were grown. The best crop yields were obtained from lea ground where the grass sod was not broken overall but simply turned or folded into strips which formed the ridges – a method of cultivation which has been practised for millennia. These old patches are particularly common among the hills.

Linen and livestock

Ulster, and in particular the eastern part of the province, has been distinguished from other parts of Ireland by a long-established tradition of industrial development. This reflects the area's close historical links with Great Britain and was originally based on the home production of flax for the manufacture of fine linen. Flax was a crop which thrived under the attention that a family-farming system could devote to its cultivation, and most of the growing processes and subsequent preparations for spinning were conducted by hand. Every little farm in the flax-growing areas had its own retting pit, a pool of stagnant water where the harvested crop was left to rot. An innocent stranger enquiring into the fascinating smell of decay that thus permeated the countryside during late summer was often told that it was the 'whiff of Donegal violets'. Modern farming in Northern Ireland is quite different and relies largely on the rearing of livestock and production of associated products. About 70 per cent of the functioning farm units are involved with animals, so it is not surprising to find that only one seventh of the available land is tilled, or that livestock and dairy produce make the largest single contribution to the Northern Irish economy in both production and export. This also explains why so much of the land is put down to grass. By English standards the size of an average farm here appears less than economically viable. Animals have been grazed on the hills for centuries, which is one of the reasons why the denuded forests never re-established themselves by natural propagation. Over the centuries, livestock has browsed on any vegetation that was remotely palatable, leaving a legacy of inedible thorn, holly, and an abundance of prickly furze on drier ground. For hundreds of years the cattle, more abundant in the past than sheep, were moved to summer hill pastures situated at a moderate altitude and typically scattered between patches of blanket bog. This custom is known as 'booleying' from the Irish word *buaile*, meaning 'milking place', and the largely unenclosed grazing areas were generally held in common – an arrangement which saved both manpower and fencing.

Empty farmlands

A great deal of the settled lowland was not enclosed until the 19th-c agrarian revolution, and the boundary thorn hedges that ring the fields with May blossom in early summer are usually little more than a century old. Trees that occasionally occur in the hedges are small and stunted because they are young compared to the great hedgerow oaks and vanishing elms of England, and because they are rooted in dry earthen banks which provide scant nourishment. Steady depopulation has left large areas of Co Donegal almost empty but for 'fossil' landscapes, criss-crossed with neglected earthern banks or tumbled stone walls that generally predate the days of permanent enclosure and are known throughout Ulster as 'ditches'. These structures mark the boundaries of settlements which might have been abandoned at any time between the Great Famine and today. Throughout Ulster and as far back as can be traced there has always been a marked preference for the isolated farmhouse and the independence associated with such a mode of existence. This is still the case, and the most representative holdings in the province remain the lone steadings, with their attractive clusters of buildings half-hidden in sheltering sycamores, beeches, or conifers – depending on the area. The average modern farm covers about 35 acres. Because every farm must have its access road the Ulster countryside is a tangle of lanes or 'loanings', attractive little thoroughfares that skirt tiny fields which have not generally changed in size since they were first enclosed during the first half of the 19thc. Farms at this time averaged about 15 acres in extent and were divided into a number of 2-acre fields to allow crop rotation. The most productive modern agricultural techniques cannot be successfully implemented in such minute areas, and it is generally considered that the amalgamation of holdings and grubbing of hedges is a prime economic need for future development.

Cottage life was centred on the hearth, where a turf fire was kept burning to provide continuous heat for comfort and cooking.

The rural house

About one quarter of all rural houses were thatched until as recently as 1950. Since then their numbers have decreased rapidly, and the visitor is hard pressed to find examples even in areas where they were once very common. Good examples do, however, exist in Co Donegal, where the old ways of life linger on and the skills of thatching with rye straw or flax are not entirely forgotten. Rye and flax are considered the best materials for this purpose (but oat straw is more commonly used), and houses sited near the windy coasts have their thatches securely roped down like the covering over a ship's hold. The most common style of farmhouse was built on a simple rectangular plan and included small windows, a chimney at the gable end, and a low-pitched roof. A typical 19th-c Donegal house comprised a single room to accommodate the entire family at the chimney end, and a byre for cattle under the same roof at the other. A little projecting wing or 'outshot' near the fire, examples of which can still be seen in mid and west Ulster, enclosed the family bed. The Ulster Folk and Transport Museum at Cultra Manor, near Holywood in Co Down, displays various types of traditional housing in 175 acres of attractive parkland. Included amongst the exhibits is an example of the kitchen-byre or open longhouse removed from Donegal – perhaps the only structure of its type now to be found in the province.

An interesting characteristic of the north-western house was the provision of a back door immediately opposite the dwelling's front entrance. Both doors had additional half-doors on the outside, and according to the state of wind the draught which fed the ever-burning turf fire – the life and soul of the home – could be controlled by opening or shutting the doors. The rubble or field-stone walls with which such buildings were constructed were thickly whitewashed both inside and out. It was rare for a dwelling of this nature to exceed one storey, and they were traditionally without ceilings. More sophisticated dwellings were divided into two or three rooms, and those that still exist generally keep to their original ground plan – although they have often gained an additional storey and a slated roof. Few areas in Ulster are able to provide serviceable roofing slates, and until cheap transport became available in the 19thc the only structures to include them were mansions, churches and public buildings, the houses of farmers and wealthy merchants, and dwellings in the main streets of some towns.

Another form of rural house existed south of a line between Glenarm and Enniskillen. This followed the general Irish model of a rectangular plan and single storey, but was roofed with scalloped (*ie* pegged-down) thatch and had a hearth in the centre of the house. The hearth separated the kitchen from the bedroom. This house had no outshot, and although it retained the half-door idea it had no back entrance. A cross wall known as the jamb or 'hollan' wall, erected between the door and fire, included a spyhole through which the housewife could keep an eye on the outside world from her fireside. The clay walls of these structures were heavily whitewashed and the scalloped thatch of their steep, hipped roofs displayed distinctive patterns formed by the securing rods used in this method of thatching. The central-chimney house is often hip-roofed but this type is rare in Ulster, though a few examples can be seen in counties Monaghan, Cavan, and southern Fermanagh. The developed central-chimney house is more typical of the province of Leinster, and in both areas appears to be associated with a more orderly and gracious way of life which evolved from historic English settlements.

The former distribution of the central-chimney house in Ulster roughly corresponds with the strongest areas of mid-Ulster dialect, derived from the speech of planters from the west of England. Similarly, the buildings with gable chimneys find their nearest parallels in the 'but-and-ben' cottages of south-west Scotland and are characteristic of the areas where Ulster-Scots dialects are spoken. The two Ulster dialects share certain common features because they retain old forms and have their roots in the heritage of a Gaelic substratum. For much the same reasons the traditional farmhouses of the province shared certain features and rarely departed from the elemental simplicity of functional plan and design. The heart of the home was always a turf fire which provided warmth and the means by which thin bread was baked, potatoes boiled, and meat and tea stewed in iron pots and pans. In all cases the houses were sited close to the main source of sustenance – the byre and midden.

Facets of living

The essentials of material culture show a large measure of adaptation to the Ulster environment, but it is possible to detect some regional differences in the cultural landscapes of areas where Irish, Scottish, or English traditions predominate. For instance, the English predilection for roses, flower gardens, and orchards is strongly reflected in the usage of the north Armagh countryside. A victim of adaptation was the half-timbered English yeoman's house, and the fireside bread oven gave way to open hearths where potato bread and soda 'farls' – quartered thin bread – were baked on the griddle, or oatcakes toasted on wrought-iron 'harnen stands'. Perhaps the most regrettable recent change in the countryside is the replacement by concrete posts of massive stone gate pillars which marked the entrances to fields and farmsteads all over Ulster. These pillars were once so common that they were chosen as a provincial symbol for the Northern Ireland Womans' Institute, for the Ulster Folk and Transport Museum, and have been used on commemorative postage stamps. In the past they were treated with an almost superstitious reverence which manifested itself in the care with which their annual coats of whitewash were applied. Their prevalence can be linked with the province's virtual lack of oak timber, which also explains the absence of oaken five-barred gates and the popularity of wrought iron gates. These could once be found in an infinite variety of styles which reflected the tastes of various landlords and the skills of scores of country blacksmiths, but they are fast vanishing in favour of mass-produced monotony.

The visitor to one of the isolated peninsulas around the Donegal coast will occasionally come across a little clustered settlement which has managed to survive in a virtually unchanged condition. Such places, including Malin Beg in the extreme west or Kearneystown in Inishowen, provide an insight into the old rural order – or rather, disorder. A feature of the old land-tenure system which went with the formless, clustered farm settlements was the changing size and ownership of minute, unfenced arable patches scattered within a demarcated area, the infield.

Situated close to the settlement – which was variously known as a town, village, or *clachan* – the infield plots were kept under almost permanent cultivation with the help of abundant animal manure, seaweed, or a combination of both. Land farther afield was held in common as rough grazing and left unenclosed. This method of land distribution was known as the rundale system, and was akin to the Scottish 'runrig' in that it was designed to ensure that all the joint tenants had a share of the better as well as the poorer land. All the tenants were kinsfolk who lived in a settlement usually named after a common ancestor. Inside his own community of 'friends' *ie* kin – one man was as good as another, and there was a rough equality. The custom of partible inheritance ensured that no matter how small a land holding was it would be subdivided amongst the tenant's co-heirs. This system eventually gave rise to diminutive holdings that were often the subject of disputes and rival claims which were stubbornly contested. The word used to describe the resulting confusion of scattered plots and access ways was 'throughother', a term now employed in Ulster to describe anything untidy or slovenly.

The 'Protestant' land-use system was based on moderately sized independent holdings and came to replace the rundale system from the 17thc onwards, but under the pressure of population after the adoption of the potato this too developed into a system where holdings became subdivided between co-heirs. The eventual result was that various parts of Ulster became characterized by very small farms and fields. In such areas as Co Down and Co Armagh the subdivision of land was economically practicable because food crops were supplemented by flax growing and the weaving of linen, but in the end it led to the existence of uneconomic holdings and keen competition for land. By 1841 the amount of arable ground per head of the population had fallen to $1\frac{1}{4}$ acres in Co Armagh.

Towns and townlands
The scale of urban development in Co Donegal can be judged by the following reference to the village of Falcarragh in a recent Development Report on the Gaeltacht area. The settlement is described as 'one of the other larger towns' of the county, although the last census showed it to have a population of only 366. In Ulster the word 'town' need not have any urban implications but can refer to a cluster of houses of any size, and it is in this sense that the term 'townland' should be understood. In areas where there has been little change both town and townland may bear the same name – *eg* Kellystown might refer to a collection of houses and at the same time to an area of ground. Townland is not a term usually found in English dictionaries, but it has much the same meaning as the word 'township' had in medieval England. Areas so designated are little territorial subdivisions, normally not much more than 300 acres in extent, into which Ulster as well as the other three Irish provinces are demarcated. Most Irish families are directly or historically connected to a particular townland and will extol the virtues of their ancestral townland with enthusiasm. Another interesting survival is the Anglo-Norman barony, a parcel of land which comprised between one sixth and one twelfth of a county and was given legal and administrative functions which it exercised through the Grand Juries. In the British Isles the criminal functions of the baronies lasted longest in Northern Ireland – in fact until 1969 – but throughout Ireland as a whole they lost most of their powers when County Councils were set up under the Local Government Act of 1898. It was partly because of the historic weaknesses of parishes and boroughs, especially in Ulster, that the Grand Juries exercised such considerable power. They represented the landed gentry and were responsible for roads, bridges, and public buildings such as courthouses. In area, and to some extent in function, the baronies corresponded with the *tuaths* – subdivisions under the old Gaelic system – but almost all traces of these petty kingdoms had disappeared by the 17thc. The kingdom of Mourne is an example of a barony based on an ancient *tuathe* which retains its proud title in popular speech. In ecclesiastical organization both Protestant and

Wrought-iron gates and whitewashed stone pillars were once typical of the Ulster countryside, but nowadays these have been largely replaced by mass-produced units and concrete posts.

THE FACE OF SOLITUDE

Cookstown, in Co Tyrone, is a 17th-c plantation settlement built along a single long street.

Catholic dioceses are approximately equal in both size and number to the counties of Ireland, although they do not precisely correspond with each other.

The evidence of names

The townlands of Ulster may be younger than the landscape but they are almost as venerable, and like the hills they keep their Gaelic names, often in anglicized or otherwise corrupted forms. When the townlands came to acquire legal title their recording in deeds and maps resulted in standardized spellings, and because only the larger farms and houses in the countryside ever bore individual names the townland's title became the postal address of most people living in it. The names thus became well known and the best means of identifying one district from another. The townland network in Ireland is the only administrative framework to have existed in a workable form through historic times. Townland names often include a prefix or suffix taken from some topographical feature such as drum or knock(hill). A smaller group of names incorporates a word indicating the nature of the local vegetation, thus the term *doire* (derry) points to the survival of many oak trees in some areas at the time when a town incorporating this word in its name was first established. Londonderry city, still known as Derry to its inhabitants, is built on a hill which was selected by St Columba for the establishment of a monastic settlement in a grove of oaks during the 6thc. In 1566 the same site was chosen for a city by English forces, and later the London Companies gave it its present name. The most frequent and widely-distributed of all elements in the names of townlands is the word bally or *baile,* meaning a place or piece of land. This is followed closely in order of frequency by other cultural designations such as 'kill' or *cill* – a cell or church – and *lis, rath,* or *dun,* an enclosure or fort. The amazing frequency with which Irish townland names are repeated, often within short distances, suggests that early society was intensely local in its organization and outlook. Also suggestive of such localism is the fact that a river such as the Co Tyrone Strule, which is itself in fact a combination of a number of other named streams, becomes the River Mourne below Newtownstewart and ultimately the River Foyle of Co Londonderry. In townland names which are English, the commonest element by far is the word 'town', which can be taken as the equivalent of the Gaelic *baile,* but its occurrence in Ulster is rare compared with other provinces. Leinster has many English-type names because of its heavy involvement with Great Britain in the middle ages, but the conquest of Ulster came much later and thus the province boasts an extremely high proportion of Gaelic placenames – higher even than Munster or Connacht. Thus Ulster, in some ways the most 'British' of all Irish provinces, retains certain elements of folk culture and idiom which hold an unexpectedly strong Irish flavour. There is another strange paradox here in the exasperation with which the fervent Ulsterman will regard an Englishman who fails to stress the correct syllables when trying to get his tongue round such Ulster placenames as Aughandunvarran, or who refers to Lond*err*y as *Lon*don'dry.

Towns are not native to Ireland but were established by Norsemen, Normans, Elizabethans, and the Stuart planters. In recent years the populations of some of the country towns have dropped, but at the same time the number of people living in towns in general has increased to the point where half the inhabitants of Ulster now reside in the urban areas. During the 17thc, a time when no settlement in the province had a population of more than 3,000, the best-known towns were Londonderry, Coleraine, Newry, Carrickfergus, Downpatrick, and Armagh. The first two were laid out on an unusual plan which indicates that they were established by London companies in the form of medieval *bastides* – walled towns intended as defence points and market places, containing a central square surrounded by a grid-pattern of streets. Market houses later erected at these places have not survived; the one at Londonderry was demolished, while that in Coleraine was replaced by a 19th-c town hall which still stands. A feature of the town hall is the Coleraine coat of arms which it displays, in which a salmon is prominently figured as a reminder of the importance of this fish to communities sited on the River Bann since prehistoric times. In fact excavations on the banks of this river, described by Edmund Spenser as the 'fishy fruitful Bann', have revealed fisherfolk dwellings which are the oldest known habitations in Ireland. As in other Ulster towns the market square in Coleraine is known as the Diamond, and the fact that many similar rectangular squares in Pennsylvanian towns are also known by this enigmatic name is a reminder of the floods of Ulster-Scots – many from Co Derry – who left for the New World in the 18thc and played a leading part in both the shaping of the American frontier and the fight for independence.

Armagh's ground plan is unique in Ulster because the curving streets in the heart of the city are a reflection of the barely-traceable rath ditch which once encircled the site of St Patrick's Cathedral. Monks and scholars reputedly thronged the settlement which existed here in early Christian times, but its wealth and fame attracted the Norsemen and later attackers who repeatedly pillaged its treasures and fired its buildings. It also suffered from

The 18th-c Lagan Canal contributed a great deal to the development of Belfast as Ulster's major east-coast port.

inter-monastic feuds and had little time to recover from successive devastations until plantation times, when it was given a new lease of life by being incorporated as a borough. Armagh Royal School was set up following a royal decree of 1608 and the community became a borough in 1613, but it was not until Archbishop Robinson – later Lord Rokeby – succeeded to the primacy in 1765 that the city began to assume much of its present character. The 18th-c imprinted its Georgian ideas of elegance on the city, and Robinson himself was responsible for building and endowing both the Armagh Library and the Observatory. The latter developed into an astronomical museum, planetarium, and lively research centre. This and the Armagh County Museum are both well worth a visit.

Shaping the towns
Apart from the port and industrial city of Belfast, most of the other Ulster towns bear the stamp of 17th- or 18th-c market communities and are laid out around a broad street or diamond which once served as a market place. Examples of the latter include some of truly ambitious dimensions, such as can be seen at Cookstown in Co Tyrone and Crossmaglen in Co Armagh. As a general rule the rival towers and spires of town churches represent at least three dominations, with the Episcopalian building in a fairly central position in the market place or high street and discreetly late-gothic in architectural style. Nonconformist meeting houses and Roman Catholic chapels are generally to be found some distance away on roads leading to the centre. It has been suggested that this arrangement prevented the devil from entering the town and disturbing episcopalian privilege. Earlier Presbyterian churches in Ulster were usually barn-like in plan and soberly classical in style, while the chapels – the building of which was proscribed under penal laws until the Emancipation of 1829 – display tall spires and ornate examples of medieval French or English gothic which reflect the romanticism of the period and the release from centuries of oppression. Thus it can be seen that churches and chapels in Ulster feature various styles which express the history and traditions of the three main elements in the province's population, *ie* Irish Catholic, English Protestant, and Scottish Presbyterian. It is only in recent years that a native style of ecclesiastical architecture has re-emerged in such chapels as those in Burt and Creeslough, Co Donegal, the designs of which mirror the clear lines of the Ulster Hills and exhibit the same qualities as the early-Christian oratories and traditional farmhouse styles.

Court and market houses are, like the churches, a typical feature of the province's towns, and being nominally undenominational they display less variation in architectural style. As a group these buildings are among the best of their period, and all the more noticeable because of the relative scarcity of other public structures in small towns where the domestic and commercial buildings are generally undistinguished. If it can be said that the various styles of church architecture reflect the divisions in Ulster's society, then it can be equally well stated that the court and market houses represent the integrating forces of the province's life. In the smaller towns these two important functions were often served by the same building, a structure usually erected between 1750 and 1850, and it is these combined court-and-market houses, in their austere, neo-classical dignity, that come closer than any other style of construction to being indigenous to urban Ulster. Most have become superfluous and many have been destroyed, damaged, or put to baser uses. Some, such as the one at Portaferry, now serve as community centres. Perhaps the two most outstanding court houses still surviving are Francis Johnson's graceful structure of 1809 at Armagh and the charming, late 18th-c building at Hillsborough in Co Down. The latter was taken into state charge in 1959 and subsequently tastefully restored. The splendid 18th-c market house at Newtownards now serves as a town hall and retains an old stone lock-up with an interesting corbelled roof. Corbelling is a prehistoric technique of building which is illustrated in several megalithic tombs, the chambers of many souterrains, and in sweat houses – the traditional Ulster equivalent of a Turkish bath. Typical examples of the latter can be seen at Tirkane and Ballydonegan in Co Londonderry.

Industrial growth
Industrial towns and villages are virtually unknown to the majority of Irish people living outside the north-east part of the country. In 1961 40 per cent of the insured population in Northern Ireland were employed in manufacturing occupations, compared with only 17 per cent of the working population in the Irish Republic. As recently as 1950 the manufacture of linen in Northern Ireland formed an industry which employed some 60,000 people, or a third of the manufacturing labour force, and linen products comprised the largest single item of export. Linen was the best-known product of Ulster for so long that it deserves more than a passing mention in any realistic account of the province. As a domestic industry based on the home cultivation of flax linen goes back many centuries, and the Ulster area was more favourable for its production than any of the other provinces because of an abundance of lime-free water such as is necessary for the

THE FACE OF SOLITUDE

process which separates the raw fibre from the flax stem. The association of Ulster with the linen industry also owes something to the encouragement given by William of Orange, and in particular to his introduction of Huguenot refugees to the province from the linen country of Flanders. Other advantages that the area had to offer included wide expanses of smooth pasture ideal for use as bleach greens, and – as the manufacture became mechanized – a ready supply of water power.

The most favoured region was the Lagan Valley. This had ready access to the developing port and market of Belfast, which replaced Carrickfergus as the chief port of the north east, particularly after the construction of the Lagan canal in 1763. In common with the seaports of western Britain Belfast developed new industries based on colonial and other overseas imports, and by 1780 the city had attracted cotton spinning. When steam power came to supplement the forces of running water the port quickly took advantage of cheap imported coal to keep abreast of the times, but it was not until after 1825 and the discovery of the wet-spinning process for the treatment of the more intractable flax that the town became a great linen metropolis. Today Northern Ireland provides one fifth of the United Kingdom's output of shirts, collars, and pyjamas, and also has factories which produce carpets, knitting, a variety of hosiery products, twine, nets, and ropes.

Ulster at work

Belfast's linen industry was securely bound to its equally-famous shipyards by numerous ropeworks and by the fact that it employed women whose wages supplemented those of the men who worked in the yard. It was not, however, until Harland and Wolff perfected the iron ship in 1862 that the shipyards acquired their world-wide reputation. The textile industries that were once so widespread throughout the province have kept their hold on towns remote from the metropolis by concentrating on the manufacture of specialized goods. The most striking example of this adaptation to changing times and needs is Londonderry, where a linen weaver called William Scott invented the ready-made shirt in the 1830's and ensured high production by employing out-of-work spinsters in the hinterland. He organized the collection and finishing of these garments in Derry which became – and still remains – a leading centre of shirt manufacture. The numerous shirt factories operating here today, as varied in shape and style as the garments which they produce, are as famous in Ulster as the old city's 17th-c walls. Another outstanding Ulster enterprise which depended on a colonial import and the deft fingers of former textile workers was the tobacco industry. This is now centred on Belfast and Ballymena, but it was a Derry man called Tom Gallaher who laid the foundation of the firm which bears his name by 'rolling' tobacco in 1857. Since 1950 the government has encouraged many new industries to put down roots in Northern Ireland, thus reducing the tragically-high level of unemployment which resulted from the decline of the older concerns and a lessening need for land workers. Growth centres such as Ballymena and Craigavon, the latter a new town formed by the amalgamation of two old linen centres (Lurgan and Portadown), have played a great part in revitalization of the province's industrial scene.

The Ulsterman

An Ulsterman may not differ physically from his fellow countrymen, but the visitor is bound to notice marked speech characteristics which immediately identify his home province. Surviving Gaelic dialects in Ulster differ from those found in other parts of Ireland in that they are more akin to the language spoken in the Hebrides, a language which was in fact taken to Scotland from the north of Ireland in the dark ages. Regional dialects of Ulster-English owe some of their characteristics to the influence of Gaelic idiom during the long period in which the two languages co-existed in the province, and their best-known form is probably the Ulster-Scots typical of areas where Scottish immigration predominated. These areas form a belt which runs from north-east Donegal, through Co Londonderry and north Tyrone, to Co Antrim and east Down. The dialect heard here has a distinctly Scottish flavour but retains archaic words and sounds which give it an unmistakable regional stamp, and it has helped to shape the general pattern of Ulster speech. The other main dialect to be heard in the province is that of mid Ulster. This is spoken over an area extending from Co Fermanagh to south Antrim and south Down, and is mainly derived from the speech of planters who came here from western England. It too includes a number of archaic features, some of which have been described as Elizabethan or Shakespearean. In west and south Ulster the mid Ulster dialect passes into sub-forms which show a stronger Gaelic influence. These include the dialect which is heard among the hills and drumlins of the border areas and which was again largely of English west-country origin. This border dialect differs both from the mid Ulster and from the form which spread north from the Irish Republic's capital city of Dublin. Despite these regional variations the common speech of Ulster has a distinctive flavour which entirely separates it from the Anglo-Irish of southern Ireland.

Cultural expression in Ulster takes the form of highly-personalized arts which have developed from centuries of folk literature and music as attractively simple as the old way of life. The essence of Ulster cannot be expressed in terms of the elaborate works produced elsewhere in the world, but is distilled in the words of its poets, the music of its country fiddlers, the instinctive touch of its painters, the uncompromising slogans of its people, and the energy of its men of action. The visitor to this ancient province will find infinitely varied landscapes largely untouched by urban sprawl. Industrial development and inventive adaptation show that this is not a backward province; yet a sense of the past is never far away.

Ulster's country fiddlers maintain a cultural tradition that has flourished for centuries.

The Sister Capitals

DUBLIN

Dublin, the capital city of the Republic of Ireland, stands at the head of Dublin Bay and encloses a large bight of the Irish Sea with two pincer-like arms. The city is divided by the River Liffey, and its Irish name – *Baile Atha Cliath,* meaning the 'town of the ford of the hurdles' – provides a clue to its early importance as a river crossing. The word 'hurdles' probably refers to a wicker structure which spanned the Liffey near the point where 19th-c Father Matthew Bridge now stands. Views to the south of the city are bounded by the Dublin Mountains, which cross the border and merge with the venerable peaks of the Wicklow range. Kippure rises to 2,473ft from the border itself and is a noted landmark. Part of Dublin's success as a community is due to its beautiful surroundings, but the city owes much of its prosperity to the sea and the river. Such products as stout, whiskey, biscuits, man-made fibres, and paper are exported from its extensive quays, and the amenity value of Dublin's estuary and waterways is being developed for leisure activities. The city's communications system includes an airport, which lies 6m north at Collinstown.

Besides its natural advantages, Dublin has the added benefit of an architectural homogeneity which has largely survived the intrusion of necessary modern development. Few medieval buildings still stand, and the overall impression is one of Georgian completeness. Efforts have been made to preserve the old fronts of buildings which have required interior modernization, but many beautiful plaster ceilings and exquisite staircases have been lost in the process of reconstruction. However, Dublin can still rejoice in the elegance of such squares as Merrion, Parnell, Fitzwilliam, and others where many interiors preserve tasteful stucco executed by masters of the craft.

In spite of its relatively small size and population of 850,000 or so, Dublin still has the feeling of a European capital. It has an atmosphere which is entirely its own, includes large areas for leisure and relaxation – *eg* St Stephen's Green and the Phoenix Park – and offers excellent facilities for shopping. In addition it provides the hotels and restaurants to be expected of a capital city, plus entertainments which include the famous Abbey Theatre. Although the typical Dublin 'Jackeen' is fast being obscured by an increasing wave of provincials, the city is still known for its characters – highly-individualistic people who can be met at any time in the markets, on the streets, or in the pubs. One of the real assets of Dublin is that the visitor can find everything that the city has to offer in a small area.

The Norsemen were the founders of the city. During the 9thc they built a fortress on the high ground now occupied by Christ Church Cathedral and Dublin Castle, south of the Liffey, and their settlement extended to the black pool *Dubhlinn* from which the city took its Norse and English name. From this and other Viking strongholds the invaders sent raiders all over the country, with the intention of completing the conquest. They ravaged monasteries and churches and left a wake of terror behind, but their legacy was not entirely one of destruction. These were the first people to establish trading centres and develop commerce in Ireland. The Norsemen found allies among the native Irish, and it is known that there were Irishmen on both sides in the 11th-c Battle of Clontarf when 'Brian Boru and the Irish' won a decisive victory. Although the Vikings were no longer masters at this time, they kept a tight hold on Dublin. Later they became converted to Christianity and built the city's first church on the site now occupied by Christ Church Cathedral, and even managed to extend their rule to the area north of the Liffey. St Michan's, the one-time parish church of this area, was founded in 1095; Oxmantown Road still preserves the name by which the invaders were generally known – Ostmen.

In 1171 the Anglo-Normans, under the Earl of Pembroke (Strongbow), and with the help of Leinster's King Dermot McMurrough, successfully took and held the city. Henry II established his feudal rights over the invaders and their conquests in 1172, and received the submission of Irish chieftains on the site of the present College Green, which was formerly known as Hoggen Green. To consolidate, Henry then gave Dublin to the men of Bristol by charter and made it the centre of English government and The Pale – a fortified Anglo-Norman territory. Dublin was attacked many times by the O Tooles and O Byrnes, who had hidden in the Wicklow Mountains, and King John ordered the building of a castle. Later the city was encircled by strong walls, fragments of which can still be seen at St Audoen's Arch and Dublin Castle.

During the English civil war the city remained loyal to King Charles until 1647, when it surrendered to parliament.

The city of Dublin grew up round a strategic ford on the River Liffey.

Some two years later the Marquess of Ormonde made an ill-fated attempt to regain the city at the Battle of Rathmines. During the Williamite wars Dublin remained loyal to the Stuart King James II, who struck his debased coinage – 'brass money' – at a mint which stood on the site now occupied by 27 Capel Street.

The 17thc saw Dublin's rise to commercial importance, increased development of trade with England, and the building of new houses for noblemen and commoners alike. The Duke of Ormonde – the Viceroy – planned the Phoenix Park to: 'keep up the splendour of the government.' Although the 17thc saw a great deal of growth, Dublin owes its great public buildings and the best of its residential mansions to the 18thc. Both native and imported architects of unusual skill and vision, stucco workers, and sculptors vied to erect and embellish the fine buildings which are still admired today. Even though many of the structures have been restored and remodelled after destruction by bullet and fire, they still amaze and please the first-time visitor.

After the bitterly-contested Act of Union was established in 1800 the city began to decline. The old aristocratic influence began to die, parliament ceased to exist, and any reasons the noblemen had to maintain their beautiful mansions in Dublin vanished. Resentment and the danger of revolution were aggravated by an erosion of identity and dignity.

This situation resulted in the rise of numerous patriots, whose names live on in the public memory, on statues and wall plaques, and in the names of streets and squares. Many buildings are associated with these times. Leinster House, seat of *Dáil Éireann* (the Irish Parliament), was once the home of Lord Edward Fitzgerald, who was arrested during the 1798 Insurrection and died of wounds received during his capture. A tablet at St Catherine's Church marks the site of the scaffold on which Robert Emmet was hanged in 1803. In 1873 the Rotunda was the venue for the first great Home Rule

DUBLIN

conference. These events had little effect on the outward appearance of the city, but the uprising of Easter week in 1916 marked the start of a new and more destructive phase.

The General Post Office in Lower O Connell Street was seized for use as the headquarters of the Rising, and in the ensuing struggle this building and several adjoining streets were swept by fire. In the immediate years which followed the conditions of civil war were never absent. May 1921 saw the seizure and burning of the Custom House. As far as Great Britain was concerned the conflict was brought to an end with a treaty which was ratified by *Dáil Éireann*, the representative parliament of Ireland, in 1922. However, a substantial number of leaders in the Irish movement were not satisfied, and took up arms against their former comrades. The Four Courts were seized and held for two months in 1922, and were bombarded by troops of the newly-constituted government of the Free State. During this conflict between the national government and the anti-treatyites the east side and some parts of the west side of Upper O Connell Street were completely destroyed by fire.

The fine buildings that were damaged during this period have since been restored, although some have been modified to suit new purposes. Some of their original grandeur has been lost, due to necessary modern developments in the city, but along the river's fine quays the splendid proportions and fine domes of Gandon's masterpieces, the Custom House and the Four Courts, can still be seen. To the north in O Connell Street is the impressive frontage to the General Post Office, a survival of Francis Johnston's work. The splendid façade of Trinity College and the Bank of Ireland – the latter formerly the parliament buildings – form a noble pair beside College Green on the other side of the Liffey.

Dublin's suburbs and environs are listed under their own names in the main gazetteer section of this book. See these and the Touring Atlas for further information.

STATUES, BRIDGES, PARKS, AND SQUARES

Most of the statues which commemorate the country's past liberators and heroes are to be seen in O Connell Street. At the north end is the Parnell Monument, a bronze statue of 19th-c Charles Stewart Parnell which stands on a pedestal in front of a tall shaft of Galway granite. South of this is a statue to Father Theobald Matthew, who lived between 1790 and 1856 and was a pioneer of the total abstinence movement in Ireland.

On opposite sides of a junction between Abbey Street and O Connell Street are statues of William Smith O Brien and Sir John Gray. The former was the leader of the Young Ireland Party, responsible for the uprising of 1848, and Sir John was the proprietor of *The Freeman's Journal*. The O Connell statue by Foley shows 19th-c Daniel O Connell 'The Liberator' – a Kerry advocate and Member of Parliament who secured Catholic emancipation for Ireland in 1829. Thomas Brock's 'Victories' around the statue represent Fidelity, Eloquence, Courage, and Patriotism. Historic College Green, on the other side of the river at the end of Westmoreland Street, features a number of fine statues by John Foley. These include representations of Henry Grattan, Edmond Burke, and Oliver Goldsmith, the last two being sited in front of Trinity College. Also here is a statue of Thomas Moore by Christopher Moore.

The oldest and one of the most beautiful of Dublin's bridges is Queen's, which was constructed between 1764 and 1768. Sarah or Island Bridge was built by Alex Stephens (or Stephenson) in 1791, and the original O Connell Bridge was by Gandon in the same year. The last-mentioned, once known as Carlisle Bridge, was replaced by the present structure in 1880. Huband Bridge spans a canal in Upper Mount Street, and both Old Bridge and Ormonde Bridge were replaced after a serious flood in 1802. Also built in the early 19thc were Richmond Bridge and Whitworth or Father Matthew Bridge. The Metal or Halfpenny Bridge was named from a toll levied to cover the cost of its construction, and its delicate tracery makes a valuable contribution to the city's architecture. Other iron bridges in Dublin are Kingsbridge and Barrack Bridge.

The largest and perhaps the best known of the city's famous squares is St Stephen's Green. Originally a common outside the city wall, this was laid out in building plots in 1663 and the centre was enclosed as a public park to be munificently laid out at the expense of Lord Ardilaun in 1880. Its various memorials include works by John Henry Foley, Seamus Murphy, and Oliver Sheppard. The fountain known as the Three Fates, given in thanksgiving for Irish relief of distress after the second world war, was by Josef Wackerle. The attractive Garden of Remembrance in 18th-c Parnell Square was designed by Waithi P Hanley. Merrion Square, the second largest, was laid out by John Ensore in 1762 but was not completed until the end of the century. It is now a public park. The Rutland Memorial, executed by Henry Aaron Baker in 1791, can be seen on the west side but is bereft of its fountain and much of its stone ornamentation.

Mountjoy Square was created between 1792 and 1808. Several of its houses retain good interiors by Michael Stapleton and Charles Thorpe, and number 61 features a particularly fine doorway. Fitzwilliam is the smallest and best-preserved of the squares, and includes fine buildings which are largely used as doctors' consulting rooms. It dates from 1820.

Phoenix Park, named from a spring of clear water known as *Fionn Uisge*, originally covered some 2,000 acres and formed the confiscated demesne of the Knights Hospitallers at Kilmainham. The Duke of Ormonde allotted 250 acres on the south side of the river for the construction of the 17th-c Royal Hospital for aged war veterans. At the north-east side of the park are Zoological Gardens which were created by the 19th-c Royal Zoological Society of Ireland and are the second oldest in the world. A racecourse occupies the north-western corner. A particularly well-known feature of the park is the beautiful 'Phoenix' memorial, which was erected by Lord Chesterfield and is surmounted by a carving of the fabulous phoenix itself. This tends to perpetuate the misconception that the park was named after a bird rather than a spring. Other interesting items include the Knockmaree megalithic tomb, which is situated near the Knockmaroon Gate, and an imposing obelisk which was erected as a monument to the Duke of Wellington.

The old Viceroy's residence is now that of the President of Ireland and dates from 1751. It is now known as *Arus an Uachtarain*. Lord Frederick Cavendish and Mr Burke were assassinated within sight of the house in May of 1882. The US Embassy stands among trees to the left. In 1932 the 31st Eucharistic Congress was held here on a 200-acre plain modestly known as the 'Fifteen Acres'. Just inside the main entrance on Parkgate Street are the attractive Peoples' Gardens.

CATHEDRALS AND CHURCHES

CHRIST CHURCH CATHEDRAL (CI)
Christ Church Place
This cathedral of the united sees of Dublin and Glendalough was so heavily restored in 1875 that it is difficult to envisage it as an old foundation. A clue to its ancient origins can be seen outside on the south side of the transept, where remains of an old, 13th-c chapter house and traces of the cloister and garth are visible. Sitric, Norse king of Dublin, created the foundation in 1038, and the first bishop was Donat – an Irishman. It is claimed that the crypt dates back to these early times, but this is unlikely. At first the Danes looked to Canterbury

Daniel O Connell 'The Liberator' was a member of parliament who secured Catholic emancipation for Ireland in 1829. His statue is by Foley.

rather than Armagh for the consecration of their bishops, but when St Laurence O Toole became bishop a formal attachment to the Irish church was forged. St Laurence became Archbishop of the province as a result. In 1163 he replaced the secular clergy with a community of Aroasian Canons. A new church was begun in 1172 by the Anglo-Normans under Strongbow, the Earl of Pembroke, and it is to this that the Norman-arched crypt probably belongs.

O Toole's successors, John Comyn and Henry de Londres, attempted to move their influence outside the jurisdiction of the city. They built a new cathedral on the site of the little wooden Church of St Patrick, but over the succeeding years Christ Church continued to share the Archbishops' favours. It took precedence from seniority first, then in 1300 by Papal decree. Richard II received the homage of Ireland's provincial kings here in 1394, and in 1487 Lambert Simnel was crowned Edward VI of England in the cathedral. Simnel was the Pretender to the throne during the reign of Henry VII. James II stopped here to hear mass on his way to the Battle of the Boyne, and after the battle William III came here to give thanks.

By 1569 the south wall of the nave had collapsed and was roughly rebuilt; the entire building was in a poor state of repair. Six new bells were fitted in the cathedral during 1670, but the necessary structural work was not forthcoming. After the disestablishment of the church in Ireland in 1869 the cathedral was found to need large-scale restoration. The resulting work left very little of the older building intact, apart from the crypt. The west bay of the choir and north wall of the nave and transepts are of medieval origin, while the groin-vaulted crypt which extends under the entire church dates from the 12th or 13thc. Inside the crypt are the altar tabernacle and candlesticks used when James II heard mass here, plus the oldest secular statues in Dublin. The latter, probably by William de Keyser, depict Charles II and James II and came from the old Tholsel or City Council House – demolished in 1806. Also of interest are the city stocks, and the Sneyd monument by Thomas Kirk. These historic vaults were used as wine cellars and drinking taverns during the 16th and 17thc.

The transepts date from c1170 and preserve choir-aisle arches, arcade capitals, and parts of the north nave wall – all in transitional style. One of the effigies in the south arcade may be of the Earl of Drogheda, c1340, and is said to stand on the site of Strongbow's tomb. A small effigy near by is sometimes called 'Strongbow's Son', but this may be a viceral monument commemorating the burial of Strongbow's bowels. A 12th- or 13th-c Archbishop and the sister or wife of Strongbow are respectively commemorated by two effigies in the St Laurence O Toole Chapel. The south-east chapel, dedicated to the Archbishop St Laud, contains what is believed to be the embalmed heart of St Laurence. Dublin's Huguenot colony once made extensive use of the Lady Chapel, in the north-east part of the cathedral, but this now houses the library, chapter house, and music school.

The Synod Hall, which stands on the site of the medieval parish church of St Michael the Archangel and incorporates the old church tower, is linked to the cathedral by a bridge. This is the meeting place for the General Synod of the Church of Ireland.

METHODIST CENTENARY CHURCH
St Stephen's Green
Only the Carlow-granite façade of this interesting and dignified church has survived a fire which destroyed the major part of the building. It was once the main Methodist church in Dublin, and was built to replace John Wesley's chapel in Whitefriar Street in 1843. The design was by Isaac Farrell.

ST ANDREW'S CHURCH (RC)
Westland Row
This church was built by James Boulger between 1832 and 1837, and is one of the largest neo-Grecian churches in the city. The distinguished exterior features a heavy Doric portico, and inside are two fine examples of Hogan's sculpture – The Transfiguration and a monument to Elizabeth Farrell.

ST ANN'S CHURCH (CI), Dawson St
This church was started in 1720 to a design by Isaac Wills, then refronted in Romanesque style by Sir Thomas Deane in 1868. Its gallery is supported by square, unfluted Ionic columns, and the curved apse features six magnificent gilt-plaster drops flanking the three east windows. On either side of the chancel are curved shelves used for holding loaves of bread. These are here as a result of a bequest made by the Rt Hon Theophilus 'Lord' Newtown of Newtownbutler, father of Lord Lanesborough, who died in 1723. He left £13 per year to be distributed to the poor in the form of weekly bread doles, a practice which is still continued though with much smaller loaves. Also of interest in the church are the Elizabeth Phibbs memorial by Edward Smythe, the St Christopher window by Wilhemina Geddes, and the grave of 19th-c poetess Felicia Hermans.

The beautiful Phoenix Monument, erected by Lord Chesterfield, tends to perpetuate the misconception that Phoenix Park was named after a fabulous bird rather than a spring (see page 46).

ST AUDOEN'S CHURCH (CI), High St
St Audoen's is Dublin's only surviving medieval church and is named after the patron saint of Rouen. All that remains of the original Norman building is the nave, which is now used as a parish church and was once a Guild Chapel. The transitional west door dates from c1190, but the rest is of late-pointed style. Both the south aisle and the chancel are roofless. The tomb of Roland FitzEustace – Baron of Portlester and the builder of the south-east chapel – and his wife can be seen in the porch. Of interest in the ruined parts of the building are medieval floor tiles and a 16th-c mural monument depicting kneeling parents and rows of children. The tower was restored in the 19thc and houses three 15th-c bells which are considered to be the oldest in Ireland. North of the church is St Audoen's Arch, the only surviving fragment of the city's medieval gates. The lower part of this dates from 1275, but the upper section is a 19th-c reconstruction.

ST AUDOEN'S CHURCH (RC), High St
Patrick Byrne designed this 19th-c church, which has two internal storeys of niches and is lit by lunettes in the plaster barrel-vault. A dome which rose over the crossing collapsed in 1884 and has been replaced with a flat plaster circle which some consider to be out of character. The portico of 1898 was by Stephen Ashlin and H Byrne, and the impressive exterior uses the site to full advantage.

ST FRANCIS XAVIER'S CHURCH (RC)
Upper Gardiner St
Built in the form of a Latin cross, this church belongs to the Jesuit Order and was built by Joseph B Keane in 1832. Its front features a tetrastyle Ionic portico, and the building is in a good state of decoration. One of its features is a wooden figure of St Joseph by Oisin Kelly.

ST GEORGE'S CHURCH (CI), Temple St
Although this magnificent church gives an impression of neo-Grecian architecture, its 200ft steeple is definitely Renaissance in style. The interior of the building is wider than the length, and the galleries arrayed on three of its sides are cantilevered on an inner wall. Francis Johnston designed the decorations and woodcarvings, which were executed by a number of carvers, including Richard Stewart. The church stands at the focus of three streets on one of the most magnificent sites in Dublin.

ST MARY'S ABBEY, Meetinghouse Lane
No longer in use as a church, this vaulted, four-bay building was once the chapter house of the 12th-c Abbey of St Mary. The abbey was founded as a daughter house of Savigny in Normandy, and it

DUBLIN

adopted the Cistercian reforms in the second half of the 12thc. It was often the venue for meetings of the English Council in the middle ages. The chapter house is now half underground, but it was here that 'Silken Thomas' of Offaly – Thomas Fitzgerald – made his dramatic declaration of rebellion against Henry VIII in 1534. A beautiful wooden statue of Our Lady of Dublin that once stood here can now be seen in the Church of the Carmelites in Whitefriar Street. A blocked underground passage which starts in the abbey is said to have led under the River Liffey to Christ Church Cathedral.

ST MARY'S PRO-CATHEDRAL (RC), Cathedral Street

Built between 1816 and 1825 to a design by John Sweetman, this church is a monumental Greek-Doric building featuring an internal colonnade, dome, and apse. Its hexastyle portico is large, and the pediment is surmounted by figures of the Blessed Virgin, St Patrick, and St Laurence O Toole. The white-marble altar is by Turnerilli, and the roof above displays a fine stucco representation of the Ascension. During the 19thc John Henry Newman came here to make his public profession of the Catholic faith before Cardinal Cullen, whose statue now adorns the nave. The Pro-Cathedral's Palestrina choir was endowed by Edward Martyn, a friend of the writer George Moore. John Count McCormack, the famous tenor, was a member of the choir for a while.

ST MARY'S CHURCH (CI), Mary St

This is the oldest unaltered church in Dublin, and the first galleried church to be built in the city. Outside features include a dignified west door and an east window with mouldings enriched with scrolls, but the building is mainly noted for its fine interior. The internal cornices are of richly-carved wood, and the organ case is splendidly adorned with figure-sculpture and friezes. Also of interest are the unusually deep churchwardens' pews, pew doors to the window embrasures, and an additional gallery above the main gallery on either side of the organ – perhaps intended for charity children. The architect of the church was Thomas Burgh, and the building is associated with many famous men. The Volunteer Earl of Charlemont and Wolf Tone were both baptized here, and John Wesley came here to preach for the first time in Ireland in 1747.

ST MICHAN'S CHURCH (CI), Church St

Situated in the old Norse district of Ostmantown, this 19th-c restoration occupies the site of an 11th-c church and incorporates a great deal of 17th-c work. It is thought the effigy that stands in the churchyard may represent the Norse founder, Bishop Samuel O Haingli. The 120ft tower dates from around the 12thc, and the interior of the building includes a gallery which displays fine carvings of musical instruments. The old organ is dated 1724 and is said to have been played by Handel.

Also of interest is the 'stool' on which repentant sinners are supposed to have asked forgiveness in front of the congregation – more probably a moveable litany desk. The yellow limestone with which the building was constructed has moisture absorbing properties, and bodies deposited in the crypt are preserved in a mummified state. Several corpses can be seen by the visitor, including the bodies of the brothers Sheares, who were executed for their part in the 1798 Insurrection. A stone marks the supposed burial place of Robert Emmet, who was executed in 1803. Edmund Burke was born near by at 12 Arran Quay. It is probable that he was baptized here.

ST PATRICK'S CATHEDRAL (CI), Patrick St

St Patrick's is the national cathedral of the Church of Ireland. Its site was once a small island in the River Poddle, where St Patrick is traditionally held to have baptized converts, but the river now flows underground and the island only exists in history. A small church which stood near by was called St Patrick de Insula. The saint's holy well, near the west tower of the present structure, was marked by an inscribed stone which is now preserved in the south-west corner of the nave.

The entry concerning Christ Church Cathedral has shown that the erection of St Patrick's was due to Archbishop Comyn's ecclesiastical ambition to be unrestrained by city confines. Hence he built his collegiate church outside the city walls on a holy – if marshy – site with the aim of superseding the older Christ Church. Henry de Londres, his successor, raised the church to cathedral status in 1213.

It is thought that the two west bays on the south side may preserve some of this original church, which was consecrated in 1192, but most of the present cruciform structure is of early-English style and dates from a century later. In 1300 the precedence of Christ Church was recognised by papal decree, which meant a decline in the fortunes of St Patrick's. Over the years the building declined, suffering damage at the hands of the O Tooles and O Byrnes of Wicklow, and in the 14thc the north transept became the church of the newly-formed parish 'St Nicholas Without the Walls.' It remained as such until 1961. The great tower was built by Archbishop Minot in 1381, and measures 147ft in height. It is slightly out of square with the cathedral walls, and is surmounted by an 18th-c spire. The reduction of status to parish church occurred at the Reformation, and part of the building became a courthouse. The associated Palace of St Sepulchre was taken into the possession of the Viceroy, and the Archbishop moved to the Deanery. St Patrick's regained cathedral status for a while during the Catholic Restoration under Queen Mary Tudor, but Huguenots were still allowed to worship in the Lady Chapel.

Most people associate St Patrick's with Johnathan Swift, who was Dean here for 32 years. He and his wife Stella are buried at the foot of a pier near the south-west entry, and their resting place is marked by a brass plate. Near by is a bust of Swift, and a slab carrying his own epitaph: 'He lies where furious indignation can no longer rend his heart'. His pulpit is also preserved here, plus the altar table from the church at Laracor, in Co Meath, where he was appointed rector in 1699. The altar table is kept in the Chapel of St Peter.

The south-west corner also features the Boyle Monument, which was erected by the Earl of Cork and displays painted figures of his family. The removal of this huge monument from its original position at the east end of the choir by Lord Deputy Strafford aroused the Earl's hatred and contributed to Strafford's execution. The best-preserved portion of the ancient fabric is the choir. Over the stalls are the helmets, swords, and banners of the Knights of St Patrick, an order instituted in 1783 by George III. The flags of disbanded Irish regiments which distinguished themselves on European battlefields hang round the walls. After disestablishment the ceremony of institution was transferred to the castle. A holed door near the south-east entrance of the cathedral is a relic of the time when the reconciled Butler and Geraldine chiefs clasped hands after their conflict in 1492 – at a safe distance, with timber between them. The south transept is the part of the building that was used as a

Heavy 19th-c restoration – although pleasantly executed – disguises the 12th-c origins of Christ Church Cathedral (CI) (see page 46).

chapter house for many years. It contains the tomb of Swift's servant McGee, plus the 18th-c Simon Vierpyl monument of Lady Doneraile.

Many other monuments can be seen in the cathedral, including a supposed effigy of St Patrick, a representation of 13th-c Archbishop Fulk de Saundeford, and a 15th-c memorial to Archbishop Tregury. In the north aisle are a bust of John Philpot Curran, the orator; a monument to Samuel Lover, the novelist; and another commemorating Carolan, the best-known and loved of the Irish bards. A monument to the many-times married Dame St Leger can be seen in the corner of the north transept and choir. A tablet in the north choir aisle commemorates the Duke of Schomberg, who was killed at the Battle of the Boyne, and bears a biting epitaph composed by Swift at the expense of the dead general's indifferent family. The south aisle features memorials to Sir Henry Wallop (1599), who was Queen Elizabeth's Deputy; Dean Sutton (1528); Sir E Ffiton (1579); and Charles Wolfe, who won fame overnight by writing *The Burial of Sir John Moore*. Also in this part of the cathedral is a brass in memory of John Henry Bernard, who became Archbishop of Dublin and Provost of Trinity College.

Restoration work conducted in the 19thc was financed by the Guinness family, and Sir Thomas Drew – the architect – paid more attention to the original fabric than was shown in the case of Christ Church. The statue of Sir Benjamin Guinness – near the south-west door outside the cathedral – was executed by Foley. A fine peal of ten bells was donated by Lord Iveagh, who also granted a bequest to ensure the upkeep and maintenance of the building. His benefactions are commemorated by a stained glass window. The Deanery – rebuilt since Swift stayed there in 1781 – stands across the street on the south side. A programme of restoration was commenced in 1970.

ST SAVIOUR'S CHURCH (RC), Dominick St
J J MacCarthy designed this French-gothick church in 1858. Good carvings and sculpture can be seen on the façade, and the interior features Hogan's Dead Christ and beautiful altar carving. The priory attached to the church is sited to the north of the building, as is usual in the case of Dominican foundations.

ST STEPHEN'S CHURCH (CI), Mount St Crescent
Built *c*1820, this beautifully-sited structure is the last of Dublin's neo-Grecian Protestant churches. The design by John Bowden was completed by Joseph Welland, and the appearance of the fine portico was inspired by the *Erechtheum*. This influence is also seen in the Tower of the Winds, the clock tower belfry, and the monument of Lysicrates. The building has been described as 'a delicate and scholarly' composition.

ST WERBURGH'S CHURCH (CI), Castle St
The site on which this building stands was once occupied by an Anglo-Norman foundation, which in turn had replaced an even older church. Its dedication is to St Werburgh, a daughter of Wulfhere, one-time King of Mercia. After a fire in 1745 the structure was largely rebuilt. John Smith, or Smythe, designed the gracious interior and incorporated a new upper gallery for schoolchildren, plus a carving of the Royal Arms in front of the Viceregal pew. The beautiful pulpit was designed by Francis Johnston and carved by Richard Stewart.

The present structure dates from 1784 and was erected to a design by Thomas Burgh. Inside in the south wall is the sculptured altar tomb of the Fitzgerald family. The exterior front of the building is an impressive mixture of Ionic and Doric architectural orders. Before the Chapel Royal was built inside the walls of Dublin Castle, this was the place where the Viceroy was sworn to office and where the Lord Lieutenant attended divine worship. It also served as the city's parish church. Lord Edward Fitzgerald is buried in the church vault, and his captor – Major Sirr – lies outside in the graveyard. The church's lovely tower and spire were falsely declared unsafe and demolished during the 19thc.

THE AUGUSTINIAN CHURCH (RC), Thomas St
Edward Welby, Pugin, and C Ashlin designed this gothic-revival church. The imposing exterior features an elaborately-carved doorway and a 160ft tower. Also of interest is a four-light window of St Augstine by Michael Healy.

UNIVERSITY CHURCH (RC), St Stephen's Green South
Irish marble can be seen at its best in this 19th-c, neo-Byzantine basilica. The architect, John Hungerford Pollen, was commissioned by Cardinal Newman. Inside is a bust of Newman by Farrell.

FAMOUS AND HISTORIC BUILDINGS

The buildings of Dublin are known for both their architectural importance and their associations with famous men. In many cases the birthplaces or residences of the city's celebrities have vanished beneath the tide of progress, but their occupants are still remembered in the names of streets or by metal plaques set into the walls of existing buildings. Dean Swift's birthplace at 7 Hoey's Court no longer exists, but his name is recorded in many parts of the city. The house in which composer Michael Balfe was born has also gone, but the street in which it stood is now known as Balfe Street. Edmund Burke was born at 12 Arran Quay, Thomas Moore at 12 Aungier Street, and the Duke of Wellington at 24 Upper Merrion Street – and so it goes on. Richard Brinsley Sheridan was born at 12 Dorset Street; Oscar Wilde at 21 Westland Row; James Clarence Mangan at 3 Lord Edward Street; Wolfe Tone at 44 Wolf Tone Street; George Bernard Shaw at 33 Synge Street; and James Joyce at Brighton Square, Rathgar.

St Audoen's Church (CI), the only medieval church to have survived in Dublin. The tower was restored in the 19th-c (see page 47).

Famous people who were not Dubliners by birth but made their homes in the city are also honoured. These include Daniel O Connell, who lived at 58 Merrion Square, and the famous poet W B Yeats, who lived at 42 Fitzwilliam Square. Sir William and Lady (Speranza) Wilde resided at 1 Merrion Square; John Philpot Curran at 4 Ely Place – where George Moore also lived; Samuel Lover at 9 d'Olier Street; and George Petrie at 21 Great Charles Street. Many buildings not necessarily associated with personalities are famous by virtue of their architectural excellence, and include ordinary houses as well as the larger, monumental type of buildings. A selection follows.

ALDBOROUGH HOUSE, Portland Row
The brick main block of this 18th-c house, which has been attributed to Sir William Chambers, features granite facings on the east front. The surviving wing is trimmed with Portland limestone and is decorated with a sphinx and lion in Coade stone. It is thought that this ornamentation was originally intended for a theatre. When this house was first built it was in a rural situation, as indicated by the inscription on the portico – *RUS IN URBE*, 'The country in the town'. It is now occupied by government offices.

BANK OF IRELAND, College Green
This magnificent building, the former Parliament House, was begun in 1729 and built to a design by Sir Edward Lovett Pearce. Its main front faces south, and the building originally had an open colonnade which extended round three sides of the square and ended in lofty entrance arches. It also had four

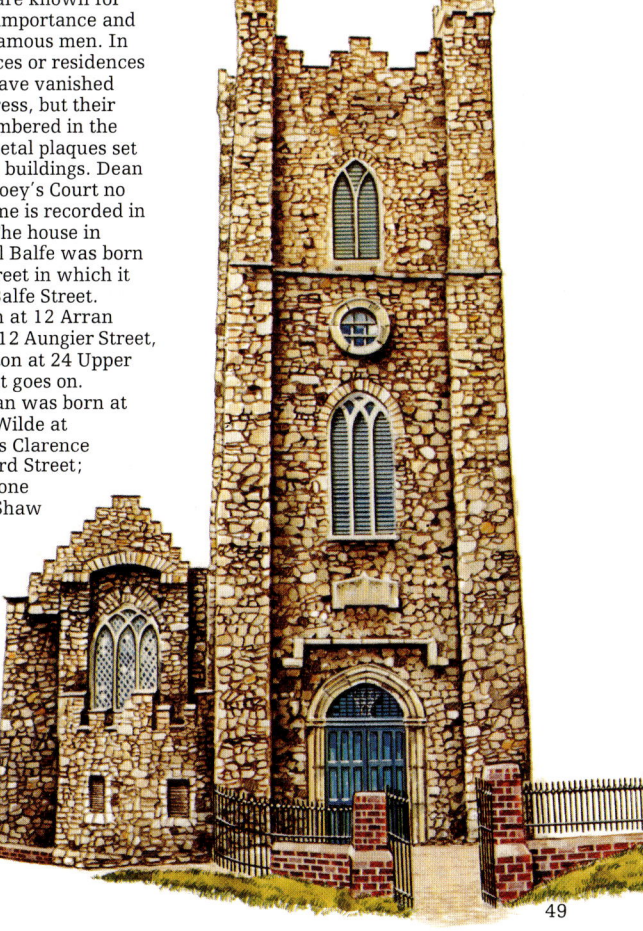

DUBLIN

Central Plan
1. Abbey Theatre
2. Aldborough House
3. Bank of Ireland
4. Belvedere House
5. Christ Church Cathedral (CI)
6. City Hall
7. Civic Museum
8. Clonmel House
9. College of Physicians
10. Custom House
11. Dublin Castle
12. Ely House
13. Four Courts
14. General Post Office
15. Green Street Courthouse
16. Iveagh House
17. King's Inns
18. Leinster House
19. Mansion House
20. Marsh's Library
21. Methodist Centenary Church
22. Mornington House
23. Municipal Gallery of Modern Art
24. Music Hall
25. National Gallery
26. National Library
27. National Museum and Natural History Museum
28. Newman House (University College)

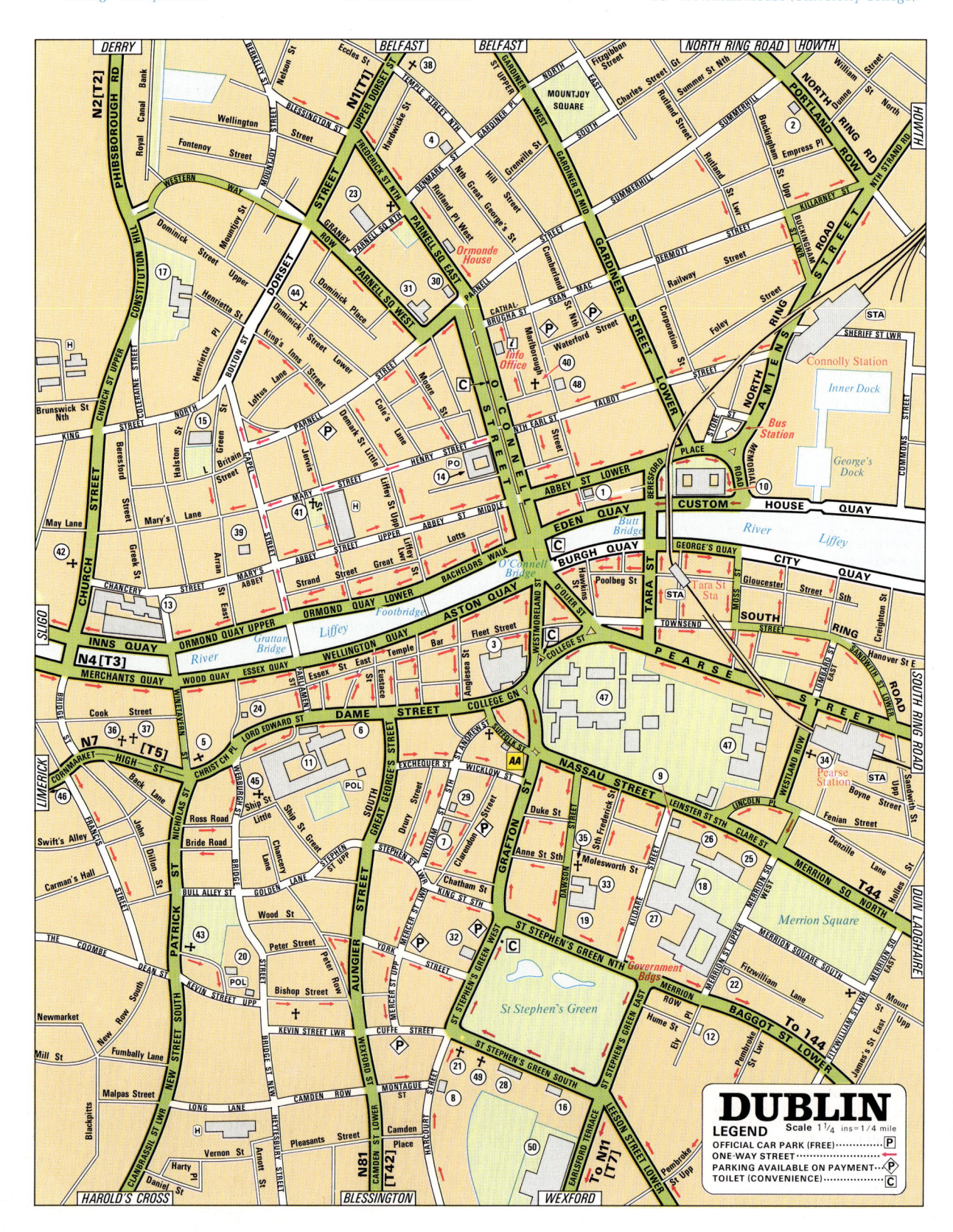

29 Powerscourt House
30 Rotunda
31 Rotunda Hospital
32 Royal College of Surgeons
33 Royal Irish Academy
34 St Andrew's Church (RC)
35 St Ann's Church (CI)
36 St Audoen's Church (CI)
37 St Audoen's Church (RC)
38 St George's Church (CI)
39 St Mary's Abbey
40 St Mary's Pro-Cathedral (RC)
41 St Mary's Church (CI)
42 St Michan's Church (CI)
43 St Patrick's Cathedral (CI)
44 St Saviour's Church (RC)
45 St Werburgh's Church (CI)
46 The Augustinian Church (RC)
47 Trinity College
48 Tyrone House
49 University Church (RC)
50 University College, Dublin

Ionic columns to support the principal portico, a tympanum which featured splendidly-carved Royal Arms by John Houghton (who also carved the capitals), and statues by Edward Smythe. Inside were the House of Commons, House of Lords, and the Court of Requests.

There was no longer any need for a Parliament House after the Union, and this superb building was sold to the Bank of Ireland, who commissioned Francis Johnston to make the alterations they considered necessary. The House of Commons has now gone, although its corridor remains, and the Court of Requests serves as the cash office. The Court's carvings by Thomas Kirk and fine stucco work by Charles Thorpe have been preserved. The Director's Luncheon Room boasts a beautiful rococo ceiling from Touche's Bank in Castle Street. This is dated prior to 1735, and the unknown artist has exhibited extraordinary skill in his execution of the theme 'Venus Wounded by Love'.

Fortunately it is still possible to see and admire Pearce's lovely House of Lords, which is apsidal and top-lit with Diocletian windows. Pearce did not live to see the completion of this building, and in 1782 James Gandon was employed to make an extension. He placed a grand hexastyle portico to the east, extending it over the pavement and connecting it to Pearce's south colonnade by a curved wall with seven niches – using Corinthian columns to gain the extra height needed. Inside is his beautiful circular hall, which features an oxhead frieze by Edward Smythe and survives almost in its original form. Two early 18th-c tapestries respectively depicting the Siege of Derry and the Battle of the Boyne are preserved in the House of Lords, but the throne has been replaced by a statue of George III and is now kept in Northland House – the Royal Irish Academy. Descendants of the last Speaker sold the silver-gilt mace of the House of Commons to the bank.

By 1792 Robert Parke and others had made a similar extension to the west. This too was altered by Johnston, and features a superb, carved trophy by Thomas Kirk. The Central Bank of Ireland is now at the west end, in Foster Place.

BELVEDERE HOUSE, Gt Denmark St
Features of this 18th-c, five-bay mansion built by Michael Stapleton – include a fine situation, a fluted frieze and cornice, and a noble elevation. The handsome interior decoration uses geometric arabesques and brightly-coloured plaster. A mahogany organ and bookcases can be seen in the Diana Room, and the ceiling of the Apollo Room is considered exceptional. The Venus Room has lost its centrepiece, but the splendid staircase still exists. This house has been a Jesuit school since 1841. James Joyce was one of its more famous pupils.

CITY HALL, Lord Edward St
Built between 1769 and 1779, this structure was designed by Thomas Cooley and was originally intended as the Royal Exchange. Cooley, who won the commission in a competition for a prize of £100, designed the building with a central ring of columns which was to be the ambulatory – where the Dublin merchants could discuss their business. Outside there was a deep entablature, a copper dome, and many windows. Interior decorations were by Simon Vierpyl. When the building became the City Hall in 1852 it was substantially altered. The Victorians changed the glass and porticos, and the ambulatory was filled with statues. Included among the latter are works by Sir Francis Chantrey and Hogan. Housed in the Muniment Room is the Lord Mayor's regalia, including a gold S-collar which was presented by William III, plus the charters of the city. The central hall is known for its dignified design.

CLONMEL HOUSE, Harcourt St
Number 17 Harcourt Street once formed the central block of Clonmel House, a brick-built structure which was erected for the Earl of Clonmel. It is possible that the architect was Stapleton. At one time the building included low side wings, and interior features of the surviving block include good ceilings and mantels. This block has been divided into two since 1830.

Renaissance-style St George's Church occupies a fine position at the junction of three streets (see page 47).

COLLEGE OF PHYSICIANS, Kildare St
Completed in 1864, this building was designed by William Murray and incorporated in 1867. Inside are portraits of famous medical men.

CUSTOM HOUSE, Custom House Quay
The architect James Gandon worked alone to raise this fine building on its marvellous river-side site, but was constantly beset by critics and money problems. The site boasted a 375ft frontage and was 204ft deep, while the Custom House itself – completed in 1791 – carries an elegant dome which rises 125ft above the ground. On top of the dome is Edward Smythe's statue of Commerce, and the tympanum features his sculpture of Hibernia and Britannia, with Neptune brandishing Famine and Despair. Also by Smythe are the fourteen carved keystones, each representing an Irish river, and the Arms of the Kingdom of Ireland on the end pavilions. These works put the sculptor in the forefront of architectural figure carving, and have been preserved in spite of the interiors having been gutted by fire during the War of Independence in May 1921. The building was reconstructed after this damage. It now houses the Department of Local Government and the Customs and Excise offices.

DUBLIN CASTLE, Cork Hill
At first sight Dublin Castle may prove a disappointment to visitors, but it has several excellent features and occupies a very historic site. It is almost certain that the ridge on which it stands – enclosed by the Upper Castle Yard – was crowned by a Celtic rath and later by a Norse stronghold before King John erected his stronghold. All that remains of the medieval structure, which had a curtain wall flanked by four sturdy towers and surrounded by a deep moat, are two much altered towers and a fragment of the wall. During the reign of

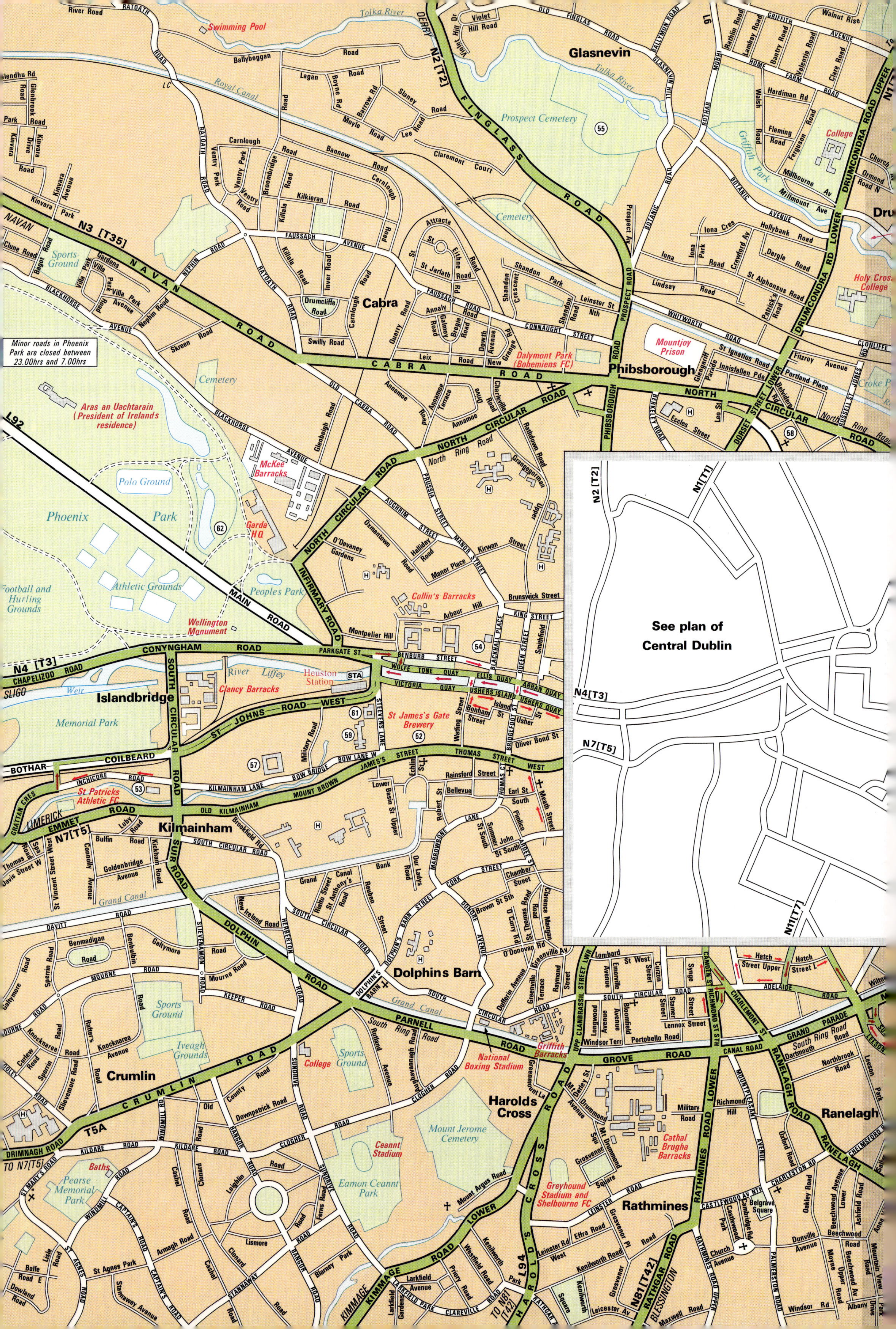

Glasnevin
Cabra
Phibsborough
Islandbridge
Kilmainham
Dolphins Barn
Crumlin
Harolds Cross
Rathmines
Ranelagh
Phoenix Park
Minor roads in Phoenix Park are closed between 23.00hrs and 7.00hrs
Aras an Uachtarain (President of Irelands residence)
Polo Ground
Athletic Grounds
Football and Hurling Grounds
Wellington Monument
Peoples Park
Garda HQ
McKee Barracks
Cemetery
Sports Ground
Swimming Pool
Tolka River
Royal Canal
Prospect Cemetery
Griffith Park
College
Holy Cross College
Mountjoy Prison
Dalymont Park (Bohemians FC)
Collin's Barracks
Heuston Station
River Liffey
Weir
Memorial Park
Clancy Barracks
St James's Gate Brewery
St Patricks Athletic FC
Grand Canal
Sports Ground
Iveagh Grounds
College
National Boxing Stadium
Griffith Barracks
Mount Jerome Cemetery
Ceannt Stadium
Eamon Ceannt Park
Baths
Pearse Memorial Park
Greyhound Stadium and Shelbourne FC
Cathal Brugha Barracks
See plan of Central Dublin
N3 [T35] NAVAN ROAD
CABRA ROAD
NORTH CIRCULAR ROAD
FINGLASS ROAD
DERRY N2 [T2]
DRUMCONDRA ROAD LOWER
DRUMCONDRA ROAD UPPER
PROSPECT ROAD
PHIBSBOROUGH ROAD
CONYNGHAM ROAD
CHAPELIZOD ROAD
N4 [T3]
SLIGO
MAIN ROAD
INFIRMARY ROAD
ST JOHNS ROAD WEST
SOUTH CIRCULAR ROAD
BOTHAR COILBEARD
INCHICORE ROAD
KILMAINHAM LANE
OLD KILMAINHAM
EMMET ROAD
N7 [T5]
LIMERICK
SUIR ROAD
DOLPHIN ROAD
CRUMLIN ROAD
T5A
DRIMNAGH ROAD
TO N7 [T5]
PARNELL ROAD
GROVE ROAD
HAROLD'S CROSS ROAD
KIMMAGE ROAD LOWER
L94
TO N81 [T42]
N81 [T42] RATHGAR ROAD BLESSINGTON
RATHMINES ROAD LOWER
RANELAGH ROAD
CHARLEMONT ST
ADELAIDE ROAD
GRAND PARADE
THOMAS STREET WEST
JAMES'S STREET
BENBURB STREET
WOLFE TONE QUAY
VICTORIA QUAY
USHERS ISLAND
USHERS QUAY
ELLIS QUAY
ARRAN QUAY
PARKGATE ST
BLACKHORSE AVENUE
L92
N11 [T7]
N1 [T1]
N4 [T3]
N7 [T5]
N2 [T2]

DUBLIN

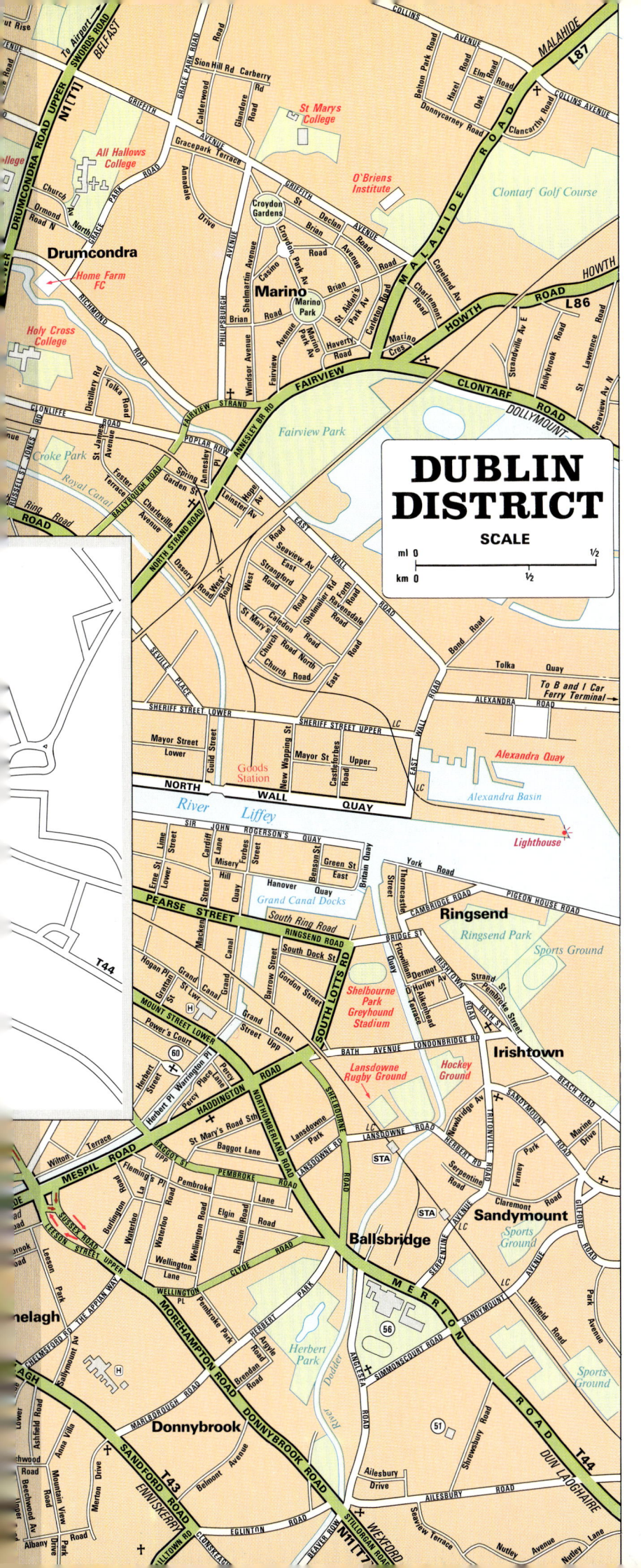

Elizabeth I the castle became the residence of the Lord Deputy, or Viceroy, and from that time until the establishment of the Irish Free State it was the headquarters of British Administration in Ireland.

The main entrance at Cork Hill is on the site of the old main gate. Apartments formerly occupied by the Lord Lieutenant are sited on the south side of the Upper Castle Yard, and in recent years were used as Courts of Justice during the rebuilding of the Four Courts. The impressive Throne Room has a fine ceiling and contains the great, canopied chair of state, which is over 200 years old. The walls of picturesque St Patrick's Hall are hung with the banners of the Knights of St Patrick. The panelled ceiling features paintings depicting St Patrick, Henry II, and George III. The Bermingham Tower dates from 1411 and was rebuilt in 1775. It was once the state prison, and held the almost legendary Red Hugh O Donnell during the 16thc – until he escaped, was recaptured, and escaped again to fight the English occupation.

Lower Castle Yard adjoins the Upper and is bounded on the south side by the Record Tower and the Church of the Most Holy Trinity. The church was formerly the Chapel Royal. The Record Tower, one of the four original towers which stood at the angles of the curtain wall, has walls 16ft thick. In 1813 the upper storey was rebuilt and the parapet added, but the ancient lower portion is in such an excellent state of preservation that it still gives a good idea of the stronghold's original appearance. Heraldic work is conducted in the Genealogical Office, in Upper Castle Yard, and the interesting Heraldic Museum is located on the other side of the courtyard. Francis Johnston designed the 19th-c Church of the Most Holy Trinity, which has an exterior which features over 90 carved heads of ecclesiastics, sovereigns, and other notables. Carved panels inside the church display the arms of all the Viceroys since 1173. This series is continued in the stained-glass windows. The east window, a gift of one of the Viceroys, has four compartments which respectively feature the arrest of Christ, Christ before Caiphas, Christ before Herod, and Christ before Pilate.

ELY HOUSE, Ely Place
Situated at number 8 Ely Place, this fine house was built for the Earl of Offaly by Michael Stapleton in 1770. Its stucco and other decorations are considered very fine, and the building is now the headquarters of the Knights of St Columbanus.

District Plan
51 Chester Beatty Library
52 Guinness's Brewery
53 Kilmainham Gaol (see Kilmainham entry)
54 King's Hospital
55 National Botanic Gardens (see Glasnevin entry)
56 Royal Dublin Society Showgrounds (see Ballsbridge entry)
57 Royal Hospital (see Kilmainham entry)
58 St Francis Xavier's Church (RC)
59 St Patrick's (Swift's) Hospital
60 St Stephen's Church (CI)
61 Steeven's Hospital
62 Zoological Gardens (Phoenix Park)

DUBLIN

Belvedere House is a huge, five-bay mansion designed by Michael Stapleton. It has served as a Jesuit school since 1841 and was attended by James Joyce (see page 51).

FOUR COURTS, Inns Quay
The old Courts of Law were originally within the walls of Dublin Castle, then for a century and a half they were located in the precincts of Christ Church Cathedral before being moved to the Four Courts in 1796. This splendid pile, designed by Thomas Cooley and completed by James Gandon at a cost of almost a quarter of a million pounds, has a frontage of 450ft. The first stone was laid in 1786. The great portico features six Corinthian columns and includes statues of Moses, Justice, and Mercy on the pediment. This leads to a large, circular hall, off which are situated the original Four Courts. A circular lantern and dome surmount the central block.

In 1922 this important centre was a focal point of the conflict between the new Free State Government and the Anti-Treatyites. Happily the solid granite walls were able to withstand fire and explosion, so the external appearance of the structure was little affected. The damaged interior was reconstructed by the government, and the courts re-opened in October 1931. Ten Courts are accommodated by the restored structure. Of these, the Supreme Court is finished in walnut panelling, and the others in polished Austrian oak.

GENERAL POST OFFICE, O Connell St
Although the interior of this building was severely damaged in 1916 – when it was used as the headquarters for the Rising – its monumental façade has survived. The building was designed by Francis Johnston in the early 19thc, and the 220ft-long by 56ft-high front features a Greek-Ionic style portico – with six columns – which extends over the pavement. John Smythe's statues of Fidelity, Hibernia, and Mercury are mounted above the pediment. Inside the public office is Oliver Sheppard's excellent 1916 memorial, the Death of Cuchullain. Padraic Pearse read the Proclamation of Independence from this bullet-scarred portico in 1916.

GREEN STREET COURTHOUSE, Capel St
Although not architecturally distinguished, this building is of considerable historical interest as it was the scene of state trials in 1848 and 1867. It was designed by Francis Johnston in the 18thc.

GUINNESS'S BREWERY, James's St
This famous Dublin landmark, with its tulip domes, incorporates St James's Gate and was bought by Sir Arthur Guinness in 1759. Nowadays its extensive buildings cover some 40 acres, but the complex preserves some pleasant late 18th- and early 19th-c houses. Regular tours give visitors the chance to visit an interesting museum and to sample the world-famous stout.

IVEAGH HOUSE, St Stephen's Green
Now the Department of Foreign Affairs, this fine house was built for Bishop Clayton of Killala in 1730. The designer was Cassells, and some of the original 18th-c interior has survived. John Philpot Curran lived here for a while.

KING'S HOSPITAL, Blackhall St
This school, also called The Blue Coat Boys School, was founded in 1669 and granted a charter by Charles II in 1670. By the 1770's it was in need of new accommodation. Thomas Ivory was commissioned to design new buildings and produced a grand scheme which was embarked upon with the laying of a foundation stone in 1773. He used the finest craftsmen available, including Vierpyl for the stone work, Semple for supervision of the brickwork, Thorpe for the plaster, Cranfield for carving, and Chambers for the woodwork. By 1780 the Dining Room, Board Room, and façade were complete, but the government refused to grant money for building the cupola top, and ordered economies which even affected the chapel furnishings. Ivory resigned in disgust. A dome was added in 1894 – a poor substitute for the original concept – and a splendid window was created by Evie Hone. The ancient school or 'hospital' has now moved to a new location in the city's outer suburbs. The old building is now owned by the Incorporated Law Society.

KING'S INNS, Bolton St
Commenced in 1795 and finished in 1817, this complex was designed by James Gandon and comprises a central block surmounted by an octagonal cupola and flanked by two later wings. The Dining Hall is a magnificent apartment ornamented with fluted Ionic columns, and contains stucco figures executed by Edward Smythe. Also by Smythe are the figures carved in the caryatid doorways of the pedimented wings. The fine library contains a unique collection of books and was designed by Frederick Darley in 1827. This area was the most fashionable part of the city in the 18thc.

LEINSTER HOUSE, Kildare St
Cassels built this, the largest of the city's great town houses, for the young Earl of Kildare in 1745. Its situation was then remote and semi-rural, but the Earl was confident that others would follow where he led. The building is based on a long, central corridor and includes a two-storey entrance hall which features a deep, plaster-coved ceiling. Redecoration work carried out towards the end of the 18thc included contributions by Wyatt. The east and west fronts are both formal, and the last-mentioned is in Ardbraccan limestone. Lord Edward Fitzgerald lived here before and after his marriage. Purchased by the Royal Dublin Society in 1815, the house passed – a little over a century later – into the possession of the government for the accommodation of both *Dáil Éireann* and *Seanad Éireann* – the two houses of the Republic of Ireland parliament. A memorial to Arthur Griffith, Michael Collins, and Kevin O Higgins can be seen on Leinster Lawn, and Foley's statue of Prince Albert stands near by.

MANSION HOUSE, Dawson St
It is not known who designed this house, which was built in 1705, but it was bought from Joshua Dawson to serve as the Lord Mayor's residence in 1715. An 'Oak Room' was added at this time, and still features brackets which were once used to hold swords and maces. These are positioned on either side of the fireplace. The two-storey exterior was originally of red-brick construction, but this was greatly altered in the 19thc when the Round Room was

added as accommodation for a ball given in honour of George IV. It was again the scene of an important occasion 100 years later, when it was used for the signing of the 1919 Declaration of Independence and the Treaty of 1921. The room was designed by John Semple and contains several notable portraits, including one of the Duke of Northumberland by Reynolds.

MORNINGTON HOUSE, Upper Merrion St
Once known as Antrim House, this structure was built by John Ensor for Lord Antrim in the 18thc. Lord Mornington moved here in 1765, and the child that was to become the famous Duke of Wellington was born here in 1769. The Land Commission now occupies the building.

MUSIC HALL, Fishamble St
The Charitable society's Music Hall, designed by Cassels in 1741, was sited at the east end of Christ Church Cathedral in this once-fashionable street. The ground on which it was built is now occupied by Kennans Iron Works. The first performance of *The Messiah* was held here on April 13, 1742 – with Handel himself as Conductor.

POWERSCOURT HOUSE, South William St
Designed for Viscount Powerscourt by Robert Mack, this house was built between 1771 and 1774. Its impressive frontage extends for 130ft, and its 73ft height is crowned with a tall, blind attic which may have been intended for use as an observatory. The granite exterior contrasts pleasantly with the delicate inside decoration. James McCullagh was responsible for the fine hall and staircase, while the reception rooms were by Michael Stapleton. One of these rooms features a shallow-dome ceiling which meets the walls in charming arcs. The building now houses commercial offices, but is open to visitors.

ROTUNDA, Parnell St
Built with the object of making money – which it successfully did – this lofty, round hall has a diameter of 80ft and was erected to a John Ensor design in 1755. Later James Gandon improved its appearance by adding a frieze and Coade-stone plaques by Edward Smythe. The hall has been the scene of many memorable events, including the Volunteer Convention of 1783, but now houses a cinema. To the north east of the Rotunda are the New Assembly Rooms, which were by Frederick Trench and Richard Johnston. These now house the Gate Theatre.

ROTUNDA HOSPITAL, Parnell Sq West
This, the first maternity hospital in Ireland or Great Britain, was designed by Cassels for Dr Bartholomew-Mosse in 1751. Its Doric façade is joined to the end pavilions by curved flanking colonnades, and a three-storey tower is surmounted by a cupola. A fine interior staircase features stucco work by William Lee and leads to the chapel. This measures 86ft square by 30ft high and has a magnificent baroque ceiling which presents mythological, allegorical, and biblical figures in whole relief – the work of Bartholomew Cramillion.

ROYAL COLLEGE OF SURGEONS, Stephen's Green
Edward Parke designed this building in 1806, and it was completed in 1827. Its west façade, facing on to Stephen's Green, was later extended north by four bays and re-centred. The original York St elevation remains largely unaltered, although a large modern extension has been built to the rear. Over 30,000 volumes are kept in the impressive library.

ST PATRICK'S (SWIFT'S) HOSPITAL, Bow Lane
Dean Swift left the legacy by which this hospital was founded, and the ground on which it stands was granted by the governors of Steeven's Hospital. The architect was George Semple, and the building was opened – some eight years after its commencement – in 1757. Enlargements carried out in 1778 were by Cooley. The seven-bay entrance front is constructed of mountain granite and features a central pediment. The wings were designed by Cooley.

STEEVEN'S HOSPITAL, Steeven's Lane
Steeven's is one of the oldest hospitals in Ireland. It was founded by 'Madame' Steevens, designed by Thomas Burgh, and opened in 1733. Dean Swift became a member of the committee of trustees set up by the foundress, in 1721. Features of the hospital include a courtyard and piazza, some charming wrought-iron, and a delightful little clock tower. The general effect is one of quaintness. Swift's Stella endowed the chaplaincy. The interesting Worth Library is contained within the hospital.

TRINITY COLLEGE, College Green
All that remains of the first college buildings, founded by Elizabeth I in 1591, is the representation of the Royal Arms near the library entrance. The splendid, 300ft façade of 1759 is attributed to Henry Keene and John Sanderson of London, while David Sheehan was responsible for the fine stone-carving. Foley executed the statues of two of the college's famous graduates, Oliver Goldsmith and Edmund Burke.

The 18th-c City Hall by Thomas Cooley was originally intended to house the Royal Exchange. It was subsequently changed by the Victorians when it came into use as the City Hall (see page 51).

The visitor entering the great gateway between the lodges approaches Front or Parliament Square, which dates from between 1752 and 1759 and was so called because its construction was financed by parliament. The square is flanked on each side by two buildings respectively designed by Sir William Chambers and Graham Myers. The structure to the right is the Public Theatre or Examination Hall, and the one to the left is the Chapel. Inside the Public Theatre is beautiful stucco decoration by Michael Stapleton, the case of an organ which was taken from Spain in 1702, the gilt-oak chandelier from the House of Commons, portraits of Queen Elizabeth, Archbishop Ussher, Bishop Berkeley, and Edmund Burke, and a monument to Provost Baldwin. The late 18th-c Chapel also features stucco work by Stapleton, plus good woodwork and three memorial windows. Of particular note is its 17th-c plate. The mid 18th-c Dining Hall was designed by Cassels and contains a portrait by Grattan among its many pictures. The next buildings encountered by the visitor are known as Botany Bay and the Baths. The former dates from 1810, and the latter were given by Lord Iveagh in 1924. A statue of Lecky by John, and a figure by Henry Moore, can be seen near by.

The oldest structural part of the college still standing is The Rubrics, which dates from the early 18thc and is situated beyond the restored, red-brick range. Goldsmith once resided in the top corner rooms near the library. The library itself was built to a Thomas Burgh design between 1712 and 1732. It originally had three storeys, an open ground arcade, and a central wall to support the weight. Its great, 270ft length is divided into 27 bays, and the present roof was erected in the mid 19thc. The original roof was concealed behind the parapet.

The ground floor was enclosed in 1892. Inside this are preserved Cassels' gracious stairway and beautiful rococo plaster by Edward Semple. During the 19thc the flat plaster ceiling of the main Long Room was replaced by a wooden, barrel-vaulted structure designed by Benjamin Woodward.

Of the 3,000 ancient manuscripts preserved in the Library, the most interesting are probably the masterpieces of Celtic art such as the *Book of Kells,* the books of Durrow, Armagh, Dimma, Mulling, and Leinster, and the *Yellow Book of Lecan.* Among its printed books is a first folio Shakespeare, and it is entitled to a copy of every book published in Great Britain or Ireland if it stakes its claim within a year of publication. Other precious items exhibited in the Library include a gold fibula and 'Brian Boru's Harp'. Carving displayed here includes busts of Dean Swift, Dr Delany, Thomas Parnell, and Dr Clements. The New Library of 1967 is a striking example of modern architecture, erected to the prize-winning design of Paul Koralek. The external wall is faced with Wicklow granite, and the overall impression of the structure is softened by curved expanses of plate glass.

The early 20th-c Graduates' Building stands opposite Library Square, and New Square contains the 19th-c Museum Building by Thomas Deane and Benjamin Woodward. The carvings outside the latter structure are by the O Shea brothers, and the building contains a magnificent entrance hall and staircase. The 18th-c University Printing House is a delightful little building with a Doric portico which was designed by Cassels, and stands in the north-west corner of New Square. To the east and south of the complex are College Park and the playing fields, and east of the park are the Medical School buildings and Laboratories. The Moyne Institute of Preventive Medicine occupies the south corner of the park, and was presented by the Marchioness of Normanby in memory of her father Walter Edward Guinness – the first Baron Moyne.

The Provost's House of 1760 was designed by Lord Cork and includes low wings by John Smythe. Inside are an interesting octagonal staircase and a superb saloon which features a coved ceiling and columnar screens. This is the only one of the great Dublin houses which is still used for its originally-intended purpose. Also of interest at Trinity is the Fellows' Garden, a small, elegant, neo-Grecian magnetic observatory by Frederick Darley. Trinity is constantly expanding – as are most other progressive educational establishments – and the college's old buildings are gradually being supplemented by a variety of modern structures. A new Arts' block by Paul Koralek is under construction.

TYRONE HOUSE, Marlborough St
This was the first Dublin town house to be built of cut stone – *ie* Irish granite – and was designed by Cassels for Sir Marcus Beresford, the 1st Earl of Tyrone. It dates from 1740 and is split into seven bays. The cornice is situated immediately below the top windows, and the interior features a fine staircase hall, mahogany balusters, and good examples of plaster work. The house is now occupied by the Department of Education.

UNIVERSITY COLLEGE, DUBLIN, Earlsford Terrace
Originated in the Catholic University of Ireland, this college was founded in 1852 and opened in 1854. Dr John Henry Newman was the first rector, and its principal seat was University House – now known as Newman House. The foundation later became University College, and was conducted by the Jesuits in connection with the Royal University of Ireland. The poet Gerald Manley Hopkins came here to be professor of Greek, and it was here that he wrote some of his most searching sonnets. Another celebrated literary figure, James Joyce, was a student here. University College became a constituent college of the National University of Ireland in 1908.

The university has outgrown the Renaissance-style buildings designed for it by R M Butler, and these – sited in Earlsfort Terrace – now house the Faculties of Medicine and Architecture. A large new campus which has been developed at Belfield, some 5m south of the city, displays several striking examples of modern architecture in the varied styles of its blocks. Newman House is now two houses on St Stephen's Green, numbers 85 – formerly Clanwilliam House – and 86. Number 85 was built by Cassels in 1740 and includes fine ceilings

King's Inns stands in a once-fashionable part of Dublin. It was started in 1795 and built to a design by James Gandon (see page 54).

and rococo work. Of particular note are the fine figure sculptures and arabesques, which were executed by the Francini brothers. Number 86 was built by Richard West for the notorious Richard Chapell Whaley, father of 'Buck' Whaley. Richard Whaley's intention of 'outdoing' the house next door has resulted in many fine features. These include excellent stucco work, probably by West himself, and a lead lion in the portico by John Van Nost Jr. Both 85 and 86 have been used as student club rooms for some time.

MUSEUMS, ART GALLERIES, AND LIBRARIES

CHESTER BEATTY LIBRARY, 20 Shrewsbury Rd
Features of this superb library include a fine collection of Oriental manuscripts, prints, and books, plus early Western Biblical manuscripts and exquisite Books of Hours from the Continent. Also on display in the foundation's two galleries are Chinese snuff boxes and famous papyri of both the *Old* and *New Testaments.*

CIVIC MUSEUM, South William St
This fine 18th-c house was originally built for the Society of Artists, but it later became the Assembly House and was where the Irish Bar voted against the Act of Union in 1799. The museum which the building now houses is in the custody of the Old Dublin Society, and its fine collection of antique and otherwise historical items includes a good collection of early prints.

MARSH'S LIBRARY, St Patrick's Close
The oldest of Ireland's public libraries, Marsh's was designed by William Robinson *c*1702 for Archbishop Narcissus Marsh. It is a little L-shaped building beside St Patrick's Cathedral, featuring a steeply-pitched roof and an unspoiled interior. The books are arranged in bays between the windows, and the library's collection includes many early editions, manuscripts, and a large number of autographs. The former residence of the archbishops lies to the south of the library and now serves as barracks for

the *Garda Siochana.* The structure's noble ancestry is shown by the stone gate pillars, an old west doorway which has been converted into a window, and a representation of the archbishop's arms dated 1523.

MUNICIPAL GALLERY OF MODERN ART, Parnell Sq North
This gallery was the first to be established exclusively for the exhibition of modern art – including foreign work – in Ireland or Great Britain. At its opening in January of 1908 it was temporarily accommodated in 17 Harcourt St, once the town residence of John Scott, Earl of Clonmel. In 1927 the government presented Charlemont House, in Parnell Square, to the city, whereupon the Corporation expended the sum of £35,000 on the provision of an art gallery. This was formally opened by the Lord Mayor on June 19, 1933. Charlemont House, completed in 1763, was the only town house to be built in Ireland by Sir William Chambers.

The gallery owes its fine collection of paintings largely to the generosity and public spirit of Sir Hugh Lane. Time has fully justified his prescience and flair as a connoisseur, and the reputations of most artists represented in the collection have steadily appreciated. When the gallery opened it kept a room empty and prepared for the eventual return to Ireland of the famous Lane pictures, which were held in London following a dispute over Sir Hugh's will. An agreement concluded between the Government of Ireland and the Trustees of the National Gallery in London in 1959 makes provision for half of this outstanding collection to be seen in the gallery for twenty years. The collection is divided into groups, each of which is loaned to Dublin alternately for five-year periods. The first group, which has been exhibited since 1971, includes 'Les Parapluies' by Renoir, 'Eva Gonzales' by Manet, and works by Boudin, Corot, Daumier, Ingres, and others. Modern Continental and Irish schools are represented in the permanent collection.

In 1970 an exchange of pictures was carried out between the National Gallery of Ireland and the Municipal Gallery of Modern Art. By this agreement all works painted by artists born after 1860 are to be housed in the Municipal Gallery, and those of artists born prior to this date are to be kept at the National Gallery in Merrion Sq. It was also agreed that the arrangement should be brought up to date every 10 years. A collection of historical portraits which could once be seen here has also been moved to the National Gallery.

NATIONAL GALLERY, Kildare Place
Although Clarendon's elevation for the Natural History Museum was used as a basis for the design of this structure, the columnar portico and middle galleries were added by Sir Thomas Manly Deane. Those responsible for the actual building work were Sir Richard Griffiths and Captain Francis Fowke, who were employed by the Board of Works.

The gallery's collections of pictures by Old Masters were begun in 1856 – although the gallery was not formally opened until 1864 – and include outstanding examples of works from all major schools. Irish works include a superb series of national portraits by John Butler Yeats the Elder, and the landscapes of Nathaniel Hone.

One of Yeat's sons, Jack, is represented by a dozen brilliantly characteristic works covering his painting life of 50 years. Jack B Yeats died in 1957 and was considered the most imaginatively poetic of all Irish painters. The National Portrait Gallery, housed in the same building, covers many religious, political, literary, and artistic figures who have played parts in Irish history from the 16thc to the present day. Also of interest is a cabinet of prints, water colours, and drawings.

NATIONAL LIBRARY, Kildare St
Founded in 1877, the National Library was built up round a nucleus formed by the library of the Royal Society of Dublin, and housed in its fine, Renaissance-style building during 1890. Its Department of Printed Books keeps over 500,000 volumes, and the extensive Department of Manuscripts includes microfilm copies of manuscripts existing in other countries. Particular emphasis is laid on the collection of material relating to Ireland, including maps of the country, a unique collection of Irish newspapers, and the Joly Collection of some 70,000 prints. The foundation is well-used as a general reference library by research workers.

NATIONAL MUSEUM, Kildare St; Merrion St
The national collections relating to Ireland's antiquities, fine arts (exclusive of painting and sculpture), history, folklife, and natural history (exclusive of botany) are housed in this museum. The natural history collection is accommodated in a separate building entered from Merrion St, while the others are in the main building – entered from Kildare St.

The exhibition of antiquities illustrates the history of man in Ireland from remote prehistoric times to the end of the middle ages. Of particular interest is a large collection of personal gold ornaments dating from the bronze age; a number of reconstructed bronze-age graves; and decorated iron-age metalwork. The early-Christian period was remarkable for the production of highly-decorative metalwork, and is represented in the museum by a series of richly-ornamented brooches, shrines, and miscellaneous objects of an ecclesiastical nature. The most noteworthy of these items are the 8th-c Tara Brooch, 8th-c Ardagh Chalice, 11th-c Shrine of St Patrick's Bell, and 12th-c Cross of Cong.

Included in the art collections are Irish silver, glass, coins and medals, costumes, textiles, lace, musical instruments, arms, and material relating to the main historical movements and personalities from the late 18thc to recent times. Also on exhibition are ceramics from Irish, English, and Continental factories, plus Irish and European furniture and examples of religious wood sculpture.

Specimens of all the native Irish mammals, birds, and fishes are represented by the natural history collection, together with many examples of other life forms and an extensive display of animal life of all kinds from all parts of the world.

ROYAL IRISH ACADEMY, Dawson St
It is thought that this late 18th-c house, built for the Knox family of Dungannon, may have been designed by John Ensor. Originally it was known as Northland House, and although it is mainly brick-built the structure includes stone quoins, string-courses, window cases, and cornice. The remarkable interior features elaborate 'Chinese' plaster in white on a green ground. Other features include the throne and some of the benches from the old House of Lords. The Royal Irish Academy took the house over to accommodate its priceless collection of Irish manuscripts in 1852. Included in this collection are the *Book of the Dun Cow,* the *Book of Ballymote,* and an autograph copy of the *Annals of the Four Masters.* In addition to its many other activities, the Academy supports scientific research and has been responsible for many important investigations.

Dublin's 18th-c Mansion House has an illustrious history. The adoption of the Declaration of Independence took place here in 1919, and the Truce was signed here in 1921. (See page 54).

BELFAST

Few cities in the British Isles can boast the varied and beautiful countryside which surrounds Belfast, the capital of Northern Ireland. It stands at the point where the River Lagan empties into the 12m-long and 4m-broad expanse of Belfast Lough, and is guarded to the north and west by the 1,000ft basalt plateau of Antrim. Examples of the variation in scenery around the city include 1,182ft Cave Hill to the north, the richly-wooded Lagan Valley to the west, and the undulating green hills which rise to the south and south east of the lough. Environment plays such a large part in the shaping of a people that it might be relevant to compare Belfast folk with the landscape. The contrast between Co Antrim's hard rock and the gentle slopes of Co Down is reflected in a way of life which includes both the warm, Celtic contribution of ready speech and the dramatic Ulster-Scots strain of endurance, invention, purpose, and the relegation of pageantry to a few annual occasions.

Belfast as it is today is a typical example of a 19th-c town where rapid and unplanned development has resulted from a sudden urgent need for housing and industry. It may lack the timeless graciousness of a city which has gradually evolved over hundreds of years, but its atmosphere of purposeful progression might be considered ample compensation. Its huge industries and commercial enterprise provide employment for almost half the population of Northern Ireland.

The name Belfast is derived from *Bealfeirste*, meaning the Mouth of the Sandy Ford, and refers to a crossing on the little River Farset – on the banks of which the early town was sited. This river is now culverted, but it used to flow down what is now the centre of the High Street and empty into an arm of the lough which was large enough for the berthing of marine vessels. Much of the city's early history is centred around this ford. The earliest mention of the crossing appears in the *Annals of The Four Masters,* which records a battle fought here between the Ulidians and Picts in AD 665. Prehistoric man was originally attracted to the mouth of the Lagan by the abundance of wildfowl and fish in the area, and remains of early tools and weapons have been discovered in the raised beaches on both sides of the lough. Belfast's development as a town can be traced back to 1177, when John de Courcy built a castle to command the ford from a strong position in a settlement which stood between the modern city's Donegall Place and Corn Market. The memory of this first stronghold is perpetuated in the names of Castle Street, Castle Lane, and Castle Place.

In 1315 the castle was destroyed by Edward Bruce. In the early 16thc Belfast was little more than a fishing village - although still described as a fortress – in the hands of the O Neills. This family were the Earls of Tyrone, and ruled the Lagan Valley from their stronghold of Castlereagh. Belfast continued to be a place of strategic importance however, and it was attacked twice during Edward Fitzgerald's risings of 1503 and 1512. Fitzgerald was the Earl of Kildare. The O Neills finally relinquished their hold over the town and fortress in 1571, after the assassination of Brian O Neill and the subjugation of his son. The property passed into the hands of Sir Thomas Smith, at that time a favourite of Queen Elizabeth, but was later forfeited by him to the Lord Deputy Sir Arthur Chichester. In 1612 Sir Arthur was made Baron Chichester of Belfast.

At this time the town consisted of 120 houses, a partly-ruined church, a brewhouse, and a mill in the area now known as Millfield. Chichester immediately brought a large number of colonists from England and Scotland and built himself a palace on the site of the old castle. The appearance of the Chichester family on the Belfast scene marked the start of an intensive growth period. The town received a charter of incorporation from James I in 1613, with the right to return two members to parliament, and in 1632 Thomas Wentworth – the Earl of Stafford – was appointed 1st Lord Deputy of Ireland with fiscal rights of the monopoly of imported goods for Belfast. This right had formerly been held by Carrickfergus, hitherto a more important town and garrison, and the associated prosperity was a major factor in the capital's development.

After the 1641 rebellion the town was surrounded by a deep ditch and rampart which were pierced by gates on the land side. North gate stood at the junction of Hercules Street, North Street, and John Street, while Millgate stood near the point where Chapel Lane intersects Castle Street. Colonization by Chichester's followers necessitated the building of houses and led directly to the introduction of a brick-making industry from the area's abundant clay. In the course of Sir Arthur's own building operations he requested the manufacture of 1,200,000 good bricks 'whereof, after finishing the castle, there will be a good proportion left for the building of other tenements within the saide towne of Belfast'.

James II anulled the original charter, but this was restored by William III in 1690. Industry continued to develop – for instance, the establishment of letterpress printing by James Blow in 1696 – and Belfast's commercial interests began to take precedence over its strategic importance. This development had been considerably aided by an influx of French Huguenots in 1685, who introduced many improvements in the already well-established linen industry under the leadership of the distinguished Louis Crommwelin. Another significant advance was the appearance of the Belfast News Letter in 1737. This was the world's first daily newspaper, and its records present a unique history of social life from the time of its foundation to the present day. In 1788 the Belfast Library, now known as the Linenhall Library, was founded and accommodated in the old White Linen Hall. A developing interest in education resulted in the foundation of the Belfast Academy in 1785, followed by that of the Belfast Academical Institution in 1815. Both of these institutions later earned the prefix 'Royal'. Belfast's growth was confirmed by the foundation of Queen's College between 1845 and 1849, and the granting of city status by Queen Victoria in 1888. An outstanding school for girls, founded in 1859, was first called the Ladies Collegiate School but changed its name to Victoria College by royal command in 1887.

The 'sleech' or slobland on which the town rests required some ingenuity in building. This was provided by the blind engineer Alexander Mitchell, whose invention of screw-piling became the accepted method of foundation construction in other parts of the world where similar conditions prevailed. Belfast's ship-building industry began with the enterprises of William Ritchie of Ayrshire, and dates from 1791. The earliest records of this type of work, on a somewhat smaller basis, date back to the building of the 150-ton 'Eagle Wing' on the shores of Belfast Lough in 1636 by a group of Presbyterians who sought refuge in the 'New World' of America. In 1858 Mr Harland was joined by Mr Wolff of Hamburg to found the famous Harland and Wolff shipbuilding yard. This highly-successful industry pioneered many new techniques and was responsible for the construction of some of the great, record-breaking ocean liners. The shipyards and the famous Short Bros aircraft factory were prime enemy targets during the second world war, when Belfast shared

Cave Hill, so-called because of its interesting caves, rises to 1,182ft outside Belfast and is surmounted by the earthwork of MacArt's Fort. On the lower slopes are 19th-c Belfast Castle, the Floral Hall, Bellvue Park, Hazlewood, and the Zoological Gardens.

the agony of the blitz with Britain and lost 1,000 civilians. Belfast also lost its city centre during that period.

The corner of Castle Place and Corn Market is a vantage point from which both streets, which formed the nucleus around which the city grew, can be seen simultaneously. In the early part of the 17thc the boundary wall of the castle ran along the south side of Castle Place, and the area where the Ulster Club now stands was occupied by the small houses of shopkeepers and tradesmen. At this time the castle was the home of the 3rd Earl of Donegall, who owned Belfast and its environs and was killed fighting in the Duke of Marlborough's army. After his death the property came into the hands of his wife and six daughters, but in 1706 the castle was destroyed by a fire which claimed the lives of three of his daughters. The inheritance was taken over by the Duke's nephew, who adopted an energetic approach to his task of extending the town. His initial steps included a survey, an arrangement for the surrender of old leases, and the issuing of new leases in 1767. The new agreements included an obligation on the part of the owners to replace old building with a 'good and substantial Messuage or tenement of Brick and Lime, or Stone and Lime . . . to be built Twenty-eight Feet high and fourteen inches thick at least' within 14 years. This was, in fact, an attempt at town planning. High Street grew up on the curving banks of the Farset River, which flowed down the centre of the road, but the original design intention has been diminished since the river was culverted. The junction of the Farset with the more important Lagan is near the Custom House, considered the finest public building in the city.

The corner of High Street and Corn Market is the site of an old market house, where the idealistic Henry Joy McCracken was hanged as a rebel. He was buried in the churchyard of St George's. Waring Street became an alternative way to the docks in old Belfast and thereby attracted merchants to choose it as a centre for trading. It was named after a merchant whose daughter became the object of one of Jonathan Swift's eccentric passions. Swift lived between 1667 and 1745, and a fellow literary figure – Thackeray – wrote of him 'To think of him, is like thinking of the ruin of a great empire.' A meeting house for the United Irishmen once stood in the passage of Sugarhouse Entry, which ran between Waring Street and High Street. A main feature of Waring Street is the excellent stonework displayed by the head office of the Ulster Bank.

Donegal Quay is the heart of the city and the starting point for various cross-channel steamers. Liverpool ships which came here at low tide up until c1839 had to land their passengers by means of small boats. They had no choice, because this was the only quay in existence before the Harbour Commissioner created the Victoria Channel and the docks and basins that have made Belfast a great port. The position of Harbour Commissioner was established in 1831, and the person who held it was responsible for all port facilities.

Towards the end of the 18thc Belfast supported numerous little industrial and commercial enterprises, including linen mills, cotton mills, warehouses, and small shipbuilding yards, but the buildings associated with these have vanished. Survivals from this period include several churches and the old Charitable Institute of 1771, now known as Clifton House, but many fine structures have been lost. The original layout of Donegall Place and Donegall Square – in which the White Linen Hall was built between 1784 and 1787 – included a series of broad streets which were lined with houses of the late-Georgian style. Some of the other streets also show definite signs of embryonic – if accidental – town planning. Wellington Place, Chichester Street, Howard Street, and May Street are the main east-to-west thoroughfares. The limiting north and south lines are formed by Cromac and Great Victoria Streets. The entire system thus defined forms a framework in which the linen merchants established themselves. The wide, tree-lined streets of Bedford, Adelaide, and Alfred run south from Donegall Square South and feature several good warehouses of brick construction. Also here is the 19th-c Ulster Hall, south of which are the University and Botanic Gardens.

It is not surprising that a city with such a long and involved history as Belfast should have reared and nurtured many famous men. Among these was Dr William Drennan, who was born the son of a Presbyterian minister in 1754 and became a poet infected by the spirit of free thought that was sweeping Europe during his lifetime. He became a leader of the United Irishmen, and coined the term 'Emerald Isle' in his poem *When Erin First Rose*. Other eminent men from the city include the poet and antiquary Samuel Ferguson, born 1810; the 19th-c scientist Lord Kelvin; the statesman Lord Bryce, born 1838; and Sir Almroth Wright, who was born in 1861 and became a famous physician. Belfast's men of letters include Canon Hannay, who was also known as George Birmingham and died in 1950; John Ervine the dramatist; Forrest Reid the novelist, born at the pleasant Georgian house of Mount Charles in 1875; and the 20th-c poet Louis Mac Neice. Mac Neice was the son of Bishop of Down, Connor, and Dromore, who wrote 'I was born in Belfast between the mountain and the gantries'. W R Rodgers the poet and C S Lewis the philosopher were also born in the city, and local painters include Sir John Lavery and Paul Henry.

The Harland and Wolff shipyard is representative of the thriving industry which has brought so many Ulster people to Belfast and the east coast.

The city's hospitals have pioneered some remarkable medical techniques with the aid of brilliant men like Professor J F Pantridge of the Royal Victoria, who evolved the invaluable cardiac unit. This consists of an ambulance, called the Mobile Cardiac Resuscitation Unit, which is fully equipped to commence treatment on emergency heart operations from the first moment of contact. Similar units exist at other hospitals. Internationally-known names such as MacAfee, Fraser, Lowry, and many others are in the fine tradition of medicine built up by the university and hospitals.

Although Belfast is without training facilities of international standard, the city still manages to produce many distinguished athletes. These include Mike Bull, the pole-vaulter who gained a gold medal in the Commonwealth Games; David Larmour, the gold medalist fly-weight boxer, and Mary Peters – Olympic gold medalist for the pentathlon, and one of the great names in modern athletics.

CATHEDRALS AND CHURCHES

The churches of Belfast are many and varied, but as with the city's other buildings they are nearly all of fairly recent date. One of the earliest is the Knockbreda parish church (CI) of 1747, which stands at the end of Ormeau Road. Richard Cassels designed this as a short cruciform plan with an apsidal chancel and transepts. Both the Carlisle Memorial Church of 1875 and St Peter's Pro-Cathedral (RC) of 1886, in Derby Street, display an interesting gothick style. St Patrick's Church (RC) stands in Donegall Street and contains a tryptych which was painted in the pre-Raphaelite manner by Sir John Lavery. Sir John was baptized in this church, which dates from 1877.

Behind the Presbyterian Assembly College, near the Botanic Gardens, is the striking Christian Science First Church

BELFAST

Central Plan
1. Albert Memorial Clock Tower
2. Belfast Bank
3. Carlisle Memorial Church
4. Christ Church (CI)
5. City Hall
6. Clifton House (Old Charitable Institute)
7. Custom House
8. Linenhall Library
9. Municipal College of Technology
10. Old Museum
11. Old Presbyterian Oval Church
12. Royal Belfast Academical Institution
13. Royal Courts of Justice
14. St Anne's Cathedral (CI)
15. St George's Church (CI)
16. St Malachy's Church (RC)
17. St Patrick's Church (RC)
18. Ulster Bank
19. Ulster Hall

by Clough Williams Ellis. Its black and white exterior is certainly unusual. Also in this area of the city, on Malone Road, is St John's Church (CI) of 1894. This was designed by Henry Seaver and features beautiful examples of the work produced by artists Wilhelmina Geddes and Evie Hone. St Molua's Church (CI) stands in east Belfast and is a pleasing modern structure by Denis O D Hanna.

James MacKendrey produced the bronze over the door of the parish hall, and inside the church itself is an apse mural by Desmond Kinney.

CHRIST CHURCH (CI), College Sq North

This 18th-c church is a brick building with an Ionic stone, unpedimented front which was completed later than the main building in 1833. This good example of Georgian classicism was by William Farrel, who was also the architect of Colebrook in Co Fermanagh. Inside the structure are some delicate cast-iron columns, and a three-decker pulpit in pitch-pine. The latter was by William Batt in 1878.

OLD PRESBYTERIAN OVAL CHURCH, Rosemary St

Roger Mulholland completed this beautiful Unitarian church in 1783. The overall design theme of the interior is elliptical, and its flowing lines have been preserved in spite of an extension which was necessary to accommodate the organ. The oval pattern is repeated in the enclosed box pews and the gallery, and an elegant curving staircase mounts to the pulpit. Other features include a radial-plastered ceiling and examples of fine woodwork. When John Wesley preached here in 1789 he pronounced it the 'completest place of worship I have ever seen'. Distinguished members of the church's congregation included Henry Joy McCracken, his uncle Robert, his sister Mary, and Dr William Drennan.

ST ANNE'S CATHEDRAL (CI), Donegall St

Some people consider that the effect of this building, when set against the considerable period of time taken for its construction, is disappointing. It was erected to replace the old parish Church of St Anne by the two architects Thomas Drew and W H Lynn, who began work in 1899. The west front was completed in 1927 as a memorial to the Ulstermen who gave their lives in the 1914 to 1918 war. The tall nave is plain and contains nave columns and corbels displaying carvings by Morris Harding. W H Lynn was responsible for the baptistry, which contains mosaics by Gertrude Stein and a font carved with angel heads by Rosamund Praeger. The font was presented to the church by the children of the diocese.

The interesting nave pavement is a harmonious blend of black marble from Kilkenney and Galway, white marble from Recess, Clifden, and Dunlewy, plus the red marble of Cork. Rose windows opening into the north and south aisles portray biblical scenes, and the mosaic roof is formed of 150,000 pieces of glass arranged to represent the Creation. The tomb of Lord Carso, the Northern Unionist Leader who died in 1935, is in the nave.

ST GEORGE'S CHURCH (CI), High St

Originally erected as a chapel of ease but now used as a parish church, St George's stands on a site which was once occupied by the ancient Chapel-of-the-Ford-of-Belfast. The present structure was opened for worship in 1819. Dublin architect John Bowden was responsible for the body of the church, which is considered a fine example of Georgian stonework. Its portico of Corinthian columns, probably designed by Michael Shanaghan, was transferred from the front of a palace which was being built at Ballyscullion by the eccentric Bishop of Derry – Earl of Bristol. Bishop Alexander presented the front to the church; it would be interesting to know what it would have looked like at its intended location on the shores of Lough Beg. The churchyard contains the grave of the idealistic rebel Henry Joy McCracken, who was hanged on the site of the city's old market house.

ST MALACHY'S CHURCH (RC), Alfred St

Designed by Thomas Jackson and completed in 1848, this unusual church has a strangely eccentric exterior which displays numerous turrets and battlements. The interior is undoubtedly the most sumptuous in Belfast. Of particular note is the fan-vaulted ceiling.

ST MARK'S (CI), Dundela

The hilltop situation of this late 19th-c church by William Butterfield makes it an interesting landmark on the road between Holywood and Bangor. Its red-sandstone construction and tall, square belfry are very distinctive, and the building has been greatly admired by Sir John Betjeman – the Poet Laureate.

FAMOUS AND HISTORIC BUILDINGS

CASTLE AND CAVE HILL, Antrim Rd

Belfast's modern castle was built c1870 by the 3rd Marquess of Donegal. It was designed by Sir Charles Lanyon in true Scottish baronial style, and stands on the lower slopes of Cave Hill. Features include a six-storey square tower and an outside staircase which was added in 1894. The castle and its grounds were presented to Belfast Corporation by Lord Shaftesbury. Adjacent are Hazlewood, with the Floral Hall; Bellevue Park, with the Zoological Gardens and a fine view over the city; and the 1,182ft summit of Cave Hill.

Cave Hill is noted for its five caves and is surmounted by the earthwork of MacArt's Fort, which was once known as Ben Madagan after a local chieftain who lived c AD 933. This flat-topped stronghold is guarded by cliffs which

Belfast Castle was built by the 3rd Marquess of Donegal c1870, and was presented to the Corporation of Belfast with a large extent of ground by the Earl of Shaftsbury.

drop from its east, north-east, and south-east sides, while the vulnerable land side is scored by a great ditch measuring 25ft wide by 10ft deep. In clear weather the view from this summit extends over the city and lough, sometimes reaching as far as the Isle of Man and the Scottish coast.

CITY HALL, Donegall Sq

White Linen Hall was replaced in function by this large quadrangular building of Portland limestone, which was designed by Brumwell Thomas in 1906. It is Renaissance in style and is ranged round a central courtyard. The great dome which rises at its centre is balanced by towers at each of the four corners. Italian marble was used to line the walls of the impressive entrance hall, which is floored with black and white marble and includes a fine staircase lit by stained-glass windows. The latter portray various scenes from Irish history. The most handsome of the four halls that comprise the structure is considered to be the Great Hall.

A stone statue of Queen Victoria in the fine gardens was executed by Sir Thomas Brock and unveiled by King Edward VII in 1903. Works by Brumwell Thomas, apart from the building itself, include the Cenotaph, the Garden of Remembrance, and a striking monument to the Royal Irish Rifles. Thomas and Frederick Pomeroy were jointly responsible for the exceptionally fine memorial to the 1st Marquis of Dufferin. A simple plinth stands in front of the City Hall to commemorate the arrival of the American Services into the second world war. In the grounds of the hall is a memorial to the Belfast-built liner 'Titanic', which struck an iceberg and sank with tragic loss of life in 1912.

CLIFTON HOUSE or OLD CHARITABLE INSTITUTE, North Queen St

Said to have been the work of Robert Joy, a Belfast paper merchant, this fine structure is considered a good example

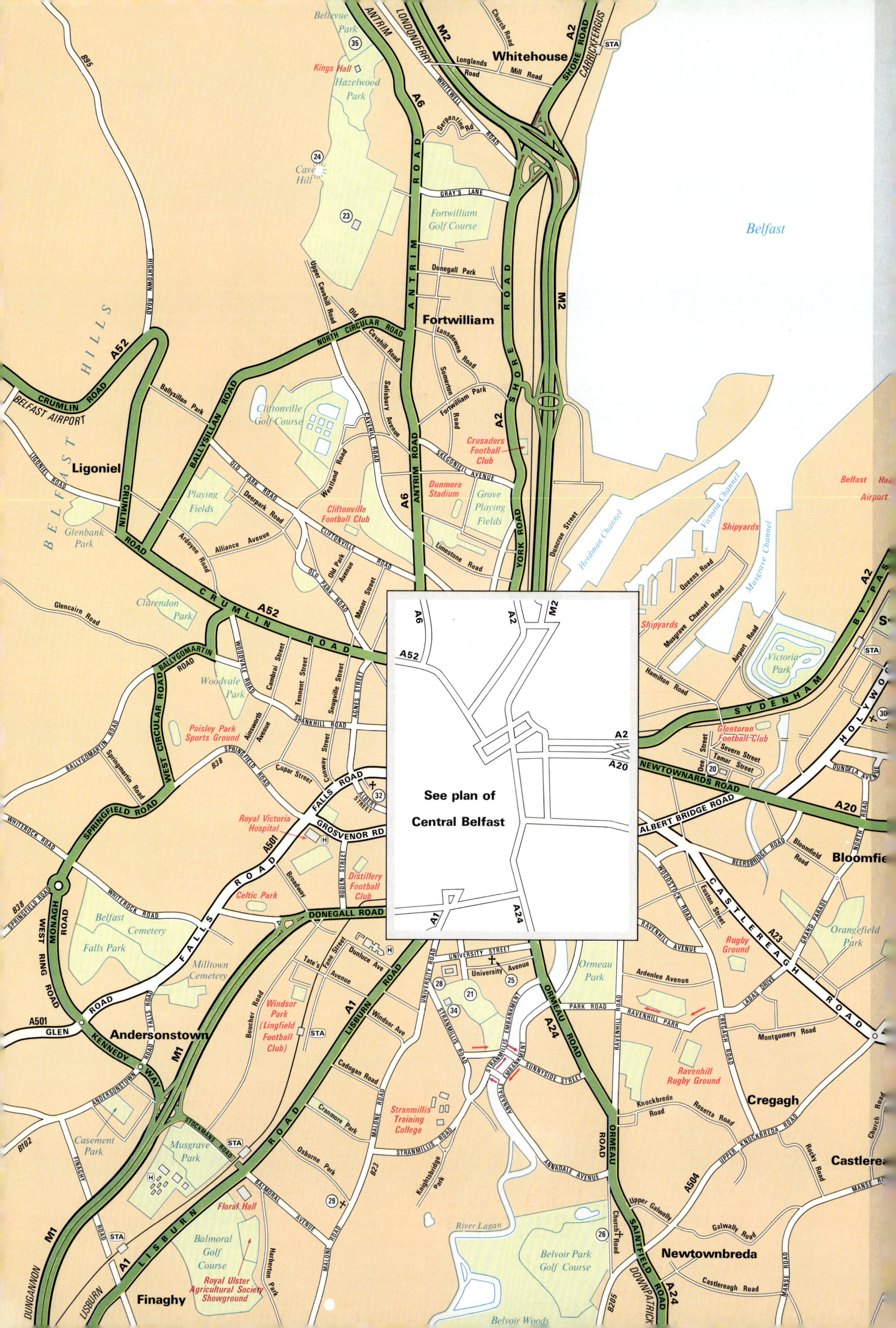
Bellevue Park
35
Kings Hall
Hazelwood Park
ANTRIM ROAD
LONDONDERRY
M2
Church Road
Whitehouse
A2
SHORE ROAD
CARRICKFERGUS
STA
Longlands Road
Mill Road
WHITEWELL ROAD
A6
Serpentine Rd
24
Cave Hill
B95
HIGHTOWN ROAD
GRAY'S LANE
Fortwilliam Golf Course
Belfast
23
Donegall Park
Upper Cavehill Road
Fortwilliam
Old Cavehill Road
NORTH CIRCULAR ROAD
Lansdowne Road
Somerton Road
Fortwilliam Park
A52
BELFAST HILLS
CRUMLIN ROAD
BELFAST AIRPORT
Ballysillan Park
BALLYSILLAN ROAD
Cliftonville Golf Course
Salisbury Avenue
CAVEHILL ROAD
Crusaders Football Club
SKEGONEILL AVENUE
Ligoniel
LIGONIEL ROAD
Playing Fields
OLD PARK ROAD
Deerpark Road
Westland Road
Dunmore Stadium
Grove Playing Fields
YORK ROAD
Belfast Ha
Airport
Herdman Channel
Victoria Channel
Shipyards
Musgrave Channel
Glenbank Park
Ardoyne Road
Alliance Avenue
Cliftonville Football Club
CLIFTONVILLE ROAD
Limestone Road
Duncrue Street
Old Park Avenue
Manor Street
Queens Road
Musgrave Channel Road
Clarendon Park
Glencairn Road
WOODVALE ROAD
Cambrai Street
Tennent Street
Snugville Street
AGNES STREET
Airport Road
Victoria Park
BALLYGOMARTIN ROAD
Woodvale Park
Hamilton Road
SYDENHAM BY-PASS
Paisley Park Sports Ground
Ainsworth Avenue
SHANKHILL ROAD
Glentoran Football Club
Severn Street
Dee Street
Tamar Street
20
HOLYWOOD
30
Springmartin Road
WEST CIRCULAR ROAD
SPRINGFIELD ROAD
B38
Cupar Street
Conway Street
FALLS ROAD
ALBERT STREET
32
NEWTOWNARDS ROAD
DUNDELA AVENUE
A20
See plan of Central Belfast
A1
A24
WHITEROCK ROAD
Royal Victoria Hospital
H
GROSVENOR RD
A501
ALBERT BRIDGE ROAD
BEERSBRIDGE ROAD
Bloomfield Road
Bloomfie
NORTH ROAD
Broadway
RODEN STREET
Distillery Football Club
WOODSTOCK ROAD
CASTLEREAGH ROAD
Euston Street
GRAND PARADE
Celtic Park
DONEGALL ROAD
MONAGH ROAD
Belfast Cemetery
Falls Park
RAVENHILL AVENUE
Rugby Ground
Orangefield Park
A23
WEST RING ROAD
FALLS
Milltown Cemetery
Tate's Avenue
Fane Street
Dunluce Ave
UNIVERSITY STREET
University Avenue
25
Ormeau Park
Ardenlee Avenue
UNIVERSITY ROAD
28
21
34
STRANMILLIS EMBANKMENT
ORMEAU ROAD
PARK ROAD
RAVENHILL ROAD
RAVENHILL PARK
LADAS DRIVE
Montgomery Road
GLEN ROAD
KENNEDY WAY
Andersonstown
Boucher Road
Windsor Park (Lingfield Football Club)
LISBURN ROAD
Windsor Ave
STRANMILLIS ROAD
SUNNYSIDE STREET
Ravenhill Rugby Ground
CREGAGH ROAD
M1
Cadogan Road
ANNADALE EMBANKMENT
Cregagh
Knockbreda Road
Rosetta Road
ANDERSONSTOWN ROAD
Cranmore Park
Stranmillis Training College
STOCKMANS ROAD
Casement Park
B102
Musgrave Park
FINAGHY ROAD
MALONE ROAD
Osborne Park
B23
Knightsbridge Park
ANNADALE AVENUE
UPPER KNOCKBREDA ROAD
Rocky Road
Castlerea
A504
MANSE ROAD
BALMORAL AVENUE
29
Floral Hall
River Lagan
Upper Galwally
Galwally Road
Balmoral Golf Course
Haberton Park
Belvoir Park Golf Course
26
Newtownbreda
SAINTFIELD ROAD
DUNGANNON
Royal Ulster Agricultural Society Showground
Finaghy
LISBURN
Belvoir Woods
B205
DOWNPATRICK
Castlereagh Road

BELFAST

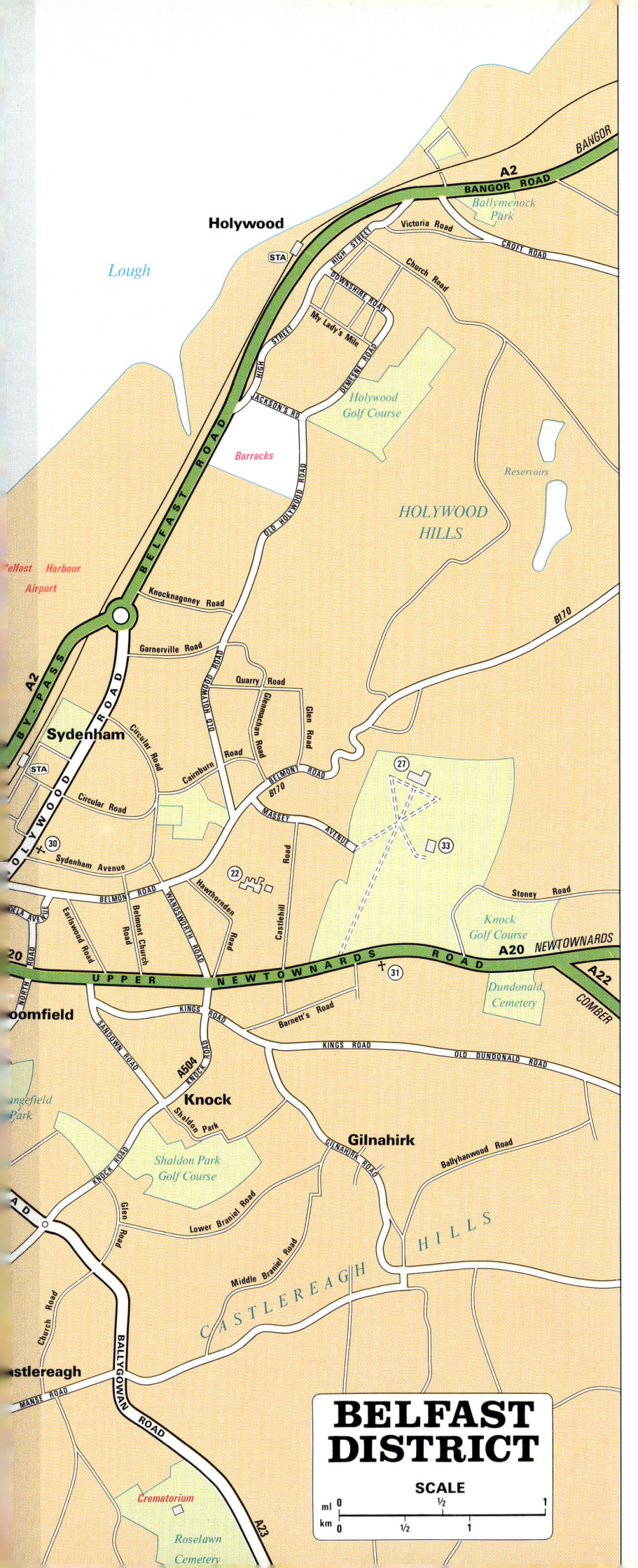

of Irish-Georgian public building. It features a fine, pedimented brick-built façade with a stone spire, and wings that were added and extended in 1821 and 1829. The main body of the building dates from 1771.

CUSTOM HOUSE, High St
This Corinthian-style structure is often considered the city's finest public building, and stands near the point where the culverted River Farset flows into the Lagan. It dates from 1857 and was designed by Sir Charles Lanyon in the 'Italian style after Palladio'. The outer arms of its E-shaped plan are joined by a staircase and high platform, and the portico is a fine composition by Thomas Fitzpatrick. The main fabric of the building comprises a fine, golden stone. Anthony Trollope, the 19th-c novelist, worked here as a surveyor's clerk in 1841. His many experiences during this period are often related through his books.

PARLIAMENT BUILDINGS, Stormont
Some 300 acres of gardens surround this English-Palladian style complex of buildings, which forms the administrative centre of the province and lies 5m E of the city. Materials used in the construction of the group include Portland stone and unpolished granite from the Mourne Mountains of Co Down. Six pillars above the main entrance are surmounted by a figure of Britannia with two lions. The vestibule leads to the central hall. To the left of this is the House of Commons, which is enriched with Travertine and Botticino marbles, plus polished walnut. The Senate Chamber, which lies to the right of the hall, is decorated with Botticino marbles and ebonized mahogany. Also in the complex are the Members' Library, Dining Room, and Conference Rooms.

ROYAL COURTS OF JUSTICE, Chichester St
This impressive building of Portland Stone was opened in May 1933 as a gift from the British parliament. It was designed by J G West and includes accommodation for the 'Four Courts', including the Court of Appeal.

STORMONT CASTLE, Stormont
Formerly the official residence of the Prime Minister of Northern Ireland, this 'essay in the Scottish baronial style' is now occupied by government offices. It is situated some 5m E of the city.

ULSTER and BELFAST BANKS, Waring St
The headquarters of the Ulster Bank occupy a yellow-stone building designed in an Italian-romantic variation on the classic theme by James Hamilton of

District Plan
20 Belfast Transport Museum
21 Botanic Gardens
22 Campbell College
23 Castle
24 Cave Hill
25 Christian Science First Church
26 Knockbreda Church (CI)
27 Parliament Buildings
28 Queen's University
29 St John's Church (CI)
30 St Mark's Church (CI), Dundela
31 St Molua's Church (CI)
32 St Peter's Pro-Cathedral (RC)
33 Stormont Castle
34 Ulster Museum
35 Zoological Gardens

BELFAST

Parliament House, Stormont, is English-Palladian in style and is considered the finest building in Northern Ireland. The floor space covers some 5 acres (see page 63).

Glasgow. It was completed in 1860, and features excellent stonework by Thomas Fitzpatrick. The Belfast Bank's offices, also in Waring Street, are the oldest public buildings in Belfast. They occupy the old Exchange and Assembly Rooms, where the Harp Festival of 1792 took place, and were transformed into a handsome building of Renaissance-revival style by Lanyon.

ULSTER HALL, Bedford St
This vast building by Barre dates from 1860. Nowadays it caters for boxing and wrestling matches, orchestral concerts, religious meetings, and political gatherings.

MUSEUMS AND LIBRARIES

BELFAST TRANSPORT MUSEUM
Witham St
The many interesting exhibits collected by this museum, which is currently occupying temporary premises in Witham Street, include the original horse-drawn Fintona tram. Also of interest is the Southern Irish locomotive 'Maeve', which dates from 1939 and has now been replaced by modern diesel units.

BOTANIC GARDENS, Stranmillis Rd
After their formation in 1827, the Belfast Botanic and Horticultural Society purchased a small piece of ground for the establishment of a garden. Judicious acquisition of land over the years has swelled this to 38 acres. Of particular interest among the associated buildings is the Palm House, which has two wings flanking a bold, elliptical dome. It is considered one of the earliest examples of a curvilinear glass house in Great Britain, and was designed by Charles Lanyon. Although the foundation stone for this fine structure was laid in 1939, the garden's full range of glass-houses was not complete until the 1950's.

LINENHALL LIBRARY
Donegall Sq North
This fine library was founded in 1788 as the Belfast Society for Promoting Knowledge, and was housed in the city's old White Linen Hall – hence the name. Its superb collection of books relates to Ireland in general, the linen trade in particular, and many other subjects of general and historic interest. The first librarian was scholarly Thomas Russell – 'The Man from God Knows Where' of Florence Wilson's ballad – who was a prominent leader of the United Irishmen. He was hanged at Downpatrick in 1803 for his attempt to rouse the north in support of Emmet's Rising.

OLD MUSEUM, College Sq North
Old Museum, a four-storey stucco building erected in 1831 by Duff and Jackson, was the first of its kind in Ireland. It was the inspiration of the Natural History and Philosophical Society, a group of distinguished scholars founded in 1821. Some of the famous names connected with the society are: Sir James Emerson Tennant, Robert Patterson, George Hyndman, James Macadam, Dr Drummond, and W Thompson the naturalist. The latter's collections of wild birds and the society's Irish antiquities formed the nucleus of the modern museum. A great deal of valuable field work is conducted by the Belfast Field Club, who share the building with allied groups.

ULSTER MUSEUM, Stranmillis Rd
The old building occupied by this museum was by J C Wynne and stands in a fine position adjoining the Botanic Gardens. A modern extension by Francis Pym of London houses an art gallery which displays sculpture, Irish metalwork and glass, ceramics, embroideries, and historic silver. Also here are a representative collection of British water colours; works by Turner, Lawrence, Steer, Sickert, Matthew Smith, and Stanley Spencer; and those of such notable Irish artists as Sir John Lavery and Wilhelmina Geddes. All the American presidents of Ulster descent are represented by portraits painted by Frank McKelvey, who was also responsible for a number of old Belfast scenes.

Other sections of the museum house comprehensive collections of archaeological, technological, and natural history exhibits. A major attraction is the skeleton of a huge, extinct species of deer popularly known as the Irish elk. The museum's policy is to provide a stimulating source of interest for the young.

ACADEMIC FOUNDATIONS

CAMPBELL COLLEGE, Belmont Rd
Ireland's largest public school, Campbell College, lies 3m E of Belfast and comprises a block of impressive, Tudor-style buildings in beautiful grounds.

MUNICIPAL COLLEGE OF TECHNOLOGY
College Sq East
This school is housed in a Portland-stone building which is situated in grounds belonging to the Royal Belfast Academical Institute (designed by Sir John Soane) – a body more popularly known as 'Inst'. It was founded in 1807 by the Presbyterians and included a small medical department in its curriculum. Famous ex-pupils include Lord Kelvin and Viscount Bryce. The College of Technology, built between 1900 and 1907, is equipped with all the machinery necessary to train young people in various manufacturing techniques.

QUEEN'S UNIVERSITY
South of Castle Junction
The central tower of this red-brick, Tudor-gothick building is a replica of the Founder's Tower at Magdalen College in Oxford, and is balanced by several smaller towers. Founded in 1849, Queen's was formerly associated with the old colleges of Cork and Galway until the University of Belfast was incorporated separately in 1909. Buildings recently added to the foundation include the David Keir complex of 1958, which houses the Zoological Museum plus the Departments of Chemistry, Biology, and Civil Engineering. A Redwing figure by F E McWilliam stands in the central court. The Ashby Institute, by Cruikshank and Seward, was built between 1954 and 1964.

Galleons, Gold, and Graves

Many creatures live beneath the surface of the waters that wash the coastline of Ireland, including anemones, sea squirts, starfish, spider crabs and cuttlefish to name but a few. These remarkable animals create a living collage of colour and movement against a backdrop of sand, rock, and weed. In addition to fauna native to Irish waters, foreign species inhabit the coastal areas from time to time, carried on the three ocean currents that flow round and about Ireland. An icy stream flowing down from the Arctic brings cold-loving marine life, while warming tides from the Mediterranean and the Gulf of Mexico propel more tropical visitors to the coast in much the same way as the sea has brought successive waves of settlers, traders, and invaders to Ireland.

For the best part of 8,000 years men have braved the ocean to reach this land. Beginning with mesolithic man, who hunted in the dense forests of the country and fished in its coastal waters, society developed through neolithic farmer and bronze producer to Gaelic-speaking, iron-age man. Each new influx came to Ireland over the sea, probably by means of a timber-framed, skin-covered vessel. Although these frail craft have long since disappeared, a latter-day derivative exists in the *currach*, commonly used in the west of Ireland until quite recently. Such boats were doubtless adapted to various purposes; small ones for fishing in the rivers and along the shore, and larger ones for importing the neolithic farmer's stock and exporting the distinctive metal products of the bronze age. Even in the absence of relics, it takes little effort to imagine the courage and purpose required to undertake the sea voyage to what was then a wild and remote land. Its proximity to Scotland in the north and Wales in the south probably did little to detract from the daunting passage, however short. The sea has always held a forbidding fascination for man, and there is no reason to think that Ireland's early settlers were any less awed by its power and unpredictable nature than today's voyagers.

The peoples from the east brought more than their courage, however. They brought ideas too, and Ireland owes much to the cultivating influence of England, Scotland, Wales, and the European mainland. Tempered and moulded by the indigenous population, these thoughts emerged as the court cairns of the stone age, the copper halberds and gold neck ornaments of the bronze age, the hillforts of the iron age, and the high crosses and round towers of the early-Christian period. Such monuments and antiquities abound in Ireland today; countless other relics lie beneath its waters, unseen reminders of the maritime movement which made the island's cultural development possible.

At a time when Roman ships – 100ft or more in length and built of stout ribs overlaid with fir planking – were plying the Mediterranean, there is evidence of ocean-going vessels off the Irish coast. A remarkable hoard of gold objects – discovered in the 19thc by a ploughman in the townland of Broighter, near Limavady in Co Derry – included a model boat. Although only 7½in in length, it is complete with oars, a steering oar, a mast with yard-arm, and a hold in the central rowing bench for stepping the mast. The find also included a splendid gold collar, decorated in superb La Tène style and dating from the 1stc BC. The gold boat model almost certainly

Many of the prehistoric peoples who settled in Ireland arrived in small, sea-going vessels such as the *currach* (below). Currachs, extensively used from the Aran Islands and the west coast even today, are made of tar-impregnated canvas stretched over a wooden frame. Prehistoric builders probably used animal skins.

The currach oars, shown in the bottom left-hand corner of the picture, are of particular interest. Each is shaped from a length of sturdy timber and includes a block fixed near the handgrip. An eye in the block fits over a wooden pin fixed in the top side frame of the vessel, and the slender blade provides manoeuverability in rough seas.

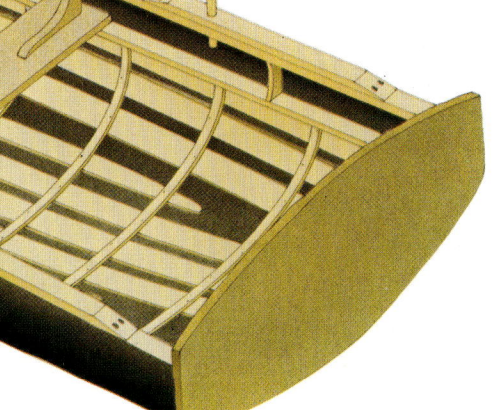

GALLEONS, GOLD, AND GRAVES

represents a large, sea-going craft similar to those used by the famous sea-faring *Veneti*. It may have been deposited on shore as an offering of thanks for safe delivery from shipwreck.

The Romans for their part never extended their empire to Ireland, although they did contemplate an invasion of the country in the 1stc AD. During the period when Agricola was governor of Britain, between 78 and 86, he was informed by Tacitus that 'Ireland's interior parts are little known, but through commercial intercourse and the merchants there is better knowledge of the harbours and approaches.'

During Ireland's early-christian period there was considerable maritime activity in the country's coastal waters, and a corresponding amount of information to detail such activity. For instance, the *Annals of the Four Masters* record one of the earliest Irish shipwrecks AD 728. At this time, there were scores of petty kingdoms in Ireland. Dal Riata's ruling stock, originating in the north, had overflowed into Scotland in the 5thc. According to the account, a fleet from Dal Riata in Scotland was summoned by Flaithbeartach, the Irish High King, to participate in a campaign in Inishowen. The flotilla was defeated and 'countless' crew members were drowned in the River Bann. Four years later it was recorded that Failbhe, son of Guaire, was drowned together with his 22-man crew in a second wreck. Irish ships fought near their own coast during this period, but trade took them far beyond their country's shores. St Filibert of Jumieges recorded visits by Irish vessels to the Loire region of France in the 8thc, and in return Gaulish ships carried cargoes of wine up the River Shannon as far as Clonmacnoise.

With the coming of the Vikings in 794, naval activity in Irish waters inevitably quickened. The Norsemen struck not only at coastal points like Cork, Dunseverick in Co Antrim, Bangor in Co Down, and Waterford, but carried the attacks inland to places like Armagh, Kildare, Devenish in Lough Erne, and Clonmacnoise on the Shannon. The Vikings berthed their ships and established camps on rivers and inland loughs over a wide area, surely striking terror into the heart of a people who had known centuries of relative peace. Early Irish society saw its monasteries plundered, its churches burned, and the erosion of its old Gaelic order. The rivers Liffey and Boyne, the sea-loughs Foyle and Strangford, and the inland loughs Neagh and Ree on the Shannon were just a few of the places that knew the Viking sword. Although these invaders from the north brought devastation and destruction, they also left their mark on the country's trading affairs, its architecture, and its art. Many places – such as Waterford, Wexford, and Dublin – became the sites of Viking towns, and many of the sea-loughs, such as Carlingford and Strangford, have retained Scandinavian names rather than their original Gaelic

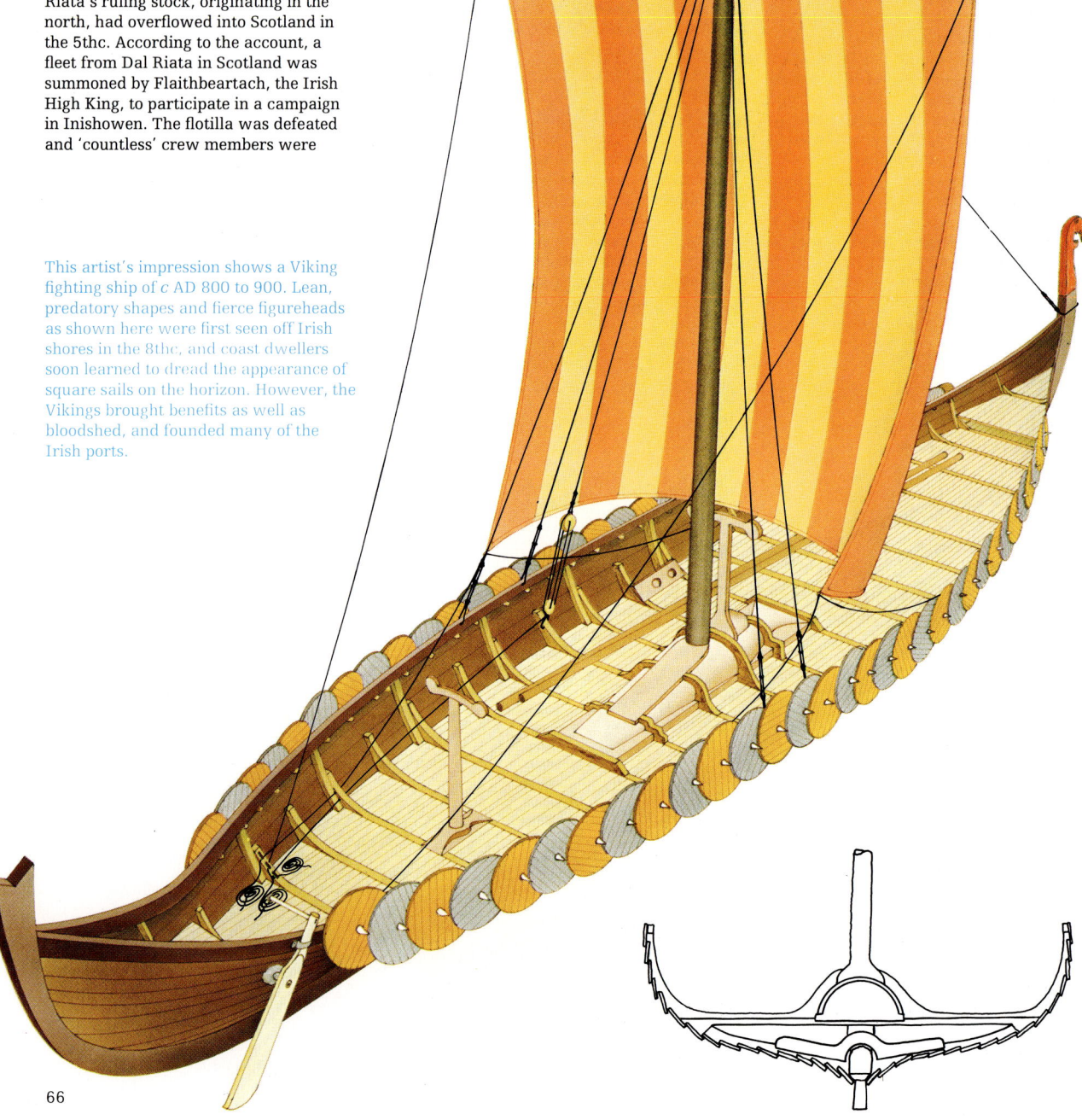

This artist's impression shows a Viking fighting ship of *c* AD 800 to 900. Lean, predatory shapes and fierce figureheads as shown here were first seen off Irish shores in the 8thc, and coast dwellers soon learned to dread the appearance of square sails on the horizon. However, the Vikings brought benefits as well as bloodshed, and founded many of the Irish ports.

GALLEONS, GOLD, AND GRAVES

ones. The Norsemen were not always the victors, however. Notable routes of their ships are recorded at Lough Foyle, Carlingford Lough, Dublin, and Lough Neagh, among others, and in 923 an entire fleet was sunk in Dundrum Bay in Co Down. To date, however, no wrecks of either moored or defeated Viking ships have been recovered. There are at least two reasons for this, the first being that underwater archaeology is a relative newcomer to Irish waters. Secondly, the wooden hulls of these ships will only have survived if buried beneath protective sand, where their low iron content renders them virtually undetectable save by chance.

Roughly a century and a half after the power of the Vikings was broken, the Normans made the first move in a campaign which was to place them in control of three-quarters of Ireland. From the very beginning of English involvement, good use was made of the many seaport settlements developed by the Norsemen. A multiplicity of ships shuttled between the ports of England and those of Ireland, ferrying Norman bowmen, armoured knights, and subsequently, colonists. One of the Irish annals contains an early reference to the conquest: 'In 1171 Henry, King of England, Duke of Normandy and Aquitaine came to Ireland with 240 ships.' The size of the king's fleet was probably not a direct reflection on his status; according to existing documentation, the involvement of large numbers of ships was commonplace at that time.

The Irish were no match for the enemy's troops or statecraft. Henry's son John conceded Connacht to Cathal Crobhderg O'Conchobhar in the hope that it would help to achieve effective authority for the English crown. This and other such moves only served to crystallize the discontent which had existed since the coming of the English. King Cathal, for example, may well have been hunting the Anglo-Norman foe in 1190 or 1191, when he 'went to Clonmacnoise on that night and early next morning embarked in his fleet and sailed up the Shannon until he came to Lough Ree. A violent storm arose on the lake and so agitated the vessel in which O'Conchobhar sailed that it foundered, and all crew, except O'Conchobhar himself and six others, perished.' According to a second source, '36 men were drowned' in this incident. King Cathal most definitely crossed swords with the English in 1199. Some time before then the invaders had seized a castle which was guarding a Shannon crossing to Meath near present-day Athlone. O'Conchobhar burned the castle bawn and carried off booty.

The Gaelic magnates understood the value of naval warfare. By the end of the 12thc many of the small kingdoms maintained fleets, and attack by sea was recognised as a powerful weapon – as evidenced by this 13th-c account: 'Thomas Mac Uchtry and the sons of Randal McSorely came to Derry with a fleet of 71 ships and plundered and destroyed the town.' By means of this assault they were able to 'pass thence into Inishowen and ravage the entire peninsula.'

An interesting reference in the *Annals of Loch Ce* supports the view that the devices and stratagems of naval warfare were quickly adopted in Ireland. In this instance the annalist might actually have been an eye-witness to the event, since it took place on Loch Ce (on the River Boyle, a tributary of the Shannon). The account notes that in 1235 'a fireship was used to take Port na Cairge on Loch Ce', which may well be the first record of the use of this tactic in Irish waters.

During the 13thc, small plundering excursions round the Irish coasts were a recurrent feature. Shipwrecks would have been a continuing and inevitable hazard of such activity, particularly on the west coast – an unwelcome expanse of rocky promontories, sheer cliffs, and wind-tossed waves. Records of the time rarely pinpointed the location of vessels claimed by Neptune, and most are thus lost to time. One report which is more precise is that recounting a manoeuvre in 1247, during which 'O'Dowda and O'Boyle brought a fleet to plunder Carbury; the crew of one ship, under the command of Manus O'Boyle, was drowned at Inis Tuathrass.' The wreck of that craft must lie in the vicinity of Cruit Island, off the north-west coast of Co Donegal.

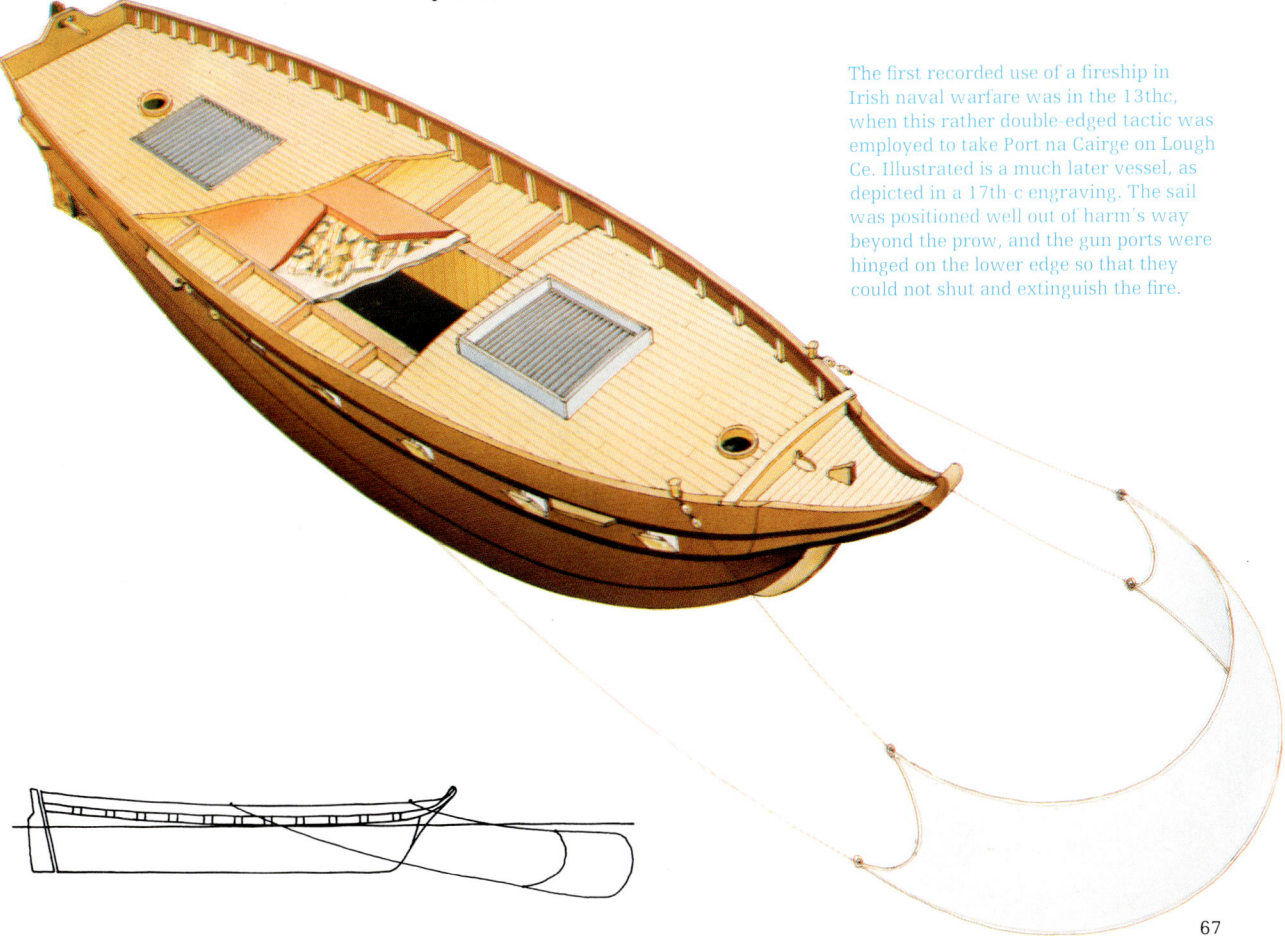

The first recorded use of a fireship in Irish naval warfare was in the 13thc, when this rather double-edged tactic was employed to take Port na Cairge on Lough Ce. Illustrated is a much later vessel, as depicted in a 17th-c engraving. The sail was positioned well out of harm's way beyond the prow, and the gun ports were hinged on the lower edge so that they could not shut and extinguish the fire.

GALLEONS, GOLD, AND GRAVES

In addition to sea-borne raids on the land, the Irish waters saw numerous acts of true piracy, particularly in Connemara. One incident in 1258 is recorded: 'Mac Somhairle and a great fleet robbed a merchant ship of all its goods, both wine and clothing, and copper and iron.' Brigandage afflicted the seas regardless of war and conflict. Gaelic resurgence, on the other hand, owed much to England's involvement in Continental wars and domestic strife. With this resurgence came renewed conflict, both on land and sea. Hoping to forge a Scottish-Irish-Welsh alliance against the Anglo-Norman invaders, Edward Bruce, son of Robert, 'came to Ireland, on the coast of *Uladh* [Ulster] in the North with a fleet of 300 ships.' He campaigned successfully in several regions of the country and sparked a series of uprisings.

Acts of God shared responsibility with those of men for the ships lost or damaged in Irish waters. War ships and trading vessels alike were subject to the destructive force of the wind and waves. In 1365, for instance, 'a very great storm in this year threw down several churches and houses, and also sank many ships and boats'. According to an English source Sir John Arundel's fleet, with reinforcements from Brittany, was scattered by a storm in 1379; 26 ships were wrecked on the Irish coast, including the flagship, and there was great loss of life. Then, as now, nature sometimes dealt a kind of rough justice. The following description concerns a shipwreck off the Aran Islands in 1560, the sequel to a campaign of plundering undertaken by Mahon, the son of Turlough. 'On his return with his spoils, the wind became rough and the sky angry, and the ship and boat were separated from each other. When the ship was making for Aran in the beginning of the night, the sail was swept away from the hands of the men and warriors, and torn to rags off the ropes and tackle, and blown skywards. The ship struck upon a rock, which is at the mouth of Cuan-an-fhir-mhoir, in west Connacht, where she was lost, with her crew, except Mahon and three others. Upwards of one hundred were drowned in that harbour.'

The erosion of the English crown's authority left turbulence in its wake. Petty sniping occurred, one example being the predatory foray of Conor, the son of Owen O'Malley, into west Connacht in 1396. His ship was 'loaded with the riches and prizes taken by that adventure. But all, save one man only, were drowned between Ireland and Aran.' Even the presence of an English fleet was no deterrent to pirates, this time Welsh, who swept into Dublin in 1453, plundering the town and capturing Michael Tregury, Archbishop of Dublin. The timing of Irish pirates was somewhat amiss on one occasion in 1477. A London merchant, Bartholomew Couper, had taken merchandise to the value of 6,000 marks to Ireland in his ship, the *Mary London*. Having discharged his cargo he took on board hundreds of pilgrims bound for Santiago de Compostella in Spain. While he was on his way back from Ireland he was captured by an overwhelming force of pirates, allegedly 500 in number.

Pilgrims could play a more active role, however, as shown by this 1516 account. 'A French knight came upon his pilgrimage to Lough Derg, and on his arrival, and at his departure, he visited O'Donnell, from whom he received great honours, gifts and presents. They formed a great intimacy and friendship with each other. The knight, upon learning

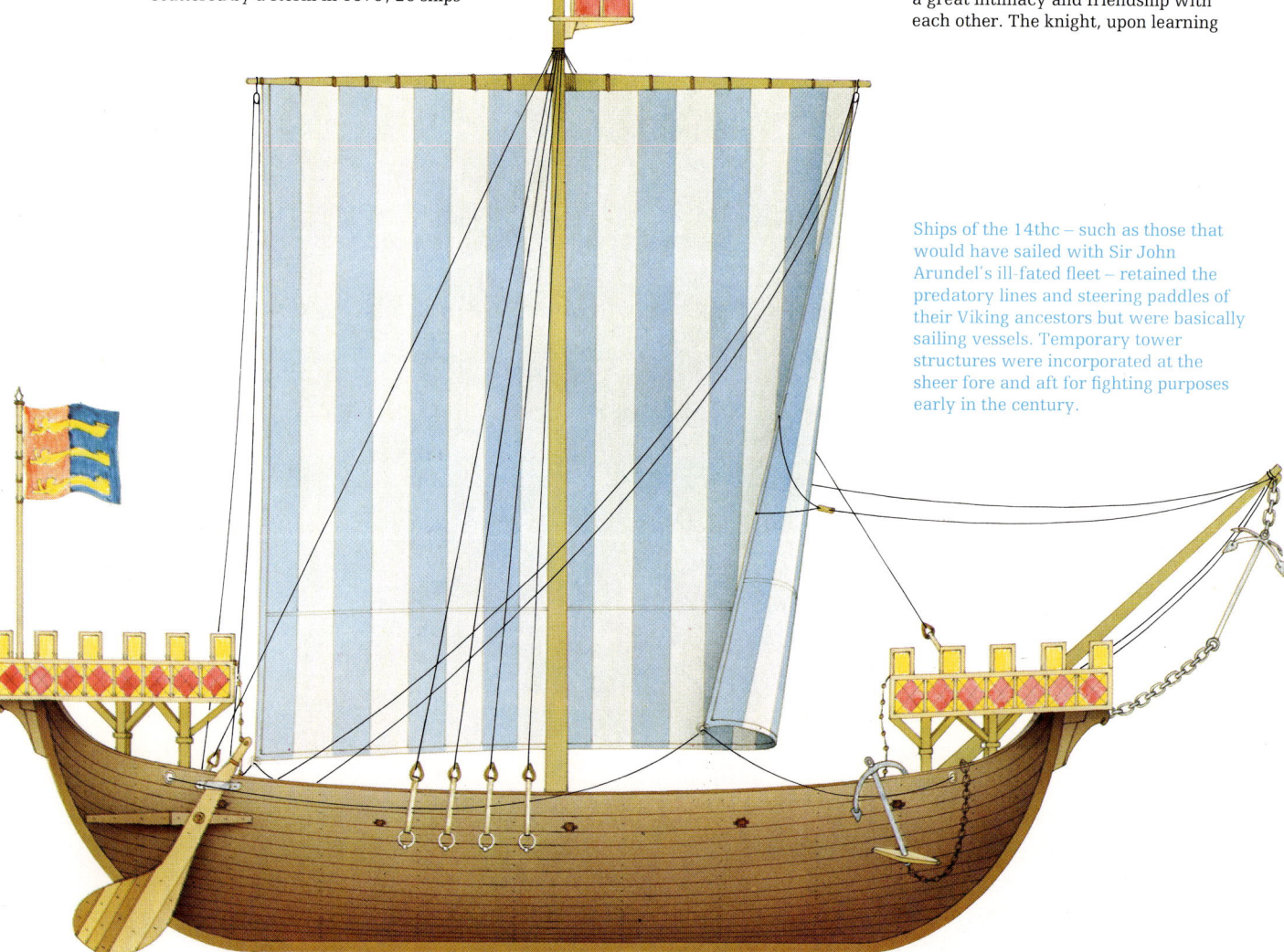

Ships of the 14thc – such as those that would have sailed with Sir John Arundel's ill-fated fleet – retained the predatory lines and steering paddles of their Viking ancestors but were basically sailing vessels. Temporary tower structures were incorporated at the sheer fore and aft for fighting purposes early in the century.

GALLEONS, GOLD, AND GRAVES

that the Castle of Sligo was defended against O'Donnell, promised to send a ship with great guns.' True to his word, the knight sent a ship, which 'arrived in the harbour of Killybegs.' With the aid of the ship's 'great guns', the castle was taken and much of the town destroyed.

Ships sometimes carried cargo more lethal than great guns or armoured knights. According to a grim entry in the annals, in 1478 'a great plague was brought by a ship into the harbour of Assaroe.' This plague spread through the whole of Ulster, leaving behind a trail of death. Previous outbreaks of plague, including the Black Death in 1348–49, must have been occasioned by the arrival in Ireland of contaminated goods or infected travellers.

The Tudors strove to bring another kind of affliction to Ireland, that of subjugation to the English Crown. In support of this aim, a fair number of ships were maintained in Ireland, as instanced by this 1539 account. Lord Leonard, the English Lord Justice, 'made muster of all the English in Ireland . . . and all the fleets in the adjacent harbours and especially the large fleet in the bay of *Carlinne* [Carlingford].' The strength of this force takes on greater significance in light of the accounting of the Royal Navy under Henry VIII in 1546: some 20 ships, 15 galleasses (warships), 10 pinnaces (small craft intended for reconnaissance, dispatch service, and inshore work) and 13 row-barges.

Resistance to English rule came from many quarters. James Fitz Maurice fled to the Continent after leading an unsuccessful rebellion in 1569 against an English adventurer. He returned with 'an Italian fleet of the Pope's people'; prepared to fight for the supremacy of the Catholic religion. These forces landed at Dun-an-oir in Co Kerry, where Fitz Maurice was defeated for the second time, and the hundreds of Italians and Spaniards accompanying him were massacred on the orders of the Lord Justice, Lord Grey. Some of the ordnance used to fortify Dun-an-oir on this particular occasion has been recovered.

In 1588 the Spanish Armada set sail for England. The *Annals of the Four Masters* describe it thus: 'A great fleet, consisting of eight score ships, came from the King of Spain, upon the sea in this year. Some say that their intention was to have taken harbour, and landed on the coasts of England, if they could get an opportunity. But this did not happen to them, for they were met on the sea by the Queen's fleet, which captured four ships; the rest of the fleet was scattered and dispersed along the coasts of the neighbouring countries. Great numbers of the Spaniards were drowned and their ships were totally wrecked in those places.'

Routed by the English fleet, the surviving Spanish ships – hounded by enemy galleons – made for the west coast of Ireland in the hope of taking on sufficient

Vessels typical of the pinnace and row-barge types used in Henry VIII's Royal Navy during the 16thc. The name 'pinnace' (top) was given to almost any small boat that could not be fitted into a particular class, while the row barge was a service vessel for ship-to-shore duties.

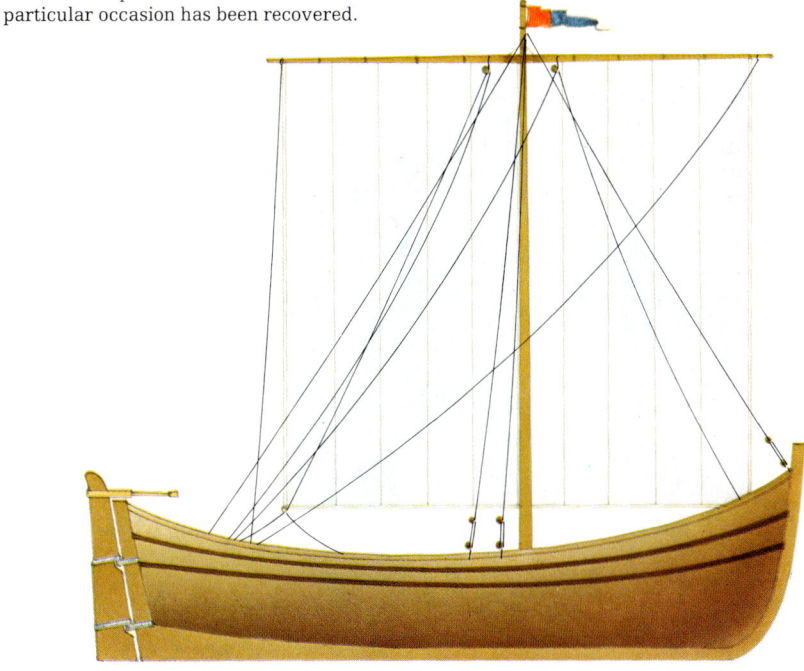

St Brendan's Voyages

According to the *Navigatio Sancti Brendani*, or *Voyage of St Brendan*, the saint made a series of journeys around the Atlantic and returned to two islands after each voyage. The manuscript names these as the Island of Sheep and the Paradise of Birds, but they can fairly accurately be identified as Streymoy and Vagar in the Faeroes. The different journeys marked on this map are intended to show the stages in the 'Voyage', which culminated in Brendan's landfall upon the 'Land of Promise'.

— First stage
— Second stage
--- Third stage
--- Fourth stage
--- Fifth stage
--- Sixth stage

GALLEONS, GOLD, AND GRAVES

THE SAILOR SAINT

St Brendan – 'the Navigator' – was born in AD 484. His life was dedicated to God from a very early age, and a body of stories gradually accumulated about his life and travels. Sometime before the 10thc these were collected into two manuscripts – the *Life of St Brendan*, and the *Voyage of St Brendan*. The *Voyage* concerns Brendan's search for the 'Land of Promise'. He set sail in a specially built currach from Brandon Creek in Co Kerry with a company of monks. They travelled back and forth across the ocean for seven years, seeing on the way many strange and wonderful things. At last they made a landfall on the 'Land of Promise', but after only a comparatively short time spent in exploration St Brendan decided that their quest had been accomplished, and they returned to Ireland.

This may simply be a delightful rendering of a spiritual journey, with a few identifiable places added as spicing, but several modern scholars have pointed out that very many of the places mentioned in the *Voyage* can be pin-pointed with remarkable accuracy on a map of the Atlantic. It has been suggested that the 'Land of Promise' was, in fact, the coast of America.

The map opposite is based upon the work of these researchers. It is entirely hypothetical of course, and it is quite likely that Brendan himself sailed no farther than the Faeroes. What makes the *Voyage* so tantalizing is that it is possible to make a fairly accurate map from it, which implies that the author, or authors, had access to a large amount of information about the geography of the Atlantic – perhaps including the Americas – hundreds of years before Columbus. The Irish may even have been to America before the virtually-proven Norse discovery of that continent.

---

food and water to ensure their return to the homeland. But off the north-west coast of Ireland they encountered storms and variable headwinds. Most of the ships approached the Irish coast in a crippled condition, with crippled crews, and either broke up on the rocks, wedged on reefs or were hurled against sea cliffs. The galleas *Girona* was the last to survive. She fled Ireland on the morning of October 27 with those rescued castaways she had been able to collect. Her original complement was some 550 men, but on that morning she carried 1,300. 'A cruel talon of rock' known as Lacada Point made a final claim on the galleas, however, and only five survived the wreck. The *Girona* was the last of the Armada ships off the Irish coast to go down, and it was the first to be totally excavated.

In June 1967 a young Belgian underwater archaeologist by the name of Robert Sténuit slipped into the chilly waters of Port na Spaniagh, and swam underwater along the eastern face of Lacada Point. He came upon a boat-shaped ingot of lead, the first object from the *Girona* to be discovered in nearly 400 years. Shortly afterwards he found first one bronze gun, then a second, and then a series of breech-blocks and a scatter of cannon balls. The following year, Sténuit returned to the site with a properly equipped team. He spent two seasons and some 6,000 hours diving time, on excavating the wreck. The finds are displayed in the Ulster Museum in Belfast, which in 1972 became the first museum in the world to show a representative collection of material from an Armada wreck. As well as providing a great deal of information about life on an Armada ship, the collection forms a

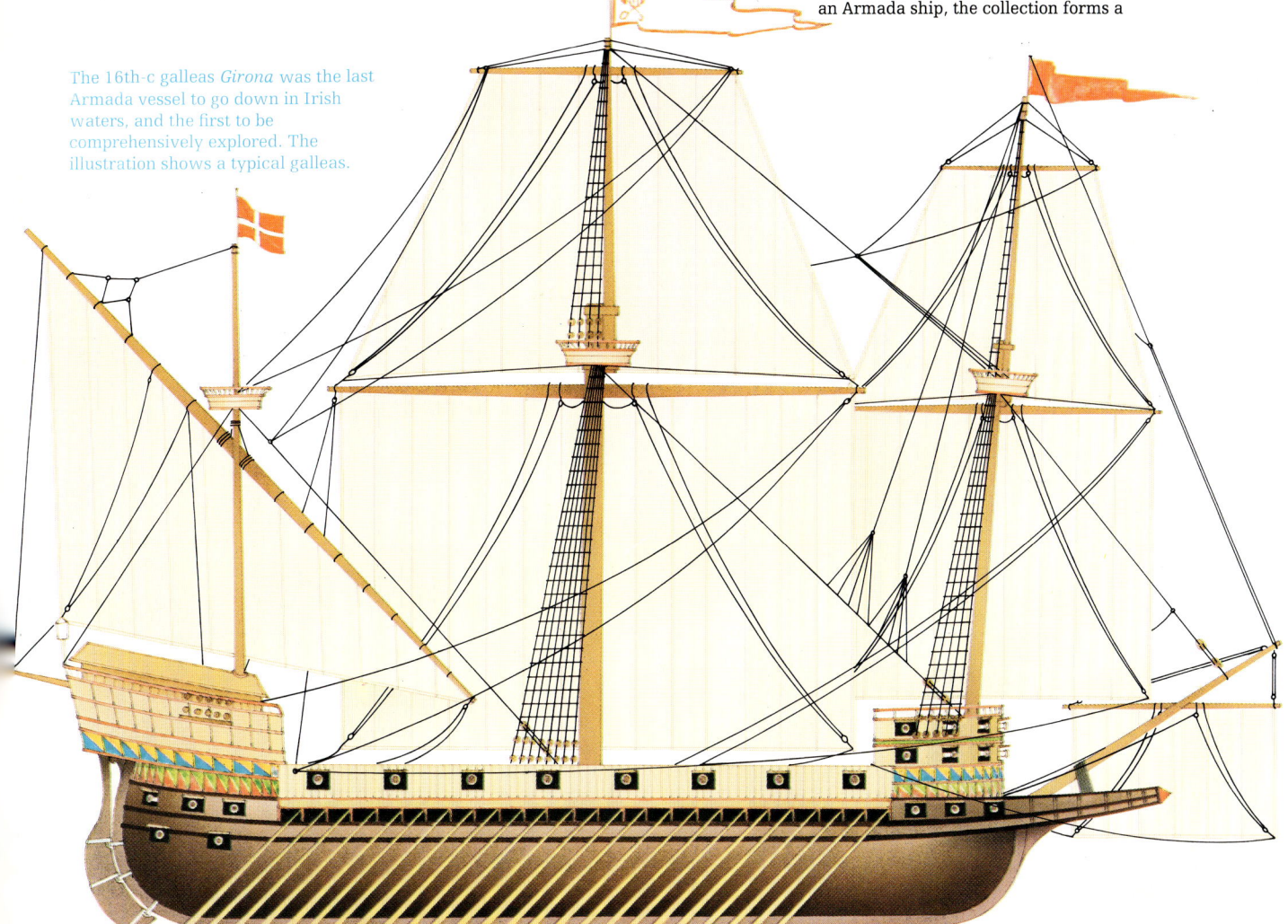

The 16th-c galleas Girona *was the last Armada vessel to go down in Irish waters, and the first to be comprehensively explored. The illustration shows a typical galleas.*

GALLEONS, GOLD, AND GRAVES

splendid spectacle. The guns – a breech-loading Esmeril and a muzzle-loading Half-Saker – are only two of the fifty the *Girona* originally carried. Three are known to have been salvaged in 1588 by the MacDonnels from nearby Dunluce Castle, and the remaining ones are probably scattered over the bed of Killybegs Harbour. Other items from the wreck include navigational instruments – two bronze astrolabes, five pairs of navigational dividers, and a fantastic collection of Renaissance gold jewellery, including a Cross of a Knight of Malta that probably belonged to Fabricio Spinola, Captain of the *Girona*, and a fabulous salamander set with rubies. One of the most poignant finds was a gold ring decorated with a hand holding a heart, bearing the inscription *No tengo mas que dar te* – 'I have nothing more to give thee'. This was probably a gift to a departing lover from his beloved. Another gold ring, inscribed 'Madame de Champagney, 1524' provided conclusive proof that the wreck was that of the *Girona*. Nicole Bonvalot – Madame de Champagney – was the grandmother of Don Tomas Perrenoto, who is recorded as having perished on the *Girona*. Vast numbers of everyday articles such as knives, daggers, forks, a musket-stock, and fragments of silver and pottery dishes have also been recovered, as well as 400 gold and 750 silver coins, their mints covering the whole Spanish world at that time.

To the west of the Giant's Causeway in north Antrim lies another Armada wreck, the *Trinidad Valencera*. She is currently being excavated by the Derry Sub-Aqua Club under the supervision of a leading British underwater archaeologist, Colin Martin. The first finds from the *Trinidad* were uncovered in 1972. Buried in sand at Glenagivney, on the west side of Lough Foyle, were two 50 pound siege-guns bearing the Royal Arms of Philip II of Spain, one of which is remarkably well preserved. Portions of their field-carriages, a superb swivel gun, and other assorted ordnance have been recovered. Among the more extraordinary finds are a half-barrel of gunpowder and, in a different vein, the leather boot of a small boy.

The next located wreck site is that of the *Duquessa Santa Ana,* which was driven ashore at Loughros More, near Ardara in Co Donegal. According to local tradition, until a hundred years ago or so the ship's timbers were visible at extremely low tides. Today, however, nothing can be seen of the wreck, although up to 1968

Marine archaeology is a young but effective science. A few of the fascinating items recovered from the *Girona* wreck are illustrated here.

A lover's ring inscribed *No tengo mas que dar te* – 'I have nothing more to give thee'.

One of two astrolobes discovered on the *Girona* site.

Two examples of navigational dividers from several found on the wreck.

This Cross of the Knights of Malta is thought to have belonged to Captain Fabricio Spinola.

An exquisite *Agnus Dei Reliquary* box in the form of a book.

GALLEONS, GOLD, AND GRAVES

one relic of the *Duquessa* was still there – a cast-iron falcon left on O'Boyle's Island in Kiltoorish Lake by Alonso de Leiva. One of the most celebrated of Armada commanders, de Leiva had established himself on the island before he heard that the *Girona*, on which he was to perish, had put into Killybegs some 20m to the south.

Two smaller, unnamed Armada ships arrived at Killybegs at the same time as the *Girona*. One had run onto the rocks just outside the harbour and the other had run aground just inside; the latter was almost certainly extensively cannibalized in the emergency refitting of the damaged *Girona*. The remains of these two ships, as well as the 45 guns probably jettisoned from the *Girona* to make room for surviving castaways, lie here off the south-west coast of Co Donegal.

Streeda Point in Co Sligo is directly across Donegal Bay from Killybegs. Three large ships of the Armada, one of them the *San Juan de Sicilia* – a converted merchant ship belonging to the Levantine squadron – put in here, perhaps to ride out a storm. Francisco Cuellar, formerly captain of the *San Pedro*, was on board the *San Juan*. For four days the three ships strained at their anchors. Then, according to a letter written by Cueller in 1589 following his escape to the Continent, 'on the fifth day there came a great tempest which took us on the quarter, with a sea running as high as Heaven, so that neither could our hawsers stand the strain nor could the sails be of any service. The ships were driven on a beach of fine sand, and in the space of an hour the three vessels went to pieces. Of their crews, not more than 300 escaped, while more than 1,000 were drowned.' In the same letter Cuellar also recounts the great sufferings of many of his ship-mates and other members of the Spanish fleet. He writes of the atrocities meted out, by both English and Irish, to those Armada crewmen who reached the coast of Ireland, attributing the Irish actions partly to English threats of reprisals and partly to greed. He describes the Irish thus: 'These savages liked us very much, for they knew that we were great enemies to the heretics and had come to fight them. Had it not been for these people, not one of us would now be alive. These savages got a great quantity of jewels and money from us and from those ships of our fleet that were cast ashore, for there were many people of great possessions on board who were drowned.'

Just along the coast from Streeda Point, in the neighbouring county of Mayo, a singularly gruesome fate awaited the exhausted survivors of another Armada

Portrait of a Roman emperor, one of eleven *lapis lazuli* cameos in gold frames set with pearls.

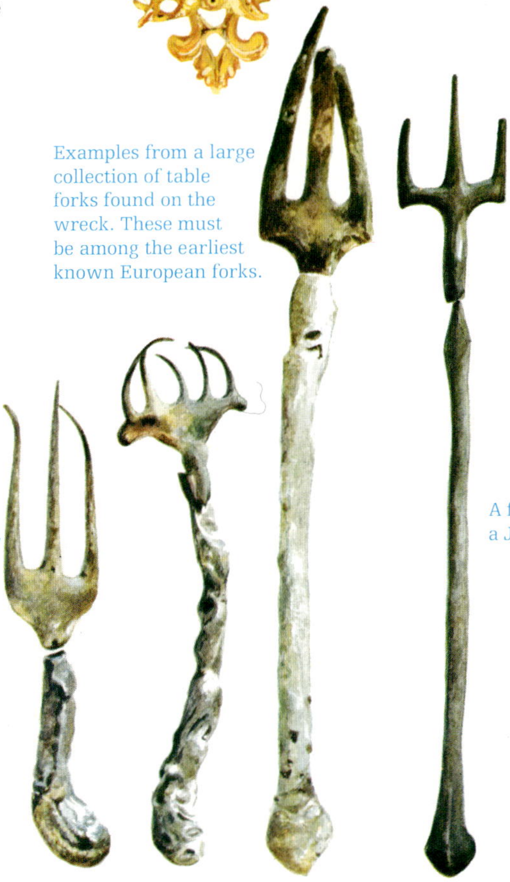

Salamander pendant beautifully executed in solid gold and set with rubies.

Examples from a large collection of table forks found on the wreck. These must be among the earliest known European forks.

Battered medallion, once the treasured possession of an unknown Knight of Alcántara.

Obverse and reverse of a gold ducat bearing the head of Charles V, Holy Roman Emperor.

A four-escudo coin decorated with a Jerusalem cross.

73

GALLEONS, GOLD, AND GRAVES

ship. Somewhere on the stretch of coast between Killala and Belderg, 80 crewmen were massacred as they crawled up the strand. The killer was a Scot by the name of Melaghlen McCabb, a psychopath armed with a gallowglass axe.

Sometime earlier the *Santa Maria Encoronada* had rounded the north-west corner of Co Mayo and entered Blacksod Bay. In command of the *Santa Maria* was the same Alonso de Leiva who was subsequently to sail on the *Duquessa Santa Ana* and finally on the *Girona*. On board was the body of Maurice Fitzgerald, son of the 'late arch-traitor Fitz Maurice,' who engineered the ill-fated Dun-an-oir venture. Fitzgerald had been dead for the last 40 leagues of the passage. Once the ship had anchored in Blacksod Bay, fourteen men were sent ashore to get fresh water. They were seized by Richard Burke and then freed by Bryan O'Rourke. On the following day a storm broke. The *Santa Maria*, a huge, lumbering converted merchant vessel with high castles fore and aft, was particularly vulnerable to wind. She dragged her anchor and ran firmly aground on the beach. Don Alonso calmly disembarked his men, fired the wreck, and fortified the small castle of Fahy at Doona. He remained there only until he had made contact with another Spanish ship, anchored somewhat farther north in Elly Bay on the Mullet Peninsula. This was the *Duquessa Santa Ana*. James Machary, an Irishman who sailed with the Armada, was captured and interrogated. According to his account, 'Don Alonso and all his company were received into the hulk of the *Santa Ana* with all the goods they had in the ship of any value, as plate, apparel, money, jewels, weapons and armour, leaving behind them victual, ordnance, and much other stuff which the hulk was not able to carry away.' Alas for Don Alonso – wrecked once in the *Santa Maria*, twice in the *Duquessa*, his luck ran out on the *Girona*.

To the south, two other Armada ships approached the coast of Galway – the *Concepcion* and a transport known as the *Falco Blanco*. Both were forced into Galway Bay, followed by an unnamed ship. According to local tradition the *Falco Blanco* ran aground at Barna, not far from the seaside resort of Salthill, and most of her complement of soldiers and sailors reached shore in safety. The *Concepcion* ran aground at Duirling na Spainneach, near Carna, and it is said that she was lured aground by false signals made on the instructions of Tadg na Buile O'Flaherty. The survivors of these two ships – 300 in number – were subsequently executed in Galway, and instructions were given 'to take view of

Representation of the 16th-c *Santa Maria de la Rosa*, a Mediterranean merchantman which was converted to a fighting galleon for the Armada and became vice flagship of a squadron.

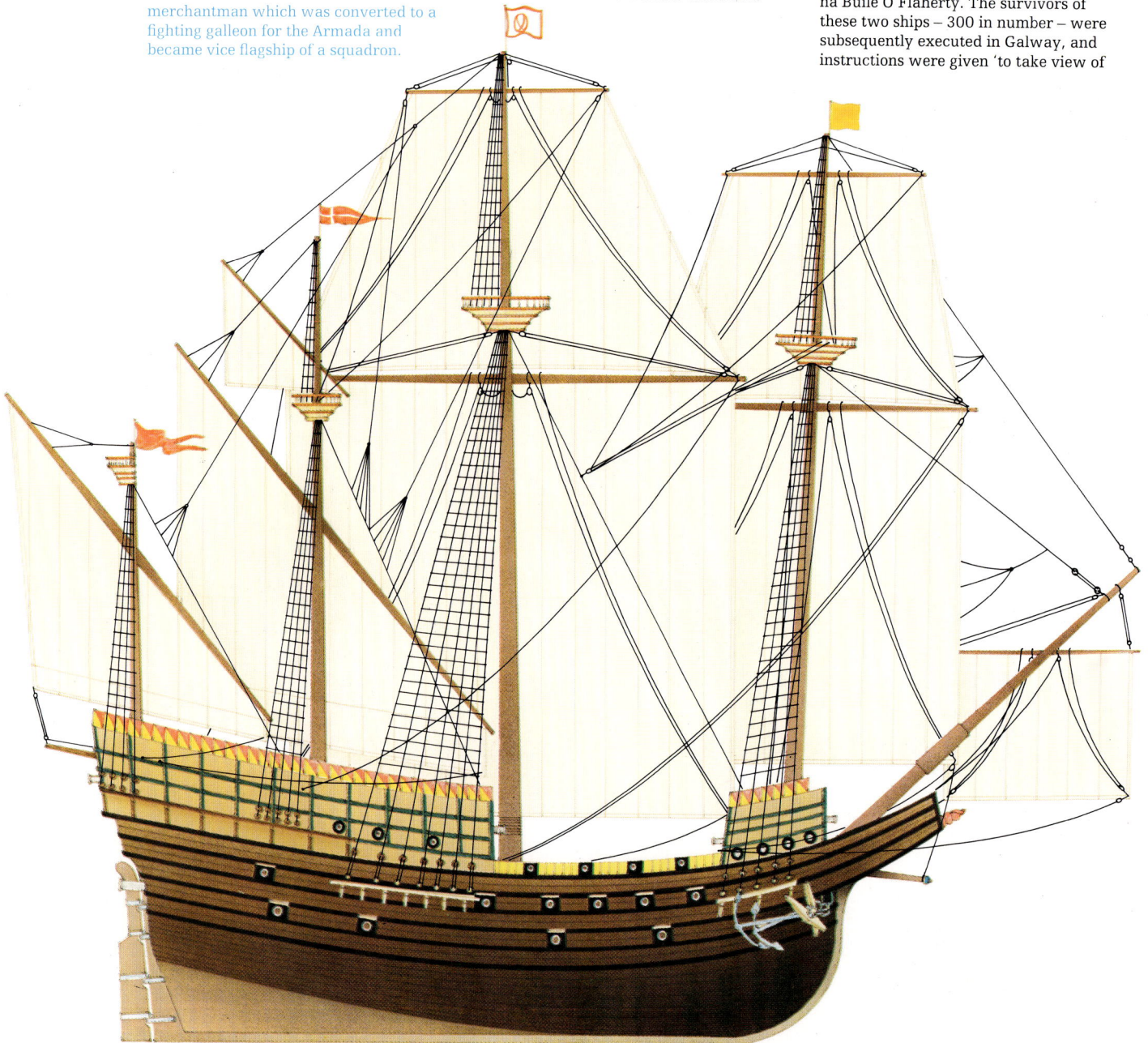

GALLEONS, GOLD, AND GRAVES

the great ordnance, munitions and other things which were in the two ships that were lost in that country, and to see how it might be saved for the use of Her Majesty.' The 70 survivors from the third ship shared the fate of their fellow countrymen. It is ironic that the man in charge of this massacre of helpless prisoners, Sir Richard Bingham, had previously fought alongside the Spaniards against the Turks at the celebrated naval battle of Lepanto.

At least two ships perished along the coast of Co Clare: one, probably the *San Marcos*, at Spanish Point near Milltown Malbay, and the other, possibly the *San Esteban*, farther south at Doonbeg. All surviving Armada vessels were hopelessly in need of food and water, and it was the dregs of green slime in water barrels and the mouldy biscuits which forced the ships so dangerously close to the Irish coast. The search for sustenance was in most cases a fatal one. Occasionally, however, the ships were spared, as was the case with four galleons and three small zabras anchored in the mouth of the Shannon. Their need for supplies was so desperate that they finally turned to the local English commander, offering to exchange one of the ships – guns, gear, and all – for provisions. The commander refused, so the *Annunciada* was stripped and fired by the Spanish. Her crew was taken aboard the *Barca de Danzig* which, with the other ships, sailed from the Shannon on September 11.

The final site of Armada wrecks in Ireland is off the Blasket Islands in Co Kerry. Here, thanks to the superb seamanship of Juan Martinez de Recalde, Vice Admiral of the entire Armada, two ships – Recalde's *San Juan de Portugal* and the *San Juan Bautista* – weathered a terrible storm, eventually to return safely to Spain. Two other ships, the *Santa Maria de la Rosa* – vice-flagship of the squadron of Guipuzcoa and commanded by Martin de Villafrance – and the *San Juan de Raguza* – a converted merchant ship – were not so fortunate. The remains of the *Santa Maria* were located in 1967 by Sidney Wignall. Of the treasure said to be on board, variously defined as 50,000 ducats, 30,000 ducats and three chests of gold and silver, there was no trace.

The many shipwrecked survivors of the Armada were not the last Spanish sailors to meet their 'doom off the Irish coast.'

In 1601 a Spanish fleet put into Kinsale in Co Cork and seized the town. The English Lord Deputy countered by laying seige to Kinsale, but the Spaniards held out, awaiting support from Irish in the north. On December 9, however, 'one ship of the enemy was sunk, and the Spanish Admiral, with 9ft of water in the hold, drove to the shore upon the rocks. The vice-admiral, with two others, likewise drove aground and most of the Spaniards quit their ships.' In fact, because of its importance as a trading port, Kinsale was to prove a notorious place for shipwrecks. A report of 1634 notes: 'Ireland, Kinsale, 17th March. Then followed a storm when a ship bound for Liverpool was lost. Three French corn and wine ships were also cast away at the harbour mouth.' It is not surprising, therefore, that a petition was drawn up in 1661, calling 'for the liberty to erect lighthouses,' and stating that 'there is as yet no lighthouse in any part of Ireland.' In August 1663 this was followed by the draft of a Royal Warrant for the erection of lighthouses at Dublin, Waterford, Londonderry, and Kinsale.

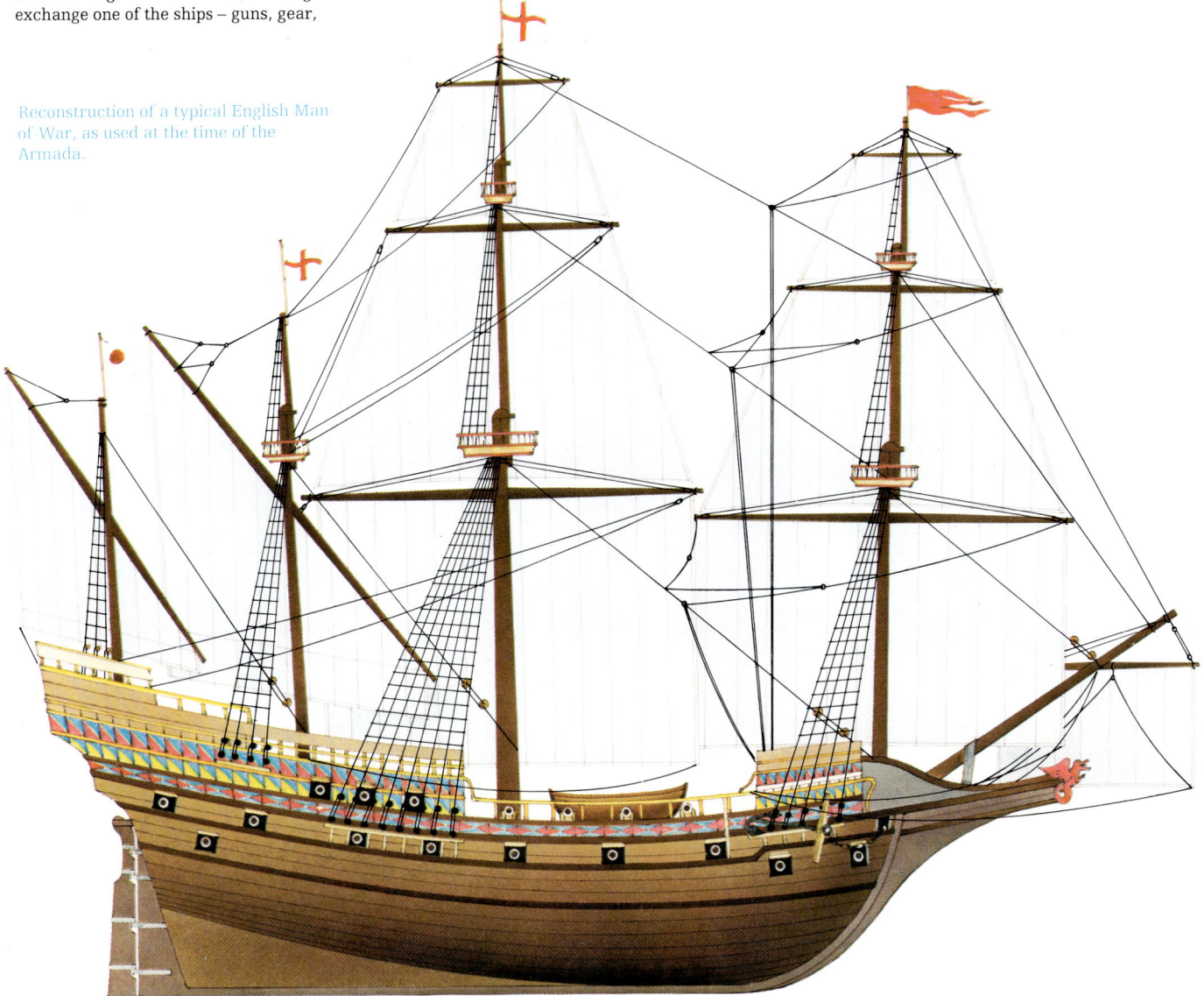

Reconstruction of a typical English Man-of-War, as used at the time of the Armada.

GALLEONS, GOLD, AND GRAVES

Although Ireland's dependence on commerce with England continued to grow, the country retained strong trading ties with the Continent during the 17thc. There are numerous accounts of ships which went down with valuable cargo. It was reported that in December 1665 'a ship has lately run ashore in the County Mayo. She is richly laden and supposed to be a Dutchman.' A salvage attempt was made on her in August 1666: 'One of the prize ships taken into Crookhaven has been sent to Sligo to recover anchors, cables, etc, left by the Dutch ship that was lost on the Mayo coast eight months ago.' During the same period a vessel called the *Bonadventure* went down in Bantry Bay, and 'a rich ship, laden with wines from France' had her cables broken by another ship at Dublin in 1667; she 'sunk downright.' The same year the *Hope* of Dublin, arriving from Barbados, was forced on to the Bar in Dublin harbour and 'bulged' in the sands. Attempts to float her off with the tide the next day failed, and the *Hope* 'was lost'.

Meanwhile Kinsale harbour claimed new victims. An eight-gun ship from Matigoe sank here, 'this side of the Old Head of Kinsale.' In 1668, four ships – the *Betty* of Dublin, the *Providence* of Kinsale, the *Reformation* of Barnstaple, and the *John* of Bristol – ran aground in the harbour during a vile storm. Attempts to raise the *Betty* were successful, but the *Providence* was sunk in 6 fathoms and 'will never be got up.'

A great deal is known about 18th- and 19th-c ships wrecked off the Irish coast, because official documents and newspaper reports have made it possible to more accurately establish the resting places of some of these vessels. Even so, salvage attempts during this period were only partially successful. The wreck of the warship *HMS Temple* is a case in point. In 1762 a strong British force captured and looted Havana. The proceeds from this effort totalled approximately £1,000,000 in money, church plate, and other valuables. A portion of the treasure was loaded onto the *Temple* the following year, but after safely crossing the Atlantic she sank off the Irish coast. Her crew and captain made it safely to shore as the ship and cargo went straight to the bottom. Some of her guns and treasures were recovered, but a fair share of wealth probably remains on board. An English steamship named the *Crescent City* also sank with a valuable cargo. In 1869 she went down off Galley Head, in Co Cork with some £200,000 in gold. Only a fraction of the precious metal was ever recovered.

The value of some ships' cargo could not be measured in monetary terms. The Dublin branch of the Irish Sub-Aqua Club succeeded in locating the wreck of an Australia-bound emigrant ship known

During the 17thc the Dutch operated more than 10,000 merchantmen of various types. The craft most commonly seen in European waters was the *fluyt*, a round-sterned vessel with narrow decks and a flat bottom.

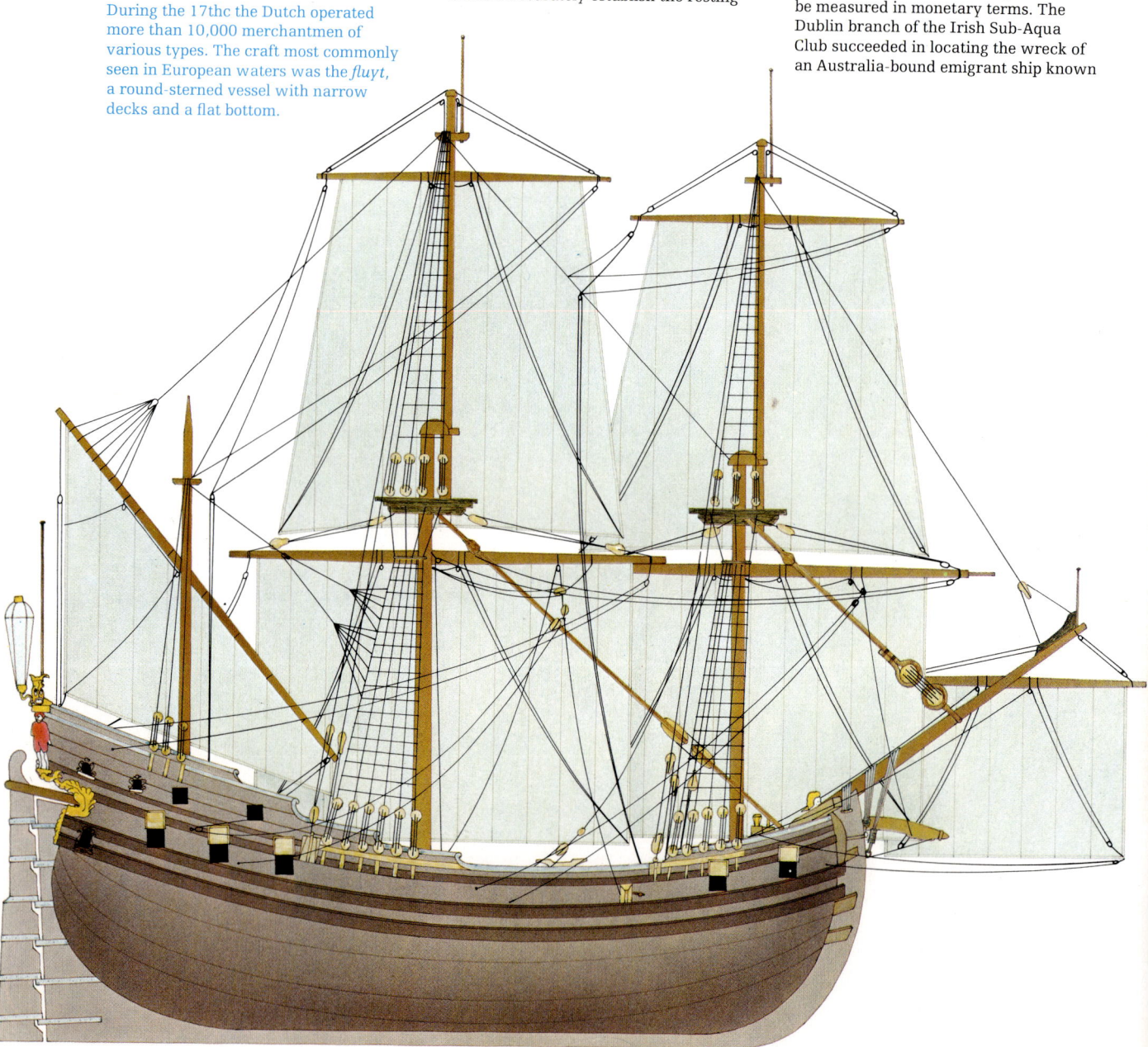

GALLEONS, GOLD, AND GRAVES

as the *Tayleur*. She sank off Lambay Island in 1854, with 650 men, women, and children on board. Only 282 of the passengers were rescued. In addition to the emigrants she carried another, prophetic cargo – slate tombstones.

Through the centuries the vagaries of nature have sent many ships to their death, but the actions of men have frequently heightened these losses. The steamship *Lusitania* sank after a German torpedo exploded inside her on May 7 1915. Described as 'a shot heard round the world,' it resulted in the loss of 1,198 lives. The ship was supposedly carrying up to £250,000 in bullion and lies about 11m off the Old Head of Kinsale, the graveyard of many ships. Another wreck, that of the *Aud*, lies in the approaches to Cork harbour. This vessel was carrying German arms for use in the Easter Rising of 1916, but she failed to make the arranged contact with a shore party. She was arrested by the Royal Navy, and while being escorted to Cobh her commander, Karl Spindler, scuttled her. The cargo of 20,000 rifles ended up on the seabed. Yet another victim of war

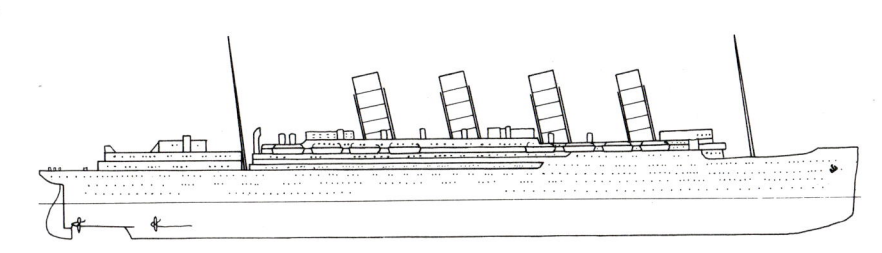

The tragic Lusitania was sunk, with massive loss of life, by a German torpedo in 1915. Below is a detail of the section which suffered the first – and fatal – explosion.

GALLEONS, GOLD, AND GRAVES

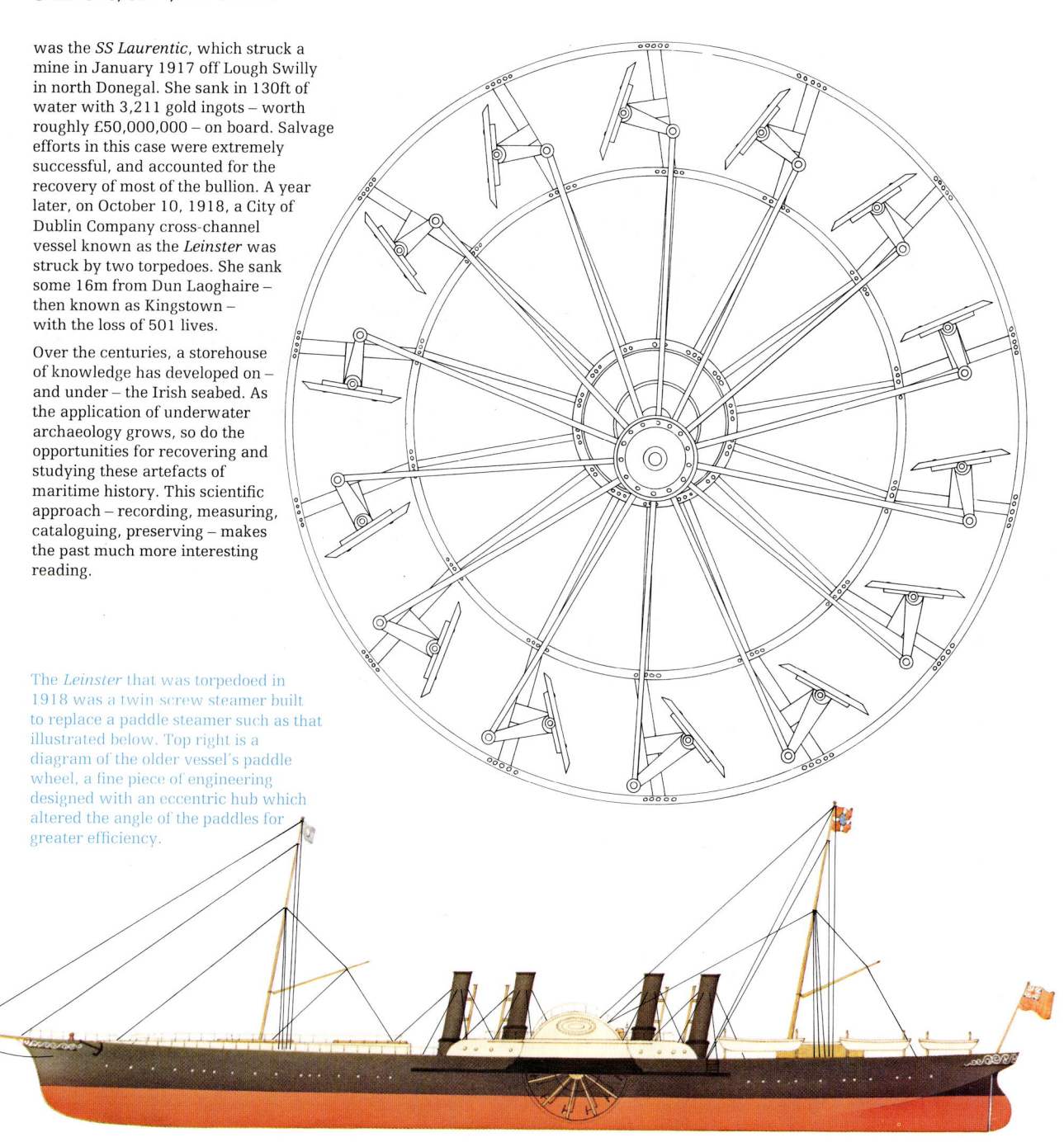

was the *SS Laurentic*, which struck a mine in January 1917 off Lough Swilly in north Donegal. She sank in 130ft of water with 3,211 gold ingots – worth roughly £50,000,000 – on board. Salvage efforts in this case were extremely successful, and accounted for the recovery of most of the bullion. A year later, on October 10, 1918, a City of Dublin Company cross-channel vessel known as the *Leinster* was struck by two torpedoes. She sank some 16m from Dun Laoghaire – then known as Kingstown – with the loss of 501 lives.

Over the centuries, a storehouse of knowledge has developed on – and under – the Irish seabed. As the application of underwater archaeology grows, so do the opportunities for recovering and studying these artefacts of maritime history. This scientific approach – recording, measuring, cataloguing, preserving – makes the past much more interesting reading.

The *Leinster* that was torpedoed in 1918 was a twin-screw steamer built to replace a paddle steamer such as that illustrated below. Top right is a diagram of the older vessel's paddle wheel, a fine piece of engineering designed with an eccentric hub which altered the angle of the paddles for greater efficiency.

SS Laurentic (below) struck a mine and sank in 130ft of water in 1917. Her cargo of 3,211 gold ingots was recovered by an efficient salvage operation.

Day Drives

Key to Day Drives

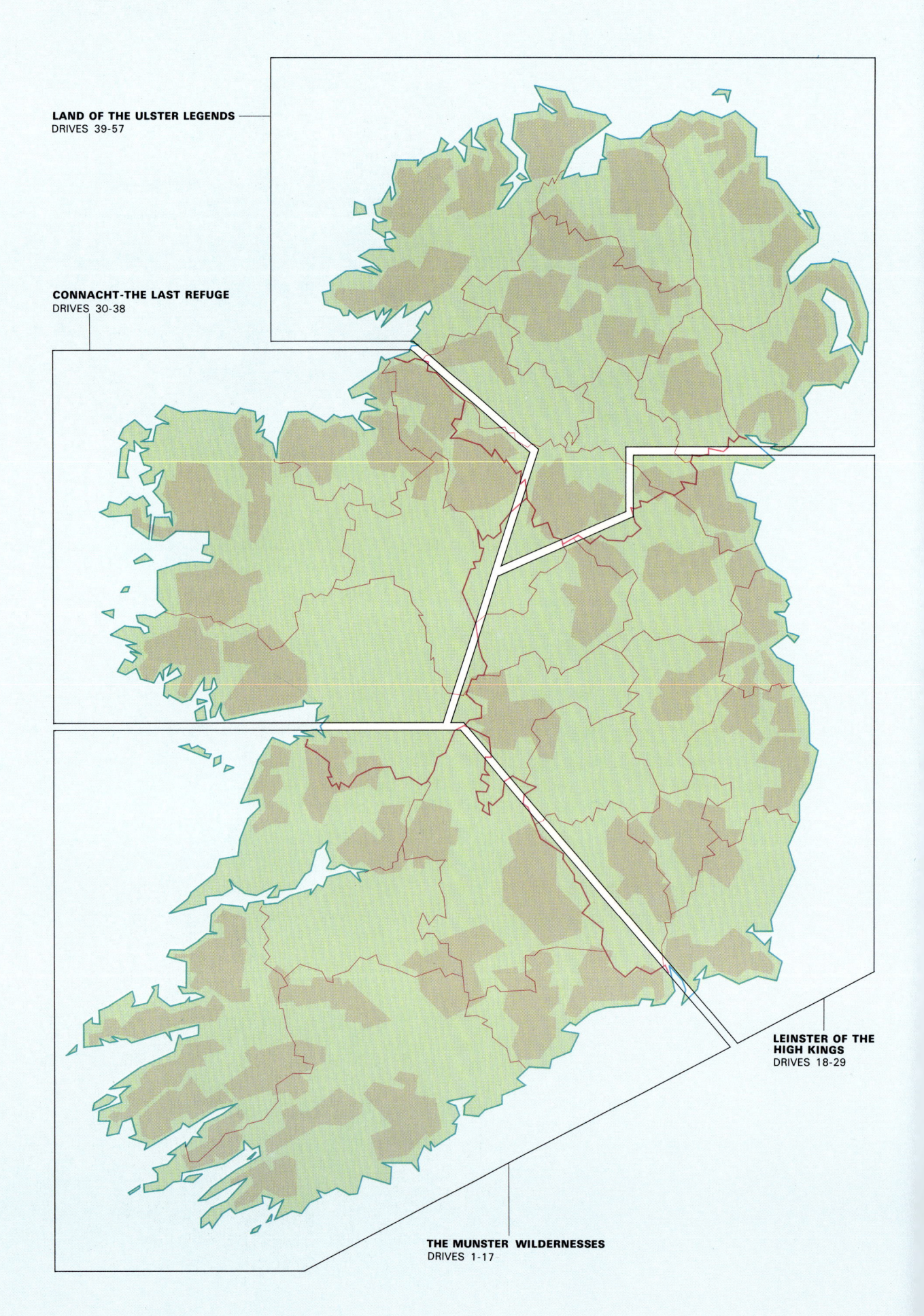

LAND OF THE ULSTER LEGENDS
DRIVES 39-57

CONNACHT-THE LAST REFUGE
DRIVES 30-38

LEINSTER OF THE HIGH KINGS
DRIVES 18-29

THE MUNSTER WILDERNESSES
DRIVES 1-17

The Munster Wildernesses

Wild, unlikely Munster is a place where high moorlands roll towards horizons suddenly jagged with peaks; where the skyline is always disconcertingly close until an unexpected chink reveals the moody immensity of the Atlantic Ocean. Its face is scored by numerous river valleys enriched by soil washed from the high lands by an omnipresent rain, and its coast is a chaos of inlets and peninsulas – startling fjords that water the roots of mountains, and quiet bays where grey seals have their nurseries. Spectacular cliffs drop many hundreds of feet to little green islands that dot the sea like a scattering of leaves on the face of a lake, or guard the mouths of estuaries populated by gulls and waders.

The province comprises six counties, each of which carries proof of its individuality in the folds and wrinkles of its landscape. Co Clare, in the north-west part of Munster, is an area of flat lakelands and low hills extending north from the Shannon estuary to Galway Bay and east to higher ground on the western shores of Lough Derg. The county's Atlantic coast gathers itself into folds and cliffs which culminate in the superb, 700ft Cliffs of Moher north of Liscannor Bay. To the north of this is the Barony of Burren, 50sqm of shale and limestone that has been crushed, eroded, and folded into a surrealist moonscape of shattered rock riddled by the caverns of subterranean streams. Rare Alpine plants flourish in this strange environment, and the works of ancient man crouch amongst the Burren's rocks like sleeping legends. Lisdoonvarna town stands at the southern edge of its influence, secure in the fame and elegance inevitably attracted to its fine mineral springs.

East of Clare is Tipperary, the largest – and some say the greenest – inland county in Ireland. A large, fertile plain which covers its central area is ringed by hills and ranges that include the splendid Galtee group and part of the Knockmealdown Mountains, while rich grasslands of the Golden Vale extend north west from the Comeragh Mountains on the Waterford border. Deep in the soft curves of the vale is Cashel, where the Rock of Cashel thrusts to 300ft high in unmistakable dominance and is crowned with the architectural debris of centuries. King Cormac had his Munster capital on the rock in the 4thc, and Christianity rooted here when St Patrick used a shamrock to demonstrate the Trinity in the 5thc. Nowadays the wild creatures hold court in Cormac's ancient stone fort, and the rock's 13th-c cathedral is choired by winds laden with the damp scent of growing grass.

The vast, rugged area south of Clare and east of Tipperary encompasses the counties Limerick, Kerry, and Cork. Here the scattered uplands and mountain groups of north Munster regroup like a gathering of giants before marching troop-like to the tips of Kerry's peninsula wildernesses. Northern Limerick, with its tiny stretch of shoreline on the south side of the Shannon estuary, offers the exquisite Georgian proportions of its elegant city namesake and the river-webbed northern termination of the Golden Vale. In Kerry and Cork the mountains mass, and the coast pushes long, rocky fingers far out into the island-studded sea. Dingle Peninsula is strung along a backbone formed by the Slieve Mish Mountains and terminates opposite the Blasket Islands – the most westerly land in Europe. Early man found this fortress-like landscape to his liking, and the peninsula abounds with remains so old that they have become accepted by the countryside as natural extensions of itself. South of Dingle and Dingle Bay is the Iveragh Peninsula. This is completely encircled by a scenic route known as the Ring of Kerry, which affords excellent views of the Lakes of Killarney and 3,414ft Carrauntoohill, the highest mountain in Ireland. Valentia Island hangs from the tip of the Iveragh like a disjointed fragment of the mainland and defiantly faces the open sea with the 700ft cliffs of Bray Head.

Farther south the Kenmare River pushes hills and mountains aside as it rushes into the Atlantic alongside the north shore of Kerry's last peninsula, the Beara, which carries the Slieve Miskish Mountains at its shattered toe and shares the Caha range with Co Cork. Picturesque Bantry Bay separates the Beara from the last of the west-coast peninsulas, two ragged little tongues of land that protectively extend from the Cork coast to shelter Clear Island – the most southerly point in Ireland. Munster's lonely west coast is a haven which supports flourishing colonies of rare Alpine and American plants, plus the only wild red deer to have survived past slaughter by people who lived under the shadow of consecutive famines.

Cork itself is the largest county in Ireland. Two parallel groups of mountains throw up high natural barriers from east to west across its central area, but south of the River Lee the landscape softens into hills and uplands which gradually merge into lower ground near the wave-fretted southern coastline. One of the best-known features of the county is Blarney Castle, where the Blarney Stone waits to bestow the traditional 'gift of the gab' upon anyone willing to risk life and limb by kissing it. East of Co Cork and south of Co Tipperary is Waterford, the last of Munster's counties and a gateway through which marauding Vikings once swept in their ruthless search for monastic wealth. To the north and mid-west it is a land of rounded heights which have been scraped and moulded by ice-age glaciers, indiscriminate artists literally capable of moving mountains and changing the courses of mighty rivers. Some of their finest work can be seen in the Commeraghs, where the tiny gem of Coumshingaum Lake is set in a circlet of 1,350ft cliffs which shoot skywards in a tremendous display of sheer permanence. Waterford Harbour washes the low, eastern extremes of the county and guides the River Suir away from its long border route.

The visitor to Munster should learn to expect sudden heights and long drops; tiny cameos of green meadow, the constant prattle of running water, and mellow landmarks from every period of Irish history.

DAY DRIVE ABBREVIATIONS & MAP SYMBOLS

AA Viewpoint	
Abbey	
Airport	
Avenue	Av
Battle Site	
Border Crossings	
Northern Ireland	
Republic of Ireland	
Bridge	
Castle	
Century(ies)	c
Circa	c
Crags	
Drive Route	T68
Feet	ft
Heights in Feet	2413
Houses Open to the Public	
Industrial Building	
Lighthouse	
Mile(s)	m
Motorway	M1 3
National Boundary	
National Monument	(NM)
National Trust	(NT)
Other Roads	L62
Places off Main Route	Kenmare
Places of Interest	
Places on Route	Ballin
Racecourse	
Railways	
Rivers and Lakes	R Maine
Road	Rd
Signpost(s); Signposted	SP
Street	St
Tower	
TV or Radio Mast	
Waterfall	
Windmill	
Yard(s)	yd(yds)

THE MUNSTER WILDERNESSES

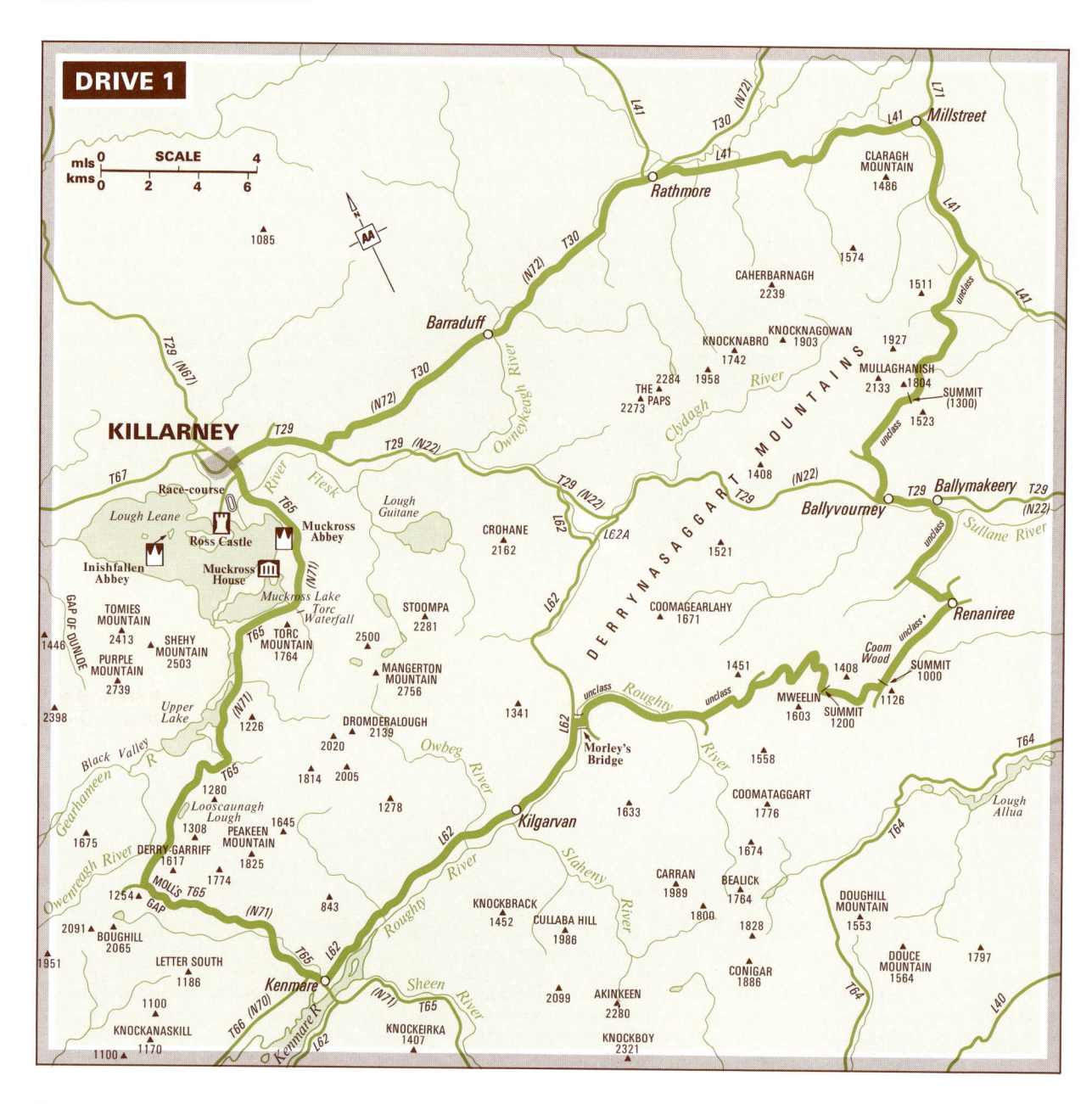

Peaks of Three Ranges

From Killarney

Drive 1   86 miles

Leave *Killarney* via the T29(N22) 'Cork' road, and in 2½m bear left on to the T30 (N72) SP 'Mallow, Rathmore'. Proceed with the Mangerton Mountains on the right, and in 5½m pass through *Barraduff*. Drive to *Rathmore*, in ½m branch right on to the L41 SP 'Millstreet', and in 7m reach *Millstreet*. On meeting the memorial, turn right, and immediately bear right on to the L41 SP 'Cork, Macroom'. In 4m turn sharp right on to an unclassified road SP 'Ballyvourney'. Climb steadily through forestry plantations to the 1,340ft road summit, then descend through dense forest.

In 2m turn left SP 'Ballyvourney', and in 1½m meet a T-junction and turn left on to the T29(N22). Pass through *Ballyvourney*, and in 1½m reach *Ballymakeery*. Turn right on to an unclassified road SP 'Ballingeary, Renaniree', and shortly enter the Douglas River valley. In 2¾m turn left SP 'Renaniree', pass through rocky countryside, then in 1m meet a T-junction and turn right. In ¼m reach *Renaniree* and turn right. Ascend gradually for 3m to a 1,000ft summit and turn right SP 'Kilgarvan, Kenmare'. Follow the mountain side to a 1,147ft summit and make a long, winding descent. Climb to a 1,055ft pass and continue down into the Roughty Valley. Cross Inchee Bridge and drive alongside the river for 2½m to Morley's Bridge. Turn right across the bridge, then left on to the L62. Proceed to *Kilgarvan* and follow SP 'Kenmare' through the village.

Continue down the Roughty Valley to reach *Kenmare*. Follow SP 'Killarney' on the T65 (N71) to drive along the Finnihy River valley and ascend between low hills. Climb to the summit of an 860ft pass known as Moll's Gap and bear right. Descend into the Owenreagh Valley; after 1½m pass the famous *Gap of Dunloe* — separating 2,739ft Purple and 2,503ft Shehy Mountains from the main part of the *Macgillycuddy* range — to the left. Beyond Looscaunagh Lough (on the right) pass Lady's View viewpoint, which lies to the left. Proceed through extensive woodland for several miles to the shores of Upper Lake, then pass the conical 1,103ft Eagle's Nest Mountain before skirting the base of 1,764ft Torc Mountain with Muckross Lake on the left. Shortly pass the entrance to magnificent *Torc Waterfall* on the right. Continue through dense woodland, and after 1m (from the waterfall) pass the entrance to *Muckross* House and Gardens on the left. In another ¾m pass ruined Muckross Abbey (NM) on the left, and shortly catch sight of Lough Leane.

In 1¾m cross the Flesk, and after ½m pass a left turn leading to ruined Ross Castle. Continue to Killarney town centre.

THE MUNSTER WILDERNESSES

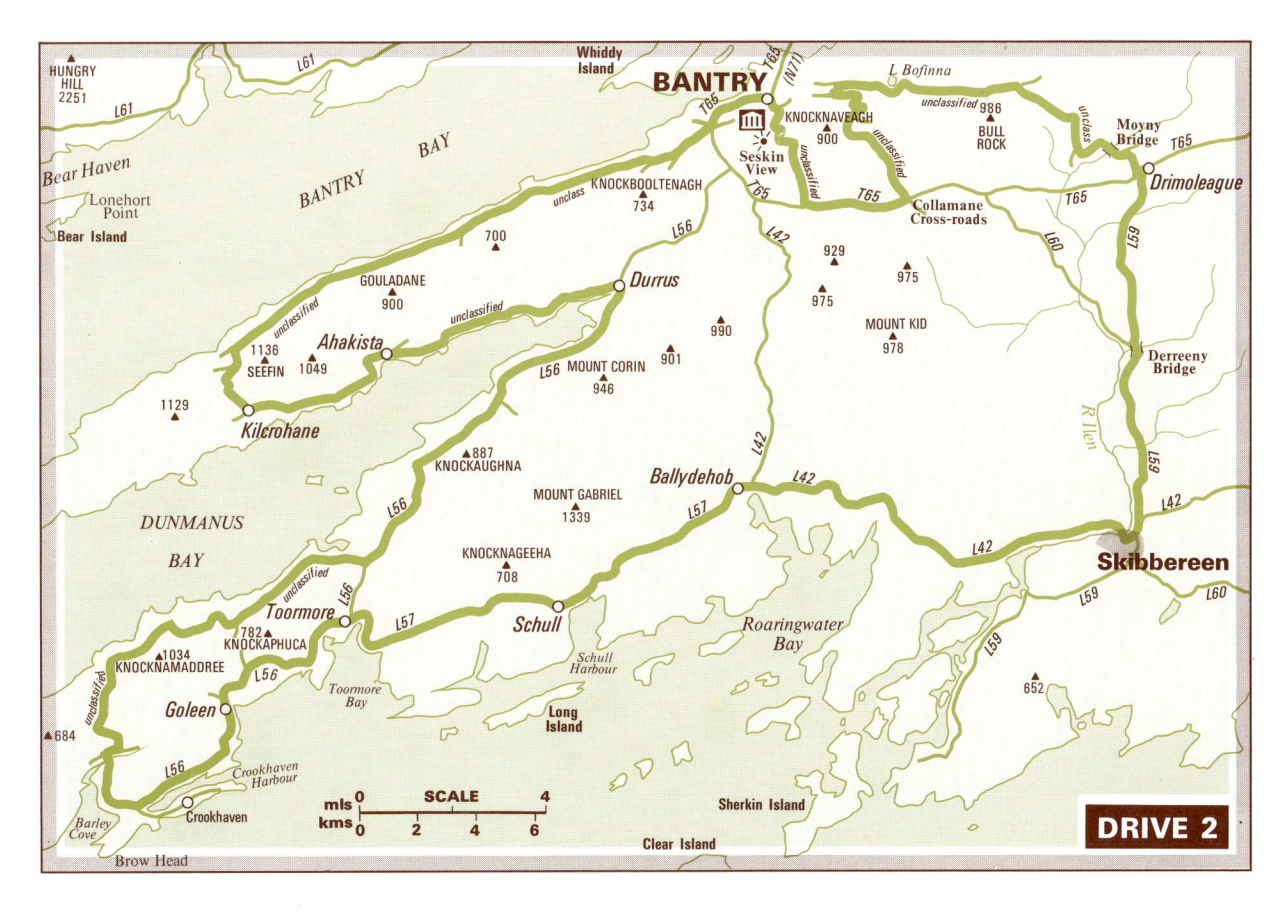

Among the Bays and Coves

From Bantry

Drive 2 98 miles

Start from the Square in *Bantry* and follow SP 'Cork' on the T65(N71), passing the entrance to Bantry House on the left. In 1¼m pass West Lodge Hotel and take the second turning right on to an unclassified road SP 'Rooska, Goat's Path'. In ¾m bear right to wind between low hills before reaching the S shore of Bantry Bay. Views across the water take in the Caha Mountains. In 5¼m bear right SP 'Goat's Path' to remain on the coast and ascend to over 200ft. The 1,887ft Sugarloaf Mountain, 2,169ft Knockowen, and 2,251ft Hungry Hill rise from the Caha range to the right. Left are the 800ft hills which form the peninsula's spine. After 4¾m follow the road inland and ascend to the 600ft summit of a pass between 1,136ft Seefin (left) and 1,129ft Caher Mountain.

Wind steeply down to *Kilcrohane*, with views of Dunmanus Bay, and drive to the church. Turn left to follow the coast road, then after 3¾m reach Ahakista and bear right SP 'Durrus, Bantry'. This road affords views of 887ft Knockaughna, 946ft Mount Corin, and 1,339ft Mount Gabriel across the bay. Proceed to *Durrus*, on the Four Mile Water at the head of Dunmanus Bay, and turn sharp right on to the L56 SP 'Goleen, Barley Cove'. Follow the S shore of Dunmanus Bay and after 3¾m bear right SP 'Crookhaven, Mizen Head'. Pass below the slopes of Knockaughna, then turn inland and drive through farming country for several miles. In 4¾m turn right on to an unclassified road SP 'Coast Road'. Shortly join the rocky coastline before passing beneath 782ft Knockaphuca, and later climb over the slopes of 1,034ft Knocknamaddree Hill. Magnificent views extend across Dunmanus Bay to the Kilcrohane Peninsula. After 9¼m turn right SP 'Barley Cove', then shortly left and cross a causeway. Ascend with 765ft Mizen Head and the fine sandy beaches of Barley Cove on the right. Meet a junction and turn left on to the L56 SP 'Schull, Goleen'. Follow the shoreline of Crookhaven Harbour, with the hamlet of *Crookhaven* visible across the inlet to the right. Approach *Goleen*; fine views from this section take in Cape Clear, with the islands of Roaring Water Bay in the distance. Enter Goleen, and at the far end of the village bear right. In 1m bear right to pass through rocky countryside, with the *Fastnet Rock* visible in the distance. After 2m bear right and cross a bridge, then in 1m reach *Toormore*. Keep forward on to the L57 SP 'Schull'. Continue with rocky hill scenery to the left and agricultural land to the right. Views ahead extend to 708ft Knocknageeha, in front of Mount Gabriel.

Descend gradually to *Schull* on the shores of Schull Harbour, go forward SP 'Skibbereen', then continue through bleak and uninteresting countryside. Proceed to *Ballydehob*, a small village at the head of Roaring Water Bay, and go forward on to the L42. Continue for 7m through farming country, then join the estuary of the Ilen River and follow it up to the market town of *Skibbereen*. Turn left through the main street, drive to the 1798 memorial at the end of the town, and turn left SP 'Clonakilty'.

In ¼m bear left on to the L59 SP 'Bantry', pass through the pleasant River Ilen valley to Derreeny Bridge, and on crossing the bridge bear right SP 'Cork'. In 4m reach Drimoleague. Turn sharp left on to the T65, then immediately right on to an unclassified road. In ¾m bear left, and after another ¼m cross the Clodagh River at Moyny Bridge.

Ascend steadily, passing between high hedges at first and later enjoying panoramic views. Bull Rock rises to 986ft on the left, and 1,629ft Mullaghmesha can be seen on the right. In 2m bear left SP 'Bantry' and continue to the 700ft summit for views of Bantry Bay. Follow a long descent past young forestry plantations (left), with the Caha Mountains W and N. Skirt Lough Bofinna on the right, and in 1m bear left. In ¼m double back to the left SP 'Colomane', and begin a long, winding ascent below 900ft Knocknaveagh (right). Descend from the summit, meet Colomane X-roads, and turn right on to the main T65(N71) 'Bantry' road. In 2¼m turn right on to an unclassified road SP 'Vaughan's Pass'. Climb steeply along a narrow hill road to the Seskin View carpark and viewpoint, which is sited at over 600ft. Magnificent panoramic views can be enjoyed from here. After the steep, winding descent meet a T-junction and turn left to re-enter Bantry.

Placenames in *italic* type are worth stopping at; each is listed and described in the main gazetteer section.

THE MUNSTER WILDERNESSES

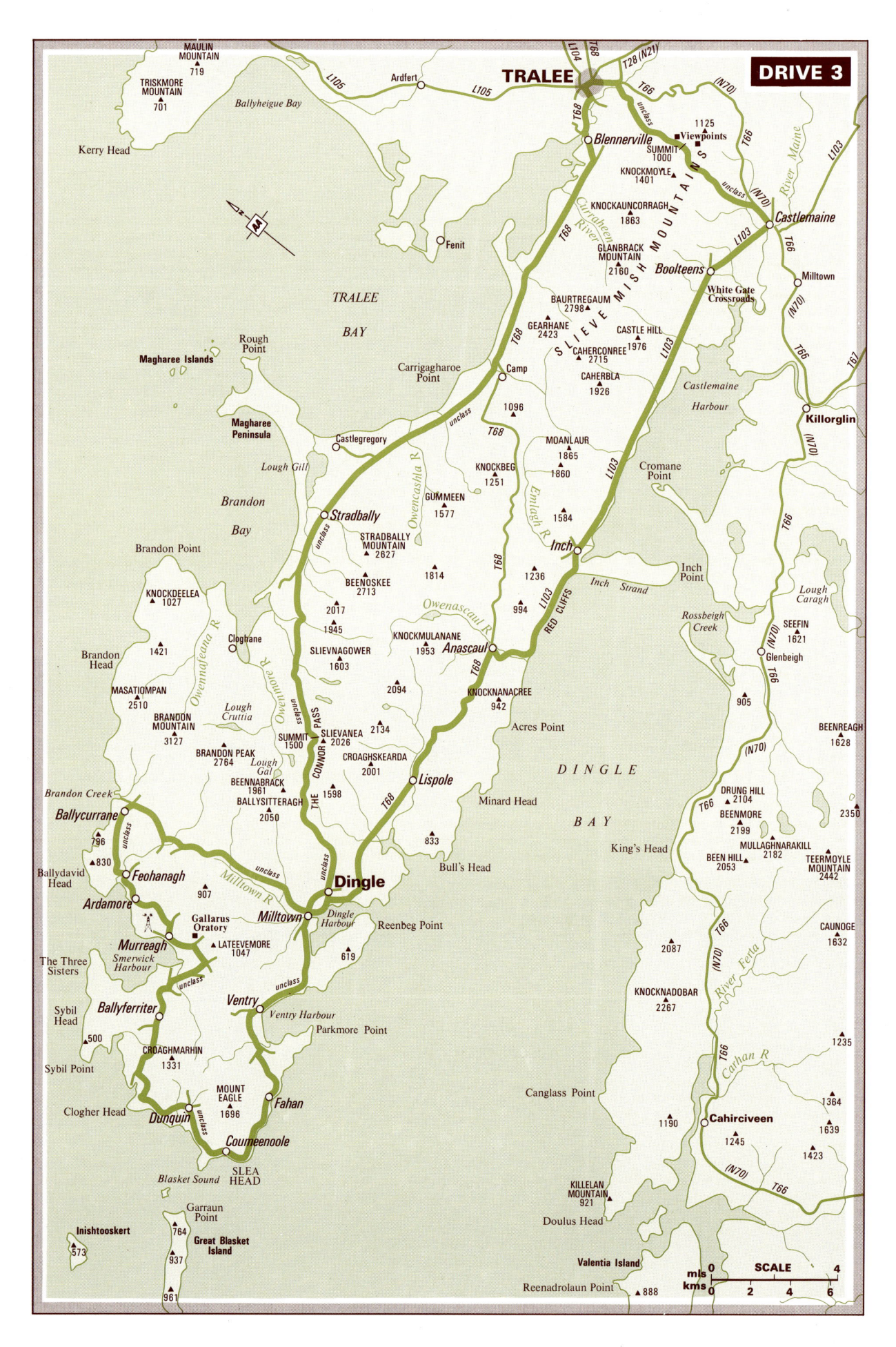

DRIVE 3

THE MUNSTER WILDERNESSES

The Dingle Peninsula

From Tralee

Drive 3   104 miles

Leave The Mall in *Tralee* by turning left into Bridge St, then follow SP 'Dingle T68' along Princes Quay for ¼m before turning right. Drive between a ship canal on the right and the River Lee, and in 1¼m turn left over the river to enter Blennerville. The *Slieve Mish Mountains* are visible in the background.

Proceed along the T68 with Tralee Bay on the right and four mountains on the left. The latter are 2,160ft Glanbrack Mountain, 2,795ft Baurtregaum, 2,713ft Caherconree, and 2,423ft Gearhane. Continue for about 5m until the Stradbally Mountains can be seen ahead and *Fenit* Harbour can be made out across the bay. In 2¾m reach the edge of *Camp* village and turn right on to an unclassified road SP 'Stradbally, Connor Pass'. In 5m pass a road to the right which leads to *Castlegregory*, situated in the Magharee Peninsula between the bays of Tralee and Brandon. In 1¾m the drive affords distant views of *Lough Gill* to the right, with 2,627ft Stradbally Mountain and 2,713ft Beenoskee to the left. Proceed through *Stradbally* village, and continue with views ahead of 2,764ft Brandon Peak rising from the Brandon range. In a short distance the route offers right-hand views over Brandon Bay, Brandon Point, and the fine strand which extends along the W side of the Magharee Peninsula. After 2m (from Stradbally village) bear left SP 'Dingle, Connor Pass', and in 1½m cross the end of deep Glennahoo Valley below 2,017ft Coumbaun – which rises to the left. In 2m climb steeply away from the Owenmore River valley to the upper slopes of 2,026ft Slievanea. Brandon Peak and *Brandon Mountain* – at 3,127ft the fifth-highest peak in Ireland – are visible to the right; also to the right and beside the harbour is *Cloghane* village. Continue forward and shortly enjoy views ahead of numerous small loughs, then meet a sharp bend where a small waterfall provides a high outlet for tiny Lough Doon.

After a further 1m reach the dramatic, almost knife-edged summit of the 1,500ft *Connor Pass*, with Slievanea rising to 2,026ft on the left. To the right are the impressive bulks of 1,579ft Beenduff and 1,961ft Beennabrack. Follow a long descent for panoramic views which extend across Dingle Bay to encompass 2,267ft Knocknadobar and *Valentia Island*, with *Dingle* town and Harbour in the foreground. On entering Dingle turn left and immediately right, then in ¼m turn right on to an unclassified road SP 'Ventry, Ballyferriter'. Drive out of the town and proceed alongside Dingle Harbour, then after ¾m reach *Milltown* and turn left SP 'Murreagh, Ballydavid' across the Milltown River. In ¼m keep straight ahead SP 'Slea Head', and in ½m keep forward again SP 'Slea Head' – with Dingle Harbour visible on the left. In 1½m continue along a stretch of route which affords views on Mount Eagle, rising to 1,696ft beyond Ventry Harbour. After another 1¾m enter *Ventry*, in ½m turn left SP 'Slea Head, Dunquin', and in 1¼m turn right. In ¼m turn left again, then after 1¼m rejoin the coast. Continue for a short distance and pass through *Fahan* – the site of some 400 of the stone bee-hive huts known as clochans, plus numerous other ancient remains. Some of the huts are modern farm buildings, and opposite the village is the interesting Dunbeg promontory fort. Views S from here take in Bray Head on distant Valentia Island, with the remote *Skellig Islands* far beyond. After another 1m pass SP indicating 'Fahan prehistoric bee-hive huts' on the right. In a further 1½m drive round *Slea Head*, high above the shore and below the towering bulk of Mount Eagle. This section of the drive affords dramatic views of *Dunmore Head*, Blasket Sound, 961ft *Great Blasket Island*, and farther out to sea the smaller islands of Inishnabro and *Inishvickillane*.

Proceed for another 1m and pass through Coumeenoole. Pass behind Dunmore Head, before rejoining the coast, with views which extend beyond Beginish and Young's Island to distant *Inishtooskert*. Continue to *Dunquin* – claimed to be the farthest W place of habitation in Europe. Meet X-roads and turn left. In 1½m pass Clogher Head on the left, with views ahead extending across a small bay to take in Sybil Point and a curious rock formation known as the Three Sisters. *Smerwick* Harbour and, to the N, 830ft Ballydavid Head can be seen to the right. Meet a T-junction and turn right SP 'Ballyferriter', then in 2m keep forward through *Ballyferriter* village. In 1m meet another T-junction and turn left SP 'Murreagh, Ballydavid', then in ¼m turn right SP 'Dingle, Feohanagh'. Cross a bridge and keep forward. In 1¼m turn left SP 'Murreagh, Feohanagh, Gallarus Oratory', and proceed through barren, rocky countryside. In ½m meet a T-junction and turn left; the road to the right here leads to the ancient *Gallarus Oratory* – the only perfect example of its type in Ireland. After a further 1m enter Murreagh, turn right, and keep forward with SP 'Feohanagh'. Pass a radio transmitter on the left beyond the village, and after 1½m drive past Ardamore. In a further ¾m keep forward for views to the left of the Dooneen Cliffs. In ½m enter Feohanagh and turn sharp left SP 'Ballycurrane'. Pass Ballydavid Head on the left, with fine forward views of 2,509ft Masatiompan and 3,127ft Brandon Mountain, and proceed to Ballycurrane. Continue for ½m, meet X-roads, and turn right SP 'Dingle'. The road to the left here leads to Brandon Creek. Climb to a low pass, with views of the Brandon Mountains to the left, and continue to the summit for views which extend along the valley of the Milltown River to Dingle Harbour. Ballysitteragh rises to 2,050ft on the left. In 4m reach Milltown and turn left, then in ¾m drive into Dingle via the main street. Proceed to the end of this street, cross a bridge, and immediately turn right SP 'Tralee'. In ¼m turn left on to the T68 SP 'Tralee, Anascaul'.

Ascend gradually for several miles, then descend to cross a wide valley which surrounds a coastal inlet. Slievanea and several other 2,000ft-plus summits rise to the left. After 5½m pass Lispole and follow a long, winding climb to a low summit, then descend to the edge of *Anascaul*. At the nearside of the village turn right on to the L103 SP 'Inch' and follow the Owenascaul River between high hills. Meet the coast and drive along the Red Cliffs, with Dingle Bay on the right and views of the mountains which rise from the *Iveragh Peninsula*. The Inch Peninsula, with its fine sandy beach extending 3m out into the estuary, can be seen ahead. *Rossbeigh* Strand and Creek occupy the opposite shore of the estuary.

Pass through the village of *Inch*, which lies at the base of the peninsula, then meet a forked junction and bear right SP 'Castlemaine'. In a short distance drive close to the shores of Castlemaine Harbour. Pass 1,860ft Knockmore and 1,865ft Moanlaur on the left before meeting the main group of the Slieve Mish Mountains – the peaks Baurtregaum, *Caherconree*, and Glanbrack – on the approach to Whitegate Crossroads.

After 1¼m (from Whitegate) reach *Boolteens* and bear right with the main road. Continue for another 2¼m and enter *Castlemaine*. Turn left on to the T66(N70) SP 'Tralee', then immediately left again. In ¾m turn left on to an unclassified road SP 'Viewing Park', and climb over the lower slopes of the Slieve Mish range. In 2½m reach a carpark and 1,000ft viewpoint on the left. Features that can be identified from here include the Maine Valley, Castlemaine Harbour, the Laune Valley as far as *Killarney*, and the *Macgillycuddy's Reeks* mountains. Continue, and after a short distance reach a second carpark which affords fine views to the N. Tralee Bay can be seen to the left, with Tralee town and the Stack's Mountains ahead. Descend to X-roads and keep forward, then in 1½m meet a T-junction and turn left on to the T66(N70) for Tralee. In ¾m turn left into Castle St and drive into the centre of the town.

85

THE MUNSTER WILDERNESSES

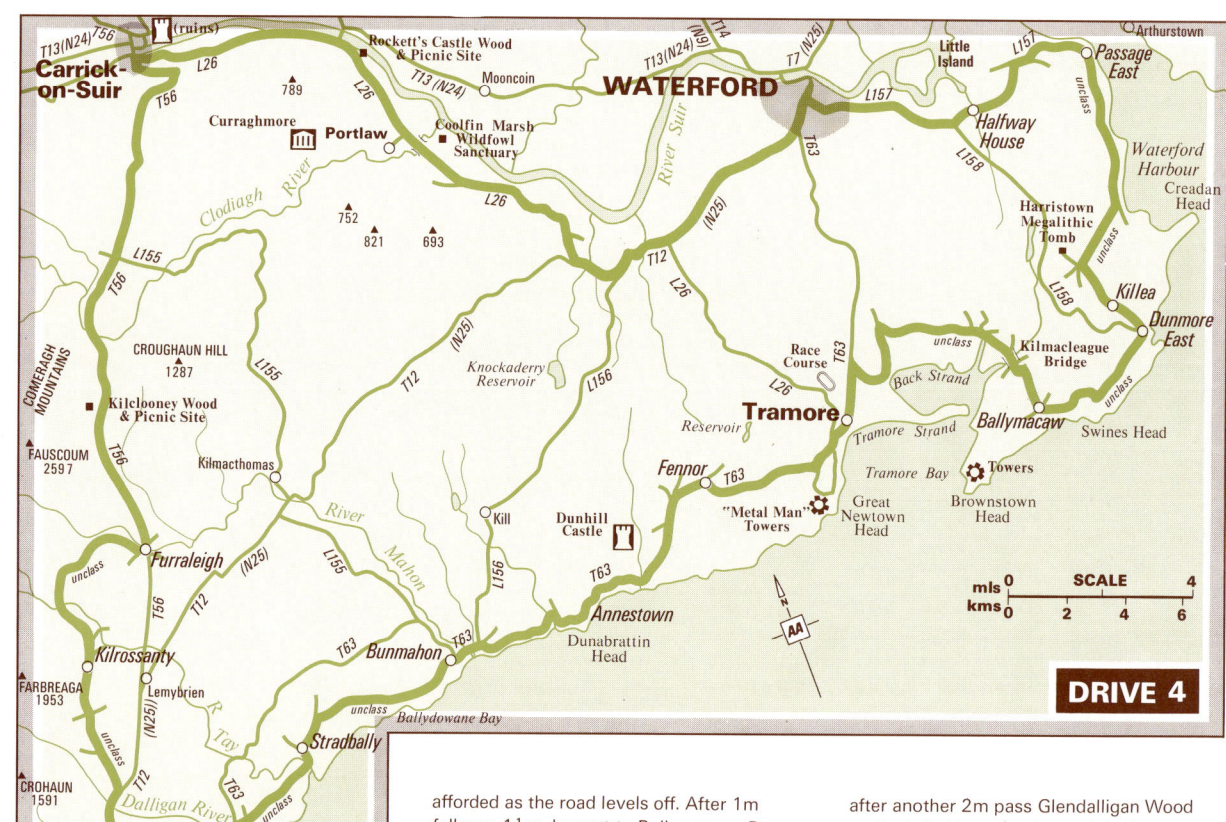

Southern Shorelines

From Waterford

Drive 4   93 miles

Leave *Waterford* Quay by turning right into The Mall, then meet traffic signals and turn left into Lombard St. Continue through Newtown Rd to join the L157 'Dunmore' road. Ascend along the S bank of the River Suir, then after 3½m turn left SP 'Passage East'. In ½m pass an unclassified road leading right to the 436ft viewpoint of *Cheekpoint*. In 1¾m bear left, and after another 1m start the descent into *Passage East*, with estuary views to the left; *Ballyhack* and distant Waterford Harbour can be seen as the drive approaches the town. Turn right and immediately left, then shortly turn right again on to an unclassified road SP 'Woodstown'. Follow the W shores of the estuary S for 3m to pass Woodstown Beach on the left, then continue with the Dunmore East road. In ¼m keep forward SP 'Tramore'.

After 1½m meet X-roads and turn left SP 'Dunmore East'. A right turn here leads to the Harristown Megalithic Tomb. In 1m drive through Killea. Descend to *Dunmore East*, then on reaching the shore keep forward and ascend. Meet staggered X-roads at the road summit and continue forward, passing a church on the left. Ascend, and in ½m keep forward to enjoy wide views afforded as the road levels off. After 1m follow a 1½m descent to Ballymacaw. Bear right SP 'Tramore'; Brownstown Head and the E side of Tramore Bay lie to the left. In ¼m bear right, and after another ¾m reach Kimacleague Bridge. Keep forward SP 'Tramore', then in 3½m turn left SP 'Tramore' for views over Back Strand and the waters of Tramore Bay. After 2m meet a T-junction, turn left on to the T63, then continue into *Tramore*. Keep forward through the town, climb Gallwey's Hill, and shortly turn left into Church Rd. In ½m turn left SP 'Dungarvan Coast Road', continue for ½m to the next T-junction, then turn right on to the T63 SP 'Annestown, Dungarvan'. The distant *Comeragh Mountains* are seen as the drive nears Fennor, where the route turns left.

After 1¼m pass SP 'Dunhill Castle' on the right. Descend to the coast and turn right, then after 1½m pass through Annestown. Keep forward SP 'Dungarvan, Bunmahon' to cross an old copper-mining area which affords fine coastal views, and after 4½m enter *Bunmahon*. Turn left on to an unclassified road SP 'Ballydowane Cove, Stradbally', and ascend to enjoy views of the Monavullagh Mountains. About 1½m from Bunmahon pass SP 'Ballydowane Cove' on the left. The cove is visible from the road. Continue for 2m to a T-junction, turn sharp left SP 'Stradbally', and in 1m enter *Stradbally* village. Turn left SP 'Stradbally Cove, Dungarvan', and descend. In 2½m meet a T-junction and turn left on to the T63 to cross the Dalligan River. Ballyvoyle Head can be seen to the left, and a sharp right-hand bend affords views across Dungarvan Harbour to the Drum Hills and ruined Clonea Castle (on the shores of Clonea Bay). In 2m turn right over a bridge and continue for 2¾m to the edge of *Dungarvan* (castle and abbey left). Turn right on to the T12(N25). After 2¾m ascend through the Monavullagh's foothills, and after another 2m pass Glendalligan Wood on the left. About ½m beyond the latter (and 5¼m from the edge of Dungarvan) turn left on to an unclassified road SP 'Kilrossanty'. Climb forested foothills with views of the Comeragh Mountains ahead. Descend through Kilrossanty and in ¼m keep forward SP 'Mahon Bridge'. After another ¼m branch left and climb the lower slopes of the Comeraghs. Reach 700ft before following a long descent to Furraleigh. Turn left here, then left again on to the T56 'Carrick-on-Suir' road. Climb to a forested gap between the hills; Kilcloony Wood and Picnic Site lie to the left. Descend through hairpin bends and continue to *Carrick-on-Suir*.

Drive to the nearside of the river bridge and turn right on to the L26 SP 'Tramore', then keep forward. In ½m castle ruins can be seen across the river, and in 6m Rockett's Castle Wood and Picnic Site are passed on the left. A road on the right leads to *Portlaw*, beyond which lies *Curraghmore* Mansion. This is a magnificent 18th-c house which incorporates greatly-altered remains of a medieval castle. Fine, contemporary interior decorations include good stucco and wood carving. In 1m cross the Clodiagh River, with the Coolfin Marsh Wildfowl Sanctuary on the left, and continue along the L26 with SP 'Waterford'. In 4½m meet a T-junction and turn left on to the T12 SP 'Tramore'. Follow a tree-bordered road for the return to Waterford.

THE MUNSTER WILDERNESSES

Valleys of the Knockmealdowns

From Dungarvan

Drive 5   96 miles

Follow SP 'Youghal T12(N25)' from the Square in *Dungarvan*, turn right and shortly left into Youghal Rd, then in ½m join the shores of Dungarvan Harbour. In 1¾m cross the River Brickey and climb to 919ft at Carronadavderg. Pass through the gap and continue to a viewpoint just over 12m from Dungarvan. After a further 4¼m turn left to cross the Blackwater, then turn right on to an unclassified road SP 'Cappoquin, Lismore, Scenic Route'. Follow the Blackwater, and after 1½m pass a ruined castle (right). Continue with SP 'Cappoquin, Scenic Route', and in ½m bear right. Shortly cross a bridge and turn left, then after a further ½m bear right and ascend steeply. In ¾m descend, keep left to cross a bridge, then keep left again to follow a small valley. After another 1m climb past Carnglass Wood (right).

Shortly meet X-roads and keep forward, then bear left. Continue for 1m to a T-junction and turn right SP 'Cappoquin, Scenic Route'. Descend for ½m to pass Strancally Wood on the left, and rejoin the Blackwater Valley. After a further ½m turn left, and in ¼m pass the entrance to Strancally Castle on the right. Meet a T-junction and turn right. In 1m turn right SP 'Cappoquin, Scenic Route, Lismore' and shortly cross the River Bride. In 1m enter a gap and continue above the Blackwater for 1m. Killahaly Wood (left) faces Dromana Forest across the river. After ¼m (from the river) keep forward SP 'Lismore' for forward views of the *Knockmealdown Mountains*. In 2¾m meet a T-junction and turn left into *Lismore*. Drive to the monument in the town centre and turn right SP 'Clogheen', then pass Lismore Castle on the left and cross the Blackwater.

Take the second turning left on to the L34 SP 'The Vee, Cahir, Scenic Route' and enter the Owennashad Valley. Climb steadily to a 1,114ft summit at *The Gap*. Descend to a hairpin bend known as The Vee, where a carpark affords views of the *Galtee* and *Comeragh* ranges. Negotiate The Vee and enter Bohernagore Wood. Descend through numerous sharp bends and later enter Killballyboy Wood. Within ½m of *Clogheen* turn sharp right on to an unclassified road SP 'Newcastle' and continue along the Tar Valley. In 5½m meet X-roads and go forward with the River Tar now on the left, and in 1¼m turn left. In 1m meet a T-junction and turn right, then in ½m turn left into *Newcastle*. Follow SP 'Clonmel' and in 2½m meet Ballymakee X-roads. Turn left SP 'Clonmel'. In ¾m reach Ballydonagh X-roads, cross the main road, and ascend. In 1¾m reach Kilmanahan Bridge, go forward on to the T27, and turn right. In 2m pass through a valley between Mountneill and Cannon Woods, then 1½m farther meet a T-junction and turn right. In ½m go forward on to the L27, and in a further ½m turn left then right. Shortly run alongside the river, meet X-roads, and turn right on to an unclassified road SP 'Nier Scenic Route'. Shortly climb along the Comeragh Mountain foothills, then turn S up a small valley. After 3½m pass Lyreanearca Wood (right). In a further ¾m turn right SP 'Comeragh Drive', and in 1m — after a pair of hairpin bends — reach a carpark offering mountain views across the Suir Valley from 1,100ft. Ascend to 1,300ft, then descend towards the Nier Valley. After 2½m pass Nier Wood (left), shortly cross the River Nier, and turn right SP 'Ballymacarbry'. Continue for 3m to the edge of *Ballymacarbry*, meet X-roads and turn sharp left, then climb to 800ft. After 5¾m meet a T-junction and turn left, then shortly right. In ¼m turn left and in 1¼m meet a T-junction and turn left SP 'Kilbrien, Comeragh Drive'. Descend to Scart Bridge, bear right, and after ½m farther reach Kilbrien Church; keep forward SP 'Dungarvan'. In 1¾m keep forward again. In ¼m turn right and cross a bridge. In 1¼m turn right again and cross another bridge, then in ¾m meet X-roads and turn right — still with SP 'Dungarvan'. Descend, and after 1¾m cross the Colligan River and turn left SP 'Dungarvan'. In ¾m pass through Colligan Wood, and in ½m turn left on to the T75. In 1m meet a T-junction and turn left. Continue along this road to reach Dungarvan in 2½m and finish the drive.

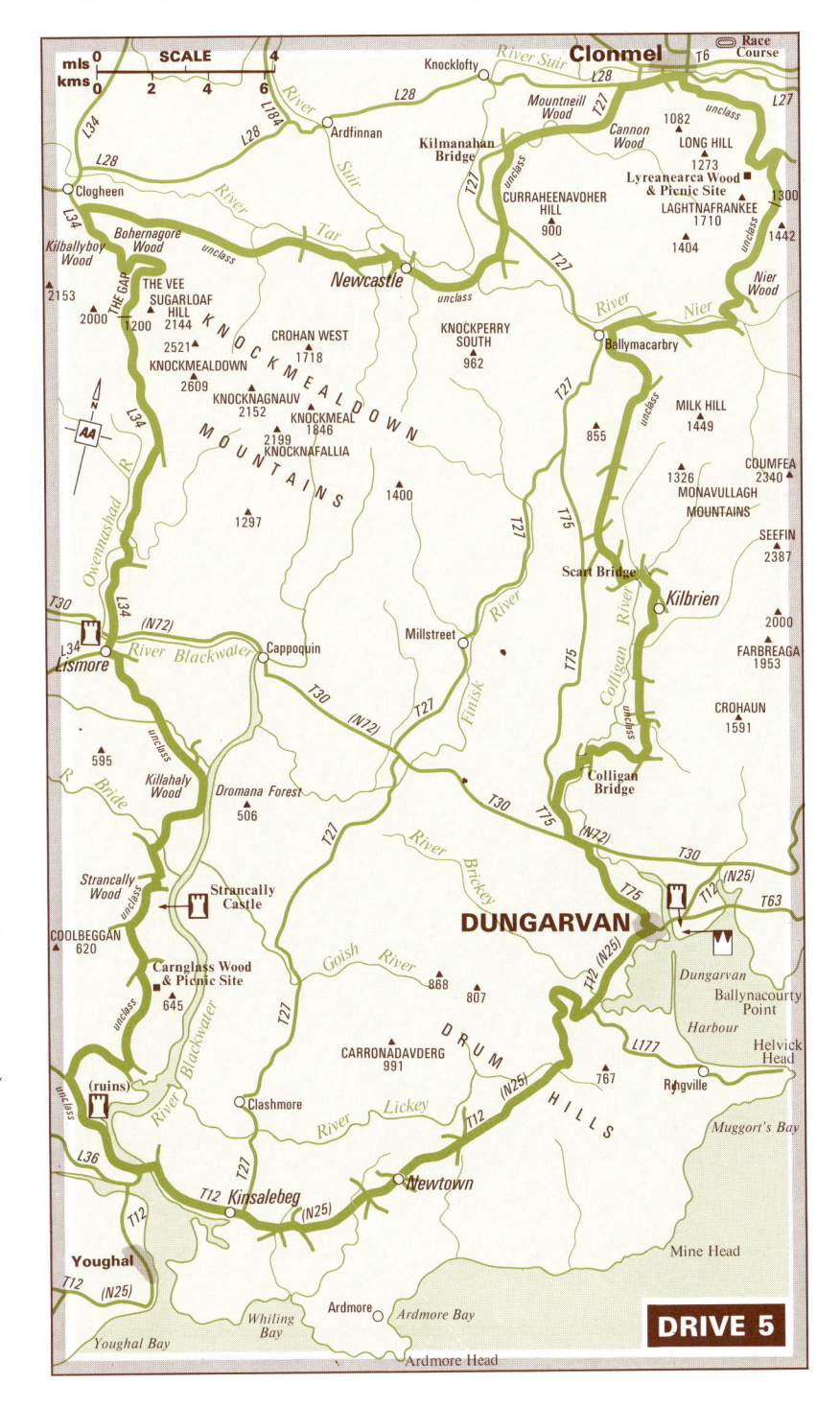

Placenames in *italic* type are worth stopping at; each is listed and described in the main gazetteer section.

THE MUNSTER WILDERNESSES

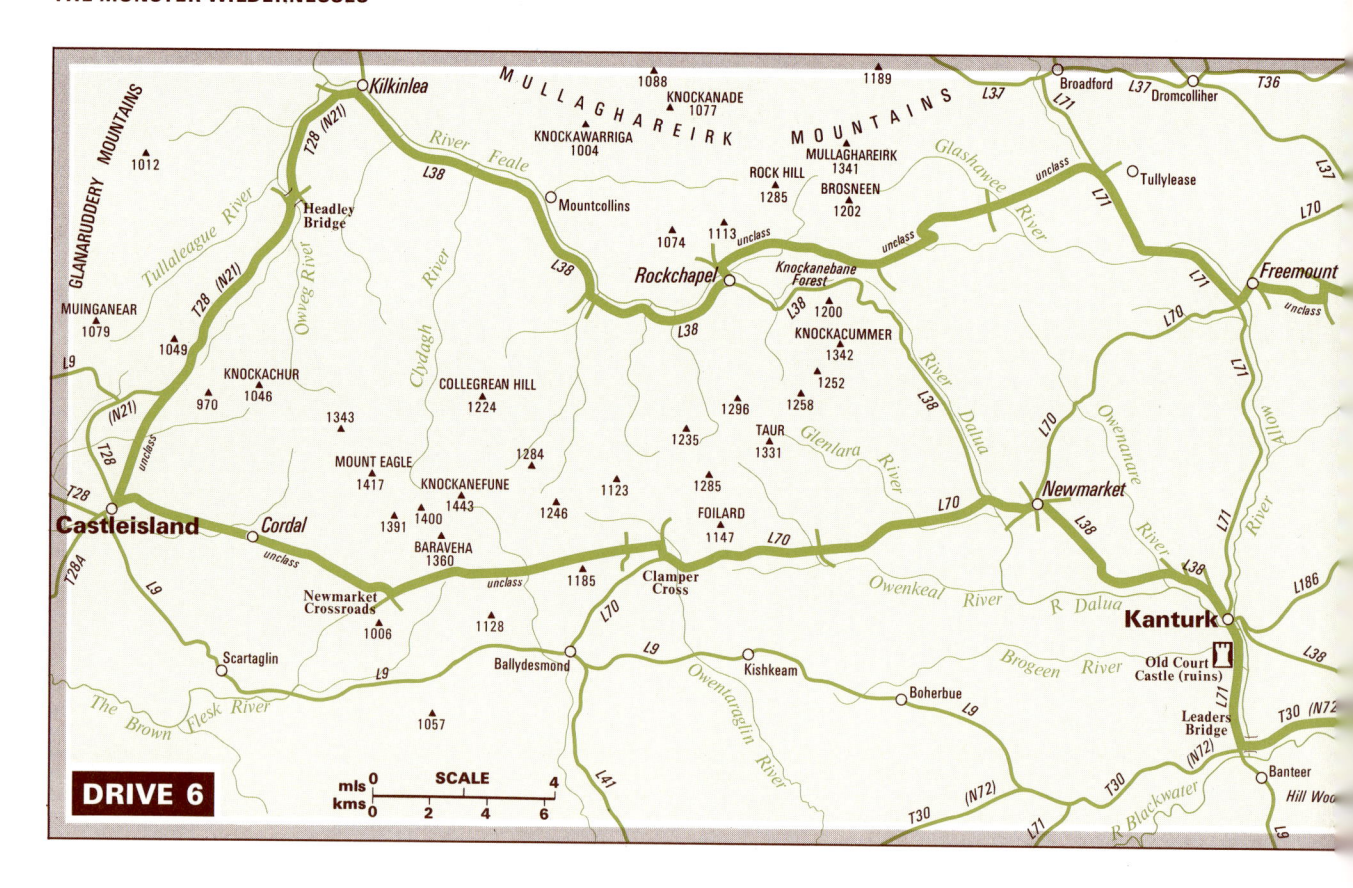

Rivers, Rocks, and Woodland

From Mallow

Drive 6   95 miles

Leave *Mallow* on the T30(N72) 'Killarney' road. Follow the River Blackwater, with dense woodland on the right at first and then distant lefthand views of the Boggeragh Mountains. In 2m pass Mallow Racecourse on the left, and in another 6¾m bear left SP 'Killarney'. Mount Hillary rises to 1,288ft across the valley. In 3½m cross the River Allow via Leader's Bridge, then meet X-roads and turn right on to the L71 SP 'Kanturk'.

Follow the river N and in 2m pass the ruins of Old Court Castle on the left. After 1m enter *Kanturk*. Meet a T-junction, turn right SP 'Newmarket', then cross a river bridge and immediately turn left on to the L38 SP 'Newmarket'. Enter well-wooded country and in 1m bear left. In a further 4¾m reach *Newmarket* and turn right SP 'Listowel, Tralee', meet the town centre X-roads and keep forward, then shortly bear right SP 'Tralee'. In 1¼m turn left on to the L70 SP 'Tralee', and follow the Glenlara River for several miles. Enter hilly country, with Taur rising to 1,331ft on the right, and after 8m (from Newmarket) enter the Owentaraglin Valley. Cross the river, meet a road junction at Clamper Cross, and turn right on to an unclassified road. In ¼m meet X-roads and turn left. Ascend, then in ½m meet X-roads and drive forward. Continue to a 1,100ft road summit for views to 2,239ft Caherbarnagh, 1,958ft Knocknabro, plus the 2,273ft and 2,284ft Paps in the distance on the left. Farther on are 2,162ft Crohane, 2,281ft Stoompa, and 2,756ft Mangerton Mountain. Descend into the Blackwater Valley, cross a small river bridge with 1,441ft Knockanefune to the right, then ascend through open moors to 1,157ft. This section should be taken at very low speed. Descend to Newmarket X-roads, with the Mangerton Mountains to the left, and turn right SP 'Cordal'. Descend, then climb to 855ft for views ahead over *Castleisland* and to the distant *Slieve Mish* range, *Tralee*, and Tralee Bay. Right are the relatively low Stack and Glanaruddery Mountains. Descend through Cordal village and continue along this road for 3m to reach Castleisland. Drive to the Carnegie Library on the nearside of the town and turn right. In 1m begin an ascent, with the Glanaruddery Mountains ahead, 1,097ft Knight's Mountain on the left, and 1,046ft Knockachur on the right. Climb over the scarp and pass Tonbaun Wood on the right, with Dooneen Wood stretching away to the left. Shortly turn right on to the T28 (N21) SP 'Abbeyfeale', and proceed to an 810ft summit. Make the long descent to Headley Bridge, on the Owreg River, with extensive forestry plantations on the right.

Turn right across the bridge, then left, and continue through moorland to the edge of Kilkinlea in the Feale Valley. Reach the nearside of the village, turn right on to the L38 SP 'Rockchapel, Newmarket', and drive alongside the River Feale with extensive afforestation on the right. After 11m reach the remote village of Rockchapel. Turn left on to an unclassified road SP 'Toornafulla', then in ¼m meet X-roads and turn right. Drive along a winding, undulating road which affords pleasant views of the valley and forests. In 3m pass Knockanebane Forest at 1,100ft and shortly turn left. Forested, 1,341ft Mullaghareirk can be seen to the left, and bleak moorland extends to the right. In 1½m turn sharp left and ascend the wooded slopes of 1,092ft Banane, then descend to enjoy views over the surrounding countryside. Meet X-roads and keep forward, then in 2½m turn right on to the L71.

Proceed through countryside which gradually changes to an agricultural aspect, and in 4¾m meet X-roads and turn left on to the L70 SP 'Freemount'. Cross the River Allow and in ½m enter *Freemount*. Drive to the village centre, turn right on to an unclassified road, then keep left. Climb to over 700ft, and after 1½m turn left. In ¼m meet a T-junction and turn right, then descend with further views of the countryside and distant Ballyhoura Mountains ahead. Meet a T-junction and turn right SP 'Liscarroll'. In 1m meet X-roads and keep forward on the L37 SP 'Buttevant' to enter *Liscarroll*. Drive through the main street, with the castle ruins on the left, and turn right SP 'Buttevant'. After a further 1m meet X-roads and go forward on to an unclassified road SP 'Lisgriffin'. Ascend once more, and descend with views of the distant Boggeragh Mountains. In a further 1m cross a main road, and in 2½m meet Kilmaclenine X-roads and go forward. In 1¼m turn right, then meet Copsetown X-roads, keep forward and turn left SP 'Mallow'. Proceed through well-wooded countryside. In 2½m drive under a railway bridge and turn right on to the T11 (N20) for Mallow. In 1½m meet a T-junction and turn left for the town centre.

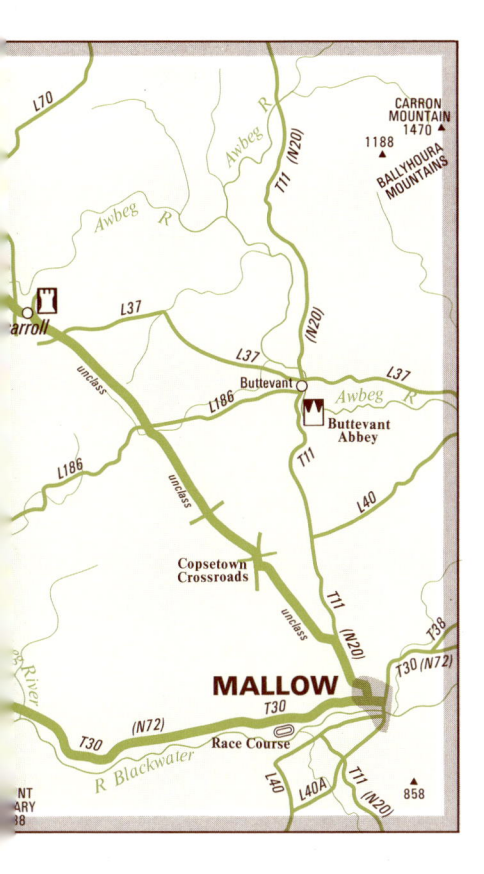

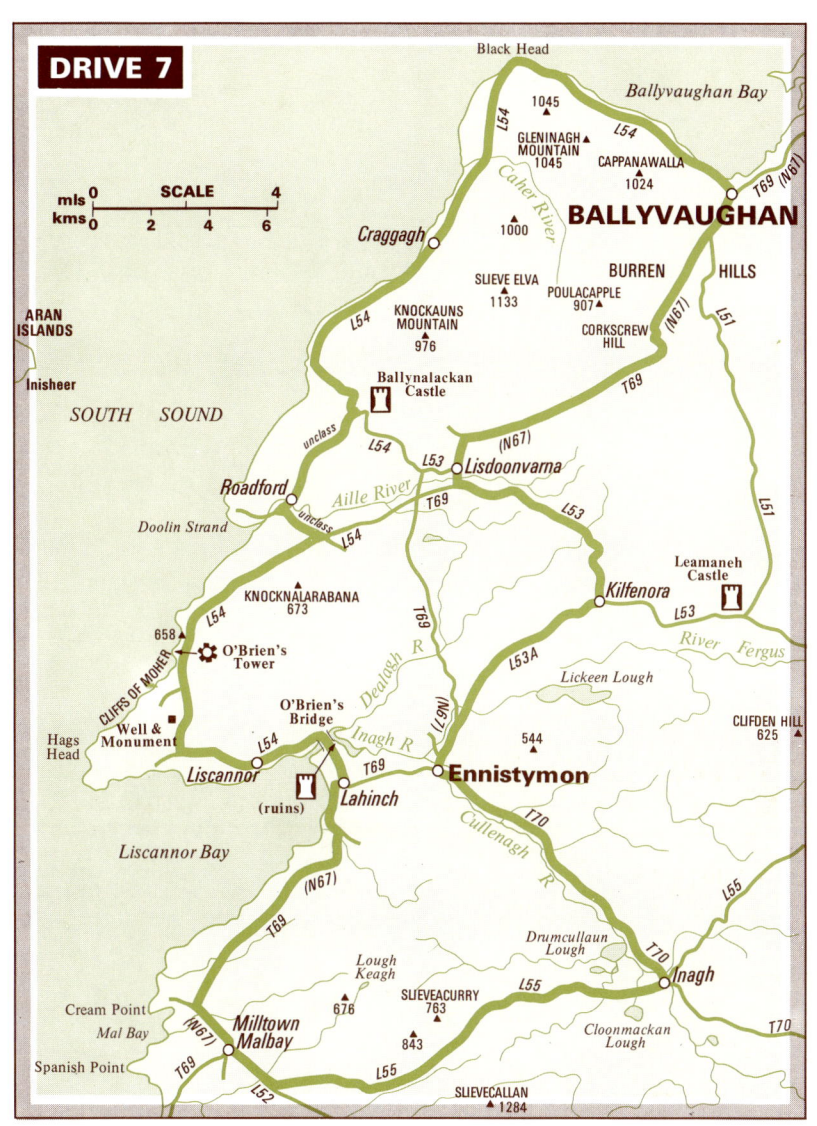

THE MUNSTER WILDERNESSES

Burren Moonscapes

From Ballyvaughan

Drive 7   79 miles

Depart from the monument in *Ballyvaughan* with SP 'Black Head' on the L54 and drive along the shores of Ballyvaughan Bay. Pass beneath 1,024ft Cappanawalla and 1,045ft Gleninagh Mountain, then after 6m round *Black Head* for views of the *Aran Islands*. After 4½m pass Craggagh Post Office on the right, with 1,134ft Slieve Elva to the left.

Continue, passing 976ft Knockauns on the left, then after 4m (from Craggagh) turn inland and ascend with 15th-c Ballynalackan Castle visible ahead. *Galway* Bay and the Aran Islands can be seen behind during the climb. After 1¾m reach the castle gates and turn right on to an unclassified road SP 'Cliffs of Moher'. Pass through farmland with distant forward views of the famous, 600ft *Cliffs of Moher*. Descend to Roadford, cross the River Aille, and in ¼m turn left SP 'Cliffs of Moher'. The road ahead leads 1m to Doolin Strand. In 1¼m meet X-roads and turn right on to the L54. Ascend with fine views right and 678ft Knocknalarabana on the left, then after 4½m pass a right turn leading to the Cliffs of Moher carpark. Steps from here lead up to cliff-top O'Brien's Tower, which affords magnificent views of the 3m cliff range. After another 2m along the L54 pass St Bridget's Well and a monument on the right. In ¾m meet a T-junction and turn left SP 'Liscannor, Lahinch', then in 1½m enter *Liscannor* on the shores of Liscannor Bay. Continue along the shore with the L54 and in 1m pass a fine (but dangerous) beach. Follow SP 'Lahinch', cross the Inagh River by *O'Brien's Bridge* with castle ruins on the left, then skirt Lahinch Championship Golf Course among the sand dunes on the right. Meet a T-junction, turn right on to the T69, then immediately left into the main street of *Lahinch*. Drive to the church, turn right, then immediately left SP 'Kilkee, Milltown Malbay'. Ascend, with views back and to the right over Liscannor Bay, and in 1m turn right SP 'Kilkee' to continue along the coast road. Views right extend across Liscannor Bay to the Cliffs of Moher. Proceed through farmland with hilly country to the left, and in 4m enjoy views of *Mutton Island* ahead.

After a further 2¼m turn right into *Milltown Malbay*, continue to the end of the town, and turn left on to the L52 SP 'Inagh, Ennis'. In 1½m turn left on to the L55 SP 'Inagh' and follow a winding road between 843ft Slieveacurry (left) and 1,284ft Slieve Callan. After another 4m pass between several loughs as the drive approaches Inagh. Enter the village and turn left on to the T70 SP 'Ennistymon' to follow the valley of the Inagh or Cullenagh River. Drumcullaun Lough is glimpsed to the left. Reach *Ennistymon*, go forward through the town and climb on the T69 SP 'Lisdoonvarna', and in 1m branch right on to the L53A SP 'Kilfenora' to enter low, hilly country. In 4½m enter *Kilfenora*, drive to the end of the village, and turn left on to the L53 SP 'Lisdoonvarna'. Climb steadily with views ahead and right of the *Burren* – a vast moonscape of bare limestone. After about 2m pass bogland. Continue, and in another 1m turn right on to the T69(N67) across the Aille River. Enter the well-known spa town of *Lisdoonvarna*, follow SP 'Galway, Ballyvaughan', and in ¼m bear left. In another ½m meet a T-junction and turn right SP 'Galway' to follow a narrow road between stone walls with rocky fields on both sides. Slieve Elva – the highest point in the area – rises to the left as the route climbs steadily into the heart of the Burren.

After 6m (from Lisdoonvarna) reach Corkscrew Hill, which affords magnificent views over the Burren area to Ballyvaughan and Galway Bays, plus *Lough Corrib*. Descend steeply through hairpin bends, and in 3½m re-enter Ballyvaughan.

89

THE MUNSTER WILDERNESSES

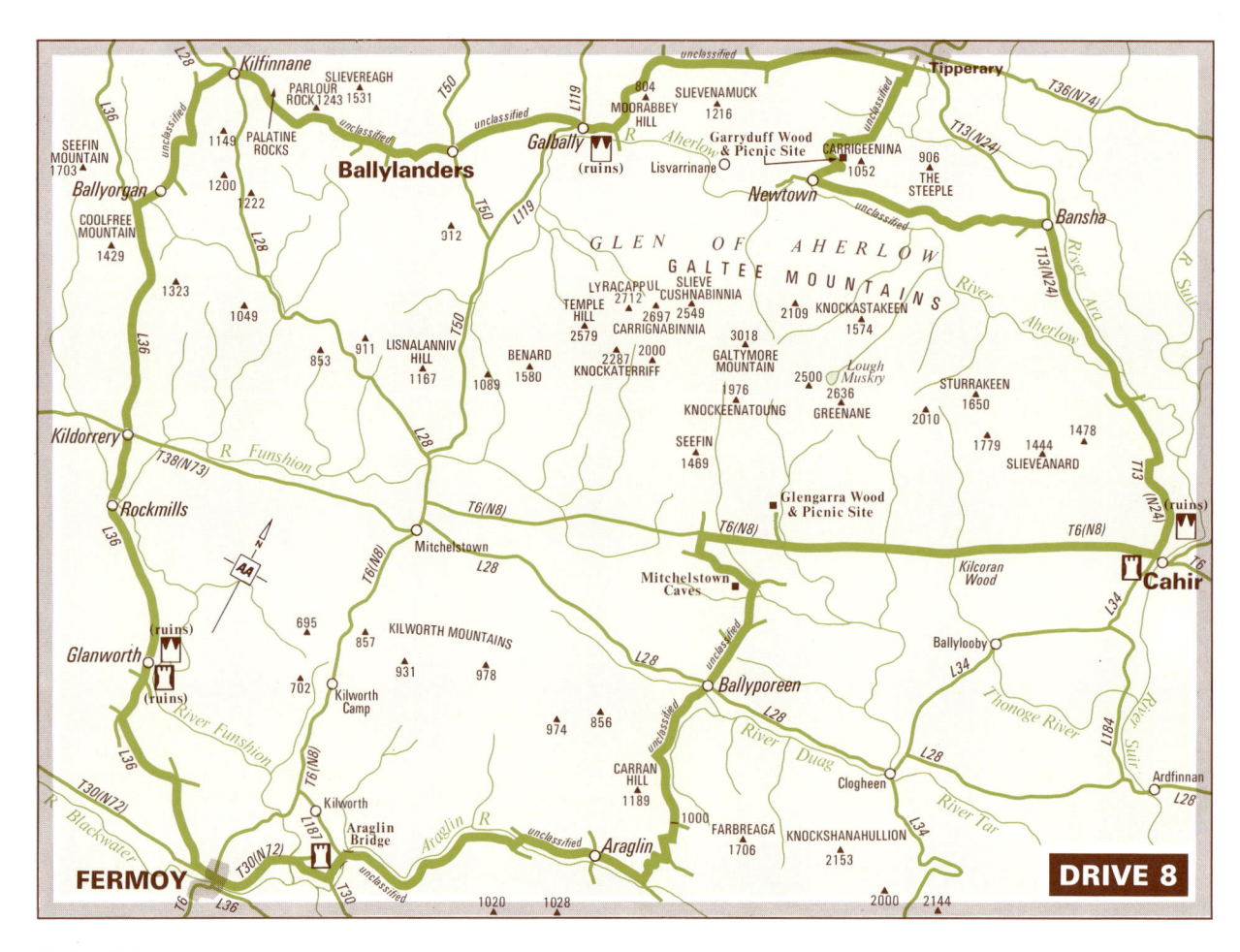

Ancient Ruins

From Fermoy

Drive 8   92 miles

Depart *Fermoy* town centre on the T6(N8) SP 'Dublin, Mitchelstown'. Cross the River Blackwater, turn right on to the T30(N72) SP 'Waterford', then follow the Blackwater Valley. After 1½m pass ruined Licklash Castle, then after 1m cross the River Funshion and turn right SP 'Lismore'. In ¾m pass Ballyderoon Castle (left), branch left on to the L187 SP 'Araglin', and in ¾m turn right on to an unclassified road SP 'Araglin'. Cross Araglin Bridge and turn left to follow the river. In 1¾m descend to cross a stream, and in 1m pass ruined Castle Cooke on the left. In 2m turn left to recross the Araglin, then bear right. In ¼m bear right again, and in 1½m keep forward through *Araglin* village. In 1¼m turn left SP 'Ballyporeen', and shortly ascend over hills between the Kilworth and *Knockmealdown Mountains*. The latter rise to the right. After 1¼m turn sharp left for good views, and in ½m turn sharp right. In ¾m reach the 1,000ft road summit for forward views across a valley to the 3,000ft *Galtee Mountains*. Descend the valley of a small stream. Reach *Ballyporeen*, meet X-roads, and go forward SP 'Burncourt'. In 1m bear right SP 'Mitchelstown Caves', and in ½m turn left.

Descend into a small valley, then in ½m meet a T-junction and turn left. In ¼m pass the house of Jack English, owner of the famous *Mitchelstown Caves* – which can be visited on application to the house. In 1¼m turn right, then in ¼m meet X-roads and turn right on to the T6(N8). Follow a straight road, and in 1½m pass the entrance to Glengarra Wood and Picnic Site on the left. Far ahead and to the right are the *Comeragh Mountains*. After 3¼m (from Glengarra Wood) enter Kilcoran Wood. After another 5½m reach the edge of *Cahir* and turn left on to the T13(N24). SP 'Tipperary'. Pass Cahir Abbey on the right and skirt the wooded slopes at the E end of the Galtee range. In 5m cross the River Aherlow, and in 3½m enter *Bansha* village. Proceed to the village centre and turn left on to an unclassified road SP 'Glen of Aherlow Scenic Route'. In ½m bear right SP 'Glen of Aherlow, Galbally', and follow SP 'Galbally' along the glen for 5½m. Reach Newtown and turn right SP 'Tipperary and Scenic View'.

Ascend, then in 1m negotiate a hairpin bend and pass a carpark and viewpoint overlooking the glen and the Galtee Mountains. Continue the ascent, and in ¾m reach an 800ft summit with the Garryduff Wood and Picnic Site on the right. Descend through woods, and in 1m – at the bottom of the descent – turn left SP 'Tipperary'. In ¾m cross a small river, then after 1m reach the edge of *Tipperary*. Meet X-roads and turn left SP 'Galbally'. In ½m keep left, then after 5m meet a T-junction and turn left again. In ¾m ascend 804ft Moorabbey Hill. Descend, and in 1m turn right. Ruined Moor Abbey stands on the left. In ¾m enter *Galbally*, drive to the square, and turn left on to the L119 SP 'Mitchelstown'. In ¼m branch right on to an unclassified road SP 'Limerick'. In ½m bear left SP '*Ballylanders*', and proceed to this village. Cross a main road with SP 'Kilfinnane', and in 1½m keep forward. In ¾m meet a fork and bear right, then ascend to over 900ft. After another ¾m pass the Palatine Rocks on the right and descend into *Kilfinnane* village. Meet X-roads, turn right, then shortly turn left into the main street.

Drive to the top of the main street and branch left on to an unclassified road SP 'Kildorrery, Ballyorgan'. Ascend to 800ft, then in ¾m on the descent bear right to drive through Ballyorgan village. Cross a small valley and meet a T-junction. Turn left on to the L36 SP 'Kildorrery', and skirt the Ballyhoura Mountains. Pass through a gap between two mountains, and in 3½m reach *Kildorrery*. Cross the main road SP 'Glanworth' and continue on the L36 to *Glanworth*, with its ruined castle and abbey. Keep forward through the village SP 'Fermoy'. In 5½m rejoin the Blackwater Valley and meet a T-junction. Turn left on to the T30(N72) to re-enter Fermoy, and in ½m turn right for the town centre.

THE MUNSTER WILDERNESSES

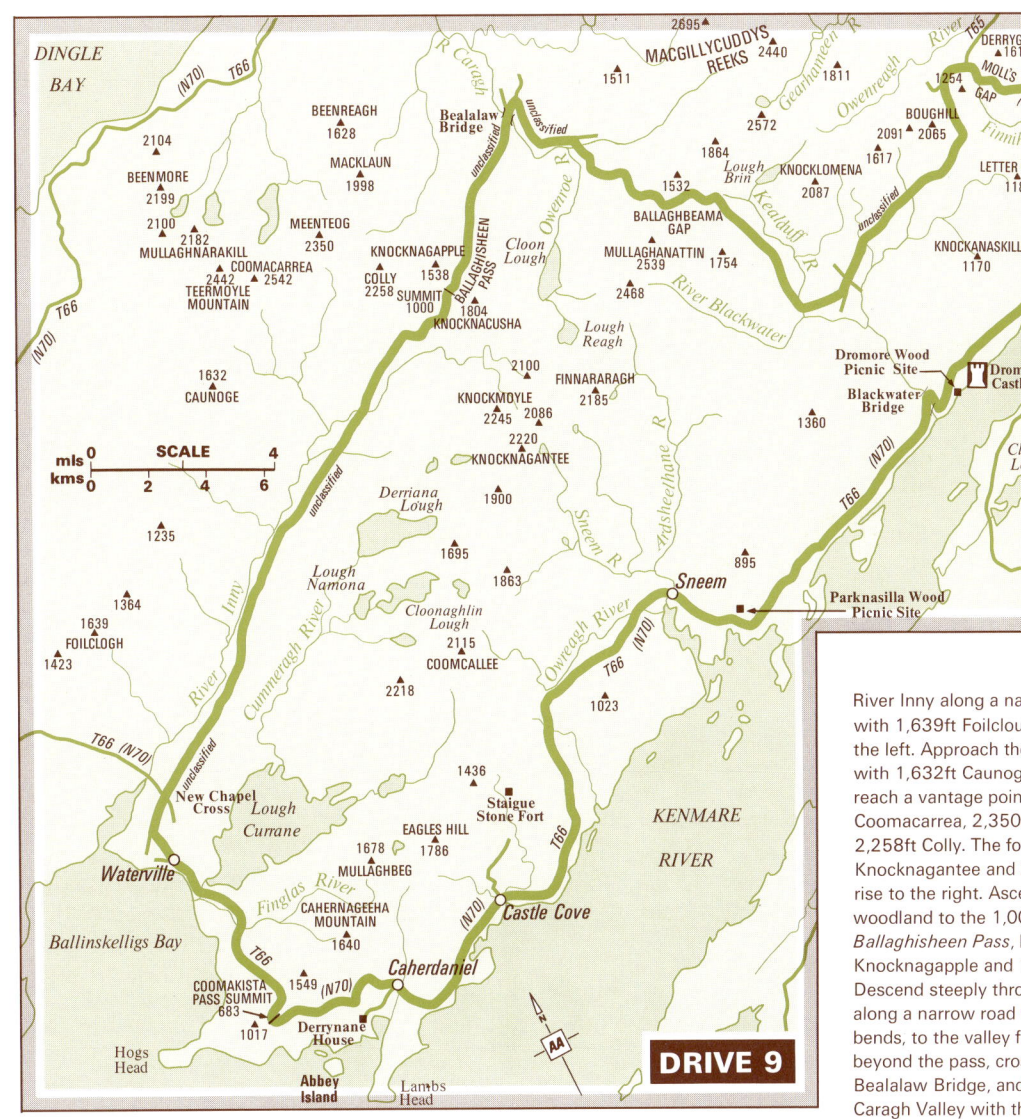

Through the High Passes

From Kenmare

Drive 9   80 miles

Take the T65(N71) and follow SP 'Killarney, Ring of Kerry' to leave *Kenmare*. In ½m bear left on to the T66(N70), then follow the N shore of Kenmare River with views of the Caha Mountains to the left. To the right the 1,186ft hills of Letter South and 1,170ft Knockanaskill rise above the waters of the bay. After 5m (from Kenmare) pass the entrance to Dromore Castle on the left, and 1¾m farther pass Dromore Wood Picnic Site on the left. In another 1m cross *Blackwater Bridge* and continue alongside the bay.

After 7m pass another picnic site at *Parknasilla* Wood. Continue from here to *Sneem* along a tree-lined road, with glimpses of Kenmare River to the left. Approach Sneem with views of mountains which ring the town. This group is dominated by 2,155ft Coomcallee, which rises to the W. Cross the Sneem River by a narrow bridge and turn inland. Ascend along an afforested valley to the summit of a low pass, with Coomcallee on the right. Descend through wild, rocky scenery to rejoin Kenmare River.

Views afforded by this stretch extend across the bay to the Slieve Miskish Mountains, which rise from the *Beare Peninsula*. Continue to Castle Cove, situated beneath 1,786ft Eagles Hill; an unclassified road here leads to *Staigue Fort* (NM). Follow the coast below the mountain to reach *Caherdaniel*. Restored, 17th-c Derrynane House (NM) can be visited from here.

Ascend on the main road, and pass beneath 1,640ft Cahernageeha and 1,549ft Farraniaragh. Magnificent seaward views include Scariff and Deenish Islands. Continue to the summit of Coomakista Pass, where Beenorourke rises to 1,017ft on the left. Descend gradually to the small resort of *Waterville*, with magnificent views over Ballinskelligs Bay and 1,350ft Bolus Head. Approach the town and pass Lough Currane on the right. Proceed to the N end of the town and bear left, then right. In 1¾m reach New Chapel Cross and go forward on to an unclassified road SP 'Ballaghisheen, Glencar'. Follow the broad valley of the River Inny along a narrow but level road, with 1,639ft Foilclough in the distance to the left. Approach the head of the valley, with 1,632ft Caunoge to the left, and shortly reach a vantage point for views of 2,541ft Coomacarrea, 2,350ft Meenteog, and 2,258ft Colly. The foothills of 2,250ft Knocknagantee and 2,245ft Knockmoyle rise to the right. Ascend past extensive woodland to the 1,000ft summit of *Ballaghisheen Pass*, between 1,538ft Knocknagapple and 1,804ft Knocknacusha. Descend steeply through desolate bogland, along a narrow road with several difficult bends, to the valley floor. Continue for 4m beyond the pass, cross the Caragh River at Bealalaw Bridge, and bear right. Follow the Caragh Valley with the foothills of *Macgillycuddy's Reeks* on the left. After 1¾m turn right SP 'Ballaghbeama, Parknasilla', and recross the Caragh River.

Ascend between towering rock faces, with 2,539ft Mullaghanattin on the right, to reach the 1,000ft summit of *Ballaghbeama* Gap. The 1,532ft summit on the left is part of Knockaunanattin. Pass the road summit and descend along the valley of the River Kealduff, with 2,097ft Knocklomena ahead and Lough Brin to the left. On reaching the valley floor, continue through forestry plantations and cross the river. After 1m turn left SP 'Killarney, Moll's Gap', and follow a wide valley with Knocklomena on the left, 2,091ft Boughil and 1,825ft Peakeen Mountain ahead, and the low hills of Knockanaskill and Letter South on the right. Climb to over 700ft and join the top end of the Finnihy Valley, with Boughil towering on the left. Shortly pass little Lough Barfinnihy on the left, then skirt an unnamed, 1,254ft hill for views of the Owenreagh Valley to the N. Meet the main road and turn right on to the T65(N71). Pass through Moll's Gap, situated between the unnamed hill and 1,617ft Derrygarriff at a height of over 900ft. Complete the drive by returning to Kenmare via a long, winding descent, which affords excellent views of Kenmare Bay and the surrounding mountains.

Placenames in *italic* type are worth stopping at; each is listed and described in the main gazetteer section.

THE MUNSTER WILDERNESSES

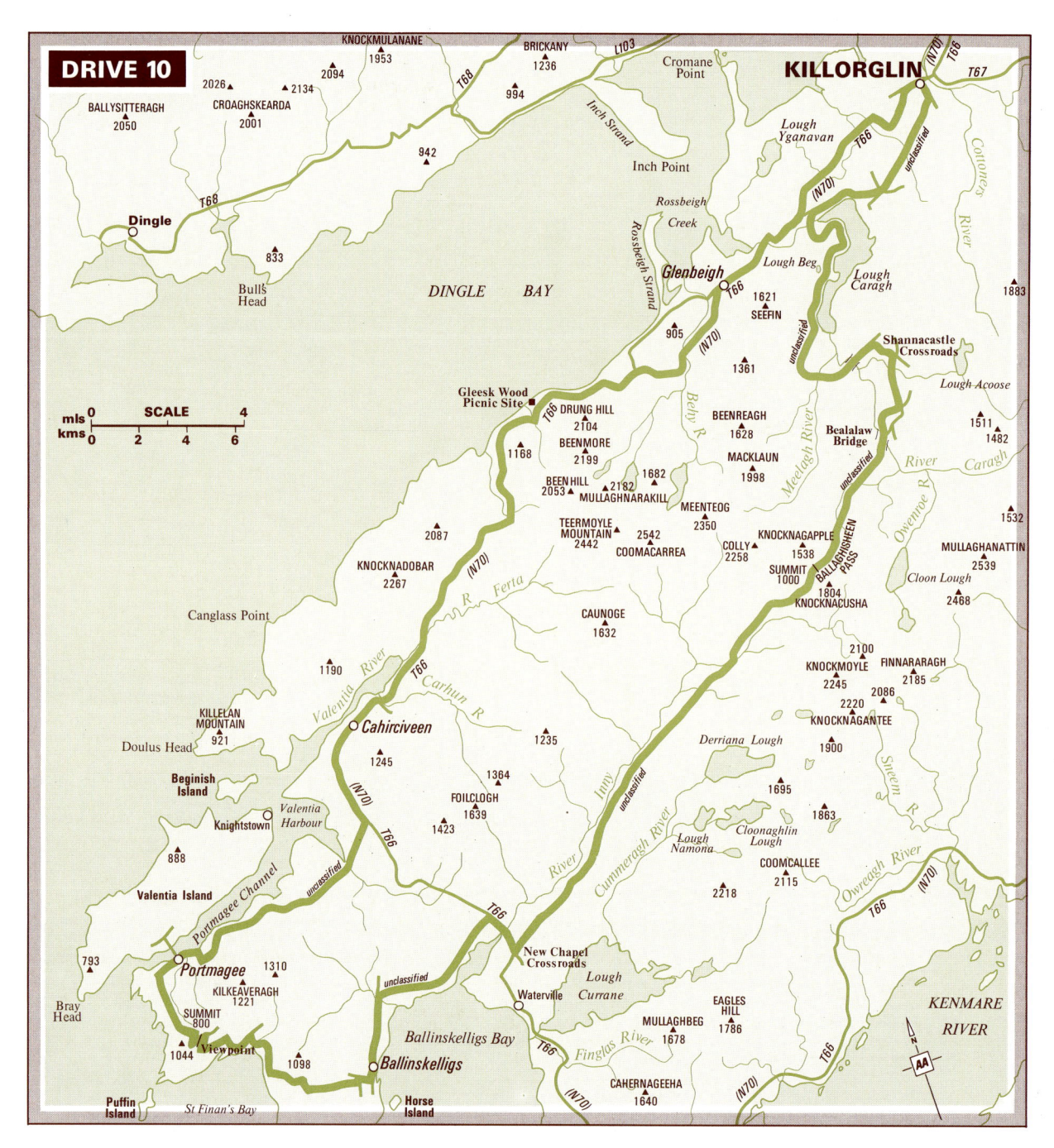

Over Ballaghisheen Pass

From Killorglin

Drive 10   88 miles

Depart *Killorglin* via the T66(N70) SP 'Ring of Kerry, Glenbeigh', and in ½m bear left. In 5m pass the Caragh River and Lough on the left. Continue to *Glenbeigh*, below the W slopes of 1,621ft Seefin, then after the village pass an unclassified right turn leading to beautiful Rossbeigh Strand. Stay on the T66 and follow the River Behy valley between high hills to enjoy mountain views ahead and to the left.

Pass below 2,104ft Drung Hill and emerge on to the coastline of Dingle Bay, with views N to the high mountains of *Dingle Peninsula*. Turn slightly inland and pass a small picnic site and carpark at Gleesk Wood. Leave the coast and turn inland, passing between Been Hill and an unnamed 2,087ft mountain. Descend the Ferta Valley (with 2,267ft Knocknadobar on the right) to *Cahirciveen*, situated near the head of the Valentia River. Pass through this town and shortly reach a vantage point for views to the right over Valentia Harbour and *Knightstown*, the main settlement on *Valentia Island*. After 3m (from Cahirciveen) turn right on to an unclassified road SP 'Valentia, Portmagee'. Cross flat bogland, with views of Valentia Island S, and enter *Portmagee*. Turn left SP 'Ballinskelligs', and ascend with hill views to the left. Views right and behind encompass Bray Head on Valentia Island.

Climb steeply to an 800ft summit, with an unnamed hill rising to 1,044ft on the right. The views from here are panoramic. Turn right and descend steeply to enjoy seaward views of the *Skellig Rocks*, St Finan's Bay, and 1,350ft Bolus Head. Descend steeply, turn sharp right at a church, then drive close to the shores of St Finan's Bay. Climb to a low pass, and descend with fine views over Ballinskelligs Bay and the distant resort of *Waterville*. Proceed to Ballinskelligs School, turn left and immediately right into *Ballinskelligs*, then turn left SP 'Waterville'. In 2¼m cross a river and turn right, then in 3¾m turn right on to the T66(N70). After 1m meet New Chapel X-roads and turn left on to an unclassified road SP 'Ballaghisheen, Glencar'. Continue along the broad River Inny valley. As the drive nears the head of the valley the hills become much higher, with 1,632ft Caunoge on the left before the backs of 2,542ft Coomacarrea, 2,350ft Meenteog, and 2,258ft Colly come into view. To the right are the foothills of 2,220ft Knocknagantee and 2,245ft Knockmoyle. Ascend past extensive woodland to reach the *Ballaghisheen Pass*, reaching a road summit of over 1,000ft between 1,538ft Knocknagapple and 1,804ft Knocknacusha.

Descend steeply, along a narrow road with

THE MUNSTER WILDERNESSES

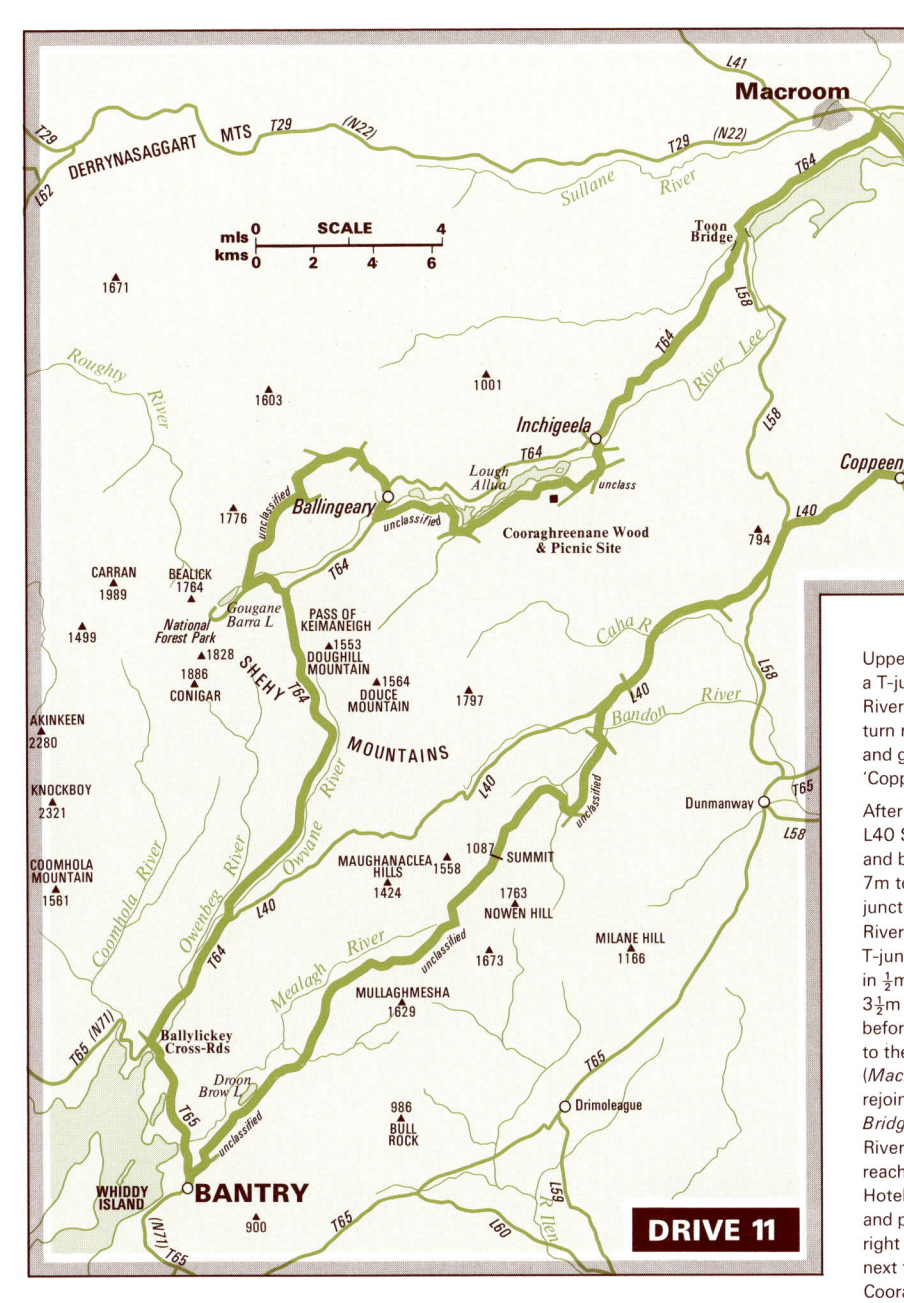

Drive 10 continued

several difficult bends, to the valley floor. After 4m (from the summit of the pass) cross the Caragh River at Bealalaw Bridge, then bear left SP 'Glencar, Killorglin'. After a further 1m turn sharp left uphill along a narrow road SP 'Glencar'. Distant views to the right take in the high summits of *Macgillycuddy's Reeks*. In 1½m meet Shannacastle X-roads and turn left. Descend to the Caragh River valley. Recross the river at Blackstones Bridge, pass through forestry plantations, then join the shores of Lough Caragh below the E slopes of Seefin. Views from this section are often from a considerable height above the water and take in the surrounding hills. Pass craggy slopes on the left and drive through an arch of trees.

Skirt tiny Lough Beg on the left, then after several miles recross the Caragh River. After ¼m turn right SP 'Killorglin', then in 2m pass a school and bear left. Follow a gradual descent to Killorglin.

A Riverbank Tour
From Bantry
Drive 11 82 miles

Take the T65(N71) 'Glengarriff' road from the Square in *Bantry*, in ½m pass a telephone box on the left then turn right on to an unclassified road and in ½m bear left.

Climb along the Mealagh Valley, then continue beyond the valley head to a 1,087ft pass. Descend, and in 1¾m meet X-roads and turn left. Descend into the Upper Bandon Valley, then after 1¾m meet a T-junction and turn left. Cross the Bandon River, turn right SP 'Inchigeela', and in ½m turn right on to the L40. In ¾m meet X-roads and go forward, then in 2¾m bear left SP 'Coppeen'. In 1½m turn left on to the L58.

After another 1m branch right on to the L40 SP 'Crookstown'. In 3m reach Coppeen and bear left SP 'Macroom'. Continue for 7m to Bealnablath, bear left through the junction SP 'Cork', then follow the Bride River down to *Crookstown*. Meet a T-junction and turn left SP 'Macroom', and in ½m turn left on to the L41. After another 3½m follow the River Lee reservoir for 2½m before crossing this river. In ¾m turn left on to the T64 SP 'Inchigeela, Glengarriff' (*Macroom* lies 1¼m ahead), and shortly rejoin the reservoir. After 3m reach *Toon Bridge*, then turn left and right over Toon River. Continue on the T64 and after 5½m reach *Inchigeela*. Drive to Creddon's Hotel, turn left on to an unclassified road, and proceed to the end of the village. Turn right SP 'South Lake Road', bear right at the next three junctions, and later pass Cooraghreenane Wood (left). After a further 1¼m descend to Lough Allua, then in 1¼m turn right and cross a river. In another ¼m turn right and drive beside the lake. In 2½m turn right on to the T64 SP 'Macroom' to reach *Ballingeary*. Shortly cross a bridge and turn left on to an unclassified road SP 'Macroom, Killarney', then climb. In 1¼m turn left across a bridge on to a narrow road. After a further 1m bear left SP 'Gougane' and ascend to 800ft. After 1¼m turn right SP 'Gougane Barra', then after another ¼m bear left. Descend steeply to *Gougane Barra* Lake and branch left.

In ¼m meet a T-junction and turn left SP 'Ballingeary'. The right turn here leads to the Gougane Barra national forest park. In 1¼m meet another T-junction and turn right on to the T64 SP 'Bantry, Glengarriff'. Ascend the Pass of Keimaneigh to 662ft, then descend alongside the Owvane River valley to reach *Ballylickey* X-roads – at the edge of Bantry Bay. Turn left on to the T65 (N71) SP 'Bantry', cross the river, and skirt the E end of the bay. Continue into Bantry.

THE MUNSTER WILDERNESSES

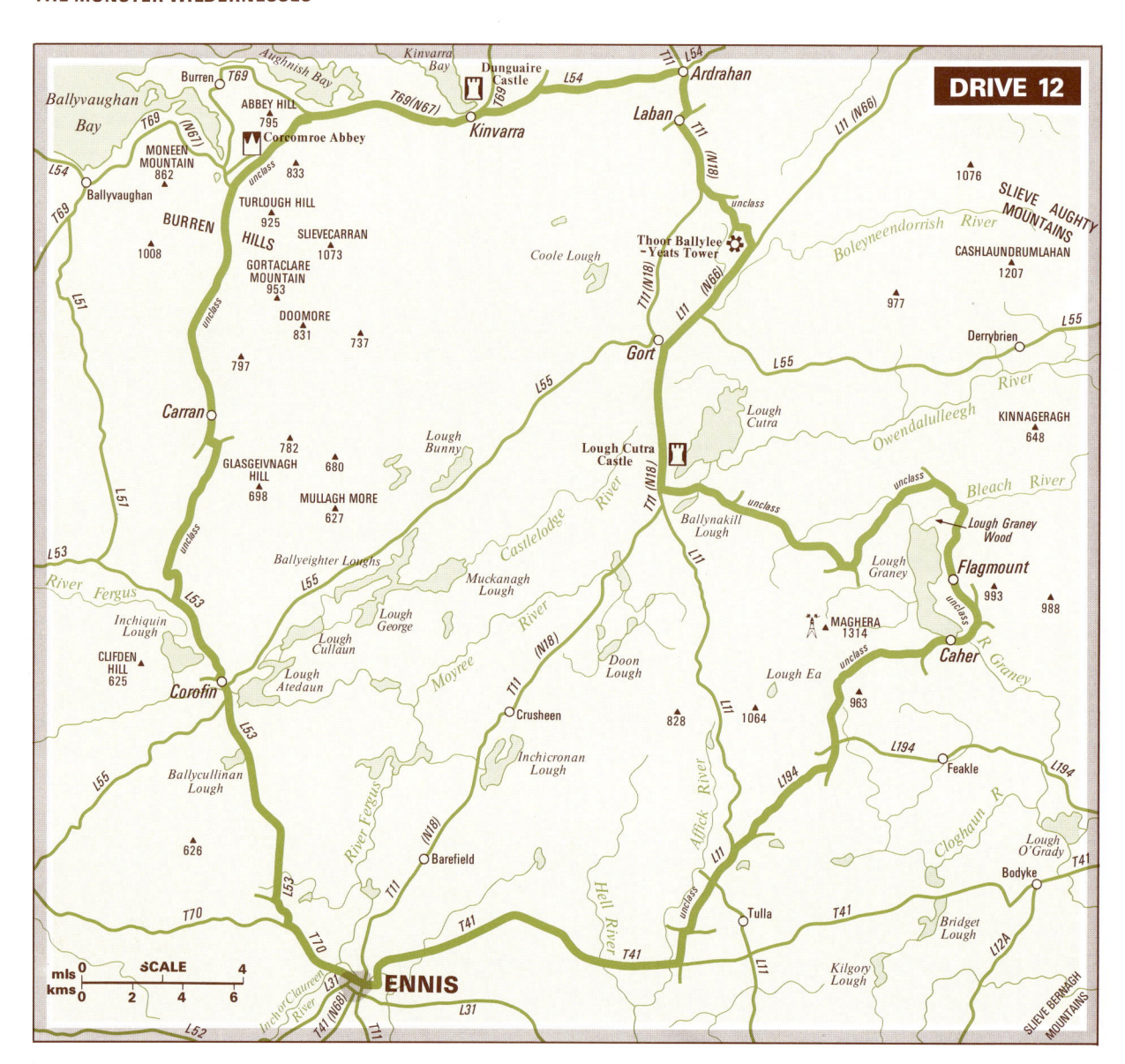

Landscapes of Clare and Galway

From Ennis

Drive 12 84 miles

Follow SP 'Ennistymon T70' from *Ennis*, and in 2¼m branch right on to the L53 SP 'Lisdoonvarna, Corofin'. In ¾m turn right. Reach *Corofin* and keep forward to the Grotto, then bear right SP 'Ballyvaughan, Kilfenora'. Shortly pass Inchiquin Lough and 15th-c castle ruins (left). After 2½m (from Corofin) turn right on to an unclassified road.

In ½m ascend through several hairpin bends, and 3¼m farther bear left. In ½m meet a T-junction and turn right. In ½m pass through the hamlet of *Carran*, and in a further 2m begin a long descent. Pass through a deep, rocky gorge into a wide valley, then later drive between 862ft Moneen Mountain and 925ft Turlough Hill. Lough Luick lies a short distance from the road on the left. Shortly beyond this pass the *Bealaclugga* left turn which leads to the entrance to *Corcomroe Abbey* (NM). After another 1m pass close to the abbey buildings and climb to a low pass. The summit affords forward views over the islands in Galway Bay. In ½m turn right on to the T69(N67)

'Galway' road and continue with fine views of the *Burren* hills on the right. After 4m reach *Kinvarra*. Follow SP 'Galway' to round the head of Kinvarra Bay, with 16th-c *Dunguaire Castle* ahead to the left. Reach the castle gate and turn right on to the L54 SP 'Ardrahan'. Continue, and in 1¾m bear right. In a further 3¾m enter Ardrahan and turn right on to the T11(N18) SP 'Ennis, Gort', then in 1¼m reach *Laban* and turn left to follow a main road with views to the Slieve Aughty Mountains on the left. In 1¾m meet X-roads and bear left on to an unclassified road SP 'Thoor Ballylee-Yeats Tower'. In ½m bear right, then after 1m pass the entrance to the *Thoor Ballylee*-Yeats Tower (right). In ½m meet a T-junction and turn right on to the L11(N66) SP 'Gort'.

Proceed for 3½m to the edge of *Gort*, turn left SP 'Shannon, Ennis' to rejoin the T11 (N18), and in 2¼m pass the entrance to *Lough Cutra Castle* (left) beside Lough Cutra. After another 1¼m turn left on to an unclassified road SP 'Scarriff', and shortly

follow SP 'Lough Cutra Drive' to pass close to Ballynakill Lough (right). In just over 1¾m bear right SP 'Feakle, Scarriff'. In 2½m bear left, and in ¼m left again. In 3¼m meet a T-junction and turn right, with views of Lough Graney to the right. Descend and shortly cross the Bleach River, then bear right and in ½m pass the entrance to Lough Graney Wood on the right. After another ¾m reach the shores of the lough and continue between high hedges. Shortly pass Flagmount Post Office on the left, turn away from the lough, and in 1m bear right. In a further ½m meet a T-junction and turn right SP 'Feakle', then in ¾m rejoin the shores of Lough Graney and enter Caher village. Continue for ¾m and turn right SP 'TV Station'. Ascend steeply for 1¾m to the entrance of Maghera TV Station, then continue the climb to an 800ft summit.

Descend, then in 1m meet X-roads and go forward on to the L194. In ½m bear right, with views left of the 1,750ft Slieve Bernagh Mountains. In 2½m meet a

THE MUNSTER WILDERNESSES

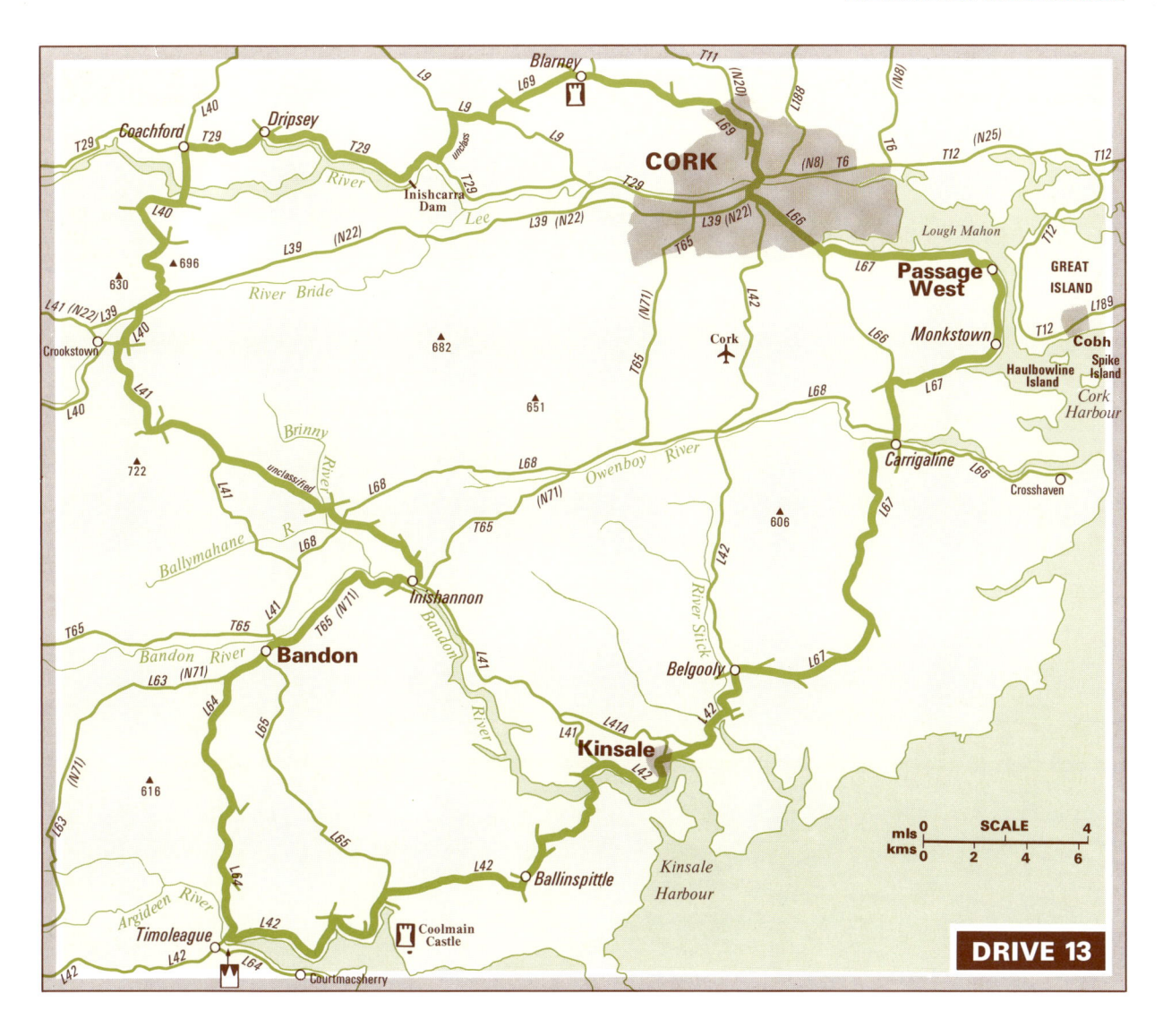

Seascapes and the Lee Valley

From Cork

Drive 13   95 miles

Drive from St Patrick's Bridge with SP 'Limerick T11(N20)' along Watercourse Rd. After ¾m reach Blackpool Church, turn left, then immediately right SP 'Killarney' into Commons Rd L69. In 1¼m bear right and drive to Blarney. At the end of Blarney pass a hotel and bear left SP 'Killarney, Macroom'.

Drive 12 continued

T-junction and turn right, then in 1m bear left on to the L11 SP 'Tulla'. After another 1m meet X-roads and go forward on to an unclassified road SP 'Quin'. In 1¼m reach a T-junction and turn right, then in ¼m bear left and continue for 1m to X-roads. Turn right on to the T41 SP 'Ennis' and follow a broad road for 9m to re-enter Ennis.

In 1¾m bear right then left. In ¾m turn right on to the L9, and in 1m left (unclassified) SP 'Inishcarra'. Descend for 1¼m and turn right on to the T29 SP 'Killarney, Macroom'.

Shortly follow the River Lee to *Dripsey* and turn left over a bridge SP 'Coachford'. In 2m at *Coachford* X-roads turn left on to the L40. Descend, cross the River Lee, and meet a T-junction. Turn right SP 'Crookstown, Bandon' and ascend. In 1¼m bear left; after 1m at X-roads turn right. Descend to a T-junction, turn right on to the L39, and in ¾m turn left on to the L40 SP 'Bealnablath'. Cross the river, and in 1m meet a T-junction. Turn right, then in ¼m left on to the L41 SP 'Bandon'. Climb to X-roads and bear left. In 2m branch left (unclassified). After 3m reach the Old Mill Bar and bear left. Cross the Brinny River, meet X-roads, and turn right SP 'Bandon'. In ½m cross a main road SP 'Upton', then in ½m branch right. In 1¼m bear right, then in ¾m descend to *Inishannon*. Turn right on to the T65(N71) and in ½m cross the Bandon River and bear right. In 3¾m meet a T-junction and turn left then right on to the L63 to keep forward through

Bandon. In 1½m bear left on to the L64 SP 'Timoleague'. After 1¼m reach the edge of *Timoleague* and turn left on to the L42 to run alongside the Argideen estuary. After 3½m meet X-roads, turn right, then in ¼m bear right SP 'Kinsale'. In 1m turn right, then ¾m farther cross a bridge and turn left.

In ½m right SP 'Ballinspittle'. Within 2m descend to a T-junction, turn left, then bear right into *Ballinspittle*. Continue along the L42 SP 'Kinsale'. Cross Kinsale Western Bridge, bear right, then in ½m bear right over a bridge. Drive to the Trident Hotel in *Kinsale*, turn right and immediately left, and follow SP 'Cork' through the town. Meet a fork, bear left uphill, then in 2m cross a bridge. In a further ½m cross another bridge and turn left SP 'Cork'. Reach *Belgooly*, meet X-roads, and turn right on to the L67 SP 'Carrigaline'. Continue on the L67 for 9½m to a T-junction in *Carrigaline* and turn left to go forward on the L66. In 1½m meet X-roads. Turn right on to the L67 SP 'Monkstown' and proceed to *Passage West* via *Monkstown*. After 5m turn right on to the L66 to re-enter *Cork*.

Placenames in *italic* type are worth stopping at; each is listed and described in the main gazetteer section.

THE MUNSTER WILDERNESSES

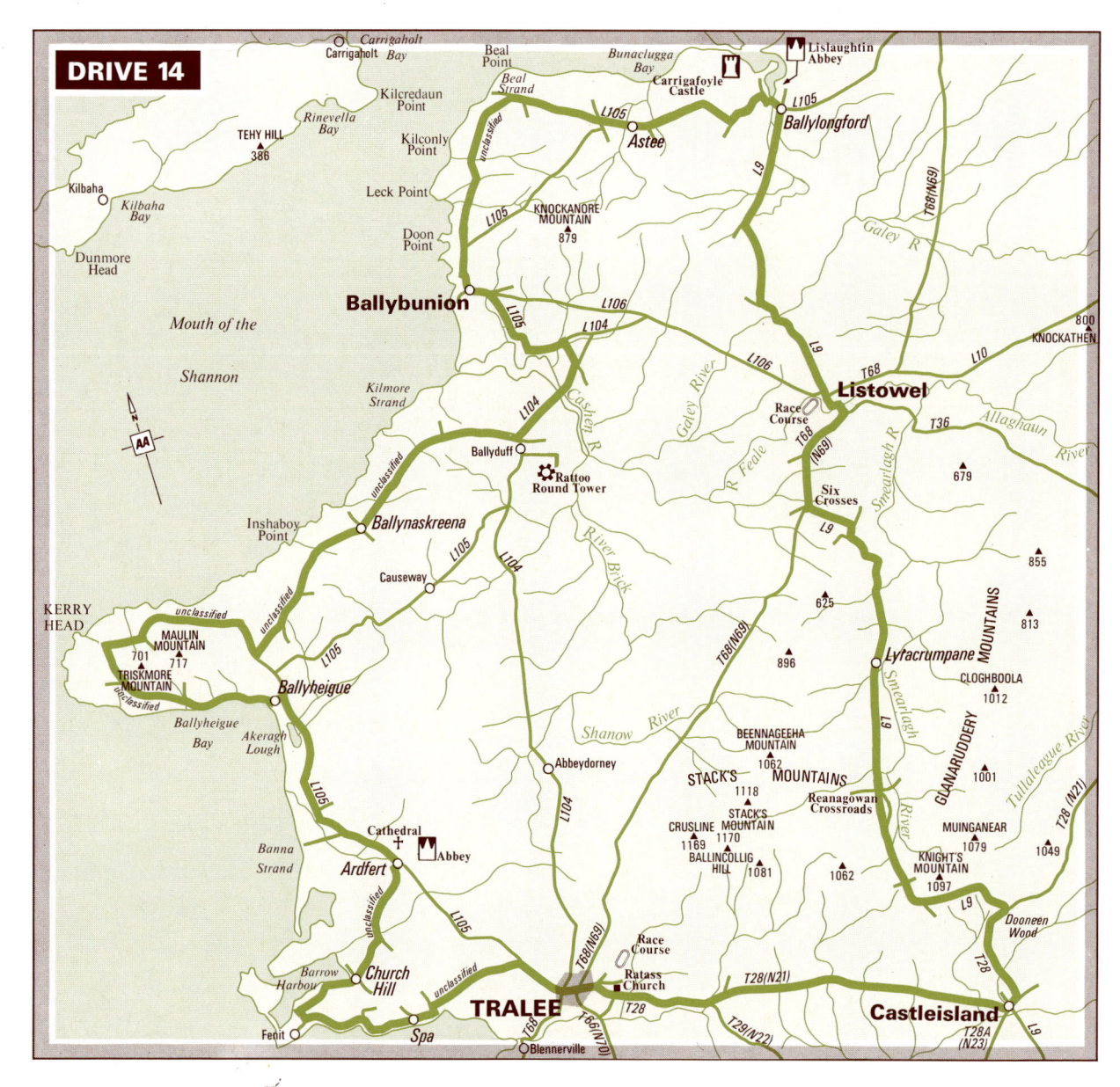

DRIVE 14

Mouth of the Shannon

From Tralee

Drive 14   98 miles

From *Tralee* follow SP 'Ardfert, Ballyheigue L105', and in 1¼m turn left on to an unclassified road SP 'Spa, Fenit'. In 2½m reach Spa village. Turn left and shortly turn sharp right at the edge of Tralee Bay. In ½m bear left SP 'Fenit'. After 3¼m turn right SP 'Church Hill, Ardfert'. In ½m bear right, then in 1m right again. In ¾m enter Church Hill and turn right SP 'Ardfert', then left. Ascend, and in 1½m meet a T-junction and turn left.

In 2m enter *Ardfert* and turn sharp left on to the L105 SP 'Ballyheigue, Banna'. In 1½m keep forward, and in a further 1m bear left SP 'Ballyheigue, Ballybunion'. In 3m turn left on to an unclassified road SP 'Kerry Head Ring' and enter *Ballyheigue*. In 4m meet a fork and bear right to reach the N side of Kerry Head. Pass ruined Ballygarry Castle (left), then in 1m meet a T-junction and turn left. After another 4m turn left SP 'Ballyduff, Ballybunion'. In 1m turn left then right, still with SP 'Ballyduff, Ballybunion',

and in 3½m meet X-roads at Ballynaskreena. Go forward, and after 5m meet X-roads at the edge of *Ballyduff* and turn left on to the L104 SP,'Listowel, Ballybunion'. In 1½m cross the Cashen River and in ¾m meet X-roads. Turn left on to the L105 SP 'Ballybunion', then after 3m meet a T-junction and turn left with the L105. In ½m enter *Ballybunion*. Drive through the town and turn right on to an unclassified road SP 'Beal, Ballylongford'. In ½m follow SP 'Ballylongford, Tarbert' to rejoin the L105, and in ¾m bear left on an unclassified road. In 4¼m bear right SP 'Limerick', then in 2½m meet X-roads and go forward on the L105 SP 'Ballylongford'. Pass Astee, then in 2½m meet a T-junction and turn left. In 1m farther reach a T-junction and turn right.

Drive to the centre of *Ballylongford*. Meet X-roads and turn right on to the L9 SP 'Listowel, Tralee'. Follow these signposts and in 3m turn left. After another 2m bear left, and in a further ½m cross the Galey River. Proceed to the square in *Listowel* and follow SP 'Tralee T68(N69)'. In ½m cross the River Feale and immediately turn right SP 'Tralee, Lixnaw'. In 1½m bear left, and in

1¼m reach Six Crosses X-roads. Turn left on to the L9 SP 'Castleisland, Crumpane' and ascend. In 1¼m meet a T-junction, turn right, then in ¼m turn left SP 'Lyracrumpane, Castleisland'. In 4m pass Lyracrumpane. Continue along the L9, and after 3m meet Reanagowan X-roads. Keep forward on an unclassified road SP 'Castleisland'. In ¾m go forward to rejoin the L9, and in 2m meet X-roads. Go forward and in ½m reach an 800ft-plus summit. Bear left and descend, and in 2½m meet a T-junction. Turn right on to the T28(N21) SP 'Killarney'.

In 2½m reach *Castleisland*, turn right for 'town centre', then follow SP 'Tralee T28 (N21)' and at the end of the main street bear right. In 7¼m drive under a railway bridge and shortly bear right. In 2½m pass *Ratass* Church (NM) on the right, then enter the outskirts of Tralee. Follow SP for the town centre and re-enter the town via Castle St.

THE MUNSTER WILDERNESSES

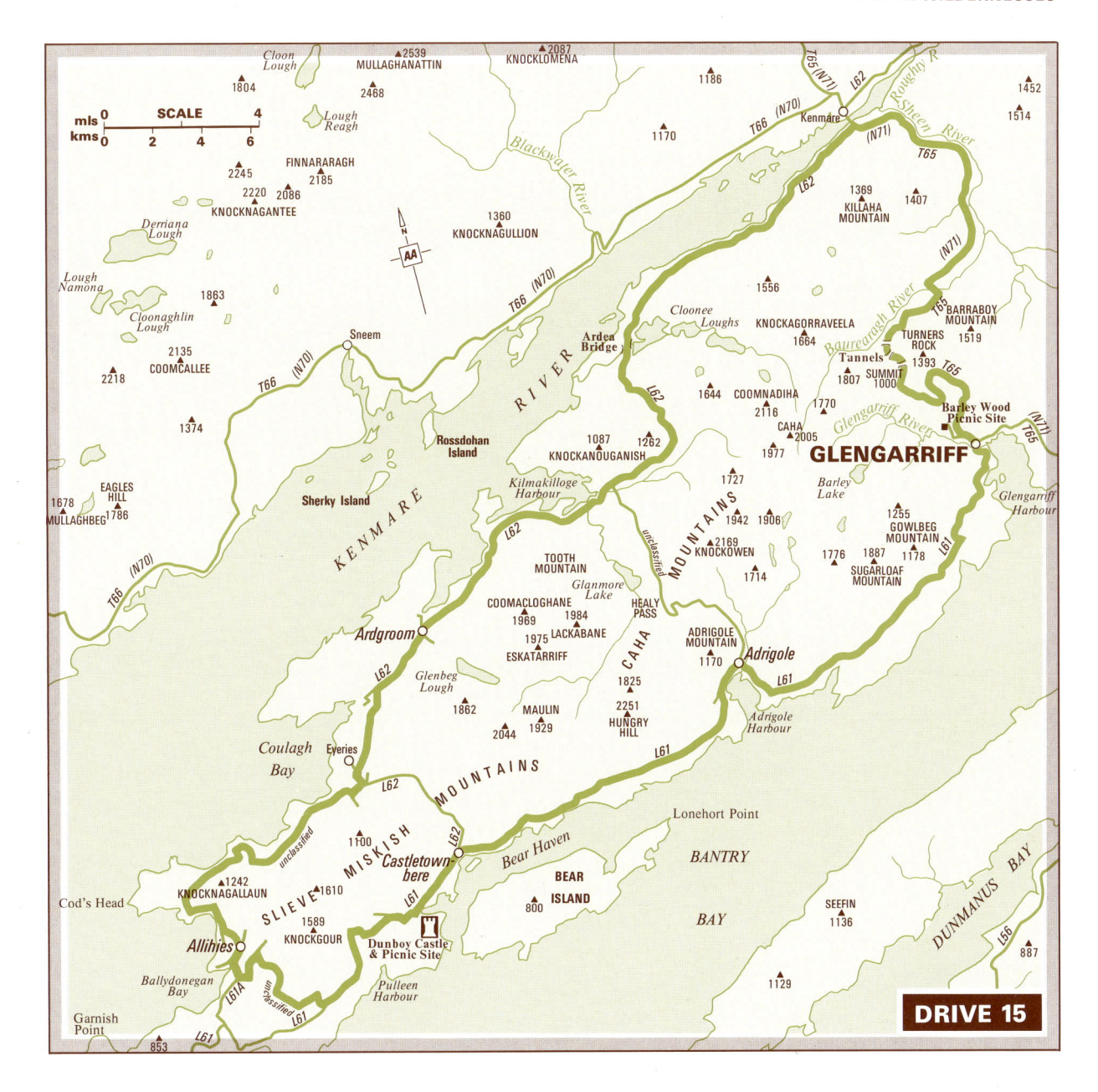

Around Bear Haven

From Glengarriff

Drive 15   84 miles

From *Glengarriff* follow SP 'Castletownbere, Healy Pass' on the L61, skirting Poul Gorm pool and Glengarriff Harbour on the left. Continue above the Bantry Bay coast with the 1,887ft Sugarloaf, highest of the Caha Mountain foothills, to the right. Descend and skirt Adrigole Harbour. Continue to *Adrigole*, cross the river, and turn left SP 'Coast Road'.

After 2½m ascend with forward views of 800ft Bere Island, then follow the shores of *Bear Haven* with the Slieve Miskish Mountains on the right. Enter *Castletownbere*, keep forward through the town on the L61 coast road, and in 1½m pass Dunboy Castle and Picnic Site on the left. After 1m bear left and ascend to a 500ft summit. Descend for 1¼m and turn right on to an unclassified road SP 'Allihies'. Climb to a low pass and in 1¼m bear left. In 1m turn right on to the L61A, and after ½m turn sharp right. In ½m enter *Allihies*, turn left on to an unclassified road SP 'Eyeries', and in ¾m turn right. Climb to another low pass and descend steeply. Follow SP 'Eyeries', with the Slieve Miskish range on the right, and after 6m reach Kealincha River bridge and bear left.

Meet X-roads and turn left on to the L62. In ¼m bear right SP 'Killarney, Kenmare' and continue on the L62 to Ardgroom. Bear left, then turn right SP 'Kenmare'. To the right rise 1,969ft Coomacloghane and Tooth Mountain. Shortly enjoy views of *Kilmakilloge* Harbour; in 3m reach Lauragh Bridge and pass an unclassified right-turn leading to 1,000ft *Healy Pass*. Ascend the Glantrasna River valley to a 600ft pass, with mountain views to the right, and follow a long descent to Ardea Bridge. The mountain-ringed Cloonee and Inchiquin Loughs can be seen to the right. Continue along the river for another 8m to *Kenmare* Suspension Bridge, then turn right on to the T65(N71) SP 'Glengarriff'. Drive along Sheen Valley, and after 7½m cross the Baurearagh River.

Climb through several short tunnels to reach a long tunnel which marks the summit of a 1,000ft ridge. Descend, with the Caha Mountains to the right, into the densely-wooded valley bottom and pass the entrance to Barley Wood Picnic Site on the right before re-entering Glengarriff.

THE MUNSTER WILDERNESSES

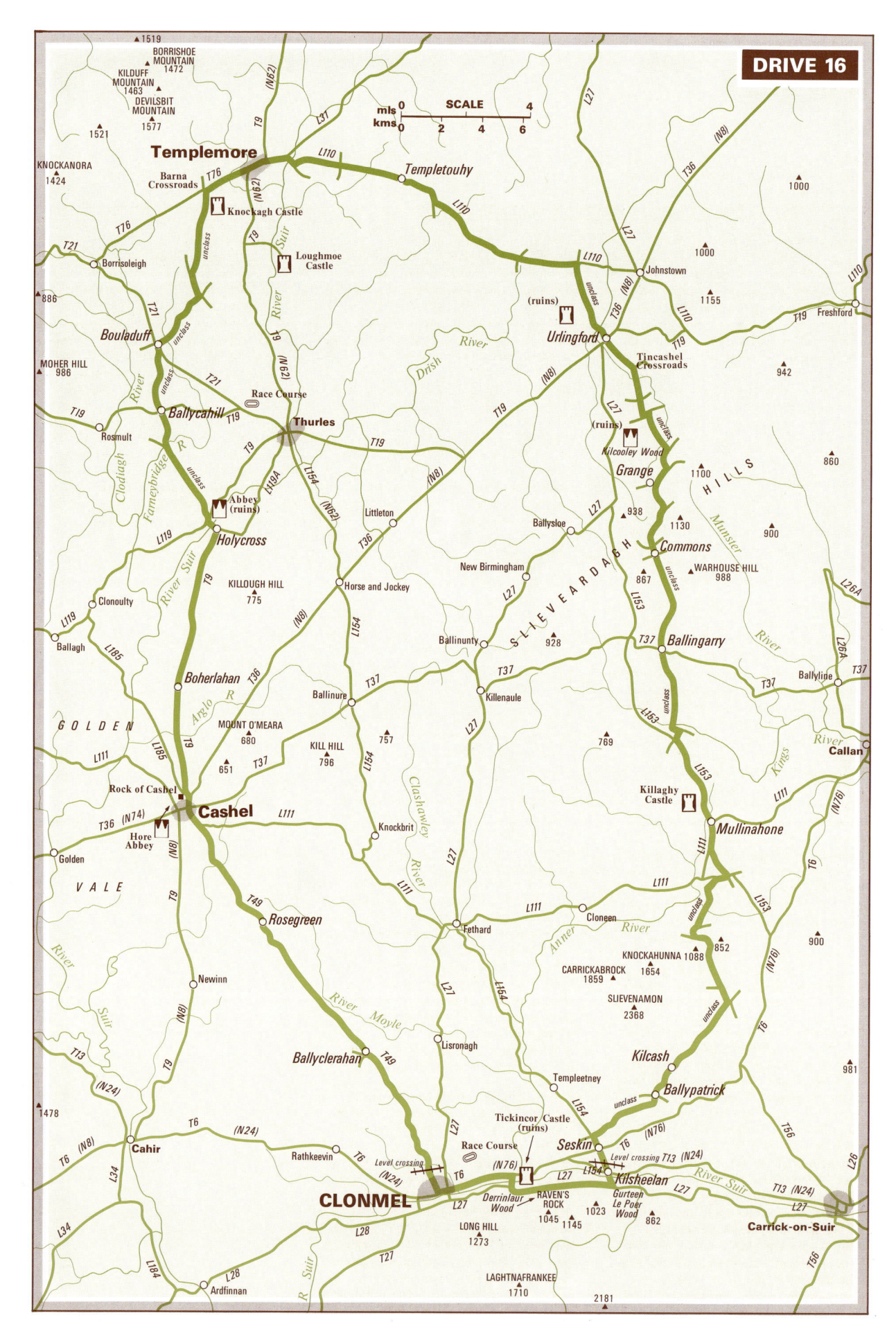

DRIVE 16

THE MUNSTER WILDERNESSES

Into the Slieveardagh Hills
From Clonmel
Drive 16   90 miles

Clonmel is an ancient town which was once walled and has seen periods of fierce military action, including an engagement in which Cromwell lost over 2,000 men. Leave the centre of Clonmel by Gladstone St and follow SP 'Cashel T49'. After $\frac{3}{4}$m pass over a level crossing. Some 2m from Clonmel the road affords views of conical, 2,368ft *Slievenamon* to the right, and attractive countryside dominated by the 3,000ft *Galtee Mountains* to the left. Drive to Ballyclerahan, bear right, then proceed along the E edge of the *Golden Vale* – an area of rich agricultural land in the Suir Valley. Continue through Rosegreen, with views of the Slieveardagh Hills to the right and the *Galtee Mountains* to the left, then in $3\frac{1}{2}$m reach a section of road which offers good views of the Rock of Cashel on the approach to *Cashel* town.

Continue for 1m and enter Cashel, then proceed to the Celtic Cross, turn right, and in a short distance turn left SP 'Dublin' into Ladyswell St. Meet a fork and bear left into The Kiln – passing the Rock of Cashel and cathedral ruins on the left – then bear right SP 'Thurles, Holy Cross', into Thurles Rd T9. In $1\frac{3}{4}$m views to the left extend across the Suir Valley to a range of 1,400ft hills.

Attractive open country stretches to the right. After a further 2m pass through Boherlahan village. Continue for 5m, passing thickly-wooded Killough Hill on the right before reaching *Holycross*. At Holycross turn left SP 'Thurles', and on crossing the River Suir pass the ruins of Holycross Abbey on the right. This abbey is a 12th-c foundation named after a relic of the True Cross. Its buildings show additions from many periods and were partly restored in the early part of this century. The infirmary block lies on the SE side of the complex and is unusually large. Bear right, and in $\frac{1}{4}$m turn left on to an unclassified road SP 'Nenagh'. In $\frac{1}{2}$m cross a railway bridge and proceed through rich farmland, with views of 1,404ft Knockalough and 1,398ft Ring Hill to the left. After $2\frac{1}{4}$m (from the bridge) bear right SP 'Ballycahill, Borrisoleigh', and ascend for a short distance. In $\frac{3}{4}$m reach the road summit, then descend with views of the *Devil's Bit Mountain* ahead. In $\frac{1}{2}$m meet staggered X-roads at Ballycahill and turn right, then turn immediately left SP 'Nenagh'.

In 2m meet a T-junction and turn left on to the T21. In $\frac{1}{4}$m enter Bouladuff, proceed to the school house, and turn right on to an unclassified road SP 'Templemore'. Drive on through well-wooded country, and in $2\frac{1}{2}$m meet staggered X-roads. Turn left SP 'Drom', and follow a narrow winding road to enjoy views of the 1,577ft Devil's Bit Mountain ahead. In 1m bear right and in 2m pass the five-storey, circular keep of Knockagh Castle. After a further $\frac{1}{2}$m meet Barna X-roads and turn right on to the T76 SP 'Templemore', then in $1\frac{1}{2}$m enter *Templemore*. Keep forward along the main street and proceed to the E end of the town, then bear right on to the L110 SP 'Templetouhy'. In $\frac{3}{4}$m turn right SP 'Templetouhy, Kilkenny', cross a railway bridge, then turn left and proceed through farming land. In 2m meet Strogue X-roads and keep forward. Continue, with views over the surrounding countryside, and drive into Templetouhy. Turn left along the village street, proceed to the end, then bear right SP 'Johnstown, Urlingford'. Continue and enter an area of forestry plantation and peat bog. Peat-extraction operations in this area are often conducted with the aid of machinery. Views ahead take in the 1,000ft Slieveardagh Hills. Meet X-roads after 4m (from Templetouhy) and keep forward, then in 2m reach another set of X-roads and turn right on to an unclassified road SP 'Urlingford'. Follow an undulating, winding road through fertile agricultural land, and in $2\frac{1}{4}$m pass ruined Urlingford Castle (right).

Continue into *Urlingford*, then drive forward across a main road and descend gradually through wooded country, with views of the Slieveardagh Hills ahead. In $1\frac{1}{2}$m meet Tincashel X-roads and keep forward. Continue for 1m to another set of X-roads and keep straight on, then in $\frac{1}{2}$m meet a T-junction and turn left. In $\frac{1}{4}$m turn right, passing the wooded grounds of ruined *Kilcooley Abbey*. This Cistercian foundation was first created *c*1200 by King Donagh O'Brien as a daughter house of the better-known abbey at *Jerpoint*. Its church includes 15th-c additions. In $1\frac{1}{4}$m meet a T-junction and turn right, then in $\frac{1}{4}$m meet another T-junction and turn right again SP 'Grange, Commons, Ballingarry'. Continue, with good views towards Templetouhy on the right and dense woodland to the left. In $\frac{3}{4}$m reach Grange and bear left, then ascend through thick woodland into the Slieveardagh Hills via a narrow, winding road. As the drive clears the woodland it affords good views both to the right and behind. Climb to 1,000ft, meet a T-junction and turn right, then gradually descend along a winding road into a small valley. Views ahead embrace distant Slievenamon Hill. Meet X-roads and drive forward into the village of Commons, then keep forward SP 'Ballingarry, Mullinahone'. Climb gradually with hilly country on the left and good views to the right. Proceed to the exposed village of *Ballingarry*, which is situated at an altitude of 700ft, and on meeting X-roads continue forward SP 'Mullinahone' to begin a long descent. In $2\frac{3}{4}$m cross the King's River, and in $\frac{1}{4}$m turn right. In $\frac{1}{4}$m meet X-roads and turn left on to the L153.

Pass over fertile farming country, and in $2\frac{1}{2}$m pass Killaghy Castle and Wood on the right. In $\frac{1}{4}$m enter Mullinahone. Bear left and immediately right on to the L111 SP 'Clonmel, Cloneen, Fethard', and in 1m bear left on to the L153 SP 'Clonmel', with Slievenamon rising to the right. After a further 1m keep forward on to an unclassified road SP 'Fethard, Cloneen', then bear right. In $\frac{1}{2}$m meet a fork and bear left, then in 2m bear right. After another $\frac{1}{2}$m meet a T-junction and turn right, then immediately turn sharp left. Climb steeply through dense woodland on the lower slopes of Slievenamon, with good views to the left afforded by the first part of the ascent. In 1m meet X-roads and drive forward, then descend to cross a valley bottom. In $1\frac{1}{2}$m meet X-roads on an ascent and turn right. After a short distance the road affords panoramic views over part of the Suir Valley, with *Carrick-on-Suir* to the left, the *Comeragh Mountains* dominated by 2,478ft Knockanaffrin and 2,597ft Fauscoum ahead, and Clonmel to the right. Continue, and follow a steep descent from the forest-covered escarpment to pass through the hamlet of *Kilcash*, with Kilcash Wood on the right. The blind poet Raftery immortalized this famous wood in Irish folk lore. Continue forward over Ballypatrick X-roads, and in $1\frac{1}{2}$m pass Ballyglasheen Wood on the right. After a further 1m meet X-roads and turn left on to the L154 SP 'Kilsheelan, Clonmel'. In $\frac{1}{2}$m reach Seskin and cross a main road. Views ahead take in the wooded slopes of the Comeragh Mountains. After another $\frac{1}{2}$m drive over a level crossing and proceed to *Kilsheelan*. Cross the main road SP 'Rathgormuck', then cross the River Suir.

In $\frac{1}{2}$m turn sharp right on to the L27 SP 'Clonmel', then follow the river valley with dense woodland on the left and views over the valley to the right; Slievenamon rises in the background. In 1m pass the grounds of Gurteen le Poer House – home of the 19th-c statesman Richard Lalor Shiel – adjacent to a wood of the same name on the left. After another 2m pass Derrinlaur Castle on the right, with Derrinlaur Wood high up on the left. In $\frac{3}{4}$m the route affords views of ruined Tickincor Castle to the right of the road. At this point keep forward on to an unclassified road to cross the river by a narrow bridge.

In $\frac{1}{4}$m meet a T-junction and turn left on to the T6(N76). Follow this road into Clonmel, and complete the drive by keeping forward for the town centre.

Placenames in *italic* type are worth stopping at; each is listed and described in the main gazetteer section.

THE MUNSTER WILDERNESSES

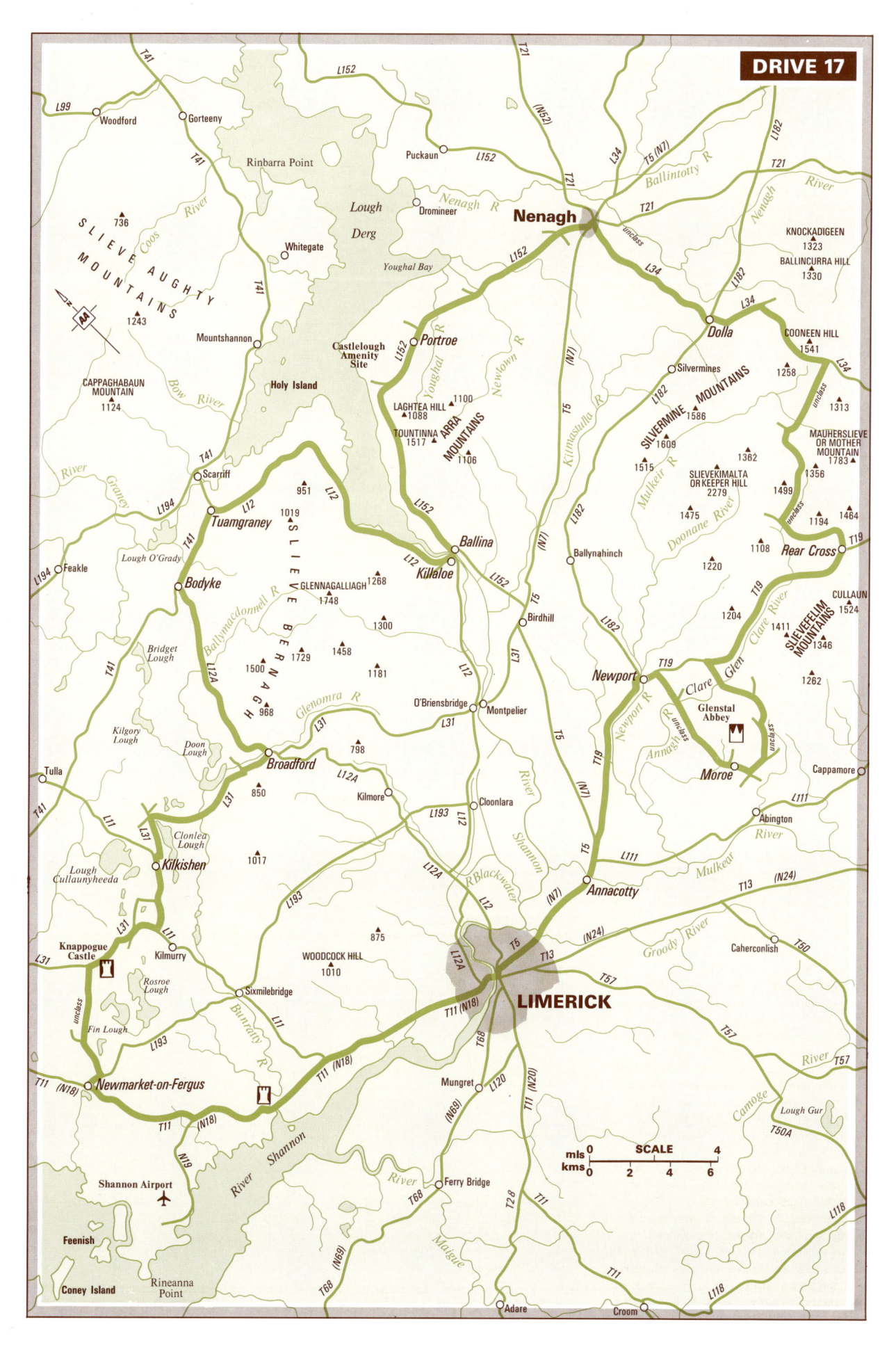

DRIVE 17

THE MUNSTER WILDERNESSES

Mountains and Castles

From Limerick

Drive 17   108 miles

Follow the T5(N7) 'Dublin' road out of *Limerick*, and in 4½m cross the Mulkear River at Annacotty Bridge. In ¾m turn right on to the T19 SP 'Thurles, Newport', and after a further ½m drive over a level crossing. Continue along this pleasant, narrow road through well-wooded countryside, with views of the Silvermine Mountains ahead. In 5m pass through Newport, and in ½m turn right on to an unclassified road SP 'Clare Glen'. In 1½m pass the entrance to the glen – an amenity area which offers interesting forest walks, rapids, etc – on the left. In 2½m pass the attractive grounds of *Glenstal Priory* on the left, then enter Moroe. Go forward through the village, and at the monument turn left SP 'Cappamore' to skirt the grounds of the priory. This recent foundation is based on 19th-c Glenstal Mansion, which was originally built for the Barrington family, and is now known as the St Columbia Abbey. The monks run a secondary school for boys here, and operate a small craft industry for the production of hand-wrought, artistic metalwork. In ½m branch left, with views of the Slievefelim Mountains ahead, then in 1½m enter an area of dense woodland and bear right. In ¾m branch left and follow a gradual descent which affords good views into the Clare Valley. In 1m meet a T-junction and turn right on to the T19. Follow the Clare River, with a rocky hill rising to 1,200ft on the left and the Slievefelim Mountains standing at over 1,400ft on the right. In 6m reach *Rear Cross*, pass the local church, then turn left on to an unclassified and unsignposted road and ascend. Ahead on the T19 road is a fascinating collection of prehistoric remains. Features of the site include a bronze-age pagan burial ground dating from c1500 BC and neolithic remains of c2000 BC. Continue to an 800ft road summit for pleasant mountain views. Ahead is 2,279ft Slievekimalta (or Keeper Hill), and to the right is 1,785ft Mauherslive – also known as Mother Mountain. In 2½m turn sharp right to ascend a narrow road between the two mountains. Beyond the mountains the countryside to the left of the road is covered with dense forest. Continue at an altitude of over 900ft for several miles, with 1,541ft Cooneen Hill rising ahead. Meet a T-junction below the hill and turn left on to the L34, then continue along the 'Nenagh' road through a low pass which affords fine views. In 5m reach Dolla and drive to a public house called the Eagles Nest, then turn left and right. In 4¼m cross a railway bridge, and after a further ¼m keep left to enter Nenagh. Meet traffic signals in the town centre and turn left on to the T5 SP 'Limerick'. In ¼m turn right on to the L152 SP 'Killaloe, Lake Drive'. Continue to the next X-roads and turn left, then in 4m reach Newtown and go forward SP 'Lake Drive' to reach Portroe. The Arra Mountains rise to the left of the road and culminate in 1,517ft Tountinna. Continue along the L152, and in 1¼m pass a right turn to the Castlelough Amenity Site on the shores of *Lough Derg*. This site includes a picnic site and playground among its facilities. Shortly meet the shores of the lough. Fine views from this section of the drive extend over the lake and its picturesque islands to Slieve Bernagh, which rises from the opposite shore. The highest point of Slieve Bernagh is 1,746ft Glennagalliagh. Continue along the shore to the end of the lough and enter Ballina. Turn right and cross the River Shannon via a 13-arch bridge to enter *Killaloe*, then turn right again on to the L12 SP 'Scarriff, Lake Drive'. Follow the W shore of Lough Derg beneath the Slieve Bernagh range. After 5m follow the drive away from Lough Derg, climbing to a 400ft road summit before descending – with further views of the lake – to enter *Tuamgraney*. An interesting 10th- or 11th-c church and the ruins of an O Grady castle can be seen here. At Tuamgraney turn left SP 'Ennis', then left again on to the T41. In 2¾m reach *Bodyke*, turn left on to the L12A SP 'Broadford, Limerick', and follow a level road through agricultural land. This section of the drive affords occasional views of Slieve Bernagh to the left. After 6¼m enter *Broadford*, which is attractively situated at the mouth of the Glenomra River valley. Turn sharp right on to the L31 SP 'Galway', and in 1m turn left SP 'Shannon Airport'. In ¼m turn right and continue with SP 'Kilkishen'. Shortly pass Doon Lough on the right, and after 3m (beyond the lough) meet X-roads and turn left. Clonlea Lough is glimpsed to the left at this point. After 1½m meet a T-junction and turn left on to the L11 SP 'Limerick' to enter *Kilkisheen*. In 2¼m turn right on to the L31 SP 'Quin, Ennis', and in 1¼m bear right SP 'Knappogue Castle'. In 1¼m pass *Knappogue Castle* on the left, then in ¼m turn left on to a narrow, unclassified road. This restored castle is used for medieval-style banquets and features curious pillars inscribed with local distances in both English and the rarely-used Irish miles. In 1¾m drive over X-roads, and after a further ½m bear left. In 1¼m meet a T-junction and turn right to enter *Newmarket-on-Fergus*. Turn left on to the T11(N18) 'Limerick' road follow this broad, level highway through pleasant farmland. After 6¼m (from Newmarket-on-Fergus) pass *Bunratty* Castle and Folk Village on the left. The castle dates from the 13thc, but most of the impressive structure seen here today is of 15th-c origin. It has been well restored and includes several notable features. Follow the final section of the drive, with pleasant views of Cratloe Wood and 1,010ft Woodcock Hill to the left, for the return to Limerick.

Leinster of the High Kings

The forces that crumpled Munster into a time-frozen explosion of rock also touched Leinster, but with subtler fingers that nudged the landscape into gentle waves and jagged miniatures of the west-coast mountains. East Leinster counterbalances its violent compatriot with the Wicklow Mountains, but elsewhere the province rolls from valley to vale in merging shades of green pasture, brown marsh grasses, and the bright splashes of purple loosestrife. Ancient lakes, turned to bogland by their own fertility, lap glacial ridges that once provided dry sites on which prehistoric and early-Christian men could build their precarious communities. In other areas the province gathers itself into lazy folds which afford surprisingly wide views, or drops to succeeding miles of deserted strand punctuated by the occasional puffin-populated headland.

This is a land where legend is entangled with history, an amalgam of two ancient kingdoms whose people counted gods amongst their ancestors and wove heroic epics as magical as any from Arthur's Britain. It is also a backwater where the flotsam of time has gathered in a haphazard collection of monuments, religious buildings, veteran castles, and demesnes carved from the wilderness by invaders long since absorbed by the enchanted Irish landscape.

Northern Leinster, the lowest and greenest part of the province, was once the powerful kingdom of Meath. It was here that the High Kings sat enthroned in power over provincial monarchs, where a Leinster king received judgement which was to result in invasion from Norman Britain, and where the early monks came to found some of the greatest of their religious houses. Counties Longford and Westmeath extend east from the River Shannon and Lough Ree to cover north-west Leinster in a confusion of bogland and meadow through which the Royal Canal cuts a determined path to Longford town. Athlone occupies a glacial ridge at the provincial border and has been an important military centre for centuries. Mullingar, county town of Westmeath, stands in a beautiful arc of loughs at the centre of Lakeland. Louth – the smallest Irish county – extends flat landscapes dotted with reminders of a splendid monastic past over the province's north-eastern corner. Its low northern hills face Ulster's peaks across Carlingford Lough, and its coast is a gentle progression of golden strands.

County Meath, bearer of a name which echoes down centuries of Irish history, is an archaeological storehouse of treasures which testify to its illustrious past. Close to the River Blackwater in the north is Ceanannas Mor or Kells, where the fabulous *Book of Kells* was written in the 8thc, and where the High Kings ruled from their Tara Palace centuries before the flowering of Irish Christianity. South east of this the vast motte of An Uaimh asserts the waned power of The Pale, a defensive ring erected to discourage Ulster tribes who objected to the Anglo-Norman occupation of their neighbours' lands. From here the River Boyne, swelled by the waters of the Blackwater, flows east towards Drogheda and the coast through dense woodlands, splendid demesnes, the royal Tara burial grounds, and over gravels scattered with the artefacts of prehistoric man. Meath's tiny, uninspiring stretch of coast drops south from the Boyne estuary to meet the northern border of Dublin – a busy county of flat coastal plains that blanket some of the oldest rock formations in Ireland before rising gradually south to meet the Wicklow Mountain foothills. Midway along the Dublin coast is Dublin city, a strange mixture of Georgian restraint and 20th-c materialism which crowds the River Liffey and extends long pincers of development to capture a sizeable bight of the Irish Sea. In keeping with the ancient eminence of the area in which part of its county is situated, Dublin is the capital of the Irish Republic, the most important commercial centre in the country, and a major seaport on the ocean highways of the world.

Mid-Leinster combines Offaly, Laois, Wicklow, and Kildare in a comfortable – if remarkable – mixture of scenic contrasts. Wet lowlands common to Longford and Westmeath continue into Co Offaly, while the thousands of quivering acres which form the vast Bog of Allen spread a peaty blanket across Westmeath, Offaly, and Kildare boundaries north of Edenderry town. Across the River Shannon to the west is Connacht, and the two provinces are linked by a one-time ford which marks the site of Clonmacnoise – an extensive collection of monastic remains that survive from the most important early-Christian centre in Ireland. Near Banagher the provincial boundary drops south-east to Birr and turns east to the border of Co Laois, taking a short cut over a large piece of Offaly and skirting the gentle Slieve Bloom Mountains. East of Tullamore, county town of Offaly, the countryside rises to merge with an enormous, even area known as the Central Plain. This extends over the whole of Kildare to the massive east-coast barrier presented by mountainous Wicklow.

Kildare is a county of wide horizons, where its magnificent racehorses have room to build the muscle and stamina necessary to maintain their reputation as world champions. Sometimes these superb animals race at The Curragh near Kildare town, a course set amid gallops which cross the largest consecutive area of arable land in the country. Beyond Naas, one-time seat of the Leinster kings, the great Central Plain crashes headlong into the mountains which cover Co Wicklow with startling ranks of old granite and coruscating white-quartzite peaks. Foothills on the inland side of the Wicklows guard Dublin's water in Poulaphouca Reservoir, then soar to the high peaks before dropping in careful stages to the flat, golden sands of the east coast. Deep glens which penetrate far into the seaward side of the range enclose some of the most attractive mountain scenery in Ireland; Glendalough, with its twin lakes and important ecclesiastical remains, is particularly famous.

Between the western Leinster border and Co Wicklow is Co Laois, a long, flat vale which runs between the isolated Slieve Bloom Mountains and low groups of hills which rise from Co Kilkenny in the south. Much of the lowland is webbed by rivers and scattered with little patches of bogland, while long esker ridges of glacial gravel produce the undulations familiar in other parts of the country. Historic Mountmellick, which grew to prominence as a textile-manufacturing community, lies in a fertile semi-circle formed by the infant River Barrow east of the Slieve Bloom range.

South Leinster tries to emulate the rugged dominance of Wicklow with groups of hills and a little range of high peaks known as the Blackstairs Mountains, but its main features are four great rivers that carve fertile valleys through counties Kilkenny, Carlow, and Wexford on their eccentric journeys to the sea. Kilkenny's southern border, shared with the provincial boundary, is marked by the River Suir's meandering course from Munster to its confluence with the Barrow at the head of Waterford Harbour. The Barrow runs due south along the east border of Co Kilkenny and is swelled by the Nore – which forms a vertical division through the county – near New Ross in Co Wexford. The last great river in this area is the Slaney, which flows across Wexford from the Blackstairs Mountains and empties into the east-coast Wexford Harbour.

West of the Nore the horizon is corrugated by the Slieveardagh and Booley Hills, and a spine of hills running between the Nore and Barrow terminates in 1,694ft Brandon Hill to the south. The east bank of the Barrow is in Carlow, a tiny county bordered by the Blackstairs range in the south east and guarded by foothills of the Wicklow Mountains in the north east. Flat Wexford eases towards the south and east coasts in a gradual descent from high outriders of the Blackstairs and Wicklow ranges, fringing the sea with a smooth, sandy shoreline interrupted only by Wexford Harbour and the odd headland. After Carnsore Point the coast makes a sudden, right-angled change of direction from due south to east, at the same time undergoing a change of personality from smooth progression to a hiccoughing series of small bays, tiny islands, and almost land-locked lagoons.

Leinster's easy-going landscape of rolling plains and mountains that build gently from the horizon forms an antithesis to the sudden visual shocks of jagged Munster. Its beauty relies on the soft graduation of colour across wetlands rusty with wind-dried seed-heads, the green folds of pastures curving down into river valleys, and the peaceful isolation of long, deserted strands between widely-spaced headlands.

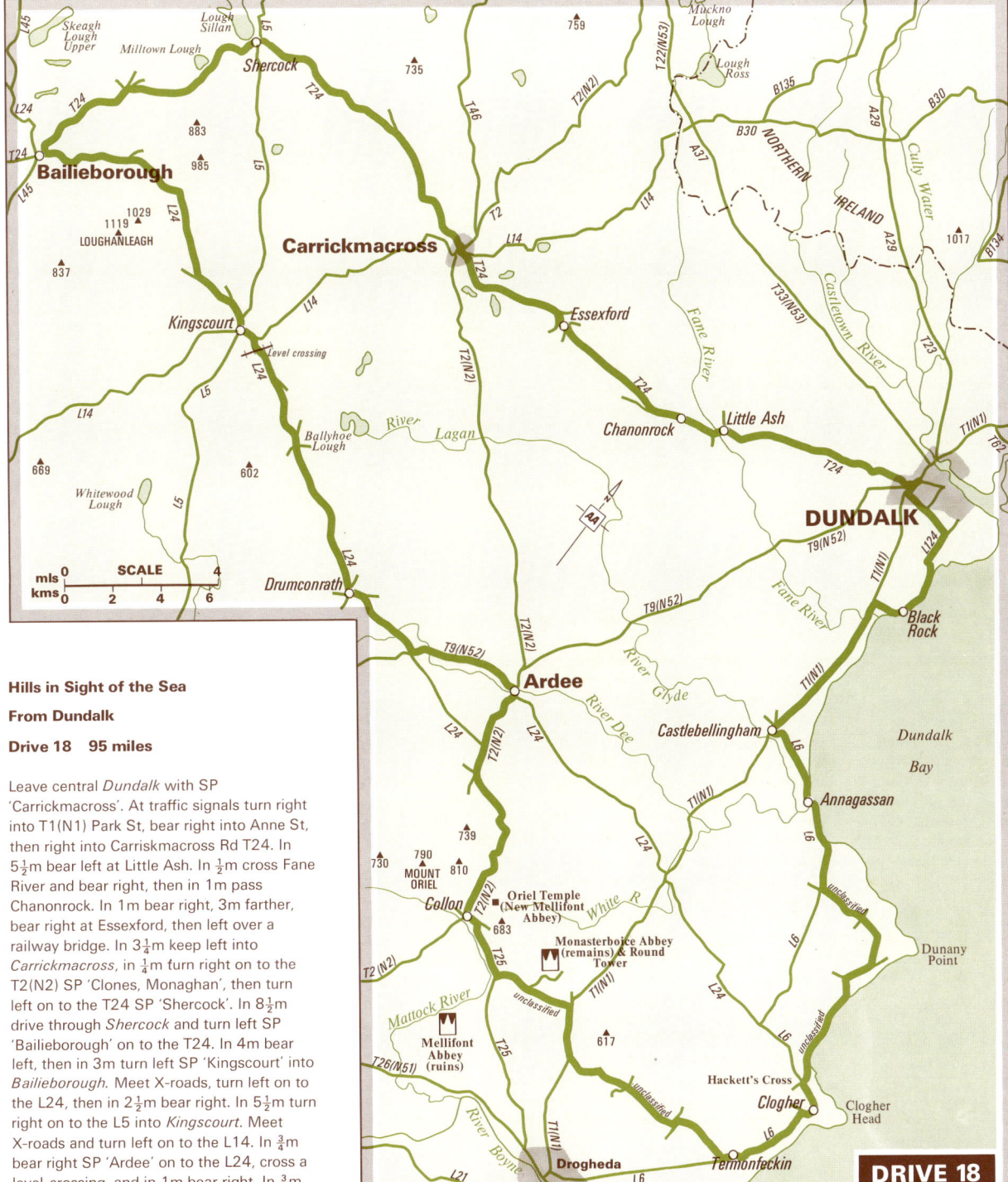

LEINSTER OF THE HIGH KINGS

Hills in Sight of the Sea

From Dundalk

Drive 18   95 miles

Leave central *Dundalk* with SP 'Carrickmacross'. At traffic signals turn right into T1(N1) Park St, bear right into Anne St, then right into Carriskmacross Rd T24. In 5½m bear left at Little Ash. In ½m cross Fane River and bear right, then in 1m pass Chanonrock. In 1m bear right, 3m farther, bear right at Essexford, then left over a railway bridge. In 3¼m keep left into *Carrickmacross*, in ¼m turn right on to the T2(N2) SP 'Clones, Monaghan', then turn left on to the T24 SP 'Shercock'. In 8½m drive through *Shercock* and turn left SP 'Bailieborough' on to the T24. In 4m bear left, then in 3m turn left SP 'Kingscourt' into *Bailieborough*. Meet X-roads, turn left on to the L24, then in 2½m bear right. In 5½m turn right on to the L5 into *Kingscourt*. Meet X-roads and turn left on to the L14. In ¾m bear right SP 'Ardee' on to the L24, cross a level-crossing, and in 1m bear right. In ¾m meet X-roads. Go forward SP 'Drumconrath'; in 4m enter *Drumconrath*, meet X-roads, and turn left. In ½m turn right SP 'Ardee'. After 2¼m meet X-roads, turn left to the T9(N52), and in 2½m enter *Ardee*. Turn right on to the T2(N2) SP 'Drogheda', cross the River Dee, and after 6¼m enter *Collon*. Meet X-roads and turn left on to the T25 SP 'Drogheda'. In ¼m bear right. In 1½m meet a T-junction and turn left on to an unclassified road SP 'Monasterboice'.

In 1m keep forward, then in 1m meet a T-junction and turn right to the T1(N1) SP 'Drogheda'. In 1¼m turn left and immediately left on to an unclassified road SP 'Ballymackenny'. In 2m meet X-roads and go forward SP 'Termonfeckin', then in 1½m turn left on to the L61 and enter *Termonfeckin*. Meet X-roads, turn right on to the L6 SP 'Clogerhead', then in 2¾m left into Clogher.

Turn left SP 'Dunleer'. In ¾m turn right on to an unclassified road SP 'Dunany' at Hackett's Cross. In 2¾m meet a T-junction and turn right. In 1m turn left SP 'Annagassan'. In 2¾m meet X-roads and turn right to the L6 SP 'Annagassan'. In 1½m bear left. After 1m enter *Annagassan*, turn left at the end, then immediately right SP 'Castlebellingham'. In 2m turn left and in ½m enter *Castlebellingham*. Turn right on to the T1(N1), and in 4½m right on to the L124 SP 'Blackrock'. Pass Blackrock, then in 2½m turn left SP 'Dundalk'. In ¾m go forward, then in 1¾m enter Dundalk. Meet a T-junction, turn right on to the T1(N1), and return to the town centre.

Placenames in *italic* type are worth stopping at; each is listed and described in the main gazetteer section.

103

LEINSTER OF THE HIGH KINGS

Sea Views and the Wicklows
From Arklow
Drive 19   84 miles

Leave *Arklow's* main street with SP 'Dublin L29(N11)' and cross the Avoca River. In ½m branch right on to an unclassified road SP 'Brittas Bay', and continue with the sea visible to the right. Ballymoyle Hill rises to 923ft on the left, and low *Mizen Head* can be seen ahead. After 6m reach the shores of *Brittas Bay*, and 5m farther turn right SP 'Coast Road' to pass Wicklow Head and lighthouse on the right after 3m. At this point the road becomes the L29A and affords views to the coast and mountains of N Wicklow. Shortly descend into *Wicklow*.

Go forward through the town on the L29A, and on reaching the hotel bear right on to the T7 SP 'Dublin, Rathnew'. In 2m enter *Rathnew* and bear right on to the T7(N11) SP 'Dublin'. After another 1½m approach *Ashford* and pass the *Mount Usher* Gardens and Carriage Museum on the right. Shortly cross the Vartry River into *Ashford*. Turn left on to the L161 SP 'Devil's Glen, Roundwood', and in just over ¼m turn left on to an unclassified road. In ½m descend and bear left, then recross the Vartry River. In ¾m pass the entrance to Glanmore Castle on the right, and in a further ¼m bear right SP 'Annamoe' up an ascent. Carrick Mountain rises to 1,256ft on the left. Shortly pass the entrance to the Devil's Glen Woods, gorge, and waterfall on the right. Continue the steep ascent through dense woodland to a summit of 700ft and continue for several miles with the Vartry River and Devil's Glen on the right. Ahead are views of the hills around *Annamoe*. Descend, with fine views down the Avonmore Valley to *Laragh* ahead, and turn left on to the T61 into Annamoe.

Cross the Avonmore River and follow a broad main road which affords tree-framed views of the Wicklow Mountains. After 2m pass the entrance to Trooperstown Wood, which offers forest walks, a carpark, and a picnic site, on the left. Proceed to Laragh, with a magnificent view into the Vale of Glendalough ahead, and bear left across the Glenmacnass River – then left again with the T61 SP 'Rathdrum, Wexford'. In ½m pass the *Glendalough* Craft Centre and Museum on the right. Bear right SP 'Glenmalure, Rathdrum' and cross a river bridge, then in ½m branch right uphill on to an unclassified road SP 'Aghavannagh'. Climb along an old military road with views along the Vale of Clara (Owenmore Valley) ahead, 1,654ft *Great Sugarloaf* distantly left, and 1,419ft Trooperstown Hill across the valley. Reach a 1,245ft summit, with 1,559ft Kirikee on the left and 1,538ft Cullentragh right, then descend towards the Avonbeg River with 2,179ft Mullacor to the right. Reach the valley bottom, meet X-roads, and go forward SP 'Aghavannagh, Rathdrum'. Cross Drumgoff Bridge; right is 3,039ft *Lugnaquilla*, the highest mountain in the Wicklows. Climb through forestry to a 1,480ft summit, with 2,181ft Croaghanmoira on the left and Slieve Maan on the right. Descend to *Aghavannagh* X-roads, turn left SP 'Aughrim', and in ½m bear left. Left is 1,658ft Carrickashane. Ascend through heavy woodland on the slopes of Croaghanmoira to a 1,212ft summit. In 2m descend and meet X-roads. Go forward SP 'Ballinaclash' and continue the descent into the Avonbeg Valley. After 3m keep forward, and in ¼m reach Ballinaclash. Turn left on to the L32 and cross a river bridge, then turn left again SP 'Rathdrum'. In 1m turn right on to an unclassified road, and in ¼m cross a main road SP 'Avondale House'. After a further ¼m bear right; the road on the left leads to *Avondale* House. Follow a ridge between the Avonmore and Avonbeg Rivers, then make a steep descent through woodland with the mansion of Castle Howard visible across the river on the left. Meet a T-junction, turn left on to the T7, and shortly cross the Avonbeg River at the Meeting of the Waters.

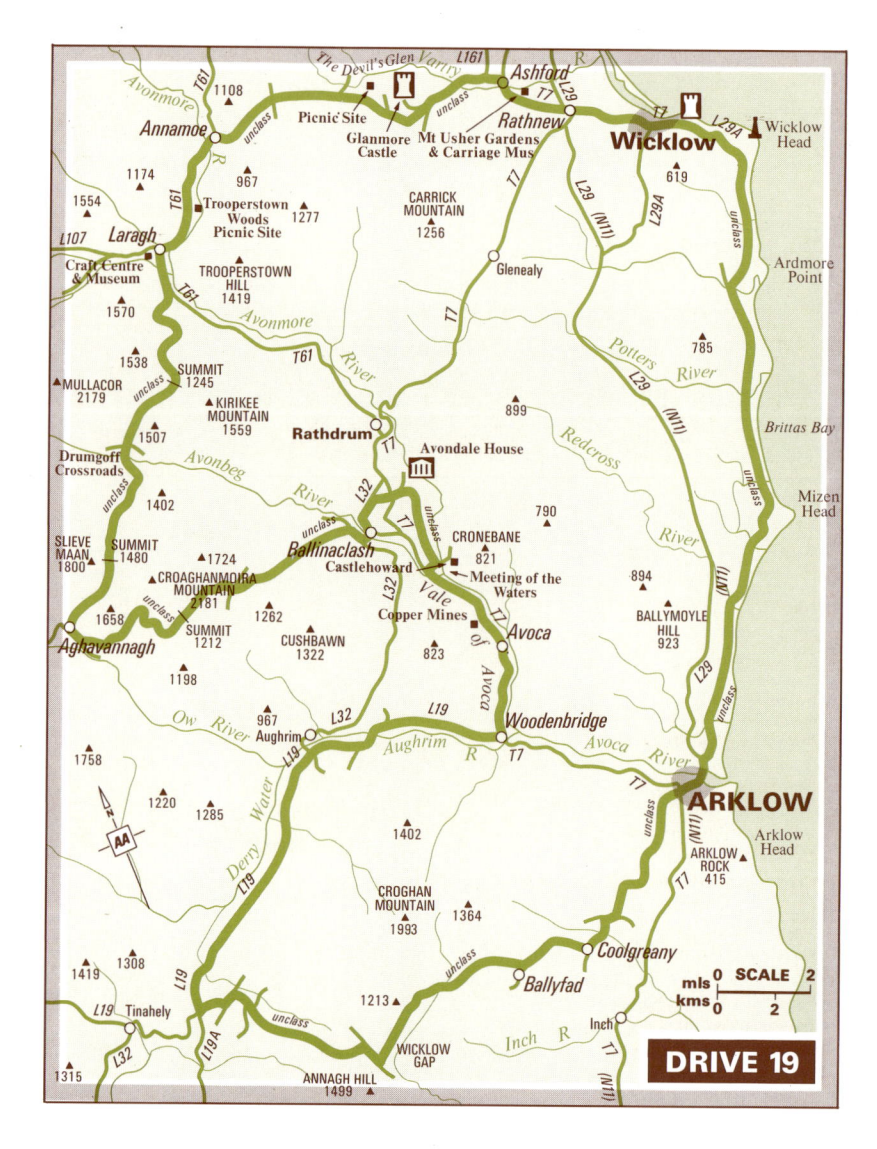

Enter the Vale of Avoca and pass a former copper-mining area on the right after 1½m. In another ¾m reach the edge of *Avoca* village and turn right SP 'Woodenbridge'. Continue, and in 2m reach *Woodenbridge*. At the hotel, turn right on to the L19 SP 'Aughrim', and follow the Aughrim River. In 2¼m bear left, and after another 1m turn left then right across the Aughrim River. In ¼m bear right again and in 1¼m pass the edge of *Aughrim* town. Continue forward with the L19 to follow the Derry Water, with 1,993ft Croghan on the left. In 6½m (from Aughrim) meet X-roads and turn left on to an unclassified road SP 'Gorey'. Ascend, and in 3½m bear left SP 'Gorey'. Enter the low *Wicklow Gap* with 1,499ft Annagh Hill on the right, then descend and meet X-roads. Turn left, ascend to over 800ft, then descend. Climb again to 800ft with coastal views, then descend and continue for 1¼m to Ballyfad Post Office. Meet a T-junction here and turn left SP 'Coolgreany'.

Continue the descent and in 1½m enter Coolgreany. Meet a T-junction, turn left SP 'Arklow', and in 1m turn right. In ¼m bear left along a quiet road, with views of Ballymoyle and other hills beyond Arklow. After 3¼m meet a roundabout and bear left to re-enter Arklow.

LEINSTER OF THE HIGH KINGS

DRIVE 20

Castles of the Coast

From Wexford

Drive 20 90 miles

Follow the T8(N25) SP 'Rosslare' from *Wexford* Quay. In 5½m cross a railway bridge, in ½m at Killinick turn left, and in 1m branch left on to an unclassified road SP 'Rosslare Strand'. In 1¾m branch left, then in ¼m turn right for the coast. Turn right and follow the shore for ½m, with views of *Rosslare Harbour* ahead, before turning inland. In ½m meet a T-junction and turn left SP 'Rosslare Harbour' to continue along a winding, narrow road, and enter *Tagoat*. On reaching this village turn left on to the T8(N25) SP 'Rosslare Harbour'. Take the next turning right on to an unclassified road SP 'Lady's Island'. In 2m turn right SP 'Wexford', with Lady's Island Lake ahead.

At the head of this lake is *Lady's Island*, site of an ancient Augustinian priory which was dedicated to Our Lady and formed a place of pilgrimage for centuries. Enter Broadway, take the first turning left, and in 1¾m pass through *Tacumshane*. In ½m meet X-roads and keep forward. After another 1m pass a ruined 13th-c castle before catching sight of Tacumshane Lake on the left. After a further 1m meet a T-junction and turn left, then shortly keep forward. In 1¼m pass castle ruins, and in ½m enter *Tomhaggard*. Turn right, then in ½m meet X-roads and turn left SP 'Bridgetown'. In ½m meet a T-junction and turn left on to the L29 SP 'Kilmore Quay'. After 2¼m pass through *Kilmore* and continue for 3m to reach *Kilmore Quay*. Bear right SP 'Wellington Bridge' on to an unclassified road which turns inland, and in ¾m pass ruined Ballyteige Castle on the right. This 15th- to 16th-c edifice has a well-preserved bawn and high tower. In 1¾m turn left SP 'Duncormick', then in 1¾m turn left again. After 2m turn left on to the L128A for *Duncormick*. Drive through the latter and turn right on to an unclassified road SP 'Wellington Bridge', and in 1¼m bear left SP 'Wellington Bridge'. In ¾m pass ruined *Coolhull Castle* on the left. Coolhull is an unusual little stronghold which dates from the late 16thc. In 1m turn right, and after a further 1¼m meet a T-junction. Turn right then shortly turn left. In 1m meet a T-junction and turn right on to the L128A for Wellington Bridge, then go forward on to the L159 SP 'Duncannon, Fethard'. Cross the Corock River and keep left SP 'Fethard', then in 3¾m meet X-roads and take an unclassified left turn SP 'Saltmills, Fethard'. After 1m pass ruined *Tintern* Abbey (NM) on the right, and shortly enjoy views of *Bannow* Bay ahead. After a further 1m cross an inlet of Bannow Bay to reach Saltmills. Drive through the village and in 2m turn left on to the L159A SP 'Fethard'. In 1¼m enter *Fethard*. Continue to the village centre and turn right on to an unclassified road SP 'Hook Head'. In 2m meet X-roads and turn right SP 'Duncannon', then in 1m reach Templetown T-junction and turn right. After 1¼m the drive affords views of Booley Bay on the left. Continue for ¾m and turn left SP 'Duncannon', then in ¾m turn left to descend towards the *Duncannon* sands.

Meet a T-junction and turn left, then in ½m turn right SP 'Arthurstown'. Skirt Duncannon, then in 1½m meet a T-junction and turn left on to the L159 SP 'Arthurstown'. Continue for ¾m to Arthurstown and go forward on to an unclassified road SP 'Ballyhack', with the harbour on the left. Follow the shore to *Ballyhack*, drive to the harbour and keep right, then ascend sharply past a ruined castle. At the top of the ascent bear right and descend. In ¾m meet X-roads and turn left on to the L159. In 1½m reach X-roads and go forward SP 'New Ross', and in ¾m pass *Dunbrody's* ruined abbey on the left and castle on the right. The abbey is considered the finest medieval ruin in Wexford. In ¼m cross a bridge and bear left, then in ½m turn right SP 'New Ross'. In ½m turn left SP 'New Ross, JF Kennedy Park', then after 2m meet X-roads and turn right on to an unclassified road SP 'JF Kennedy Park'. Ascend to the lower slopes of 888ft Slievecoiltia, and in 1m pass the entrance to the JF Kennedy Memorial Park. Continue along the Wexford road and descend. In 1½m meet X-roads and go forward SP 'Ballynabola', then in ½m bear right. After another 1m bear left SP 'Wexford', and in a further 2¾m meet a T-junction. Turn right on to the T12 SP 'Rosslare', then take the next turning right on to the L160 SP 'Foulksmill'.

After a further 5¼m descend into Foulksmill, cross the Corock River with the mill on the left, and bear right. Drive another 1m and bear right SP 'Wexford', with views ahead of 779ft Forth Mountain; later the Blackstairs Mountains are distantly visible (left). After 3½m enter *Taghmon* and turn right SP 'Wexford'. Pass a ruined castle on the right, drive to the end of the town and keep left, then continue with Forth Mountain and 729ft Shelmaliere Commons on the right. In 3¾m turn right on to the T12. In ½m keep forward with the L160, and after 2½m pass an unclassified left turn leading to the Slaney Gorge Promontory Fort (*Ferrycarrig* Castle). Continue, with views over the River Slaney valley, and pass Wexford racecourse on the right before descending into the town.

105

LEINSTER OF THE HIGH KINGS

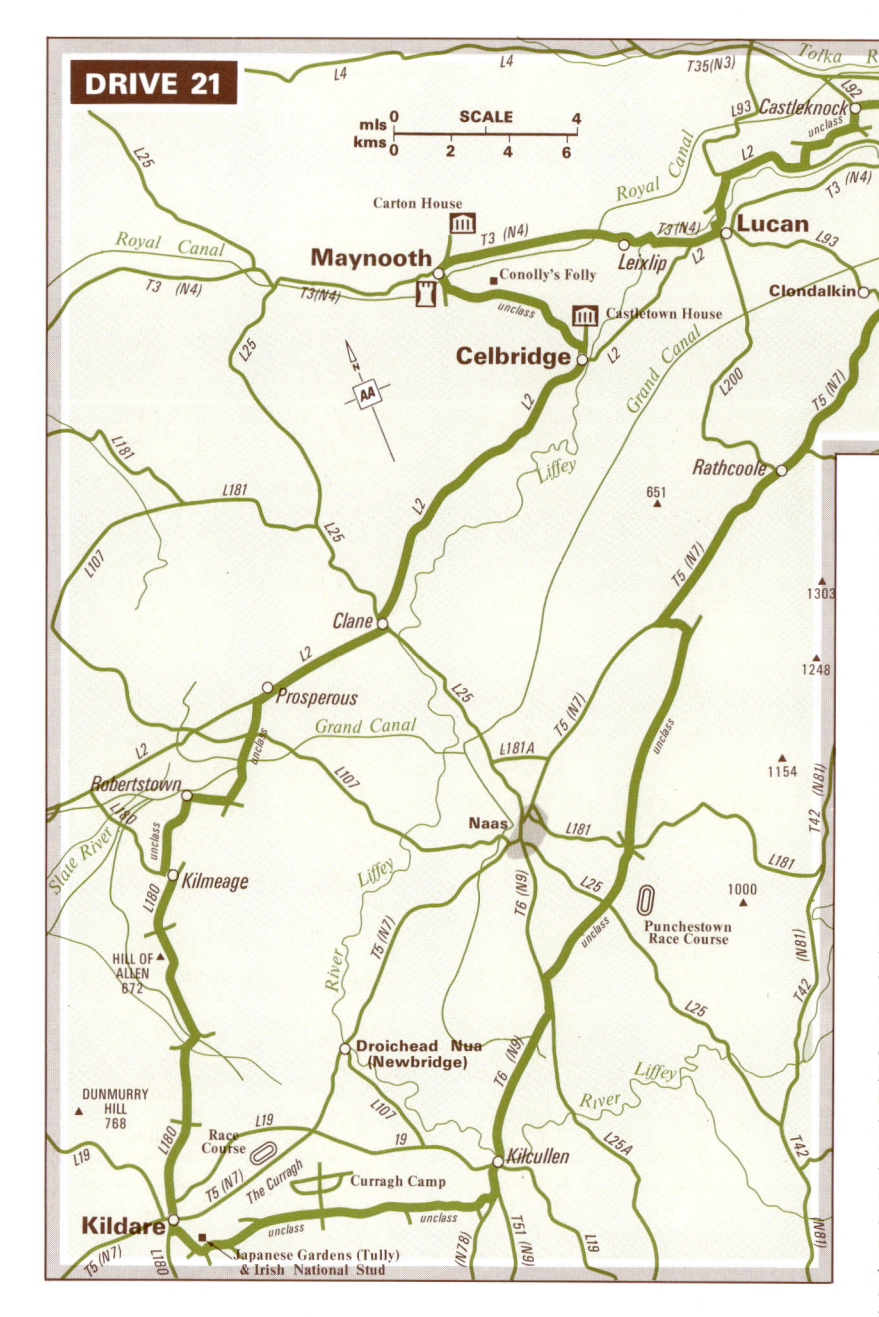

Heaths of The Curragh

From Dublin

Drive 21   80 miles

Drive along the N bank of the River Liffey from *Dublin* city centre, and after 1½m join Parkgate St. Continue past traffic signals, then branch right on to the L92 and enter attractive Phoenix Park. After 2½m leave the park and continue to Castleknock. At Castleknock turn left on to an unclassified road SP 'Chapelizod'. In ½m meet X-roads and turn right SP 'Clonsilla' to leave the city's built-up areas behind in favour of rural scenery. After 1m turn left into a narrow lane and descend, then meet a T-junction and turn right on to the L2. Rejoin the N bank of the Liffey and follow the river through well-wooded country. In 2¾m turn left across the river bridge SP 'Lucan', then turn right into *Lucan* itself. Bear right along a one-way street and meet traffic signals, then turn right on to the main T3 Dublin–Sligo road. Continue, and recross the Liffey at *Leixlip*. Leave this village, and after 3m pass the grounds of Carton House on the right. After 1½m keep left into *Maynooth* and pass the entrance to Carton House on the right. This building replaced a winged manor house which originally occupied the site, and was once a seat of the FitzGeralds. Take the first turning left on to an unclassified road. In ½m bear left SP 'Celbridge', and after 1¼m pass the Conolly's Folly obelisk on the left. Proceed to *Celbridge* and turn right, passing the entrance to *Castletown House* on the left, then keep forward to rejoin the L2, SP 'Clane'. Pass through mainly agricultural, though occasionally well-wooded, country to reach *Clane*. Keep left into the village, pass the church, and turn right to remain on the L2. Follow a straight road to *Prosperous*, pass through the village, and after 1¼m turn left on to an unclassified road SP 'Robertstown'. In ¾m cross the main road, and ½m farther cross the *Grand Canal* via a hump-back bridge. After 1m meet X-roads and turn right for *Robertstown*, which stands beside the canal. Near by is the Falconry of Ireland.

Enter the village and turn left, then in 1¾m turn left on to the L180 and drive into the village of Kilmeage. Turn right here, then in 1¾m meet X-roads and go forward SP 'Kildare'. Cross the low *Hill of Allen* to enjoy distant views of the Wicklow Mountains. In 2m turn right, then cross a canal bridge and keep left. After a further 1½m keep forward to cross open heath on the way to *Kildare*. Proceed to Kildare town centre and cross the main road SP 'Japanese Gardens'. Continue to the church and keep left on to an unclassified road, then immediately bear right. The Irish National Stud and the Japanese Gardens at *Tully* lie to the left after 1m. In ½m keep left, and in ¾m join the 'Kilcullen' road to cross the heathland of *The Curragh*. After 1m the military township known as Curragh Camp lies to the left. Meet X-roads and keep forward, then in 1¼m keep forward again. After ¼m fork left to enter more agricultural country and once more have the chance to enjoy distant views of the Wicklow Mountains.

In 1¾m keep left, meet a main road, and turn left on to the T6 for *Kilcullen*. The Liffey is crossed for the third time here. Continue along the T6 for 4m and turn right on to an unclassified road SP 'Punchestown'. In 2m cross a main road. Pass *Punchestown Racecourse* and look out for a standing stone in a field on the right. In ½m keep left, then bear right over X-roads SP 'Rathcoole'.

Continue along an undulating road; after 2m pass through a gravel-quarrying area, and in a further 2¼m branch left. In ¾m meet a T-junction and turn right on to the T3. Follow a dual-carriageway main road to the outskirts of Dublin before returning to the city centre.

LEINSTER OF THE HIGH KINGS

Wicklow Summits

From Dublin

Drive 22   72 miles

Follow the T42(N81) Rathmines Rd to leave *Dublin* and proceed to the suburb of *Rathmines*. Bear right, and in 100yds bear left into Rathgar Rd. In ¾m bear right through *Rathgar* on to Terenure Rd East, and in a further ½m enter Terenure. Meet traffic signals and turn left, then in ¾m reach *Rathfarnham*. Bear left into Main St, drive to the church, and turn right on to the L94 SP 'Glencree'. In 1¼m turn right SP 'Sally Gap', then shortly left into Stocking Lane and ascend. Views to the left take in 1,540ft Tibradden and 1,339ft Kilmashogue. Pass close to Mount Pelier, or Hellfire Club Hill, and the entry to the Hellfire Club Wood on the right. Continue the ascent, and in 1m reach Killakee carpark and viewpoint. Bear right up an ascent, then in ¾m pass a left turn leading to Cruagh Forest and carpark.

Continue along the side of 1,761ft Killakee Mountain and emerge high above the Dodder Valley. Within 1½m reach a 1,600ft summit between 1,929ft Glendoo and 2,475ft Kippure. Descend to a minor road junction known as *Glencree* Cross. Magnificent views from this 1,300ft point extend along the Glencree Valley to the conical, 1,654ft Great *Sugarloaf* in the distance. The Welsh mountains can be seen in clear weather. Continue along the L94 to a 1,714ft summit between Kippure and the two Tonduff hills – 2,042 and 2,107ft respectively. A right turn here leads to a TV transmitter on 2,475ft Kippure. In ½m cross the Liffey Head Bridge, with the source of the River Liffey on the left. In a short distance the drive affords panoramic views of the Liffey Valley as far W as *Blessington*. A 2,244ft hill rises ahead, above *Sally Gap* and in front of 2,352ft Gravale. In a short distance gradually descend to X-roads at Sally Gap and drive forward on to the unclassified 'Glendalough' road. Views from this old military road extend left across the Clochoge Valley to 2,250ft War Hill and 2,385ft Djouce. In about 1m descend, then later pass through plantations below 2,364ft Duff Hill and an un-named, 2,615ft summit. Climb to 1,400ft at the head of the Glenmacnass River. In ½m descend to a carpark at the head of *Glenmacnass* Waterfall. Continue along this unclassified road for 4¾m and reach *Laragh*.

Turn right on to the T61, cross a bridge, then branch right again on to the L107 SP 'Glendalough'. In 1¼m bear right up an ascent. The L107A left turn here leads to the Vale of Glendalough. Ascend the Vale of Glendasan, with rocky slopes on the right and views of the *Glendalough* lakes to the left. Climb past 2,296ft Camaderry, with 2,686ft Tonelagee rising on the right, and after 4m pass a left turn leading up to the Turlough Hill pumped-storage electricity station. Immediately beyond this reach the 1,500ft summit of *Wicklow Gap*. Descend into the King's River valley, and after 3¾m turn right on to an unclassified road SP 'Valleymount'. Climb through a plantation at first, then after 1¾m reach a summit and descend with views over the *Poulaphouca* Reservoir – or Blessington Lakes. After 2m turn right SP 'Lake Drive', and continue above the reservoir with 2,313ft Moanbane on the right. In 7¼m meet a T-junction and turn left. In ¾m reach a bridge and keep forward SP 'Manor Kilbride'.

Follow the shore for another 1¼m, then later cross the River Liffey. After 1¼m (from the river) reach Manor Kilbride and turn right on to the L161 SP 'Sally Gap'. After another ½m turn left up an incline on to an unclassified road. Climb to over 1,000ft, then descend to meet the L199 – 3½m from Manor Kilbride. Turn right on to the L199 SP 'Dublin, Rathfarnham' and climb to about 1,000ft. Descend into the Dodder Valley, cross a river bridge, then in 1½m meet X-roads and turn left into the L93 Old Bawn Rd for *Tallaght*. Recross the River Dodder, in 1m enter Tallaght, then turn right on to the T42(N81) to pass along the main street. Return to central Dublin via *Templeogue, Terenure,* Rathgar, and Rathmines.

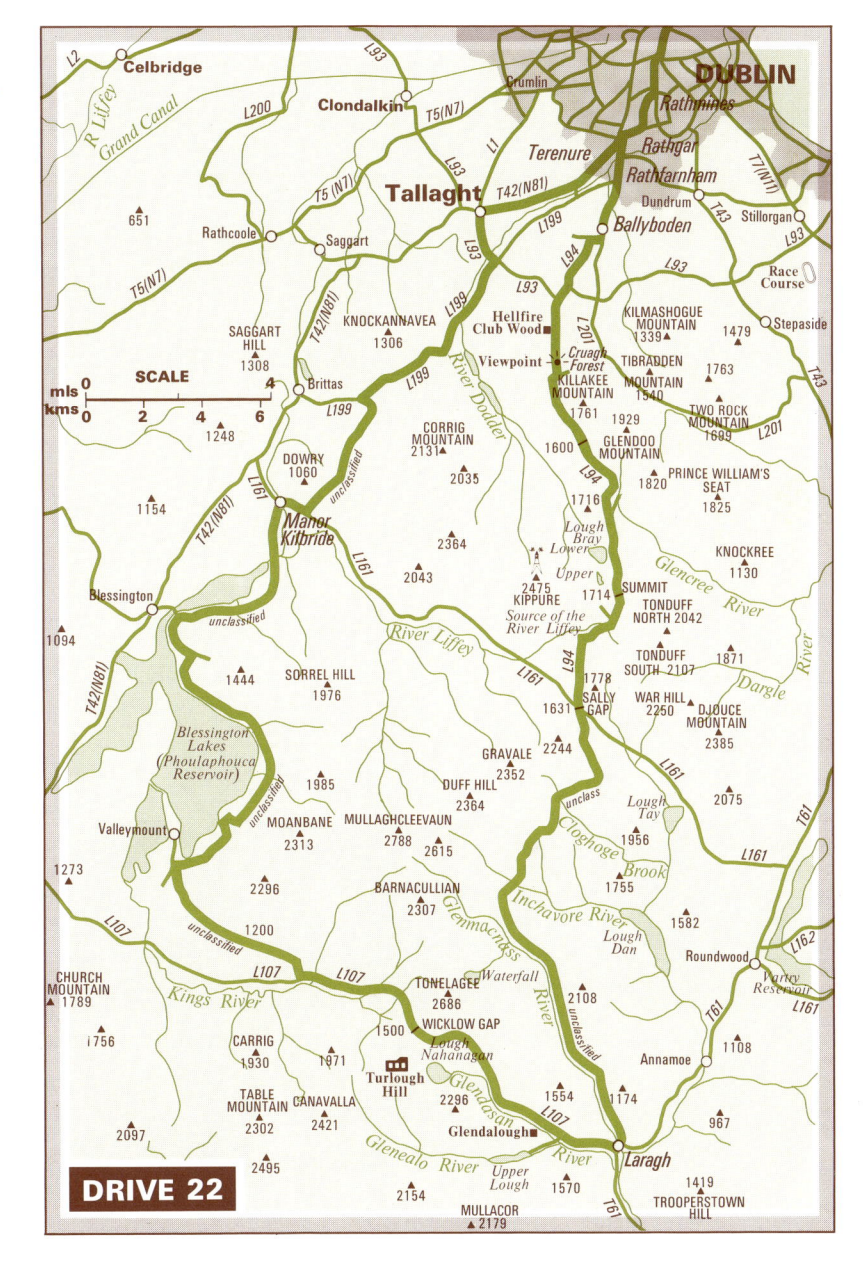

Placenames in *italic* type are worth stopping at; each is listed and described in the main gazetteer section.

LEINSTER OF THE HIGH KINGS

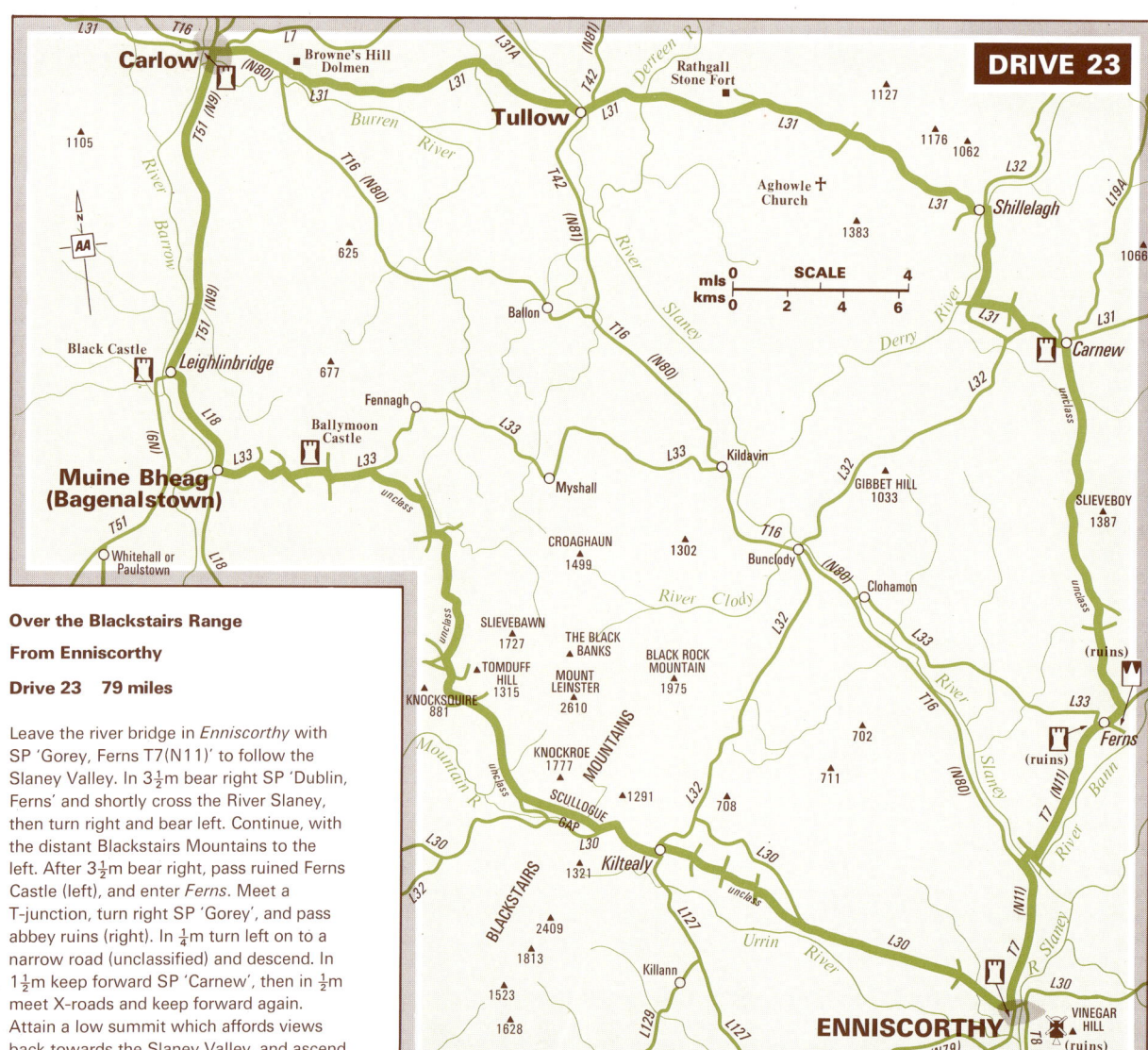

DRIVE 23

**Over the Blackstairs Range
From Enniscorthy
Drive 23 79 miles**

Leave the river bridge in *Enniscorthy* with SP 'Gorey, Ferns T7(N11)' to follow the Slaney Valley. In 3½m bear right SP 'Dublin, Ferns' and shortly cross the River Slaney, then turn right and bear left. Continue, with the distant Blackstairs Mountains to the left. After 3½m bear right, pass ruined Ferns Castle (left), and enter *Ferns*. Meet a T-junction, turn right SP 'Gorey', and pass abbey ruins (right). In ¼m turn left on to a narrow road (unclassified) and descend. In 1½m keep forward SP 'Carnew', then in ½m meet X-roads and keep forward again. Attain a low summit which affords views back towards the Slaney Valley, and ascend to 743ft with 1,387ft Slieve Boy on the right.

Descend steeply and continue to Carnew, then turn left on to the L31. Pass a castle (left) and keep forward, then in 1m branch right on to an unclassified road. In ¼m meet X-roads and bear left SP 'Shillelagh'. After a further 1m meet X-roads and turn right on to the L31 'Shillelagh' road to follow the Derry River. In 2½m turn left and cross the river into *Shillelagh*. Follow SP 'Tullow L31' to the end of the village and bear right. After 3½m enjoy distant views of 1,993ft Croghan, rising from the S Wicklow mountains to the right. In another 1m drive over X-roads where an unclassified left-turn leads to *Aghowle* Church (NM), and in 1¼m pass an unclassified right-turn SP 'Ring of the Rath', leading to Rathgall Stone Fort (NM). In 2¾m cross the Derreen River; in a further 1¼m go forward on to the T42(N81) and descend through the main street of *Tullow*. Cross the River Slaney and turn right on to the L31 SP 'Carlow'. In ¼m bear left, then in 7¾m meet X-roads and go forward on to the T16(N80). An unclassified right turn here leads to Browne's Hill Dolmen, which features the largest capstone in Ireland. In 1½m enter *Carlow* and follow SP 'Waterford' to leave by the T51(N9) Kilkenny Rd. In 1¼m join the River Barrow (right) and drive along its valley with 1,000ft hills to the right. Ahead in the far distance is 1,703ft Brandon Hill, and the 2,610ft Blackstairs range rises to the left. After 8m (from Carlow) enter *Leighlinbridge*, meet a T-junction, and turn left on to the L18. Follow the river for a further 2¾m to *Bagenalstown* (Muine Bheag), and turn left on to the L33 SP 'Bunclody, Enniscorthy'.

In ¼m cross a railway bridge and bear left. In just over ½m bear right, and in a further 1½m pass ruined *Ballymoon Castle* (left). In ½m meet a T-junction and turn left SP 'Bunclody, Fennagh', then in 1m branch right on to an unclassified road SP 'Borris'. In 1¼m turn right SP 'Borris', then in 1m meet X-roads and turn left SP 'Myshall, Tullow'. In ¼m turn right and gradually ascend to a 600ft summit, with 1,727ft Slievebawn ahead. Descend, then after 1¼m meet X-roads and turn left. Shortly turn left again on to the unclassified Bagenalstown to Kiltealy road. Climb to a 700ft pass between 1,315ft Tomduff Hill (left) and 881ft Knocksquire.

Descend to X-roads, and drive forward SP 'Enniscorthy, Kiltealy'. After another 2½m meet X-roads and bear left, then skirt the base of Mount Leinster and follow a gradual climb past 1,777ft Knockroe to the low *Scullogue Gap* between Knockroe and the 2,409ft Blackstairs Mountain (right). Turn left on to the L30, shortly descend to *Kiltealy*, and turn left on to the L30 SP 'Bunclody, Enniscorthy'. Drive to the post office and branch right on to an unclassified road, then in ¾m meet X-roads and go forward. In a further ¾m bear right and immediately left at Mocurry X-roads. Descend to the Urrin River valley and turn right on to the L30. Continue towards Enniscorthy, and after 5m re-enter the town.

LEINSTER OF THE HIGH KINGS

Around the Sugarloaf

From Dublin

Drive 24   73 miles

Leave *Dublin* by the T44 Merrion Rd and in 2¼m reach Ballsbridge. The Royal Dublin Society complex is seen to the right. After a while continue close to the shores of Dublin Bay at *Merrion* Strand, with views of the Dublin port area and *Howth* Head to the left. After 3m (from Ballsbridge) reach the resort of *Blackrock*, bear left SP 'Dun Laoghaire' into Newtown Av, and in ½m turn left into Seapoint Av SP 'Dun Laoghaire Pier'. Drive alongside the seashore. Fine views are afforded across Dublin Bay and *Dun Laoghaire* harbour on the approach to the town. This magnificent, granite-built harbour was designed by famous John Rennie in the 19thc. It is the terminal for a ferry which crosses from Holyhead in Wales. Pass the car ferry on the left, meet traffic signals, and go forward SP 'Dalkey'. Continue along the shore, then in 1¼m meet a T-junction and turn right. The left turn here leads to the famous Forty Foot bathing place for men, plus a martello tower which houses a James Joyce museum and was once the poet's home. In 100yds meet X-roads and turn left on to the T44 SP 'Dalkey'. In ½m pass Bullock Castle on the approach to *Dalkey*. Meet a T-junction and turn left along Castle St. At the end of the street bear right SP 'Killiney' into Railway Rd, then bear left into Sorrento Rd. In ¾m turn right into Vico Rd. Ascend with views of Dalkey Head behind and *Killiney*, *Bray*, and Bray Head visible ahead. Pass wooded Killiney Hill, which is surmounted by an obelisk, and in ¼m turn left SP 'Coast Road, Bray'.

Descend steeply into Station Rd, Killiney, passing the station on the left. In ¼m meet staggered X-roads and go forward SP 'Bray, Wicklow'. After another ½m meet a T-junction and turn left on to the T44. In ¼m keep forward with the main road, then in ¾m go forward on to the T7(N11). Pass through *Shankill* and continue along a tree-lined road. In 1¾m keep forward on to the L29, then cross the River Bray to enter Bray. Keep forward through the main street to the town hall, then at the top of an ascent branch right SP 'Glendalough, Roundwood'. In 1¾m turn right on to the T7(N11) dual carriageway SP 'Dublin', and in ½m turn left on to the T43 SP 'Enniskerry'. Continue along the wooded Glencullen River valley to *Enniskerry*. Turn left SP 'Powerscourt', then on reaching a clock tower, bear left on to the T43A to ascend past the entrance of *Powerscourt* Demesne (right). The house was gutted by fire, but the magnificent gardens are open. Continue with SP 'Kilmacanoge', and in ¾m bear right; both the Great and Little *Sugarloaf* Mountains can be seen ahead. After 1m turn left on to the main T61 road and descend through fine rock scenery with the 1,654ft Great Sugarloaf on the right. Drive to *Kilmacanoge*, turn right on to the T7(N11) SP 'Wexford', and follow a main road between 1,123ft Little Sugarloaf and Great Sugarloaf. In 2m enter the *Glen of the Downs* and shortly pass the access to Bellevue Woods – with nature trails and a picnic site – on the left.

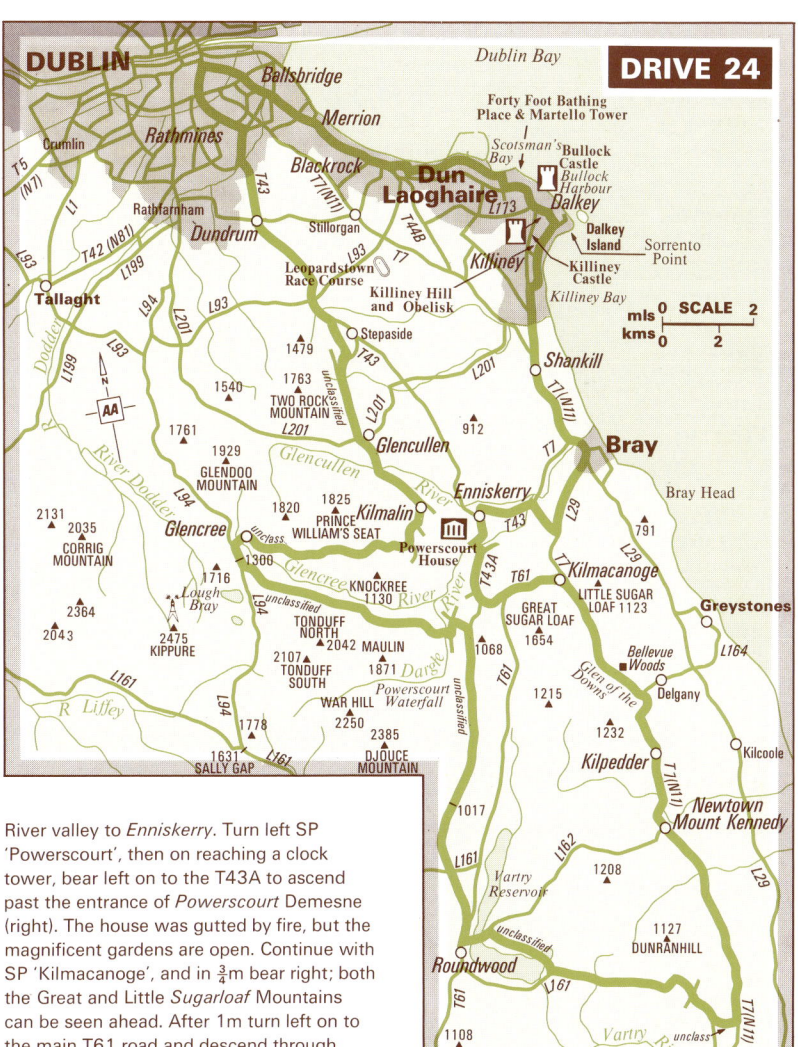

After 2m pass the edge of Kilpedder, from where the lower slopes of the Wicklow Mountains can be seen to the right. In 1½m pass through *Newtownmountkennedy*, and 5m farther turn right on to an unclassified road SP 'Roundwood'. In ½m meet a T-junction and turn right on to the L161. In ¾m meet X-roads and keep forward to pass through a gap between low hills. Continue to the edge of Varty Reservoir and bear right on to an unclassified road SP 'Sally Gap'. Follow the shores of the reservoir, with mountain views ahead. In 1½m meet a T-junction and turn left on to the L162. Cross the reservoir and in ½m reach the edge of *Roundwood*. Turn right on to the T61 SP 'Sally Gap, Bray', and in ¼m turn left on to an unclassified road SP 'Sally Gap, Enniskerry'. After a further 1½m go forward over X-roads SP 'Enniskerry'. Djouce Mountain rises to 2,385ft on the left, and Great Sugarloaf stands on the right. In 3¾m pass Djouce Wood on the left, and shortly enjoy a fine view over Bray Head and the coast (right). Some ¾m beyond this point, and 5½m from the X-roads, turn left SP 'Waterfall'. Descend steeply along a narrow road, then in ¼m meet X-roads and turn left to continue the descent. In ½m pass the access to magnificent Powerscourt Waterfall (left) and bear right across the Dargle River SP 'Glencree'. Climb through forest, then after 5½m reach the 1,300ft head of Glencree Valley and turn right on to the L94 SP 'Rathfarnham'. A magnificent view to the right extends down the Glencree Valley to the distant Great Sugarloaf. In ¼m branch right on to an unclassified road SP 'Glencree'. Descend to the area known as *Glencree* and shortly pass a world-war II German cemetery on the left.

Descend gradually below 1,825ft Prince William's Seat (left), with pleasant mountain and hill views across the valley. After 3¼m (from Glencree) drive past Curtlestown Church on the left. In 1¼m bear left SP 'Glencullen', pass the edge of Kilmalin on the right, and climb again to over 800ft. Descend steeply, cross the Glencullen River, and climb steeply. Meet Glencullen X-roads and keep forward SP 'Stepaside' to a 1,000ft summit below 1,763ft Two Rock Mountain. In ¾m descend, with views over Dublin Bay to the right, and after another 2m turn left on to the T43. Continue to *Dundrum* and go forward over X-roads. Follow SP 'City Centre' for the return to central Dublin.

109

LEINSTER OF THE HIGH KINGS

Wetlands and Mountains

From Birr

Drive 25   91 miles

Follow SP 'Roscrea' from the Square in *Birr*, and in 100yds bear left on to the L116 SP 'Mountmellick'. In 1m go forward on an unclassified road, and in a further 1¼m meet X-roads. Bear left and continue with the distant *Slieve Bloom Mountains* ahead. In 3¼m reach *Clareen*, meet X-roads, and turn left on to the T9. In 4m reach *Kinnitty*. Cross X-roads, and in ¼m branch right on to an unclassified road SP 'Slieve Bloom Mountains'. Continue, and pass the grounds of Castle Bernard (left) before crossing the Camcor River. Ascend into the heart of the Slieve Bloom range. After 6m (from Kinnitty) reach a 1,500ft summit, with 1,659ft Barna and 1,677ft Baunreaghcong to the left. On the right is an un-named hill which rises to 1,696ft – one of the highest points in the range – and panoramic views extend ahead towards *Mountrath* and the Nore Valley.

Descend, with fine views of the surrounding countryside, and at the foot of the descent cross the Delour River. In ½m reach a school and bear left SP 'Mountrath', then after another ½m turn left SP 'Mountain Drive, Clonaslee'. Proceed through the Delour River valley and in 2½m cross a river bridge. This is the location of a very attractive picnic site, shadowed to the right by Barna and Baunreaghcong hills. Follow a gradual ascent through plantations, with fine views across the valley to the higher parts of the range, and after 2½m reach a 1,400ft summit. This point, known as The Cones, affords views of 1,584ft Wolftrap Mountain and 1,533ft Knockachorra to the left, with Barna on the right. Descend along the Gorragh River valley, with fine forward views extending to the plains around *Tullamore*. After 5m (from the summit) meet a T-junction and turn left on to the L116 SP 'Birr, Clonaslee'. Cross the Gorragh River into Clonaslee. Shortly cross the Clodiagh River and immediately turn right on to an unclassified road SP 'Tullamore'. Follow the river for several miles.

In approximately 4¼m reach *Gorteen* Bridge and turn left SP 'Mountbolus', then 3m farther turn right and immediately left SP 'Mountbolus' across a main road. In 2m meet a T-junction at Black Lion and turn right. Shortly pass a church on the right and continue along this tree-lined road. In 1m pass Pallas Lough, which lies close to the road, and after another ½m meet Blue Ball X-roads. Drive forward across a main road on to the L2, and in ½m turn left SP 'Cloghan'. Later cross extensive bogland with views of the Slieve Bloom range to the left. Cross Boora Bog and later pass a peat-fired power station on the left. After 1m meet X-roads and turn right on to the L114 SP 'Ferbane'. Continue through further bogland, and in 2¼m cross the *Grand Canal*. In another ½m turn right on to the T32 (N62), then in ¾m cross the River Brosna into *Ferbane*. Continue along the T32 SP 'Athlone', and after 4½m meet X-roads. Turn left on to an unclassified road SP 'Clonmacnoise' and continue along a narrow route through marshy land. After 2¾m bear left SP 'Clonmacnoise', then after 4½m farther reach *Clonmacnoise* – one of the most important Christian sites in Ireland. Features here include a castle, cathedral, round tower, crosses, churches, and several hundred grave slabs. Turn left, shortly pass St Ciaran's Well on the right, and in 3¾m meet a T-junction at the edge of *Shannonbridge*. Turn left on to the L27 SP 'Cloghan, Tullamore', and in 5½m cross the River Brosna. In ¼m turn right on to an unclassified road SP 'Shannon Harbour'. Clonony Castle (NM) can be seen ahead on the main road. In 1½m reach *Shannon Harbour* and cross a bridge over the Grand Canal, then in a further 1½m meet X-roads and turn right on to the L2 SP 'Banagher'.

Continue, with views of the River Shannon on the right, and after 2m reach *Banagher*. Meet a T-junction and turn right, then immediately left on to an unclassified road SP 'Cloghan Castle'. After another 2m meet X-roads and keep forward, then in ¼m pass a road on the right leading to Cloghan Castle. In 3½m meet X-roads and turn right on to the L113, then cross the Little Brosna River. In ¾m turn sharp left on to an unclassified road SP 'Birr' and enter well-wooded countryside, with forestry plantations on the right. In 3½m the drive affords views of Birr Castle on the right. Recross the Little Brosna River, turn right on to the L115, and re-enter Birr.

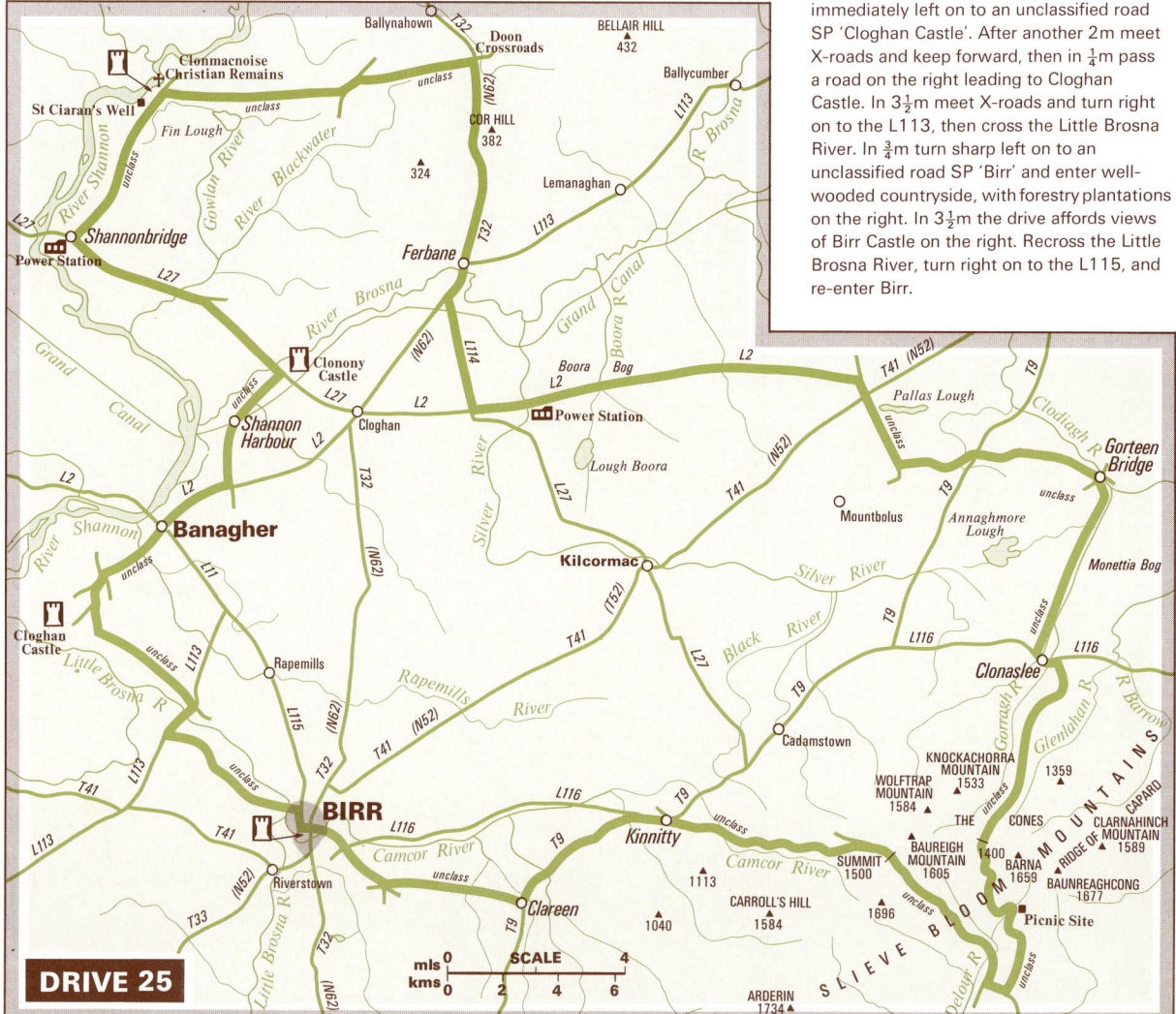

LEINSTER OF THE HIGH KINGS

Islands and Farms
From Dublin
Drive 26   86 miles

From *Dublin* (see town plan) follow Fairview to leave the city by Clontarf Rd. Pass through the N suburbs and drive alongside the shore of Dublin Bay. After 4m pass the Bull Wall on the right. This leads to the interesting Bull Island Bird Sanctuary, and there are views of the *Howth* peninsula ahead. In 3¾m meet traffic signals and turn right with the L86, SP 'Howth Head'. Gradually ascend to the summit of Howth Head. A road from the Summit Inn leads to a carpark which affords views over Dublin Bay to the distant Wicklow Hills.

Descend to Howth, enjoying fine seascape views which include a small island known as *Ireland's Eye*. Continue to Howth Harbour and turn left, then after ½m pass the entrance to medieval Howth Castle. In 1½m meet traffic signals and turn right, still with the L86, SP 'Baldoyle'. Drive over a level crossing, and in another ½m reach Baldoyle. Turn right here, then after a further 1½m turn right again on to the L87 for the resort of *Portmarnock*. The fine expanse of sandy beach here is known as the *Velvet Strand*. Continue along the coast to *Malahide*, with seaward views of *Lambay Island*. Enter Malahide and keep forward through the town, then in 1m turn right on to the L143 SP 'Swords'. Stay inland and pass through agricultural country to reach the ancient town of *Swords*. Meet traffic signals and turn right on to the main T1 'Dublin–Belfast' road, then after 3¾m turn right on to the L90 SP 'Skerries'. In another 2m bear right into the village of *Lusk*. Once in the village, turn right on to the L96 'Rush' road and enter the market-gardening area for Dublin. Proceed to *Rush* and turn left on to the L89 SP 'Skerries'. Rejoin the coast and follow a section of the drive which affords seaward views of the *Rockabill* lighthouse, with Shenick's Island in the foreground. Enter *Skerries*, turn left at the obelisk, then meet X-roads and go forward. Turn right SP 'Balbriggan' to remain with the L89. Continue along the attractive coast, with views of the distant Mourne Mountains Enter *Balbriggan*, cross a railway bridge, then turn right SP 'Drogheda'. Still in the town, turn right to rejoin the T1 and drive inland. Cross the county border just beyond the town and enter Co Meath. Proceed to *Julianstown*, turn right on to the L125 on an ascent SP 'Laytown', and in 1½m bear right. Rejoin the coast for the last time at *Laytown*, then continue along the coast road to *Bettystown*. At Bettystown bear left and left again SP 'Mornington', then in ¼m bear right SP 'Drogheda'. After ¾m turn right, then in 1m keep left and immediately right. Continue to *Mornington*, turn left, and cross a river bridge. Follow the Boyne Estuary, then later pass beneath a viaduct which carries the main 'Dublin–Belfast' railway line.

Enter the historic town of *Drogheda* (see gazetteer town plan). Leave Drogheda via Mary St, meet a T-junction, turn left SP 'Dublin', then turn right on to the L88. In 5m branch left SP 'Ardcath, Garristown', and after another 2m meet X-roads. Turn left, bear right, and continue to Ardcath. At Ardcath keep left and drive through undulating farming countryside to Garristown. Keep forward with SP 'Dublin', and in 1m bear left. The Dublin Mountains can be seen in the distance. In 5m meet X-roads and go forward, then in 2¾m turn left on to the T2. After another 2½m pass a left turn leading to *Dunsoghly* Castle. This massive structure is situated on a small hillock in a marsh and dates from the 15thc. Its keep still retains the roof timbers and is flanked by four angle towers. Continue through the built-up areas around Finglass, and return to Dublin through the suburbs.

Placenames in *italic* type are worth stopping at; each is listed and described in the main gazetteer section.

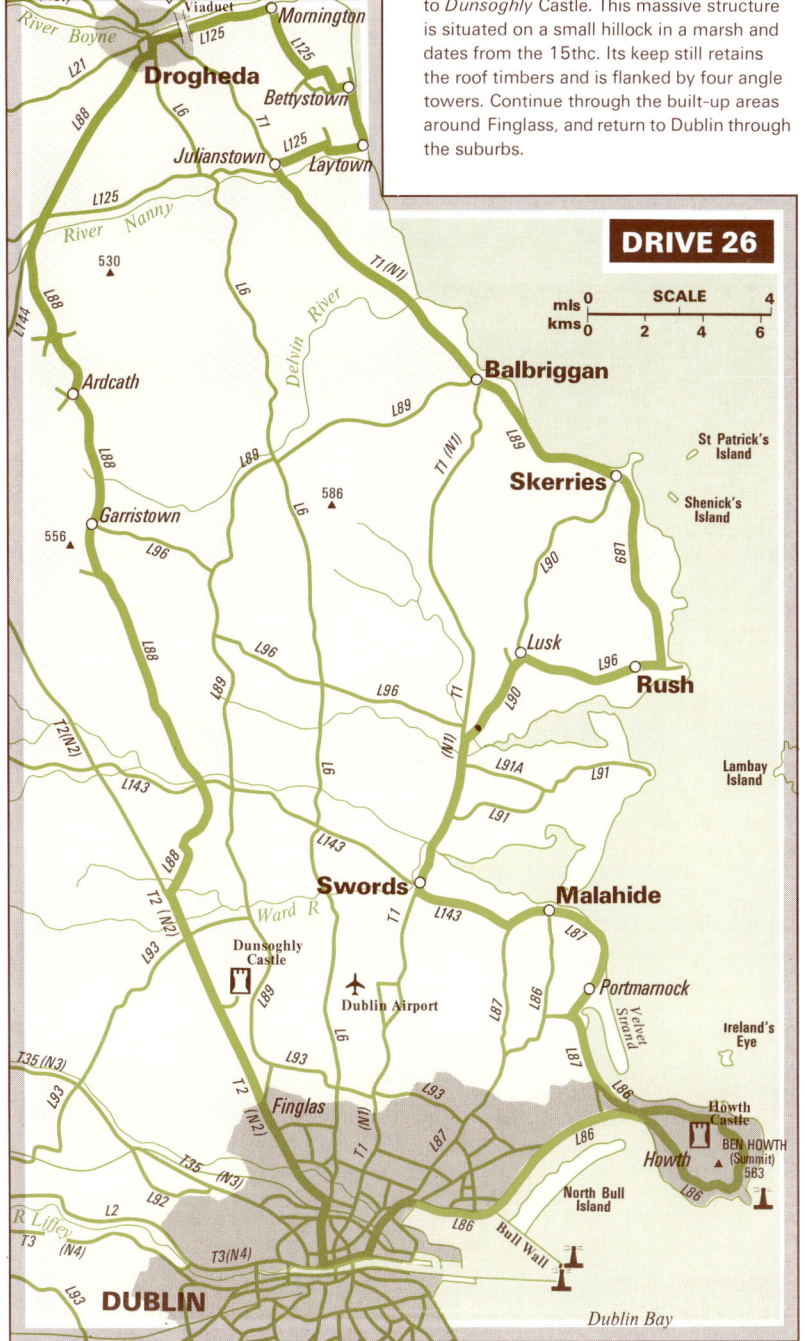

LEINSTER OF THE HIGH KINGS

DRIVE 27

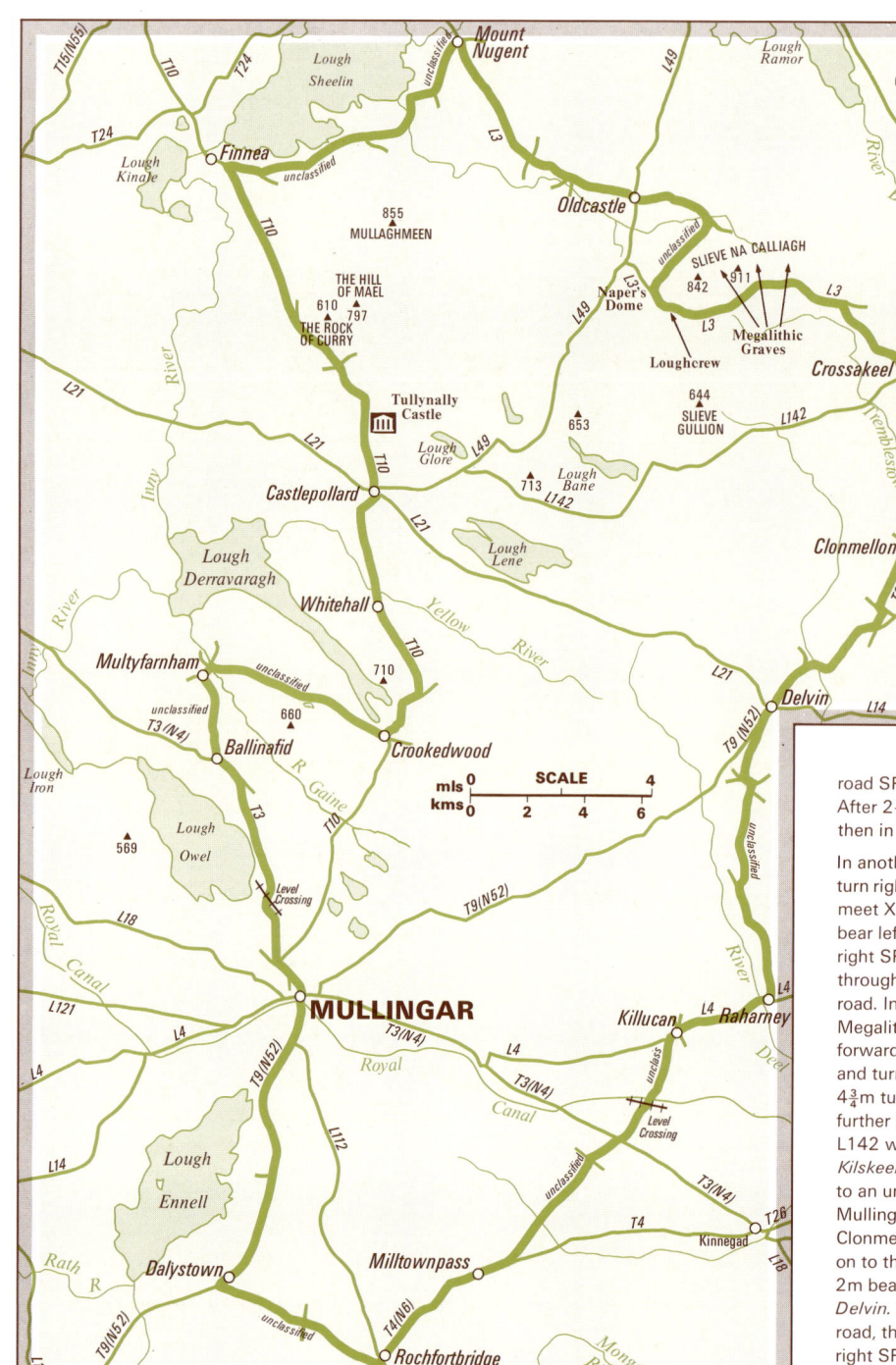

Westmeath Lowlands

From Mullingar

Drive 27   92 miles

Depart central *Mullingar* via the T3(N4) Castle St SP 'Longford'. In ¾m go forward SP 'Longford, Multyfarnham' and bear right. In 1¼m drive over a level crossing, and in a further 1½m pass Lough Owel (left). After a further 2m reach Ballinafid and turn right on to an unclassified road SP 'Multyfarnham'.

In another 2m enter *Multyfarnham* and turn right SP 'Crookedwood'. Cross the River Gaine and turn right. In 1¾m pass tiny Lough Patrick (right). After another 3m reach *Crookedwood* and turn left on to the T10 SP 'Castlepollard'. In a further 1¼m bear left SP 'Castlepollard', and in 2¼m pass Whitehall. Continue to *Castlepollard*, turn left SP 'Finnea' to remain on the T10, and in 1½m pass a right turn leading to Tullynally Castle. After another 6¾m reach the edge of Finnea, turn sharp right on to an unclassified road SP 'Mount Nugent', and in ¾m turn left. After 2½m meet a junction and keep forward, then in 1¼m cross the Upper Inny River.

In another 2m enter *Mount Nugent* and turn right on to the L3 SP 'Oldcastle'. In 3¼m meet X-roads and keep forward, then in 1m bear left over a bridge and immediately right SP 'Oldcastle'. In 1½m follow SP 'Kells' through *Oldcastle* to leave by an unclassified road. In 2m turn right SP 'Loughcrew, Megalithic Graves', and in 1m keep forward. After another 1m meet a T-junction and turn left on to the L3 SP 'Kells'. After 4¾m turn right SP 'Crossakeel', and in a further 2½m enter Crossakeel. Cross the L142 with SP 'Athboy', and in 2½m reach *Kilskeer*. Pass the church and turn right on to an unclassified road SP 'Clonmellon, Mullingar'. After another 2½m reach Clonmellon, meet X-roads, and go forward on to the T9(N52) SP 'Delvin, Mullingar'. In 2m bear right, and in 3½m drive through *Delvin*. In ¾m turn left on to an unclassified road, then in 1¼m turn left and immediately right SP 'Raharney'. In 1½m enter woodland and follow the River Deel. Continue for another 3½m to Raharney, turn right on to the L4 SP 'Mullingar', and cross a bridge into the village. Keep forward along the L4 for 2¼m to reach *Killucan*, drive to the end of this village, then turn right SP 'Mullingar'.

In ¼m turn left on to an unclassified road SP 'Milltownpass'. After 1½m cross the Royal Canal and drive over a level crossing. In 1m turn right on to the T3(N4) and immediately left on to an unclassified road. In 3½m reach the Pass of Kilbride, turn right on to the T4(N6) SP 'Rochfortbridge', and in a further ½m drive through Milltownpass SP 'Athlone'. In 3¼m enter *Rochfortbridge* and, near the centre of the main street, turn right on to an unclassified road. In 1¾m meet X-roads and go forward. In 2¼m reach Dalystown, turn right on to the T9(N52) SP 'Mullingar', and in 6¾m re-enter Mullingar.

LEINSTER OF THE HIGH KINGS

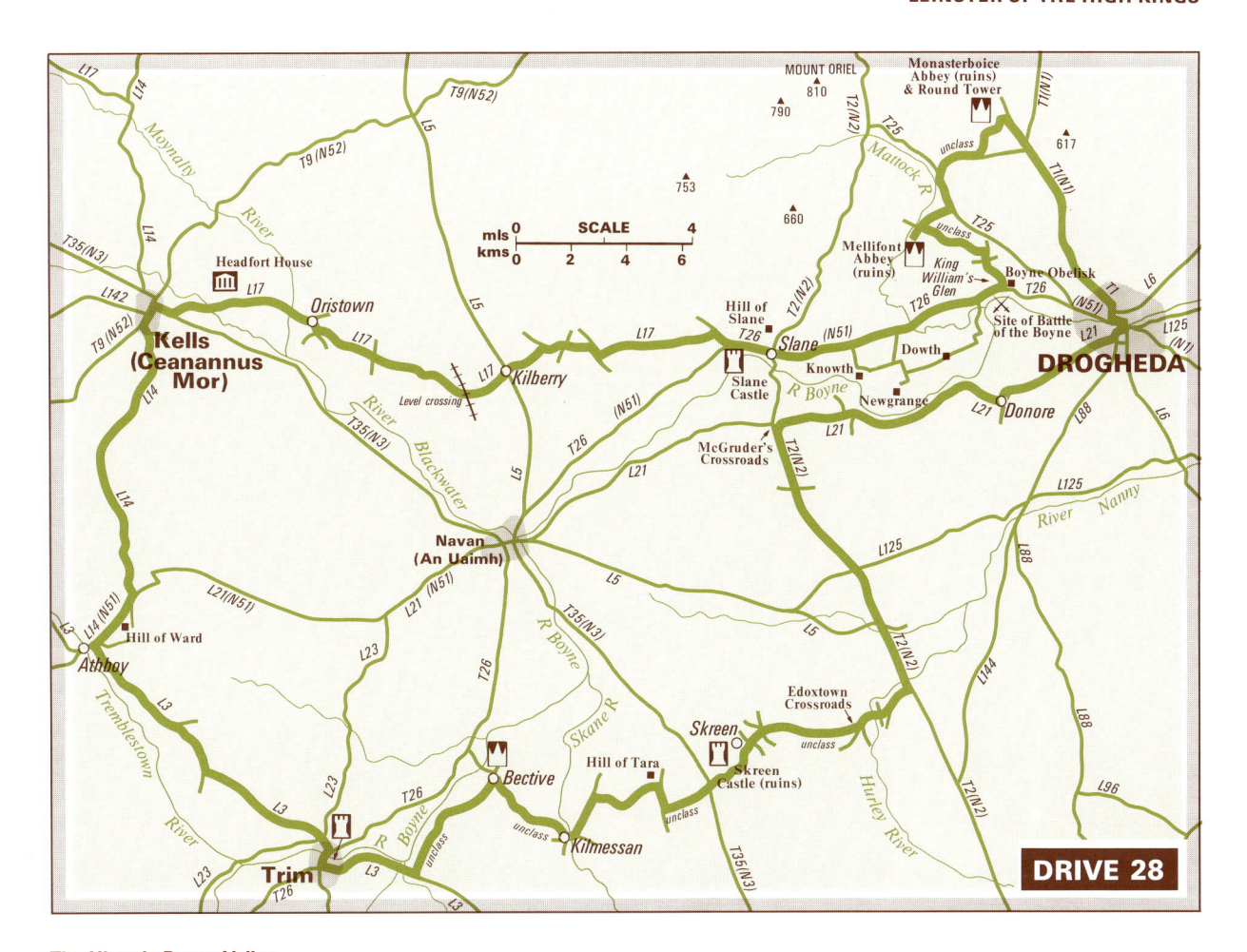

DRIVE 28

The Historic Boyne Valley

From Drogheda

Drive 28 85 miles

Leave central *Drogheda* via West St and turn right into George's St T1(N1) SP 'Dundalk, Belfast'. In 4½m turn left on to an unclassified road SP 'Monasterboice Abbey, Round Tower', and in ½m turn left again. In ¾m pass ruined *Monasterboice* Abbey on the right. Continue with SP 'Mellifont Abbey' and in 1m turn right. After another 1m go forward on to the T25 SP 'Dublin, Drogheda'. In 1m turn right on to an unclassified road SP 'Mellifont Abbey', and in another 1m meet X-roads. Go forward for ¼m to ruined *Mellifont Abbey*, beside the Mattock River. Return to the X-roads and turn right. In 1¾m meet X-roads and go forward into King William's Glen, then in ¾m turn right on to the T26(N51) SP 'Slane'. In ¾m pass an unclassified left turn leading to the prehistoric tumuli at *Dowth, Newgrange,* and *Knowth*.

Follow the main road along the Mattock Valley and after 1¾m cross the River Mattock. After ¼m (from the bridge) pass another left turn leading to Knowth and Newgrange, then in a further 1¼m pass a third, similarly signposted road. After another 2m enter *Slane,* meet X-roads, and keep forward on to the T26(N51) SP 'Navan'. In 1m, with the Slane Castle estate on the left, turn right on to the L17 SP 'Kells'. In ½m turn left, and in 2½m meet a T-junction. Turn right, then in ¼m turn left SP 'Kells'. In 1¼m bear left, and in a further 1m reach *Kilberry*. Meet X-roads, go forward, and in 1m drive forward over a level crossing. In 4m meet X-roads and bear right then shortly left through Oristown. In a further 2½m cross the River Blackwater, and in 1¼m bear right into the town of *Kells*. Pass the Headfort Hotel, branch left, then turn left on to the T9(N52) SP 'Athboy'. In ½m reach the edge of the town and branch left on to the L14. Bear right, and after another 6½m bear right SP 'Athboy'. The L21 left turn here leads to Rathmore Church (NM). In 1¼m, on entering *Athboy*, pass an unclassified left turn which leads to the Hill of Ward. Immediately beyond this road turn left on to the L3 SP 'Trim' and follow the line of the Athboy River. In 2½m bear right, and after a further 4½m enter the town of *Trim*.

Continue forward, and on meeting a T-junction turn right into the High St. Cross the River Boyne into the town square, and follow SP 'Dublin L3'. Pass castle ruins (left) and in ½m bear left to follow the River Boyne. After 1¾m turn left, cross a bridge, then turn left again on to an unclassified road SP 'Bective'. Continue along the Boyne Valley, then after 3m enter *Bective* and proceed to X-roads. Turn right SP 'Kilmessan'; the left turn here leads to a ruined fortress abbey. In 2¼m reach *Kilmessan* and turn left SP 'Tara' to cross a river bridge. Keep straight ahead, and in 1¼m turn right SP 'Tara'. Climb towards the ancient, royal hill of *Tara*, then in 1¾m meet a T-junction and turn right. In ½m turn left, and in 1¼m cross the T35(N3) SP 'Skreen Cross Church'. In a further 1¼m pass the ruins of Skreen Castle on the right. Shortly pass Skreen Church and Cross (NM) on the left, meet X-roads and go forward, then in ½m meet the next X-roads. Drive forward and later descend. After 2¼m reach Edoxtown X-roads and turn left, then in ¾m meet more X-roads and drive forward, in ¼m bear left SP 'Duleek, Drogheda'.

Keep forward for ¾m, meet X-roads and turn left on to the T2(N2) SP 'Slane'. Keep forward for 6¾m along the T2 to McGruder's X-roads and turn right on to the L21 SP 'Drogheda'. In 1¾m pass an unclassified left turn SP 'Battle of the Boyne' – site of a crossing made by part of the Williamite force. Shortly bear left to reach the Boyne, then in 4m enter Donore and turn left SP 'Drogheda'. After another ½m pass another unclassified left turn SP 'Battle of the Boyne' – the site of the main battlefield. In 2¾m re-enter Drogheda.

113

LEINSTER OF THE HIGH KINGS

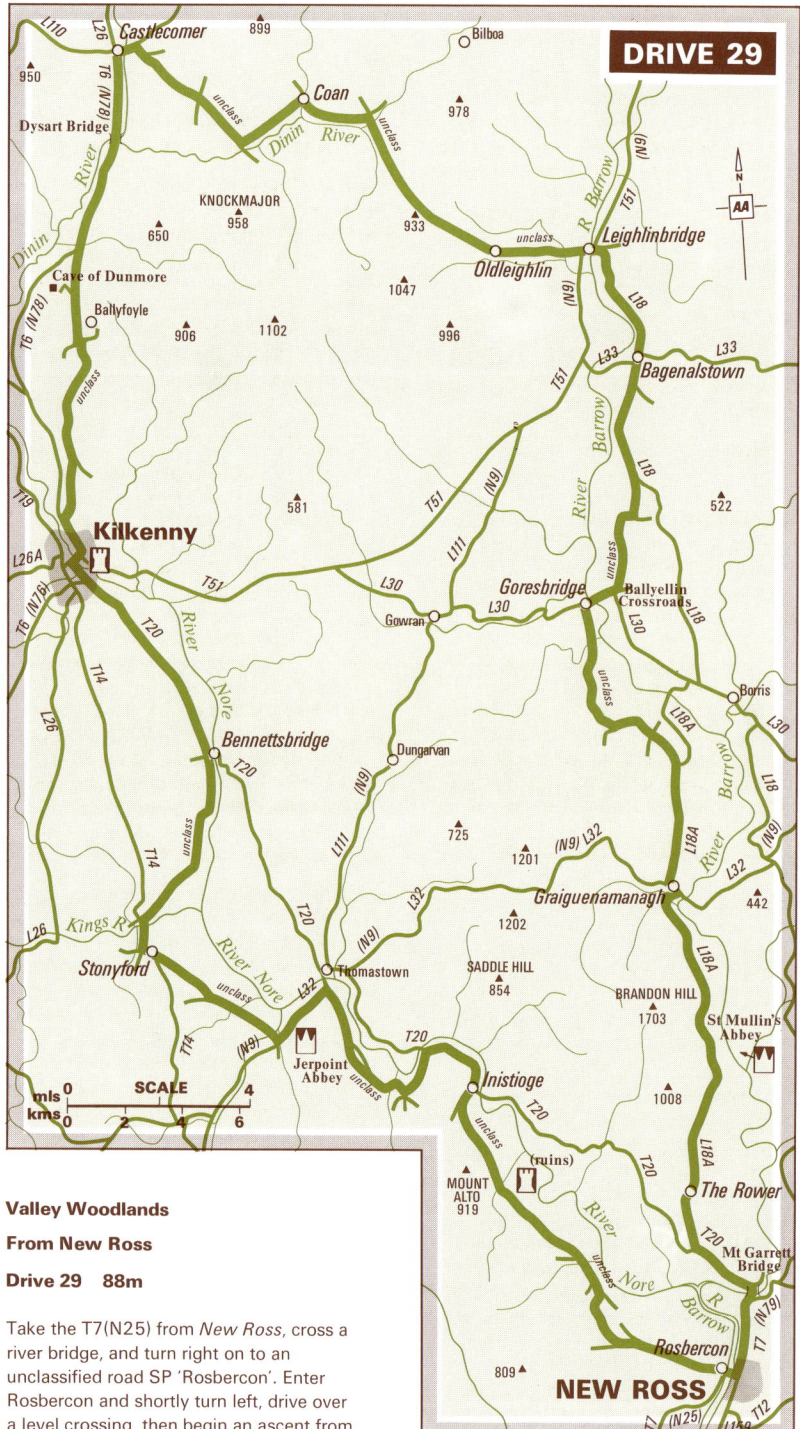

Valley Woodlands
From New Ross
Drive 29 88m

Take the T7(N25) from *New Ross*, cross a river bridge, and turn right on to an unclassified road SP 'Rosbercon'. Enter Rosbercon and shortly turn left, drive over a level crossing, then begin an ascent from the Barrow Valley. In 2m bear left, and in ½m bear right SP 'Inistioge'. In ¾m descend through wooded country into the Nore Valley, with 1,703ft Brandon Hill ahead. Shortly bear left, keep forward, and in ¾m begin a long ascent with SP 'Inistioge'. In 2m the route affords panoramic views over the Nore Valley ahead and to the right. From this point descend for about 1m, passing a ruined castle on the right, and shortly climb round the heavily-wooded lower slopes of 919ft Mount Alto. Once clear of woodland the route affords good views before a further descent. In ¾m bear right and in ½m descend steeply into *Inistioge*. Turn left on to the T20 'Thomastown, Kilkenny' road, follow the River Nore for 1¾m to Brownsbarn Bridge, and at the nearside of the bridge turn left on to an unclassified road SP 'Tullogher'. Enter dense woodland and in 1¼m meet a road junction. Bear right and descend through more woodland, then shortly bear left across the Arrigle River. In 1m keep forward to enjoy good views ahead along the valley towards *Thomastown*. In 2m reach the edge of Thomastown and turn left on to the L32. Ascend, with views of 2,368ft *Slievenamon* ahead, and in 1¼m pass the remains of 12th-c *Jerpoint Abbey* on the left. This is considered one of the most interesting first-generation Cistercian houses in Ireland, and carries typically-Irish battlements. The church which serves this monastic complex incorporates many interesting features, including a number of fine early carvings. In a further ½m turn right SP 'Stonyford' and cross the Little Arrigle River. In 1½m enter heavy woodland, with *Mount Juliet* Wood on the right, then in ¼m meet a forked junction and bear right SP 'Stonyford'. In 1½m enjoy further views over the attractive countryside towards Kilkenny. In ¼m turn right on to the T14(N9) SP 'Kilkenny' to enter the village of Stonyford. In ¼m turn right, and in ½m cross the King's River. Meet X-roads and turn right on to an unclassified road SP 'Bennettsbridge'. Continue along an undulating, partly tree-bordered road which affords distant hill views to the right. Later continue alongside the River Nore, with dense woodland to the left of the road. After 4¼m reach *Bennettsbridge*, meet X-roads, and go forward on to the T20 SP 'Kilkenny'.

Continue along the Nore Valley, and in 4¼m reach Quarry Hill. Fine views extend over the city of *Kilkenny* from here. In ¾m enter the city — passing the castle on the right — then proceed to traffic signals and turn right into Rose Inn St. Follow SP 'Carlow, Dublin' to cross the River Nore via John's Bridge. Keep forward, and in ½m go forward under a railway bridge on to the T6(N78) Castlecomer Rd. Bear left, and in ¾m turn right on to an unclassified road SP 'Ballyfoyle'. Shortly meet a T-junction and turn left to follow a narrow, hilly road through dense woodland. After 2m a scenic section of the drive affords good views, which include the Slieveardagh Hills in the distance on the left. After another ½m turn left and shortly right SP 'Castlecomer'. In 1½m pass a road on the left leading to the Cave of *Dunmore* (NM), a natural limestone cave which is considered one of the finest to be found anywhere in the country.

In ¾m go forward on to the T6(N78) SP 'Caslecomer' and follow the valley of the Dinin River. In 2½m cross Dysart Bridge, and in a further 1¾m enter *Castlecomer* — a pleasant town which serves as a centre of the Leinster anthracite coalfield. Meet X-roads and turn right SP 'Athy, Carlow', then in a short distance recross the Dinin River and enter dense woodland. In ¼m turn right on to an unclassified road SP 'Coan, Bagenalstown'. Ascend gradually, with good views extending over the landscape behind and to the left. In 1½m meet X-roads and keep forward SP 'Coan, Paulstown' to enter more woodland. Descend gradually into the valley of another Dinin River, and at the nearside of the bridge turn left SP 'Coan, Carlow'. Follow the valley and climb steadily for 1¾m to reach the village of Coan. Turn right SP 'Bilboa, Carlow' and cross a river bridge, then keep forward to enjoy good views over the surrounding countryside. In 1½m meet X-roads, turn right SP 'Oldleighlin', and climb out of the river valley. Drive to a height of 933ft to enjoy fine forward views of the Blackstairs Mountains and prominent, 2,610ft Mount Leinster. Follow a long, straight descent for 1¾m to Oldleighlin village, where remains of a 12th-c Protestant cathedral can be seen to the right of the road. Continue through the village, and after 2m reach *Leighlinbridge*. Drive forward along the main street SP 'Dublin, Carlow', cross the River Barrow with the ruins of Black Castle on the right, then keep forward

Connacht – The Last Refuge

Connacht's landscape is a shifting kaleidoscope of extremes, where vast tracts of deserted mountain country suddenly give way to rolling moors carpeted with springy Irish heath. Stoney flats and fertile grasslands slide gracefully into acres of bog marking the senility of a lake, or stop abruptly at the shores of beautiful loughs rich with fish and wildfowl. The coasts of Connacht are jigsaw-like complications of peninsulas, ragged headlands, and clustered islands – little emissaries of Ireland that crowd close to the parent shore in their hundreds and carry crumbling evidence of man's rise to Christianity. It was from here that ambitious men set out to take over Tara and the High Kingship of Ireland in the 3rdc; here that the last Irish Celts faced Anglo-Norman treachery across the Shannon.

Co Mayo's fractured coast faces north to the Arctic Circle and west across the Atlantic Ocean in a welter of sheer headlands, detached stacks, long sandy beaches, and gull-crowded cliffs riddled with caves. North west are the almost treeless flats of the Mullet Peninsula, while farther south narrow Achill Sound separates Achill Island from the west coast's peaked Corraun Peninsula. Achill Head defends the tip of the island in a 2,192ft display of obstinacy which falls sheer to the erosive sea. The northern part of inland Mayo features long horizons of moorland bordered by hills which rise south to join 200sqm of the loneliest, most desolate countryside in Ireland – the magnificent Nephin Beg range. There are no roads, farms, or houses here; only high peaks which face east towards the Ox Mountains across the fertile flatlands of Lough Conn. Farther south Croagh Patrick rises from the convoluted Murrisk area with all the aplomb expected of a Holy Mountain. St Patrick is said to have fasted on the summit for the 40 days of Lent, during which time he banished all 'venemous' creatures from Ireland. South-east of Croagh Patrick the Partry Mountains tower above Lough Mask, Lough Corrib, and an expanse of damp flats that rise north to the Plains of Mayo.

It is said that every stage of the country's prehistory is represented in the frantic cycles of Irish legend and tangible archaeological evidence preserved in Co Sligo. Its mountains still hold echoes of Queen Maeve's turbulent journey to steal the fabulous Brown Bull of Cooley, its towns are graced by ancient monastic remains, and its loughs are dotted with island-bound ruins. East of Co Mayo the west-to-east Sligo shoreline abruptly bends north and zig-zags up to Donegal Bay, running west of fretted spires and cliffs that form the limestone Dartry Mountains. Sligo town nestles in the angle formed by the coast's sudden change of direction, sheltered on the seaward side by Coney Island and comfortable in the knowledge that it raised the celebrated 19th-c poet W B Yeats. Several of the poet's works were inspired by Lough Gill, an exquisite, tree-shrouded lake sited east of the town.

South of this the county is split almost in two by a valley which pushes north from Lough Arrow and marks the edge of a low-lying central plain which rolls west to the Ox Mountain foothills. Volcanic activity in these foothills during the 15thc resulted in the creation of the country's youngest lake.

Connacht's eastern border runs south from Donegal Bay and along the edges of counties Leitrim and Roscommon before rounding a small piece of south-east Galway. It was to the boggy mountains of northern Leitrim and flat grasslands of Shannon-side Roscommon that the last Irish Celts were driven when Henry II's barons broke their king's faith by pushing Anglo-Norman occupation into Connacht. The mountains are riven by secretive, lough-scattered valleys which once provided refuge for tragic Dervorgilla, who sparked off the initial Norman invasion of Ireland by eloping from a persistent Leinster king. The most southerly hill groups of the range are divided by Lough Allen, a wide expansion of the infant Shannon from which the river re-emerges to forge south through low bogland and lakes to Georgian Carrick-on-Shannon. The damp character of the countryside continues south through Roscommon, first following the Shannon and later the shores of Lough Ree before meeting Co Galway. Stony grasslands ringed to the north by an arc of tree-shaded loughs cover the rest of the county, providing a relatively dry site for ancient Boyle below the Curlew Mountains.

Most of southern Connacht comprises Galway, a county where stark peaks dominate a fractured, north-western coastline which seems unable to make up its mind whether to be land or water. Long fingers of the Atlantic penetrate far inland, joining the boggy valleys which split this jagged land into unofficial but totally accepted regions such as Connemara in the west, Iar Connacht alongside spectacular Lough Corrib in the south west, and Joyce's Country in the east. The latter was named after a 13th-c immigrant Welsh family whose descendants still live here. Connemara's lake-scattered coastal plain rises north in ranks of granite mountains formed by intense volcanic activity in the geological past. These merge north into the gleaming schists and white quartzite peaks which tower over the rock-strewn plains of south Mayo. Iar Connacht rises gently above its western circlet of tiny loughs and Lough Corrib in the east, dropping to the smooth north coast of Galway Bay in restrained undulations.

Many of the islands that speckle west Galway's coastal waters and inland loughs provided security for holy men who sought isolation in which to contemplate their faiths. Their epitaphs are written in gull-haunted ruins and the salt-rimed granite of ancient crosses. East of Lough Corrib and tide-washed Galway town the county's low plains roll across Ireland in easy, fertile waves which cross southern Roscommon and slide lazily into the Shannon.

Biologists revel in Connacht's unique collection of wildlife, and walkers reflect on the lifetimes they would need to explore its landscapes.

Drive 29 continued

on the L18 SP 'Bagenalstown, Graiguenamanagh'. Proceed through rich pasture land along the Barrow Valley to enjoy fine views of Mount Leinster ahead. In 2½m reach *Bagenalstown* and follow SP 'Kilkenny' and 'Borris', then shortly turn left into the main street. In ¼m turn right on to the L18 SP 'Borris', then meet X-roads and go forward. After a short distance cross a railway bridge, and in ¼m bear right. In 2m go forward on to an unclassified road, and after a further 1m meet a T-junction. Turn right, then shortly turn sharp left.

In 1¾m reach Ballyellin X-roads, turn right SP 'Goresbridge, Kilkenny', and go forward on to the L30. In ½m recross the River Barrow into *Goresbridge*, meet X-roads in the village centre, and turn left on to an unclassified road SP 'Graiguenamanagh'. Continue along an undulating road and in 2m pass Mount Loftus Wood on the left, with Brandon Hill rising ahead. In 1¼m descend to the valley bottom, and in a further 1½m turn right on to the L18A SP 'Graiguenamanagh, New Ross'. The Blackstairs range can be seen to the left. In 2m begin a descent into *Graiguenamanagh*, with the wooded slopes of Brandon Hill directly ahead. Meet a T-junction, turn left into the town SP 'New Ross, Enniscorthy', and continue to the town centre. A signpost to the left here indicates 'Duiske Abbey, Castle, and Church ruins'. Turn right SP 'New Ross', and in ¼m keep forward on to the L18A SP 'New Ross, Waterford'. Continue alongside the River Barrow with dense woodland on the right. Mountain views are afforded to the left, and views ahead extend along the valley towards New Ross.

After a while pass directly beneath Brandon Hill, which rises to the right. After 7m (from Graiguenamanagh) reach the curiously-named village of The Rower. Descend from here along a road which offers more views, and in 1½m turn left on to the T20. In a further 1½m turn right and cross *Mountgarrett Bridge,* which spans the River Barrow, then immediately turn right on to the T7(N79). Pass through woodland, rejoin the river, and descend into New Ross.

Placenames in *italic* type are worth stopping at; each is listed and described in the main gazetteer section.

CONNACHT – THE LAST REFUGE

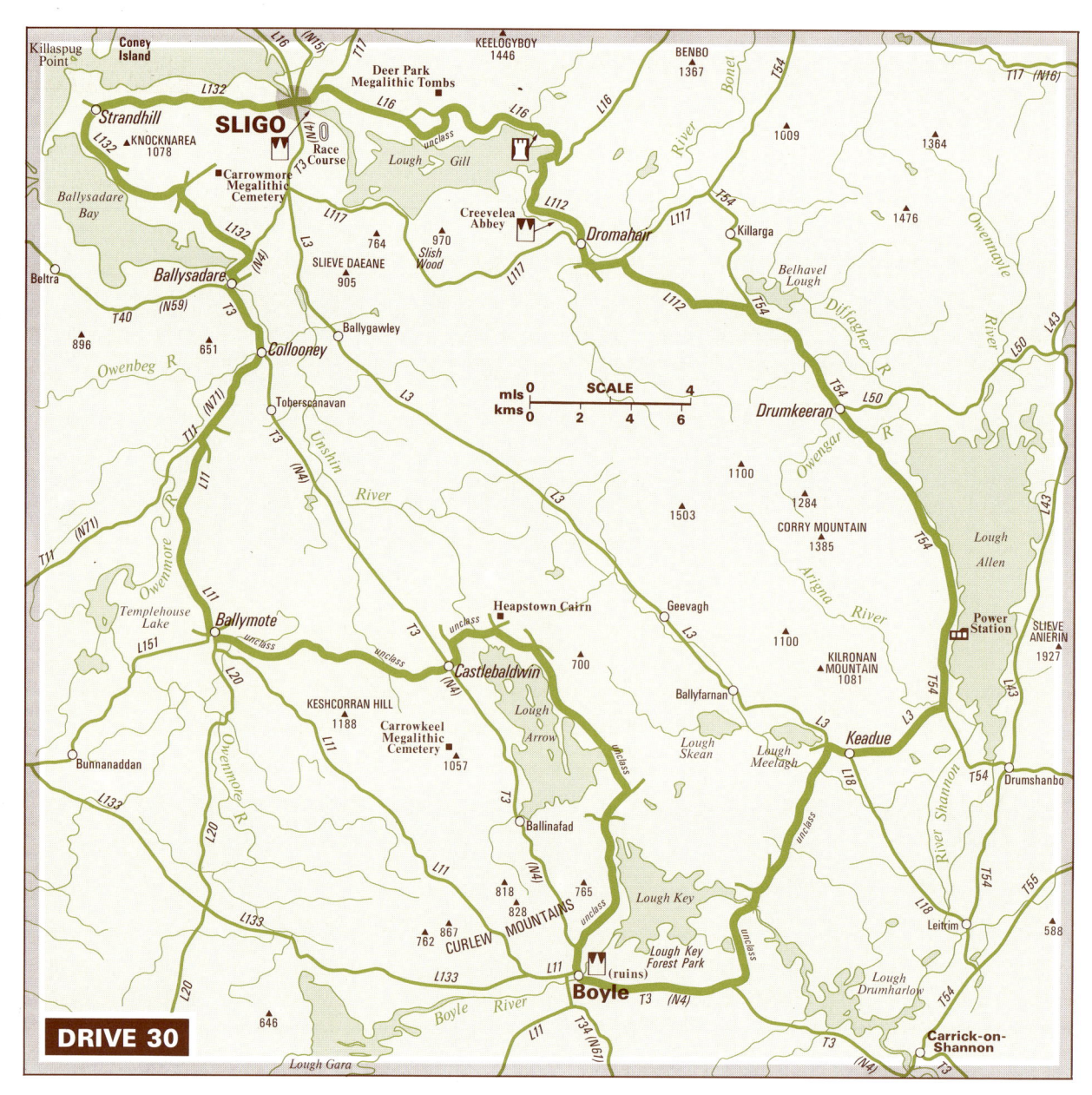

Lakes of Three Counties

From Sligo

Drive 30 87 miles

Follow SP 'Strandhill' to leave central *Sligo* via the L132 Knappagh Rd. After 5m bear left through *Strandhill*, and in 1½m continue alongside Ballysadare Bay. Shortly bear right, then in 2m meet X-roads and turn right SP 'Ballysadare'. In 2½m drive beneath a railway bridge and turn right on to the T3(N4), then bear right. In 1¼m turn right, cross the Ballysadare River into *Ballysadare*, turn left, and continue along the main road.

After 1¾m enter *Collooney*, cross the Owenmore River, and bear left. In ¼m turn right on to the T11(N17) SP 'Galway' into the town centre, then drive forward and bear right SP 'Galway, Ballymote'. After 2½m turn left on to the L11, cross a railway bridge, and immediately turn right SP 'Ballymote'. After another 5m turn left into *Ballymote*; in the town centre turn right with an ascent. Reach the church and turn left on to an unclassified road SP 'Lough Arrow'. Ascend, then after 6½m reach Castlebaldwin. Meet X-roads and go forward, then in ¼m bear left. In a further ½m turn right, and in 1¼m meet X-roads and turn right again. After another 1m meet X-roads and descend to the shores of Lough Arrow, then follow SP 'Boyle'. After 2m turn right, then leave the lough and in 1m turn right. In ¾m meet X-roads and drive forward. In another ¾m run close to Lough Key, and in 3m turn left on to the T3(N4). After ¾m meet X-roads at *Boyle*, go forward, and shortly bear left. In 3¾m go forward on to an unclassified road.

After another 1½m pass Fin Lough (left), then 1m farther cross the Boyle River at Knockvicar Bridge and immediately bear left. In ¼m turn right SP 'Keadue', and in ½m bear right. Continue with SP 'Keadue', then in 3¾m reach the edge of Lough Meelagh and turn right on to the L3. In ½m bear right into *Keadue*. Keep forward through the village, bear left on to the L3 SP 'Drumshanbo', and after 2¾m turn left on to the T54 'Manorhamilton' road. Cross the Arigna River and follow a main road, with glimpses of nearby Lough Allen (right). After 8½m enter *Drumkeeran* and keep forward SP 'Dromahair'. In 3¾m branch left to the L112, leave the hills, and gradually descend towards the Bonet Valley. After 3¾m meet X-roads and turn left then in ¾m turn right. Shortly bear right, and in ½m right again.

Cross the Bonet River into *Dromahair* and continue along the L112 SP 'Sligo' for 2m to *Lough Gill*. Meet a T-junction and turn left on to the L16 SP 'Sligo'. Continue alongside the lough, then after 2½m pass a lakeside carpark (left). In a further 1¾m ascend and branch left (unclassified) uphill SP 'Lough Gill Loop'. Descend and turn left to rejoin the L16, then in 2½m turn left on to the T17(N16) to re-enter Sligo.

CONNACHT – THE LAST REFUGE

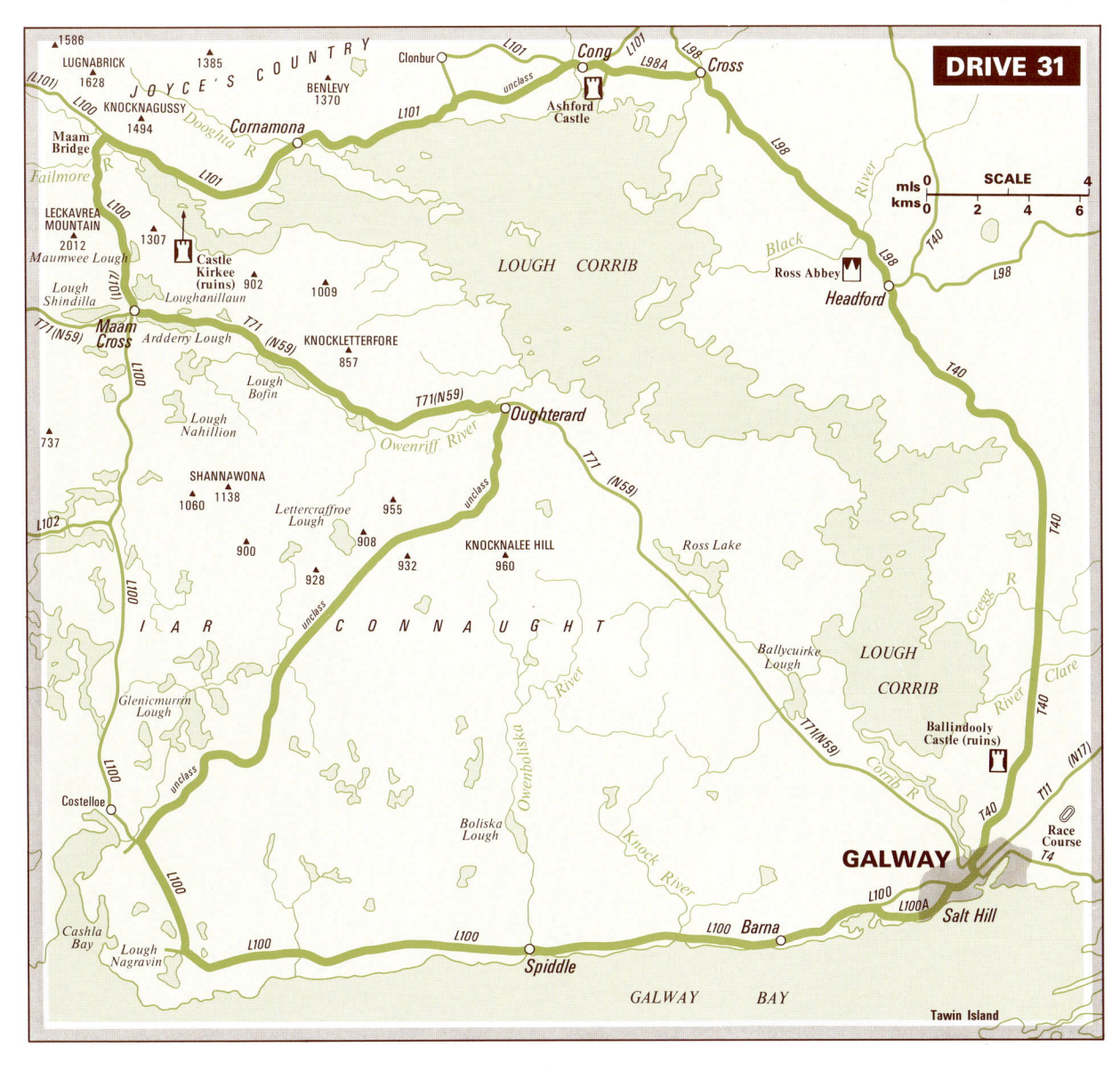

DRIVE 31

The Shores of Lough Corrib

From Galway

Drive 31   92 miles

Follow SP's 'Salt Hill' to leave *Galway* via the L100, and drive to the seaside resort of *Salt Hill*. Continue on the 'Spiddle' road, and in 1½m keep left SP 'Carraroe'. Follow the N coast of Galway Bay and pass through Barna before reaching the small angling resort of *Spiddal*. Views afforded by this part of the drive extend across the waters of the bay to the distant mountains of Co Clare.

Seascapes beyond Spiddal encompass the *Aran Islands*, while landward views take in a patchwork of little stone-walled fields – a prominent feature of this part of Ireland. After 9m branch right SP 'Costelloe', and turn inland to pass through barren rocky countryside. In 2¾m turn right on to an unclassified road SP 'Oughterard'. After a short distance the scenery becomes mountainous and the drive route affords views of numerous small lakes as it winds through the hills of the Iar Connaught district. After 8m enter a newly-afforested pine plantation, and later make a gradual descent towards *Oughterard* for fine views of distant *Lough Corrib*. On reaching Oughterard turn left on to the T71, then immediately right SP 'Westport'. Cross the Owenriff River and drive alongside it for a short distance. Enter the *Connemara* district, then after 10m reach *Maam Cross* and turn right on to the L100 SP 'Maam Bridge'. Drive over barren, open countryside before crossing higher ground with 2,012ft Leckavrea Mountain prominent to the left.

Continue to Maam Bridge with the Maumturk Mountains rising to the left and the hills of *Joyce's Country* ahead. Cross the Bealanabrack River at Maam Bridge and turn right SP 'Cong' to remain on the L101. After a short distance there are views of Lough Corrib's W arm – including the island-ruins of *Castle Kirke*, which is also known as *Hen's Castle*. After 1½m turn inland for a short distance and cross more high ground before continuing to *Cornamona*. Drive beyond this village and parallel the shore of attractive Lough Corrib for 2½m before once again turning inland. Make a winding ascent and turn right on to an unclassified road SP 'Cong', then continue through agricultural country criss-crossed with stone walls and studded with little farms. In another 2½m pass through Cong Woods, then keep forward to reach *Cong*. One of the major features offered by this interesting village is its largely-rebuilt Augustinian friary, a royal foundation dating from the 13thc. Drive to the old Market Cross in Cong and keep left SP 'Galway'. Leave the village, and after ½m pass the impressive gates of 19th-c *Ashford Castle*, which now serves as a hotel but was originally built for Arthur E Guinness. Keep forward with the L98 'Headford' road, and in 2½m turn right for the village of Cross. Continue along the L98 through undulating livestock-grazing country, and after 1½m keep left. After another 4¾m pass the ruins of Ross Abbey on the right and proceed into the small country town of *Headford*.

Join the T40 SP 'Galway', and continue the drive through flat, rather uninteresting countryside for almost 11m before crossing the River Clare. This river flows into Lough Corrib, which lies only 1m to the right but is not clearly visible from the road. In 2¾m pass the remains of Ballindooly Castle, then complete the drive by continuing along the T40 to Galway.

117

CONNACHT – THE LAST REFUGE

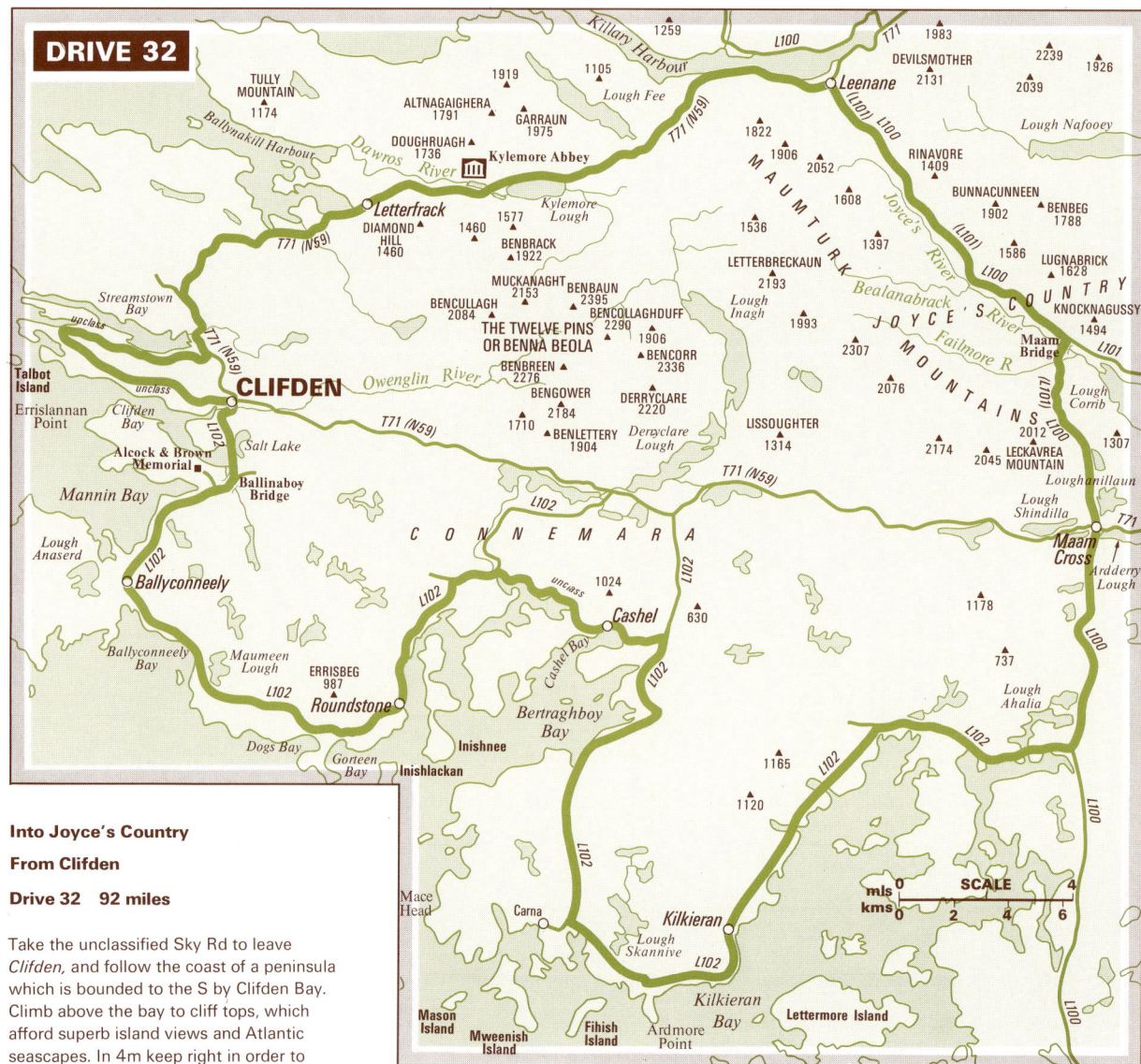

Into Joyce's Country

From Clifden

Drive 32   92 miles

Take the unclassified Sky Rd to leave *Clifden*, and follow the coast of a peninsula which is bounded to the S by Clifden Bay. Climb above the bay to cliff tops, which afford superb island views and Atlantic seascapes. In 4m keep right in order to return along the N side of the peninsula, and later follow the shore of Streamstown Bay. This part of the drive affords distant views of the *Twelve Bens*, or *Pins*; the highest of these mountains rises to 2,395ft. After 3¾m turn left on to the T71 SP 'Letterfrack, Leenane', and continue through barren countryside. In 1¾m bear right to cross open moorland, with further views of the Twelve Bens to the right. After another 1¾m the views to the left take in Ballynakill Harbour, backed by 1,174ft Tully Mountain. Continue, and later drive alongside Barnaderg Bay to reach *Letterfrack* in the shadow of 1,460ft Diamond Hill. Leave Letterfrack and continue, with 1,736ft Doughruagh ahead, before following the valley of the Dawros River and entering the Pass of Kylemore. The late 19th-c *Kylemore Abbey*, a castellated granite structure which was one of Ireland's last castle houses, is later passed on the left. This was built in 1860 for a rich Liverpool merchant and is constructed of stone from Dalkey.

Proceed to the attractive shoreline of Kylemore Lough. The stretch after the lough affords views of the Maumturk Mountains to the right. After 3m it is possible to catch a glimpse of Lough Fee to the left. Descend to the shores of picturesque *Killary Harbour*, from which views of the Mweelrea Mountains can be enjoyed. The 2,688ft Mweelrea dominates the range to which it gave its name and is the highest peak in Connacht. Continue to *Leenane*, which is pleasantly situated near the head of Killary Harbour, and branch right on to the L101 SP 'Maam Cross and Galway'. Cross higher ground for a while, then gradually descend through moorland scenery to enter the area known as *Joyce's Country*. This unofficially-named region derives its title from a Welsh family who moved here in the 13thc. Many of the local people count these early settlers among their ancestors. Follow the valley of Joyce's River with the Maumturk Mountains prominent to the right. Later on keep forward with the L100 to Maam Bridge, then turn right on to the L101 SP 'Maam Cross'. Cross Joyce's River and continue over higher ground with 2,012ft Leckavrea to the right.

Proceed through rather barren countryside to *Maam Cross*, then meet X-roads and go forward SP 'Screeb'. In 5½m keep forward on to the L102 SP 'Carna', and skirt the numerous inlets of the Atlantic Ocean which form a main feature of the S *Connemara* coast. In 4¾m cross a river bridge, then keep left and later follow the W shores of Kilkieran Bay to reach the village of *Kilkieran*. Continue with the L102 to the outskirts of *Carna*, meet a T-junction, and turn right SP 'Cashel' to turn inland. More views of the Twelve Bens are offered ahead. After 3½m rejoin the coast and skirt Bertraghboy Bay.

In a further 4m turn left on to an unclassified road SP 'Cashel and Roundstone', then after 1m pass Cashel Bay. In 4m turn left SP 'Roundstone' and rejoin the L102, then in 1m turn left again. The next section of the route offers extensive coastal views before taking the drive to the little fishing village of Roundstone. Continue along the Clifden road and later skirt Dog's and Ballyconneely Bays to reach *Ballyconneely*. Proceed N and shortly pass Mannin Bay. In 3¼m pass a track to the right which leads to the spot where famous aviators Alcock and Brown landed after the first trans-Atlantic flight in 1919. A memorial and viewpoint commemorating the event lie ½m to the left. In order to complete the drive, cross Ballinaboy Bridge and turn left, then later pass Salt Lake before returning to Clifden.

CONNACHT – THE LAST REFUGE

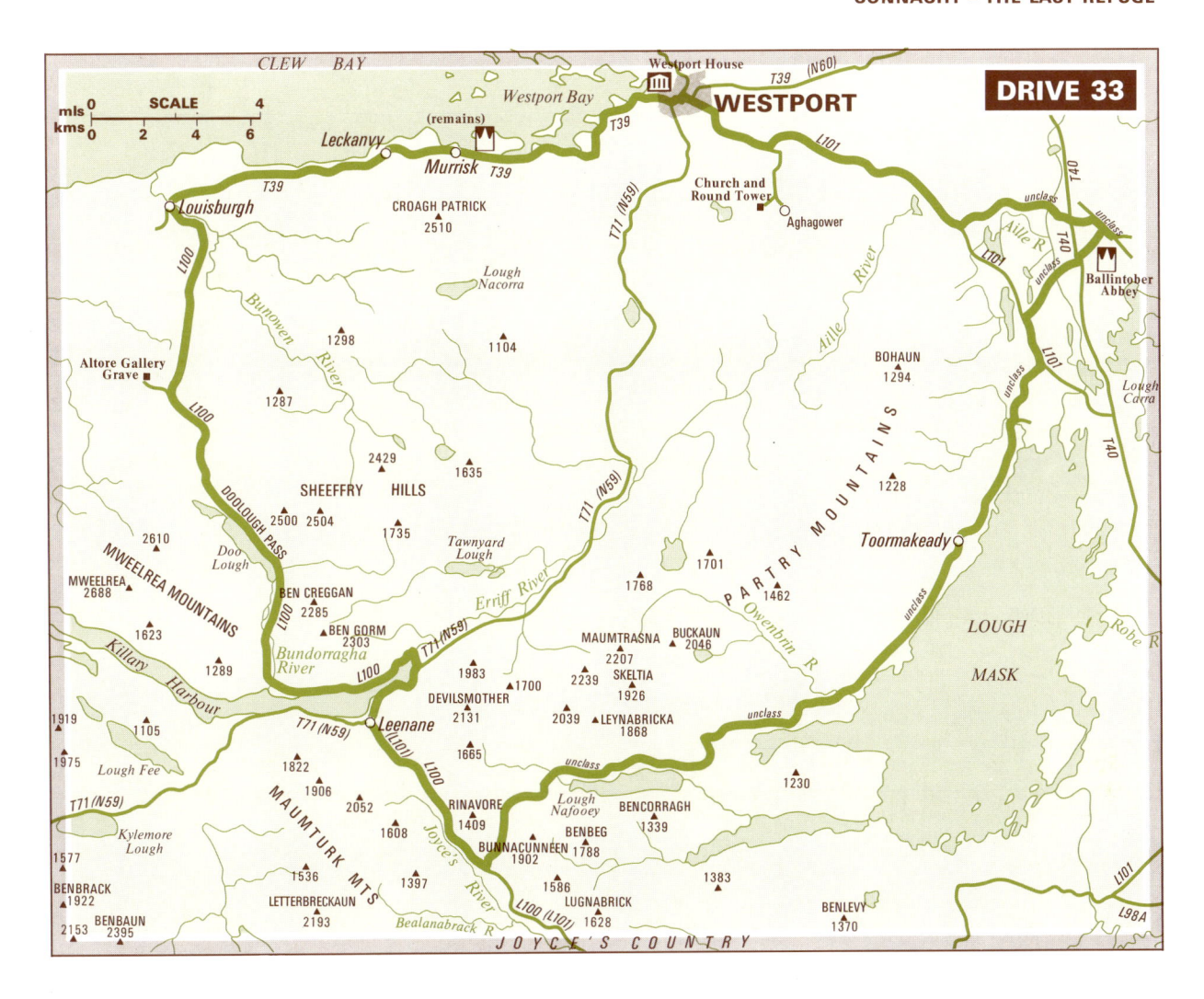

DRIVE 33

Pilgrimage to Croagh Patrick

From Westport

Drive 33   74 miles

Take the L101 'Ballinrobe' road to leave *Westport*. Drive through undulating farming country, and in 2¾m bear left. The side road to the right leads to *Aghagower*, where there is a 60ft round tower and ruined church which once formed part of a monastery – remains worth the detour. Continue with the L101 for 2½m to enjoy views of the distant Partry Mountains to the right. In another 2½m turn left on to an unclassified road SP 'Ballintober', then after 2¾m cross the T40 and continue to *Ballintober* Abbey (NM). This foundation was created in 1216 for the Augustinian order of monks, and the nave of the church was rebuilt in 1270 after fire damage. During the 19thc there was massive restoration of the structure, a process which has continued up to the present day.

Return along the road and in 200yds turn left; in 1¼m meet a main road and turn left and immediately right. Continue through scenery which becomes barren and open, offering more views of the Partry Mountains. Later turn left on to the L101 SP 'Partry', and after 1¼m turn right on to an unclassified road SP 'Toormakeady'. In 1½m keep forward and continue alongside *Lough Mask*. The Partry Mountains now rise to the right.

On reaching Toormakeady continue with the 'Leenane' road and shortly run along the shore of Lough Mask. After 2½m turn inland, then after more fine views of the lough cross higher ground before descending to the shores of Lough Nafooey. This picturesque, mountain-encircled lake is set in the heart of *Joyce's Country* – an unofficial area named after a 13th-c immigrant family from Wales. Cross the River Fooey and ascend through hills, with the peak of 1,902ft Bunnacunneen prominent to the left. In 2¾m meet a T-junction and turn right on to the L101 SP 'Leenane'. Follow the valley of Joyce's River through moorland, with the Maumturk Mountains to the left. Continue to Leenane, a village near the head of *Killary Harbour* with 2,303ft Ben Gorm ahead.

Turn right in the village on to the T71 SP 'Westport'. Follow the S side of the harbour, with 2,131ft *Devil's Mother* to the right, and after 2m turn left on to the L100 SP 'Louisburgh'. Cross the Erriff River, with Aasleagh Falls to the right. Proceed along the N side of Killary Harbour for 4m, then turn inland and continue along the Bundorragha River valley. To the left the Mweelrea Mountains are dominated by 2,688ft Mweelrea, which is the highest peak in Connacht. Drive to *Delphi* Bridge and follow the shores of Doo Lough through the Doo Lough Pass, which was constructed in 1806. Continue over open moors with the Sheeffry Hills to the right. After 4¾m pass a left turn leading to the Altore wedge-shaped gallery grave. Beyond this turning the route affords first views of *Croagh Patrick* – the Holy Mountain (right). St Patrick is said to have fasted on the mountain for 40 days, and the tradition of pilgrimage is still maintained here on the last Sunday in July. Many of the pilgrims complete the arduous course in bare feet. At the N base of Croagh Patrick's cone is a ravine known as Log-na-nDeamhan. Legend maintains that it was here that Patrick rang his bell to rid Ireland of all venomous creatures. Near the S base is Lough na Corra, said to have risen when St Patrick hurled the demon Corra from the mountain. In 4½m turn right on to the T39 to enter *Louisburgh*, then continue with the 'Westport' road and later run alongside the S shore of Clew Bay.

Continue, passing through Leckanvy to *Murrisk*, a small village under the shadow of Croagh Patrick. A footpath from Murrisk leads to the mountain's 2,510ft summit, where there is a chapel in which mass is celebrated on special occasions. Continue, passing the remains of Murrisk Abbey on the left, and skirt Westport Bay. Later pass the entrance to Westport House and return to Westport.

Placenames in *italic* type are worth stopping at; each is listed and described in the main gazetteer section.

CONNACHT – THE LAST REFUGE

The Giant Horseshoe

From Bundoran

Drive 34   104 miles

Leave central *Bundoran* with SP 'Manorhamilton T54', pass a church on the left, and bear right SP 'Kinlough, Melvin'. Cross the Drowes River, then in ¾m bear left SP 'Kinlough'. After another ½m enter *Kinlough*, and on the nearside of the village centre turn left on to an unclassified road SP 'Lough Melvin' to continue through well-wooded countryside with high ground rising to 1,720ft on the right. After 5m reach the shores of Lough Melvin. Views here extend over the island-scattered lake to the hills of N Ireland. Proceed to the end of the lough, cross the Glenaniff River, and in ½m turn right on to the L16. Shortly enter *Rossinver*.

At X-roads turn left on to an unclassified road. Proceed to *Kiltyclogher*, meet X-roads near the memorial, and go forward SP 'Glenfarne, Blacklion'. Continue through wooded country at the base of 1,425ft Thur Mountain, and later drive high above Lough Macnean Upper (left). After 6m (from Kiltyclogher) meet a T-junction and turn left on to the T17(N16) 'Blacklion' road. In 2¾m turn right on to the L43 SP 'Dowra, Carrick-on-Shannon', and after some 4m join the Shannon Valley. This river rises from the slopes of 1,949ft Tiltinbane, seen to the left. Continue for 4m, passing 1,787ft Slievenakilla (left), to reach Dowra. Keep forward along the L50 through Dowra, following the River Shannon for some distance. After 3½m (from Dowra) pass fairly close to Lough Allen, then in a further 3½m enter *Drumkeeran*. Turn right on to the T54 SP 'Manorhamilton' and in 3¾m bear right. In ½m pass the edge of Belhavel Lough, then in a further 1¾m drive through Killarga.

In 4¾m turn left to enter *Manorhamilton*. Turn left and shortly left again on to the T17(N16) 'Sligo' road, cross the Bonet River valley, and shortly pass 1,367ft Benbo Hill (left). Continue along a valley with mountain views to the left, and in 7½m (from Manorhamilton) turn right on to an unclassified road SP 'Glencar and Glencar Waterfall'. Continue along the Diffreen River valley for 1¾m to reach *Glencar* Lough. A footpath to the right leads to the Glencar Waterfalls. Continue along the shore, then in 2m – just beyond the end of the lough – bear left SP 'Sligo' and cross the Drumcliff River. In 1m turn right to rejoin the T17 (N16). In 1½m meet a T-junction, turn sharp right on to an unclassified road, and in 2m meet X-roads. Turn right on to the T18 (N15) 'Sligo–Bundoran' road and in 1m pass through *Drumcliff*. Shortly recross the Drumcliff River, and in ¼m turn left on to an unclassified road SP 'Lissadell House, Carney'. In 1¼m reach Carney and turn left SP 'Lissadell House'. In 1¼m pass the entrance to *Lissadell* House, and in a further 1¼m – near another entry – turn right. In 2½m go forward across a main road SP 'Ballinatrillick' and drive along the lower slopes of 1,730ft *Benbulben*. In 1½m bear right, then in 4m turn right SP 'Gleniff Horseshoe'. Benweskin rises to 1,702ft on the right, and 2,120ft Truskmore is visible to the left across the bowl-shaped valley. Climb to an 800ft summit, with the sides of the bowl rising to 2,000ft above sea level on the right. Continue round the valley's horseshoe rim and later pass a right turn leading to a TV transmitter on the summit of Truskmore. Magnificent views are available from here. Descend, and in 2½m – on leaving the mountains – meet X-roads and keep forward. In 3m reach *Creevykeel* X-roads and cross a main road SP 'Mullaghmore'. To the right of this point is the Creevykeel Court Cairn (NM). In ¾m pass Bunduff Lough on the right, then in a further ¾m reach the entrance to Classie Bawn Castle and bear left. In ½m reach the shores of Donegal Bay, with the castle and *Inishmurray* Island clearly visible. Continue round a headland, reach the small resort of *Mullaghmore* on the edge of Bunduff Strand, and proceed through the village. In 1m, at the entrance to Classie Bawn Castle, turn left. Pass Bunduff Lough (left) again, meet Creevykeel X-roads, and turn left on to the T18(N15) 'Sligo – Bundoran' road. Return to Bundoran.

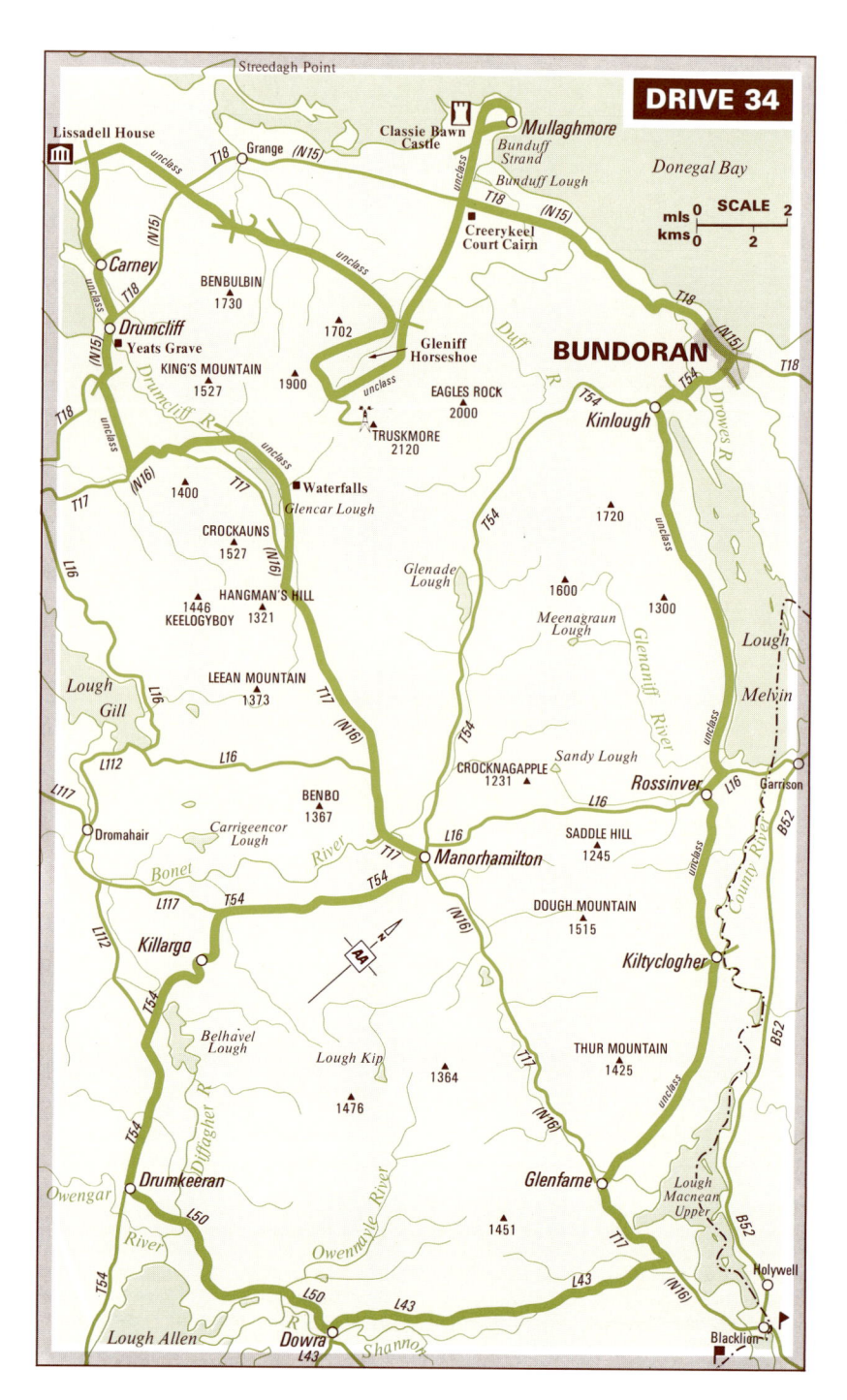

CONNACHT – THE LAST REFUGE

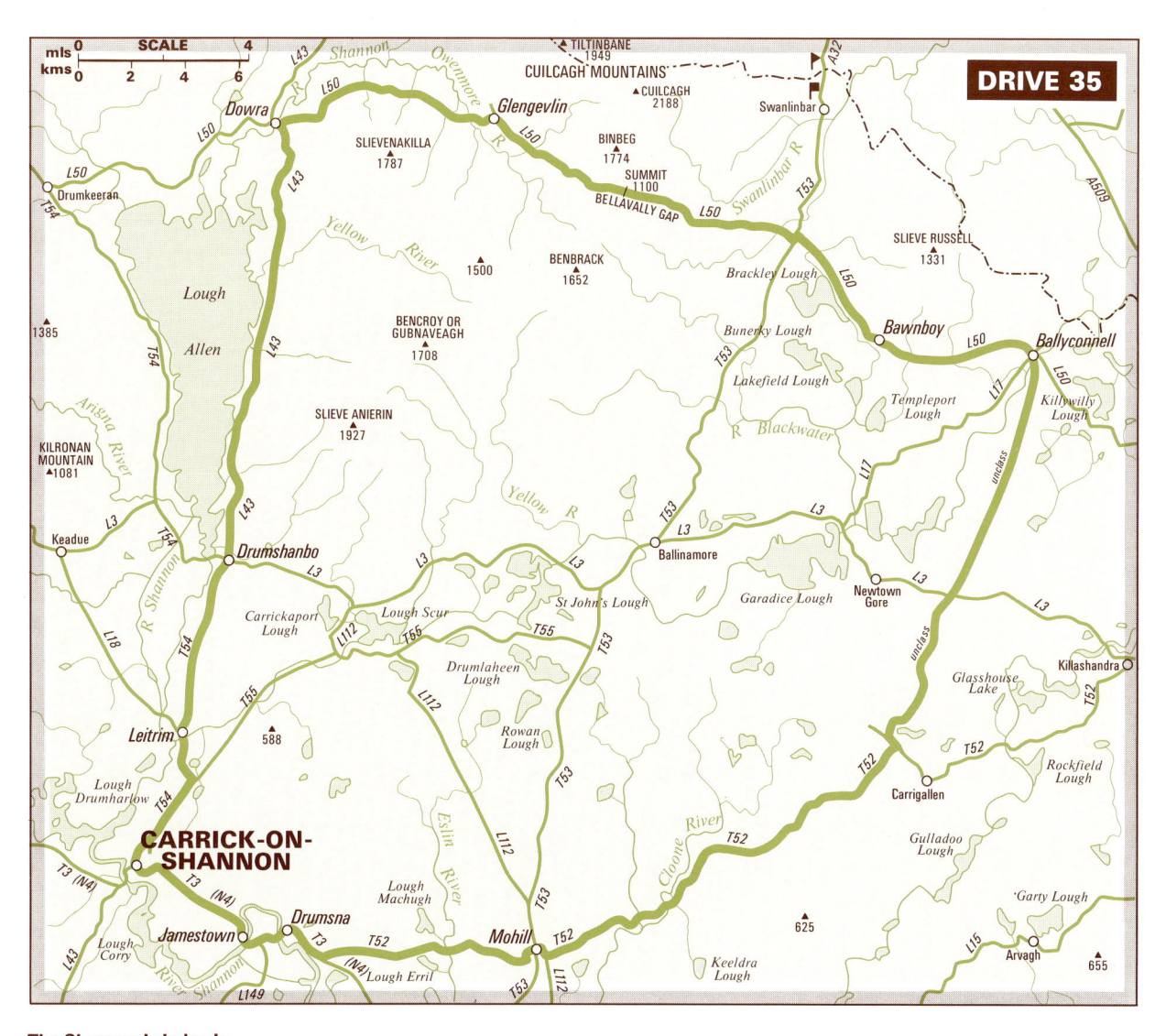

DRIVE 35

The Shannon Lakelands

From Carrick-on-Shannon

Drive 35   73 miles

Carrick-on-Shannon, the county town of Leitrim, is a major centre for boating and various other water sports. Its massive locks and water works date from the 1800s and were built by the cheap labour which flooded the market during successive famines. Depart Carrick-on-Shannon via the T3(N4) 'Dublin' road and in 3m pass through *Jamestown,* which stands on the River Shannon. In ½m bear left to cross the river, then in ¾m recross the Shannon to reach *Drumsna –* where there is a prehistoric earthwork measuring some ½m in length.

After 1½m (from Drumsna) turn left on to the T52 SP 'Mohill'. Proceed through level, well-wooded countryside and pass several small loughs on both sides of the road. After 5½m reach Mohill and follow SP 'Monaghan' through the village. In ¼m bear left SP 'Carrigallen' and continue along the T52 with SP 'Carrigallen', passing through well-wooded countryside. In 11¼m meet a T-junction and turn sharp left on to an unclassified road. After a short distance turn right SP 'Ballyconnell', then proceed through hilly and well-wooded farmland. Distant views take in 1,331ft Slieve Russell and the Cuilcagh Mountains. In 10m reach *Ballyconnell,* turn left into the village, then go forward on to the L50 SP 'Bawnboy'. Skirt Slieve Russell on the right, and in 4m reach Bawnboy. Keep forward SP 'Glengevlin', and in 1m skirt Brackley Lough on the left. Views ahead take in Cuilcagh – which rises to 2,188ft from the Cuilcagh Mountains – plus 1,652ft Benbrack standing in front of 1,708ft Bencroy and 1,927ft Slieve Anierin to the left. Reach the end of the lake, then after 1m turn left on to the T53. In 200yds turn right on to the L50 SP 'Glengevlin'. Begin an ascent and pass through bogland with forestry plantations visible to the right. Views from the higher ground extend left over the lake-studded area around *Ballinamore,* and to the right of the gap in which *Swanlinbar* is situated.

Climb steadily to the 1,100ft summit of the *Bellavally Gap,* which affords fine forward views along the broad valley of the Owenmore River to distant mountains. Binbeg stands at 1,774ft on the right of the pass, opposite an un-named hill which rises to 1,600ft. Descend into the valley and after 4m reach Glengevlin. Bear left, cross the valley, then climb to slightly higher ground below 1,787ft Slievenakilla – which can be seen to the left. Views right take in 1,949ft Tiltinbane, the extreme W summit of the Cuilcagh range. The lower slopes of this mountain feature the *Shannon Pot,* which is the source of the River Shannon. Views of another wide gap to the N, beyond which are Lough Macnean Upper and N Ireland, can be enjoyed as the route runs above the Shannon and swings round to the SW.

Descend into Dowra, meet a T-junction, and turn left on to the L43 'Carrick-on-Shannon' road. Descend to the edge of mountain-ringed Lough Allen, with Slievenakilla and the valley of the Yellow River on the left, and continue along a level stretch of the route which affords views across the lough. Approach *Drumshanbo,* at the S end of the lough, with Slieve Anierin rising to the left. Enter the village and turn left on to the T54 SP 'Carrick-on-Shannon', then turn right to follow a broad road through well-wooded agricultural country. In 4m pass the small village of *Leitrim,* which stands on the Ballinamore and Ballyconnell Canal. In a further 3½m re-enter Carrick-on-Shannon.

121

CONNACHT – THE LAST REFUGE

To the Shores of Lough Conn

From Castlebar

Drive 36   60 miles

Historic *Castlebar* is the county town of Mayo and has many interesting associations with Ireland's past. It was here, at the Imperial Hotel, that Michael Davitt founded the Land League during the time when the notorious Lord Lucan was forcing eviction on his tenants. Lucan was a member of the hated Bingham family. Leave the town centre via the L136 Shamble St and cross a river bridge. Turn right SP 'Foxford, Ballina' into Chapel St and pass a church on the right, then meet X-roads and turn left into an unclassified road. Keep straight on to enter hilly, rather infertile country, then in 2m look left for distant views of 2,510ft *Croagh Patrick* and the *Connemara* mountains. Croagh Patrick is one of the most famous mountains in Ireland, and is traditionally the place where St Patrick withdrew to fast for the Lent period. After a further ½m pass through extensive forestry plantations, and shortly ascend to the top of a low rise. This affords views of Lough Sallagher to the left. Some 4m from Castlebar is a right turn which leads up to the TV transmitter on the 1,412 summit of Croaghmoyle, the highest peak of its range and an excellent viewpoint.

The next section of the route becomes undulating and offers forward views of Lough Beltra, which lies in front of the Nephin Beg Mountains. The main heights visible from here include 1,912ft Bengorm above Lough Feeagh, 1,935ft Buckoogh, and 2,295ft Birreencorragh. Pass Glenisland Wood on the left and descend to reach the L136. Meet this junction and go forward, then in 1m cross a river bridge to reach the shores of Lough Beltra. To the right are the wooded slopes of 1,078ft Birreen, while 1,695ft Knockaffertagh and the conical peak of 2,646ft Nephin rise ahead. Birreencorragh is visible to the left. Pass the end of the lake and continue for ¾m, with the Crumpaun River valley separating the two mountains ahead, and meet staggered X-roads at the edge of *Beltra* hamlet. Turn right on to an unclassified road SP 'Lahardaun, Crossmolina', and drive along Glen Nephin with bogland stretching back to the forested slopes of Nephin Mountain to the left. Rocky slopes rise to the right. Make a small ascent for forward views over *Lough Conn*, and in 1½m meet a T-junction and turn left. In 1m drive straight ahead, and again in 1m keep forward. Pass extensive forestry plantations to the right, and beyond these enjoy good views over Lough Conn. Shortly go forward on to the L140 SP 'Crossmolina', and pass through the village of Lahardaun. In 2m bear right to cross undulating grazing land, then in 1½m meet a junction and bear right. In ¼m pass an unclassified road to the right allowing access to ruined Errew Abbey on a long, narrow peninsula in the lough.

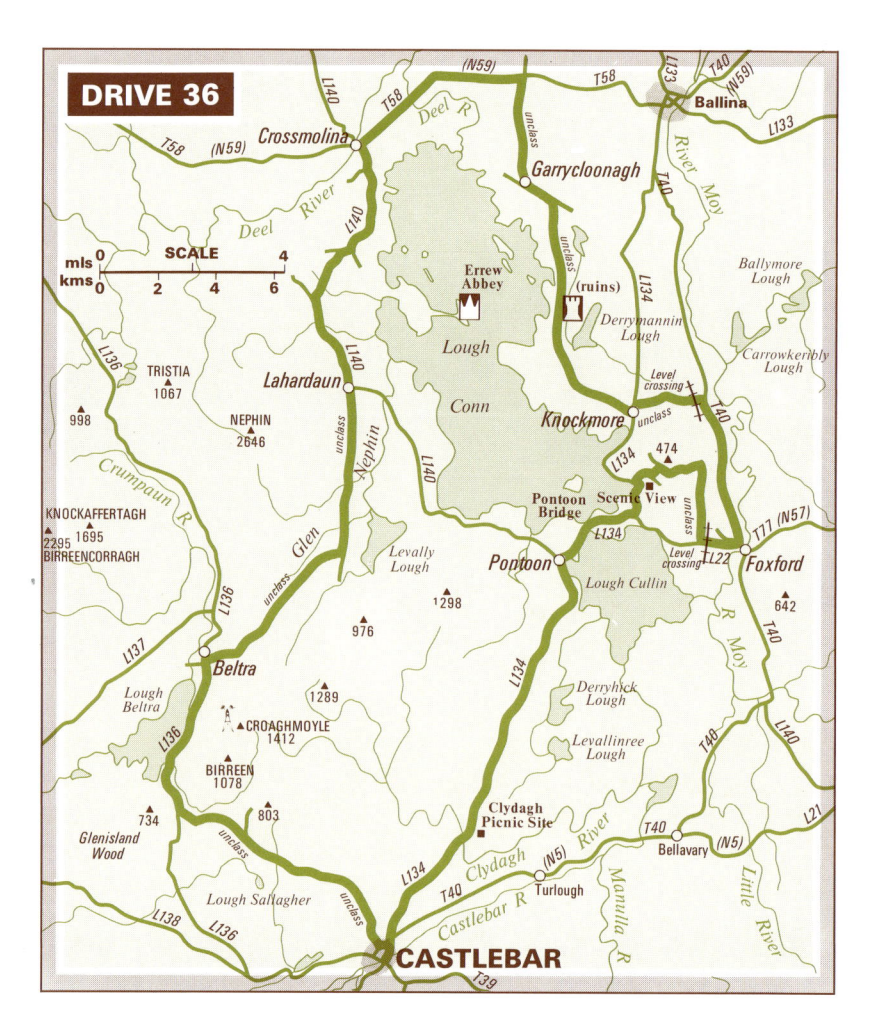

Continue the drive through pleasant countryside and scrubland, then after 2¾m reach *Crossmolina* on the River Deel. On reaching the centre of the village turn right on to the T58(N59) SP 'Ballina'. Drive over more grazing land at the N end of Lough Conn, and in 2m enter a belt of dense woodland. After a further 2m meet X-roads and turn right on to a narrow unclassified road, with Nephin Mountain visible to the right. In 2m meet a T-junction and turn left, then in 1m bear right to pass fairly close to the shores of Lough Conn. In 2m go forward and pass a ruined castle on the left, then continue across predominantly flat grazing land. In 3½m reach Knockmore village and turn left on to the L134, then right on to an unclassified road. Climb this narrow section of the drive through scrubland, crossing the edge of Stoneparkbrogan Hill before descending to pass over a level crossing. Meet a T-junction and turn right on to the T40(N58). Proceed through boggy countryside, with the Moy River to the left in front of the distant Ox Mountains, and dense forest to the right. Drive to the edge of *Foxford* and before reaching the river bridge turn sharp right on to the L22 SP 'Pontoon', then bear left. In ¾m go over a level crossing, then immediately turn right on to an unclassified road SP 'Scenic Route'. Follow this narrow road and gradually ascend through extensive woodland, with good views over Foxford to the right. After 1½m turn sharp left and continue to climb. After a further ¾m reach the road summit below the top of Stoneparkbrogan Hill. Panoramic views from here take in Lough Conn and the Nephin Beg Mountains ahead, with Lough Cullin to the left. In just over ½m turn left SP 'Scenic View Carpark' and ascend. Meet a T-junction and turn right, then in ½m reach the Scenic View carpark. Descend steeply to the lake shore and meet a T-junction. Turn left on to the L134, and in 1m keep forward SP 'Pontoon'. After 1m cross the stream which separates Lough Conn from Lough Cullin, via *Pontoon Bridge*.

Follow the shores of Lough Cullin to the forest-backed village of Pontoon, meet a T-junction, and turn left SP 'Castlebar'. In 1m follow the route away from the lake, through scenery which gradually changes to moorland and hills to the right and poor grazing land to the left. After 5m (from Pontoon) climb a rise in the road for views ahead over Castlebar to the distant Partry Mountains. Croagh Patrick rises to the right. Pass bogland to the right, with Clydagh Wood and Picnic Site on the left, and cross the Clydagh River. Gradually descend past Tucker's Lough. After a while go forward on to the T40(N5) to re-enter Castlebar.

CONNACHT – THE LAST REFUGE

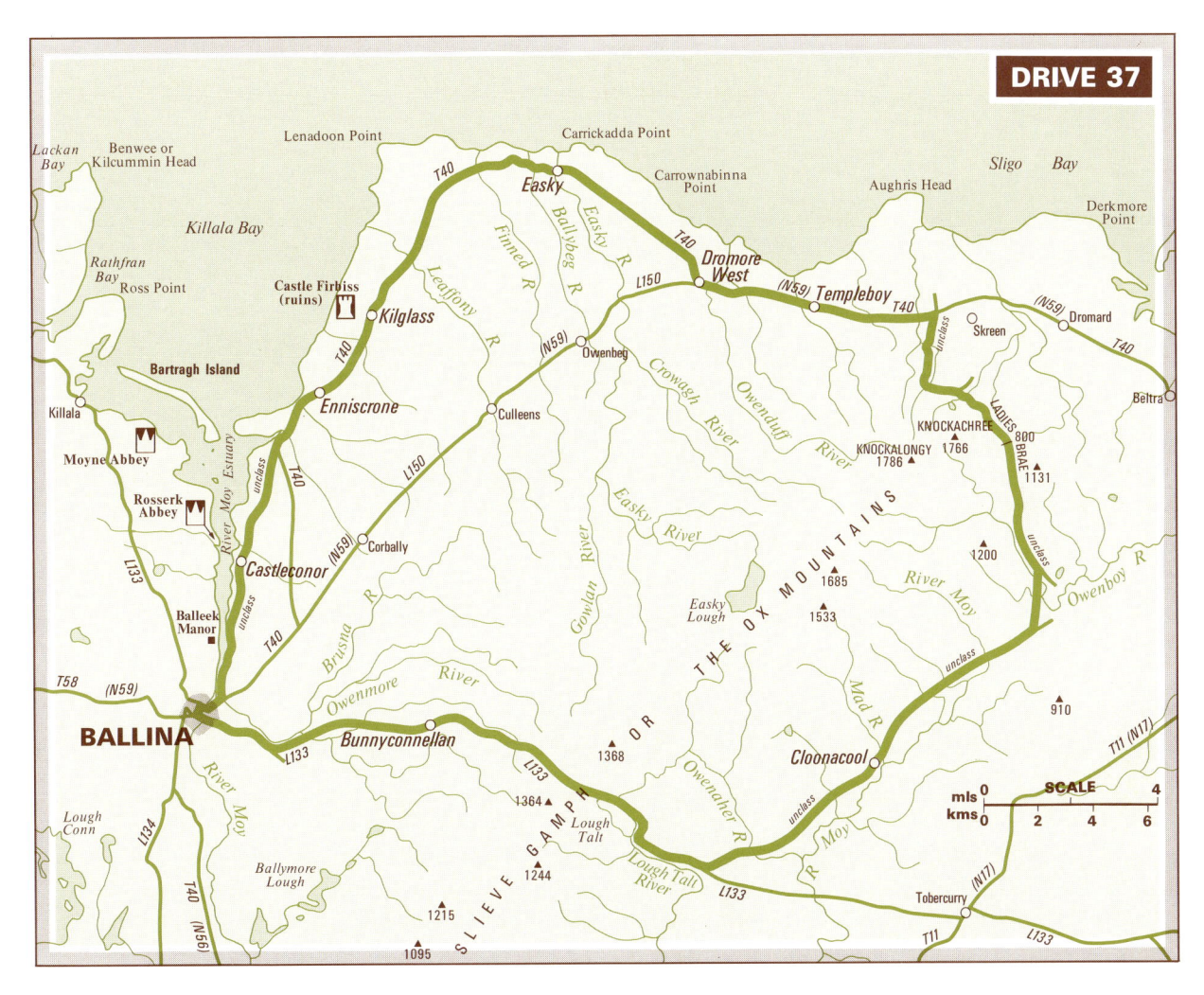

DRIVE 37

Tour of the Ox Mountains

From Ballina

Drive 37   58 miles

This town stands on the River Moy and is the largest in Co Mayo. Of interest here are the remains of a 15th-c Augustinian Friary, which can be seen near the RC cathedral. Leave *Ballina* by following Bridge St and the L133 Abbey St, a wide level road which affords distant views of the Ox Mountains. After 1¼m reach the Owenmore River, and in ½m bear left. After another 4m pass Bunnyconnellan and follow SP 'Lough Talt'.

Gradually ascend into the Slieve Gamph, also known as the Ox Mountains, and reach a 600ft road summit. Descend past Lough Talt. Good views ahead extend over the Moy basin towards *Tobercurry*. Continue to the foot of the descent and branch left on to a narrow unclassified road. In 1m cross the Owenaher River, then after a further 4m enter Cloonacool. Drive on with SP 'Coolaney' and skirt the Ox Mountains, which rise to 1,683ft on the left. The Moy Valley can be seen to the right of the road. After 4½m turn left SP 'Skreen', and in 1½m cross the Owenboy River before turning left to follow it into the mountains. Ascend past the head of the river, following SP 'Ladies Brae' and pass extensive forestry plantations on the surrounding slopes. To the left the mountain range is dominated by its highest peaks – 1,786ft Knockalongy and 1,766ft Knockachree. Continue to the 800ft pass known as Ladies Brae, then descend to enjoy a magnificent panoramic view which extends across the waters of Sligo Bay to *Ben Bulben* and King's Head (on the right). *Inishmurray Island* and the Donegal coast are visible ahead, while further views take in the coast as far as *Easky* to the left, plus 1,078ft Knocknarea and *Strandhill* on the right. Meet a T-junction and turn left, then in 2½m meet X-roads and turn left on to the T40(N59) 'Ballina' road. To the right of this road is the village of *Skreen*. An interesting feature of the area is Lough Achree, which lies 2m S of Skreen in the foothills of the Ox Mountains and is sometimes refered to as Ireland's youngest lake. It was formed by a volcano during the 15thc. Proceed along the coastal plain, and in 5½m enter *Dromore West*. This village is situated on the short Dunneill River, and boasts the ruins of a medieval church which was used by the Church of Ireland during the 18thc.

Bear right on to the T40 SP 'Enniscrone'. Follow a reasonably level road through agricultural country to enjoy views over Sligo Bay. Continue to Easky, where a curiously split rock known as Finn Mac Cool's Fingerstone can be seen. It is thought that this may be a relic of the ice ages. In 2m follow the route SW to skirt the E side of attractive Killala Bay. Proceed to Kilglass, where ruined Castle Firbis can be seen in the distance to the right. This castle was once one of the many strongholds held by the Mac Firbis family. Duald Mac Firbis was one of the greatest Irish genealogists and came from a long line of ancestors who had made their names in the same field. The famous *Great Book of Lecan* and *Yellow Book of Lecan* were both compiled here, the latter in the 15thc. Kilglass itself is a resort near several prehistoric sites, and offers good surf bathing.

After a further 3m enter the village of *Enniscrone*. Leave this village, still with the T40, and in 1½m branch right on to an unclassified road SP 'Ballina'. Follow the estuary of the salmon-rich River Moy, and after 4½m drive along the river bank. The well-wooded grounds of Belleek Manor can be seen on the opposite side of the Moy. After a further 1½m turn right on to the T40(N59), to re-enter Ballina.

Placenames in *italic* type are worth stopping at; each is listed and described in the main gazetteer section.

CONNACHT – THE LAST REFUGE

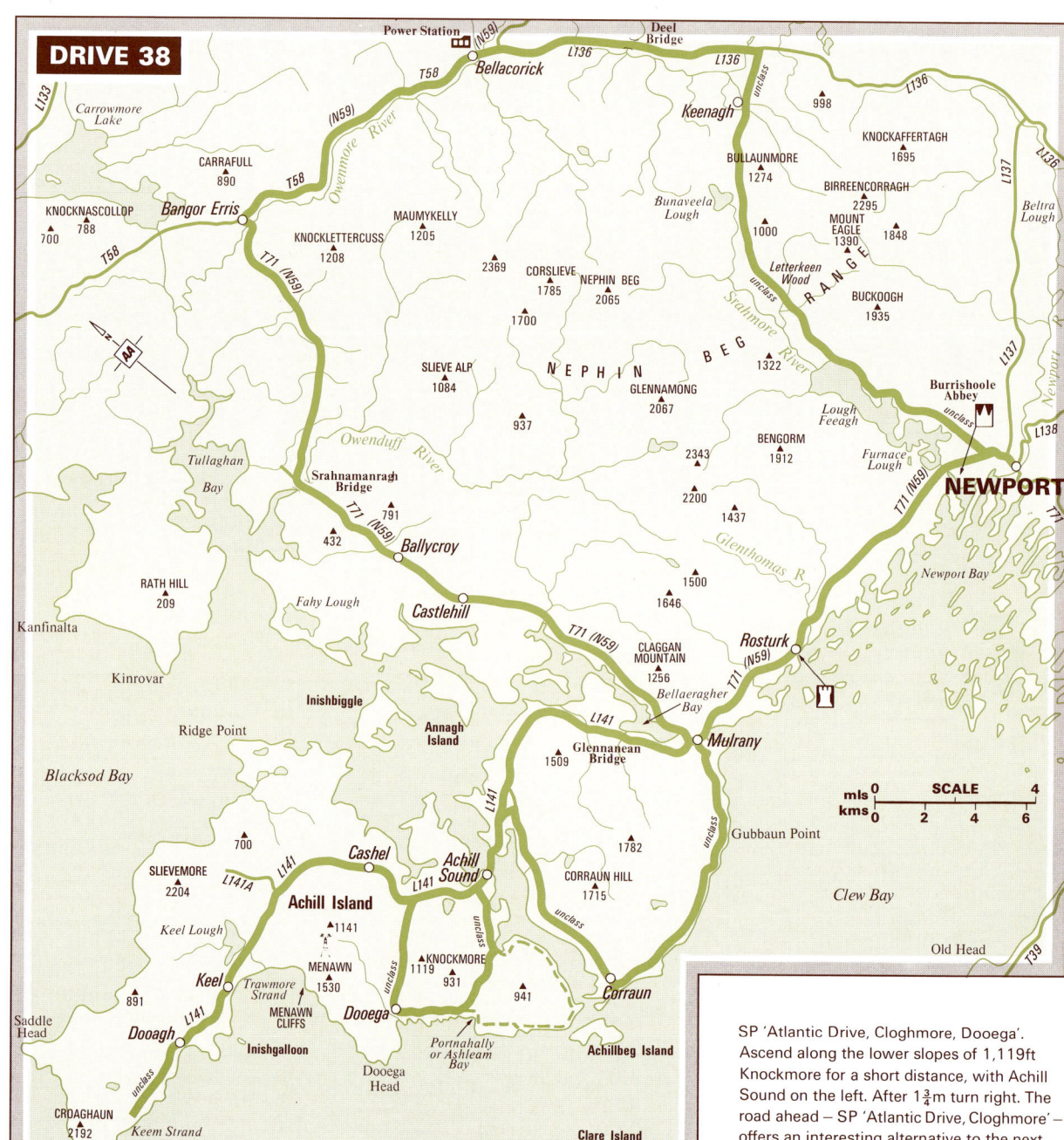

Into Achill Island

From Newport

Drive 38   119 miles

Follow SP 'Achill T71(N59)' from *Newport* and shortly bear left SP 'Achill, Mulrany'. The Nephin Beg range is visible ahead and to the right, while famous *Croagh Patrick* rises to 2,510ft from the S shores of Clew Bay (left). After 1½m pass SP 'Burrishoole Abbey' on the left. Carrigahooly Castle (NM) stands adjacent to the abbey. In a further ½m cross Burrishoole Bridge and continue with views of the 1,784ft Corraun Peninsula ahead. After 3m the drive affords views left of island-studded Clew Bay. In another 2m pass Rosturk Castle on a headland to the left, shortly drive through a plantation, and in a further 2½m enter *Mulrany*. Views from here extend across the strand to Croagh Patrick and the *Connemara* mountains, right to 1,256ft Claggan, and ahead to the Corraun Peninsula. Drive through Mulrany and turn left on to an unclassified road SP 'Corraun Coast Road'. Continue close to the shore of the Corraun Peninsula, and after about 4m note *Clare Island* rising to 1,520ft offshore. The smaller island of Achill Beg is visible after several more miles. In 8m (from Mulrany) turn right into Corraun and follow Achill Sound N, with Kildownet Castle standing opposite on the shores of *Achill Island*. Pass beneath 1,715ft Corraun Hill, and in 2¼m negotiate a bend which affords fine views over the sound. Descend gradually and in 3m turn left. In ½m turn left again on to the L141 SP 'Achill Sound'. In 1½m cross the sound to reach Achill Island, enter the village of Achill Sound, and keep forward along the main street. Shortly beyond the village turn left on to an unclassified road SP 'Atlantic Drive, Cloghmore, Dooega'. Ascend along the lower slopes of 1,119ft Knockmore for a short distance, with Achill Sound on the left. After 1¾m turn right. The road ahead – SP 'Atlantic Drive, Cloghmore' – offers an interesting alternative to the next section and can be followed alongside the sound, past Kildownet Castle, Cloghmore, and Achill Beg Island, thence along the Atlantic shoreline to rejoin the main drive after 7m. If following the main route, drive along a valley between two 900ft hills, and in 1¼m meet a road junction (the termination of the alternative section). Keep forward SP 'Keel, Dooega' and proceed along the coast for 1½m with 818ft Dooega Head on the left and Knockmore again on the right. Reach *Dooega*, meet a T-junction and turn right SP 'Keel, Doogort', then follow a long, gradual climb inland between Knockmore and 1,530ft Menawn (left). After 2¾m descend to the L141 and turn left SP 'Doogort, Keel'. In ¾m pass a narrow left turn SP 'Menawn Heights', leading to a transmitter and view vantage point. Continue along the L141 with SP 'Keel', pass Cashel, and later climb over a low ridge. Views right and ahead take in the conical, 2,204ft bulk of Slievemore Mountain. In 2½m pass Keel Lough on the

Land of the Ulster Legends

In Ulster the counties of Northern Ireland are divided from the Republic by a strange, eccentric boundary which wanders aimlessly through the province in complete ignorance of ancient or natural limits.

Drive 38 continued

right, with views left over Trawmore Strand to the impressive, 800ft Menawn Cliffs – behind Cathedral Rocks. After another 1m enter *Keel* and continue forward on the L141. In 2m pass the village of *Dooagh* – where the road loses its classification – and in a further $2\frac{1}{2}$m reach Keem Strand. The high sea cliffs of 2,192ft Croaghaun Mountain rise from the waters of this secluded bay. Return to Dooagh – where the road becomes the L141 – and proceed through Keel and Cashel to Achill Sound.

Recross the sound to leave Achill Island and keep forward on the L141 SP 'Mulrany', then continue along the N side of the Corraun Peninsula. After a while skirt Bellacragher Bay beneath Claggan Mountain (left) and approach Mulrany. After 8m (from Achill Sound) meet a T-junction and turn left on to the T71(N59) SP 'Bangor Erris, Ballycroy'. Follow Bellacragher Bay for several miles. Once clear of Claggan Mountain the route affords views of the coast to the left and the distant Nephin Beg range to the right. After 12m (from Mulrany) cross the Owenduff River at *Srahnamanragh Bridge*, and in $7\frac{1}{4}$m cross the Owenmore River into *Bangor Erris*. Meet a T-junction and turn right on to the T58(N59) SP 'Ballina, Bellacorick'. Follow the Owenmore Valley for 8m to reach *Bellacorick*. Views left of the approach to this village encompass bogland which is mechanically worked to supply fuel for a local peat-fired power station. In $\frac{1}{2}$m (from Bellacorick) branch right on to the L136 SP 'Castlebar' and continue with distant views of the Nephin Beg range.

After $3\frac{1}{2}$m cross the Deel River, then in a further $3\frac{1}{2}$m meet X-roads – with 1,067ft Tristia and 2,646ft Nephin directly ahead – and turn right on to an unclassified road SP Newport'. Climb the foothills of 2,295ft Birreencorragh for $2\frac{1}{4}$m to a 700ft summit. Descend past Lough Bunaveela, and in another 1m enter Letterkeen Wood. This section of road is poorly surfaced and frequently restricted by gates. After $2\frac{1}{2}$m leave the forest and enter the Srahmore River valley. In $1\frac{1}{2}$m reach Lough Feeagh and follow its shores for several miles. Leave the lough and after $\frac{1}{2}$m meet X-roads; keep forward SP 'Newport', with occasional views of Lough Furnace (right). In $2\frac{1}{4}$m meet a T-junction and turn left on to the T71(N59) SP 'Newport'. In $\frac{3}{4}$m re-enter Newport village.

Prehistoric boundary markers stand aloof from modern adaptations, ignoring them with all the pride of an iron-age aristocracy who valued poetry and battle-glory higher than life itself. This was the land where bloody and incredible deeds from *The Tain* were enacted some 1,200 years ago, when heroic Cuchulainn defended his king's border single-handed against Queen Maeve's armed pursuit of the fabulous Brown Bull of Cooley.

The Ulster countryside – sparsely-populated landscapes that shift between extremes with bewildering rapidity – exudes an atmosphere redolent of cloudy legend and populated by the memories of warrior kings. Across the border in the north west of the province is Co Donegal, a giant peninsula wrinkled with hills and mountains that slope to a coastline fragmented into bays, islands, and headlands by incursions of the ocean. A minor peninsula north of Donegal Bay extends west from the Blue Stack Mountains and culminates in the cliffs of 1,972ft Slieve League – stern sentries which guard the sea route to Donegal town. A hilly central mass punctuated by occasional peaks rolls north from the Blue Stacks to the Derryveagh Mountains, a lough-encircled range which overlooks northern and western coastal waters where majestic Armada vessels once sailed to almost certain disaster.

East of this range the long, sinuous finger of Lough Swilly extends far inland along the western shores of the Inishowen Peninsula, a cluster of high mountains bordered to the east by Co Londonderry's Lough Foyle and tipped by Malin Head – the most northerly point on the Irish mainland. East of Donegal and across the Northern Ireland border the Co Tyrone countryside masses into a long spine of hills which arcs north to surround the moorland Sperrin Mountains. The farmland that cradles prosperous Omagh town in a curve of the hills continues south into the lush Clogher Valley, while the eastern heights drop away to blend into flats bordering the western shore of Lough Neagh – 135sqm of inland water fed by thirteen rivers and shared between five counties.

Hilly Londonderry extends north west from Lough Neagh to Lough Foyle, sharing the high Sperrin Mountains with north-east Tyrone on one side and dropping away to the wide Bann Valley on the other. Its northern shoreline offers 6m of golden beach at Magilligan Strand, while the hills south of Londonderry town and Lough Foyle disguise deep valleys noisy with the chatter of running water. Lough Foyle's eastern rim curves gently beneath towering slopes and crags that condense upwards to form spectacular Benvenagh.

County Antrim climbs from the eastern banks of the River Bann in a succession of folds which sweep across the county to a range of hills majestically strung along the east coast. Between the hills and the sea is the Antrim Coast Road, a route which opens up some of the finest marine views in Europe. At intervals the hills are cut across by deep wooded valleys containing rivers that rush seawards from the summits of the range. These are the renowned Nine Glens of Antrim, of which Glenariff – with its salmon-rich river and picturesque waterfalls – is generally considered the finest. At the northern end of the range Fair Head affords distant views of Scotland and rises opposite Rathlin Island, where exiled Robert Bruce was taught the value of perserverence by a spider. West of Fair Head some 40,000 geometric columns of basalt descend to the shore in stepped ranks and march into the Atlantic to form one of the most impressive sights in Ireland – the Giant's Causeway. South of the east-coast hills Belfast Lough shelters a narrow sea route to the capital of Northern Ireland, and west are the eastern shores of vast Lough Neagh.

Co Armagh's 'Orchard of Ulster' extends south from Lough Neagh in a flat, fertile plain which is covered with apple blossom or roses at the appropriate times of year. After Armagh town, the ecclesiastical capital of all Ireland, this plain rises into small hills which continue east to Carlingford Lough – on the border with Leinster. North of Carlingford's salt reaches the Ulster skyline is corrugated by Co Down's superb Mourne Mountains, a range which includes some of the highest peaks in Ireland and is encircled by a scenic route. A hilly area north of the Mourne range extends east to lowlands which almost enclose island-scattered Strangford Lough with the fertile Ards Peninsula. Downpatrick town is set like a jewel at the southern extreme of the lough and is revered throughout the world as the burial place of St Patrick.

Ulster undergoes a complete change of character west of Armagh. Its east-coast hills and lowland intermingle in a switchback landscape which expands over the Northern Ireland border and through counties Monaghan and Cavan, gathering rivers and lakes by the hundred before dropping sharply to the outstanding Lough Erne system in Northern Ireland's Co Fermanagh. An incredible riot of lakes, boglands, and waterways centred on Lough Outra in Co Cavan creeps north to a junction of valleys on the Northern Ireland border, then continues through Fermanagh below the eastern flanks of Ulster's south-west mountains as Upper Lough Erne. After the island-town of Enniskillen this tortuous network resolves itself as the wide, placid acres of Lower Lough Erne, linked to Donegal Bay by the River Erne. Many of the system's tree-clad islands are graced by the ruins of strongholds built by men who once hunted solitude in these watery mazes.

The chameleon landscape of Ulster challenges the traveller to capture each of its many moods – to venture from its soft farmlands in search of hidden places sculpted by water, woodland cathedrals grown from the banks of clear streams, and wave-flattened strands where human intrusion is a barely-tolerated exception.

LAND OF THE ULSTER LEGENDS

To the Blue Stack Mountains
From Donegal
Drive 39   100 miles

Leave *Donegal* from The Diamond and follow SP 'Killybegs, Mountcharles' on the T72(N56). Drive alongside Donegal Bay, passing *Mountcharles* after 3¾m, and ascend inland for several miles. Rejoin the coast at Inver Bay. After 7m (from Mountcharles) pass through *Dunkineely*, which lies at the base of a narrow peninsula separating Inver and McSwyne's Bays. This peninsula can be explored by an unclassified road. In 4½m turn left on to the T72A and drive alongside *Killybegs* harbour before entering the town. In ¼m bear right and ascend, then in 1m descend to the edge of sandy *Fintragh Bay*. After 4m bear right SP 'Kilcar', and climb a low pass between 864ft Croaghbeg and 1,621ft Crownarad Hill. Descend along Glenaddragh Valley into *Kilcar*. Meet X-roads and keep forward SP 'Coast Road' on to an unclassified road. In ½m ascend steeply, with distant views of the Co Mayo mountains to the left. Summit views extend across Teelin Bay to the famous 1,972ft *Slieve League*.

Rejoin the T72A at the edge of *Carrick*, a village which provides access to *Teelin* and *Slieve League*. Pass through Carrick, shortly enter the Owenwee Valley, then climb to 600ft before descending towards *Glencolumbkille*. At the edge of the village keep forward on an unclassified road SP 'Ardara': A left turn here allows a detour to the Folk Village. In ¼m bear left over a river. Meet a T-junction and turn right SP 'Glengesh', then in 1m cross a river and bear right. Climb to a 700ft pass between 901ft Croaghnaleaba and 1,026ft Croaghloughdivna, then descend to the Glen River valley. Bear left SP 'Ardara' then drive forward to cross the river and enter the Crow River valley.

Follow an easy ascent past Crow village, with mountains ahead and to the right, and climb to 900ft below 1,228ft Croaghavehy at the head of Glen Gesh. Descend, with maximum gradients of 1 in 4 and hairpin bends. Meet a T-junction and turn left on to the T72(N56) for *Ardara*. Enter the town and bear left SP 'Glenties', then ascend and bear right. Continue for 6½m to reach *Glenties*. Pass the school and church on the right, and immediately turn right on to an unclassified road, keeping the town to the left. Follow the Owenea Valley. After 4m the road affords views of 1,961ft Aghla Mountain on the left, plus 1,713ft Carnaween and 1,979ft Silver Hill. Lough Ea lies to the right after several more miles. In 3m reach an 800ft summit, then make an easy descent into the Reelan Valley. Ahead is 1,865ft Gaugin Mountain, and views to the right include the Blue Stack Mountains. Continue for 4m and bear right across a river, then in 1m join the valley of the River Finn. Follow the river for 3½m and drive forward on to the L75, then proceed to *Ballybofey*. Turn right here on to the T18(N15) SP 'Donegal', and skirt Lough Mourne after 5½m. The mountains beyond this include 1,793ft Croaghnageer on the right, plus 1,724ft Croaghconnellagh and 1,491ft Barnesmore ahead. Drive between the latter two mountains via *Barnesmore Gap*. Once clear of the range pass Lough Eske (right), and later re-enter Donegal.

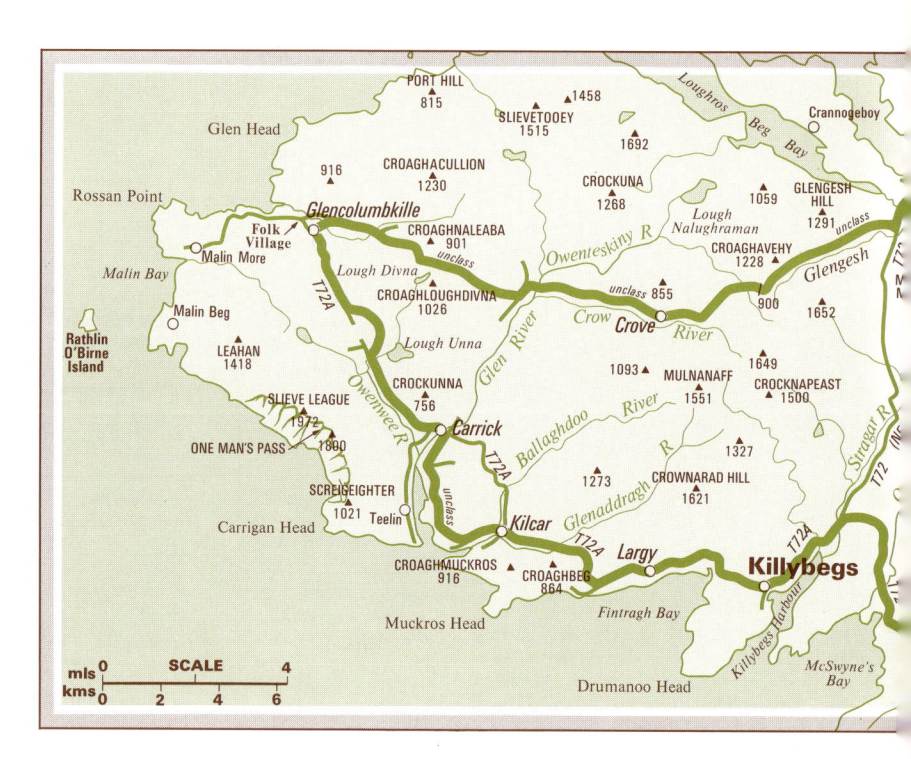

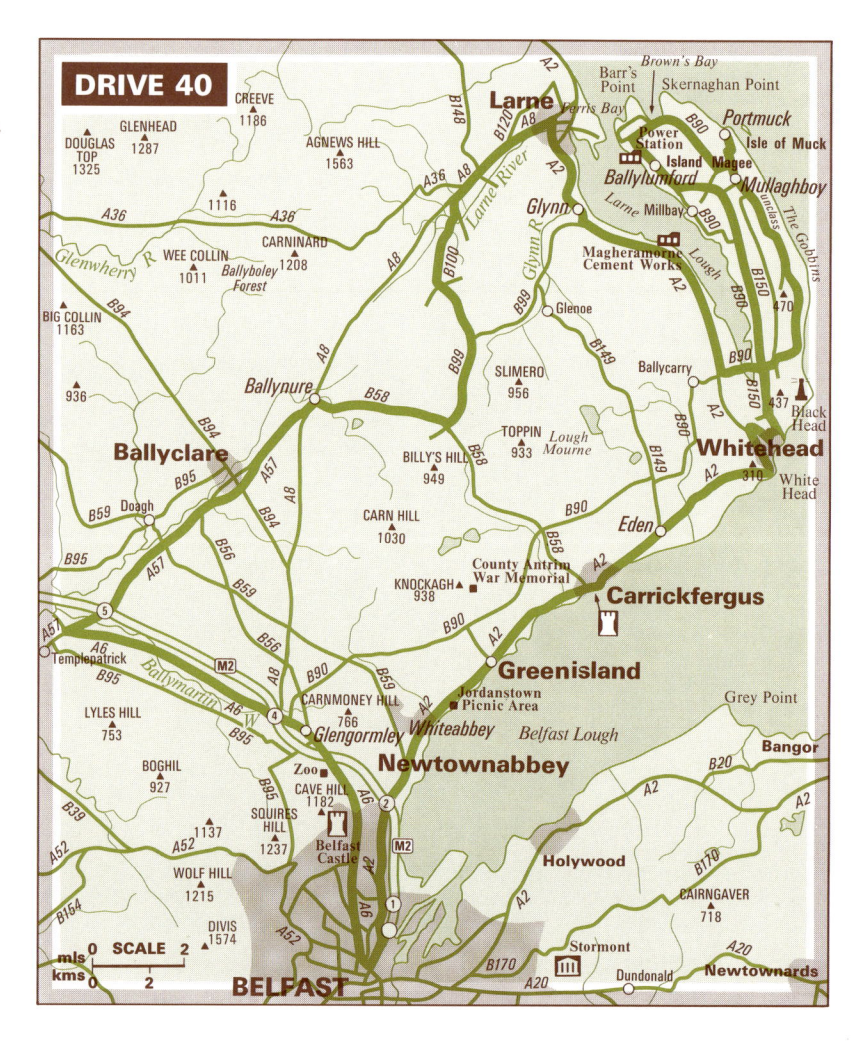

LAND OF THE ULSTER LEGENDS

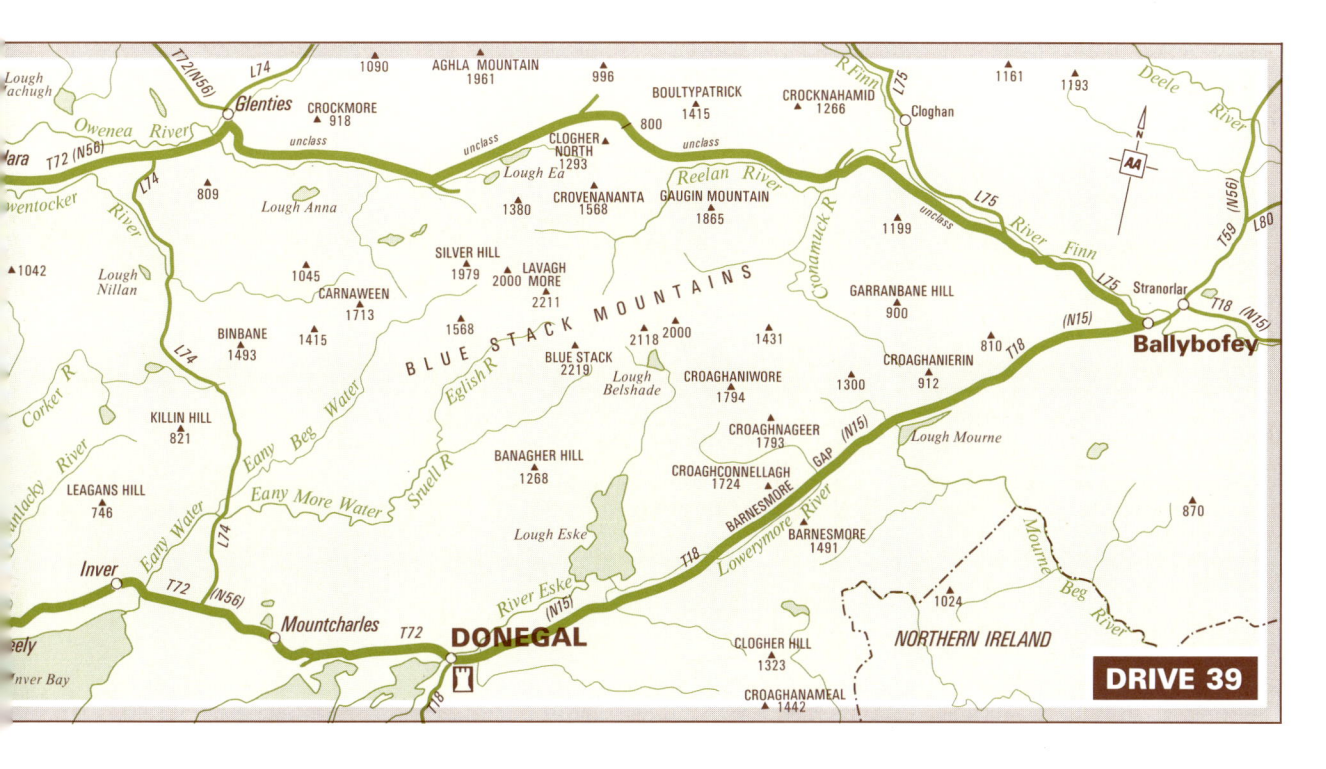

Seascapes of Islandmagee

From Belfast

Drive 40   72 miles

Leave *Belfast* via York St and Shore Rd A2 with SP 'Carrickfergus', drive through the N suburbs of the city, and after 3½m meet a junction with the M2 motorway. Keep forward under road bridges and proceed to *Whiteabbey*. Follow the N shore of coastal Belfast Lough and pass the Jordanstown Picnic Area on the right, with 938ft Knockagh surmounted by the Co Antrim War Memorial to the left. In 2¼m follow a dual carriageway for a short distance with views of Carrickfergus Harbour. Enter historic *Carrickfergus*, well known for its ancient and well-preserved castle — which dates from between 1180 and c1205. This is possibly the first structure of its type to have been erected in Ireland, and was founded by either John de Courcy or Hugh de Lacy. Its fine keep stands between the inner and outer courts. After passing the harbour and castle drive along the promenade with SP 'Larne'. Beyond Carrickfergus town leave the lough shore and pass through Eden, then follow a winding, well-wooded road before crossing higher ground which affords intermittent sea views to the right. Rejoin the coast at Bla Hole and veer left with the road to enjoy views which extend over *Whitehead* to the lighthouse on Black Head.

Descend, and in ¾m turn right on to an unclassified road SP 'Whitehead'. Continue to this resort and follow SP 'Islandmagee', then cross a railway bridge, meet a T-junction, and turn left. After another ¼m bear left, then in ½m turn right on to the B150 SP 'Islandmagee'. In another ¼m turn left, then in 1m meet X-roads and keep forward on to the B90 SP 'Ballylumford'. Ascend across the W side of the *Islandmagee* Peninsula, with views of Larne Lough to the left, and after 2½m bear right SP 'Ballylumford'. In 1½m meet X-roads and go forward on to an unclassified road, then descend. Ascend, and after another ¾m reach a T-junction and turn right on to the B90. This section of the route affords further views over Larne Lough. After 1¼m pass Ballylumford Power Station on the left; in another ½m meet a T-junction and turn right. Proceed, with views of Ferris Bay to the left, then pass a golf course and continue to Brown's Bay. Ascend beyond the bay and drive through pleasant countryside along an undulating road. After another 2m turn left on to the B150 SP 'Portmuck'. In ½m turn left on to an unclassified road, then bear right and descend to *Portmuck*.

This whole area offers very fine seascape views which include the Isle of Muck. Return to the B150 and continue forward through Mullaghboy. At the end of this village bear left, then in ½m turn left on to an unclassified road SP 'The Gobbins' and return along the E coast of the Islandmagee Peninsula. Fine sea views are available over the 250ft-high basaltic cliffs known as The *Gobbins*. A path cut into the face of these cliffs a few feet above sea level has deteriorated to a dangerous condition, but once allowed access to over 1m of rugged scenery via bridges and tunnels. Continue along the hilly road, then after 4m meet a T-junction and turn left on to the B150 SP 'Whitehead'. Take the next turning right, continue to X-roads, and drive forward on to the B90 SP 'Ballycarry'. Cross the S tip of Larne Lough and in another ½m turn right on to the A2 SP 'Larne'. Drive along the shores of Larne Lough, pass through the village of Magheramorne, and continue with fine views of Larne Harbour. In 1½m cross the Glynn River to reach the picturesque village of *Glynn* and continue to *Larne* — the car-ferry port for Stranraer in Scotland. The harbour entrance here is guarded by a modern copy of a round tower, and a fine dolmen can be seen near the landing place. Leave the town with SP 'Belfast' along the A8 dual-carriageway, and in 2½m turn left on to the B100 SP 'Carrickfergus'. Follow a pleasant road through hilly, pastoral countryside or 3¾m, then meet staggered X-roads and proceed with SP 'Carrickfergus'. After another 1½m branch right to join the B58 SP 'Ballynure'. On reaching *Ballynure* turn left SP 'Ballyclare' to join the A8, then in ¼m turn right on to the A57 SP 'Ballyclare'.

Follow the course of the Six Mile Water and after 2m skirt the small linen-bleaching town of *Ballyclare* on the right. Continue with SP 'Templepatrick' through mainly agricultural country, driving forward at all road junctions for 5m, to reach the outskirts of *Templepatrick*. At a roundabout take the first exit SP 'Belfast' to join the A6. Drive alongside the M2 motorway, and after 4m pass the Chimney Corner Hotel on the right. In ¾m negotiate roundabouts with SP 'Glengormley' to remain on the A6, then on reaching *Glengormley* meet traffic signals and keep forward. After a while reach a section of route which affords views of Cave Hill, then pass the entrance to the Belfast Zoological Gardens. Pass the road to Belfast Castle on the right, then continue through the N suburbs of Belfast and re-enter the city via Antrim Rd.

Placenames in *italic* type are worth stopping at; each is listed and described in the main gazetteer section.

LAND OF THE ULSTER LEGENDS

**Through the Mourne Mountains
From Newcastle
Drive 41   63 miles**

Leave *Newcastle* with SP 'Bryansford B180'. First the forested slopes of 2,796ft *Slieve Donard* and later *Tollymore Forest* Park beneath 2,203ft Shan Slieve are visible to the left. After 1¾m (from Newcastle) pass the park entrance, then in ½m meet a T-junction and turn left. In a further ½m follow SP 'Hilltown' through *Bryansford* and pass Tollymore Forest Park below the *Mourne Mountains*. After ¾m pass a road to 'Drumena Cashel and Souterrain' (AM) on the right. In ½m pass the entrance to the Tollymore Mountain Centre (left), with 817ft Moneyscalp on the right. Gradually ascend with further summits on the left and views of Lough Island Reavy below 927ft Tullynasoo Mountain on the right. After several miles reach a 680ft summit and descend along the Kinnahalla Valley, then after 1½m pass the road to Goward Dolmen (AM) on the right. Views to the left extend across the upper Bann Valley to 1,189ft Hen and 1,666ft Cock. In ½m turn right on to the B27 SP 'Hilltown', and in 1m turn left on to the B8. Shortly cross the River Bann to enter *Hilltown*, then continue on the B8 SP 'Newry' and proceed with high ground on the left. After 1½m bear right and continue the ascent for ¾m, then descend into Mayobridge. Meet X-roads and turn left on to the B7 SP 'Warrenpoint', then climb through hilly country beneath 949ft Craignamona and 977ft Slieveacarnane. Descend, bear left and shortly right, then after another 3m meet X-roads and turn left SP 'Warrenpoint'. After 1½m enter *Warrenpoint*. The Carlingford Mountains rise to over 1,500ft on the S side of Carlingford Lough and include the isolated summit of 1,935ft Slieve Foye. Turn left on to the A2 and follow SP 'Rostrevor' through Warrenpoint. Proceed along the lough shores with mountain views to the right and Rostrevor Forest on the slopes of 1,597ft Slievemartin ahead. After 1m cross the Moygannon River, and in a further 1¼m cross the Ghann River into *Rostrevor*.

Here the main drive route keeps forward with SP 'Hilltown B25', and in ½m branches right on to an unclassified road before crossing the Kilbroney River in ½m. However, Rostrevor town centre offers an attractive alternative route through the Rostrevor Forest Park. To follow this turn right on to the A2 'Kilkeel' road SP 'Forest Scenic Drive', and in ½m turn left on to an unclassified road SP 'Rostrevor Forest'. Enter the forest and follow the signposted, one-way route. Climb steeply, with views of Carlingford Lough, and cross several mountain streams on the way through the forest. After 1¼m reach a picnic area and descend with fine views over Rostrevor, Carlingford Lough, and the Republic of Ireland. Warrenpoint can be seen in the distance. After 2m leave the forest and turn right on to an unclassified road SP 'Hilltown' to rejoin the main Drive. Climb the Kilbroney Valley, with part of Rostrevor Forest ahead and to the right; 1,162ft Leckan More rises to the left. After 1¾m cross a bridge and enter the forest. In ½m pass a picnic area SP on the right, then in another 1m leave the forest and reach a 684ft summit. Gradually descend along the valley of Shanky's River, with views of 1,328ft Rocky Mountain ahead, and after 1½m meet a fork and bear right SP 'Spelga Dam'. Pass Rocky Mountain on the right and in 1¼m cross the Rocky River. In ¾m cross the River Bann, meet X-roads, and turn right on to the B27 SP 'Spelga Dam, Kilkeel'. Follow the Bann River past Hen Mountain and the wooded lower slopes of 975ft Kinnahalla, then ascend steeply (1 in 10) into barren country between 1,500ft Spelga and Cock Mountain. This section of road is part of the *Spelga Pass* hillclimb route. Shortly reach the edge of the Spelga Dam reservoir, with some of the higher points in the Mourne range ahead. In ¾m meet a T-junction and turn right SP 'Kilkeel' to continue at over 1,250ft above sea level.

In ¾m cross the infant River Bann, then pass between Slieve Muck and 1,753ft Pigeon Rock Mountain to start the long descent towards 'Kilkeel'. After 1¾m skirt a small forest, with picnic areas SP on the right, and in another 1¾m branch right on to an unclassified road SP 'Newry'. Descend through agricultural country, and in ¾m pass the small village of Attical. After another ½m cross the White Water River, with 1,889ft Finlieve ahead and the wooded slopes of 1,015ft Knockchree on the left. Follow the White Water past Knockchree and the woods of the Mourne Park Estate, then continue the descent with some views of Carlingford Lough to the right. Meet a T-junction, turn right on to the A2 SP 'Newry', and in 1½m turn sharp left on to the unclassified 'Cranfield' road. Skirt Mill Bay with views of the Carlingford Mountains, and after 1m (from the A2) meet a fork and bear right. In a further 1½m cross the White Water bridge, then meet X-roads and turn left for 'Kilkeel'. In ¾m meet a fork and bear right, then turn right SP 'Kilkeel'. In ½m meet a T-junction and turn left to proceed to *Kilkeel*. Enter this town and follow SP 'Newcastle' to join the A2. The road to the right leads to Kilkeel Harbour. Reach the end of the town, cross the Kilkeel River, and in ¼m pass an unclassified road on the left leading to the *Silent Valley* reservoirs — situated deep in the Mourne range. The lower reservoir lies to the left of 2,449ft Slieve Bignian. In 1¾m pass through *Ballymartin*, descend almost to the shore, then after 2m (from Ballymartin) enter the straggling fishing village of *Annalong*. In ¾m pass the harbour (right).

Cross the Annalong River and continue along the A2 with views of Slieve Bignian to the left and 2,152ft Chimney Rock Mountain ahead. Follow the coastline, with views across Dundrum Bay to St John's Point, and after 5m (from Annalong) cross *Bloody Bridge*. *Slieve Donard*, the highest of the Mourne Mountains, rises to 2,796ft on the left. Rejoin the cliff edge, and in ¾m pass a ravine known as Maggie's Leap. Beyond this is the edge of extensive Donard Lodge Forest, and to the right are further views over Dundrum Bay. After 1m (from Maggie's Leap) pass Newcastle Harbour, and in ¾m re-enter the town.

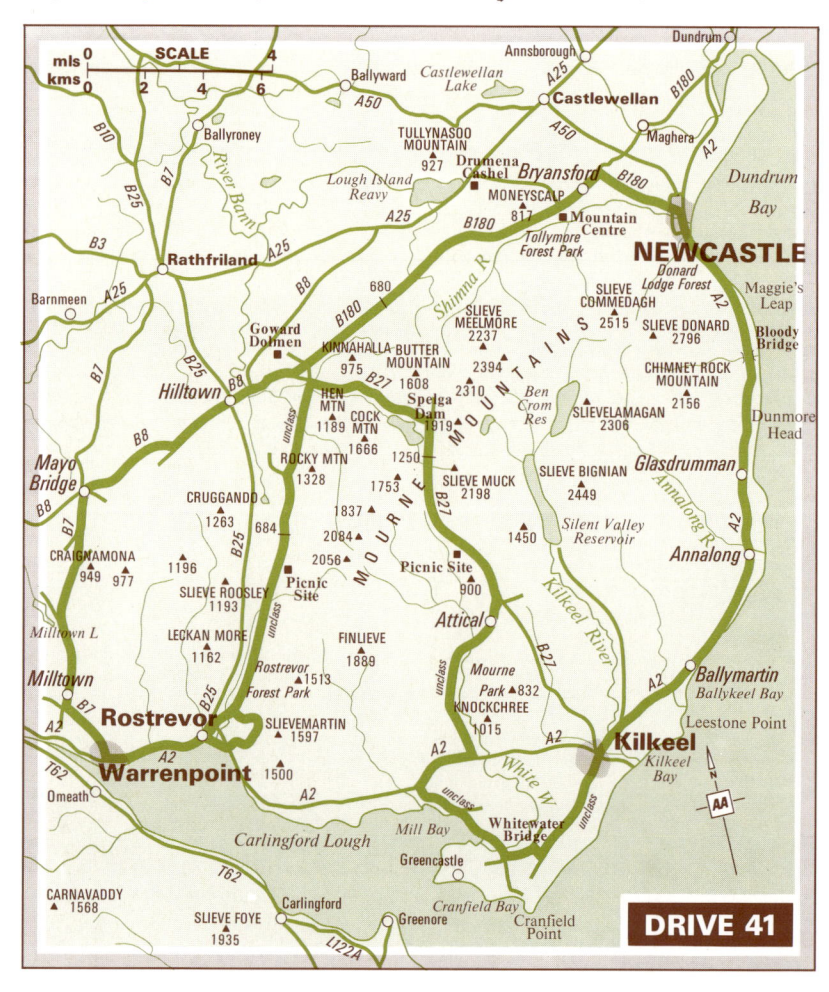

LAND OF THE ULSTER LEGENDS

A Spectacular Sea Drive

From Larne

Drive 42   58 miles

This route follows part of the *Antrim Coast Road* – rightly considered to be one of the finest marine drives in the whole of Europe – through some of the spectacular scenery around the famous nine *Glens of Antrim*. Most of these glens are accessible from the road and comprise a series of deep, wooded rifts which cut across a range of coastal hills. The most distinctive is *Glenariff,* which extends 5m inland from *Red Bay* and includes attractive waterfalls.

From *Larne* follow SP 'Glenarm' to leave by the A2 along the Antrim Coast Road. In 2m pass through Black Cave Tunnel to drive along the bays of Drains and Carnfunnock, then round 300ft Ballygalley Head and continue to *Ballygalley.* The fine fortified manor house in this village is now used as a hotel. Continue along the coast for 6½m to enjoy lovely hill and sea views before reaching *Glenarm,* a village on the Glenarm River at the head of one of the Nine Glens of Antrim. The village's chief attraction is the beautiful park and glen which adjoin its imposing castle, built by the Earl of Antrim in 1636 but subsequently altered. Leave the village by following SP 'Carnlough' and cross the Glenarm River, then continue along the coast to *Carnlough*. The latter is beautifully situated at the foot of Glencloy – famous for its waterfalls – and features one of the mesolithic raised beaches for which this coast is famous. On leaving Glencloy pass beneath a stone arch, with the harbour to the right, then follow SP 'Cushendall, Waterfoot'. In 4m pass Garron Point Post Office, where *Garron Point* itself towers above the road and offers views which extend to the Scottish coast.

Veer W with road to follow shoreline of Red Bay. After 4m reach *Waterfoot*. Drive to the end of the village, cross the Glenariff River, and on meeting a T-junction turn left on to the A43 SP 'Glenariff, Ballymena'. Begin the ascent of Glenariff, often considered the most beautiful of the nine Glens. A particularly attractive feature of this place is the contrast between the green of cultivated land and the black of basalt cliffs. Keep the Glenariff River on the left and wind along the cultivated, tree-shrouded slopes of 1,154ft Lurigethan Mountain, which rises to the right. This road affords fine views across the glen to the left, and to imposing cliffs with several waterfalls on the right. After 3m bear right and continue the ascent, then in 1¼m pass the entrance to Glenariff Glen on the left. *Parkmore Forest* is later seen to the right, and N of this is 1,817ft Trostan Mountain – the highest of the Antrim Hills. Proceed through rugged hill country with views of Cargan Water to the right, then descend through pastoral scenery to reach the village of Cargan. In 2¾m cross the Clough River, and after another 1¾m meet X-roads and turn left on to the B94 SP 'Broughshane'. Continue through undulating countryside for 4m, then cross the Braid River and join the A42 to enter Broughshane.

Leave the latter by following SP 'Ballyclare' along the B94. Drive through pleasant, hilly country along a stretch of road which affords views of 1,437ft *Slemish Mountain* to the left, then after 6m meet X-roads and turn left on to the A36 SP 'Larne'. Follow the valley of the Glenwhirry River to *Glenwhirry,* then after this village bear right and in 2m cross the Glenwhirry river. Ascend through hilly countryside with fine views of the river, now on the left, and in another 1¼m reach Ballyboley Forest. Beyond the forest climb for a short distance and attain a 1,025ft summit, then descend over bleak moorland. Later pass the Kilwaughter House Hotel, and in 1m turn left on to the A8 for the return to Larne.

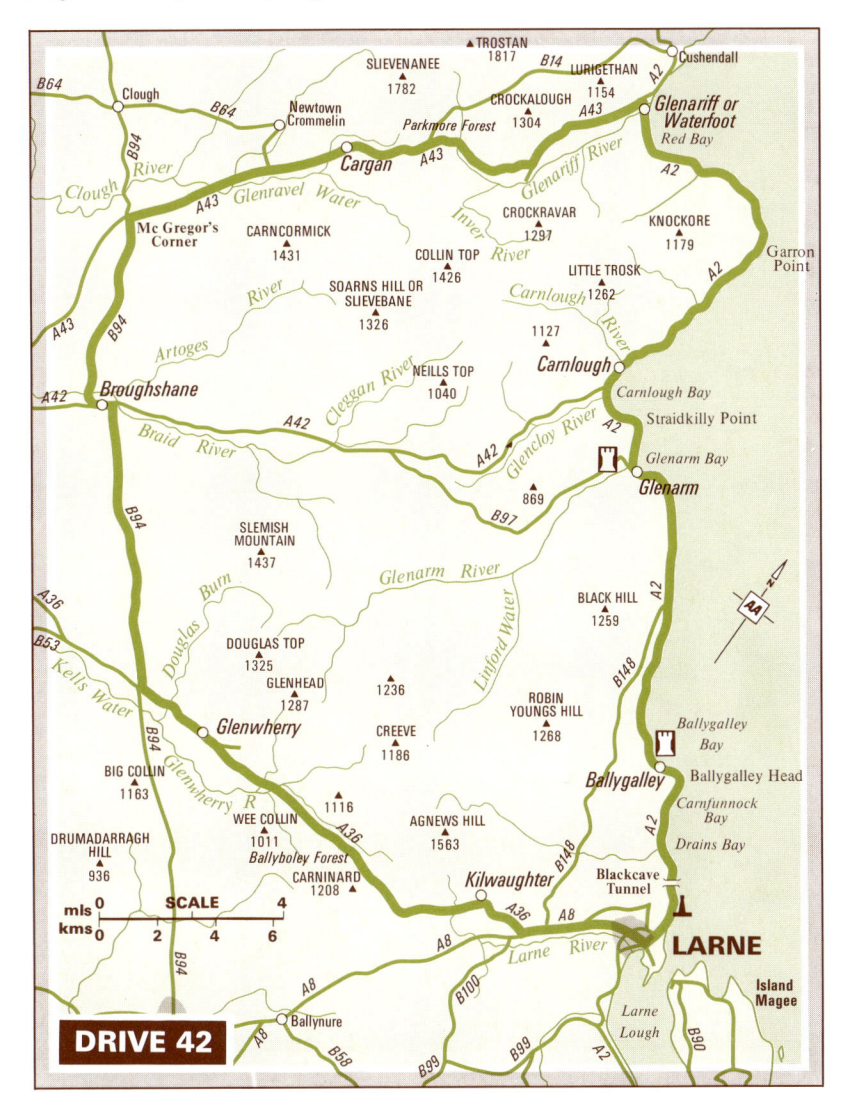

LAND OF THE ULSTER LEGENDS

Forests in the Armagh Hills

From Newry

Drive 43   55 miles

The name 'Newry' means 'The Yew', and is said to have been derived from a yew tree planted at the head of Carlingford Lough by St Patrick. According to tradition this tree stood for 700 years. Interesting buildings in the town include several churches, a fine Catholic cathedral, and an imposing town hall. The first Irish mail-coach service is said to have been established here in 1790.

Depart *Newry* via Monaghan St, then follow SP 'Camlough, Newtownhamilton A25' and in 1m pass under a railway bridge known as the Egyptian Arch. This carries the main Dublin to Belfast line. In ¼m pass the B113 on the right, which is SP 'Bessbrook and Ballymoyer (NT)'. The latter is a wooded glen situated 7m NW of Newry. After about 1m farther pass *Derrymore House* (NT) on the right. Continue in sight of Camlough Mountain, which rises to 1,389ft on the left, and proceed through hilly country to reach *Camlough*. An unclassified road leading left here runs S to Killery Church and Ballymacdermot Cairn, both AM. Continue on the A25, and after 1m pass the end of Camlough Reservoir with views left of 1,893ft *Slieve Gullion*. Drive along a winding road through rolling pastoral countryside and climb steadily for 3m to pass *Belleek* village. Continue the ascent through hills and moorland, reaching summits of 782ft and 845ft before descending through scrubby bogland along a section of route which affords good views over the surrounding landscape. Reach the market town of *Newtownhamilton*, proceed to the town centre, and turn right on to the A29. Leave the town with SP 'Keady', and in ¾m bear left to follow the valley of the White Water into hilly country. Views to the right from this part of the route take in the forested slopes of 1,176ft Deadman's Hill. After 1½m pass through a forested area SP 'Fews Forest', with Carrigatuke Viewpoint on the right, and attain a 1,060ft road summit. Descend, with further hill views to the left, and after 2½m (from the summit) pass Aughnagurgan Lough (left).

Continue through hill country for 3m to reach *Keady*. Meet X-roads and turn right SP 'Armagh' and proceed through the town, continuing on the A29 for 'Armagh'. In 1m bear right, and in 2½m bear right again to cross the Callan River. Continue through undulating, pastoral country, and in 4m enter the city of *Armagh*. This county town is the ecclesiastical capital of all Ireland and has been an important cultural centre for hundreds of years. It has two cathedrals which offer a pleasant contrast between ancient and modern styles of building. The Protestant structure includes parts dating back to the 13thc, and the Catholic building was erected during the last century. Notable among the city's fine Georgian buildings are the Protestant Archbishop's Palace and the famous Observatory. The latter is one of the oldest of its type in the British Isles. Leave the city on the A3 'Portadown' road, passing a regimental museum on the right and the famous Planetarium on the left while ascending steep College Hill. Proceed along a good main road through undulating countryside dotted with apple orchards, and after 7½m cross the boundary into the Craigavon New Town area. In 1¼m enter a roundabout and take the second exit SP 'Portadown Centre', then after ¼m reach the outskirts of *Portadown*. This town is a centre of Ulster's greatest fruit-growing area, and was made prosperous by the building of the Newry Canal. At the edge of Portadown turn right SP 'Tandragee, Newry' and drive along the B78 'Mahon' road. In 1¾m turn left, and after another ¼m turn right on to the A27.

Continue through more agricultural country, and in 2m pass Tandragee Power Station on the left. After a further 1m bear right into *Tandragee* and shortly pass the town's modern castle on the right. Proceed to the end of the town and follow SP 'Newry A27', then bear left. The B2 road on the right leads to the Clare Glen Scenic Point on the Cusher River. After a short distance bear right and cross the Cusher River, then follow a pleasant road through pastoral countryside. In 1¾m pass the small graveyard of Relicarn on the right; a local highway man was buried here after being caught and hanged in 1681. In a further ¼m pass the curiously-shaped Aughlish Cottages on the right. The valley to the left contains both the disused Newry Canal – which was opened in 1741 and ran from Newry to Lough Neagh – and the Belfast to Dublin railway line. These stay with the drive for the remainder of the journey back to Newry. After another 1½m the route affords views left of Lough Shark – or Acton Lough – and the distant *Mourne Mountains*. In 1¼m proceed through *Poyntzpass*, still with SP 'Newry', and in a further 2m skirt the Drumbanagher Estate on the right. Ahead are views of Camlough Mountain. In 1¾m drive underneath the railway line via the main road and run between the track and canal. Pass through *Jerrettspass*, and after another 1m pass the disused Goraghwood Quarries. Bear away with the road to join the valley of the Newry River. Fine mountain views open up ahead as the drive approaches Newry. After 2½m (from Goraghwood) turn left on to the A28, and in 1m re-enter Newry via Armagh Rd.

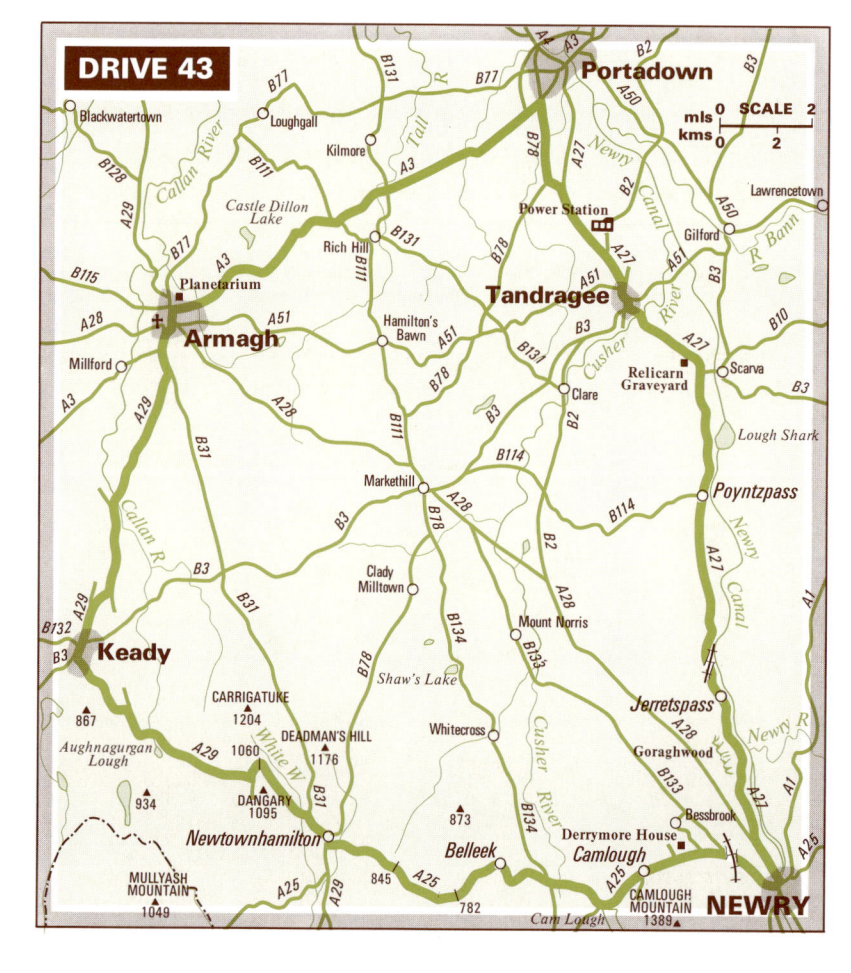

LAND OF THE ULSTER LEGENDS

The Lower Erne Shoreline
From Enniskillen
Drive 44 64 miles

Enniskillen is an island town strategically sited in the River Erne between Upper and Lower Lough Erne. Its position has made it of great military importance for hundreds of years; as such it has been the centre of numerous battles and the site of several castles.

From Enniskillen follow SP 'Omagh' to leave the town on the A32. In 3¼m branch left on to the B82 SP 'Kesh' and pass the road to *Devenish Island*. This is situated in beautiful Lough *Erne* and boasts one of the most complete monastic settlements in Ireland. St Molaise first founded a monastery here in the 6thc, and the small, rectangular oratory which carries his name is typical of many such structures built by the early-Irish church. Other interesting remains to be seen on the island, which can be reached by passenger ferry, include the Great Church and an 85ft round tower of 12th-c date.

After another 1½m pass Ballycassidy Post Office and cross the Ballymallard River via a hump-backed bridge. Beyond this the road affords a fine view over the island-studded waters of Lower Lough Erne. Continue through the small angling resort of *Killadeas* and follow the wooded shores of attractive Rossclare Bay, then after a further 1m pass the road to Rossigh Bay Picnic Area on the left. Continue through the village of Lisnarrick and in 1m turn left on to an unclassified road SP 'Kesh Scenic Route', passing the entrance to *Castle Archdale* on the way. This castle now serves as a Ministry of Agriculture Grassland Experimental Centre. Ascend through part of the Castle Archdale Forest and reach a stretch of road which offers further excellent views of Lough Erne. Drive through more open, undulating countryside, still with views of the lough, and in 3m meet a T-junction. Turn left here SP 'Kesh' and proceed to the sailing and angling centre of *Kesh* village, then turn left on to the A47 and cross the Kesh River. In a further 1m turn left SP 'Boa Island, Belleek' to pass through pleasant scenery alongside the N shore of Lower Lough Erne. In 2¼m cross a bridge on to narrow *Boa Island*, the largest of the many islands in the lough, and in another 4½m cross over to the mainland.

Meet a T-junction and turn left SP 'Belleek, Castle Caldwell', and in 3½m pass the entrance to *Castle Caldwell* Forest Wildlife Park (left). Beside the park gate is the 18th-c Fiddle Stone, which carries a curious inscription. The castle which gave its name to this park was one of the numerous 'Plantation' structures which dot the shores of Lough Erne. Continue to *Belleek,* which is noted for its pottery, then leave this small town on the A46 – passing the Hotel Carlton on the right. Follow SP 'British Customs, Enniskillen'. After a further ¼m follow SP 'Garrison, Scenic Forest Drive' on to the B52.

Ascend, and in 1½m turn left on to an unclassified road SP Derrygonnelly Forest Drive. Continue through barren, hilly countryside with distant views of Lough Navar Forest and Corral Glen Forest ahead, plus Big Dog Forest to the right. After 6¾m proceed along a pleasantly tree-lined road, first passing the Lough Navar Forestry Office and then the entrance to the circular Lough Navar Forest Drive. The latter offers an interesting diversion from the main drive and visits a viewpoint situated at about 900ft on Magho Cliffs.

The magnificent panorama which spreads from here includes Lough Erne, the distant Donegal Hills, and far-off Donegal Bay on the W coast. The signposted return follows a descent past Lough Achork and rejoins the main road, where a left turn is made to complete the circuit and once again pass the forestry office. A road opposite the entrance to the Forest Drive leads into wooded Glen Corral.

Continue along the unclassified road which forms part of the main route, and in ¾m pass picturesque little Carrick Lough. Follow SP 'Lough Erne', then in 2¼m meet X-roads and keep forward. After another 1½m turn right on to the A46 SP 'Enniskillen'. In 1m pass the road to Camagh Bay on the left, then after another 1½m pass the road to Carrickreagh Viewpoint on the right. Skirt the shore of Lower Lough Erne and pass the entrance to Ely Lodge Forest Loughshore Trail and Picnic Area on the left, then drive through part of the Ely Lodge Forest. Later pass a road leading right to *Monea* Castle ruins, and continue along the A46 for the return to Enniskillen. Portora Royal School can be seen on the hill before the route enters the town.

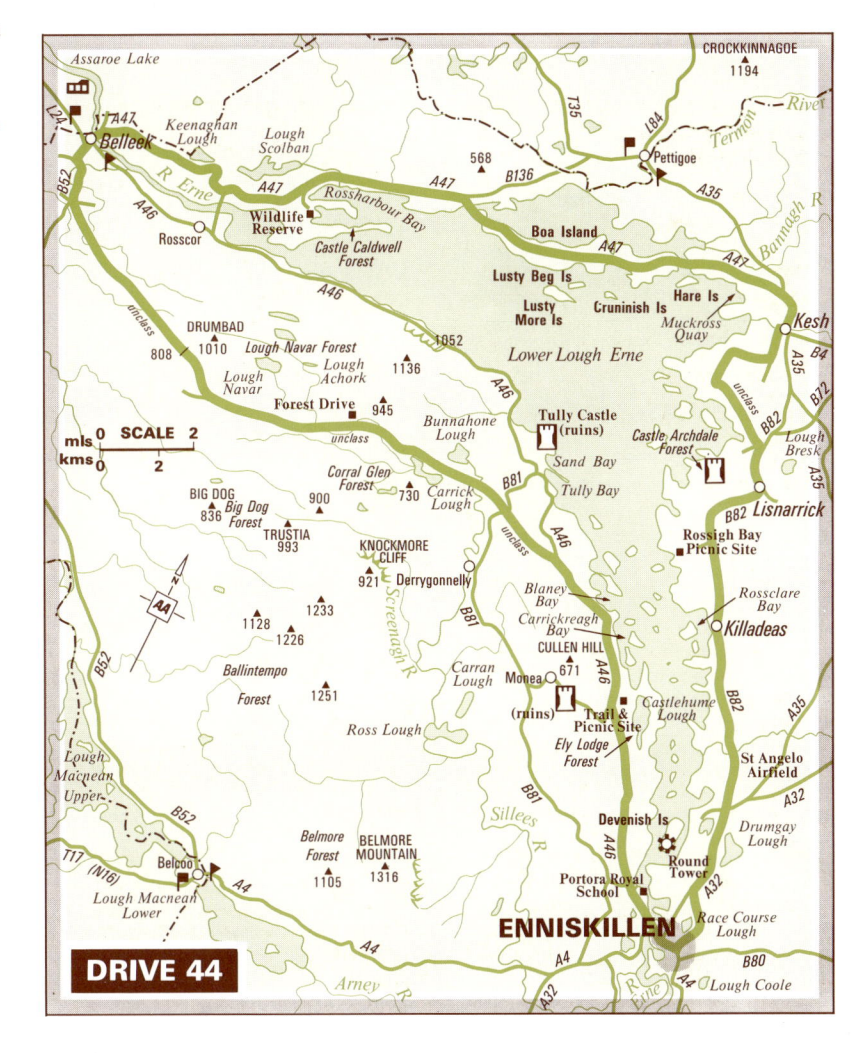

Placenames in *italic* type are worth stopping at; each is listed and described in the main gazetteer section.

LAND OF THE ULSTER LEGENDS

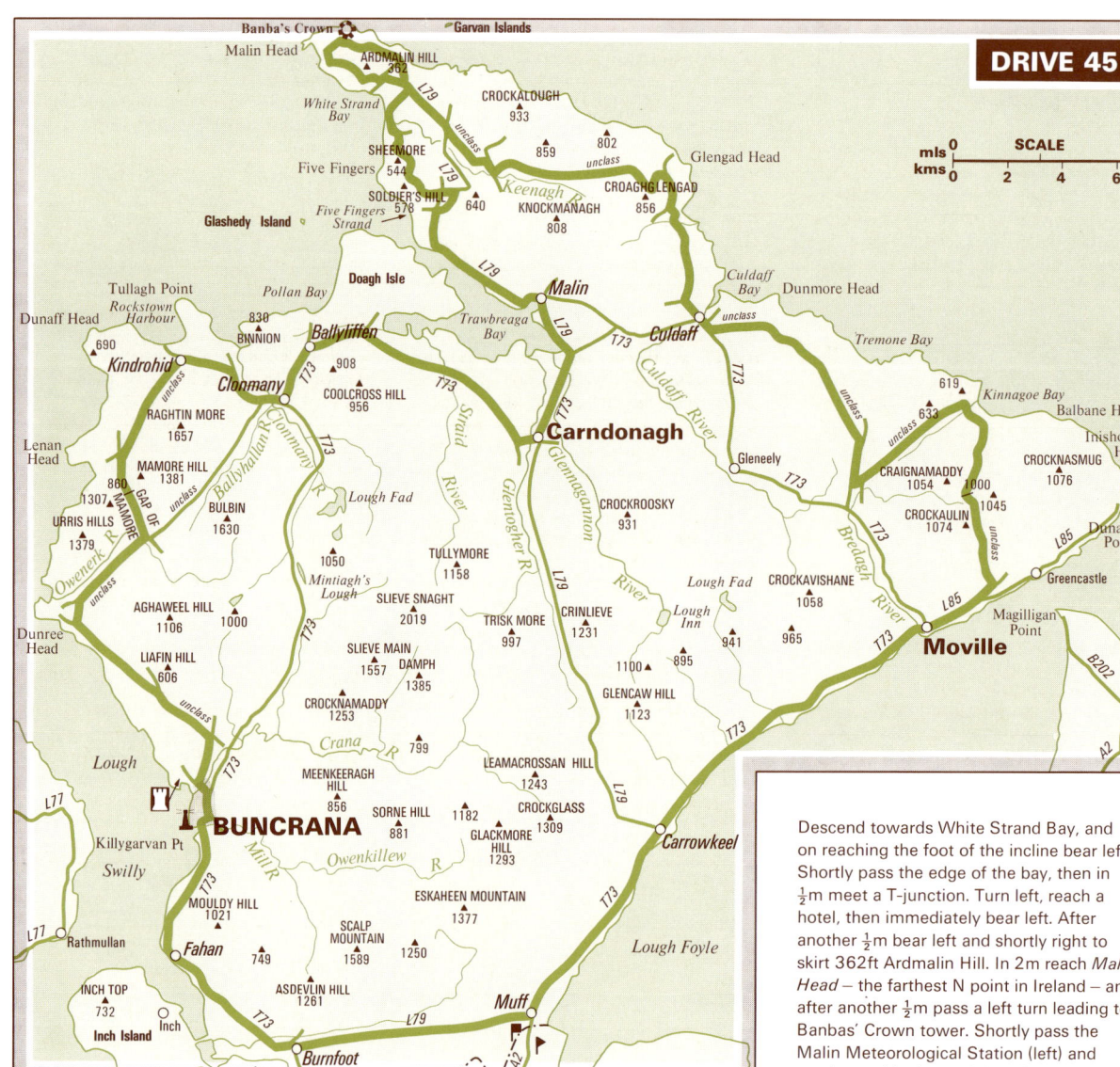

DRIVE 45

Over the Mamore Gap

From Buncrana

Drive 45 96 miles

Leave *Buncrana* with SP 'Carndonagh T73'. In ½m turn left on to an unclassified road SP 'Gap of Mamore', and in ¼m bear right. After another 1m meet X-roads and bear left SP 'Dunree'. Ascend gradually, and in 1½m bear left SP 'Dunree, Mamore Gap'. The 1,200ft Knockalla Mountains can be seen on the far side of *Lough Swilly* (left), and the Urris Hills rise to 1,379ft ahead. Aghaweel Hill stands at 1,106ft on the right. After 2¾m turn right, then in ¾m meet a T-junction and turn right. Drive along the Owenerk River valley and in 2m meet X-roads, then turn left for the Gap of Mamore. To avoid the gap's gradients, keep forward along the direct road to 'Clonmany'.

Climb to the gap's 860ft summit, with 1,381ft Mamore Hill on the right and 690ft Dunaff Head ahead, then descend steeply through hairpin bends. Views extend left over the mouth of Lough Swilly to Fanad Head, right across Rockstown Harbour and Tullagh Point, and ahead to Dunaff Head.

In 1m reach the foot of the descent and bear right SP 'Clonmany'. Continue, with Rockstown Harbour on the left, then in 2¾m reach Kindrohid. Bear right here and enjoy views of Tullagh Bay (left) before entering the Clonmany River valley. After 2¼m (from Kindrohid) meet X-roads and turn left. Cross a river into *Clonmany*, turn right in the village, and in ¼m turn left on to the T73 SP 'Ballyliffin'. Pass between Binnion and 908ft Crockaughrim, and in 1½m reach *Ballyliffin*. Bear right SP 'Inishowen' and continue with Doagh Isle and Trawbreaga Bay on the left. In 6½m reach *Carndonagh*, turn left SP 'Malin Head' to remain on the T73, and in 2m keep forward on to the L79. Skirt the edge of Trawbreaga Bay, then in 1½m reach *Malin*.

Turn left SP 'Malin Head' to follow the bay's N shore, then after 3½m pass a left turn leading to Five Fingers Strand. In another 1m meet a T-junction and turn left on to an unclassified road, then in ¼m meet X-roads and drive forward SP 'Knockamany Bens'. Climb past 578ft Soldier's Hill to a carpark and viewpoint. Panoramic views from here extend over Pollan Bay towards Dunaff Head, and inland to 2,019ft Slieve Snaght.

Descend towards White Strand Bay, and on reaching the foot of the incline bear left. Shortly pass the edge of the bay, then in ½m meet a T-junction. Turn left, reach a hotel, then immediately bear left. After another ½m bear left and shortly right to skirt 362ft Ardmalin Hill. In 2m reach *Malin Head* — the farthest N point in Ireland — and after another ½m pass a left turn leading to Banbas' Crown tower. Shortly pass the Malin Meteorological Station (left) and continue with views of the offshore Garvan Islands. Farther along, this road becomes the L79. In 1½m (or 4m from Malin Head) meet X-roads and drive forward SP 'Malin'.

In another 1½m turn left SP 'Glengad', then proceed through farmland with views of 933ft Crockalough (left) and 809ft Knockmanagh (right). After 4½m bear right, then in 1m meet a T-junction and turn left SP 'Culdaff'. Climb, then descend with Culdaff Bay on the left. Reach *Culdaff* village and turn left on to the T73 SP 'Moville', pass a hotel, then bear right. In ½m turn left on to an unclassified road and gradually ascend. In 4¾m bear right, then in a further 1m turn left and immediately left again. Reach a low summit, descend to Kinnagoe Bay, then turn sharp right and climb to a 1,000ft summit. Follow a long descent which affords magnificent views across the mouth of Lough Foyle to Magilligan Point, 1,260ft Binevenagh, other Co Londonderry hills, and the N Ireland coast as far as *Portrush*. Meet a T-junction, turn right to follow the shores of the lough, and in ¾m turn right on to the L85. In 1½m enter *Moville*, go forward on to the T73, and continue alongside the lough for 13½m to reach Muff. Drive to the end of this village and turn right on to the L79. Continue through farming country, and after 5¾m

LAND OF THE ULSTER LEGENDS

Donegal Bays and Lakes

From Letterkenny

Drive 46   89 miles

Leave *Letterkenny* on the 'Rathmelton' road. In ½m turn left on to the T72 SP 'Rathmelton' and later climb the lower slopes of 757ft Carn Hill, with the River Swilly estuary on the right. After 8m (from Letterkenny) descend steeply into *Rathmelton* and turn left. In ¼m cross a river and turn right on to the L77 SP 'Rathmullan'. Continue, with views across *Lough Swilly* to the *Inishowen Peninsula* mountains, then drive along the shore. Right is 732ft Inch Top on *Inch Island*, while 1,137ft Crockanaffrin and 1,008ft Croaghan Hill rise to the left. In 5m (from Rathmelton) pass the entrance to Rathmullan Wood Picnic Site (left), and in a further 1¾m enter *Rathmullan*. Drive through the village, and near the end turn left SP 'Knockalla Coast Road'. In ½m bear left, and after 2½m turn right on to an unclassified road SP 'Knockalla Coast Road'. Follow Lough Swilly with hill views across the water and 1,203ft Knockalla Mountain ahead. In 2¼m bear right, then in a further 1¼m meet a T-junction and turn right. Proceed along the foot of Knockalla, in 1m reach a headland, then climb to a 400ft viewpoint. Descend, and after 1¾m turn right SP 'Portsalon'. In another 1m turn right on to the L78. In ¾m meet X-roads, turn right, and in ½m enter *Portsalon*. Drive through the village on the unclassified coastal road and in 2m bear right. In a further 2¾m turn right, and after another 1½m meet a T-junction; turn left, with Fanad Head 1m to the right. This section affords fine views along the N coast towards the Rosguill Peninsula, distant *Horn Head*, and *Tory Island*. In 3m turn left again SP 'Kindrum, Kerrykeel', with Ballyhiernan Bay on the right and several loughs on the left. In 1m pass the end of Kindrum Lough (right), and in ¾m join the N shore of *Mulroy Bay*.

Follow the shore for 1¾m, then in another 1m pass Rosnakill village. Skirt the bay and in 2m (from Rosnakill) bear right. In a further ½m turn right on to the L78, following the shores of Mulroy Bay, and in 1½m reach *Kerrykeel*. Turn right SP 'Milford' and follow a broad, level road with rocky hills on the left and good views across Mulroy Bay (right). After 3m turn right on to an unclassified road SP 'Milford', then in 1m reach the edge of *Milford* and turn right on to the T72 SP 'Carrigart'. Continue round the head of Mulroy Bay and later follow the W shore. After 3m (from Milford) pass Woodquarter Wood Picnic Site entrance (right). After 7m reach *Carrigart*, bear left at the end of the village to remain on the T72, and in 1½m branch left on to an unclassified road SP 'Glen'. Ascend, with views right of *Sheep Haven* and 2,197ft Muckish Mountain.

After 2½m enter *Glen* and bear right SP 'Lough Glen'. Continue for 4m, partly along the shore, and meet a T-junction. Turn right on to the L76, in ¼m cross the Owencarrow River, and after another ½m turn left on to an unclassified road. Follow the river's line and in 1m turn left to recross it. The Derryveagh Mountains, with *Glenveagh* Deer Forest above Lough Beagh, can be seen to the right. Pass through bogland, and after 2m go forward on to the L82 SP 'Kilmacrenan'. In ½m bear right SP 'Gartan, Church Hill'.

Descend with views over Lough Akibbon (right), then after 2m meet X-roads and bear right. Shortly skirt the shores of Lough Akibbon. After 1½m turn left across a river bridge, then in ½m turn right on to an unclassified road and follow the shores of *Gartan* Lough. Views from this section encompass 746ft Brown Mountain (left) and 1,461ft Leahanmore (right). After 1¼m reach the entrance to Church Hill Wood, then in ¾m turn left SP 'Letterkenny'. In 2m turn right on to the L82 SP 'Letterkenny'. In 3¾m enter the Swilly Valley and turn left on to the L74, then proceed along the valley and return to Letterkenny.

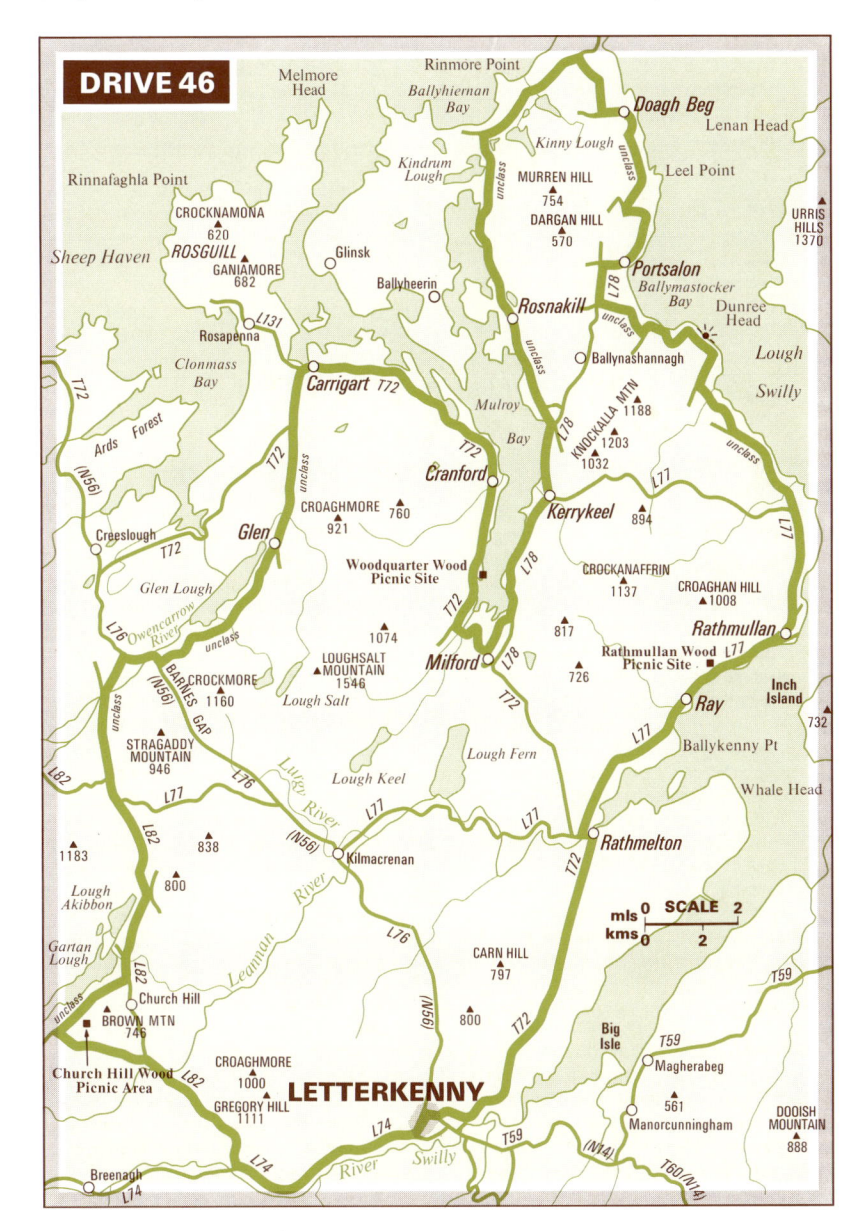

Drive 45 continued

reach Burnfoot. Meet a T-junction, turn right on to the T73 'Buncrana' road, and in ¼m bear left. In 2½m rejoin the shores of Lough Swilly, with Inch Top rising to 732ft from *Inch Island* (left), and proceed to *Fahan*. Continue alongside Swilly and in 3½m re-enter Buncrana.

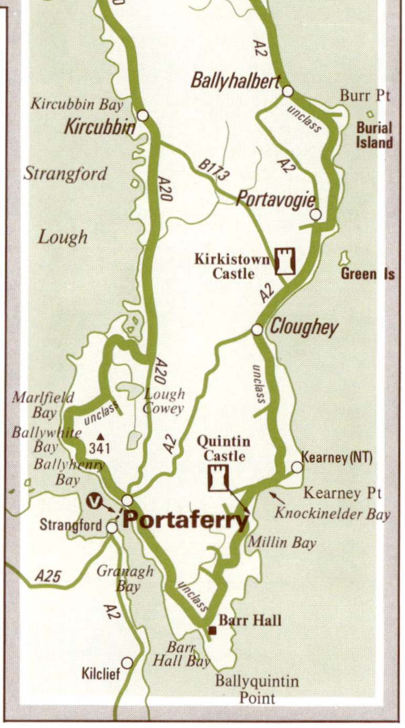

LAND OF THE ULSTER LEGENDS

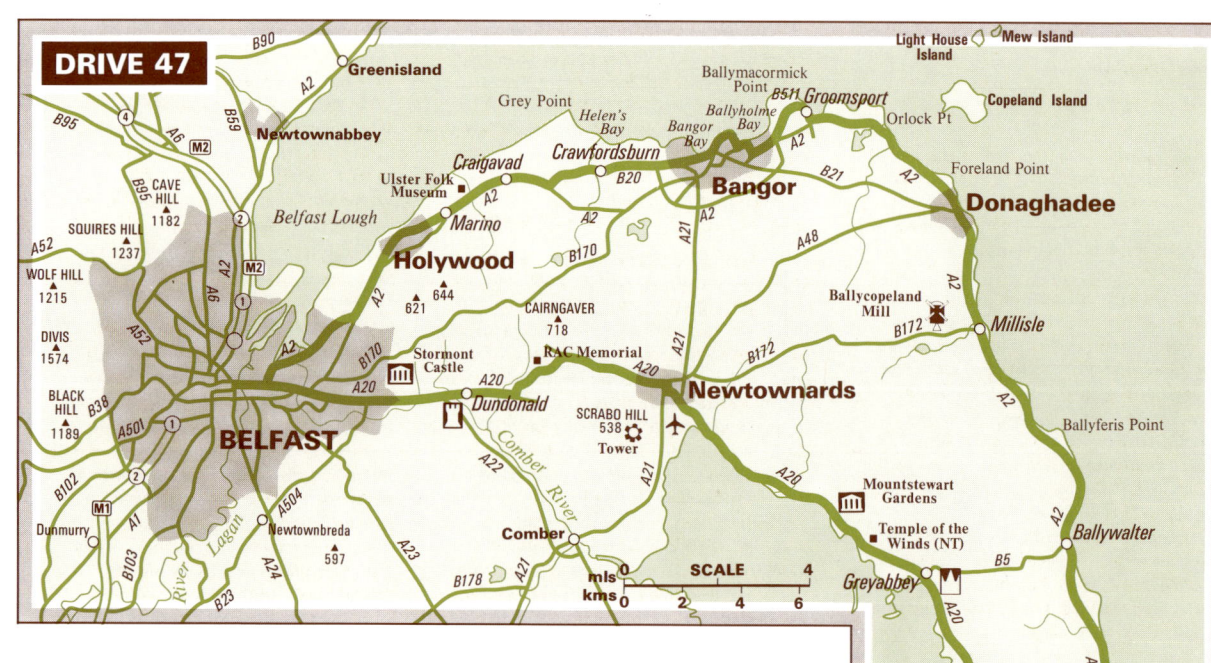

Peninsula Villages

From Belfast

Drive 47   81 miles

Leave *Belfast* by following SP 'Bangor A2' and join the Sydenham Bypass. In 3¼m enter the Tillysburn Roundabout and take the first exit, then continue along a stretch of road which affords views over the coastal Belfast Lough to the left. Skirt *Holywood* and stay on the 'Bangor' road to pass through Marino village. After another ¾m pass Cultra Manor on the left. The manor and its grounds form the *Ulster Folk Museum*, which was originally created to illustrate traditional Ulster life. Re-erected buildings in the 136-acre park include a thatched barn, a farm, and a spade foundry.

Paintings by William Conor can be seen inside the house, and other interesting exhibits include a fine collection of transport vehicles. Adjacent to the museum is the proposed site of the projected Transport Museum. Proceed through Craigavad and in 2m turn left on to the B20 SP 'Crawfordsburn', then follow a pleasantly tree-lined road to the attractive village of this name. At the Crawfordsburn Inn bear left and drive to the outskirts of *Bangor*. This town is Northern Ireland's largest seaside resort and boasts all the usual amenities, including good sandy beaches and the annual regatta of the Royal Ulster Yacht Club.

Drive into the town, cross a railway bridge into Bryansburn Rd, and at the ensuing roundabout keep forward. On meeting a T-junction turn right along the sea front. Views from here extend over Bangor Bay. In a further 1m pass Ballyholme Yacht Club on the left, then at the end turn left on to Ballyholme Esplanade to run alongside *Ballyholme Bay*. In almost ½m turn right into Sheridan Drive, then left into Groomsport Rd. In ¾m enter a roundabout and take the first exit SP 'Groomsport' on to the B511 to reach the small resort of *Groomsport*. Leave the latter with SP 'Donaghadee' and turn left on to the A2. Fine seascape views which now open up to the left include the off-shore *Copeland Islands*. Enter the resort of *Donaghadee*, leave by following SP 'Millisle' to stay on the A2, then continue along the E coastline of the fertile *Ards Peninsula* to *Millisle*. To the W of this small resort is the restored Ballycopeland Windmill of 1784, which stands on the B172. Remain on the A2 and continue, with fine sea views, for 5m to pass through *Ballywalter* – a little resort noted for its extensive sands. Proceed to *Ballyhalbert*; on entering this village the drive affords views of the off-shore Burial Island, which marks the extreme E limit of Irish soil. Leave Ballyhalbert and keep forward on to the unclassified Portavogie Coast Road, then in 1m bear right and continue into the small fishing village of *Portavogie*. On entering the village turn right then left and drive to the harbour.

After ½m turn left to rejoin the A2 SP 'Cloughey'. Follow a stretch of road which offers views of *Kirkistown Castle* to the right, and reach the little resort of *Cloughey* – situated on Cloughey Bay. Drive through the village, then at the church turn left on to an unclassified road SP 'Kearney'. Continue along this undulating road for 1¾m, then turn left on to the 'Newcastle' road SP 'Quintin Bay'. After another 1½m meet a T-junction and turn right SP 'Portaferry'. A diversion can be made from this point by turning left to visit the restored fishing village of *Kearney* (NT). Drive alongside Knockinelder Bay for ½m and turn left to continue along the coast. Pass the much-restored Norman stronghold of *Quintin Castle* on the left, and in ¾m keep left. Meet a T-junction and take the 'Quintin Bay' road for Barr Hall. After another 1¼m pass the Ballyquintin Point Road on the left and continue along the 'Barr Hall' road.

On reaching the shores of Barr Hall Bay turn right on to the 'Portaferry' road and proceed N along the narrow straights of *Strangford Lough*. In some places the lough is as deep as the section of English Channel between Dover and Calais. Continue, with fine views across the water, and drive into the small port of *Portaferry*. Leave this town via the unclassified Lough Shore Road, pass *Strangford* car ferry on the left, and skirt the edge of Strangford Lough. In 3¼m meet a T-junction and turn left. In another 2¼m turn left on to the A20, and after a further ¾m reach *Ardkeen* Post Office. Proceed along the W arm of the Ards Peninsula. Views from here take in part of Strangford Lough which has broadened to form an inland sea studded with numerous small islands. In 4m pass through the village of *Kircubbin* and continue to *Greyabbey*, which features one of the most complete Cistercian abbeys in Ireland. Drive to the Police Station and turn left SP 'Newtownards', then after 1¼m pass the *Mountstewart* Estate on the right. Skirt the wall of the estate for 2m before passing the entrances to the 18th-c Temple of the Winds and beautiful Mount Stewart Gardens (both NT). The estate grounds are rich in prehistoric remains, including three raths and a perfect dolmen. Continue along the 'Newtownards' road with views which extend across the lough to the

LAND OF THE ULSTER LEGENDS

Londonderry's Northern Hills

From Coleraine

Drive 48 71 miles

Follow the A2 from *Coleraine* SP 'Castlerock' and 'Downhill'. After 3m pass through the Quilley Picnic Area, and in 1¼m cross Dartress Bridge to reach *Articlave*. Continue along the A2, and in 1m pass the B119 to *Castlerock* on the right. In a further ¾m pass an unclassified road leading right to the *Mussenden Temple* (NT). Shortly pass the Bishop's View Picnic Area on the left, and beyond this continue for ½m to descend steeply into *Downhill*. Pass the Downhill Hotel and turn left on to the unclassified Bishop's Rd SP 'Gortmore Picnic Area'. Climb a steep hill, at first passing Downhill Forest on the left, for views to the right of Magilligan Strand, Lough Foyle, and Inishowen Head. After 2¾m reach the Gortmore Picnic Area and 800ft Bishop's View (AA Viewpoint). Continue along the hillside and head towards Ballyleighery Forest on the slopes of 1,260ft Binevenagh.

After 1½m turn right and follow a steep descent with the forest on the left. In 1m meet X-roads and keep forward, then in ½m drive over a level-crossing. In a further ½m meet X-roads and turn left on to the A2 for Limavady. After 1m pass the B202 leading right to Magilligan Point, and in a further 1½m recross the railway at *Bellarena*. After 1¼m meet a road junction and bear left SP 'Limavady'. In 2m meet a T-junction and turn right, then in a further 1½m reach another T-junction and turn right again SP 'Limavady' to enter Artikelly. Drive to the end of this village and bear left, cross Artikelly Bridge, then bear right. After another 1m enter *Limavady*; in ½m turn left and follow SP 'Dungiven' to leave Limavady by the B68. Follow this road along the Roe Valley and pass a road leading right to O'Cahan's Rock (NT). Gradually ascend, then after 6m descend to cross the Gelvin River.

In 1m meet a T-junction and turn left SP 'Dungiven'. Continue, with 1,535ft Benbradagh visible to the left, and approach *Dungiven*. Meet a T-junction, turn left on to the A6, and drive through this town with SP 'Maghera'. Continue along the Roe Valley and shortly pass a road leading right to Dungiven Priory (AM). Follow a long, steady climb past 1,479ft Carn Hill and 1,306ft Craigmore on the left, plus 1,278ft Brown Hill, 1,774ft White Mountain, and 1,391ft Corick Mountain on the right. After 6½m cross Currudda Bridge beneath 1,521ft Carntogher and enter the *Glenshane Pass*. Continue the ascent past Glenshane Forest, which lies to the right, and reach a 996ft summit. Cross the summit and descend steeply, with Ranaghan Picnic Area on the left, and in 2m keep forward on to the A6 Maghera Bypass. In a further 2m cross the A29, then in ½m turn left SP 'Maghera A29' to leave the A6. Shortly pass the Mullagh Bridge Picnic Area on the right. In ¾m meet a T-junction and turn right SP 'Maghera'.

Proceed forward into the town of *Maghera*. Leave the latter by the A29 SP 'Kilrea, Garvagh', and in 1¾m branch right on to the B75 SP 'Kilrea'. In 1m pass *Upperlands*, and in a further 6m turn right into Kilrea, meet X-roads, and turn left on to the A54 'Coleraine' road. In 6½m cross a bridge over the Agivey River, then in ¼m meet a T-junction and turn right. In ¾m recross the river and bear left, then after another 3m pass woodland to the right. In 1½m enter the Castle Roe Wood of Somerset Forest. In 1m meet a T-junction and bear right. Complete the drive by re-entering Coleraine via Strand Rd.

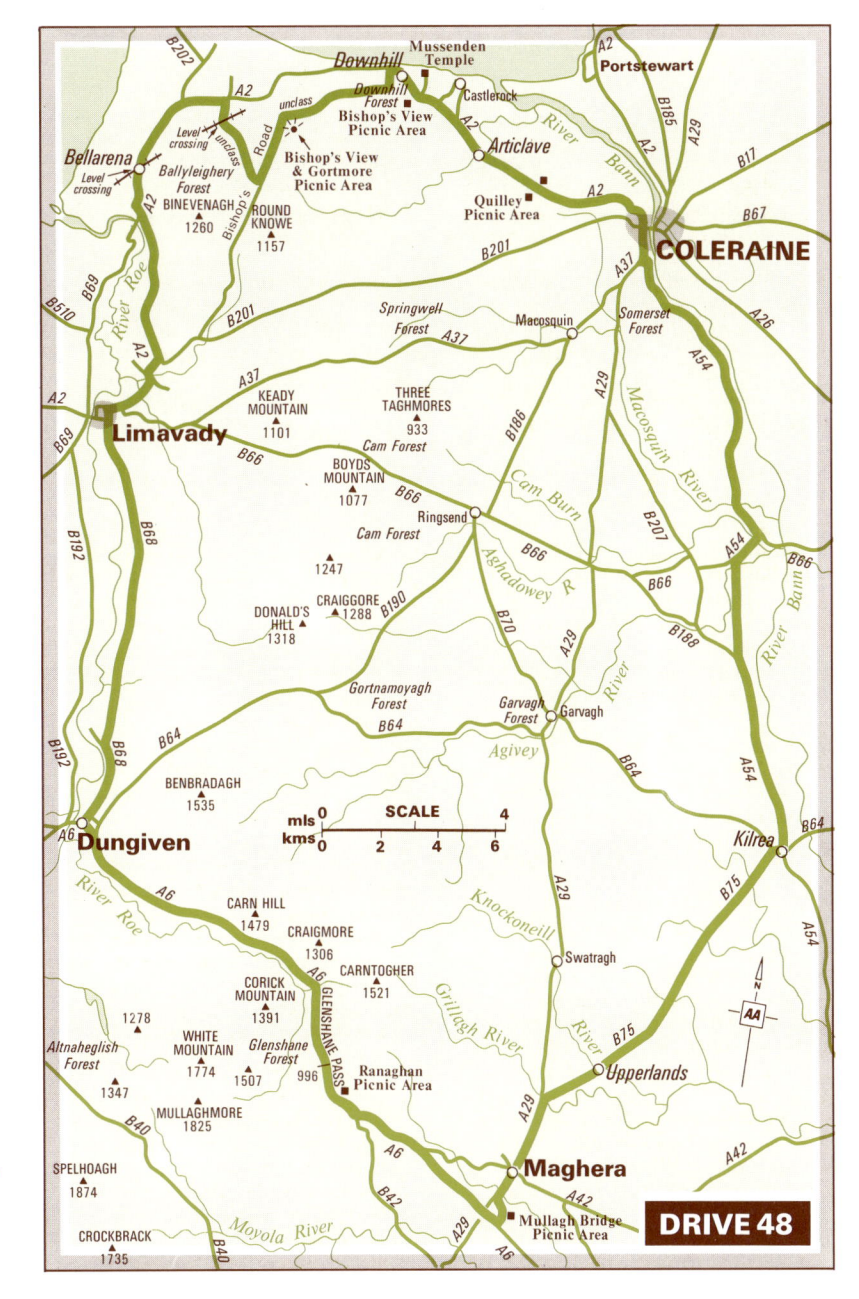

Drive 47 continued

Londonderry Monument on distant *Scrabo Hill*. Enter *Newtownards* and follow SP 'Belfast' to leave by the A20. Pass through undulating countryside, and after 5m reach *Dundonald*. Beyond Dundonald drive through increasingly urban areas to a point where views to the right take in Stormont — the parliament buildings of Northern Ireland. Proceed to Belfast city centre.

Placenames in *italic* type are worth stopping at; each is listed and described in the main gazetteer section.

LAND OF THE ULSTER LEGENDS

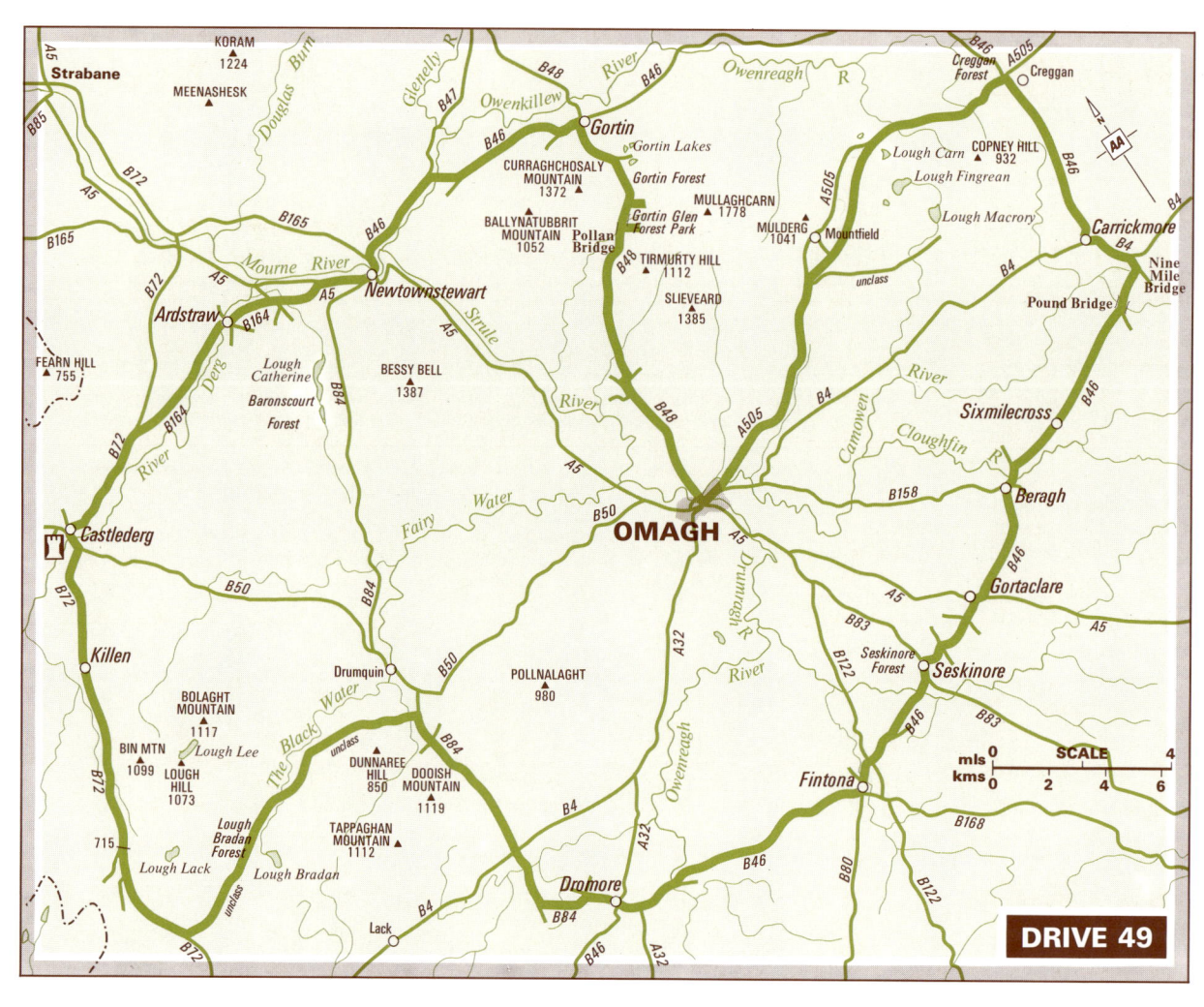

The Tyrone Forests

From Omagh

Drive 49   93 miles

Take Mountjoy Rd B48 for 'Gortin' to leave *Omagh*, and follow SP 'Gortin Glen Forest Park'. After 3m bear right and continue with 1,385ft Slieveard and 1,112ft Tirmurty Hill on the right. In $3\frac{1}{2}$m enter the Gortin Forest, in $\frac{1}{4}$m cross the Pollan Burn, and in a further $\frac{1}{4}$m pass the entrance to Gortin Glen Forest Park (right). A signposted, $4\frac{3}{4}$m forest drive can be taken through the park's fine scenery, which boasts numerous carparks and planned forest walks. The park exit joins the B48 on the 'Omagh' side of Pollan Bridge.

To continue with the main drive, ascend through the forest on the B48 to an 850ft summit between 1,372ft Curraghchosaly Mountain and a high spur of 1,778ft Mullaghcarn. In $\frac{3}{4}$m descend past an unclassified road (right) SP 'Scenic Drive' leading right to the small Gortin Lakes. In $1\frac{1}{4}$m reach the edge of *Gortin* and turn left on to the B46 SP 'Newtownstewart'. Proceed along the valley of the Owenkillew River, and after $3\frac{1}{4}$m bear right. In $\frac{1}{2}$m cross the river, then meet a T-junction and turn left SP 'Newtownstewart'. In $2\frac{1}{2}$m reach another T-junction and turn left. Cross Abercorn Bridge into *Newtownstewart*, which is situated beneath 1,387ft Bessy Bell. Leave this town on the A5 'Strabane' road and in $\frac{1}{2}$m bear right. In $\frac{3}{4}$m turn left on to the B164 SP 'Ardstraw', and $2\frac{1}{2}$m farther bear right into Ardstraw. Meet X-roads and go forward to cross the River Derg, then bear left SP 'Castlederg'. Continue along the valley with glimpses of the Derg on the left. After $3\frac{1}{4}$m meet a T-junction, turn left on to the B72 SP 'Castlederg', and in a further $2\frac{1}{2}$m enter Castlederg. Leave this town via the B72 'Ederny' road. Shortly cross the river, then climb out of the valley and after $3\frac{1}{4}$m pass through Killen. High ground to the left includes 1,099ft Bin Mountain, 1,117ft Bolaght Mountain, and 1,073ft Lough Hill. Continue the gradual ascent, and after 4m reach a 715ft summit at a fork in the road. Bear left here SP 'Ederny' to remain on the B72. Gradually descend, and after 1m skirt Lough Bradan Forest on the left. In a further $1\frac{1}{2}$m turn left on to an unclassified road SP 'Drumquin, Lough Bradan'. Continue through hilly country with forested areas which give way to peat bogs.

Pass Lough Bradan Forest and Lake on the right after $2\frac{3}{4}$m, then begin a descent into the valley of the Black Water and skirt part of the forest for about 1m. After 4m (from Lough Bradan) cross a small bridge, meet a T-junction, and turn right on to the B84 SP 'Dromore'. Ascend, and after $1\frac{1}{4}$m reach a low summit between 980ft Pollnalaght and 1,119ft Dooish. In $2\frac{1}{4}$m meet X-roads and drive forward, in $1\frac{1}{4}$m bear left, then in a further $1\frac{1}{4}$m reach X-roads and bear right. In $\frac{3}{4}$m enter *Dromore*. Leave the latter via the A32 'Enniskillen, Fintona' road and in $\frac{1}{2}$m go forward on to the B46 SP 'Fintona'. After 1m cross a river bridge, turn left SP 'Fintona', and in a further $4\frac{3}{4}$m enter *Fintona*. Proceed to a T-junction and turn left along the main street on to the B122 'Omagh' road. Pass an old church on the right and bear right with SP 'Omagh', then in $\frac{1}{2}$m turn right across a river. Meet X-roads and drive forward on the B46 SP 'Seskinore, Beragh', then in $\frac{3}{4}$m bear left SP 'Beragh'. In $1\frac{1}{4}$m proceed through Seskinore and shortly skirt the wooded grounds of Seskinore House on the left. After $\frac{3}{4}$m meet X-roads and turn right. In another $1\frac{1}{2}$m meet staggered X-roads and turn right on to the A5, then left on to the B46 SP 'Beragh'. In $2\frac{3}{4}$m reach Beragh, meet X-roads, and turn right into the village. Continue along the B46 with SP 'Sixmilecross' and cross the Cloughfin River. After 2m enter Sixmilecross, then leave by following SP 'Carrickmore' on the B46. Pass high ground on the right.

After 3m bear left across Pound Bridge. In a further $1\frac{1}{4}$m cross Nine Mile Bridge, meet a T-junction, and turn left on to the B4

LAND OF THE ULSTER LEGENDS

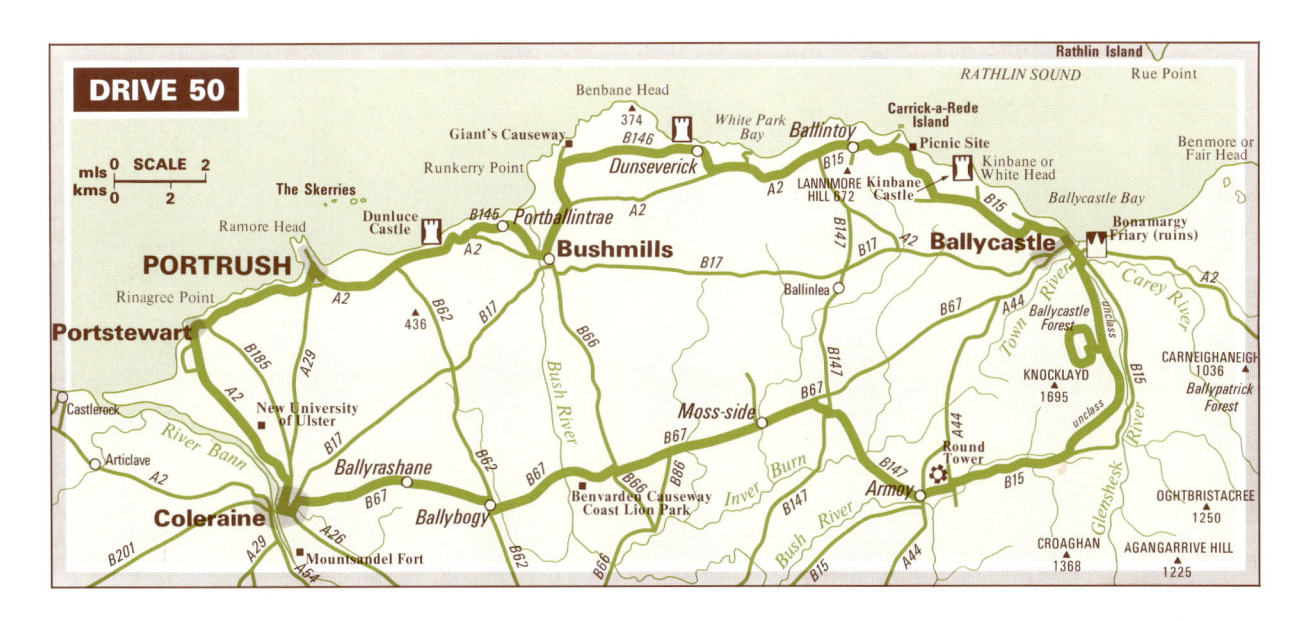

To the Giant's Causeway

From Portrush

Drive 50   74 miles

Follow SP 'Portstewart' to leave *Portrush* on the A2. Continue, with seascape views which include *Ramore Head* and Co Donegal's Inishowen Head, and reach the Derry resort of *Portstewart* – noted for its extensive sands. Follow SP 'Coleraine' to remain on the A2 and turn inland with the road along the Bann estuary. Pass the new University of Ulster on the left and enter the commercial and market centre of *Coleraine*, on the River Bann. Leave the town by following SP 'Ballycastle B67', and on reaching the Railway Arms Hotel turn left. Drive over a level crossing, immediately turn right into Ballycastle Rd, then continue through pleasantly pastoral country. After 4m cross the county boundary to enter Co Antrim, then ½m farther meet a T-junction and turn right then left, still following SP 'Ballycastle B67'. In 1¾m cross the Bush River, then pass the Benvarden Causeway Coast Lion Park on the right. This 62-acre reserve holds free-ranging lions and other species of wild animals. In ¾m meet staggered X-roads and turn right, then immediately left. Proceed along a straight but undulating road and pass through pleasant countryside to reach Moss Side. Drive through this village and in 1½m turn right SP 'Armoy B147'. Ascend to a T-junction and turn right, then immediately turn left on to the B147. Continue through hilly country, with views left of 1,695ft Knocklayd Mountain before *Armoy*.

To leave Armoy follow SP 'Glenshesk B15', then in ¾m meet staggered X-roads and follow SP 'Ballycastle', still on the B15. Cross a river bridge, and after another 2¾m turn left on to an unclassified road SP 'Forest Scenic Drive'. Climb through picturesque hill country with Knocklayd Mountain to the left and the Glenshesk River below. To the right is Ballypatrick Forest, while fine seaward views to the N encompass *Rathlin Island*. Here exiled Robert Bruce was taught a lesson in perseverance by a spider.

In 4½m reach the entrance to Ballycastle Forest. A worthwhile diversion from the main drive can be made by taking this signposted circular route, which affords exceptionally fine views as it passes through picturesque forest scenery. For the main drive, continue along the 'Ballycastle' road and descend, then in 2m meet a T-junction and turn right then immediately left on to the B15. Enter the resort of *Ballycastle*, passing Ballycastle Golf Course and the ruins of *Bonamarghy Friary* on the way. Leave this resort by the harbour road and follow SP 'Portrush B15'. In 1½m meet a T-junction and turn right SP 'Ballintoy, Bushmills' in order to continue through hilly country with intermittent sea views to the right. After another 2m bear right, then in 1½m pass a picnic area on the right. Fine views of Rathlin Island are afforded from here. After another ¼m pass the entrance to *Carrick-a-Rede* rope bridge, a precarious bridge which links Carrick-a-Rede island to the mainland across a coastal chasm measuring 60ft wide and 80ft deep. The shore scenery in the vicinity of the bridge is very picturesque.

Continue through the village of *Ballintoy*; beyond this the route offers good views of *White Park Bay* and Benbane Head. In a further 1m join the A2 SP 'Bushmills, Giant's Causeway', and in 1¼m pass the entrance to White Park Bay. In another 1m turn right on to the B146 SP 'Dunseverick, Giant's Causeway', continue through *Dunseverick*, and beyond the latter pass the ruins of Dunseverick Castle to the right. Veer inland with the road for 2¾m, then pass the entrance to the world-famous *Giant's Causeway*. This feature is one of the most remarkable natural phenomena known in Britain, and comprises a virtual cascade of geometric basaltic columns which march down the cliff to the sea in their thousands. Continue with the 'Bushmills' road, and in 1m turn right to rejoin the A2. Proceed to *Bushmills*, a community noted for its distillery and fishing, and turn right SP 'Portrush'. Cross the Bush River, then turn right again on to the B145 for *Portballintrae*.

Leave this pleasant little resort by following SP 'Portrush', and in 1m turn right to rejoin the A2 once again. After ¾m pass the ruined, cliff-top *Dunluce Castle* on the right. This strange structure is precipitously perched on a detached basaltic rock far above the sea. Complete the drive by returning to Portrush.

Drive 49 continued

'Carrickmore' road. Proceed through wooded country for 1¼m to reach Carrickmore, and turn right on to the B46 'Gortin' road. Ascend into wild hill and bog country, with 932ft Copney Hill on the left, and after 4m meet X-roads. Turn left on to the A505 'Omagh' road and pass Creggan Forest on the right, then continue with magnificent hill and forest views. Proceed, with views of 1,778ft Mullaghcarn ahead, and in 3¼m (from the X-roads) drive between a series of small lakes. In 3m views to the right take in Mountfield village beneath 1,041ft Mulderg. In a further ¾m pass an unclassified road on the left leading 4m to Lough Macrory.

Continue past Mullaghcarn, gradually descending towards Omagh. In 5m cross the Camowen River on the outskirts of Omagh. After another 1m re-enter the town centre.

LAND OF THE ULSTER LEGENDS

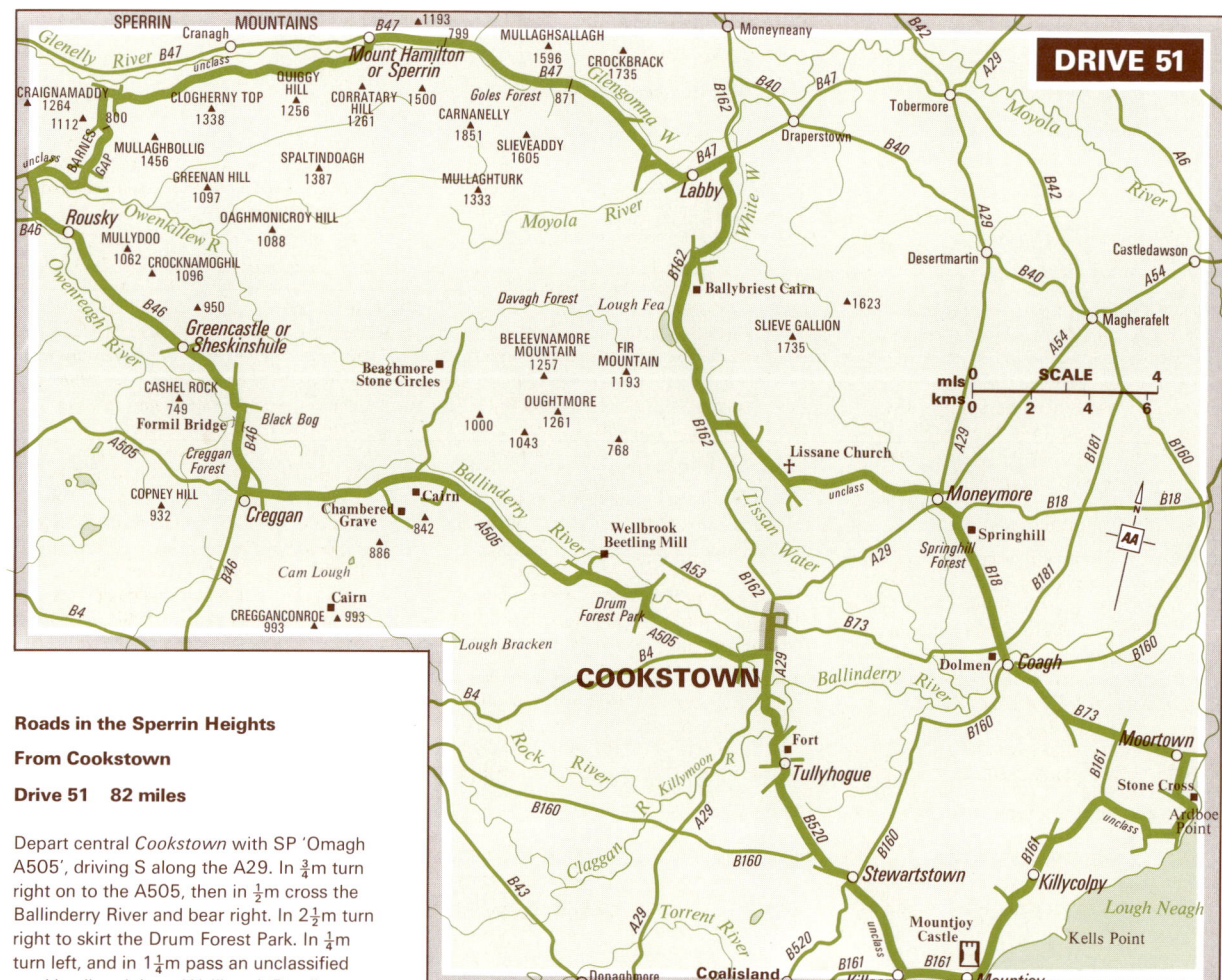

Roads in the Sperrin Heights

From Cookstown

Drive 51 82 miles

Depart central *Cookstown* with SP 'Omagh A505', driving S along the A29. In ¾m turn right on to the A505, then in ½m cross the Ballinderry River and bear right. In 2½m turn right to skirt the Drum Forest Park. In ¼m turn left, and in 1¼m pass an unclassified road leading right to Wellbrook Beetling Mill (NT) on the Ballinderry River. Follow the Ballinderry Valley, and after 5m pass an unclassified road leading right to Beaghmore Stone Circle (NT). Left of the main road is the Cregganconroe Chambered Cairn (AM). Proceed through moorland with the Black Bog away to the right. In 4m reach the second X-roads N of Creggan village and turn right on to the B46 SP 'Greencastle, Gortin'. Skirt Creggan forest on the left, with the Black Bog on the right, and in 1½m cross Formil Bridge. In ½m bear left SP 'Gortin', and in another ½m bear left again to follow the upper Owenreagh Valley.

In 1½m pass through *Greencastle* and continue along the B46 'Gortin' road alongside the river. Left is 1,776ft Mullaghcarn, and right are 1,096ft Crocknamoghil and 1,062ft Mullydoo. After 3¾m pass through *Rousky*, and in 1m reach the nearside of Drumlea Bridge. Turn right on to an unclassified road SP 'Barnes Gap'. Ahead are the Sperrin foothills. In ¾m cross the Owenkillew River, then in ¼m meet a T-junction and turn right to follow SP 'Barnes Gap'. In ½m cross Laragh Bridge, and in a further ½m keep left, then meet X-roads and drive forward SP 'Barnes Gap, Plumbridge'. Ascend between 1,112ft Mullaghbane and 1,456ft Mullaghbollig. After 1½m reach a height of 800ft, then descend through *Barnes Gap* into the Glenelly River valley. Fine views ahead take in the Sperrin range, with 1,896ft Mullaghclogher, 1,904ft Mullaghasturrakeen, and 2,088ft Mullaghclogha directly ahead.

In ½m meet a T-junction, turn right SP 'Draperstown', and ascend. In ¼m meet another T-junction and turn right, then sharp left. Proceed along the side of the Glenelly Valley to enjoy magnificent views of the river below, plus 1,870ft Mullaghdoo with 2,040ft Dart Mountain and 2,240ft Sawel Mountain lined up beside the other Sperrin peaks. Sawel is the highest mountain in the range. After 6m descend to cross the much-reduced Glenelly River and enter Sperrin village. Turn right on to the B47 SP 'Draperstown' and continue up the valley past the prominent hill spur of 1,193ft Mullaghrawer on the left. After 1m cross Glenerin Bridge and climb with the spur of 1,577ft Oughtvabeg on the left. Carnanelly rises to 1,851ft on the right.

Reach a summit and descend to Goles Bridge, dominated to the left by 2,061ft Meenard Mountain, 1,596ft Mullaghsallagh, and 1,878ft Oughtmore. Ascend, and after ¾m enter the Goles Forest. In ½m leave this woodland and continue for a further 1¼m to an 871ft summit. Descend along the Glengomna Water, with 1,735ft Crockbrack on the left, and after 2½m from the summit turn right SP 'Draperstown'. In ¼m turn sharp left, and in ¾m cross the Moyola River. In ¼m meet a T-junction and turn left SP 'Draperstown'. Proceed through Labby village, then in ¾m meet X-roads and turn right on to the B162 SP 'Cookstown, Lough Fea'. Ascend along the White Water Valley,

and in 2¾m turn left across a bridge over the Black Water. Bear right, and in 1¼m join Lough Fea and follow its shores. In ½m (beyond the lake) descend through hills, and in 1¼m turn left on to an unclassified road. In ½m cross Claggan Bridge, meet a T-junction, and turn right SP 'Moneymore'.

In 1¾m reach Lissane Parish Church and turn left SP 'Moneymore'. Continue, and in 3½m cross a bridge to enter *Moneymore*. Turn right on to the A29 to reach the town centre, then follow SP 'Coagh' to leave via the B18. In ½m bear right to pass Springhill Estate (NT) on the left, and Springhill Forest on the right. In 2½m meet X-roads and drive forward, then in ¼m bear left to cross the Ballinderry River into Coagh. Keep forward SP 'The Battery' on to the B73. After 1½m bear left, then in a further 1m meet X-roads and keep forward SP 'The Battery'. Ascend steeply for ½m and descend to enter Moortown in 1m. At the end of the village turn right on to an unclassified road SP 'Ardboe Cross'. In 1m meet a T-junction and turn left, then in ½m turn right with the magnificent *Ardboe* Cross (AM) on the left. Good views are afforded over *Lough Neagh* from this point. In ½m meet a T-junction and turn right, in ¾m meet another T-junction and turn right again, then in 1m at a further T-junction turn left on to the B161. In 1½m meet X-roads and turn left for *Coalisland*, then in 1m pass through Killycolpy and in ¾m reach a T-junction. Turn left here SP

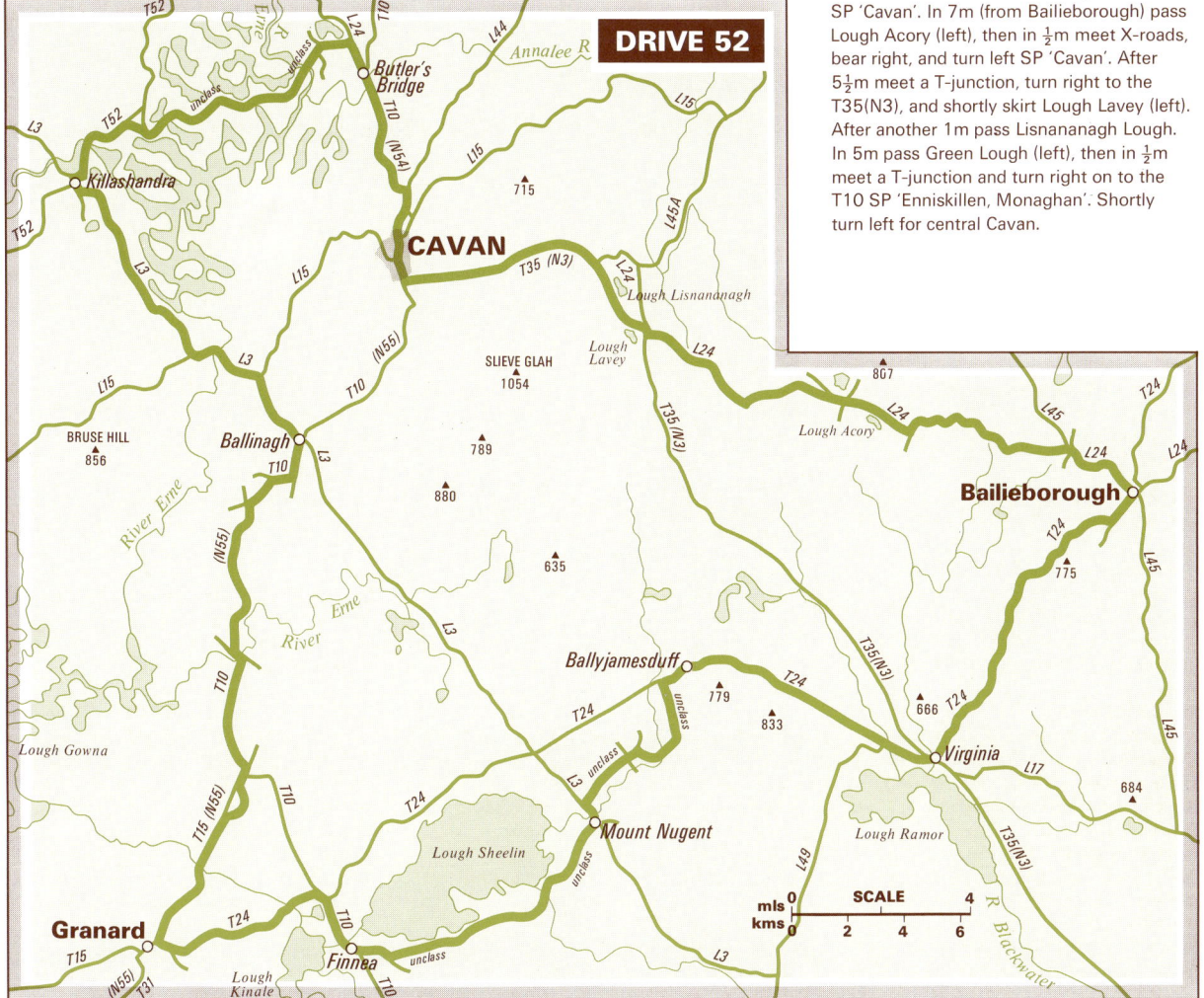

LAND OF THE ULSTER LEGENDS

Loughs of the Erne Valley

From Cavan

Drive 52   89 miles

Follow the T10(N3) 'Enniskillen, Monaghan' road from *Cavan*, in 1¼m bear left, and in ¾m bear right SP 'Belturbet'. After another 2m cross the Annalee River, enter Butler's Bridge, and turn left on to the L24 SP 'Belturbet'. In 1m turn left on to an unclassified road SP 'Killashandra'. In ½m bear left, in ¼m bear right with SP 'Killashandra', and later cross the River Erne. After 5m bear left SP 'Killashandra' and in ¼m drive forward on to the T52. In 1m turn left across the Newbridge River, and in ½m skirt Town Lough (right). Enter *Killashandra*, turn left into the main street, then keep forward on to the L3 SP 'Ballinagh'. In ¼m turn left, and in another 1½m bear left SP 'Ballinagh'. In 3¾m cross the River Erne, and in ¼m bear right SP 'Ballinagh'. After another 1m reach Crossdoney and bear right. In 2m reach Ballinagh, turn right on to the T10(N55) SP 'Granard, Athlone', and in ¾m bear right.

After a further 1½m reach X-roads and turn left SP 'Granard'. In 3½m recross the River Erne and shortly bear right, then in 2½m keep forward on the T15(N55). After ½m bear left, and in another 2m meet X-roads and turn left. In 1¾m reach the outskirts of *Granard* and turn sharp left on to the T24 SP 'Lough Sheelin'. After ½m bear left, and in a further 3¾m turn right on to the T10 SP 'Finnea'. Continue for 1¼m, cross the River Inny into Finnea, then in ¼m turn left on to an unclassified road SP 'Mount Nugent'. After ¾m meet X-roads and turn left to drive close to Lough Sheelin. After 2¼m meet a road junction and keep forward. In 1¼m cross the Upper Inny River. After another 2m meet *Mount Nugent* X-roads and turn left on to the L3 SP 'Kilmacrott Abbey' then in ¼m turn right on to an unclassified road SP 'Kilmacrott Abbey'. In 1½m meet X-roads and keep forward, then in ¼m bear right SP 'Ballyjamesduff'. In 2½m turn right on to the T24, then in ¾m enter *Ballyjamesduff*. Meet X-roads and drive forward to the square, turn right opposite the hotel, and immediately left SP 'Virginia'.

After 5¾m turn right on to the T35(N3) to enter *Virginia's* main street. Cross a river and shortly turn left on to the T24 SP 'Bailieborough'. In 2½m turn left SP 'Bailieborough', climb to 700ft, then in 4¼m reach *Bailieborough*. Meet X-roads and turn left into the main street; drive to the end and branch left on to the L24 SP 'Cavan'. After 2m meet X-roads and keep forward SP 'Cavan'. In 7m (from Bailieborough) pass Lough Acory (left), then in ½m meet X-roads, bear right, and turn left SP 'Cavan'. After 5½m meet a T-junction, turn right to the T35(N3), and shortly skirt Lough Lavey (left). After another 1m pass Lisnananagh Lough. In 5m pass Green Lough (left), then in ½m meet a T-junction and turn right on to the T10 SP 'Enniskillen, Monaghan'. Shortly turn left for central Cavan.

Drive 51 continued

'Coalisland', and in 1¾m pass a road leading right to Mountjoy Castle (AM). In ¼m go through *Mountjoy* village, and in 1½m meet Killeen X-roads. Turn right on to an unclassified road SP 'Stewartstown', and in 2½m reach *Stewartstown*. Turn right on to the B520 to enter the town, drive to the town centre, and turn left on to the B520 'Cookstown' road. In ½m turn right, and in a further 2¾m enter *Tullyhogue*.

Proceed to end of village and turn left SP 'Cookstown', passing the road to Tullyhogue Fort on the right, then bear right and in ¾m join the Killymoon River. Turn left across the river bridge, then in 1m enter a roundabout and take the second exit on to the A29 SP 'Crookstown'. In ¼m cross the Ballinderry River via the King's Bridge. In a further ¼m re-enter Cookstown, and drive forward for ¾m to reach the town centre.

Placenames in *italic* type are worth stopping at; each is listed and described in the main gazetteer section.

LAND OF THE ULSTER LEGENDS

Apple Blossom in Armagh

From Armagh

Drive 53   80 miles

From *Armagh* town centre follow SP 'Loughgall' and in $\frac{1}{2}$m enter a roundabout. Take the third exit on to Loughgall Rd B77. This winding road forms part of the well-known Apple Blossom Drive through fertile orchard country around *Loughgall* and *Portadown*. After 5m reach Loughgall, continue on the B77 SP 'Portadown', and in $1\frac{3}{4}$m bear left to pass through rich apple orchards. In $1\frac{3}{4}$m meet X-roads and drive forward, then in a further $2\frac{1}{4}$m cross the boundary into the new-town area of Craigavon. In a short distance bear right across the Ballybay River, and in $\frac{3}{4}$m enter the outskirts of Portadown. Continue to the town centre and follow SP 'Dungannon' to leave by Obin's St A4. In 1m meet X-roads. Turn left on to B28 SP 'Annaghmore, Moy'. Proceed forward through low, undulating pastoral and orchard country. In $4\frac{3}{4}$m bear right SP 'Moy', then in $\frac{1}{2}$m meet X-roads and bear left. After another $\frac{1}{2}$m pass a road leading left to *Ardress* House (NT). Shortly bear left, then in $\frac{1}{4}$m meet X-roads and drive forward. In $1\frac{3}{4}$m cross a canal bridge and curve round to run alongside the canal itself. In $\frac{3}{4}$m turn right, then in $\frac{1}{2}$m reach the nearside of Callan Bridge and pass an unclassified road on the right leading to Derryscollop Grave (NT). Cross the bridge and bear right SP 'Moy'.

Ascend through orchards, and in $1\frac{1}{2}$m enter Charlemont. Meet a T-junction and turn right on to the A29 SP 'Moy, Dungannon', passing the ruins of *Charlemont Fort* on the right.

Cross a bridge over the Blackwater River to enter *Moy*, and continue forward through the village on the A29 SP 'Dungannon' to pass through hilly agricultural country. In $3\frac{1}{4}$m at a roundabout take the first exit on to the A29. In a further $1\frac{1}{2}$m enter *Dungannon*. Leave this town by the A4 'Enniskillen' road, and in 1m turn right on to an unclassified road SP 'Castlecaulfield'.

Continue along a winding course through hilly country and in $\frac{1}{2}$m bear left, then in a further $1\frac{1}{2}$m pass a ruined castle (AM) on the left and enter *Castlecaulfield*. Cross a bridge, then drive to the Memorial Hall and turn right. Continue through pleasant country for 2m to reach *Donaghmore*. At the ancient stone cross turn left on to the B43 SP 'Pomeroy', then in $\frac{1}{2}$m meet X-roads and bear left and left again on to an unclassified road SP 'Cappagh'. In $\frac{3}{4}$m pass Mullygruen Lough on the left, and in a further $1\frac{1}{4}$m meet a fork and bear right. Gradually ascend into hilly country, and after $2\frac{1}{2}$m meet X-roads and turn left SP 'Cappagh'. Descend into a small valley and cross a river bridge, then in $\frac{1}{4}$m meet a T-junction and turn right SP 'Cappagh'. After $\frac{1}{4}$m enter Cappagh village, with Cappagh Mountain rising to 948ft on the left. Drive beyond the village and shortly cross the river via Cappagh Bridge. In $\frac{1}{4}$m pass a small lake on the left and a forested area on the right.

Continue the ascent on a stretch of road which affords pleasant views over the valley and surrounding hills. After 1m meet X-roads and turn left. Proceed through bogland, with some hill views to the right; 901ft Shane Barnagh's Hill and Cappagh Mountain rise to the left. After 1m reach a summit of 782ft, then descend and in a further $\frac{1}{2}$m cross Caroll's Bridge. Climb again, this time through a forested area with fine panoramic views, to a 754ft summit. Descend, with more fine views, then in $1\frac{3}{4}$m meet a T-junction and turn left. In $\frac{1}{2}$m cross Altanagh Bridge, then climb steeply through pastoral country along a section of the route which offers hill views on both sides. After $1\frac{1}{2}$m reach a height of 794ft, then shortly begin a descent into the valley of the Owenbrack River. Follow another long ascent for 2m, with a forested area on the right and bogland to the left, to reach a 730ft summit. Descend again, cross White Bridge, and turn right SP 'Ballygawley' to leave the forested area behind. Ascend through pleasant countryside with newly-planted forests ahead and attain a final, 760ft summit. Descend from the hills, with fine views extending over open country ahead, and drive into *Ballygawley*.

Go forward through the village with SP 'Aughnacloy A5'. Enter a roundabout and take the second exit, then almost immediately turn left on to the A5. Proceed through hilly, mainly pastoral country for 4m to reach *Aughnacloy*. The Republic of Ireland lies $\frac{1}{2}$m to the S of this village. Turn left on to the B35 'Dungannon' road, then in $\frac{1}{4}$m meet X-roads and turn right on to the B128 SP 'Benburb'. Continue along a winding road through hilly country. In $4\frac{1}{2}$m bear left SP 'Benburb', and after a further 1m reach Holland's X-roads. Minor roads to the left and right are respectively SP 'Brantry Lough' and 'Creeve Lough' scenic places. Proceed along a tree-edged section of road, and after $2\frac{1}{4}$m little Tullygiven Lough on the right. In $\frac{1}{4}$m meet a T-junction and turn left SP 'Benburb', then shortly reach X-roads and turn right to continue on the B128. In $\frac{1}{4}$m cross a bridge over the Oona Water, then after another $\frac{1}{4}$m meet X-roads and drive forward. Continue along a road which winds through hilly, pastoral country and in $1\frac{1}{4}$m pass the site where the Battle of Benburb was fought in 1646 (right).

In another $1\frac{1}{2}$m enter *Benburb*, passing its ruined 17th-c castle on the right, and continue forward on the B128 SP 'Blackwatertown'. In $\frac{3}{4}$m bear right, in a further $1\frac{1}{4}$m cross the River Blackwater into *Blackwatertown*, then immediately bear right SP 'Armagh' to follow the banks of the river for a short distance. After $\frac{1}{2}$m cross Mullyleggan Bridge and continue along a winding, undulating road. After $2\frac{1}{2}$m (from

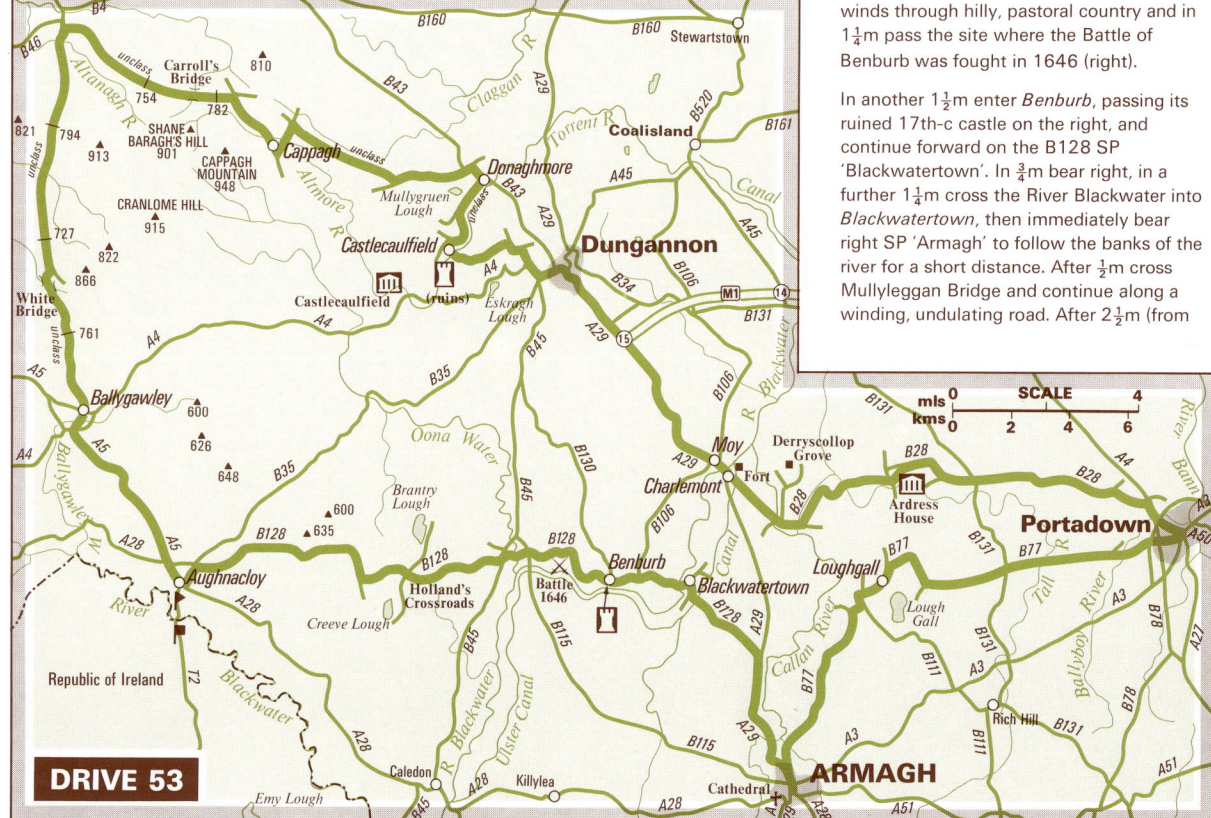

LAND OF THE ULSTER LEGENDS

Over the Derryveagh Range
From Dunfanaghy
Drive 54   77 miles

Leave *Dunfanaghy* via the T72(N56) with SP 'Portnablagh and Carrigart', then in 1¾m reach *Portnablagh*. In ¼m reach a garage and turn left uphill on an unclassified road SP 'Marble Hill Strand'. After 1¾m join *Marble Hill* Strand (left) and shortly pass a well-wooded hillside (right) as the route turns away from the beach. In 1½m turn left to rejoin the T72(N56), and in ¼m pass through *Ballymore*. After a further 1m pass the Ards Forest Park entrance (left). In 2m — close to a new church at the edge of *Creeslough* — branch right on to an unclassified road and ascend. Later pass beneath 2,197ft Muckish (right), and in 4¾m meet a T-junction. Turn left; the right turn here leads to 800ft Muckish Gap. In ¾m cross the Calabber River and immediately turn left on to the L82. Skirt 1,068ft Kingarrow on the right, cross the Owencarrow River at the end of Lough Veagh, and in ¼m pass the *Glenveagh* Castle Estate entrance. Continue for 1½m, reach a T-junction, and turn right. In ½m bear right SP 'Gartan', then in 1¾m reach the bottom of a small valley and turn sharp right uphill.

Continue above the W shore of Lough Akibbon, later enjoying views of *Gartan* Lough, then descend past another Glenveagh Estate entrance (right). Bear left, pass between the two loughs, then in ¼m drive forward on to the L82. Cross a river, bear right, and in ½m turn right on to an unclassified road to follow the shores of Gartan Lough. Brown Mountain stands at 746ft on the left, and 1,461ft Leahanmore rises to the right. After 1¼m reach the entrance to Church Hill Wood. Drive forward past the end of Gartan Lough and enter the Bullaba Valley. Later climb to an 800ft pass, with Leahanmore and 1,388ft Farscollop to the right and the *Glendowan* range left. Ahead the peaks of 2,147ft Dooish and 2,240ft Slieve Snaght rise from the Derryveagh Mountains, and views right extend towards Lough Veagh. Follow the road left and descend into the Barra Valley between Moylenanav and Slieve Snaght, then continue past Lough Barra with high ground to the right. In 5½m reach the nearside of *Doochary*. Turn sharp right on to the L75, then ascend steep Corkscrew Hill.

Isolated Croaghleconnell rises to 882ft on the left. Proceed, with small lakes on both sides of the road, and after 5½m turn right on to the T72(N56) 'Dungloe' road. In 2½m reach a garage on the nearside of *Dungloe* and turn right on to the L130(N56) SP 'Gweedore'. Follow a broad road, and after 5m pass Loughanure village and lough. In 2½m turn right to rejoin the T72, then continue and shortly pass through Crolly. In 1m keep forward on to the L130 and gradually ascend. After 1¼m cross the end of Lough Nacung Lower, then in ¼m reach *Gweedore* and meet a T-junction. Turn right here on to the L82 SP 'Gortahork', follow the shores of Lough Nacung Lower, and pass the peat-fired Gweedore Power Station. In ½m keep forward on the L130 and ascend; the L82 right turn here leads to *Dunlewy* and the famous *Poisoned Glen*. Magnificent views right extend over Lough Nacung Upper and take in the highest mountain in Co Donegal — conical, 2,466ft *Errigal*.

Continue to a low summit, with Tievealehid and 1,300ft Carntreena on the left, then gradually descend and turn right on to the T72 (N56). Views from this section extend down the Glenna River valley towards *Gortahork* and the coast. In 1m pass through Gortahork, then in 2¼m proceed through *Falcarragh* and re-enter Dunfanaghy in a further 8m.

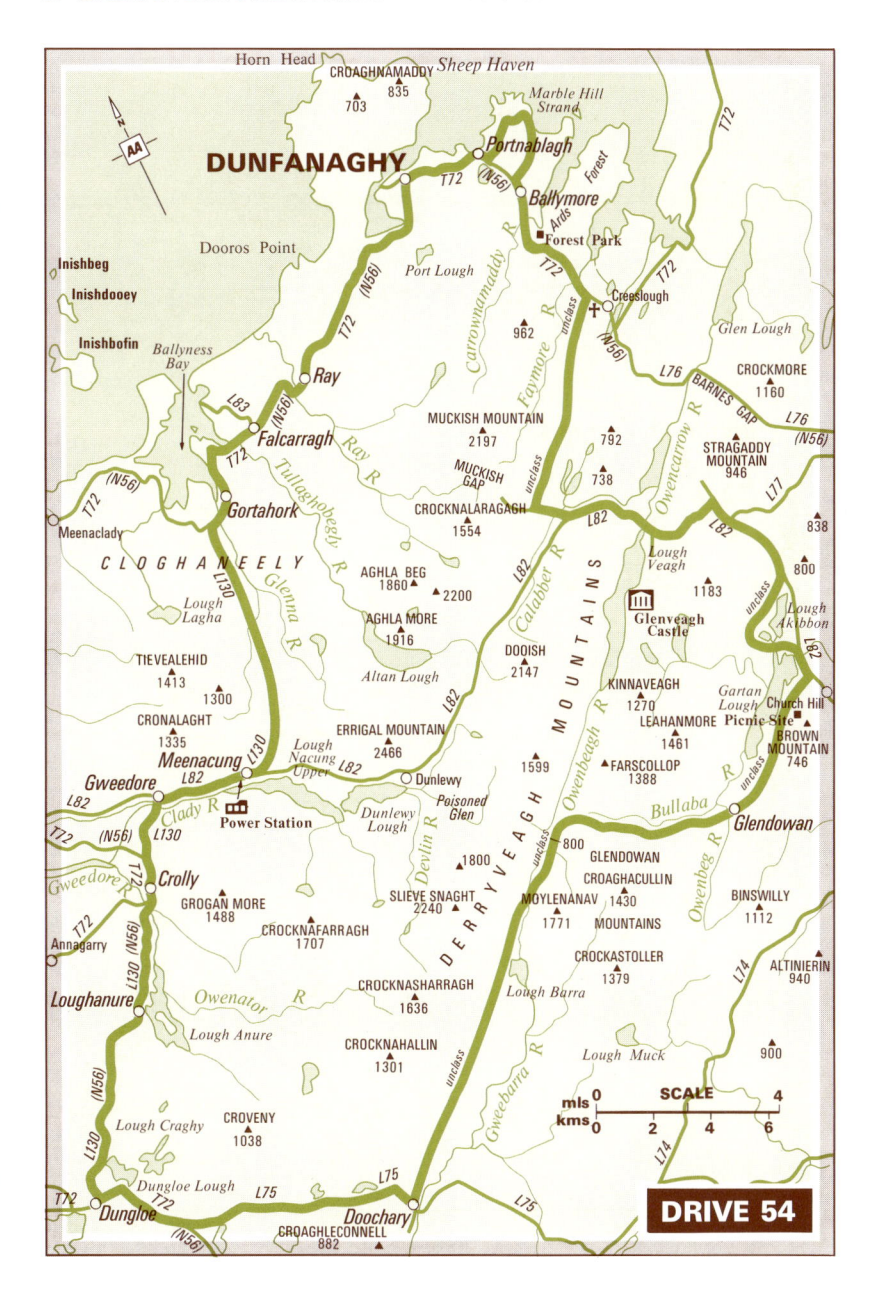

Drive 53 continued

Blackwatertown) meet a T-junction and turn right on to the A29 SP 'Armagh'. Proceed through pleasant countryside dotted with apple orchards for 3m and re-enter Armagh.

LAND OF THE ULSTER LEGENDS

Lonely Northern Coasts

From Cushendall

Drive 55   56 miles

Leave *Cushendall* with SP 'Golf Club' along an unclassified road. In ¼m bear left SP 'Cushendun' and ascend along a hill road with sea views to the right. Climb for 2m to reach a 560ft summit, then descend quite steeply into the Glendun Valley. Meet a T-junction and turn right on to the B92 SP 'Cushendun', then pass through *Knocknacarry*. In ½m cross the Glendun River to *Cushendun* (NT). Continue through the village on the B92 and run alongside the shores of Cushendun Bay. After ½m meet a T-junction and turn right on to an unclassified road SP 'Ballycastle by Torr Head Scenic Route'. Climb steeply along this narrow road at first and enjoy fine coastal views as the route winds along the hillside below 1,000ft Cushleake Mountain. Continue high above the shore beneath 880ft Carnaneigh, and after 3½m pass Runabay Head. Farther on Loughan Bay can be seen to the right.

Climb to a 750ft summit at Green Hill, overlooking Crockan Point; the Scottish coast is only 12m away from here. Descend steeply with 1,253ft Carnanmore on the left, then after ½m cross the Altmore Burn and shortly bear right SP 'Torr Head'. Continue the descent, then after ½m cross a small bridge and turn right for *Torr Head*. Descend steeply to reach the Torr Head carpark in ¼m. A footpath to the top of this 200ft-high headland affords fine views of *Fair Head* and *Rathlin Island*, the Scottish coast, and Port-aleen Bay. Return along the approach road, and in ½m bear right to begin a steep ascent. In ½m meet a junction and drive forward SP 'Ballycastle'. Continue the ascent through hilly country to an 873ft summit, then follow a long, gradual descent.

After 2¾m pass a road SP 'Murlough Bay' on the right. This leads to the NT-owned Murlough Bay, which is dominated by towering cliffs. After another 1m meet a T-junction and turn right SP 'Ballycastle', then in ¾m pass a road to the right SP 'Fair Head NT Property'. In another ¾m turn right on to the A2 and gradually descend towards *Ballycastle*. In 1¾m pass the road to the Corrymeela Conference Centre on the right, and shortly note ruined *Bonamargy Friary* (AM) on the left. In ¼m cross the Margy or Glenshesk River, meet a T-junction, and turn right into Ballycastle. In a further ¼m turn left for the town centre. On leaving Ballycastle return along the A2 for ¾m, then meet a junction and keep forward on to the B15 SP 'Glenshesk'. In ¼m cross the river and ascend, with views of the Glenshesk River valley to the right. Follow the Glenshesk to enjoy good views of 1,695ft Knocklayd and Ballycastle Forest.

Distant Ballypatrick Forest clothes both 1,036ft Carneighaneigh and 1,321ft Crockaneel to the left. In 3½m (from the previous bridge) recross the river at Glenshesk Bridge, then ascend gradually to enter a low, wide pass between 1,368ft Croaghan and Knocklayd. After 4½m cross a bridge and bear left SP 'Lough Guile, Clogh', then immediately left again over another bridge on to an unclassified road.

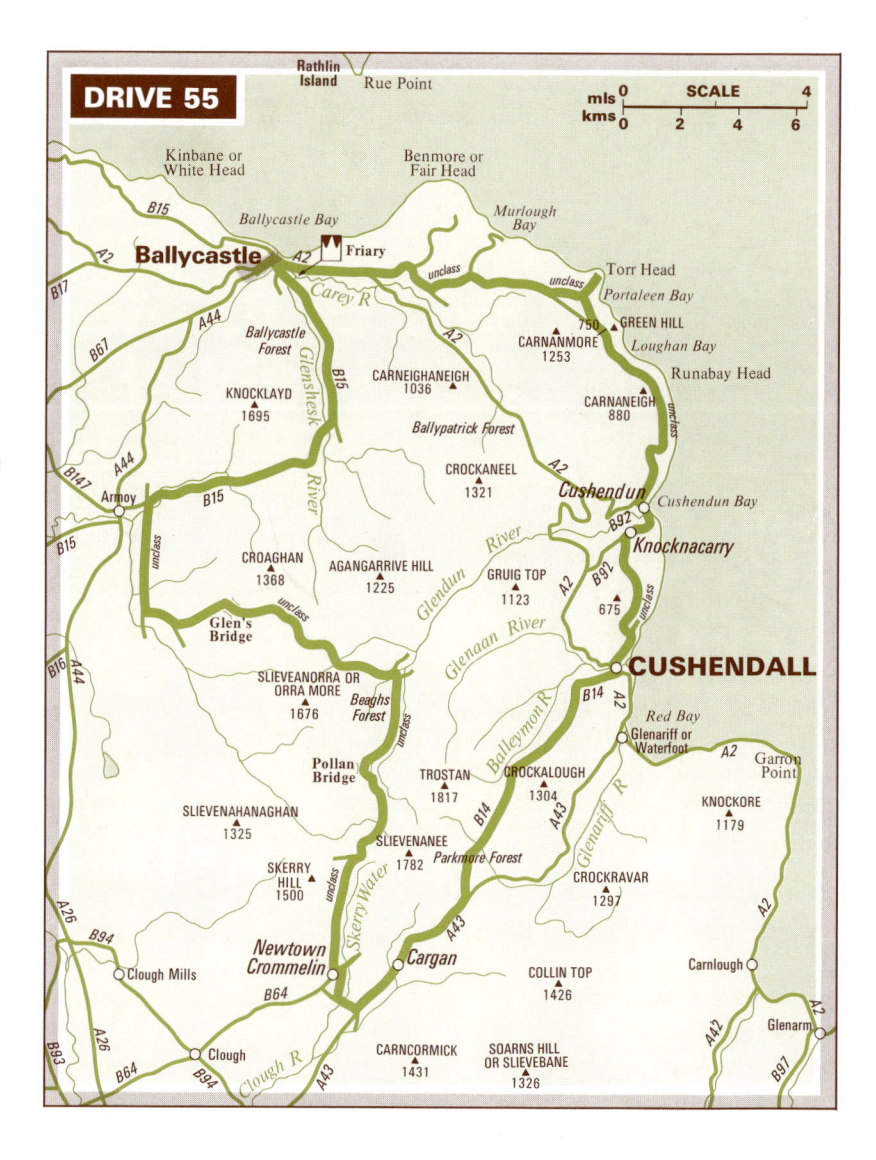

Continue along this undulating and almost entirely straight road to follow the line of the Bush River through pastoral country. Views left encompass 1,368ft Croaghan. After 2½m turn left SP 'Cushendall and Cushendun Scenic Route', and in ½m bear left. Ascend with pleasant views of forested, 1,676ft Slieveanorra to the right. After 1½m bear right over Glen's Bridge and drive along a section offering good forest views.

Ascend along a winding hillside stretch which affords views. In 3m (from Glen's Bridge) reach a 1,141ft summit, and in a further ½m cross a small river bridge with wooded land to the left and views of Beaghs Forest to the right. Descend past the forest into upper Glendun Valley, meet a T-junction, and turn right. Cross a small bridge and keep forward SP 'Newtown Crommelin, Ballymena' to follow the upper Glendun River. Trostan rises to 1,817ft on the left, and Slieveanorra – or Beaghs Forest – can be seen to the right. After 2½m cross Pollan Bridge and bear left. Leave the forest behind in another ¼m and continue to climb with 1,782ft Slievenanee visible to the left and Slieveanorra – or Glenbush – Forest on the right. After 2¼m (from Pollan Bridge) attain a 1,364ft summit and descend. In ½m meet a fork and bear left SP 'Newtown Crommelin'. Descend gradually at first, then

after 1m drop more steeply as the route follows the line of Skerry Water into the Clogh Valley, offering fine views over the surrounding countryside. After 2½m reach the foot of the descent, meet a T-junction, and turn left on to the B64. Enter Newtown Crommelin, shortly turn right SP 'Cushendall, Waterfoot', and descend with views of 1,431ft Carncormick to the left. After ¾m meet X-roads and turn left. Cross a bridge over the Skerry Water, then in ¼m meet a T-junction and turn left on to the main A43 'Cushendall' road. Shortly enter a tree-edged section which offers fine hill views both to the left and right, and in 1½m pass the village of Cargan. Climb through hill country with Cargan Water on the left – beneath Slievenanee – and *Parkmore Forest* ahead.

Some 2m beyond Cargan reach a 947ft summit and branch left on to the B14 SP 'Cushendall'. Climb through Parkmore Forest for 2m and pass between Trostan on the left and 1,304ft Crockalough on the right at a height of 1,000ft-plus. Follow a long descent across the side of the Ballyemon Valley, with distant coastal views, then re-enter Cushendall.

LAND OF THE ULSTER LEGENDS

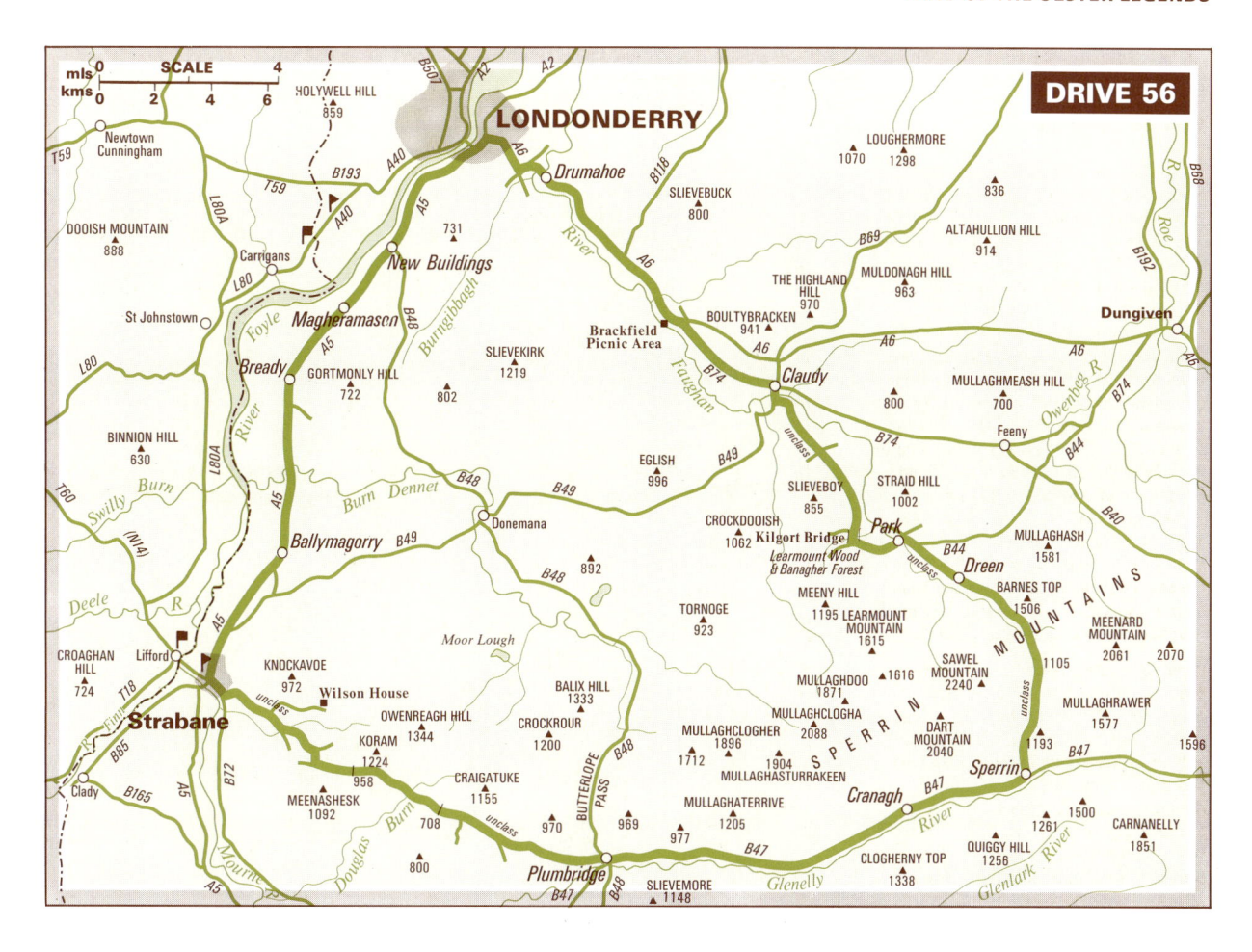

DRIVE 56

Rivers among the Mountains

From Londonderry

Drive 56   60 miles

Leave *Londonderry* by the A5 'Strabane' road and pass Victoria Bridge – which spans the River Foyle – on the right. Follow a good, wide road alongside the Foyle. In ¾m meet a junction, bear right, and pass Londonderry Golf Course on the left. In a further 1¾m reach the village of New Buildings, meet a junction, and branch right SP 'Strabane'. Later on pass boundary SP to cross into Co Tyrone and enter the small village of Magheramason. Continue along the valley of the River Foyle. In 2m drive through Bready, beneath 722ft Gortmonly Hill, on a section of road which affords distant views of the River Foyle to the right. Drive through more hilly country and in 2m cross the River Dennet. Continue through pleasantly wooded country and proceed to *Strabane*, situated near the point where the Rivers Finn and Mourne combine to form the Foyle.

Enter the town of Strabane, turn left, then drive forward on to the B72 and in ½m turn left on to the unclassified 'Plumbridge' road. Pass the Fountain Bar on the right and ascend. In 1½m pass the entrance to President Wilson's House (NT) – traditionally the home in which the ancestors of the American president of this name lived. Cross Cavanalee River and bear left SP 'Plumbridge'. Continue to ascend through wild hill country to reach a 958ft summit between the foothills of the Sperrin Mountains. Descend and pass through a forested area, and in ½m bear left. In a further 1¾m cross a bridge and bear right for *Plumbridge*, picturesquely situated in the Glenelly Valley and dominated by the Sperrin Mountains. Enter the village, meet a T-junction, and turn left on to the B47 SP 'Glenelly Valley Scenic Drive'. Continue along the valley between the Sperrin Mountains to enjoy wonderful views of the river winding below and the peaks of 2,088ft Mullaghclogha, 2,040ft Dart, and 2,240ft Sawel rising to the left. In 2m (from Plumbridge) bear right and cross numerous bridges spanning tributaries of the Glenelly River. After 6m reach Cranagh, then continue along the B74 to reach Sperrin village and turn left on to an unclassified road SP 'Park'. Ascend along a narrow, winding road between the mountains, with Sawel prominent on the left and both 2,061ft Meenard and 2,070ft Mullaghaneany to the right, to reach a 1,105ft road summit.

Descend through the village of Dreen, then in 1m cross a small bridge and meet a T-junction. Turn left here, then in a further ¼m turn left again SP 'Claudy' and cross a river bridge into Park. Drive through this village, then pass Learmount Wood and Banagher Forest. Meet a junction and bear right SP 'Claudy', and immediately turn left over Kilgort Bridge, then bear right. Continue along the perimeter of the forest between 855ft Slieveboy and 1,002ft Straid Hill. In 1½m pass Tullintrain Post Office on the left, meet X-roads, and drive forward. In 2m meet a T-junction, turn right, and cross the River Faughan to reach *Claudy* – situated at the head of a wooded valley. Meet X-roads and turn left on to the B74, then in 2½m meet more X-roads and turn left again on to the A6. Drive along a fast main road through the Faughan Valley, with views of the river on the left. Enter *Drumahoe* and recross the River Faughan. To the N is Fincairn Glen, a notable gorge which measures 100ft in depth and extends for more than ½m. Pass an AA Road Service Centre, then meet traffic signals and turn right to return to Londonderry.

LAND OF THE ULSTER LEGENDS

Hills and an Inland Sea

From Newcastle

Drive 57   105 miles

Take the A50 'Castlewellan' road out of Newcastle and ascend. In 2m pass a road leading right to Maghera Old Church and Round Tower, and one leading left to Tollymore Forest Park. In 2m enter Castlewellan and turn right on to the A25 SP 'Downpatrick', then descend to Annsborough and turn left on to the B175 SP 'Ballynahinch'. Ascend, and in 1½m turn left on to an unclassified road. Continue the climb with views extending left to 1,755ft Slieve Croob. Reach a 1,183ft road summit and descend with magnificent views. In 2m meet X-roads, turn right on to the B7 SP 'Dromara', and in ¾m turn right again. Drive through Massford to reach Dromara, go forward, then in ½m cross a river bridge and turn right SP 'Ballynahinch'. Climb and then descend through pleasantly wooded areas.

In 3m meet a T-junction and turn right on to the B2. Enter Ballynahinch, turn left on to the A24, and follow SP 'Belfast'. In 1m turn right on to the A21 SP 'Saintfield' and continue through hill country. Pass Dairy Lough and Long Lough (left), then in 2¾m reach Saintfield, meet X-roads, and turn left on to the A7 SP 'Comber'. In a further ½m bear right on to the A21, and in 2¾m enter Ballygowan. Enter a roundabout, leave by the second exit, and enjoy distant views of Scrabo Tower before reaching Comber.

Leave this town via the A22 'Downpatrick' road. In ½m turn left on to an unclassified road SP 'Ardmillan', and in 3m reach Ballydrain. Meet a T-junction and turn left SP 'Mahee Island', then after another 1¾m cross a quay on to Reagh Island and drive over a bridge on to Island Mahee. Return to the outskirts of Ballydrain and turn left SP 'Ardmillan'. Drive through the village, then cross a bridge and turn left SP 'Ballydorn'. In ¼m turn left again. Drive alongside Strangford Lough to pass Sketrick Island and enter Whiterock. Leave the lough with SP 'Killinchey' and ascend, then in 2m meet X-roads and turn left on to the A22 SP 'Killyleagh'. Continue, and in 4m drive through Toye to reach Killyleagh. Go forward on to the 'Downpatrick' road.

Proceed with views of the Mourne Mountains and Strangford Lough. In 5m turn left, cross the Quoile River, then turn left again SP 'A25 Strangford'. Drive alongside the river, then in ½m meet X-roads and turn left on to the A25. In a further ¼m bear right, and in 3½m bear right again. In 1¾m pass a road leading left to Castleward, then later descend to Strangford. At Strangford turn right on to the A2 SP 'Ardglass' and drive alongside the lough. In 2m reach Kilclief Castle (right) and turn left on to an unclassified road SP 'Ballyhornan'. Continue alongside the lough, with views which extend over Ballyhornan Bay to Guns Island, and proceed to Ballyhornan. In ½m meet a T-junction and turn left on to the A2 SP 'Ardglass'. In a further 1½m pass a road leading left to St Patrick's Well and Ardtole Church, then enter Ardglass. Leave the latter on the 'Killough' road, passing Jordan's Castle (right) and the harbour, then continue with the A2 and drive through Coney Island. In ¾m bear left SP 'Killough', enter the village, and drive alongside the harbour. Go forward on to an unclassified road SP 'St John's Point', and in ¼m turn right. In 1¼m turn right SP 'Clough' and drive along Dundrum Bay. In a further 1¼m meet a T-junction and turn left on to the A2 to continue along the shoreline. In 2m bear left, and in another 2m bear right to reach the outskirts of Clough. Meet a T-junction and turn left SP 'Dundrum', then continue with views of the Mournes. In 2m drive through Dundrum for the return to Newcastle.

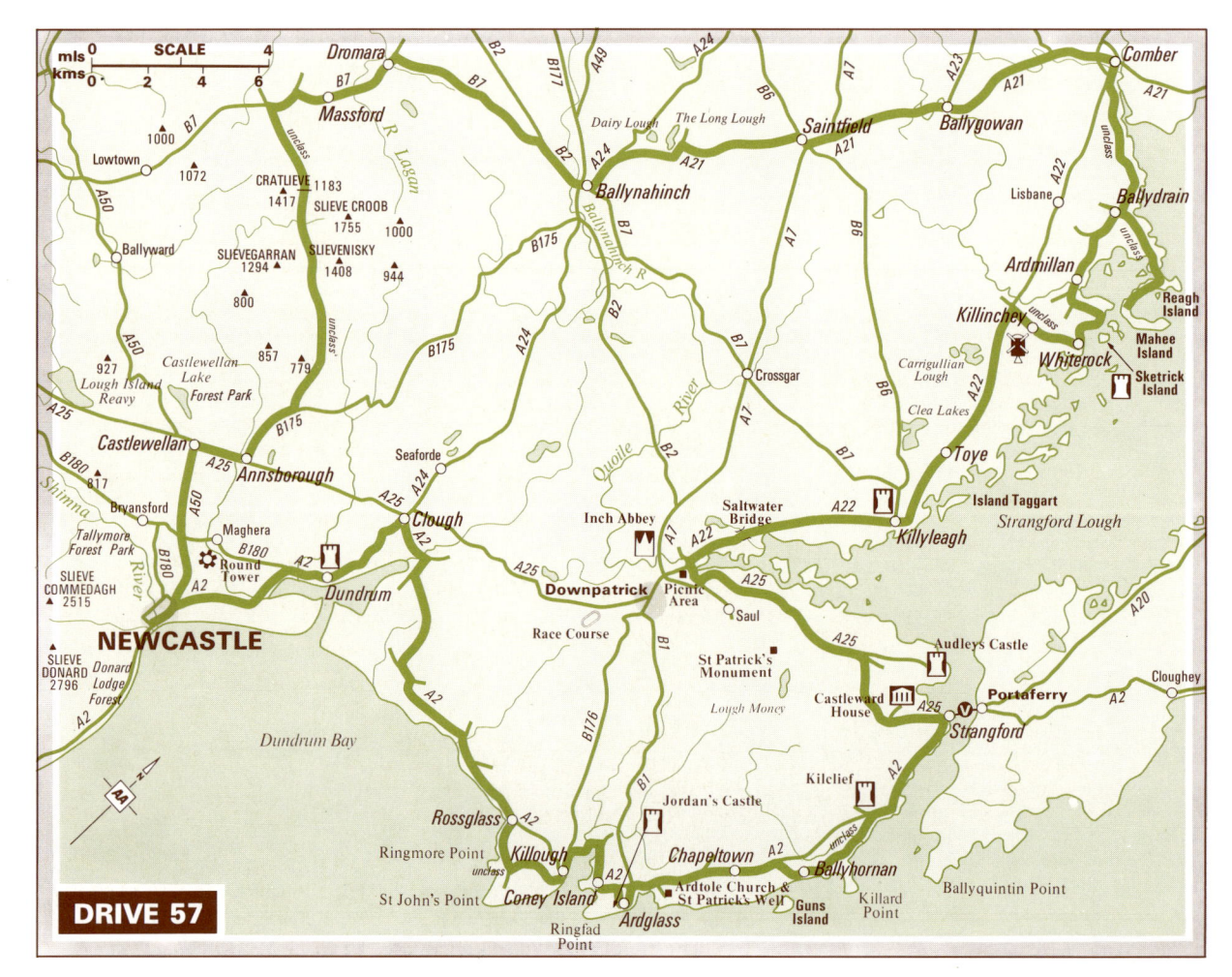

Gazetteer

Key to Town Plans

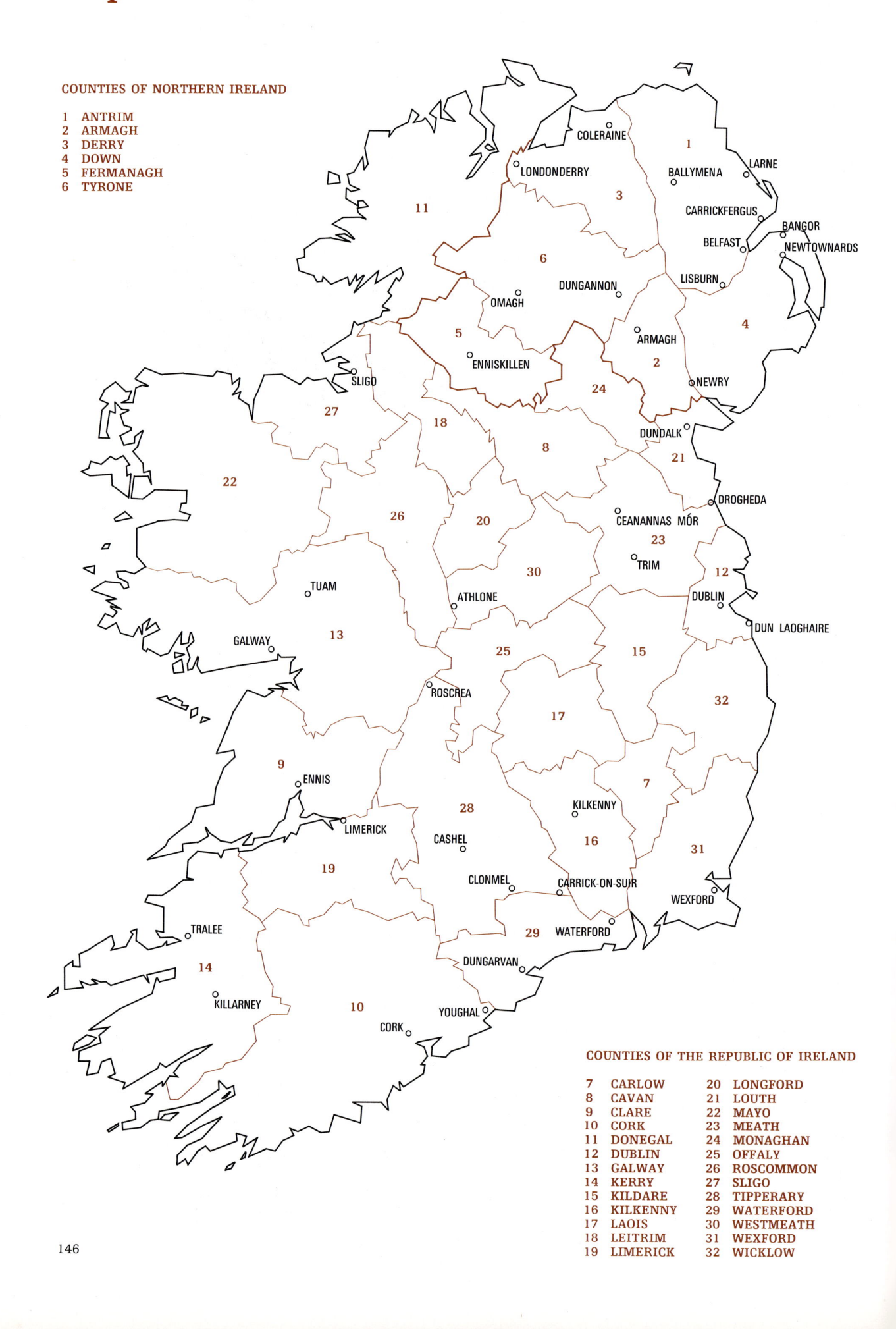

COUNTIES OF NORTHERN IRELAND

1. ANTRIM
2. ARMAGH
3. DERRY
4. DOWN
5. FERMANAGH
6. TYRONE

COUNTIES OF THE REPUBLIC OF IRELAND

7	CARLOW	20	LONGFORD
8	CAVAN	21	LOUTH
9	CLARE	22	MAYO
10	CORK	23	MEATH
11	DONEGAL	24	MONAGHAN
12	DUBLIN	25	OFFALY
13	GALWAY	26	ROSCOMMON
14	KERRY	27	SLIGO
15	KILDARE	28	TIPPERARY
16	KILKENNY	29	WATERFORD
17	LAOIS	30	WESTMEATH
18	LEITRIM	31	WEXFORD
19	LIMERICK	32	WICKLOW

ABBEY, *An Mhainistir:*
the Abbey, Galway **16 M70**
Abbey is thus named because of its close proximity to the Franciscan Kilnalahan Friary. The original monastery was founded here by John de Cogan for the Carthusian Order, but the monks abandoned it *c*1370 and the 30-year-old buildings were taken over by the Franciscan Order. Memorials to the important Anglo-Norman Burke family survive in the ruins, and the tomb of the founder was discovered in 1779. Other finds included de Cogan's family arms and a long broadsword.

ABBEYDORNEY, *Mainistir Ó dTorna:*
the Monastery of the Uí Torna, Kerry **20 Q82**
Remains of the mainly 14th-c Cistercian abbey from which Abbeydorney derives its name lie to the N of the village.

ABBEYFEALE, *Mainistir na Féile:*
Abbey of the River Feale, Limerick **21 R12**
This small market town crouches amongst the foothills of the Mullaghareirk Mountains, on the banks of the River Feale. The community takes its name from a Cistercian abbey which was founded by Brian O Brien in 1188. Nearly all traces of the original foundation, which was later annexed to Monasteranenagh near Croom, have disappeared. The only easily discernible remains extant are of the abbey church, and these have been incorporated in the structure of the RC village church. About 1½m NW, on the N banks of the Feale, are the ruins of the Geraldine castle of Portrinard. These fragmentary remains date from the 14thc.

TOWN PLAN SYMBOLS

† ✝	Church/Cathedral
H	Hospital
▬▬	Major Road
──	Minor Road
P	Official Carpark (Free)
←	One-way Street
Park	Parks & Open Spaces
ⓟ	Parking Available on Payment
ⓘ	Point of Interest
POL	Police
PO	Post Office
▬▬	Recommended Route
STA	Station
C	Toilet
i	Tourist Information Centre
○	Traffic Roundabout

GAZETTEER ABBREVIATIONS

AM	See NM (below)
c	Century
CI	Church of Ireland
c	*Circa*
*	Day Drive Starting Point
ft	Foot (Feet)
m	Mile(s)
N,S,E,W	Points of the Compass
NM	National Monument
NT	National Trust
OACT	Open At Certain Times
RC	Roman Catholic
sqm	Square Mile(s)
yds	Yards

ABBEYKNOCKMOY, *Mainistir Chnoc Muaidhe,* Galway **16 M54**
Nearby Collis Victoriae is a Cistercian abbey (NM) from which this village derived its name. The abbey was founded by Cathal O Conor – King of Connacht during the 12thc – in memory of a battle victory over Anglo-Norman forces. The nave is refreshingly simple, but the chancel displays rib vaulting, beautifully-carved stonework, plus fine capitals and east windows. The pointed chancel arch contrasts pleasingly with the other arches at the crossing, which are round. The corbels in the chancel suggest that there was once a room overhead. The interesting trans-early gothic church is noted for its frescoes. These include depictions of the Holy Trinity, the Martyrdom of St Sebastian, and the Three Dead and Three Living Kings.

ABBEYLARA, *Mainistir Leathrátha:*
Monastery of the Half Ring-fort, Longford **17 N37**
Remains of a 13th-c Cistercian abbey survive here, and nearby Loughs Kinale and Gowna are separated by a 3m section of the ancient Black Pig's Dyke (see entry).

ABBEYLEIX, *Mainistir Laoise:*
the Monastery of Laois, Laois **23 S48**
Named after a Cistercian abbey which has since disappeared, this pleasant town is an excellent example of the type of work carried out by an 'improving' landlord. In this case the landlord was the first Viscount de Vesci, who built the community during the mid 18thc. It is based on a well-planned network of tree-lined streets and includes a number of elegant Georgian houses. Other buildings of interest include the Protestant church and the market house. Nowadays it is a known centre for angling on the River Nore and its tributaries.

Immediately SW is the home of Viscount de Vesci – the demesne of Abbey Leix (OACT). This was built by Sir William Chambers in 1773, to a design by James Wyatt, for the enlightened first Viscount. Early 19th-c terraces slope through unusually attractive parkland to the banks of the Nore, and afford views of the Kilkenny Hills. Remains of an ancient oak wood (OACT), and a 12th- to 13th-c monks' bridge survive in the grounds. Other interesting features – which can only be seen by appointment – include an effigy of Malachi O More from the abbey, and a fragment of a medieval font. O More was once Lord of Laois.

ABBEYSHRULE, *Mainistir Shruthla:*
Monastery of the Stream, Longford **17 N25**
Remains of the Cistercian abbey standing on the E bank of the Inny River at Abbeyshrule include the choir and part of the nave of an aisleless church, dating from the 12th or 13thc. The foundation was colonized by monks from Mellifont *c*1150, but the earliest buildings date from *c*1200. The graveyard NNE of the ruins features the broken shaft of a small early cross, which displays a five-strand plait and other patterns.

ABBEYSTROWRY, *Mainistir Shruthra:*
Monastery of the Stream, Cork **27 W13**
The ruined Cistercian abbey which stands 1m W of Skibbereen on the bank of the River Ilen here was a cell of the Abbey of Maune during the 14thc.

ACHILLBEG, *Acaill Bheag,* Mayo **8 L79**
Achillbeg is a small island measuring about 1sqm, situated opposite the S entrance to Achill Sound. An elaborate promontory fort (Doon Kilmore) exists on a small peninsula which extends from the W shore. This was defended by a ditch and stone-revetted rampart built across the outer neck of the promontory, inside which there are remains of graves, huts, and a bullaun. Two smaller defended promontories can be seen on the island, the larger (The Dún) of which displays triple ramparts. The other (The Daingean) boasts the remains of a medieval castle.

ACHILL ISLAND, *Acaill,* Mayo **8 F60**
Access to the island – the largest off the Irish coast – is via a swivel-bridge built in 1888 which spans the narrow channel known as Achill Sound. The mainland end of the bridge is approached through the tiny village of Achill, and to the W of the island end is the community of Achill Sound. The small proportion of the island's 36,248 acres suitable for cultivation is centred mainly on the coast or in the sheltered valleys. The rest of the land is a dazzling combination of magnificent cliffs, golden strands, purple moors, precipitous hillsides, and scattered white cottages. It is an ideal holiday resort for seekers after solitude.

Slievemore is a 2,204ft viewpoint from which the whole island can be seen, and is easily climbed from Doogort. A slightly smaller but finer hill is 2,192ft Croaghaun, situated in the extreme W, which can be approached from Dooagh via Lough Acorrymore. Its summit comprises a 2m ridge which falls sheer to the sea on two sides, offering breathtaking cliff scenery. Rock-climbing enthusiasts may like to attempt the W descent to the knife-edge projection of Achill Head, but it must be stressed that this is an adventure for experts only. The less proficient can enjoy a fine walk from Dooagh to Keem Bay, which is sheltered by Moyteoge Head, and may be lucky enough to see choughs flying up from the grassy hillsides. This walk can be continued W beyond Keem Bay to a 1,000ft precipice which affords views of Achill Head.

Slievemore and its immediate vicinity are rich in prehistoric remains. A megalithic gallery grave can be seen 100ft up on the S slope of Slievemore, and there is a chambered tomb known as the Giant's Grave at Doogort West. About 600yds W of the latter is Keel East Cromlech, a cairn with an elliptical court and three-chambered gallery grave. A chambered tomb known as Cromlech Tumulus can be seen in the same area, and close to the deserted village of Slievemore is the Keel East Giant's Grave. This is a ruined court cairn.

Achill Sound 8 L79
This village is a convenient shopping centre, and offers boat-hire facilities for scenic trips and deep-sea fishing.

Dooagh 8 F60
Corrymore House, once occupied by Captain Charles Boycott, stands near the slopes of Croaghaun. The village itself is a delightful scatter of houses near a fine strand.

Doogort 8 F60
Sited at the foot of Slievemore, this community comprises Doogort itself plus the Missionary Settlement to the SW. The former stands at the E end of Pollawaddy Cove, and the latter was settled in the 19thc by a Protestant clergyman. It once

contained schools, an orphanage, and a printing house, but is now primarily a holiday resort with the attraction of a fine strand at nearby Pollawaddy. Hired boats can be used to visit the seal caves under Slievemore.

Keel 8 F60
The magnificent 2m strand near this attractive cluster of whitewashed buildings is bounded to the E by the cliffs of 1,530ft Menawn. This height affords a splendid view of Clew Bay, encompassing Clare Island and distant Croagh Patrick – St Patrick's Mountain. Cathedral Rocks form an interesting example of erosion. Keel is the HQ of a deep-sea fishing industry, and Keel Lough, lying NE of the village, offers good trout fishing.

Kildownet 8 L79
Situated on the Atlantic Drive beside Achill Sound, Kildownet features the ruins of a small 12th- to 13th-c church. Near by is the keep of a small 15th-c tower house (NM) which was associated with Grace O Malley, a 16th-c freebooter whose exploits have joined the tales of Irish legend.

ACHONRY, *Achadh Conaire*:
Conaire's Field, Sligo 10 G51
Ruins of an ancient church link Achonry with the distant past, when 7th-c St Nathy established his bishop's seat here. The bishopric still exists. The ruins of 15th-c Court Abbey, a Franciscan foundation, can be seen at nearby Lavagh and include a lofty tower.

ACOOSE LOUGH, Kerry 26 V78
See Carrantuohill entry.

ADARE, *Áth Dara*:
Ford of the Oak, Limerick 22 R44
Sited on the River Maigue, this delightfully tranquil village of carefully thatched cottages and broad, tree-lined streets owes its unique qualities to Edwin, 3rd Earl of Dunraven. He lived during the 19thc and was considered one of the best 'improving' landlords; he was also an authority on early-Irish architecture.

The community's story starts in the 13thc, when the occupying Normans found themselves confronted by a formidable castle built by the O Donovan family. This was rebuilt in 1326 by the Earl of Kildare, enlarged and strengthened at various times by his successors, and finally dismantled by Cromwellian troops in 1657. During its turbulent history it suffered assault by both native and foreign forces. Surviving remains (NM) include a ruined square keep surrounded by a battlemented rampart with semi-circular bastions. Access to the south gate was by drawbridge across a fosse which may have formed part of a ringfort. The castle's Great Hall stands near the river and displays interesting 13th-c windows. To the E of this are the remains of a second, more recent hall, including traces of a 15th-c kitchen and bakery.

The castle complex is one of several important medieval sites which exist within the demesne of Adare Manor. Also within the grounds (OACT) are remains of a Franciscan friary, and two medieval chapels.

The friary was founded by the 7th Earl of Kildare in 1464, and the reasonably complete remains include a nave, choir, and south transept of late Irish-gothic origin. A graceful, tapering tower rises to a considerable height from the crossing, and there is a fine sedilia. Also of interest are several well-preserved windows, and a cloister which lies a little to the N. The friary was restored by the Earl of Dunraven in 1875. The larger chapel, dedicated to St Nicholas of Myra, is a ruinous building dating originally from the 13thc. Near to it is a ruined 15th-c chapel of the Desmond family.

In the village, close to the fine 14-arch bridge which spans the Maigue, are the remains of an Augustinian friary which was founded c1316. The choir was converted into a CI parish church by the Earl of Dunraven in 1875, and was restored and opened to the public in 1937. The refectory was restored for use as a school by the 1st Earl's wife, and the cloisters were converted into a mausoleum. On the outside of the south aisle, which was formerly the lady chapel, is what is thought to be the only example of a Tudor rose in the whole of Ireland. In the centre of the village is the Trinitarian Monastery, founded by Lord Ossory in 1230. This now serves as the present parish church (RC), and is the only dedication to the Trinitarian Canons of the Redemption of Captives known to have survived in Ireland.

Adare Manor has been the family home of the Earls of Dunraven since the mid 17thc. The present neo-gothic building stands on the site of a smaller Georgian house and was begun by the 2nd Earl of Dunraven in 1832. The 2nd Earl was an amateur architect and conducted much of the work himself, but important contributions were made by such celebrities as the brothers Pain of Limerick, Alexander Pugin, and P C Hardwick. The latter was commissioned after Pugin fell ill, and was responsible for the whole west end of the south front. James Conolly, an Adare mason, was responsible for much of the stonework and is commemorated by an inscription on the east front – a part of the building which was the work of the 3rd Earl. Features inside the house include fine local-stone fireplaces, the minstrel's gallery, the staircase, and the dining room, all of which were commissioned from Pugin. A fine collection of paintings is also of interest.

Some 2m SW of Adare are the ruins of 15th-c Garraunboy Castle, a one-time stronghold of the Faltagh family.

ADVENTURER'S HOUSE, Tyrone 12 H76
Situated 2m SW of Donaghmore is a good example of a defensive structure dating from the time of James I. The remains are picturesquely situated on a limestone shelf.

AFFANE, *Áth Mheáin*:
Middle Ford, Waterford 29 X19
Affane House, a plain Georgian mansion which occupies the site of a medieval castle, is the main feature of this River Blackwater village. The first cherry trees to be cultivated in the British Isles were planted here by Sir Walter Raleigh, who brought them from the Canary Islands. In 1565 a battle was fought here between the rival houses of Desmond and Ormonde, resulting in a victory for the latter.

AGHABOE, *Achadh Bhó*:
Field of the Cow, Laois 23 S38
Small and well kept, this village lies W of Abbeyleix and is the site of a monastery which was founded in the 6thc by St Cannice, who is buried here. Successive raids reduced the foundation to ruins, and after it was rebuilt as an Augustinian priory in 1234 it again suffered considerable damage. The only parts of the original fabric extant are the tower and an arcade in the present parish church (CI). A nearby Dominican friary founded in 1382 by the MacGillapatricks displays a long nave and a south chapel. Aghaboe was once the principal church of the Kingdom of Ossory. A square, tree-covered Anglo-Norman motte can be seen in a field to the N.

AGHADA, *Achadh Fhada*:
Long Field, Cork 28 W86
Aghada is a pleasant resort overlooking Cork Harbour, which was defended in the S by Davis Fort and in the N by Fort Meagher. Rostellan chambered grave stands 100yds below high-water mark on the shore, and is almost submerged at high tide. The sides of the grave are slotted into the cracks of an E–W natural limestone pavement, a fact which suggests submergence of the coastal shelf after the settlement of the megalith builders in S Ireland. Set amidst woodlands to the NE is Rostellan Castle, which was the first to be built by Robert de Marises at the time of the Anglo-Norman invasion. It was later adopted and remodelled by the Fitzgerald family.

AGHADOE, *Achadh Deo*:
Field of the Two Yews, Kerry 27 V99
The demesne of Aghadoe, once known as the maiden estate, is situated at the foot of Glenbower on the N shore of Lough Leane. Up until 1932 it had been in the hands of the Capell family for almost 700 years, but the land now serves as a state forestry centre. As well as being naturally attractive and interesting, Aghadoe also features interesting architectural remains in the shape of a round tower and church (NM). These structures formed part of a monastery which was founded by St Finian the Leper in the 7thc. The 22ft tower has been greatly altered and truncated through the ages, and the church similarly shows work from many periods. The oldest part of the church lies to the W and was completed by a member of the O Donoghue family in 1158. This benefactor was buried here eight years later in 1166, and the only outstanding work that remains is a fine Romanesque doorway. An ogham-inscribed stone can be seen amongst the 13th-c work; the latter includes a window at the top of a south wall.

To the SW of the church is Parkavonear Castle (NM), a two-storey, circular structure which dates from the 13thc. It is located within a square, walled enclosure surrounded by a moat, and is known as the Bishop's Chair or Pulpit. The two storeys are linked by a staircase inside the wall, and the remains of a fireplace can be seen on the first floor. Aghadoe Hill affords panoramic views of the Killarney district, with the E to W chain of mountains overshadowing the Lower Lake.

AGHAGOWER, *Achadh Fhobhair*:
Field of the Well, Mayo 15 M08
The area around this small village is rich

church (NM) and 12th-c round tower (NM). These buildings once formed part of a monastery which was founded by St Senach, who was created Bishop of Aghagower by St Patrick himself. The church displays a three-light east window, and the tower has a round-headed doorway.

AGHAMARTA, Cork   **28 W 76**
See Crosshaven entry.

AGHOWLE, Wicklow   **24 S 96**
Close to Aghowle cemetery is the village's 12th-c church (NM), a long, rectangular building which displays a remarkable west door with a distinctive double architrave on the outside and a round arch within. The holes on each side of the door were intended for locking bars. Features of the east wall include two round-headed windows, with exterior hood moulding supported by pillars. Interesting gravestones, an unfinished granite cross (NM), and a water font can be seen in the grounds. This church is considered to have been part of a monastery which was founded by St Finian of Clonard in the early 6thc. Views from here extend over the lowlands around Tullow and Bunclody, to a 1,381ft peak rising from the Wicklow Mountains behind the village.

AGLISH, *An Eaglais:*
the Church, Kilkenny   **24 S 51**
To the E of this lovely little River Suir-country village are the picturesque ruins of a stronghold once held by the Ormondes of Granny, or Granneagh. The castle, which withstood an assault led by the Cromwellian leader Axtel in 1650, is particularly noted for its 17th-c oriel window.

AHENNY, *Áth Eine,* Tipperary   **23 S 42**
Ahenny is an attractive village situated between two ranges of hills on the Kilkenny border. Its old graveyard features two superb 8th-c high crosses (NM), the shafts of which are finely sculptured with intricate interlacing and abstract designs. These are said to be among the finest of their type. The N cross is the better preserved of the two, and the design on its base depicts a procession which includes a cleric carrying a ringed cross, a pony carrying a headless man, and a scene composed of animals and a palm tree. The S cross displays horsemen and Daniel in the Lion's Den. Both crosses are capped by curious 'hats'. Also here is the socket of a third cross, the shaft of which is supposed to have been stolen and subsequently lost at sea c1800.

AHERLOW, *Eatharlach*
Tipperary   **22 R 92**
Known as the Glen of Aherlow, this beautiful and secluded valley lies between the Galtee Mountains and the wooded ridge of Slievenamuck. The Galtees form the highest inland range in Ireland and are of particular interest to walkers and botanists. A 16ft statue of Christ the King stands on the lower slopes of Slievenamuck. The glen itself was once an important pass between the Golden Vale of Tipperary and Limerick, and it was also the scene of numerous battles between the O Briens and Fitzpatricks. This constant strife eventually resolved itself with the emergence of the O Briens as overlords for three centuries. On the S side of the glen is an oval enclosure called St Berraherb's Kyle (NM) which contains many early gravestones. At the head of the glen, near Galbally village, are the ruins of Moor Abbey (NM; see Galbally).

ALLENWOOD, *Fíodh Alúine*
Kildare   **18 N 72**
A large, turf-fired power station which was completed in 1952 is situated here. This vast area of turf and water covers much of the Central Plain from Kildare westward to the Shannon. Close to the power station are the Lullymore turf-producing works, an industry concerned with the production of briquettes from milled peat.

ALLUA LOUGH, Cork   **27 W 16**
See Inchigeelagh entry.

ANASCAUL, *Abhainn an Scáil:*
the River of the Hero, Kerry   **26 Q 50**
This village lies inland from Dingle Bay and is dominated by peaks which rise to over 2,000ft from the range of mountains behind it. A village inn called the South Pole was so named to commemorate Tom Crean, its one-time owner and the member of Scott's polar expedition who discovered the bodies of Scott and his companions. The countryside around Anascaul is of great interest to the botanist, particularly in May and early June when the banks of local streams and ditches are golden brown with the lovely royal fern. Other interesting plants to be found in the area include the green-gold Irish spurge, large-flowered butterwort, and a variety of orchids.

About 1½m NW at Knockane hamlet are the remains of a multiple-cist cairn, with a boulder displaying an inscribed Chi-Rho cross near by. Remains of Minard Castle, a stronghold of the Knights of Kerry, can be seen on the coast 3m SW. This structure was virtually destroyed by Cromwellian troops in 1650.

ANNAGHDOWN, *Eanach Dhúin:*
Marsh of the Fort,
Galway   **15 M 23**
This small village is sited on the shores of Lough Corrib, which is a well-known game- and coarse-fishing venue. The lough is studded with small wooded islands, and there are extensive enigmatic remains in the area. According to tradition, St Brendan of Clonfert founded a monastery here in the 6thc and governed it until his death in 577. It is also said that he set his sister Brigid over a nunnery here just prior to his death. There is no doubt that a monastery and nunnery did exist here, but all evidence yet discovered points to 12th-c origin. It seems that a convent of Augustinian nuns also existed here in the 12thc, but it is thought to have dissolved at the turn of the 12th/13thc and become a monastic institution c1225.

Ecclesiastical remains that can be seen today are mainly of the cathedral, nunnery, and priory. The cathedral dates from the 13thc and may stand on the site of an earlier church. It is a simple, rectangular structure with a gothic doorway in the north wall and a good Romanesque window from the nearby priory. Scant remains of the nunnery lie NW of the cathedral and comprise survivals of a 12th- to 13th-c church. To the W of the cathedral are the priory ruins (NM). These are mainly of 15th-c origin and include fine windows, plus sculptured pilasters which were evidently the side posts of a Romanesque doorway. To the S of the priory church is a cloister with surrounding buildings of a distinctly military aspect, perhaps indicating a fortified monastery. The 15th-c remains of a castle can be seen near by.

ANNAGHMORE, *Eanach Mór:*
Big Marsh, Sligo   **10 G 62**
Renowned for its rare trees and shrubs, the lovely demesne of Annaghmore is situated on the W bank of the River Owenmore 2½m SW of Collooney and has been in the hands of the ancient O Hara family since the middle ages. Ruined Moymlough Castle stands near by and was once an O Hara fortress.

ANNALONG, *Áth na Long:*
the Ford of the Ships, Down   **13 J 32**
Annalong is a bustling little town on the coast road between Newcastle and Kilkeel. Its strong stone houses stand around a deep-water harbour and in front of an awesome backdrop supplied by the lofty Mourne Mountains. In the heart of these mountains is the giant Silent Valley Reservoir, which was completed in 1933. The main industries of the town include fishing, the dressing of Mourne granite for export, manufacture of jewellery from local gems, and embroidery. The area has a strong attraction for walkers. One particular route follows the Annalong

Adare owes its charm and tranquility to the 3rd Earl of Dunraven, a 19th-c 'improving' landlord.

ANNALONG/ARAN ISLANDS, THE

River to Dunny Water Bridge, by way of Glassdrumman, and passes the cliff-encircled Blue Lough tarn on the rocky side of Slieve Lannagan. The energetic can climb the granite crags of 2,449ft Slieve Bignian from here.

ANNESTOWN, Waterford **29 X49**
See Tramore entry.

ANTRIM, *Aontroim*, Antrim **7 J18**
This pleasant county town stands on the site of an ancient monastery at the confluence of the Six Mile Water river and Lough Neagh. Its history is splashed with stormy episodes. During the 17thc the town was burned by Scottish Covenanters under the leadership of General Munroe, and in 1798 it was the scene of battles between English troops under Lord O Neill, and the United Irishmen under Henry J McCracken. McCracken was almost successful, but was eventually caught and hanged in Belfast. The earlier, 17th-c battles even included a naval engagement on the lake.

A building which saw and participated in much of the fighting is Antrim Castle. The castle's demesne, which is noted for its fine trees, rhododendrons and other shrubs, is situated at the W end of the town and encloses a motte-and-bailey, plus the burnt-out shell of a 17th-c house. The house was originally built by Sir Hugh Clotsworthy between 1613 and 1662, and was later enlarged by Sir John Clotsworthy. The latter was created Viscount Massereene and Ferrard by Charles II. Further alterations were made through the 19th and early 20thc, until in 1922 the building was completely burnt out. The cut-stone features surrounding and surmounting the door are the oldest parts of the building. Some Jacobean elements managed to survive 19th-c restoration.

The town's broad main street contains most of Antrim's interesting buildings, including fine terraces of stone houses and the parish Church of All Saints (CI). This dates from 1596, was destroyed by fire in 1649, and rebuilt in 1720. The best features from the 18th-c work are the square stone gate piers, which are surmounted by ball finials. The distinctive tower and spire were added in 1812 and 1816 respectively. Both are attributed to John Bowden. A monument to the 4th Earl, by John Flaxman, is one of the many commemorative stones erected inside the church to the Lords Massereene. Other interesting churches in the town include the 19th-c First Presbyterian Church, with its striking Greek-revival exterior; The High Street Presbyterian Church, with its black basalt masonry and gothick sandstone decorations; the gothick Methodist Church and Hall of 1867; and St Comgall's RC Church, an impressive structure of white-painted stone round an Italianate tower.

An interesting group in the Market Square comprises the courthouse, Castle Gate, and Castle Gardens. The courthouse is of early 18th-c origin, and has a doorway which is considered one of the richest 18th-c classical conceptions extant in N Ireland. The Castle Gate is a 19th-c neo-Tudor structure which is attributed to John Bowden, and comprises octagonal turrets above a tower. Castle Gardens are attributed to Le Notre, creator of the famous Versailles Gardens, and are sheltered by numerous mature trees. Also here is a double canal, and the 10th-c round tower (NM). The latter is one of the two most perfect in Ireland and has a doorway set 7½ft above ground level. Another interesting building in the town is Pogue's Entry, a carefully-restored 18th-c cottage which was the birthplace of author Alexander Irvine. He is particularly well known for his work *My Lady of the Chimney Corner*.

ANTRIM COAST ROAD, Antrim **7 D30**
The 60m stretch of road between Larne and Portrush is known for its magnificent and often startling scenic contrasts. Designed by Sir Charles Lanyon in 1834, it was built with the intention of providing famine-stricken farm workers with employment, and is considered one of the finest projects of its kind. Its course takes in superb cliffs of black basalt and dazzling chalk, wooded escarpments, picturesque bays, and the famous Nine Glens of Antrim. Glenariff is considered the most attractive of the latter. The horizontal bands of flint which are so much a feature of the chalk cliffs along this route were greatly sought after by stone-age tool makers. Part of the road S of Glenarm was washed away during a storm in recent years, but massive reconstruction work has kept the route open.

AN UAIMH, *An Uaimh*:
the Cave, Meath **18 N86**
See Navan entry.

ANURE LOUGH, *Loch an Iúir*:
Lake of the Yew, Donegal **4 B81**
See Dungloe entry.

ARAGLIN, *Airglinn*, Cork **28 R90**
Sited on the banks of a river of the same name, this little hamlet stands at the head of beautifully-secluded Araglin Glen which carves its way through the heart of the impressive Knockmealdown Mountains. The picturesque ruin of Ballyderoon Castle stands at the confluence of rivers Araglin and Blackwater.

ARAN ISLAND, *Arainn Mhór*:
Big Aran, Donegal **4 B61**
Also known as Aranmore, this island lies opposite Burtonport and to the W of the low-lying Rosses coast. There are regular ferry sailings between Burtonport and Leabgarrow, the island's main harbour. Although the E coast of this 4m-long by 3m-wide island is fairly heavily populated, the wild and heathery central plateau falls away to terminate in rugged, 535ft cliffs on the W shore. These cliffs are at their highest near the lighthouse, and both these and the cliffs on the N coast provide nesting sites for colonies of seabirds. The E shore has fine sands and is the haunt of waders. Various plants of interest to the botany enthusiast can be found in the central area.

ARAN ISLANDS, THE, *Oileáin Árann*, Galway **14/15 L71**
Inishmore, Inishmaan, and Inisheer – the three islands that make up this group – are the high peaks of a submerged limestone reef that runs out to sea from the coast of Co Clare. The terrain is rocky and unfriendly, scattered with glacial erratics and almost entirely without natural soil or sand. The scenery is enlivened by a wide variety of limestone-loving wild flowers, ranging from cowslips to honeysuckle, and orchids to wild thyme. Food in the form of potatoes and cereals is grown in little walled enclosures in which the hardy islanders have gradually built up their own soil from fragments of stone, mixed with layers of sand and seaweed. Fish are caught from small craft, of a very ancient design, known as *currachs*. These are constructed by stretching tarred canvas over a framework of laths – rather like the Welsh coracle – and in the hands of an expert are made to weather the often mountainous seas off the Irish coast. The islanders themselves have long been thought of as living examples of Gaelic culture, although some sources maintain that their way of life has been shaped by necessity rather than pure tradition. Their community existence is certainly self sufficient. Each family has its own plot of artificial soil, has its own fishing craft, and makes some of its own clothes from the wool and hides of local sheep. The principal port and village of the group is Kilronan, which stands on the SE coast of Inishmore.

Various studies of island life have been published over the years, including *The Aran Islanders* by J M Synge, and the play *Riders to the Sea* by the same author; *Man of Aran* by Pat Mullen; *Aranmen All* by Tom O Flaherty; and the film *Man of Aran* by Robert Flaherty.

Even though it is not certain that the present life pattern is a reflection of ancient times, the remains that exist on all three islands prove that they were inhabited from earliest eras. These include defences of indeterminate age – possibly built as protection against Norse raiders – and rich monastic survivals. The latter are mainly churches, high crosses, and round towers. Christianity was brought to the islands in the 5thc by St Enda, who established a monastic school here which became so famous that it earned the Arans the nickname the 'Islands of the Saints'. A brief description of each island follows.

Inishmore 14 L80
This is the largest of the three islands and has so many sites of interest that it is not possible to mention them all here. The most famous of its historical sites is the Dun Aengus stone fort (NM), which is situated in the townland of Kilmurvy and is considered one of the finest prehistoric structures in W Europe (see inset on page 203). Also in Kilmurvy townland is the massive stone fort called Dun Oghil, which comprises an inner citadel and outer defensive wall of truly remarkable strength.

About 1m N of Kilmurvy is one of the best preserved of the many clochans to be found on the Aran Islands – Clochan-na-Carraige (NM). This little stone beehive house is unusual in that it has an oval outline but a rectangular interior. A short distance SW of Kilmurvy is Templemacduagh (NM), a small, pre-Romanesque church with an early cross, a holy well, and the remains of an enclosing cashel (NM). The chancel displays 16th-c additions. To the S of Cowrugh village is a holy well, and S of this is *Teampall an Cheathrair Alainn* – 'Church of the Four Beautiful Saints' (NM). This is a 15th-c, rebuilt structure with a trefoil-headed east window and pointed north door. The *Leaba* or 'Bed' of the saints (NM) is at the east gable. Still in Kilmurvy townland, Templebrecan (NM) is an interesting early church which was greatly altered in medieval times. An inscribed stone here recalls seven Roman saints who fled before the tide of barbarism which swept Britain.

The Killeany townland also has its fair share of interesting monuments, including Arkin's Castle, Doocaher (the Black Fort), Tighlagh Eany, Turmartin and Temple Benan. Arkin's Castle was originally built c1587, but was later occupied by Cromwell's troops who plundered several monuments in order to repair it. The promontory fort of Doocaher displays a 200ft-long stone wall with inner terracing and exterior *chevaux de frise*. Tighlagh Eany is an early church which is noted for its antae and round-headed east window. It is the most venerated spot on the islands and is said to stand amidst the graves of 120 saints. Turnmartin, the stump of a round tower, is reputed to mark the grave of St Gregory. Pope Gregory the Great endeared himself to the Irish people, and legend has it that his tomb floated to this island after having been set adrift on the Tiber in Rome. Temple Benan is an early church which is unique in that it is orientated N–S, although the only window faces E. There are several other monuments in the immediate vicinity. All the aforementioned are NM.

Inishmaan 15 L 90
This is the middle island and was the setting for J M Synge's *Riders to the Sea*. Carrownlisheen townland features Kilcanonagh Church (NM), a little oratory with an angular east window, plus several other interesting remains. Dun Moher (NM) is an ancient stone fort with interior steps, Dermot and Grainne's Bed (NM) is a dolmen comprising two orthostats surmounted by a capstone, and Templesaghtmacree (NM) is a ruined stone church dedicated to Seven Sons of Kings. Dun Conor (NM) is a fine oval fort within which are several restored hut sites.

Inisheer 15 L 90
The farthest E of the three islands, Inisheer has remains which include several forts and a number of old churches. Creggankeel (NM) is a large, irregular, stone-built cashel which is often misnamed a fort, surrounding a ruined church known as the Grave of the Seven Sisters. On top of a rocky hill are sparse remains of a 15th-c tower set in a stone ringfort known as O Brien's Castle (NM), and NW of the Post Office is a small cairn with nearby ruins of a chamber tomb. St Cavan's Church (NM) is an early building with later additions, and St Cavan's grave lies beneath drifting sands to the NE. Kilgobnet Church (NM) is a small oratory which displays many of the features which make early Irish church architecture so distinctive.

ARDAGH, *Ardach*:
High Field, Limerick 21 R 23
Some time during 1868 a number of valuable relics were found in the incomplete Reerasta ringfort (NM), near Ardagh. The hoard included items of personal jewellery and a bronze cup which has since become famous as the Ardagh Chalice. This can be seen in Dublin's National Museum. Thought to date from the 8thc, the chalice consists of many different precious materials and is considered a masterpiece of early design and metalwork. Some of the other items found on the site were of later date. Ringforts and earthworks are a common feature of this area.

ARDARA, *Ard an Rátha*:
Height of the Ring Fort, Donegal 4 G 79
Artists are among the most frequent visitors to this village, which is set in a deep, wide valley near the confluence of the Owentocher River and Loughros More Bay. The village's name is derived from a ringfort which is situated on the nearby clifftops. A beautiful peninsula extends from the settlement and divides the bays of Loughros More and Loughros Beg. Spectacular natural features within easy reach of Ardara include Maghera Caves and falls and 1,458ft Slievetooey Mountain – all of which lie to the W of the village. Tormore Point offers fine cliff scenery. Homespun Ardara Tweed is made by local girls, and is only a little more famous than the local hand knitting, fine hand embroidery, and hosiery. The quality of the colouring is maintained in spite of the occasional use of substitute chemical dyes.

ARDBOE, *Ard Bó*:
Cow Height, Tyrone 6 H 97
Ardboe's main claim to fame is its magnificent 10th-c churchyard cross (NM). This richly-sculptured monument stands 18½ft tall, and although severely weatherbeaten is considered the finest high cross in the whole of Ulster. Its 22 panels depict various scenes from the scriptures. Also of interest in this Lough Neagh hamlet are the ruins of a 10th-c monastery, of which the remains of a church form the main part. The foundation was established by St Colman.

ARDEE, *Baile Áth Fhirdhia*:
the Town of Ferdia's Ford, Louth 12 N 99
This ancient River Dee town is an angling resort and the market centre for the surrounding districts. It is strategically sited and was a place of importance in pre-Christian times, having stood at the heart of ancient Muirthemne. This historic territory covered much the same area as that encompassed by the boundaries of present-day Louth. The town also has a niche in Irish legend as the place where the great warrior Cuchullain fought his friend Ferdia for four days, in an attempt to stop the forces of Queen Maeve entering Ulster. The well-matched battle ended when Cuchullain carried Ferdia's body across the Dee to show that he had reached his objective. This event is commemorated by a plaque on the bridge over the Dee.

A feature of the town are the substantial remains of the quadrangular castle, guarded by projecting towers on the east and west walls. This was originally built by Roger de Pippard in the early 13thc, marking the Anglo-Norman occupation of the town and their acquisition of a Charter of Incorporation for it. Both James II and William III lodged at the castle, the former during his journey to the Battle of the Boyne. Part of the structure, which contains a small museum, has been restored and now serves as a courthouse. Hatch's Castle, in Market Street, is also of 13th-c origin.

Ardee features several fascinating churches, of which St Mary's (CI) is probably one of the most interesting. This building incorporates part of an ancient church and contains an old, beautifully-carved font. A staircase leading to the rood screen is built into the church wall. St Mary's (RC) is a 19th-c structure built on the site of a monastery which was founded by de Pippard in 1209. Some 2m E of Ardee are sparse remains of Stickillen church, with three interesting souterrains near by. One of these underground passages is almost tall enough for a person to pass through either of the two entrances in an upright position.

ARDFERT, *Ard Fhearta*:
the Height of the Grave, Kerry 20 Q 72
Perhaps the most important ecclesiastical site in Kerry, Ardfert lies inshore from Ballyheige Bay and features the remains of an imposing 13th-c cathedral (NM). A cathedral was founded here by St Brendan the Navigator in the 6thc, but the existing survivals are mainly from the 13thc. One interesting aspect is the incorporation of a fragment of a 12th-c church's west wall into the fabric, including a Romanesque doorway with blind arcading on each side. The fine nave is lit by beautiful lancet windows and shows 15th-c extensions. Two interesting episcopal effigies exist in the chancel.

To the NW of the cathedral is Temple na Hoe (NM), a 12th-c Romanesque church with the unusual ornamentation of quoin shafts with carved capitals. To the NW of this is Temple-na-Griffin (NM), a 15th-c church named after the griffin effigies kept inside. Ardfert Abbey, Georgian home of the Earls of Glandore, lies to the E. Ruins of a Franciscan friary (NM) founded by Thomas FitzMaurice, the 1st Lord Kerry c1253, can be seen to

The demesne of Antrim Castle is noted for its fine trees and shrubs.

the N of the house, including a 13th-c nave and chancel, and a 14th- to 15th-c south transept, west tower, and cloisters.

A field 1m W of Ardfert contains McKenna's Fort, one of the many prehistoric monuments in the area. It was in this single-rampart earthen structure that Sir Roger Casement was arrested after landing from a German submarine in April 1916. The submarine had been escorting a gun-running ship which was carrying arms for the Easter Rising.

ARDFINNAN, *Ard Fhíonáin:*
St Fíonán Height, Tipperary **23 S01**
A 15-arch bridge spans the River Suir at this picturesquely-sited village, and a 12th-c Anglo-Norman castle stands on the river bank. The castle was first built by Prince John of England in 1186, but the oldest surviving part of the structure is a fragment of the late 13th-c keep. Two of the later square towers on the curtain wall are still intact, in spite of a cannon assault from a neighbouring hill by General Ireton in the 17thc. When the general took the castle he dispelled a local myth that the stronghold was impregnable. A monastery was founded at Ardfinnan during the 7thc by St Fionan the Leper, but no trace of this has survived. Sparse remains of a Carmelite lady's abbey can be seen 1½m SW of the village. A deep gorge carved by the Suir divides the area's low hills.

ARDGLASS, *Ard Ghlais,* Down **13 J53**
Ardglass is built on gentle slopes which run down to a small deep bay. It is a place of great charm and character, and a recently revived interest in its fishing industry and architecture has restored much of the community's vitality. The village was founded by the Vikings, and its continuing importance is attested to by the fact that between the 14th and 16thc several small castles were built here. The deep, safe harbour formed an ideal base for English forces who would otherwise have been cut off from their Downpatrick HQ and Carlingford troops.

Henry IV provided a trading company with a grant to establish themselves in Ardglass, and two early 15th-c buildings built by London traders for storage are incorporated in Ardglass Castle. These early warehouses were known as New Works. The castle also includes the structure of Horn Castle, with its 50ft, slab-constructed tower, and was rebuilt in 1790. To the NW of this imposing conglomerate is Cowd Castle, a smaller, 16th-c structure which is thought to have once served as a storehouse. Even farther N is 15th-c Margaret's Castle, which preserves an interesting original doorway between the corner turrets on the north-west wall. There is an aperture designed to allow the discharge of stones and scalding water on the heads of invading troops, and the west tower contains a spiral staircase.

Jordan's Castle (NM) is the most perfect of these fortified stores and strongholds, and is thought to commemorate Jordan de Saukeville – a Norman who settled here in 1177. It is built of blue-stone rubble masonry, with freestone quoins and window jambs, and is considered an excellent example of the pele-tower type of defended dwelling. The outer shell of the building, which houses a small museum, is complete. The O Neills held the castle under siege for three years, but the garrison held out and was finally relieved in 1601.

Isabella's Tower stands on the lovely Ardglass Downs and affords a view N over the town to the Ward of Ardtole. The latter is a hill crowned by the ruins of old Ardtole Church (NM), which is dedicated to St Nicholas and was formerly the parish church of Ardglass. It fell into disuse after a neighbouring clan massacred the townsmen. To the N of this is a mound of earth and stones surmounted by a central flat slab known as the Cross of Ardtole. This measures 3 by 2ft, is mounted on a 6ft-long wall of stones, and is of unknown origin. A little to the SW of the church is an exceptionally well-preserved souterrain.

ARDKEEN, *Ard Caoin:*
Pleasant Height, Down **13 J65**
Close to this village and lapped by the waters of Strangford Lough is a 130ft knoll surmounted by a well-preserved Norman motte-and-bailey castle. This was built c1180 by William, Baron le Savage, who was a follower of de Courcy. Ardkeen was contemporary with the de Courcy castle at Skreen, and remained the seat of this branch of the Savage family for a long period. The knoll also carries a 17th-c mansion, and near its foot are the ruins of a church which replaced an older Church of St Mary.

ARDMILLAN, *Ard an Mhuilinn:*
the Height of the Mill, Down **13 J56**
Situated at the edge of an island-studded bay on the W side of Strangford Lough, this little hamlet still has the ruins of a mill as a reminder of the origins of its name.

Some 2m E is Sketrick Island, which is approached via a causeway and carries the remains of 15th-c Sketrick Castle (NM). Storm damage to it in 1896 was so extensive that only parts of the north and east walls survived. The north wall contains a series of closets or sleeping chambers within its thickness, and the less-massive east wall is 4½ft thick. *The Annals of the Four Masters* relate how, in 1470, the son of Owen O Neill took the castle from the Clandeboye branch of the family and restored it to the MacQuillans. Later on it was garrisoned by the 9th Earl of Kildare. To the S of Ardmillan is White Rock, a residential area where the Strangford Lough Yacht Club is based.

ARDMORE, *Aird Mhór:*
Big Height, Waterford **29 X17**
Ardmore Bay, on which this resort is sited, is edged by a fine sandy beach and rugged cliffs. The area also boasts a good group of monastic remains on the 5th-c site of St Declan's settlement. St Declan's Oratory, 'The Little Peaked Building', is a small early church displaying high-pitched gables and a west door with inclined jambs. The 96ft Round Tower (NM) is one of the most complete of its kind in Ireland. Four separate storeys are indicated by projecting string courses and slight rebates on the outside. Projecting stones on the inside are ornamented with carved grotesques.

The cathedral was built in the early 13thc, but incorporates earlier work and includes some later additions. Of particular interest are the beautiful, pointed arch and nave of Irish-Romanesque style in the chancel; a recessed Romanesque west window; and a row of Romanesque sculptures set in two tiers on the exterior of the W wall and displayed in a series of arcades. The top series is contained in a number of small arches, while the bottom effigies are grouped inside two larger arches. Although the upper series has suffered the ravages of time, there is still one piece which is reasonably complete – a depiction of the Archangel Michael weighing souls. Clearly visible in the lower part are Adam and Eve, The Judgement of Solomon, and the Adoration of the Magi. There are also two Ogham-inscribed stones preserved in the church.

About ½m E of the main group is Teampull Deiseirt (NM), which displays a west gable, a south side wall, and the fragments of a larger church's east gable. Traces of a crannog can be seen on the beach. Ardmore had its first bishop in 1170, was leased to Sir Walter Raleigh for a two-year period, and in 1642 the church and round tower were used to shelter the Confederate Catholic Army. The latter eventually surrendered to the English. Whiting Bay lies to the W of Ardmore, and just beyond it is the pleasant bathing beach of Monatrea.

ARDNACRUSHA, *Ard na Croise:*
the Height of the Cross, Clare **22 R56**
This is the site of the Shannon Hydro-electric Scheme, which was begun in 1925 and completed in 1929. The turbines are powered by the harnessed waters of the Shannon, which drops nearly 100ft in 18m between Lough Derg and Limerick. The fall, and more important the consistent level of water throughout the year, made this river ideal for such a scheme after considerable adaptation. Sufficient fall was ensured by the construction of a 7½m feeder canal to Ardnacrusha, and a weir was built across the river between Killaloe and O Briensbridge to maintain the required head. The vast storage reservoir which backed up behind the weir includes part of the river and the whole of Lough Derg. Embankments had to be built round the lough to contain the extra depth.

Water for the turbines is regulated by three sluices, with the surplus cascading over the weir and into the river bed. After it has been used the water leaves the power house and re-enters the river via the mile-long tail race. Part of this project was the provision of access for barges and salmon. Boats navigate the head and tail races, and cross from one to the other by means of navigation locks. A barge passage has been constructed at the weir intake, and fish ladders cater for the migrating salmon.

Of particular interest to the visitor are the massive plant at Ardnacrusha Power Station; the barge-navigation locks; the head and tail races, constructed by the removal of 252 million cu ft of earth; the Weir and Intake at O Briensbridge; the salmon ladder at the east end of the weir; and the huge embankments which bound parts of the race and contain the river between Killaloe and the weir.

ARD OILEAN, *Ardoileán:*
High Island, Galway **14 L55**
Also known as High Island, this desolate little place lies 2m W of Aughrus Point off the Connemara coast. It is now uninhabited, but features the very complete remains of an ancient monastery founded by St Fechin of Fore in the 7thc. The ruins (NM) include a 12 by 10ft church with a flat-headed

doorway containing a grave slab for a lintel, and a number of the beehive-shaped huts known as clochans. A number of cross slabs can also be seen round the church, and the entire complex is surrounded by an amazingly intact wall. At the highest point of the island is a holy well and an incised cross slab. Access to Ard Oilean is by boat from Cleggan, weather permitting.

ARDPATRICK, *Ard Pádraig:*
St Patrick's Height, Limerick 22 R 62
The hill which gave this small village its name rises above the community and bears monastic remains on a site where St Patrick is said to have created an earlier foundation. The remains which exist today comprise the stump of a round tower – seen outside the cemetery wall – and a church with antae and a plain, round-headed doorway. This church dates from *c*1200. Seefin, the highest point of the Ballyhoura Mountains, rises to 1,702ft S of the village. This is one of the many Irish hills named after the legendary warrior, Finn MacCool.

ARDRESS, *Ard Dreasa:*
Height of the Brambles, Armagh 12 H 95
George Ensor, a Dublin architect, remodelled the 17th-c farm dwelling known as Ardress House (NT) when he moved into the building during the latter half of the 18thc. Of particular note is the beautiful plasterwork in the drawing room, which was executed by Michael Stapleton – also from Dublin.

ARDSCULL, *Ard Scol:*
Height of Schools, Kildare 18 S 79
This place is noted for its massive Norman motte, a 35ft-high earthwork encircled by a ditch and bank entrenchment. There are traces of a bailey on the north side, and it is likely that the castle which topped this mound was built in the late 12thc. It was burnt down in 1286. Near by is the site of a battle in which Edward Bruce defeated an English force in 1315.

ARDS HOUSE, Donegal 5 C 03
See Creeslough entry.

ARDS PENINSULA, *An Aird:*
the Point, Down 13 J 66
Small fields, white cottages, and winding roads combine to form a landscape in miniature on this delightful, low-hilled peninsula. It extends for 20m and varies from 3 to 5m in width. To the W are the island-studded waters of Strangford Lough, while the E coast is washed by the Irish Sea. Archaeological remains abound here and include abbeys, churches, raths, castles, and cromlechs. The lough is the winter home for duck, geese, and many other species of wildfowl, and the Strangford coastline is an Eldorado for the marine biologist.

ARDTOLE, Down 13 J 53
See Ardglass entry.

ARIGNA, *An Airgnigh:*
the Despoiling (river), Roscommon 10 G 91
Situated at the foot of a valley in the mountain range of the same name, this village was once known for its iron-mining industry. It is now the site of coal-mining operations, which have gained new importance with the construction of a 15,000kw coal-fired electricity-generating station near by.

The 96ft-high round tower which marks the site of St Declan's 5th-c foundation at Ardmore is one of the most complete in Ireland.

Magnificent views are afforded from the road which crosses the hills from here to Geevagh in Co Sligo.

*ARKLOW, *An tInbhear Mór:*
the Big Estuary, Wicklow 25 T 27
Arklow is a bustling resort which overlooks the sea from the mouth of the Avoca River at the foot of the Wicklow Mountains. Its fine sands extend N and S of the river, providing access for safe sea bathing, and the town was once known as a shipping port. Local skills still include the construction of small boats.

Legend has it that both Palladius and St Patrick first set foot in Ireland in the Arklow district, but there is little evidence to support this. However, there are equally interesting historical connections which can be proved. Arklow was founded by the Norsemen and later became the property of the Fitz Walters – ancestors of the Butler family – after the Anglo-Norman invasion. One of the strongest of all Ormonde castles was built here, but in 1649 this was partially demolished after having resisted centuries of attack from native and foreign forces alike. The battered remains of this stronghold overlook the Avon River from a raised bluff. In 1798, during the abortive Wexford Rising, Father Michael Murphy led a band of patriots into battle at Arklow and was killed. A monument marks the spot where he fell.

Remains of a 13th-c Dominican friary can be seen in a field near the parish priest's house. The CI parish church is a gothick structure built by Sir Arthur Bloomfield in 1900, featuring a three-light window by Henry Clarke. The handsome RC church of 1840 is by Patrick Byrne. Shelton Abbey, 2¼m NW, a mock-Tudor structure by Sir Richard Morrison, stands in fine grounds which are noted for their shrubs – in particular the magnificent rhododendrons. The abbey now serves as a state forestry school, and is appropriately set in the most productive commercial forestry area in the Republic. Famous beauty spots within easy reach of the town include Glendalough, the Vale of Clara, Glenmalure, and the Meeting of the Waters.

*ARMAGH, *Ard Mhacha:*
Macha's Height or Height of the Plain, Armagh 12 H 84
Ancient Armagh has been an ecclesiastical focal point for some fifteen centuries, and is one of the most venerated of Irish cities. The visitor can stand here and feel the atmosphere which prompted St Patrick to cry out 'It is Armagh that I love, my sweet thorp, my sweet hill'.

The city's name is derived from the Irish *Ard Mhacha*, meaning the 'Height of Macha'. General opinion puts this naming down to the fact that Queen Macha founded Emain Macha (see entry) – the 'Great Fort' – on a hill W of the present community *c*300 BC. This is known as Navan Fort and was once the palace of the Ulster kings. It was also the HQ of the mighty Knights of the Red Branch, and is associated with the legend in which Cuchullain harried a giant invasion force while King Conor and his forces were recovering from a druidical sickness.

King Daire was ruling when St Patrick first came to Armagh, and the present Protestant cathedral stands on a site once occupied by the king's hall. The saint made it known that he desired this land for his first church, but initially King Daire refused to move his court. He gave Patrick another site, on which the Bank of Ireland now stands, but after his baptism he relented and allowed the saint on to the hilltop occupied by his court. This, the second church, very soon became the Christian centre of Ireland and a famous seat of learning. Scholars came from near and far, and there were so many from England that part of the city was named the Saxon Ward.

In 1004 Brian Boru, the High King of Ireland, came to St Patrick's Cathedral and was allowed to hold the precious *Book of Armagh*. He donated 20oz of pure gold in tribute as he was kneeling at the altar. Some ten years later both Brian and his son Murrough were killed in their hour of victory over the Danes, and their bodies were brought to rest in the shadow of the cathedral. The *Book of Armagh* is a Latin manuscript of the New Testament, combined with the Confessions of St Patrick, Two Lives of St Patrick, and various other writings translated by the scribe Ferdomnach in 807. The documents are enclosed in a leather satchel of ancient Celtic design, and are kept in the library of Trinity College, Dublin.

The Shrine of St Patrick's Bell is another of the city's treasured heirlooms. The bell which it was built to contain is constructed of rivetted iron plates bronzed on both sides. It is beautifully

Entries marked * are the starting point of drives included in the Day Drive section of the book (pages 79 to 144).

ARMAGH

engraved with a request for a prayer for Cumascach, a steward of the monastery of Armagh who died in 908. The shrine, which was commissioned between 1094 and 1105, is constructed of bronze and silver plates ornamented with enamel, gold-filigree work, and crystal. Both relics are housed in the National Museum, Dublin.

Because of its strategic situation and great wealth, Armagh has been the centre of political and martial strife for many centuries. Successive wars during the 17thc destroyed all of the medieval buildings, and the only structures to have survived to the present day are those which were too strong or too holy to be successfully assaulted. The town is dominated by the two cathedrals, both of which are built on hilltops. The Protestant St Patrick's Cathedral which is seen now is the result of rebuilding during the 19thc, and it is known that at least seventeen predecessors stood on the same site. During the 18thc the wealthy Archbishop Richard Robinson transformed the slum into which Armagh had degenerated to a beautiful Georgian city, and employed Thomas Cooley to repair the cathedral. He also commissioned the brilliant young architect Francis Johnston, who was responsible for the building's tower and spire. Further restoration work was conducted by Lewis Cottingham in the late 19thc, this time under the instructions of Archbishop Beresford. The term rebuilding would be a more apt description of this work, because the so-called restoration entailed the removal of surviving medieval stone and carving, plus the dismantling of Johnston's spire. Most of the excellent monuments inside the cathedral date from the 17th and 18thc, but there is also a broken 11th-c cross preserved here. A number of sculptures, some of which date from the early iron age, can be seen in the north transept. The tower affords a view which reveals the old city layout – streets radiating from the cathedral like the spokes and rim of a wheel, following the lines of the original rath.

The other St Patrick's Cathedral is an RC church in 19th-c decorated-gothick style, built of Armagh limestone and Dungannon freestone. Its distinctive twin towers dominate a hill to the N of the CI cathedral, and the people are called to worship by a mid 20th-c carillon of 32 bells. Several Italian artists were employed for the interior decoration of the building.

Near the older of the two cathedrals is the well-proportioned Public Library (by Thomas Cooley) of 1771, which boasts a valuable collection of manuscripts and books. Fine paintings can be seen in the 18th-c former Archbishop's Palace, designed by Cooley and later extended by Francis Johnston. Beside the palace is a small classical chapel, the exterior of which is by Cooley and the interior by Johnston. The grounds of the palace contain the remains of a 13th-c Franciscan friary (NM) built by Primate O Scannail. As well as restoring the cathedral, the generous Archbishop Robinson founded the Public Library, laid the foundations of the Royal School in 1773, built the County Infirmary in 1774, and from a chance meeting with the great astronomer William Herschel was inspired to build the Observatory in 1789. Again it was Francis Johnston who was responsible for the design of the latter, and the three-storey building has an interesting interior. A feature of the Observatory grounds is the Planetarium, which plays a role in the city's leisure activities. Also of interest in the city is the Military Museum.

The Mall, an attractive green constructed on the old racecourse, has a good cricket pitch at its centre and is bordered by mature trees. It is flanked by a number of excellent Georgian buildings, including the courthouse (by Johnston) and imposing Charlemont Terrace. The County Museum is sited on the E side of The Mall. Other fine examples of Georgian design include the prison and the Savings Bank. The Royal School, another of Robinson's legacies, stands on College Hill and replaces a building founded by James I in 1608, in Abbey Street. Of interest in the latter street are the 18th-c iron gates of the old Presbyterian church.

To the SW of Armagh are the buildings of 18th-c Drelincourt's School, and 2m N

1 Archbishop's Palace (former)
2 Bank of Ireland
3 County Museum
4 Courthouse
5 Emain Macha or Navan Fort
6 Franciscan Friary Remains
7 Military Museum
8 Observatory & Planetarium
9 Old Presbyterian Church
10 Prison
11 Public Library
12 Royal School
13 St Patrick's Cathedral (CI)
14 St Patrick's Cathedral (RC)
15 St Patrick's Well
16 Savings Bank
17 The Mall

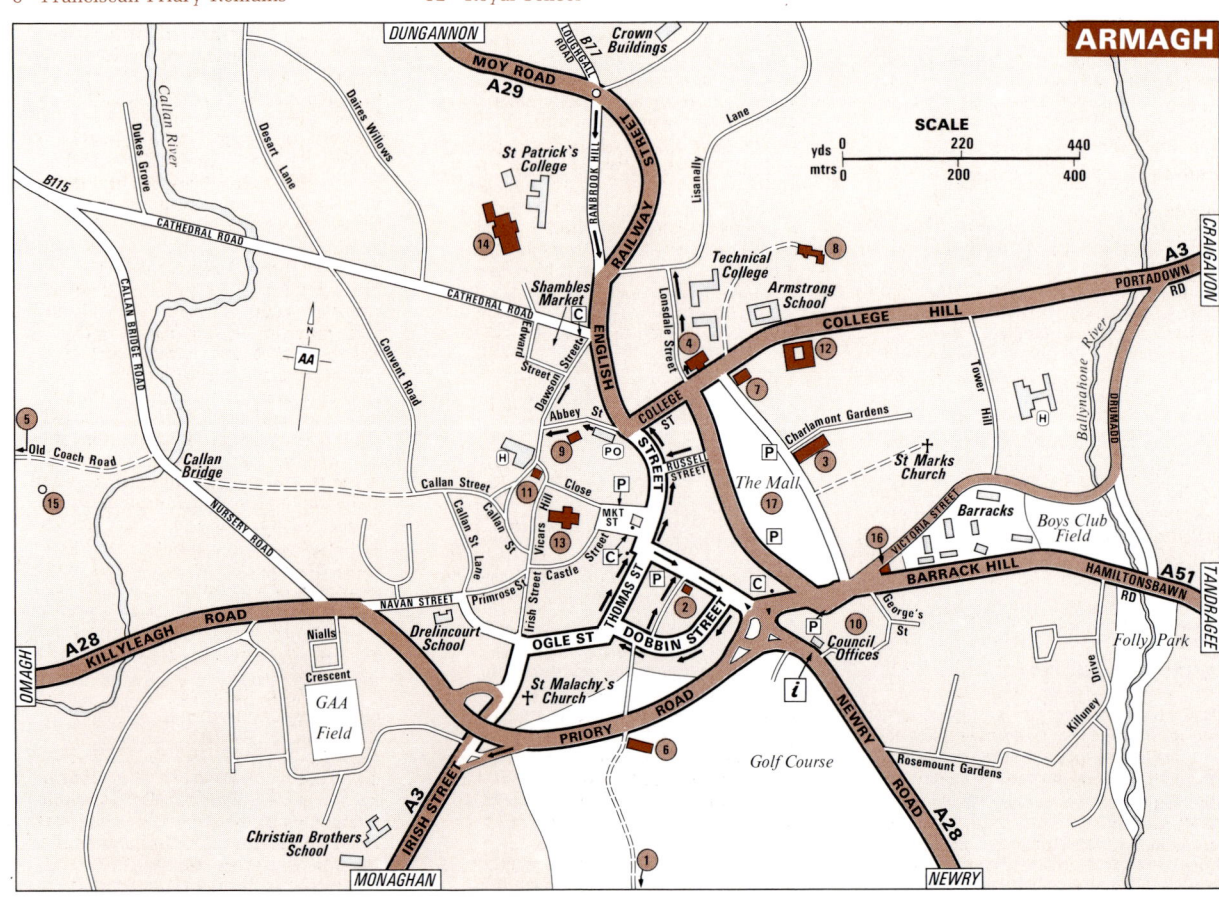

on the River Callan is the Yellow Ford. It was here, in 1598, that Hugh O Neill defeated and killed Sir Henry Bagenal in battle. Just W of Armagh, halfway between the city and Navan Fort, is St Patrick's Holy Well.

ARMOY, *Oirthear Maí:*
East of the Plain, Antrim **7 D03**
This pleasant village lies some 6m SW of Ballycastle and is noted for its ruined, 10th-c round tower (NM). The door of this is of particular interest, being 5ft high by only 19in wide. The top of the doorway is formed from a single stone which has been cut into a semi-circular arch and shaped on its outside face to fit the curve of the wall. A World Ploughing Match held here in 1959 is commemorated by the Cairn of Peace. Flat-topped Knocklayd rises to 1,695ft NE of the village.

ARROW LOUGH, Roscommon **10 G71**
See Ballinafad entry.

ASHBOURNE, *Cill Dhéagláin:*
St Declan's Church, Meath **19 O05**
A monument unveiled here in 1959 commemorates those who fell at Ashbourne during the 1916 Rising. An obelisk raised in 1880 to Charles Brindley, a local huntsman of long standing, is located 2m to the SE of Ashbourne. The 2nd Baron Ashbourne lived in the village until his death in 1942. A patriot and an eccentric, he insisted on speaking Irish in the House of Lords, and upon wearing a saffron kilt which he considered to be the ancient national dress. A local Pattern takes place 2m E at Palmerstown in July.

ASHFORD, *Áth na Fuinseoige:*
the Ford of the Ash, Wicklow **19 T29**
Devil's Glen is a narrow, rocky defile through which the River Vartry flows, and is a major feature of the beautiful countryside around this village. To the N is the Glen of Dunran, and close to the village are the Walpole Gardens of the Mount Usher demesne. On the banks of the river in Devil's Glen are the celebrated Mount Usher Gardens. The gardens were the inspiration of Edward Walpole in 1860 and originally covered a single acre. From this small beginning they have developed into the 20 acres of rare trees and shrubs which exist today. Also of interest here is a fascinating carriage museum (OACT).

ASHFORD CASTLE, Galway **15 M15**
See Cong entry.

ASKEATON, *Eas Géitine:*
the Waterfall of Géitine, Limerick **21 R35**
Askeaton stands on the River Deel and was once the stronghold of the powerful Desmond family. The Desmonds achieved a position of virtual independence during the middle ages, and strongly resisted English forces. The town and castle were eventually taken in 1580, and the Earl of Desmond was forced to take refuge in the Kerry Hills.

The castle (NM) is built on an island in the River Deel, near a bridge, and was originally founded by William de Burgo in the late 12thc. The finest surviving building is the 15th-c Great Banqueting Hall, which measures 90ft long by 30ft wide and was built by the 7th Earl. Features of this fine monument include superbly-executed windows, a blind arcade, and vaulting which shows evidence that basketwork was used during construction. A ward above the one in which the Great Hall stands contains a natural limestone outcrop which carries the ruins of the principal 15th-c tower. This replaces a 13th-c tower which occupied the same site. Near the tower is a tall, possibly 16th-c house.

Remains of a 14th-c Franciscan friary (NM) can be seen on the E bank of the river, but most of the surviving buildings date from the 15thc. These include the cloisters, which are enclosed by twelve pointed arches fashioned from black marble and supported by cylindrical columns. Also of interest are the nave, chancel, north transept, refectory, and a statue of St Francis in the north-east corner. Portions of a 13th-c church of the Knights Templar are preserved in the walled-off south transept of the CI parish church.

ASSEY CASTLE, Meath **18 N86**
See Bective entry.

ATHASSEL, *Ath Aisil:*
Aisil's Ford, Tipperary **23 S03**
Remains of one of the largest medieval priories (NM) in Ireland can be seen here on the picturesque banks of the River Suir. The foundation was originally created for the Augustinian Order by William de Burgo at the end of the 12thc, and the ruins cover more than 4 acres of ground. The church is basically Cistercian in plan, but the great tower, of which only the base remains, is of Augustinian origin. The 13th-c doorway leading from the nave to the choir is an especially fine piece of architecture. Adjoined to the east end of the church are four small chapels, and the larger Lady Chapel. The south wall displays a 13th-c tomb with an effigy of the founder. Other 13th-c buildings enclosed by the priory wall include the usual cloisters, sacristy, refectory, and labourers houses, etc. Several of the buildings stand upon vaults. Nothing remains of the town which grew up around this once immensely rich foundation. The Baronry of Clanwilliam, in which Athassel is situated, was granted to William de Burgo by King John. William was more interested in the fertile lands of the Golden Vale, and left the subjugation of Connacht to his son. The Baronry of Clanwilliam in which Athassel is situated still preserves de Burgo's name.

ATHBOY, *Baile Átha Buí:*
the Town of the Yellow Ford, Meath **18 N76**
The church (CI) in this small market town is built on the site of a 15th-c Carmelite priory, and the west tower of this is incorporated in the present structure. Also of interest is a 15th-c effigy of a knight and his lady. Near the church are parts of the medieval town walls, which date from the time when Athboy was a stronghold of the Pale.

About 1m E of the town is the celebrated Hill of the Ward (NM), a hilltop fort comprising a central enclosure surrounded by four pairs of banks and ditches. In ancient times this was *Tlachtga*, one of the principal assembly places of the kingdom of Meath. It is named after the sorceress *Tlachtga*, who died in childbirth and is buried under the hill. On Samhain Eve the rituals connected with the beginning of winter were performed here. It is said that on some occasions human sacrifice was carried out on a hideously large scale. Cromwell's army camped here in 1649. Some 3m NE of Athboy are the ruined church and castle of Rathmore (see entry). Father O Gramhna, the Irish language revivalist, spent his boyhood 1½m S of Athboy at Ballyfallon.

ATHCARNE CASTLE, Meath **19 O06**
See Duleek entry.

ATHENRY, *Baile Átha an Rí:*
the Town of the King's Ford, Galway **16 M52**
Meyler de Bermingham founded this town in 1235, after the land had been granted to him by William de Burgo. The castle (NM), built by de Bermingham between 1235 and 1250, is a typical Anglo-Norman stronghold comprising a keep and a walled court or bawn. The keep has three stories and is entered at the first floor via steps. The steps are modern, but the handsome door is original. Although the enclosing wall has been restored it still retains its original corner turrets.

Phelim O Conor, King of Connacht, met Anglo-Norman troops under William de Burgo and Richard de Bermingham outside the castle walls in 1316. During the battle the king and many Irish nobles were killed, and this marked the last O Conor attempt to oust the invaders. The Irish defeat also had an important effect on Edward Bruce's campaign in Ireland.

De Bermingham founded a Dominican friary (NM) in 1241, but the church is the only part of this to have survived. A large number of the many people concerned with the enlargement and edification of the friary were Irish, which is surprising when it is considered that this was an Anglo-Norman foundation. The church has been greatly altered through the years. It was largely rebuilt by William de Burgo in 1324, gutted by fire in 1423, burned again in 1574, restored in the early 17thc, closed by Cromwell in 1652, and finally wrecked while in use as barracks during 1750. Some of the most prominent people of the W were buried here during the middle ages, and original 13th-c windows can be seen in the choir. Athenry's parish church (CI) is built on part of a site once occupied by a 13th-c collegiate church. An interesting feature of the town's market place is a ruined 15th-c cross with a representation of the Crucifixion on one side and the Virgin and Child on the other. Parts of the old walls mark the limits of the medieval community. The town's most priceless treasure, the Shrine of St Patrick's Tooth, is now in the National Museum, Dublin. This was commissioned by Sir Thomas de Bermingham in the 14thc and comprises richly-ornamented silver with a full relief of the Crucifixion on the front. The ruins of 15th-c Derrydonnell Castle are located 3½m SW of Athenry. There are also several other castles within easy reach.

ATHLEAGUE, *Áth Liag:*
Ford of the Standing Stones, Roscommon **16 M85**
This village stands on the River Suck and features remains of a 13th-c castle known as the Fort of the Earls. A ditch which divides the structure in half was, according to tradition, cut because of an insoluble argument between two noblemen. In the demesne of Castle

Strange, 1½m NNW of Athleague, is an ancient ritual object known as the Castle Strange Stone (NM). This dates from *c*200 BC and is decorated with ornamentation in the Celtic iron-age La Tène style. Castle Strange itself is a ruined house with extensive stables.

ATHLONE, *Baile Átha Luain*:
the Town of the Ford of Luan, Westmeath 17 N04

Athlone is a busy commercial and communications centre on the main Dublin to Galway road, at one of the most important crossings of the River Shannon. Most of the modern town occupies the river's E bank. Because of its strategic position the town has played an important part in Irish history from earliest times. The river crossing was frequently the scene of battles against the western tribes, who were continually attempting to gain access to the rich midland plains. In 1001 the High King Brian Boru marched his army from his palace at Kincora to a great hosting at Athlone. His ships sailed to the gathering via Lough Derg and the Shannon. In 1129 Turloch Mor O Conor built a fort on the W bank of the river to protect a new bridge, but both of these structures were frequently destroyed. Towards the end of the 12thc the Anglo-Normans constructed a motte-and-bailey here, and in 1210 the Justiciar John de Gray erected a strong castle. Remains of the latter can still be seen in the ruins.

During the Elizabethan wars the town was considered to be of such importance that serious consideration was given to the idea of moving the Lord Deputy from Dublin to Athlone. The great battle of 1690 saw the town attacked by 10,000 troops under King William's commander Douglas, but Colonel Richard Grace's Jacobite forces repelled the assault and a further attack was made in 1691. This too was thwarted, when a small band of defenders successfully destroyed the bridge in the face of heavy artillery fire. However, a small party from William's force made a surprise crossing via a deep ford below the bridge, and the Jacobite commander failed to use his troops in time. The defence collapsed, and the Jacobites withdrew.

The castle (NM) overlooks the bridge and has a history as interesting and varied as the town itself. In 1211, the year after it had been completed, the tower fell in. However, the many-sided keep has survived to the present day, and is the oldest part of the present structure. Repair work was carried out several times during the 13thc, and the angle towers were built during one of these 'overhauls'. Although the towers still stand they do not bear much similarity to the original design, because they were rebuilt to support heavy guns during the 19thc. The seige of 1691 resulted in a great deal of damage to the fabric of the castle, and a series of subsequent rebuildings has considerably changed the appearance of the building, whose keep houses a museum.

St Mary's CI Church incorporates the tower of an earlier building and is associated with Oliver Goldsmith's family. The wife of Dean Goldsmith, the poet's brother, was buried in the tower in 1769. It is said that Colonel Grace, commander of the defending Jacobite forces in 1690, is also interred here. The Church of SS Peter and Paul (RC), built on the site of an old military barracks yard, was opened in 1937. This Roman-Renaissance style building carries twin towers and a dome and features stained-glass windows depicting famous men contemporary with its time of erection.

A bronze plaque on a house in The Bawn marks the birthplace of celebrated tenor Count John McCormack, and a plaque which was unveiled in 1937 marks the site of a house which was the birthplace of journalist and politician T P O Connor. The corner of Church Street is occupied by a house – now greatly altered – in which William's Dutch commander Ginkel stayed during the siege of 1691. Also of interest is the house in which the Duke of Wellington lived as a young man when quartered in Athlone. Other places worth a visit are the fragments of a 16th-c town wall, the remains of an abbey, and a Franciscan friary. The latter was completed in 1241 and abandoned at the Dissolution.

To the W of the town are ruins of 19th-c defences which were erected to guard against a possible attack from the French. Places within easy reach of Athlone include the island-scattered Lough Ree, Goldsmith Country, and the ecclesiastical centre of Clonmacnoise.

ATHY, *Áth Í*:
the Ford of Ae, Kildare 18 S69

Set in a fine agricultural district round the River Barrow, where it is joined by a branch of the Grand Canal, Athy is an important market centre for the surrounding district. The town's historical importance stems from its strategic position at a ford – a dubious asset in the light of the many past battles which have been fought for control of the crossing. King Ae of Munster was killed during an 11th-c engagement here, which is how the town acquired its name. Towards the end of the 13thc an Anglo-Norman baron, probably Richard

1 Abbey Ruins
2 Castle and Museum
3 Church of SS Peter & Paul (RC)
4 Franciscan Friary Remains
5 John McCormack's Birthplace (The Bawn)
6 St Mary's Church (CI)
7 Town Wall Remains

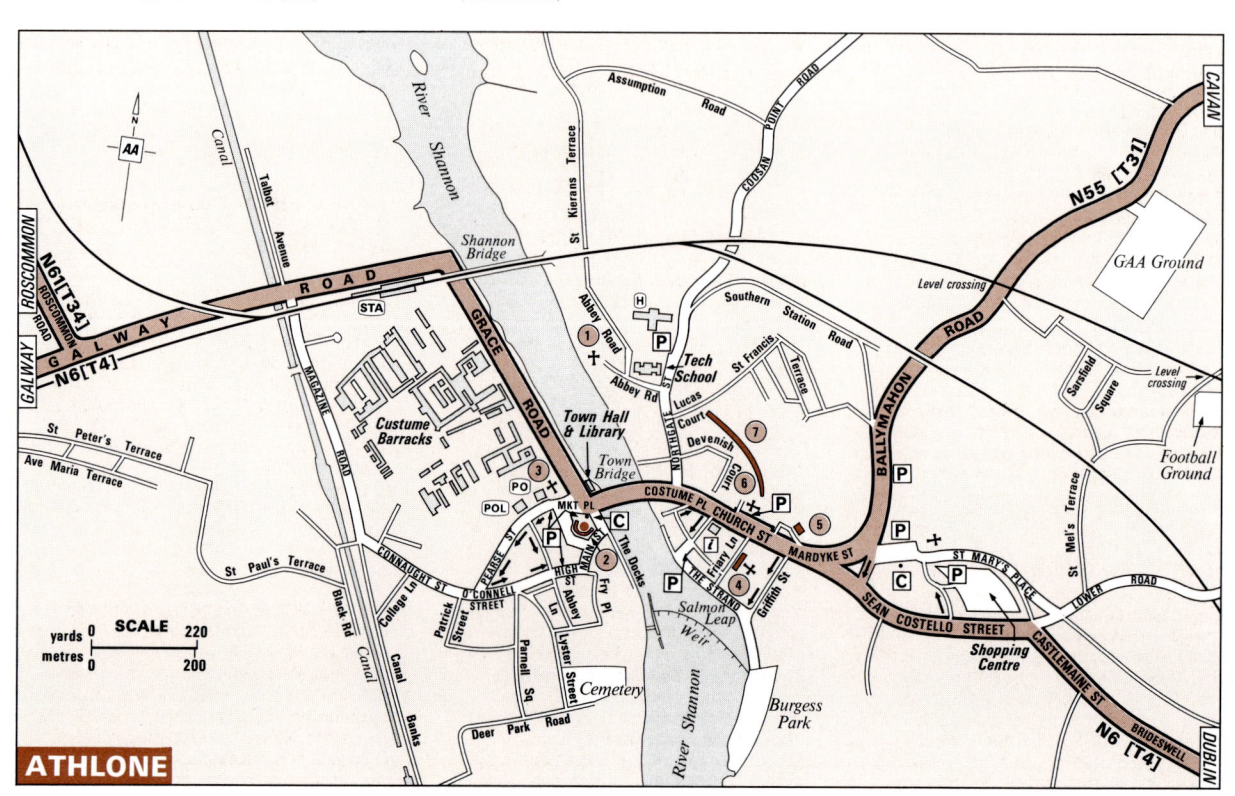

de St Michael, erected Castle Woodstock to guard the ford. This was badly damaged in 1649, but remains of the massive structure can still be seen on the N side of the town.

White Castle dates from 1575 and was likewise built to defend the crossing, this time by the Earl of Kildare. Its massive, rectangular wall carries a turret at each corner and overlooks an 18th-c bridge called Crom-a-boo, a peculiar name derived from the war cry of the Desmond family. Both castles participated and suffered damage in the Stuart and Jacobite wars.

The Dominican Church in Athy is an interesting modern structure. Several contemporary artists contributed to the interior, including Bridget Rynne, Breda O Donoghue, and George Campbell RHA. The latter was responsible for the windows and Stations of the Cross.

There are many other places of interest within easy reach of the town. The ruined O More fortress of Ballyadams preserves a turretted tower and 16th-c wings, and can be seen 4m SW. Some 6m SE is Belan House, an example of work by 18th-c architect Richard Cassels, now in a dilapidated state. Ruined Castle Inch can be seen 3m E of Athy. The foundations on which this stands were laid in the reign of King John, and the structure was enlarged during the 15thc. Gracefield Lodge, situated about 6m SW, was designed by John Nash for the Grace family. The Graces were descended from Raymond le Gros, who accompanied Strongbow into Ireland. About 3m NW are the ruins of the 13th-c Richard de St Michael stronghold known as Reban Castle. Reban, or Righban, is marked on Ptolemy's 2nd-c map as one of the inland towns of Ireland.

ATLANTIC DRIVE, Donegal **5 C14**
See Rosguill Peninsula entry.

AUBURN, Westmeath **17 N15**
See Ballymahon entry.

AUDLEY'S CASTLE, Down **13 J55**
See Castleward entry.

AUGHER, *Eochair:*
Border, Tyrone **12 H55**
This Clogher Valley village is delightfully set on the River Blackwater. Castlehill demesne occupies an area at the W end of the village and contains Spur Royal, or Augher, Castle, which was built in 1611 by Lord Ridgeway as a plantation stronghold. It is a square, three-storeyed structure built on the site of an earlier fortress, and carries a triangular tower in the middle of each side. Fire destroyed part of the building in 1689, and when it was restored in 1832 a new north front was added to enclose the old north wall. A circular tower of the castle bawn or walled court stands SW of the main structure. Knockmany Hill lies 1¾m NW.

Some 4m NE is Errigal Keeroge, which is thought to have been a 15th-c Franciscan foundation. Of interest are the remnants of a gable and fragments of walls belonging to St Kieran's Church (NM), plus traces of an earlier round tower. Errigal Keeroge Cross (NM), a 6ft-high monument with the arms projecting slightly from a solid ring, can be seen to the W.

AUGHNACLOY, *Achadh na Cloiche:*
the Field of the Stone, Tyrone **12 H65**
Part of the border with Monaghan is formed here by the River Blackwater, which also provides good fishing and enables this small market town to double as an angling resort. About 3m W of the town is the large bawn of Favour-Royal, an area 25yds square with a tower at each corner. It was built by Sir Thomas Ridgeway in 1611 and displays several interesting relics from the far more distant past. Among these is a carved head with a flat face and outlined features, brought here from Errigal Keeroge near Augher, plus a stone 'chair' which was found S of Clogher on Ashban Mountain. A state forest in the area offers recreational facilities which include a picnic site.

AUGHNANURE, Galway **15 M14**
See Oughterard entry.

AUGHRIM, *Eachroim:*
Horse Ridge, Wicklow **25 T17**
Two tiny rivers known as the Ow and the Derry join to the W of this village to form the Aughrim River. The village itself, set amid attractive countryside, lies at the junction of several mountain valleys and forms a good base from which to climb 3,039ft Lugnaquilla Mountain. This, Wicklow's highest peak, can be approached via Aghavannagh Valley. A route which crosses the watershed between the sources of the Ow and Slaney leads to beautiful Glen of Imaal. In the valley of the Ow River, some 3m NW of Aughrim at Ballymanus, is a splendid farmhouse of elegant Georgian proportions. This was the birthplace of Billy Byrne, who led a force of Irish insurgents against the king's army in 1798. The house carries a memorial plaque to Byrne.

AVOCA, *Abhóca,* Wicklow **25 T27**
Immortalized by Thomas Moore, the Vale of Avoca is part of a beautiful area extending from Rathdrum to Woodenbridge. It is delightful throughout the year and is particularly lovely in spring and autumn. Castle Howard stands in its demesne overlooking the Meeting of the Waters – the confluence of the Avonmore and Avonbeg rivers which forms the Avoca River. This first 'Meeting' can be seen from the Lion Bridge, which was once the access to the castle and spans the Avonmore. Below the Meeting Bridge is an old tree stump known locally as Moore's Tree. It is said that this is where the poet sat to contemplate the lovely scene which inspired his poem *Meeting of the Waters*, composed here in 1807. The poet is commemorated by a bust near the spot. The second 'Meeting' – of the Avoca and Aughrim rivers – is at Woodenbridge.

Copper mining is carried on to the N of Avoca and there are also traces of other mineral deposits. Cronebane is an 816ft ridge which rises above Castle Howard and affords magnificent views along the Avonmore, Avonbeg, and Avoca valleys. In the middle distance are Glenmalure and Glendalough, with Lugnaquilla and Kippure Mountains in the background. An interesting relic on the summit of the ridge is the Mottha Stone, a 14ft-long boulder traditionally held to be the hurling stone of Finn MacCool. This amply illustrates the remarkable strength attributed to legendary Irish heroes.

AVONDALE, Wicklow **25 T18**
Birthplace of Charles Stewart Parnell in 1846, Avondale is an 18th-c house, lying 1½m S of Rathdrum, which now serves as a Government forestry school (OACT). It is situated in the Avonmore Valley and the grounds contain a nature trail.

BAGENALSTOWN, Carlow **24 S76**
See Muine Bheag entry.

BAGINBUN HEAD, Wexford **24 S80**
The first Norman invasion fleet arrived here in May of 1169.

BAILE-ATHA-CLIATH, Dublin **19 O13**
See Dublin feature on page 45.

BAILIEBOROUGH, *Coill an Chollaigh:*
the Wood of the Boar, Cavan **12 N69**
Most of this town's interest is centred upon the wide main street. Two buildings are of special note, both the work of a 19th-c improving landlord, Colonel William Young. The first is the three-bay, two-storey, hipped roofed courthouse of 1817. It is succeeded with contrasting quoins, and a county brideswell was added to the rear of the building c1833. The second of Young's buildings is the now neglected market house of 1818. In design it is similar to the courthouse, but is dressed in a random blackstone.

Also of interest in the town is the Catholic church, which contains stations of the cross by the painter George Collie. At Killinkere, 6m SW, is the reputed birthplace of General Philip Sheridan, 19th-c American Civil War hero who became commander of the US army.

BALBRIGGAN, *Baile Brigín:*
Brigín's Homestead, Dublin **19 O26**
Sheltered sandy beaches to the N and S of the River Delvin are a major feature of this resort. The Delvin is a good trout stream, and it was in its estuary that St Patrick is supposed to have baptized his disciple and successor St Benignus. Prosperity was brought to Balbriggan by the Hamilton family, who used parliamentary grants to build a pier, dock, cotton factory, and facilities for the manufacture of hosiery during the 18thc. Of interest is the RC church, which has two good two-light windows by Henry Clarke. King William III broke his march to Dublin and set up camp near the town after the Battle of the Boyne.

BALDONGAN CASTLE, *Baile Dhonnagáin:*
Donnagán's Homestead, Dublin **19 O25**
See Skerries entry.

BALLA, *Balla:* a Well, Mayo **15 M28**
Situated in the district known as the Plains of Mayo, Balla is a good centre for brown-trout fishing. A neglected graveyard here contains the stump of a round tower (NM) and a medieval altar, the sole surviving remains of a 7th-c monastery foundation created by St Mochua. The latter was a pupil of St Comghall of Bangor. Tobar Muir, or the Blessed Well, lies to the W and is claimed to have curative powers for the lame.

BALLAGHADERREEN, *Bealach an Doirín:*
the Road of the Little Grove,
Roscommon **10 M69**
The Lung River, near the head of which this little market and cathedral town is sited, flows NE into nearby Lough Gara. The town includes several charming Georgian houses, plus a gothic-revival cathedral of dubious aesthetic merit.

BALLAGHBEAMA PASS 26V77
This lonely pass lies in the shadow of the MacGillycuddy's Reeks mountain range. The road here is dangerously narrow and steep in places.

*BALLINA, *Béal an Átha:*
Mouth of the Ford, Mayo **9G21**
Cathedral town of the Killala RC diocese and the largest centre of population in Co Mayo, Ballina stands on the River Moy near the NE shores of Lough Conn. The S extension of this lake is known as Lough Cullin, and both reaches are shadowed by 2,646ft Nephin Mountain. The town is the market centre for the surrounding area, and is a well-known resort for game fishing.

During the 1798 Insurrection General Humbert landed at Killala Bay with a force of 1,100 French troops, and Ballina was the first Irish town to be captured in his subsequent campaign. The defending garrison retired to Castlebar and the general occupied the town. The RC cathedral here displays a beautiful stained-glass window, and near by is Augustinian Ardaree Friary. This 15th-c foundation was created by the O Dowdas, princes of Fiachrach, and the church which stands here was built a short time after the rest of the complex. Features of the church include a finely-ornamented west doorway, and a window decorated with two sculptures of human heads.

On a hill to the SW of the church is the *Clogh-ogle*, or Dolmen of the Four Maels (NM). This comprises three uprights supporting a capstone, with the displaced fourth stone lying near by. Legend claims this to be the grave of four brothers who murdered their master Bishop Ceallach of Killala, and were hanged by his brother. About 1m NW is the site of Kilmoremoy – the 'Great Church of Moy' – which was founded by St Olcan, who was a disciple of St Patrick. Remains include an ancient church inside an enclosing rampart, with a cross-incised rock surface known as the *Liag* near its centre. On the W bank of the River Moy, N of Ballina, may be seen the wooded grounds of Belleek Manor. The long, serrated ridge of the Ox Mountain range rises to the E of Ballina.

BALLINAFAD, *Béal an Átha Fada:*
Mouth of the Long Ford, Sligo **10G70**
Famous for its tranquillity, this small town is sited at the SW corner of Lough Arrow, with the low Curlew Hills to the S and the Bricklieve Mountains rising to 1,057ft in the NW. Curlieus Castle (NM) was built to guard a pass over the Curlew Hills *c*1519. It was modelled on the plan usually adopted by 13th-c castles, and displays a small, central square block flanked by four massive corner turrets. The latter are curved on the outside but have square interiors. There are numerous raths in the area, and the giant, possibly bronze-age Heapstown Stone Cairn (NM) can be seen near the N shores of Lough Arrow. It is thought that this 20ft-high mound of stones and earth may cover a passage grave, but this is purely conjectural as the cairn has never been excavated. In the Bricklieve Mountains is the famous Carrowkeel passage grave cemetery (see entry).

In Aghanagh, ¾m N, are the remains of a small pre-Romanesque church which was originally founded by St Patrick. Some 3m beyond this is 17th-c Castle Baldwin (NM). To the NE of Ballinafad on the NE shore of Lough Arrow are the ruins of Dominican Ballindoon Friary, which was founded by the MacDonaghs in 1507. Features of the church here include entrances in the north and south walls, plus a central tower and belfry.

BALLINAKILL, *Baile na Coille:*
the Homestead of the Wood, Laois **23S48**
Fragmentary ruins are all that remain of a once-important castle which guarded this Kilkenny-border community. The stronghold was unsuccessfully stormed by Cromwellian troops in 1641, then rebuilt but left unoccupied in 1680. Haywood House, situated 1m NNE of Ballinakill was built in 1773 and partially destroyed by a disastrous fire. It was rebuilt in 1950 and now serves as a Salesian missionary college. The grounds in which the house stands include sunken gardens designed by Sir Edward Lutyens.

BALLINALACK, *Béal Átha na Leac:*
the Fordmouth of the Flagstones, Westmeath **17N36**
The River Inny flows through this village as it makes its 6m way from Lough Derravaragh to Lough Iron. Near the latter are 12th-c remains of Tristernagh Abbey, which was destroyed in 1783, plus the almost-perfect Templecross Church. This interesting little building dates from the 15thc and incorporates a priest's room.

BALLINASLOE, *Béal Átha na Sluaighe:*
the Ford-mouth of the Host, Galway **16M83**
The famous October fair held here is the largest livestock market in Ireland, and in the days of the cavalry and horse-drawn transport it was the largest horse fair in Europe. The town, which has some fine 18th-c houses, stands at the crossing of the River Suck, in an area which yields a type of limestone once prized as a superior building material. There are still numerous quarries in the district. Garbally Park estate adjoins the town and surrounds a Georgian mansion which was once the home of the Earls of Clancarty. This elegant 19th-c building, now a school, shows enlightened use of the local stone. Beside the Suck is a 19th-c house known as Ivy Castle, so-called because it was built around the remains of a genuine medieval stronghold. Unfortunately the more recent work has completely obscured the original structure, which was the scene of many armed encounters during the Elizabethan wars. The Catholic parish church of 1852, designed partly by Pugin, contains some excellent modern workmanship. The mental hospital was built in 1838 from designs by Francis Johnston. Ballinasloe is the W terminus of the Grand Canal.

BALLINCOLLIG, *Baile an Chollaigh:*
the Homestead of the Boar, Cork **28W57**
Both the Bride and the Lee flow near Ballincollig, which is situated in the Lee Valley, and provide excellent fishing. Ballincollig Castle, 1m SW, is a 14th-c keep from the reign of Edward III and the one-time stronghold of the Barretts. Remains include an irregular bawn with flankers, traces of a tower which contained unusually small rooms, a great hall, and an encircling moat. The remains of 14th- to 17th-c Carrigrohane Castle lie approximately 2m ENE of the village. They stand upon a cliff overlooking the River Lee.

BALLINDERRY, *Baile an Doire:*
the Homestead of the Oak Grove, Antrim **13J16**
A somewhat scattered village near the SE corner of Lough Neagh, Ballinderry is associated with 17th-c Jeremy Taylor, the English divine and author who became Bishop of Dromore. At first he declined the position because he was expected to share the duty with a Presbyterian, but he eventually accepted and retreated to Viscount Conway's mansion on Lough Neagh. He was appointed to the see of Down and Conor, to which the diocese of Dromore was later added, and his remains were interred at Dromore. About 1m WNW of the village are the remains of Ballinderry First Church, where Taylor preached. To the E is 17th-c Middle Church, which was built by Taylor and still preserves the original oak fittings. This was restored in 1896. Taylor wrote some of his best-known books while in residence here.

BALLINDERRY, *Baile an Doire:*
the Homestead of the Oak Grove, Westmeath **17N23**
Remains of two crannogs – or lake dwellings – may be seen in Ballinderry bog, which is situated 1½m NE of the village of Moate.

The first, called by archaeologists Ballinderry I, was discovered in 1928 and excavated during 1932. Construction began in the 10thc, and the site was occupied intermittently up to the 17thc. The first building upon the site consisted of a large round house, almost as big as the crannog itself. This was eventually abandoned, probably because the foundations sank. New foundations were laid upon the old surface and two smaller houses were built. These too were abandoned, and a fourth house was built upon yet another foundation layer. Many interesting finds were made on the site, including wooden objects which the damp atmosphere had kept in a remarkable state of preservation. Of these the most fascinating was a carved 10th-c wooden gaming board, which is now in the National Museum, Dublin.

About 2,000yds SE in Co Offaly is the second crannog, Ballinderry II. This was first noticed during drainage operations for a railway in 1844, and was subsequently excavated, after much looting, in 1933. The site was originally occupied in late bronze age times, and was not at first, strictly speaking, a crannog, as the structures were built directly upon the surface of the island. Later, however, the surface was artificially raised. The site was reoccupied *c*800, and has yielded a considerable number of finds.

BALINDOON FRIARY, Sligo **10G71**
See Ballinafad entry.

BALLINEEN, *Béal Átha Fhínín:*
Fínín's Ford-mouth, Cork **27W35**
This village is attractively situated on the River Bandon.

BALLINGARRY, *Baile an Gharraí:*
the Homestead of the Garden, Limerick **21R43**
Places of interest in and around this town include a castellated dwelling known as Parson's Castle, the ruins of two other houses, and the tower of a Franciscan friary.

Heapstown Cairn, a 20ft-high heap of stones near Ballinafad, may be of bronze-age origin.

BALLINGARRY, near Birr,
Baile an Gharraí:
the Homestead of the Garden, Tipperary
17 R99
This village is situated on the main Birr to Borrisokane road. About 1½m to the E is 700ft Knockshigowna, a hill celebrated in Irish fairy legends as the 'Otherworld Seat of Una'. Una is the fairy-queen guardian of the O Carrolls of Eile, and the summit of the hill used to be the scene of Lughnasa celebrations on Bilberry Sunday.

BALLINROBE, *Baile an Róba:*
the Homestead of the (River) Robe, Mayo
15 M16
Anglers come to this Plains of Ellerton market town, which is situated on the Robe River, for the excellent fishing offered by nearby Loughs Mask and Carra. Mask measures 10m long by 4m wide and is the largest lough in Co Mayo. On the E shore, 4m SW of the town, is ruined Lough Mask Castle, a 15th-c Mac William fortress built on the site of a 13th-c Fitzgerald stronghold. The structure was restored by Sir Thomas Burke in the 17thc. Across the lough the Partry Mountains are dominated by the peaks of 2,239ft Benwee and 2,207ft Maumtrasna. During the 19thc nearby Lough Mask House was the residence of Captain Boycott, whose name became part of the English language after he was ostracized for treating his tenants badly. On the N edge of the town are the slight remains of the church of an Augustinian friary founded c1313.

BALLINSKELLIGS, *Baile an Sceilg:*
the Homestead of Skellig Island, Kerry
26 V46
This seaside resort is situated in an Irish-speaking area on the W side of Ballinskelligs Bay, and boasts a 4m strand. Fine coastal scenery, boating, and fishing are also offered. To the W are remains of a MacCarthy castle and the ruins of Augustinian Ballinskelligs Monastery (NM). The monastery was founded by monks from Skellig Michael (see entry) in the 12thc. Although the existing remains have been badly eroded by the sea, it is possible to date the two churches to the 15thc. Both have windows and doors of dressed stone, and one has an adjoining cloister garth with a large hall on the far side. To the SW lies 1,330ft Bolus, which overlooks St Finan's Bay and the Skelligs. Rewarding boat trips can be made (weather permitting) to the Skellig Rocks and Puffin Island. A variety of traces of past occupation may be seen upon the slopes of Bolus, including stone alignments, ringforts, and a monastic settlement.

BALLINSPITTLE, *Béal Átha an Spidéil:*
the Ford-mouth of the Hospital, Cork
28 W54
This village is noted for ancient Ballycatteen Fort, a trivallate rath with a 400ft diameter earthwork, sited about ½m WSW. This defensive system covers some 3 acres of ground and occupies the SE end of a ridge. The three fosses are cut through shale to a depth of 6ft, leaving a solid causeway as the south-east entrance. This was defended by a series of wooden stakes. Three souterrains were constructed in the centre of the rath, and there is evidence that the complex was occupied during the medieval period. Pottery discovered here dates back to c600. Garrettstown Strand lies 1¾m to the S, beyond which are the Bays of Holeopen East and Holeopen West on either side of the remote Old Head of Kinsale.

BALLINTAGGART, *Baile an tSagairt:*
the Homestead of the Priest, Kerry
26 Q40
Interesting Ogham stones (NM) can be seen in the circular graveyard here, and the townland itself is situated near Dingle Harbour in one of the richest areas of archaeological interest in Ireland. Three of the five stones bear incised crosses and they are all worked from sandstone. This graveyard is probably a killeen – *ie* a walled enclosure commonly used until recent times for the burial of unbaptised children.

BALLINTOBER, *Bail an Tobair:*
the Homestead of the Well, Mayo
15 M17
The abbey (NM) for which this little village is famous was founded by Cathal O Conor, King of Connacht, in 1216. It was built by the side of a previous 5th-c foundation and is unique in being the only church of the English-speaking world to have held Mass continuously for 750 years. Henry VIII's suppression was merely nominal, and the abbey continued to flourish through the 16thc until the Cromwellians unroofed it in 1653. Despite this despoliation the abbey continued in use.

The internal stone-vaulted chancel roof remains intact, as do the four side chapels and 13th-c sacristy, and complete restoration of the abbey begun in 1963 by the Office of Works was completed in 1966. Archaeological investigation which accompanied the restoration revealed the original 15th-c cloisters, which were subsequently re-erected. The Chapter House has a beautiful four-order west doorway with a pointed arch. The original 15th-c west doorway and window have been returned to the nave, which has been re-roofed. A three-light east window is surmounted by a smaller window and resembles others in the Cistercian churches of Abbey, Knockmoy, and Corcomroe.

BALLINTOBER, *Baile an Tobair:*
the Homestead of the Well, Roscommon
16 M77
This village derives its name from a local holy well dedicated to St Brigid. Extensive ruins of a keepless castle dating from the 13thc can be seen, complete with a twin-towered gatehouse and polygonal corner towers. From c1300 to 1652 this was a stronghold of the O Conors, Kings of Connacht, and it played an important part in the Stuart and Tudor wars. The local churchyard includes the O Conor mausoleum, in which the 18th-c Irish scholar and antiquary Charles O Conor of Bellanagere is buried.

BALLINTOY, *Baile an Tuaighe,* Antrim
7 D04
Ballintoy is set on the Ballycastle to Bushmills road near a magnificent section of coast. Downing Fullerton, one-time landlord of the village, endowed the Cambridge college which carries his name. The oak panelling and staircase in the college came from a castle which used to stand on the W side of the village. The local parish church was used as a place of refuge during the strife-torn 17thc, and in 1663 was rebuilt to a design by Henry Wynne. This work was not completed until 1831. Features of the church, which is two bays long, include a rich stained-glass east window depicting the Resurrection and dedicated to the 19th-c Rev Robert Traill. St Joseph's is a plain basalt RC church which was financed by Fullerton and considerably altered in 1966.

Templastragh Old Church is built on the site of a 7th-c church and was possibly dedicated to St Lassara. Its present form dates from the 16thc, and the material used in its construction includes pentagonal-section blocks of basalt from a local quarry. These are similar to the geometric basalt stacks seen in the Giant's Causeway. Mount David House is a five-bay mansion of 1791, built in two stories and with a harled exterior.

The natural features of the area are by far the most interesting. A precipitous road leads to the small harbour between raised-beach caves to the W and Larry Bane Head to the E. This magnificent, white-limestone headland was captured by Paul Henry in one of his paintings, but inadequate planning regulations in the past have allowed much of the rock to be quarried away. About ½m out to sea is Sheep Island, a breeding ground for various species of sea birds. The rats which once infested the island have been cleared and the birds are allowed to breed in peace. To the E is the famous Carrick-a-Rede rope bridge, which spans a deep, 60ft-wide chasm between the

BALLINTOY/BALLYBUNION

A many-arched bridge spans the River Finn to link Ballybofey with Stranorlar.

mainland and a rock stack after which the bridge takes its name. The bridge is made of ropes and planks, and hangs 80ft above the chasm. It is used by salmon fishermen, who carry baskets of fish from one side of the chasm to the other in all weathers. This is a hair-raising venture even on calm days. The bridge is removed at the end of the fishing season.

To the W of this rope bridge is Kinbane Head, which is surmounted by a castle (NM) built by Colla Dubh – elder brother of Sorley Boye MacDonnell. Sorley Boye granted it to a captain of his Scottish troops, a MacAllister, as a reward c1850. Remains of this structure include a huge, rectangular gate tower which rises to 30ft and has flanking walls that extend to the cliff edge. Whole rooms are contained within the massive thickness of the south-east wall.

White Park Bay (NT) is a natural amphitheatre on the coast to the W of Ballintoy. An appeal by the Youth Hostel Association of N Ireland resulted in the NT's acquisition of the bay in 1939, and a new hostel was built to replace the 'wee white cottage' that had served before. Raised beaches here have yielded abundant prehistoric relics, with the bones of the great auk and red deer amongst those of domestic animals which had undoubtedly ended their days in the cooking pot. Excavations conducted during 1933 and 1934 centred on Potters Cave and uncovered a clay female figure. Many examples of bronze-age pottery, artefacts, and kilns have been discovered in the bay. To the W of the bay is Portbradden, a cluster of houses nestling under a cliff, including a thatched, white-washed cottage adjoining a little thatched chapel. This has been restored and developed. The waters of this entire area are known for their salmon.

BALLINTRA, *Baile an tSratha:*
the Homestead of the Holm, Donegal
10 G96
Numerous small, rounded hills called drumlins combine to form the soft landscapes around this village, which is built on the banks of a river bearing the same name. A swift stream called the Blackwater River cuts its way through the soft limestone hills, disappearing underground in some places and flinging itself over steep cliffs in others before rising from a meadow and tumbling into a deep chasm known as The Pullins. Some 300yds E of the village is the attractive waterfall of Aghadullagh Mill, and about ½m S of the village is Racoon, the site of a monastery founded c440 by St Patrick. Part of the complex was later used as a church, and the remains that exist here comprise a flat, rectangular mound of earth and stones. The Seven Bishops of Rath Cunga, mentioned in the *Litany* of Aengus Ceile De, are associated with this area.

The ancient royal seat of Ard Fothadh is situated 2m SW of the village. Also known as McGonigle's Fort, this is 870ft in circumference and is protected by a 20ft-high earthen rampart. There is another rampart below this, and a wide fosse separates the two. Inside the fort is a 20ft-high by 190ft-round mound shaped like a beehive. This is said to have been dug into and to have revealed a stone chamber which tradition states to have been the burial place of the 6th-c High King Hugh MacAinmare. This S part of Donegal is known as *Tirhugh*, after the high king. Of the district's many megalithic remains, two tombs are of special interest; these are the one 1m W near Connor's Bridge, and one 2m SW on the slopes of 492ft Lurgan Cairn.

BALLON, *Balana,* Carlow   **24 S86**
During the mid 19thc an important bronze-age cemetery was discovered on prominent Ballon Hill, a 430ft granite knoll. A large number of cremated burials were found, most accompanied by food vessels and urns. Associated with the burials were a considerable number of ritual pits, which contained burnt bones and charcoal. The discoveries were made in and around large entrenchments which surmount the hill. These may be the remains of a hilltop cairn, though the local name for these entrenchments – The Walls of Troy – may suggest that this was the site of a bronze-age ritual maze.

BALLSBRIDGE, *Droichead na Dothra:*
Dodder Bridge, Dublin   **19 O13**
Good, early 19th-c houses are a feature of this elegant residential suburb of Dublin. The Royal Dublin Society, originally founded in 1731 to promote practical economics, is situated on the main Merrion road. Nowadays it is best known for the famous Dublin Horse Show, which is held in August, and the Spring Show and Industrial Fair held in May. The society has provided a very fine library for its members, and arranges music recitals by international artists. Lectures on popular scientific themes are also given here (see Dublin district plan on page 48).

BALLYBEG, *Baile Beag:*
the Small Homestead, Cork   **28 R50**
Augustinian Ballybeg Friary (NM) is situated just S of Buttevant and was founded by a de Barry in the early 13thc. De Barry dedicated the foundation to St Thomas and commemorated himself with a brass equestrian statue. The church was built shortly after the foundation and displays two fine west windows. The central tower has an interior staircase, and both this and a tower to the W were added to the structure in the 15thc. The friary dovecote or pigeon house can be seen ESE of the church and is considered by some to be the best example of its type in the country.

BALLYBOFEY AND STRANORLAR, *Bealach Féich:*
the Homestead of Fiach's Cattle and *Srath an Urláir:*
the Holm of the Floor, Donegal   **5 H19**
A many-arched bridge spans the River Finn and connects the small market town of Ballybofey with Stranorlar. Both places stand at the junction of two particularly scenic roads. One of these runs up the Finn Valley to Fintown and thence along the shores of Lough Finn to Glenties, while the other climbs through the Barnesmore Gap and affords views of the Blue Stack Mountains and lovely Lough Eask on its way to Donegal. The grave of Isaac Butt, founder of the Irish Home Rule movement, lies beside Ballybofey's Protestant church. This district is noted for its game fishing.

BALLYBRITTAS, *Baile Briotáis:*
the Homestead of the Brattice, Laois
18 N50
This quiet village was the scene of a battle in the 16thc when the Earl of Essex led English troops against the Irish under O Dempsey. The battle site itself became known as the Pass of the Plumes after the victorious Irish cut the plumes from the English helmets. To the SW is the Great Heath of Maryborough, near which is the ruined Fitzgerald stronghold of Morretta Castle. About 3m W is Emo Court, an 18th-c house which was built by the Earl of Portarlington to a design by James Gandon. Inside the house is a fine collection of paintings, glass, and sculpture, and the fine demesne is noted for its Wellingtonia firs. The grounds are maintained by the Forestry Division of the Department of Lands. Work by the architect James Gandon can also be seen in the CI church at Coolbanagher, 5m to the W.

BALLYBUNION, *Baile an Bhuinneánaigh:*
Bunyan's Homestead, Kerry   **20 Q84**
Excellent surfing and bathing are offered from the fine strand of this popular Atlantic-coast resort. A promontory which divides the strand into two carries a lofty, ruined wall of the Fitzmaurice family's castle, and the castle itself stands on Castle Green. Under the green is a complicated network of souterrains. Fine caves can be seen near the S end of the strand, and there are precipitous, cave-riddled cliffs towards the N. These, and the magnificent seascapes, were enjoyed by the poet Tennyson in 1842. To the S of picturesque Doon Cove are the remains of a promontory fort, and remains of a similar structure at Doon Point include fragments of a Geraldine castle. Farther N

is the Fitzgerald Lick Castle. The 880ft summit of inland Knockanore Hill to the E affords superb views across the River Shannon to the far-distant spires of Limerick city. Railway enthusiasts may be interested to know that Ballybunion was once the proud owner of the only Lartigue mono-rail single line railway in Ireland or Britain. No trace of it remains.

BALLYCARRY, *Baile Cora*:
Weir Homestead, Antrim 7J49

Now ruined, the first Presbyterian church ever built in Ireland was erected in this small industrial town early in the 17thc. The churchyard contains the grave of James Orr (1770 to 1816), a weaver and United Irishman poet who wrote the song *The Irishman*. The town itself lies just inland from the coast road. Nearby Old Mill Glen was the scene of a battle in 1597 in which Sir John Chichester was defeated and killed by the MacDonnells.

BALLYCASTLE, *Baile an Chaistil*:
the Town of the Castle, Antrim 7D14

This important coastal resort stands on the Glenshesk River and is dominated by 1,695ft Knocklayd, which rises to the S and incorporates a forest park. A certain Hugh Boyd spent his lifetime in building the town into a flourishing centre of commercial and industrial interests, but at his death these activities entered a slow but steady period of decline. The town is divided into two parts, each of which is almost a separate community and wears its own distinctive air of individuality.

Old Upper Town is dignified and spacious, and is linked to the busy Lower Town by a terrace of Victorian houses. Its area includes The Diamond, where the ancient Lammas Fair is still celebrated on the last Tuesday in August. A block of Georgian buildings here stands on the site once occupied by Randall MacDonnell's 17th-c castle. Although the stronghold is no longer standing it lives on in the town's name. Also in The Diamond is the CI Holy Trinity Church, a Greek-revival structure which displays a façade with a pedimented doorcase, semi-engaged Doric columns, and a Vitruvian door opening. Inside is the burial place of the town's benefactor, Hugh Boyd.

The fine buildings of the Lower Town are grouped around the harbour and softened by a grove of mature trees. Antrim Arms Hotel is a fine building with a fanlight, elegant porch, and fluted, free-standing columns capped with floral Ionic capitals. Franciscan Bonamargy Friary (NM) was founded by Rory MacQuillan in 1500, burnt in 1589, repaired and re-occupied until 1642, and restored in 1931 at a cost met by public subscription. The church features 17th-c family vaults of the Earls and Marquesses of Antrim, and the gatehouse carries a high, cut-stone chimney. An aerial survey has shown that the friary stands on a rampart which encloses a rectangular space around the complex. The foundation is named after the little River Margy – formed by the confluence of Glenshesk and Carey Rivers – which itself is associated with the Children of Lir legend in which three brothers and a sister were changed into swans and condemned to roam the waters of Ireland for 900 years.

Dunaney Castle stands ruined on a cliff edge to the W of the town, and was one of the first strongholds to be built by the MacDonnell family. It may have been the birthplace of famous Sorley Boye, who died in 1590. On the coast is spectacular Fair Head, which rises 636ft from a talus of huge blocks which slope away to deep water. Some of these columns are up to 50ft in girth and stand hundreds of feet high. On top of the head are three small loughs. Lough-na-Cranagh is the site of a crannog-type lake dwelling. This is oval in shape and includes an interesting dry-built revet 5 to 7ft above the water. The steep cliffs of Rathlin Island, to which Marconi transmitted his first radio message from Ballycastle in 1905, rear up from the sea opposite the head, providing many species of seabirds with a safe breeding ground. The island (see entry) can be reached by boat from Ballycastle Harbour. Doon Fort, a motte-and-bailey structure dating from c1180, may be seen ½m W of Lough-na-Cranagh. The motte is carved from a natural outcrop and encircled by a winding ramp that leads to the summit.

BALLYCASTLE, *Baile an Chaisil*:
the Homestead of the Stone Fort, Mayo 9G13

The Ballinglen River flows N through this pleasant resort to join Bunatrahir Bay, where there are sand dunes and a small beach. A major feature of this district is the spectacular sandstone-cliff scenery some 4m NE near Downpatrick Head, where the Atlantic storms have eroded the rocks into fantastic shapes. A good example of this natural sculpting is Doonbristy Rock, which is separated from the head by a deep channel. The blowholes along this part of the coast shoot great spouts of brine into the air during stormy weather.

Some 2m NW of the resort is an enclosure which contains the Pillar Stone of Doonfeeny. This measures nearly 18ft in height and is decorated with two crosses. The area is rich in prehistoric graves, of which perhaps the most interesting is situated 4m WNW at Behy overlooking the sea. It is set amidst extensive blanket bog at over 500ft. Most of the cairn was protected by peat, and on excavation between 1963 and 1964 it revealed many items of interest.

BALLYCLARE, *Bealach Cláir*:
Road of the Plain, Antrim 7J29

The annual fair for which this town is particularly noted takes place at the beginning of May and is second only to the Lammas Fair at Ballycastle. Ballyclare itself stands on the Six Mile Water river between Antrim and Larne at the S end of the Antrim Plateau, and was once the centre of a thriving linen industry. It was also noted for its paper manufacture, but today these traditional industries have given way to the manufacture of synthetic fibres and woollen yarn.

Pre-Christian settlement of the area is indicated by numerous forts, some of which incorporate natural caves. The War Memorial Park features a motte without a ditch or bailey, plus a 15ft-high by 54ft-long flat-topped earthwork which may have been constructed as a sepulchral mound. Lisnalinchy Fort (NM), a circular structure which rises to 25ft above its surrounding ditch, can be seen about 2m SE of the town, W of the Belfast road. Its saucer-shaped top measures 146ft across, and a souterrain is preserved close to the rampart on one side. This fort was once a stronghold of the O Loingsech family, who are historically linked with the O Leethlobhains. Members of both these families became kings of Dalradia during the period between the 8th and 11thc.

Dunamoy Motte, situated some 250yds W of the Ballymena to Ballyclare road, comprises a 60ft diameter, flat-topped mound encircled by a ditch which varies between 25 and 30ft in width and from 8 to 10ft in depth.

BALLYCONNELL, *Béal Átha Conaill*:
the Ford-mouth of Conall, Cavan 11H21

This village lies in a noted coarse-fishing area at the foot of the Slieve Rushen Hills, a range dominated by a 1,331ft main peak. The Protestant church dates from the 17thc, and there are earthworks to be seen in the churchyard. Ballyheady Mountain, 2½m SW, features a cave which has yielded skeletons dating from the bronze age, and is traditionally held to have been the burial place of Connail Cearnach – a hero of the Red Branch Knights. Cearnach is said to have been killed by the men of Connacht in revenge for the death of their king. About 3m SW of the village is the Killycluggin Decorated Stone, a monument which displays well-executed Celtic spirals and lies outside the remains of a disturbed stone circle which is probably all that remains of a megalithic grave. Small circles of boulders can be seen on many hilltops in the area, and although their

Lough na Cranagh lies near Ballycastle (Antrim) and features a crannog with a drystone revet.

function is enigmatic it is thought that they may mark burial sites. Also to be seen are a number of standing stones, one of which may be the *Crom Cruaich* – a stone god – overthrown by St Patrick. The area was one of religious importance from bronze-age to Celtic times.

BALLYCOWAN BRIDGE, *Baile Cobhainn:*
Cobhann's Homestead, Offaly   17 N32
Although the nearby ruins of a 16th-c castle bear the same name as this River Clodiagh bridge, which lies 1½m W of Tullamore, the castle itself is situated on the banks of the Grand Canal. Most of the remains are of a 17th-c fortified house built by Sir Jasper Herbert, and their most notable feature is a collection of unusual chimney stacks.

BALLYCROVANE HARBOUR, *Béal an Churraigh Bháin:*
Mouth of the White Marsh, Cork   26 V65
See Eyeries.

BALLYDUFF, *An Baile Dubh:*
the Black Homestead, Kerry   20 Q83
A lane at the end of this village leads to Rattoo Church (NM) and Round Tower (NM), which occupy an old monastic site. The 15th-c church stands in the graveyard and was constructed with stones from an earlier building. Features displayed by the well-preserved, 92ft-high round tower include an interesting round-headed doorway surrounded by an architrave in raised relief. At the base the tower is 48ft in circumference. To the E of the round tower, near the demesne gates, are the remains of a 15th-c abbey. Originally founded in the 13thc, it has a three-light east window.

BALLYDUFF, *An Baile Dubh:*
the Black Homestead, Waterford   28 W99
Situated on the banks of the River Blackwater, this small village features a fortified manor house dating from 1628 known as Ballyduff Castle. To the S of the village are the remains of Mocollop Castle, including a circular keep and square flankers.

BALLYFERRITER, *Baile an Fheirtéaraigh:*
Ferriter's Homestead, Kerry   26 Q30
This small village beneath 1,331ft Croaghmarhin has a fine strand 1m N on the edge of Smerwick Harbour. The hills known as the Three Sisters are located 3m N of the village. This area is beautiful and of exceptional historical interest. Ferriter's Castle, a 15th-c structure situated 2m NW, was the birthplace of distinguished scholar, poet, and soldier Pierce Ferriter – the last Kerry commander to submit to Cromwell. The castle ruins occupy a site which formed part of earlier defences across the neck of Doon Point. A second line of defence lies about 180yds to the W, and there are some interesting hut sites at the extremity of the point.

At Reask, 1¾m ENE of the village, is an old walled enclosure containing the remnants of a beautifully-decorated, cross-inscribed pillar (NM), two smaller cross slabs, and the foundations of two beehive huts. The first of these monuments has decoration reminiscent of late La Tène art. Traces of a cashel about 3m E at Lateevemore mark the site of ancient Templenacloonagh, and within the enclosure are the shell of an oratory and two early cross pillars.

Ballywiheen Townland lies close by and features an interesting ogham stone, which has been placed inside a small cashel known as Cahernagat Old Church (NM). To the N of this is a killeen with a ruined oratory, and E is a pillar stone beside St Molaga's Well. An exceptionally-fine standing stone measuring 17ft in height can be seen 150yds to the NE.

BALLYGALLEY, *Baile Geithligh:*
Geithleach's Homestead, Antrim   7 D30
Picturesquely set on the celebrated Antrim Coast Road, this village is close to the spectacular 300ft mass of columnular basalt which makes up Ballygalley Head, upon which may be seen Cairncastle. Inland the Sallagh Braes rise to join 1,268ft Robin Young's Hill, affording views of the Scottish mainland and islands from the tops of their vast basalt cliffs. The braes, or heights, surround a huge natural amphitheatre.

Ballygalley Castle now serves as a hotel, but was built by James Shaw of Greenock in 1625 and is considered a fine example of period Scottish baronial construction. Additions of 1760 can be seen next to the main structure, which features a flanking tower with an entrance and a spiral staircase at the north-east angle of the rectangle. The building has four stories, and the 5ft-thick walls are perforated with musketry holes. There is a circular tower with a conical roof at each end of the surrounding bawn. On the moors 4m W of the village, near Dunteige Bridge, is Dunteige, a wedge-shaped gallery grave; ¼m N of this is a court cairn with a ruinous chamber tomb.

BALLYGAWLEY, *Baile Uí Dhálaigh:*
O Daly's Homestead, Tyrone   12 H65
Fertile Clogher Valley, in which this village is situated, is particularly rich in archaeological relics. Remains of chambered graves, and of another grave of unusual type, can be seen 2m WNW at Sess Kilgreen (NM; see entry). On a hilltop 3m W of Ballygawley are the remains of Errigal Keeroge monastic site (NM; see Augher entry). Monuments include a crude early cross (NM).

BALLYGLASS, *An Baile Glas:*
the Grey Homestead, Mayo   15 M27
Excavations carried out near this village by a Harvard University archaeological team in 1933 yielded several artefacts and remains of bronze-age date. The well-preserved remains of a court cairn lie ¾m WNW of the village. The cairn is some 30yds long and consists of two double-chambered galleries (in which the burials would have been made) facing one another across the court from which this type of monument takes its name.

BALLYHACK, *Baile Shac,* Wexford   24 S71
Wexford   24 S71
Ballyhack is a fishing village which faces Waterford Harbour and has a ferry service to Passage East. The castle here stands on the site of a structure which was a preceptory of the Knights Templar, but the present 15th- to 16th-c remains probably had nothing to do with this famous Order. Cromwellian forces attacked and wrecked the building in 1649. Features of this ruined, five-storey stronghold include a number of deep recesses in the third floor – including one on the east wall that served as a chapel, and an inaccessible prisoners' cell on the third floor.

BALLYHAISE, *Béal Átha hÉis,*
Cavan   11 H41
Statesman George Canning favoured this village for the excellent fishing offered by the River Annalee. Ballyhaise House was built by Brockhill Newburgh to a design by Richard Cassels, a German architect who changed his name to Castle. A mid 18th-c mansion which is vaulted on all floors, it now serves as an agricultural college. Also of interest in the village is the derelict arched market house, a two-storey, five-bay structure which probably dates from the first years of the 19thc.

BALLYHALBERT, *Baile Thalbóid:*
Talbot's Homestead, Down   13 J66
This village features a rocky shoreline and an attractive small harbour. About 1½m SE is Burial Island, the farthest E point of Ireland and an area scheduled as a place of special scientific interest. The rocks of which the island is composed date from the Silurian era and form a breeding ground for seabirds and seals. The mainland coast to the S includes rocky reefs and cliffs where patches of softer rock have been eaten away by the sea to form inlets and small, sandy bays.

To the S of the village are ruins of the old parish church, a tumulus, and a standing stone. The Moat can be seen to the N of Ballyhalbert, and is a ditch which has been cut in the centre of a natural ridge which runs parallel to the sea. On the land side the ditch slopes down from a height of 25ft; there is no sign of a bailey.

BALLYHALE, *Baile Héil:*
Howel's Homestead, Kilkenny   24 S53
The local parish church is dedicated to St Martin of Tours and incorporates a structure known as the Castle of Ballyhale. The latter is, in fact, the west tower of the medieval church of Kiltorcan, which contains two medieval fonts. Kiltorcan Quarry has yielded various prehistoric remains.

BALLYHAUNIS, *Béal Átha Hamhnais,*
Mayo   16 M47
An attractive market town set in a district of small lakes, Ballyhaunis features an Augustinian friary which incorporates parts of a church from an earlier foundation. The earlier friary was created by Jordan Duff MacCastello in 1348, and the present structure of 1641 was burned by Cromwellian troops in 1650. It was restored in 1938. Bracklaghboy Ogham Stone is a 6ft-high relic standing in the centre of a round, 21ft-diameter mound some 2½m WNW of the village at Lisvaun, which is in the townland of Island. It is thought to mark the burial place of the person whose name is carried in the ancient inscription. The whole of this area is rich in prehistoric remains, and 2m NNW in Coolnaha South is a pillar stone inscribed with a ringed cross and surrounded by a low earthen mound.

BALLYHOOLY, *Baile Átha hUlla:*
the Town of the Ford of the Apples, Cork   28 W79
Views of the attractive, upper River Blackwater country in which this village stands can be enjoyed from the tower of ancient Ballyhooly Castle – a former stronghold of the Roche family. It was restored in the 19thc by Lady Listowel. The Nagles Mountains can be seen to the S.

BALLYJAMESDUFF, *Baile Shéamais Dhuibh:* James Duff Town, Cavan **12 N59**
Made famous by the Percy French song *Come Back Paddy Reilly to Ballyjamesduff,* this small town, which has unusually wide streets, takes its name from an English officer who fought in Ireland during the 1798 Rising. The fine market house of 1813 carries a plaque which records Wellington's victories, and is of granite and random-rubble construction. It has been well restored. To the NE of the town are the twin loughs of Nadreegeel.

BALLYKELLY, *Baile Uí Cheallaigh:* Kelly's Homestead, Derry **6 C62**
This interesting village was established by the Fishmongers Company, and includes a fortified manor which was erected by this body in 1619. Remains of Walworth Church (NM), built by the company in 1629, can be seen at the N end of the village. Of interest is the plain, Norman-style arch of red sandstone, and the 18th-c chancel. Remains of a church destroyed in 1641 and said to occupy the site of a 6th-c monastery dedicated to St Columcille can be seen 1½m ESE of the village at Tamlaght-Finlagan.

BALLYLANDERS, *Baile an Londraigh:* Lander's Homestead, Limerick **22 R72**
To the S of this pleasant village are the Ballyhoura Hills, while to the E are the loftier Galtees with the dominating peaks of 3,018ft Galtymore and 2,712ft Lyracappul. The local church is built of red sandstone and is roofless. A massive tower forming the west end of the building was begun by the Earl of Kingston in the 17thc – as a castle. Some time later the tower was completed, and with the addition of an eastern extension became the CI parish church.

BALLYLARKIN, *Baile Uí Lorcáin:* Larkin's Homestead, Kilkenny **23 S36**
The rectangular-shaped church of Ballylarkin Abbey (NM), located 1m SW of Freshford, is probably of 13th-c origin. Its massive though small build gives the church an almost military appearance. This functional aspect is lent by the single small door, and the one small window in the east wall. Notable features include good carved stonework on the interior and exterior corbels, and on the 14th-c triple sedilia. Seven bishops are said to have been murdered at an ash here known as the Bishops' Tree.

BALLYLESSON, *Baile na Leasán,* Down **13 J36**
Situated on a twisting road just 4m S of Belfast, this little village features interesting remains of a structure known as Farrell's Fort. This oval defence complex includes double ditches and an outer rampart. The east side of the rampart has been breached by modern road and house-building operations, but the rest of the fort is well preserved. It is thought to have been a residence of the MacSherries, one-time chiefs of Dalmboyne.

Giant's Grave, a late-neolithic henge monument, stands ½m NNW of Ballylesson. This very impressive monument encloses 7 acres with a 12ft-high bank measuring some 60 to 70ft wide at the base. In the centre of the ring is a dolmen, or single chamber grave, which comprises five uprights supporting a capstone 7ft across.

The massive tower at the west end of Ballylander's roofless church was begun as part of a castle in the 17thc.

Excavations within the burial chamber yielded quantities of cremated bones. At Drumbo, 1½m SSW, are the stump of a round tower (NM) and the remains of an early church (NM).

BALLYLIFFIN, *Baile Lifín:* Liffin's Homestead, Donegal **5 C34**
A secluded resort on the lovely Inishowen Peninsula, Ballyliffin is within easy reach of 2m-long Pollan Strand. It is situated between 830ft Binnion and 908ft Crockaughrim. Pollan Bay and, to the E, Trawbreaga Bay, are separated by the Doagh Isle peninsula. At the NW extremity of this are the ruins of Carrickbrahey Castle, comprising a 16th-c square tower, an additional circular tower, and the remains of a 16th- to 17th-c bawn. This was once a stronghold of the MacFauls and the O Doherty family.

BALLYLONGFORD, *Béal Átha Longfoirt:* the Ford-mouth of the Fortress, Kerry **21 Q94**
Situated on the Shannon estuary and a bay of the same name, this village is the starting point of an occasionally submerged path which leads 2m along the Shannon shore to the ruins of 15th- and 16th-c Carrigafoyle Castle (NM). It is a five-storey building of layered stone sited on a beautiful inlet, and when first built by O Conor of Kerry formed a heavily-defended island. The original fortifications included a square bawn with rounded turrets on the landward side, and on the seaward side another bawn with square towers at each corner guarding a dock for boats. A spiral staircase allows access to the battlements. During the 16thc the castle was subjected to frequent attacks, and in 1649 it was partially destroyed by Cromwellian cannon fire.

Remains of the Franciscan Lislaughtin Abbey (NM), founded by John O Conor of Kerry in 1477, can be seen to the N of the village and include several items of architectural interest. Examples of these are a four-light east window executed in the pointed style, a beautifully-carved sedilia on the south side of the altar, and three fine windows in the south wall of the choir. A fine, 15th-c processional cross from Ballylongford is preserved in the National Museum, Dublin. Field Marshall Kitchener was born at Crotter House in 1850.

BALLYMACODA, *Baile Mhac Óda:* the Homestead of the Mac Oda Family, Cork **29 X07**
Ballymacoda and its immediate area form the last Irish-speaking district in E Cork. The village itself stands close to Youghal Bay and offers road access to the cliffs of Knockadoon Head. Beyond the head is Ballycotton Bay, with Ballycrenane Castle at its E end. This stronghold was built by the Tyntes, a family who acquired lands and property in the area during the 17thc.

BALLYMAHON, *Baile Uí Mhatháin:* Ó Matháin's Homestead, Longford **17 N15**
A fine, five-arch bridge spans the River Inny in this small town, which is a known angling resort and stands in the heart of the Goldsmith Country. Oliver Goldsmith was born 3m E of the town at Pallas in 1728. In 1730 his father moved to Kilkenny West and took up residence in the village of Lissoy, or 'Sweet Auburn', which lies some 5m SW in Westmeath. Ruins of his house can still be seen, and it was here that Oliver is said to have received the inspiration for the *Vicar of Wakefield* and the *Deserted Village*. Various places mentioned in the poet's works – *ie* 'The Three Jolly Pigeons Inn', 'the apple tree', 'the never-failing brook', 'the busy mill' and 'the decent church that topped the neighbouring hill' – can be identified with landmarks in the area.

Oliver Goldsmith was educated in the village school by Thomas Byrne, a schoolmaster who had soldiered in the Peninsular Wars for several years. After leaving school Goldsmith went to Athlone to prepare for university, and afterwards to Mostrim.

BALLYMALIS CASTLE, *Béal Átha Málais:* Málas' Ford-mouth, Kerry **26 V89**
Occupying a site on the peaceful banks of the River Laune 4m S of Killorglin, this 16th-c tower affords views of 3,414ft Carrantuohill – the highest mountain in Ireland. The castle (NM) is rectangular in shape and has four floors. Its features include fine, triple-mullioned windows on the north and south walls of the third floor, and bartizans, or projecting defences, perforated with musketry holes on two opposite corners of the tower. One of the third-floor windows displays representations of doves on the outside.
cont overleaf

BALLYMALIS CASTLE/BALLYMONEY

The tower eventually passed into the hands of Alexander Eager after confiscation in 1677.

BALLYMASCANLAN, *Baile Mhic Scanláin*: MacScanlan's Homestead, Lough   13 J01

Notable Proleek Dolmen (NM) is the main feature of this little Dundalk Bay village, and can be reached via a path through the grounds of the Ballymascanlan Hotel. It is a good example of a portal dolmen and comprises a 40-ton capstone supported on three legs. According to legend, anybody who throws a stone which stays on the dolmen's capstone will be attended by good luck. Situated 100yds to the SE are the remains of a wedge-shaped gallery grave.

BALLYMENA, *An Baile Meánach*: the Middle Town, Antrim   7 D10

Ballymena stands on land received by William Adair of Kinhilt (in Scotland) from Charles I. In the 18thc the Adair and Hickey families introduced a linen industry which ensured the town its continuing importance and prosperity. Today Ballymena is a thriving community set at the convergence of many roads, and a resort to which anglers are attracted by the salmon and trout to be had from the Rivers Main, Braid, Clough, the Kells Water, and numerous small streams. The town has not always been this quiet, however, and in 1798 a body of United Irishmen battled through the streets with English forces and held the community for a full three days.

Much of the region around the town is rich in historical remains, and the history of the whole Braid Valley is associated with St Patrick. It was here that the saint is said to have tended the sheep of his master Miliuc, whose dun or fort is thought to have stood on the site now occupied by ruined Skerry Church. The O Neills of Clandeboye were buried in the barrel-roofed vault at the east end of this church. An extinct, grass-sloped volcano known as Slemish is one of the hills on which St Patrick is said to have wandered with his flock, and nearby Skerry has the same reputation.

Most of the town's major developments took place in the 19thc. This is particularly the case with the churches, which include three built within 60 years of each other. The oldest of these is the First Presbyterian, which was built on a 17th-c site between 1805 and 1812 and features an interesting interior with pine galleries and cast-iron lotus-flower columns. St Patrick's CI Church of 1855 was rebuilt in 1881 after a serious fire, and is a large gothick building of basalt decorated with sandstone trim. Inside are encaustic tiles, two art-nouveau windows, and chamfered arcading, and it carries a prominent tower. All Saints' RC Church was consecrated in 1860 and includes a square, buttressed tower.

Two handsome banks in the town are the early 19th-c, classically-styled Bank of Ireland, and the Provincial Bank of Ireland. The former is a single-storey building, and the latter is a late-Georgian town-house type of building in red basalt, with red-brick surrounds and painted quoins. Both Church Street and Mill Street display fine 19th-c commercial buildings of architectural merit, and one particular basalt-built block boasts a shop front which may be the finest of its period in Ireland. The upper floors of the block include Georgian glazed windows, and the front itself is complete with a long entablature supported on five fluted Ionic columns. The 1928 town hall is an imposing building in Portland stone, the neo-Tudor Adair Arms Hotel is of interest, and the courthouse of 1846 is in the Elizabethan style.

Roger Casement was born in Ballymena, and this is the home town of Willie John MacBride, who holds the record number of international Rugby Union caps in the world. The Royal Ulster Rifles have a regimental museum in the grounds of St Patrick's Barracks.

BALLYMOE, *Béal Átha Mó*: the Ford-mouth of Mó, Galway   16 M67

This small village is situated on the Roscommon border, which at this point is formed by the River Suck. The 17th-c ruins of Glinsk Castle (NM) stand 4m SE, and 1m W is ruined Ballynakill Church, which has a 16th-c effigy of a knight.

BALLYMONEY, *Baile Monaidh*: the Homestead of the Moor, Antrim   6 C92

Within easy reach of the excellent fishing offered by the rivers Bann, Ballymoney, and Bush, this attractive market town is said to have developed from a huddle of houses around two medieval castles. One of these sites is said to be near Castle Street, and the other to the N of the town. The main erection of the town, and the building or extension of all the churches, took place in the 19thc. The town hall dates from 1866 and is a red and yellow-brick edifice in Ruskinian Romanesque style. Very slightly earlier is the basalt and brick courthouse, and even earlier is the Masonic Hall of 1775. This was originally the town hall, but has been considerably changed since it served this purpose.

A street known as Cockpit Brae includes interesting terraces of small Georgian houses and is said to take its name from the sport beloved of local carters – cockfighting. These drivers used to take passengers and goods from here to Belfast in the days of the stagecoach.

Several famous people are connected with Ballymoney, including two sons of a local Presbyterian minister. These were John and David MacBride; the former died in 1800 after having achieved the rank of Admiral and defeating a Spanish flagship, while his brother David became a famous physician. Among other things David is known for having produced a potion which was successfully used against scurvy during Captain Scott's expedition to the South Pole a hundred years later. James McKinley, born in 1783 3m N at Conagher, was grandfather to the 25th president of the USA – William

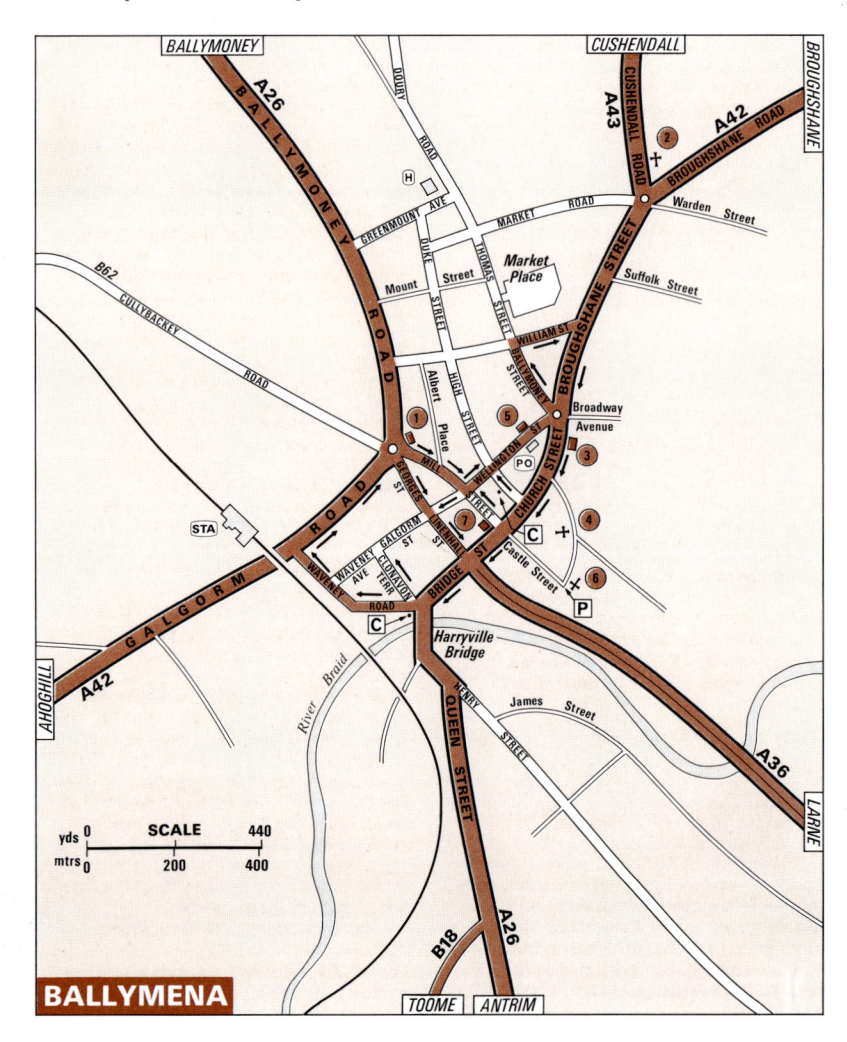

1 Adair Arms Hotel
2 All Saints' Church (RC)
3 Bank of Ireland
4 First Presbyterian Church
5 Provincial Bank of Ireland
6 St Patrick's Church (CI)
7 Town Hall

McKinley. Sir Charles Lanyon made his mark on the area with a beautiful line of firs, which he had planted to stabilize a section of roadway across bogland between Ballymoney and Ballymena. His solution was both technically effective and aesthetically pleasing – a combination which does not seem to occur often these days. The Garry Bog, near the River Bush to the N, is one of the largest in Ireland.

BALLYMOON CASTLE, *Bealach Múna:* Múna's Road, Carlow **24 S76**
See Muine Bheag entry.

BALLYMORE EUSTACE, *An Baile Mór:* the Big Homestead, Kildare **18 N91**
A River Liffey village in which the river is spanned by an attractive bridge, Ballymore Eustace derives its name from the Fitz Eustace family. Members of this family were constables of the Archbishop of Dublin's manor from 1373 until c1524, a position which was handed down from father to son. The village was burnt by the Leinster Irish in 1572. An early 16th-c armoured tomb effigy of one of the family can be seen in the Protestant church, but this was originally housed in New Abbey. Features of the churchyard include a granite high cross, a smaller granite cross, and the remains of an ancient church. Several very fine houses and demesnes exist in the district. In an attractive setting 1½m S of the village is the Piper's Stone Circle.

BALLYMOTE, *Baile an Mhóta:* the Homestead of the Mound, Sligo **10 G61**
Richard de Burgo, Earl of Ulster, built a keepless castle of great strength here in the early 14thc. This stronghold (NM) passed successively into the hands of the O Conors, the MacDermots, the Mac Donaghs and in 1598, the O Donnells. It was from here that Red Hugh O Donnell marched to the Battle of Kinsale in 1601. The O Donnells surrendered the castle to the English in 1602 but in the Williamite wars it was back in Irish hands for a time until finally surrendered to Lord Granard in 1690. After this the castle fell into ruin. The structure is square in plan with round towers at each corner of the 10ft-thick curtain walls and D-shaped towers in the middle of the east and west walls. Also of interest in Ballymote are the remains of the Franciscan friary where the 14th-c *Book of Ballymote* was written. Now in the Royal Academy, Dublin, this document contains valuable historical information and supplied the key to the deciphering of ancient ogham script. Temple House stands in lake-watered grounds 3m NW of the town. A ruined house of the Knights of St John standing by the lake dates from 1303.

BALLYNACARRIGA CASTLE, *Béal na Carraige:* the Ford-Mouth of the Rock, Cork **27 W25**
This 16th-c castle was originally built either by the O Herlys or McCarthys to guard a strategic pass; its remains stand near the River Bandon. It was taken and garrisoned by the English in the rebellion of 1641. The 6ft-thick walls contain a spiral staircase which provides access to the battlements, and there are some curious sculptured stones in the windows. Of particular note is a representation of Our Saviour on the Cross between the Two Thieves. High up on the external wall is a *Sheila-na-gig*, or fertility figure. The river is spanned by Manch Bridge here and is known for its good angling prospects.

BALLYNAHINCH, *Baile na hInse:* the Homestead of the Holm, Down **13 J35**
Low, rounded drumlins abound in this area and have prompted comparisons between the district and a basket of eggs. The town itself is of great character and is a market centre for the surrounding countryside. It was laid out in the first half of the 17thc by the Rawdon family, but its church and many of its domestic buildings were seriously damaged in the Battle of Ballynahinch which took place in 1798. During this engagement the invading British troops occupied the town under General Nugent, and very soon were totally intoxicated and disorganized. Henry Munro, a Lisburn linen merchant and commander of the Irish force, refused to allow his pikemen to take advantage of this situation and made them wait until daybreak for the counter-attack. As the pikemen pursued the militia out of the town they heard a bugle call, and thinking it was a retreat command they fell back and were caught by the enemy. Fatalities included Betsy Grey, a heroine of the battle, and Henry Munro, who was executed in front of his Lisburn home. Much of the fighting took place round the Windmill Stump of 1773.

In 1802 the town and nearby Montalto House passed into the hands of the Ker family, who – like the Rawdons – were improving landlords. They had a great effect on the appearance of the town. Today Ballynahinch displays pleasant terraces of houses, large shops with good façades, and roads which have no particular uniformity as they rise and fall to blend with the drumlin country. Ballynahinch Mill is a 19th-c complex of blackstone buildings on the Newcastle Road, with an adjacent scutch mill of 1820 and a prominent red-brick chimney.

Montalto House is a fine mansion which was built by John Rawdon, who was created Baron in 1750 and Earl of Moira in 1761. When the family seat was moved from Moira to Montalto, the earl brought many of his hot- and greenhouse plants to install in the new grounds. Thus the beautiful demesne is full of rare shrubs, plants, and magnificent trees – plus a herd of red deer. As to the house itself, the only unaltered part of the original two-storey building is the Lady's Sitting Room. The ceiling of this small room is possibly the work of Robert West, and displays fiddle-shaped arabesques with birds modelled in high relief. In 1837 the house was extended by the creation of an under-storey supported by numerous arches and pillars.

There are four main churches in the town. St Patrick's (RC) is a classical building which was erected before the emancipation of Catholicism, and is one of the few large Catholic churches in the N. Magheradroll CI parish church dates from 1772, but only part of the original building can still be seen – the tower and spire. The Second Presbyterian Church of 1841 has an annexed schoolhouse, and both buildings are in a restrained classical style. A pleasant interior is displayed by the First Presbyterian Church.

Although sadly neglected, the courthouse is a well-proportioned building which is worth a visit. Some 2m S of the town is The Spa, two springs of chalybeate and sulphurous waters which were once well-used by people who believed in their medicinal properties. Legananny Dolmen (NM), one of the most famous and photographed prehistoric sites in Ireland, can be seen on the S slopes of Cratlieve Mountain. It comprises a tapering capstone supported by two 6ft portal stones at the front, and a single, smaller stone at the rear. This distinctive arrangement, of which Legananny is a classic example, has led to this class of monument being called Tripod Dolmens. Surprisingly, the monument has not been fully investigated. To the SW of the town is the earthen fort known as Dunbeg (NM), which lies near to the source of the River Lagan. The fort is a small but good example of its type, and excavations made in 1956 disclosed the remains of a small house, within which were shards of dark-age pottery. Loughs Aghery (5m W) and Henney (4m NNW) are just two of the district's lakes and are popular venues for water ski-ing. Some 5m SW of the town is 1,755ft Slieve Croob.

BALLYNAHINCH LAKE, *Loch Bhaile na hInse:* the Lake of the Homestead of the Holm, Galway **14 L74**
Set at the foot of 1,904ft Benlettery, one of the Twelve Bens of Connemara, this lovely lake mirrors the mountain's quartzite cone and is the farthest S in a girdle of lakes which partially encircles the Twelve Bens to the S, SE, and E. One of the wooded islands in this lake carries the ancient keep of a castle once belonging to the Martin family. It is possible that this may have served as a prison for their enemies.

Ballynahinch Castle is a greatly altered 18th-c house superbly set on a site overlooking the River Owenmore S of the lake. This was once a home of the Martins, an extraordinary clan whose best known member was Richard. Also known as Humanity Dick, Richard was born in 1754 and was one of the founders of the RSPCA. Always a forthright man, he had at one time another nickname – Hairtrigger Dick – gained from his fondness for dueling. It is also reported that he treated his tenants in a very high handed fashion. Thackeray mentions him in *An Irish Sketch Book,* Maria Edgeworth's *Letters* refer to him, and Charles Lever wrote about the whole family in *Martins of Cro Martin.* The family lost their home in the great famine, and in 1926 it became the home of famous cricketer Ranjit Singh. It was converted into a hotel in 1945.

BALLYNOE, *An Baile Nua:* the New Homestead, Down **13 J43**
A fine stone circle (NM) ½m NW of this village was excavated between 1937 and 1938. The outer ring of the monument is 100ft in diameter and is made up of over 50 large stones, some of which exceed 6ft in height. The incomplete inner circle is eliptical in shape and measures 90 by 40ft. A burial cairn is also enclosed. About ½m W is a rath surrounded by a deep, water-filled fosse and protected by an earthen rampart which rises to 30ft in places. The ruins of Castle Skrene, former home of a 12th-c De Courcy, lie 1¼m to the W. The hill on which this building stands affords a commanding view over the surrounding countryside.

BALLYNURE, *Baile an Iúir:* the Homestead of the Yew, Antrim **7 J39**
To the NW of this village are the sparse remains of Ballynure Old Church, which contains several interesting ark-shaped

stone vaults containing the remains of many old families. The stone-vaulted watch house in the graveyard is a reminder of the days when body snatching was prevalent. This church appears as *Ecclesia de Ywes* on the 1300 *Taxation Roll*, and the district is particularly rich in ancient remains.

BALLYRAGGET, *Béal Átha Ragad*:
the Ford-mouth of Ragget, Kilkenny **23 S47**

This little River Nore town boasts the 15th- and 16th-c remains of a former Ormonde castle, which was once the home of the great Countess of Ormonde. The countess is famous for leading her own troops into battle. Surviving parts of the stronghold include four round towers linked by crenellated curtain walls to form a rectangle round the strong keep. Closer to the river is an 80ft-high motte with a deep fosse – thought to be the site of one of the first Anglo-Norman motte-and-bailey castles in Ireland. When complete, this would have comprised an archers' tower enclosed by a stout palisade, in turn surrounded by a deep, wide trench.

BALLYSADARE, *Baile Easa Dara*:
the Homestead of the Waterfall of the Oak, Sligo **10 G62**

Pleasantly situated and very popular, this town stands at the point where the Owenmore River cascades off a series of shelving rocks to enter nearby Ballysadare Bay. The river offers excellent angling prospects, and the migrating salmon are helped over the falls by means of a fish ladder. Below the bridge are the remains of a monastery founded in the 7thc by St Fechin of Fore. Remains include a 12th-c church which has a later Romanesque doorway, and 300yds from that another church of 13th-c date, which was built after the monks had accepted the Augustinian discipline. At a spot about 1m SE of the town the French (who landed at Killala in 1798) defeated a small militia force under Colonel Vereker.

BALLYSHANNON, *Béal Átha Seanaidh*:
the Ford-mouth of the Hillside, Donegal **10 G86**

This is a busy town finely set on a hill overlooking the River Erne. Two hydro-electric stations in the area supply over 250 million units of electricity to the national network – one at Cathleen's Fall above the town, and one at Cliff – downstream from Belleek. The Assaroe Reservoir was completed in 1952.

Ballymacward Castle stands outside the town on the Bundoran road and was the home of the Colleen Bawn. About 3½m NW, the ruins of Kilbarron Castle stand on the coast and proclaim the one-time might of the ancient O Clery family. Michael O Clery, chief of the *Four Masters*, is famous as one of the authors of the *Annals*. These traced the history of Ireland and its major families from remotest times to O Clery's own time, the 17thc. About ¾m NW of the town centre are the ruined 12th-c Cistercian Abbey of Assaroe and nearby St Patrick's Well. Also in the vicinity are numerous raths and two bullauns on the banks of the river.

A bridge which connects the town with a suburb known as The Port carries a tablet commemorating the birthplace of poet William Allingham. He lived in the 19thc and is famous for such works as *Adieu to Ballyshanny* and *The Winding Banks of Erne*, which refers to this town. A bronze head has been raised to him outside the Allied Irish Bank, and his grave is NW of Mullaghnashee – in St Anne's churchyard.

BALLYTRENT HOUSE, Wexford **25 T10**

John Redmond, famous politician and the leader of the Irish Party, was born in this seaside house, situated 3m SW of Rosslare Harbour, in 1856. The grounds of the house include a perfect bivallate ringfort with an outer circumference of 650yds. Out to sea is lonely Tuskar Rock, surmounted by a lighthouse which was built in 1815 and improved in 1885.

BALLYVOURNEY, *Baile Bhuirne*:
the Homestead of the Stony Place, Cork **27 W17**

Once a noted resort for students of the Irish language, this village is set in the attractive Sullane Valley within easy reach of the high Derrynasaggart Mountains. The village is very popular as a place of pilgrimage, for here in the 7thc lived St Gobnat, a lady saint who was able to cure the ailments of her nuns and the local folk. There are many early-Christian remains in and around the village, most of which are visited as part of the pilgrim's round of prayers.

The round starts at St Gobnat's house or kitchen (NM), a circular dry-stone hut with 5ft-thick walls and an internal diameter of 20ft. A central post supported the roof, and the site was occupied by metal-workers in the early-Christian period. Artefacts found here include iron tools, pottery fragments, crucibles, and whetstones. St Gobnat's Holy Well lies to the S and near by is the 1951 statue of the saint by Seamus Murphy.

St Gobnat's Grave can be seen across the road in the graveyard of a small medieval church which incorporates earlier fragments, including a *sheila-na-gig*, a fertility figure. The grave itself is a small mound surmounted by three bullaun stones. The grave and well of St Abban can be seen a short distance ESE of the village. In this instance the grave comprises a small cairn with a single bullaun and three ogham stones. The townland of Killeen boasts Gobnat's Stone, an early cross slab which bears a circle enclosing a Maltese cross on each face. Above one of the crosses is a figure of a cleric carrying a crozier.

BALLYWALTER, *Baile Bháltair*:
Walter's Homestead, Down **13 J66**

Composed of old houses grouped round a wide main street and small harbour, this pleasant village holds a music festival in May and a festival in June. The music week attracts major celebrities and is held in the parish church. Power-boat races are held in the off-shore waters during the summer.

Adjoining the village is Ballywalter Park. This is the demesne of Lord Dunleath, a member of the old Irish Mulholland family and a prominent figure in the cultural and musical life of N Ireland. The present mansion was begun by Sir Charles Lanyon in 1846, who transformed the appearance of the original 18th-c house to produce a building of neo-classical style and fine proportions. The central three-storey block is balanced by two slightly-advanced wings, each displaying a good recessed window. A Roman Doric *Porte Cochère* was added at a later date, and the interior reflects Lanyon's predilection for high-Renaissance detail. One of the additions to the 18th-c structure was the stable block of 1810.

A short distance away from the CI Holy Trinity Church are the interesting remains of Templefinn – the White Church. These include two fragmentary and one perfect Anglo-Norman grave slabs, attached to the north end of the east gable. About 1m NW of the village is circular Dunover Motte, a 36ft-high, flat-topped mound considered a good example of a minor Anglo-Norman castle without a bailey. Dunover is mentioned as the caput of a manor belonging to Lucian D'Arquilla, unsuccessful defender of Carrickfergus against King John. The king later granted the castle to Godfrey de Serland, and it passed to the De Coyly family during the inquisition of 1333.

BALRATH, *Baile na Rátha*:
the Homestead of the Ringfort, Meath **19 O06**

The fine mansions at Balrath, which is 4m SW of Duleek, was built for the Nicholson family in 1761. Beside the road is Balrath Wayside Cross (NM), a late 16th-c monument re-erected in 1727, bearing the inscription *Orate-p-aia-Johanis Broin* – Pray for the soul of John Broin. Its east face carries a representation of the Pieta, and its west face displays gothic decoration and a depiction of the Crucifixion. Aylmer Cross (NM) can be seen to the N of Balrath crossroads. The fortified mansion of Athcarne Castle is 2m E.

BALTIMORE, *Dún na Séad*:
the Fort of the Jewels, Cork **27 W02**

Situated on sheltered Baltimore Bay, this small fishing port and resort operates a well-established boat-building industry and is known as a sea-angling centre. Sherkin Island acts as a breakwater for the bay and features Dunalong Castle and a Franciscan friary (NM). The former was an O Driscoll fortress and the latter, still in a fair state of preservation, was founded by the same family. A rock near the pier on the mainland carries the O Driscoll's castle. The family were sea rovers, and the castle has been in ruins since it was sacked by the men of Waterford in 1537.

BALTINGLASS, *Bealach Conglais*:
the Road of Cúglais, Wicklow **24 S88**

Baltinglass Hill rises to 1,258ft above this River Slaney town, and as well as being a fine viewpoint is crowned with the remains of a burial mound and a hillfort (NM). The burial mound is a cairn 90ft in diameter within which are the remains of five burial chambers. The mound is surrounded by a double row of kerb stones. Of the chambers, the most impressive is the northern, which is a 12ft passage with a chamber at the end containing a decorated basin-stone. This chamber was probably the last to be built. In the SW of the cairn is a passage grave with five recesses off a central chamber and two decorated stones, while to the NW of the ring is an earlier interment. There are two smaller chambers within the cairn. The hillfort, which is called Rathcoran, was constructed in the early iron age, and consists of a large stone wall surrounding the hilltop, and lower down the hill, two further walls.

An abbey known as *Vallis Salutis* (NM) was founded here by Dermot

MacMurrough, a king of Leinster and the man who paved the way for Ireland's subjugation. It is a Cistercian foundation dating from the 12thc, and a sister house of Mellifont. Its remains include the lower parts of the transept, chapel, and cloisters, and the site occupies a fine position overlooking the River Slaney. The ruins can be reached through the grounds of the parish church. The demesne of Grange Con, 5m NNW, boasts a herd of white fallow deer unique in Ireland. These animals are said to have been brought over from Welbeck Abbey, part of the Duke of Portland's Nottingham estate.

BALTRAY, *Baile na Trá*:
the Homestead of the Strand, Louth **19 O17**

Noted for the championship-class County Louth Golf Club and unique Beaulieu House, this little town has good sands and is sited at the mouth of the River Boyne. Beaulieu House, 1m SW, is the earliest and finest example of a completely unfortified country house in Ireland. Its style is Dutch-inspired, and the most obvious feature is the extreme width of the eaves. It is built of rubble stone, plastered over and with brick dressings. Possibly the only exterior alteration is the replacement of the windows, which may originally have been of the mullioned casement kind. The interior of the house also remains remarkably well preserved; of special note are the stairways and elaborate 18th-c wood carvings. The house was constructed between 1660 and 1666 for Sir Henry Tichbourne, who had acquired the land from Oliver Plunkett at the time of the 1641 rising. The nearby church houses a cadaver tomb and a medieval coffin slab displaying a floriated cross.

BANAGHER, *Beannchar*, Derry **6 C60**

Beautiful Banagher Glen, 2m S of Dungiven, covers some 75 acres and was declared a national nature reserve (OACT) in 1974. It includes a deep river valley filled with sessile oak, birch, and rowan, and the bryophite growth is considered among the richest in the province. The glen is also of considerable geological interest, and the entire district is rich in prehistoric remains in various states of preservation.

Ancient Banagher Old Church (NM) is probably of 12th-c origin and was founded by St Muiredach O Heney. The square-headed doorway displays inclined jambs and massive lintels, and is of great antiquity. It is thought that the date of the nave is *c*1100. Near the church is a remarkable stone tomb (NM) in the form of a miniature oratory, carrying a figure of the saint in carved relief. The sand which lies beneath this tomb is said to have been prized by the O Heneys, who believed that it brought them luck in battle or other forms of conquest. Features of the graveyard include a termon cross and a highwayman's grave. About ½m S of Banagher Old Church, in Carnanbane Townland, is a double-court cairn with two unconnected chambered galleries. Many sherds of neolithic pottery were found in ritual pits underneath the E grave. Over these were the remains of a great fire and burnt offerings.

BANAGHER, *Beannchar*, Offaly **17 N01**

A long bridge spanning the Shannon in this market town dates from 1843 and replaces a structure which had stood for 400 years. The town itself is famous for its fairs. The author Anthony Trollope once worked here as a Post Office surveyor, and Rev A B Nicholls – husband to the authoress Charlotte Brontë – died at local Hill House in 1906. Ruined Garry Castle, 1m SE, a large MacCoghlan stronghold, and Castle Inver stands in the neighbourhood. Georgian Cuba Court, built by a former governor of Cuba, can be seen to the E. A sculptured, 9th-c cross shaft from Banagher is now kept in the National Museum, Dublin.

BANBRIDGE, *Droichead na Banna*, Down **13 J14**

The name of this busy and attractive town is derived from the bridge which carries the main Dublin–Belfast road across the River Bann at this point. Banbridge was once an important centre for the linen trade, and is famous for its remarkable main street. The central part of this wide road is at a lower level than the two sides, which are connected by a bridge, in effect producing an underpass. The river, Corbet Lake (3m E), and Lough Brickland (3m SW) all offer excellent game and coarse fishing. Many fine mills can be seen in the surrounding district, proving the town's former commercial importance. A successful Civic Trust scheme carried out in 1962 has brought about a new awareness of the town's scenic and historical qualities.

Crozier House stands in Church Square and was the 18th-c home of Captain Francis Crozier, who was second-in-command to Sir John Franklin during the famous voyage in search of the Arctic North West Passage. Features of the building include a stuccoed basement and rusticated ground floor.

The random-blackstone market house of 1832 includes heavy granite quoins at the corners and to a central projection, and the century-old gothick-Italian courthouse has been carefully restored. Banbridge's Unitarian Church of 1846 was once Presbyterian, and is considered one of the last and best of classical Presbyterian buildings left in Ulster. Its interior is of particular merit.

The Bannside Presbyterian Church displays an unusually fine compartmented ceiling decorated with feathery plaster rosettes in the Rococo style. Seapatrick CI parish church and the RC St Patrick's Church are both built in blackstone. The Primitive Methodist Church now fills a commercial function and displays an imposing façade. Fine, early 19th-c terraces can be seen in Church Street, and the attractive Lancastrian School of 1826 is sited in a bend of the river.

BANDON, *Droichead na Bandan*:
the Bridge of the (River) Bandon, Cork **28 W45**

Founded in 1608 by Richard Boyle, the Great Earl of Cork, this town is situated on the river of the same name and is a popular angling resort. The Earl acquired large estates in Munster after successfully dispossessing many ancient families, including the MacCarthys, the O Mahonys, the O Driscolls, and the Desmond Geraldines. Roman Catholics and Non Conformists were not allowed within the town walls. Parts of the latter are still visible, and there is a monument to the men who fell in the rebellions of 1798, 1848, and 1867.

Town stocks dating from the 18thc can be seen at the courthouse, and the early 17th-c church 1m N at Kilbrogan is traditionally the first Protestant church to be built in Ireland. Many ruined castles line the Bandon River between the town and Inishannon, the most important of which is Downdaniel, 3m NE. This was built in the 15thc for Barry Og, and later purchased by the East India Company to form part of a community settled for the exploitation of local iron ore.

BANGOR, *Beannchar*, Down **7 J58**

Built on a site overlooking Belfast Lough, this large seaside resort has a front which extends over 4m round Smelt Mill Bay to the W, Bangor Bay, and Ballyholme Bay to the E. Part of the town's attraction is in the way it has grown on steeply rising ground over the waters and well-used quays of Bangor Bay, but the clean air and wooded surroundings also have a great deal to do with the popularity of the resort. Shore works include two quays, Central and North Piers, and an inner quay dominated by a small square tower of 1637. This tower (NM) was built in the Scottish style by Lord Clandeboye as a custom house, and was later equipped with windows for use as a dwelling. On the opposite side of the bay are the sheltered Marine Gardens and Pickie Pool, one of the finest open-air swimming pools in Ireland. A path which runs beside the rocky shore leads to Strickland's Glen and Connor Park, both of which form sections of a coastal walk from Bangor to Holywood.

cont overleaf

Near Banagher Old Church is a remarkable stone tomb built in the shape of an oratory.

BANGOR

The Seacliffe Road runs E to a 1m beach at Ballyholme Bay. Ballyholme Yacht Club is situated on this road, and the Royal Ulster Yacht Club is sited on the shores of the bay. Near the E end of the beach is a strip of coast (NT) which includes a scenic path round Ballymacormick Point to Groomsport. General Schomberg landed at Groomsport with 10,000 men in 1689.

Ward Park includes a stream which has been widened to form two large ponds, which support an interesting collection of wildfowl and provide visiting greylag and pinkfoot geese with a place to rest. The ponds also have a resident flock of barnacle geese. Castle Park covers some 150 acres and includes over 100 different species of trees. A nature trail which starts at the Post Office crosses Castle Park and finishes in Ward Park. As well as the usual activities to be expected from a seaside resort, the town offers other entertainment in the form of Highland Gatherings, sheepdog trials, and folk-dance festivals.

Historically, Bangor is very rich, and the town occupies a remarkable niche in Irish ecclesiastical development as well as in the evolution of Christianity in Britain and Europe. It is known as Bangor Mor (the Great) to distinguish it from the Welsh town of the same name, and grew from an abbey founded here in 559 by St Comgall. This saint was a native of Magheramorne, on the shores of Larne Lough, and had studied under many famous schools. The monastery flourished under his rule and that of his successor Carthagus, and students were attracted here from all over Ireland, Britain, and the Continent. Missions from Bangor started when St Comgall first began to send his disciples off from a little reef of rocks near the present N Pier, protected against the sea by nothing but the flimsy sides of their coracles and their implicit faith. The despatching of missionaries from Bangor became an established tradition which lasted for eight centuries and covered the known world.

Because it was so rich and famous, the monastery at Bangor attracted predators – namely the Danes. It suffered many raids and attacks, but these were as nothing compared with the massive assault of 824 when 3,000 people died, records and manuscripts were destroyed, and the monastery itself was utterly wrecked. Early 18th-c building operations on the raised beach at Ballyholme Bay revealed relics which may have been associated with the disaster. These included a pair of Norse brooches and a bronze bowl, all dating from the early 9thc and now preserved in the National Museum, Dublin. When St Malachy came to Bangor in 1121 he was so horrified by what he saw that he vowed to restore the abbey to its former splendour in honour of those who had suffered. He died before he could realize his grand intention, and the foundation declined. In 1469 the Franciscans were ordered to take over the monastery, and it remained in their hands for the next 150 years.

The next phase came with the confiscation of estates from Clandeboye O Neill, and the granting of the foundation to Sir James Hamilton by James I in 1604. Sir James, 1st Viscount Clandeboye, built a church by extending the east end of the tower of the old Franciscan church. This decayed, and in 1832 a larger church was erected against the old tower – which was adorned with a wooden spire. The CI Abbey Church as it stands today incorporates medieval fragments and contains interesting 17th- and 18th-c memorials. One of these, raised to a Hamilton-Mordaunt, was executed by the Dutch sculptor Peter Scheemakers. There must have been hundreds of early tombstones here from the graves of monks, but apart from one example in Lord Dufferin's Chapel at Clandeboye there is no trace of these. It is thought that Sir James and his Scottish followers may have used the stones for building during their thorough occupation of the district. However, at least one priceless relic of old Bangor has survived in the shape of the 7th-c *Antiphonarium Benchorense* – a manuscript which is preserved with other ancient Irish papers in the Ambrosian Library, Milan. It comprises a unique collection of forms of service and was intended to be used by the abbots.

A 14th-c seal of the Abbot of Bangor was discovered in the ruins of Saul, near Downpatrick, and its design was adopted as the corporate seal of the Belfast, Holywood, and Bangor Railway. This interesting bronze relic depicts an abbot standing in a niche of gothic architecture. From the time of James Hamilton until the 19thc there was little change in the town, but the growth of Belfast and the extension of the railway from Holywood to Bangor changed all this. Suddenly the town became a favourite resort for people from the city.

Bangor Castle was opened as a town hall by primeminster Viscount Brookeborough in 1952. The present building of 1852 stands in a beautiful demesne, and was built in the style of an

1 Abbey Church (CI)
2 Ballymacormick Point
3 Bangor Castle (town hall)
4 Custom House (old tower)
5 First Presbyterian Church
6 Northern Bank
7 Pickie Pool & Marine Gardens
8 Royal Ulster Yacht Club

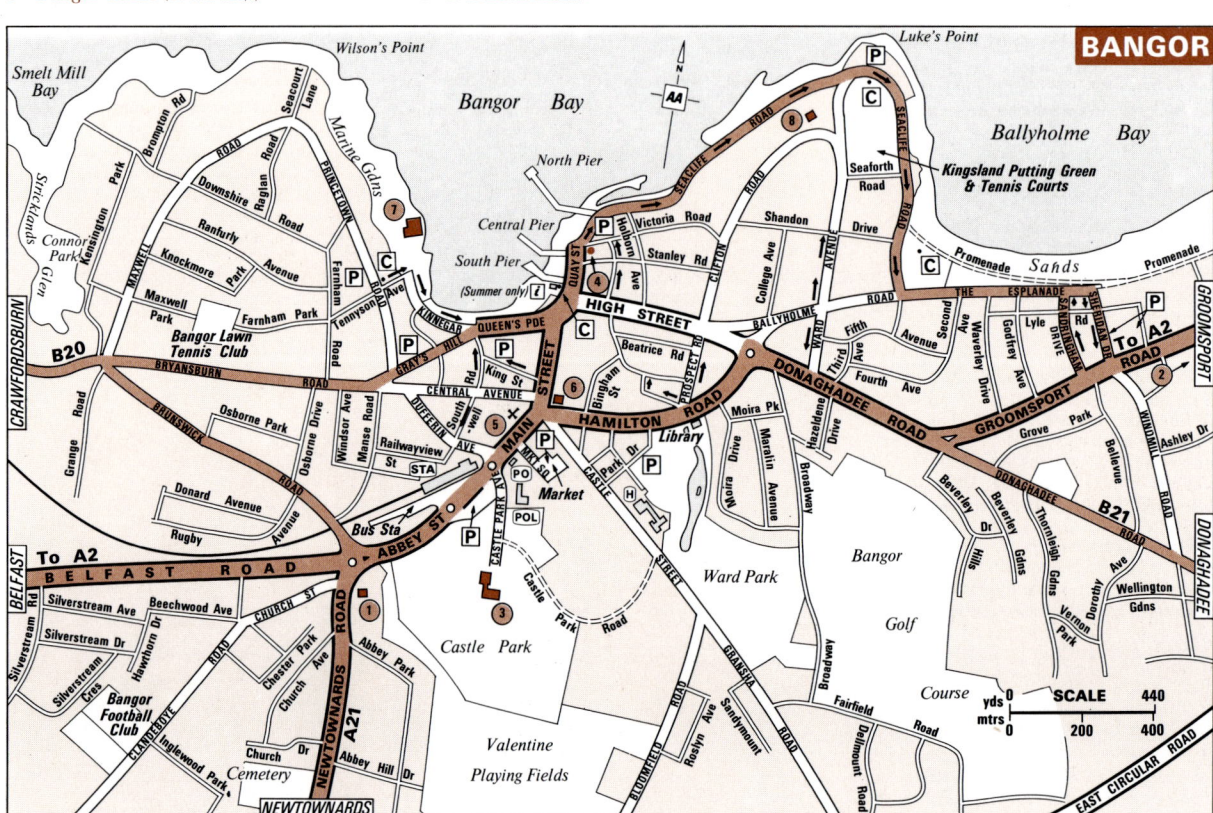

English manor house by Robert Edward Ward. It occupies a site on which two castles have stood, and is constructed in Scrabo stone. The first of the castles, also in Scrabo stone, was built by Sir James Hamilton in the early 17thc. At the junction of Main Street and Hamilton Road is a fine building which is now occupied by the Northern Bank. This dates from *c*1780 and was originally built as a market house. It was later used as the Ward School, and between 1933 and 1952 it served as the town hall. Features of the building include a façade of well-painted stucco, a hipped roof behind a parapet ornamented with balusters, and first-floor Georgian-glazed windows. There are many fine churches in the town, and the First Presbyterian Church of 1831 is among the most notable. It is built on a typically Presbyterian 'barn' plan and has a D-shaped two-storey auditorium. The spire was added in 1881. The red-brick clubhouse of the Royal Ulster Yacht Club dominates the seafront and was built in 1898 by Vincent Craig, younger brother of Lord Craigavon. The town has three 18-hole golf courses.

Several famous architects adapted and extended Baronscourt House after its completion in 1781.

BANNOW, *Cuan an Bhainbh*:
the Harbour of the Suckling Pig, Wexford **24 S 80**
The site of an ancient town which is said to have operated a mint during its occupation by the Danes lies near the head of Bannow Bay, at the mouth of a small estuary. The first corporate town here was built by the Anglo-Norman invaders. This community evolved naturally enough and existed in the reign of Charles I. By the end of the 17th-c the town had been buried beneath drifting sands, and all that now remains of the 'Lost City of Bannow' are the ruins of St Mary's Church – a simple, 13th-c nave-and-chancel structure with later north and south porches, plus the remains of a small chapel.

BANSHA, *Báinseach*:
Grassy Spot, Tipperary **22 R 93**
This village is delightfully situated below the E end of a wooded ridge known as the Slievenamuck Hills, at the mouth of the Glen of Aherlow. The local graveyard contains the remains of poet Darby Ryan, who lived between 1770 and 1855. Bansha is closely linked with *Muintir na Tire*, an organization promoting the social and cultural life of the rural community.

*BANTRY, *Beanntraí*, Cork **27 V 94**
Set amongst hills and within easy reach of fine bathing beaches and caves, Bantry includes a harbour large enough to accommodate a number of coasting vessels and with anchorage for ¼million-ton tankers. An oil terminal on Whiddy Island copes with the unloading of super tankers. The sheltered aspect of the harbour is lent by Whiddy Island, on which there are the remains of an O Sullivan stronghold and three redoubts.

Bantry House (OACT) is situated in exquisite surroundings at the head of Bantry Bay and was remodelled in 1771 for Richard White – 1st Earl of Bantry. It is a brick- and stone-built Georgian mansion with a fourteen-bay south front added by the 2nd Earl Richard in 1840. Many of the numerous art treasures inside the house were collected from all over Europe by the 2nd Earl. These include Russian icons, Gobelin tapestries, French furniture and Aubusson carpets, etc. In the fine demesne, which includes Italian-style terraces and statuary as well as a fine stable block, are the remains of a cross-inscribed pillar with an engraving of a currach or skin-boat. The demesne is set against a background of low hills and the wide sweep of Bantry Bay. The house was the first in Ireland to be opened to the public. The bay itself was the scene of French invasion attempts in 1689 and 1796. The smaller bays along the road to Glengarriff contain thousands of tons of limestone coral. This material was worked and used by local farmers as fertilizer.

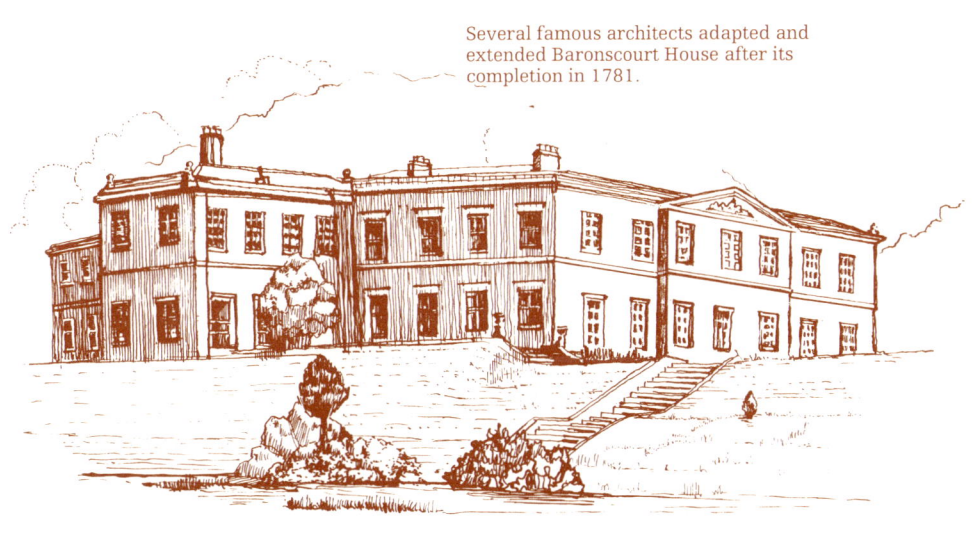

Tim Healy, 1st Governor General of the Irish Free State, was born in Bantry and is commemorated in the name of the Healy Pass.

BARGY and FORTH, *Uí Bairche* and *Fotharta*, Wexford **24 S 91**
These two baronries are situated in the extreme S of Wexford and are of particular interest to students of dialect and folklore. It was here that the Anglo-Normans first landed, and their followers and retainers – mostly of Welsh extraction or originally from the Low Countries – left their dialects in the area. Until recently this unique survival of an archaic speech form could still be heard. Bargy Castle is a much modified structure which is still occupied.

BARNAGEERA, *Barr na gCaorach*, Dublin **19 O 26**
See Skerries entry.

BARONSCOURT, *Cúirt an Bharúin*:
the Baron's Court, Tyrone **5 H 38**
Baronscourt, located 3½m SW of Newton Stewart, is the seat of the Duke of Abercorn. It is a fine building situated in a lovely valley below 1,387ft Betsy Bell. The 8th Earl of Abercorn commissioned the architect George Stewart to build him a new seat, and this was completed by September 1781. In 1790 the 8th earl's successor, his nephew, decided to change the appearance of the house and for this work he employed Sir John Soane (who later designed the Bank of England). Soane literally turned the place around, making the back the front, and vice versa. One of the results of this was to create the gallery which runs the whole length of the house. The building was extensively restored during the 19thc by W V Morrison. The gardens are open to the public, but the house is not. Near the estate office is the delightful Agent's House – a long, single-storey brick building with a central Doric portico and pediment. Stone paving leads to a heavy door flanked by circular windows. About ½m NNE of Baronscourt is Derrywoone Castle, a ruined L-shaped building with the shell of a three-storey tower at the south-east corner. This was replaced as a residence – by the Agent's House – in 1690.

The demesne of Baronscourt includes fine gardens, and there are three lakes on the estate. Lough Catherine boasts a crannog, or artificial island dwelling, known as Island MacHugh's Castle. On excavation this site proved to have been inhabited during neolithic, bronze age, early-Christian, and medieval times. Many finds were made but analysis is difficult because the stratification is confused. The 16th-c keep was deserted in favour of Derrymoone Castle in 1600. Cloghogle, a small cairn probably dating from megalithic times, can be seen on Altar Hill.

BARRYSCOURT CASTLE, *Cúirt an Bharraigh*: Barry's Court, Cork **28 W 87**
Strategically sited within the inner reaches of Cork Harbour, the remains of this castle include a quadrangular keep with square towers, surrounded by a bawn. It was rebuilt in 1585 and displays an interesting chapel and a chimney piece dated 1588.

BEAGHMORE, Tyrone **6 H 68**
See gazetteer inset overleaf.

BEALACLUGGA, *Béal an Chloga*, Clare **15 M 20**
Built at the head of the almost land-locked Poulnaclogh Bay, the main feature of this little village is Parkmore Fort. This is situated 3m NW on Finvarra Head, and comprises two concentric ramparts with a souterrain at the centre. The ruined Castle of Muckinish is 2m NW. To the S a broad valley surrounded by hills leads into Burren country.

BEALIN, *Béal Linne*:
Mouth of the Pool, Westmeath **17 N 14**
A sculptured high cross (NM) found here now stands on a hill N of the school in Twyford demesne. Thought to date from *c*800, this carries representations of three animals with bird-like heads on the east face. The north face depicts a

Entries marked * are the starting point of drives included in the Day Drive section of the book (pages 79 to 144).

hunter with a spear, and a dog biting the leg of a deer. The cross also displays interlacing geometric patterns and an inscription in Irish.

BEARA or BEAR HAVEN PENINSULA, *Bearra*, Cork   26 V64

This is the farthest W of the Cork peninsulas. It stretches for over 30m in a SW direction, separating Bantry Bay from the estuary of the Kenmare River, and carries a spine of rugged mountains. These form the Caha and Slieve Miskish ranges. The former rises to 2,251ft at Hungry Hill and makes a natural border between Cork and Kerry. The only flat land on the peninsula is the narrow coastal strip. Dursey Sound separates the peninsula from Dursey Island, its furthest extremity. The peninsula is linked to the island by cable car.

BEAR HAVEN, Cork   26 V64
See Castletownbere entry.

BEAR ISLAND, Cork   26 V64
See Castletownbere entry.

BEAGHMORE STONE CIRCLES, ALIGNMENTS, AND CAIRNS

Archaeologists frequently have cause to bless the preservative qualities of peat, which can hold objects in a perfect state for thousands of years. The extraordinary complex of stone circles, cairns, and alignments at Beaghmore near Cookstown in Co Tyrone is a case in point. Until about 30 years ago the existence of these prehistoric monuments was completely unsuspected. It was only when peat cutters began work in the area that the stones started to come to light. A deterioration in the climate during and after the monuments had been constructed caused the gradual growth of the peat bog. This eventually covered all the monuments, ensuring that they remained undisturbed until the 20thc.

An aerial view of the site, which covers about 1½ acres, gives the best idea of the layout of the various structures.

Altogether there are three pairs of circles and a single circle, all of which have associated alignments (or rows of stones) which run NE, and all of which have cairns either in direct relationship or set close by.

The circles marked A and B on the accompanying illustration have a small cairn set between them; this was found to contain a small cist in which a polished stone axe was discovered. To give some idea of the size of the monuments, the alignment of small boulders set at a tangent to circle B is 78ft long. Circle C hardly merits the name circle, being very irregular, but it is of special interest. Within it were found hearths with fragments of neolithic pottery. These form one of the factors which lead archaeologists to say that the site was utilized by neolithic peoples before the construction of the circles etc – which date from the early-bronze age. The cairn associated with circles C and D was found to contain an empty cist. An alignment of large boulders and another of small boulders lead from it.

Circle E differs from the other monuments on the site in that it does not form a pair, and its interior is filled with hundreds of small upright boulders. A small cairn, which has two alignments, is set into the edge of the circle. This was found to contain two cremated burials. Circle G is special in that it has a clear entrance of two large boulders. This circle and the rest of its group – circle F and a cairn – have only one alignment leading from them.

There are various other cairns on the excavated site, as well as heaps of stones which give further evidence of neolithic use. The area surrounding the site promises to be just as rich in monuments, but as yet has not been excavated. At the present state of knowledge it would be dangerous to attempt to put a meaning to the stone complex at Beaghmore. It has been suggested that the circles and alignments have some connection with astronomy, but they might equally well have served some function in fertility rites.

BEAULIEU HOUSE, Louth   19 O17
See Baltray entry.

BECTIVE, *Beigteach*, Meath   18 N86

Known for its fine fortress abbey (NM), this hamlet stands on the W bank of the River Boyne amid attractive countryside. The abbey was founded in the 12thc by O Maoleachlain, King of Meath, and grew to be a very important sanctuary under the rule of an abbot who was a spiritual lord. It was also a daughter house of Mellifont. Nothing of the original foundation survives, but remains of the

12th- to 13th-c buildings include parts of the chapter house, west range, and church alcove. In the 15thc the buildings were fortified and many changes took place. The cloister, tower and great hall date from this time. The main plan of the abbey is rectangular. On the other side of the river, 2m NE, is Ballinter House, considered one of the best large houses in Co Meath. This was built by Richard Cassels for John Preston MP during the 18thc. Assey Castle, which stands 1m NNE, comprises a square tower with circular flankers. Near the castle is the old church of Clady, which has a feature unusual in early churches – a transept; it was probably a later addition. A brook beside this small church is crossed by a very ancient footbridge, and near the church are two subterranean passages of beehive shape which have fallen in and become ruinous. Trubley Castle, of the same type as Assey, is situated close to the River Boyne, 1m SW of Bective.

BELCOO, *Béal Cú:*
Mouth of the Narrow Neck, Fermanagh **11 H03**
This village is situated between Loughs Macnean Upper and Lower, which are connected by a short stream. High, partly forested hills lie to the N and S. To the SE of Belcoo is a region of limestone swallow-holes, caves, and collapsed caverns. Perhaps the best known of the caves is the Marble Arch, which lies 3m SE at the head of the attractive wooded Cladagh Glen. Streams flowing N from the face of 2,188ft Cuilcagh Mountain sink into the beds of soluble carboniferous limestone at about 650ft through swallow-holes – vertical joints in the strata – such as Cat's Hole and Pollasumera. These streams flow underground along the joints, eroding them into passages and caverns. Where there has been a change of course, their former routes can be traced on the surface by dry valleys or tree-grown gullies, and gorges – the latter formed by the collapse of cavern roofs. These streams combine underground to emerge at the base of the limestone strata as the Cladagh River, which flows beneath the Marble Arch (a fine natural arch caused by the collapse of an adjacent cavern roof) and through Cladagh Glen to reach the Arney River a little to the E of Lough Macnean Lower. Several of the caves display formations of stalagmites and stalactites. The caves and glen form part of a nature reserve. Hanging Rock, a 600ft cliff overhanging the lough-side road which connects Belcoo with Cladagh Glen, is composed of Carboniferous deposits and was declared a nature reserve in 1974. This escarpment and its adjoining slopes support flourishing natural woodlands of ash, rowan, birch, and hazel.

Some 8m SE, on the E side of 1,221ft Benaughlin, is a prehistoric single-court grave and multiple cist cairn called Doohatty Glebe, which was excavated in 1882. A remarkable feature of the cairn is the fact that it is built of sandstone, even though the area abounds with local limestone. The excavation revealed fifteen small cists in the body of the cairn, some of which contained burnt earth and fragments of bone. Of the court cairn, only the chamber is easily recognisable. About 1m E of Belcoo are the remains of Templenaffrin Church (NM), near which is a fine bullaun stone. This boulder displays three deep, large cup-shaped marks at the top.

BELDERG, *Béal Deirg:*
Dearg's Estuary, Mayo **9 F93**
Coastal scenery around Belderg is of unsurpassed beauty, and the W seaboard all the way to the 829ft viewpoint of Benwee Head is a succession of magnificent cliffs. These are riven by steep precipices, and stacks that have been separated from the parent rock by sea erosion are rich with varied seabird life. The Stacks of Broadhaven rise from the sea as a series of pinnacles 2m N of Portacloy Bay. One of the best views of the area is afforded by 1,002ft Glinsk Hill, 4m WNW, and the whole district is ideal for the walker. Some 5m to the WNW of Belderg is the cliff-encircled bay of Moista Sound.

*****BELFAST,** Antrim **7/13 J37**
See feature starting on page 58.

BELGOOLY, *Béal Guala:* Entrance of the Hill-shoulder, Cork **28 W65**
To the S of this village the waters of Oyster Haven are spanned by a bridge which carries the road to Kinsale. The impressive ruins of Mount Lang Castle, built in 1631, stand on the E side of the haven 1¾m SSE. This fortified house figured in the wars of the 17thc.

BELLACORICK, *Béal Átha Chomhraic:*
the Ford-mouth of the Confluence, Mayo **9 F92**
Slieve Car rises to 2,369ft to the SW of this little hamlet. A feature of Bellacorick is its 'musical bridge', so called because a series of notes is produced if a large stone is run along the parapet. Lough Dahybaun lies to the ESE off the Crossmolina road. There is a turf-fired power station on the N side of the village.

BELLARENA, *Baile an Mhargaidh:*
the Town of the Market, Derry **6 C63**
The splendid basalt cliffs of Binevenagh rise sheer to 1,260ft above Bellarena, and the rock stacks that tower over the wooded countryside are alive with ravens and other birds. Views from the summit of this massive outcrop encompass the plain of Magilligan, Lough Foyle, the Atlantic Ocean, and the Inishowen Peninsula. It is situated close to the River Roe and supports a flourishing colony of Alpine flora. Near the village are Tamlaghtard Church and Well (NM). The church is possibly of 11th- or 12th-c date and is constructed of schist, basalt, and a little sandstone. Its gables are 25ft high, and nearby St Aidan's Well is still visited by pilgrims.

BELLEEK, *Béal Leice:*
the Ford-mouth of the Flagstone, Fermanagh **10 G95**
Angling resort and border village, Belleek is situated on the Erne at a point where the river's bed has been adapted to prevent flooding. The Erne was deepened by the extraction of many tons of rock, and giant sluice gates were fitted to regulate the flow of water. The river course between here and Ballyshannon features a picturesque gorge and several rapids.

Famous Belleek pottery is manufactured locally from felspar. This mineral is imported from Norway, but it was originally worked in the area. To the NE of the village is interesting Rathmore Fort. A road which runs along the S side of Lough Erne and near the edge of a limestone plateau is dominated by the sheer cliff of Magho, which rises in front of the Lough Navar forest park (NT).

BELLEEKS, *Béal Leice:*
the Ford-mouth of the Flagstone, Armagh **12 H92**
Close to Belleeks is Carrickananny Souterrain (NM), an unusually complex system of tunnels a little to the SW of a bridge of the same name. The structure measures 60ft in length and includes several defensive devices. Access to the chambers is from the central rooms, and the chamber closest to the entrance features a curious peephole, which commands a view of the central chamber.

BELLEVUE AND HAZELWOOD,
Antrim **7 J38**
See Belfast feature on page 58.

BELMULLET, *Béal an Mhuirthead:*
Entrance of the Mullet Peninsula, Mayo **8 F73**
Belmullet is one of the most remote villages in Ireland and is situated on the narrow neck of land which connects the Mullet Peninsula with the mainland. The area offers good angling prospects and there are beaches and sandhills at Elly Bay, between Belmullet and Blacksod Bay. The peninsula and the islands dotted around its coast are very rich in ancient remains. At Doonamo Point, 5m NW, are the remains of Doonamo Promontory Fort (NM), which was protected by rows of upright stones called *chevaux de frise*. The early-Christian site of Kilmore Erris is situated 4m W amongst sand dunes; the remains include a small enclosure, a cross slab, and some small cist-like mounds. About 2m W of Binghamstown are the remains of a small church called Cross Abbey. At the S tip of the peninsula is Falmore, which has the remains of St Derivla's Church (NM) and various associated structures. *La Rata*, the largest of the Armada galleons, sank in Blacksod Bay in 1588. See also Duvillaun More, Inishglora, and Inishkea Islands.

BEN BULBEN, *Binn Ghulbain:*
Beak Pinnacle, Sligo **10 G64**
The unmistakable 'table topped' shape of Ben Bulben rises to 1,722ft and dominates the surrounding countryside as it extends W to drop in a 1,500ft cliff and talus to the low Atlantic coast. The summit of the plateau affords fine views and is rich in Alpine plantlife.

BENBURB, *An Bhinn Bhorb:*
the Rough Peak, Tyrone **12 H85**
A battle fought here in 1646 resulted in a victory for the Irish forces under Owen Roe O Neill over General Munro's Scottish troops. O Neill's Castle (NM) stands high above the Blackwater River and was once the home of the Longfield family. It is a Plantation castle dating from c1615 and consists of a large bawn, or enclosure, and two rectangular flankers, or corner towers. On the cliff edge to the SE is a small circular tower. The site on which this structure stands was once occupied by an ancient O Neill stronghold. A modern mansion in the demesne of the castle was opened in 1949 as the Priory of Our Lady of Benburb by the Servite Order. The Protestant church dates from 1618, but contains medieval stonework, possibly from Clonfeakle.

Entries marked * are the starting point of drives included in the Day Drive section of the book (pages 79 to 144).

BESSBROOK, *An Sruthán:*
the Brook, Armagh 13 J02
This delightful model village is conveniently situated for tours of the S Armagh mountains. It owes its past prosperity and fortune to John Grubb Richardson – a member of a well-known Quaker family – who was responsible for its foundation in 1855. Bessbrook was used as a model for the Cadbury garden township of Bourneville, near Birmingham in England.

BETTYSTOWN, *Baile an Bhiataigh:*
Betagh's Homestead, Meath 19 O17
Usually referred to as the twin seaside resorts of Bettystown and Laytown, this small seaside resort offers a 6m sandy beach and is well known as the place in which one of the country's most valuable archaeological treasures was found. The relic, a late 17th-c bronze ornament known as the Tara Brooch, was found on a strand near the mouth of the River Boyne in 1850 and is said to rank with the Armagh Chalice in importance. It is exquisitely worked in bronze, with gold filigree settings of amber, enamel, and glass. The whole effect is of minute perfection. The Tara Brooch can be seen on display at the National Museum in Dublin. On the coast near Mornington (see entry) is the Maiden Tower.

*BIRR, *Biorra:*
Watery Place, Offaly 17 N00
Birr is strategically set on the River Camcor in the lovely countryside of central Ireland, and once served as a garrison town. The Camcor and the Little Brosna rivers join here and provide an attractive setting for the town's well-planned streets. Birr Castle was a stronghold of the O Carrolls until the last member of this clan was outlawed in 1620, and withstood many sieges. After 1620 it passed into the hands of Lawrence Parsons, who gave Birr its original name – Parsonstown. The Earl of Rosse, a descendent of Parsons, still occupies the castle. During the 18th and 19thc the 2nd Earl, who was an amateur architect, enlarged the structure after fire damage and created both the courtyard facade and the 'Strawberry Hill' saloon. The 3rd Earl was an internationally famous astronomer and the discoverer of the spiral nebulae. The mountings for the giant telescopes which he designed and set up here in the 19thc can be seen in the Science Museum, London. From the mid 19th to the early 20thc the castle was the residence of the 4th Earl, whose brother Charles was the inventor of the steam turbine.

As to the town itself, its road pattern is formed around four principal streets which open off Emmett Square and feature good buildings. Excellent examples of 18th- and 19th-c architecture can be seen in the Georgian houses and terraces in Oxmantown Mall and St John's Mall. Two interesting monuments in Birr are the Cumberland Pillar, which commemorates the Battle of Culloden, and the Manchester Martyrs' Memorial.

BLACK PIG'S DYKE, THE
10 G94, 11 G92, 17 N38
This name encompasses a series of earthworks which extend across Ireland in a broken line from a point near Tullaghan, S of Bundoran in Co Donegal, to S Armagh. Parts of the series are variously named the Worm Ditch and the Black Pig's Dyke or Race, while structures connected with the dyke include the Dane's Cast earthwork and the great Dorsey enclosure of S Armagh – possibly constructed as part of the fortification system. The stretches in Monaghan are among the best preserved, but there are interesting features along the entire route of the series.

An earthwork known as Duncla or the Black Pig's Race extends for 6m from 1m NE of Granard in Longford, and protects the important route between Loughs Kinale and Gowna. The bank here has a base width of 30ft, a height of up to 20ft, and generally a fosse on either side with a small bank outside. On sloping ground there is only a single deep fosse with a bank on the downhill side, a type of construction similar to that of Irish hill forts. There is some evidence that the Black Pig's Dyke and the Dorsey were both strengthened with timber in places.

Lengths of the dyke seem to have been built to control the passage of cattle in areas between natural obstacles such as water and drumlins. According to tradition the dyke replaced the Dane's Cast, a similar earthwork which runs W and S near the border between Co Armagh and Co Down, after the fall of the Navan Fort *c*330. The stretch between Loughs Melvin and MacNean, near Kiltyclogher, is the best-preserved part of the dyke and extends for 6m in a discontinuous line from Gubmanus to Lough MacNean Upper – effectively controlling all routes which come from the SW and pass between the lakes. At this point the present N Ireland border is only ½m from the Worm Ditch or Black Pig's Race. A damaged section of the dyke runs 2m from Dowra to Lough Allen. The Dun of Drumsna, a 1m-long earthwork enclosing a 1sqm loop of the River Shannon, is of a different construction to the Black Pig's Dyke.

Construction of the various parts which make up the series may have taken place over a considerable period, possibly from 300BC to AD300. A legend which is associated with the building of the Black Pig's Dyke occurs most frequently in the places through which the earthworks run, and concerns a schoolmaster who tampered with magical things. He is supposed to have used a magic book to turn one of his pupils into a hare, and the rest of the class into hounds to chase him. The ailing victim informed his father of the cause of his exhausted state, and the father challenged the master to prove his powers by turning himself into a pig. The master assumed the required form, and the father forced him to stay in the shape of a pig by burning the magic book. In a fit of rage the pig rushed and rooted across the countryside until it reached the ocean at Tullaghan and drowned.

BLACKROCK, *An Charraig Dhubh:*
the Black Rock, Dublin 19 O22
Blackrock was a very fashionable watering place during the 18thc, and still features very fine swimming baths. Among the many interesting buildings here are two notable houses – Frascati and Rockfield. The former was once the residence of Lord Edward Fitzgerald, and Lord Townsend lived in Rockfield while he was Lord-Lieutenant. Also of interest is Leoville, home of the father of the poet James Joyce during the late 19thc. All Saints' Church (CI) features two windows by Wilhelmina Geddes, and gothick St John's Church was erected by Patrick Byrne in 1842. St John's was constructed on the basis of drawings of the church of Stanton St John in Oxfordshire, executed by the famous architect Pugin.

BLACKWATERTOWN, *An Port Mór:*
the Big Fort, Armagh 12 H85
Associated with one of the most decisive of all the Elizabethan battles, this village is the site where the Earl of Sussex built his Portmore Fort in 1575 – in spite of the opposition of Hugh O Neill, Earl of Tyrone. Hugh's own great stronghold was sited at Dungannon, and some 20 years after the erection of Portmore he attacked the fort and razed it to the ground. The structure was rebuilt and occupied by the English, then in 1598 it was so successfully blockaded by O Neill that the garrison was reduced to eating grass from the rampart walls. An English army under Sir Henry Bagenal – whose sister eloped with O Neill – marched to relieve the fort but on reaching Yellow Ford were attacked by Irish forces and forced into a bog. They were unable to extricate themselves, and were mercilessly slaughtered by O Neill's men. However, the heroic band of defenders were allowed to leave the fort and make their way to Newry unmolested.

BLARNEY, *An Bhlarna,* Cork 28 W67
Although noted for its tweed industry, which was established in 1750, this attractively set village is better known for the Blarney Stone. The latter is said to bestow the gift of eloquence to anybody with the agility to kiss its rough surface, and as it still forms one of the machicolations of Blarney Castle this is no mean feat. According to tradition this gift was used by Cormac MacCarthy, the Lord of Muskerry, to successfully avoid acceptance of Queen Elizabeth I's authority. The Queen is held to have said 'This is all Blarney; what he says he never means'.

The castle itself (OACT) is of 15th-c origin and was the strongest in Munster. Its walls are 18ft thick, and the massive square keep or tower features a battlemented parapet 83ft above the ground. The first keep was a tall, narrow tower, but a heavy structure of oblong plan was later added to this and blended with the original structure to form the building that exists today. Blarney Castle remained in the hands of the persuasive MacCarthys until it fell to Lord Broghill in 1646. In 1703 it was bought by the Jefferys family, whose descendants still own it.

The top of the castle affords fine views over the wooded hills of Muskerry, and close by are the celebrated Groves of Blarney. The caves and rock-close of the latter, and Blarney Lake, are particularly attractive. There is also an interesting vintage-car museum here.

BLASKET ISLANDS, *Na Blascaodaí,*
Kerry 26 V29
Access to these rocky islands is first by a precipitous road to the tiny harbour of Dunquin, and then by currach across the wild seas which separate the group from the mainland. Before depopulation the islands formed a mecca for scholars of Irish language and folklore, and although

nobody now lives here the mini-culture survives in the lyrical tales so carefully recorded in translations, recordings, and books. Some of the books which allow an insight into the lives of the islanders include Flower's translation of Thomas O Crohan's *The Islandman*, Bryan MacMahon's translation of Peig Sayers *Peig*, and Maurice O Sullivan's *Twenty Years A-growing*. Life on the islands seems to have been pretty nearly idyllic, and the people are supposed to have been the 'happiest in the world'.

Great Blasket Island, the largest of the group, forms a ridge measuring 4m in length, 1m in width, and nearly 1,000ft high at the peak of its knife-edged backbone. Views from her include the rugged splendour of the Kerry coast, and the island itself features the remains of an old church (NM). The Armada vessel *Santa Maria de la Rosa* was lost in the sound which separates Great Blasket from the mainland in 1588. Interesting remains on Inishtooskert Island comprise an early church, beehive huts, and three crosses (NM). Inishvickillane Island preserves the remains of a stone oratory, a beehive cell, and an old cross (NM). A lighthouse stands on Tearaght, at the W end of the group.

BLESSINGTON, *Baile Coimín*:
Comyn's Town, Wicklow   18 N 91
Built on a site near the N arm of the Poulaphouca Reservoir, this town was granted a charter of incorporation by Charles II in 1669. Before the Act of Union it returned two members to the Irish parliament. The town's church dates from the year in which the charter was granted. To the W of Blessington are the remains of Downshire House, a building which was destroyed by fire during the 1798 rebellion, and at the SE corner of the reservoir are the quarries of Ballyknockan. Stone from the latter was used in the construction of the Nelson Pillar, which formerly stood in O Connell Street, Dublin. Fine views over the local countryside are afforded by 2,788ft Mullaghcleevaun, one of the highest mountains in the Wicklow range.

BLOODY BRIDGE, *Droichead na Fola*:
Bloody Bridge, Down   13 J 32
The name Bloody Bridge was given to the path here after a massacre took place at the old road bridge, a little to the W of the present road bridge and carpark, in 1641. Also known as the Brandy Pad, this track, on the coast 2m S of Newcastle, leads into the heart of the Mourne Mountains and links the coast road with the head of the Trassey Valley, towards Rathfriland. The latter was once a destination for contraband brandy, which was collected from the many little coves below the Newcastle road and carried inland via the track. After joining a quarry road beneath the shoulder of 1,410ft Slievenagarragh, the track climbs alongside a tumbling stream to pass the 2,152ft Chimney Rock and 2,796ft Slieve Donard.

A hostel built on a site which comprises the only level ground along the route of the track was constructed by weekend workers from the Youth Hostel Association. The resulting 'haven' has already served several generations of walking enthusiasts, who would otherwise have had to rely on tents.

The 'Stone' in 15th-c Blarney Castle is said to bestow eloquence on anybody with the nerve and agility to kiss it.

BOA ISLAND, *Inis Badhbha*:
Island of the Scald-Crow, Fermanagh   11 H 16
A 4m-long road crosses this Lower Lough Erne island, and bridges at each end provide links for a route between Kesh and Belleek. Caldragh Graveyard is sited on the S shore of the island and features two unusual statues (see gazetteer inset on page 179).

BOG OF ALLEN, *Móin Alúine*:
Bog of Allen   18 N 63
See Edenderry entry.

BOHER, *An Bóthar*:
the Road, Offaly   17 N 13
Of interest here is the local RC church, which contains the 12th-c Shrine of St Manchan. This comprises a yew-wood box containing some of the saint's bones, encased in a metal shrine decorated with zoomorphic ornamentation and cast-bronze figures.

BOHERLAHAN, *An Bóthar Leathan*:
the Wide Road, Tipperary   23 S 04
Charles Bianconi, who lived from 1786 to 1875 and gave Ireland its first regular transport service, is buried beside the local RC church.

BOHO, *Botha*: Huts, Fermanagh   11 H 14
Colonies of Daubenton's bat can be seen in the cave series carved beneath the local countryside by an underground stream, and the moorland NW of Boho features many pot and swallow holes. These include the deepest pothole in Ireland – Noon's Hole. About 1m SW of Boho crossroads is Coolarkan Cave, a swallow hole which engulfs a surface stream and features a large chamber. Evidence that the caves were occupied by man in prehistoric times has been supplied by finds at Clogherbog Cave (on the Belcoo to Garrison Road) and Aghanaglack Cave (1½m NW of Boho crossroads). In the graveyard of the RC church is the shaft and base of a 9th- or 10th-c high cross with some figure sculpture. About 1m N of the church, beside a holy well known as Tober St Ferber, is an ancient stone font associated with the saint after which the spring was named. This site is said to have been occupied by a very early church.

To the SW of the village is the Aghanaglack Dual-Court Cairn, an imposing structure belonging to that group of monuments collectively ascribed to the Clyde-Carlingford Culture. It comprises two twin-chambered galleries in a cairn nearly 80ft long and 35ft wide. Each of the 20ft-long galleries includes a forecourt, and they are set back to back – separated only by a common end orthostat (or upright stone). Finds here included the cremated bones of a child, cremated remains of a youth accompanied by the teeth of a pig and red deer, pottery, several hollow scrapers, a stone bead, a flint javelin, and two barbed and tanged arrowheads. It is possible that this monument dates from the early bronze age, but it is more likely to have been of late-neolithic origin.

BONAMARGY FRIARY, Antrim   7 D 14
See Ballycastle entry.

BOOTERSTOWN, *Baile an Bhóthair*:
the Town of the Road, Dublin   19 O 23
Well-known Blackrock College boys' school is situated here. One of Blackrock's more famous pupils was Eamon de Valera, who later returned to the school as a teacher of mathematics. The actual building displays three early 20th-c armorial and decorative windows by Evie Hone, who was also responsible for a fine lunette. Two pairs of single-light windows in the school chapel were by Michael Healy, and a three-light window in the Senior House was, again, the work of Evie Hone. A local house known as Glena was the residence of singer Count John McCormack before his death in 1945.

BORRIS, *An Bhuirios*:
the Borough, Carlow   24 S 75
Known as a convenient place from which to climb 2,610ft Mount Leinster, this attractive Georgian village is situated to the E of the River Barrow and at the head of a valley which separates Brandon Hill from the Blackstairs Mountains. Between the river and the village is the beautiful demesne of Borris House. This is the seat of the MacMurrough Kavanagh family, once Kings of Leinster.

BORRIS-IN-OSSORY, *Buiríos Mór Osraí*:
Big Borough of Ossory, Laois   23 S 28
Strategically set on one of the principal highways into Munster, this place was once of great defensive importance. It was commonly known as the Gate of Munster, and was guarded by a great Fitzpatrick castle which now lies in ruins.

BORRISOLEIGH, *Buiriós Ó Luigheach*:
Borough of Uí Luigheach, Tipperary **23 S06**
A village on the hill road from Thurles to Nenagh, Borrisoleigh includes the remains of an old castle built by the de Burgo family. Also of interest here is a table tomb inscribed to the memory of a member of this family, which can be seen 1½m NW in Glankeen Church.

BOURN VINCENT PARK, Kerry **27 V98**
See Killarney entry.

BOVEVAGH, *Both Mhéabha*:
Maeve's Hut, Derry **6 C61**
The ancient local church (NM), said to have been founded by St Ringan, stands about 1m NW of Burnfoot Bridge. The walls are 54ft in length, 34ft broad, and measure up to 3ft thick. There is a small arched doorway in the south wall, and near the west end is a miniature oratory with a stone-flag roof. The latter structure is of uncertain date, but is said to be the saint's tomb.

BOYLE, *Mainistir na Búille*:
Monastery of the River Boyle, Roscommon **10 G80**
Beautifully situated on the banks of the River Boyle, this town is built at the base of the impressive Curlew Hills between two loughs – Gara and Key – connected by the river. Also on the banks of the Boyle, to the N of the town, is a well-preserved Cistercian abbey (NM) which is considered one of the finest in the country. Colonized from Mellifont in 1161, the foundation was plundered by the Anglo-Normans under Richard de Burgo and Maurice Fitzgerald in 1235, and much later suffered considerable damage at the hands of Cromwellian soldiers. Remains that have survived to the present day are abundant, however, and include a gatehouse with a porter's lodge, a cloister, kitchen, sacristy, and the cellars beneath the refectory. The notable church was consecrated in 1218 and shows various additions of later date. It is considered a good example of the Irish transition from Romanesque to gothic design, and is a cruciform structure with a 131ft nave. The north side features three early pointed arches, and the south side features eight arches in the Norman style – probably of early origin. Four of the eight are supported by columns and the other four by piers with fine capitals. The arches under the central tower are of different styles; the chancel arch is an early pointed structure, while the nave and transept arches are round. Of particular note are the beautiful capitals.

Near the S end of Lough Key is the ancient church of Asselyn, and 2m W of the town – on a site 300yds N of the River Boyle is the Drumanone Portal Grave. This is surrounded by the remains of a circular cairn and is one of the largest in the country. Around 360 crannogs (an almost fantastically large figure) were discovered during draining operations on the shores of Lough Gara in 1952. Several of these lake dwellings were excavated by Dr J Raftery in subsequent years, revealing a large number of prehistoric relics. As the lake level fell, many artifacts were exposed; these included 40 dug-out boats, several bronze implements, and numerous Bann flakes. The latter, also known as Bann points, are leaf-shaped implements with trimmed butts believed to have been used as fishing tools in late mesolithic and neolithic times. Excavation of some of the sites showed that the area had been more or less continually inhabited from c3000BC up to cAD500.

BRANDON MOUNTAIN, *Cnoc Breánainn*:
St Brendan's Hill, Kerry **20 Q41**
Dingle Peninsula, considered one of the finest of the great mountain promontories in Ireland, has a high E to W backbone which turns N and rises to form the 3,127ft bulk of Brandon Mountain. This massive pile extends 8m from Brandon Point to a pass above Kilmalkedar, and is up to 5m broad. Its E side is deeply sculptured with spurs and valleys. Directly above the tiny settlement of Cloghane is a deep transverse gash which extends from the base to the summit of the mountain. One side of this rift is overshadowed by a huge cliff, while at the bottom of the other side is a series of rock steps. Each one of these shelves is occupied by a lake.

Access from Cloghane is via a little track which runs beside the RC church before climbing to a low lip of the coomb and meeting a zig-zag path which leads to the summit. This latter path was made by pilgrims who regularly climbed the mountain slopes to visit the cell of St Brendan the Navigator; here he had his retreat, and from here, the legend says, he set sail in order to discover the earthly paradise. Brendan was born in 484, ordained in 512, and died in 577. After his death his fame spread far and wide; there are place-name dedications to him throughout Ireland and Great Britain. The foundations of the stories told about him can be traced back to two ancient manuscripts – *The Life of St Brendan* and *The Voyage of St Brendan*. St Brendan was certainly an adventurous sailor, but whether he discovered America, as some say, is a matter that must remain, for the present at least, in dispute (also see special feature on page 71). On the mountain's summit may be seen the remains of St Brendan's oratory, cell, and well, in addition to a number of other clochans.

Views to the W from the summit include the Blasket Islands beyond Mount Eagle and are considered among the finest in Ireland. Further views can be enjoyed from the splendid road which climbs through Connor Pass between 2,026ft Slievanea and 2,050ft Ballysitteragh. The area which lies in the shadow of the Brandon, from Dingle to Smerwick, was extensively colonized by both prehistoric peoples and later men of learning. Consequently it is rich in stone forts, beehive huts, oratories, and ogham stones.

BRAY, *Bré*, Wicklow **19 O21**
Perhaps one of the best-known holiday resorts in Ireland, Bray boasts a 1m esplanade which extends from the harbour in the N to the approaches of 791ft Bray Head. The summit of the latter forms a good viewpoint, and a path from the esplanade affords more views as it winds round the lower slopes of the head in the direction of Greystones. The landward side of this path rises in precipitous cliffs. Bray is situated within easy reach of many interesting places and makes a good base for touring.

Killiney Hill and a public park lie to the N beyond Killiney Bay, and a deep, densely-wooded glen known as The Dargle can be seen to the W. The River Dargle flows through this valley. In the SW the Great and Little Sugar Loaf Mountains rise to respective heights of 1,659 and 1,120ft. In the same direction is the Glen of the Downs, and a little farther afield are Loughs Tay and Dan. Kilruddery (OACT), seat of the Earl of Meath, is situated in a lovely valley between Bray Head and the Little Sugar Loaf. This house was designed by Sir Richard Morrison and his son William, and built in 1820. Farther S is 19th-c Hollybrook, a house which stands on a site once occupied by the residence of sportsman Robin Adair – hero of a well-known song. The building is surrounded by fine gardens.

Features of the old road to The Dargle include the Cross of Fassaroe, which carries a representation of Our Saviour. The ancient Church of Rathmichael (NM) about 2m NW of Bray may originally have been founded by St Comgall of Bangor. Although the building which currently occupies the site may have been built or rebuilt in the 16thc, it still incorporates part of the older structure. A number of unusual early-Christian grave slabs and a cross are attached to the south wall, and the stump of a round tower can be seen at the south-west end of the building. Other old churches near Bray include Raheenaclig, on the side of Bray Head, and Templecarrig, S of Windgates. Ancient crosses can be seen at Killiney, Tullow or Tully, and Kill of the Grange, while old castles survive at Shankill, Shanganagh, Old Court, and Puck's Castle. Of the many dolmens in the district, Kilternan is the biggest and Glendruid the most picturesque.

BROADHAVEN, STACKS OF, *Na Stácaí*:
the Stacks, Mayo **8 F84**
See Belderg entry.

BROOKEBOROUGH, *Achadh Lon*:
Field of Blackbirds, Fermanagh **11 H34**
Well-maintained houses and a broad, tree-lined main street are features of this pleasant village, which is situated below a wooded ridge. The surrounding countryside is dotted with little black-and-white farmhouses crowned by hipped roofs and displaying dripstone window decoration. About 2m NE is Colebrooke, a fine example of the Georgian manor houses to be found in Ulster. It is the ancestral home of the 1st Viscount Brookeborough – Prime-minister of N Ireland between 1943 and 1963 – and Field Marshall Viscount Alanbrooke. The house was built by William Farrell of Dublin. As well as its fine hall and main staircase, it features a well-proportioned drawing room which retains its original 18th-c wallpaper. St Ronan's Church (CI) stands on a knoll at the edge of the well-wooded estate, which supports a herd of sika deer and an abundance of wildlife, and was built in 1762. The chancel was added during the 19thc, and the beautifully-redecorated interior contains the 1st Viscount Brookeborough's Garter Banner. Also here are the Garter and Order of the Bath Banners of Lord Alanbrooke.

BRUGH NA BOINNE, Meath **19 O07**
See gazetteer inset on pages 176 and 177.

BRUREE, *Brú Rí*:
King's Mansion, Limerick **22 R53**
Remains of an impressive fortress with

a rampart which measures 120yds in circumference – a one-time stronghold of the de Lacy family – can be seen here. Near the church are the ruins of a strong castle said to have been built by the Knights Templar in the 12thc. A picturesque, six-arched bridge spans the River Maigue at Bruree, and the village is a noted hunting centre. The village was the venue for half-yearly meetings of the Irish Bards up to 1746.

BRYANSFORD, *Áth Bhriain*:
the Ford of Brian, Down   13J33
Shadowed by the impressive Mourne Mountains, this attractive little village is known as the location for Ulster's first national forest park, the Tollymore. This comprises some 2,000 acres of forest, offering hill climbs, walks, and facilities for caravan parking. Special features include pony-trekking routes and a small public museum with displays relating to the local wildlife. The River Shimna, on which the village stands, is noted for its cascades.

*BUNCRANA, *Bun Cranncha*:
Mouth of the River Crannach, Donegal   5C33
Buncrana, the chief town of the Inishowen Peninsula, stands on the E shores of Lough Swilly and is sheltered by hills on three sides. A prominent member of the range, 2,019ft Slieve Snaght, rises in the NE. Swilly is also known as the Lough of Shadows and is seen to the W of the town with the hills of the Fanad Peninsula in the background. To the S is 3m Lisfannon Strand, and to the NE, a road to the lighthouse at Dunree Head affords fine views over the lough. A number of megalithic monuments exist within a 3m radius of Buncrana, including a bronze-age burial cairn 1m N at Crockcashel and two pairs of pillar stones ¾m SE. O Doherty's Keep (NM) stands near Castle Bridge and is the 14th- to 15th-c tower of a castle built by the O Doherty family – Lords of Inishowen. This structure was rebuilt in the 17thc and is in a very good state of preservation. Beyond the bridge is the now-decaying Buncrana Castle, built in 1716 by Henry Vaughan. It is a handsome building, especially noted for its panelled interior. Buncrana itself is a popular seaside resort.

*BUNDORAN, *Bun Dobhráin*:
Mouth of the River Dobhrán, Donegal   10G85
Picturesquely set on the shores of Donegal Bay, with the Sligo-Leitrim Mountains to the S and the hills of Donegal across the water, this major resort offers a good range of recreational facilities. The bathing is good, golf and tennis enthusiasts are well catered for, and there is good fishing 1½m W in the River Drowes. The bay offers excellent prospects to the sea angler. Strange rock formations along the cliffs beyond Aughrus Head include the Fairy Bridge and the Puffing Hole. As its name suggests, the latter funnels and ejects water in an impressive display, particularly in rough weather. The rocks along the shoreline are rich in fossils.

To the N is Tullan Strand, a fine beach which extends for 1½m towards the mouth of the River Erne. Ruined Finner Church dates from the 15thc and can be seen on the Ballyshannon road, while Finner Hill features an interesting chambered cairn. Near by are a dolmen and a stone circle. Franciscan friars from Donegal town sheltered in a convent at Bundrowes, and between 1630 and 1636 compiled the *Annals of the Four Masters* here. Bundrowes means the Foot of the Drowes and refers to the river of this name.

BUNMAHON, *Bun Machan*:
Mouth of the River Mahon, Waterford   29X49
Natural amenities offered by this pleasant coastal resort include a sandy, sheltered beach backed by impressive, 200ft cliffs. There are traces of copper workings in the area, and natural stone walls containing strange formations of interest to the aspiring geologist. During the summer these walls are covered with colourful blankets of thrift, or sea pink. Near by at Gleann an Earbaill is the site of the first modern college of Irish, which was opened in 1835.

BUNRATTY, *Bun Raite*:
Mount of the River Raite, Clare   22R46
A castle has stood on this site since 1251, and the present building (NM), which dates from 1425, was once the home of the O Briens of Thomond. Faithfully restored as a medieval fortress in the 1950's under the auspices of Viscount Gortin, the building contains furnishings from the 15th and 16thc and nowadays frequently plays host to people attending 'medieval' banquets. Bunratty Castle was the first to hold feasts of this nature in modern times, and the idea has since caught on in many other parts of the country.

As to the building itself, it is oblong in plan and has a square tower or turret at each corner of the lofty walls. A broad arch unites the south turrets, but a similar arch on the north face of the structure is hidden by a brick-built house which was erected between the turrets in the 18thc. The original entrance doorway penetrates this N wall and leads into a large vaulted hall in the body of the building. Beneath the hall is a vaulted store, and above it is a magnificent apartment which still retains some of the stucco work – a popular method of ornamentation in the 17thc. The turrets exceed the main block's three floors and are honeycombed with passages, stairways, and chambers. A chapel with rich stucco ceiling decoration dating from *c*1619 is housed in the south-east turret. A folk park behind the castle displays six authentically-furnished examples of Co Clare thatched cottages, plus an old forge.

BURNCOURT, *An Chúirt Dóite*:
the Burnt Court, Tipperary   22R91
Certainly the latest and perhaps the most perfect example of an English Tudor fortified house in Ireland, Burncourt was built in 1641 and burnt nine years later. The fire was purposely set by its chatelaine, Lady Everard, to prevent the building being used by the approaching Cromwellian army. Features of the structure include tapering walls, several tall chimneys, and interesting windows.

BURREN, THE, *Boirinn*:
Stony Place, Clare   15M10
Some 50sqm of N Clare ground is taken up by this great upland wilderness of limestone, which faces Galway Bay and constantly reveals its rocky skeleton in natural ridges and pavements. Surface streams that run into this territory vanish into pot- and swallow-holes as soon as they cross from the shale to the limestone. An excellent example of this phenomenon can be witnessed near Slieve Elva, where a number of streams disappear into underground caverns which often extend for many miles. The cave known as Polnagollum, which penetrates the E side of the hill, has been explored for nearly 7m from the 100ft pothole from which it is entered. Potholers should be warned that although many of these caves are easy to enter, they can be very dangerous for the inexperienced or poorly equipped.

Corkscrew Hill, on the road which links Ballyvaughan with Lisdoonvarna, is characteristic of the whole region. Fissures and cracks in the rocks of The Burren support rare colonies of Alpine plants, including gentians, cranesbill, and the highly-coloured saxifrages. Prehistoric remains in the area include numerous stone forts and dolmens.

BURRISHOOLE ABBEY, *Buiríos Umhall*:
The Borough of Umhall, Mayo   9L99
See Newport entry.

BUSHMILLS, *Muileann na Buaise*:
the Mill of the River Bush, Antrim   6C94
A small and prosperous town noted for its game fishing and distillery, Bushmills stands on the River Bush SW of the

cont on page 178

Burncourt House was built in 1641 and is often considered the most perfect example of an English fortified Tudor mansion in Ireland.

BRUGH NA BOINNE

Situated in a great bend of the River Boyne between Slane and Oldbridge in Co Meath is the most famous concentration of prehistoric monuments in Ireland. Brugh na Boinne, as this necropolis is collectively entitled, poses many questions, the first of which could easily be – why here? What made this particular spot so important? The cairns and other features that make up Brugh na Boinne are not situated on prominent hill-tops as are many monuments of their kind. In fact they are placed on very low ground – between the 100 and 200ft contours – and archaeology has shown that at the time the monuments were built this area was blanketed in dense woodland and scrub. This would not only have concealed the tombs, but would have made the job of clearing the area much more difficult than if a relatively barren upland region had been chosen.

The most plausible theory put forward for the siting of Brugh na Boinne is that this is where the people who built the passage graves first landed upon their arrival in Ireland. They travelled, of course, in boats – coming either from Iberia or from Brittany. It is easy to imagine them edging up the E coast of Ireland, looking for a suitable place to land. The River Boyne is tidal up as far as the great bend. What more natural action than to sail as far as here then pitch camp? And what more natural place to establish a temple, or at least a place of special sanctity, than the place where the first footfall was made? It is only a theory, but an attractive one nonetheless.

The visitor will probably arrive with three names uppermost in his mind – Newgrange, Dowth, and Knowth. These indeed are the largest and most impressive monuments on the site. They are by no means the only structures, for there are numerous other burial cairns, henge-type monuments, standing stones, and unidentified earthworks. Individually the smaller monuments may not be of tremendous interest to the layman, but taken together they become astonishing; a vast complex of structures, some of which are not understood at all, and all of which still have some mystery about them. The three large cairns are of course world famous for the way in which many of the stones from which the tombs are built are decorated with a range of symbols and motifs that may fulfil the term art.

Newgrange is the most famous mound – or more precisely cairn – here. Now grass covered where once it had a gleaming coat of quartz pebbles, it is estimated that 180,000 tons of stones were needed to build it. The cairn is still 44ft high in parts – it was probably once 50ft – and its diameter is about 300ft. At a small distance from the cairn are twelve standing stones, all that remain of a probable 36 which once surrounded it. This circle is probably not contemporary with the construction of the cairn. The cairn was originally partly held in place by a ring of kerb-stones, and the debris that had slipped from the cairn over the centuries, covering the curb, has now been cleared, enabling the symbols with which some of them are decorated to be seen. The circular cairn has a slight dent in it which marks the entrance to the tomb. This entrance was discovered at the end of the 17thc, when a lone standing stone still stood on the summit of the cairn.

At the entrance to the passage is the most renowned of all Newgrange's decorated stones. It is covered in a swirl of spirals, and from the way in which the pattern runs off the stone it can be speculated that it was considered as a complete design, not simply as a surface upon which to engrave a series of unrelated motifs. Above the entrance is another decorated stone which shields a sort of box which has a slit in its bottom opening into the tomb's passage. The function of this slit is not clear, but it has been surmised that it was used to pass offerings into the tomb after the entrance had been sealed.

The passage itself is 62ft long, and for most of its length it is possible to walk upright. It is lined with 43 orthostats (or upright stones) which vary in height from 5 to 8ft. Many of these stones are decorated, and excavation has shown that a large number of the decorations could only have been applied before the stones were placed in situ. Indeed, many of the decorations were only seen at the time of excavation, and are now no longer visible. It seems that it was not as important to see the decorations as it was to know that they were there. The passage leads to the magnificent central chamber, which is corbelled and attains a height of nearly 20ft. Directly connected to the large chamber are three smaller chambers, which form, with the passage, an overall cruciform plan to the tomb. Each of these side chambers has a stone basin in it (the right-hand chamber has two, one on top of the other), the function of which was presumably to contain the ashes of the dead. The construction of the cairn itself has been shown by archaeology to have comprised alternative layers of turf and stones capped by quartz pebbles collected from the river. A considerable amount of sophisticated detailing went into the construction of the monument. For instance some of the stones forming the roof of the passage have grooves cut into them, their function clearly being to channel water percolating through the cairn away from the passage. So effective was this piece of engineering that the chamber and passage are still remarkably dry. Several mounds near the Newgrange cairn have turned out to be smaller tombs of the passage grave type.

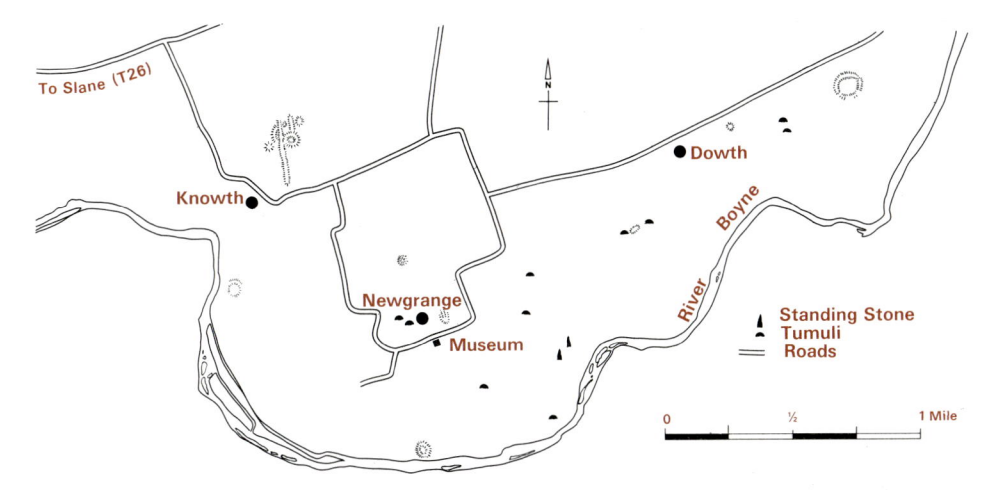

Nearly 2m NE of Newgrange is another great passage tomb, that of Dowth. The cairn here is 280ft in diameter and about 50ft high. The tomb has been plundered many times through the centuries, not least by the Vikings, who seem to have had a predilection for such activities. It was 'excavated' in the 19thc, and as was often the case in such digs, more harm than good was done. Many of the so-called antiquaries of the 19thc were only interested in finding exactly the same thing that the much maligned Vikings had looked for – gold. Three passages have so far been discovered in the cairn (there may be more), all on the W side. Two of these are prehistoric passage graves, and one is a souterrain probably dating from early-Christian times. Of the passage graves, one is cruciform in plan and its chambers are approached along a passage 27ft in length. The main chamber here, which has a stone basin, has three side chambers opening from it. From the right-hand side of the chamber leads another passage with two small chambers. The other passage grave in the cairn has a short passage, and its circular stone chamber, from which only one side chamber opens, has a modern concrete roof. Several of the stones at Dowth are decorated.

Knowth, the third of the great cairns of Brugh na Boinne, is situated about 2mNW of Newgrange. It is in many ways the most fascinating of all the monuments which make up this neolithic cemetery, for it has been, and continues to be, the subject of intensive and painstaking excavations which have already yielded rich rewards in the shape of the discovery in 1967 and 1968 of two passage graves within the cairn. These are placed almost back to back, one with an entrance on the W, and the other with its entrance on the E. The W tomb is 114ft long, and terminates in a single chamber. The E tomb is of the cruciform type, and its passage is 130ft long. The N recess of this tomb has a particularly magnificent stone basin. The cairn also has several souterrains cut into it. It was adapted for use as a tribal seat in early iron-age times, and as motte by the Anglo-Normans. Excavations carried out between 1941 and 1965 revealed not only the complex structure of the cairn – alternate layers of stones and turfs – but also the magnificently-decorated kerb stones, which are said to be the finest examples of their type in the world. The Knowth tomb has numerous satellites, several of which have been excavated and shown to be small passage graves.

No doubt there will always be mysteries about Brugh na Boinne, but as excavation continues and our knowledge of the monuments and their builders grow, many will conclude, if they had not concluded so already, that that glib phrase 'our primitive ancestors' has no meaning and is an insult to the achievements of our forefathers.

world-famous talus of huge, geometric basalt columns known as the Giant's Causeway (NT). The first hydro-electric tramway was built between the causeway and Portrush in 1883, but this was abandoned in 1947. About 2½m W of the town is ruined Dunluce Castle, a formidable structure built c1300 by Richard de Burgh – Earl of Ulster. The castle occupies the top of a detached basaltic rock and is separated from the mainland by a deep, 20ft-wide chasm. Its stormy history in the hands of the de Mandevilles, who are better known by their Irish name of McQuillan, came to an end when it was taken and reconstructed by the Scottish McDonnells c1560. The Earl of Antrim, who lives in Glenarm Castle and is the representative McDonnell today, handed the ruins (NM; OACT) over to the N Ireland government.

The castle is a good example of Anglo-Norman architecture and features five circular towers joined by a strong curtain wall. A platform on the inside of the wall allowed archers to fire through openings in the battlements. Remains include two of the original towers and fragments of two others, plus a large rectangular gatehouse at the south-west angle as well as extensive domestic buildings. The gatehouse dates from c1600 and takes the place of the keep which the castle never had – probably because of its cliff-top position. Round turrets of the Scottish type still crown the outer angles of this later structure.

BUTTEVANT, *Cill na Mallach*, Cork 22 R50
The name of this important River Awbeg town is derived either from the Norman-French word *botavant*, meaning defensive outwork, or from *Boutez en avant*, meaning push forward – a de Barry warcry. A rock overhanging the river carries the ruins of a castle built by the de Barry family, and the town's strong monastic tradition is supported by remains of a 13th-c Franciscan friary (NM). Of the original monastic complex, only the church has survived; this includes a long nave and choir with a south transept. An interesting feature of the church is the way in which a crypt was built below the choir to support it on the site's steep incline towards the river. The windows show the respective preferences of 13th- and 15th-c stone masons for sandstone and limestone. Two early de Barry tomb recesses can be seen in the walls of the nave. To the S of the town are the fragmentary remains of two castles.

CAHERCONREE, *Cathair Conraoi*: Cúraoi Fort, Kerry 26 Q70
See Camp entry.

CAHERDANIEL, *Cathair Dónall*: Dónall's Stone Fort, Kerry 26 V55
This attractive Derrynane Bay village is derived from the caher or fort near the roadside. Some 2m E of Caherdaniel are the remains of St Crohane's Hermitage, a curious little structure hewn from solid rock. To the W of this are the remains of Kilcrohane Church. Derrynane House lies 1½m SW and was the home of Daniel O Connell (1775–1847). His introduction of a totally new spirit into Irish affairs resulted in his being named the 'Liberator'.
His beliefs included emancipation of the upper and middle classes of Irish society, plus the liberation of peasants from local tyranny. His ideal was the union of all Irishmen into a single nation, and he was totally opposed to force or rebellion. Derrynane was his home for many years and has many objects of historical interest (OACT). Near by are the remains of Derrynane Abbey. An ogham stone (NM) found below the waterline has been erected in a new position beside the road.

CAHIR, *An Chathair*: the Stone Fort, Tipperary 23 S02
This busy market town straddles the River Suir at the E end of the Galtee Mountains, at the junction of the Dublin to Cork and Limerick to Waterford roads. The town is a noted hunting and fishing centre, and is a good base from which to explore the Galtees. It is also within easy reach of lovely Glen of Aherlow to the NW, the Suir Valley upriver, and Clonmel downriver.

The rocky islet in the river here was recognised as a natural vantage point from earliest times, as proved by a record of Dun Iascaigh Fort's 3rd-c destruction in the *Yellow Book of Lecan*. The present castle, which was restored in the 1970's (NM; OACT) dates mainly from the 15thc and is the largest of its period in Ireland. Its high walls enclose several irregular courtyards, a hall, and the massive keep, while a strong curtain wall follows the contours of the ground and is strengthened by seven towers – three large and four smaller. It was partially restored in 1840. The stronghold had a part to play in the Elizabethan wars, and it was here that Essex achieved the only important military success of his campaign by capturing Cahir in 1599. Remains of Cahir Abbey, founded in the reign of King John for Augustinian Canons Regular, occupy the banks of the river. The town has some good Georgian architecture, notably the CI church and the *cottage orne* in Cahir Park, both of which were designed by John Nash. Some 3m N off the Cashel road is the Anglo-Norman motte of Knockgraffon, which dates from 1192, and the nearby ruins of an early nave-and-chancel church display a 15th-c window. Most of the remains date from the 13thc, and close by is a tower which was built by the Butler family in the 16thc.

CAHIRCIVEEN, *Cathair Saidhbhín*: Little Sadhbh's Stone Fort, Kerry 26 V47
Bentee rises to 1,245ft from the outskirts of Cahirciveen, overlooking both the town and the waters of Valentia Harbour. The town's main building is a RC church which was erected to the memory of Daniel O Connell – the 'Liberator' – in 1888. Both the cornerstone and arch keystone were gifts from the Pope; the keystone came from the house of St Clement in Rome. Ashlin the architect was responsible for the interesting stone-groined roof, which was the first to be constructed in Ireland after the Reformation, and his overall design of the church is pleasing.

Ballycarbery Castle lies in ruins 1¾m W, and N of this is the stone fort of Cahergall (NM). This light-coloured structure is plainly visible on the mountain slope and encloses two dry-masonry buildings. One of these is a beehive hut, and the other a rectangular house built against the ramparts. To the W of this is the carefully-restored stone fort of Leacanabuaile (NM), which has three terraces and an enclosure which contains the foundations of a square house. Excavation revealed that this had been built upon two earlier round houses. Touching the foundations of the square house are those of a round house, from where a souterrain leads to a chamber in the fort's wall. Finds from the site date its occupation to the 6th to 8thc. There are two other impressive ringforts in the area.

CALEDON, *Cionn Aird*: High Head, Tyrone 12 H74
Formerly known as Kenard, this historic village stands on the River Blackwater and takes its present name from the Earls of Caledon. Sir Phelim O Neill had a castle here, and an inscribed stone from this is preserved in the demesne of 18th-c Caledon House. Built by Thomas Cooley in 1779, Caledon House is considered one of the finest Georgian mansions in the country. Its colonnade and domed pavilions were added by John Nash in 1812, the second floor was raised in 1835, and the interior is decorated with Wyatt-like plasterwork. Nash's splendid state chambers include an elegant round drawing room. A feature of the park is the Bone House, which has pillars and arches faced with ox bones and is the sole surviving remnant of one of Ireland's earliest rococo gardens. These gardens were created by Lord Orrery, the biographer of author Jonathan Swift, in 1740. A 19th-c doric column by William Murray is surmounted by a statue of the 2nd Earl of Caledon.

CALDRAGH CEMETERY FIGURES, Fermanagh 11 H16
See gazetteer inset opposite.

CALLAN, *Callainn*, Kilkenny 23 S44
Callan is a busy market town situated close to the Tipperary border. Its CI parish church is the adapted chancel of a church (NM) which was built in 1460. The west tower is the only remnant of a church built c1250. There are fine sculptured details on the doorways, and a good collection of 16th- and 17th-c tombstones in the nave. The town also has remains of a 15th-c Augustinian friary (NM). The sacristy and domestic buildings of this foundation have long since gone, but the rectangular church carries a central tower and preserves a sedilia which is considered one of the most ornamental in the country in the south wall of the choir. A decorative doorway and window can be seen in the east wall. The town's RC church dates from 1836 and features an ionic portico. Its west tower, in the form of a pedimented lantern, is surmounted by an obelisk-like spire. Brother Rice, founder of the Irish Christian Brothers, is commemorated by a handsome memorial of Kilkenny limestone in the main street. A well-preserved Norman motte with traces of the bailey can be seen in the town.

CAMP, *An Com*: the Hollow, Kerry 20 Q60
Sited at the seaward end of Glen Fas, this small cluster of houses lies W of the Slieve Mish range and is a good starting point from which to explore one of the highest peaks – 2,713ft Caherconree. A

stone fort (NM) built at 2,050ft on a promontory, possibly the highest structure of this type in Ireland, comprises a 350ft-long and 14ft-thick stone wall which cuts off and defends the tongue of land. It is associated with an ancient story which relates how hero and champion Cuchullain fell in love with the 1st-c King of Munster's wife, Blanaid. Legend has it that Blanaid returned Cuchullain's feelings, and at an opportune moment poured milk into a nearby stream as a signal for the champion to attack. Cuchullain killed Curaoi the king and carried off his queen. The fort is named after Curaoi, and the stream which flows through Glen Fas is still known as Finglas – White Stream.

CAPPOQUIN, *Ceapach Choinn:*
Conn's Plot, Waterford   **29 X 19**
Glenshelane River joins the River Blackwater near the foot of the Knockmealdown Mountains, a range which is accessible from this small market town. The town itself is situated on the Dungarvan to Lismore road and is a good base from which to explore the lovely Blackwater Valley. Woodland and the flanking hills combine to make the valley scenery some of the finest in the country. Some 4m N is the Mount Melleray Cistercian abbey, a heavy, gothick building which was founded in 1833.

CARAGH LAKE, *Loch Cárthaí:*
Lake of the Caragh, Kerry   **26 V 79**
Measuring 5½m long by up to 1m in width, this lake offers excellent fishing and superb waterside scenery. The banks and well wooded, and mountains which rise from the lake shore include 1,621ft Seefin to the W. MacGillycuddy's Reeks culminate in 3,414ft Carrantuohill, the highest mountain in Ireland, in the distant SE.

CARBURY, *Cairbre,* Kildare   **18 N 63**
Extensive ruins of Carbury Castle occupy the summit of Carbury Hill, overlooking the great central plain and the River Boyne Valley. It is a castellated manor house of the time of James I, with the characteristic features of pointed gables, graceful clustered chimneys, and mullioned windows. The massive walls of the west end and the stone-roofed donjons, however, show that a good deal of the original castle built by the de Berminghams in the 14thc was incorporated in the later building. In 1652 it was granted to ancestors of the Duke of Wellington. Pre-Christian remains can be seen near the castle, and the ruined church of Temple Doath lies to the S.

CARLINGFORD, *Cairlinn:*
Hag's Bay, Louth   **13 J 11**
Cooley Peninsula, on which this little seaside resort is situated, separates Carlingford Lough from Dundalk Bay. The lough's name originated from Viking forces, who quickly recognised the strategic importance of the position and built a fortified trading centre from which to harass the surrounding countryside. The castle which dominates the town today from a rocky cliff above the harbour is a massive D-shaped structure (NM) of 13th-c origin. Much changed and now in ruins, this stronghold is attributed to King John – who stayed here for three days in 1210 – but may well have been founded by Hugh de Lacy. The outer wall includes an inner platform from which archers could fire. The dividing wall and entire east half of the castle were added in 1261. Near the castle is a small building supported by an arch, originally one of the town gates. This is said to have been the Tholsel, or Corporation House, where the sovereign and burgesses once met. In the 18thc it also served as a gaol. A narrow street just off the town square features The Mint (NM), a 15th- to 16th-c town tower house with an extended turret over the door. The exterior of the house features remarkable mullioned windows displaying pre-Norman Celtic motifs amongst the decoration. These include interlacing, a horse, and a human head. None of the three storeys has a fireplace, and the building is said to occupy the site of a mint which was established in 1467. Opposite the railway station, and attached to a modern house is Taaffe's Castle, a 16th-c fortified town house. The tower of the CI church was originally part of the town walls. Near the church are the remains of a 14th-c Dominican friary which was rebuilt in the 16thc. Both Ghan House and the CI Rectory date from the 18thc.

CALDRAGH CEMETERY FIGURES

Boa Island is situated on Lower Lough Erne in Co Fermanagh. It measures 4½m long, and both ends are linked to the N shore of the lough by bridges. At the W end of the island on the S shore is an ancient graveyard in which two carved stones stand amongst the ferns and undergrowth. The larger, more compelling stone, has been here for a very long time, but the other came originally from the nearby island of Lusty More. Each stone has been shaped to form two figures standing back to back, and their stylized features have been sketched in with a superb economy of line.

The larger stone stands 2½ft high. The bodies, which only survive above the waist, are crossed by diagonal bands which have been variously interpreted as crossed arms, crossed legs, or simply abstract designs. The waists (if such they are) are circumscribed by a band which may or may not be a belt. The heads have long pointed chins, giving the faces a triangular shape. Again interpretation is called for – are the chins simply pointed chins or are they intended to represent beards? In the end it does not matter for the unknown sculptor has created an image that is powerful and somehow significant.

Some see the stone not as two separate figures, but as one figure with two faces – a sort of Janus. Those who put forward this theory cite various Celtic multi-faced carvings in support of their argument. The larger stone has a socket in the top which, along with similarities of style, link it to the carvings on White Island – also on Lough Erne. The close proximity of all these island figures hints at some sort of school of thought and design. It is impossible to put an accurate date to the figures in Caldragh cemetery. It is assumed that they were executed after the introduction of Christianity into Ireland, but whether they are wholly pagan, or Christianized idols, no one can say for sure.

CARLOW, *Ceatharlach,* Carlow 24S77

Capital of its county, and attractively situated on the E bank of the River Barrow, Carlow is the cathedral town of the RC diocese of Kildare and Leighlin. A sugarbeet factory established in this busy communications and marketing centre during 1926 was the first of its kind in the country.

The town's strategic position made it an important Anglo-Norman and English stronghold in the middle ages, and 13th-c Carlow Castle (NM) still suggests the power that its rulers must once have wielded. All that remains of this once large fortress is half of the keep, which is the earliest of its kind in Ireland. It was probably built between 1207 and 1213 by William Marshall. The keep, which is now surrounded by factory buildings, was not destroyed in some desperate siege; it was accidentally blown up by a Dr Middleton, who had hoped to reduce the thickness of the walls in order to adapt the place for use as a lunatic asylum. Carlow's classical-style courthouse is probably one of the finest in Ireland, and was built in 1830 by either Sir Richard Morrison or his son Vitruvius. The 19th-c gothick RC cathedral was constructed to the designs of Thomas A Cobden and houses a good monument by John Hogan. This memorial was raised to Bishop Doyle, one-time champion of Catholic emancipation. St Patrick's Training College, opened in 1795, is one of the earliest such in Ireland. In Graiguecullen churchyard may be seen a memorial in the shape of a Celtic cross, which commemorates 417 men killed here in the 1798 insurrection.

Drainage work on the River Barrow has revealed numerous stone and bronze artifacts, most of which are now on display in the National Museum, Dublin.

Browne's Hill dolmen stands 2m E of Carlow near the Georgian mansion after which it is named. It is reputed to be the largest dolmen in Europe, and its mighty capstone, supported on five upright granite blocks, is estimated to weigh 100 tons. The Georgian mansion is a handsome greystone building of 1763.

CARNDONAGH, *Carn Domhnach:* Cairn of the Church, Donegal 5C44

Hills shelter this thriving Inishowen Peninsula town on three sides, and Trawbreaga Bay lies 2m N. The main sources of employment in Carndonagh are shirt making and an industrial alcohol factory. The Donagh Cross (NM; about ½m W) is said to date from the 7thc, which would put it at the very beginning of the high-cross tradition. At the top of the east face is a cross comprising two broad, interlaced ribbons with birds beneath the arms, and the centre bears a figure with arms outstretched in benediction. The figures of three ecclesiastics adorn the foot of the east face. The west face is covered by an interlacing pattern. Two small flanking pillars carry representations of human figures, a bird, David and his harp, and spirals. Near by is a CI church with a door dating from the 15thc, and the churchyard contains a cross-inscribed pillar stone known as the Marigold Stone.

CARRA LOUGH, *Loch Ceara,* Mayo 15M17

Ruined Moore Hall, birthplace of playwright George Moore in 1852, stands near the vivid green waters of this lake. Like the poet James Joyce, Moore left Ireland and went to work in London, where he produced a number of plays in collaboration with Edward Martyn. One of his most celebrated works was the three-part, autobiographical trilogy *Hail and Farewell*, which recounted his experiences in Dublin with a splendid lack of accuracy. His ashes are contained in an exact replica of a bronze-age urn found in Co Wexford, and this is buried in a cist on Castle Island – in the centre of the lake. Stones taken from the remains of the island's ancient castle have been used to raise a cairn above the cist. An underground river links Carra Lough to the larger Lough Mask.

CARRAN, *An Cairn:* the Cairn, Clare 15R29

Early prehistoric and medieval remains abound in the area around this small, isolated village, and the community itself is situated on the edge of a limestone basin known as a *polji*. The well-known karsts of the rocky Burren wilderness can be seen to the W. The village's fine medieval church features a 15th-c south doorway and a contemporary east window. Three corbels at the east end of the north wall are decorated with carved heads, and there is evidence that an upper storey at the west end was once used as a fortified residence.

Poulawack multiple cist cairn is situated 1½m WSW of the village and comprises a large cairn within which were found a total of 16 burials. Cahercommann stone fort (NM) lies 3m S. It is a huge structure with two outer walls and an inner wall; the walls are 28ft thick in places. The fort was found on excavation to contain the remains of a number of stone buildings. Finds made on the site indicate that it was occupied during the 9thc. The ruins of a 12th-c church called Temple Cronan (NM) are situated 1m NE at Termon. It is beautifully situated in a little dell, and has been restored at least twice. The west doorway is square headed and has inclined sides, and there is a later, pointed doorway on the north side.

CARRANTUOHILL, *Corrán Tuathail:* Tuathal's Curved Mountain, Kerry 26V88

This 3,414ft mountain dominates the MacGillycuddy's Reeks range and is the highest in Ireland. Views from the summit encompass the sea, lakes, and hills of Co Kerry. The ascent can be made from Beaufort Bridge via the Devil's Ladder. The school lies on the N side of the mountain at the mouth of Hag's Glen. Lough Acoose lies at the W end of the range and is the starting point for the finest ridge walk in Ireland – a circuit of Caher, Carrantuohill, Beenkeragh, and Skregmore.

CARRICK, *An Charraig:* the Rock, Donegal 4G57

A good base from which to explore Slieve League and the spectacular local cliff scenery, this small coastal village lies 3m NW of Kilcar. A drive to Teelin, 2m S of Carrick on the W side of Teelin Bay, and thence on foot to Bunglass and 1,024ft Eagle's Nest affords views NW to Slieve League which at 1,972ft is the highest marine cliff in Europe. Farther along is the notorious One Man's Pass, a narrow ledge which drops 1,800ft to the sea on one side and almost as steeply to a lonely tarn on the other. This should not be walked except by people with

1 Carrickfergus Castle
2 Church of St Nicholas (CI)
3 North Gate
4 Town Hall
5 Town Wall Remains

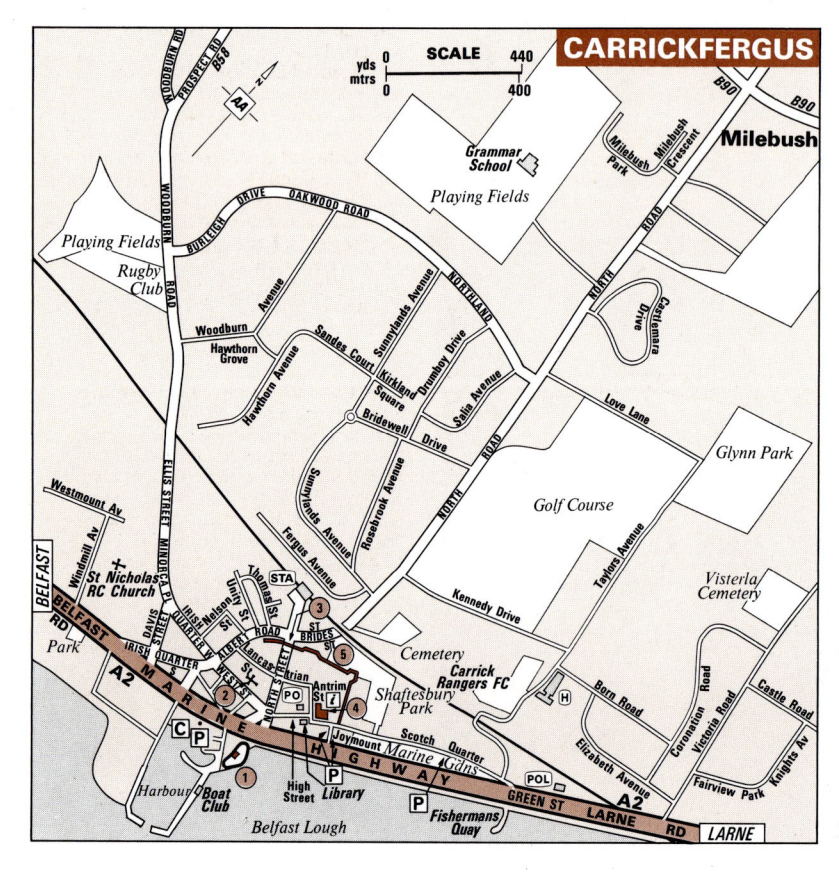

suitable footwear and an excellent head for heights. On the summit of Slieve League are the slight remains of a hermitage. Several good trout lakes are drained by Rivers Glen and Owenwee, and both offer fine game fishing. Teelin Bay and other local coastal waters offer good prospects to the sea angler.

CARRICK-A-REDE, *Carraig an Riada*, Antrim **7 D04**
See Ballintoy entry.

CARRICK CASTLE, *Caisleán na Carraige*: the Castle of the Rock, Kildare **18 N63**
Remains of this castle, 3m N of Edenderry, stand on the top of isolated Carrick Hill, a 387ft limestone outcrop which also carries the Witch's Rock. In 1305 Pierce de Bermingham came here and treacherously slew O Conor, Prince of Offaly, and about 30 of his relatives. Near the castle are the ruins of a 13th-c church.

CARRICKFERGUS, *Carraig Fhearghais*: Fergus' Rock, Antrim **7 J48**
Historic Carrickfergus was once an important port, but today is well known for its industry and its superb Norman castle (NM; OACT). This structure may have been the first true castle to have been erected in the country, and it is certainly the most impressive. It was built between 1180 and c1205 by either John de Courcy or Hugh de Lacy, and stands beside the harbour on a rocky peninsula enclosed by curtain walls. A modern reconstruction of the portcullis and its machinery is to be seen in the double-towered entrance on the landward side. Access to the massive, 58 by 56ft keep is between two half-round towers. It is entered – as is usual – at first floor level. Originally the keep had only four storeys, but at some time the topmost portion was raised to provide a fifth floor. The interior is ascended via a masonry staircase in the thickness of the wall. The third floor comprises one large room – the great hall of the castle – which has relatively large windows. From the 16thc onwards the defences of the castle were altered in order to accommodate artillery.

The CI Church of St Nicholas was built towards the end of the 12thc and rebuilt in 1614. Fragments of the original arcades can be seen in the truncated nave, and the interesting north transept features an elaborate, early 17th-c monument to Sir Arthur Chichester – virtually the founder of modern Ulster. Remains of the 17th-c town walls include North Gate, which was restored in 1911. Houses and shops in High Street retain some of their 18th- and 19th-c appearance, but the main feature of this road is the town hall. This retains the old County Court House front of 1779. Excavations in recent years have revealed traces of the medieval town and its defences; there have been many finds from the medieval and Plantation periods.

CARRICKMACROSS, *Carraig Mhachaire Rois*: the Rock of the Plain of Ross, Monaghan **12 H80**
Famous for its hand-made lace, some of which is still produced, this busy market town is situated on the Ardee to Monaghan road and includes slight remains of a castle. Queen Elizabeth I granted the town to the Earl of Essex, who built the castle while he was in control. The stations of the cross in the RC church are of interest. Lough Fea House stands in well-wooded grounds to the SW of Carrickmacross, and some 1½m W are the interesting limestone caverns of Tiragarvan. Local lakes offer excellent coarse fishing.

*CARRICK-ON-SHANNON, *Cora Droma Rúisc*: Weir of the Ridge of the Crust, Leitrim **10 M99**
The River Shannon, which is navigable to a short distance above this town, and the River Boyle, which runs W to Lough Key near Boyle, are responsible for this town's importance. Both the rivers and the local lakes offer good mixed angling, while Carrick, which is the county town, has facilities for tennis and golf. Several of the town's buildings, notably the 19th-c courthouse and the CI church, are of interest.

CARRICK-ON-SUIR, *Carraig na Siúire*: Rock of the River Suir, Tipperary **23 S42**
Carrick-on-Suir is situated on one of the most beautiful stretches of the lovely River Suir. This town is a well known angling centre and a good base from which to explore the Comeragh Mountains, a range which includes several peaks of over 2,000ft in height. The splendid Manor House stands in front of a ruined castle whose origins go back to 1309. The Manor House (NM) is a gabled and mullioned Elizabethan structure built by Black Tom – the 10th Earl of Ormonde. On first appearance it seems to have been built without thought of defence, but the firing holes around the main door belie this. The interior has some fine plasterwork, and the gallery hall, in its day, was the finest and most sumptuous in Ireland. The town's old Tholsel was originally the west gate and is surmounted by a clock tower. Across the river in the suburb of Carrickbeg is an RC church which incorporates the tower and north wall of a 14th-c Franciscan friary. The river is spanned by a bridge which dates from medieval times.

CARRIGADROHID, *Carraig an Droichid*: the Rock of the Bridge, Cork **27 W47**
An island in the lake which borders this attractive village carries the remains of a castle which was once considered the strongest in the country. Its present condition is a result of trickery by Cromwellian forces, who forced the garrison to surrender by placing cannon-like baulks of timber in sight of the defences. Before the defenders gave up the castle the Bishop of Ross exhorted them not to surrender, but they ignored him and he was later hanged. A hydro-electric power station and dam were built here in 1953.

CARRIGAHOLT, *Carraig an Chabhaltaigh*: the Rock of the Fleet, Clare **20 Q85**
Situated on the estuary of the River Shannon, this quaint village includes the O Curry Irish Language College and a ruined 14th-c castle (NM). The latter, built by the McMahon family, passed into the hands of Donal O Brien in the 17thc after a four-day siege by his renegade brother the Earl of Thomond.

CARRIGALINE, *Carraig Uí Leighin*: Lyon's Rock, Cork **28 W76**
A 12th-c castle built on a rocky cliff overlooking the Owenboy River can be seen near this fast-growing town, which lies on the Cork to Crosshaven road and is known for its pottery. The castle was first built by Milo de Cogan in 1177 and later taken over by the Desmond family. The CI church has a remarkable leaden effigy of Lady Newenham, who died in 1754. Ballea Castle, perhaps the oldest inhabited castle in Ireland, stands 2m NW. The present building is of 17th-c date.

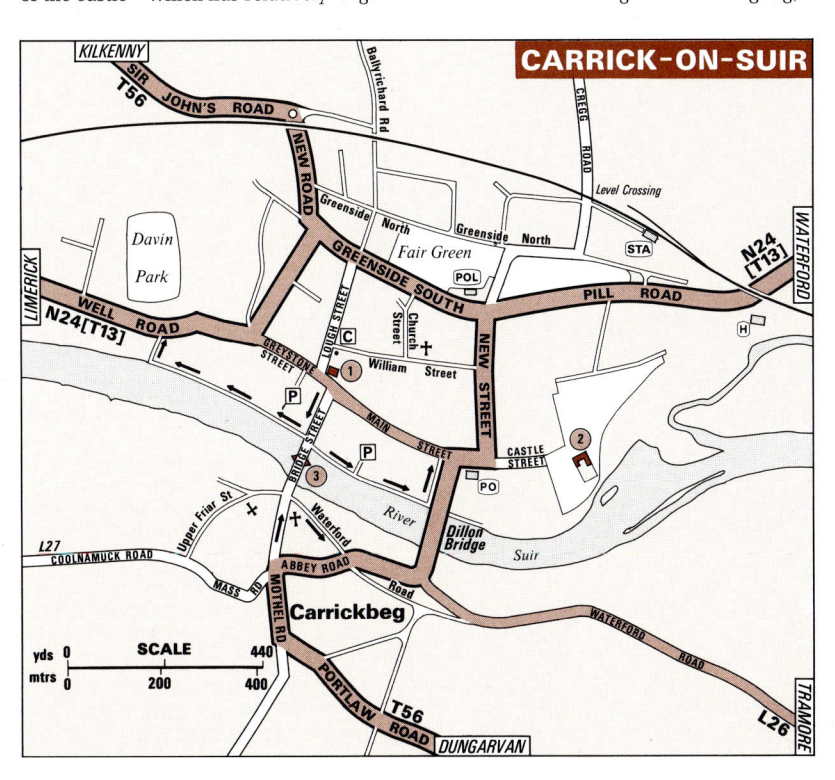

1 Clock Tower
2 Manor House & Castle
3 Medieval Bridge

Entries marked * are the starting point of drives included in the Day Drive section of the book (pages 79 to 144).

CARRIGAPHOOCA CASTLE/CASHEL

CARRIGAPHOOCA CASTLE, *Carraig an Phúca:* the Púca's Rock, Cork   **27 W 27**
Noted for its four-storey elevation, this massive 15th-c or earlier tower (NM) occupies a rocky perch 3m W of Macroom and appears to have been constructed with neither fireplaces nor chimneys.

CARRIGOGUNNELL CASTLE, *Carraig ó gConaill:*
O Connell's Rock, Limerick   **22 R 45**
Ruins of this fine castle occupy the top of a basaltic rock above the River Shannon. It was originally built by William de Burgo in the early 13thc, but was rebuilt *c*1336 by the O Brien Lord of Thomond. In 1691 General Ginkel blew it up after the siege of Limerick. The remains consist of parts of walls, keep, tower, and domestic buildings.

CARROWKEEL, *An Cheathrú Chaol:* the Narrow Quarter, Sligo   **10 G 71**
This cemetery (NM) of megalithic passage graves, 2m NW of Ballinafad, is situated on a series of extraordinary limestone ridges in the 1,057ft Bricklieve Mountains and overlooks Lough Arrow. There are a total of 16 tombs on the site, 13 of which are of the passage grave type. Of the remaining three, two are cist burials and one (called cairn E) displays an amalgam of passage-grave and court-cairn features. This is fascinating because it supplies evidence of the mixing of two very distinct cultures. The site was badly excavated in 1911, but many finds were made, including the famous pottery type now called Carrowkeel. The material found – bone pins, stone beads, and pendants – dates to the neolithic period. Near by is a cluster of almost 50 stone rings, called perhaps erroneously 'The Village'. It has been suggested that these are the remains of shelters used by the tomb builders.

CARROWMORE, *An Cheathrú Mhór:* the Great Quarter, Sligo   **10 G 63**
Carrowmore lies 2½m SW of Sligo and is the largest megalithic cemetery (NM) in the whole country. Although its tombs are widely spread in many directions, the majority are reasonably close to the road. It is thought that there may once have been over 200 graves on the site, but only about 60 can now be traced. Many of these have been destroyed or damaged by gravel workings. Most of the graves are of the small passage type, and were originally covered by stone mounds enclosed by boulder kerbs. In many cases both kerbs and mounds have disappeared. Also in the area are ancient forts, standing stones, and – near the Sligo road in Tobernaveen townland – a curious stone with a hole in it.

CARRYBRIDGE, Fermanagh   **11 H 23**
See Erne, Upper Lough entry.

CASHEL, *Caiseal:*
Stone Fort, Tipperary   **23 S 04**
Prosperous and noted for its River Suir angling, Cashel forms an excellent base from which to explore the surrounding countryside and is shadowed by the famous Rock of Cashel (NM). The rock rises from the Plain of Tipperary, forming a striking landmark which can be seen from all roads leading to the town, and carries a complex of buildings of immense historical significance. From the 4th to the 12thc it was the principal stronghold of the kings of Munster, but after being visited by St Patrick in the 5thc it acquired a religious significance which was soon to outshine its political importance. Many of the early kings were also bishops, and in 1101 it became a foundation of entirely ecclesiastical purpose.

Remains on the rock comprise the 92ft round tower, Cormac's Chapel, the roofless cathedral, the Archbishop's Palace, the Hall of the Vicars Choral (presently being restored), and the Cross of St Patrick – all knit together in a tightly-grouped architectural unit. The plain but extremely well-built round tower dates from the 11thc and is complete. It occupies a site at the north-east corner of the 13th-c cathedral's north transept. Roofless and without aisles, the cathedral carries a central tower and features a choir lit by five rows of lancet windows to the north and south. The choir is twice the length of the nave, and the transepts include east chapels and wall passages. Miler McGrath, Archbishop here from 1571 to 1622, is buried in the cathedral's most notable tomb. Fire and the sword arrived with Murrough O Brien, Earl of Inchiquin, in 1647. Many of the buildings were damaged, but the cathedral continued in intermittent use until its final abandonment in 1749.

During the early 15thc Archbishop O Hedigan constructed a tower house in the west half of the cathedral's nave. The uncertainty of the times is evident from the large number of passages which honeycomb the walls of this structure. The Hall of Vicars Choral adjoins the entrance to the rock and dates from the same time as the 'castle'. Cormac's Chapel lies in the angle between the cathedral choir and north transept, and is considered both the largest and most fascinating example of Irish Romanesque art in the country. Built by Cormac MacCarthy – king and bishop – it was consecrated for use in 1134. Some of its outstanding features are the high stone roof; nave, chancel, and transeptal pillars; and a pyramidal stone roof. Inside is a broken but still magnificent 11th-c sarcophagus with Scandinavian ornamentation. Part of the east wall of the chapel was reconstructed in 1875.

The 11th-c Cross of St Patrick stands S of the nave and is unusual in having the arms linked to the base by a rectangular frame. A 12th-c high cross on a pedestal stands near the cathedral and carries a sculptured Crucifixion scene on one side. The other side displays the effigy of a bishop. Close to the ruins of the main complex are remains of the 13th-c Cistercian Hore Abbey (NM). Most of the abbey's plan conforms to the usual layout of Cistercian houses, but it differs from the norm in that the cloisters lie to the N of the church. The church comprises a nave, chancel, and two transepts. Each of the latter originally included two chapels, but only those of the north transept survive. The 13th-c domestic buildings include the chapter house, which is one of the few units to

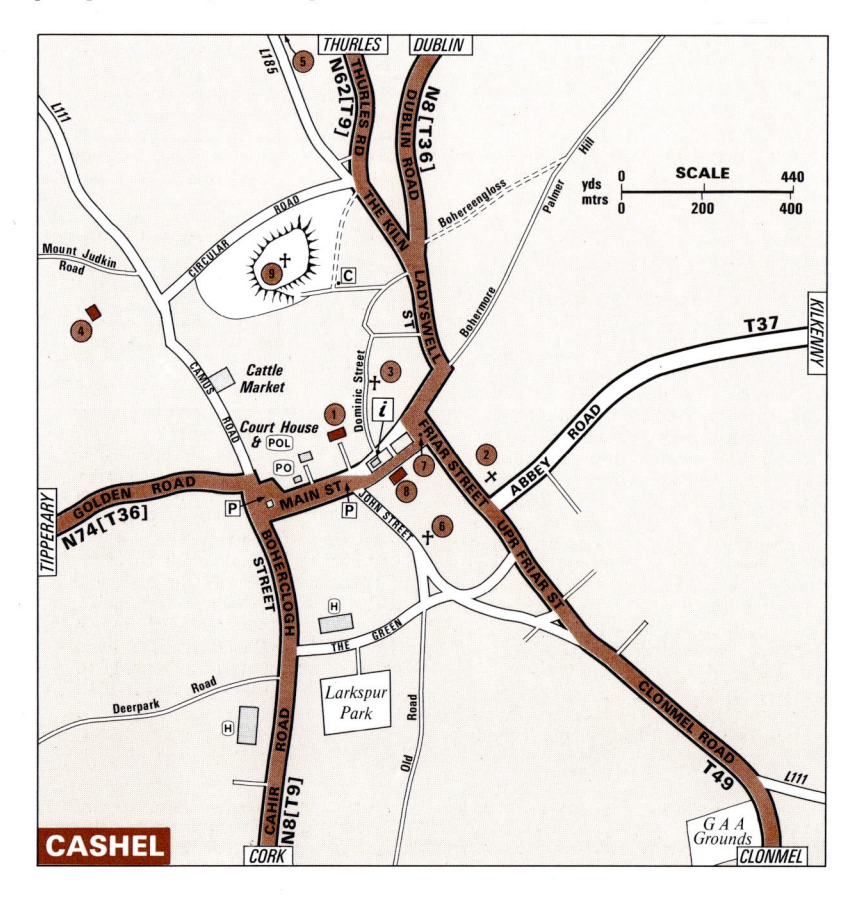

1 Cashel Palace Hotel (former Palace of Protestant Archbishops)
2 Church of St John the Baptist (RC)
3 Dominican Friary Church
4 Hore Abbey
5 Longfield House
6 Protestant Cathedral of St John the Baptist, & Diocesan Library
7 Memorial Cross to Archbishop Croke
8 Quirke's Castle (Grant's Hotel)
9 Rock of Cashel

have remained relatively intact. The tower was added to this structure during the 15thc, and the original lancet windows were replaced by smaller fittings. A new wall was added to the church to form a rood screen, and alterations were made to the wall of the choir.

Although the town of Cashel is largely eclipsed by its important rock, it too features several interesting buildings. Quirke's Castle, a 15th-c tower in the main street, is now a hotel. The former Palace of Protestant Archbishops dates from 1730. Now a hotel, this is considered one of the finest houses of its period in the country and is tastefully furnished in 18th-c style. Remains of a 13th-c Dominican friary just off the town's main street include a beautiful east window and several lancets. Some of the latter have been blocked, while others were replaced by windows with flowing tracery in the 15thc. The cloisters have disappeared, and a south wing was added to the church c1270. Founded by Archbishop David MacKelly, whose seat was immediately above the abbey on the Rock of Cashel, this was probably one of the first Dominican churches to be built in Ireland. General chapters of the Dominican Order in Ireland were held here in 1289 and 1307.

Another interesting building in the town is the 19th-c St John the Baptist Cathedral (CI) in John Street. This is a good little classical building which was erected after the historic cathedral on the Rock of Cashel was abandoned in the 18thc. The site on which it stands was formerly occupied by a medieval church. A fine series of medieval tomb effigies from the old cathedral and some of the town churches has been built into the church wall. The Diocesan Library is situated in the precincts of the cathedral and contains a fine library bequeathed to the archdiocese by Archbishop Bolton in 1741. The building was erected in 1835 and houses one of the finest collections of 16th- and 17th-c books in Ireland. The Catholic parish church of St John the Baptist, in Friar Street, is a building in the classical style with later additions. It stands on the site of a 13th-c friary of which only fragments survive. Also of interest in the town is a memorial cross to Archbishop Croke. Some 5m N of Cashel is Longfield House – one-time home of Charles Bianconi, who started Ireland's first public transport system during the 19thc.

CASTLE ARCHDALE, Fermanagh 11H15

Situated at the edge of a 200-acre country park on the E shore of Lower Lough Erne, the ruins that can be seen here today are the remains of one of the Plantation castles that every 17th-c planter or 'undertaker' was required to build. It was erected by John Archdale of Suffolk between 1615 and 1618, in accordance with the 1609 rules of Plantation. Unlike many other landowners Archdale actually occupied his castle, but the structure was destroyed and the Archdale children killed by Rory Maguire in 1641. The only child to escape was the heir, who had been hidden by his nurse. After having been rebuilt the castle (NM) was occupied until 1689, when it was again attacked and destroyed. Queen Wilhelmina was brought to the 18th-c Georgian house in the country park by Sunderland flying boat during the second world war. At this time the building was known as Rossfad House and belonged to the Richardson family.

Castle Archdale Deerpark is situated in the Kiltierney townland and features à number of both prehistoric and Christian remains. Among these is a multiple cairn comprising a central cairn surrounded by a circle of 22 smaller ones. Two of the six large stones which form the central cairn carry bronze-age carvings. A raised platform in the area carries an incomplete stone circle of seven large and one smaller boulders. Friar's Walk is a grassy track which borders two sides of the multiple cairn and is said to be associated with Cistercian monks. Close by are slight remains of a grange of the Cistercian abbey of Assaroe. This measures about 68ft long by 24ft wide, has a 3ft-thick partition wall, and features gables. The farthest W building of the complex stands at right-angles to the other two, and the church appears to have been the farthest building to the S. It is believed that the site was occupied by an early monastery, and there are still traces of a circular earthen enclosure which may once have surrounded it.

*CASTLEBAR, *Caisleán an Bharraigh*: Barry's Castle, Mayo 9M19

The pleasant, tree-lined Mall is the focal point of this busy country town, which is situated close to Castlebar Lough. Several smaller loughs lie to the SW, and the excellent coarse fishing of the area is free. Other leisure activities offered by the town include tennis and golf. The Claremorris road crosses a district known as the Plains of Mayo to the SE. James I granted a charter to the town in 1613, and the community was captured by the Confederate Irish in 1641.

CASTLEBELLINGHAM, *Baile an Ghearlánaigh*:
Gernon's Homestead, Louth 13O09
Formerly known as Garlandstown – after the Anglo-Norman Gernon family – this village is sited on the main Dublin to Belfast road about 1½m from the shore of Dundalk Bay. The Gernons occupied a castle here until their estates were confiscated by the Cromwellians and granted to Henry Bellingham. Castle Bellingham is now a hotel, but the grounds are noted for their yews and a picturesque reach of the River Glyde.

CASTLEBLAYNEY, *Baile na Lorgan*:
the Town of the Strip of Land, Monaghan 12H81
James I granted Sir Edward Blayney land on the sloping W shore of Lough Muckno, where the town which bears Edward's name now stands. The S boundary of the town is formed by the Hope demesne, which was held by the Blayneys from 1641 until it was sold to the Hope family in 1856. The building hére is now the guest house of a Franciscan convent. The largest of several lakes at the head of River Fane, which offers good trout fishing, are Lough Muckno and Lough Ross. Both offer shooting (with permission) for mallard, teal, and widgeon. Woodcock can be found on the lakes' islands and in the surrounding woodland.

CASTLECALDWELL, Fermanagh 11H06

Originally known as Castle Hasset, ruined Castlecaldwell is a Plantation structure built between 1610 and 1619 by Francis Blennerhasset as one of a series of strongholds guarding the Lough Erne road. In 1662 the Blennerhasset family sold the castle to James Caldwell, who renamed it and whose descendants lived there for over 200 years. The remains include two of the bawn's flankers, a boathouse and quay, and a ruined Protestant church. The latter was built by Francis Blennerhasset in 1641, and during later use as a family chapel acquired some interesting monuments. The English traveller Arthur Young enjoyed the hospitality of James Caldwell in 1776. Beside the road is the Fiddler's Stone, a monument raised to a drunken fiddler who fell from a boat and drowned while travelling with Sir James' band in 1770.

The whole of this area at the NW corner of Lough Erne is classed as a region of outstanding natural beauty. As well as being a forest park, it is also a reserve under the control of a RSPB warden who watches over the thriving local bird life.

CASTLECAULFIELD, *Baile Uí Dhonnaíle*:
O Donnelly's Town, Tyrone 12H76
This fine Jacobean mansion (NM) was built in 1614, only to be destroyed by fire in 1641. It was a three-storeyed building, and its layout is reminiscent of a medieval hall, suggesting that it may have been built on the site of such a hall. The porch of the nearby church was erected by Lord Charlemont in 1685, and the church's tower carries a dated sundial.

CASTLECOMER, *Caisleán an Chomair*:
the Castle of the Confluence, Kilkenny 24S57
This town takes its name from a castle which was erected here during the Anglo-Norman invasion. Its apt Irish name refers to the nearby confluence of the River Dinin and a tributary. The town itself lies in the lovely wooded valley of the Dinin, which cuts into the hilly N region of Kilkenny. The town is at the centre of the Leinster coalfield, which yields a high grade anthracite.

CASTLECONNELL, *Caisleán Uí Chonaill*:
O Conaing's Castle, Limerick 22R66
This popular resort stands on the E bank of the River Shannon, some 8m NE of Limerick, and was noted for its spa during the 18thc. Today it is better known for the game fishing offered by the Shannon. The wooded demesnes that fringe the river banks include that of Mount Shannon. Now ruined, the house here was once the stately home of Lord Clare, who played a prominent part in the events which surrounded the legislative Union of 1800. Below the village and near an old de Burgo castle is a reach where the great river suddenly throws itself over a series of limestone shelves, swirls round the rock promontory of Doonass, and then races over a long stretch of shallows before resuming its sedate course to Limerick.

CASTLE COOLE, Fermanagh 11H24
See Enniskillen entry.

CASTLECOR, *Caisleán na Cora*:
Castle of the Weir, Cork 28R40
Dr Croke, Archbishop of Cashel and the

co-founder of the Gaelic Athletic Association, was born in this village. Mid 18th-c Castlecor House is a strange building with wings that were modelled on baroque plans. Inside is a beautiful ballroom with a central chimney piece.

CASTLEDERMOT, *Díseart Diarmada*: Dermot's Hermitage, Kildare 24 S78
Diarmait, a grandson of the King of Ulster, founded a monastery here during the 9thc and was honoured in the original Irish name of this well laid-out town. Later the community was walled and under the protection of the Fitzgerald family. Hugh de Lacy built an Anglo-Norman castle here in the 12thc; the 60ft round tower (NM) carries a modern crenellated top and occupies the site of the old monastery. Relics from Diarmait's foundation include two 9th- or 10th-c granite crosses (NM) depicting such subjects as saints Paul and Anthony, the Apostles, the Crucifixion, the Fall, the Sacrifice of Isaac, and Daniel in the Lions' Den. A reconstruction of the church's fine Romanesque doorway can be seen in a nearby church of later date. In Abbey Street are the remains of a Franciscan friary (NM) which was founded in the 13thc, but enlarged in 1302 and rebuilt in 1317. St John's Tower, or the Pigeon Tower (NM), is situated at the N end of the town and is the only remnant of a 13th-c hospital of the Crutched Friars.

Kilkea Castle, once the seat of the Marquess of Kildare, lies 3m NW of the town. The present building is a 19th-c restoration of the medieval castle, which was partly destroyed in 1798. Features include several interesting medieval carvings and fragments of a figured cross commemorating John Fitzgerald of Narrabeg. Near the castle stand the ruins of Kilkea Church, close to a motte which was erected by the first Anglo-Norman proprietor, Walter de Riddlesford. Today the castle serves as a hotel, but its impressive exterior is preserved.

CASTLE GRACE, Tipperary 23 S01
See Clogheen entry.

CASTLEGREGORY, *Caisleán Ghriaire*: Gregory's Castle, Kerry 20 Q61
This quiet seaside resort is situated at the foot of a narrow neck of land which divides Tralee Bay from Brandon Bay. The village derives its name from a 16th-c castle built here by Gregory Hoare. Beautiful countryside surrounding the resort includes Lough Gill to the W and the Magharee or Seven Hogs Islands to the N. Illauntannig, the largest of the islands, features the remains (NM) of a small monastic settlement surrounded by a stone wall. One of the two oratories inside the walls has a doorway with sloping jambs and a south wall which displays herring-bone masonry; the other has a white cross over the door. There are also three beehive huts and three burial places. Striking views of the area around the village are afforded by the summit of 2,713ft Beenoskee, which rises to the S of Castlegregory.

CASTLEISLAND, *Oileán Ciarraí*: the Island of Kerry, Kerry 21 R00
The colour of the red marble for which this market town is noted is due to the natural infiltration of iron oxide. There is a ruined 13th-c castle in the town, and 1,097ft Knight's Hill rises N of Castleisland from the Glannaruddery range. Interesting marine caves can be seen 2m E at Ballymouth, and the Abbeyfeale road affords fine views as it crosses 810ft Glonsharoon Hill.

CASTLE ISLAND, *Oileán an Chaisleáin*: Castle Island, Mayo 15 M17
See Carra Lough entry.

CASTLE KIRKE, *Caisleán na Circe*: Hen's Castle, Galway 15 L95
See Hen's Castle entry.

CASTLELYONS, Cork 28 W89
See Fermoy entry.

CASTLEMAINE, *Caisleán na Mainge*: the Castle of the River Maine, Kerry 26 Q80
The castle after which this small market town was named guarded the River Maine crossing before being sacked and destroyed by Cromwellian troops under Ludlow. Castlemaine Harbour lies SE of the Slieve Mish range of mountains and is almost cut off from Dingle Bay by the Inch, Rossbeigh, and Cromane peninsulas. An old burial ground some 1½m W in Ardcanaght contains a standing stone and two ogham stones (NM).

CASTLEMARTYR, *Baile na Martra*: Town of the Relics, Cork 28 W97
To the W of this town, which is situated on the Youghal to Midleton road, is Castlemartyr House. This now serves as a Carmelite priory and shares its demesne with the remains of 15th-c Seneschal's Castle. This was built for the Earl of Desmond's Seneschal, and the ruins include a 15th-c bawn with angle towers, a keep, and 17th-c domestic quarters. About 3m SE is 17th-c Ighter-murragh Castle, and 15th-c Castle Richard lies 3m E.

CASTLEPOLLARD, *Baile na gCros*: the Town of the Crosses, Westmeath 17 N47
A good touring and angling centre for the Westmeath Lakelands, Castlepollard lies NE of Lough Derravaragh in a region of small hills. Tullynally Castle (OACT), 1½m NW, is a 17th-c structure – residence of the Earls of Longford – which was formerly known as Pakenham Hall. In 1775 it was classicized by Myers, and between 1804 and 1806 Francis Johnston transformed it into a flamboyant gothick edifice. Johnston's work was extended with picturesque additions by James Sheil in 1825 and Sir Richard Morrison in 1842. The kitchen, museum, and various relics here are associated with the Duke of Wellington, and the building stands in 1,500 acres of parkland. Another famous name associated with the house is that of the novelist Maria Edgeworth.

CASTLEREA, *An Caisleán Riabhach*: the Striped Castle, Roscommon 16 M68
Castlerea stands in the Sandford demesne, now a public park, on a wooded reach of the River Suck. The park offers pleasant woodland scenery, a sports ground, and a swimming pool. Sir William Wilde, father of the controversial dramatist and wit Oscar Wilde, was born here. Sir William's wife, Lady Wilde, often contributed to the Young Ireland Movement newspaper *The Nation* under the pen-name Speranza. Clonalis House contains the Harp of Carolan – the last of the Irish bards – and was formerly the home of the legendary O Conor Don. The 11th-c Emlagh High Cross (NM) lies 2m S and features decoration comprising loosely-knit geometric patterns and interlacing.

CASTLETOWNBERE, *Baile Chaisleáin Bhéarra*: the Town of the Castle of the Bear, Cork 26 V64
The natural harbour of this small town and angling resort is sheltered by Bear Island, which is situated almost directly opposite in Bantry Bay. To the NE of the town the Slieve Miskish range of mountains includes 2,044ft Maulin, and 2½m SW are the slight remains of Dunboy Castle. This ancient fortress of the O Sullivan Bere family resisted Sir George Carew's force of 4,000 men in 1602, after the battle of Kinsale, until the walls were shattered and all the defenders killed. An excellent sailing school is administered from Bear Island, and the town itself is being developed into a modern fishing port. Offshore Dinish Island is to become a fisheries industrial estate.

CASTLETOWN (COX), Kilkenny 23 S42
The house built here for Archbishop Cox of Cashel between 1767 and 1771 was by the Sardinian architect Davis Ducart, and is considered a masterpiece. This richly-detailed, cut-stone building features pilastered centrepieces on both fronts, plus arcaded wings which are placed cornerwise to the main block and terminate in octagonal, domed pavilions. The wings define and partly enclose the forecourt. Inside are examples of fine plasterwork by Patrick Osborne of Waterford, and the structure as a whole can be compared with the Kilshannig and Limerick custom houses, which are also by Ducart.

CASTLETOWN GEOGHEGAN, *Baile Chaisleáin na nGeochagán*: the Town of the Castle of Mac Eochagáin, Westmeath 17 N34
A large Anglo-Norman motte and bailey can be seen in this village, which is situated SW of Lough Ennell, but the place takes its name from a castle built by the Mac Eochagáins. This family held local lands up until Cromwellian times. Remains of a medieval priory can be seen on the W side of the village, and there are numerous ringforts in the area – particularly S and SW. Middleton House is a fine classical building sited 1m SE.

CASTLETOWN HOUSE, *Baile an Chaisleáin*: Town of the Castle, Kildare 18 N93
This is the largest and undoubtedly the most architecturally important private house in the country. Built between 1719 and 1732 for William Conolly, speaker in the Irish House of Commons, this interesting structure (OACT) was the combined result of designs by Sir Edward Lovett Pearce and the Florentine architect Alessandro Galilei. Conolly was the son of an innkeeper and was born in Donegal in 1662. By careful business deals and use of money he made himself the richest man in Ireland.

The layout of the building, with twin pavilions linked to the central block by colonnaded curtin walls, was completely new to Ireland and became the model and inspiration for many other houses, though none ever surpassed it in design and appearance. The central block resembles the typical Italian Renaissance town-palace façade, while the curved, coloured quadrants are of Palladian influence. The magnificent entrance hall contains a fine staircase and 18th-c plaster work by the Francini brothers, and the first floor features a Pompeian-style long gallery by Thomas Riley. A view towards the N end of the house includes what is probably the most fantastic folly in Ireland. This edifice, which comprises an obelisk supported by superimposed arches, was built by Conolly's widow in order to provide work for people affected by the hard frost of 1740. It is almost certainly the work of Richard Cassels, who was working at nearby Carton at the time. To the E of the house is the Wonderful Barn, a conical five-storeyed structure with an external spiral staircase. This was built in 1743, again to provide work for famine-distressed people.

Between 1759 and 1765 the interior of the house was remodelled by Conolly's grand nephew, Thomas Conolly. The magnificent staircase by Vierpyl and the Francini stucco work date from this time. The house passed out of the hands of the Conolly family in 1965, and was bought two years later by Desmond Guinness to serve as a headquarters for the Irish Georgian Society and be preserved for posterity.

CASTLETOWNROCHE,
Baile Chaisleáin an Róistigh:
the Town of Roche's Castle, Cork **28 R60**
Named after a Roche-family stronghold, this picturesque Awbeg River village was included in Spenser's *Faerie Queene* as 'Mulla'. The keep of the fortress, which was defended against Cromwell's army by Lady Roche in 1649, is now incorporated in the structure of Castle Widenham, which stands in fine gardens. Another feature of the village is ruined Bridgetown Abbey, which was founded by Fitzhugh Roche during the 13thc. The remains include a church with fine lancet windows and a good 15th-c tomb niche, plus a good refectory with 13th-c lancet windows and portions of other domestic buildings. Annes Grove, 2m N, is noted for its fine grounds.

CASTLETOWNSHEND,
Baile an Chaisleáin:
the Town of the Castle, Cork **27 W13**
The village lies on the W of the inlet of Castle Haven. To the ENE of the village are ruins of Bryans' Fort, a small Plantation stronghold erected c1650 by Colonel Richard Townsend from England. Drishane House, home of 19th-c authoress Edith Somerville, is situated SW of the village. Knockdrum Fort is ¾m NW (see entry).

CASTLEWARD, Down **13 J54**
Bernard Ward, 1st Lord of Bangor, and his wife built this fine Georgian mansion (NT) in the 1760's. The couple could not agree on the style of the building, so they compromised. The strictly Palladian front reflects Lord Bangor's taste, while his wife's preference is displayed by the 'Strawberry Hill' gothick north-east front overlooking Strangford Lough. Admirable plastering and panelling can be seen in the classical rooms, and parts of the gothick interior show remarkable fan vaulting. The beautiful grounds and gardens feature an interesting collection of waterfowl, a Victorian laundry, an 18th-c summer house, and two 15th-c castles. Of the latter, Old Castle Ward is situated in a farmyard and Audley's Castle stands on the shore 1m N of the house.

CASTLEWELLAN, *Caisleán Uidhilín:*
Uidhilin's Castle, Down **13 J33**
Well-wooded countryside containing a number of demesnes surrounds this charming village, from which good views of the Mourne Mountains can be enjoyed. Some of this countryside forms the Castlewellan national forest park, which features a tree-shrouded lake and offers facilities for angling, pony trekking, and camping. Also here are fine gardens and an interesting arboretum. The CI parish church of 1853 is in the early-perpendicular style, and William Annesley's 18th-c market house carries a later tower. The main block of this structure comprises five bays and two storeys. Access is by four arched openings.

*CAVAN, *An Cabhán:*
the Hollow, Cavan **11 H40**
Chief town in the county of the same name, Cavan lies in a pleasant district of low-lying hills and numerous lakes. The lakes are within easy reach and offer both game and coarse angling, while other recreational facilities include golf on a course about 1m from the town. Some 3m NW of Cavan is the fine demesne of Farnham House – seat of the Maxwell family, Lords Farnham. Although the house originally dates from 1700, it was enlarged to a design by Francis Johnston in 1801. Cavan's neo-Renaissance cathedral was built in 1942 by Ralph Byrne and contains sculptures by Albert Power.

In ancient times the town was the seat of the O Reillys, who were rulers of E Breffni and had their principal residence on the outskirts of Cavan at Tullymongan Hill. Shantemon Hill, which lies 3m to the NE, was the ancient inauguration place of the O Reillys. The 14th-c Franciscan friary around which the town grew was founded by Giolla Iosa Rua O Reilly. All that remains is the belfry tower.

CEANANNAS MÓR, *Ceanannas Mór,*
Meath **18 N77**
Also known as Kells, Ceanannas Mór is one of the most interesting and historic of all Irish inland towns. It is situated near the wooded banks of the River Blackwater, and occupies a site originally granted to St Columba for the foundation of a monastery in the 6thc. Monks fleeing from the Viking harassment of Iona, another of this saint's foundations, refounded the monastery and built a new church to mark the event. Reliquaries of the saint were transferred here in 807, but the Viking marauders followed the fugitives and sacked the foundation in 919, 950, and 969. The richest treasure surviving from the monastery is the Book of Kells, a Latin copy of the gospels believed to have been written here in the 8th or early 9thc. In 1007 the book was stolen from the west sacristy of the church, but two and a half months later it was recovered – minus its gold – from beneath a sod. Now preserved by Trinity College in Dublin, the book's marvellous colouring and exactness of detail lead many experts to consider it the most beautiful object of its kind in the world. A replica of the book may be seen in St Columba's Church (CI), Ceanannas Mór. Arrangements for the finalization of

1 Churchyard (round tower & high crosses)
2 Market Cross
3 Medieval Church Tower
4 Parish Church of St Columba (CI)
5 St Columba's House

Entries marked * are the starting point of drives included in the Day Drive section of the book (pages 79 to 144).

the country's dioceses were made at a famous synod which met here in 1152.

The signposted churchyard at the top of a local hill contains the round tower and a number of high crosses. The 100ft-high tower (NM) was built in 1076 and features five windows (which face the five ancient roads into the town) at the top. The original conical cap is missing. Severe weather erosion has almost destroyed a series of carved heads which once ornamented the doorway. Near the tower is the S cross, which is dedicated to Saints Patrick and Columba and was erected some time during the 9thc. The base includes interlacings, representations of a deer and other animals, and a chariot procession. Adam, Eve, Cain, and Abel are depicted on the south face, plus the Three Children in the Fiery Furnace and Daniel in the Lions' Den. The left arm displays the sacrifice of Isaac, the right shows Saints Paul and Anthony in the desert, and the top features David playing his harp and the Miracle of the Loaves and Fishes. The west side shows the Crucifixion, above which is the Judgement of Christ. Respective carvings showing David killing a lion and a bear can be seen on the south and north arms. Additional decorations on the cross include a number of ornamental panels, interlacing, and a vine scroll with animals. Some 20yds N of this is the stump of what must have been a fine and very tall cross. An unfinished cross with a Crucifixion on one face stands near the parish church and shows the various stages involved in the carving of this type of monument. Although the town's parish church is recent, it includes an ancient detached tower which was built in three stages and displays a black-letter inscription on the west side. Inside the church are two early sepulchral slabs and a 13th-c Anglo-Norman tombstone. An interesting little museum is housed in the gallery. The rounded base of another high cross stands near the tower.

The town's market cross stands at the intersection of two streets, but it is thought that this may not have been its original location. The base carries representations of horsemen, a battle, and various animals, while the east side displays biblical scenes. An inscription on the west side records that the cross was re-erected here by Robert Balfe in 1688. Above this and also on the south side are many more fine representations of biblical scenes and personages. St Columba's House (NM) is an ancient oratory with a steep stone roof. Access to the interior is via a modern entrance, and its barrel-vaulted room was originally at two levels. The present ground floor served as a basement, while the original church proper was entered through a door in the west wall. Now blocked, this door was positioned some 7 or 8ft above ground level. A small chamber above the vault was included to stop the rock fabric of the building collapsing. Both the courthouse and the Catholic church were designed by Francis Johnston.

Adjoining the town on the NE side is the Headfort demesne, which affords good views of the River Blackwater and is the ancestral seat of the Marquesses of Headfort. Part of the 18th-c Georgian mansion now serves as a school for boys and features several rooms decorated with stucco and plasterwork by Robert Adam. About 1½m N is Dulane Church, a massively-built structure which includes a west doorway with inclined jambs. Its walls project beyond the gables as antae, and the entire building is thought to be of 9th-c origin.

Some 3½m NW on the banks of a River Blackwater tributary is the church of St Kieran, a plain 14th-c building (NM) which preserves the remains of three termon crosses (NM) once used to mark the boundary of its land. In the river and close to the bank farthest from the church is the stump of a fourth cross. A fugitive seeking sanctuary had only to jump into the river to be immediately 'under the protection of God and St Kieran'. A small inscribed stone can be seen NW of the church, and nearby St Kieran's Holy Well is the venue for a holy pattern held on the first Sunday in August. Some 4m SE on the N bank of the Blackwater near Donaghpatrick, at Tailltenn, or Teltown, was the place where the Royal Games were held each August. Overlooking the town on the Hill of Lloyd is a commemorative tower erected by the Marquis of Headfort in 1791.

CELBRIDGE, *Cill Droichid:*
the Church of the Bridge, Kildare   18 N93
Esther Vanhomrigh, the ill-fated 'Vanessa' made famous by Dean Swift, lived at Celbridge Abbey in this picturesque River Liffey village. The Dean often visited her here, and a seat beneath rocks at the river's edge is often pointed out as having been one of their favourite retreats. About 1m SW is the 18th-c house of Killadoon.

CHAPELIZOD, *Séipéal Iosóid:*
Yseult's Chapel, Dublin   19 O13
The name of this Liffey-side village, which is situated on the Dublin to Lucan road, is said to have been derived from Yseult – daughter of an Irish king and tragic heroine of the famous *Tristram and Yseult*. The CI church preserves a medieval belfry tower. Chapelizod is the scene of Le Fanu's 'House by the Churchyard', and was the birthplace, in 1865, of the first Lord Northcliffe. There are fine parklands and excellent scenery near the River Liffey. On the S bank of the river 1m NW is Palmerston House, residence of John Hely Hutchinson during the 18thc. Hutchinson was Prime Sergeant-at-Law and later became Provost of Trinity College in Dublin. The house now serves as a children's home. Remains of an early little nave-and-chancel church featuring a trabeate west door, plain round-headed chancel arch, and round-headed east window can be seen ¼m NE.

CHARLEMONT, *Achadh an Dá Chora:*
the Field of the Two Weirs, Armagh
12 H85
See Moy entry.

CHEEKPOINT, *Pointe na Síge:*
Point of the Streak, Waterford   24 S61
After leaving Waterford city the attractive River Suir winds E and divides to flow round Little Island. From there it continues to the village of Cheekpoint, where it meets the combined waters of Rivers Barrow and Nore. From this confluence the three united rivers flow S to the great estuary of Waterford Harbour. Cheekpoint or Faithlegg Hill affords superb views over the junction of rivers and the harbour. About 1m SW of the hill are the ruins of a church and several castles.

CHURCH ISLAND, *Oileán an Teampaill:*
Island of the Church, Antrim   6 H99
See Toome Bridge entry.

CHURCH ISLAND, *Oileán an Teampaill:*
Island of the Church, Kerry   26 V56
See Waterville entry.

CLADAGH GLEN, *Gleann na Cladaí:*
Valley of the Cladagh, Fermanagh
11 H13
See Belcoo entry.

CLAGGAN, *An Cloigeann:*
the Head, Donegal   6 C63
Features of this small Bredagh River village 1m NW of Moville include remains of a tomb slab with an Irish inscription, and the ornamental shaft of a high cross.

CLANDEBOYE HOUSE, *Clann Aodha Buí:*
Descendants of Yellow Aodh, Down
7 J47
See Crawfordsburn entry.

CLANE, *Claonadh:* Sloping Ford, Kildare
18 N82
A fine six-arched bridge spans the River Liffey in this busy village, which lies on the Kilcock to Naas road. Ruins of a Franciscan friary founded in 1258 by Sir Gerald Fitzmaurice Fitzgerald lie to the SE, and the noted Jesuit school of Clongowes Wood College is situated 2m N. The nucleus of the school complex is formed by medieval (but greatly-changed) Castle Brown. The old school chapel, now used as a church, is an interesting example of 19th-c classical work. The new chapel contains stations of the cross by Sean Keating. Michael Healy and Evie Hone designed the very fine series of 19th-c windows. A 10th-c bachall shrine found in a bog in Prosperous and known as the Prosperous Crozier is housed in the school museum. In the vicinity is Bodenstown, where Wolfe Tone is buried.

CLARA, *Clóirtheach,* Offaly   17 N23
This busy manufacturing town stands on the River Brosna and was originally a Quaker settlement. Its interesting Protestant church dates from 1770. A souterrain can be seen 2m N in the grounds of Doone House.

CLARA CASTLE, *Caisleán an Chláraigh:*
Castle of the Level Place, Kilkenny
24 S55
Clara Castle, 4½m ENE of Kilkenny, is a 16th-c house (NM) which is considered one of the best-preserved of its type in the country. From it much can be learned about the construction and use of these tower houses. The entrance, preceded by a forecourt with early gun holes beside the gate, leads to a hall situated below a murder hole. There is a fine fireplace on the third floor, plus a secret room which can be reached from the garderobe on the fourth. Freestone Hill, 2m SSE, is surmounted by a bronze-age cairn. The hill is encircled by two defensive earthworks, and finds made here date the occupation of the hillfort to the 4thc.

CLARA, VALE OF, Wicklow   25 T19
See Rathdrum entry.

CLARECASTLE, *Droichead an Chláir:*
Bridge of Clare (*ie* the Plain), Clare
21 R37
The Fergus, a tributary of the River

Shannon, flows through this small town and round an island which carries an O Brien castle. A little way from the Ennis road are the remains of Augustinian Clare Abbey (NM), which was founded in 1195 by Donal O Brien. The abbey was dedicated to St Peter and St Paul in 1278, and later became the scene of great slaughter in the internecine war between factions of the O Brien family; the church and charter were reconfirmed in 1461. Parts of the single-aisle church date from the 12thc, but most of the surviving remains are of 15th-c origin. These include a well-preserved east window, the tower, and domestic buildings – with an unusual floral window – to the SE. To the SE of the village is mid 18th-c Carnelly House.

Ruined Clare Abbey, at Clarecastle, has a mainly 15th-c church which incorporates fragments of the original 12th-c structure.

CLAREEN, *An Cláirín:*
the Little Plain, Offaly   **17 N 10**
A Celtic cross and a carved stone head are housed in Clareen's Church of St Ciaran. Apart from the great earthen banks, these are virtually all that remain of the early monastery founded here by St Ciaran. In Seirkieran parish, a little to the S of Clareen crossroads, a whitethorn tree known as St Ciaran's bush grows in the middle of the road.

CLAREGALWAY, *Baile an Chláir:*
the Town of the Plain, Galway   **15 M 33**
Perhaps the chief feature of this small, well-kept village is the finely-preserved, 13th-c Franciscan friary (NM) which was founded here by John de Cogan. This retains its 80ft tower, plus other remains which include a nave-and-chancel church and parts of a cloister. The chancel displays six side windows and a triple sedilia of *c*1300. The north aisle was added to the nave at a later stage, and the lancet windows in the east wall were incorporated during the 15thc. It is probable that the north transept was also built in this period. After the suppression the friary was granted to Richard de Burgo, but the Franciscan monks lingered on here until 1765. A primitive tombstone inside the church carries the representation of an early plough. Now a tangled ruin, the 15th-c de Burgo castle which dominates the river crossing was garrisoned by the Marquess of Clanricarde in the 1641 Rebellion.

CLARE ISLAND, *Cliara,* Mayo   **14 L 68**
On bright days there are beautiful views of this island from neighbouring Achill Island and the mainland shores around Clew Bay. Clare is a green and pleasant place, and unlike many other Irish islands its population remains stable, partly because the Congested Districts Board – which bought the island in 1895 – made the local holdings far more efficient in size and layout. The island's highest point is 1,520ft Knockmore. It can be approached from Roonah Quay. Cistercian monks from Knockmoy in Co Galway established a cell here in 1220, but the present nave-and-chancel church of St Bridget – called the 'Abbey' – has its origins in the 16thc. The building (NM) includes a sacristy and features interesting paintings in the chancel – some of the very few medieval frescoes surviving in Ireland. Amongst other subjects, these depict animals, people, and the Archangel Michael.

It is said that the famous pirate queen Grace O Malley is buried in the church. Her massive tower castle (NM) may be seen near the harbour. It is a three-storey building, but was much altered in 1831 when it was adapted for use as a coastguard station. Grace's exploits have passed into legend, and while they may have grown with the passage of time, there can be no doubt that she was an extraordinarily daunting and strong-willed person who apparently earned the grudging respect of Elizabeth I. A lintel-roofed holy well, a cashel enclosing a beehive hut, and an altar are situated ½m NE. A promontory fort occupies a striking position on the SW side of the island, and another structure of this type can be seen on the NW side.

CLAUDY, *Clóidigh:* the Washer, Derry   **6 C 50**
Situated in a lovely wooded valley on the River Faughan, this small village lies on the Dungiven to Derry road and is near the River Burntollet. The White Stone, an interesting prehistoric pillar of quartz (NM), can be seen ½m NNW near the Derry road – in Cregg. To the SE of the village the Sperrin Mountains culminate in 2,240ft Sawel, over which lies the Tyrone and Derry county boundary.

CLEAR ISLAND, *Cléire,* Cork   **27 V 92**
Clear Island measures about 3m square and is separated from the little mainland port of Baltimore by Sherkin Island. About 4m SW is Fastnet Rock, the most southerly point of Ireland and a rounding point for one of the toughest sailing races held in these waters. There are many early-Christian monuments on the island, including the remains of St Ciaran's Church (NM), situated near North Harbour. St Ciaran is said to have been born on the island. Near by is a cross pillar (NM). Within the remains of a promontory fort on the NW coast are the ruins of an O Driscoll fort.

*CLIFDEN, *An Clochán:*
the Stepping Stones, Galway   **14 L 65**
One of the most popular and attractive market towns in Ireland, Clifden is set at the head of the N arm of Clifden Bay and in front of the tremendous Twelve Bens – or Pins – mountains. The range offers days of walking and climbing, and all roads out of Clifden afford superb views of some of the loveliest scenery in the country. To the SW a road skirts the bay and leads to the entrance of the now derelict Clifden Castle, which was built in 1815 by the d'Arcy family. During August or September the town is the venue for the well-known Connemara Pony Show. The Protestant church contains a silver copy of the Cross of Cong. John Alcock and Arthur Whitten Brown crash-landed 5m SW in Derrygimlagh Bog after their historic W to E Atlantic flight in 1919. This feat is commemorated by a cairn close to the landing place at the edge of the bog, and a monument on high ground about 1½m away. Below the town the Owenglin River falls steeply over heavy boulders to form the Owenglin cascade.

CLOGHAN, *An Clochán:*
the Stepping Stones, Offaly   **17 N 01**
On the Shannonbridge road NW of this village is the well-preserved keep and bawn of Clonony Castle. A ruined church marks the site of an early monastery 1½m W of the castle.

CLOGHEEN, *An Cloichín:*
the Little Stone, Tipperary   **23 S 01**
Clogheen is a small market town situated in the foothills of the Knockmealdown Mountains. Anglo-Norman Castle Grace lies 2m E near the River Tar and probably dates from the 13thc. It is a quadrangular structure with a tower at each angle, one of the towers being square in shape and the others circular. An erratic road to the S ascends through hairpin bends to the 1,114ft Gap in the Knockmealdowns. To the W of this is 2,153ft Knockshanahullion, and 2,609ft Knockmealdown dominates the range a little to the SE. The view from this, the highest peak in the range, takes in the fertile Plain of Tipperary backed by the lofty Galtees, with Slievenamon to the NE and the Comeraghs to the E. Sugar Loaf Hill is where Samuel Grubb, one-time owner of the Castle Grace, chose to be buried in an upright position. The place is now known as Grubb's Grave. After descending from the gap the road divides, with one branch leading to Lismore and the other to Cappoquin. Both of these routes afford splendid views.

CLOGHER, *Clochar:* Stony Place, Tyrone   **12 H 55**
Sited 2m W of Augher, this village was the original cathedral town of the diocese in which St Macartan was first bishop. This saint was a disciple of St Patrick. The first Protestant bishop here was Myler Macgrath the pluralist, who held the see of Clogher and other bishoprics after his appointment as Archbishop of Cashel by Queen Elizabeth I. The present CI cathedral occupies the site of an ancient monastery, the only remains of which are two 9th or 10th-c

high crosses. Both of these have been reconstructed, and a small cruciform-incised pillar stands close by. The present cathedral building was rebuilt in the early 18thc and reconstructed in the classical manner in 1818.

Also of interest in the area is Park House, which is also known as the Old Palace and dates from c1800. William Carlton the novelist was born at nearby Prolusk in 1794. About 2½m away is the Daisy Hill demesne, which boasts one of the two stone 'chairs' found on Ashban Mountain, and the Findermore Abbey Stone (NM) – a cross-incised pillar. There are a considerable number of prehistoric monuments in the vicinity, and Fardross Forest lies SW.

CLONAKILTY, *Cloich na Coillte:*
Stone of the Woods, Cork   **27 W34**
Founded in 1614 by the 1st Earl of Cork, this small market town is strategically sited on an arm of the sea which is almost landlocked to the S by the Inchydoney Peninsula. The latter is low lying and sandy, and is connected to the mainland by two causeways. At low tide the broad, sandy beach of Main Strand becomes enormous and seems to cover the whole bay. The town itself is the centre of a strong agricultural community which works the fertile local countryside. At Templebryan, 1½m N of the town, is the enclosed site of an ancient church which has a souterrain, holy well, and pillar stone. A stone circle SE of the church comprises five stones encircling a central white stone.

CLONARD, Cluain Ioraird:
Iorard's Pasture, Meath   **18 N64**
During the early ages of the Irish church Clonard was the centre of a strong monastic complex with a splendid college which attracted thousands of students from all over Europe. Notable names amongst the scholars here were St Columba, St Brendan, and St Ciaran. St Finnian held a seat here as bishop of the diocese. Today there is nothing left of the abbey, churches, chapels, and round towers which were so much a feature of this remarkable place little more than a century ago. The modern CI church in Clonard houses a 15th-c font made of grey marble and displaying biblical scenes on the external panels. It is thought that this may be a relic of the abbey. A nearby mound may have served a sepulchral function. Remains of a structure that may have once been a motte and bailey can be seen to the NW.

CLONDALKIN, *Cluain Dolcáin:*
Dolcán's Pasture, Dublin   **19 O03**
A modern industrial complex a little to the W of Dublin has this little old-world village at its heart. Preserved here is a round tower from the ancient monastery founded by St Cronan. This tower (NM) rises to 84ft, still retains its conical cap, and features a plinth and outside stair which are probably original. Opposite this fine specimen is a graveyard which preserves two granite crosses (the larger is NM), a granite baptismal font, and the remains of a medieval church which was largely destroyed by a gunpowder explosion in a nearby mill in 1787. Tully's Castle (NM) – remains of a narrow 16th-c tower at the end of the town – displays crenellations and incorporates a lean-to building of later date.

CLONES, *Cluain Eois:*
the Pasture of Eos, Monaghan   **12 H52**
Clones grew from a monastery which was founded here by St Tighearnach in the 6thc, and extensive remains of this complex have survived to the present day. The Market Place includes an interesting high cross (NM) which displays biblical scenes, and the 'Abbey' in Abbey Street is a ruined 12th-c nave-and-chancel church. Also of interest is a 75ft round tower (NM) featuring a square-headed door and windows. The two graveyards in which the ruined church and round tower stand contain a number of highly individualistic gravestones. Near the round tower is St Tighearnach's Shrine, a house-shaped structure with finials, which has been carved from a single stone. On the NW side of the town is a motte-and-bailey structure with well-defined concentric earthworks.

CLONFERT, *Cluain Fearta:*
the Pasture of the Grave, Galway
16 M92
Remains of this ancient ecclesiastical settlement lie 2m W of the River Shannon. The monastery was founded by St Brendan the Navigator in 563, and the earliest portions of the partly-ruined CI church date back to the 12thc. The church doorway is a superb example of Irish Romanesque art and has six receding planes which are decorated with a profusion of heads, foliage, and abstract designs. The triangular pediment above the door gives it its unique appearance. Within this are five arcades from which sculpted heads peer, and above the arcades is a series of ten receding triangles within which are more sculpted heads. The chancel's east windows are fine examples of late-Romanesque work, and the 15th-c chancel arch is decorated with angels, rosettes, and a mermaid carrying a mirror. Arches supporting the tower at the west end of the building were also decorated during this period, and the sacristy is contemporary. Clonfert's Catholic church houses an interesting late 13th-c wooden statue of the Madonna and Child. Near by beside the road is a 16th-c tower house.

CLONKEEN, Limerick   **22 R65**
Little Clonkeen Church (NM), ¾m E of Barringtonsbridge, features antae and a well-preserved Romanesque doorway which – despite its simplicity – may be assigned a late date, probably mid 12thc. An ancient round-headed window can be seen in the north wall.

CLONMACNOISE, *Cluain Mhic Nóis:*
the Pasture of the Descendants of Noas, Offaly   **17 N03**
Situated S of Athlone and N of Shannon Bridge, Clonmacnoise lies on the pastoral E bank of the River Shannon. One of the most important and interesting of Ireland's monastic sites, all of its priceless treasures are now in state care. Although it is best visited by boat from Athlone, a number of quiet roads eventually lead here from Birr and other main centres.

Some time between 545 and 549 St Ciaran abandoned his cell on Hare Island in Lough Ree and came here in search of peace. A local prince named Diarmaid helped him build the first outlines of his new church, and generously endowed the monastery after being elected High King. Although the saint lived only about 7 months after the initial foundation, his settlement grew to become one of the most important monastic foundations in the country. Because of this it attracted a great deal of undesirable attention, and the Vikings plundered its riches six times and burnt it 26 times between 834 and 1012. In 844 the Viking King Turgesius, who was bitterly opposed to Christianity, had his wife pronounce pagan oracles from the high altar.

Clonmacnoise was patronized by the greatest in the land, many of whom lie buried here. As a centre of learning it was unsurpassed, and many manuscripts were produced here. Two of the more famous of these are the 11th-c *Annals of Tighearnach* and the 12th-c *Book of the Dun Cow*. The history of harassment was continued by the Normans, who attacked the foundation in 1179, and it was plundered often over the next 400 years. In 1552 the English garrison from Athlone dealt the death blow by removing all that was in any way transportable, including the window glass. From this supreme act of vandalism there was no hope of recovery.

A great number of early-Christian grave slabs have been re-erected along the wall inside the enclosure, and have been grouped to show the various types of graves used from about the 8thc to the 11th or 12thc. This vast collection of Christian memorials – over 400 in number – is arguably Clonmacnoise's greatest treasure. At the end of this astonishing gallery is a round tower which is said to have been built by Fergal O Rourke in the 10thc. It was partially restored in 1135 after having been struck by lightning. In front of the cathedral is the famous Flann's High Cross, also known as the Cross of the Scriptures, which dates from the early half of the 10thc. It includes depictions of the Last Judgement and the Crucifixion, and a scene which is interpreted as St Ciaran and King Diarmaid erecting the original wooden church. Various unidentified figures can be seen amongst the carvings on the east face, and the base is adorned with animal figures. The South Cross lies to the S of this high cross and features a Crucifixion plus panels of interlacing interspersed with animal representations. This is of 9th-c origin, and it is thought that the shaft of a cross to the N of the cathedral may date from the same period.

Features of the cathedral itself include antae and parts of a Romanesque doorway which was replaced in the 15thc. At one time – probably during the 15thc – the chancel was divided into three chapels. The fine doorway, displaying figures of saints Francis, Patrick, and Dominic, was incorporated in 1460. Two churches lie S of the cathedral. The W church is divided into two, and the west half of the building is known as Teampull Doolin. Prior to its restoration by Edmund Dowling in 1689 it had antae and a round-headed east window; Dowling inserted a new door. Teampull Hurpan was added to the east part of Teampull Doolin during the 17thc. Teampull Ri, or Teampull Melaghlin, is a fine 12th-c church to the E of the dual building in the W. It features fine lancet windows, a gallery at the west end, and a possibly 16th-c south door. To the N of Teampull Ri is tiny ruined Teampull Kieran, reputedly the burial place of St Ciaran. Early in the 19thc various finds were made here, including the superb crozier of the Abbots of Clonmacnoise – now in the National Museum, Dublin. Near by is Teampull Kelly, of 12th-c date. Farther down the slope is Teampull Conor, an 11th-c building said to have been endowed with lands by Cathal O Conor. Both the west doorway and south window are original, but the building is locked. It is occasionally used for services by the Church of Ireland. Teampull Finghin is a fine nave-and-chancel church which lies NE at the edge of the cemetery. It shows traces of a Romanesque south doorway, and a small round tower is incorporated in the structure of the building beside the fine Romanesque chancel arch.

An 11th-c stone-lined causeway which leads E from the cathedral passes through the east gate of the cemetery to join an unsurfaced road. About 300yds along this road, and over a stile on the right, is the Nun's Church of 1167. This beautiful ruin, typically Romanesque in its construction, has a decorative doorway and chancel arch. The doorway displays four orders and includes capitals adorned with carvings of terrifying beasts, while the heavily-decorated chancel arch is of three orders and displays heads and interlacings. In 1170 Dervorgilla (who, because she was abducted from her husband by Dermot McMurrough was the immediate cause of the Norman invasion), retired here in penance. The church was restored in 1867. A field to the N of the local carpark contains a Norman castle which was built c1212. These remains include a gateway, courtyard, and tower.

*CLONMEL, *Cluain Meala*:
Pasture of Honey, Tipperary   **23 S22**

1 Church of SS Peter & Paul (RC)
2 Courthouse
3 Franciscan Church
4 Main Guard
5 Municipal Library, Museum, & Art Gallery
6 St Mary's Church (CI)
7 St Mary's Church (RC)
8 Town Hall
9 Town Walls
10 West Gate

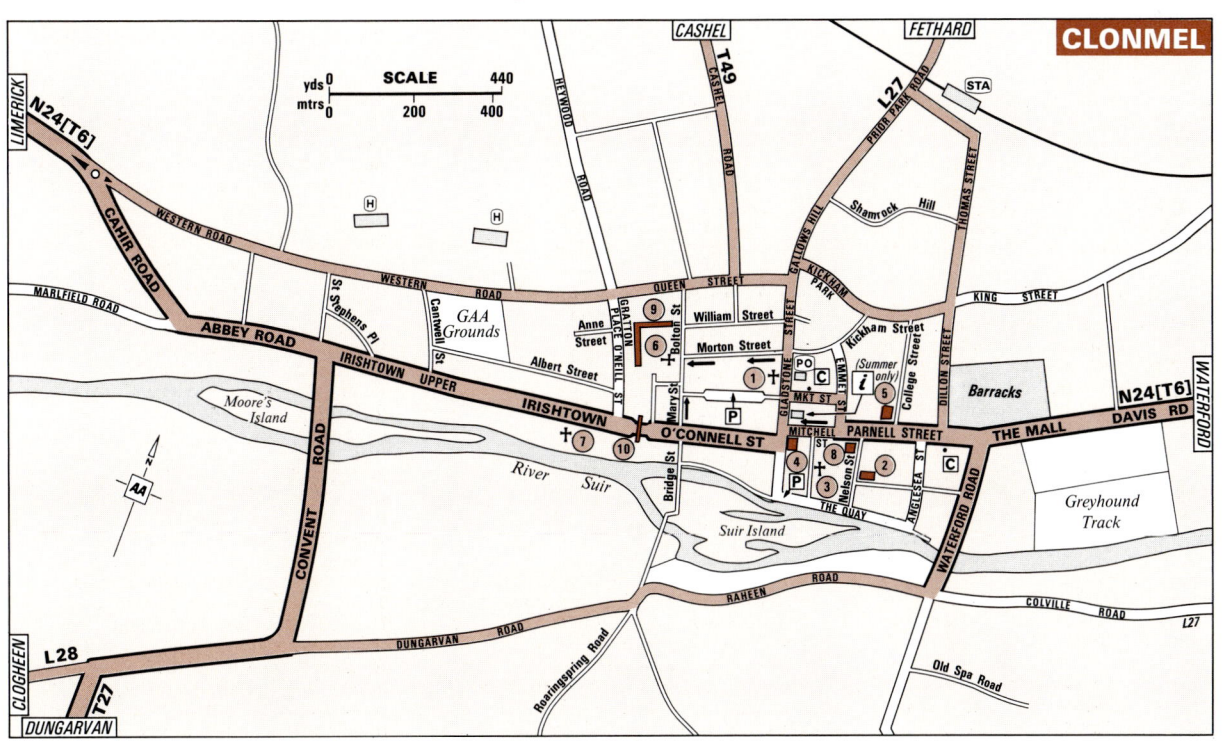

Principal centre of S Tipperary, Clonmel is a market town which is also concerned with industries such as cider making and the manufacture of footwear and perambulators. Its splendid situation on the banks of the River Suir allows easy access to superb scenery upstream towards Cahir and downstream in the direction of Carrick. The Comeragh Mountains rise in the distance, and the Knockmealdown range can be seen in the SW.

The town still retains portions of its originally 14th-c walls – including the West Gate, which was completely rebuilt in 1831, and three square towers on the N and W sides of St Mary's graveyard. A Georgian house behind railings W of the West Gate once housed a grammar school and was attended by George Borrow in 1815. Borrow is famous for his books *Wild Wales* and *Lavengro*. He first learnt Irish here, and his passion for the language continued until he died. At the far end of Abbey Street, beyond the Main Guard (said to have been built to a design by Wren), is a 19th-c Franciscan church which has a 15th-c tower and a 13th-c choir wall; the church contains a carved Butler tomb of 15th-c origin. The CI St Mary's Church of 1857 incorporates parts of a 13th-c church which was rebuilt in the 15thc, and the mid 19th-c RC St Mary's displays a classical facade. Inside the latter building is a fine stucco ceiling. The courthouse was designed by Sir Richard Morrison and built in 1800.

Inside the recent town hall is the Corporation regalia, including a gold chain to which each mayor contributes a link. The 19th-c Church of SS Peter and Paul (RC), in Gladstone Street, is the largest non-cathedral Catholic parish church in the diocese.

One of the town's historical focal points was the establishment of a passenger transport system between towns by Charles Bianconi. The network grew to cover most of S Ireland and used horse-drawn cars which carried people at a rate of somewhere around 2d per mile. Italian-born Bianconi arrived at Clonmel as a picture framer, became rich, and was eventually elected mayor. His transport system survived until the introduction of the railways. Another famous man from this town was Laurence Sterne, author of *Tristram Shandy*, who was born here in 1713. Recreations offered by the town include greyhound and horse racing, fishing in the local waters, and pony trekking in the surrounding countryside. The Municipal Library, Museum, and Art Gallery are in Parnell Street. The area is famous as a racehorse-breeding centre. The huge bulk of Slievenamon rises to 2,368ft 7m NE, and tradition has it that the legendary Finn MacCool watched while Irish girls raced to the mountain's summit to win him for a husband. Graine, daughter of the Irish King Cormac, proved to be the winner; the name of the mountain means 'Mountain of the Women'.

CLONTARF, *Cluain Tarbh*:
Pasture of Bulls, Dublin   **19 O13**
The name of this prosperous Dublin suburb means 'Pasture of the Bulls', and a nearby tract of land known as North Bull now serves as a nature reserve for birds. The community itself is situated on the inner N shore of Dublin Bay and was the site where Brian Boru defeated Norse marauders in 1014. Of all the buildings here the most notable is the Marino Casino (NM), which was designed for Lord Charlemont by William Chambers between 1765 and 1771 in what was then the Marino Estate. This charming little building is in the classical style and is considered

Entries marked * are the starting point of drives included in the Day Drive section of the book (pages 79 to 144).

one of the finest examples of 18th-c architecture in the British Isles. It is exquisitely decorated. The corner corinthian columns were made to function as drain pipes, and the chimneys were designed as roof urns so that the classical symmetry would not be marred by 'extras'.

CLONTUSKERT ABBEY, Galway **16 M82**
See Laurencetown entry.

CLOUGHEY, *Clochaigh:*
Stony Place, Down **13 J65**
This pleasant resort has a good strand and is close to the early 17th-c Kirkistown Castle of the Savage family. Circular towers defend the castle's south wall, and the square keep and bawn have survived. A nearby airstrip is occasionally the venue for motor racing.

CLOYNE, *Cluain:* Pasture, Cork **28 W96**
St Colman founded a monastery here in the 6thc which was destroyed many times by the Vikings. In the 12thc it became the seat of a bishopric. The 86ft round tower, perhaps of 9th-c date, survives from the early monastery. It is of the usual design, but lost its cap in a thunderstorm in the 18thc. Also surviving from the early monastery is the building known as the Fire House, which stands in the cathedral churchyard. Nothing much is known about it, but it was probably an oratory. The name, according to folklore, comes from the fact that a flame was kept constantly alight within it.

The cathedral itself is based upon a building of c1270. Of interest within the church are the carvings round the north door, the Fitzgerald family tomb of 1612, the monument to the astronomer John Brinkley, and the fine monument by Bruce Joy of the illustrious philosopher George Berkeley. Berkeley was Bishop of Cloyne from 1734 to 1753, and he lived in now-ruined Cloyne House.

COBH, *An Cóbh:* the Cove, Cork **28 W86**
Several interesting geological features combine to form Cobh's fine harbour, which was once a port of call for transatlantic liners. Three parallel slate ridges run respectively N of Cork city, through Great Island (on which Cobh stands), and across the mouth of the harbour. Limestone troughs between these ridges have been eroded by the solvent action of river water, thereby creating long E to W strips of water to the N of Great Island and a main harbour to the S. River-cut passages across the width of the ridges join the two main stretches of water at Great Island, and a 1m-wide opening in the S ridge leads to the sea. Views S from the hill above Cobh take in the land-locked harbour, with the naval depot of Haulbowline Island and the Islands of Rocky and Spike in the foreground.

The town itself boasts a fine 19th-c cathedral (RC) which is dedicated to St Colman and has a 47-bell carillon – the largest in these islands. An adjacent Diocesan Museum displays an interesting collection of ecclesiastical antiquities. Boats for sea fishing can be hired from the harbour, and the shore at Cobh offers excellent sea bathing. An old churchyard at Clonmel on the outskirts of the town contains the grave of Charles Wolfe, writer of *The Burial of Sir John Moore.* Also buried in the churchyard are many victims of the Lusitania disaster; they are commemorated by a memorial on the Quay.

COLEBROOKE, Fermanagh **11 H44**
See Brookeborough entry.

*COLERAINE, *Cúil Raithin:*
Fern Recess, Derry **6 C83**
A Plantation town built on land granted to the London Company by James I of England, this industrial and seafaring community on the River Bann is the seat of N Ireland's second university. The CI Jacobean parish church has been rebuilt and modified, but the unchanged town hall of 1859 displays a restrained Italianate style in warm sandstone. Other interesting 19th-c buildings here include the Methodist Church of 1854 by Isaac Farrell, which takes the form of a Roman corinthian temple; Charles Lanyon's railway station of 1855, a single-storey stucco building with round-headed windows and a five-bay arcaded porch; the gothick RC St John's Church of 1834; and the University College. A large rath known as Mount Sandel Fort lies about 1m S of the town.

COLLOONEY, *Cúil Mhuine:*
the Recess of the Thicket, Sligo **10 G62**
Close to this small town, which lies 7m from Sligo, the Owenmore River combines with the Unshin from Lough Arrow and forces its way through Collooney Gap between the E spurs of the Ox Mountains and Slieve Daeane. A monument here commemorates Captain Teeling, a hero of a skirmish between Militia and French forces in 1798. The fine Georgian mansion of Markree Castle overlooks the River Unshin and displays modifications carried out by Francis Johnston in 1801, including castellations. Some 2m SW beside the Owenmore River is the lovely Annaghmore demesne, which includes fine gardens filled with exotic trees and shrubs. The O Haras, one of this region's notable families, have lived here since the middle ages. Cormac O Hara was a patron of the celebrated poet Tadhg Dall O Huiginn in the 16thc.

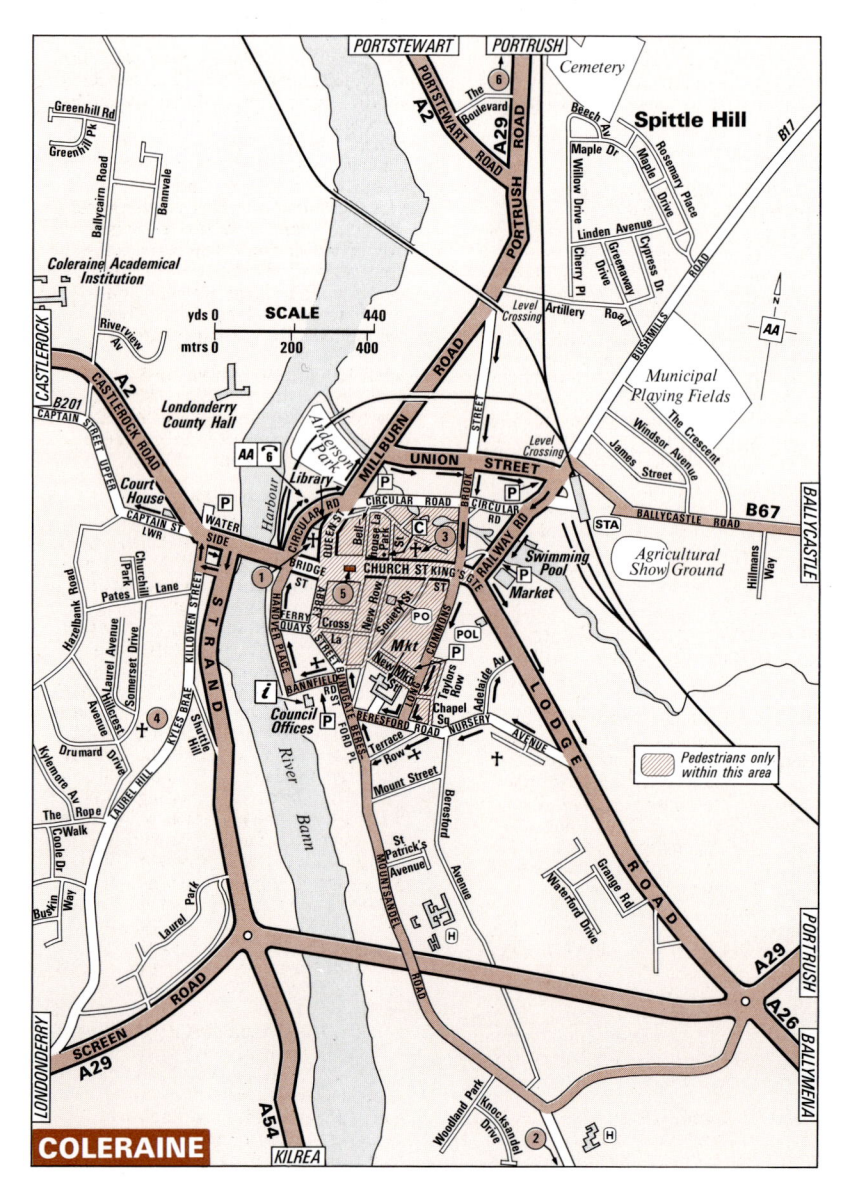

1 Methodist Church
2 Mount Sandel Fort
3 Parish Church (CI)
4 St John's Church (RC)
5 Town Hall
6 University College of Ulster

COMBER, *An Comar:*
the Confluence, Down **13 J46**
Grouped around a pleasant square, this village stands near the NW corner of Strangford Lough and is concerned with the linen trade. The CI church was built c1610 but has since been greatly altered. Its site was once occupied by an ancient abbey that was founded in the 13thc. A monument to Sir Robert R Gillespie, a native of the town associated with Nepal, stands in the Market Square.

COMERAGH MOUNTAINS, THE,
Waterford **23 S21**
See Kilmacthomas entry.

CONG, *Conga:* Isthmus, Mayo **15 M15**
This Galway-border village is well known for its fishing and shooting prospects, and has a strong monastic tradition. Ashford Castle was once the home of the Guinness family and now serves as a hotel. This vast and imposing building was constructed by J H Fuller around an earlier tower house and mansion in 1870. To the W of Cong is the picturesque district known as Joyce's Country. Derived from Joyce of Wales, this name refers to a family in which the men were of much greater than average stature; they are said to have settled in Galway during the 13thc, and the name is still found in the district.

Both the walker and archaeologist will find a great deal to interest them here. A number of marvellous caves near the village include Poll na gColm and Kelly's (NM, with some traces of prehistoric occupation). Because of the nature of the local limestone countryside, many of the rivers that feed Loughs Mask and Corrib are underground for much of their courses. Many years ago, government engineers started to build a canal to allow navigation between Galway and Ballinrobe, but as soon as it was flooded the water just disappeared through the porous rock at the bottom. Poll na gColm is the most accessible of a number of caves in which there is a steep rise and fall of water.

Cong Abbey (NM) occupies the site of a 6th-c abbey which was founded by St Fechin of Fore. The only remainder of this early foundation is a bullaun (or mortar) at the SE end of the village. The market cross is constructed upon the base of a medieval cross. The present abbey ruins are basically of an Augustinian abbey founded by King Turloch O Conor in the 12thc. The magnificent north door was reconstructed from an original doorway during the restoration of 1860, which was carried out by Peter Foy for the Guinness family. Very fine sculpture can be seen in this doorway. The cloister, which was erected c1200, has been reconstructed and contains several capitals also carved by Foy. A fine transitional doorway of the same period can be seen beside the cloister. This leads to the Chapter House, which features some very fine windows plus decorated stone work which is possibly the finest of its type in the W of Ireland. In the grounds is an island upon which stands the ancient Monks Fishing House.

The famous Processional Cross of Cong, now preserved in the National Museum, Dublin, is an oaken object covered with bronze plates and decorated with beautiful zoomorphic ornamentation in gilt and bronze. The large crystal in the centre probably covered the holy relic, a splinter of the True Cross, and the shaft and arms carry thirteen jewels. Both sides of the 2½ft cross display Latin and Irish inscriptions. Of the large number of ancient remains near Cong, space permits mention of only a few: four stone circles (NM) stand 1¼m NE in Glebe Townland; N of this are the ruins of a 15th-c castle (NM); and E of Cong is Ballymacgibbon passage grave (NM).

CONNA, *Conaithe,* Cork **28 W99**
During the 16thc a Fitzgerald earl built the notable towered castle which stands in this River Bride village. James Fitzgerald, known as the 'Sugan' earl, was born here.

CONNEMARA, *Conamara:*
the Conmaicne Tribe of the Sea, Galway
14 L75
Considered one of the most unspoilt and spectacular regions in Ireland, Connemara is dominated by the Twelve Bens (or Pins) range and the Maamturk Mountains. Views afforded by the peaks of the latter take in striking landscapes of lake, moorland, and coastal water. Several beautiful and very deep lakes in the region include Derryclare, Lough Inagh, Kylemore Lough, and Lough Nafooey, all of which offer excellent fishing, bird watching, and boating. Much of the area resembles the hilly limestone of the Burren, but as far as antiquities are concerned the similarity ends here. There are relatively few ancient sites in Connemara.

CONNOR PASS, *An Chonair:*
the Path, Kerry **27 Q50**
This mountain pass crosses the Dingle Peninsula from Dingle to the bays of Brandon and Tralee. Its rapid climb between 2,050ft Ballysitteragh and 2,026ft Slievanea culminates in a 1,354ft summit, which affords marvellous views and makes this road one of the highest in the country. Several small loughs can be seen far below to the N, and even farther N is the impressive bulk of Brandon Mountain. Tiny, rock-encircled Lough Doon occupies a corrie above the pass on the E side of the road. The descent from the road summit leads NE and runs above the valley of the Owenmore River as it makes its way towards the shores of Brandon Bay.

***COOKSTOWN,** *An Chorr Chríochach:*
the Boundary Hill, Tyrone **6 H87**
Situated on the Dungannon to Maghera road W of Lough Neagh, this market town is a good base from which to explore the interesting Sperrin Mountains. This range is particularly rich in megalithic remains. The town itself, which has an exceptionally long main street, was laid out and built by an early 17th-c planter named Alan Cook, but it owes much of its present aspect to the Stewart family. Amongst its finest buildings are two attractive 18th-c houses. The Stewarts lived in the fine mansion of Killymoon, which lies to the SE on the N bank of the Ballinderry River and was designed by John Nash in 1803. Nash also built Lissan Rectory, an Italianate villa situated some 2m NNE. An 18th-c, water-powered beetling mill (NT) survives 3m W at Wellbrook.

COOLEY, *Cuaille,* Donegal **6 C53**
An interesting graveyard at Cooley, which lies about 2m NW of Moville, is well known for its extensive archaeological remains. These include an ancient ruined church, an unusual stone cross, and a small structure known as the Skull House. Sparse remains of the church occupy a site on which St Patrick is traditionally held to have founded an earlier place of worship. The monolithic cross stands outside the graveyard entrance and is a slender, 10ft-high monument of ancient origin. Although undecorated by the usual carvings, it displays a perforated ring and includes a hole through the upper portion of the shaft. The Skull House is a curious form of tomb associated with one of Ireland's many saints. Also of interest in the area are a number of souterrains and a sweat house at Leckeny – used as a type of Turkish bath in ancient times. Numerous ringforts, standing stones, and megalithic-tomb remains can be seen in the area.

COOLEY PENINSULA, *Cuailgne,*
Louth **13 J20**
Incorporating the Cooley Mountains, from which Slieve Foye rises to 1,935ft, this peninsula forms a barrier which divides Dundalk Bay from Carlingford Lough. Riverstown is sited near Giles Quay on the S shore and boasts the most successful of five government-established factories concerned with the manufacture of industrial alcohol from potatoes.

The peninsula is closely linked with the Irish epic known as *The Tain,* in which Queen Maeve plunges Connacht and her allies into war with Ulster in an attempt to steal the great Brown Bull of Cooley. The hero of the tale is legendary Cuchullain, the Hound of Ulster, who resisted Maeve's armies single handed while the warriors of Ulster lay in a bewitched sickness. This story is the central part of the 8th-c Ulster heroic cycle, and a number of the locations mentioned in the legends have been associated with this part of Louth.

COOLHULL CASTLE, Wexford **24 S80**
Built during the late 16thc, this long, low, two-storey building situated 2m WNW of Duncormick is in an excellent state of preservation.

COOTEHILL, *Muinchille:*
Sleeve, Cavan **12 H61**
The Coote family founded this prosperous town, which lies between the Annagh River and its tributary the Dromore, after gaining possession of confiscated O Reilly lands in the 17thc. Part of the acquired ground N of the town was known as Bellamont Forest, and the house of Bellamont is considered one of the finest Palladian structures in Ireland. It was designed by Sir Edward Lovett Pearce for Thomas Coote, who was his uncle by marriage, in 1729 or 1730. Built of red brick and boasting a fine doric portico, the house has suffered very little change during its history and contains attractive rooms with coffered-plasterwork ceilings. The top-floor bedrooms open from the earliest lanterned lobby in Ireland. Extensive lake-watered and wooded grounds surround the house, which is connected to its detached stable block by an underground passage. In an area dotted with prehistoric remains, Cohaw dual-court grave may be singled out for description. The cairn of this monument (NM) is 85ft long, with forecourts at each end leading into two pairs of chambers. A fifth chamber was constructed between the end-stones of

each gallery. The remains of two young people were found in one of the chambers.

COPELAND ISLANDS, THE,
Down 7J58
This group of off-shore islands is situated at the entrance to Belfast Lough and comprises Copeland, Lighthouse, and Mew islands. So-called Lighthouse Island (NT) has a bird observatory. Boat trips to the group leave from Bangor and Donaghadee.

COPPINGER'S COURT, *Cúirt Choipineár*,
Cork 27W23
A ruined, four-storey Jacobean building 1½m NW of Rosscarbery, this semi-fortified mansion includes two projecting wings with machicolations for defence. Surviving features include lovely mullioned windows, tall gables, well-preserved turrets, and elongated chimneys.

CORCAGUINEY PENINSULA,
Kerry 20 & 26Q40
See Dingle Peninsula entry.

CORCOMROE ABBEY, *Corca Mrua*:
the Sept of Mrua, Clare 15M30
Founded c1180 by either the King of Thomond or his son and namesake Donal O Brien, the remains of this Cistercian abbey (NM) date from the 14th or 15thc. The church was originally a cruciform-shaped building without a tower, and the present inadequate tower was inserted between the choir and nave during the 15thc. The excellent masonry features delicate floral ornamentation, and inside the building are the stylized figure of an abbot and a recumbent effigy of Conor O Brien. Remains of other buildings on the site are scanty. Nearby Oughtmama boasts three ancient churches (NM), the largest of which features a flat-headed doorway and plain Romanesque arch. Inside is an interesting stoup carved with representations of two stags with interlaced antlers. The second-largest church has a round-headed doorway and a good window, but the last building is fragmentary.

*CORK, *Corcaigh*: Marsh, Cork 28W67
This city stands on the River Lee on the S coast of Ireland and is the second largest city in the Republic of Ireland. The river flows through the city in two channels, both of which are spanned by numerous bridges, and the name 'Cork' – meaning marsh – presumably refers to the state of the immediate area in ancient times. During the 18thc ocean-going vessels docked in the deep waters over which Patrick Street and Grand Parade are now built. Today the city is still an important sea port, but it also receives air traffic and is a centre for commerce and industry. On the ecclesiastical and academic side, it is the cathedral city of both Protestant and RC dioceses, and the seat of a constituent college of the National University of Ireland. Cork is admirably situated as a touring base.

The city's turbulent history starts with the foundation of a monastery by St Finbarr in the 6th or early 7thc. The saint, who died c630, sited his ecclesiastical complex on a small island surrounded by swampland. Part of a round tower that existed until the foundations of the present CI St Finbarr's Cathedral were laid suggests that this church occupies the old monastic site. Probably commenced as a small hermitage, the monastery rapidly grew into an extensive and wealthy foundation which attracted scholars and the not so welcome attentions of Norsemen. They often came to plunder, but civilization had a calming influence and they eventually realized that trade was more profitable than destruction of the source of the riches. It was these sea-bandits who laid down a basis for the strong tradition of commerce on which the city still flourishes.

The Desmond chieftain Dermot MacCarthy was in possession of Cork when Henry II arrived in Ireland in 1172. He submitted to the English forces, who threw him and his followers out and strongly fortified the city against possible reprisals. A long and deadly struggle for possession which then ensued continued well into Tudor and Stuart times, and more often than not Cork was on the losing side. This tradition of ignominious defeat continued when it stood up for Charles I and was quickly taken by Cromwell.

Because of all this trouble there is scarcely a fragment of the medieval city extant, and nothing at all from the 16th or 17thc. The 18thc produced a few good Georgian houses but there was nothing of really great merit here until the arrival of James and George Richard Pain – both pupils of the famous John Nash – c1818. This duo was sent to Ireland to supervise the erection of several country houses on which Nash himself was working. George stayed in Cork on completion of his work and greatly improved the local architecture. William Burgess designed 19th-c St Finbarr's Cathedral (CI) in the fashionable French-gothick style. Striking features of the building include the west front and its three recessed doors, its elaborate carving, its beautiful rose window, and the graceful twin spires that complete and compliment its design. The rose window on the west front is just one example of the many and varied stained-glass works displayed by the cathedral. A fine Bishop's Throne which is supported by a plinth of the red marble quarried in Co Cork carries the carved profiles of 20 past bishops on three of its sides. A cannon ball fired in the siege of 1690 and found embedded in a wall of the old cathedral tower is mounted on display in the south transept. Italian artists working in Paris executed the choir's mosaic pavement, and the 22-bay sanctuary roof displays decorations specified by Burgess as a memorial to the 20th-c Bishop Dowse. A painting of Christ in Glory, seated on a throne and surrounded by angels, occupies the apex of the roof. Mrs Aldworth, said to have been the only female Freemason ever, lies in a grave marked by a tablet inside the cathedral. The graveyard includes a tombstone marked Henry Murrough over the grave of 19th-c painter Samuel Forde.

About ½m W of the cathedral is University College Cork, which was founded in 1845 and occupies a fine, Tudor-style building of Carboniferous limestone. At first the college was created as one of the Queen's Colleges, but the original buildings by the firm of Sir Thomas Deane I were never completed. These occupy three sides of a quadrangle overlooking the Lee Valley, on a site where 7th-c Gill Abbey once stood. The west wing was rebuilt after a fire in 1862 and the science laboratories were added later by Arthur Hill. Although recent development of the college facilities has entailed expansion over the site of the former County Gaol, the 19th-c classical gate by James and George Richard Pain has been preserved. Two of the college's main assets are a fine library and an important collection of ogham stones. A nearby Romanesque-style building contains the Honan Chapel and students residence, and features a miniature round tower at one end. The architect for this was James F McMullen, and the superb interior includes stained-glass windows by Sarah Purser and Harry Clarke. A statue of St Finbarr in the gable of the west doorway was executed by Oliver Sheppard, and an interesting pavement illustrates the story of the *Canticle of the Three Children in the Fiery Furnace*.

St Ann's CI church in Shandon, on the N side of the city, is chiefly known through the doggerel written about its bells by 19th-c Father Prout. The building was erected during the 18thc on the site of medieval St Mary's Church, which had been destroyed in the siege of 1690, and has a tower with graduated turrets. Two sides of the tower are faced with red sandstone and two with limestone. Inside are the famous eight bells, the sixth of which bears the inscription 'We were all cast at Gloucester in England, Abel Rudhall 1750'. Father Prout's grave can be seen near the tower.

St Mary's pro-Cathedral (RC) of 1808 stands N of Shandon and serves as a pro-cathedral of the Cork diocese. After fire damage in 1820 the interior was remodelled by George Richard Pain, and the tower dates from c1826. Noteworthy figures of 27 Apostles and saints and a bas-relief of 'The Last Supper' seen here were all based on engravings by John Hogan. About ½m N of St Mary's Cathedral is the Church of the Assumption, which features statues carved by the Cork sculptor Seamus Murphy. Some ¾m E of the cathedral, in Old Youghal Road, are interesting Collin's Barracks with their fine, three-light chapel window. This early 20th-c stained glass was the work of Evie Hone. St Finbarr's RC church stands on the S side of Cork and includes transepts that were added later than its 18th-c origins. A monument to Bishop Florence MacCarthy in the south transept was by Derry-born sculptor James Heffernan. The altar piece shows Hogan's Dead Christ, and The Crucifixion painting was by local artist John O Keefe. The RC Church of Christ the King at Turner's Cross is an interesting modern edifice by Chicago-born Barry Byrne. This elliptical building can hold 1,200 people and is entered via a great doorway designed by the American sculptor John Storrs. Other striking features of the structure include an imposing entrance tower and high altar.

Crawford Municipal School of Art and Art Gallery in Emmet Place are housed in a building which was based on the old, 13th-c custom house. Exhibits include Rodin bronzes, sculpture by John Hogan, and works by Irish artists. Included is a collection by Sir John Lavery. Washington Street boasts the fine court-house, which was erected in 1835 to a design by the brothers Pain. To the SE of this is the CI Church of the Holy

Trinity. Its site was occupied by the city's second medieval church until this was demolished in 1717, and the present building of 1720 was designed by Coltsman. The aisled crypt of the old structure has survived. In 1825 the building was modified and given a new west front by George Richard Pain. Many of Cork's leading families are buried here. A surviving remnant of the city's former Augustinian Abbey, Red Abbey Tower, was used as a vantage point by John Churchill, later to become the Duke of Marlborough, during the 1690 Siege of Cork.

cont overleaf

1 Bachelor's Quay
2 Church of Christ the King (RC)
3 Church of the Assumption
4 Church of the Holy Trinity (CI)
5 Collins Barracks
6 Cork Public Museum
7 Courthouse
8 Crawford Municipal School of Art & Art Gallery
9 Father Matthew Memorial Church (RC)
10 Father Matthew Statue
11 Gaol Gate
12 Mardyke
13 Marina
14 National Monument
15 Red Abbey Tower
16 St Ann's Church (CI), Shandon
17 St Finbarr's Cathedral (CI)
18 St Finbarr's Church (RC)
19 St Mary's Pro-Cathedral (RC)
20 University College, Cork

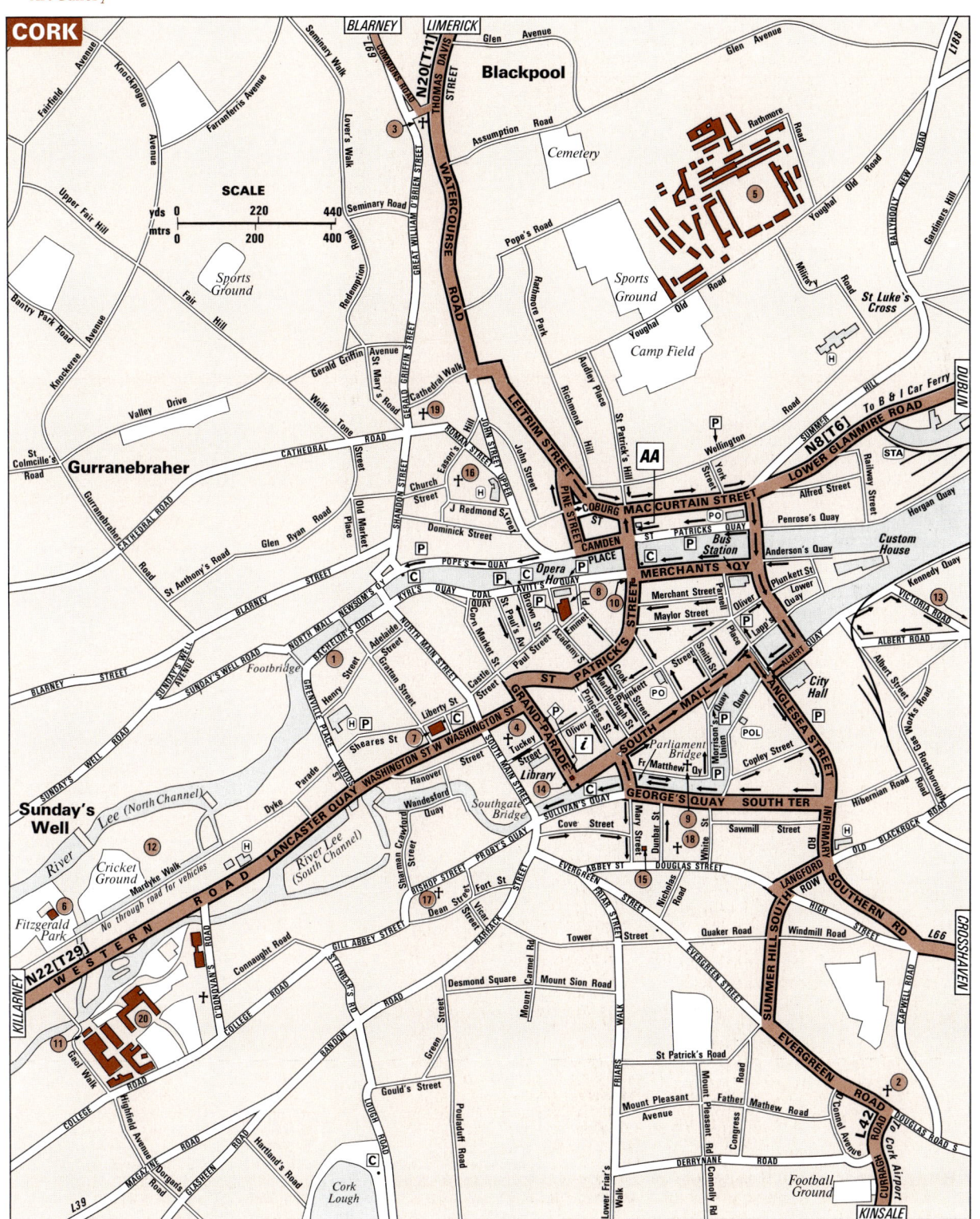

Cork Public Museum was presented to the people of the city by the Lord Mayor in 1945 and is housed in Fitzgerald Park. Exhibits include collections which illustrate the history and archaeology of the city, Cork glass and lace, locally-printed books, development of the coopering industry, and the growth of the Cork merchant banks. The main business area of the city is sited on an island between the N and S branches of the river, close to the 4m of quays which line both channels. Bachelor's Quay includes several fine Georgian Houses and there are two splendid promenades. The older of these lies to the W and is known as the Mardyke. This once-fashionable walking place was admired by Thackeray, but today it has been supplanted by the Marina on the E side of the city. This tree-lined walk affords views of the River Lee and the well-wooded suburbs on its far bank. Many other buildings in Cork are worthy of attention. Space prohibits detailed remarks here, but some of them are: the Catholic Church of SS Peter and Paul by Pugin; the 19th-c custom house; the 1953 Church of St Francis; the Catholic Church of St Paul in Lower Glanmire Road; the Old Market in Cornmarket Street; the 18th-c Mercy Hospital; and Elizabeth Fort, parts of which are 17thc. The National Monument, at the end of Grand Parade, was erected to 18th- and 19th-c Irish patriots.

During the 18th, 19th, and early 20thc Cork was the home of many famous men. Among these were George James Allman, 19th-c zoologist and botanist; James Barry, 18th- and 19th-c historical painter; Edward Dowden, 19th- and early 20th-c Shakespearian scholar; Dr Hincks, the 18th- and early 19th-c Egyptologist; and Dr Salmon, mathematician and divine of the 19th and early 19th c. Sir Walter Scott was presented with the freedom of the city in 1825. Next to O Connell, Theobald Matthew was the best-known Irish figure of the 19thc and is commemorated by both a church (the Capuchin Church of the Holy Trinity on Charlotte Quay) and a statue (the N end of St Patrick St). This zealous priest was generally unknown until his middle years, when he took up the unpopular cause of Temperance. Father Matthew's energy turned an idea into a crusade.

CRAIGAVON, Armagh 13 J05
Craigavon is the first New Town in Northern Ireland and is named after Viscount Craigavon, the first Prime-minister. It is set in well-wooded countryside to the S of vast Lough Neagh and encompasses the existing towns of Portadown, and Lurgan – already major communities in their own rights. The area's present population of 62,000 is expected to double to about 120,000 by 1981. The boundary of the new area will extend for approximately 10m from NE to SW, and in the N will come as far as the S shores of Lough Neagh. It is planned that the main areas of population and industry will be contained in a 3m-deep parallel zone. Great care is being taken to preserve the natural features of the landscape, and both factory and housing districts will include large areas of woodland and open space.

CRANFIELD, *Maigh Chreamhchoille:*
Plain of the Wood of Wild Garlic, Antrim 7 J08

A ruined church (NM) here dates from 1258, and a holy well in the village is still the object of pilgrimage. The village is situated $3\frac{1}{2}$m SW of Randalstown, on the N shore of Lough Neagh.

CRAWFORDSBURN, *Sruth Chráfard:*
Crawford's Stream, Down 7 J48
Close to Belfast and 1m from the sea, Crawfordsburn is sited at the head of the glen from which it takes its name and is considered by some to be one of the most attractive villages near the city. Its little thatched inn was a staging post during the 17thc. A country park to the N of the village comprises woodland, parkland, and foreshore, and includes a modern fort at Grey Point which was used during both world wars. The park, with its attractive bays and beaches, is within easy reach of half the population of N Ireland. Records show that one million visitors availed themselves of its amenities during 1973, and a considerable area is leased as camping ground to the Scouts' Association.

To the S is the Clandeboye Estate, seat of the Marquis of Dufferin and Ava, with its much-altered 17th-c house. Most of the changes made to the building were effected by the 1st Marquess during the 19thc. Helen's Tower stands at the S end of the demesne and was erected by the 1st Marquess in memory of his mother. Lord Dufferin's private chapel houses a cross which displays nimbus and rich interlaced carving, and originally belonged to Bangor Abbey.

CREESLOUGH, *An Craoslach:*
the Gullet, Donegal 5 C03
Creeslough village lies near an inlet of Sheep Haven and is a convenient centre from which to ascend 2,197ft Muckish. Favourite stopping places for tourists in this area are the Duntally Bridge and Waterfall, and mountain-shadowed Glen Lough. Doe Castle, once the chief stronghold of the MacSwiney family, perches on a low promontory which is defended on three sides by the sea and by an artificial ditch on the fourth. The powerful, 55ft-high keep is surrounded by a bawn protected by a high curtain wall carrying spaced round towers. Although the castle (NM) was modernized and occupied within living memory it still retains the essential features of its 15th-c origin. A graveyard which adjoins the castle contains a tombstone to the memory of the MacSwineys. Nearby Ards House is sited on a superbly-wooded peninsula and is occupied by the Capuchin order.

CREEVELEA, *An Chraobh Liath:*
the Grey Branch, Leitrim 10 G73
Considerable remains of a Franciscan friary (NM) founded by Margaret O Rourke in 1508 can be seen here, on the left bank of the Bonet River opposite Dromahair. Although the foundation was burnt down in 1536 it was later rebuilt, and the cloister arcades display some interesting carving.

CREEVYKEEL, *An Chraobhaigh Chaol:*
the Narrow Wooded Place, Sligo 10 G75
This little hamlet has lent its name to one of the most impressive of Irish prehistoric monuments. It lies immediately off the Sligo to Bundoran road, near Cliffony, and was excavated by the Harvard Archaeological Mission in 1935 (see gazetteer inset opposite).

CROAGH PATRICK, *Cruach Phádraigh:*
St Patrick's Mountain, Mayo 15 L98
Ireland's Holy Mountain, 2,510ft Croagh Patrick is a beautiful quartzite cone and ridge which rises steeply from the S shore of Clew Bay and affords striking views over the surrounding countryside. St Patrick is reputed to have spent 40 days fasting and praying on the summit c441. The tradition of pilgrimage to the summit still continues, and on the last Sunday in July – Garland Sunday – people from all over the country undertake the arduous climb, often in bare feet, to join in the prescribed religious patterns at the summit.

The first part of the climb from Murrisk is relatively easy, but the upper section over scree and the cone proper is extremely difficult – even with shoes on. A modern chapel now occupies the site of the old summit shrine. NE of the chapel is a heap of stones known as *Leaba Phadraigh*, or Patrick's Bed. Legend has it that the deep ravine known as Log na nDeamhan at the N base of the cove was where St Patrick rang his bell to rid Ireland of all venomous creatures. Lough na Corra, near the S base of the mountain, is said to have burst from the earth when St Patrick threw the demon Corra from the summit.

CROM CASTLE, Fermanagh 11 H32
See Newtown Butler entry.

CROOKEDWOOD, *Tigh Munna:*
Munna's House, Westmeath 17 N46
Set in woodland on the shores of Lough Derravaragh, this village lies about 1m W of 15th-c St Munna's Church (NM) of Taghmon (see entry). To the N of the village is the good viewpoint of 707ft Knockeyon. The lough is associated with the legend of the Children of Lir.

CROOKHAVEN, *An Cruachán:*
the Little Round Hill, Cork 26 V82
A safe anchorage protected from the fury of the Atlantic makes this remote village a popular meeting place for yachtsmen. The local coastline and peninsula divides into three separate forks respectively known as Brow Head, Mizen Head, and Three Castles Head, between which are Barley Cove – a beautiful sandy beach – and cliff-girdled Dunlough Bay. Brow Head carries a wireless station, and Mizen Head is known for the massive, sheer cliffs which officially form the extreme SW point of Ireland. Three Castles Head derives its name from three towers that have survived from an O Mahoney Stronghold. Dunmanus Bay bounds the peninsula to the N and terminates at Muntervary, or Sheep's Head, where there are more castle remains. The great O Malley chieftain Granuaile (or Grace) is associated with these parts. During her life of political and personal intrigue she was a sea captain, pirate, and rebel who faithfully followed her motto *Terra marique potens* – 'powerful on both land and sea'.

CROOKSTOWN, *An Baile Gallda:*
the English Town, Cork 27 W46
This village lies off the southern road from Cork to Macroom, near the head of the striking Bride Valley. A monument to the SW on the Dunmanway road, at Bealnablath, commemorates the death of General Michael Collins in an ambush here during 1922. To the SE near Templemartin are the remains of a large fort called Garranes, which incorporates

triple ramparts and is often referred to as Rath Raithleann (NM). It is said to have been the 6th-c birthplace of St Finbarr, whose father was a metal worker in the service of the ruling chief. Interesting remains discovered during excavation of the site are now on display in Cork University College Museum. These include a 7th-c bronze button, an unfinished brooch, objects of iron and glass, crucibles, and sherds of pottery. The ruins of Castlemore are 1¼m NE.

CROOM, *Cromadh:*
Crooked Ford, Limerick **22 R 54**
Because of its proximity to the old Thomond border, Croom and its 13th-c castle have had a turbulent history of battles and bloodshed. During the 17thc in particular it was frequently attacked, and the local countryside rang with the O Briens' war cry of *Lamh laider abu* in reply to the Geraldines' *Cromadh Abu* – ie 'The strong hand for ever' and 'Croom for ever'. Of the castle only shattered fragments survive. About 1m W at Carrigeen are the rectangular church (NM) and incomplete round tower (NM) of the ancient monastic foundation of Dysert. The 65ft-high round tower has five storeys, each lit by a window, and is 54ft in circumference with walls measuring 4½ft thick. Its Romanesque doorway is situated 15ft above the ground. The lovely octagonal tower of 15th-c Glenogra Castle can be seen 6m E, while 4m NE is Ballycahane House. This was once the home of Scanlon, who was executed in 1819 for murdering his young wife – the famous 'Colleen Bawn'.

CROSSHAVEN, *Bun an Tábhairne:*
Lowland of the Tavern, Cork **28 W 76**
Shady country lanes and a superb beach are the main attractions offered by this Owenboy River resort, which also boasts a sheltered yacht anchorage and good sea bathing at Church, Myrtleville, and Graball Bays. Templebreedy church is a ruined building attractively situated on a headland. It dates from 1778 and includes a modern tower on the east side. To the W of the village a ruined Desmond stronghold overlooks the river from the grounds of Aghamarta. This reach of the Owenboy is known as Drake's Pool, from an incident in which

CREEVYKEEL COURT CAIRN
Court cairns are amongst the earliest-known megalithic structures in Ireland. On present evidence they would seem to date from between 3,000 and 2,500BC, but who the people were who built them, or where they came from is not known. Collectively, court cairns belong to the type of monument called gallery graves, which are found throughout Ireland and Europe, though court cairns are a peculiar development confined to the north of Ireland. Until recently the accepted theory was that the megalith builders originated in the Mediterranean lands and gradually spread outward. This theory has now been called into question by some experts, partly because of discrepancies recently discovered in the Carbon 14 method of dating – the result of which has been to push many previously established dates back, and partly because it seems likely that certain cultures developed along far more independent lines than had once been thought. It still seems reasonable to state, however, that even if the court-cairn builders in Ireland were not directly governed by Mediterranean trends, then at least they were influenced by cultural movements from that area.

The Creevykeel court cairn, near the hamlet of the same name in Co Sligo, was the first to be properly excavated and is one of the most complex of its type. It was originally covered by a 200ft-long cairn and faces roughly E. The court is entered via a passage which is set slightly off centre in a straight kerb, and is a rounded oblong measuring approximately 30ft by 50ft. It was originally covered by a flooring of stones. The large stones which make up the wall of the court increase in size on the west to make an impressive entrance to the actual grave gallery. This is 30ft long and is divided by a stone sill so as to form two chambers. In the cairn to the west of the previously-mentioned gallery are the remains of three other graves, which were entered independently via entrances set into the sides of the cairn. These appear to have been built at the same time as the rest of the monument, but may have been introduced at a later date.

Finds from the monument included traces of four cremations in the main chambers, plus fragments of various types of pottery vessels, arrowheads, axes, and two clay balls. This material was not of much use in dating the monument. Some of it appeared to belong to the early neolithic period, and some of it to the bronze age. At some time during the early-Christian period a structure that has been variously interpreted as a kiln or an iron smelter was built into the north-western corner of the court.

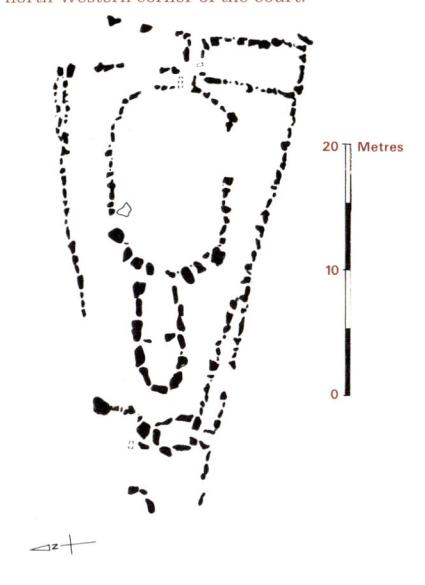

CROSSHAVEN/DAINGEAN

Sir Francis Drake hid here while being pursued by a Spanish coastal patrol. Although their search was exhaustive the Spaniards missed this little haven.

CROSSMAGLEN, *Crois Mhic Lionnáin:*
Mac Lionnáin's Cross, Armagh **12 H91**
The huge market square in this border town seems entirely disproportionate to the size of the place, and the fairs that were once held here became notorious for the undesirables that frequented them.

Numerous small lakes and the River Fane offer excellent boating and fishing, and a crannog in the middle of Lough Ross is said to have been the place where plans for the 1641 Rebellion were discussed. Lissaraw, about 1¼m S, is a fine ringfort with an open souterrain, and a similar complex (NM) can be seen 2m NW at Corliss. The well-preserved prehistoric grave of Annaghmare lies 1½m N of Crossmaglen. It comprises a horseshoe-shaped court from which leads a 23ft gallery; the gallery is divided into three chambers. The monument (NM), which was excavated in 1963, is especially noteworthy for the fine drystone walling to be seen in the court. Two smaller chambers were inserted into the cairn behind the main gallery at a slightly later date. The tomb had been used for both cremated and inhumed burials. Further N is Lisleitrim Trivallate Rath (NM) which has a souterrain. Nearby Lisleitrim Lake has a crannog.

CROSSMOLINA, *Crois Mhaoilíona:*
Maoilíona's Cross, Mayo **9 G11**
Considered one of the most progressive towns in N Mayo, this Lough Conn and River Deel community owes its prosperity to Bord na Mona and the Electricity Supply Board. These bodies have been intelligently exploiting the local boglands without detrimental effect to the countryside. The lakes and scenery of 2,646ft Nephin are a major attraction to the area, and the lough offers fishing and boating. On the shore of Lough Conn SE of Crossmolina are the remains of Errew Abbey (NM), built for the Augustinians in the 15thc. Near by are the remains of a church (NM) which is probably built on the site of a 6th-c foundation. Near the point where the Deel enters Lough Conn are the remains of 16th-c Deel Castle, which stands in the grounds of 18th-c Castle Gore.

CULDAFF, *Cúil Dabhcha,* Donegal **6 C54**
Several safe sea-bathing places and long sandy beaches can be found near this pleasantly-secluded village, and the Culdaff River offers good game fishing. Good catches can be made in the coastal waters here. Fine local coastal scenery includes a range of cliffs which rise to nearly 800ft in the N and extend from Glengad to Malin Head. Clonca, between Culdaff and Carrowmore, features a ruined church containing a beautifully-carved sepulchral slab bearing an inscription in Irish. A translation of this reads 'Fergus MacAllen made this stone; Magnus MacOrriston of the Isles lies under this mound'. The armless but elaborately-carved High Cross of St Buadan (NM) stands outside the graveyard.

Carrowmore, the site of an ancient monastery, features a group of stone crosses. Close to Culdaff at Bocan is a church which preserves St Buadan's Bell, an interesting artifact dating from the 9th or 10thc. Black Hill rises near Bocan Church and is surmounted by a horned cairn known as the Temple of Deen. Remains of a stone circle can be seen on the summit of a low hill about ½m away.

CULMORE, *An Chúil Mhór:*
the Big Recess, Derry **6 C42**
A fort built here by the London Companies in the 17thc was erected to guard the mouth of the River Foyle, and replaced by the present structure (NM) in the 19thc. Amelia Earhart landed at Culmore after completing her epic solo flight across the Atlantic in 1932. Near the Protestant church are the ruins of a 17th-c church which was also built by the London Companies.

CURRAGH, THE, *An Currach:*
the Racecourse, Kildare **18 N71**
The Curragh of Kildare is world famous as the home of Irish racing and the venue for such important events as the Irish Derby. It is basically a long plain which lies immediately E of Kildare and measures 6m long by 2m wide. Sheep and cattle are put out to take advantage of its fine grazing, and most mornings the visitor can see the finest Irish bloodstock being exercised on the carefully-maintained gallops. The military importance of this large plain has been known for centuries, and it has been the scene of many encampments. The Irish army took it over from the British in 1922. A curious feature on the Kilcullen road is Donnelly's Hollow, where the footprints of Dan Donnelly – who defeated the English Boxing Champion George Cooper here in 1815 – have been preserved.

CURRAGHMORE, *An Currach Mór:*
the Big Marsh, Waterford **23 S41**
A 12ft-high demesne wall which bounds this 4,000-acre estate, 4m SE of Carrick-on-Suir, was built to provide employment during a famine. More than half of the estate land, which is a seat of the Beresford family, has been put down to arable farming. The rest is occupied by market gardens, a stud farm, grazing for pedigree herds, and woodland. The square castle which now forms the central core of Curraghmore House dates from the 12thc and has been continuously occupied by the family, while the beautiful Georgian house itself includes one of the finest courtyards in Ireland. The details of this are reminiscent of the work of Inigo Jones, and although the overall plan recalls the work of 18th-c architect Vanbrugh it was in fact by John Roberts of Waterford. The stucco, carved-wood, and painted interior decoration was supervised by James Wyatt. Lady Catherine Poer designed the charming Shell House (OACT), which stands in the grounds (OACT) and contains a statue of her by J Van Nost Jr.

*****CUSHENDALL,** *Bun Abhann Dalla:*
Mouth of the River Dall, Antrim **7 D22**
Cushendall is an attractive village, situated on the scenic Antrim Coast Road at the mouth of the River Dall. Four pleasant streets of late-Georgian and Regency houses meet at the Curfew or Turnley's Tower, which was built by landlord Francis Turnley in 1809. His intention was that it should 'Be manned by a single guard' as a place of confinement for idlers and rioters. Sandstone taken from the cliff at Red Bay during the construction of the Red Bay tunnel was used to build the 19th-c courthouse. The tunnel itself is entered 1½m S via the Coast Road, near 1,100ft Lurigethan, and on the nearby cliffs to the N of Red Bay are the remains of a 16th-c O Donnell fortress.

Two of the well-known Glens of Antrim – Ballyemon and Glenaan – meet at Cushendall. Glen Ballyemon and 1,346ft Tievebulliagh feature the sites of ancient neolithic weapon factories and have yielded fine-grained dolerite remains of axes, spear points, hammers, and scrapers. Megalithic *Cloghbrack Lubitavish,* or Ossian's Grave (NM), can be seen 2m NW of the village, near the Glenaan River. The ruined church of Layd on the minor coast road to the village was in use up to 1790 and contains monuments to the MacDonnells.

CUSHENDUN, *Bun Abhann Duinne:*
Mouth of the River Dunn, Antrim **7 D23**
Considered one of the most attractive villages in N Ireland, Cushendun lies at the mouth of the Dun River and occupies both banks. A few black-and-white houses, cottages, and hotels occupy the S side of the Dun, and the part of the village on the N side of the river is composed mainly of cottages designed by Clough William-Ellis. These were built by Ronald MacNeill – Lord Cushendun – and his wife, and have been acquired by the NT with the aid of the Ulster Land Fund, as has much of the village and surrounding countryside. Miniature Glencorp lies SW of the village, and to the W as a complete contrast is a deep river gorge spanned by a 19th-c viaduct which carries the main Ballycastle road.

To the N of the village is a steep, narrow road which affords fine views as it winds to the top of Green Hill before passing near lonely Torr and Fair heads and rejoining the inland road to Ballycastle. The Harvard Archaeological Mission claims to have found the key to the chronology of the entire Irish stone age near here. This takes the form of a riverside site about 150yds W of the village in which tools from all four principal stone-age cultures were found lying on top of each other at various levels, thus proving a previously assumed order. The excavation was made by paring the face of the 35ft cliff down to reveal the different layers, and was of high geological as well as archaeological importance. Professor Jessen of Copenhagen has said that the post ice-age information contained in this cliff makes it one of the most valuable examples of its type in W Europe. Impressions of shells and leaves that have long been extinct were found in the clay strata, and of the eight distinct layers uncovered, four revealed flints dating from c6000 to 2000 BC.

Close to the village are the remains of two megalithic tombs, and interesting caves formed by the action of waves on the old red sandstone can be seen to the S of the village. Of the tombs, the most interesting is Carnamore, which lies 4m NNW of Cushendun. It is the best preserved of a distinctive group of Antrim passage graves. A souterrain and the Mass Rock, an altar of the Penal times also known as the Altar in the Woods, can be seen 1½m W at Innispollan.

DAINGEAN, *An Daingean:*
the Fortress, Offaly **17 N42**
This village stands on the Grand Canal and was once a seat of the country's

chief family, the O Conors. At the S end of the village is 18th-c Fort Castle, and 3½m N is the good viewpoint of 769ft Croghan Hill – which has several prehistoric and early-Christian remains.

DALKEY, *Deilginis*:
Thorn Island, Dublin **19 O22**
Now a popular seaside resort and residential area, Dalkey was once a busy Dublin port of prime commercial importance. During the middle ages its business interests were protected by a defensive ring of castles, two of which are still standing and can be seen in the main street. One of these is incorporated in the town hall and the other – directly opposite – is known as Archbold's Castle (NM). Both structures appear to date from the 16thc. Archbold's features a three-storey granite tower with a vault over the second floor and displays parapet machicolations.

The ancient parish church of St Begnet stands in the same street as the castles and includes a pre-Norman north wall. Its lintelled west door is of note, and there is an ancient stone inscribed with a Celtic cross near the south wall. The clear, deep waters of Coliemore Harbour provide a safe anchorage in the shelter of Dalkey Island, to the S of the town. The old church (NM) on the island, also dedicated to St Begnet, includes antae at each corner, a flat-headed west doorway, an unusual two-tiered south window, and a more recent belfry. Builders involved in the construction of a nearby martello tower during the 19thc lived in the church and constructed a fireplace in the east gable. Excavations here have revealed roof slates and glazed tiles which prove the church was used in medieval times. A rock opposite the west gable features a Greek equal-armed cross.

During the last quarter of the 18thc Dalkey Island was the seat of a burlesque court presided over by 'his facetious majesty the King of Dalkey, Emperor of Muglin's and Elector of Lambay and Ireland's Eye, Defender of his own faith and respecter of all others, sovereign of the Illustrious Order of the Lobster and Periwinkle.' This parody of a court of law attained such size and importance that a coronation was attended by some 20,000 people. The custom died out for a while but was revived in 1935.

Superb views are offered from the small park which has been laid out S of the town on Sorrento Point, and close to the town is the excellent bathing beach of White Rock Strand. The Vico road curls round Killiney Bay between magnificent sea cliffs to the E and bracken-covered hills to the W, offering a pleasant scenic drive. Killiney Hill is surmounted by an obelisk built during the 18thc to provide work for the unemployed and affords views which encompass the Wicklow Hills, Killiney Bay, and the Vale of Shanganagh. Bullock Harbour lies less than a mile N of the town and, during the middle ages, was a fishing port belonging to one of the religious houses. The fishing was protected by a strong castle built during the 12thc. Mesolithic remains found in the area of the town and island can be seen in the National Museum, Dublin. Granite used for the construction of the well-known Dun Laoghaire piers was taken from Dalkey Quarry, which is now a favourite and demanding test for amateur rock climbers. George Bernard Shaw spent his boyhood years at Torca Cottage on Dalkey Hill.

Curraghmore House stands on an ancient site amid the woods and farmlands of its 4,000-acre estate.

DALWAY'S BAWN, Antrim **7 J49**
See Whitehead entry.

DANE'S CAST, THE, Down and Armagh **13 J03**
This series of ancient earthworks is believed to have formed a border between the kingdoms of Oriel and Ulaidh. Good sections of it may be seen near the village of Poyntzpass in Down; near Lough Shark in Down; NE of Meigh in Armagh; and 4m S of the city of Armagh.

DANGAN, *An Daingean*:
the Fortress, Meath **18 N85**
The Duke of Wellington spent part of his boyhood here and attended a diocesan school in Trim. Dangan's modern castle, which once belonged to the Wellesleys, incorporates the keep of an old fortress. Don Ambrosio O Higgins, who was Spanish Viceroy of Chile and Peru during the 19thc, was born here.

DARTRY MOUNTAINS, THE
Sléibhte Dhartrái, Leitrim and Sligo **10 G74**
Although this limestone range is not one of the highest in Ireland it is certainly among the most spectacular. Its rocks have been eroded into high cliffs, isolated spires, and curious shapes – all of which challenge the aspiring rock climber. The 1,722ft Ben Bulben, sometimes called Ireland's Table Mountain, is by far the best-known peak in the range and forms a landmark which can be seen for miles around. The highest mountain is 2,113ft Truskmore. Valleys such as beautiful Glencar, Gleniff, and Glenade offer easy and pleasant routes by which to explore the range.

DELGANY, *Deilgne*:
Thorny Place, Wicklow **19 O21**
Sheltered in a wooded hollow in the foothills of the Wicklow Mountains, this pretty village lies 10m S of Bray near the Glen of the Downs. The village church contains a magnificent 18th-c monument to the banker David la Touche.

DELVIN, *Dealbhna*, Westmeath **18 N56**
Delvin Castle (NM), a 13th-c stronghold situated at the top of this picturesque village's main street, was built by the Nugent family but later abandoned in favour of Clonyn Castle. The latter lies in ruins to the W of the village in the grounds of a 19th-c castle. The village itself is set in pleasantly-wooded surroundings W of the Stoneyford River. This area is best known through the controversial and very unpopular works of 20th-c author Brinsley McNamara, who was born 1¾m NE at Ballinvalley, and included the district in his novels. His most famous book, *The Valley of the Squinting Windows*, was publicly burnt in the village. A similar reception was waiting for *The Clanking of the Chains*, which discarded the romantic image of the drive for national independence and emphasized the disillusionment that could set in. McNamara died in 1963.

DERGALT, Tyrone **5 H39**
This farming townland lies between Strabane and Plumbridge and includes a typical Tyrone farmstead (NT) which was the home of Woodrow Wilson's ancestors.

DERREEN HOUSE, Doirin:
Little Wood, Kerry **26 V75**
See Kilmakilloge entry.

DERRY **5 C41**
See Londonderry entry.

DERRYGONNELLY, *Doire Ó gConaile*:
the Oak Grove of the Connollys, Fermanagh **11 H15**
Close to this small village are the Knockmore Caves, which feature strange figure markings and designs known as rock scribing on their walls. Ruins of a 17th-c Plantation church built by Sir John Dunbar can be seen near by. Lough Navar Forest offers angling, picnic sites, and a 7m forest drive which leads to the top of the Magho Cliffs. These cliffs afford a spectacular panorama of Lough Erne. Remains of interesting Aghamore Church can be seen 2m NW of the village on the shores of Carrick Lough.

DERRYHIVENNY CASTLE,
Doire hAibhne: River Oak Grove, Galway **16 M80**
Most of the L-shaped bawn surrounding this well-preserved, four-storey tower (NM) built by Daniel O Madden has survived, including the round towers guarding the opposite corners. Three of the floors include good fireplaces, and the main windows are of two- and three-mullioned type. The Jacobean-style chimney stacks are an attractive feature of the castle, as is the stonework of the doorway to the tower. An inscription on one of the corbels states that the castle was built in 1643 and distinguishes the building as one of the few Irish castles to have been accurately dated. It was probably the last of its kind to be built.

DERRYMORE HOUSE, *An Doire Mór:*
the Big Oak Grove, Armagh **13 J02**
Erected by Isaac Corry, last Chancellor of the Irish Exchequer, this little thatched manor house (NT; OACT), 2m NW of Newry, dates from 1780 and may have been the place where Corry and Lord Castlereagh drafted the 1800 Act of Union. The drawing room is known as the Treaty Room.

DESMOND'S GRAVE, Kerry **21 Q91**
Accessible from either Tralee or Castleisland, this grave contains the remains of Gerald Fitzgerald – an Earl of Desmond who was killed by Ormonde soldiers in 1583 – and lies 4½m NW of Castleisland in Glanageenty Glen. The glen is 2m WSW of 1,097ft Knight's Mountain, which forms part of the Glanaruddery range.

DEVENISH ISLAND, *Daimhinis:*
Ox Island, Fermanagh **11 H24**
The island's setting combines the waters of Lough Erne, a skyline jagged with low mountain peaks, and a wealth of historical monuments from the Irish age of saints and scholars. Access to the island is either by ferry or one of the cruise boats that begin their daily tours from the Round O Quay in Enniskillen.

The island's monastery is said to have been founded by St Molaise in the 6thc, and the buildings that exist today are all national monuments. Teampull Mor, the Priory Church of the Culdees or Companions of God, dates from c1200 and later became the parish church of Devenish. Its south wall contains a good window and features the 16th- or 17th-c burial chapel of the Maguires of Tempo. Two representations of this family's arms can be seen outside the church. St Molaise's House, a small, 12th-c oratory, retained its steeply-pitched stone roof until the end of the 18thc and features Romanesque pilaster bases designed to match the cornice of the nearby round tower. The tower itself is of 12th-c date and is a superb example of its kind. Over 80ft high, it carries four enigmatic carved heads below its pointed cap. The richly decorated book-shrine of St Molaise is in the National Museum, Dublin.

Farther up the island is the 12th-c and later Augustinian Abbey of St Mary. Most of the structure that can be seen today is of 15th-c origin, and a Latin inscription on a stone near the bottom of its spiral staircase records reconstruction work conducted in 1449. The abbey tower was added in the 16thc, and the church has a nave and choir. A door in the north wall of the church has a carving of a bird pecking at vine leaves. To the S of St Mary's is a graveyard featuring a 15th-c high cross depicting the Crucifixion on its east face.

DEVIL'S BIT MOUNTAIN, *Bearnán Éile:*
the Gap of Éile, Tipperary **23 S07**
See Templemore entry.

DEVIL'S PUNCHBOWL, *Poll an Diabhail:*
the Devil's Hole, Kerry **27 V98**
See Killarney entry.

DINGLE, *An Daingean:*
the Fortress, Kerry **26 Q40**
Often referred to as the last parish before America, this small town is beautifully set among the hills of the Dingle Peninsula or *Corca Dhuibhne* on the triangular inlet of Dingle Harbour. It was important as the site of a fort even before the Norman occupation and has had an eventful history. It suffered greatly during the Desmond troubles, and as a consolation for this Queen Elizabeth I donated £300 for the repair of defences and granted it a charter of incorporation. Throughout the middle ages Dingle operated as one of the prosperous W ports that traded with Spain. Irish is still the everyday language of the area. The parish church dates from 1804 and occupies the site of an older structure. A Geraldine tablet to a Knight of Kerry, dated 1741, can be seen in the transept, and the graveyard features a carved Desmond tomb of 1540 and several interesting carved stones from the town walls. Remains of the walls can be seen in Green Street.

DINGLE PENINSULA, Kerry
20/26 Q40 etc
Also known as the *Corca Dhuibhne*, or Corcaguiney Peninsula, this is the farthest N of the three picturesque Kerry peninsulas that extend W into the Atlantic to enclose the inlets of Dingle Bay and the Kenmare River. At the root of the peninsula is the wild Slieve Mish range, the highest points of which are 2,796ft Baurtregaum and 2,713ft Caherconree. This range is encircled by roads to the N and S. The N of the peninsula is dominated by 3,217ft Brandon Mountain, and to the S off Slea Head are the lonely Blasket Islands. The whole peninsula has superb mountain and coastal scenery, and there are extraordinary numbers of prehistoric and early-Christian remains. Places on the peninsula are listed under their own names in the gazetteer.

DOE CASTLE, *Caisleán na dTuath:*
Castle of the Territories, Donegal **5 C03**
See Creeslough entry.

DONABATE, *Domhnach Bat,* Dublin
19 O24
This small town – situated between Balbriggan and Dublin, with a fine sandy beach 1½m E – is a popular holiday resort. The Protestant parish church of 1758 contains a private gallery complete with fireplace. Near the station are the remains of the square keep of Donabate Castle. In the grounds of nearby Newbridge House, designed by Richard Castle c1737, are the ruins of Landestown Castle. To the SW is 18th-c Seafield Hall. Ruins of a 15th-c castle with a small, square west tower can be seen 1½m NE at Portrane, and Portrane House was once the home of Dean Swift's beloved Stella. The demesne now contains a large mental hospital, near which is a fairly recent round tower. See also Turvey House entry.

DONAGHADEE, *Domhnach Daoi,* Down
7 J58
This pleasant town and port, which is the nearest to the Scottish mainland, was once a port for the ferry service to Portpatrick in Scotland. This link was abandoned in 1849 in favour of the Larne to Stranraer route. Historical features of the town include a prehistoric mound or rath topped by a castellated structure added in the 19thc, and the restored parish church. The latter includes a Jacobean tower of 1641 and shares its grounds with a holy well. Parts of the foreshore at Coalpit Bay have been designated an area of special scientific interest because of the valuable rock succession displayed here.

DONAGHMORE, Meath **18 N86**
See Navan entry.

DONAGHMORE, *Domhnach Mór:*
Big Church, Tyrone **12 H76**
A beautifully-carved, 16ft high cross (NM) is all that remains of an ancient monastery which once stood here. The Rev George Walker, who distinguished himself during the Siege of Londonderry, was rector of this parish.

DONAGHPATRICK, *Domhnach Phadraig:*
St Patrick's Church, Meath **18 N87**
St Patrick's Church (CI) with its 15th-c tower stands on the site of an early monastery. Near by is a motte. Across the River Blackwater are the remains of a 17th-c fortified building. At Teltown, 1½m W of Donaghpatrick, are the remains of a ringfort (NM) where a great public assembly was held in the days of of the Ui Neill kingship.

DONARD, *Dún Ard:*
High Ring-fort, Wicklow **18 S99**
Remains of a medieval church here contain a recumbent tombstone of the same period, and close by is a 20ft-high mound topped by a low, circular bank. This is known as Ball Moat. An ogham stone can be seen in the garden of the former Garda (Police) Station. A walk 4m to the SE of the village leads to lovely Glen of Imaal and starting places for climbs on 3,039ft Lugnaquilla – the highest mountain in Wicklow. The NE slopes of the glen are used as an artillery firing range, and near by stands the rebuilt Dernamuck Cottage, with its folk museum commemorating Michael O Dwyer's refuge here after the 1798 Uprising.

*****DONEGAL,** *Dún na nGall:*
the Fort of the Foreigners, Donegal
4 G97
The heart of this thriving and pleasantly laid-out market town is The Diamond, a wide triangular space in which the three main roads from Derry, W Donegal, and Sligo converge. Donegal's position on the mouth of the River Eske and at the head of Donegal Bay made it strategically important in ancient times. Up to the 17thc it was the chief seat of the O Donnell family, princes of Tir Chonaill.

The castle (NM), situated on a rocky eminence above the quay, is based upon a 15th-c tower but was enlarged and improved by Sir Basil Brooke in the 17thc. Windows and gables were inserted in the tower, and a very handsome house was added to it. Of particular note in the building is the vast Jacobean fireplace, which incorporates the arms of Brooke and Leicester. The gatehouse and the wall on either side of the entrance was built by Sir Basil, but the tower at the west end of the wall is contemporary with the O Donnell's original tower.

On the seashore S of the town are the sparse remains of a Franciscan friary (NM) founded by Red Hugh O Donnell in 1474. Only the chancel and a gable of the south transept remain of the church, but the remains of the cloister arcade are better preserved. The community became famous after four of the friars compiled the 17th-c *Annals of the Four Masters,* one of the most important sources of early-Irish church history available. An obelisk in The Diamond commemorates their achievement. The town itself makes an excellent base from which to explore the region's mountains, rivers, and hills – especially for the keen walker or angler.

DONEGORE, *Dun na gCuradh:*
Heroes' Fort, Antrim 7 J28

Donegore is a little village particularly noted for its 'Mote' (NM), one of the most conspicuous man-made features of the S Antrim landscape. Clearly visible from the M2, this structure is based on an almost circular outcrop of basalt and is shaped like an inverted flowerpot. On the south-west side it rises to 120ft, although it is only half this height on the opposite side. The flat top measures 105 by 85ft. Preliminary excavations conducted here revealed alternating layers of cremated human bones and suggest that this was once a sepulchral mound. The Anglo-Normans appear to have adapted it for use as a motte castle – a purpose for which it was ideally suited as its natural defences precluded the need for a ditch and bailey.

Close to the south-east side of the mound is the first chamber of a rock-hewn souterrain similar to others found in Ireland, and this is linked to a second chamber by a rising passage. Evidence suggests that the second chamber was used as a pit dwelling, and excavation has yielded relics dating from the early-Christian era.

Irish poet and antiquary Sir Samuel Ferguson was born in Belfast and buried in the CI Donegore churchyard in 1886. His most important antiquarian work, published in 1887, was *Ogham Inscriptions in Ireland, Wales, and Scotland*. Buildings of interest in the village include the parish church, the first Presbyterian church of 1627, and 19th-c Craig House.

DONERAILE, *Dún ar Aill:*
Fort on a Cliff, Cork 28 R50

Kilcolman, the house where Edmund Spenser lived and worked for eleven years between 1587 and 1598, lies ruined on the edge of a small lake some 3m NNW of this attractive River Awbeg town. Spenser came to Ireland in 1580 as Secretary to Lord Deputy Grey of Wilton, and on taking possession of Kilcolman became Clerk to the English Council of Munster. His outrageous views of the Irish people made him extremely unpopular, and when the castle was attacked and burned in 1598 he barely escaped with his life. While here he wrote *View of the Present State of Ireland*, the first three books of *The Faerie Queene*, the *Amoretti* sonnets, *Colin Clout's Come Home Again*, and *Epithalamion*. All that remains of the house is a 40ft tower in which narrow turret stairs link a vaulted chamber with a vacant area once occupied by the upper rooms. Poet and novelist Canon Sheehan was parish priest here from 1895 to 1913, and it was at Doneraile that he did most of his work on the relationship between Irish clerical life and the problem of rural population. A statue of the canon was erected in front of his church in 1925. Doneraile Court was built c1730, but was altered in the 19thc. The fine entrance arch was designed by the brothers Pain.

DOOAGH, *Dumha Acha,* Mayo 8 F60
See Achill Island entry.

DOOGORT, *Dumha Goirt:*
Bitter Mound, Mayo 8 F60
See Achill Island entry.

DOONBEG, *An Dún Beag:*
the Little Fort, Clare 21 Q96

An old fortress of the Mac Mahon's and later the O Brien family stands on the edge of this village, where the Doonbeg River joins the bay. The W shores of the bay rise in 100ft-high sandhills. White Strand is a good beach 1½m NE, and the coastal scenery W as far as Baltard and Farrihy Bays is exceptional.

DORSEY, THE, *Na Doirse:*
the Entrance, Armagh 12 H91

The Dorsey, situated in the townland of Dorsey and Tullynavall, some 4m NE of Crossmaglen, is the largest entrenched enclosure in the whole country. The earthwork encloses some 300 acres and comprises a rampart with a ditch on each side and a smaller rampart on the outside. At the points where it crossed boggy land or rivers it was built on a foundation of piles strengthened by horizontal beams and flat stones. About 1m NW of Silverbridge the rampart measures 120ft in width by 20ft in height from the base of the inner ditch and is particularly impressive.

Associated with the series of earthworks collectively known as the Black Pig's Dyke, The Dorsey is traditionally held to mark the S limit of territory controlled by Navan Fort – or Emain Macha (see entry) – near Armagh.

DOWNHILL, *Dún Bó:* Fort of Cows, Derry 6 C73

This tiny resort lies under the shadow of basaltic cliffs to the W of Castlerock, and includes a castle which was built in 1780 by John Adam for the eccentric Lord Bristol – Bishop of Derry. The bishop was a traveller and collector of art and literature who was devoted to the improvement of relations between different religious groups. He erected several fine buildings in Ireland, and during his time at Downhill organized races between clergy of all denominations on nearby Magilligan Strand. Remains of the castle, which was almost completely demolished in 1949, include the Mussenden Temple (NT), Bishop's Gate (NT), Lion Gate, and parts of the walls. It is probable that designer Michael Shanahan created the Temple, which was built in c1783 on the lines of the Temples of Vesta in Tivoli and Rome. It occupies a cliff-top site which commands a view of the Magilligan Strand, the hills of Inishowen, Co Donegal, the N Antrim coast, and some of the W Isles of Scotland. South of the entrance gate is ruined Dumboe Church. The Bishop's View Viewpoint is 2½m SW on an unclassified road.

DOWNPATRICK, *Dún Pádraig:*
St Patrick's Fort, Down 13 J44

For centuries this historic River Quoile town has been the ecclesiastical and administrative centre of Co Down. It is said that the dun or rath from which the town takes its name occupied the site on which the CI cathedral now stands, and that a monastery was founded inside the dun during the 6thc. This was yet another of the early foundations to suffer at the hands of Norse raiders.

After the Norman occupation Anglo-Norman John de Courcy established English Benedictine and Cistercian monks in religious houses which he founded in Ireland. To do this he had to conciliate the local clergy. His problem was solved by the local discovery of relics of St Patrick, St Brigid, and St Columba, justifying his transference of the see from Bangor to Downpatrick.

The present cathedral is almost a complete 18th- and 19th-c rebuilding by Charles Lilly, with only the choir and chancel of the original church to testify that it ever existed. A 10th-c high cross found in fragments was re-erected outside the east end of the cathedral in 1897, and the original Norman font from the old building was rescued from a local farmyard. This now stands at the east end of the church. A fine 20th-c memorial window raised to the memory of Lord and Lady Dunleath illustrates events in the life of St Patrick. An enormous slab of granite that can be seen in the churchyard was placed there in 1900 by Francis Joseph Biggar for reasons best known to himself.

The town itself is a charming collection of late-Georgian and early-Victorian buildings grouped around interesting roads such as the cobbled English Street, which climbs the hill to the cathedral. Denvir's Hotel is a partly 17th- but mainly 18th-c building with a Georgian stairway and a small Victorian public bar. The structure housing the Charity Schools and Almshouses was built by Edward Southwell in 1733, and is one of the most pleasing Georgian buildings in Ulster. Other interesting buildings in English Street include the 19th-c courthouse, the Downe Hunt Rooms, the Old Gaol group, and the clergy widows' houses.

Remains of John de Courcy's enormous motte-and-bailey castle lie to the NW between the town and river. St Patrick is said to have landed in Ireland some 1½m away in AD 432 at the mouth of the River Slaney – now called Fiddler's Burn. Near here is an old church which is said to stand on the site of a barn given to the saint by Dichu, one of the earliest converts, for the erection of a church. The saint's crossing to this country is commemorated by a CI memorial church of hammer-dressed Mourne Mountain granite. A hill overlooking Strangford Lough is surmounted by a giant statue of St Patrick, executed by Francis Doyle Jones in 1937. About 1m NW of the town near the banks of the Quoile is Inch Abbey, which stands on the site of an early monastery plundered and destroyed by Viking raiders. After this another foundation was created in this beautiful spot, by John de Courcy in atonement for the destruction of the Irish Erenagh Abbey. The latter lay 3m S. Little of Inch Abbey (NM) has survived, except the east end of the second church, but the entire foundations have been excavated. The east wall of the choir displays three late-Romanesque lancet windows of c1200, and the transept includes two chapels in each arm. A 15th-c well and bakehouse were included in the choir, and remains of what may have been the old infirmary lie to the NW.

The church of the old monastery stood in a graveyard to the N of the Cistercian abbey. A rude Crucifixion slab from the west doorway of this building is preserved in the vestry of the Protestant parish church. Struel Wells (NM) lie 1½m E of the town and are traditional objects of pilgrimage. Slievenagriddle hill has remains of a chambered cairn. About 1m E of Struel in Ballyyalton is an elliptical court cairn (NM) with a pillar stone. The marshes to the W of the town are the winter home for great numbers of greylag geese.

**DOWNPATRICK HEAD, ** Mayo 9 G 14
See Ballycastle entry.

**DOWTH, ** *Dubhadh, * Meath 19 O 07
The great mound of Dowth (NM) belongs to the tremendous collection of burial mounds and other monuments which form a prehistoric necropolis on the banks of the River Boyne and are called collectively *Brugh na Boinne* (see inset on page 176).

**DRIMNAGH CASTLE, ** *Droimeanach:*
Place of Ridges, Dublin 19 O 13
Work of the 16th and subsequent centuries is displayed in the structure of this attractive castle, which lies off the Dublin to Naas road. Many of the castles built at this time, when the O Tooles and O Briens made frequent raids from the Dublin Hills, included cattle bawns for the protection of stock. The bawn and fosse at Drimnagh are remarkably well preserved. The castle has been incorporated into a later structure and is now a house of the Irish Christian Brothers.

**DRISHANE CASTLE, ** *An Driseán:*
Place of Briars, Cork 27 W 29
Dermot MacCarthy, Lord of Munster, built this tower house (NM) in 1450. The building, which is 1m NE of Millstreet, has a modern top and an interesting ogee-headed window on the third floor. Additions made in 1641 included a number of fireplaces, each of which bears the monogram 'W' for Wallace. This family took over the castle in 1643 and remained here until the end of the 19thc. The building is currently the property of the Holy Child nuns.

***DROGHEDA, ** *Droichead Átha:*
Bridge of the Ford, Louth 19 O 07
Now a thriving and progressive industrial town, Drogheda has had a turbulent history which began before its capture by the Vikings in 911. This seaport, 4m from the mouth of the River Boyne, and its immediate environs offer the visitor a wide range of historical and architectural interest. St Laurence's Gate (NM) is the only entrance in the 13th-c walls to have survived and comprises two battlemented, circular towers linked by a wall. The Dominican friary of St Mary Magdalene carries a 15th-c two-storey belltower which still bears the scars of Cromwellian artillery, and was first founded by Lucas de Netterville in 1224. It was here that Richard II of England received the submission of the families who ruled Ulster and Leinster in 1395. St Mary's is an Augustinian friary founded in 1206 by Ursus de Swemole. It occupies a site said to have been connected with St Patrick and St Columba, includes a 15th-c tower, and features a fine arch which spans Abbey Lane.

The parish Church of St Peter stands in William Street and displays good rococo decoration. Inside is a medieval font which was damaged by Cromwellian troops, but still shows the Baptism of Christ and the Twelve Apostles. A church that previously occupied this site was burnt, with its 100 defenders still inside, by Cromwell. The present building dates from 1748 and includes a classical tower and spire designed by Francis Johnston. Graves in the churchyard include those of Oliver Goldsmith's uncle Isaac, and the father of Swift's Vanessa – Humphrey Vanhomrigh. St Peter's RC church is a 19th- and 20th-c gothick building erected as a memorial to the Blessed Oliver Plunkett. Plunkett was martyred at Tyburn in 1681, and his embalmed head is preserved in the north transept.

In the NW part of the town is the Butter Gate, an octagonal tower which includes a pleasant, round-arched passage. Other interesting buildings in Drogheda include the Cornmarket and market hall, both of which were designed by Francis Johnston. Close to St Laurence's Gate is a group of 18th-c buildings belonging to Drogheda Grammar School, and the Tholsel of 1770 is now occupied by a bank. This small classical building includes a cupola and was originally built as a corporation and law courts meeting place. The courthouse stands in Fair Street.

Millmount lies on the S side of the river and features a tower erected on the site of an Anglo-Norman motte, which in turn had been built over a prehistoric tomb. A large cross here commemorates the Holy Year of 1950, and is illuminated at night. Sir John MacNeill built the Boyne Viaduct to carry the Dublin to Belfast railway line in the 19thc; this was reconstructed in 1931. There are good bathing beaches at Baltray (4m NE) and Mornington (3m ENE), and an obelisk 3m W of the town marks the place where King William III was wounded during the Battle of the Boyne in 1690. The night before the battle James, claimant to the English throne, slept in the now-ruined Donore Church. Although the Jacobite army was enthusiastic it was no match for William's trained troops, and Drogheda surrendered the following day. About 4m WNW of the town is the Georgian mansion of Townley Hall, which was designed by Francis Johnston in 1794. A passage grave and neolithic dwelling site on a nearby ridge are so sited as to afford views of the great Boyne tombs of Newgrange, Knowth, and Dowth. The grave (NM), which was excavated during 1960 and 1961, has a NE-facing passage and was built on top of the neolithic site. Francis Johnston's first exercise in church building can be seen 4m N in Ballymakenny. The interior of the church is beautifully preserved.

**DROICHEAD NUA (NEWBRIDGE), ** *Droichead Nua:* New Bridge, Kildare
18 N 81
This busy town on the River Liffey, contains a cutlery factory, rope works, and offices of *Bord na Mona* (the Irish peat board). The latter organization is responsible for the working and utilization of Ireland's massive turf deposits. Scanty remains of Great Connell Priory, an important foundation where the priors ranked as Lords Spiritual in parliament, can be seen 1m SE. It was founded in 1202 and occupied by the Augustinian Order. The granite Long Stone, which dates from prehistoric times, is in the same townland. A fine 40ft-high motte known as Old Connell can be seen near the Dominican College NE of the town.

**DROMAHAIR, ** *Drom Dhá thiar:*
Ridge of the Two Demons, Leitrim
10 G 83
This was once the royal seat of Breffni, and it was here that the chain of events which resulted in the Anglo-Norman invasion of Ireland started. In 1152 Dervorgilla, wife of Tiernan O Rourke, fled with her lover the King of Leinster – Dermot MacMurrough. MacMurrough

1   Boyne Viaduct
2   Courthouse
3   Dominican Friary
4   Millmount
5   St Laurence's Gate
6   St Mary's Friary
7   St Peter's Church (CI)
8   St Peter's Church (RC)
9   Site of the Battle of the Boyne
10 Tholsel
11 Townley Hall

was subsequently banished by the High King and sought the aid of Henry II of England for his reinstatement. The help was granted and the invasion began in 1169. The site of the O Rourke Castle adjoins the Old Hall, built by Sir William Villiers in 1626, and part of a Plantation bawn can be seen here. To the NW of Dromahair is Lough Gill, and a flat-topped hill known as O Rourke's Table rises 3m N. Views S from the hill take in Dromahair, the valley of the River Bonet, and Lough Gill. For Creevelea Abbey see entry.

DROMANEEN CASTLE, *An Dromainín:* the Little Ridge, Cork **28 W59**
Square mullioned windows and gable ends are the main features of this ruined 16th- to 17th-c mansion (NM), which stands on a steep escarpment overlooking the S bank of the River Blackwater 4m W of Mallow.

DROMBEG, Stone Circle, Cork **27 W23**
See inset below.

DROMINEER, *Drom Inbhir:* Estuary Ridge, Tipperary **22 R88**
Dromineer is a small boating, fishing, and shooting centre on the shores of Lough Derg and features the remains of an old lakeside castle. Killodiernan Church lies 3m NE of the village and preserves a 12th-c Irish-Romanesque

DROMBEG STONE CIRCLE

Stone circles and similar monuments draw attention and attract considerable speculation. They also exercise a strange fascination over many people. This may be because they are mysterious – their function and history are largely obscured by time and seem likely to remain so.

The facts about the circle at Drombeg, which is situated 1¾m E of Glandore in Co Cork, are in themselves fairly scanty, although certain inferences may be drawn from some of the details. Drombeg belongs to a type of recumbent stone circle found only in W Cork, and is the best preserved and best excavated of its type. It is 30ft in diameter, and is made up of 17 stones. On the NE side of the circle, facing the recumbent stone from which this type circle takes its name, are two 6½ft portal stones. The

doorway and east window. Its mortuary chapel dates from 1677.

DROMISKIN, *Droim Ineasclainn,* Louth **13 O09**
A 55ft-high round tower (NM) here has been recapped and used as a belfry for the local CI parish church. Its doorway is only 4ft 3in high and features an elaborate round arch. The monastic foundation that existed here was originally Patrician, but its most famous abbot was St Ronan. This saint's holy well exists near by. The ancient head of the local high cross (NM) is said to have been brought here from Baltray, and is mounted on a modern base. Also to be seen is a fragment of an early church. Near the village are the castles of Darver (3m W) and Milltown (1m NW). The latter is a square 16th-c fortress with round towers and an adjoining tower house. Interesting Killencoole Castle is a well-preserved fort which stands 3½m NW of the village.

DROMOLAND CASTLE, Clare **21 R37**
William Smith O Brien, a leader of the Young Ireland party, was born in this huge mansion. It was built in 1830 by the brothers Pain, is now a hotel, and lies 2m NNE of Newmarket on Fergus. The grounds of the house contain an old tower and an ancient stone fort known as Mooghaun. The fort encloses

recumbent stone is decorated with two egg-shaped cup marks, which are simple depressions carved out of the rock.

The axis of the circle runs between the portal stones and over the recumbent stone, and is aligned to the setting sun at the winter solstice. This marked association with a cardinal position of the sun, noticed in Stonehenge and Newgrange among many others, strongly indicates that the movements of heavenly bodies were of interest and importance to the builders of such monuments.

The interior of the circle at Drombeg was carefully covered with a layer of gravel. During excavations two pits were discovered near the centre, one of which contained an urn in which the cremated remains of a youth had been placed. The significance of this burial is not clear, but it may have been a dedicatory offering. The circle is very difficult to date. Radio-carbon tests give the 1st-c BC, but other evidence suggests a much earlier origin.

over 27 acres within its three great walls. The famous 'Great Clare Find' of late bronze-age objects was made in the vicinity in 1854.

DROMORE, *Droim Mór:* Big Ridge, Down **13 J25**
The diocesan cathedral built here *c*1661 by Bishop Jeremy Taylor replaced a medieval structure which was burnt down during the 1641 Rebellion. Restoration work conducted during the 19thc was initiated by Bishop Percy, author of the work *Reliques of Ancient Poetry*. Taylor is buried beneath the altar, and the remains of Percy lie in the transept. A cross-inscribed stone in the south wall is known as St Colman's Pillow and is thought to be a relic of a monastic foundation created here by the saint *c*600. Also of interest in the cathedral are a 17th-c font and a poor-man's box. Dromore House, the Bishop's Palace, is of late 18th-c date.

Near Regent Bridge is a restored 9th- or 10th-c high cross (NM), and the parish stocks are still preserved in the Market Square. A splendid motte-and-bailey known as The Mount (NM) rises NE of the town and dates from the 12thc. The mound is about 200ft in diameter and is linked to the banks of the River Lagan by a sunken way. Earthworks and the scanty remains of a castle can be seen in Castle Street.

A little to the W of the circle is a group of hut circles, and a cooking place. The larger (west) hut is 15ft across and has walls 4ft thick. It is linked by a doorway to the other hut, which has a roasting oven. Both of the huts have been dated to about AD200. The cooking place consists of a well, a hearth, and a lined pit into which stones heated on the hearth were thrown to boil water. A date of sometime before AD500 is given for this construction.

The widely differing dates given for the construction of stone circle, cooking place, and huts, suggest that the site was of some importance over a considerable length of time. It is possible however that it was only occupied periodically – perhaps at the time of the winter solstice.

DROMORE, *Droim Mór*:
Big Ridge, Tyrone 11 H36
A local Cistercian abbey which was destroyed by fire in 1690 is said to have been built on the site of a nunnery founded by St Patrick. To the W of the village are the ivy-clad remains of a Protestant church built in 1694, and the area around Dromore features a number of ancient earthen forts.

DROMORE CASTLE, *Drom Mór*,
Limerick 21 R45
This Victorian fairy-tale castle is perched on a hill-top site overlooking the Shannon near Pallaskenry. It was designed, with infinite attention to detail, by Edward William Godwin for the 3rd Earl of Limerick. The castle was completed in only two years, between 1867 and 1870, and although the work was of a high standard the damp was so bad that it was unbearable to live in. That the castle was intended to function as a castle if need be may be ascertained from the fact that the walls are over 6ft thick. The castle has a bit of everything from early Irish architecture – stepped crenellations, trefoil windows, corbelling, even a round tower. After its final abandonment in 1950 the castle was stripped of much of its detail.

DROMORE WEST, *An Droim Mór Thiar*:
the Big West Ridge, Sligo 9 G43
Situated close to an attractive waterfall on the Dunneill River, this village lies NW of 1,786ft Knockalongy and the smaller peaks of the Ox Mountains. Ruined Kilmacshalgan parish church, used for Protestant worship from 1616 until it was abandoned in 1812, stands near by.

DRUMACOO, *Droim an Chú*:
Hounds' Ridge, Galway 15 M31
The most notable feature of the small early church (NM) here is the south doorway, which is considered to be one of the masterpieces of the transitional style. The doorway was inserted in the 13thc, when the church was enlarged. This was an early monastic foundation, and near by are a holy well and a cross slab.

DRUMBO, *Droim Bó*:
Cow Ridge, Down 13 J36
Features of this attractive area, near the River Lagan, include the stump of a round tower (NM) and the remains of an early church (NM). A little to the N is the Giant's Ring (NM), a late-neolithic ritual henge monument with a chambered grave. This very impressive monument encloses 7 acres with a 12ft-high bank measuring some 60 to 70ft wide at the base. The five uprights of the dolmen form a 5ft-diameter polygon and support a capstone measuring 7ft across. Excavations within the chamber yielded quantities of cremated bones. Farrel's Fort, which lies 1½m NE, may be the Rath of Drumbo mentioned in 11th-c annals.

DRUMCLIFF, *Droim Chliabh*:
Ridge of Baskets, Sligo 10 G64
Sited at the head of Drumcliff Bay and dominated by Ben Bulben, Drumcliff is traditionally the site of a monastery founded in 574 or 575 by St Columba. Two local relics which may be survivals of this are the stump of a round tower (NM) and a 10th-c high cross decorated with scenes from the Old and New Testaments. The 19th- and 20th-c poet William Butler Yeats was buried – at his own request – in the graveyard of the CI parish church where his father had served as rector during the first half of the 19thc. Some 200yds W of Cowney Bridge on the N bank of the River Cowney is a wedge-shaped gallery grave known as the Giant's Grave. The peaks which rise above Drumcliff include 1,527ft King's Mountain and 1,730ft Ben Bulben, and form part of the Dartry range. Beautiful Glencar Lough and its lovely waterfalls lie to the E, and the remarkable cliffs of 1,472ft Lugnafaughery can be seen to the S. Picturesque Swiss Valley is an attractive natural feature formed by a large landslip.

Nearby Lissadell House was where the Countess Markievicz, daughter of Sir Henry Gore-Booth and a leader of the Irish Republican forces in the 1916 Rising, spent her youth (see entry). Other features of the area include Dunfore Castle, a cashel containing four souterrains, and a dolmen with a stone circle in a field adjoining the cashel. Dunfore Castle occupies the site of an ancient dun.

DRUMCONDRA, *Droim Conrach*,
Dublin 19 O13
James Gandon, designer of the custom house and other fine Georgian buildings, was buried in the parish church of this N Dublin suburb in 1823. Drumcondra House was erected by Marmaduke Coghill in 1720 and now serves as the Missionary College of All Hallows. It is well preserved and displays several good interior features. The church has an elaborate monument to Coghill. St Patrick's Training College incorporates late 17th-c Belvedere House and includes a fine, mid 18th-c drawing room among its later additions.

DRUMHALLAGH, *Droim Shalach*:
Ridge of Willows, Donegal 5 C23
This village, 1¼m N of Rathmullan, is situated on the shores of Lough Swilly. A dolmen can be seen near the golf course, and a field in the area contains an early cross slab believed to mark St Garvan's grave.

DRUMLANE, Cavan 11 H31
Of interest here are carvings of birds displayed on the north face of a 12th-c round tower (NM) 3½m SSW of Belturbet. Its round-headed doorway and windows are of interest. Next to the tower is a church which may date from the late 13thc but was altered in the 15thc. Its good stonework includes carved heads of ecclesiastics.

DRUMLOHAN, Waterford 29 S30
Several ogham stones found built in to a souterrain here have been rescued and re-erected inside a fence above ground. They had previously formed part of the underground passage's roof.

DRUMSHANBO, *Droim Seanbhó*:
Ridge of the Old Cow, Leitrim 11 G91
This small angling resort is situated at the S end of Lough Allen, with Slieve Anierin, highest point of the Iron Mountains, rising to 1,922ft 4m NE. Drumshanbo is noted for its Franciscan Convent of Perpetual Adoration, created in 1864 and still the only foundation of its kind in the world.

DRUMSNA, DOON OF, *Droim ar Snámh*:
Ridge over the Swimming Place, Leitrim and Roscommon 11 M99
This feature, known as a travelling earthwork, measures 1m in length and extends across the Leitrim and Roscommon borders. It cuts off an area of nearly 1sqm in a loop of the River Shannon between Drumsna and Jamestown, and is thought to have been built to control river crossings. In some places the main rampart is 100ft in width at the base and rises to a height of 16ft; at least six raths lie S of the ramparts. Whether these fulfilled some defensive function, or were merely farmsteads is not clear. This mysterious collection of monuments may be seen in superb scenery 3½m SE of Carrick-on-Shannon.

*DUBLIN, *Baile-Átha Cliath*:
The Town of the Ford of the Hurdles, Dublin 19 O13
See feature article beginning on page 45.

DULANE, *Tuileán*, Meath 18 N77
See Ceanannas Mor entry.

DULEEK, *Damhliag*:
Stone Church, Meath 19 O06
The name of this small village, pleasantly situated on the River Nanny, is derived from an early stone house or church which stood in the bishopric founded by St Patrick and later assigned by him to the care of St Cianan. The site of this ancient structure (said to have been the first stone-built church in Ireland) was then occupied by an Augustinian church, which was later replaced by the present CI parish church. Monastic relics (NM) here include three early gravestones, the remains of St Cianan's Church, and two 10th-c high crosses. The north cross is a stumpy object, with figures on one side and abstract designs on the other. The south cross is without its shaft and is placed in the ruined, 15th-c church of St Mary's Augustinian Priory (NM). The latter boasts a massive 80ft-high west tower, which was built against the monastery's round tower. All traces of the round tower have disappeared, except an impression in the north wall of the west tower. In the church are several interesting monuments, including a 17th-c Bellew tomb decorated with biblical scenes. The cross (NM) in the village marketplace was erected by Genet de Bathe to the memory of her husband William in 1601. A very fine memorial cross to this family stands 3m SW at the roadside and is known as the White Cross (NM). A third memorial cross to the de Bathe family may be seen 1¾m S beside the entrance to Annesbrook. Aylmer Cross (NM) can be seen to the N of Balrath crossroads and is of late-medieval origin. This bears representations of the Crucifixion and a saint. Some 3m SSW of Duleek is the fortified Elizabethan mansion of Athcarne Castle, which dates from 1587. Good trout fishing is offered by the River Nanny, which is spanned here by an old bridge dating from 1587.

DUNADRY, *Dún Eadradh*, Antrim 7 J28
Although most of the industrial development in this busy community is modern, Dunadry is no stranger to mechanization. In the early 17thc Daniel Blow founded a paper mill here. This was succeeded by a linen mill, and until the 1920's the village was involved in all the stages that go towards the manufacture of fine linen.

Prior to industry the area was still important, and the name is derived from The Dun of Eadradh – a great ringfort which was a major Irish stronghold on the road between Tara and Dalriada. Also in the area are the ringforts of Rathmore of Magh Linne (NM), 1¾m NW, and Donegore (see entry). The former is an oval structure with a souterrain and an Anglo-Norman motte which was added to the east end, and was once the seat of the Kings of Dal Araide. A notable stone circle can be seen at nearby Kilmakee.

DUN AENGUS, *Dún Aonghasa:*
Aengus' Fort, Galway **14 L80**
See inset below.

DUNAMASE, *Dún Másc:*
Másc's Fort, Laois **18 S59**
The 200ft-high Rock of Dunamase is the superb site of a dun or fort occupied by a Leinster chieftain in early-Christian times. This stronghold was later acquired by Strongbow through his marriage to Eva MacMurrough, and a motte-and-bailey castle subsequently erected here was enlarged and strengthened c1250 by William de Braose. In the 15thc it became an O More stronghold, and after many attacks during the civil war it was finally reduced to ruins by Cromwellian troops in 1650. The remains on the rock include curtain walls, bastion towers, and a tower of 13th- to 16th-c date guarding the south-west angle. The whole is surrounded by the ramparts of the earlier fort. Opposite the rock is the ruined Dysert Enos church, which was built on the site once occupied by a 9th-c hermitage of St Aengus. The castle is overlooked to the E and S by a series of isolated hills rising to 850ft.

DUNBRODY ABBEY, *Dún Bróithe:*
Brody's Fort, Wexford **24 S71**
Cistercian monks from St Mary's Abbey in Dublin built this monastic complex c1182, and the substantial remains that have survived add greatly to its picturesque setting. The very large cruciform church includes an aisled nave with six transept chapels and a fine central tower dating from the 15thc. Also of interest are ruins of the sacristy, refectory, chapter house, and other buildings, all of which reflect the plainness of Cistercian design – relieved only by the striking windows. The lancets of the nave, trefoil clerestory windows, and the three-light early-English great east window are generally well preserved. A massive bronze seal which may have been the seal of the abbey was discovered in the ruins in 1810.

Some 2m to the NW on Great Island is the circular earthwork of Kilmokea. The 'island' is no longer separated from the mainland, and the 1,000ft-diameter earthwork is bisected by the road to Ballinlaw Ferry. The ancient church and graveyard of Kilmokea can be seen in the south-west quadrant of the complex, and elsewhere are remains of other earthworks, bullauns, and various internal buildings. It is thought that this may have been a fortified Anglo-Norman village. A large, rectangular earthwork to the E is probably the site of a manor house.

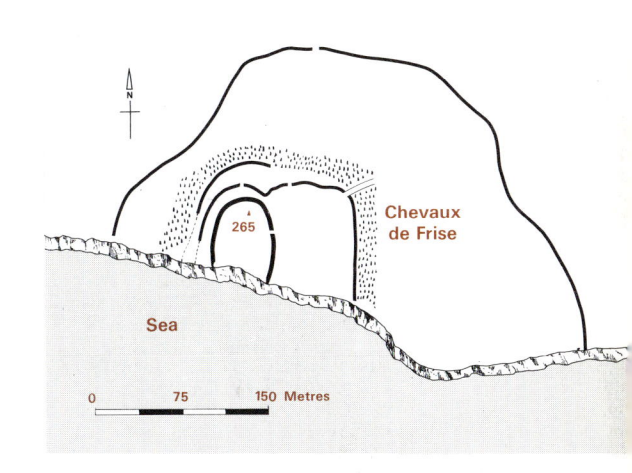

DUN AENGHUS STONE FORT

No really satisfactory reason has been given to explain the existence of the magnificent stone forts, such as Dun Aenghus, with which the Aran Islands are dotted. Legend has it that they were built by a dispossessed people on the run from a conquering invader, and that the Arans were their last refuge. There may be a grain of truth in this, but the legend is very sketchy and the known facts about Dun Aenghus are almost as brief. The archaeologist does not have much to go on at Dun Aenghus – in order to put dates and names to places he needs artifacts, and because of the nature of the terrain (bare limestone for the most part) very few objects have, or are likely to, come to light. From the finds that have been made and from studies of related sites, it has been estimated that the fort dates from the first few centuries AD. Even a study of the fort's construction could be misleading, as it was extensively restored in the 19thc: the buttressing on the inner wall, for instance, dates from this time.

The fort, which is situated ½m S of Kilmurvy on Inishmore Island, is perched on the edge of a vertical 200ft cliff. It has been suggested that originally it was round in plan, but that the sea has eroded away the cliff, and consequently parts of the fort. This theory is not really tenable (though a protective wall built on the very edge of the cliff may have disappeared) as the fort was no doubt built in this position in order to make the best possible use of the perfect defence offered by the cliff. When the fort was first constructed it had four roughly semi-circular defensive walls. The outer wall is very badly preserved, but it once stood 8ft high and 8ft wide. This outer defence encloses an area of some 11 acres. Next in the defensive system comes a barrier composed of thousands of upright limestone pillars, the technical name for which is *chevaux de frise*. Their function was similar to that of modern tank traps in that they would have severly hindered the approach of any intruders. An avenue 80ft long leads through these.

The next two walls have at some time been amalgamated, so that the defences as they now stand comprise three complete walls. The innermost wall of the fort is entered through a low lintelled doorway, and is 13ft thick at the base. This wall is built in three sections, one on top of another, forming a sort of terrace arrangement on the interior. The terraces are approached by sets of steps, beneath some of which are small wall chambers. Dun Aenghus's superb position and its structural perfection, have prompted many experts to pronounce it one of the finest prehistoric monuments in Europe.

DUNCANNON/DUNDALK

DUNCANNON, *Dún Canann:*
Canann's Fort, Wexford **24 S70**
Nothing is known about 'Canann', whose name was adopted by this little seaside village, but the pre-Norman fort on the village's W promontory could have been his 'dun'. An Anglo-Norman castle erected here was strengthened by successive rulers, and during the civil war changed hands before falling to Cromwellian forces after the fall of Waterford. The present structure was completed in 1590. James II, claimant to the English throne, sailed for Kinsale and France from here after his defeat at the Battle of the Boyne. Later William III himself embarked for England from Duncannon. Ruined Geneva Barracks are sited on the other side of the harbour.

***DUNDALK,** *Dún Dealgan:*
Dealgan's Fort, Louth **13 J00**

King John made the town a borough in 1220, by which time it already had a strong garrison. A Franciscan friary was founded by John de Verdon c1240. A survival of this is the high, square building known as Seatown Tower. Two features of Seatown Place are a seven-storey windmill and Kincora House – birthplace of 19th-c Arctic explorer Sir Francis McClintock. Interesting St Patrick's Cathedral (RC) was built by T J Duff in 1848 after the style of King's College Chapel in Cambridge, England. The CI Church of St Nicholas features a 14th-c tower but was rebuilt in both the 17thc and 19thc, latterly by Francis Johnston. Two interesting 16th-c memorials to the Bellew and Field families, plus a monument to Robert Burns' sister Agnes, can be seen in the churchyard. Behind the library, with its archaeological exhibits, are slight remains of a hospital of the Crutched Friars which was founded by Bertram de Verdon c1190.

The town's fine courthouse is a granite building in doric style designed by Edward Park and John Bowden in the 19thc. The 19th-c town hall originally functioned as a corn exchange. St Nicholas' RC Church and St Mary's College are also of interest. To the W of the town is Castletown Hill, a splendid viewpoint which features a Norman motte and has been identified with the birthplace of mythological warrior Cuchullain – it used to be called Dun of Dealga. Access to the hill is via a short climb, with Captain Byrne's folly striking an incongruous note at the summit. To the SE of the hill is 15th-c and later Bellew's Castle. The town itself has a strong shipping trade and is involved in

1 Castletown Hill
2 Courthouse
3 Kincora House
4 Library & Hospital Remains
5 St Mary's College
6 St Nicholas' Church (CI)
7 St Nicholas' Church (RC)
8 St Patrick's Cathedral (RC)
9 Seatown Tower
10 Town Hall
11 Windmill

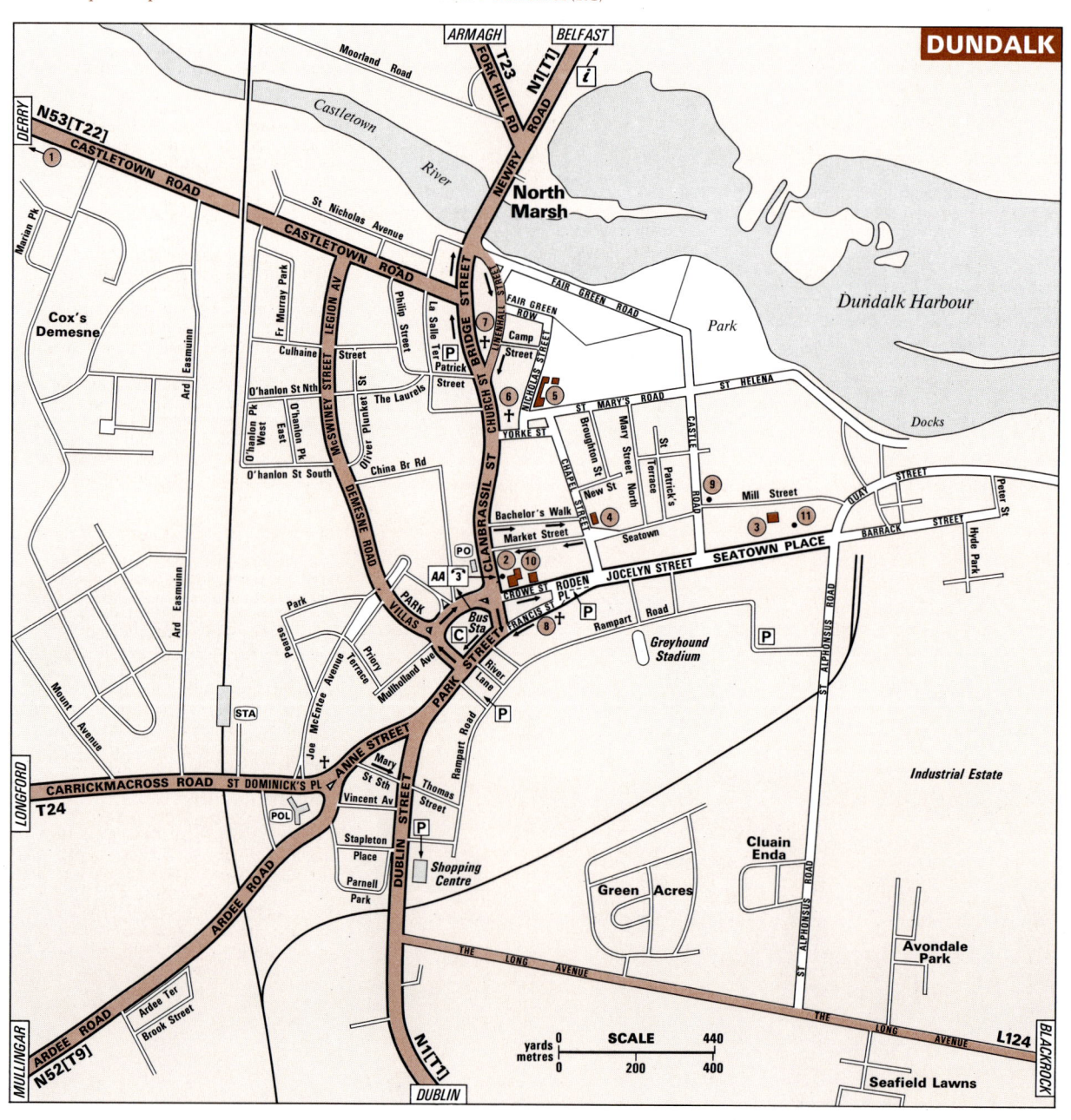

Entries marked * are the starting point of drives included in the Day Drive section of the book (pages 79 to 144).

various industries requiring imported materials. Castletown Castle, a 15th-c four-storey building modified in the 16th and 17thc, stands 1½m NW of the town.

DUNDONALD, *Dún Dónaill*:
Dónall's Fort, Down 13 J47
Situated in a narrow trough of land on the main roads E from Belfast to Newtownards and Comber, Dundonald is rapidly expanding into an industrial community. The Anglo-Norman motte (NM) known as Dundonald Fort can be seen near the CI parish church, and a fine portal grave called Kempe Stones (NM) lies in the townland of Greengraves about 1½m E of Dundonald. Inside the grave is a 5ft-square chamber which faces E and is entered over a high sill. The huge capstone, measuring 8½ by 7½ft, rests on a smaller horizontal roofing slab at the rear and the two vertical portal stones at the front. Stormont Castle is 1m W.

DUNDRUM, *Dún Droma*:
Fort of the Ridge, Down 13 J43
Situated on the almost land-locked Dundrum Bay, this picturesque little fishing village lies NE of the Mourne Mountains and features a magnificent ruined castle (NM). An Anglo-Norman stronghold that preceded the present building was a motte-and-bailey castle built by John de Courcy c1177 and taken by King John in 1210. The oldest parts of the castle are contained within the early 13th-c upper ward. This ward contains the great circular keep of c1230. In the basement of the keep is a funnel-shaped pit into which subsoil water percolated. The lower ward was first built towards the end of the 13thc, but most of the existing structure is 15thc. In the lower ward are the remains of a 17th-c house. The castle changed hands several times during the 17thc, and was eventually slighted by Cromwellian troops in 1652. Also of interest here are the Dundrum or Murlough Dunes, a stretch of sandhills that extend from Dundrum Bay to Newcastle and have yielded relics dating from neolithic to medieval times. A particular type of bowl with a heavy rim has been named the Dundrum Bowl after this site. About 475 acres of the dunes now form the Murlough nature reserve (NT), which offers many specimens of botanical and zoological interest. One of its main features is a signposted nature trail. At the entrance to Dundrum Bay is one of the three 'tonns' or waves of Ireland, which are frequently mentioned in ancient Irish literature, and whose melancholy sound – caused by the movement of water upon sand and rock – was said to foretell the death of a great personage.

*DUNFANAGHY, *Dún Fionnachaidh*:
Fort of the White Field, Donegal 5 C03
Views from here extend across the inlet of Sheep Haven to the Rosguill Peninsula, and the local beach is excellent. Stray finds dating from the early-Christian period have been found on the golf courses E of the village. The coastal scenery in this area is very fine. Horn Head to the N and 835ft Croaghnamaddy offer magnificent cliff views and can be reached by a pleasant walk from the village and round the Little Horn. To the W of the head is the natural feature Templebreaga Arch, and 2m W of Dunfanaghy is a blowhole known as MacSwiney's Gun. The latter is particularly impressive at certain states of the tide and weather. The 600ft cliffs of the head offer a demanding challenge to the experienced rock climber. Good sands and fine cliff scenery are offered by Port-na-Blagh Cove, which lies 2m E of the village. Columbkille's Lake is a holy well situated 2m S.

DUNGANNON, *Dún Geanainn*:
Geanann's Fort, Tyrone 12 H86
Up until the castle and town were burnt to prevent them falling into the hands of English forces in 1602, Dungannon was one of the chief seats of the O Neill family. Nothing survives of the original stronghold started by Hugh O Neill in 1567, and the remains of a structure of 1790 – wrongly called O Neill's Castle and built by Thomas Knox Hanyngton – are sparse. Two corner towers surviving from the latter were late additions.

The Royal Schools in Dungannon were originally founded in the 17thc. A bronze statue of Brigadier General John Nicholson, who died in 1857, stands in front of the original block. The present buildings were erected in 1786. An 18th-c building erected in William Street by Richard Taylor was intended as 'A new gaol and session house'. This is now occupied by a printing firm which produces the *Tyrone Courier* newspaper, but still displays its interesting pediment and four-columned portico. George's Street features the impressive 19th-c courthouse by John Hargrave. The CI parish church dates from 1790.

DUNGANSTOWN, Wexford 24 S62
See New Ross entry.

*DUNGARVAN, *Dún Garbhán*:
Garbhán's Fort, Waterford 29 X29
Plan overleaf
An important town even before the Anglo-Normans came to Ireland, Dungarvan is situated in a fine position overlooking Helvick Head. Part of the castle keep has survived from the stronghold built here in 1185 by King John, and although this structure suffered in Cromwellian times it is said that Cromwell himself spared it after seeing a woman drink his health at the town gate. Parts of the town walls also exist. Some of the Anglo-Norman castle remains are incorporated in the British military barracks, which were destroyed in 1921. The town's CI church stands in a graveyard which features a curious stone gable with five circular openings. St Augustine's Church (RC) of 1828 stands in Abbeyside on the E bank of the Colligan River and incorporates remains of an Augustinian church erected by the McGrath family in 1295. These include a tower and part of the old choir. Also in Abbeyside is the curious Shell Cottage.

The single-arched, 75ft-span bridge across the river in Dungarvan was built by the Duke of Devonshire in 1815 at a cost of £50,000. Some 2½m NW of the town is the 19th-c Master McGrath Memorial to a famous greyhound. Local scenery includes the charming glen of the Colligan River and the lovely landscape that accompanies the 8m trip to Helvick Head. To the N the Monavullagh Mountains culminate in 2,387ft Seefin, and the Drum Hills rise to the SW.

DUNGIVEN, *Dún Geimhin*:
the Fort of the Hide, Derry 6 C60
Dungiven Castle (NM) dates from 1839, but the Plantation castle built here by the Skinners Company dates from the 17thc. Survivals of the latter structure are the bawn walls (NM). About ¾m S on a cliff above the River Roe are the remains of an Augustinian priory founded in 1100

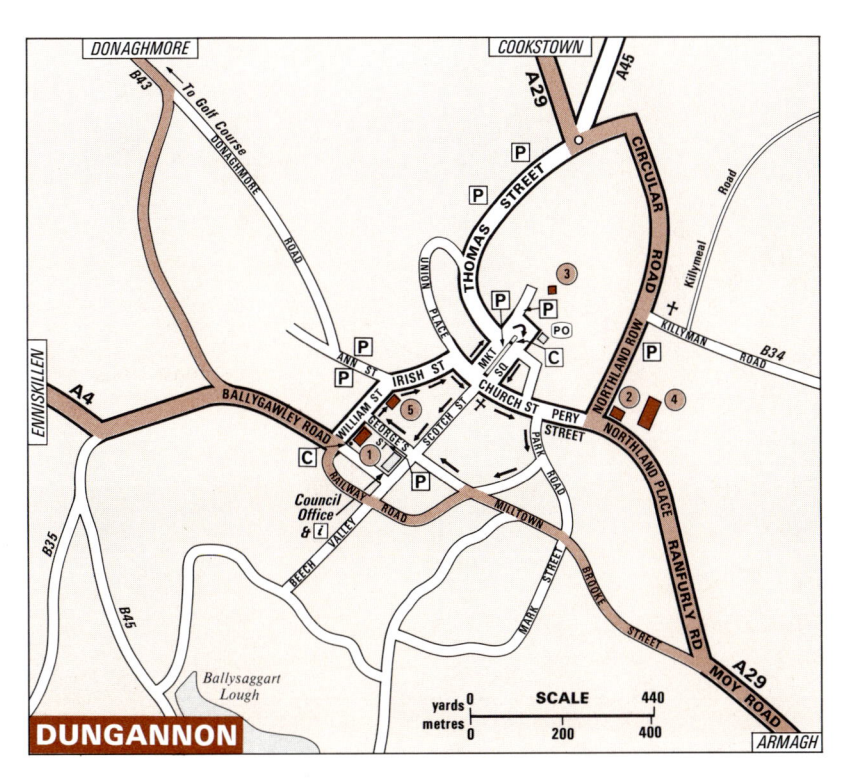

1 Courthouse
2 Northland House
3 O Neill's Castle
4 Royal Schools
5 *Tyrone Courier* House

Entries marked * are the starting point of drives included in the Day Drive section of the book (pages 79 to 144).

by the O Cahan family. They include a ruined church (NM) containing a largely 12th-c Romanesque chancel and a 14th-c nave. The main feature of the church is the beautiful 15th-c tomb of Cooey-na-Gall O Cahan, who died in 1385. This is situated in the south wall of the chancel and features an effigy clad in Irish armour, plus six mourning 'weepers'.

Dungiven itself, a small market town, lies at the foot of 1,535ft Ben Bradagh with the Sperrins rising to the 2,240ft peak of Sawel in the S. The picturesque Maghera road leads through the shadow of 1,825ft Mullaghmore and over the wild Glenshane Pass in lonely countryside to the SE. About 2½m ESE on this road is the Boviel wedge grave. This is known locally as *Cloghnagalla*, meaning the 'Hag's Stone' and was excavated in 1938. It comprises a 22ft-long by 7ft-wide gallery which is segmented into jambs that carry a lintel and form a 6ft-long antechamber. Originally this grave was corbel-covered and included an oval cairn.

DUNGLOE, *An Clochán Liath*:
the Grey Stepping Stones **4 B 71**
This is the only town in the Rosses, a region which lies to the N and consists of grey rocks, small lakes, and tiny fields surrounded by characteristic dry-stone walls. It is a small fishing port and angling resort situated near an inlet of the sea within sight of several little offshore islands, some 5m NE of the cliffs and caves of Crohy Head. Near the head, at Maghery, is a fine beach and N of the village is the interesting ancient church of Templecrone. Those interested in the action and progress of ancient glaciers should visit Lough Anure and the surrounding district. The lough itself is situated 4½m NE of Dungloe on the Gweedore road and displays good evidence of the ice age.

DUNIRY, *Dún Daighre*, Galway **16 M 70**
To the ESE of this village is the well-preserved 16th-18th-c Burke stronghold of Pallas Castle (NM). Features of the structure include the bawn, a rebuilt gatehouse, a five-storey tower with a vaulted third storey, and part of a large 17th-c house which was erected when the castle was assigned to the Nugent family. Members of this family were buried 3m E at St Corban's Church in Kilcorban, which stands on the site of a Dominican friary founded in 1466.

DUNKINEELY, *Dún Cionnaola*:
Kenneally's Fort, Donegal **4 G 77**
The name of this village is derived from Kenneally's Dun, or Fort, which is sited at the W end of the community. The village itself stands on the road between Donegal and Killybegs, at the base of a long narrow peninsula – ending in St John's Point – that separates Inver and McSwyne's bays. McSwyne's Castle stands on the shore 1½m SW of the village. A graveyard at Killaghtee overlooking McSwyne's Bay contains an interesting 6 by 2½ft cross slab displaying a Maltese cross cut in relief within a circular border. It is possible that the circular cut in the top arm of the cross represents the Chi-Rho symbol. A threefold knot or *triquetra* is carved below the cross as a symbol of the Trinity. A similar slab can be seen at the Relig 1½m WNW of Dunkineely in Bruckless townland. The area around Dunkineely is noted for its fishing.

DUN LAOGHAIRE, *Dún Laoghaire*:
Laoghaire's Fort, Dublin **19 O 22**
After a visit by King George IV in 1821 this well-known Dublin Bay port, residential suburb and major holiday resort, was renamed Kingstown, but it re-assumed its original Irish name in 1920. This is derived from Laoghaire, 5th-c High King of Ireland and a convert of St Patrick. The magnificent granite harbour with its two huge piers, which enclose an area of 250 acres, was built by John Rennie between 1817 and 1821. The East Pier is a popular promenade. Among its numerous bathing places is the famous Forty-Foot sea-bathing spot. Dun Laoghaire is a major ferry port with regular passenger, mail, and car ferry services to Holyhead in Wales. It is also the most important yachting centre in Ireland, having three yacht clubs, and is the venue for the Dublin Bay Week Regatta. Fragments of Monkstown Castle are all that remain of a 15th-c stronghold. Monkstown CI Church is an interesting gothick structure. James Joyce once lived in a martello tower at Sandy Cove. This now houses a Joyce museum.

DUNLEER, *Dún Léire*:
Léire's Fort, Louth **13 O 08**
This was once an important town, but has now decreased in size so much that it is only a village. Transitional features are displayed by the west tower of the local 19th-c Protestant church, and its hall contains three early gravestones. The latter are relics of an early monastic site known as Lann Leire, which was associated with St Brigid. John Foster, Lord Oriel and last speaker in the Irish House of Commons, is buried in the churchyard. About 3m SE is Rokeby Hall, a mansion designed for Primate Robinson of Armagh by Francis Johnston in 1794.

DUNLEWY, *Dún Lúiche*:
Lughdhach's Fort, Donegal **4 B 91**
Situated by the shores of Dunlewy Lough, Dunlewy is a small village in the heart of the Donegal Mountains. Errigal Mountain, Donegal's highest summit, rises to 2,466ft above the village to the N, and the Derryveagh Mountains form a line to the E and S. SE of Dunlewy is the Cronanly Burn leading into the Poisoned Glen. Slieve Snaght, at 2,240ft the highest point in the Derryveagh range, rises to the S beyond Dunlewy Lough. Crocknafarragh (1,707ft) and Grogan More (1,488ft) lie to the SW, and to the NW the long narrow Lough Nacung stretches away towards Gweedore and the slopes of 1,335ft Cronalaght. At the head of Lough Nacung, near Dunlewy, stands the disused parish church (CI) of local white marble. The newer RC church has a picturesque – though modern – round tower, and an interesting early cross slab can be seen 4m to the S on the ancient church site of *Trian na Cille*. The village is a well-known centre for the manufacture of home-spun tweed.

The most scenic approach to Dunlewy is from the NE along the road from Creeslough and Glenveagh. Following the Calabber River from the area of Glenveagh, 2,197ft Muckish Mountain is seen ahead. Bearing left at Calabber Bridge, a wide valley is entered with 1,554ft Crocknalaragagh, 1,860ft Aghla Beg and 1,916ft Aghla More on the right, and Dooish, the 2,147ft northernmost summit of the Derryveagh range, on the left. A long gradual climb reveals a view of Altan Lough to the right before reaching the 900ft summit of the Gap of Dunlewy. On the descent the magnificent quartzite cone of Errigal Mountain is seen before passing above Dunlewy village.

DUNLUCE CASTLE, Antrim **6 C 94**
See Bushmills entry.

DUNMORE, *Dún Mór*:
Big Fort, Galway **16 M 56**
Features of this market village include a wool weighhouse and weighbridge. Remains of an Augustinian Hermits' friary founded here in 1428 include The Abbey (NM), a church which

1 Castle & Town Walls
2 Holed Gable in Parish Churchyard (CI)
3 Master McGrath Memorial
4 St Augustine's Church (RC)
5 Shell Cottage

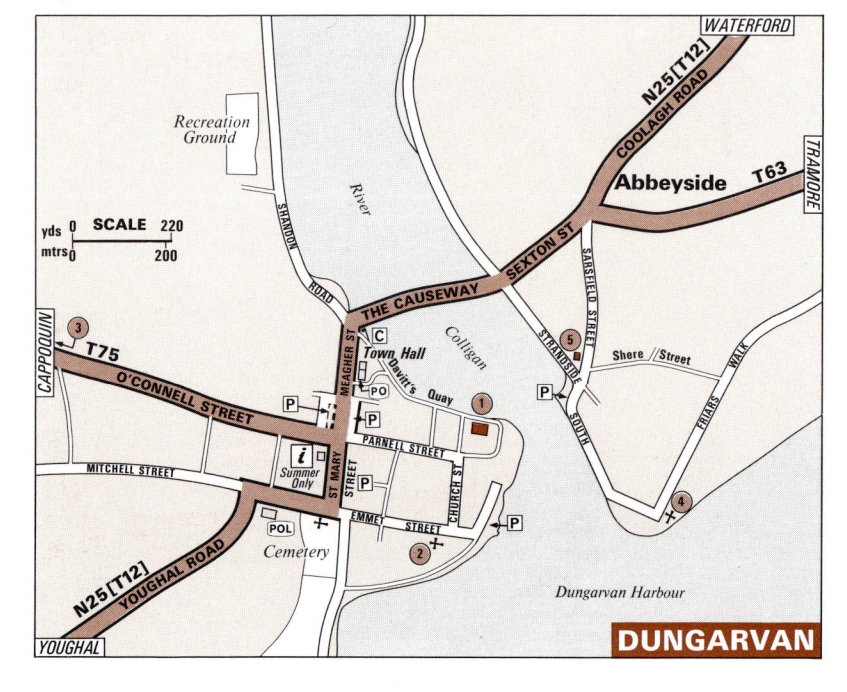

DUNGARVAN

displays an interesting perpendicular west doorway and also retains its central tower. Dunmore Castle, ½m NW, dates from the 13thc and was built by the de Bermingham family on a site once occupied by King Turloch O Conor's fort. The ruins are bisected by a road, on one side of which are remains of an upper ward and keep, with the lower ward or bailey on the other. A mound to the W on an esker known as Knockmannanan or Rathcol is called King Turloch's Grave. There are a great many archaeological sites in the area.

DUNMORE CAVES, *An Dún Mór:*
the Big Fort, Kilkenny   24 S56
See Kilkenny entry.

DUNMORE EAST, *Dún Mór:*
Big Fort, Waterford   29 S60
A small angling and seaside resort at the mouth of Waterford Harbour, Dunmore East faces the long peninsula of Hook Head and derives its name from the great dun which partially survives here. Black Knob Cliff with its promontory fort known as the Shanooan can be seen on the S side of the village, and access to Merlin's Cave beneath the Black Knob is via a footpath. About 2½m NNW is the Harristown passage grave. Excavations carried out here in 1939 revealed that this is an undifferentiated type with a 22ft-long passage which widens to a maximum of 4½ft at the west end. The whole structure was originally roofed with stone slabs, and the orthostatic kerb within which it lies is 30ft in diameter. The 430ft viewpoint of Knockadirragh lies 2½m NW.

DUNMORE HEAD, *Ceann an Dúin Mhóir:*
Big Fort Head, Kerry   26 V39
Situated at the extreme W end of the Dingle Peninsula at the foot of massive 1,696ft Mount Eagle, Dunmore Head is the most westerly point of the Irish mainland. At one time some 80 acres of the headland were cut off from the main coast by a 1,300ft rampart, thus forming a well-defended site. The 328ft summit of the head carries a 6ft-tall ogham stone with a long inscription. To the SE is Slea Head, and to the W across Blasket Sound rise the Blasket Islands. Of these Great Blasket is the largest and most prominent, being a long narrow ridge rising to 961ft.

DUNMURRY, *Dún Muirigh:*
Muiríoch's Fort, Antrim   13 J26
Belfast's expansion has stimulated the similarly rapid growth of this village, which is situated close to the Lagan Valley country park. The Presbyterian church is typical of the Ulster barn-type of building and was erected in the style of James Gibbs in 1779. A notable old packhorse bridge can be seen in the village. Collin Mountain rises to 1,086ft NW of Dunmurry, near the beautiful wooded slopes (NT) of Collin Glen.

DUNSANY CASTLE, *Dún Samhnaí:*
Samhnach's Fort, Meath   18 N95
See Tara entry.

DUNSEVERICK, *Dún Sobhairce:*
Sobhairce's Fort, Antrim   6 C94
According to tradition, St Patrick blessed the very early Irish fort which once stood on the site now occupied by Dunseverick Castle (NT), and the stronghold was subjected to frequent Viking attacks. Remains of the 11ft-thick walls seen here today survive from an Anglo-Norman invasion castle built by the de Mandevilles, whose name was subsequently Gaelicized as MacQuillan. Later it came into the possession of the O Cahans, who lost it to Sean O Neill in 1565 but recovered it a little while later. After this the family held the castle until it was captured by Cromwell. The last O Cahan was executed in 1653. The stronghold was frequently mentioned in Irish annals and played a large part in the history of the country, but all that remains today are fragments of the gatehouse walls. Dunseverick itself is a small village close to the N Antrim coast, between Benbane Head and White Park Bay.

DUNSHAUGHLIN, *Dún Seachlainn:*
St Secundinus' Church, Meath   18 N95
This village is named after St Seachnal, or Secundinus, who came to Ireland to help St Patrick in his missionary work. The local CI church features a list of pastors from St Patrick to 20th-c John McClenaghan, and its graveyard preserves the lintel (NM) of a pre-Romanesque church. This carries a carved representation of the Crucifixion.
cont overleaf

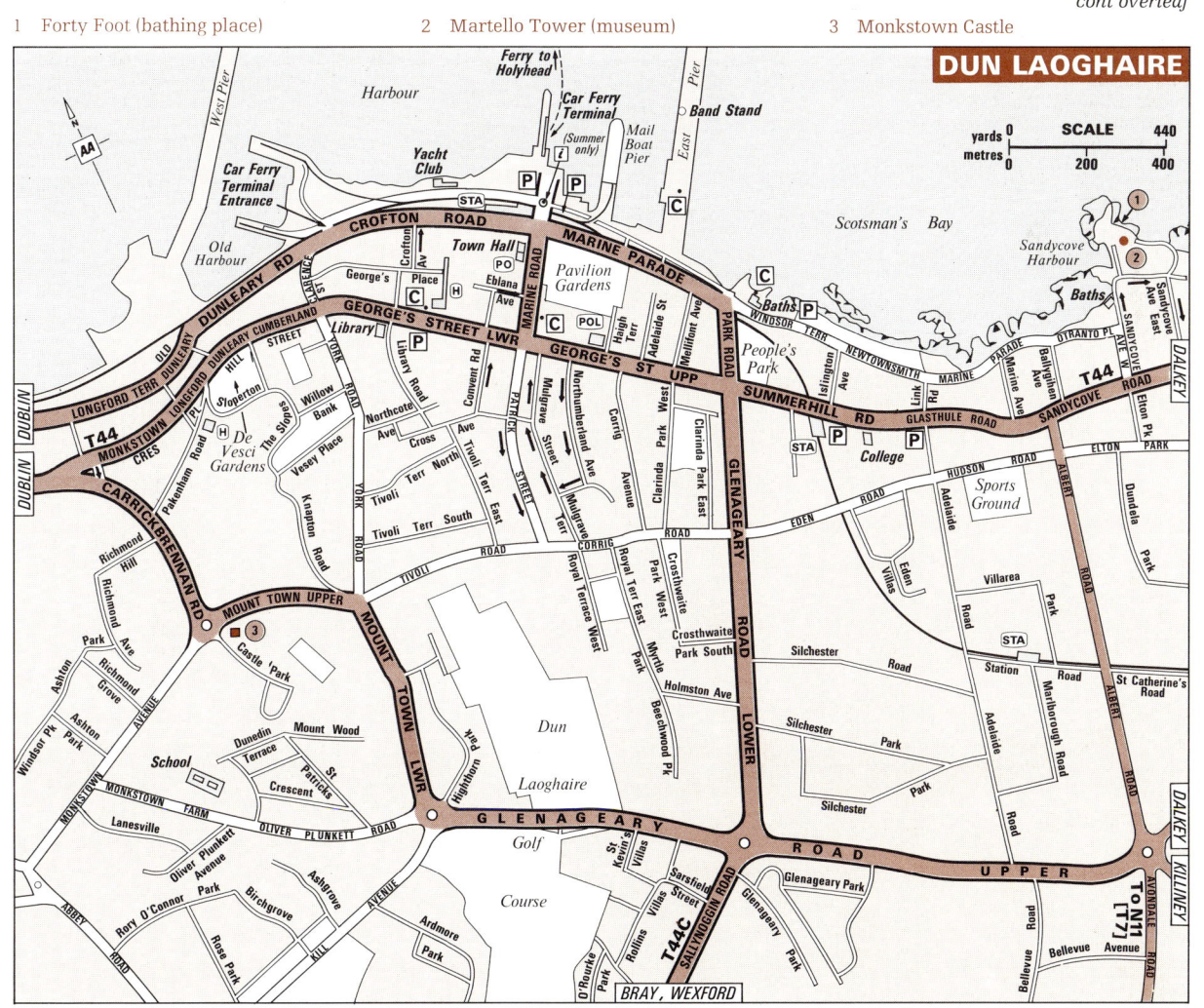

1 Forty Foot (bathing place)   2 Martello Tower (museum)   3 Monkstown Castle

Also of interest in the village are the nave arcade of a medieval church and a small courthouse by Francis Johnston.

DUNSINK, *Dún Sinche:*
Sineach's Fort, Dublin **19 O13**
Situated in the NW suburbs of Dublin 1½m W of Finglas is the Dunsink Observatory (OACT), which was founded in 1788 as a faculty of Trinity College in Dublin. Sir William Rowan-Hamilton, whose important *Lecture on Quaternions* was published in 1835, was one of the foundation's distinguished early Directors. Shortly after 1921 the observatory was closed down, but the Irish government re-established it under the auspices of the Institute for Advanced Studies in 1947. It specializes in research connected with the sun and the effect of solar influences on the earth. Its equipment includes electronic devices for the measuring of star brightness. A 36in telescope mounted in Bloemfontein, S Africa, is jointly owned by the Dunsink and Armagh observatories.

DURROW ABBEY, *Darú:*
Oak Plain, Offaly **17 N33**
See Tullamore entry.

DUVILLAUN MORE, Mayo **8 F51**
This little cliff-guarded island is situated some 3m WSW of the S tip of the Mullet Peninsula and is uninhabited. People did live here once, and the island, which is only accessible in calm weather, features several early-Christian monuments in a fair state of preservation. Many of these are contained within a cashel which is split by a cross wall. In the eastern half of the enclosure are the foundations of an oratory, a long cist, and at the head of the latter a cross pillar displaying a Greek cross inside a circle. A Crucifixion scene is also represented on the pillar. Elsewhere are the remains of several beehive huts.

DYSERT O DEA, *Díseart Ui Dheá:*
O Dea's Hermitage, Clare **21 R28**
St Tola, 8th-c Bishop of Clonard, founded a hermitage on the site where the local 15th-c church (NM) now stands. Although all traces of the original structure have disappeared, a well to the SE still bears the saint's name. The present church features a reconstructed Romanesque doorway of unusual and elaborate style. The famous 12th-c high cross (NM) here carries representations of a fully-clothed Crucified Christ, various ecclesiastics, and pleasing abstract patterns which include zoomorphic ornamentation. Also of interest is the 40ft-high stump of a round tower and 15th-c O Dea Castle, ruins of which lie to the N on the site of a battle in which the Irish defeated the Anglo-Normans c1318.

EASKY, *Iascaigh:*
Abounding with Fish, Sligo **9 G33**
The name of this small, Easky River resort means 'abounding with fish', and its angling reputation lives up to its description. It lies between Killala and Sligo Bays, and features a curious split rock known as Finn MacCool's Finger Stone, which is a relic of the ice age. The rocks near the beach are well known for their fossiliferous nature. There are two martello towers – one at each end of the village. Roslee Castle stands on the shore about ¾ N of the resort and was once a stronghold of the MacDonnell family. The MacDonnells were the galloglas servitors of the O Dowds, who were chiefs of the area. Prehistoric remains in the area include two court cairns in Fortland, ½m SSE, and the remains of a gallery grave in Bookaun ½m SSW of Fortland.

EDENDERRY, *Éadan Doire:*
Hill-brow of the Oak Grove, Offaly **18 N63**
Many of this market town's buildings were constructed by the Marquess of Devonshire after he had acquired Blundell's Castle by marriage. This hilltop castle lies to the S of the town; 1m S of the castle is the Grand Canal. Sir John de Bermingham founded the Monasteroris Friary for the Franciscans some 2m W in the 14thc, and beside the ruins of this is a small parish church which features a dovecote on a mound. Carrick Hill rises to the N (see Carrick Castle, Kildare entry). The source of the River Boyne lies at an altitude of 290ft above sea level near the town, and the 240,000-acre Bog of Allen extends to the W.

EDGEWORTHSTOWN (MOSTRIM), *Meathas Troim:*
Frontier of the Elder Tree, Longford **17 N27**
Authoress Maria Edgeworth, a member of the family which gave their name to this market town, is known for her novel *Castle Rackrent.* She lived between 1767 and 1849, and was visited here by such famous literary figures as Sir Walter Scott and William Wordsworth. The steeple of the local CI church is a curious edifice built by another member of the family. The family vault is in the church, as are some of their personal effects. The Georgian mansion built by Maria's father, Richard Lovell, is now a convent. Abbé Edgeworth, who attended Louis XVI on the scaffold, lived 2m N at Firmount.

ELPHIN, *Ail Finn:*
the Rock of the Clear Spring, Roscommon **10 M88**
St Patrick founded the first bishopric here, but nothing now remains of either the buildings associated with this or the Augustinian and Franciscan houses which followed it. The local CI church was a cathedral until the diocese was amalgamated with Ardagh and Kilmore. Oliver Goldsmith was born at Pallas but attended the diocesan school when he was eight years of age. His grandfather the Rev Oliver Jones lived 1m NW at Smith Hill.

EMAIN MACHA, *Eamhain Mhacha,* Armagh **12 H84**
Also known as Navan Fort (NM), this romantic hillfort palace of Ulster's Gaelic kings is a place where legend and known history meet. The huge circular bank measures 40ft in width and encloses 18 acres of ground. The internal fosse is 10ft deep, and these defences encircled two mounds. One of these is hardly visible and yielded evidence of dark-age occupation when excavated. The other has a diameter of 200ft and is 20ft high. It contained a ritual temple-like structure and was covered with a cairn measuring 10ft high and 120ft in diameter. Legend says that this is the burial place of Queen *Macha,* or Maeve.

Basically a ritual site, Emain Macha was the scene of an annual assembly or *Eonach* and may have been covered by a huge mound before it was abandoned at the approach of the Ui Neill clan in the 4thc. At this time Fergus was King of Ulster, and according to legend the fort-palace was the seat of Conchobar mac Nesa and his fabled Red Branch Knights. The chief of this band was the great warrior Cuchullain, who appears often in the *Ulster Cycle* legends. The name of the site means the 'twins of Macha' and may refer to the twin raths of Navan and Armagh. Legend offers a different interpretation and tells of a woman who was forced to run a race when pregnant. After the race she gave birth to twins and cursed both the site and the Ulster heroes. Tradition aside, the site is truly ancient and had been abandoned for 100 years when St Patrick arrived at Armagh.

EMLY, *Imleach:*
Lake Border, Tipperary **22 R73**
A small village set in undulating country, up to the Reformation Emly was an episcopal see, with a cathedral standing on the site now occupied by the CI parish church. Relics preserved in the churchyard include the Well of St Ailbhe and a low stone cross (said to mark St Ailbhe's grave) – all that remains of a monastic foundation dedicated to St Ailbhe, a contemporary of St Patrick.

*****ENNIS**, *Inis:* Holm, Clare **21 R37**
Ennis is a busy market and county town situated on the River Fergus. Its streets are narrow and tortuous. A column on the site of the old courthouse commemorates Daniel O Connell, its representative in the House of Commons from 1828 to 1831. Steele's Rock in the River Fergus at Newbridge Road is carved with a lion and recalls O Connell's friend 'Honest Tom'. Ruins of a Franciscan friary (NM) founded in 1242 by Donough O Brien, King of Thomond, can be seen at the end of Church Street. The church includes a transept lit by long, pointed windows and contains a McMahon tomb of 15th-c date. Known as the Royal Tomb, this splendid monument displays carvings representing the Passion of Our Lord. An Inchiquin tomb against the south wall carries beautifully carved floral designs, and a small 15th-c carving in a pier recess poignantly depicts Christ with his hands bound and head crowned with thorns. This carving includes the crowing cock arising from a pot, sometimes interpreted as a symbol of the resurrection, or alternatively as the bird intended for the High Priest's supper – the one that crowed at Peter's denial. Perhaps the most striking work in the church is the carving of St Francis with the stigmata.

Thomas Dermody the 18th-c poet lived at Ennis, and Harriet Smithson – who married the famous French composer Hector Berlioz – was born here in 1800. The town has preserved an interesting narrow-gauge locomotive from the former West Clare Railway. The CI parish church, the RC cathedral and some of the Georgian buildings are also of interest. There is a municipal museum in Bindon Street. Ruined Clare Abbey (NM), which lies 1m SE, is an Augustinian foundation of 1189 with a prominent central tower.

*ENNISCORTHY, *Inis Corthaidh*,
Wexford 24 S93

Well situated on the steep W bank of the River Slaney, this important market town includes a restored and modernized castle which contains the county museum but still retains many of its ancient features. This stronghold was built in the 13thc by the Prendergast family, and features a keep flanked by three drum towers and a turret. Edmund Spenser the poet lived in the building after it had been restored by Sir Henry Wallop in 1586 after the Tudor wars. During its history the castle was captured by Cromwell, who spared it out of respect for its strength. It was then taken by insurgents during the 1798 Rising. The rebels used the windmill on Vinegar Hill as a fort, making a brave stand there before both it and the castle were recaptured by General Lake. The Earl of Portsmouth, a descendant of Sir Henry Wallop, restored the structure for the second time during the 19thc. Views N from the ruined windmill (NM) take in the Wicklow Mountains, Ferns, and Ferns Castle. To the E is Oulart Hill, where the King's forces received a setback in 1798, while NW are 2,610ft Mount Leinster and the Blackstairs Range. Hills of the Barony of Forth rise in the S, from beyond the estuary.

The local CI parish church deserves a visit, as does 19th-c St Aidan's Cathedral (RC). This cathedral was designed in gothic-revival style by Pugin. Earl Beatty was born at nearby Borodale 2m S (see entry). A road leads NW from here towards the Scullogue Gap S of Mount Leinster.

ENNISCRONE, *Inis Crabhann*:
Holm of the Esker of the River, Sligo 9 G22

Good surf bathing is offered by this Killala Bay resort. There is a 3m long beach, and medicinal baths are available. About 2m NE of the village is famous Castle Firbis. Built in 1560, this was a stronghold of the MacFirbis family, a member of which compiled the 15th-c *Book of Lecan* – a treasure preserved by the Royal Irish Academy in Dublin. The 17th-c ruins of a Plantation castle can be seen ¼m NE, and the remains of a chamber tomb lie between the castle and the shore.

ENNISKERRY, *Áth na Sceire*:
the Ford of the Reef, Wicklow 19 O21

This delightful little village stands on the Cookstown River in attractive country a little N of the magnificent 34,000-acre Powerscourt Estate. The pedimented entrance gate to the estate lies ½m S of Enniskerry. The Georgian mansion was designed by Cassels in 1731 and altered and enlarged in the 19thc; it was badly damaged by fire in 1974. It is reached by an avenue of trees nearly 1m in length. King George IV was entertained in the ballroom and banqueting hall. It is probable that the site on which the house stands was once occupied by an Anglo-Norman stronghold built by the de la Poer family.

The beautiful gardens (OACT) include Italian and Japanese sections and lead up to a vantage point for superb views of the Great Sugar Loaf Mountain. A point just beyond the entrance to the Deer Park affords magnificent views of 2,473ft Kippure rising above the lovely Glencree Valley. Farther S are the impressive heights of 2,385ft Djouce Mountain and 2,250ft War Hill. The horseshoe-shaped Deer Park Glen leads to a famous waterfall where the Dargle River plunges over a precipice. At 398ft it is one of the highest in Great Britain and Ireland. Close to the entrance of the Powerscourt demesne is Tinnahinch House, a fine building which was presented to the patriot Henry Grattan by the grateful Irish parliament in 1782. Tinnahinch Bridge spans the Dargle and is a well-known beauty spot, as is Dargle Glen. A megalithic tomb can be seen at Parknasilloge, 1m NW of Enniskerry.

*ENNISKILLEN, *Inis Ceithleann*:
Ceithle's Island, Fermanagh 11 H24

Enniskillen, the county town of Fermanagh, is beautifully situated on an island in the River Erne which here forms the boundary between the historic Irish provinces of Ulster and Connacht. Some authorities claim that the town's name was taken from the ford here, but others say that it is a derivation of the 'Island of Ceithleann' – wife of Balor of the Mighty Blows. Enniskillen Castle, which was for long used as a military barracks, commands the old ford, now replaced by the West Bridge. The castle houses an interesting museum. It has been greatly changed over the years since its 15th-c origins, but still retains the original batter of its lower courses. More famous than the stronghold itself is the castle's Water Gate, which may be a 17th-c rebuilding of an early Maguire feature by Sir William Cole.

St Macartan's Church was raised to cathedral status in 1924 to be the second of the CI Clogher diocese, but was originally built as a parish church in the 17thc. The tower carries the date 1637 and a representation of the Lamb and Flag over the main entrance, but the main building was entirely rebuilt in 1840. Included is the Fusiliers' Regimental Chapel, which was dedicated in 1970. Enniskillen has the distinction of being the only town in the British Isles to have raised two regiments. These are the Royal Inniskilling Dragoon Guards and the Royal Inniskilling Fusiliers, which is now amalgamated with the Irish Rangers. Notable features inside the cathedral include an old font of 1666 and the Porkrich Stone of 1628.

On the NW edge of the town is Portora Royal School. This was one of five such foundations created by Charles I in 1626, and today it is one of the leading Irish public schools. Its fine Georgian buildings, dating mainly from 1777, have witnessed the rise of several famous men. These include Oscar Wilde, Sam Beckett, and the Rev Henry Francis Lyte, author of *Abide With Me*. Portora Castle in the school grounds is a ruined Plantation

1 Cathedral of SS Peter & Paul (RC)
2 Franciscan Friary Ruins
3 Narrow-gauge Steam Locomotive
4 O Connell Memorial

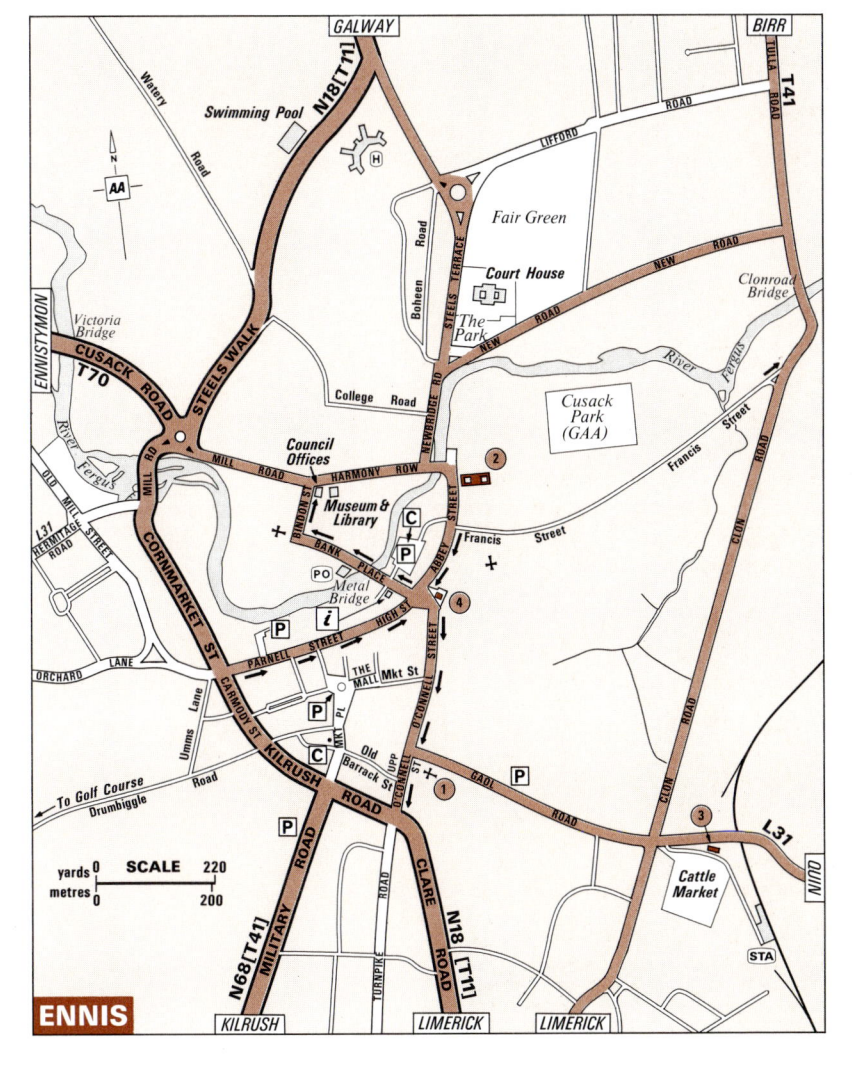

stronghold which was built c1616 by Sir William Cole to guard the meeting of the River Erne and Lower Lough Erne. Part of the bawn is intact and parts of three corner flankers have survived. This castle now presides over sluice gates which control the flow of water from the upper lough. Both Irish governments participated in this project, which has resulted in the control of winter flooding in the N and a supply of hydro-electric power to the S. About 1½m SE of the town is Castle Coole (NT), a Georgian mansion built by Sir James Wyatt for Lord Belmore in 1748. It was enlarged by Francis Johnston in 1818 and is said to be the finest structure of its kind in Ireland. The building comprises an oblong central block emphasised by a pedimented portico and flanked by colonnades which terminate with small pavilions. A feature of the rear is its semi-circular bay, and the interior shows plasterwork by Joseph Rose and Dominic Bartoli, and carvings by David Sheehan and John Houghton. A lake in the 1,500-acre wooded demesne supports a breeding colony of greylag geese. In the grounds is a stone with four bullauns. In Fort Hill Park is a column which commemorates Sir Galbraith Lowry-Cole; it stands on the site of a star fort.

ENNISTYMON, *Inis Díomáin*:
Dioman's Holm, Clare **21 R18**
This holiday and small market town grew up around a castle built by Turlough O Brien in 1588. Situated on the River Cullenagh, it is noted for its fishing. At this point in its course the river rushes over a rocky bed before joining the sea at Liscannor Bay. The poet Brian Merriman was born here c1749. A hill above the town is surmounted by a ruined church which dates from 1778, and the town's notable modern RC church dates from 1953.

ERNE, LOUGH, *Loch Éirne*, Fermanagh **11 H23/H06**
The Erne complex comprises the Upper and Lower loughs, of 1,505 and 10,450 acres respectively, connected by a 10m river which contains the island town of Enniskillen. Both lakes offer beautiful landscapes of drumlins and islands, forested shores, and encircling cliffs and hills. The islands in the Lower Lough, including Boa, Devenish, White Island, and Inishmacsaint, feature a number of important archaeological sites (all NM).

Of the islands in the Lower Lough, Lusty Beg is an attractive tourist centre and Ely Island is the home of the Duke of Westminster. The old house on Ely belonged to the Marquess of Ely and was destroyed c1870. Carrickreagh is a fine viewpoint which rises from the Ely Lodge Forest on the western shore and dominates the island's attractively-sited jetty. Below this hill is the delightful Perch Path walk. The shores of the Lower Lough also have a great deal to offer, including an ancient church site at Killadeas and ruined Plantation castles at Castle Archdale (NM), Castle Caldwell, Crevenish near Kesh, Tully, and Portora near Enniskillen. Magnificent views of the lower lake and its islands are available from Goblusk, which also boasts the Lough Erne Yacht Club. Nearby Rossfad House occupies a well-chosen site which was once occupied by a 17th-c building owned by Lancelot Carleton. Boat-hire stations and marinas are available at Enniskillen, Killadeas, Aghinver, and Muckross near Kesh.

Upper Lough Erne is more easily definable as a series of flooded islands, less populated, and remoter than the lower lake. A number of the islands here feature ancient church sites, but of these Cleenish, Inishkeen, and Galloon display little more than badly-weathered crosses and are only of interest to archaeologists. Bell Isle, now connected to the lake shore by a bridge, is the 17th-c Seanad MacManus where the famous *Annals of Ulster* were compiled. Near the E shore of the lake's Tamlaght Bay, in Derryvullen townland, is a holy well dedicated to St Patrick and traditionally associated with healing. A hilltop near Derryvullen is surmounted by a ruined church which occupies the site of a medieval parish church. It is thought that the carved-stone head built into the east gable of the local Protestant parish church came from the original building.

1 Castle Coole
2 Enniskillen Castle & Water Gate
3 Portora Castle
4 Portora Royal School
5 St Macartan's Cathedral (CI)
6 Sir Galbtaith Lowry-Cole Memorial
7 West Bridge

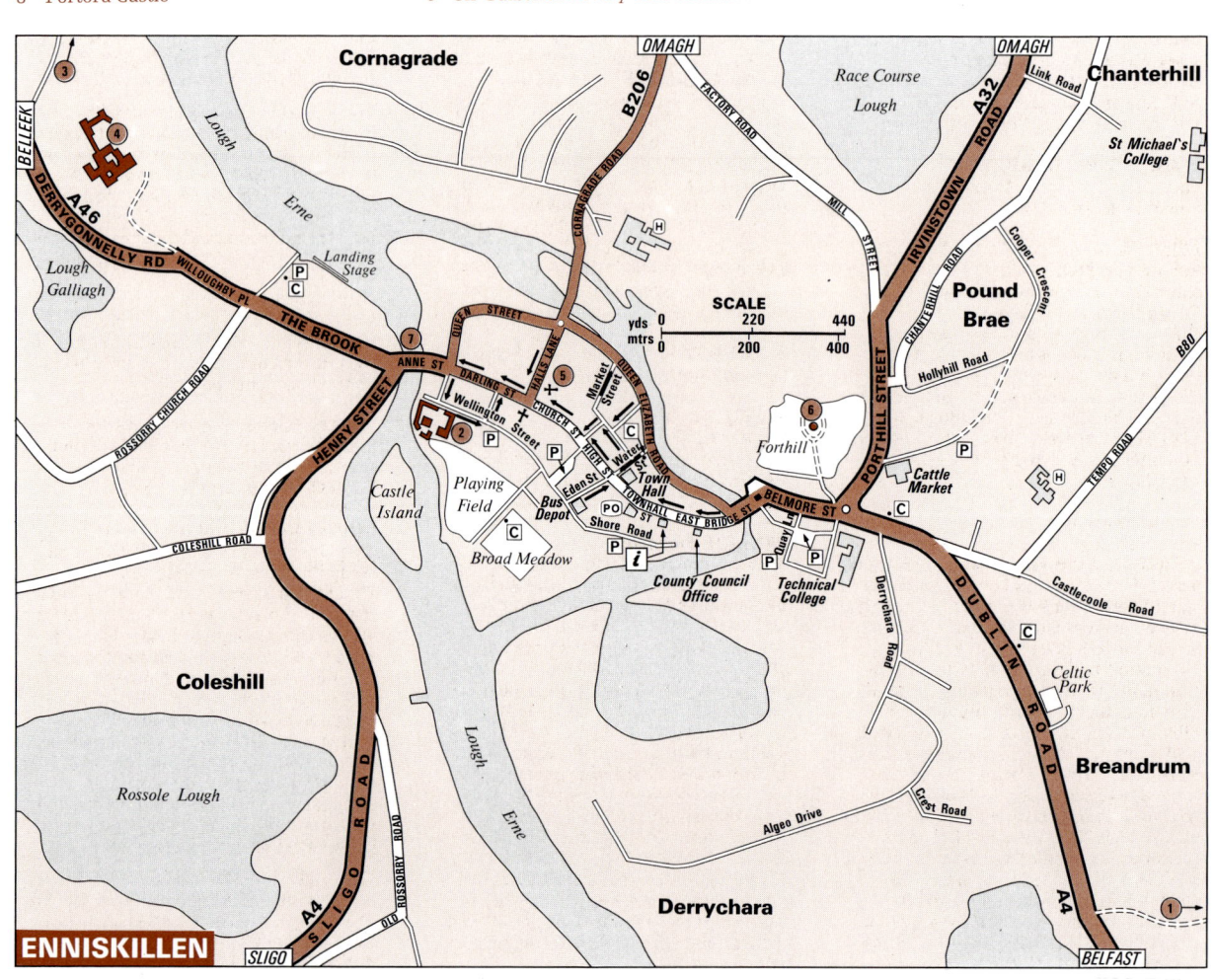

About 1m S in Fyagh townland is a well-defined rath enclosing Derrybrusk Old Church. The latter features a two-light window in perpendicular style, with two carved heads acting as finials.

Bird life on the Upper Lough is prolific, and the waters of the lake are alive with both game and coarse fish. Boat-hire companies exist at Carrybridge and Bellaneek, while a regular boat service from the Round O Quay in Enniskillen offers tours of the lake and its islands. Mountains which are particularly prominent from the Upper Lough include 1,316ft Belmore, 2,188ft Cuilcagh, 1,221ft Ben Aughlin, 630ft Knockninny and 1,331ft Slieve Rushen. Scenery around the Lower Lough includes the 1,000ft Magho Cliffs, Church Hill and 835ft Breesy Hill rising from Co Donegal. Both Erne lakes have been declared areas of outstanding natural beauty and scientific interest. Further information concerning places mentioned in this entry can be found elsewhere in the gazetteer.

ERRIGAL KEEROGE, *Aireagal Dachiaróg:*
St Dachiaróg's Oratory, Tyrone **12 H 65**
See Augher, Tyrone entry.

ERRIGAL, MOUNT, *An Earagail,*
Donegal **4 B 92**
This superb white quartzite cone rises to a height of 2,466ft above Dunlewy Lough and Lough Nacung. It is the highest peak in Donegal and from its summit views of most of the Ulster peaks may be obtained.

ERRIL, *Eiréil,* Laois **23 S 27**
Remains of a foundation created here by St Ciaran of Saighir include St Kieran's Church (NM) and the monastic site (NM). The base of a stepped cross (NM) standing at nearby crossroads was raised to Florence Fitzpatrick and his wife Katherine O More, who both died in 1613.

ESKE or EASKLOUGH, *Loch Iasc:*
Fish Lake, Donegal **4 G 98**
See Ballybofey entry.

EYERIES, *Na hAoraí,* Cork **26 V 65**
Situated in the Beara Peninsula near the shores of Coulagh Bay, this well-kept little village lies slightly S of Ballycrovane Harbour. Near by in Faunkill is an ogham-inscribed pillar (NM) which, at 17½ft, is the tallest yet discovered. A stone fort and souterrain can also be seen near the village. The Slieve Miskish range lies to the S and E, culminating in 2,044ft Maulin 4m E of the village.

FAHAN, *Fathain:*
Grave, Donegal **5 C 32**
A ferry links this village with Rathmullan, which faces it across Lough Swilly. Inch Island peninsula lies to the S. A cross slab which survives from the early monastic site in the local CI churchyard is associated with St Mura, who was the first abbot of this Columban foundation. The magnificent slab displays broad-ribbon interlaced crosses on two faces, and a unique Greek inscription on the north edge. The latter may refer to a doxology of 633. Two ecclesiastics are featured on the west face, and two birds on the east. Near the churchyard entrance is a small cross slab. St Mura's Well can be seen near by; his bell is included in the Wallace Collection in London, and his crozier is preserved in the National Museum, Dublin. Mouldy Hill rises to 1,021ft in the NE.

FAHAN, *Fán:* Slope, Kerry **26 V 39**
Sometimes called the Ancient City of Fahan, the huge concentration of beehive huts in Fahan townland, about 3½m SW of Ventry, includes about 400 of the clochans themselves, 19 souterrains, 18 standing stones, and several cashels with killeen graveyards for the burial of unbaptised children. It is thought that this settlement began in the early-Christian period and thrived between the 6th and 10thc. Stone is plentiful and wood scarce in this area, with the result that many of the clochans are recent structures built for farming purposes.

FAIR HEAD, *An Bhinn Mhór:*
Big Peak, Antrim **7 D 14**
See Ballycastle, Antrim entry.

FALCARRAGH, *An Fál Carrach:*
the Rough Enclosure, Donegal **4 B 93**
Local Ballyconnell House stands in pleasant grounds which feature the Cloghaneely Stone, a red-veined rock which traditionally formed the block used by Balor – the one-eyed king of Tory Island – to decapitate MacKineely, chieftain of the district. Errigal rises to 2,466ft S of Falcarragh, and 2,197ft Muckish can be seen to the SE. The latter can be ascended from Muckish Gap.

FALLS OF DOONASS, *Eas Danainne:*
Danann's Waterfall, Clare and Limerick
22 R 66
See Castleconnell entry.

FASTNET ROCK, *Carraig Aonair:*
Lone Rock, Cork **26 V 81**
See Clear Island entry.

FAUGHART, *Fochaird,* Louth **13 J 01**
St Brigid is said to have been born here, 2m NNE of Dundalk, in the 5thc; remains of an old church can be seen on the site of an ancient monastery which she is popularly held to have founded. An annual pilgrimage to her shrine, which is situated near Brigid's Well and the base of a high cross, takes place in July. A large stone in the local churchyard covers the King's Grave, where Edward Bruce was traditionally buried after being killed in battle against Sir Edward de Bermingham on Faughart Hill in 1318.

FAVOUR ROYAL, Tyrone **12 H 65**
See Aughnacloy entry.

FEENY, *Na Fíneadha:*
the Woods, Derry **6 C 60**
Four interesting standing stones can be seen here, and the Sperrin Mountains culminate in 2,240ft Sawel to the S.

FENAGH, *Fíonacha:*
Wooded Places, Leitrim **11 H 10**
Two ancient churches (NM) which can be seen here occupy an ancient religious site associated with St Killian. *The Book of Fenagh* was copied from an even older document in 1516 and is now held by the Royal Irish Academy. One of the churches features a good 14th- to 15th-c east window, carved gable brackets, and a barrel-vaulted west end which once included first-floor living quarters. The 17th-c mausoleum at the south-east end was erected by Torna Duignan, one-time rector of Fenagh, for his brother and family. The second church also has a barrel-vaulted west end, and includes a corridor along the south side – an unusual feature in this type of building. A large megalithic tomb can be seen in the village.

FENIT, *An Fhianait:*
Wild Place, Kerry **20 Q 71**
This small port is situated on Tralee Bay. Fenit Castle stands 2m NNW on Fenit Island. McKenna's Fort, where Sir Roger Casement hid after landing on Irish soil in 1916, is an overgrown ringfort which stands above this small village. To the W is the fine Banna Strand.

FERBANE, *Fearbán,* Offaly **17 N 12**
Gallen Monastery, which is said to have been founded here by St Canoc in the 5thc and is mentioned in the 9th-c *Irish Annals*, has completely disappeared. Gallen Priory is a gothicized Georgian house which now serves as a convent. Its outbuildings preserve early cross slabs and gravestones which may have come from the first foundation, and the shaft of an early stone cross can be seen. Ruins of a 15th-c church can be seen to the S, and Jacobean Kilcolgan House stands E of the village. Ferbane is the site of a large turf-powered electricity generating station.

*****FERMOY,** *Mainistir Fhear Maí:*
the Monastery of the Men of the Plain,
Cork **28 W 89**
Scottish-born John Anderson built this River Blackwater community as a garrison town towards the end of the 18thc, but today Fermoy is chiefly known for its excellent salmon fishing. Knocknaskagh rises to 1,406ft from the Nagles Mountains in the W, and 2m NW is Labbacallee or the Hag's Bed – considered to be the finest wedge-shaped gallery grave in Ireland (see inset on page 240). Near by on the banks of the Blackwater are the castles of Carrigabrick, Cragg, Licklash, and Hyde. The latter is the ancestral home of Douglas Hyde, 1st president of Ireland.

The village of Castlelyons with its friary, castle, and ruined church lies 5m SSE. The friary was founded in the 14thc by John de Barri, and its ruins (NM) comprise church and outbuildings. The castle, now an ivy covered shell, was built in Tudor times and burnt down in 1771. The ruined Protestant church stands in an overgrown and decrepit churchyard. Hidden in the undergrowth is the mausoleum of the Barrymore family. About 2¼m NE of Castlelyons, in the grounds of Coole Abbey, are the ruins of two early churches (NM).

FERNS, *Fearna,* Wexford **25 T 04**
Once the ancient royal seat of Leinster, Ferns boasts a 13th-c castle (NM) which probably stands on the site of King Dermot McMurrough's stronghold. The building's south-east tower contains a chapel which is generally accepted as being the finest of its kind in Ireland. Excavation in recent years has revealed traces of the outer defences of the castle. The town's present cathedral (CI) is a 19th-c edifice which incorporates nave arcading and portions of chancel walls (NM) from a previous, 13th-c structure. Fragments of a high-cross shaft (NM) said to mark Dermot's grave can be seen in the churchyard, and parts of two plain high crosses (NM) have been included in the fabric of the wall – along with other relics. St Moling's holy well can be seen near the cathedral.

The Augustinian monastery (NM) here was founded by King Dermot on the site of St Mogue's original foundation, and the ruined belfry became a round tower at the level of the church roof. This

Entries marked * are the starting point of drives included in the Day Drive section of the book (pages 79 to 144).

church measured some 64ft in length. St Peter's Church (NM) lies to the NE of the cathedral and is a smaller building featuring a Romanesque window in its south wall. Ruins of an 18th-c episcopal palace which was pillaged in the Insurrection of 1798 are also of interest. An effigy of an ecclesiastic discovered here during the 19thc is preserved in the cathedral and is presumed to depict St Moling.

FERRYCARRIG, *Glascharraig:*
Grey Rock, Wexford   25 T02
The tower which stands on the N bank of the River Slaney here dates from the 15thc, and it is not, as some claim, the ruin of the first Anglo-Norman castle to be built in Ireland. A much more likely contender for this title is the nearby bank and ditch called Carrick on Slaney, where Robert Fitzstephen took refuge after the death of Dermot McMurrough in 1171. A tower on the S bank of the river commemorates Wexford men who died in the Crimean War, and the village was the scene of a clash between insurgents and British troops in 1798. At Ferrycarrig the River Slaney rushes through a narrow gorge.

FERTAGH, *Feartach:*
Place of Graves, Kilkenny   23 S36
The 100ft-high round tower (NM) here was repaired in 1881 after having stood in ruins since it was burnt by O Loughlin, King of Ireland, in 1156. Both the round tower and the nearby ruined chapel stand on the site of a monastery founded by St Ciaran in the 7thc.

FETHARD, *Fiodh Ard:*
High Wood, Tipperary   23 S23
During the 14thc Fethard was a fortified town, and remains of this stage in its development include walls, gates, and tower-house type 'castles'. Everard's Mansion, which was incorporated in the British military barracks, still carries the town's armorial bearings. A castle stands E of the parish church (CI), which incorporates the west tower and nave of a medieval structure, and two other strongholds can be seen to the S. Fethard was besieged by Cromwellian troops in 1650. Interesting remains of an Augustinian friary founded here in 1300 include a *sheila-na-gig* carving built into a wall at the east end. There are several notable Georgian houses in the town.

Some 5m S of Fethard at Donaghmore is a ruined church (NM) with a finely-carved Irish-Romanesque doorway. Some 3m NE is Knockelly Castle, which includes a bawn and a 16th-c tower. About 3m SE is tri-towered Kiltinane Castle. Dating from the 13thc, it was captured by Cromwell in 1649 and is still inhabited. Slievenamon rises to 2,368ft SE of the town and is a good viewpoint.

FIDDOWN, *Fiodh Dúin:*
Wood of the Fort, Kilkenny   23 S41
Charming river scenery and a long, elegant bridge are features of this village, which stands on the E bank of the Suir. A font in the old churchyard is a relic of a monastery which was founded in the area during the 6thc. Other notable survivals here include the Ponsonby Mausoleum and Bessborough Monument, both of 18th-c date. The Mount Bolton Woods can be seen on the W bank of the river.

FINGLAS, *Fionnghlas:*
Clear Stream, Dublin   19 O13

The 'Fair Rill' or holy well from which this place takes its name is well known among people who suffer from eye diseases. During the 19thc a quack doctor called Dr Achment Borumborad built a pump room over the well and turned Finglas into a health resort. Of more interest here are medieval church ruins which occupy a site on which St Canice's monastery stood in the 6thc. This foundation was in the forefront of the Culdee movement for church reform in the 8th and 9thc. Ruins that survive include a nave and chancel, a later south aisle, and a vaulted north porch. A high cross which stands in the churchyard was buried for its own protection while Cromwell was in Ireland.

The surrounding countryside is known for its large bulb farms and features several interesting historical sites. Dunsoghly Castle (NM) lies NNW of Finglas and was built by Chief Justice Plunkett in the 15thc. The remains include earthworks, fragments of outbuildings, and the ruins of a chapel which was erected in 1573 by Sir John Plunkett. The three-storey tower carries corner turrets and features an original oak-timbered roof – a very unusual survival in Ireland. It is thought that a room at the top of the south-west turret may have been used as a prison or hide-out, and the earthworks may date from the turbulent period between 1641 and 1653. The castle was an English garrison at this time. To the W of the castle is the Dunsink Observatory.

FINTONA, *Fionntamhnach:*
White Field, Tyrone   11 H46
Once a stronghold of the O Neill family, this small market town includes a ruined Protestant church which incorporates the east window and several carved stones from a medieval structure. Remnants of the latter church stands 1½m N at Donacavey, where a decorated shaft known as St Patrick's Cross (NM) – traditionally held to have come from a foundation created by this saint – can be seen.

FIVEMILETOWN, *Baile na Lorgan:*
Town of the Shank, Tyrone   11 H44
The curious name of this town is explained by the popular supposition that it is 5m equidistant from Clabby, Clogher, and Colebrooke – a myth sustained by hearsay rather than accurate measurement. Sir William Stewart built a Plantation castle here during the time of James I, and remains of this can be seen on the N side of the main street. Hand-crocheted lace is still produced in the district. The border between Fermanagh and Monaghan is marked by Slieve Beagh, which rises to 1,221ft in the SE.

FLAGSTAFF, THE, Armagh   13 J12
The view from famous Flagstaff Viewpoint, 4m ESE of Newry, extends over Carlingford Lough to the Mourne and Carlingford Mountains. Amenities here include the Forest Recreation Area, and Fathom Wood, a bird sanctuary designated an area of special scientific interest.

FLORENCE COURT, *Mullach na Seangán:*
the Hilltop of the Ants, Fermanagh   11 H13
Home of the Earls of Enniskillen (whose ancestor Sir William Cole founded the island town of Enniskillen) this house (NT), which is 7m SSW of Enniskillen, was completed in 1764 and is beautifully sited under the brow of Ben Aughlin Mountain. The design was by an unknown architect and basically comprises a large central block from which colonnaded wings lead to pavilions. The facade measures 300ft long, and the interior displays good rococo plasterwork. This was restored after a serious fire in 1955. The entrance hall is symmetrical and includes a dummy door added solely to balance another on the opposite side. Also of interest is the fine staircase. Florence Court Yew, a tree now found all over the world, was propagated here from a parent tree which can still be seen. This was found on the mountain by a local farmer c1767. Numerous fine trees of other species can be seen in the pleasant gardens and grounds.

FOATY ISLAND, *Fóite,* Cork   28 W77
Great Island lies to the S of Foaty, and the waters of Lough Mahon extend to the W. The island itself is well wooded and features Fota House, which stands in extensive gardens containing exotic trees and shrubs.

FORE, *Baile Fhobhain:*
Town of the Spring, Westmeath   18 N57
St Fechin founded a monastery for 300 monks here in the 7thc. The village name refers to water which rises in the valley beside the old church, and is dedicated to the saint. Remains of the settlement comprise the church (NM) and a few fragmentary survivals. The former dates from the 9th or 10thc and includes a fine trabeate doorway which has a huge cross-inscribed lintel with Syrian affinities. Later additions include the chancel and the 15th-c east window. A stone cross (NM) can be seen in the graveyard, plus remains of St Fechin's Mill and the Anchorite's Cell. The latter was adapted to serve as the Greville-Nugent Mausoleum in the 19thc.

An abbey (NM) founded here by Sir Walter de Lacy for the Benedictines during the 12th or 13thc has also left impressive reminders of its existence, and the village itself has preserved traces of defensive walls and gateways. Several termon crosses have survived here. The so-termed Six Wonders of Fore are: the monastery on a screw; the mill without a race; the cyclopean stone above the doorway of St Fechin's Church; the well water which will not boil; the ash tree which will not burn; and the stream which flows uphill.

FOUR KNOCKS, *Fuarchnoc:*
Cold Hill, Meath   19 O16
Three major prehistoric monuments discovered here during excavations conducted between 1950 and 1952 have been respectively designated Four Knocks 1, 2, and 3. Four Knocks 1 (NM) is the most remarkable of these and comprises a cruciform passage grave inside a circular mound measuring 65ft in dimater and 10ft high. Access to the 21 by 18ft pear-shaped chamber – which includes three offset chambers – is via a 17ft passage. Although the chambers are corbelled as if to form a domed roof, it is probable that the top was covered with a timber frame supported by a central wooden post. A socket consistent with this form of construction was identified during investigation. Discoveries in the grave included fragments of over 60 burials and goods of the type commonly found in

this sort of monument. All the finds from here are preserved by the National Museum in Dublin. Twelve of the chamber and passage structural stones are decorated with Boyne-style ornamentation, but also include fine-line incised decoration and face motifs. It is thought that Four Knocks 1 dates from c1800BC. Four Knocks 2 revealed a crematorium and a multiple-cist mound, while site 3 comprised a round barrow of bronze-age origin.

FOYNES, *Faing,* Limerick **21 R25**
Although Shannon Airport has now superseded the former transatlantic seaplane base at Foynes, the town continues to flourish and boasts a fine pier and extensive oil-storage installation. A 25ft-high limestone cross on a nearby hill commemorates Stephen Edmund Spring Rice, brother of the 1st Baron Monteagle. To the S is Knockpatrick Hill, which rises to 572ft and commands extensive views over the Shannon Valley. The summit of the hill is crowned by early church ruins that survive from a foundation said to have been created by St Patrick; a holy well is near by. Ringforts can be seen in both this townland and Croaghane.

FRENCHPARK, *Dún Gar,*
Roscommon **10 M79**
Dr Douglas Hyde was born at the rectory and became the 1st president of the Republic of Ireland. Ruins of 14th-c Cloonshanville Abbey include a small tower and a rough stone cross; they can be seen in a field $\frac{3}{4}$m E. Remains of a brick-built Jacobean and 18th-c mansion exist in a local demesne owned by Lord de Freyne, which also features a notable souterrain.

FRESHFORD, *Achadh Ur:*
Fresh Field, Kilkenny **23 S46**
St Lactin, of royal descent and a disciple of St Comgall of Bangor, created a religious foundation here in the 7thc. The church attached to this was replaced by another building in the 12thc, which was subsequently rebuilt in the 18thc to form the present parish church. This incorporates the west gable and beautiful Romanesque porch of the 12th-c structure, and displays an Irish inscription which asks for a prayer for the builders. To the E of the church is St Lactin's Well. The saint's 12th-c shrine still exists and is preserved in the National Museum, Dublin. Freshford itself is distinguished by its Georgian houses and pleasant green, and lies between the Slieveardagh Hills and River Nore valley. The banks of the local Clashacrow stream were the scene of a battle between Dermot McMurrough and Donal MacGillapadraig – Lord of Ossory in 1169. At Rathealy, $2\frac{1}{4}$m SSW of Freshford, are the remains of a ringfort with houses and a souterrain.

FURNESS, *Fornocht:*
Bare Hill, Kildare **18 N92**
The 13th-c church (NM) in Furness, which is 3m ENE of Naas, was granted to St Thomas' Abbey by Richard de Lesse and displays a number of interesting features. These include a simple Romanesque chancel arch, a square medieval font, and a low side window unique in Ireland in the chancel's south wall. Nearby Furness House dates from the 18thc. Close to Furness, but in the townland of Forenaghts Great, are the Longstone Rath Sanctuary and standing stone. The rath is situated at an altitude of 560ft and is in the form of a perfect circle measuring some 190ft in diameter. Its defences include a well-preserved, 10ft-high ring bank and a 5ft-deep outer fosse. 'Rath' is really the wrong term for this monument, as it is actually a sanctuary – the Irish version of a henge monument. The central granite monolith marked a roofless long-cist grave which was partitioned by a slab and contained the cremated remains of two adults. Various relics discovered here put an early bronze-age date to the remains.

GALBALLY, *An Gallbhaile:*
the Foreigner's Homestead, Limerick
22 R72
Near to this village, which is pleasantly situated on the River Aherlow, are the remains of the Franciscan friary of Moor. The friary, in fact in Co Tipperary, was founded by Donough O Brien in c1210. At that time O Brien was king of the ancient territory known as Thomond. During the late 15thc a successor to the church was built, but it was destroyed by fire in 1472 and finally rendered completely unusable in 1569 by English troops. It was a simple building dating from 1470, with a later belfry, and was further damaged by troops in 1920 during the War of Independence. Local people have bestowed the name of Dermot and Grania's Bed on Corderry wedge-shaped gallery grave 1m NE, a title which has also been given to a roofless chamber tomb at the top of 1,215ft Slievenamuck, which is 3m NE. Duntryleague Hill rises to 922ft NW of the village and features a passage grave (NM) which has also been named after the two above-mentioned legendary Irish characters.

GALGORM CASTLE, Antrim **7 D00**
The castle's 17th-c bawn, or fortified enclosure, is clearly visible and each corner is defended by projecting salient bastions. Only the oak stair, turned balusters, and round-headed newels of Rev Dr Alexander Colville's mid 17th-c house survived 19th-c modernization by Lord Mountcashel. It was the latter who supplied the large sash windows, Flemish gables, and curved battlements. Sir Charles Lanyon designed the present front door, interior door cases, and dining-room fireplace. It is somewhat intriguing to note that the Rev Dr Colville was once accused of practising sorcery. The small 17th-c church in the grounds has a circular-headed south doorway, a small mullioned window in one gable, and a large arched opening in the other. A vaulted chamber exists under the east end. The building was sacked during the rebellion of 1641.

GALLARUS ORATORY, *Gallaras,*
Kerry **26 Q30**
A corbelled stone oratory which is without doubt the most important piece of early-Christian architecture of its type remaining in Ireland, this little building (NM) measures 10 by 15ft inside and shares its graveyard with a 4ft cross pillar. The high, ridged roof of the oratory resembles an upturned boat, and the $3\frac{1}{2}$ft-thick walls were built with very little mortar. A small round-headed window can be seen in the east end of the structure. The trabeate west doorway has inclined jambs, and the entire building, which is situated 1m inland from Smerwick Harbour, probably dates from the 8thc. The ruins of Gallarus Castle, once a Fitzgerald stronghold, stand $\frac{3}{4}$m NW. For more details concerning Gallarus in particular and early-Christian architecture in general see the feature article beginning on page 289.

GALLEN PRIORY, *Mainistir Ghailinne,*
Offaly **17 N12**
See Ferbane entry.

GALTEE MOUNTAINS, THE, *Na Gaibhlte,*
Limerick and Tipperary **22 R82**
Perhaps the best-known inland mountains in Ireland, the Galtee range extends from Tipperary across the Limerick border to merge with the Ballyhoura Hills. The range culminates in 3,018ft Galtymore, which straddles the Tipperary and Limerick border, with 2,712ft Lyracappul rising to the W. Fine N views from the summit ridge of Galtymore extend towards the Glen of Aherlow and the Golden Vale. A fine ridge walk offers a pleasing, if arduous means of exploring the range. Several small lakes lie on the N slopes, including Lough Curra beneath Galtymore and Lough Muskry below 2,636ft Greenane – near a rock known as O Loughnan's Castle. Pigeon Rock Glen is a good viewpoint on the S side of the range. The Mitchelstown to Limerick road crosses a low col in the foothills between the Galtee and the Ballyhoura ranges. Views to the S extend across a broad valley to the Kilworth and Knockmealdown Mountains, the latter rising to 2,600ft. There are many easy routes to the summit from the main Mitchelstown to Cahir road, on the S side.

***GALWAY,** *Gaillimh:*
Stony River, Galway **15 M32**
County town and the principal community in Connacht, Galway city stands at the mouth of the salmon-filled River Corrib and is a gateway to the attractive Connemara and Joyce's Country areas. It is thought that the city started as a fishing village. Substance is lent to this theory by the Claddagh district, once an independent community of fishermen who lived here under their own laws and had their own mode of dress. The thatched cottages of these people have now been replaced by modern buildings, but their distinctive Claddagh finger ring – carrying a crowned-heart motif between two hands – is widely copied in modern jewellery. Nowadays fishing is just one of the many commercial enterprises carried on in the city. The most recent of these is the tourist industry, which caters for the thousands of visitors who come to sample the local fishing, boating, and sea bathing, and to enjoy the horse racing. On the more serious side, Galway has a cathedral, university, and is a centre of Gaelic language and culture. It has also had a very colourful history.

The Anglo-Norman conquest of the local O Flaherty – O Halloran lands in the 13thc was led by the de Burgo family, who initially fortified the town and then through succeeding generations became Gaelicized themselves. The Irish version of their name is still in evidence as Burke. Before the end of the 14thc they had developed a flourishing trade with Spain and Portugal, but in 1396 Richard II granted the town a charter which made its inhabitants his loyal subjects – at the expense of native Irish and the Burkes alike. The townspeople continued to expand their Continental trade and became a community of loyal RC Anglophiles

GALWAY

directed by a prosperous merchant class. A disastrous fire severely damaged the town in 1473, but offered the opportunity for a rebuilding effort which produced many handsome dwellings for the ruling class – which comprised fourteen families, or so-called tribes. Many of the houses were built round courtyards in Spanish style, and Browne's Gateway, which was built in 1627 and re-erected in 1905 in Eyre Square (which contains the J F Kennedy Memorial Garden), gives a fragmentary idea of the comfort in which these merchants lived. The Brownes, along with the Joyces and Frenches, were almost as well known as the chief 'tribe' of Lynch. These families maintained their position by remaining loyal to one another, so the Lynch Stone's inscribed story about the mayor who hanged his own son is somewhat dubious. This stone can be seen in Market Street. Although the town's loyalty to the English crown stood it in good stead for many years, it cost dear during the civil war and resulted in the demolition by Cromwell of fourteen churches and their towers. So-called Spanish Arch, near the quay, is the only remnant of the old town walls. The great mace and sword of the city, each of silver gilt and 4ft long, containing 230 ounces of silver and made in 1660, were restored to the city in 1961.

The modern RC cathedral dedicated to St Nicholas and Our Lady Assumed into Heaven was designed by architects Robinson, Keefe, and Devan and opened in 1965. Materials used in its construction include limestone and Connemara marble, and it measures 300ft long by 158ft wide. Splendid mosaics can be seen in the side chapels. The CI Church of St Nicholas was founded in 1320 and is a cruciform building with three naves and a pyramid-like spire. Despite many changes it remains the largest medieval church in Ireland. Gargoyles adorn the outside of the building, and the 15th-c west doorway is considered very fine. Although many of the monuments both in and outside the church were mutilated by Cromwellian soldiers, there are still interesting floor memorials displaying symbols depicting the crafts of those who are buried here. Other features include a 16th-c wall tomb in the south transept; a 15th-c reading desk known as the Confessional at the entrance of the Blessed Sacrament Chapel; a Lynch-Fitzstephen memorial; and a 12th-c French tombstone. The peal includes two notable bells – one dated 1590 and one of 1631 displaying four medallions.

Galway's Franciscan friary was originally founded by William de Burgo in 1296 and contains the fine tomb of Sir Peter French – again damaged by Cromwellian troops. Near the chapel entry is a monument carved with representations of the Apostles and several saints, and the notable Clanricarde Stone dates from 1645. The wealth of the 16th-c Galway merchants is again evident in Lynch's Castle, which stands at the corner of Shop and Abbeygate Streets and displays lynx medallions. Gargoyles decorate the exterior of the building, which now houses a bank. The town hall stands in St Vincent Avenue. Sir Richard Morrison designed the courthouse of 1800 in classical style, and behind this is one of the town's three bridges. This is known as Salmon Weir Bridge. It dates from 1818, and from it fine views of the salmon on the riverbed may be obtained. The oldest bridge is O Brien's Bridge, the fabric of which may include stones from the original structure erected in 1342. Claddagh Bridge spans the Corrib River farther down and is able to swing open to allow the passage of river traffic. University College in a handsome gothick style occupies a site on the W bank of the river and is a constituent college of the National University of Ireland. Originally named Queen's College, it was founded in 1849, and its new buildings were designed by Michael Scott. St Mary's College buildings were first constructed in 1911, but have been much altered. In 18th-c Eyre Square is a statue of local Irish-language poet, novelist, and short-story writer Padraic O Conaire.

Taebhdhearc Theatre is dedicated to promoting the Irish language and culture through the medium of native plays, concerts, and *feiseanna*. The popular

1 Ballindooly Tower
2 Browne's Gateway
3 Cathedral of St Nicholas & Our Lady Assumed into Heaven (RC)
4 Claddagh Bridge
5 Courthouse
6 Franciscan Friary
7 J F Kennedy Memorial Garden
8 Lynch's Castle
9 Lynch Stone
10 Menlough Castle
11 O Brien's Bridge
12 Roscam Round Tower
13 St Mary's College
14 St Nicholas' Church (CI)
15 Salmon Weir Bridge
16 Spanish Arch
17 Taebhdhearc Theatre
18 Town Hall
19 University College

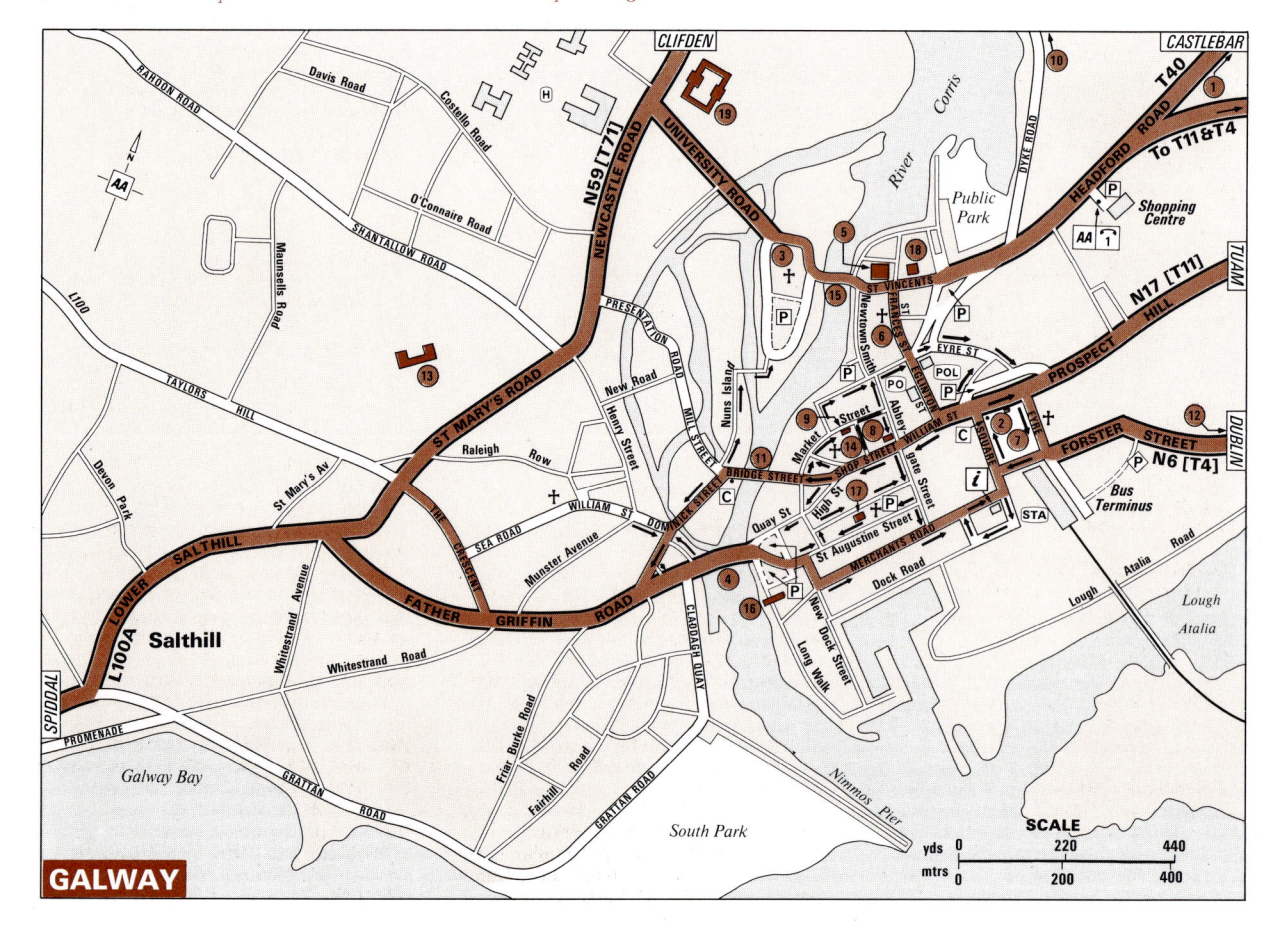

tourist resort of Salthill lies a little to the SW of Galway. Some 4m NE is 15th-c Ballindooly Tower. A 30ft-high stump 4m E survives from Roscam Round Tower. Near this is a 14th-c church (NM) which has two bullauns in its graveyard. Ruined Menlough Castle can be seen 2m NW of the town near the River Corrib. Scanty remains of 13th-c Tirraleen (or Terryland) castle stand 1m N on the banks of the Corrib.

GARINISH ISLAND, *Garinis*, Cork   **27 V95**
See Glengariff entry.

GARTAN (LOUGH), *Gartán*:
Small Field, Donegal   **5 C01**
This 2½m-long lough, the larger and lower of two lakes (the other being Lough Akibbon) is situated 5m E of the Derryveagh Mountains in N Donegal. Leahanmore rises 1,461ft above the W shore, with 746ft Brown Mountain on the E side. The area is famous as the supposed birthplace of St Columba in 521. The site, said to be on the W hillside above Lough Akibbon, is marked by a flagstone. Within the enclosure is a modern Celtic cross erected by Mrs Adair, a former owner of the neighbouring Glenveagh Estate. About ½m N is the site of the saint's monastery, on the approach to which is a holy well and ruined chapel. The latter is the burial place of the O Donnells of Tyrconnell. The site of the monastery is marked by a walled graveyard, outside which stand two severely-eroded stone crosses, possibly marking the limits of sanctuary. Half a mile from the N end of Gartan Lough, on the Letterkenny road and to the NE of Brown Mountain, is the small village of Church Hill, which caters for anglers.

GARVAGH, *Garbhachadh*:
Rough Field, Derry   **6 C81**
This small town lies to the NE of 1,521ft Carntogher Mountain and has recently become the site of a Local Enterprise Development Unit. It is also a forest touring-caravan site, and the Agivey River, which flows through the town, is a favourite spot for anglers. A former Primeminister of England George Canning was born at Garvagh House in 1770. A 5ft dolmen known locally as the Daff Stone (NM) can be seen at Moneydig Crossroads 3m E, and the Gortnamoyan Inauguration Stone (NM) lies 3m W. The latter is also known as the Giant's Track, and St Adamnan's Footprints. St Adamnan was the biographer of St Columba and the patron saint of this district. Garvagh Forest lies on the W side of the town. Denis O Hempsey, a famous harpist, was born in Garvagh in 1695 and died here aged 112.

GEASHILL, *Géisill*, Offaly   **17 N42**
A pleasant village associated with the O Dempsey family, Geashill includes an interesting Anglo-Norman motte which features obscure indications of earlier occupation. Sparse ruins of Digby Castle, an O Dempsey stronghold which eventually passed into the hands of the Digby family, can still be seen.

GEEVAGH, *An Ghaobhach*, Sligo   **10 G81**
This is a very lovely village situated in a valley between high ridges. About 3m WNW lies Lough-na-Suil, 1,000yds in circumference and estimated to contain 32 million cubic feet of water. In 1933 the water disappeared completely through an opening beneath the lake known as Balor's Eye, leaving a muddy bed for three weeks; at the end of this period the water flowed back into the lake. According to local tradition this disappearance of the lake occurs every 100 years.

GENEVA, Waterford   **29 S60**
In 1785 Geneva was the scene of a short-lived experiment in which craftsmen in gold and silverwork from Geneva in Switzerland were established in a community on the W shore of Waterford Harbour. The project failed, in spite of aid from the Irish parliament, and the colony buildings were converted into a military barracks. The now ruined buildings were used as a prison in the 1798 uprising and as such were connected with the trial and execution of Irish folk character 'The Croppy Boy'. The term *Croppy* was applied to all Irishmen who fought the English in the '98 uprising.

GIANT'S CAUSEWAY, THE, *Clochán an Aifir*:
The Giant's Stepping Stones, Antrim   **6 C94**
This marvellous formation of polygonal basalt columns (NT) was formed by the slow cooling of lava which erupted through the earth's crust in the distant geological past. The surface of the lava decayed during the periods between eruptions, forming a red bank of iron ore which can be seen halfway up the cliffs at the causeway. Various formations that form the causeway are known by such fanciful names as The Giant's Organ, The Giant's Grandmother, The Amphitheatre, and The Wishing Chair. Many visitors consider the latter a prime feature of their tour. Close to the entrance of the area is a well of pure water.

At the E bend of the bay and beyond Roverin Valley Head are several isolated columns of basalt known as the Chimney Tops. These were fired on by the Spanish Armada in the mistaken belief that they were the chimneys of Dunluce Castle. Port-na-Spania bay lies beyond the Chimneys and is the resting place of the Armada vessel *Girona*, which was dashed to pieces during a storm which broke while she was making her way back to Spain. Finds recovered from the wreck are preserved in the Ulster Museum, Belfast, and their recovery opened up many new techniques in the field of marine archaeology. Spectacular caves along this stretch of coast can be explored by boat, including the 700ft-long Runkerry Cave and 450ft-long Portcoon cave.

GIANT'S RING, Down   **13 J36**
See Drumbo entry.

GLANDORE, *Cuan Dor*, Cork   **27 W23**
This is an attractive resort and fishing village overlooking the coastal inlet of Glandore Harbour. Drombeg Stone Circle lies about 2m E of this well-known beauty spot (see inset on page 201). Glandore Castle, which is built on the site of a Barret castle, is now part of a private house. Near by are the ruins of a medieval church. Kilfinnan Castle on the SE side of the village has massive defensive walls and was a seat of the Townshend family. It has been incorporated into a hotel. The attractive village of Unionhall stands on the opposite side of the inlet. Dean Swift lived at Rook Cottage here in 1723. The area round Glandore is noted for its beauty.

GLANWORTH, *Gleannúir*, Cork   **28 R70**
This pleasant woollen-manufacturing village is situated SW of the Kilworth Mountains and has an old, thirteen-arch bridge spanning the River Funshion. The ruined 13th-c castle, once a stronghold of the Roche family, was destroyed by General Ireton's artillery in 1649. The church of the Dominican friary, which was founded by the Roche family, is a 13th-c structure of early-English style. The Elizabethan mansion of Ballyclough House lies E of Glanworth. In nearby Killeenemer are the remains (NM) of a small early church. Moneen, 1m SSW of Glanworth, has remains of a multiple cist cairn which had been erected on a neolithic ritual enclosure. There are many castles along the banks of the River Funshion in the vicinity of Glanworth.

GLASLOUGH, *Glasloch*:
Grey Lake, Monaghan   **12 H74**
Sited on the shore of a lough which bears the same name, Glaslough village is overlooked by the house and beautiful wooded demesne of Castle Leslie (OACT). The present 19th-c building here was the home of author Sir Shane Leslie, and includes an earlier gate lodge by John Nash. An ancient ecclesiastical site 1¼m WSW called Donagh features a small high cross and the base of a medieval stone cross. The former was retrieved from Donagh Bog in 1911.

GLASNEVIN, *Glas Naíon*:
Stream of the Infants, Dublin   **19 O13**
Of prime interest here are the superb Botanic Gardens, which were founded in 1795 and brought under state control in 1878 (see Dublin district plan, page 53). Various exotic plants flourish under glass, and the cast-iron Palm House is an important architectural milestone by Richard Turner. The entire property was once owned by the 18th-c poet Tickell, whose house is now the Director's residence, and many great literary figures of the day met here. These included Sheridan, Swift, Delany, Steele, and Thomas Parnell. An ancient yew walk is still pointed out as one of Addison's favourite promenades. Another meeting place of this illustrious circle of friends was Dr Patrick Delany's Delville House, where Swift's Stella was a frequent visitor. Prospect Cemetery lies to the W of the gardens and contains the graves of O Connell, John Philpot Curran, and Charles Stewart Parnell.

GLASSAN, *Glasán*:
Streamlet, Westmeath   **17 N04**
Locally known as the 'Village of the Roses' because of the profusion of these flowers that once grew here, Glassan is a small community near Lough Ree. Nearby ruins of Waterstown House, by Richard Cassels, include an octagonal dovecote. A hill 1½m E of the village on an unclassified road to Kilkenny West is said to be the geographical centre of Ireland, and is surmounted by a circular structure known as The Pinnacle; it was built in 1769. Portlick Castle stands on the shore of Lough Ree 2¾m W and is one of the few medieval castles in the country still habitable.

GLASS PISTOL CASTLE, Louth   **19 O18**
This castle is best known as the home of Archbishop Oliver Plunkett before his

execution at Tyburn in 1681 on a false charge of treason. The castle was once the home of the Dowdall family and stands ½m S of Clogherhead village. A well-preserved square tower is all that remains of the structure.

GLEN, *An Gleann:*
the Valley, Donegal **5 C13**
Glen Lough, considered one of Donegal's most attractive lakes, extends S from this small village and is connected to Sheep Haven by the salmon-packed Lackagh River. Lough Veagh lies to the SW and is connected to Glen Lough by the Owencarrow River. About 3m SE and nearly 800ft above sea level, in the crater of an extinct volcano, is Lough Salt. This lies at the foot of Salt Mountain, which rises sharply to 1,546ft at its E end.

GLENARIFF, *Gleann Aireamh:*
Ploughmen's Valley, Antrim **7 D22**
Shaped like a symmetrical shallow funnel extending inland some 5m from Red Bay, this cliff-girt glen is possibly the most beautiful of Antrim's famous Nine Glens. The seaward end is dominated by the flat-topped mountain of Lurigethan, which rises to 1,154ft above sea level. Several attractive waterfalls can be seen in Glenariff, and its cultivated lower slopes contrast pleasantly with its black basalt cliffs. The village of Glenariff, or Waterfoot, is situated on the coast road at the foot of the glen.

GLENARM, *Gleann Arma,* Antrim **7 D31**
Glenarm village stands on the S bank of the Glenarm River, near a cliff-bound bay on the scenic Antrim Coast road. On the W bank is Glenarm Castle and demesne, which has been a seat of the MacDonnells – Earls of Antrim – since 1636. The mid 18th-c body of the present house stands on the foundations of an Elizabethan keep and displays Tudor-style chimneys, minarets, and cupolas of early 19th-c origin. Jacobean dripstones can be seen above the windows. The richly-planted demesne occupies most of the glen, which is one of the famous Nine Glens of Antrim.

St Patrick's Church (CI) was described by Thackeray and stands on a promontory between the road and the sea. This site was formerly occupied by a 15th-c Franciscan friary founded by Sir Robert Bisset, and the church's graveyard contains the decapitated body of Shane O Neill. Shane was the 16th-c Gaelic chief of Ulster. The Harvard Archaeological Expedition of 1934 recovered over a ton of palaeolithic flint implements from a raised beach at the nearby point of Cloney, suggesting that this was an important centre for early man *c*1000 to 2000BC. Street names such as Toberwine and The Vennel may indicate that the layout of Glenarm today is largely medieval. This was the birthplace of Eoin MacNeill, the distinguished historian, Celtic scholar, founder of the Gaelic League, and both co-founder and commander-in-chief of the Irish Volunteers (1914). His brother James became the 2nd Governor-General of the Irish Free State. Two local industries, the mining of iron ore and chalk, have detracted somewhat from the appearance of the surrounding countryside.

GLEN BALLYEMON, *Gleann Bhaile Eamainn:*
the Glen of Eamann's Homestead, Antrim **7 D22**
This fine but almost treeless glen parallels Glenariff and opens out towards Cushendall. Finds made in the glen indicate that it was an axe factory during the neolithic period. Lurigethan (rising to 1,154ft) and the coast lie to the E.

GLENBEIGH, *Gleann Beithe:*
Valley of the Birches, Kerry **26 V69**
This small fishing and bathing resort nestles beneath 1,621ft Seefin Mountain near the River Beigh. The scenery is magnificent. One of Kerry's finest walks follows a great amphitheatre of mountains, known as the Glenbeigh Horseshoe, from Seefin to Drung Hill. Here are fine views of a series of glacial corries and loughs, the largest of which is Coomasaharn. The road from Glenbeigh SW to Kells affords splendid views of Dingle Bay and the mountains of the Dingle Peninsula.

GLENCOLUMBKILLE, *Gleann Cholm Cille:*
St Columba's Valley, Donegal **4 G58**
Glencolumbkille is one of the most inaccessible villages in Donegal, lying in a deep, secluded valley (formerly named 'the Old Glen') at the head of Glen Bay. It is now perhaps best known for the work of Glencolumbkille Development Cooperative Society in developing co-operative enterprises in tourism and cottage industries. The village has a Folk Museum consisting of four cottages, the interiors of which illustrate Irish peasant life through the centuries. Historically, the village's most famous associate is St Columba, a dominant figure in the 6th-c Celtic church. All the Christian remains in the area are of a later date, although many, such as the Oratory, the Saint's Well and Bed, bear the name of St Columba. There is a large group of structures, including megaliths, cashels with cells, and penitential stations with incised crosses. Pilgrims perform their devotions at about a dozen such crosses, covering a distance of 3m in the act. Many of the numerous prehistoric remains in the area are associated in some way with pilgrim practices.

In the graveyard of the CI parish church there is a large souterrain, probably of the 9thc, roofed with immense slabs of stone; two chambers and a long passage open out from the entrance. A walk is recommended to Glen Head, a sheer precipice over 700ft high which lies a little to the N of Glen Bay. Along the coast is some splendid rock scenery and a good strand. Sturral, a high promontory farther N, drops steeply to the sea.

GLENCREE, Wicklow **19 O11**
See Enniskerry

GLENDALOUGH, *Gleann dá Loch:*
Valley of the Two Lakes, Wicklow **19 T19**
In addition to being one of the most picturesque glens of Wicklow, Glendalough boasts the extensive remains (all NM) of a monastery that developed from the 6th-c foundation of the hermit St Kevin. He first built a church on the S side of the Upper Lake, but later, when his followers increased in number, a monastery was founded in the lower part of the glen. This foundation flourished for six centuries, although – like other Irish monasteries – it was repeatedly plundered by the Norsemen. Signs of the earliest monastic buildings and walls have been largely obliterated as a result of continual use for burials and employment of the surrounding land for agriculture. There is also no trace of the considerable dependent community that grew up around the monastery. However, there are remains of numerous churches, some with Romanesque carving, as well as monastic cashels and boundary walls, crosses and inscribed grave-slabs, a monastic cell, and two tall round towers – one at the gable of a stone-roofed church.

On approaching Glendalough via Laragh, the first of the glen's churches – Trinity Church – is seen. Its construction is primitive; the west door with slightly inclined jambs leads into a small vaulted chamber, above which a round tower once rose. The church has a small chancel, and the jambs of the chancel arch and the windows are inclined like the west door. There is a large holed stone within the church. Across the river, near Derrybawn, is St Saviour's Monastery, which was restored in the 19thc by the Board of Works. It is perhaps the most attractive as well as the latest of the monastic buildings in the valley, and is believed to have been founded by Archbishop Laurence O Toole in 1162. The remains consist of a church with nave and chancel, and a small part of the domestic buildings on the north side. The chancel arch is an interesting specimen of Romanesque architecture. It is of three orders resting on large clustered piers, and is decorated with dog-tooth, chevron, and floral ornamentation. The fantastic sculptures of human heads and animals on the capitals and bases are noteworthy. The site of St Kevin's final settlement is close to the Royal Hotel. The most prominent feature of the group of ruins is the round tower, which stands to the NW of the enclosure. It is entered by the ancient monastery archway, and is 103ft high by 52ft in circumference. The walls are of mica-slate, and the doorway and windows of granite. The doorway is round-headed with inclined jambs. Each of the five storeys has one window, and under the cap are the usual four windows facing the cardinal points. The conical roof fell in many years ago, but was rebuilt with the original stones in 1876.

The cathedral is the largest and most important building in the valley, and probably dates from the 7thc. It was used as a cathedral church until the 13thc, when the See of Glendalough was united with Dublin. It consists only of a 10th-c nave with a 12th-c chancel. The most notable features are the east window built of oolite stone and the chancel arch. There are some early tombs with incised Celtic crosses. Kevin's Cross, an 11ft-high granite monolith, is on the S side of the cathedral. St Kevin's Church, commonly called St Kevin's Kitchen, is a good example of the double-vaulted oratory with high-pitched stone roof. A chancel and belfry were later additions. The chancel has disappeared, but the belfry is still prominent. To the W of the cathedral is St Mary's Church, probably 10thc, with a chancel of later date. Its massive doorway and lintel with incised cross are the most remarkable features. To the S is the Priest's House, the mortuary chapel for the surrounding cemetery. Of note is the tympanum over the doorway, with its carving depicting three figures – one with a crozier and another with a bell. Close to St Kevin's

GLENDOLLAGH/GLENVEAGH

Church are the slight remains of a very small church dedicated to St Cieran. This was burnt down in 1163. Just across the River to the S are the Deer Stone and St Kevin's Well.

The Lower Lake presents a tranquil scene, while the Upper Lake, with 2,296ft Camaderry and 2,154ft Lugduff rising in bold escarpments from the edge of the water and the Glenealo Stream tumbling down the mountain side, forms a more imposing picture. Reefert Church, which stands on the SE bank of the Upper Lake, consists of a ruined nave and chancel. It was the ancient burial place of the O Tooles, and contains many Irish and Latin crosses and incised tombstones of ancient date. A little farther on is *Teampull na Skellig* – the 'Church of the Rock' – sited on a ledge between two cliffs. This small, rectangular oratory has been restored. A short distance to the E of the church is the narrow cave known as Kevin's Bed, excavated from the rock 30ft above the lake. It was visited by Sir Walter Scott in 1825. In this hermit cave St Kevin passed the earliest days of his solitary life upon his renunciation of human love. As the approach from the cliff above is difficult, it is more usual to reach the Bed by boat. This excursion gives an opportunity for appreciating the many beauties of lake and mountain, provided the start is made from the NE corner of the lake. There are several fine crosses in the glen, as well as the remains of buildings other than those already mentioned.

The Upper Lake area offers several enjoyable walks. At the back of the Lake House is a path which leads up the Lugduff brook to Pollanass Waterfall. There is also a fine woodland walk along the S bank of the Upper Lake, but best of all is the path through the fir plantation. The latter runs for almost 2m on the N side of the lake, offering beautiful vistas through the openings in the trees. Glendalough is a good centre for several very enjoyable drives. Ascending the valley of the Glendasan to 1,567ft Wicklow Gap, extensive views of the mountains can be obtained. The Wicklow Mountains can be seen from 2,686ft Tonelagee; this road can be followed as far as Hollywood. The lonely Vale of Glenmacnass, with hills rising on both sides of the Military Road, is worth exploring as far as the fall.

GLENDOLLAGH, *Loch na Garman:*
Lake of the Ridge, Galway **14 L84**
Glendollagh (sometimes spelt Glenalough) is one of four lakes – the others being Ballynahinch, Derryclare, and Inagh – which curve like a string of pearls round the foothills of the Twelve Bens (or Pins) and the Maamturk Mountains. St Patrick's Bed and Blessed Well are at Maumeen, in the pass between the Maamturks and the Corcogemore range to the NE.

GLENDUN, *Gleann Duinne:*
Valley of the River Dunn, Antrim **7 D23**
One of the prettiest of the Nine Glens of Antrim, Glendun is steep, narrow, and tree-lined. Its few substantial farm houses are accessible only by footbridges across the Glendun River. Glendun viaduct, designed by Charles Lanyon in 1839, is the most impressive structure on the Antrim coast road. Its reddish, dressed-stone arches rise 80ft above river and glen.

Ancient St Kevin's Church exists among the remains of a monastery which was founded in beautiful Glendalough during the 6thc.

*****GLENGARRIFF**, *An Gleann Garbh:*
the Rough Valley, Cork **27 V95**
A remarkable transformation has taken place since the time Glengarriff's name was appropriate. The huge masses of rock which covered the glen over its entire 6m length are now relieved by the most luxuriant foliage of holly, arbutus, fuchsia, yew, and other shrubs and trees down to the very edge of the bay. The glen and the harbour, with its winding coastline, are hemmed in on the N, E, and W by lofty hills, including the beautiful outlines of 2,321ft Knockboy and 2,280ft Akinkeen. To the W rise the lofty Caha Mountains, forming the border with Co Kerry. This natural shelter has endowed the place with the most genial climate in Ireland. Glengarriff is one of the loveliest spots in the country and provides facilities for excellent boating, fishing, and bathing. Swimming at night in the phosphorescent water is a memorable experience. On the outskirts of the resort is the picturesque Blue Pool, or Poulgorm. Set in wooded crags, it provides fine views of the island-studded inlet.

On nearby Garinish Island the vegetation is sub-tropical. The island was transformed from a barren rock into a 'dream garden' by Mr and Mrs Annan Bryce. Today it belongs to the nation (OACT). Whiddy Island, largest of the many islands in Bantry Bay, is used as an oil terminal and storage depot.

GLENGAVLEN, *Gleann Ghaibhle:*
Glen of Gaibhle, Cavan **11 H02**
This wild glen lies on the steep and narrow road traversing NW Cavan from a point near Swanlinbar to Belcoo, on Lough Macnean Lower. To the SE of Glengavlen, Bellavally Gap attains a height of 1,100ft, and to the N rise 2,188ft Cuilcagh and 1,949ft Tiltinbane – the latter sheltering Shannon Pot where the great river rises. W from Glengavlen is the high point of 1,793ft Slievenakilla, beyond which lies the expanse of Lough Allen.

GLENMACNASS, *Gleann Log an Easa:*
The Valley of the hollow of the Waterfall, Wicklow **19 O10**
See Glendalough and Laragh entries.

GLENMALURE, *Gleann Maolúra:*
Maolura's Valley, Wicklow **19 T09**
This deep mountain gorge, drained by the Avonbeg River, is very wild and picturesque. Lugnaquilla, at 3,039ft the highest point in the Wicklow Mountains, overlooks Glenmalure to the SW, and 2,154ft Lugduff in the NW. At the end of the gorge is Ess Waterfall. The valley is interesting to the geologist owing to the two moraines formed during the glacial period, when the snows on the heights of Lugnaquilla and the surrounding peaks were melting. The lower moraine is near Strand Bridge, where a side valley enters from the S. The second moraine is 2m higher up, and has the appearance of an irregular embankment across the valley. The ascent of Lugnaquilla is best made by the Carrawaystick Waterfall, which is 1m above Drumgoff Barracks on the Military Road from Laragh.

GLEN OF THE DOWNS, *Gleann Dá Ghrua:*
The Valley of the two Brows, Wicklow **19 O21**
Close to Delgany, the Glen of the Downs is a glorious heritage of the post-glacial period. Its steep banks rise to a height of over 1,200ft on the W side and are clad with fine timber. This beautiful ravine extends for almost 1m.

GLENQUIN CASTLE, Limerick **21 R22**
A well-preserved tower house (NM) of seven storeys, Glenquin Castle was built in 1462 by the O Hallinans and restored by the Duke of Devonshire in the early 19thc. It stands 1½m W of Killeedy.

GLENS OF ANTRIM, Antrim **7 D22**
One of the most picturesque features of Co Antrim is the well-known series of narrow valleys known collectively as the Glens of Antrim. Traditionally they are regarded as nine in number, although there are more. The nine are Glenshesk, Glencorp, Glendun, Glenaan, Glenballyemon, Glenariff, Glencloy, Glentaise, and Glenarm. The finest is Glenariff. Most of the glens can be conveniently visited from various points on the famous Antrim Coast Road, or from roads fanning out NE from Ballymena.

GLENSTAL ABBEY, *Gleann Státhail:*
Státhál's Valley, Limerick **22 R75**
See Moroe entry.

GLENVEAGH, *Gleann Bheatha:*
Birch Valley, Donegal **5 C02**
A glance at the map of Donegal will show that the country is strongly folded from NE to SW. Erosion along the axis of folding has resulted in rock ridges alternating with deep gorges. Glenveagh is the most beautiful of these gorges. A lake extends for 5m along the trough of the valley, and at the SW end the

Entries marked * are the starting point of drives included in the Day Drive section of the book (pages 79 to 144).

mountains rise precipitously from its edge. Two peaks – 1,220ft Keamnacally on the W side and 1,270ft Kinnaveagh on the E side – are covered with fine timber up to a considerable height. Several streams tumble 1,000ft down the precipitous rocks of 2,147ft Dooish Mountain into the River Beagh. The Derryveagh range dominates the background to the W. The streams form magnificent waterfalls, of which Astellion is the most striking. Glenveagh Castle, a castellated mansion completed in 1870 by John Adair, stands about half-way up the E side of the lake. It was visited by Lord Kitchener, Arthur Balfour, and members of the Royal Family before world war I. (Gardens and house grounds only OACT.)

GLIN, *An Gleann*:
the Valley, Limerick   **21 R14**
The town is beautifully situated on the S bank of the River Shannon, which is nearly 3m wide here. Once known as the greatest salmon fishery depot of the Shannon and its tributaries, it is now mainly a centre for the dairy industry. The district was granted by Henry II to the Fitzgerald family, Lords O Decies and Desmond. Their descendants, the Earls of Desmond, were created princes palatine in Ireland with the power of creating barons. By this authority they created the Knight of Glin and others. The property has descended in virtually uninterrupted succession through the male line for more than 700 years to the present Knight of Glin.

Close to the Shannon estuary stands a fragment of the old Castle of Glin, a storm centre in Tudor times. Adjacent to the town is the fine Glin Castle demesne, with its 18th-c mansion. The 19th-c structure called Hamilton's Tower overlooks the pier.

GLINSK CASTLE, *Glinsce,*
Galway   **16 M76**
This shell of a fine castle (NM) displays well-preserved mullioned windows and chimneys. It stands $3\frac{1}{2}$m SSE of Ballymoe, and was built by the Burke family $c1647$.

GOREY, *Guaire*, Wexford   **25 T15**
Gorey is a market town built mainly along one long street. The courthouse and church (CI) were built in 1819. The convent and the Church of St Mark (RC) are both by Pugin, and the Protestant church contains superb stained glass by Harry Clarke. Gorey was a storm centre in the Insurrection of 1798, and the town was alternately held by the royal forces and the insurgents. Both 418ft Gorey Hill, just SW of town, and 833ft Tara Hill $2\frac{1}{4}$m NE are good viewpoints. To the N rise the S foothills of the Wicklow Mountains.

GORMANSTON, *Baile Mhic Gormáin*:
Mac Gormáins Homestead, Meath
19 O16
The hamlet of Gormanston has a fine 18th-c castle that replaced a structure which was the home of the Preston family for more than six centuries. The family was exceptional among Irish landed proprietors in remaining Catholic at the Reformation and refusing inducements to conform. On the lawn at the east end of the castle grounds is a notable yew walk, which takes the form of an equilateral triangle with 100yd-long sides. Near by is a perfectly spherical tea-house of yews. The property was bought by the Franciscans in 1947, and the grounds contain a boarding school.

About $1\frac{1}{2}$m SW at Stamullen in St Christopher's chapel is the Gormanston family vault, with unusual carvings of human heads on the walls.

GORT, *An Gort*:
the Field, Galway   **16 M40**
Gort is a well-planned market town held under perpetual lease from Viscount Gort. Built on rising ground with a large square in the centre, Gort was for a long time a garrison town. The church (CI) was built in 1828 and the chapel (RC) in 1825, both on sites given by Lord Gort. Near the town is the subterranean River Beagh, which emerges to flow spectacularly through a ravine called the Ladle and circular basins called the Punch-bowl, the Beggarman's Hole, and the Churn. SE of the town is Lough Cutra and the well-planted demesne of Loughcutra Castle (see entry). About 2m N is the entrance to Coole Park, former home of Augusta Lady Gregory and a one-time centre of the Irish Literary Revival. It was a favourite haunt of W B Yeats. The house was demolished in 1941, but the Autograph Tree inscribed with the initials of George Bernard Shaw, Yeats, and many others still remains. Yeats lived at the Castle of Thoor, 4m NE in Ballylee, which has been restored and contains a collection of Yeats memorabilia (see entry). In the vicinity is the extensive and imposing ruin of the 13th-c castle of Kiltartan or Ballinamantaine (NM), with a strong courtyard defended by towers. Nearby Kiltartan church is a ruined building with primitive architectural details. Tulira, a gothic-style mansion to the N of the town, was once the home of art patron Edward Martin. About 5m SSW is the 16th-c Fiddaun Castle (NM), a fine tower house of the O Shaughnessy family with a large six-sided bawn.

GORTIN, *An Goirtín*:
the Little Field, Tyrone   **6 H48**
This little village consists of one irregular street and is situated in the deep valley of the Owenkillew River – in the Munterlony Mountains. A major attraction is the national forest park, which offers camping and recreational facilities plus a magnificent forest drive. Near by is the fine demesne of Beltrim Castle, which is owned by the Blakiston-Houston family.

GOSFORD FOREST PARK,
Armagh   **12 H94**
See Markethill entry.

GOUGANE BARRA, *Guagán Barra*:
St Finbarr's Cleft, Cork   **27 W06**
The romantic mountain lake of Gougane Barra, the source of the River Lee, lies off the road a little to the NW of the Pass of Keimaneigh. It is 1m long by about $\frac{1}{4}$m wide, and is bounded to the N, S and W by precipitous mountains which include 1,764ft Bealick on the Kerry border to the NW, 1,698ft Foilastookeen to the S, and 1,886ft Conicar to the SW. Winding down the precipices are numerous streams which become foaming cataracts after heavy rains. The whole scene, now forming part of a 1,000-acre national forest park, is one of the most striking in Ireland. St Finbarr, a native of the locality, founded a monastery in this desolate region in the 7thc. Subsequently he established a monastery 'where the waters of the River Lee meet the tide' in the marshy

land of Cork. In the middle of Gougane Barra lake is an island approached by a causeway, at the entrance to which is St Finbarr's Well and an ancient cemetery held in great veneration. On the island, which measures about $\frac{1}{2}$ acre in extent, are a cluster of buildings, a tiny chapel, and a large court which survives from an 18th-c building. The court is set with stations of the cross and has a large cross at its centre. The small modern church is by Samuel F Hynes.

GOWRAN, *Gabhrán*, Kilkenny   **24 S65**
This village was of considerable political and strategic importance in medieval Ireland. It was constituted a parliamentary borough by James I in 1608 with the right to send two members to the Irish parliament until disfranchised by the Act of Union. James, the 3rd Earl of Ormonde, built a strong castle and lived there until he bought Kilkenny Castle in 1391. No trace of the old castle survives, though the ruins of Ballyshawnmore Castle may be seen S of the town. The present Gowran Castle was built in 1815. Edward Bruce penetrated as far S as Gowran and took possession of it in 1317. The Collegiate Church (NM) of Gowran, $c1275$, is one of the finest parish churches in Ireland and is in the early-English style. The tower was added in the 14th or 15thc and is now incorporated in a 19th-c church which occupies the site of the older building's chancel. Features of the church include a finely-pointed arch of black marble leading into the chancel, a series of similar arches supported by circular and octagonal columns, elegant windows delicately ornamented in quatrefoil, and an ogham stone.

GRACEHILL, *Baile Uí Chinnéide*:
Kennedy's Homestead, Antrim   **7 D00**
This little settlement of Moravians or United Brethren, situated on the River Main, was founded by Rev John Cennick in 1746. It is built on a small elongated grid-plan, with the church, school, and halls occupying one side of one of the two longer streets. The village is unspoiled and the original street plan remains. The Georgian character of the houses is very little changed, and the tradition of using random and coursed basalt stonework with pebble infill to the pointing has been well maintained. The church of 1765 has a central square clock turret and two-storey house with wings at the extremes. The interior consists of a long hall with galleries at either end, and includes a central pulpit which is approached by a double flight of steps. Two houses in the square were set aside for unmarried brethren and sisters who supported themselves by managing the houses as boarding schools for boys and girls, and also by doing needlework. Also of interest is a graveyard with a fine avenue of trees. In 1975 the town was designated the first conservation area in N Ireland. Gracehill is connected to Galgorm by bridge.

GRAIGUENAMANAGH, *Gráig na Manach*:
The Hamlet of the Monks, Kilkenny
24 S74
Situated on the River Barrow near the Carlow border, this small market town is best known for its Cistercian monastery. The town was once called Duiske, a name which the monastery retains. Duiske Abbey was founded by William le Mareschal – Earl of Pembroke – in 1207,

and was apparently modelled on the abbey of Strata Florida in Wales. Even the measurements match, making Duiske the largest Cistercian church in Ireland. It was built between 1150 and 1250, and although rather spoilt by 19th-c restoration is still considered one of the best-preserved examples of Cistercian building in Ireland. In 1536 the abbey was suppressed, but monks continued to live in the precincts for many years afterwards. In 1813 a portion of the abbey church was roofed and is now in use as a place of worship (RC). Interesting monuments in the churchyard include two granite high crosses with biblical decorations. These were brought from Ballyogan and Aghailta. An effigy of a cross-legged knight wearing 14th-c armour used to be in the churchyard and is now in the church.

GRALLAGH CASTLE, Tipperary 23 S14
Grallagh Castle is a well-preserved 16th-c tower house (NM) situated 7m SSE of Thurles. It is four storeys high, and part of the bawn wall survives.

GRANAGH CASTLE, Kilkenny 24 S51
The fine 13th-c ruin of Granagh Castle (NM) stands high on the N bank of the River Suir 2½m NW of Waterford. It was once the home of the Le Poer family, but most of the building was probably conducted under the ownership of the Ormondes between 1375 and 1650. The remains include 13th-c towered curtain walls, a 14th- to 15th-c keep, and a 16th-c hall. A circular building at the NW corner of the enclosure may have been a windmill.

GRANARD, *Gránard,* Longford 17 N38
Granard is a marketing and angling centre which, in former times, was celebrated for an Irish Harp Festival endowed by a native by the name of Dungan c1784. The town was burnt in 1315 by Edward Bruce on his march S. To the E of Granard are Loughs Kinale and Sheelin, to the N is Lough Gowna, and between the first and last named of these are parts of prehistoric earthworks known as the Black Pig's Race (see Black Pig's Dyke entry). The Motte of Granard (NM) lies SW of the town and is said to be the largest in Ireland. It has an extensive bailey, a deep ditch, and a bank.

GRAND CANAL 17 & 18 N32 & N92
This 80-m link between Dublin and the River Shannon was started in 1756. Together with all its branches the canal covers 150m, and crosses the great central plain of Ireland. It passes through Tullamore – which was reached in 1798 - and terminates beyond the Shannon at Ballinasloe. The other end of the canal is on the SE side of Dublin, where it joins the River Liffey. Not far from this point – at Portobello – the company which constructed the canal built a large hotel in 1807. One of the canal's branches runs S from Robertstown to join the River Barrow at Athy. The waterway is no longer in commercial use.

GRANGE, *An Ghráinseach:*
The Grange, Sligo 10 G64
Grange lies 9m N of Sligo and once formed part of the estate of Lord Palmerston, an improving landlord who lived in the first half of the 19thc. To the W of the village is a beach sheltered by Streedagh Point. Here three Spanish Armada ships were wrecked, resulting in great loss of life. Slight remains of the ancient Church of Staad can still be seen. Off-shore and accessible by boat is the island of Inishmurray, where there is a wealth of antiquities. To the E of Grange are the Dartry Mountains, including the remarkable 1,722ft Ben Bulben.

GRANGEFERTAGH, Kilkenny 23 S36
Remains on the site of a monastery founded here by St Ciaran in the 6thc include a 100ft-high round tower (NM) with eight floors in good condition. The nearby Kilpatrick Chapel has a double-effigy tomb.

GREENCASTLE, *An Caisleán Nua:*
The New Castle, Donegal 6 C64
The bathing is good in this small Inishowen resort. Extensive remains of a castle built in 1305 by Richard de Burgo, Red Earl of Ulster, possibly occupy the site of a 13th-c stronghold. The fortress is dominated by a great gatehouse fronted by polygonal towers, and is the only example of 14th-c English defensive building in the province. Its purpose was to subjugate the O Donnells of Tirconnell and the O Dohertys of Inishowen; it also served as a port of supply for English armies in Scotland. Greencastle was once a meeting place for emigrants bound W on Atlantic-crossing ships. The cliffs of Inishowen Head rise to over 300ft NE of the resort and afford views E to N Derry and Antrim. A shipwreck was discovered 3m N at Kimagoe Bay by members of the City of Derry Sub-Aqua Club in 1971. Found some 200yds off-shore, the *La Trinidad Valencera* was a Venetian merchantman which sailed as a warship in the Spanish Armada of 1588. It was the largest ship in the fleet, and with 42 guns one of the most heavily armed. Apart from the armaments found during the preliminary excavations, there were a fine pair of navigator's dividers, pottery, a brass bucket, and a boy's leather boot. Because of the peculiar nature of the muddy sea floor, all the items were wonderfully preserved.

GREENCASTLE, *Caisleán na hOireanaí,*
Down 13 J21
Once the ancient capital of the Kingdom of Mourne, Greencastle is strategically sited in a position which commands the entrance to Carlingford Lough. The Anglo-Normans built a castle (NM) here in the 13thc. Remains of the stronghold include a 14th-c keep, lofty crenellated corner turrets, and outworks. The building was originally of great strength and often served as one of the few English outposts in Ulster. De Burgo (the Earl of Ulster) garrisoned it, but in 1315 it fell to Edward Bruce. To the S of the castle are the remains of a 16th- to 17th-c church and a motte.

GREYABBEY, *An Mhainistir Liath:*
The Grey Monastery, Down 13 J56
The building from which Greyabbey takes its name is one of the most complete Cistercian abbeys in Ireland. The village itself is attractively situated on the E shore of Strangford Lough. The abbey (NM) was founded in 1193 by Affreca, the wife of John de Courcy, and served by monks from Holme Cultram in Cumbria. The community was dissolved in c1541. In 1572, the building was burned down by the O Neills to prevent English colonists, who were trying to claim Ards Peninsula under a grant of Elizabeth I's, from sheltering there. The abbey church was re-roofed in the 17thc and used as a parish church until 1778. The abbey buildings follow the usual Cistercian plan, with the church to the N. The great west door with its beautiful mouldings, and the great east window with its three graceful lights, reflect the former grandeur and dignity of the ancient church. Most of the work is early English. The windows on either side of the chancel, however, were added in the perpendicular period shortly before the Dissolution. The small window over the west door and the disfiguring bellcote were added when the church was re-roofed. In the N wall of the chancel there is a recumbent figure, and in the N transept is a mutilated statue of a man in armour. The gable of the refectory stands complete, with three beautiful lancet windows, and its west wall contains a flight of stone steps which apparently led to a lectorium. A few of the 13th-c architectural fragments preserved on the abbey site bear mason's marks.

GRIANAN OF AILEACH, *Grianán Ailigh:*
Sun-palace of Aileach, Donegal 5 C31
This royal seat and stronghold (NM) of the O Neills, Kings of Ulster, is perhaps Ulster's best known and most conspicuous antiquity. Set on top of an 800ft-high hill at Carrowreagh near the Donegal and Derry border, the fort commands a view over Loughs Foyle and Swilly. Carrowreagh lies 11m S of Buncrana. The fort was built c1700BC, occupied until the 12thc, but drastically restored between 1874 and 1878. Three greatly dilapidated concentric ramparts encircle a strong stone cashel. The cashel is a circular wall about 17½ft high, with an average base thickness of 12½ft. The diameter of the enclosed area is 77ft. The entrance doorway is narrow and easily defensible. Galleries cover half the circumference on the inside of the wall.

GROOMSPORT, *Port an Ghiolla Ghruama:*
The Harbour of the Gloomy Individual, Down 7 J58
There are few modern buildings to spoil the old-world atmosphere of Groomsport, and the attractive sandy beach is well-suited for bathing. At the village's small quay in 1689 Schomberg landed with his army of 10,000 men. A monument commemorates the event. The soldiers bivouacked for the night on the sea-front. In 1631 the 150-ton *Eagle Wing*, with her cargo of persecuted Presbyterians, set sail from Groomsport for America. Storms forced her return. Off-shore to the E lie the Copeland Islands. There is a good view of these from Orlock Point.

GWEEDORE, *Gaoth Dobhair:*
Dore Inlet, Donegal 4 B82
Gweedore is well known to fishermen by virtue of the good sport found in the River Clady and nearby loughs. The village itself is prosperous and has three modern hotels, a large college, and many small industries. The Irish language is widely spoken in the district and the Irish language summer school is very popular. In 1838 Lord George Hill bought 23,000 acres of local land, introduced a reformed system of land tenure, and improved the quality of the land. He financed the building of roads, a church, a school, and a post office. At the little port of Bunbeg, a few miles to the W, he

established a store. It is at Bunbeg that the Clady enters Gweedore Bay. To the N of Gweedore rise 1,335ft Cronalaght and 1,413ft Tievealehid, while SW is a bleak district known as The Rosses.

HAMILTON'S BAWN, *Bábhún Hamaltún:*
Hamilton's Enclosure, Armagh **12 H94**
The name of this village is derived from a bawn built by John Hamilton in 1619 and almost entirely destroyed in the 1641 Rebellion. It was the subject of a humorous poem by Dean Swift called *The Grand Question debated whether Hamilton's Bawn shall be a Barrack or a Malt-House.* Swift probably composed this when he visited nearby Gosford Castle. A castle which stood on a hill above the town was regularly garrisoned until the early 19thc. The most interesting example of a crannog in the county is to be found 2½m E on the Tandragee road, by Marlacco Lake. The Earl of Tyrone kept his family and their treasures there for safety in c1595.

HARRYVILLE, *Baile Éinrí:*
Henry's Town, Antrim **7 D10**
One of the best surviving feudal motte-and-bailey castles in Ulster is to be found in this Ballymena suburb. Built in the de Courcy period, the circular motte is 140ft in diameter and 40ft high. A bridge across the River Main links Harryville with Ballymena.

HAZELWOOD, *An tEanach:*
The Marsh, Sligo **10 G73**
Little Hazelwood House is one of the finest small 18th-c country houses in Ireland. Situated on a peninsula at the W end of Lough Gill, it was designed for the Wynne family by Richard Cassels.

HEADFORD, *Áth Cinn:*
The Ford of Ceann, Galway **15 M24**
Headford is a market village and angling resort. On its outskirts is Headford Castle demesne and to the W is Lough Corrib. About 1¼m NW is the Franciscan friary of Ross Errilly (NM), on the banks of the Black River. The ruins are extensive and beautiful. They probably date from the late 15thc, although the friary was probably founded c1351 by Sir Raymond de Burgo. As in many similar Irish religious establishments, the friars lived within the sacred precincts until long after the Dissolution. The buildings were not abandoned until 1753. It was used as a fort at one time, and plundered by Cromwell's troops in 1656. The church has a nave with aisles, a choir, and a south transept. A chapel runs parallel to it. Features of special interest include the tracery of the east window and the moulding of the west doorway. The cloisters, with ten beautiful pointed arches, are in good condition. The conventual buildings are fairly complete and afford an excellent illustration of the arrangements of a medieval friary. Some ¾m N of the friary and 2m NW of Headford are the ruins of Moyne Castle and Church (see entry).

HEADFORT HOUSE, Meath **18 N77**
See Ceanannas Mor, Kells entry.

HEALY PASS, Bealach Scairte, Cork, Kerry **26 V75**
Considered one of the finest mountain roads in Ireland, this pass crosses the Berehaven Peninsula and climbs in carefully-graded bends from Adrigole Bridge on Bantry Bay, to a height of 1,084ft on the summit ridge of the Caha Mountains. The descent passes Glanmore Lake and reaches Lauragh Bridge at the head of Kilmakilloge Harbour, on the peninsula's N side. There are magnificent views N over Glanmore towards the Kenmare River, and S over Bantry Bay to Sheep's Head and Mizen Head – guarding the approach to Dunmanus Bay.

HEAPSTOWN CAIRN, Sligo **10 G71**
Situated near the N end of Lough Arrow, this great mound of loose stones (NM) possibly covers a passage grave. It is bounded by a stone kerb.

HELEN'S BAY, *Cuan Héilin:*
Helen's Bay, Down **7 J48**
The pleasant residential area of Helen's Bay lies a short way to the S of Grey Point and Helen's Bay, at the mouth of Belfast Lough. It is named after Helen, Lady Dufferin. The beach and adjoining belts of trees planted by the Dufferin family now form part of Crawfordsburn Country Park. A 3m-long overgrown avenue connects the beach and the railway station with Clandeboye House. The station buildings and adjoining coachyard were built to designs by Benjamin Ferrey in the 1860's.

HEN'S CASTLE, *Caisleán na Circe:*
The Hen's Castle, Galway **15 L95**
The extensive ruins of Hen's Castle (NM), also known as Castle Kirke, cover nearly the whole of a small island in an arm of Lough Corrib. Legend has it that the castle was built by a witch and her hen in one night. The witch presented it to a certain O Flahertie, with the warning that his life depended on the hen. Should he ever be besieged, it would lay sufficient eggs to sustain him. But O Flahertie put the hen in the pot when the castle was cut off by his enemies, and was shortly forced to capitulate through starvation. The castle was, in fact, built by the sons of Rory O Conor, the last king of Ireland, in the 13thc. It took the form of a Norman fortress, with a strong keep and projecting towers on the longest sides of the rectangular curtain walls.

HIGH ISLAND, Galway **14 L55**
See Ard Oilean entry.

HILL OF ALLEN, *Cnoc Alúine,*
Kildare **18 N72**
The hills of Allen, Naas, and Dun Aillinne were three residences of the kings of Leinster. Straight lines linking them form an equilateral triangle with a 9m-long sides. 676ft Allen is immediately to the S of the Naas to Rathangan road. On its summit is a tower, decorated with Latin inscriptions, which was erected by Sir Gerald Aylmer in 1859. There are still some traces of the original fort – which is said also to have been a residence of the legendary warrior Finn MacCool.

HILL OF SKREEN, *Scrín Choluim Chille:*
St Columcille's Shrine, Meath **18 N76**
See Tara entry.

HILL OF WARD, *Tlachtga,*
Meath **18 N96**
See Athboy entry.

HILLSBOROUGH, *Cromghlinn:*
Crooked Valley, Down **13 J25**
This charming Plantation town was named after Sir Arthur Hill, whose family first obtained land here in 1611. Hillsborough developed mostly in the 18thc, however, when there was some attempt to foster the linen industry. There are more good 18th- and early 19th-c houses here than in any other Ulster town of comparable size. The courthouse (NM) is a particularly fine example and dates from c1790. It was originally a market house and referred to as the Tholsel. There are a number of characteristic Georgian houses, notably in the steep main street and in the square. Hillsborough is probably the most English looking of Ulster towns, and today is largely inhabited by the descendants of the original English settlers.

The fort (NM) in the centre of a park to the S of the town was probably built in the 1650's by Col Sir Arthur Hill to command the road from Dublin to Belfast and Carrickfergus. It was refurbished in the mid 18thc. A massive building, it is defended by four quadrangular bastions and has a pointed arched gateway. There are good 'Strawberry Hill' gothick ogee-headed windows in the north-east and south west faces. Charles II made the fortress a royal one, appointing Sir Arthur and his successors hereditary constables with 20 warders. William III stayed at the fort on his way to the Battle of the Boyne. Until recently the garrison was maintained at full strength, the members wearing uniforms of the original pattern. The Marquess of Downshire, the lineal descendant of Sir Arthur Hill, bore the title of Marshal of Ulster and Hereditary Constable of Hillsborough Fort. The 1st Marquess of Downshire is commemorated by a monument on a hill overlooking the town; a statue of the 4th Marquess stands at the foot of the main street. Also in the park is the official residence of the Governor of N Ireland, Government House. The fine wrought-iron gates (NM) were brought from Richhill Castle.

Hillsborough was the birthplace of the eminent conductor Sir Hamilton Harty (1880–1941), who is buried in the parish churchyard. Sir Hamilton's father was organist at the local church (CI), a handsome, gothic-styled edifice erected by the Downshire family in 1774. Many interesting monuments can be seen here.

HILLTOWN, *Baile Hill:*
Hill's Town, Down **13 J22**
Situated on the River Bann in the shadow of the Mourne Mountains, this attractive angling village owes its development to the work of the Downshire family as improving landlords in the early 19thc. The market house (designed by Thomas Duff in 1828), and the Downshire Arms Hotel (designed by R F Brettingham and Charles Lilly) were built at this time. The parish church (CI) of Clonduff was completed in 1776 at the expense of Wills Hill, Earl of Hillsborough. It replaced the former church, which was destroyed in the Rebellion of 1641. The style is classical, with a gothic survival in the western pinnacled tower.

HOLLYMOUNT, *Maolla,* Mayo **15 M26**
The entrance to this little town on the River Robe is very pretty. The church (CI) is a handsome one, and the grounds of Hollymount House are beautiful. The house was the home of the Lindsays – a 19th-c family of improving landlords who provided and supported two public schools. They also obtained the site for a model agricultural school which was built by the Mansion House Relief Committee in 1822. Also of interest are

the ruins of a 17th-c church (CI) built by Archbishop Vesey. The present church was built in 1816.

HOLLYWOOD, *Cillín Chaoimhín*:
St Kevin's Little Church, Wicklow **18 N90**

This hamlet is situated on the edge of the Wicklow Mountains, near the Poulaphouca Reservoir. The name of the hamlet recalls a hollywood which figures in the life of St Kevin of Glendalough, and near by are various sites associated with him. At Athgreany, 1½m SSW, is a circle of fourteen large stones commonly called The Piper's Stones (NM). It is said that this is a group of dancers who were turned to stone for dancing on the Sabbath. A solitary stone a short distance away is said to be the Piper himself. The road running SE from Hollywood crosses the mountains by means of the well-known 1,567ft Wicklow Gap, leading to Rathdrum and the coast.

HOLY CROSS ABBEY, *Mainistir na Croiche*:
The Monastery of the Cross, Tipperary **23 S05**

This is one of the most picturesque Christian monuments in Ireland, with a charming setting beside the banks of the River Suir. The abbey founded in 1169 by Donal O Brien (King of Thomond) for monks of the Cistercian order was built on the site of an earlier Benedictine settlement. The Monastery of the Cross took its name from a portion of the True Cross which was contained in a golden shrine set with precious stones. It is believed to have been presented by Pope Pascal II to Donogh O Brien, the grandson of Brian Boru, in 1110. The relic attracted multitudes of pilgrims, especially in the 15th and 16thc, and their offerings greatly enriched the abbey. It is now to be found in the Ursuline Convent in Blackrock, Cork.

The Cistercian Abbey Church (NM) incorporates late 12th- and 15th-c architecture, with exceptionally well-preserved stone carving and traceries. It lay neglected and roofless from c1650, but during the period 1971 to 1975 was completely restored and brought back into use for public worship. The rooms above the church are in use as a local museum. The church, and in particular the chancel, is one of the finest pieces of 15th-c architecture in Ireland. Much altered and rebuilt in the 15thc, only the aisled nave contains some of the original late 12th-c inscription. The church is cruciform in shape, consisting of nave, choir, transepts with eastern chapels, and a square tower at the junction of the choir and nave. The nave is separated from the north aisle by round-headed arches, and from the south aisle by pointed arches. It is lighted by a fine six-light west window inserted in the late 15thc. The east portion of the church has two storeys, the upper having probably served as a scriptorium. The choir is lighted by a beautiful six-light window which is reticulated. On the right side of the high altar is a remarkable structure known as the 'Tomb of the Good Woman's Son'. This is probably the sedilia.

The north transept has two chapels with windows having flowing tracery of flamboyant type. There is also a wall-painting – one of the few to be seen in an Irish church – portraying a hunting scene of the 15thc. A stone staircase leads to the roof and to the top of the tower. This tower contains the oldest-known tower bell in the country, dating from the 13thc. This bell and another less ancient one were found in 1890 during grave-digging at the small ruined church of Boulick near Urlingford 12m NE. The south transept is the finest feature of the church; it has two chapels on the east with windows of flamboyant type, but its most interesting aspect is a remarkable structure between the two chapels. This has an elaborately groined roof and a double row of supporting pillars showing twisted shafts without capitals. Its carved foliage is similar to that of the sedilia, and it is probably of the same date. This was very likely where the relic of the True Cross was displayed.

The remains of the conventual buildings are scanty, and those on the S side of the cloister have disappeared altogether. On the W side is the cellarium, with the dormitory of the lay brothers overhead, and on the E are some remains of the sacristy, chapter house, and common room of the monks. Nearer the river are the very dilapidated remains of the abbey infirmary and guest house, plus the partially preserved early-Tudor style Abbot's House. The water mill on the site of the former abbey mill went out of use in 1947, but has been partially restored with its timber water wheels, sluice-gates, mill race, and weir. Restoration of Holy Cross Abbey and village was chosen as part of Ireland's presentation for European Architectural Heritage Year.

On a wall of the River Suir bridge outside the abbey precincts is an inscription. Surmounted by the arms of the Butlers and the O Briens, it relates to the rebuilding of the bridge by Lord Dunboyne and his wife in 1626. About 2m SE is the old keep of Killough Castle, at the foot of isolated Killough Hill, and 3m SW there is a group of castles – Milltown, Clonyharp, Graigue, and Clogher. These stand within a short distance of each other, and are relics of the unsettled days of the Tudors and Stuarts.

HOLY ISLAND, Clare **22 R68**
See Inishcealtra entry.

HOLYWELL, Fermanagh **11 H03**
This village 1m NW of Belcoo is noteworthy for the ruins of the small early-Irish church of Templerushin. It has three penitential station stones adjoining, one with a deep bullaun or cup mark. St Patrick's Holy Well on the roadside opposite is mentioned in Camden's Britannica as being the best cold bath in the kingdom, with healing powers for nervous and paralytic disorders. The church and stations are visited by pilgrims between the last Sunday of July and August 15.

HOLYWOOD, *Árd Mhic Nasca*:
The Height of Nasca's Son, Down **7 J37**

This pleasant residential town lies on the E side of Belfast Lough. John de Courcy tried rather unsuccessfully to found a town here in the late 12thc. It was not firmly established until Sir James Hamilton received a grant of the area in 1606. The town was laid out to the W of the 13th-c friary, which was renovated as a parish church. By 1800 Holywood was a seaside resort for Belfast, and with the building of the railway c1850 it became a residential suburb of the city. The town's Latin name, *Sanctus Boscus*, probably derives from a 7th-c church foundation of St Laisren or Laserian. The 13th-c church here was in the hands of the 3rd Order of St Francis at the Dissolution and was burned down by Sir Phelim O Neill in 1572 to prevent the realization of Sir Thomas Smith's scheme for colonization. The town has a large maypole in its High Street, probably the only one in Ireland. Robert Lloyd Praeger, author and naturalist who died in 1953, was a native of the town. His sister Rosalind was the sculptress whose work, 'Johnny the Jig', stands in the High Street. Just S of the town is the Redburn estate – including a fine wooded escarpment – which is being developed as a country park. About 2m NE is Cultra Manor, now the Ulster Folk Museum (see entry).

HORE ABBEY, Tipperary **23 S04**
See Cashel (Tipperary) entry.

HORN HEAD, *Corrán Binne*:
Curved Headland of the Peak, Donegal **5 C04**
See Dunfanaghy entry.

HORSELEAP, *Baile Átha an Urchair*:
Homestead of the Ford of the Cast, Westmeath **17 N23**

This village takes its Anglicized name from Hugh de Lacy's leap, with his horse, over the moat of the now-vanished Ardnurcher Castle while being pursued by his enemies. This castle, literally 'the fort of slaughter', was one of a chain of frontier posts – like nearby Donore Castle 2m E – constructed in the 15thc along that part of Co Meath

The picturesque ruins of Holy Cross Abbey as they were before extensive restoration.

within the English Pale. Their task was to protect new settlers and check the incursions of the Irish. Standing on a hill above the village is an ancient CI church in good repair. A spire was added to this in 1822. A large chapel (RC) was built in the village in 1809.

HOSPITAL, *An tOspidéal:*
The Hospital, Limerick **22 R73**
This little town derives its name from a hospital for the Knights Hospitallers, founded in 1215. The original church (NM) still survives and features three magnificent effigy tombs, one of which is thought to be of the founder Geoffrey de Marisco. The 537ft hill of Knockainy rises to the W of Hospital. It was said to be the otherworld seat of the goddess Anu. Rituals connected with this place were continued late into the 19thc.

HOWTH, *Beann Éadair:*
Eadar's Peak, Dublin **19 O23**
Howth is one of the most charming of Dublin's residential quarters and is a popular resort in the summer, offering excellent bathing from a number of strands, coves, and creeks. The resort lies within one of Ireland's lowest rainfall areas. Howth is a Norse name (*Hofuth*, a Head) for the rocky promontory which was known before the coming of the Norsemen by the Irish name *Beann Éadair*, or *Ben-na-dair*. The promontory is connected with the mainland by a low spit of land which is simply a gravel beach of comparatively recent formation. Prior to the creation of this beach Howth was an island. The Head is formed of the oldest rocks in Ireland – quartzite and slate. The highest point is 560ft Shelmartin, or Hill of Howth, on which stands a cairn which is referred to by Sir Samuel Ferguson in his poem *The Cromlech of Howth*. It is said to cover the remains of King Crimthan, who died towards the end of the 1stc. The tomb itself is said to be much older. The carpark near the summit of the head affords magnificent views and attracts many motorists in fine weather. The old town, with its large, 52-acre artificial harbour built under the supervision of John Rennie during the 19thc, is picturesquely situated on the N side of the peninsula and is now incorporated in the city of Dublin. Howth was formerly a packet station but, owing to the silting up of the harbour, it was abandoned in favour of Dun Laoghaire. The harbour is now used principally by the fishing fleet.

Restored Howth Castle stands on the W side of the town and is a long, irregular, battlemented building dating from 1564. It is flanked by square towers – perhaps the only remains of the ancient castle – and the hall contains a collection of interesting relics. These include the great sword of Sir Almericus Tristram – the 1st Lord of Howth – who conquered and took possession of the peninsula in 1177. His surname 'St Lawrence' was acquired following his victory over the Norsemen on St Lawrence's Day. Also of interest are the three bells of St Mary's Church, a full-length portrait of Dean Swift, and a collection of weapons. In the dining room is a painting representing the abduction of the young Lord of Howth by the infamous 'Seaqueen' Grace O Malley in 1575. Landing at Howth on her return from visiting Queen Elizabeth I, she found the castle gates closed at dinner time. To mark her displeasure at what she considered a breach of Irish hospitality she carried off the young heir and refused to restore him to his family until a promise was made that the gates of the castle would henceforth be left open at dinner time. The custom was preserved until recent times. Near the castle is a very old tree with only a few branches, carefully propped. According to legend, whenever a branch falls a member of the St Lawrence family dies. Howth demesne contains the remains of 16th-c Corr Castle and is noted for its attractive gardens containing rhododendrons (OACT). Also in the demesne is a fine dolmen known as Aideen's Grave, consisting of ten enormous masses of quartzite. The capstone is estimated to weigh 70 tons. Tradition says that Aideen, the wife of Oscar, slain near Tara at the end of the 3rdc, lies buried beneath it.

The Collegiate Church of St Mary (NM), commonly known as Howth Abbey, is situated on a precipitous bank above the harbour. It is usually considered to have been founded in 1235 by Luke, Archbishop of Dublin, on an earlier Norse foundation. The Archbishop is said to have erected the church to take the place of St Nessan's, the abbey on Ireland's Eye, an islet lying off the N shore of the promontory and accessible by motor boat. The church has been very much altered and extended. The oldest parts are the porch and the west end of the nave, probably 11thc; the side chapel, 13thc; and the chancel and mortuary chapel, 15thc. The altar tomb in the mortuary chapel is also 15thc. Its sides are decorated with panels ornamented with foliage, with figures of the Crucifixion, and with angels. Effigies of Sir Christopher St Lawrence, Lord of Howth, and his wife Anne Plunkett are carved in low relief on the covering slab. A late 15th-c house which was used as a residence for the clergy who served St Mary's stands on the street front and is still occupied. Howth College dates from the 16thc. There is a beautiful cliff walk from the town round the N side of the Head to the Bailey Lighthouse, with good views of the coast. The lighthouse, erected in 1814, occupies the site of an ancient fortress. The walk can be continued round the S side of the Head and past the tiny Oratory of St Fintan, which is probably of 9th-c date but was altered in later years. The CI church was built in 1816 and the RC chapel c1820.

HUNTINGTON CASTLE, Carlow **24 S96**
Ancient yew trees form a feature of the grounds in which this 17th-c fortified house stands. The modernized building dominates the village of Clonegal.

HYNE LOUGH, *Loch Oighin,* Cork **27 W02**
This small and richly-wooded inlet of the sea, known locally as Lough Ine, is located 3½m SW of Skibbereen. It forms a picturesque sheet of water, with the ruins of an old O Driscoll castle on an island. The lough is roughly rectangular in shape, about ½sqm in area, and connected with the sea by a channel ⅔m long. At the entrance to the lough the channel is only a stone's-throw wide, with a sill of rock across it which prevents the water of the lough from dropping below half-tide level.

ILLAUNTANNIG, *Oileán tSeanaigh:*
St Seanach's Island, Kerry **20 Q62**
See Castlegregory entry.

IMAAL, GLEN OF, *Uí Máil:*
Descendants of Mál, Wicklow **18 S99**
See Aughrim (Wicklow) entry.

INCH, Donegal **5 C32**
Formerly an island in Lough Swilly, Inch is now joined to the mainland as a result of drainage works. On the N side is a battery erected in 1813 at the threat of French invasion. Another can be seen on the Rathmullan shore. There is a fine new church (RC) by Liam McCormick at Burt, and a small neat church (CI) on the E side of the island. The remains of two portal dolmens can be seen here.

INCH, *Inis Chumhscraigh:*
Cumhsrach's Island, Down **13 J44**
See Downpatrick entry.

INCH, *Inse:* Holm, Kerry **26 Q60**
At the base of the Inch Peninsula – a long sand spit which extends into Dingle Bay – lies the sheltered seaside resort of Inch. The spit is a magnificent 4m strand backed by sandhills which are well known to archaeologists for old habitation sites with kitchen middens. This was the location for the filming of *The Playboy of the Western World*.

INCH CASTLE, *Caisleán na hInse:*
The Castle of Inch, Kildare **18 S79**
See Athy entry.

INCHAGOILL, *Inis an Ghaill:*
The Foreigner's Island, Galway **15 M14**
This Lough Corrib island contains some ecclesiastical remains, including the 12-c Romanesque *Teampull na Naomh* – noted for its fine elaborately-carved west door. The building has a rounded chancel arch and a small round-headed east window. There is also the exceptionally tiny Templepatrick, a small oratory of the early mortar-built type (NM).

INCHBOFIN, *Inis Bó Finne:*
Island of the White Cow, Westmeath **17 N05**
This island in Loughree had a 6th-c monastic foundation of St Rioch. Much plundered by the Danes, it later became an Augustinian abbey. There are remains of two 12th- or 13th-c abbey churches (NM), one with a beautiful Romanesque window, as well as a number of fine early-Christian grave slabs with Irish inscriptions.

INCHICRONAN LAKE, *Loch Inse Chrónáin,* Clare **21 R38**
Attractively situated at the end of a peninsula in Inchicronan Lake are the remains of the 15th-c O Brien castle and ruins of a late 12th-c Augustinian friary (NM). The latter shows an unusual original east window and 15th-c additions.

INCHIGEELAGH, *Inse Geimhleach,* Cork **27 W26**
Inchigeelagh, a resort of anglers and artists, is situated on the River Lee near the E extremity of Lough Allua. Carrynacurra Castle, one of the McCarthy strongholds, is situated 1m ENE of the village. Lough Allua and the other expansions of the Lee present a charming picture, with their white water lilies. In the background to the SW is prominent 1,797ft Shehy Mountain, which has its lower slopes cloaked with fir trees and is best climbed by way of Pipe Hill.

INISHANNON, *Inis Eonáin:*
Eonán's Holm, Cork **28 W55**
This little village, picturesquely situated on the River Bandon, was a walled town

of considerable importance in the 15thc. There are ruins of several castles near by, including Dundanier Castle, dating from 1476, which stands at the junction of the Rivers Brinny and Bandon.

INISHBOFIN, *Inis Bó Finne:*
The Island of the White Cow, Galway **14 L56**
This island off the Connemara coast has a small harbour and some good coastal scenery. There are traces of a monastery founded by St Colman $c660$, and sparse remains of a Cromwellian castle. In the sandhills are remains of clochans, and on the W shore of the harbour there is a cliff-top fort – Doon Grannia. The SE end of the island is guarded by the promontory fort of Doonmore. The smaller island of Inislark lies to the W. Inishbofin is accessible by boat from Cleggan.

INISHCEALTRA, *Inis Cealtrach:*
Island of Churches, Clare **22 R68**
Known as Holy Island and Island of the Churches, this tiny island – 1m SE of Mountshannon village – lies in Scarriff Bay, the most picturesque arm of Lough Derg. Originally founded by St Caimen, this well-known 7th-c monastic site (NM) is made conspicuous by its tall round tower. The monastery was rebuilt and extended by King Brian Boru in 1027 after it had been ravaged by the Danes from Limerick in 834.

Starting from the landing place on the N side, the first interesting feature is a small $10\frac{1}{2}$ by 8ft building, with a rude cell at the west end. To the S of this is a cemetery with the remains of a small, 15 by 10ft oratory. To the W is a larger church with a chancel, called St Caimen's Church. The nave is considered to contain the main features of the original church restored by Brian Boru, who added the chancel. The variety of the windows is noteworthy – semi-circular, square-headed, and triangular, the last-named being unique in an ancient Irish church. The west doorway must have been a striking feature, but comparatively little of it is left. To the S of St Caimen's Church is St Brigid's Church, a 20 by 12ft building standing within an enclosure which is entered from the W by a doorway of three orders with zigzag design. To the E of St Brigid's Church is the Church of St Mary, a 55 by 22ft structure. On the E part of the island there are ruins of several churches, many grave slabs – some with inscriptions in early Irish dating from the 8th to the 11thc, fine sculptured crosses and bullaun stones, and a well-marked system of enclosures.

St Mary's Well is close to the church of the same name on the E shore. The round tower, which is incomplete, stands about 80ft high, with a doorway 12ft from the ground. A paved way leads from the tower to a small enclosure with a tiny cell. This structure was once associated with a 10th-c anchorite called St Cosgraich, but it is now known to be of more modern date. The outer, mortar-built part probably dates from $c1700$.

INISHEER, *Inis Oirthir:*
Eastern Island, Galway **15 L90**
See Aran Islands entry.

INISHGLORA, *Inis Gluaire:*
Island of Brightness, Mayo **8 F63**
This low-lying island is situated 1m from Erris off the W coast of the Mullet peninsula. On it are extensive ecclesiastical remains (NM) of the mid 6th-c monastic foundation of St Brendan the Navigator, surrounded by a cashel 156ft in diameter. The most interesting building is the 12 by 8ft St Brendan's Chapel. Built of dry stone masonry with 3ft-thick walls, it slopes inwards and has a flat-headed doorway with inclined jambs. There are two other churches – *Teampull na Naomh* (the Church of the Saints), built of stone and mortar, and *Teampull na mBan* (the Church of the Women). Three beehive cells built of dry stone masonry, some inscribed crosses, and a holy well can also be seen.

INISHKEA ISLANDS, *Inis Ge:*
Ge's Island, Mayo **8 F52**
To the SSW of Inishglora are the twin islands of Inishkea North and Inishkea South, both of which are uninhabited. On Inishkea North may be seen the remains of a village deserted in 1931, and to the SW of this is ruined St Columcille's Church (NM). There are many early crosses on the island. Inishkea South also has several early crosses.

INISHKEEN, *Inis Caoin:*
Pleasant Island, Monaghan **12 H90**
The most striking feature in this village is the modern parish church (RC), which stands on a slightly raised site. The novel circular shape of this small building blends into the gently rolling countryside. There are some remains of the 6th-c monastery founded here by St Deagh. These include part of a round tower (NM), 42ft high with a doorway 14ft above the ground. An inscribed cross dated 1729 and bearing the MacMahon arms is embedded in a wall.

INISHMAAN, *Inis Meáin:*
Middle Island, Galway **15 L90**
See Aran Islands entry.

INISHMAAN, *Inis Meáin:*
Middle Island, Mayo **15 M16**
Situated in Lough Mask, the island of Inishmaan (more commonly known as Inishmaine) contains the remains of a small Augustinian monastery (NM). St Cormac founded a monastery here in the 6thc. On the site of his foundation is a small, early 13th-c cruciform church with good transitional carvings in the stonework of the chancel arch pier, and a square-headed doorway of an early Irish type. The nearby gatehouse is probably of 15th-c date. There are ruins of a typical Irish sweat-house near the W shore.

An ancient fortification once guarded the shores of Howth from the site now occupied by 19th-c Bailey Lighthouse.

INISHMACSAINT, Fermanagh **11 H15**
On this island, which is situated off the W shore of Lower Lough Erne, there is an early cross and the ruins of an 11th- or 12th-c church.

INISHMORE ISLAND, *Árainn Mhór:*
Big Aran, Galway **14 L80**
See Aran Islands entry.

INISHMURRAY, *Inis Muirígh:*
Muiríoch's Island, Sligo **10 G55**
Inishmurray lies 4m off the coast of Co Sligo at the entrance to Donegal Bay. Although this vast rock is precipitous on the side facing the Atlantic, it shelves gradually towards the mainland and is accessible by boat from Grange. The island was inhabited until comparatively recently, with fish providing the main subsistence and income. The 100 acres of profitable land were mainly used for grazing since tillage was always poor, despite the use of sea wrack for manure.

The well-preserved monastery (NM) on the island was founded by St Molaise during the 6thc. The 7th- and 8th-c buildings that remain were kept in reasonable order by the islanders, who used them for housing their cattle. The monastery was frequently raided by the Vikings and was finally abandoned in the 9thc, but the buildings that remain provide an exceptional insight into the appearance and even way of life of an early-Christian monastery in Ireland.

The monastery is surrounded by a well-preserved cashel built of drystone masonry and measuring 175ft long by 135ft broad. The massive surrounding walls vary in height from $7\frac{1}{2}$ to almost 10ft, and the base is between 7 and 15ft thick. Five entrances through the wall lead to the central area, which is divided into four enclosures. The largest of these contains *Teampull na bhFear* (The Men's Church), $25\frac{1}{2}$ by 12ft and used as a burial place for men. The NW enclosure contains *Teach Molaise*, 9 by 8ft, a more primitive church with stone roof, flat-headed doorway, and round-headed east window. In the same enclosure is *Teach na Teineadh* (The Fire House). This has a hearth from which fire was believed to be miraculously kindled, and probably dates from the 14thc. The cashel also contains three altars and three beehive cells (clochans). The oval clochans are constructed with very large stones, and the largest, called the Schoolhouse, was used as such by the island's inhabitants at one time.

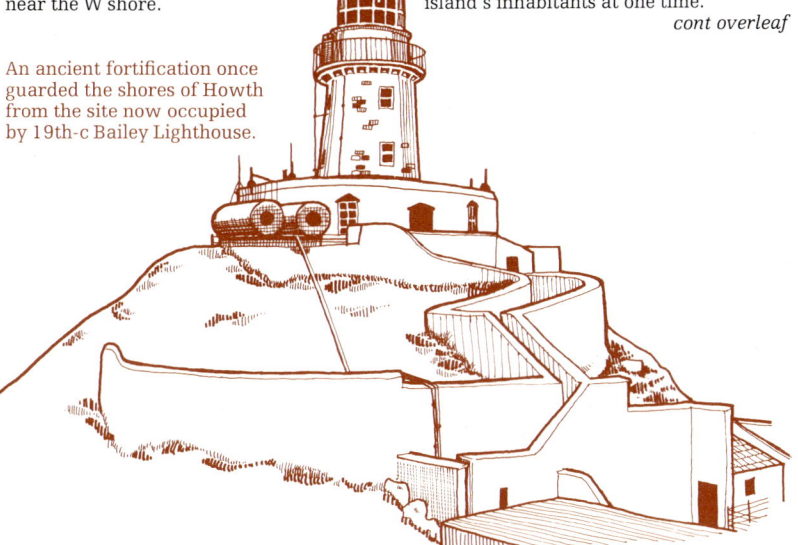

cont overleaf

Outside the cashel to the NW is the *Teampull na nBan* (The Women's Church), a burial place for women. The islanders are said to have believed that if a man was buried in the women's place the corpse would be mysteriously transferred, and vice versa. Also outside the cashel there are about 50 cross-slabs, some of which have early Irish inscriptions and one with the Latin inscription *hic dormit*. In addition there are three fine pillar stones, two of which are holed, two bullauns, and two holy wells.

INISHOWEN PENINSULA, *Inis Eoghain:*
Eoghan's Island, Donegal **5 & 6 C 33**
This peninsula separates the two large inlets of Lough Swilly and Lough Foyle. Within its comparatively small area the peninsula contains some remarkably fine scenery, notably on the W and N seaboard.

INISHTOOSKERT, *Inis Tuaisceart:*
North Island, Kerry **26 Q 20**
Situated 3m N of Great Blasket Island, this lonely uninhabited island contains the ruins of a boat-shaped stone oratory (NM). The oratory was dedicated to St Brendan. Although only three stone crosses and four beehive cells remain, there are traces of others.

INISHVICKILLANE, Kerry **26 V 29**
This member of the Blasket group lies 2m SW of Great Blasket Island. On the island are an oratory cell (NM) and cross (NM). Inishnabro is adjacent to the N end of the island.

INIS PATRICK, *Inis Phádraig:*
St Patrick's Island, Dublin **19 O 26**
See Skerries entry.

INISTIOGE, *Inis Tíog,* Kilkenny **24 S 63**
Charmingly situated on the banks of the River Nore, this pretty town has a square lined with lime trees. The river flows under a handsome 18th-c bridge and, S of the town, through a delightfully-wooded stretch of countryside.

The motte on a rock overlooking the river is all that remains of a motte-and-bailey castle erected by the first Anglo-Normans to arrive in the area. The Protestant parish church incorporates part of an Augustinian monastery founded in 1210 by Thomas Fitzanthony, Seneschal of Leinster. The ruins consist of the nave and tower of the church, and the adjoining lady chapel. The tower, which is square at the base and octagonal above, probably dates from the foundation and was converted into a mausoleum by the Tighe family. 18th-c Woodstock house was once held to be one of the finest houses of its era in the country, but has not been occupied since 1922. Within the boundaries of the Woodstock demesne are the ruins of two ancient castles, Brownsford and Cloon.

Brandon Hill rises to 1,703ft NE of Inistioge. On the summit are a cairn and stone circle. The hill can be easily climbed from the town, and there are superb views of the Barrow and Nore valleys from its summit. Mount Leinster and the Blackstairs range can be seen to the E. At Clonamery, 2½m SE of Inistioge, are the remains of a church (NM) which formed part of an early monastery. Its most notable feature is the massive lintel of the west door.

INNISFALLEN, *Inis Faithleann:*
Faithle's Island, Kerry **27 V 98**
See Killarney entry.

INNISFREE or INISHFREE, *Inis Fraoigh:*
Heather Island, Sligo **10 G 73**
This island near the SE shore of Lough Gill has been immortalised in W B Yeats' poem *The Lake Isle of Innisfree*.

INVER, *Inbhear:* Estuary, Donegal **4 G 87**
Inver is a small holiday and fishing resort with good sands. The town is situated at the point where the Eany river enters Inver Bay, an inlet of the larger Donegal Bay. Inland, to the NE, rise the Blue Stack Mountains. Thomas Nesbitt, who invented the harpoon-gun, was born near Inver in 1730 and is buried in the graveyard of the ruined church.

IRELAND'S EYE, *Inis Mac Neasáin:*
The Island of the Sons of Neasán, Dublin **19 O 24**
A wedge-shaped mass of quartzite resting on beds of slate forms this fantastic islet, which provides a natural breakwater for Howth Harbour. The islet lies a little to the N of Howth, from where it can be reached by motor boat. The tiny church of St Nessan stands on the site of an older foundation dating from the 7thc. Near the W end of the islet is a martello tower.

ISERTKELLY, Galway **16 M 51**
Isertkelly is a fine, mid 16th-c house (NM) which was built by the MacHubert Burkes. It has a fine arcaded second-floor room. In the room is a carved stone chimney-piece of 1604 with a Latin inscription praying that the builder (initials WH) may be preserved from all evil. Near the house is a ruined church.

ISLAND MAGEE, *Oileán Mhic Aodha:*
Magee's Island, Antrim **7 D 40**
A low undulating peninsula 7m long by 2m wide, Island Magee extends NW from the area of Whitehead. On its W side is Larne Lough. This lough is almost entirely enclosed. It expands from a narrow channel between Larne Harbour and the peninsula's NW tip into a wide strip of water before tapering again near Whitehead, where it is narrow and marshy. Very little is known of the history of the peninsula before Queen Elizabeth I's time, but it is supposed to have got its name from the Scottish family Magee, to whom it once belonged.

The cliff scenery on the E side of the peninsula is fine, particularly the Gobbins – basalt cliffs almost 250ft high. A path cut in the face of the rock a few feet above sea level extends for over 1m, passing over bridges and through tunnels. The path has been allowed to deteriorate and is dangerous in places, but provides a splendid view of the cliffs and rocks. The Gobbins is the reputed scene of an unpleasant incident during the rebellion of 1641. According to the story members of the garrison at Carrickfergus were inflamed by the reported sufferings of Protestants. In retaliation they massacred Roman Catholic inhabitants of the peninsula, throwing live and dead bodies over the cliffs into the sea. Like most reports of atrocities during the 1641 rebellion, this account is doubtless much exaggerated.

Ballyharry townland, close to Larne Lough, contains the small parish church of St John (CI), one of the best examples of an early-Jacobean church in Ulster. The church was probably built in 1609 and measures 60 by 30ft. The windows are of the square-topped late-Tudor style and all appear to be original. In the townland of Ballykeel, ½m S, there is the ruin of a similar but older parish church. A passenger ferry plies between Larne and Ballylumford at the NW point of the peninsula, where there is an oil-fired power station. Near the landing place, standing in the front garden of a private house, is a fine dolmen – a small single-chambered grave. A number of spiral gold ornaments and a gold collar were dug up close by in 1817 and 1824. Near by, in the pleasant little cove and small resort of Brown's Bay, is a rocking stone of glacial origin. The last witch tried in Ireland came from Island Magee.

ISLAND MAHEE, *Inis Mochaoi:*
St Mochaoi's Island, Down **13 J 56**
This island has an almost idyllic setting in Strangford Lough. Because of this it has become the place of residence of a few discerning city workers. A feature of the island is ruined Nendrum Abbey (NM; see entry).

IVERAGH PENINSULA, *Uíbh Ráthach,* Kerry **26 V 56**
Iveragh Peninsula is the central and largest of Co Kerry's three peninsulas. It is 35m long by 15m wide, and is encircled by a splendid coast road called the Ring of Kerry. The road traverses the picturesque shores of Dingle Bay and the Kenmare River. The interior of the peninsula contains the rugged MacGillycuddy's Reeks.

JACK'S HOLE, Wicklow **25 T 38**
This pleasant little cove is situated N of attractive Brittas Bay.

JERPOINT ABBEY, *Mainistir Sheireapúin,* Kilkenny **24 S 54**
Although ruined, these picturesque abbey buildings (NM) are fairly complete and form one of the finest groups in the country. The abbey was once surrounded by a town, but there is little trace of this now. It was founded in 1180 as a daughter house of the Cistercian abbeys of Baltinglas, Mellifont, and Clairvaux, and was built on the site of a Benedictine house – traces of which remain. By the Dissolution the abbey had attained a position of great wealth and influence, and with 6,500 acres was granted to the Marquis of Ormonde.

The church is cruciform, with the usual Cistercian arrangement of two chapels in each transept. The oldest remaining parts of the abbey are the chancel and the transepts in the Irish Romanesque style. The stone roof over the rough barrel vault of the chancel is still in a good state of preservation. The tower is supported on arches – the one leading to the choir being circular-headed, while the others are pointed. The fine, battlemented central tower is of perpendicular style and dates back to the 15thc. The battlements give a foreign look to the group of buildings and are similar to those found in the north of Italy. The 14th-c east window is in decorated style, while the earlier west window consists of three lights with semi-circular heads. The cloisters, which were rebuilt in the 15thc, incorporate some exceptionally-fine sculpture and have been excellently restored. Of particular interest are the site's many outstanding 13th- to 16th-c monuments with effigies. The carving on some of these stands comparison with the best in Europe. One tomb has the effigy of Bishop O Dullany, who died in 1202, and shows a serpent at the end of his crozier. In the south transept is a damaged 16th-c tomb. Another 16th-c tomb can be found under the tower, while in the chancel near the sedilia is a notable 15th-c tomb. At Newtown Jerpoint, ¼m NW, is the interesting parish church of St Nicholas, noted for its groin-vaulted rood gallery. At Ballylowra, 1½m SW, are two megalithic tombs and the re-erected Liaghan ogham stone.

JIGGINSTOWN, *Baile Shigín:*
Jiggins' Homestead, Kildare **18 N81**
Ruined Jigginstown was one of the largest mansions ever built in Ireland, and had a frontage of 380ft. It was one of the earliest brick buildings in the country. The red brick used is possibly Dutch in origin. Thomas Wentworth, Earl of Strafford, built the mansion between 1632 and 1639 for entertaining Charles I. Work stopped when Wentworth was executed, and the building was never completed. The groin-vaulted basement has rows of panelled and moulded brick columns. Behind the house there is a sunken garden with a gazebo in the SE corner. Adjacent to Jigginstown is two-storey Castlerag Castle.

JOHNSTOWN, *Baile Eoin:*
St John's Town, Kildare **18 N73**
At one end of the village is Palmerston House, a great early 19th-c mansion and seat of the Earl of Mayo. The ruins of a small early nave-and-chancel church are ¼m NE. On the summit of a hill near by is a large, strongly-built circular entrenchment with a huge upright block of granite in the centre.

JOHNSTOWN, *Baile Sheáin:*
John's Homestead, Kilkenny **23 S36**
This village, dating from *c*1700, is best known for the nearby spa of Ballyspellan (2m NE). Several treatises were written on the medicinal properties of the water, which was stated to be of 'great efficacy in obstructions, relaxations, and recent dropsies'. Sheridan and Dean Swift wrote humorous lines about the spa. In the 19thc the west doorway and east window of the 13th- to 16th-c Augustinian abbey of Grangefertagh were installed in the parish church (CI). The baptismal font and a representation of the crucifixion are in the Catholic church. An ogham-inscribed 8th-c silver brooch found in the village is now in the National Museum, Dublin. Foulkscourt Castle, W of Johnstown, dates from *c*1450. The castle stands in the demesne of the ruined mansion of Foulkscourt House, built in 1715.

JOHNSTOWN CASTLE, *Baile Sheáin:*
John's Town, Wexford **25 T01**
Johnstown Castle is a 19th-c gothick mansion standing in beautiful grounds (OACT). The building is now state-owned and is used as an agricultural college. It incorporates the tower of a 13th-c fortress built by Esmonde – one of the Anglo-Norman settlers – and destroyed by Cromwell in 1649 before he attacked Wexford.

JONESBOROUGH, *Baile an Chláir:*
The Town of the Plank, Armagh **13 J01**
The village of Jonesborough stands near the Louth border. To the W is the Moyry Pass, the scene of many bloody contests between Ulster's invaders and defenders. Elizabethan troops tried to wrest

More of a mansion than a castle, 19th-c Johnstown is a fine example of the gothick style and incorporates a 13th-c tower.

possession of the pass from Hugh O Neill, who stubbornly held it for six years. In 1600 Mountjoy momentarily triumphed, but eventually retreated to Dundalk severely wounded. Moyry Castle lies 2m S of Jonesborough and was built by Lord Mountjoy in 1601. It played an important part in the fierce struggles, but only an unroofed rectangular tower now remains. SE of Jonesborough, in the Carlingford Peninsula, is 1,674ft Clermont Carn.

JORDAN'S CASTLE, *Caisleán Shiurdán:*
Jordan's Castle, Down **13 J53**
See Ardglass entry.

JOYCE'S COUNTRY, *Dúiche Sheoigheach:*
Joyce's District, Galway **15 L95**
The Joyces of Wales, men noted for their great stature, came to Galway in the 13thc and gave their name to this area of picturesque mountains, glens, and lakes. Their descendants still live in the locality. Joyce's Country lies between Connemara and Co Mayo, and extends E to the narrow strip of land separating Lough Mask from Lough Corrib. The principal mountains bordering Joyce's Country are the Maamturks to the SW and the Partrys to the NE. The heart of this country is traversed by the Maam Cross to Leenane road, which is paralleled by Joyce's River. To the E a range of hills in Bunnacunneen rises to 1,902ft.

KANTURK, *Ceann Toirc:*
The Head of the Boar, Cork **27 R30**
Kanturk is a market town situated at the junction of the rivers Allow and Dalua, tributaries of the Blackwater. Impressive Old Court Castle was a stronghold of the McCarthys during the Elizabethan period. Dermod MacOwen MacDonagh MacCarthy built the castle in 1601 like an Anglo-Norman castle, with a large 120 by 80ft quadrangle, and a massive, square, four-storey tower in each corner. The castle was probably never completed however, since the strength of the structure aroused the suspicions of the Government and the builder received an order to cease work on it. The castle is let on long lease to the Irish National Trust *(An Taisce).*

KATESBRIDGE, *Droichead Cháit:*
Kate's Bridge, Down **13 J24**
Katesbridge village features the scanty remains of a motte. A large circular cairn stands 2¾m ENE on the summit of 1,054ft Deehommed Mountain. A magnificent bronze-age cemetery was found 3m E at Closkelt in 1973.

KEADUE, *Céideadh:*
The Hill, Roscommon **10 G91**
Turlough O Carolan, the last Irish Bard, lived at Keadue during the late 17th and early 18thc. His grave is in the ancient cemetery of Kilronan (see entry).

KEADY, *An Céide:*
The Hill, Armagh **12 H83**
This market town is sited on high ground near the Monaghan county boundary, a little to the NE of Clay Lake. It was a major centre of the Irish linen industry until the 1930's and had manufacturing facilities at Dundrum, Annvale, Darkley, New Holland, and Balleer. An adequate water supply has been ensured by the damming of three local lakes – Clay, Tullynawood, and Aughnagurgan. The local CI church is a neat, plain building which was erected by Primate Robinson in 1776. A tower was added as part of a general enlargement scheme in the 19thc. Some 2m NE of Keady is an old burial ground associated with the Culdee Priory of Armagh.

KEEL, *An Caol:*
The Isthmus, Mayo **8 F60**
See Achill Island entry.

KEEM BAY, *An Choim,* Mayo **8 F50**
See Achill Island entry.

KEIMANEIGH, PASS OF, *Céim an Fhia:*
The Deer's Pass, Cork **27 W16**
This picturesque pass extends for over 1m and is bounded by steep, rugged precipices on each side. Wild flowers and ferns rooted in rocky crevices relieve the stern surroundings of the road as it climbs to an altitude of 662ft, shadowed to the E and W by the respective heights of 1,555ft Doughill and 1,698ft Foilastookeen. After the summit the pass descends SW along the valley of the Ouvane River towards Bantry Bay.

KELLS, Antrim **7 J19**
The name 'Kells' applies to a famous and well-endowed Augustinian foundation which once thrived in the townland of Templemoy, but the only remains that have survived to the present day are the battered west gable of a church and the shaft of a high cross. The fragment of church may date from the 15thc; the building itself was known to have existed through the Dissolution until its destruction in the 1641 Rebellion.

KELLS, *Ceanannas*, Kilkenny 24 S44
Even before the 12th-c invasion of the Anglo-Normans this village was the most important centre in the ancient kingdom of Ossory. After the invasion it was granted to Geoffrey Fitzrobert de Marisco, who built a strong castle and founded an Augustinian friary to house a community which included monks he had brought over from Bodmin in Cornwall. Among these 'aliens' was Hugh de Rous, who became the 1st English Bishop of Ossory. Remains that have survived from this period include fragments of the town walls, a few tombstones from the early church, and very little else. Nothing of the original castle can be seen, but interesting later ruins of a strongly fortified priory include remains of defensive walls, towers, and church buildings dating from the 15th or 16thc. These extensive survivals (NM) cover some 5 acres of ground and comprise the largest monastic enclosure in Ireland. The large, oblong area used by the foundation was divided into two courts by a wall and moat. The heavily-fortified north court was defended by towers as well as a wall, and contained various important monastic buildings such as the church, cloisters, and a mill. The church itself consisted of a nave, choir, lady chapel, and south transept. It displays later additions which include a tower built in the perpendicular style. A strong castle attached to the south-east angle of the choir is said to have been the residence of the prior. Only the foundations of the domestic buildings are visible today. The southern or Burgher's, Court does not seem to have contained any buildings and was probably used as a protective pound for cattle. It too is fortified by towers, with the addition of curtain walls on the north and west sides. The priory and its grounds were granted to the Earl of Ormonde at the Dissolution of the monasteries.

A Norman motte close to the priory ruins stands 30ft high and commands a bridge which spans the King's River at this point. Ancient walls still partly surround the castle's bailey. About 4m S of Kells is 10th-c Sheepstown Church, an interesting structure which features a doorway with inclined jambs.

KELLS, *Ceanannas Mór*, Meath 18 N77
See Ceanannas Mor entry.

***KENMARE, *Neidín*:**
Little Nest, Kerry 27 V97
Charmingly sited where the Roughty River opens into the beautiful estuary of the Kenmare River, this town is set among the Kerry hills and is surrounded by the lofty peaks of the western mountains. The Killarney Mountains rise in front of lofty MacGillycuddy's Reeks to the N, the Caha range dominates the Cork border to the SW, and 2,280ft Akinkeen stands proud of its neighbouring mountains to the SE. Kenmare itself was founded in 1670 on land assigned to Sir William Petty by the English government, and was settled by a handful of English fighting men. These colonists withstood almost continuous assault while building up a prosperous fishery, establishing an iron works, and cutting local timber to fuel the foundry. In 1688 the town was besieged by 3,000 men. The defenders made their last stand on the little peninsula of Killowen, near Kenmare, and finally escaped the attackers in two 30-ton vessels – 'Packed like fish one upon the other.' After a fortnight's tossing on the Atlantic they managed to make a landfall at Bristol and were saved.

This was not the end of the colony however. Kenmare was re-established by William III during his campaign of pacification in Ireland, and the town's industries once more swung into production.

Industries operated here today include the manufacture of high-quality lace and woollen products. The main road through Kenmare is carried across the sound by a two-span, 'rigid-arch' concrete suspension bridge which replaces a 19th-c structure which was built with financial help from the Marquess of Lansdowne. The Marquess also contributed towards the construction of a pier below the town c1833. A developing industry nowadays is that of tourism, and Kenmare has plenty to offer the holidaymaker. Local fishing is excellent and the area around the town is rich in antiquarian relics. An interesting old bridge spans the Finnihy River, and near the river at the Shrubberies is the Druids' Circle – a circle of stones enclosing a small chamber tomb. Dunkerron Castle stands on a rock some 2m W of the town and dates from the 13thc.

KERRYKEEL, *An Cheathrú Chaol*:
The Narrow Quarter, Donegal 5 C23
Kerrykeel village is situated on the beautiful road which runs along the E coast of Mulroy Bay. To the NE is 1,203ft Knockalla, or the Devil's Backbone, a mountain ridge which extends almost to picturesque Lough Swilly and terminates at 19th-c Knockalla Fort. This stronghold was built to defend the lough against possible infiltration by French forces. A portal dolmen can be seen about 1¼m S on Knockmore Hill.

KESH, *An Chéis*:
The Wicker Causeway, Fermanagh 11 H16
Situated near an inlet of island-studded Lower Lough Erne, Kesh village stands in the heart of a lakeland area which is known for its excellent fishing prospects and rich wildlife. About 2m SW of the village are the ruins of 17th-c Crevenish Castle, a house built by Thomas Blennerhasset. The Drumskinny Stone Circle (NM) can be seen 4½m NNE.

KESH, *An Chéis*, Sligo 10 G71
Keshcorran Hill, which rises to 1,188ft near this village, features a number of caves of considerable archaeological importance. These are situated near the 600ft contour and have yielded bones of extinct animals, plus traces of human habitation.

KILBARRACK CHURCH, *Cill Bharróg*:
St Barróg's Church, Dublin 19 O23
The church here dates from the 13thc and is little more than an ivy-covered ruin, but it has interesting associations with the notorious Francis Higgins. Higgins, the 'Sham Squire' who betrayed Lord Edward Fitzgerald, was buried here; his tomb was smashed when the facts of the betrayal became known to the local citizens.

KILBEGGAN, *Cill Bheagáin*:
Beagán's Church, Westmeath 17 N33
A 17th-c charter allowed this little River Brosna market town to return two members to the Irish parliament, but this right ceased after it was disfranchised at the Act of Union. Kilbeggan's prosperity was assured by the branch of the Grand Canal which used to flow here, and many of the town buildings reflect a past, elegant way of life and work. Proprietor Gustavus Lambert erected the neat limestone-built market and courthouse, and the interesting old distillery building here dates from 1757. Newforest, a Georgian mansion situated 3m NE of the town, dates from 1749. About ½m S is a green mound which is known as the Church of the Relic, and is said to mark the site of an abbey.

KILBEHENY, *Coill Bheithne*:
Birch Wood, Limerick 22 R81
The ruined castle in this little village was assaulted and taken by Cromwell in the 17thc. To the N of Kilbeheny the Galtee Mountains culminate in 3,018ft Galtymore, which can be reached on foot via the Glengarra Valley. Access to the valley is from a point some 5m NE on the Cahir road.

KILBENNAN, Galway 15 M45
Features of the monastic site here, some 2½m NW of Tuam, include the ruins of a 15th-c Franciscan church and the remains of a round tower (NM). The church shows later additions. A foundation was first created here in the 5thc.

KILBERRY, *Cill Bhearaigh*:
St Bearach's Church, Kildare 18 S69
Kilberry stands close to the River Barrow and features the remains of an ancient abbey. Interesting Reban Castle stands to the W, on the other side of the river.

KILBERRY, *Cill Bhearaigh*:
St Bearach's Church, Meath 18 N87
Remains of an old church dedicated to St Bearach can be seen here, plus the motte of a Norman castle.

KILBOLANE CASTLE, *Cill Bholáin*:
Bolan's Church, Cork 21 R42
The design of this castle (NM) is similar to that of strongholds built in the late 13thc, but the building was erected much later in the 15th or 16thc. Its two outer walls carry a pair of circular corner turrets and are defended by a water-filled moat on the south-west side.

KILBONANE, *Cill Bhonáin*:
Bonán's Church, Kerry 26 V89
Interesting remains that can be seen here include the ruins of an old church – near the banks of the River Laune – and 16th-c Ballymalis Castle (NM). An ogham stone found in the area is preserved at Dunloe Castle.

KILBRITTAIN, *Cill Briotáin*:
Briotán's Church, Cork 28 W54
This village is pleasantly situated near the fine demesne of Kilbrittain Castle, which is undergoing restoration at the hands of a new owner (at time of printing).

KILBRONEY, *Cill Brónaí*:
St Brónach's Church, Down 13 J11
This old churchyard is sited on the E side of the Hilltown road, about 1m NE of Rostrevor, and contains the ruins of a 15th- or 16th-c church. A tree brought down by the wind in 1885 was found to contain an early-Christian bronze bell which may have dated from the times of St Bronach, to whom the ruined church was dedicated. This was recast, furnished with a new clapper, and

re-hung in the RC church at Rostrevor. The graveyard itself features two old crosses. The tallest of these is decorated with abstract designs, which can still be seen in spite of extensive weathering, and is of an early type.

KILCASH, *Cill Chais:*
Church of Cas, Tipperary 23 S 32
This small village lies under the S escarpment of 2,363ft Slievenamon and features a ruined church which preserves a good Irish-Romanesque doorway.

KILCLIEF, *Cill Chléithe:*
Wattle Church, Down 13 J 54
Situated on the W side of the narrow straight which connects Strangford Lough with the sea, this small village stands in a rich lowland area known as Lecale. The district was exceptionally prosperous as early as the 18thc, when its farms supplied Dublin city with heavy harvests of wheat and malting barley. Evidence of this wealth can still be seen in the large holdings and substantial houses that dot the countryside. One of the main features in Kilclief is the castle (NM), a rectangular tower house that was probably built c1440 by John Cely – Bishop of Down. It is a very early example of 'gatehouse' design and may have served as a model for later strongholds. Nowadays the building is used as a storehouse. Close by are very slight remains of a Norman motte.

KILCOLGAN, *Cill Cholgáin:*
Colga's Church, Galway 15 M 41
The derivation of the Irish placename for this place seems to support the local tradition that an abbey was founded here some time in the 6thc. More substantial are the interesting remains of the castle. Drumacoo Church lies about 2m SW of Kilcolgan and dates from the 13thc. The south-west part of the building is part of an earlier stone church and retains a flat-headed doorway. Most of the present structure dates from the 13thc, but a north wing was added c1830. An early monastic site 2m SE at Kilbiernan (NM) features the ruins of an early church inside a large enclosure. Also in the enclosed area are remains of houses and a souterrain.

KILCOLMAN ABBEY, *Cill Cholmáin:*
St Colmán's Church, Kerry 26 Q 80
Remains of Killagh Priory, a foundation created in the reign of King John, can be seen in the grounds of this beautiful old abbey. Near by is Fort Agnes, with the remains of a large circular stronghold and a souterrain. Several more circular forts exist near the River Maine estuary.

KILCOLMAN CASTLE, *Cill Cholmáin:*
St Colman's Church, Cork 22 R 51
See Doneraile entry.

KILCONNELL, *Cill Chonaill:*
Conall's Church, Galway 16 M 73
Kilconnell Friary (NM) is considered one of the finest examples of 15th-c Franciscan architecture in Ireland. The Franciscans totally dominated building design in Ireland during this period, in much the same way as the Cistercians did between 1150 and 1250. The friary was built by William O Kelly on the site of an earlier church which was said to have been founded by St Conall. The church stands at the south side of the cloisters, as is usual with foundations of this Order, and comprises a nave with a south aisle, a transept with an east chapel, and a choir. The groined roof is evidently of a later date than the rest of the building. Notable features include beautiful window tracery and a number of interesting tombs which recall the names and arms of influential Galway families. Two of these memorials are of particular note; the one near the west door of the nave is divided into six niches to house the effigies and names of six saints, and is surmounted by an elaborate canopy. A tablet to the Trimblestone family is inscribed 'whoe being transplanted into Connacht with others by order of the usurper Cromwell, died at Moinivae, 1667'.

The small cloister garth measures a mere 48ft square and is enclosed by pointed arches on each side. The columns of these are not carried down to the ground, but spring from a low wall to give an effect which has been described as being in keeping with a Spanish or Sicilian monastery. On the east side of the garth the cloisters are in a particularly good state of preservation, and those on the other sides are in a fair condition. This excellent state of repair probably stems from the fact that the friary was occupied as late as the reign of James I. A restored monument (NM) in the village is known as the Donnell Memorial Cross and is of 17th-c date.

KILCOO, *Cill Chua:*
Cua's Church, Down 13 J 23
Miles of stone walling round numerous little fields in the neighbourhood of Kilcoo show the amount of hard work needed to make a living off the local land. Each one of these walls has been built with stones taken out of the fields to make cultivation possible. Fragmentary remains of a late-medieval church can be seen ½m NNW in the townland of Ballymoney, which lies in the foothills of the Mourne Mountains. About ½m NE is Lough Island Reavy, a pleasant lake with an easily accessible north shore, while the interesting Drumena Cashel and souterrain (NM) can be seen 1¾m NE.

KILCOOLE, *Cill Chomhghaill:*
St Comhghall's Church, Wicklow 19 O 20
In ancient times the O Byrnes were the proprietors of the territory around this little resort. The local graveyard contains many memorials to the family, plus a small nave-and-chancel church (NM) which dates from the 12thc and stands on the site of a 6th-c foundation created by St Comgall.

KILCOOLEY ABBEY, *Cill Chúile:*
Church of the Recess, Tipperary 23 S 25
King Donagh O Brien founded this Cistercian abbey c1200 as a daughter house of the better-known Jerpoint Abbey. The ruins, mainly of a church which was reconstructed in the 15thc, are beautifully-sited in the Kilcooley demesne. Of particular note are the chancel, transepts, and a six-light east window with good tracery. Various tombs in the chancel include a 16th-c Butler effigy, and the south transept preserves an old font plus good examples of carving. A rare Irish columbarium or dovecote stands in a field near the abbey.

KILCORNAN, *Cill Chornáin:*
Cornán's Church, Limerick 21 R 45
The well-preserved 15th-c parish church of Killeen Cowpark (NM) stands on a by-road to the SW of this little hamlet. Its narrow windows and turret-like belfry give it a defensive appearance. Inside is an unusual font.

KILCREA, *Cill Chré:*
Cré's Church, Cork 28 W 56
Ruined Kilcrea Friary (NM) stands in a charming situation on the banks of the River Bride, with the Clara Hills rising in the background. It was founded in the 15thc by Cormac McCarthy – the Lord of Muskerry – for Franciscan friars, and dedicated to St Brigid. The main ruins comprise a nave with side aisles, choir, and transepts, plus an unusual multi-windowed sacristy and scriptonia to the north of the chancel. Local tradition blames the removal of the window mullions on Cromwellian soldiers.

The most striking feature of the site is the lofty, 80ft tower. The friary was the burial place of the McCarthy family, and the founder was laid to rest in a church tomb after having been murdered by his brother soon after the building of the friary. Another interesting tomb is that of Bishop Herlihy, who was one of the three Irish ecclesiastics in attendance at the Council of Trent. Kilcrea was not disturbed at the Dissolution, and the only reason for the friars eventually forsaking the foundation in 1614 was a condition attached to a grant from the Lord Deputy.

To the W of the friary is Kilcrea Castle, a one-time MacCarthy stronghold of which the bawn and outworks can still be traced in the vicinity of the keep. Wolves are recorded to have lived in Kilcrea Wood as late as the 17thc. Some 4m W of the abbey are the extensive

Kilbeggan's interesting old distillery dates from the 18thc and features a water wheel.

remains of Castle More, comprising a keep and well-preserved walls overlooking the River Bride from the S bank.

KILCRONEY, Wicklow **19 O 21**
Situated $1\frac{1}{4}$m ESE of Enniskerry on the edge of the Dargle Valley, this little place features a considerably rebuilt church (NM) of a very early type. Of particular interest is the fine, flat-headed south doorway.

KILCULLEN, *Cill Chuillin:*
Church of the Slope, Kildare **18 N 80**
New Kilcullen straddles the River Liffey some 2m NNE of Old Kilcullen, a walled town which controlled the area from a bleak eminence in medieval times. One of the old settlement's seven gates still stood on a local turnpike road until it was demolished in the 18thc. The bridge which spans the Liffey and links the two parts of New Kilcullen was built in 1319, and contributed to the decline of the old town in favour of the village which exists today.

Extensive remains of the old settlement include a round tower (NM) and parts of three 9th-c high crosses (NM) – all indications of an early monastic foundation based on the church which gave the communities their names. Also here are the remains of an abbey founded for the Franciscans by Sir Rowland Fitz-Eustace in the 15thc. This was granted to the poet Spenser by Queen Elizabeth after the Dissolution. Although the tower collapsed in the 18thc and much of the fabric was used in the construction of an RC chapel, the ruins that have survived to the present day are of considerable interest. The tomb of the founder and his wife can be seen in the overgrown churchyard.

Another major feature of the area is the hillfort known as Dun Aillinne (NM). This covers 20 acres at the summit of 600ft Knockaulin and includes a massive circular earthwork. It is thought to have been one of three residences used by the Kings of Leinster, the other two being at Naas and the Hill of Allen. Recent archaeological excavation of the site seems to indicate an iron-age ritual and ceremonial structure which had little if anything to do with habitation, industry, or defence. Dun Aillinne lies approximately $\frac{3}{4}$m NW of Old Kilcullen.

The fine 18th-c house of Castlemartin lies $\frac{1}{2}$m NW of the village, and about 3m S is Haverstown House – described in Thackeray's *Irish Sketchbook* of 1842.

KILCUMMIN, *Cill Chuimín:*
St Cuimín's Church, Mayo **9 G 23**
A 7th-c church dedicated to St Cuimín stands in this delightful area, on the NW shores of Killala Bay, and features a notable doorway with inclined jambs. Both the doorway and a window on the east side of the building have semi-circular heads. Two uprights and a small sepulchral stone incised with a cross mark the saint's grave, and there is a holy well near by. A hilltop memorial on Kilcummin Head records a French landing which occurred here during the 1798 Insurrection. The French forces managed to capture and hold Killala.

KILDARE, *Cill Dara:*
Church of the Oak, Kildare **18 N 71**
Situated in a commanding position on rising ground, this town was once an important ecclesiastical centre, but in modern times has become famous – together with the Curragh (which is $1\frac{1}{2}$m E) – as the centre of the Irish horse breeding and training industry.

St Brigid established a nunnery here in the 5th or 6thc, and a monastery founded a little later had a King of Leinster as its abbot during the 7thc. Kildare and its religious foundations were continually exposed to the ravages of the Danes, who regularly crossed the easy east coast in search of the riches they knew to exist in such settlements. After the Anglo-Norman invasion the whole area was granted to de Vesci. The castle that he built here stood on the site of an earlier stronghold and proved a formidable obstacle to those intent on taking the lord's lands. Subsequently the castle and estate fell into the hands of the Geraldine family, from which time its history was a constant story of battle and bloodshed. It was almost destroyed in the Elizabethan wars, the Parliamentarians took the rebuilt building, the Irish wrested it from Cromwell's men, and it was later carried in an assault mounted by English forces. Although it is surprising that any part of the fabric has survived, a few interesting remains can be seen near Kildare's most historic monument – a 100ft-high round tower. This has been slightly marred by the addition of a battlemented top, but its superb Romanesque doorway has been preserved and can be seen 14ft above the ground. This is thought to be one of the last round towers built in Ireland and dates from the 12thc. It is open to the public and includes a modern stairway which allows access to the top.

St Brigid's CI Cathedral stands on an ancient site which has been occupied by many churches over the centuries. The first of these was replaced by a larger structure which was destroyed by the Norsemen in the 9thc, and several succeeding churches met the same fate until Bishop Ralph began to build his cathedral in the 13thc. In the Rebellion of 1641 Ralph's cathedral was completely ruined, but 50 years or so later the choir was rebuilt for public worship. The rest of the structure remained in ruins. Nothing else was done to the building until 1875, when it was rebuilt in a sensitive manner which preserved the best features of the old church. The exterior of the nave shows buttresses linked by arches, above which are parapets of characteristic Irish design. Some of the cathedral's windows are of particular note, and the remains of an ancient cross can be seen SW of the main building.

To the S of Kildare are the remains of a Carmelite monastery which was founded by the de Vesci family in the 13thc. This is the last resting place of eight earls of Kildare. A fine viewpoint known as the Chair of Kildare can be visited in the low Red Hills, which lie NW of the town, and 1m SE are the famous 'Japanese Gardens' of Tully House. These were devised and presented to the nation by Lord Wavertree in 1906. An interesting feature of the gardens is the Path of Life, which carries out the ideal of its Japanese designer by symbolizing man's journey from cradle to grave. Adjacent to the garden is the state owned National Stud – well known as the place where many famous racehorses have been reared. Also in this area are ruined Tully Church and a holy well dedicated to St Brigid. About $1\frac{1}{2}$m W of Kildare on the Port Laoise road is a curious thatched house with outer walls which are completely covered with seashells brought from the Wicklow coast.

KILDEMOCK, *Cill Dhíomóg:*
Díomóg's Church, Louth **12 N 98**
An interesting legend surrounds local St Catherine's Church, a 13th-c building of which the remaining gable stands 2ft within the confines of its foundations. Tradition has it that this effect was caused by the church wall leaping inwards to exclude the grave of an excommunicated person from hallowed ground; the building is quite famous as the 'jumping church'. No doubt the real explanation is rather more prosaic – if less appealing.

KILDERMOT, Mayo **9 G 21**
Only the chancel walls and nave foundations of the small 12th-c church (NM) which exists here have survived, but the site is picturesquely enhanced by Ballymore Lake.

KILDIMO, *Cill Díoma:*
Díoma's Church, Limerick **22 R 45**
Kildimo's neat little CI church was rebuilt in 1705, and the remains of a tiny church built c1290 by the Knights Templar can be seen near the W boundary of the parish. The last-mentioned measures a mere 12 by 8ft. Other ruins in the area include Bollane and Cullan castles. Bollane was built by the O Donovan family in the 15thc, and Cullan – $1\frac{1}{2}$m E near the River Maigue – was built in 1514 by the Fitzgeralds.

KILFANE, *Cill Pháin:*
St Pán's Church, Kilkenny **24 S 54**
The most important feature of Kilfane's small 13th-c church (NM) is 'Long Cantwell', a great stone effigy which depicts an Anglo-Norman knight of the Cantwell family. This dates from c1320 and is considered one of the finest examples of medieval sculpture in the country.

KILFENORA, *Cill Fhionnúrach:*
Church of Fionnúir, Clare **15 R 19**
An important ecclesiastical centre with its own bishop until the middle of the 18thc, this W-Clare village has gradually declined since the rise of Ennistymon, but still has plenty to testify to its past status. St Fachtnan's Cathedral (CI) is a small building which dates from c1200 and carries a massive square tower (NM). Its roofless chancel (NM) is particularly notable and includes a 20ft-high east window of three lights, all with round-headed arches. Interesting monuments inside the building include an effigy which is said to represent St Fachtnan, the founder. Three high crosses (NM's) survive in the cathedral precincts, and a fourth (NM) can be seen in a field to the W. The last-mentioned stands 13ft high and is elaborately ornamented with designs and a carving of the Crucifixion. The finest of the three churchyard crosses is undoubtedly the Doorty Cross; all four of these limestone monuments date from the 12thc. Several stone forts exist in the district, but the finest is the great stronghold of Ballykinvarga. This lies ENE of Kilfenora, measures 155 by 130ft, and has a wall

which varies between 12 and 16ft in height. It is surrounded with a *chevaux-de-frise* of sharp stones, a form of defence which can also be seen round some of the forts on the Aran Islands.

KILFINNANE, *Cill Fhíonáin:*
Fíonán's Church, Limerick 22 R62
Mountains surround this market town on all sides except the N, where there is a small gap which opens out into the rich valley of Kilmallock. The district is known for the production of dairy goods. Palatine's Rock, situated to the E of the town, is one of the many placenames that recall the settling of Palatine Knights here *c*1740. Kilfinnane's chief claim to fame is the immense rath which rises to 130ft beside the town and has a base diameter of 50ft. It has a 20ft diameter at the summit and measures 2,000ft round the outer circumference. The top of the rath is a popular viewpoint.

Another good vantage point near the town is 1,531ft Slievereagh, which rises some 2m NNE of Kilfinnane and features an interesting collection of ancient remains. These lie on the mountain's W flank and include raths, souterrains, and graves in a large complex known as Cush. Six of the raths are joined to form an unusually-shaped group of obscure significance.

KILGARVAN, *Cill Gharbháin:*
St Garbhán's Church, Kerry 27 W07
This village is situated in a mountain-ringed valley near the confluence of the Rivers Roughty and Slaheny. A road which follows the Slaheny Valley climbs to a summit of 1,169ft and affords good views before descending the Coomhola Valley to reach Bantry Bay. The road is narrow and winding, with a sheer drop to the side at one point; it should be undertaken only by experienced drivers.

KILGOBBIN, *Cill Ghobáin:*
St Gobán's Church, Dublin 19 O12
Much of the granite used for building and flagging in Dublin came from quarries near Kilgobbin, which is situated in the N foothills of the Wicklow Mountains above the city's SE suburbs. Other features of the locality include a ruined castle and the remains of a 12th-c church. A high cross (NM) near the entrance of the churchyard displays two figures of Christ, one carved on each side of its head. Near by are the ruins of an 18th-c Protestant church.

KILKEA, *Cill Chathaigh:*
St Cathach's Church, Kildare 24 S78
Hugh de Lacy built a castle here in 1180, and defended it as a link in the chain of strongholds erected to keep the Irish out of an Anglo-Norman territory known as The Pale. Because of its position it suffered constant attack from native forces – particularly in the 15thc – and eventually passed into the hands of the Geraldines. It now serves as a hotel. Near by are remains of an old church and a mound which survives from the 12th-c stronghold.

KILKEE, *Cill Chaoi:*
St Caoi's Church, Clare 20 Q85
Attractive Kilkee is a pleasant resort with a fine strand which is sheltered from the full force of the Atlantic by the Duggerna rocks. This ledge lies to the W and extends across a third of Kilkee Bay. Visitors to the town will invariably be shown a typical one-storey cottage and proudly informed that it was the birthplace of Sir Ernest Shackleton, the 19th-c explorer. Also of interest in the area is a double-moated dun known as Sheedy's Fort, but the district's most notable asset is its magnificent cliff scenery.

Between Doonbeg in the NE and Loop Head in the SW is a 16m stretch of coast which has been carved and eroded into a spectacular confusion of caves and chasms. Of particular note is a natural amphitheatre which is used for open-air concerts. The cliff walk SW of the resort affords views of precipitous Bishop's Island, which lies beyond Intrinsic Bay and preserves ancient monastic remains. It takes in such features as the ruined tower of Doonlickas Castle and a fine stack known as Grean Rock. The walker who continues past Kilbaha to Loop Head will find even more to capture his interest, including the rocky pinnacles of Illaunlenearaun; ruined Knocknagarhoon Castle; the high natural bridges of Ross; the Puffing Hole and Caves near the remains of Cloghaunscavaun Castle; and Loop Head with its fine lighthouse.

KILKEEL, *Cill Chaoil:*
Church of the Narrow, Down 13 J31
In ancient times this town was the centre of the Kingdom of Mourne, but nowadays it is content to reap the prosperity attracted by its fine strand, busy fishing harbour, and good angling prospects. A local industry apart from tourism operates round the quarrying and dressing of Mourne granite. To the NE of the resort is a dolmen (NM) which is known as the Crawtree Stone and carries a 10 by 8ft capstone. A road which leads NW towards Hilltown affords excellent views of the Mourne Mountains as it climbs to a summit of 1,250ft before descending through the Spelga Pass. Wild and remote Silent Valley lies to the N of the town, and 1m WNW of Kilkeel is the fascinating Mass Fort. Mourne Park, seat of the Earl of Killarney, is situated 3m WNW in a demesne which it shares with a ruined court cairn known as the Giant's Grave.

KILKENNY, *Cill Chainnigh:*
St Canice's Church, Kilkenny 24 S55
Kilkenny, situated high on the E bank of the River Nore, is considered by many to be the most attractive town in Ireland. Its winding passages and lanes have the air of a medieval university town, while Georgian elegance is represented by lines of handsome houses. Its period of grandeur lasted from the 14th to the 17thc, after which the town entered a decline which accelerated in the 19thc and resulted in a population loss of two thirds.

The town is very much the creation of the Earls of Ormonde, who bought it in 1391. Edward III had divided the part of Ireland that he controlled into three great earldoms – Kildare, Desmond, and Ormonde. Kilkenny became the centre of the latter and emerged as a chief seat of government which rivalled Dublin, being an occasional residence of the Lords Lieutenant and a regular meeting place of the Irish parliament. The most famous meeting held here was that summoned by the Duke of Clarence *c*1366, at which the Statute of Kilkenny was passed. This forbade any English settler to use the Irish language, to adopt an Irish name, or to wear Irish apparel. The marriage of a settler with an Irish woman was classed as high treason, and all men of Irish blood were forbidden to live in walled towns. A measure of the town's eminence was the decision of Henry VIII, on the Dissolution of the monasteries, to grant the site of the Blackfriar's foundation to Kilkenny Corporation – on condition that free accommodation would be offered to the Chief Governor of Ireland whenever he was in the area. During the 17th-c war between the English king and parliament Kilkenny became the seat of the Confederate Parliament of the Catholics. This was the last native Irish parliament to include representatives from all the counties and important towns in the country. The upper and lower Houses met in the house of Robert Shee, which stood on the site now occupied by the gates of a new market in Parliament Street. A Supreme Council was chosen, a seal adopted, a mint established for coining new money, weapons were manufactured, and new armies were formed under the command of experienced veterans. Ambassadors received here at this time included Rinuccini, the Nuncio of the Pope, who arrived in 1645 with arms and financial aid. In 1648 the Confederation ended, and in 1650 the city was besieged and captured by Cromwell.

Kilkenny has three well-defined divisions. Irishtown lies to the N and had both a charter from the Bishop of Ossory and a distinct municipal government until the Municipal Reform Act of 1843. It sent

'Long Cantwell', an effigy in Kilfane's little 13th-c church, represents an Anglo-Norman knight in full period armour.

KILKENNY

two members to the Irish parliament until disfranchised by the 19th-c Act of Union, and is distinguished by magnificent St Canice's Cathedral. The second division of Kilkenny, High Town, is situated S of Irishtown and is divided from it by the Bregagh River. High Town held its charter from the lord of the soil and was governed, in the early days, by a sovereign. The ruling function was later taken over by a mayor, but old power is still represented by the castle. The third division lies E of the River Nore and contains the Priory of St John.

St Canice's Cathedral (CI) is one of the most famous and certainly among the most spectacular buildings in Kilkenny. It stands on a hilltop site previously occupied by a succession of early churches which may have begun with a foundation created by St Canice in the 6thc. The present structure dates from the 13thc, although its early-English style has been somewhat modified by repair work in 1661, more complete restoration in 1756, and further extensive modification in 1865. The most notable exterior features of the building include the embattled parapets on the clerestory, transept, and aisle walls, which echo a similar design on the low, massive tower. The west doorway is of note. Interesting features inside the cathedral include the groining of the tower, the fine early-English west window, the east window, and the 12th-c black-marble font at the south-west end of the nave. Many notable medieval monuments survive in the building, of which the 13th-c memorial to the son of Henry de Ponto is one of the earliest; in almost all cases the standard of workmanship is particularly fine. Close to the south transept is a round tower (NM). This relic probably survives from the foundation which occupied this site before the cathedral, and measures 100ft high with a base circumference of 46½ft. The unusual widths of the structure's eleven windows make it noteworthy. Nearby St Canice's Library preserves some 3,000 books dating from the 16th and 17thc.

Kilkenny's Franciscan or Grey Friary (NM) was founded on the angle of land formed by the confluence of the Rivers Nore and Bregagh, at the north-east corner of High Town's ancient wall, in 1234. Remains to be seen here today include a fine seven-light window, a picturesque tower supported by groined arches, and an ancient font similar to that housed in the cathedral. Excavations have been carried out in the precincts of the friary, which are now in the possession of a brewery. The Dominican or Black Friary was founded at the north-west corner of the High Town wall in 1225 by the Earl of Pembroke, and served as a courthouse after the Dissolution. The fine, cruciform church has been restored and is again in the possession of the Dominicans. Of particular note are the traceried window in the south transept, and a number of old monumental slabs and stone coffins on the left of the path from the street to the church. Black Freren Gate is the sole survivor of the town-wall access ways.

The beautifully-situated castle stands on the banks of the Nore and dominates the fine vista from John's Bridge. During the 19thc the building was completely remodelled, and the only ancient parts still in existence are three of the circular towers and fragments of the curtain walls. Anti-Treatyites took the stronghold in May of 1922, while the Earl and Countess of Ossory were in residence, and it was besieged by Free State Troopers under General Prout. It had been a seat of the Butler family since the 14thc before it was given to the city. A great collection of Ormonde manuscripts which was preserved here, some of them dating from 1200 or thereabouts, was acquired by the National Library in Dublin. Many have been published by the Irish Manuscripts Commission. Opposite the castle, in the Stables, are the Kilkenny Design Workshops (Irish Design Centre). This group has been established with the intention of improving design and finishing standards in a wide variety of crafts.

The town's courthouse occupies the site of a one-time Grace's castle. This stronghold was surrendered in 1566 by James Grace, who was appointed constable of the gaol into which it was then converted. The balcony and staircase were added in the 19thc, when it became the County and City Court. St Mary's Church (CI) in St Kieran Street is a greatly modernized 13th-c structure which contains interesting monuments dating from medieval times and the 16th and 17thc. Shee's Almshouse in Rose Inn Street dates from 1594, and the 18th-c Tholsel, or town hall, is easily distinguished by its peculiar cupola and wooden tower. This tower is locally known as the 'Lighthouse', and the

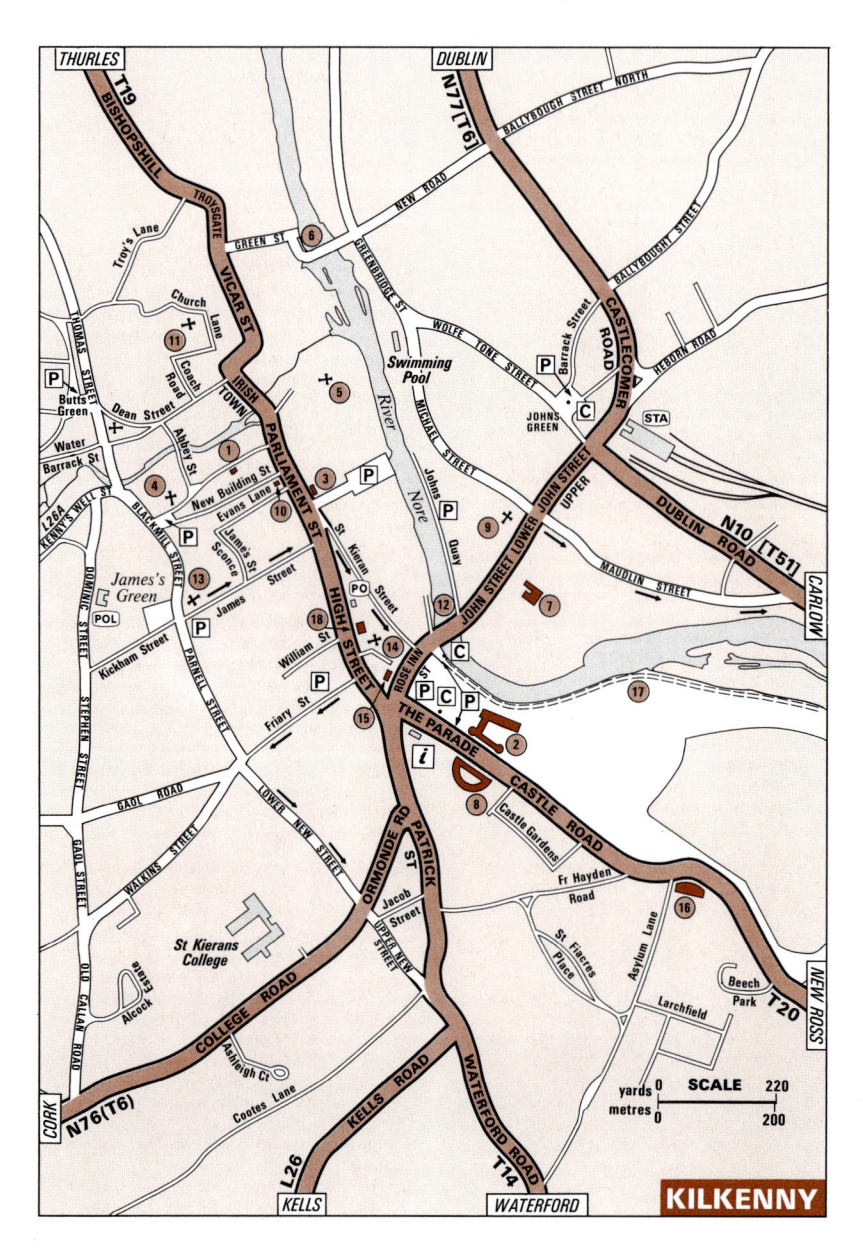

1 Black Freren Gate
2 Castle
3 Courthouse
4 Dominican Friary
5 Franciscan Friary
6 Green's Bridge
7 Kilkenny College
8 Kilkenny Design Workshops
9 Priory of St John and Parish Church (CI)
10 Rothe House
11 St Canice's Cathedral (CI), Library & Round Tower
12 John's Bridge
13 St Mary's Cathedral (RC)
14 St Mary's Church (CI)
15 Shee's Almshouses
16 Switsir's (St James') Hospital
17 The Mall
18 Tholsel

building itself stands in the High Street. To the E of the River Nore is the Priory of St John, a 13th-c foundation created by William the Earl of Pembroke for the Knights Hospitallers of the Order of St John. The Lady Chapel, known as the 'Lantern of Ireland' because of its numerous mullioned windows, is now the parish church (CI).

Kilkenny College in John Street was founded in 1666 by the Duke of Ormonde. Its late 18th-c buildings can best be seen from the Canal Walk, and the school itself is very famous as the place from which numerous eminent men have started their careers. Almshouses known as Switsir's or St James' Hospital date from 1803, and the fine, 19th-c cruciform St Mary's Cathedral stands to the W outside the old High Town. The cathedral, which is built of grey limestone and carries a 200ft-high tower, contains a statue of the Virgin by Benzoni. Some of the interesting old houses to be seen in the town are: Kyteler's in St Kieran's Street, dated 1639 and once the most famous old inn in the town; Archer's in High Street, dating from 1594; Rothe in Parliament Street, a 16th-c building now containing a museum; notable Fitzgerald's in John Street.

There are many ways to see Kilkenny. A fine walk called the Mall extends for nearly 1m along the bank of an uncompleted 18th-c canal, and good road access allows a pleasant drive along the Nore N of the town. One of the best ways to see the many mills which sprang up along the banks of the river in the 19thc is by cot, a flat-bottomed boat which is the standard vehicle on the Nore. Only the flour mills are still working, and these have been electrified. Elegant John's and Green's bridges, both by G Smith, were built across the Nore to replace structures washed away in the flood of 1763. One of the most remarkable overall aspects of Kilkenny is its use of marble as a plain building stone. Even the pavements are made of this prized material, although it is an ordinary, dull grey in colour until polished for decorative work. About ½m from the city are quarries where black marble was once extracted to be worked by water-driven machinery in a mill. In the early 19thc another great industry was the manufacture of blankets. Kilkenny's livestock and wool fairs used to be among the most important in the country. The town's once-famous private theatre was founded in the 18thc and housed in buildings now occupied by government departments. This, and the local Archaeological Society – probably the oldest in the country – are both defunct. Some 6m N of the city are the Dunmore Caves (NM), four passages and a large chamber carved from the carboniferous limestone by the solvent action of slightly acidic water. A feature of the caves, which are considered among the finest in Ireland, is the Market Cross stalactite pillar which stands in the main chamber. Access is easy.

KILKIERAN, *Cill Chiaráin*:
St Ciarán's Church, Kilkenny **23 S42**
The site of an early-Christian monastic foundation here is marked by three high crosses which may date from the 9thc (NM's). Of particular interest is the west cross, which is elaborately decorated with panels showing horsemen, animals, interlacing, geometric motifs, and bosses.

KILL, *An Chill*:
The Church, Kildare **18 N92**
This village is best known for the interesting area in which it is situated, but features the motte of an Anglo-Norman castle. About 1m NE is 18th-c Bishopscourt, the Ponsonby family mansion, while the remains of a castellated mansion encircled by a fosse can be seen 1m S at Hartwell Castle. Remains of a small medieval church and the grave of Theobald Wolfe Tone can be seen 1m N in the townland of Bodenstown, and 2¼m NE is 458ft Oughterard Hill. This fine viewpoint preserves the remains of an 11th-c round tower and church.

KILLADEAS, *Cill Chéile Dé*:
The Culdees' Church, Fermanagh **11 H25**
An angling resort facing island-studded Lough Erne, this village occupies a site on which a chapel belonging to the Culdees of Devenish once stood. In the graveyard of the 'Yellow Church' are three ancient sculptured stones. The most interesting of these is known as the Bishop's Stone and carries figure carvings; it may date from the 7th or 8thc.

KILLALA, *Cill Ala*, Mayo 9 G22
The village of Killala is a declined port town and the one-time seat of a bishopric. It is attractively situated opposite Bartragh Island on the shores of Killala Bay, and includes a quay with substantial empty storehouses. Just off the community's main street and across the road from the plain little 17th-c cathedral (CI) is a well-preserved round tower (NM). This cone-topped structure measures 84ft high, 17ft in diameter, and has a doorway let into the massive walls some 11ft from the ground. This relic survives from a 5th-c Patrician foundation, and under the graveyard is an elaborate souterrain complete with passageways and a circular chamber. The original church was replaced by a medieval cathedral which was destroyed during the civil wars. The only surviving relic of this structure is the great pointed doorway which can be seen in the south wall of the present building.

One of the most notable events to have taken place in Killala was in connection with the Insurrection of 1798. This involved the occupation of the village by French troops who had landed in Kilcummin Bay (see entry). The 'invasion' occurred under the leadership of General Humbert in August of 1798, but the occupation of Killala was short lived. The French were driven from the village by English forces commanded by General Trench. One incident – the execution of Father Conroy for assisting Humbert – was commemorated by the erection of a 16ft Celtic cross at Larhardane in 1937. Larhardane is situated near the W shores of Lough Conn, midway between Killala and Castlebar. About 2m N of Killala is Rathfran Friary (NM), a picturesque cluster of ruins near the inner reaches of Rathfran Bay. As well as the ruined nave and choir, remains here include a 15th-c south chapel and a conventual building to the N. After Dissolution the site was leased to Thomas Exeter. In 1590 the abbey was burned by Bingham, but the Dominicans stayed on. Five of them were recorded to have been living in a nearby cottage in Mullaghnacroiste as late as 1756. A stone circle (NM) can be seen in Rathfran townland, and features of Rathfran Park include two ringforts and a wedge-shaped gallery grave (NM). At Breastagh, a little to the N of the Rathfran Friary site, is a 12ft-high ogham stone (NM).

Also in the area, beside the River Moy, are the extensive ruins of a foundation which is often described as the finest Franciscan site in the country – Rosserk Friary (NM). Founded in 1441, the settlement includes a nave, chancel, south transept, square tower, and two-storey conventual buildings. Inside the church is a double piscina which displays excellent carving. A round tower is depicted in relief on one of the shafts. An indication as to the quality of this 15th-c workmanship is the excellent state of preservation of the cloisters. To the NW of Killala, at Castlereagh on the River Rathfran, are vestiges of a very strong castle. The Bourke family's massive Carrickanass Castle stands within a strong bawn 1m to the W.

KILLALIATHAN, Limerick 21 R32
Sometimes written as 'Killagholehane', this village lies 1m SSW of Broadford and features a small parish church (NM) which probably dates from the 15thc. Of particular interest in this building are a fine 15th-c tomb niche in the north wall, and an unusual arrangement of windows in the east gable.

KILLALOE, *Cill Dalua*:
St Dalua's Church, Clare **22 R67**
Pleasantly situated on the W bank of the Shannon, this town stands close to the falls of Killaloe about 1m from Lough Derg. Two of its noteworthy features are the central town square and a nine-arch bridge across the river. At one time there were obstructions to navigation above and below the bridge – *eg* eel weirs, natural shoals, etc – and the Board of Inland Navigation built a canal detour to link the navigable parts of the river. During the last century Killaloe, as the headquarters of the Shannon Steam Navigation Company, was a great communications centre linked by river to Limerick in the S, and to Dublin via the Grand Canal from Banagher in the N.

Modern Killaloe attracts the attentions of visitors who wish to sample her beautiful scenery or explore the archaeological wealth of her countryside. Glennagalliagh rises to 1,746ft from the Slieve Bernagh range in the NW, and a drive along the W and SE banks of vast Lough Derg affords exquisite glimpses of mountain and lake scenery. The famous Shannon Hydro-electric scheme is within easy reach of Killaloe.

Features of the town itself include several fascinating old buildings. Among these is 12th-c St Flannan's Cathedral (CI), a cruciform building which carries a massive square tower and was restored in 1887. Its most notable feature is a Romanesque doorway which came from an earlier church and has been built into the west corner of the nave's south wall. Beside this highly-ornamented doorway, near the main entrance, is Thorgrim's Stone – a cross shaft which displays a unique bilingual inscription in Viking runes and ogham script. Also worthy of notice are the ancient font, the carved corbel caps in the chancel, and the three-light east window. A 19th-c memorial commemorates John Grantham, who conducted the first survey of the Shannon and put steamers on the river in 1825. To the N of the cathedral is St Flannan's Oratory, a well-preserved 12th-c church with a steep-pitched stone roof. The latter is a good example of a particularly Irish feature. The carved Romanesque west doorway dates from the 11thc, the north and south walls are penetrated by deeply-splayed windows, and there is a croft between the barrel vaulting and roof.

Close to the RC parish church is pre-12th-c St Molua's Church (NM), an interesting structure which was moved here from its original site on Friar's Island in 1929. The island was later submerged by the Shannon Hydro-electric scheme. The stone-roofed chancel was added to the wooden-roofed nave at some later date. Several earthen forts can be seen on the Clare bank of the Shannon, between the bridge in Killaloe and the wide expanse of Lough Derg. That known as Beal Boru lies 1½m W of the bridge, has an external circumference of over 200yds, and in some places rises to a height of 20ft. It is covered with fine trees. Brian Boru's Kincora Palace is thought to have stood in the vicinity of the fort in the 10th or 11thc. Some 3m N of the bridge which links Killaloe with the Tipperary suburb of Ballina, just off the Nenagh road in Lough Derg, is the circular tower of Derry Castle. This is accessible by foot, depending on the tide. To the NE of Killaloe, in the vicinity of the attractive Arra Mountains, are several barrow burials known as the 'Graves of the Leinster Men'. One of the more memorable peaks in the area is 1,517ft Tountinna.

KILLALOO, Londonderry **6 C50**
Of particular interest in this little hamlet is a fortification known as the 'Stronghouse' (NM), or Brackfield Castle. This was built in the Plantation period by the Skinners' Company, and preserves reasonably complete bawn walls.

KILLAMERY, *Cill Lamhraí*:
Lamhrach's Church, Kilkenny **23 S33**
Killamery village stands on the Callan to Clonmel road and features a sandstone high cross. The cross (NM) is thought to date from the 8thc, and features a weathered hunting scene as well as the usual formal decoration.

KILLARE, *Cill Air*:
Church of Slaughter, Westmeath **17 N24**
Ruins of Killare's old parish church stand in a graveyard on a site which was once occupied by an important monastery. Opposite the churchyard is a remarkable mound surmounted by another ancient ruin. Nearby Clare Hill was the site of one of Hugh de Lacy's 12th-c motte-and-bailey castles. Remains of Killenbrack Castle can be seen near Mosstown, and the fine viewpoint of The Hill of Ushnagh rises to the NE.

*****KILLARNEY**, *Cill Airne*:
Church of the Sloes, Kerry **27 V99**
This town has become famous the world over, due more to the unsurpassed beauty of its setting than to any major historical, architectural, or archaeological background. Basically a fairly typical country town, it has been swelled by the influx of tourists from the 19thc to the present day. However, Killarney has a certain individuality and features one or two buildings of distinction. Perhaps the best of these is the 19th-c Cathedral of St Mary (RC), built to a design by Alexander Pugin and recently refurbished. This is a cruciform building which carries a massive, square tower capped by a spire. At the E end of the town on Fair Hill is the fine gothick Franciscan church (RC). This displays good decorative woodwork and an outstanding stained-glass window by Harry Clarke. Opposite the Franciscan Church is a memorial by Seamus Murphy to The Four Kerry Poets of the 17th and 18thc. The Sky-Woman depicted by the monument is an allegorical symbol of Ireland. Killarney's town hall is also of interest. Sporting facilities in the town are numerous, and transport by jaunting car is a great tourist attraction.

Most of the area's famous Lake District now forms the superb and extensive Bourn-Vincent Forest Park as a result of the generosity of Mr and Mrs William Bowers Bourn of California, and their son-in-law Senator Arthur Vincent. The Bourns and Senator Vincent presented their 11,500-acre Muckross Estate to the Irish government in 1932, including Muckross Gardens, which lie 2½m S of Killarney and form the centrepiece of the national park. These gardens are particularly splendid when the azaleas and rhododendrons are blooming in May and June. The rock garden is considered one of the finest in Europe, the grounds are rich in sub-tropical exotics, and the 19th-c Portland-stone edifice of Muckross House is being developed as the Kerry Folk Museum. Crafts in danger of becoming extinct are already preserved here. Ruined Muckross Abbey, which was founded in the 15thc for Franciscan monks by Donal MacCarthy Mor, is beautifully situated near the wooded shore of the Lower Lake. Although suppressed in 1542, the monks continued to reside in this foundation until they were driven out by Elizabethan soldiers in 1589. The buildings were restored in 1626 and are considered to form the best-preserved example of ecclesiastical architecture in Ireland. After the 16th-c raid the friars returned and remained in residence until the abbey was burned by Cromwellian troops under the command of General Ludlow. A feature of the church is its four-light east window. The nave and adjoining transept are separated from the choir by a massive tower, and the heart of the building is a 22-arch cloister which encloses an open court and features both gothic and Romanesque arches. Three stairways lead to the upper-floor domestic facilities, and a giant yew tree stands in the court.

Two of Killarney's three main lakes occupy a large glacial depression at the foot of mountains which rise SW of the town, while the third lies in a valley which runs SW from the S end of the range. To the W of the lakes are 2,413ft Tomies, 1,827ft Shehy, and 2,739ft Purple Mountain. These all rise from the E end of the highest range in Ireland – MacGillycuddy's Reeks. Mangerton Mountain rises to 2,756ft on the SE side. The Lower Lake covers some 5,000 acres, contains about 30 islands, and lies nearer to the town than the others. It is also the largest, and is separated from the 680-acre Muckross or Middle Lake by the Muckross Peninsula. A narrow, wooded strait links Muckross Lake with the 430-acre Upper Lake. There are four islands in the Middle Lake and eight in the Upper. Apart from these three main waters there is also Lough Guitane,

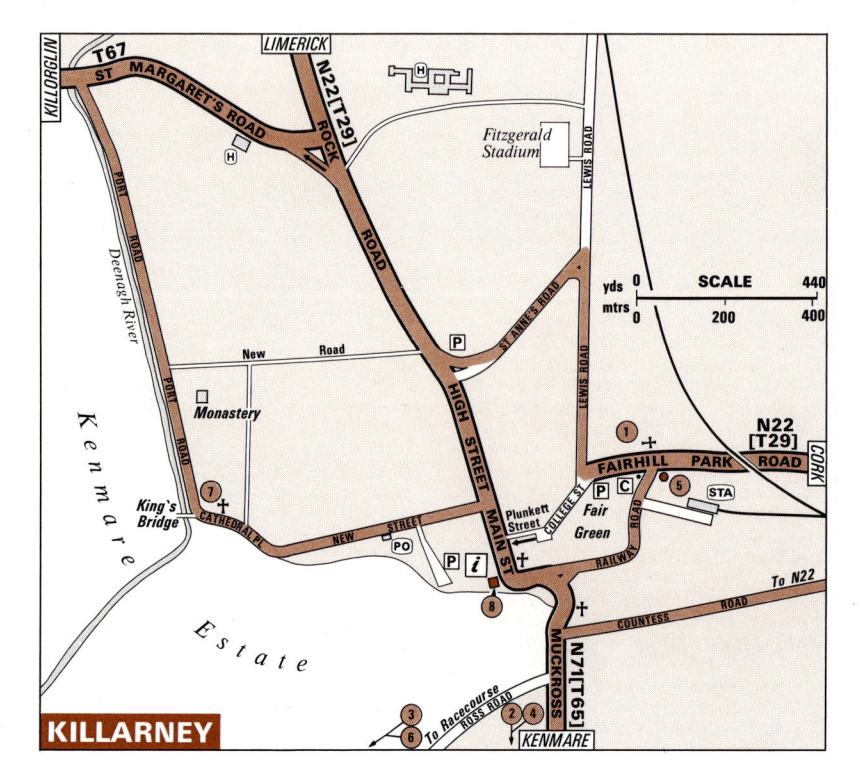

1 Franciscan Church (RC)
2 Franciscan Friary of Muckross
3 Innisfallen Abbey
4 Muckross House
5 Poets' Memorial
6 Ross Castle
7 St Mary's Cathedral (RC)
8 Town Hall

which lies 5m SE of Killarney, and numerous mountain tarns. These are mainly to be found in the Gap of Dunloe and on the slopes of Mangerton Mountain. Luxuriant woodland clothes the banks of all the lakes, and the E shores of the Middle and Lower Lakes – which both lie in a limestone trough – have been eroded into fantastic shapes and mysterious caves. Slate rock rises almost precipitously from the W shore. The effects of the ice age are particularly evident around Killarney, including ice-smoothed rocks, perched boulders, and deep corries excavated by glacial action. The Horse's Glen and Devil's Punch Bowl on Mangerton Mountain are good examples of erosion by ice. To the S of Lough Guitane is an interesting series of volcanic rocks comparable with the columns of the famous Giant's Causeway. Several rivers replenish the lakes, which drain into the Atlantic via the River Laune.

Muckross Abbey is not the only antiquarian relic to be found in the area. Magnificent Ross Castle lies SW of Killarney, at the end of an unclassified road which leads past the racecourse, and is known for its massive 15th-c keep. Suggestive of Anglo Norman origin but said to have been a 14th-c residence of the O Donoghues, the stronghold is in an excellent state of preservation and is considered one of the finest examples of castle building in the country. It is sited on a long, wooded peninsula which extends into the lake, and was defended against a large Cromwellian force under Ludlow by Royalist troops under Lord Muskerry. The castle eventually surrendered after the introduction of floating batteries, but was the last to capitulate. Close to the castle is a quay from which excursions can be taken on to the lake. Past this the peninsula broadens out to form 'Ross Island', an almost triangular area of land which partly encloses Ross Bay on its N side and is known for the strangely eroded rocks of its limestone shore. To the S of the castle are copper workings that have been exploited since prehistoric times (up to the early 19thc), and between the mines and Library Point is a pathway which leads left to a headland called Governor's Rock. This small area is particularly rich in native plant life, and has been set aside as a nature reserve. On the N side of the road which leads back to Killarney – on the W side of the town – is the vast Kenmare Estate. This was formerly owned by the Earls of Kenmare and is now the location of several luxury hotels. The mansion was burnt down in 1913, and most of the demesne was bought by an American syndicate in 1956. Features of the demesne include a fine stretch of shoreline on Lough Leane, and the magnificent Killarney Golf Club championship course in the N section.

One of the most complete views of the district is afforded by the Hill of Aghadoe, which rises to 400ft some 2½m NW of the town and overlooks the N end of the Lower Lake. Panoramic mountain views from here extend E to W to include the island-dotted waters of the Lower Lake, and can be enjoyed from a carpark and picnic site. Monastic ruins at Aghadoe include the 12ft stump of a round tower and the remains of a church which dates from the 12thc and incorporates the nave of a 7th-c structure. The chief features of the church are the elaborate Irish-Romanesque west doorway, a double-light lancet window in the east end, and an ogham stone which has been built into the south wall. To the S of the church is a massive circular castle (NM) of unknown origin. This is variously known as Parkavonear Castle, the Pulpit, and the Bishop's Chair, and is thought to date from c1200. Its design is uncommon in Ireland. A short flight of stairs in the 6ft thickness of the walls has been broken, and the floors inside the building have also been destroyed. Traces of earthworks are visible.

About 3m WSW of Aghadoe is Dunloe Castle and the entrance to the famous Gap of Dunloe. Although the castle has been modernized as a dwelling, its walls are part of the old stronghold erected by O Sullivan More to defend the entrance of the gap in the 13thc. After surviving many sieges in the Tudor Wars and the Insurrection of 1641, the stronghold was eventually taken by the Cromwellians and slighted. Modern Dunloe Castle is attractively sited in pleasant, 3,000-acre grounds noted for their rare and exotic plants. Close to the Avenue is the curious Cave of Dunloe, a circular souterrain built of mortarless field stones. The collapsed roof, also of stone, included seven rocks bearing ogham inscriptions. A short distance beyond the castle is the wild and sombre glacial overflow channel known as the Gap of Dunloe, a 4m ravine through which a rough road provides uncertain access for motor transport. Kate Kearney's Cottage is soon reached after the Loe Stream is crossed, and it is usual to continue from here by pony, jaunting car, or on foot. The original Kate Kearney's Cottage was the home of illegal poteen sellers who used to offer their wares to tourists, and is said to have been named after a local beauty. From a bend beyond the cottage the road is bordered by a string of dark, gloomy tarns, with MacGillycuddy's Reeks on the right and Tomies and the Purple Mountain on the left. The awesome solitude of the place is impressed upon the mind as the valley contracts. A point above the hamlet of Dunloe Upper is the best place from which to hear the famous Dunloe echo. The lake here is called Cuchvalley. Within 1m of the top of the gap is Black Lough, a water which tradition holds to be fishless because it contains the corpse of the last serpent to have lived in Ireland – drowned by St Patrick. Views from the top of the gap are magnificent, and the head of the ravine is a good starting point from which to ascend the Purple Mountain. From here the road descends past the Logan Stone on the left and continues through superb scenery to penetrate the heart of the Reeks. A road leading right off the gap road ascends the wonderfully scenic Cummeenduff Glen, and another right turn about 1½m farther along the gap road leads along the beautiful Glen of Owenreagh to Moll's Gap and Killarney. Straight on is the toll gate by which visitors enter for the excursion down the lakes for the return to Killarney. After the toll gate the road skirts the S side of Upper lake and continues to Queen's Cottage, built by Lord Kenmare to commemorate a visit by Queen Victoria in 1861. The cottage overlooks a charming waterfall known as Derrycunnihy Cascade. At Galway's Bridge a sharp right turn leads to the famous Ladies' View viewpoint.

The visitor approaching Killarney via the main road from Kenmare, or the unclassified road up the Owenreagh Valley from the Gap of Dunloe, starts a tour of the magnificent scenery from Moll's Gap. From here the road begins a long, undulating descent from an altitude of 838ft, passing high above the Owenreagh Valley and below the slopes of 1,617ft Derrygarriff and 1,308ft Foardal before skirting the shores of Looscaunagh Lough. After woodland on the right the road descends past 901ft Looscaunagh Hill on the left, plus the famous Ladies' View viewpoint which overlooks the Upper Lake. Further views are afforded before the road enters more of the dense woodland for which the area is known, then a small river is crossed at Galwey's Bridge and further woodland is passed on the slopes of 1,286ft Cromaglan Mountain. On reaching the lakeside the road passes through a short tunnel which penetrates a projecting spur. From the top of this tunnel there is a magnificent view of the Upper Lake set against its backdrop of lofty mountains. Mangerton dominates the scene in the opposite direction. The road from the tunnel descends towards Long Range, beyond which are the conical Eagle's Nest Mountain and 1,764ft Torc Mountain, and on reaching Middle Lake turns right to skirt the lakeshore. At Torc Bridge a detour should be made to follow the Owengarriff River through a glade which leads to the Torc Waterfall. Here the waters of the Devil's Punch Bowl, high on the side of Mangerton Mountain, fall 60ft through a series of sandstone crags to form one of the most attractive waterfalls in Ireland. The winding path which leads above the fall offers superb views. From Torc Bridge, on the main route, the road passes the entrance to Muckross House on the left after 1m and the entrance to Muckross Abbey after another 1m. After a further 1¾m the Flesk River is crossed and the route leads back into Killarney.

A visit to Killarney would be incomplete without an excursion on the lakes themselves. Starting from the landing stage near Lord Brandon's Cottage, at the W end of the Upper Lake, the water-borne traveller will pass the Lebanon cedars of MacCarthy More's Island; Eagle Island, the one-time haunt of these noble birds; and Arbutus Island, covered with the indigenous arbutus for which Killarney is famed. The lake appears landlocked, but a narrow, 10yds-wide passage opens at a narrow promontory called Colman's Eye and leads into the Long Range. Precipitous mountains clad with rich foliage rise from the banks of this beautiful river, which winds round the foot of Eagle's Nest Mountain before tumbling over rapids and rushing beneath the Old Wier Bridge. This part of the journey may be somewhat of an ordeal to the uncertain traveller. The river divides at this point – called the Meeting of the Waters – with the left branch skirting Dinish Island to enter the Lower Lake and the right passing into Muckross or Middle Lake. Dinish Island is known for its sub-tropical flora.

Middle Lake is separated from the Lower by a tapering, somewhat indented peninsula which is densely wooded in places. It is possible to walk along the peninsula from Muckross House and Abbey. The limestone on which the Middle Lake lies has been eroded into fantastic shapes along the shore, and has been dissolved away to form the Colleen Bawn Caves on the N side. After skirting Dinish Island on the right the traveller passes a whirlpool on the left known as O Sullivan's Punch Bowl, and shortly enters Lough Leane – the Lower Lake. After about 2m on the W side of the Lower Lake the traveller passes O Sullivan's Cascade, which consists of three separate falls which plummet from a total height of 70ft. A charming view of the cascade can be enjoyed from a little grotto beneath a projecting rock in the lowest basin. Fine woodlands grow near the falls, and less than a mile across the lake is the small wooded island of Innisfallen. Remains of Innisfallen Abbey (NM) can be seen near the landing stage, on a site where a foundation was created by St Finian the Leper in the 7thc. The western part of the church, including antae and a restored flat-headed doorway, belong to the early structure. The rest of the church and the other monastic buildings were added in the 13thc. To the N of this site is a small oratory which stands on a low cliff overhanging the lake. The main features of this are a small, round-headed east window and a fine Irish-Romanesque doorway. The *Annals of Innisfallen,* a chronicle of world and Irish history composed in the abbey between the 11th and 13thc, is preserved in the Bodleian Library, Oxford. An edition has been published by the Dublin Institute of Advanced Studies, and the famous Innisfallen crozier can be seen in the National Museum, Dublin. From Innisfallen the visitor can return to the landing stage of Ross Castle, which is the nearest point to Killarney town.

About 2m E of Killarney at Lissyvigeen are the Seven Sisters – a stone circle inside a rath, enclosing an area 17ft in diameter. Two large standing stones exist outside the enclosure. Some 6m ESE of the town are the ruins of Killaha Castle, an O Donoghue fortress which commands the entrance to Glen Flesk. The picturesque situation of this tower house is near the Robbers' Den, a small cave in the face of the Demon's Cliff. Tradition has it that this was the abode of a former outlaw of the MacCarthy sept. The return to Killarney can be made via Lough Guitane, which lies beneath 2,162ft Crohane and 2,281ft Stoompa. Mangerton Mountain can be approached from Muckross village, and includes a pony track which leads to the very crest. Magnificent views from the summit take in Killarney town, the surrounding countryside, and a large part of SW Ireland. Close to the summit is the source of the town's water supply, the Devil's Punch Bowl. If great care is exercised the descent can be made via Glenagappal, a magnificent gorge with precipitous sides. The popular ascent of 3,414ft Carrantuohill is from Gortbue School, at the mouth of Hag's Glen. The route is along the glen and mounts to the summit via the Devil's Ladder. This is the highest mountain peak in the country, and is of more interest to the seasoned climber than to the casual visitor. The journey from Killarney is long and arduous, sudden mountain mists can blanket the limited views and make progress even more hazardous, and the lakes cannot be seen from the summit. The best viewpoint in the district is Torc Mountain

KILLEAGH, *Cill Ia:*
Ia's Church, Cork **29 X07**
The Dissour River, on which this neat little village stands, was once noted for the bleaching properties of its water. Killeagh itself was the property of the Aghadoe estate for over 700 years, and thus under the ownership of the Capell family. The delightful wood of Glenbower begins above the village and winds several miles up into the hills. Now a state forest, this is a rare example of indigenous Irish forestry. The Dissour flows through the wood, partly in a rift known as Glaunbour or 'the deafening valley'. The 13th-c circular keep of Inchiquin Castle stands SE of the village on the estuary of the Womanagh River.

KILLEEDY, Limerick **21 R22**
Ruins of a Romanesque church stand on the site of a nunnery founded here by St Ide in the 6thc. Pilgrims still place flowers on the saint's reputed grave. Remains of a Desmond Castle can be seen in the same townland, and Glenquin Castle (see entry) lies to the W.

KILLEEN, Mayo **14 L77**
Also known as 'The Killeen', this tiny settlement lies about 5½m SW of Louisburgh and is almost alone in an isolated and beautiful area. The local churchyard features an incised cross pillar and an early cross slab. The sea and miles of attractive beach lie ½m away. Carrownisky Strand and White Strand lie to the N, Bunlough Strand is to the S, and even farther S are the sandhills and strand of Kinnadoohy.

KILLEEN CASTLE, *An Cillín:*
The Little Church, Meath **18 N95**
Hugh de Lacy erected the original castle that stood here in 1180, but the remains of this were enlarged and greatly improved after a design by Francis Johnston in the 19thc. Further alterations were made by the 3rd Earl of Fingall in 1841. In the demesne are the ruins of a 15th-c semi-fortified church (NM). This features a number of well-preserved windows, a staircase leading to the rood loft, and two double-effigy tombs of the founder and his wife. These date from the 15thc. Two fragments of a 15th-c cross can be seen to the N of the church.

KILLEEN COWPARK, Limerick **21 R45**
See Kilcornan entry.

KILLEENEMER, Cork **22 R70**
Features of Killeenemer include a small 12th-c church (NM) with an original round-headed window, part of the cashel wall from a monastic foundation which existed here, plus a standing stone and a bullaun.

KILLEIGH, *Cill Achaidh:*
Church of the Field, Offaly **17 N31**
See Tullamore entry.

KILLENURE CASTLE, *Cuil an Iúir:*
The Recess of the Yew, Tipperary
23 S04
Each of the six gables displayed by this 17th-c ruin is topped by a lofty chimney. The castle lies 4m NW of the village of Golden, and owes its ruinous state to the depredations of Cromwellian troops after one of the owners – an O Dwyer – failed to produce required levies.

KILLESHIN, *Cill Uisean,* Laois **24 S67**
Close to this pleasant village are the ruins of a 12th-c church (NM), which stands at the point where the Carlow to Castlecomber road pierces the limestone girdle surrounding Leinster's coalfield. Of particular interest among these remains is a fine Romanesque doorway displaying rich ornamentation and many typically-Irish characteristics. In the graveyard is a decorated font which may be the oldest of its type in Ireland. A local chalybeate spring was held in high esteem during the 18thc. Dr James Doyle, the liberal RC Bishop of Kildare and Leighlin, wrote his famous *Letters* at nearby Old Derig in the 1820's.

KILLESTER, *Cill Easra:*
Easra's Church, Dublin **19 O23**
Remains of an abbey, church, and round tower can be seen in this NE suburb of Dublin city. A number of cottage homes built for Irish soldiers of the first world war can be seen in the neighbourhood.

KILLEVY, Armagh **13 J01**
The area around this small village, which lies below the E slopes of 1,893ft Slieve Gullion, contains a number of interesting historical features. Some 2m NNW in Ballintemple townland are the remains of two churches (NM) which were built alongside each other; although joined, the two buildings have no means of direct communication between them. The 9th-c or earlier W church has a fine, square-headed doorway, and the E building probably dates from the 13thc. Of interest in the more recent structure is a doorway with inclined jambs. Close to Drumbanagher Castle, one-time home of the Close family, is the site where the Earl of Tyrone's army camped during the Nine Years War (1594 to 1603). The house was demolished c1950. Nearby Tuscan Pass was an important station between the territories of the Irish clans O Hanlon and Maginnis. The fine house of Killevy Castle lies 1m NW.

KILLIMER, *Cill Iomaí,* Clare **21 R05**
Killimer is situated near the N shore of the Shannon estuary. The churchyard of the local ruined church contains the grave of the 'Colleen Bawn' – Ellen Hanley, who was drowned in the river by her jealous husband in 1819. Gerald Griffin's book *The Collegians* was based on this tragedy.

KILLINABOY, *Cill Iníne Baoith:*
The Church of the Daughter of Baoth, Clare **21 R29**
Situated near the N end of Lough Inchiquin, Killinaboy features an interesting 15th- or 16th-c church, a castle, and the stump of a round tower. The church displays a good *sheila-na-gig* above the door. A famous and primitive Tau cross can be seen set in a wall 1m NW at Roughan. This is carved with two heads and may be a local version of a type of iron-age art found in France.

KILLINEY, *Cill Iníon Léinín:*
Church of the Daughters of Léinín, Dublin
19 O22
This resort is charmingly situated on one of the most picturesque bays in Ireland. Killiney Hill rises straight from the water's edge and is dotted with woodland and villas from base to summit. Fine views are afforded S to Bray Head and N to Howth Head from a road on the side of the hill. The hill was opened as a public park in 1887, and named Victoria Park to commemorate the Queen's Silver Jubilee. The resort itself has an 11th- or 12th-c church (NM) which features a

square-headed west doorway with inclined jambs, and an inwardly-splayed east window. The plain chancel arch is semi-circular, the aisle on the north side is possibly of 16th-c date, and a bullaun has been preserved near the west door. Higher up the hill is the Druid's Seat – all that remains of a dolmen and circle – and the summit is crowned by an 18th-c folly. About ½m away near the village of Ballybrack is a field containing a complete dolmen; yet another can be seen 2m N in the delightful grounds of Glendruid House.

KILL OF THE GRANGE, *Cill na Gráinsí:*
The Church of the Grange, Dublin
19 O22
The small early-Irish church (NM) to which this name applies is situated 1m SW of Dun Laoghaire and is dedicated to St Fintan. It is possible that the later chancel was added in the 16thc, and the belfry is thought to be even more recent. Fragments of a simple early cross exist near by.

KILLONE ABBEY, *Cill Eoin:*
St John's Church, Clare **21 R37**
Donal O Brien founded this Augustinian abbey (NM) in 1190, and although the buildings are ruined their situation on the banks of Killone Lake is still magnificent. The site is 3m SSW of Ennis in the grounds of early 18th-c Newhall House. Included in the remains is an east wall with two interesting round-topped windows. There is a crypt beneath the east end, the convent buildings date from the 15thc, and a holy well dedicated to St John lies E of the abbey near the lake. The well is still visited by local people for devotional purposes.

*****KILLORGLIN,** *Cill Orglan:*
Orgla's Church, Kerry **26 V79**
Killorglin town stands on a hill a little to the S of the Castlemaine Harbour headwaters, on the noted salmon-fishing River Laune. The ruined 13th-c castle here was once known as Castle Conway, as was also the town. Most of Killorglin's fame derives from its three-day Puck Fair, which is held in August and is by far the best-known of its type in the country. Its origins may date back to pagan times, and the whole occasion is centred round the puck or goat – a creature with monstrous horns set up on a platform at the head of the town. To the S are the high mountains of MacGillycuddy's Reeks.

KILLUCAN, *Cill Liúcainne,*
Westmeath **18 N55**
Three fine examples of 16th- and early 17th-c commemorative wayside crosses can be seen just outside this village. The local parish church (CI) dates from the 19thc and houses a finely-carved font. Remains of a 15th-c structure are incorporated in the east end of the building. Also of interest are the foundations and some of the outworks of Rathwire Castle, a motte-and-bailey stronghold built by Hugh de Lacy. Traces of an early bronze-age round-barrow burial complex can be seen in the nearby townland of Rathnarrow.

KILLULTA, Limerick **22 R45**
Killulta church is a very small early-Irish building which features antae and stands on a low hill. It measures 16 by 10ft, the walls are 3ft thick, and an interesting triangular-headed east window has been preserved.

KILLURSA, Galway **15 M24**
The site of a monastery founded here by St Fursa in the 7thc is now occupied by a simple, pre-Norman church (NM). This has been greatly altered by later additions.

KILLYBEGS, *Na Cealla Beaga:*
The Small Monastic Cells, Donegal **4 G77**
Industries operated by this busy fishing port, situated on a fine harbour in an inlet of Donegal Bay, include fish processing, sail making, and the manufacture of hand-knotted carpets. The latter is a famous process which was started in the 19thc by a Scot named Alexander Morton, with the co-operation of the Congested Districts Board. Carpets from Killybegs have ended up in such places as Buckingham Palace, the South African Houses of Parliament, Cape Town, and the lounges of the famous Cunard Queens. The town was incorporated by a charter granted by James I, and returned two members to the Irish parliament until disfranchised at the Act of Union. Historical relics here include slight remains of a castle and a church. A sculptured memorial slab found near St John's Point, to the S, has been incorporated in the wall of the present church (RC). The coast scenery in the immediate area is considered very fine.

KILLYCLUGGIN, *Cill an Chloigín:*
Church of the Bell, Cavan **11 H21**
Numerous ancient remains survive near this small village, which lies 3m SW of Ballyconnell. Among these is the curious Killycluggin Stone, which is carved with La Tène ornamentation and bears a close affinity to the famous Turoe Stone of Loughrea.

KILLYDONNELL FRIARY,
Cill O dTomhrair:
Church of Uí Tomhrair, Donegal **5 C21**
Monastic remains here are of a Franciscan house which was founded in the 16thc by the O Donnell family. The ruins are situated 2¼m SE of Rathmelton.

KILLYLEAGH, *Cill O Laoch:*
The Church of Uí Laoch, Down
13 J55
An interesting feature of this little Plantation town is the way in which it has been formally arranged around a grid pattern. The impressive hilltop castle is of 13th- or 14th-c date and was first restored in 1666. Much later, in 1850, it was drastically altered to a design by Sir Charles Lanyon, but the south-west tower is a survivor of the earliest structure. The south east tower, much of the bailey walls, and the square towers on the south bailey wall date from the 17thc. The local parish church dates from the Jacobean period. Sir Hans Sloane, whose immense collection was the basis for the British Museum and Library, was born at Killyleagh in 1666. The birthplace of his father is marked 'GS 1637'. Another of the town's famous residents was Sir Edward Hincks, who became a Fellow of Trinity College, Dublin before the age of 21, and distinguished himself afterwards as one of the most knowledgeable Egyptologists and Assyriologists of the time. Remains of a 15th-c church can be seen in a low marsh ½m N of the town. At Ringahaddy, situated 4m NNE on a peninsula in Strangford Lough, are the remains of a 12th-c motte, a 13th-c church, and a 15th- to 17th-c castle.

KILMACANOGE, *Cill Mocheanóg:*
St Mocheanóg's Church, Wicklow
19 O21
Sited between the 1,659ft Great Sugar Loaf and 1,120ft Little Sugar Loaf, Kilmacanoge is known for its beautiful surroundings. The larger of the two mountains offers a splendid view from its summit and can be ascended via Rocky Valley, which runs W from Kilmacanoge. The descent should be made on the SE side.

KILMACDUAGH, *Cill Mhic Duach:*
The Church of the Son of Duach, Galway
15 M40
The collection of church ruins here, about 3½m WSW of Gort, is considered one of the finest in Ireland and originates from a monastery founded by St Colman in the 6thc. The round tower (NM), one of the largest and best-preserved in the country, stands 112ft high. A doorway breaches the wall 26ft above the ground, and the structure leans 2ft from the perpendicular. The mainly 15th-c cathedral (NM) consists of a nave and chancel with transepts. The west gable, with its blocked, flat-headed doorway, and the rest of the nave dates from the 11th or 12th-c. This was probably a portion of the original building. Inside the church is an altar tomb of the O Shaughnessy's, and close to the cathedral are three small churches

This 18th-c folly stands at the top of Killiney Hill, which was made into a public park to commemorate Queen Victoria's Silver Jubilee.

Entries marked * are the starting point of drives included in the Day Drive section of the book (pages 79 to 144).

dating from the 12th and 13thc. These are St John's, St Mary's, and O Heynes (all NM's). A 15th-c tower known as Glebe House stands near by. Also of interest in the area is the stone fort of Caher Cugeola.

KILMACREEHY CHURCH, Clare **21 R08**
See Lahinch entry.

KILMACRENAN, *Cill Mhic Réanáin:*
The Church of Sons of Éanán, Donegal **5 C12**
Renowned as the 6th-c home of St Columba, who spent his childhood near by and founded a monastery in the area, this village is a noted angling resort on the River Leannan. During the 15thc the O Donnell family built a Franciscan friary on the site of St Columba's abbey, and some of the walls are still standing. To the S of the site are the remains of the old, towered, parish church. Doon Rock lies 2m W and was the inauguration site of the O Donnells, Lords of Tyrconnell. The celebrated holy well of Doon lies to the E of the rock, and is still the object of pilgrimage during the summer months. There is widespread belief in its healing properties.

KILMACTHOMAS, *Coill Mhic Thomáisín:* Mac Thomas' Wood, Waterford **29 S30**
Celebrated for its Irish tweeds, this town is situated on a steep hill astride the Mahon river and is a popular touring centre. Of particular interest is Lake Coumshingaun, which lies 6m NW in wild mountain scenery and is accessible only by foot. It is almost surrounded by precipitous cliffs which rise to 1,288ft and form one of the finest glacial cirques in Ireland or Great Britain. The only outlet is a small stream which flows into the Clodiagh River. Overshadowing the lake is 2,597ft Fauscoum, the highest peak in the Comeragh range, while near by is 2,384ft Knockaunapeebra. About 4m NW are the forest-clad slopes of 2,478ft Knockanaffrin, while N of Coumshingaun Lake is a crag-encircled Crotty's Lake. A small cave here is said to have been the hiding place of notorious William Crotty, an 18th-c outlaw who was eventually hanged at Waterford. The Monavullagh Mountains rise SW of the Comeragh range.

KILMAINHAM, *Cill Mhaigneann:*
Maighne's Church, Dublin **19 O13**
A little church which was founded here by Maighne in the 7thc gave this Dublin environ its name, and may have stood in the ancient local churchyard which now contains little more than a high cross (NM). An interesting feature of the area is the Royal Hospital, which was originally built for old soldiers during Ormonde's Viceroyalty c1680. This is the earliest secular building in Ireland – and by far the largest of its period – to survive until the present day. It was designed by William Robinson and has so many good features that it is well worthy of restoration. Kilmainham Gaol dates from the 19thc and now serves as a museum – a memorial to the many famous patriots and political prisoners who were imprisoned here (see Dublin district plan, page 52). A stark carving over the door depicts a serpent in chains. Farther W, on the S bank of the River Liffey, is the War Memorial Park. This incorporates the Garden of Remembrance, a beautifully-planned and planted area which commemorates the 49,000 Irishmen who died in the 1914 to 1918 war.

KILMAKILLOGE, *Cill Mocheallóg:*
Mocheallóg's Church, Kerry **26 V75**
The small bay of the same name on which this place is sited is an inlet of the Kenmare River. At the head of the inlet is Derreen House, which stands in a finely-wooded demesne (gardens OACT). An ancient ruined church overlooks the harbour. Close to the shores of the bay is Lauragh village, while in the background the Caha Mountains rise from the Cork border to culminate in 2,169ft Knockowen.

KILMALKEDAR, *Cill Maolchéadair:*
St Maolchéador Church, Kerry **26 Q40**
This small village lies 1m E of Smerwick Harbour and features a 12th-c church (NM) which is considered one of the best examples of Irish-Romanesque design extant. There is evidence to suggest that the original roof was corbelled, which would stylistically link this structure with the famous Gallarus Oratory. Other details link it with Cormac's Chapel at Cashel. An alphabet stone can be seen near the chancel doorway. In the graveyard are an ogham stone, an early sundial, and a stone bearing an incised cross. To the NE of the church is a two-storey medieval building known as St Brendan's House (NM), while to the S is the 14th- or 15th-c Chancellor's House. The whole area is particularly rich in prehistoric and early-Christian remains.

KILMALLOCK, *Cill Mocheallóg:*
St Mocheallóg's Church, Limerick **22 R62**
This old corporate town is pleasantly sited on the W bank of the River Loobagh, to the N of the Ballyhoura Hills in the fertile Golden Vale. Little is known of the settlement's origins, but the magnificent ruins here show that it was a place of importance. St Molach or Mocheallog founded a church or monastery here in the 7thc. The medieval town's rise to prominence was due largely to the Anglo-Norman Desmond family, who were all-powerful in Munster province for many centuries. As with all other occupying Anglo-Norman families, they organized the civic life, established defences, and made provision for religion. Edward III granted a charter, and the town was surrounded by a cut-stone wall fortified by earthern mounds and breached by four imposing gateways. Blossom's Gate, through which the Charleville road passes, survives from this time and includes a well-preserved section of the wall. King's Castle (NM) is a tall, 15th-c gate tower on the Limerick road.

The Desmond family consolidated their considerable power by shipping large Irish forces across the sea to help Edward III against the Scots. The commanders of these forces were three cousins of the great Earl of Desmond, and they so distinguished themselves on the field that the king dubbed them the White Knight, Black Knight, and Green Knight respectively – after the colours of their armour. The White Knight's descendants were particularly involved with the life of Kilmallock. The tomb of the last head of the family can be seen in the choir of the Dominican friary. During the town's period of greatest prosperity, from the 15th to the 17thc, many of the Munster gentry had their town houses within the walls of Kilmallock. These mansions were built to a uniform plan and consisted of three storeys of hewn stone – with adequate provision for defence. Very little has survived from this period of building. Another claim to fame is that Kilmallock was one of the principal towns chosen by Edward IV for the establishment of a royal mint. In Elizabethan times the town was an English stronghold held against the Desmonds, and it was sacked so many times that at one time it was deserted. Cromwell negated the town's military importance by razing all the fortifications. Up until the 19th-c Act of Union Kilmallock returned two members to the Irish parliament, and the proprietor was Richard Oliver.

Interesting buildings in the town include the collegiate Church of SS Peter and Paul (NM), a 15th-c building which stands within the town walls and features a 13th-c transept with a fine south door. Massive square pillars supporting high, pointed arches separate the nave from the aisles. The spacious and lofty choir was used as a CI parish church for many years, but was burned out in 1935 and replaced by a new structure in 1938. At the west end of the north aisle is the round tower of an older church. The aisle itself contains some rudely-sculptured 17th-c tombs of prominent early families. The modern church of SS Peter and Paul dates from 1879. Remains of the town's 13th-c Dominican friary occupy a picturesque riverside site and include a choir and nave church with a single aisle. A square tower rises 90ft or so from the junction between choir and nave. Of particular interest is a pillar in the aisle arcade which carries a ball-flower ornament; this type of decoration was common in 14th-c England, but extremely rare in Ireland. The choir window includes five slender lancets and is of early-English style, while among the fine choir tombs is that of Edmond – the last White Knight. Edmond died in 1608 and was the most notable of his line; his tomb has been broken. The conventual buildings lie to the N of the church and include a well-preserved day room and kitchen.

About $\frac{1}{2}$m N of Kilmallock at Spitalfield is the site of an old leper hospital, and traces of military encampments have been found all round the town. Large numbers of human bones were discovered at the Mount Coote demesne during the early 19thc. Ash Hill Tower, situated 1m SW of the town, originated in 1781 but was subsequently gothicized in 1837. The fine interior can be viewed by appointment.

KILMOGUE, Kilkenny **24 S42**
This particularly fine example of a large portal dolmen (NM) is situated in an overgrown hollow some $\frac{2}{3}$m W of Harristown. It features a sharply sloping capstone.

KILMORE, *An Chill Mhór:*
Big Church, Armagh **12 H95**
Kilmore's CI church stands on the site of an earlier foundation and features a remarkable tower. Externally this is square, but its 8- to 9ft-thick walls enclose the almost-perfect round tower of the previous church. Also of interest here is a memorial stone to the Rev

George Walker, who was rector here in the mid 17thc and the father of the defender of Derry – also the Rev George Walker.

KILMORE, *Cill Mhór:*
Big Church, Cavan **11 H30**
Renowned William Bedell, who translated the Bible into Irish and was bishop of this ancient bishopric in the 17thc, is buried in the old CI churchyard. The modern cathedral at Kilmore incorporates a richly-carved 12th-c Romanesque doorway which was removed from the church on Trinity Island in Lough Oughter.

KILMORE, Leitrim **10 G73**
Near here is Park's Castle (NM), a picturesquely-situated Plantation stronghold on the N shores of Lough Gill near the Sligo to Dromahair road. This well-preserved structure features a five-sided bawn, of which two sides are formed by a two-storey residence. The bawn is joined to an arched gate building, and two Scottish-type turrets overlook the lough from the angles.

KILMORE QUAY, *Cé na Cille Móire:*
Wexford **24 S90**
Situated on the E side of Crossfarnoge, or Forlorn Point, Kilmore Quay has become well known as a deep-sea angling centre. Boats can be hired here for visits to the Saltee Islands, which are visible offshore. About ½m N is interesting Ballyteige Castle, a 15th- and 16th-c stronghold which retains its bawn.

KILMURVY, *Cill Mhuirbhigh:*
Church of the Sandy Shore, Galway **14 L81**
See Aran Islands entry.

KILNASAGGART, *Cill na Sagart:*
Church of the Priests, Armagh **13 J01**
Close to the Co Louth border and about 1½m S of Jonesborough is the Kilnasaggart Stone, an 8th-c pillar (NM) which carries ten cross-inscribed circles on the north face. The south face features a barely-legible Irish inscription. This stands on an early monastic site and may be the oldest Christian field monument in Ireland.

KILREA, *Cill Ria,* Londonderry **6 C91**
Once the centre of the Mercer's Company estate, Kilrea benefitted greatly from the initiatives of its improving landlords in the early 19thc. A castle built by the company in the 17thc, to protect a ford over the River Bann 2¼m N at Movanagher, still stands but is surrounded by modern farm buildings. Kilrea itself is situated about 1m W of the Bann and is known for its salmon and eel fishing. Several small loughs exist near by. Some 5m SW is the triple-ringed Dunglady Fort, one of the largest and best-preserved earthen strongholds of this type in N Ireland.

KILREE, *Cill Rí:*
King's Church, Kilkenny **23 S44**
Of interest here are a 96ft-high capless round tower (NM) and the nearby ruin of an ancient church. The latter features a flat-headed doorway and a fine 17th-c tomb. A decorated but badly-weathered high cross (NM) standing in an adjoining field dates from the 8th or 9thc, and close by is a holy well dedicated to St Brigid. Another unusual high cross can be seen near another church ruin 1½m SW at Dunnamaggan.

KILMORE/KILTEEL

One of the fine doorways in Kilmore's (Cavan) modern cathedral.

KILRONAN, *Cill Rónáin:*
Rónán's Church, Galway **14 L80**
See Aran Islands entry.

KILRONAN CHURCH, *Cill Rónáin:*
Rónán's Church, Roscommon **10 G81**
Remains of this church stand on the NE shore of Lough Meelagh, about 2½m SE of Ballyfarnan, and include a 12th- or 13th-c west doorway. Turlough O Carolan, the famous bard and harpist who died in 1738, is buried here.

KILROOT, *Cill Rua:*
Red Church, Antrim **7 J48**
Probably best known as Dean Swift's first place of ministry in the late 17thc, this village lies 2½m ENE of Carrickfergus and has many associations with the famous man. His residence was a cottage which burnt down in 1959, and his church is now in ruins. Local tradition tells how Swift had trouble in securing a congregation here, and at one time attracted the required crowd by trundling stones along the beach. During his stay at Kilroot Swift wrote his *Tale of a Tub.* The Bishop of Down and Connor chose this village as the site of a palace c1604, and the remains of this three-storey gabled house can still be seen. The ruins stand within a fortified bawn near a modern farmhouse. During the Seven Years War the French General Thurot landed at Kilroot Point with 600 men, and proceeded to take Carrickfergus in 1760. The principal seat of the area is Castle Dobbs, the one-time home of the 18th-c colonizer Francis Dobbs. Dobbs became famous as governor of S Carolina.

KILRUDDERY, *Cill Ruairí:*
Ruairí's Church, Wicklow **19 O21**
See Bray entry.

KILRUSH, *Cill Rois:*
Church of the Wood, Clare **21 Q95**
This is a busy port and important market town on the estuary of the Shannon. Of interest here are the remains of a small, pre-Romanesque church which features a flat-headed doorway and round-headed window. The steamer pier 1m S at Cappagh is the most convenient point from which to visit Scattery Island, where there is an outstanding collection of stone monuments (all NM's) which date from the 11th or 12thc.

The earliest settlement on the island was a 6th-c foundation created by St Senan. This suffered greatly at the hands of the Norsemen during the 9th and 10thc, and the oldest building on the site is a structure designed as a refuge from these pirates – a 120ft round tower. This is probably the tallest and oldest of its type in the country, and has a unique feature – an entrance at ground level. To the E of the tower is the much altered pre-Romanesque cathedral, and N is a 12th-c Romanesque church with a fine contemporary chancel arch. St Senan's Oratory is a rude little building featuring an east window with a unique external splay, and W of this is St Senan's House or Bed. The latter is reputed to be the saint's burial place. To the SW of the cathedral is the badly-ruined Church of the Hill of Angels, or *Ard na nAingil.* Close to the landing place on the island is a cemetery containing the ruined Church of the Dead, or *Teampull na Marbh.* To the W of the monastery and close to the round tower is a holy well which still attracts pilgrims.

KILSHEELAN, *Cill Síoláin:*
Síolán's Church, Tipperary **23 S22**
The Comeragh Mountains rise to the S of this village, which is charmingly situated on the N bank of the River Suir, and the countryside to the N is dominated by Slievenamon – the legendary 'Mountain of Women'. Local ruins of an early-Irish church include a Romanesque-style chancel, arch, and doorway added in the 12th or 13thc. About ½m W is the beautifully set mansion of Gurteen le Poer, a house in a fine demesne on the S bank of the Suir. An interesting dolmen exists in the grounds. Other fine residences to the NW of the village are the castles of Newtownanner and Anner, while on the S bank of the river towards Clonmel are ruined Derrinlaur Castle and 17th-c Tickincor Castle. Poulkerry Castle lies ¾m E of Kilsheelan. Cromwell captured it in 1650 and massacred the garrison.

KILTARTAN, *Cill Tartain:*
Tartan's Church, Galway **16 M40**
Kiltartan or Ballinamantan Castle (NM) is an imposing ruin which survives from a 13th-c stronghold built by the Bourke family. Its main tower is three storeys high, and the courtyard has two massive, semi-circular towers to guard its entrance. Also of interest are the ruins of Kiltartan Church. A well-preserved earthen fort with a souterrain system can be seen NW at Lydacon, on a minor road to Kinvarra.

KILTEEL, *Cill tSíle:*
Síle's Church, Kildare **18 N92**
Near the foot of the hill on which this village stands is Kilteel Old Church.
cont overleaf

This building has a unique, reconstructed Romanesque chancel arch (NM) dating from the 12thc, which displays excellent figure sculpture. Near by are a medieval granite cross (NM) and the ruin (NM) of a 15th-c tower house and gateway. The latter consisted of five storeys and included a spiral staircase which led to the roof. It is thought to have formed part of a 13th-c preceptory of the Knights Hospitallers. Cupidstown Hill, the highest point in Co Kildare, rises to 1,248ft in the SE.

KILTERNAN, *Cill Tiarnáin:*
St Tiarnán's Church, Dublin **19 O 22**
An ancient church and a fine portal dolmen can both be found under this name in a lane off the main road near the border of Co Wicklow. The dolmen (NM) is famous for its huge capstone, estimated at 40 tons, and is thought to be of neolithic origin.

KILTYCLOGHER, *Coillte Clochair:*
Woods of the Stony Place, Leitrim **11 G 94**
Situated on the Fermanagh border, about halfway between Lough Melvin and Lough Macnean Upper, this village is surrounded by attractive hill and lakeland country. The village square contains a memorial by Albert Power to Sean MacDiarmada, the leader of the 1916 Rising. Traces of the Black Pig's Race travelling earthwork can be seen SE in the townland of Corraclona, in the direction of Lough Macnean Upper.

KILWORTH, *Cill Uird:*
Church of the Order, Cork **28 R 80**
To the S of Kilworth village is the attractive demesne of Moore Park, which is watered by the River Funshion. The Kilworth Mountains, which rise to the N, are crossed by a road which runs from Fermoy to Mitchelstown and affords fine views N to the Galtees range. Castle ruins exist in Moore Park.

KIMEGO WEST, Kerry **26 V 48**
The main feature of this area is the large stone fort called Cahergall (NM; see Cahirciveen entry).

KINDLESTOWN, Wicklow **19 O 21**
Fragments of a ruined 13th-c castle built by the Archbold family can be seen here, some ¾m N of Delgany. This type of halled stronghold, with an upper storey divided into rooms with windows, is rare in Ireland at this period – particularly in this county.

KINGSCOURT, *Dún an Rí:*
The King's Fort, Cavan **12 N 79**
Well-built stone houses dating from the period between the late 18th and mid 19thc are a feature of this town. The community, which is grouped round a single main street, was founded by the local landlord Mervyn Pratt in the late 18thc. The site was near the old village of Cabra, on the borders of counties Louth, Meath, and Monaghan. Cabra Castle is a splendid, mock-medieval structure which was the home of the Pratt family. The local church (RC) features notable stained glass by the famous Evie Hone.

KINLOUGH, *Cionn Locha:*
Lake Head, Leitrim **10 G 85**
Delightfully situated near the head of picturesque Lough Melvin, this village stands in an area of particular scenic and historic interest. The S shore of the lough is known for its beauty, and to the SE is an attractive range of hills which culminate in 1,346ft Aghabohad. Actually in the lough is a small island with the remains of a crannog and the ruin of 15th-c Rossclogher Castle and church. Rossclogher Abbey can be seen on the mainland. A sulphurated hydrogen spring which was greatly frequented in the 18thc rises near the village of Ardfarna.

KINLOUGH, Mayo **15 M 25**
Interesting ruins can be seen on both sides of the river here. On one side are the remains of a small 13th-c church (NM) with a square belfry at the west end, and on the other are the surviving parts of a 16th-c castle (NM) built by the Burke family. The tall, square tower of the castle features gables and chimneys.

KINNEIGH, *Ceinn Eich:*
Horse's Head, Cork **27 W 35**
An outstanding feature of this village is its 68ft round tower. The first 18ft of this unique structure is hexagonal, while the remainder follows the usual circular design. It is divided into six storeys and has a square-headed doorway 10½ft above the ground.

KINNITTY, *Cionn Eitigh,* Offaly **17 N 10**
Considered by many to be one of the most attractive villages in Ireland, Kinnitty lies W of the Slieve Bloom Mountains – which rise from the Laois border and culminate in 1,734ft Arderin. The attractive glens in the range include Forelacka, a place of outstanding beauty off the valley of the Camcor River. The sources of the Barrow and Nore are in these mountains. In many places the heights have been afforested. Castle Bernard demesne is picturesquely situated 1m E and features Kinnitty High Cross, which may mark the site of a monastery founded by St Finian in the 6thc. The foundation was destroyed by the Danes in 839.

KINSALE, *Cionn tSáile:*
Head of the Sea, Cork **28 W 65**
Kinsale is a town of great character sited on the slopes of Compass Hill above the estuary of the Bandon River. Its streets still exude an air of elegance, even though many of the handsome 18th-c houses have fallen into disrepair. Of particular interest is the Dutch-gabled former courthouse, which dates from the 16thc and contains an interesting museum. The Sovereign's throne of 1706 is preserved here. The Desmond Castle or 'French Prison' is a distinguished 16thc townhouse (NM) which was used to incarcerate French prisoners during the Napoleonic wars. Gift House dates from 1682 and has recently been restored.

The town has played an important part in Irish history, especially from the times when it came into the possession of Miles de Cogan during the Anglo-Norman occupation. A short time after this the district passed to the de Courcys by marriage. This family, who built the castle, are still represented by the 33rd Baron of Kinsale – the premier baron of Ireland. He retains the unique privilege of being allowed to wear his hat in the presence of royalty. Edward III granted a charter to the town in 1333. Kinsale was exposed to attack both from the land and the sea, and was often harassed or blockaded by pirates, but the most outstanding historical event was its occupation by Spanish forces under Don Juan d'Aguila in 1601. The Lord Deputy Mountjoy besieged the captured town with 12,000 men and eventually won a great victory which forced the Spaniards to surrender. This was one of the decisive battles of Ireland – the last stand of medieval Gaelic Ireland against the power of the English Renaissance state. The 'Flight of the Earls' to Europe followed soon after and closed a chapter in the country's history. The battle sites are marked. During the 17th-c wars the Irish citizens of Kinsale were expelled. Charles Fort, situated to the S of Summer Cove, was built by the Duke of Ormonde in 1677 and includes the ruins of a barracks which was occupied until the Anglo-Irish Treaty. Kinsale was the base from which James II made his attempt to recover the English crown; after his defeat he fled from here to France in 1691.

One of the most interesting buildings in the town is St Multose's Church, which was built towards the end of the 12thc and is one of the few medieval parish churches in use today. It has been greatly restored and extended at various times. The building's most notable features are the curious tower and spire, a doorway ornamented with chevron moulding, and the interesting old font. Some of the sculptured slabs in the church date from the 15thc. The RC parish church is a charming building which stands near St Multose's.

A charming river excursion can be made to Inishannon from Kinsale, passing several interesting old strongholds including the castles of Carriganass and Poulnalong. Another delightful trip can be made to the Old Head of Kinsale, from which wide views extend W to Courtmacsherry Bay. Ruins of a castle built by the de Courcy family in the 12thc can be seen at Holeopen Bay, which lies close to the head.

KINVARRA, *Cinn Mhara:*
Sea Headlands, Galway **15 M 31**
A little tidal port at the head of an inlet of Galway Bay, Kinvarra was a thriving town in the 19thc but has since lost more than half of its population. The quay was built during the late 18thc by the enlightened Baron de Basterot, who was the proprietor. Trade at this time centred on the export of local grain and the import of seaweed for fertilizer. De Basterot lived 2m NW at Doorus House. Near the shore are two extensive caverns, and a nearby rock carries 16th-c Dunguaire Castle (OACT). The castle's bawn is well preserved. To the SW of Kinvarra is the limestone landscape of the Burren district.

KIRCUBBIN, *Cill Ghobáin:*
St Gobán's Church, Down **13 J 56**
This prosperous little town stands on the E shores of Strangford Lough and owes much of its success to the Ward family – proprietors of Kircubbin in the 18th and early 19thc. Industries operated here at this time included the manufacture of fertilizer from kelp, and the production of straw hats and bonnets. Most of the interesting buildings were supplied by the Wards, including the brown-linen hall, the market house, and the quay on Strangford Lough. Of particular note is the unusually early Penal Law chapel (RC) at Ballygalget. This dates from c1780, and has been restored after a long period of disuse.

KIRKISTOWN CASTLE, *Cnapach:*
Lumpy, Down
See Cloughey entry.

KNAPPOGUE CASTLE, *An Chnapóg:*
The Hummock, Clare **22 R47**
Inscribed pillars on the back gate of this castle, which lies NE of Sixmilebridge, give local distances in both English and the rarely-used Irish miles. An Irish mile is 2,240 yards. The castle itself was bought by the Land Commission in 1927 and passed to a farmer. In 1966 it was sold to an American who, in association with the Office of Public Works and several tourist organizations, undertook extensive restoration. This work has restored the medieval atmosphere of Knappogue, and since becoming the venue for medieval-style banquets the castle has developed into a major tourist attraction.

KNIGHTSTOWN, *Baile an Ridire:*
The Town of the Knight, Kerry **26 V47**
See Valentia Island entry.

KNOCKANE, Kerry **26 Q50**
See Anascaul entry.

KNOCKAST, Westmeath **17 N24**
See Moate entry.

KNOCKBRIDGE, *Droichead an Chnoic:*
The Bridge of the Hill, Louth **12 H90**
Knockbridge is a small village which stands on the Dundalk to Louth road, close to the Fane River. About 1¼m SE is 18th-c Stephenstown House, while E of the Dundalk road at Ratheddy is the 12ft-high Cuchullain Stone.

KNOCKCOSGREY, *Cnoc Uí Choscraigh:*
O Coscraigh's Hill, Westmeath **17 N24**
Tradition holds that this low hill rises from the exact centre of Ireland.

KNOCKCROGHERY, *Cnoc an Chrochaire:*
Hangman's Hill, Roscommon **16 M95**
The mound from which this village takes its name lies to the E and once served as a place of execution. Nearby Galey Castle, at Galey Bay on the shores of Lough Ree, dates from the 14thc.

KNOCKDRUM FORT, Cork **27 W13**
Farrandau, the 480ft hill on which this ancient stronghold is sited, lies ½m W of Castletownshend. The diameter of the stone fort (NM) is 95ft, the walls are 10ft thick, and the foundations of a square building have been found in the enclosure.

KNOCKEEN, *An Cnoicín:*
The Little Hill, Waterford **29 S50**
An excellent example of the portal-grave type prehistoric burial chamber can be seen here. This monument (NM) belongs to a sub-class called closed portal graves, in which a door-like slab stands between the portal stones. In this case the 'door' reaches almost to the main capstone. The monument is thought to date from *c*2000BC.

KNOCKLONG, *Cnoc Loinge:*
The Hill of the House, Limerick **22 R73**
Ruined O Hurly's Castle and the remains of an old church can be seen on a hill to the W of Knocklong. About 2m SW in the grounds of Ryves Castle is an old graveyard which features the handsome vault of the Lowe family. The Lowes were once the proprietors of the district.

KNOCKMANY, *Cnoc Meánach:*
Middle Hill, Tyrone **12 H55**
Remains of a prehistoric grave known as Annia's Cove (NM) surmount Knockmany Hill. Decorated stones in the monument clearly link its origins to those of the passage-grave tradition. The rest of this 779ft hill, which rises 2m NW of Augher, is covered with state forestry.

KNOCKMEALDOWN MOUNTAINS, *Cnoc Mhaoldonn,* Waterford **22:23 R90**
Fine mountain scenery is a feature of this lofty range, which straddles the county border between Tipperary and Waterford. Its highest point, 2,609ft Knockmealdown, rises E of the point where the Clogheen to Lismore road crosses the main ridge. This road passes a tall cairn on the slopes of 2,141ft Sugarloaf Hill, which contains the upright burial of an eccentric Quaker called Samuel Grubb. The summits of the Knockmealdowns afford widespread views which take in the Galtee, Comeragh, and Kilworth Mountains.

KNOCKNANUSS HILL, *Cnoc na nOs:*
The Hill of the Deer, Cork **27 R40**
Materials for use in road making are quarried here, 3m E of Kanturk, and the hill is being gradually dug away. It has recently been the subject of archaeological excavation. In 1647 a battle was fought here between Lord Taafe, who held the commission of the Catholic Confederacy, and Lord Murrough O Brien Inchiquin – who was supporting the parliamentary side. The battle is noteworthy for the curious proposal, by Taafe, that the fighting should be done by 2,000 foot soldiers on each side – 'more for recreation than for any serious purpose.' Inchiquin ignored the suggestion and suddenly attacked Taafe's force of 8,000, winning an overwhelming victory with a small army. Few of Taafe's men escaped.

KNOCKNAREA MOUNTAIN and GLEN, *Cnoc na Ria:* Hill of the Executions, Sligo **10 G63**
Although this hill affords excellent views over the surrounding countryside, its chief claim to fame is the huge cairn which crowns its summit. This enormous monument (NM) measures over 200ft in diameter and is thought to cover a burial place of the passage-grave type.

KNOCKTOPHER, *Cnoc an Tóchair:*
The Hill of the Causeway, Kilkenny **24 S53**
Once a corporate town and parliamentary borough which returned two members to the Irish parliament, Knocktopher is of considerable historic interest as the chief residence of the Butlers – Earls of Ormonde. The old Church of St David (NM) served as the parish church until 1870, but is now in ruins. The remains include a tower, a north wall, and a 12th-c doorway. Near by is a private house which incorporates the remains of a Carmelite friary, and across the road is the Knocktopher Motte. The motte was built by Matthew Fitzgriffin; only a few fragments remain of the more important Butler Castle which was built on the motte. Close to the church is a holy well. Also of interest in the village is the present Carmelite priory, which is about a century old.

KNOWTH, *Cnóbha,* Meath **18 N97**
See gazetteer inset *Brugh na Boinne,* page 176.

KYLEMORE ABBEY, *An Choill Mhóir:*
The Big Wood, Galway **14 L75**
Access to Kylemore Abbey is via the Pass of Kylemore, a magnificent gap which runs E to W and is considered one of the most beautiful places in the wild Connemara district. On the N side of the pass is 1,736ft Doughruagh, while 1,577ft Benbaun rises from the N extreme of the Twelve Bens (or Pins) in the S. Kylemore Lough is a charming lake which measures over 1m in length and extends alongside the road. This highway is bounded on the N side by masses of mica-glistening rocks which are softened by creeping plants and ferns. Doughruagh, a beautifully-wooded hill, features Kylemore Abbey beside Pollacappal Lough on its lower slopes. The abbey is a magnificent, late 19th-c granite and limestone building in Elizabethan style. It was erected by a Liverpool merchant called Mitchell Henry, who reclaimed many acres of surrounding bogland and planted numerous shrubs. Fine gardens and a church are contained within the extensive grounds. The mansion once functioned as a guesthouse, but now serves as a Benedictine convent boarding school.

Kylemore Abbey is a magnificent 19th-c structure which stands near Kylemore Lough, on the slopes of Doughruagh.

LABBACALLEE, *Leaba Caillighe:*
Hag's Bed, Cork 28 R 70
See gazetteer inset below.

LABBAMOLAGA, Cork 22 R 71
A monastery was founded here by St Molaga in the 7th c, and remains on the site include a small early-Irish church (NM) with grave slabs, a flat-headed doorway, and an enclosing cashel wall.

LACKEEN CASTLE, Tipperary 16 M 90
This 16th-c four-storey tower house (NM) of the O Kennedys has an extensive bawn. On the ground floor is a round-headed doorway, and a fine fireplace survives on the second storey.

LADY'S ISLAND, *Oileán Muire:*
Our Lady's Island, Wexford 25 T 10
See Rosslare entry.

LAGORE, *Loch Gabhair:*
Horse Lake, Meath 18 N 95
Situated 1m ENE of Dunshaughlin, this is one of the most celebrated examples of a crannog (lake dwelling) in Ireland. It was discovered in 1839 when a pedlar sold several items from the site to the renowned archaeologist George Petrie. Exploration of a drained lake at Lagore revealed an artificial circular mound measuring 520ft in circumference. This had been constructed by laying down alternate layers of cut peat and brushwood matting etc, which were held firmly in place by a palisade of piles, thus also providing a defence against intruders. The crannog was occupied during the early-Christian period. Objects found on the site can be seen at the National Museum, Dublin.

LAHINCH, *An Leacht:*
Grave Mound, Clare 21 R 08
This popular resort on Liscannor Bay has an excellent sandy beach and a good golf course. The famous 5m Cliffs of Moher rise 4½m NW, with 407ft Hag's Head, and Hag's Tower at the SW end. These cliffs afford magnificent views. Two natural curiosities in the neighbourhood are the Puffing Holes – *ie* water spouts – on the coast at Freagh, and the Dropping Well. Two interesting ruins can be seen at O Brien's Bridge, near the N tip of Liscannor Bay between Lahinch and Liscannor, where the Dealagh River enters the sea. One is of Dough Castle, the other of the nave and chancel of 15th-c Kilmacreehy Church. The chancel has a deeply-splayed east window and a decorated recess in the north wall.

LAMBAY ISLAND, *Reachrainn,*
Dublin 19 O 35
Prehistoric remains have been unearthed on both the W and S shores of the island, and a promontory fort exists on the NW corner. A monastery is said to have been founded on the island by St Columba, but no trace of this now remains. The island belongs to Lord Revelstoke, from whom permission to land must be obtained. Lambay Castle, his home, was designed by Lutyens and incorporates parts of a medieval castle. The island is rich in bird life and has been made a bird sanctuary.

LANESBOROUGH, *Béal Atha Liag:*
The Ford Mouth of the Standing Stones, Longford 17 N 06
An angling centre situated at the point where the River Shannon expands into the waters of Lough Ree, this town is linked to Co Roscommon's Ballyclare by a nine-arched bridge.

LARACOR, *Láithreach Cora:*
Weir Site, Meath 18 N 85
Laracor, now only a hamlet, was the parish to which Dean Swift was appointed in 1700. Only fragments of his Glebe House remain however, and his church has long since been replaced by a modern building. The Duke of Wellington was born 2m SE at Dangan Castle, and attended school in Trim. The castle is now ruined. Silver communion vessels in the local church were a gift from the Duke of Wellington's family. Remains of a simple house near the church are known locally as Stella's Cottage. Tradition has it that Swift's 'Stella' (Esther Johnson) and her friend Mrs Dingley lived here. Willows bordering the stream where Dean Swift and the two ladies strolled together are

LABBACALLEE WEDGE SHAPED GALLERY GRAVE

The Irish name for this prehistoric tomb is *Leaba Caillighe,* which means the 'Hag's Bed'. By a strange coincidence the skeleton and skull of a female were found in the grave when it was excavated. Speculation as to whether the Irish name enshrines some folk-memory of the tomb being the last resting place of an old woman is fascinating but probably unfounded. Labbacallee, which lies 1½m SE of Glanworth in Co Cork, is the largest and most complex wedge grave in Ireland, and may well represent the beginning of the wedge-grave tradition in the country.

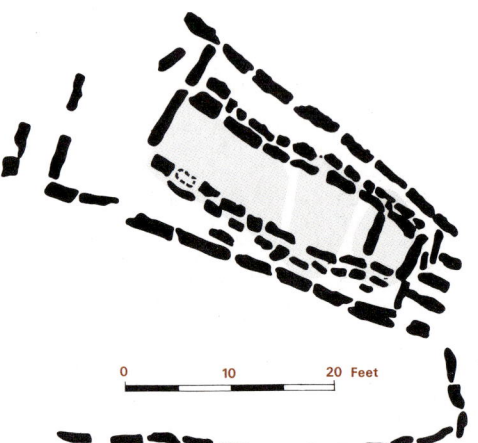

The outer plan of the grave shows quite clearly where the term 'wedge shaped' comes from, since it narrows from 20ft wide at the W end to 11ft wide at the E. It is also higher at the W end. The actual gallery is more rectangular in shape, being 25ft long and 5ft wide internally, and it is divided into two chambers by a large slab. This dividing slab has one corner broken off, apparently deliberately. It is possible that this feature (which is not uncommon in such tombs) was incorporated to enable the free passage of the soul. The roof of the gallery is formed by three very large flat capstones, the biggest of which is 26ft long and 18ft wide. The whole structure was once covered by a large cairn, which has now disappeared except for parts of the stone kerb on the S and E sides.

The headless and partially dismembered skeleton of a woman was discovered on the floor of the small chamber at the E end of the gallery. This was accompanied by burnt animal bones and a bone pin. The bone pin presumably functioned as the closing pin for a leather bag which had long since rotted away. Some cremated human bones and fragments of pottery were also discovered, and the remains of a man, a child, and a spare skull were found in the large chamber. The skull appeared to belong to the skeleton of the woman. Several secondary burials were found in the region of the portico at the W end of the gallery.

Since the primary burial was that of a woman, and the accompanying burials could have been those of her husbands and children, it is possible that the woman was a matriarch. It is not known why her head was buried apart from her body however, nor what rituals took place at the time of her burial.

the descendants of those they planted here. Nearby is Stella's Well.

LARAGH, *An Láithreach:*
The Site, Wicklow **19 T 19**
The village of Laragh is set in wooded country at the confluence of the Glenmacnass and Avonmore Rivers N of the Vale of Clara.

*****LARNE,** *Latharna,* Antrim **7 D 30**
Larne, a port and holiday resort at the narrow mouth of Larne Lough, is the S extremity of the splendid Antrim Coast Road. It is a convenient and popular centre for visiting the famous Glens of Antrim, and offers a passenger ferry service to Island Magee. The shortest steamer crossing between Scotland and Ireland is between here and Stranraer in SW Scotland. The 95ft round tower overlooking the harbour commemorates James Chaine, who founded the crossing. Besides this asset the town has engineering and linen industries. Larne was the centre for a famous gun-running operation in 1914, when Ulster organized to resist home rule being granted to Ireland.

A sickle-shaped promontory known as the Curran curves towards the S from the town. This is the S termination of a raised beach which extends round a great part of the Antrim coast. Ruined, so-called Olderfleet Castle (NM) stands at the end of the promontory. It was built in the 16thc – probably to protect merchandise – and strictly-speaking should be called Curran Castle. During mesolithic times the Curran was an important place for the manufacture of flint implements. So characteristic are these artefacts that the word *Larnian* is used to describe the culture of the period.

LAURAGH, Kerry **26 V 75**
See Kilmakilloge entry.

LAURENCETOWN, *Baile Shíl Anmach:*
Town of the Race of Anmchadh, Galway **16 M 82**
To the NW of this village, off the road which leads to Ballinasloe, are the interesting ruins of Augustinian Clontuskert Abbey. These ruins are mainly survivals of a 15th-c reconstruction. The contemporary west doorway displays fine carving, and the windows near the altar date from the 13thc.

LAYTOWN, *An Inse:*
The Holm, Meath **19 O 17**
This small resort stands at the mouth of the River Nanny and has a long stretch of fine sandy beach which connects it with Bettystown. Fortified Ballygarth Castle, situated 1½m inland beside the river, was built during the Stuart period.

LEA CASTLE, *Caisleán Léighe,*
Laois **18 N 51**
This quadrangular Norman fort is typically Irish and was built by de Vesci c1260. It has a strong, three-storey keep fortified by three-quarter round towers at each corner. After an eventful history the castle was dismantled in 1650 by the parliamentary army. The entrance gateway displays traces of the portcullis.

LEAMANEH CASTLE, *Léim an Eich:*
The Horse's Leap, Clare **15 R 29**
Fine old Leamaneh Castle (NM), also spelt Leamaneagh, lies 2½m NW of Killinaboy. Built by the O Briens c1480, it consists of a five-storey tower which was battered by Cromwell's soldiers. Remains of a large bawn can still be seen. The castle is joined to a four-storey, gabled house which has mullioned windows and dates from the 17thc.

LEAP, *An Léim:* The Leap, Cork **27 W 23**
The River Leap flows through a narrow gorge – ie the 'Leap' – in this picturesque village before entering Glandore harbour. Fine views extend across the river towards the village of Unionhall, and a nearby hill affords a charming panorama of Glandore harbour and the open sea.

LEAP CASTLE, *Léim Uí Bhanáin:*
O Banain's Leap, Offaly **17 S 19**
Remains of this stronghold can be seen

1 Chaine Memorial Tower

2 Olderfleet Castle (Curran Castle)

3 The Curran

Entries marked * are the starting point of drives included in the Day Drive section of the book (pages 79 to 144).

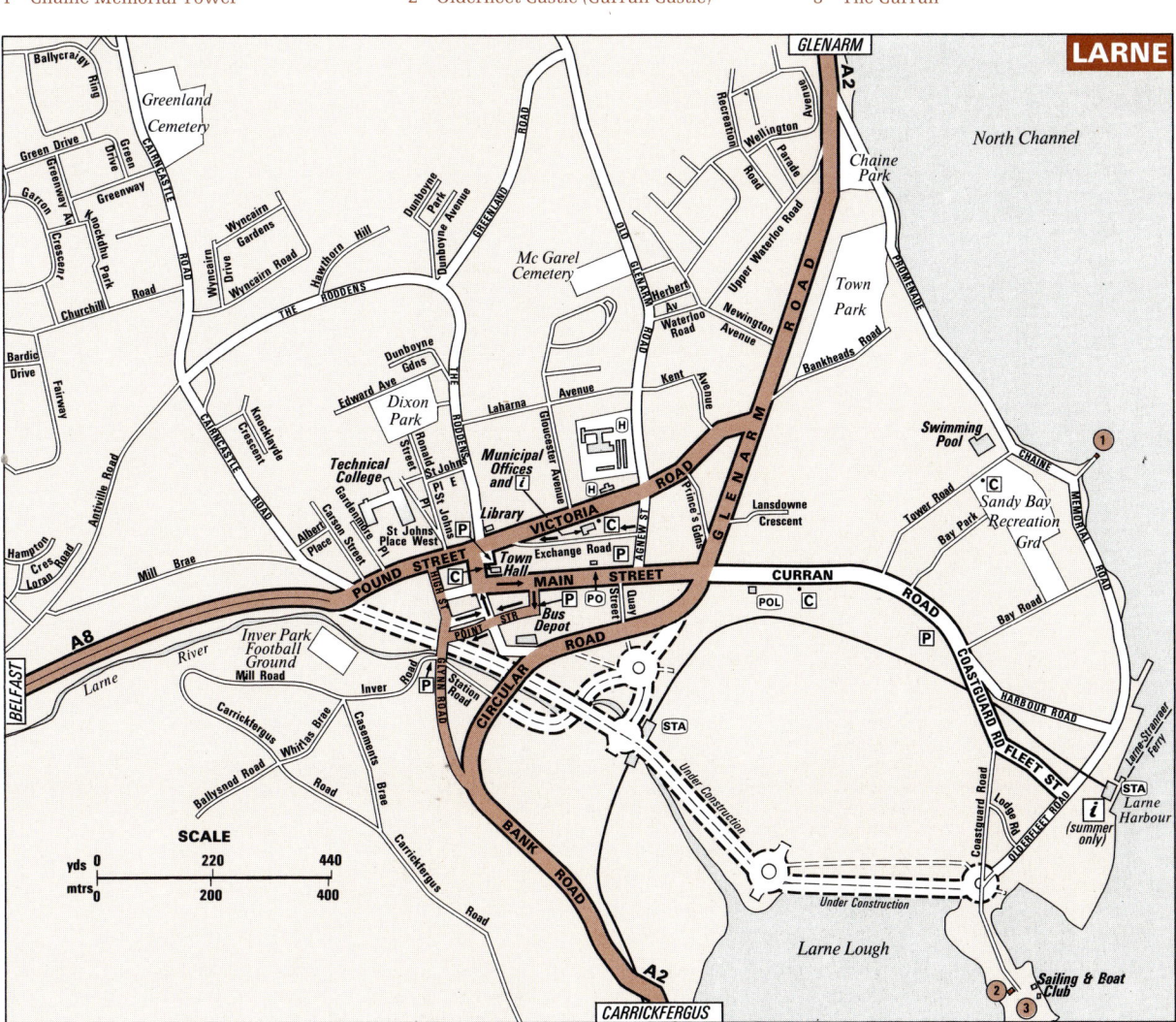

near the main road between Roscrea and Tullamore. This fortress, an O Carroll stronghold, was altered and extended during its long history. It was burnt in 1923, but the fire could not destroy the 9ft-thick walls of the massive tower.

LECARROW, *An Leithcheathrú:*
The Half Quarter, Roscommon **16 M95**
To the E of Lecarrow is the fortified peninsula of Rinndown in Lough Ree. A wall which was built in 1251 stretches across the whole peninsula, forming an enclosure in which a town developed during the 13thc. All that remains of this settlement now are a 13th-c church and a very overgrown castle.

LEENANE, *An Líonan:*
The Shallow Sea-bed, Galway **14 L86**
Leenane is a noted touring, fishing, and shooting centre on the inner reaches of Killary Harbour. It is a convenient base from which to tour Joyce's Country and Connemara, and is situated in an area of glacial moraines and terraces. The latter are rich in mineral specimens. Facilities for boating and bathing exist in the area.

To the S of Leenane are the Maamturk Mountains, while to the E is the splendid viewpoint of 2,131ft Devil's Mother with the Partry range in the background. To the N, across the waters of Killary Harbour, the Mweelrea range and Bengorm rise from Co Mayo to overshadow the picturesque defile sheltering Delphi and Doo Lough. The Westport road runs NE to the head of the inlet, passing close to the Aasleagh Falls and the important River Erriff salmon fishery. A pleasant excursion can be made past Lough Fee and Lough Muck to Salrock, on Little Killary Bay. Salrock has an ancient church, a graveyard, and a holy well to which the local people still come on pilgrimage. Views from the Pass of Salruck extend over Killary Harbour.

LEGANANNY DOLMEN, *Lag an Eanaigh:*
The Hollow of the Marsh **13 J34**
See Ballynahinch entry.

LEIGHLINBRIDGE, *Leithglinn an Droichid:*
The Valley-side of the Bridge, Carlow **24 S66**
Leighlinbridge straddles the River Barrow and was one of the earliest strongholds of the Anglo-Norman Pale – a castle built in 1181 to command an important ford across the river. The remains of Black Castle (NM), on the same site, date from the 14th to 16thc. To the S of the village in the demesne of Burgage House is a large rath known as Dinn Righ, an ancient royal residence of Leinster.

Old Leighlin lies 2m W and had a famous monastery founded in the 7thc. At this time Leighlin Bridge was only important as the site of a ford, but the monastery was the thriving centre of a bishopric until it was joined to Ferns in 1600. More recently it has been joined to Ossory. The cathedral was founded in the 13thc, but 16th-c restoration has left few traces of the original structure. It is a plain building with a nave, no aisles, and a tower. The most notable features are the gothic doorway in the north wall of the chancel, the sedilia, the ancient font, and 16th-c monument slabs with black letters. To the W of the cathedral are an ancient cross and the Well of St Laserain.

LEITRIM, *Liatroim:*
Grey Ridge, Leitrim **10 G90**
Leitrim village is situated in the low country S of Lough Allen and has given its name to the county in which it lies. Scanty remains exist of a castle which belonged to O Rourke, Prince of Breffni. The bishops of Liathdroma once had a residence here.

LEIXLIP, *Léim an Bhradáin:*
The Salmon's Leap, Kildare **19 O03**
Pleasantly set on the N bank of the Liffey, this ancient town stands at the Co Dublin border near the confluence of the Liffey and Rye. This boundary once formed the border between the ancient kingdoms of Leinster and Meath. The castle at Leixlip was erected by Adam Fitzhereford, one of Strongbow's followers in the Anglo-Norman invasion of the 12thc. The present building, the home of the Hon Desmond Guinness, dates mainly from the 18thc but incorporates parts of the original medieval building – including two towers. The parish church (CI) has a medieval west tower which served as a clerical tower house.

At Leixlip the Liffey has been harnessed to a hydro-electric scheme by a dam which has built up a 2m head of water. A fish pass now replaces the old salmon leap which gave the town its name. Farther upriver is a three-arch bridge which is a reconstruction of one built in 1308 by the mayor of Dublin, John le Decer. The old bridge had four arches, but the present structure retains some of the original's characteristics in spite of this difference. Nearby St Wolstan's demesne contains slight remains of the 13th-c Abbey of St Wolstan, which was founded by Fitzhereford.

LEMANAGHAN, *Liath Manacháin:*
St Manchan's Grey Place, Offaly **17 N12**
Remains of a monastery founded by St Manchan can be seen in this parish, including a church, a cell of St Manchan's mother, a holy well, and some inscribed stones. The River Brosna and Grand Canal both flow to the S of Lemanaghan, and St Manchan's shrine is preserved 2½m NNE in Boher Church.

*LETTERKENNY, *Leitir Ceanainn,*
Donegal **5 C11**
Chief town and ecclesiastical capital of Donegal, Letterkenny stands near the head of the River Swilly estuary and boasts one of the longest main streets in Ireland. The spire of its late 19th-c cathedral (RC) stands out silver-grey against the duller stone of other buildings. Close to the cathedral is 19th-c St Eunan's College, a castellated, stone-built boarding school which features a small cloistered courtyard and modern chapel. Some 2m to the W of the town are the scant remains of Conwal monastery.

LEVITSTOWN CROSS ROADS, *Baile Luibhéid:*
Levit's Town, Kildare **24 S78**
Grangemellon Castle, a little to the N of this junction, was the 18th-c home of Col St Leger. St Leger gave his name to the famous English horse race, which was first run in 1776 at Doncaster. The castle is ruined.

LIATHMORE, Tipperary **23 S25**
The district which carries this name boasts the distinctive remains of two old churches (NM's). These ruins, which stand to the E of the Port Laoise to Cashel road, occupy a site on which St Mochoemog founded a monastery in the 17thc. The smaller, older structure features antae, a restored west doorway, and a restored east window. The larger church was begun in the 12thc but was subsequently altered.

LIFFOCK, Derry **6 C73**
Liffock, little more than a crossroads situated 1m inland from Castlerock and the N Derry coast, features the notable Hezlett's House. This is a rare, 17th-c cottage farmhouse with a thatched roof. Until the mid 18thc it was the residence of the clergy of Dunboe parish. Its windows date from the early 19thc.

LIFFORD, *Leifear:*
Side of the Water, Donegal **5 H39**
With Letterkenny this small town is one of the two administrative centres of Co Donegal. It stands on the W bank of the River Foyle and is the twin town of Strabane, which stands on the E bank in Co Tyrone. It received a charter of incorporation in the reign of James I, when Ulster was 'planted', and preserves a number of interesting features. The 17th-c CI church houses a fine monument to Sir Richard Hansard, and the modern RC church is a good structure built 1½m WNW at Murlough in the 1950's. Lifford's mid 18th-c courthouse was designed by Michael Priestley and includes details by William Kent.

LIMAVADY, *Léim an Mhadaidh:*
The Dog's Leap, Derry **6 C62**
A small town beautifully set in the valley of the River Roe, Limavady is surrounded by mountainous horizons; notable Binevenagh rises to 1,260ft above Lough Foyle, Donald's Hill stands at 1,318ft in the SE, and the W skyline is crowded with the mountains of Donegal.

The town is unusual in that it has two main streets. It is associated with the Thackeray poem *Peg of Limavady* (Peg lived in the town's Ballyclare Street), and was the home of 19th-c Miss Jane Ross. Miss Ross made her name by noting down the famous *Londonderry Air* from a passing fiddler. The CI parish church was rebuilt in the 18thc and enlarged in 1881. To the S of Limavady is the Roe Valley Country Park, which includes a number of interesting industrial archaeological sites. One of these is the Roe Mill, which was converted home for the generation of electricity in 1896. This was the first power station of its kind in N Ireland.

About 5½m NE of the town, at Largantees, are a number of standing stones and cairns. One member of the group, the Well Glass Spring Cairn, has a double-chambered grave which yielded the first 'beaker' pottery found in Ireland. Remains of another large cairn exist about 300yds E. Ruins of 13th-c Drumachose Church can be seen 1½m E on the N side of the road to Garvagh. St Cairnech, the patron saint, is said to have been born in this district in the 6thc. Royal Fort (NT), a prehistoric ringfort in an enclosure of trees, lies 1m W of the town. About 1m S at Mullagh is a grass-covered eminence called Daisy Hill. This was where the convention of Drumceatt was held in AD 590, an important occasion attended by King Aedh, St Columbcille from Iona, and a host of minor kings, nobles, poets, and clergy. Several two- and three-chambered tombs (NM) stand 4½m SE near Donald's Hill.

*LIMERICK, *Luimneach,*
Limerick 22 R55

Limerick, the capital of its county and the third largest city in Ireland, is an important manufacturing, market, and communications centre at the head of the Shannon estuary. The town has a small but busy harbour, and Shannon International Airport is just 13m away by road. Originally the site of the city was a bare patch of hilly land on an island – now called King's Island – at the lowest ford on the River Shannon. The town itself was created early in the 10thc by the Norsemen, who used it as a base from which to plunder the surrounding countryside for over a century until the King of Thomond and his brother, Brian Boru, drove them out. After this the Norse were tolerated only as traders, and Limerick became the chief seat of the O Brien kings. King John granted the city a charter in 1197 and ordered the building of a strong castle, plus a Shannon bridge to replace the ford. The castle survives, but the bridge was replaced by the present Thomond Bridge in 1838.

One of the great historical events in the city was its siege by William III. James II had left the French General Lauzun in charge of Irish forces in Limerick, but Lauzun declared that the city walls could be battered down with roasted apples and withdrew to Galway. Responsibility for the organization of defence fell upon the Governor and Patrick Sarsfield. William brought his 26,000 troops before the walls in August of 1690, leaving his artillery to follow from Cashel. Sarsfield took a troop of horse to intercept the convoy at Ballyneety, some miles distant near Cullen, and cut its escort to ribbons. As a result of this action William was forced to abandon the siege at the end of the month. In the following year the accomplished soldier Ginkel commenced a vigorous siege and attempted to enter the town through breaches in the walls. After being foiled he made a determined onslaught across the Shannon on the Thomond Bridge defences, managing to inflict heavy losses on the defenders. By this time Limerick was hard-pressed and waiting for promised relief, but help never came and the city negotiated terms of surrender with Ginkel. The courageous Sarsfield marched out of the city at the

1 Balls Bridge
2 Church of Our Lady of the Rosary (RC)
3 County Courthouse & City Court
4 Custom House
5 Gerald Griffin Memorial School
6 King John's Castle
7 Library, Art Gallery & Museum
8 O Connell Monument
9 O Grady Memorial
10 Old Town Walls
11 St Alphonsus' Church (RC)
12 St John's Cathedral (RC)
13 St John's Church
14 St John's Hospital
15 St Mary's Cathedral (CI) (with Exchange façade in grounds)
16 St Munchin's College (Pery House)
17 Sir Peter Tait Memorial Clock Tower
18 Thomond Bridge
19 Town Hall
20 Treaty Stone

Entries marked * are the starting point of drives included in the Day Drive section of the book (pages 79 to 144).

head of 10,000 Irish troops and embarked for France – the first movement in the exile of native aristocracy known as 'the Flight of the Wild Geese'. The terms of the treaty were not honoured, however, and the Treaty Stone on which the terms are said to have been signed is known as the 'Stone of the Violated Treaty'.

Limerick was still maintained as a walled town for 70 years after the siege, but in 1760 the guns were removed and the fortifications were allowed to decay. With the abandonment of the walls the city quickly expanded S in a welter of fine business streets which criss-crossed the area now known as Newtown Pery. The most important of these thoroughfares is O Connell Street, which runs for almost 1m and terminates with the fine 19th-c O Connell monument by John Hogan in the Crescent, at its W end. Georgian buildings give this area its distinctive character – a personality which is well-represented by Mallow Street. Off Mallow Street, at the E end of Pery Street, is the Victorian Tait's Clock – a tower erected to Sir Peter Tait. Beyond in Baker Street is St Saviour's Dominican Church, which was originally built in 1817 but totally rebuilt after 1860. The Peoples' Park contains the Library, Art Gallery, and Museum. Of particular interest in the museum is the well-known 'nail' or pedestal which once stood in the exchange. The city's merchants used to discharge their debts on this. A monument in the park honours the liberal Protestant landlord Thomas Spring-Rice – Lord Monteagle of Brandon – who devoted himself to justice for the Catholics. Interesting Henry Street features the town house of the Pery family – Earls of Limerick. Pery House now serves as St Munchin's College.

The principal sights of the city are best seen from a short circular walk which starts in O Connell Street. Turn down Sarsfield Street and cross the river via Sarsfield Bridge, then turn right along Clancy's Strand. At the W end of Thomond Bridge is the Treaty Stone, and between Thomond and Sarsfield bridges are the Curragour Falls. King John's Castle, certainly built by the early part of the 13thc, stands on the far bank of the river and includes barracks built in the 18thc. The south-east bastion was built on the site of a former tower, and all the corner towers were lowered to accommodate heavy artillery. Massive drum towers stand at the north and south-west angles, and the ancient gateway penetrates the middle of the north curtain wall. Odd patches of brickwork in the 10ft-thick walls show the extent of the damage inflicted by General Ginkel's artillery in the siege of 1691. On the other side of Thomond Bridge is the old High Town. Fragments of the walls which surrounded the original town can still be seen here, sometimes surviving to a height of almost 40ft. The best sections can be seen N of the top of Castle Street, and near Island Road on the E side of High Town. Pass the castle, at the top of Castle Street, and turn right along the Parade. Continue along Nicholas Street and reach St Mary's CI Cathedral. This was originally a Cistercian foundation built in the form of a cross between 1172 and 1207 by Donal O Brien, King of Munster. The site had been occupied by the king's royal palace. Little of the original structure remains, and the cathedral has been extended by the addition of chantry chapels. One very old feature – which unfortunately fell victim to 19th-c restoration – is the Romanesque west doorway. The fine tower stands 120ft high and has four step turrets. It stands at the western end of the church, and the upper portion was rebuilt after the 1691 siege. Views from the top are excellent. Inside the cathedral are carved misericords which date from the 15thc and feature various grotesque devices. The possession of these makes St Mary's unique among Irish churches. Other notable features include many interesting monuments and a five-light window of the Ascension made by the Harry Clarke studios in 1961. The most ancient of the monuments here date from the 12thc and include the tomb of the founder. The Galway-Bultingford tomb dates from *c*1410 and is a reminder of the city's great merchant princes.

Bridge Street features parts of the old City Courthouse, now incorporated in the Gerald Griffin Memorial School, and the grounds of the Technical Institute preserve the remains of 16th-c Fanning's Castle (NM) – two walls of a merchant's house. Facing the river at the foot of St Augustine's Place is the late 18th-c City Court, a fine building which dates from 1764. The façade of the Exchange, which was built in 1673 by Alderman William York and rebuilt twice in the 18thc, stands in the grounds of St Mary's. The County Courthouse is a handsome 19th-c building designed in classical style by local architects Nicholas and William Hannan. Beyond Rutland Street in Patrick Street is the town hall of 1805, and the fine custom house of 1769 stands off Rutland Street near the S side of Mathew Bridge. The last-mentioned building was designed by the Sardinian architect Davis Ducart.

At the S end of George's Quay is Ball's Bridge, a bottleneck that once connected the old High Town with Irishtown. A 17th-c English writer compared the shape of the two connected, walled towns – linked by a bridge which stood on the site of today's Ball's Bridge – with an hour glass. Cross the Abbey River and continue straight up Broad Street and John Street to reach St John's Church. It was here that the fighting between the city and William III was fiercest. The Black Battery had made a breech in the wall opposite the church's site, but the besiegers were driven away from this vulnerable point time and again. About 200yds E of John Street, and parallel to this thoroughfare, is part of the ancient wall. This turns SW and ends near the citadel close to the end of John Street; the stonework of the angle at which the wall turns shows evidence of battering by artillery. Massive gateways which once formed part of the city's defence system can be seen inside the entrance to St John's Hospital. In Upper Henry Street is 19th-c St Alphonsus Redemptionist Church, which was designed by P C Hardwick of London in the gothick style.

St John's Cathedral (RC) is a handsome gothick building which was designed by Hardwick some time during the mid 19thc. Its graceful spire rises to 280ft, and a number of interesting items preserved in the cathedral treasury includes a 15th-c mitre and silver-gilt crozier. In Ennis Road is the wooden church of Our Lady of the Rosary, which dates from the mid 20thc and contains various modern works of art. Perhaps the most distinguished is the statue of 'Our Lady of Fatima' by Oisin Kelly. Ruins of the small, probably 10th-c Kilrush Church (NM) stand near the Ennis road.

LISBURN, *Lios na gCearrbhach:*
The Ringfort of the Gamblers, Antrim **13 J 26**
Although nowadays a thriving part of the Belfast conurbation, Lisburn maintains its own identity and operates traditional linen manufacture alongside modern industries involved in the production of steel bearings etc. It is the first town on the River Lagan upstream from Belfast. In the early 17thc Lisnagarvey, as it was then known, was colonized by English and Welsh settlers under Viscount Conway. Conway built a strong castle to defend the district, which had been granted to him by Charles I, and this stronghold bore the brunt of a siege in the Rebellion of 1641. Both the castle and the town were destroyed by fire in 1707. Remains of the castle can be seen in Castle Gardens, which were laid out after the fire to cover the area which was enclosed by the structure's walls.

The cathedral in the centre of the town (CI) was raised to its present status by Charles II in recognition of its loyalty. Built in 1623 but now mainly of 19th-c gothick appearance, this is of parish-church size and is crowded by other buildings. The recently-restored interior features a monument to Jeremy Taylor, who was Bishop of Down and Connor in the 1660's. The 19th-c spire was erected at about the same time as the cupola on the otherwise undistinctive town hall near by.

LISCANNOR, *Lios Ceannúir:*
Ceannúr's Ringfort, Clare **21 R 08**
This fishing village stands at the N end of Liscannor Bay and was once a place of strategic naval importance. John P Holland, the inventor of the submarine, was born in a cottage on Castle Street in 1841. Slight remains of an O Conor castle can be seen here, and the medieval parish church of Kilmacreely stands 1m E on the shore. Some 3m NW are the renowned Cliffs of Moher.

LISCARROLL, *Lios Cearúill:*
Cearull's Ringfort, Cork **22 R 41**
Of particular interest here are the ruins of Liscarrol Castle (NM), a 13th-c stronghold which was probably built by the Anglo-Norman Barry family. The remains of this, the third largest castle in Ireland, include a vast towered bawn.

LISCARTAN CASTLE, *Lios Cartáin:*
Cartán's Ringfort, Meath **18 N 86**
Two massive towers are carried by this 15th-c quadrangular stronghold, which stands near the W bank of the River Blackwater 2m NW of Navan. It was the birthplace of the 1st Lord Cadogan. Near by are the ruins of an old church. The 15th-c tower of Rathaldron Castle is incorporated in later Rathaldron House, which stands on the other side of the Blackwater.

LISDOONVARNA, *Lios Dúin Bhearna:*
The Enclosure of the Gap Fort, Clare **15 R 19**
A popular holiday resort and perhaps the best-known spa town in Ireland, Lisdoonvarna is sited on the edge of a strange, contorted landscape known as the Burren. A large-scale junction of limestone and shale is exhibited in a

striking manner in the district. About 3½m N at Pollnagollum is a 6¾m-long cave which is the longest in the country. To the NE are characteristic features of the Burren. Some 8m E is a church of ancient Irish type known as *Teampull Cronan* (NM), which is beautifully situated in a little dell and surrounded by fine old ash trees. The structure has been restored at two or more periods and features a square-headed west doorway with inclined jambs, plus a plain gothic doorway of later date on the north side. Grotesque heads set into the exterior walls probably date from the 12thc. St Cronan's Well rises near by. A round tower known as Doonagore faces Ballaghaline Bay 5m SW, and the 15th-c castle of Ballynalackan occupies a clifftop site 2½m NW. There is a fine bathing beach 4m WSW at Doolin. See entries for the Burren, Kilfenora, and Moher Cliffs.

LISGOOLE ABBEY, *Lios Gabhal:*
Ringfort of Forks, Fermanagh   **11 H24**
The crenellated mansion of Lisgoole Abbey gives no hint of the historic site on which it stands. The original foundation was created here by MacNoelus Mac Kenlif, the King of Ulster, for the Canons Regular of St Augustine in the 12thc. During the 16th-c the Maguire family replaced this order by Franciscans, and it was here that Brother O Clery – chief of the famous Four Masters – sought historical records and wrote the *Book of the Invasions (Leabhar Gabhála)*. After the Dissolution of monasteries the property was acquired by Sir John Davies, who built a castle from the ruins of the church. This stronghold was burnt during the Rebellion of 1641.

LISLAUGHTIN ABBEY, Kerry   **21 R04**
See Ballylongford entry.

LISMORE, *Lios Mór:*
Big Ringfort, Waterford   **29 X09**
Lismore is a charming small town and angling centre situated on the S bank of the River Blackwater, at the foot of the Knockmealdown Mountains. England's King Alfred is traditionally held to have been a student at the monastery founded here by St Carthagh in the 7thc. The town and monastery were repeatedly sacked by Viking raiders, but by the 12thc this foundation had become one of the leading centres of culture and Christianity in Ireland. Henry II visited the town in 1171, and the first permanent castle was erected here soon after in 1185. The castle and estates eventually passed into the hands of Sir Walter Raleigh, who sold it to Richard Boyle – the future Earl of Cork – in 1602. It later passed from the Boyles to the Dukes of Devonshire by marriage. The structure's superb position above the river in

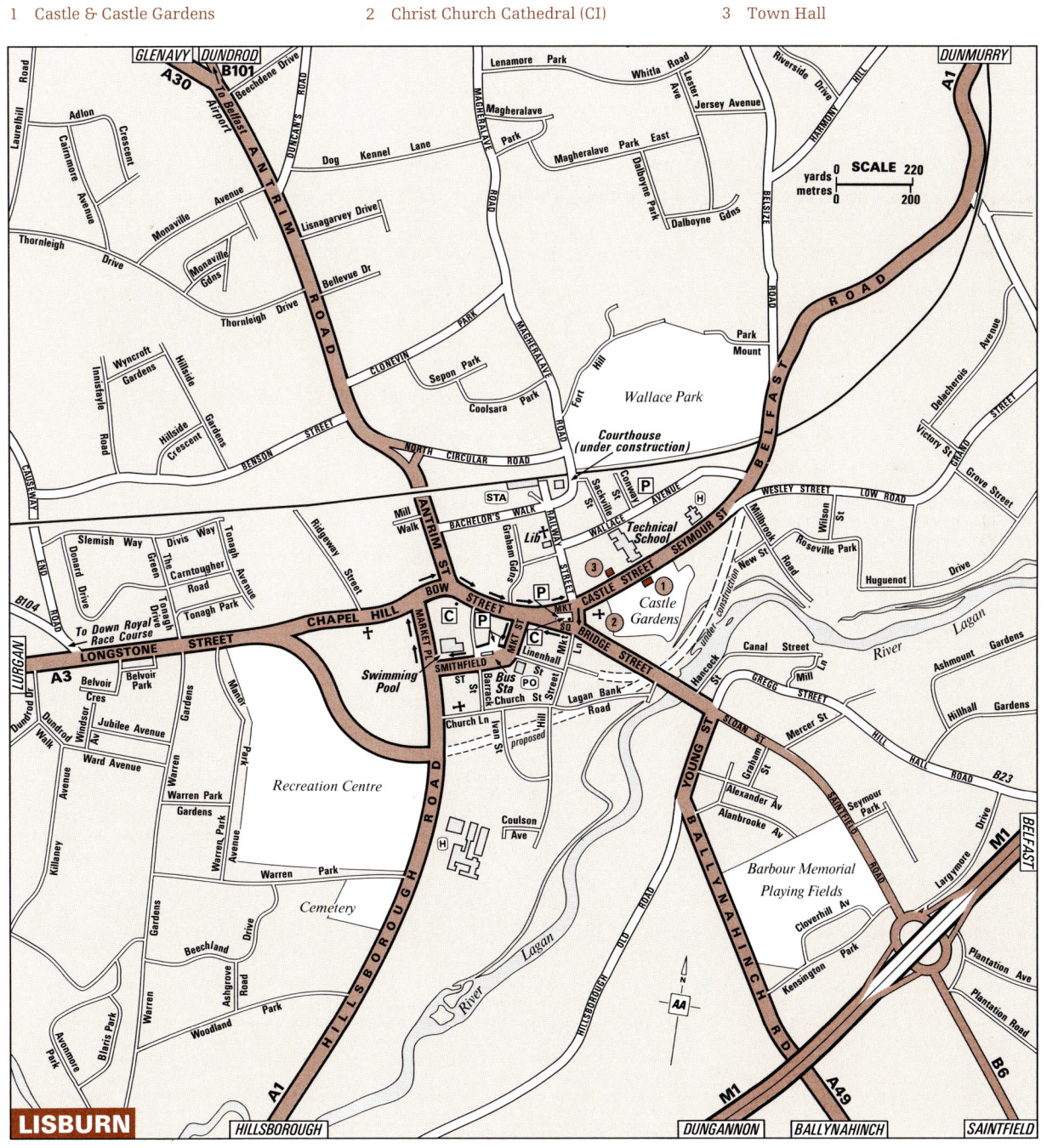

1 Castle & Castle Gardens
2 Christ Church Cathedral (CI)
3 Town Hall

attractive woodland virtually guaranteed its survival. The 6th Duke began to restore the castle in 1811, and further 'restorations' were made for him in gothic style by Sir Joseph Paxton in the 1850's. Much of the building stone was brought over from Derbyshire, and the Romanesque gateway came from a nearby 12th-c church. The famous 15th-c *Book of Lismore* and Lismore Crozier were discovered in the castle walls in 1814.

A stone bridge which spans the Blackwater here was built to a design by Thomas Ivory in 1775. St Carthagh's Cathedral (CI) was restored and rebuilt by the Earl of Cork in 1633, but includes parts of a much older building. The chancel arch and a few of the windows in the south transept probably date from the 12thc, while the slim white-limestone spire is of much more recent, 19th-c origin. Grave slabs dating from between the 9th and 11thc, some bearing Irish inscriptions, have been built into the west wall of the nave. An interesting altar tomb dates from the 16thc. Lismore's RC cathedral is a red sandstone and limestone building which was built in the Romanesque style to designs by the 19th-c architect William Doolin. About 1m E of the town is a flat-topped, conical mound separated from a bailey by a fosse – probably the site of a 12th-c castle. Several miles W on the N bank of the Blackwater are the gothick gates and bridge of Ballysaggarthore, part of a project for which the money ran out before the house could be built.

LISNASKEA, *Lios na Scéithe*:
The Ringfort of the Shield, Fermanagh **11 H33**
As well as featuring several good Georgian houses, this pleasant market town has managed to preserve a number of good public buildings. Unfortunately the handsome stone market house was destroyed by bombing, but the fine 19th-c Cornmarket dates from around the same time. The Cornmarket Cross incorporates the base section of a high cross shaft. Two Tudor-style pavilions attached to the Cornmarket have been reduced to one by demolition. A range of buildings displaying a variety of styles, including Tudor, is known as the Butter Market. Castle Balfour (NM) was built by Sir James Balfour in 1618 as a Plantation stronghold, and was re-fortified in 1652. It was burnt down in the 19thc but has since been partially restored. Also of interest are the ruins of Aghalurcher Church (NM), which stand on the site of an early foundation created by St Ronan.

LISSADELL, *Lios an Daill*:
Ringfort of the Blind Man, Sligo **10 G64**
Constance Gore-Booth – the Countess Markievicz and one of the leaders of Republican forces in the Rising of 1916 – spent her early years in this fine 19th-c house (OACT). Her poetess sister Eva also lived here, and the building is still the property of this family. It is beautifully sited at the edge of Drumcliff Bay, and affords views which extend S to 1,078ft Knocknarea in front of the Ox Mountains. Of interest inside the house are relics of the poet Yeats, who spent a great deal of time here. Near the road is a fort with a souterrain roofed with flags.

LISSOY, *Lios Eo*:
Fort of the Yew-Tree, Westmeath **17 N15**
See Ballymahon entry.

LISTOWEL, *Lios Tuathail*:
Tuathal's Ringfort, Kerry **21 Q93**
Remains of a 13th-c Fitzmaurice castle (NM) in this River Feale market town include two ivy-clad towers and little else. The Fitzmaurice's were Lords of Kerry, and the castle was the last Desmond-family stronghold to fall in the wars of the 16thc. A monorail known as the Lartigue Railway, the only enterprise of its kind ever constructed in Ireland or Great Britain, formerly ran between Listowel and Ballybunion. Gunsborough lies 4m NW of the town and was the birthplace of Earl Kitchener (of Khartoum) in 1850.

LLOYD, TOWER OF, *Mullach Laoide*, Meath **18 N77**
A magnificent view is commanded by this tower, which was built on a 428ft hill 1m W of Ceanannas Mor by the Marquess of Headfort. Many such follies were erected during the famine years, when labour was cheap.

LOHORT CASTLE, *Lubhghort*:
Kitchen Garden, Cork **28 R40**
A fine baronial residence situated 6m NW of Mallow, this castle incorporates parts of a 15th-c fort and was greatly battered during the Cromwellian wars. It was completely restored in 1876.

*LONDONDERRY, *Doire*:
Oak Grove, Derry **5 C41**
Londonderry, the second-largest city in N Ireland, is situated on a hill above the point where the River Foyle begins to broaden before entering Lough Foyle. Formerly an important naval base and garrison town, it is now a successful port and manufacturing centre. The introduction of 'London' into its name marks the granting of the city to a company of London merchants. Previously the name was Doire Columbkille, which recorded that the area had been given to St Columba for the foundation of a religious settlement by Aimire – the Prince of Hy-Neill. The monastery founded here by the saint in the 6thc prospered, but during the period from the 9th to 11thc its wealth attracted the unwelcome attentions of the Norsemen. Eventually they took possession of the place and fortified it, but were driven out during the 12thc. The Anglo-Normans never gained a foothold in Derry, but an English fort was eventually erected here as a base from which to attack powerful Hy-Neill. The fort, and the town which later grew up around it, were constantly under attack from the Irish until both were finally destroyed in 1608. James I then granted the completely ruined town to the Irish Society of London, who immediately set about rebuilding and fortifying it. Their task was finished in 1618 at a cost of £8,000, and the new walls later withstood attacks in 1641, 1649, and 1689 without breaking down. The Jacobite siege of 1688 and 1689 lasted until the boom across the river at present-day Boom Hall was broken – a full 105 days. Boom Hall dates from c1770.

The walls (NM) are in a remarkable state of preservation and are the most complete city fortifications of their type in Ireland or Britain. They measure about 1m in circumference, and were originally pierced by four gates. The Shipquay Gate of 1805 stands at the bottom of Ship Quay Street, near a 19th-c guildhall which was rebuilt in gothick style in 1912. The original design was by J G Ferguson, and the more recent embellishments are highly decorative. Ship Quay Street ascends steeply to the Diamond and is continued by Bishop Street to Bishop Gate, a triumphal arch of 1789 with keystones and panels by the Irish sculptor Edward Smythe. Streets also lead to the Diamond from the Butcher Gate and Ferryquay Gate. The top of the city wall varies in width from 14 to 30ft, and the height of the structure is between 20 and 25ft; it makes an unusual circular walk. The 17th-c cannon Roaring Meg can be seen in the Double Bastion. The Royal Bastion, a little to the N, used to hold a 90ft column erected to the Rev George Walker in 1828. The Rev Walker was governor of Londonderry during the siege of 1689. An old sentry's watch-tower can be seen on the S side of the cathedral. Most of the main shopping and business streets are within the old walls.

St Columb's CI Cathedral was built in the perpendicular architectural style, on the lines of an English parish church, by the Irish Society between 1628 and 1633. The present spire was added in 1822, and major restoration work was conducted in 1887. In 1910 the new chapter house and choir were completed to designs by Sir Thomas Drew, and in 1933 fine new entrance gates were erected in London Street. Eight of the cathedral's 13 bells date from the 17thc, two of which were gifts from James I and five from Charles I. A number of interesting exhibits in the chapter house illustrate the history of the city and the cathedral. The former Bishop's Palace in Bishop Street is said to have been largely rebuilt by Frederick Harvey – 4th Earl of Bristol and the Bishop of Derry – between 1768 and 1803. It now serves as a Masonic Hall.

Londonderry's courthouse is a handsome neo-classical building designed by John Bowden of Dublin. It dates from 1817 and features a pedimented portico. The Deanery, a brick-built Georgian house in the same street, was built in 1833. The Scot's Church in Great James Street was by Stewart Gordon in 1837 and displays a good neo-classical facade with a portico. Outside the walls are: St Eugene's (RC) Cathedral in William Street, a 19th-c design by J J McCarthy; John Bowden's 19th-c Foyle College in Strand Road, part of a college which dates back to the 17thc; the 19th-c Magee University College in Northland Road, by A P Gribbon of Dublin; St Columb's College, a 19th-c structure by Croom and Toye, in Bishop Street. Good terraces and single houses of Georgian and Victorian origin can be found in many parts of the city.

Another interesting feature is the modern bronze of Princess Macha, which stands in front of the 20th-c Altnagelvin Hospital in Dungiven Road and was executed by the Banbridge-born sculptor F E McWilliam. According to legend, Princess Macha was the foundress of the first Irish hospital. The first bridge to span the Foyle here was a wooden structure which replaced the ferry in 1790. The present Craigavon Bridge was constructed in 1933. Some 2½m NE of the city is a crannog on Rough Island, in Lough Enagh. Neolithic and later finds have been made here. St Columba's stone is a 6ft-square block which lies 2m N of Londonderry in the grounds of Belmont demesne. It features the impression of two feet, and is thought to be the inauguration stone of the Tir-Owen chiefs. Close by is Elagh Castle, a one-time stronghold of the O Dohertys.

LONGFIELD HOUSE, *Leamhchoill:* Elm Wood, Tipperary **23 S04**
Overlooking water meadows on the banks of the River Suir, this house was built by a member of the Long family in 1770 and sold to Charles Bianconi in 1846 (OACT). Bianconi was an Italian who came to Ireland just after 1800 and became famous for the nation-wide system of public transport which he developed.

LONGFORD, *An Longfort:* Fortress, Longford **17 N17**
Chief town of its namesake county, Longford was once the site of an O Farrel fortress and a Dominican friary founded by the same powerful family in the 15thc. All traces of both have completely disappeared. Fragments of the Earl of Longford's 17th-c stronghold are incorporated in old military barracks. St Mel's RC Cathedral is a classical-style building which was started in 1840 but not completed until 1893. The nearby Diocesan College houses an interesting collection of local antiquities. A branch of the Royal Canal once terminated at Longford, and the waterway's main channel joined the River Shannon some 5m W at Richmond Harbour – near Cloondara. A fine motte-and-bailey construction known as Lissardowlan can be seen 3½m SE.

LORRHA, *Lothra,* Tipperary **16 M90**
St Ruan founded a monastery here in the 6thc. The oldest surviving remains of this foundation are fragments of two high crosses, which can be seen in the Protestant churchyard. The church itself is thought to occupy the old monastic site, and is noted for a 13th-c doorway in which a 15th-c doorway has been inserted. To the NW of the church are the remains of 15th-c St Ruan's 'Abbey'

1 Altnagelvin Hospital & Princess Macha Statue
2 Apprentice Boy's Hall
3 Bishop Gate
4 Bishop's Palace (now the Masonic Hall)
5 Boom Hall
6 Butcher Gate
7 Craigavon Bridge
8 Courthouse
9 Deanery
10 Ferryquay Gate
11 Foyle College
12 Guildhall
13 Magee University College
14 St Columb's Cathedral (CI)
15 St Columb's College
16 St Columba's Stone
17 St Eugene's Cathedral (RC)
18 Scots' Church
19 Shipquay Gate
20 Town Walls (Double Bastion)
21 Town Walls (Royal Bastion)

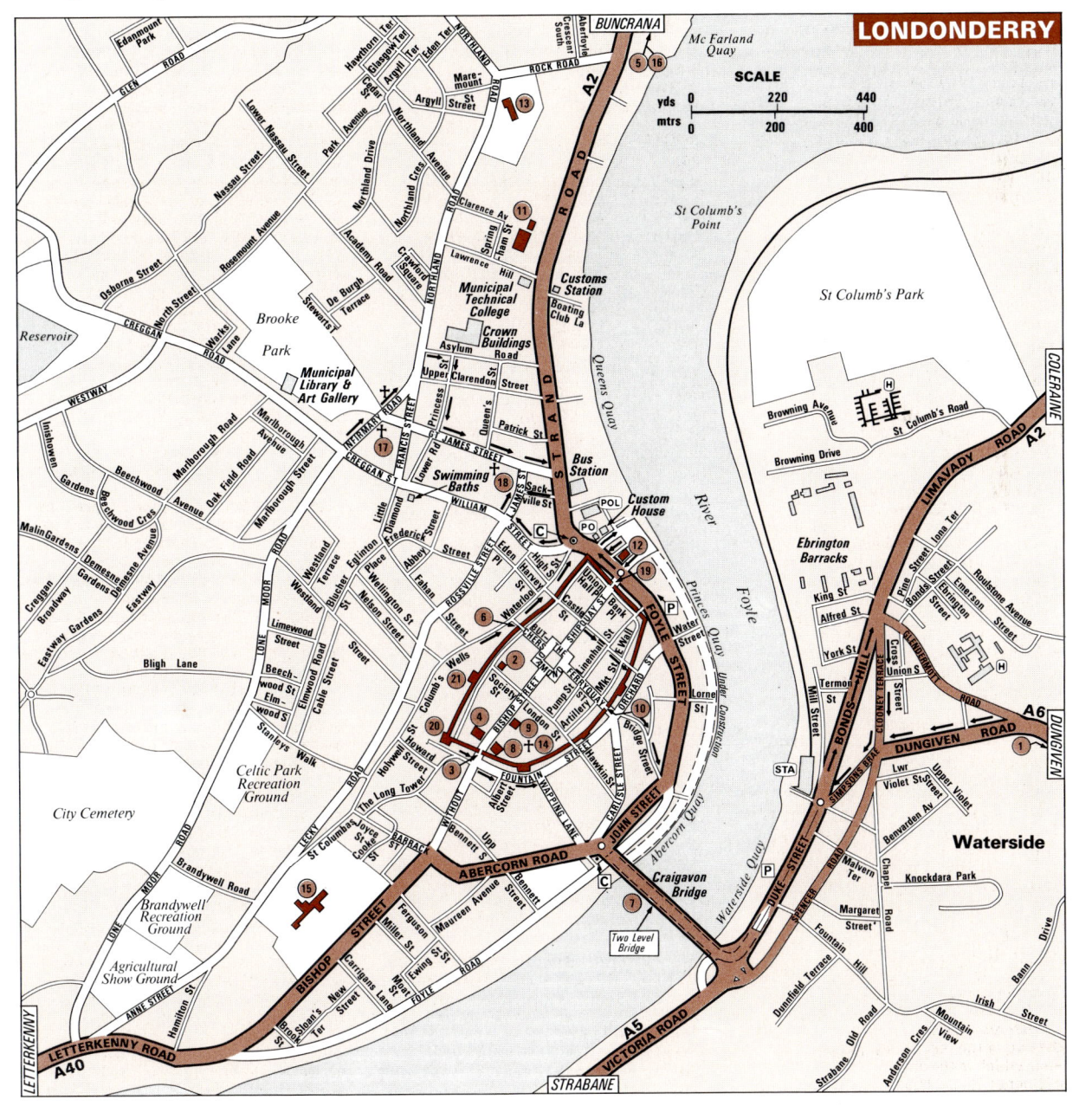

(NM). Remains of a Dominican priory founded by Sir Walter de Burgo c1269 can be seen SW of the village. Carvings from the priory are preserved in the nearby Catholic Church.

LOUGH CONN, *Loch Con:*
Hound Lake, Mayo **9 G11**
Anglers all over Europe know Lough Conn as the place where an unverified record pike of 53lbs weight was caught on rod and line in 1920. It is said that a 10lb salmon was removed from the pike's gullet before it was weighed.

LOUGH CORRIB, *Loch Coirb,*
Galway and Mayo **15 M14**
Measuring some 27m long, this beautiful lake features a picturesquely irregular shoreline and extends from the Corrib River at Galway to the edge of mountainous Joyce's Country. Fine views from the lake extend NW towards the wild Connemara heights, and its shores and islands are rich in ancient remains. One small islet is almost totally covered by the remains of Hen's Castle, or Castle Kirke. This stronghold was erected c1200 by the sons of Rory O Conor, the last King of Ireland. The N shores of the lough feature a number of interesting caves eroded by the constant passage of running water.

LOUGHCREW MEGALITHIC CEMETERY,
Meath **18 N57**
See Oldcastle entry.

LOUGHCUTRA CASTLE, *Loch Cútra:*
Cútra's Lake, Galway **16 R49**
Situated on the shores of an attractive lake dotted with wooded islands, this 19th-c castle (OACT) was built to designs by John Nash and Charles Vereker. Vereker later became Viscount Gort. In recent years the castle has been painstakingly and tastefully restored.

LOUGH DERG, *Loch Deirgeirt:*
Lake of the Red Hole, Clare, Galway, Tipperary **22 R78**
This, the largest of the lakes formed by the River Shannon, measures 25m long and contains numerous small islands. Its surroundings are interesting and varied, particularly around the SW end, and its waters are famed for their fish. Lough Derg is now harnessed in the Shannon Hydro-electric scheme, but this has neither affected its beauty nor its angling prospects.

LOUGH DERG, *Loch Dearg,*
Donegal **5/11 H07**
See St Patrick's Purgatory entry.

LOUGH ERNE, Fermanagh **11 H23**
See entry for Erne, Lough.

LOUGH GILL, *Loch Gile:*
Lake of Brightness, Leitrim, Sligo **10 G73**
Beautiful Lough Gill is a small lake in a wooded setting, sheltered by ranges of hills on its N side. It is considered to be among the loveliest of all Irish lakes. At its W end is Cairns Hill, which features numerous prehistoric remains. Church Island is the largest island in the lake and features remains of a medieval church (NM). Innisfree, the most famous island in the lake, lies near the SE shore and was celebrated in W B Yeats' poem the *Lake Isle of Innisfree*. Further old church remains can be seen towards the SW end of the lake on Cottage Island, near which is the shore-bound viewpoint of Dooney Rock. The rock was also made famous by Yeats, this time in his poem *The Fiddler of Dooney*. Hazelwood demesne lies near the W end of the lake and includes an 18th-c house which was designed by Richard Cassels, the German architect who worked in Ireland from 1728 until his death in 1751. Early 17th-c Parke's Castle stands near the NE corner of the lake and features a large bawn with two round flanking towers.

LOUGH GUR, *Loch Goir,*
Limerick **22 R64**
Lough Gur is a small lake which lies among low limestone hills and is where – according to legend – the last of the Earls of Desmond sleeps. Many antiquities came to light when the lake was drained during the 19th-c, and it is these relics which have supplied most of the information held on neolithic and bronze-age man in Ireland (see gazetteer inset opposite). Later monuments in the area include a 16th-c tower house known as Bourchier's Castle, 13th-c Black Castle, and a ruined 17th-c church.

LOUGHINISLAND, *Loch an Oileáin:*
Island Lake, Down **13 J44**
This typical Co Down lake nestles among glacial drumlins and is noted for the picturesque ruined churches (NM) which exist on one of its islands. The island, which is approached via a causeway, is sheltered by Scot's pines. The oldest remains lie in the middle of the island and may be of a 13th-c structure. The North Church, which probably dates from the 15th or 16thc, was dismantled in 1720 so that its materials could be used in the construction of a church at Seaforde. The smallest church is Phelim MacCartan's Chapel, which is situated on the S side of the island and bears the inscription 'PMC 1636'. A carved mask can be seen in its west gable.

LOUGH MASK, *Loch Measca,*
Galway, Mayo **15 M16**
An underground river links this fine fishing lake with the much larger Lough Corrib via a series of limestone caves. A canal cut across the surface of the limestone during the Great Famine dried out as soon as it was flooded, due to the porosity of the rock. Interesting remains of an old church can be seen on Inishmaan Island (see entry), and a house on the E shores of the lough was once the home of the unfortunate Captain Boycott. The captain's treatment of local people was not calculated to earn respect, and their treatment of him has given the English language an extra word. It is said that even the postman refused to deliver letters bearing his name. Lough Mask Castle is a late 15th-c structure which was altered in 1618.

LOUGHMOE CASTLE, *Leachma,*
Tipperary **23 S16**
The Purcell family, one of whom was a Jacobite signatory to the Treaty of Limerick in 1691, were formerly the owners of this ruined, castellated mansion. The castle dates from two periods. The rectangular tower at the south end dates from the 15thc and is vaulted on both the ground and first floors. Armorials and initials can be seen in the first-floor room, and there is a little prison chamber high in the south-east corner. Mullioned and transomed windows are displayed by the rest of the building, which dates from the 17thc. Purcell monuments can be seen in ruined Loughmoe Church.

LOUGH NEAGH, *Loch nEathach:*
Eocha's Lake, Antrim, Armagh, Derry, Down, Tyrone **7/13 J07**
Although the largest lake in Ireland and Britain, Lough Neagh is surrounded by relatively flat countryside and thus lacks the picturesque qualities of many smaller waters. The Upper Bann River enters the lake from the S, and the Lower Bann drains it N to the Atlantic Ocean. At one time the Lagan Canal linked Neagh with Belfast Lough. The 40ft-high remains of a round tower exist on Ram's Island, and in the SW corner of the lough is Coney Island (NT) – associated with St Patrick and the O Neill family. Lough Neagh is currently used to supplement the water supply of the Greater Belfast area, and is being developed for recreational use. Yacht clubs exist at Oxford Island and Antrim. Pleasant walking country borders the lough at both ends, and the shores are rich in wildlife. A wildfowl refuge exists in the NE section. Nature reserves have been instituted in the Shane's Castle estate (see entry), Randresham Forest, and on the W side of Longford Island.

LOUGHREA, *Baile Locha Riach:*
The Red Lough, Galway
Situated on the N bank of the crannog-rich lough from which it derives its name, this small market town includes sparse remains of a 14th-c Carmelite friary and the 19th-c RC Cathedral of St Brendan by William Byrne. Although the exterior of this building is a little dull, the interior displays rich glass by Sarah Purser, Michael Healy, Evie Hone, A E Childe, and many other early 20th-c notables from the Dublin school. The famous La Tène Turoe Stone is situated 4m NNE of the town (see gazetteer inset on page 282), and 1½m ESE is a megalithic structure known as the Seven Monuments (NM). This comprises a circle of seven stones set into a low circular bank near the remains of a square chamber tomb. Close by are the two ringforts of Rathsonny and Rahannagroagh (NM's).

LOUGHREE, *Loch Rí,*
Longford, Westmeath, Roscommon **17 N05**
One of the three large loughs formed by the River Shannon, this lake lies to the N of Athlone and is famous for the ancient remains preserved on its many islands. Ruins of a monastery founded by St Ciaran, before he created the important centre at Clonmacnoise, can be seen in the SE corner of the lough on Hare Island. The church has become the mausoleum of the Dillon family. Inchbofin (see entry), also features important monastic remains, and the peninsula of Rinndown shows several periods of fortification. St Diarmaid founded a monastery on Inchcleraun in the 6thc; surviving remains include an enclosure with a Romanesque gateway, and the ruins of five churches (NM's). The tiny oratory of *Teampull Diarmada*, which includes antae, is probably the oldest of the group. Nearby *Teampull Mor* has 15th-c additions but probably originated in the 13thc. Of the remaining structures, the most interesting is the square-towered Belfry Church. This and nearby Maeve's Solar, a cashel associated with the legendary Queen Maeve of Connacht, are sited on the highest point of the island.

LOUGH SWILLY, *Loch Súilí,*
Donegal **5 C23**
Characteristic Donegal scenery of sandy
cont on page 250

LOUGH GUR

Attractive Lough Gur in Co Limerick is remarkably rich in ancient monuments. So rich, in fact, that much of what is known of Irish prehistory – especially of the neolithic period – has been learned from finds made in this area. These finds show the remarkable continuity of man's settlement here from c3,000BC up until very recent times. The area would have been chosen for settlement by neolithic man because of its fertile, lime-rich soil, recognised by the flora typical of such regions.

During drainage operations, which eventually reduced the lough to its present size, several crannogs (or lake dwellings) were brought to light, as well as numerous objects which had probably been thrown into the waters as votive offerings. The most impressive monument, however, is undoubtedly the stone circle in Grange townland (marked 1 on the map). Its 150ft diameter makes it the largest in Ireland, and it includes an earthen bank. Some of the stones, which are placed edge to edge, are very large – the biggest having a total length of 14ft, over 5ft of which is sunk into the ground. The interior of the circle was built up with clay, partly to hide the packing stones around the base of the uprights, and partly to give a level surface. This layer of clay has yielded substantial amounts of pottery as well as flints, stone axes, and some bronze. The pottery belongs to the beaker type, which means that the circle can be dated to the early bronze age. In the vicinity of the Grange circle are several other circles, or remains of circles, two of which are marked on the map (4 and 5).

Bolin Island (6 on the map), in the NE corner of the lough, is a crannog whose foundations and surrounds were built of stone. The surface of Garret Island (7 on map) was artificially raised, also with stone, to make it suitable for habitation. Immediately above the NE shore of the lough is a group of hut sites (18 on map). The distinctive way in which these are joined together has given them the name 'The Spectacles'. The huts date back to early-Christian times, and have an associated system of small fields. The peninsula of Knockadoon has several habitation sites (16 and 17 on the map) which, according to the finds made in them, were inhabited in neolithic times. Some of the huts are square in plan, some round, and all were built of timber upon a foundation of stone.

Of the many tombs in the area perhaps the most interesting is the wedge-shaped gallery grave (11 on the map) near the SE corner of the lough. The grave, which consists of a slab-roofed gallery with a small separate chamber at the end, was found upon excavation to contain parts of twelve inhumations and traces of cremations. Pottery of various styles was also found. Among other interesting sites are the two stone forts built in a prominent position on 400ft Carraigh Aille Hill. These are respectively known as Carraigh Aille I (13 on map) and Carraigh Aille II (14 on map). Both sites yielded large quantities of objects on excavation – including several tons of animal bones – which have enabled archaeologists to date the forts to between the 8th- and 10thc AD.

1 Grange Stone Circle
2 Stone Circle
3 Stone Circle
4 Stone Circle
5 Remains of Stone Circle
6 Bolin Island Crannog
7 Garret Island Crannog
8 Crannog
9 Standing Stone
10 Standing Stone
11 Gallery Grave
12 Burial Mound
13 Stone Fort
14 Stone Fort
15 Ring Fort
16 Habitation Site
17 Habitation Site
18 Habitation Site

beaches and coves, rocky shores and fine cliffs, surrounds this large sea lough. It extends for over 25m between the rugged Inishowen Peninsula and the smaller Fanad Peninsula in the W. During the Insurrection of 1798 a French Warship which arrived here discharged Wolfe Tone with 300 French troops to aid the United Irishmen.

LOUTH, *Lú,* Louth **12 H90**
Although Louth gave its name to the county in which it stands, it is now little more than a village. St Mochta, a disciple of St Patrick, founded a monastery here in the 6thc. The small stone church known as St Mochta's House (NM) dates from the 12th or 13thc and is a single cell with a croft in the roof. Little remains of 14th- or 15th-c Louth Abbey except wall fragments of the long, narrow church. The abbey was of the Dominican Order. About 2½m N of Louth is the motte-and-bailey construction of Castlering, and a fine pillar stone (NM) can be seen 2m NE at Cloghafarmore.

LUCAN, *Leamhcán:*
Place of Elms, Dublin **19 O03**
Once a famous spa, this small town is situated in a beautiful stretch of the Liffey Valley where the river is spanned by a bridge ascribed to the well-known engineer, Isambard Brunel. Immediately W is the demesne of Lucan House, a fine building which was rebuilt by Agmondisham Vesey in 1771 and contains fine plasterwork by Michael Stapleton and Angelica Kaufmann. Remains of 16th-c Sarsfield Castle lie SE of the house, and Canon Brook was once the residence of architect James Gandon from Dublin. Luttrelstown Castle, a 19th-c castellated mansion which incorporates parts of a medieval castle, lies 2m NNE.

LUGNAQUILLA, *Log na Coille:*
Hollow of the Wood, Wicklow **25 T09**
The 3,039ft peak which bears this name is the highest summit of the Wicklow Mountains, and affords extensive views.

LURGAN, *An Lorgain:*
The Strip of Land, Armagh **13 J05**
In itself a town of some size and a centre of the linen industry, Lurgan has been linked to the considerable town of Portadown as a move towards the creation of Craigavon New Town. Christ Church is a large CI parish church sited in the centre of the town, dating partly from 1725 and partly from the 19thc. A section of the spire is the only surviving fragment of the original building. The town's broad main street was laid out towards the end of the 17thc. The 19th-c Brownlow House was designed by Edinburgh architect William Playfair, and Lurgan's attractive public park was landscaped in the 18thc. An interesting feature of the park is the grave of the racing greyhound Master McGrath; this animal won the Waterloo Cup in the years 1868, 1869, and 1871. George Russell the journalist, poet, and painter was born and reared in Lurgan.

LUSK, *Lusca:* Cave, Dublin **19 O25**
An abbey founded close to the coast here by Bishop MacCulin in the 5thc suffered many Viking raids, but still developed into a sophisticated foundation. The only part of the early monastery still to be seen is the 95ft, 9th-c round tower (NM), which has a medieval church tower standing next to it. The church, however, has long gone. Two tombs which originally stood in the chancel of the church can now be seen in the tower. Both date from the 16thc and carry interesting carved effigies. The present parish church (CI) dates from c1840 and occupies part of the monastic site. The local Catholic church features four windows by Harry Clarke.

LYONS, Kildare **18 N92**
Lyons Hill was an early royal seat and assembly place for the kingdom of Leinster. The demesne of which it now forms a part belongs to 18th-c Lyons House, which was extended by the addition of wings in the 19thc by Lord Cloncurry. Features of the interior include fine ceilings and murals by Gaspare Gabrielli, who was brought here from Rome in 1805. The house now serves as an agricultural college.

MACGILLYCUDDY'S REEKS,
Na Cruacha Dubha: The Black Peaks, Kerry **26 V88**
The highest summits in Ireland rise from this range, including 3,414ft Carrantuohill, 3,314ft Beenkeragh, and 3,200ft Caher. Several attractive corries can be seen both E and W of the first two summits, and the views from all the mountains are magnificent.

MACROOM, *Maigh Chromtha:*
Sloping Plain, Cork **27 W37**
Macroom is a market town beautifully sited on the River Sullane before its confluence with the Lee, a little way S. George Richard Pain of Cork designed the local CI church, and Macroom Castle is thought to have first been built in the reign of King John. The present ruins include a large, quadrangular keep and date from the 15thc. Restoration was conducted in the 19thc, but the structure was burnt down in 1922. Tradition has it that William Penn, the founder of Pennsylvania, was born in the castle after it had been granted to Admiral Sir William Penn by Cromwell in 1654.

MAGH ADAIR, *Maigh Adhair:*
The Plain of Adhar, Clare **22 R47**
This site is on the Tulla to Quin road and is said to have been the inauguration place of the Kings of Thomond. The main mound is surrounded by a fosse and external bank, and various associated earthworks can be seen in the district.

MAGHERA, *Machaire Rátha:*
Plain of the Ringfort, Derry **6 C80**
A small town with a venerable ecclesiastical history, Maghera boasts an old church (NM) dedicated to 6th-c St Lurach. This building is particularly noted for its remarkable square-headed doorway, which features inclined jambs beautifully carved with interlacing designs and a crucifixion scene. It is thought that the doorway, unfortunately now obscured by a later tower, dates from the 11thc. Charles Thompson, author of the American Declaration of Independence in 1776, was born in the town. Dunglady Ringfort lies 4m NE and is one of the largest, best-preserved earthen forts extant in the N of Ireland.

MAGHERA, *Machaire Rátha:*
Plain of the Ringfort, Down **13 J33**
A short distance to the S of this village are the remains of a medieval church, plus the stump of a round tower which was blown down c1714 (NM's).

MAGHERAFELT, *Machaire Fíolta:*
The Plain of Fíolta's House, Derry **6 H89**
A typical settler's town which has retained its original Irish name, Magherafelt was granted to the Salters' Company by the settlement of James I.

MAGILLIGAN, *Aird Mhic Giollagáin:*
MacGilligan's Point, Derry **6 C63**
Splendid Magilligan Strand is said to be the finest in Ireland and stretches 6m from Downhill to the narrows of Lough Foyle – facing Greencastle in Co Donegal. A Martello tower can be seen at Magilligan's Point, while about 2¾m SSE is a base-line tower used for the Ordnance Survey of Ireland. The strand constitutes the N boundary of the N Derry area of outstanding natural beauty.

MALAHIDE, *Mullach Ide,* Dublin **19 O24**
This small seaside town lies on the N side of the Broad Meadow Water estuary some 9m N of Dublin. Malahide Castle and demesne, SW of the resort, came into the possession of the Talbot family during the reign of Henry II. The castle is one of the oldest dwellings in the country and includes a multitude of styles. Parts are medieval, many portions are Georgian, and much of the old work was restored in the 19thc. To the E of the castle are the 15th- or 16th-c ruins of a chapel known as 'The Abbey'. This features fine windows and the altar tomb of Maud Plunkett. An old watchtower rises from beside the road to Portmarnock.

MALIN and MALIN HEAD, *Málainn,* Donegal **5 C44–35**
Cliffs rising to over 200ft guard Malin Head, Ireland's most northerly point. Farther to the SE, between Mailin Head and Glengad Head, the cliffs rise up to a magnificent 800ft above the sea. Malin Hall, a handsome Georgian house of 1758, stands to the N of Malin village.

MALIN MORE, *Málainn Mhóir:*
Big Malin, Donegal **4 G48**
Malin More is a remote little resort which boasts a fine strand and lies within easy reach of good cliff scenery between Glen and Malin bays. Silver Strand can only be reached by foot and is considered one of the loveliest in Ireland. To the S of the resort at Cloghanmore is an interesting wedge-shaped court grave (NM). This has a full court to the east, and there are associated graves in a long cairn to the west. Also of interest is a local site known as Dermot and Grania's Bed, where a group of six chambered graves are arranged in a straight line running east to west for a distance of 100yds. The massive west grave has pillars measuring over 10ft high, and two capstones. Rathlin O Birne Island lies 1½m off the coast near Malin More and carries a lighthouse. Older features include an early church, penitential stations, and a holy well.

***MALLOW,** *Mala:*
The Plain of the Rock, Cork **28 W59**
Situated in the beautifully wooded valley of the River Blackwater, Mallow is an important market and communications centre with the manufacture of sugar as one of its main industries. In the 18th and early 19thc it was a fashionable spa, and some of the associated buildings can still be seen. Good 18th-c houses can also be seen in many parts of the town. At the SE end of Mallow are the ruins of a

fortress (NM) built c1600 by Sir Thomas Norreys.

MANORHAMILTON, *Cluainín*:
Little Meadow, Leitrim **10 G83**
Charles I granted this town to Sir Frederick Hamilton, which explains the difference between its ancient and modern names. The remains of Hamilton's 17th-c fortified house can be seen 1m NE at Skreen.

MARKETHILL, *Cnoc an Mhargaidh*:
Hill of the Market, Armagh **12 H93**
Close to the 17th-c Plantation castle around which this town grew is Gosford Castle, the first Norman-revival castle to be built in Ireland or Britain. Thomas Hopper designed this edifice for the 2nd Earl of Gosford in 1820, and famous Dean Swift made several visits here after the death of his Stella. The Dean's Walk, Chair, and Well are still pointed out in the grounds of the house, which now form part of Gosford Forest Park.

MASHANAGLASS CASTLE, *Maigh Seanghlaise*:
Old Stream Plain, Cork **27 W37**
A single tower of this 16th-c MacSwiney stronghold has survived 2¾m SE of Macroom.

MAYGLASS CHURCH, *Maigh Ghlas*:
Green Plain, Wexford **25 T01**
Ruins of this church, which was burnt down in 1798, show interesting Norman arches. See also the entries for Tomhaggard, and Bargy and Forth.

MAYNOOTH, *Maigh Nuad*:
Nua's Plain, Kildare **18 N93**
Maynooth's main interest is in its ancient associations with the great and powerful Geraldine family, and its present-day training of RC clergy. The castle (NM) of the Earls of Kildare has a two-storey keep which probably dates from the 13thc. The keep was enlarged in the 15thc, when it also acquired towers, but was dismantled in 1647. The gatehouse is of interest. St Patrick's College stands on the site of an earlier foundation created by the 9th Earl of Kildare in the 16thc, and was instituted by the English in 1795 so that Irish priests need not go abroad for their education. It is now a recognised college of the National University of Ireland, and the greatest Catholic seminary in Ireland or Britain. The earlier of its two large quadrangles is in Renaissance style, and the later is a gothick design by the 19th-c British architect A W Pugin. College Chapel, begun by J J McCarthy and finished by his pupil William Hague, was started in 1875. Also of interest here is a small museum with a collection of antiquities and works of art.

Carton (OACT), a magnificent house which belonged to the Dukes of Leinster, stands in its demesne at the E end of the village street. The house was remodelled by Richard Cassels c1739 for the 19th Earl of Kildare, and the magnificent Saloon features superb plasterwork by the Francini brothers. During the 18thc the demesne was landscaped, which involved fishponds being formed into a lake and the building of a fine bridge by Thomas Ivory. Parts of the house were remodelled for the 3rd Duke of Leinster by Richard Morrison in 1815. A stone table which stands in the grounds and carries the date 1553 once stood in the Council House of the castle. The Shell House and Dairy date from c1770. About 3m SE is Conolly's Folly, which was built by the widow of Speaker Conolly of Castletown to give employment during the hard times of 1740. There is some indication that it may have been designed by Cassels. Slight remains of an early monastery exist 2m ESE at Donaghmore.

MAYO, *Maigh Eo*:
Plain of the Yew Trees, Mayo **15 M27**
Ruins of an abbey which was founded by St Colman in the 7thc can be seen near this village, which itself lies 2½m SE of Eyrecourt. The foundation was once famed throughout Europe as a centre of learning.

MEELICK, *Míleac*:
Place Beside Water, Galway **16 M91**
The RC church here stands on a hill above the Shannon and features considerable remains of its original medieval fabric. It was the church of a friary founded in the early 15thc by Breasil O Madden, and was used by the Franciscan Order. Close by is the site of a 13th-c motte castle.

MELLIFONT ABBEY, *An Mhainistir Mhór*:
The Big Monastery, Louth **19 O07**
Remains of this abbey (NM) which was founded in 1142 as the first Cistercian abbey in Ireland, lie in a secluded valley on the banks of the Mattock River. The one-time Archbishop of Armagh – Malachy O Morgair – had once been a monk and was very impressed with the life-style of monks at Clairvaux, which was presided over by his friend St Bernard. He sent several of his own novices there so that they could become familiar with the life of Clairvaux and, on returning to Ireland, form the nucleus of a similar community. This was the birth of Mellifont, and even the riverside site was selected because of its similarity with the other foundation. The abbey church was consecrated in 1157.

The Cistercian Order spread quickly from Mellifont and occupied new abbeys at Bective, Boyle, Monasteranenagh, Baltinglass, and Shrule. The 'home' abbey was suppressed in 1539 and came into the possession of Edward Moore, an ancestor of the Earls of Drogheda. From him it passed to the Balfours of Townley Hall. Features of the site include sparse remains of the 12th-c abbey church, a reconstructed fragment of a 12th-c cloister, and the well-preserved Chapter House and Lavabo. The Chapter House dates from the 14thc and comprises two storeys topped by a beautiful groined roof. The west end has vanished. Four sides of the 13th-c octagonal Lavabo have survived, and the corbels for supporting the roof can be seen. These ruins comprise a series of round-headed arches which spring from foliage-ornamented capitals. To the N of the abbey are the square towers of the gatehouse, and a hill to the NE carries the remains of a small 15th-c church. This was used as the parish church after the Dissolution.

MERRION, *Muirfín*, Dublin **19 O13**
Mount Merrion Estate, formerly the property of the Earls of Pembroke, lies to the S of Merrion. The local castle was once the seat of the Fitzwilliam family.

MIDLETON, *Mainistir na Corann*:
Monastery of the Weir, Cork **28 W87**
Situated at the head of the Owenacurra estuary, this small market town was founded by the Brodrick family – later the Earls of Midleton – c1670. The local abbey is much older and was founded at the end of the 12thc. Features include a good 18th-c market house in the main street, a CI church designed by the brothers Pain in the 19thc, and the long-established Midleton College. The latter, founded as a free grammar school in 1696, was attended by the Irish statesman and orator John Philpot Curran. Limestone caves can be seen ¼m NE at Fox's Quarry, and the remains of 15th-c Cahermone Castle lie 1m ENE.

MILFORD, *Baile na nGallóglach*:
The Homestead of the Galloglasses, Donegal **5 C12**
Surrounded by splendid scenery near the head of Mulroy Bay, this little fishing village and resort boasts an interesting modern church (RC) and is within easy reach of numerous antiquities. Among the latter are examples of dolmens and megalithic tombs. Lough Fern lies to the S and is well known to anglers, while the attractive waterfalls of Bunlin Glen can be seen NW of the village.

MILLISLE, *Oileán an Mhuilinn*:
The Island of the Mill, Down **7 J57**
Inland from this small Ards Peninsula resort is the Ballycopeland Windmill (NM; OACT), the only complete windmill in Co Down and one of the few existing in Ireland. It dates from c1784, ceased working in 1915, and was restored in 1958 and 1959. The internal working parts are made of wood.

The Conolly Folly at Maynooth was commissioned by the widow of Speaker Conolly to provide work for the local unemployed in 1740.

MILLTOWN MALBAY, *Sráid na Cathrach:*
The Village of the Stonefort,
Clare 21 R07
Many visitors are attracted to the sandy beaches and picturesque surroundings of this town. Nearby Spanish Point, which overlooks Mal Bay, is particularly popular. There is also excellent bathing from the Silver Strand of Freagh, which lies 2m N and features the ruins of an O Brien Castle. At least six Spanish Armada vessels were lost, with thousands of lives, off this coast in September 1588. Many of the victims were buried at Spanish Point. A turf-burning power station operates in the town. About 5½m SE of Milltown Malbay, on the slopes of 1,284ft Slieve Callan, is a fine megalithic tomb which includes a 12 by 4ft capstone.

MITCHELSTOWN, *Baile Mhistéalai:*
Mitchel's Homestead, Cork 22 R81
Mitchelstown is an important farming and market town set at the foot of the Galtee Mountains. Its present appearance is largely the creation of the Earls of Kingston, who rebuilt it during the 18th and 19thc. The Kingston College for Decayed Gentlefolk is a charming group of buildings which forms three sides of College Square. It was founded in 1780 to accommodate Protestants whom the world had treated badly – a function which the buildings still serve. The Protestant church was built to the design of G R Pain in 1823. Also of interest are the landscaped gardens of Mitchelstown Castle.

MITCHELSTOWN CAVES,
Tipperary 22 R91
These caves are sited 7m NE of Mitchelstown and about 2½m N of Ballyporeen, at Coolagarranroe. Of the two systems here – the New and the Old – the latter is the more difficult to reach and involves a descent by rope ladder. The Old Caves are sometimes called Desmond's Cave, after the Sugan Earl of Desmond took refuge here and was betrayed in the 17thc. The E cave is the largest chamber of its type in Ireland or Britain. New Cave, discovered in 1833, comprises 1½m of passages and chambers which feature well-formed stalactites and stalagmites. A rare and interesting inhabitant of the caves is the spider *Porrhomma Myops*.

MIZEN HEAD, *Carn Uí Néid:*
The Cairn of the Descendant of Niad, Cork 26 V72
Cliffs that rise to 700ft here form the extreme SW point from which the Irish mainland is measured.

MOATE, *An Móta:*
The Mound, Westmeath 17 N13
Cattle fairs are held in the wide main street of this village, which takes its name from a large rath or motte which lies SW and is known as Moatgrange. This probably dates from the Norman invasion. A 50ft-diameter cairn measuring only 4ft high can be seen on the summit of Knockast Hill, which rises 5m NE of the town. Although this monument has no central chamber, excavations conducted in 1932 revealed a number of the small burial chambers known as cists. The cairn is considered to be the cemetery of a pre-Celtic bronze-age people, dating from c2000 BC.

MOCOLLOP CASTLE, *Maigh Cholpa:*
Cholpa's Plain, Waterford 28 W99
See Ballyduff (Waterford) entry.

MOHER, CLIFFS OF, *Aillte an Mhothair:*
The Cliffs of the Ruin, Clare 21 R09
These magnificent cliffs form a 5m range which overlooks the Atlantic from a uniform height of nearly 700ft. Hag's Head marks the SW extremity, and O Brien's Tower stands at the higher NE end. This tower was built in 1835 by Cornelius O Brien, and was intended for visitors who wished to enjoy the view without being discomforted by the incredible drop. The view from here is certainly magnificent.

MOIRA, *Maigh Rath,* Down 13 J16
In recent years the broad main street of this village has suffered considerably through the felling of its trees and mutilation of its fine market house. However, the plain but elegant 18th-c parish church (CI) survives, as does the parkland of a former demesne once attached to a house owned by the Rawdons – Earls of Moira. The house itself has been demolished. Early 18th-c Berwick Hall is an interesting thatched planter's house sited close the village. The Battle of Moira, one of the most celebrated confrontations in Gaelic literary legend, was fought here in AD 637. Remains of the 15th-c church built on the site of a 7th-c monastery can be seen 1¾m SW at Magheralin.

MOLANA ABBEY, *Mainistir:*
Monastery, Waterford 29 X08
Extensive ruins of this abbey lie in the Ballinatray demesne, on an island which rises from the Blackwater estuary and is linked to the mainland by a causeway. The foundation was created for the Canons Regular of St Augustine, and built on the site of an ancient, 6th-c Celtic abbey. Among the remains are the abbey church, cloisters, and some of the conventual structures.

MONAGHAN, *Muineachán:*
Place of Thickets, Monaghan 12 H63
James I granted this administrative centre and county town a charter of incorporation, but most of the buildings seen here today date from the 18th and 19thc. The Rossmore Memorial of c1875 is a Victorian red-sandstone fountain which stands in the Diamond. St Patrick's parish church (CI) is a plain 19th-c church in gothick style, containing a number of interesting tablets to local notables. Close to the church is the courthouse of 1829, a handsome building which may have been designed by James Welland. The Dawson Memorial of 1857 is an obelisk by W J Barre of Newry, and the market house in Market Place is a small, elegant, classical building dating from 1792. The last-mentioned was designed by Col Samuel Hayes of Avondale and features carved festoons and medallions. Thomas Duff designed the solid, classical St Macartan's College of 1840, which occupies an elevated site in Emyvale Road. Off Old Cross Square is the fine Old Infirmary Building of 1768, which has recently been restored as a county museum.

St Macartan's Cathedral (RC) stands on a high site in Castleblaney Road and was begun by J J McCarthy of Dublin in 1861. After McCarthy's death the building was completed by William Hague, who was responsible for the tower and spire. The interior of the cathedral is dignified and uncluttered. A 14th- or 15th-c bronze altar cross known as the Cross of Clogher is preserved 1½m N in St Macartan's College. The fine Georgian house of Anketell Grove can be seen 4m N of the town, and Rossmore Park lies 3m SSW.

MONA INCHA PRIORY,
Tipperary 23 S18
See Roscrea entry.

MONASTERANENAGH, *Mainistir an Aonaigh:*
The Monastery of the Fair, Limerick 22 R54
Ruins preserved here are of an ancient Cistercian Abbey (NM) which was founded by the King of Thomond in 1148 as a thank-offering for the defeat of Norsemen in the neighbourhood. The foundation was a daughter house of Mellifont. Remains of the church are fairly complete, and there are surviving portions of the Chapter House, domestic buildings, the abbey mill, and an ancient bridge over the River Camoge. The main features date from the 13thc and are known for their fine stone carvings.

MONASTERBOICE, *Mainistir Bhuithe:*
St Buithe's Abbey, Louth 19 O08
High crosses on this early monastic site (NM), which is enclosed by a small churchyard, are said to be the finest in Ireland. Also in the graveyard are the remains of two small churches. The largest of these dates from the 8th or 9thc and features a primitive west doorway, while the smaller structure is of 13th-c origin. A 100ft section of the topless round tower has also survived, in spite of having been burnt – along with the foundation's books – in 1097. The tower dates from the 9thc.

St Muiredach's or the South Cross is the finest of the three and possibly the best in Ireland. It measures 17ft in height and displays numerous panels richly-carved with figure subjects. The Crucifixion is depicted on the west face, while the east face carries a representation of Christ Judging the World. The top of the cross, as is often the case, is in the form of a contemporary church with gable finials. An inscription on the base of the cross reads 'A prayer for Muiredach, by whom this cross was made'. The date of the erection of the cross is fixed by the knowledge that Muiredach was abbot from 890 to 923. The exceptionally tall West Cross measures 21½ft in height and features a Crucifixion on its head. Its 22 sculptured panels practically all represent biblical scenes, and the body of the cross is ornamented with rich decoration. Only the head and part of the shaft of the North Cross have survived to the present day, the rest having been destroyed by Cromwellian troops – according to tradition. Also of interest on the site are a grave slab and an ancient sundial.

MONASTEREVIN, *Mainistir Eimhín:*
St Eimhín's Monastery, Kildare 18 N61
St Evin founded the ancient monastery which once existed here. The site of this foundation is in the demesne of Moore Abbey, which was originally the seat of the Moores – Earls of Drogheda. Although built in the 18thc, the house was considerably gothicized in the 19th-c and has lost much of its original elegance. It was the home of the tenor John McCormack for several years until 1936, and now serves as a home for epileptic women. A cross which stands in the town square was erected

to the memory of Father Prendergast, who was hanged here for the part he played in the 1798 Rising. Several excellent 19th-c buildings can be seen in the town, and the Grand Canal is carried across the River Barrow here by an aqueduct.

MONEA, *Maigh Niadh:*
Plain of Heroes, Fermanagh **11 H 14**
Monea Castle (NM), built by rector Malcolm Hamilton of Devenish in the early 17thc, is considered to be the most picturesque and best-preserved Plantation castle in Ulster. It comprises two circular bastions which are corbelled on the top floor in Scottish fashion to become square. This Scottish air is enhanced by crow-stepped gables and un-mullioned windows. The lake beside the castle contains a crannog which, if taken with the nearby farmhouse and the castle, shows a long period of local habitation.

MONEYMORE, *Muine Mór:*
Big Thicket, Derry **6 H 88**
Moneymore is a typical Plantation town which owes its existence and development to the London Drapers' Company. A distinguished group of buildings completed by the company in 1819 still exist and include the market house, a hotel, a coach arch, and a dispensary. The latter now houses a bank. Other structures for which the drapers were responsible include the CI church, the Presbyterian church, and the corn store. Springhill (NT) lies ½m SE and is an interesting example of the type of fortified dwelling being built by settlers during the 17thc. Inside are a costume museum and an interesting cottar's kitchen.

MONKSTOWN, *Baile an Mhanaigh:*
Homestead of the Monk, Cork **28 W 76**
Anastasia Gould built 15th-c Monkstown Castle as a surprise gift for her husband on his return from foreign travel. She made an arrangement that the workmen she engaged on the project should buy all their food and clothes from her, so in the end the castle cost her a mere four pence! It now serves as a golf club. Monkstown itself is a small resort on the W side of Cork Harbour, opposite Cobh. The ruined church of *Teampull oen Bryn* stands near the castle in a graveyard which contains a monument to the crafty Anastasia. She died in 1689.

MONKSTOWN, *Baile na Manach:*
Homestead of the Monks, Dublin **19 O 22**
A gate tower and residential tower make up the 15th-c castle which stands in this Dublin suburb. The Protestant parish church is a notable gothick building.

MOOGHAUN, *An Múchán:*
The Underground Passage, Clare **21 R 47**
See Dromoland Castle entry.

MOONE, *Maoin:* The Possession, Kildare **24 S 79**
One of the most delightful high crosses in Ireland stands in the demesne of Moone Abbey House. It is very tall and slender, dates from the 9thc, and depicts a number of biblical scenes as well as a number of related themes. Examples of the latter are the Temptation of St Anthony and a panel showing lions and serpents in mortal combat. The most appealing of all the carved panels is that which shows the 12 Apostles. The 15th-c tower of Moone Castle stands near by.

MOORE HALL, Mayo **15 M 17**
See Carra Lough entry.

MORE CASTLE, *An Caisleán Mór:*
The Big Castle, Cork **28 W 46**
Considerable portions of the walls surround the keep of this castle, which stands on the S bank of the River Bride and is the second largest stronghold in the Muskerry country (after Blarney). It was built by the MacSwineys in the 15th-c and later passed to the MacCarthys, who strengthened it in the wars of 1641.

MORNINGTON, *Baile Uí Mhornáin:*
O Mornain's Homestead, Meath **19 O 17**
The splendid 6m stretch of beach for which Mornington is noted extends along the S side of the Boyne estuary. Local Maiden Tower, which derives its name from Queen Elizabeth I, was erected as an aid to shipping approaching Drogheda Harbour.

MOROE, *Maigh Rua:*
The Red Plain, Limerick **22 R 75**
This village lies under the foothills of the Slievefelim mountains and is dominated by the 19th-c mansion of Glenstal – former home of the Barrington family. This is now called Glenstal Benedictine Abbey, and is known both for its daily liturgical services and its secondary school for boys.

MOSTRIM, Longford **17 N 27**
See Edgeworthstown entry.

MOUNT BRANDON, Kerry **20 Q 41**
See Brandon Mountain entry.

MOUNT CONGREVE, Waterford **24 S 51**
See Waterford entry.

MOUNTJOY, *Muinseo,* Tyrone **5 H 47**
Mellon Cottage, a local farmhouse typical of many to be found in Ulster, is owned by the Scottish–Irish National Trust and maintained by the National Trust (OACT). Thomas Mellon was born here and grew to become a bank founder in the USA, as well as an Ambassador in London.

MOUNT JULIET, *Garrán an Bhaltúnaigh:*
Walton's Grove, Kilkenny **24 S 54**
The superb parkland of this well-known stud farm lies W of Thomastown and beyond the River Nore. The fine house was built for the Earl of Carrick c1770. Also of interest is the grave of the famous racehorse 'The Tetrarch'.

MOUNT MELLERAY, Waterford **29 S 00**
See Cappoquin entry.

MOUNTMELLICK, *Móinteach Mílic:*
Bogland of the Place Bordering Water, Laois **17 N 40**
Originally a Quaker settlement, this small market town wears an 18th-c air and preserves several good buildings. One of the county's curious esker ridges, formed by glacial action during the ice age, passes N to S near the town. About 2m NW of the town is the fine 18th-c house of Summer Grove, and attractive Cathole Glen lies at the foot of the Slieve Bloom Mountains in the W.

MOUNTRATH, *Maighean Rátha:*
Precinct of the Ringfort, Laois **17 S 39**
This quiet market town lies SE of the extensive Slieve Bloom Mountains. About 5m NNE is Ballyfin House, a 19th-c structure built by Sir Charles Henry Coote to designs by Sir Richard Morrison – a pupil of Gandon. This is now used as a boarding school. Roundwood is a handsome little Palladian villa (OACT) which lies 3m SW and dates from the 18thc. Clonenagh Church stands 2m E on the site of a monastery founded in the 6thc by St Fintan. Near by is St Fintan's Tree, a curious sycamore which contains a well.

MOUNTSANDEL, *Dún dá Bheann:*
Fort of the Two Peaks, Derry **6 C 83**
Mountsandel Fort is a large oval mound which occupies a prominent position on a promontory overlooking the River Bann. Legend links this impressive structure with heroic events of the pre-Norman age, when it was the residence of Niall of the Nine Hostages.

MOUNTSTEWART, Down **13 J 56**
Because the climate of the area in which this fine 18th-c house is built is so mild, the 7th Marchioness of Londonderry had plenty of scope when planning the features of her exquisite gardens (NT). Delicate plants and shrubs flourish in various formal arrangements, balanced by pleasant informal woodlands and lakeside plantings. The 18th-c Temple of the Winds is an elegant derivative of its namesake in Athens, and occupies a fine situation above Strangford Lough. Numerous antiquarian objects exist in the grounds of Mounstewart.

MOUNT USHER, Wicklow **19 T 29**
The famous gardens here (OACT) were

Monaghan's small, elegant market house is a classical building of the 18thc.

MOURNE ABBEY, *Mainistir na Móna:*
Monastery of the Bog, Cork   **28 W 59**
Situated on the E side of the Mallow to Cork road, this area was a walled town with a Preceptory of the Knights Templar in the reign of Edward III. After the Knights Templar were suppressed it was given to the Knights of St John of Jerusalem. Remains of the church are few and unremarkable, but a Templar tombstone can be seen 1½m SSE of Rathcormack in Kilshannig churchyard. The tower of Castle Barrett exists near the abbey site.

MOURNE MOUNTAINS, *Beanna Boirche:*
Peaks of Boirche, Down   **13 J 22**
This splendid range is the highest in NE Ireland. It is dominated by 2,796ft Slieve Donard, a fine viewpoint which rises above Newcastle and is a good 2½-hour climb from that resort. Other fine climbs include 2,512ft Commeragh, 2,448ft Bignian, and 2,394ft Bearnagh. The Silent Valley, which is overlooked by Slieve Bignian and Slieve Bearnagh, contains two reservoirs which supply Belfast and N Co Down. The lakes are respectively known as Silent Valley and Ben Crom. The massive Water Commissioners' Wall, which encloses their catchment area and links all the principal peaks of the range, marks the route of the annual Mourne Walk. This strenuous competition involves the ascent of all the main summits.

MOVILLA ABBEY, *Maigh Bhile:*
Plain of the Tree, Down   **13 J 57**
The 13th- to 15th-c church which stands here occupies the site of a monastery founded by St Finnian in the 6thc. Tradition has it that St Columba stole St Finnian's Psalter by stealthily copying it, and the resulting dispute led to the disastrous Battle of Cuildrevne. The copy retained by St Columba became the *Warrior Book* of the O Donnells, which was borne before them in battle. This is now preserved in the National Museum, Dublin. The church (NM) features a pre 13th-c window which has been incorporated into the east window, plus a number of 13th-c coffin lids arranged along the north wall (see Newtownards town plan).

MOY, *An Maigh:*
The Plain, Tyrone   **12 H 85**
James Caulfield, the Earl of Charlemont, had this village laid out to a plan based on the Lombardy town of Marengo. The pleasant tree-bordered square dates from the 18thc and forms part of the original conception. Charlemont Fort, which faces the village from the S, was built in 1602 and burnt down in 1922. Its outer-defence system is the best example of its kind in Ulster, and an 18th-c gateway bearing the Caulfield arms has survived.

MOYNE ABBEY, *An Mhaighean:*
The Precinct, Mayo   **9 G 22**
Moyne Abbey (NM) was founded for the Franciscans by MacWilliam Burke in the 15thc, on the shores of Killala Bay. Among the surprisingly complete ruins seen here today are the nave, choir, side aisle and transept, south chapel, cloisters in a perfect state of preservation, refectory, dormitories, and a tall square tower.

MOYNE CASTLE, *An Mhaighean:*
The Precinct, Mayo   **15 M 24**
Ruined Moyne Castle stands a little to the NW of Headford, near an ancient oval church site which is enclosed by a cashel. The castle's square tower has a spiral staircase which is connected to a covered passage extending round the ambit of the walls.

MOYRA, *Maighreach:*
Place of Salmon, Donegal   **4 B 93**
A large rude cross made from a single piece of rock lies in the local churchyard at Moyra. It is known as St Columba's Cross, and is said to have been carved by the saint himself. An early monastery was founded here.

MOYTURA, *Maigh Tuireadh,*
Mayo   **15 M 15**
The ancient plain of S Moytura measures about 6m square and lies NE of Cong. According to the *Annals of the Four Masters* it was the scene of a great, four-day battle between the Firbolgs and Dedanaans in the '303rd year of the world'. The Firbolgs had been in possession of Ireland for 37 years when the invading Dedanaans arrived, and the battle was won by the newcomers. Refugees from the battle are said to have fled to the Aran Islands and settled as an island population. Another confrontation between these peoples occurred seven years later in N Moytura, near Ballinafad. This consolidated the power of the Dedanaans, who ruled until the coming of the Celts some 197 years later. Five stone circles, one with a diameter of 54ft, and several large cairns exist on the battlefield. The monuments are said to indicate certain incidents in the battle.

MUCKROSS, *Mucros:*
Pig Headland, Kerry   **27 V 98**
See Killarney entry.

MUINE BHEAG, *Muine Bheag:*
Small Thicket, Carlow   **24 S 76**
Formerly known as Bagenalstown, a name given by founder Walter Bagenal of Dunleckny Manor, this is a small market town laid out on English lines. It has a good courthouse, and 2m E are the remains of Ballymoon Castle. These ruins form a remarkable survival of a square, keepless castle of the 14thc. Features include doors, fireplaces, and garderobes – all excellently preserved.

MULLAGHMORE, *An Mullach Mór:*
The Large Hilltop, Sligo   **10 G 75**
Lord Palmerston constructed the harbour here in 1842. Nowadays Mullaghmore is a popular resort, with a fine bathing beach and good cliff scenery to the W. To the SW is Classiebawn Castle, which was started by Lord Palmerston in 1842 and completed in 1872.

MULLAGHMAST, RATH OF,
Mullach Maistean:
Hilltop of Maiste, Kildare   **18 S 79**
Situated at 563ft about 2m W of Ballitore, this lonely spot was once a meeting place of the Leinster Council. Some 400 men from Laois and Offaly were treacherously murdered at a meeting held here in 1577. The scene of the massacre became known as the Blood Hole.

***MULLINGAR,** An Muileann gCearr:*
Wry Mill, Westmeath   **17 N 45**
County town of Westmeath and the market centre for Ireland's cattle country, Mullingar is sited at the heart of the ancient kingdom of Meath. Henry II granted it to Hugh de Lacy in consideration of his services, and during the middle ages the town had two religious foundations – a house for Augustinians and a Dominican friary. No trace of these buildings has survived to the present day. The principal architectural feature of the town is the Cathedral of Christ the King (RC), an early 20th-c building by Ralph Byrne. Its twin, 140ft towers form a conspicuous landmark. Both the town hall and the courthouse date from the 18thc.

Mullingar is surrounded by a ring of lakes, which explains the one-time nickname of the area as 'The district of waters'. Lough Lene is probably the most beautiful and lies about 10m NE. Church Island, 3m N in Lough Owel, boasts the interesting remains of a monastic settlement. Some 2m S is Lough Ennel, where 18th-c Belvedere House stands in fine gardens on the wooded E shore. All the lakes offer good fishing. Knockdrin Castle lies 4m NE and is a large, castellated mansion which adjoins an Anglo-Norman castle. It is likely that the ancient part of the structure was erected by a follower of Hugh de Lacy.

MULRANY, *An Mhala Raithní:*
Hill-brow, Mayo   **8 L 89**
This picturesquely-sited resort stands on the isthmus between Clew Bay and Bellacagher Bay. It has a good bathing strand, and the area is particularly noted for its mild climate. Fine views extend across island-studded Clew Bay and take in the holy mountain of 2,510ft Croagh Patrick. Immediately behind the village is the Nephin Beg range of mountains.

MULROY BAY, *An Mhaol Rua:*
The Red Hill, Donegal   **5 C 13**
Considered one of the loveliest sea loughs in Ireland, this 12m-long, almost land-locked stretch of water boasts a complicated shoreline which winds below a hilly skyline. This shore offers interesting caves and fine walks, while the lough itself contains numerous wooded islands.

MULTYFARNHAM, *Muilte Farannáin:*
Farannan's Mills, Westmeath   **17 N 46**
Remains of a 14th-c Franciscan friary exist here in the grounds of the Franciscan College, and it is said that the friars continued to inhabit their settlement until 1641 in spite of the Dissolution mandate. The church has been restored and carries a prominent tower. Some 2m NE of the village, on the E shore of Derryvarragh Lough, is Fahalty Castle. The lough is associated with the Irish legend *The Children of Lir,* which relates the tragedy of four children who were turned into swans. Wilson's Hospital is a school with good 18th-c buildings, situated 1½m to the S.

MUNGRET, *Mungairit,* Limerick   **22 R 55**
A monastery founded here by St Nessan in the 6thc grew to become one of the chief monastic schools in Ireland, but it suffered greatly at the hands of Norse raiders. Buildings here today include two churches of early mortar-built construction (NM's), and a large abbey church (NM) which dates from the 13th to 15thc. There is a Munster proverb which reads 'As wise as the women of

Mungret'. This saying arose on the occasion of a challenge being issued to the monks of Mungret to enter a competition of learning with the inhabitants of another monastery. Some of the younger Mungret monks dressed up as washerwomen and positioned themselves by the stream. As the visitors arrived the 'washerwomen' looked up from their clothes-beating and addressed the rival monks in fluent Latin. 'Let us return' said the leader, 'what hope is there to compete successfully with brethern whose very washerwomen discourse in excellent Latin'. The Jesuit College in Mungret was established in 1881.

MURRISK, *Muraisc:*
Sea Marsh, Mayo **15 L98**
Isolated Murrisk Abbey is picturesquely-sited on the S shores of island-studded Clew Bay, below the holy mountain of Croagh Patrick. It is a 15th-c foundation which was created for the Augustinian Order by the O Malley family. Its present church (NM) is a small building with a beautiful five-light east window and a tower at the west end. Inside is the tomb of the founding family – a usual feature of such abbeys. A path from Murrisk leads to the summit of venerated Croagh Patrick.

MUSSENDEN TEMPLE, Derry **6 C73**
See Downhill entry.

MUTTON ISLAND, *Oileán Caorach:*
Sheep Island, Clare **21 Q97**
Ruins of a small church connected in name with St Senan exist on this island. The island itself is the largest of a group of three situated off the Clare coast at Tromra Point.

MYSHALL, *Míseal,* Carlow **24 S86**
This village boasts a beautiful memorial church, plus an old church which preserves an 11th- or 12th-c doorway.

NAAS, *An Nás:*
The Assembly Place, Kildare **18 N81**
Several monasteries existed in this prosperous town during the middle ages, and today it is a market centre and the county town of Kildare. It is situated on the edge of the Curragh and is world-famous in racing circles. Once one of the residences of the Kings of Leinster, it was a meeting place for great assemblies of state and still features a rath which survives from the royal residence of the Fitzgeralds. The CI parish church is said to stand on the site of a camp made by St Patrick during one of his missionary journeys. It has a medieval tower. The RC Church of SS Mary and David is a gothick structure which dates from 1827. Its tower and spire were added in 1858.

NARIN, *An Fhearthainn,* Donegal **4 G79**
This small fishing village has a fine sandy beach and a pleasant outlook over Gweebarra Bay. Inishkeel Island, accessible by foot at low tide, lies close to the shore and preserves the remains of ruined churches. To the W on 418ft Dunmore Head are the remains of several forts, while S are castle ruins on Lough Doon, Lough Birroge, and Lough Kiltooris. An island in Lough Doon preserves a remarkable stone fort with walls thick enough to contain a passage.

NARROW WATER, *Caoluisce:*
Narrow Water, Down **13 J11**
Narrow Water Castle (NM; OACT) is a stone tower house which lies 1¼m NW of Warrenpoint and features a defended enclosure or bawn. It was built on the site of a 13th-c de Lacy castle c1560 and occupies a spur of rock which juts into the estuary of the Newry River. By 1580 the stronghold had passed into the hands of the Magennis family, who forfeited their estates to the Hall family in 1691. Excellent restorations were conducted in the 19thc. Near by is the handsome Narrow Water Mansion, a Tudor-revival structure dating from 1837.

NAVAN, *An Uaimh:*
The Cave, Meath **18 N86**
In recent years there has been some confusion as to the official name of this market and county town – whether it should be Navan or *An Uaimh*. A vote taken among the local people has settled the argument by proving most to be in favour of Navan. The town is set amid beautiful countryside that sweeps down to the banks of the River Boyne, itself an example of almost sylvan perfection before it flows into Navan. The town was a place of considerable strategic importance in Anglo-Norman times, and was defended by a strong castle. Although this has now disappeared, a large motte still exists on the S side of the town. The RC parish church was originally a simple classical structure erected in 1836, but at some stage it was changed into a mock-Romanesque form. Inside is a Crucifixion by the 18th-c Dublin sculptor Edward Smythe.

At Donaghmore, about 1½m NE of the town, is an intact round tower (NM) which is said to stand on the site of a church built by St Patrick. The tower stand nearly 100ft high and features interesting carving round the doorway. Near by is the fragment of a 16th-c church. About 1m E of Donaghmore is Dunmoe Castle (NM), which is splendidly sited on the N bank of the River Boyne. It originated in the 13thc but was considerably altered in the 16th, besieged in the Insurrection of 1641, and finally burned in the Rising of 1798. Athlumney Castle (NM) stands on the SE outskirts of Navan and comprises the extensive ruins of a 17th-c house which was built around a 15th-c tower house. In 1690 this building was deliberately burned down by its owner, Sir Launcelot Dowdall, so it could not be used by Williamite forces. Close by are the ruins of a church which dates from the 14th or 15thc. A little to the S of Athlumney are the remains of Kilcarn (or Cannistown) church (NM), which was built c1200 on the site of an ancient monastery. The chancel is original, but the nave was rebuilt at a later date. The old font which used to stand in the church is now kept in Johnstown Church (RC). Beyond Kilcarn is the Elizabethan mansion of Ardsallagh House, while 3m W of Navan is Ardbraccan House. The latter has wings which were built to a design by the German architect Cassels in 1747, plus a central block designed by James Wyatt in 1776. It was formerly the seat of the Protestant bishops of Meath. The nearby parish church (CI) dates from the 18thc and incorporates a medieval bell tower. White Quarry, which lies ¾m NW of the house, is the source of the famous Ardbraccan limestone of which so many Dublin buildings have been constructed.

NENAGH, *An tAonach:*
The Fair, Tipperary **22 R87**
Formerly an important centre in the Anglo-Norman settlement, this agricultural and market town features several reminders of its illustrious past. Nenagh Friary (NM), in Abbey Street, was founded c1250 by the O Kennedy family and still features a 13th-c church. The town was once the principal Franciscan centre in Ireland, and continued to thrive until the friary was destroyed by Cromwellian troops. The castle (NM) was built c1217 by Theobald Walter Butler, who came to Nenagh at the start of the 13thc and was the first of the great Butlers of Ormonde. Although the castle was the scene of a great deal of strife at various times, its remains are still imposing enough to dominate the town. The cylindrical keep or donjon, called Nenagh Round, is a remarkable structure which is considered the finest example of its kind in Ireland. It has five storeys, walls of up to 20ft in thickness, and a top section of about 25ft which was constructed by order of the Bishop of Killaloe in the 19thc.

The local RC Church of St Mary was built to designs by Doolin between 1892 and 1906, and the town's handsome courthouse is of 19th-c origin. Ruined Tyone Priory stands 1m SE, and 3m SE at Ballynaclough are the remains of a 13th-c castle and church. An interesting trivallate fort can be seen 4m ENE at Rathurles, and the ruins of a 15th-c church stand within its ramparts. The whole area round Nenagh is particularly rich in prehistoric sites, ruined castles, monastic remains, and other antiquities.

Nenagh Round is a cylindrical keep or donjon which is considered the finest of its kind in Ireland.

NENDRUM, *Naoindroim*:
Nine Ridges, Down **13 J 56**
Situated on Mahee Island in Strangford Lough, this is considered to be one of Ireland's most interesting and best-excavated early monasteries. It is said to have been founded by St Machaoi in the 5thc, but archaeological evidence so far uncovered points to a date of *c*700. The ruins were rediscovered by Bishop Reeves in 1844, while he was excavating what he believed to be an old lime kiln. This turned out to be the stump of a round tower of considerable antiquity. Extensive excavation conducted here between 1922 and 1924 have revealed a good example of the way in which early monastic sites were laid out. Remains include three concentric cashels, the foundations of a church, fragments of both rectangular and round structures, and a graveyard. Objects discovered while work was in progress include writing blocks and an iron bell coated in bronze. The bell was found hidden in a wall. These and many other relics from Nendrum are displayed in the Ulster Museum, Belfast.

NEWBRIDGE, Kildare
See Droichead Nua entry.

*NEWCASTLE, *An Caisleán Nua*:
The New Castle, Down **13 J 33**
Newcastle is a well-known seaside and golfing resort delightfully situated on Dundrum Bay, below the heights of Slieve Donard and the Mourne Mountains. The town takes its name from a castle built at the point where the River Shimna flows into Dundrum Bay in the 16thc, but this structure was demolished in the first half of the 19thc. The reason why it was removed was to make way for a hotel to serve visitors who were coming from far and wide to visit the spa which existed in the grounds of Donard Lodge. Now also demolished, this used to be the residence of Earl Annesley. The handsome parish church (CI) dates from 1832, and the modern RC church is a circular structure with a lantern which – with the central spire of the Slieve Donard Hotel – dominates the skyline.

Botanists are attracted to the area by the rare flora which grows in the mountains, especially where there is shale, and the district is full of fine examples of glaciation. Those who like the seaside will enjoy the 3m sands which face Dundrum Bay, and the rambler can take advantage of some superb countryside. A complete village is buried in the sand at Ballyvaston, and S of the town are the interesting natural features of Donard Cave and Maggie's Leap. Newcastle is a good starting point for the ascent of 2,796ft Slieve Donard, which affords excellent views. Tollymore Forest Park lies 2m NW of the town.

NEWCASTLE, *An Caisleán Nua*:
The New Castle, Dublin **19 O 02**
Situated 12m SW of Dublin, this village derives its name from a royal castle and manor which were erected here at the time of the Anglo-Norman invasion. Remains of only two of the six fortified houses which stood here in the 16thc can still be seen. St Finian's Church (CI) features a 15th-c west tower with rooms for a resident priest. The chancel is roofless, and its fine east window has been reset in the east wall of the nave. Lyons House (see entry) lies 2m W of Newcastle in the county of Kildare.

NEWCASTLE WEST, *An Caisleán Nua*:
The New Castle, Limerick **21 R 23**
Newcastle West is a busy market town in a dairy-farming district. The ruins of a great Desmond stronghold here include towers built by the Knights Templar in the 12thc, and have been incorporated in a modern house. The castle was burnt in 1642, but two 15th-c halls were preserved. Desmond's Hall is complete and includes a vaulted basement. The upper floor is still in use.

NEWGRANGE, *Sí an Bhrú*:
Fairy Mound of the Palace,
Meath **19 O 07**
See gazetteer inset for Brugh na Boinne on page 176.

NEWMARKET, *Ath Trasna*:
The Oblique Ford, Cork **27 R 30**
Statesman and Senator John Philpot Curran was born in this village in 1750, and in his later life he lived at The Priory. His daughter Sarah is buried in the nearby graveyard, but her memory is perpetuated by a song in which she is the central figure. The song opens 'She's far from the land where her young hero sleeps' – the young hero being Robert Emmet. Mrs Aldworth, said to have been the only woman freemason, is also buried here. To the NW is an area of wild, bleak countryside.

NEWMARKET-ON-FERGUS,
***Cora Chaitlín*:** Kathleen's Weir, Clare
21 R 36
This village takes its name from the English horse-racing centre. The country in which the village is situated is a flat area between the estuaries of the Rivers Shannon and Fergus. Opposite Dromoland Castle (see entry) is a belvedere from which Sir Edward O Brien used to watch local horse racing, and members of the O Brien family are buried ¾m W in the CI parish church of Kilnasoolagh. Among the interesting monuments is one by William Kidwell, a sculptor who lived in Dublin and who has recently been the subject of intensive research. The picturesque ruin of 13th-c Urlanmore Castle (see entry), once a stronghold of the McMahons, can be seen 1¾m SSW. Some 4m E in Finlough are the remains of Tomfinlough church, which stands on the site of an early monastic foundation. It was partially rebuilt in the early 14thc.

*NEWPORT, *Baile Uí Fhiacháin*:
O Feehan's Homestead, Mayo **9 L 99**
Newport is a small angling centre on the Newport River, which flows into island-studded Clew Bay. The numerous drumlins round the village are of scenic as well as geological interest. The fine parish church (RC) is a 20th-c building in Irish-Romanesque style. Its east window of 1930 is by Harry Clarke. Carrighahooly or Rockfleet Castle (NM) lies 3m W on the shores of Clew Bay, and was built by the Burke family in the 16thc. The pirate queen Grace O Malley, who was married to a Burke, withstood a siege here in 1574 and took up residence in the castle in 1583. Ruined Burrishoole Abbey (NM) lies 2m NW and includes interesting remains of the domestic buildings as well as the church. It was founded in the 15thc.

*NEW ROSS, *Rhos Mhic Thriúin*:
The Wood of Treon's Son, Wexford **24 S 72**
Once an important inland port, this town lies near the Kilkenny border on the River Barrow a little S of its junction with the River Nore. It is sited on a steep hill and is known for its numerous narrow, winding streets. Nowadays it is a manufacturing and market centre connected by bridge to the suburb of Co Kilkenny's Rosbercon. The monastery founded here by King Dermot Mac Murrough in the 6thc is thought to have stood close to the river. The town itself was created by William the Marshal, Earl of Pembroke, at the time of the Anglo-Norman settlement. Its strong castle had a formidable garrison of about 5,000 pikemen, bowmen, and horsemen, and the town walls were pierced by four gates. Bishop's Gate was once considered the finest example of its type in Ireland, but only fragments of this now remain. Both castle and town suffered greatly during the Cromwellian wars, and it was only after a heavy bombardment that New Ross finally surrendered to the parliamentary army in 1649. Three cannon balls lodged in one of the gates during the attack, and afterwards this access became known as Three Bullet Gate. Some fragments of this survive. Much of the town was destroyed by fire after an attack in the 1798 Rebellion.

St Mary's Abbey Church is a large Anglo-Norman abbey parish church of *c*1200. Surviving parts of this interesting building include the transepts and chancel (NM's), but the nave was removed to make way for a 19th-c structure. Among the sepulchral remains is a cenotaph to Strongbow's daughter Isabella, Countess of Leinster. The Tholsel is a classical building which was erected in 1749 and rebuilt in 1806. Approximately 4m SSW of New Ross at Dunganstown is the ancestral family home of the Kennedy family, and 5m S is the John F Kennedy Park. This was opened by President de Valera in 1968 and comprises 480 acres, of which 310 acres from an arboretum and 110 acres a forest garden. Also here is a Kennedy memorial. The 630ft viewpoint on Slieve Coilte can be reached by car and is well worth the drive. Annagh's Tower is of 15th- or 16th-c date and stands 2m SSE of New Ross on the banks of the River Barrow.

*NEWRY, *An tIúr*: The Yew, Down **13 J 02**
Newry is a manufacturing town and port situated 6m up-river from the head of Carlingford Lough. It lies a few miles N of the Gap of the North in a well-sheltered position protected by the Mourne Mountains in the E, the Camlough Mountains and Slieve Gullion to the W, and the Carlingford range to the S. The development of the town and port was accelerated by the opening of the Newry Canal in 1741, thereby forming a watery highway between the loughs of Carlingford and Neagh. St Patrick founded a monastery here and planted a yew tree at the head of the strand of Carlingford Lough, but both the foundation and the tree were burned in 1162. Later on Newry became an important centre in the territory controlled by de Courcey, but the castle he built was burnt by Edward Bruce in 1315. After being rebuilt it was destroyed by Shane O Neill in 1566.

At the Dissolution the Cistercian abbey here was granted to Nicholas Bagenal, who was the real founder of the town of

Newry. He colonized it, rebuilt the castle, and in 1578 erected the parish church of St Patrick (CI). This was the earliest church to be built for Protestant worship in Ireland. Bagenal's tombstone is preserved in the church porch, and his arms are in the tower. The chancel and transepts are later additions. Also of interest is the town's 19th-c courthouse, although this has suffered some damage.

The parish Church of St Mary (CI) stands close to the river and was erected to designs by Patrick O Farrell in 1810. Supervision of the building was shared between O Farrell and Thomas Duff, and the chancel was added in 1886 to designs by Sir Thomas Drew. The 19th-c Cathedral of SS Patrick and Colman (RC) was also by Duff. Good Georgian buildings in the town include the Bank of Ireland in Trevor Hill, plus various houses and shops in Hill Street, Boat Street, and Upper Water Street. John Mitchell, a leader of the Young Ireland Party in the 19thc, was the son of the town's Presbyterian minister.

NEWTOWNABBEY, Antrim 7 J 38
Parts of the Belfast suburbs have been welded together to form this new town development. The places thus affected are Glengormley, Whitehall, Whiteabbey, Jordanstown, Cavehill, Carnmoney, and Whitehouse. Newtownabbey's town hall is situated at Whitehouse.

NEWTOWNARDS, *Baile Nua na hArda:*
The New Town of the Promontory, Down
13 J 47
Plan overleaf
Founded in the very early 17thc by a Scottish Laird called Hugh Montgomery, this thriving manufacturing and market town is situated at the head of Strangford Lough in the Ards Peninsula. The Dominican friary was founded in the 13thc. Its ruins (NM) comprise a nave and north aisle, separated by an arcade of four slightly-pointed arches supported by round pillars. A handsome north tower dating from the 17thc features a good doorway and four upper storeys.

During the last three centuries the church has been used as the burial place of the Montgomery, Colville, and Stewart families. A field to the SW contains the sparse remains of a 17th-c Colville mansion, known as Old Montgomery or The Bawn.

The handsome town hall was designed by 18th-c Gloucestershire canal engineer Ferdinando Stratford. It was completed in 1770, and the cupola was added in 1778. The market cross (NM) was taken from a design by Sir James Montgomery and erected in 1635, but it was defaced by insurgents in 1653. It was restored some 13 years later and now stands in the High Street, near the priory. It is octagonal in shape and was originally surmounted by a column which protruded 20ft from the conical roof and carried the carving of a lion. The interior of the cross served as the town gaol. About 1m S of Newtownards, on the summit of a granite outcrop known as Scrabo Hill, is 19th-c Scrabo Tower. This local landmark was erected to the memory of the 3rd Marquess of Londonderry and is near the wooded NT property of Killynether. Traces of hut circles measuring 7 or 8yds in diameter have been found on the hill. About 1m E of Newtownards on the Millisle road is the site of famous Movilla Abbey (see entry).

NEWTOWNBREDA, *Baile Nua na Bréadaí:*
The New Town of Breda (*ie* The Broken Land), Down 13 J 36
Far from being just another Belfast suburb, Newtownbreda stands next to the former Belvoir Park estate and preserves the character of a small village. The park's 18th-c house was demolished fairly recently, and part of the estate has been taken for the development of a new housing scheme. During the 18thc the area now occupied by these new houses was considered a particularly attractive stretch of the River Lagan countryside. The river is still beautiful, and other parts of Belvoir Park have been afforested. Amenities here include an aboretum and woodland paths. Knockbreda parish church (CI) is a pleasant building which was erected in the 18thc to designs by Richard Cassels, the German architect. Later extensions have been sympathetically executed.

NEWTOWN BUTLER, *An Baile Nua:*
The New Town, Fermanagh 11 H 42
The outstanding event in the history of this village was the battle of 1689, in which the settlers of Enniskillen won a decisive victory over the Jacobites. The forces of James II attacked Crom Castle, which was garrisoned by settlers, but were forced to retreat to Newtown Butler. Altogether the Jacobite army lost some 2,000 men in the engagement. Crom Castle lies 4m WSW on Lough Erne Upper and was built as a Plantation stronghold by Michael Balfour in 1611. It was accidentally destroyed by fire in 1764, and its picturesque ruins can be seen alongside the present-day Crom Castle. The latter was built in 1829 by Edward Blore for the Earl of Erne, and stands in fine grounds which contain a yew tree held to be the largest in Ireland. The wooded islands and peninsulas around the castle are often said to be the loveliest in Ireland. Remains of two

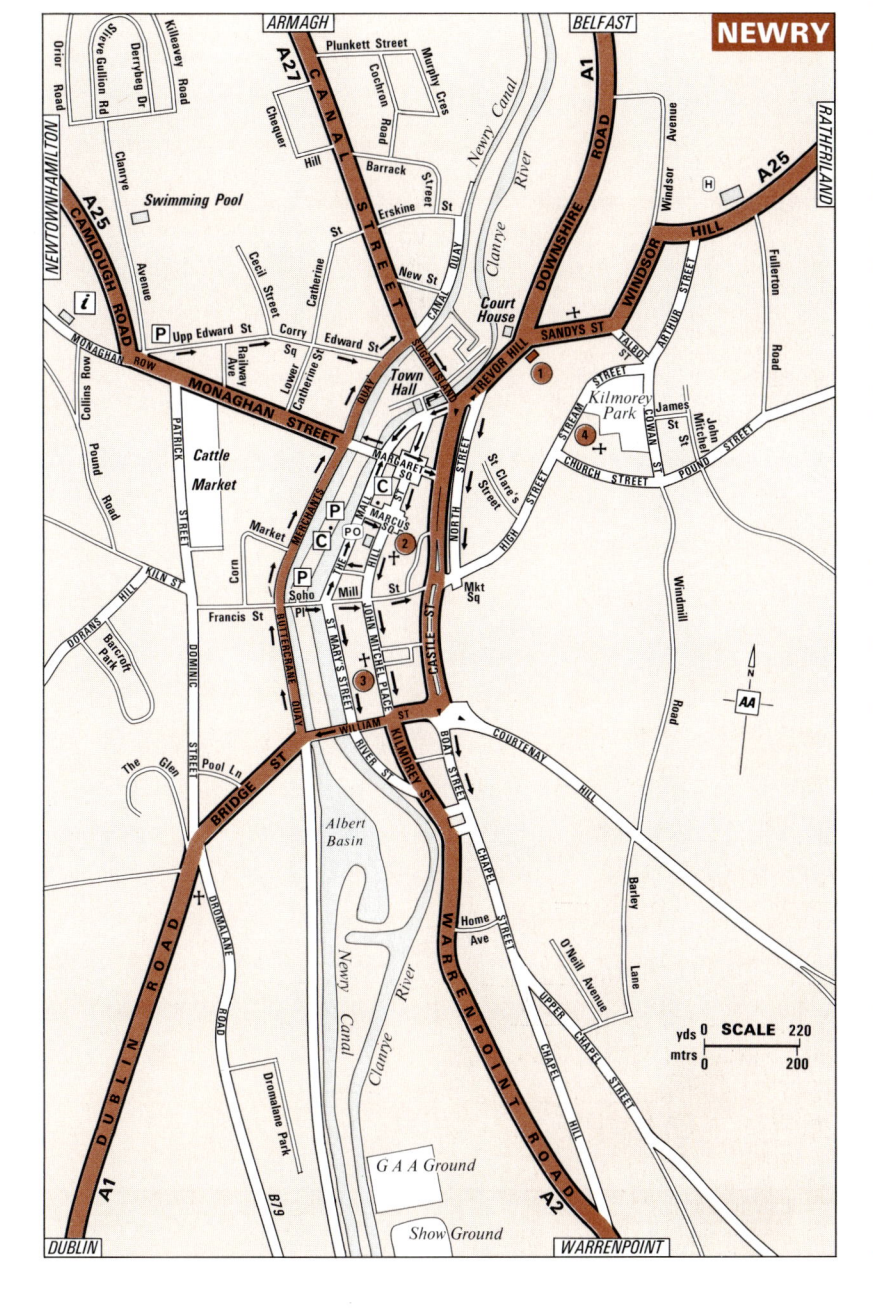

1   Bank of Ireland Building
2   Cathedral of SS Patrick & Colman (RC)
3   St Mary's Church (CI)
4   St Patrick's Church (CI)

high crosses can be seen in the churchyard on Galloon Island, in Lough Erne Upper about 3½m SW of the village. Some 3½m S is an enormous circle of stones known as the Druid's Temple (NM). This formerly surrounded a large tumulus which was removed in 1712.

NEWTOWNMOUNTKENNEDY, *Baile an Chinnéidigh:*
Kennedy's Town, Wicklow **19 O20**
The demesne of Mount Kennedy, situated in the foothills of the Wicklow Mountains on the main road between Bray and Wicklow, is considered one of the most picturesque in Ireland. The house, which lies ¾m NNW, remains one of the least spoiled in the country. It was the first to be commissioned from James Wyatt by an Irish landlord, but although arranged in 1722 it was not actually built until ten years later. Inside is superb plasterwork by Michael Stapleton.

NEWTOWNSTEWART, *An Baile Nua:*
The New Town, Tyrone **5 H48**
William Stewart, who founded this town, was given the district in 1628 during the Plantations in the reign of James I. Today this small market town is a known angling resort pleasantly grouped round the river Mourne, which is spanned by a fine 18th-c bridge of six arches. Also of interest are the remains of a 17th-c castle which James II ordered dismantled when he burned the town. Attractive Corrick Glen lies 3½m NE of the town. About ½m SW is the pre-Plantation estate of Harry Avery's Castle (NM), which may date from 1392.

NEWTOWN-TRIM, *Baile Nua Atha Troim:*
The New Town of the Ford of the Elder, Meath **18 N85**
Situated astride the River Boyne on the E outskirts of Trim, Newtown-Trim is in two parts which are linked by an old five-arched bridge. On the N bank of the river are the remains of the Cathedral of SS Peter and Paul (NM), which was founded by Bishop Simon de Rochfort in 1206. De Rochfort moved the seat of his diocese from Clonard to Trim. The building features many examples of transitional Norman work, but after a fire in the middle ages large parts of the structure were left in ruins. Also of interest are the remains of a priory which was founded at the same time as the cathedral, and the ruins of the medieval parish church. The latter contains an Elizabethan altar tomb raised to the memory of Sir Lucas Dillon and his wife. On the other side of the bridge are scanty remains of a friary and hospital.

NOBBER, *An Obair:*
The Work, Meath **18 N88**
Famous and well-loved Turlough O Carolan, the last of the Irish bards, was born here. The village itself stands on the site of an Anglo-Norman castle, the motte of which has survived. Remains of a Romanesque church (NM) can be seen 2m SW at Cruicetown, plus a 17th-c cross (NM). Near by are the ruins of the fortified 17th-c house of Robertstown (NM).

NURNEY, *An Urnaí:*
The Oratory, Carlow **24 S76**
A 6ft-high cross (NM) preserved in this village may date from the time of St Laserain. It stands on a rectangular base and features an unpierced ring.

OLDCASTLE, *An Seanchaisleán:*
The Old Castle, Meath **18 N58**
Mainly of interest to anglers and antiquarians, this out-of-the-way town stands within easy reach of Lough Sheelin, the Inny River, and the passage-grave cemetery of Loughcrew. The latter is one of the chief groups of megalithic tombs in the country and occupies the crests of two hills. The highest hill is 900ft Slieve na Calliagh, and the entire cemetery contains some 30 graves (NM's). The tombs are in two main groups – those on Slieve na Calliagh itself, and those on Carnbane West. The largest monument, Cairn 'D', has a diameter of 180ft but apparently is without a chamber. Cairn 'T' on Slieve na Calliagh has a diameter of 115ft and is a classic example of a passage-grave tomb. One of the large key stones with which it is surrounded measures 10ft long by 6ft high and is known as the Hag's Chair. Inside the tomb are 27 decorated stones. There is a considerable amount of decorative work in the Loughcrew complex, but the distinctive spiral of the Brugh na Boinne tombs is rare here. Many of the tombs have yielded artefacts which have confounded archaeologists by apparently dating from the iron age; the monuments are undoubtedly neolithic.

OLDERFLEET CASTLE, Antrim **7 D40**
See Larne entry.

OLD LEIGHLIN, Carlow
See Leighlinbridge entry.

*OMAGH, *An Omaigh,* Tyrone **11 H47**
Omagh, a prosperous market town and the home of the Inniskilling Fusiliers, stands where the Rivers Drumragh and Camowen join to form the Strule. The latter is noted for its trout and its freshwater mussel pearls. The history of the Inniskillings is traced by a regimental museum. St Columba's parish church and the RC Church of the Sacred Heart are both fine modern structures. The castle, which was a storm centre in the Tudor and Catholic Confederation wars, has vanished without a trace. The finely-sited courthouse was designed by John Hargrave in 1820 and stands on a hill at the head of High Street. Its portico is imposing. Creevenagh is the ancestral home of the Auchinleck family, of whom Field Marshall Sir Claude Auchinleck is probably the most famous member. Reasonably-preserved Cappagh Church (NM) lies 4¾m N, and a rectangular burial chamber known as the Giant's Grave can be seen 1½m to the W.

1 Colville Mansion
2 Dominican Friary Remains
3 Market Cross
4 Movilla Abbey Remains
5 Scrabo Hill & Tower
6 Town Hall

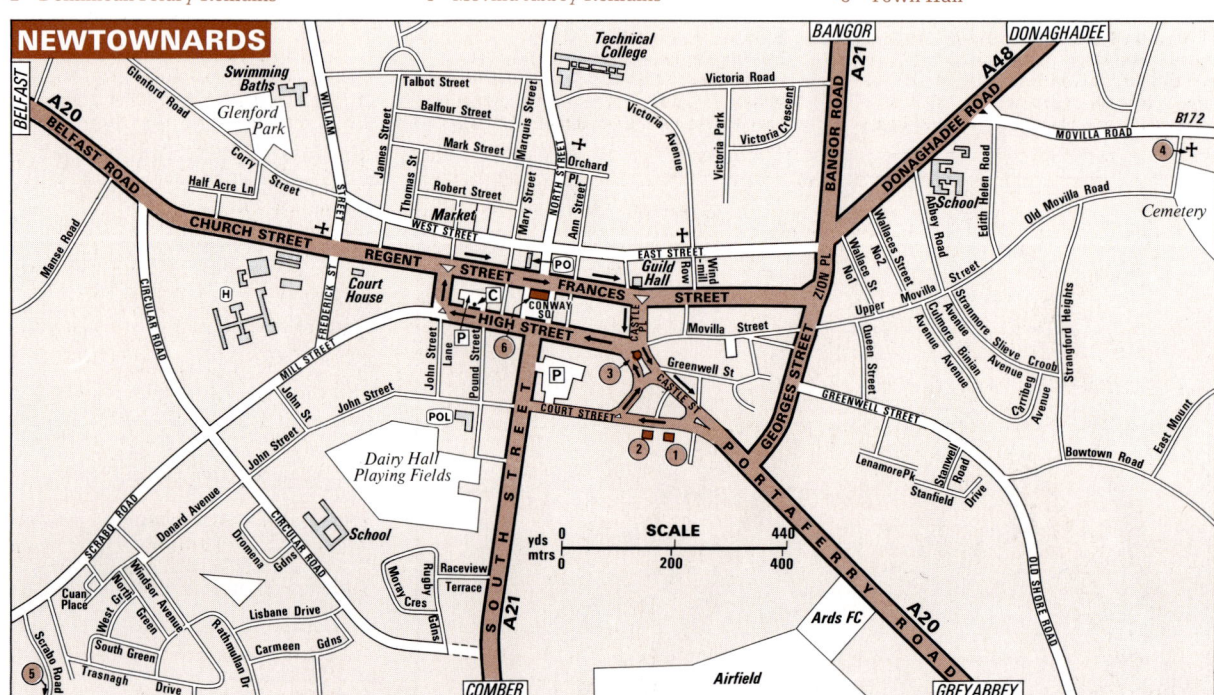

OMEATH, *O Méith:*
Descendants of Méith, Louth 13 J 11
Noted for its picturesque outlook across Carlingford Lough, this pleasant little resort has a shingle beach and nestles under the flanks of the Carlingford Mountains. A ferry connects Omeath with Warrenpoint, on the other side of the lough in Co Down. The outline of the Long Women's Grave is marked with stones at Windy Gap, which lies 2½m S of the resort. According to legend a prince once took his Spanish lover to this high point to show her the extent of his possessions. Unfortunately the view was limited to a few yards from the exact place where she stood, and the lady succumbed to shock.

OSSIAN'S GRAVE, *Uaigh Oisín,*
Antrim 7 D 22
Lying on the slopes of 1,346ft Tievebulliagh, a little inland from Cushendall, is the so-called grave of Ossian. According to tradition this hero of the Irish legends once lived here. The grave is, in fact, a megalithic court cairn which consists of a succession of chambers behind a forecourt.

OUGHTERARD, *Uachtar Ard:*
High Upper Place, Galway 15 M 14
An angling centre situated close to the shores of Lough Corrib, this village stands at the approach to the wild Connemara mountains. The district was once controlled by the O Flaherty family, who were a scourge of Galway city in the middle ages. Their depredations were finally curtailed by the government in the reign of Elizabeth I. Remains of an early 16th-c O Flaherty stronghold can be seen 2m SE of the village at Aughnanure.

PALLAS, *Pailís:*
Palisade, Galway 16 M 70
See Duniry entry.

PALLAS, *Pailís:*
Palisade, Longford 17 N 15
The celebrated poet Oliver Goldsmith was born here in 1728 (see Ballymahon entry).

PALLAS GREEN, NEW, *Pailís Ghréine:*
Grian's Palisade, Limerick 22 R 74
At Old Pallas Green, about 1¾m SW, are a motte and the remains of a manorial church. Some 3m NNE of New Pallas Green is the former O Grady stronghold of Castle Garde, a five-storey tower which is linked to a more modern wing. This is thought to be the oldest inhabited house in Limerick.

PARKNASILLA, *Pairc na Saileach:*
Willow Field, Kerry 26 V 76
The charming scenery of this well-known beauty spot is a combination of sea, islands, woodlands, and rugged mountains. It lies between the island-studded sea and 895ft Knockanamadane Hill on the magnificent coast on the Kenmare River inlet, and is an ideal place for a holiday. The area is rich in pleasant walks which follow winding paths through woods and across sparkling sea creeks via rustic bridges. Because of the warm sea its climate is mild, even in winter. One of the finest of the offshore islands is Garinish (see Glengarriff entry).

PASSAGE EAST, *An Pasáiste:*
The Passage, Waterford 24 S 70
Once fortified, this attractive village stands high above Waterford Harbour and was the place where Strongbow landed with 1,200 knights in 1170. He marched from here to Waterford, and took the town as the first stage of his invasion. Some 2½m NNW of Passage East is the splendid viewpoint of Cheekpoint. A passenger ferry runs between the village and Ballyhack, in Co Wexford.

PASSAGE WEST, *An Pasáiste:*
The Passage, Cork 28 W 76
A former dockyard town situated amid charming countryside, Passage West is sited on the narrow W passage which joins the inner division of Cork Harbour with the main outer section. The inner part is known as Lough Mahon. Passage West is a calling place for river steamers, and a favourite summer-holiday resort. The *Sirius*, which was the first steamer to cross the Atlantic, sailed from here in 1838 and took 18½ days to complete the crossing. A passenger ferry operates to Carrigaloe.

PETTIGO, *Paiteagó:*
Donegal, Fermanagh 11 H 16
This angling village is pleasantly set on the River Termon about 1m from Lower Lough Erne. It is a busy centre of activity during the season of pilgrimage to St Patrick's Purgatory (see entry), on Lough Derg. About 1½m SW is the ruined Castle Magrath, which comprises a strong keep with circular towers at the corners.

PIKE OF RUSH HALL, *An Paidhc:*
The Turnpike, Laois 23 S 38
To the NE of this village is the ruined castle of Rushall, which may date from the 17thc and was erected by Sir Charles Coote.

PILTOWN, *Baile an Phoill:*
The Town of the Creek, Kilkenny 23 S 42
Local Bessborough House was designed by Thomas Bindon in 1744 and was the property of the Ponsonby family – Earls of Bessborough. Although burnt in the early part of this century, the house has since been taken over by the Oblate Fathers and restored. Remains of a high cross mark an old monastic site 1¼m WSW in Tibberaghny, while near by are traces of a church and a 15th-c castle. Many prehistoric monuments can be seen around the village of Owning, which lies 3½m NNW of Piltown.

POISONED GLEN, *An Cró Nimhe:*
Poisoned Enclosure, Donegal 4 B 91
Steep precipices fringe this magnificent glen, which runs into the heart of the mountains S of 2,466ft Errigal and ends at the rounded heights of 2,240ft Slieve Snaght. The name of the glen is attributed to the abundance of spurge.

POMEROY, Tyrone 12 H 67
Pomeroy House stands NE of the village and now houses a Forestry School. It is a fine building which dates from the 18thc. The CI parish church was erected in 1841, extended in 1862, and gained its tower in 1877. Some 2m SW of Pomeroy near Altinagh School is the Gortnagarn horned cairn, a fine 68ft-long monument with a semi-circular horn measuring 13ft in diameter. Remains of three other chambers seen near by include jambs and sills. Cregganconroe single-court grave lies 3m NW of the village.

PORTADOWN, *Port an Dúnáin:*
The Bank of the Small Fort, Armagh 13 J 05
In ancient times Portadown was an important settlement which guarded a strategic ford across the River Bann. The first bridge was erected to replace the ford in 1708, and the prosperity of the town was assured by the construction of the Newry Canal in 1740. Nowadays Portadown is a considerable manufacturing, linen-producing, and fruit-farming centre which is linked to Lurgan to form the Craigavon New Town development. It is internationally known for its roses. In the centre of the town is St Mark's Church (CI), which was erected in 1826 and enlarged several times after 1859. The pinnacled tower dates from c1930. An interesting museum is housed in the Carnegie Library. Thackeray describes a visit he made to the town during 1842 in his *Irish Sketchbook*.

PORTAFERRY, *Port an Pheire:*
The Harbour of the Ferry, Down 13 J 55
The small seaside town and port of Portaferry is situated on the E side of

1 Church of the Sacred Heart (RC)
2 Courthouse
3 St Columba's Church (CI)

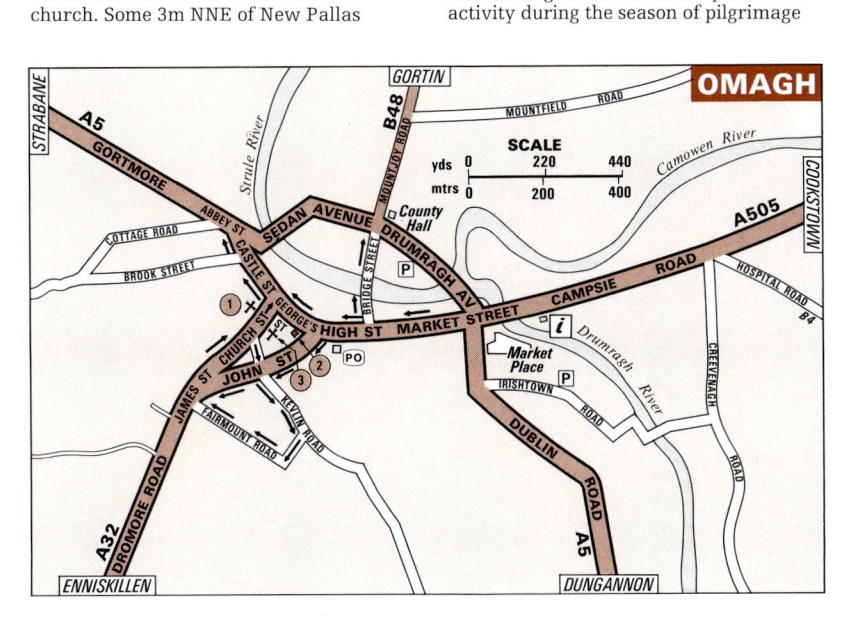

the entrance to Strangford Lough. The Celtic name for this vast sheet of water was Lough Cuan, but the Norsemen renamed it *Strang Fiord* because of the powerful tides that rush through its channel. In January of 1177 John de Courcy, 22 knights, and 300 picked men made a swift invasion of the kingdom of *Uiaidh* via the Moyry Pass, surprising King MacDunleavy and putting his army to flight. In spite of this only two of the knights succeeded in gaining a foothold in E Ulster – de Mandeville in Dalriada and William le Savage in the Ards. The Savages became the great castle-builders of the Ard Peninsula, and their linear descendants still inhabit the area – *eg* the Nugent family of Portaferry House. Portaferry Castle, the tower house of the Savage family, stands at the centre of the town and dates from the 16thc. The market house probably dates from c1800 and has recently been restored as a community centre. Also of interest are fragments of the ancient parish church, Temple Cranny.

About 1½m NE are the Derry Churches, the adjacent remains of two small churches which stand on a site thought to have been occupied by an early monastery. This would have been founded some time before the 8thc. On the shore of Millin Bay, 2½m SE of Portaferry, is the site of a unique and complex burial site. After excavation in 1953 this was re-covered, but one of the 64 decorated stones discovered here can still be seen. Also found was a long cist containing the remains of 15 people, plus several smaller cists. It is thought that the site may belong to the very beginning of the bronze age.

PORTARLINGTON, *Cúil an tSúdaire:*
The Tanner's Recess, Laois **18N51**
Lord Arlington was the owner of this town in the 17thc, and it was from him that it derived its name. At that time Portarlington was colonized by French and Flemish Huguenot refugees who were victims of the Edict of Nantes. French and English Protestant churches can still be seen here, though the latter is now disused. During the 18thc the town was bought by Henry Dawson, who was created the Earl of Portarlington, and it retains much of the character of these times. A number of the notable Georgian houses turn their backs to the street and face the river – in the French style. Portarlington's market house dates from c1800. The first turf-burning power station in Ireland was opened here in 1950.

PORTGLENONE, *Port Chluain Eoghain:*
The Bank of Eoghan's Pasture, Antrim **6C90**
This small River Bann town features the 20th-c Cistercian Abbey of Our Lady of Bethlehem – the third Irish daughter house of Mount Melleray. The 19th-c Portglenone House, which was built by Bishop Alexandra, now forms part of the abbey. The bishop purchased various parts used in the erection of this building from Ballyscullion Palace, which was built by the Bishop of Derry in the 1780's and dismantled in 1813. Alexandra retained several fine mantlepieces for his own house, and presented the fine portico to St George's Church (CI) in Belfast. The mantlepieces can still be seen in the house. The abbey church is a modern building opened in 1967.

PORT LAOISE, *Port Laoise:*
The Fort of Laois, Laois **17S49**
Formerly known as Maryborough, Port Laoise was the county town of Laois and was a corporate town in the reign of Elizabeth I. There is, however, no sign of its one-time importance because Cromwellian troops battered down its old castle in the 17thc. The courthouse was designed by Richard Morrison, and the town's gaol dates from 1830. In the burial ground behind the gaol is the former CI church. The well-known esker ridge of Maryborough is a glacial embankment of sand and gravel which runs N to S for nearly 20m, passing close to the town. The Great Heath of Maryborough lies NE on the Dublin road. James Gandon designed the CI church at Coolbanagher, which lies 5m NE, in the early 1780's; it has since been the subject of alteration. The mausoleum of the 1st Earl of Portarlington, also by Gandon, dates from 1789 and is attached to the outside of the church.

PORTMARNOCK, *Port Mearnóg:*
St Earnán's Harbour, Dublin **19O24**
The splendid expanse of sand at this small seaside resort is known as the Velvet Strand. Another attraction is the world-famous championship golf course. About 3¼m SW of Portmarnock is interesting St Doolagh's Church, which probably dates from c1200 and includes a square tower with living quarters. The church building is divided into two, the western half being for the use of a hermit. More living cells exist in the undercroft. Adjacent to the old structure is a modern CI church, and close by is an ancient holy well covered by an octagonal stone structure.

PORTNOO, *Port Nua:*
New Harbour, Donegal **4G69**
Extensive sands, rocks, and beautiful scenery which takes in mountains and various coastal features make this fishing village an ideal place for a holiday. It lies close to Narin and is known as an access point for the island of Inishkeel, a place of pilgrimage which can be reached by foot at low tide. The ruined chapel here contains a number of round stones which are believed to cure rheumatism if rubbed on the affected part for long enough. They are all highly polished with long use.

***PORTRUSH,** *Port Rois:*
Harbour of the Headland, Antrim **6C83**
Portrush lies at the N end of the famous Antrim Coast Road and is a popular resort noted for its golf and fine sandy beaches. The town is built on a basalt peninsula called Ramore Head, and its elevated situation affords views which extend from the Donegal mountains to Rathlin Island and Scotland's Mull of Kintyre. The 19th-c parish church (CI) is of interest, and the town hall dates from 1872. The former railway station is a Tudor-style building of 1872. The first electric tramway to operate in Ireland or Britain was opened from Portrush to Bushmills in 1883, and closed in 1947. Beautiful caves can be seen 2m E of the resort at White Rocks, and the handsome early house of Beariville lies 4m SE. An unusual feature of the latter is the heraldic plaque above the door, dated 1713.

PORTSALON, *Port an tSalainn:*
The Harbour of the Salt, Donegal **5C23**
Features of this delightful place include a picturesque harbour and a sandy beach which extends for 2m. The local church (CI) preserves the salvaged bell of the bullion-laden *Laurentic*, which was sunk by a German torpedo off this coast in 1917. The area around Portsalon is noted for its natural beauty. Lough Swilly is bounded to the E by the hills of the Inishowen Peninsula and to the W by 1,200ft Knockalla Mountain. Directly across the lough from Portsalon is prominent Dunree Head, which is backed by the Urris Hills. Wonderful caves and arches have been eroded from the cliffs along the coast N of the harbour, and 1½m away are the Seven Arches. This feature comprises a series of caves and tunnels accessible on foot. Some 2m farther is the interesting Doaghbeg Arch.

PORTSTEWART, *Port Stíobhaird:*
Stewart's Harbour, Derry **6C83**
Sited a few miles W of the larger Portrush, this pleasant resort offers safe, sandy bathing beaches and some interesting cliff scenery. The town was first developed in the 19thc, when Low Rock Castle was built high on the edge of a cliff. This building, described by Thackeray as a 'hideous new castle', is now St Mary's Dominican Convent.

PORTUMNA, *Port Omna:*
Port of the Tree Trunk, Galway **16M80**
Portumna is a small market town set at the head of Lough Derg. A Dominican priory (NM) to the S of the town dates from 1426 and includes the ruins of the church and conventual buildings. A few arches of the east window still exist. Adjacent to the priory is the demesne of Portumna Castle (NM), which now serves as a government forestry centre. At one time it was the seat of the Burke family, Earls and Marquesses of Clanricarde. The castle dates from the early 17thc and is an exceptionally-fine semi-fortified house; it was burnt in 1826. The house built at the other end of the demesne by Sir Thomas Deane was meant to replace it, but this too was burnt down in 1922. The keeps of many ruined castles exist in the surrounding countryside – two on the E side of the Shannon in the grounds of Belle Isle; the keep of a 13th-c Irish style castle at Old Court near Terryglass; three on the banks of Lough Derg at Cregg Point; and one at Drominagh, on the opposite side of the lough. Terryglass, which lies 7m SE, is also the site of a celebrated early monastery (see entry).

POULAPHOUCA, *Poll an Phúca:*
The Púca's Pool, Wicklow **18N90**
This is the place where the River Liffey falls 150ft in a series of cataracts. Immediately under the road bridge the finest of these falls tumbles into the pool from which the placename is derived – the 'Pool of the Pooks', or 'Puck's Hole', the home of a playful water sprite. The river and falls can be viewed from both sides of the bridge, from the wooded glen S of the hotel, and from the banks of the river above the bridge. Developments in connection with the Dublin hydro-electric scheme have reduced the amount of water in the falls. A dam and power station have been built, and a large reservoir covering more than 5,000 acres has been created.

POWERSCOURT DEMESNE,
Cúirt an Phaoraigh:
Powes Mansion, Wicklow 19 O21
See Enniskerry entry.

POYNTZPASS, *Pas an Phointe:*
The Pass of Poyntz, Armagh 13 J03
Situated in an area of tiny loughs, this village is particularly associated with an engagement that took place in 1598. English troops under Lieutenant Poyntz and an Irish force under Hugh O Neill fought through the thick forest and bogland which then covered the local countryside. The pass was held against O Neill, and this 18th-c village bears the name of the victorious officer. Rear Admiral David Lucas, the first Ulsterman to win the Victoria Cross, was born at nearby Drominargle House. About 2m S in the demesne of Drumbanagher House are Tyrone's Ditches, said to have been constructed by Hugh O Neill during his war against the forces of Elizabeth I between 1594 and 1603. About ¾m SE in the townland of Killysavan is part of a travelling earthwork which is known, in this district, as the Dane's Cast.

PROLEEK DOLMEN, *Prailíc,*
Louth 13 J01
See Ballymascanlan entry.

PROSPEROUS, *An Chorrochoill:*
The Projecting Wood, Kildare 18 N82
This small village lies N of the Grand Canal and is connected with the Rising of 1798. The latter put an end to the prosperous cotton industry which gave the village its English name. About 1m SE of Prosperous is the 18th-c Georgian building of Killybegs, a pleasant construction in red brick. The fine Queen Anne Landenstown House can be seen 2m SE.

PUNCHESTOWN RACECOURSE,
Baile Phúinse:
Punch's Homestead, Kildare 18 N91
Punchestown, one of Ireland's most famous racecourses, is where the annual three-day Kildare and National Hunt Meeting is held. Beside the medieval highway known as the Woolpack Road – which runs between Dublin and Kilkenny – is the Standing Stone of Punchestown (NM). This granite stone tapers to a height of 23ft and is considered one of the finest examples of its kind in the country. It fell in 1931, but was re-erected in 1934. A small, irregular cist grave dating from the bronze age was found at the base of the stone.

QUIN, *Cuinche,* Clare 21 R47
Set in a lovely part of the country which combines beautiful scenery with rich archaeological remains, this little village is noted for its well-preserved Franciscan friary (NM). The builders of this 15th-c foundation used the remains of an Anglo-Norman castle erected by the de Clare family, and three towers still stand at the angles of the friary buildings. The church with its high altar, cloisters, and conventual buildings on the ground floor is fairly complete. Its graceful tower is a local landmark, and the beautiful cloisters are of considerable interest. Although the foundation was suppressed in 1541, the friars continued to live in the precincts or neighbourhood until the early 19thc. Remains of several castles can be seen from the top of the friary tower. One of the most interesting is Danganbrack, a tall tower of 16th-c origin with angle machicolations and high chimneys. This lies about ¾m ENE. Many of the local remains are of MacNamara strongholds. On the opposite side of the river is 13th-c St Finghin's Church (NM), a long rectangular building with triple-lancet east windows and the remains of a richly-moulded south window.

QUINTIN CASTLE, Down 13 J65
This stronghold stands at the W end of Knockinelder Bay, on the site of an earlier structure which was known as Smith's Castle and was erected by Sir Thomas Smith *c*1580. The present building is an early 19th-c castellated mansion which incorporates a 17th-c tower house. Close to the castle is a 5½ft-high standing stone which is held to be the only survivor of a cairn's kerb.

QUOILE, *An Caol:*
The Narrow, Down 13 J44
The Quoile River flows through an island-strewn estuary to enter Strangford Lough below Killyleagh, and the neighbouring countryside has been carefully developed with facilities for picnics and angling. The construction of a controlling barrage against flooding has created a pondage area with a shoreline which has been made a national nature reserve. About ½m N of Quoile Quay is Quoile Castle, a stronghold which dates from *c*1600. Its severely-ruined state is a result of it having been built on soft foundations.

RAGHLY, *Reachla,* Sligo 10 G54
The small neck of land which supports this fishing village juts out into Drumcliff Bay, and is dominated by the fine mountain country which surrounds Sligo Bay. The local Pigeon Holes are two rock basins into which the tide rushes through underground channels.

RAHAN, *Raithean:*
Place of Ferns, Offaly 17 N22
Interesting remains of a 6th-c monastery founded by St Carthach can be seen here. There is no trace of his original church, and the three ruined churches on the site (NM's) are thought to be of 12th-c origin. The roofed church – now pebble-dashed – was begun in the 12thc and was originally cruciform in shape, but it has since lost its two transepts. It is now connected to a later, 18th-c structure, but the old building features a fine chancel arch decorated with heads. The north, south, and parts of the east wall of the chancel are Romanesque, the east window is probably 13thc, and the vault may have been built in the 15thc. A fine rose window with excellent Romanesque decoration is sited on the east gable of the exterior wall. This is thought to have once had a place in the original west gable of the church, above the door. To the E is another church with a good Romanesque doorway. This was probably rebuilt in the 16thc, at which time the doorway and other details from the previously-described church were incorporated. Scant remains of another church can be seen to the S of the main building.

RAHENY, *Ráth Eanaigh:*
Ringfort of the Marsh, Dublin 19 O23
A suburb of Dublin city, Raheny is a village situated on the Dublin to Howth road. A beautiful parish church (CI) in the early-English style occupies the site of an old fort – which can still be traced – on the N shores of Dublin Bay.

RAHINE CASTLE, *An Ráithín:*
The Little Ringfort, Cork 27 W23
Now ruined, this once-powerful O Donovan fortress lies on the E shore of the Castle Haven inlet near Unionhall.

RAHOLP, *Ráth Cholpa:*
Ringfort of the Steer, Down 13 J54
About 2m from Saul is the tiny village of Raholp, the site of one of the earliest churches (NM) extant in Ireland. The foundation was created by Tassach, a disciple of St Patrick, and built within a rath. The interior measures 33 by 21ft, and the 26in-thick walls are remarkable in having been cemented with yellow clay instead of mortar. This church was the unfortunate victim of rather inaccurate restoration work in 1915.

RAMORE HEAD, *Ráth Mhór:*
Big Ringfort, Antrim 6 C84
See Portrush entry.

RANDALSTOWN, *Baile Raghnaill:*
Randal's Town, Antrim 7 J09
A pleasant linen-bleaching and market town on the River Main, near the NE corner of Lough Neagh, Randalstown acquired its present name when it was constituted a borough by charter of Charles II. It has many fine houses, some excellent church buildings, and such interesting features as the Randalstown nature reserve.

cont overleaf

Part of a Georgian terrace in Portarlington, a good example of the period's vernacular architecture.

One of the town's most fascinating features is its 19th-c viaduct, which uses seven stone piers to carry brick-vaulted arches across the River Main. The 18th-c market house is a five-bay two-storey structure which now serves as the Public Library. The Presbyterian (Old Congregational) Church is a fine oval building which was erected in 1790. Its cupola-crowned entrance porch was added in 1829. The 19th-c 1st Presbyterian Church is a rectangular block of basalt with arcaded sides, and the old Methodist Church of c 1840 was built of squared-rubble basalt. The basalt and sandstone Drummaul parish church was built in 1831 on the site of an 18th-c church. St Macanisius' Church (RC) is a 19th-c structure built of basalt and cut granite. The west entrance to early 19th-c Shane's Castle is battlemented and features a Tudor-style entrance arch. A high turret rises to one side, and the O Neill coat of arms is displayed. See entries for Lough Neagh and Shane's Castle.

RAPHOE, *Rath Bhoth:*
Ringfort of the Huts, Donegal **5 C20**
Booths or huts which once clustered round an early monastery – possibly founded here by St Columba – are said to have given this town its name. The foundation which grew up here became the seat of a bishop in the 9thc, and it is possible that the cathedral (CI) incorporates parts of an ancient church. This building is associated with the name of St Eunan. Its transepts were added in 1702, and it gained its tower in 1738. To the SE of the cathedral are the remains of a 17th-c stronghouse erected by Bishop Leslie. Although besieged, this was not finally destroyed until it was burnt down in 1839. A hilltop 2m S of Raplhoe features the round cairn and stone circle of Beltany (NM). The summit offers splendid views.

RASHARKIN, *Ros Earcáin:*
Earcan's Wood, Antrim **6 C91**
High ground lies to the W of this village, which is sited on the edge of the lovely Bann Valley. About 100yds S of the CI parish church is Rasharkin Old Church, which has well-preserved 17th-c walls. This building was still in use until the building of the new church in the 19thc, and was mentioned at the time of the Taxation Roll – c1300.

RATASS, *Rath Teas:*
South Ringfort, Kerry **20 Q81**
Although this is a limestone district, the ancient local church (NM) has been constructed of red sandstone. The nave is the oldest part of the structure, the chancel having been added in the 12thc. A remarkable feature is the flat-headed west doorway, which is surrounded by an architrave in relief. There are antae on the W gable and a fine round-headed window with Romanesque moulding on the east wall. The church was restored c1700.

RATHANGAN, *Rath Iomgháin:*
Iomghán's Fort, Kildare **18 N61**
Several prehistoric cooking places have been found in this area, and the old rath from which the town may take its name can be seen in a field near the church. A branch of the now-disused Royal Canal flows through Rathanagan, and the Red Hills rise to the E.

RATHCORMACK, *Rath Chormaic:*
Cormac's Ringfort, Cork **28 W89**
Rathcormack is situated in the lovely countryside of the River Bride, the banks of which support numerous fine houses and demesnes. Beyond the river to the W is the hilltop site of Georgian Kilshannig House, a fine mansion built by Davis Ducart in the 18thc. Kilshannig churchyard, at Ballinterry, features a Knights Templar gravestone from Mourne Abbey. Lisnagar is another splendid Georgian mansion in the area, SW of the village, and 2m ENE on a tributary of the Bride is Castlelyons village (see Fermoy entry). A large ruined cairn and a holy well are features of 727ft Corrin Hill, which lies off the Fermoy road to the NW of Rathcormack.

RATHCROGHAN, *Rath Cruachan,*
Roscommon **16 M78**
This almost circular, flat-topped mound measures 68yds in diameter and is situated on a plain about 3m NW of Tulsk – just about in the centre of the county. It is associated with the legendary Queen Maeve – Goddess of pagan Connacht – probably one of the most colourful and romantic figures of ancient Ireland. Her husband, whose exploits caught considerably less limelight, was King Ailill of Connacht. Rathcroghan Palace figures in the country's early literature almost as prominently as the great Emain Macha. A limestone cave situated nearly ½m SW in the townland of Glenballythomas is traditionally associated with the rath as the Cave of Cruacha, an entrance to the Otherworld. The entrance of the cave is lined with dry-stone walling and is roofed with lintels for a distance of 14ft. Ogham script on two of the lintels suggests that their origin may have been early-Christian. To the SW of the mound is a monument known as Daithis Grave, which is enclosed by a bank and surmounted by a pillar stone. About ¼m S of the Rathcroghan mound is a circular enclosure called *Relic-na-Ri*, meaning 'Graveyard of the Kings'. At one time this was thought to have been the burial place of royalty, but excavations have proved otherwise. The inauguration mound of the O Conors, Kings of Connacht, lies about 6m S of the mound and is a small cairn of earth and stones called Carnfree. This stands at a height of 8ft and measures 40ft in circumference.

RATHDRUM, *Rath Droma:*
Ringfort of the Ridge, Wicklow **25 T18**
This village is beautifully set above the Avonmore River at the SE end of the gentle Vale of Clara. Its 19th-c parish church is by J J McCarthy and has several good features. A fine view of the vale can be enjoyed from Clara Bridge, which lies 3m N.

RATHFARNHAM, *Rath Fearnáin:*
Fearnan's Ringfort, Dublin **19 O12**
Rathfarnham Castle was built by Archbishop Adam Loftus in 1587 and became a prime source of contention between the royalists and parliamentarians during the 17th-c English civil war. It is now a Jesuit House of Studies and has been adapted for modern life – a process which has meant the removal of its small gothic windows. The drawing room features good ceiling panels painted by Angelica Kauffmann. To the S of the castle is the Pearse family home, where Padraic Pearse set up his famous school, *Colaiset Einne* – St Enda's. The nearby ruined priory was once the home of the Curran family, and Evie Hone had her studio in Marley House between 1943 and 1955. A feature of Marley, which was originally the home of an 18th-c banker, is the stucco work by Michael Stapleton.

Fairly close by is Columba's College, which stands in the grounds of Holly Park and was founded during the 19thc. Near Loreto Abbey is a curious 18th-c structure known as Hall's Barn, while S of the village in the Dublin Hills is the Pine Forest. The latter allows access for visitors to explore the hills which extend from 1,761ft Killakee in the W to 1,479ft Three Rock Mountain in the E. Mount Venus (3½m SSW) features a large dolmen (NM), and to the W is the charming valley of Glenasmole. Also W of the Pine Forest is the Bohernabreena Reservoir. Kippure, the fourth highest of the Wicklow Mountains, rises to 2,473ft from the Dublin and Wicklow county border, and is topped by a television mast.

RATHFRAN FRIARY, *Rath Bhranduibh:*
Brandubh's Ringfort, Mayo **9 G13**
See Killala entry.

RATHFRILAND, *Rath Fraoileann:*
Fraoile's Ringfort, Down **13 J23**
The 506ft hilltop which this village shares with its ancient castle dominates the plain of Iveagh, once owned by the Magennis family – the Lords of Iveagh. Rathfriland Castle was the chief Magennis stronghold, but all that remains of this today is a 20ft fragment of the south front and traces of the east and west walls. This tall, narrow castle dates from 1611, when James divided the baronies of Upper and Lower Iveagh among the chief families of Magennis.

RATHKEALE, *Rath Caola:*
Caola's Ringfort, Limerick **21 R34**
The market town of Rathkeale stands in the heart of the area once owned by the Desmond family, whose castle was burned by Malby in 1580. Local monastic remains are of 13th-c St Mary's Abbey, which was founded by Gilbert Harvey. The gothick RC church is by McCarthy, and the much older Protestant church contains the interesting Southwell monument of 1676.

RATHLIN ISLAND, *Reachlainn,*
Antrim **7 D15**
Situated in narrow North Channel between N Ireland and Scotland's Mull of Kintyre, this L-shaped island is the largest to be found off the Irish coast. It measures 4½m long by a maximum width of 3m, and supports a resident community of farmers who raise sheep and cattle which have to be ferried to the mainland for sale. The E corner of the island supports a dense, intricate mixture of flora and has been designated an area of special scientific interest. A nature reserve has been established in the W corner of Rathlin, where the ground rises over 447ft Slievecarn before dropping to the sea in 400ft cliffs. Detached rock stacks here provide safe, isolated nesting sites for sea birds, and the Atlantic grey seal is often seen in the area.

Also known as Raghery, the island was the *Rikini* referred to by the Greek historian Ptolemy, and was visited by prehistoric man. A stone-axe factory was established on an area of bluestone in the townland of Brockley, and among the relics to be found in the area are flakes and rough artefacts fashioned from this material. The fortified hill of Doonmore is situated 2m NE of Bull Point near the N coast of the island. Its stone-faced rampart measures 12ft in width and is broken by a 5ft entrance on the south-west side. Another entrance exists in a rock cleft to the north. An interesting sweathouse can be seen in Knockan townland, and slight remains of Robert the Bruce's Castle occupy a high promontory on the NE corner of the island, near the lighthouse. This promontory is linked to the mainland by a low neck. While hiding in a nearby cave after his defeat at Perth, Robert the Bruce was taught his famous lesson in perseverance by a spider and resolved not to give up his attempt to gain the throne of Scotland. He eventually returned and won the throne at the Battle of Bannockburn. In 1575 Rathlin castle, probably a de Courcy stronghold by that time, was battered by the guns of Sir Francis Drake.

An early church founded on the island by St Comgall in 508 developed to a more sophisticated structure in succeeding years, but the foundation was under constant attack from the Vikings between the 8th and 12thc. Rathlin has the dubious distinction of being the first place to have been raided by these pirates. In the 16thc the island MacDonnells were slaughtered by Essex's troops, and in the mid 17thc the Campbells overran Rathlin and killed the remaining members of the clan. The men were overcome at *Lag-na-vista-vor*, 'the hollow of the great defeat', and the MacDonnell women were slaughtered on the hill above – 'the hill of screaming'. Rathlin has been the home of the Gage family since the mid 18thc, when the Rev John Gage bought the leasehold. The 18th-c Manor House stands amid several other buildings associated with its maintenance.

RATHLIN O BIRNE ISLAND,
Reachlainn Uí Bhirn, Donegal 4G47
See Malin More entry.

RATH LUIRC, *An Ráth:*
The Ringfort, Cork 22R52
As a compliment to Charles II, the Lord President of Munster substituted the name Charleville in place of this town's true name. The original name has now been restored. The town itself is a market centre situated NW of the Ballyhoura Hills, near the Limerick county border. In 1690 the Lord President entertained the Duke of Berwick in his fine mansion, but the Duke repaid his hospitality by burning the house to the ground. The grave of Clarach Mac Domhnaill, the 17th-c Gaelic poet, is ¼m SSE in the cemetery of the old church of Ballysallagh.

RATHMACKNEE CASTLE,
Ráth Mac Naoi:
The Ringfort of Naoi's Sons, Wexford
25T01
This well-preserved stronghold (NM) was probably erected by John Rosseter, who was made Seneschal of the Liberties of Wexford, in 1451.

RATHMICHAEL, *Ráth Mhichíl:*
Michael's Ringfort, Dublin 19O22
See Bray entry.

RATHMINES, *Ráth Maonais:*
Ringfort of de Moenes, Dublin 19O13
In 1649 this Dublin suburb was the scene of the defeat of the Marquess of Ormonde by parliamentarians. The famous writer James Joyce was born in Brighton Square, at nearby Rathgar. The poet and dramatist J M Synge was born in a local house, that was known as Newton Villas, in 1871.

RATHMORE, *An Ráth Mhór:*
The Big Ringfort, Meath 18N76
It is thought that the ruined church (NM) here was built by members of the Plunkett family in the mid 15thc. It features interesting monuments and a fine east window. To the N of the church is a 16th-c cross erected by Sir Christopher and Lady Catherine Plunkett.

RATHMULLAN, *Ráth Maoláin:*
Maolan's Ringfort, Donegal 5C22
An attractive resort with a sandy beach, Rathmullan faces Lough Swilly and the Inishowen peninsula from a position which is sheltered by high inland hills. Close by are the ruins of a Carmelite friary (NM) which was founded by MacSwiney – Lord of Fanad – in the 15thc. Among the remains are a church with a south transept and some domestic buildings. In 1595 it was raided by George Bingham, who stole many valuable church properties, and in 1602 it passed to Captain Bingley. King James granted it to James Fullerton in 1603, and Bishop Knox acquired the building soon after. The bishop extended and restored the complex, and erected two Scottish-style turrets at the east end of the nave.

Red Hugh O Donnell was tricked into boarding a ship here, and was taken to Dublin Castle where he was imprisoned for four years before he made good his escape. After this came the 'Flight of the Earls', in which the Earls of Tyrone and Tyrconnell fled to France with their friends and relatives. Wholesale confiscation of their estates paved the way for the Plantation of Ulster with settlers from England and Scotland. A useful passenger ferry operates across Lough Swilly to the village of Fahan.

RATHVILLY, *Ráth Bhile:*
Ringfort of the Tree, Carlow 24S88
The Wicklow Mountains rise E of this neat village, which lies in the River Slaney valley near the large, Anglo-Norman Rathvilly Moate. This motte is associated with Drimhthann, a one-time King of Leinster who was baptized by St Patrick at a nearby holy well. Joseph Welland designed the fine buildings of local Disraeli School for Benjamin Disraeli in 1826. Some 3½m SE of the village is Haroldstown Dolmen, a portal grave composed of several sidestones supported by two slightly-tilted capstones. This is unusual in having served as a dwelling place until fairly recent times.

RATTOO ROUND TOWER, *Ráth Tuaidh:*
North Ringfort, Kerry 20Q83
See Ballyduff (near Ballybunion) entry.

RAY, *An Ráith:*
The Ringfort, Donegal 2B93
A monastery known as *Moyra* – the Plain of the Fort – once stood here, the site of which is marked by the ruins (NM) of a 16th-c church. The south wall of this structure features four large round-headed windows and a pointed doorway. An unfinished high cross (NM) measuring 21ft long lies before the door.

REAR CROSS, *Crois na Rae:*
The Cross of the Level Spot, Tipperary 22R85
Numerous megalithic monuments exist in the hills around Rear Cross. One of the best is Shanballyedmond, a single-court grave situated on the E spur of the Slievefelim Mountains about ¼m S. Excavations in 1962 showed this 30ft tomb to comprise a narrow funnel-shaped forecourt leading into a two-chambered gallery.

RED BAY, *Cuan an Deirg:*
Red Man's Bay, Antrim 7D22
See Cushendall entry.

REEFERT, Wicklow 19T19
See Glendalough entry.

RENVYLE, *Rinn Mhaoile,*
Galway 14L66
Safe bathing from fine beaches is offered by this promontory, which extends from the beautiful N coast of the Connemara region. The offshore islands of Crump and Shanvallybeg lie in front of the larger masses of Inishturk to the NW and Inishbofin to the W. Renvyle House Hotel was once owned by the author and wit, Oliver St John Gogarty. Small Tully Lough lies inland beneath 1,172ft Tully Mountain which, in common with all local waters, offers fine fishing. Renvyle Castle dates from the 14thc and

To the SE of Raphoe's CI cathedral is a fine 18th-c 'stronghouse' erected by Bishop Leslie.

was successively held by the Joyce, O Flaherty, and Blake families. Piratess Grace O Malley made an unsuccessful attempt to capture it. Close by is a small dolmen comprising three uprights and a 7ft capstone, plus a church and a holy well. Renvyle Hill affords panoramic views. Local people took part in the filming of Synge's *Riders to the Sea* here in 1935.

RING OF KERRY, Kerry **26 V76/68**
This name is given to a fine coast road which runs along the shores of the Iveragh Peninsula – the largest of the three great Kerry peninsulas. Starting at Kenmare in the S, the road borders the fine Kenmare River and crosses several inlets via pleasant bridges. Across the river to the S are the peaks of the Caha and Miskish Mountains. From here the road continues W through Parknasilla, Sneem, past a number of attractive inlets, and eventually through Darrynane to climb to the 700ft Coomakista Pass. Farraniaragh Mountain rises to the E. As the route descends, the surrounding countryside takes on a gentler aspect which becomes almost sylvan in the Shallow valley of the River Inny. After Cahirciveen the main route passes a side road which leads W to the rocky headlands that guard the end of the Iveragh, and to Valentia Island. The main route strikes NE to reach little Kells Bay and the wide expanse of Dingle Bay, then continues through Glenbeigh, Killorglin, and Killarney. Throughout this part of the journey the visitor can enjoy fine countryside graced by distant mountain views. The entire drive is a unique experience.

RINGSEND, *An Rinn:*
The Headland, Dublin **19 O13**
In 1647 Cromwell landed at this one-time port of Dublin with 15,000 troops, or 'Ironsides'. On the N side of the port are the North Wall quays, while to the E the granite breakwater of the South Wall extends for over 3m to the Pigeon House Fort – now a power station. Still farther E is the Poolbeg Lighthouse, which overlooks Dublin Bay.

RIVERSTOWN, *Baile Roisín:*
Town of the Little Wood, Cork **28 W77**
This village lies on the Glanmire or Glashaboy River and is noted as a fishing resort. Riverstown House was rebuilt in 1745 by Dr Jemmet Browne, Bishop of Cork. It was opened to the public in 1965 by the owners, with the help of the Irish Georgian Society. Inside is some remarkable plaster work by the Francini brothers, and the beautiful dining room is laid out as it would have been in the 18thc.

ROBERTSTOWN, *Baile Riobaird:*
Robert's Homestead, Kildare **18 N72**
Robertstown stands on the Grand Canal in the vast Bog of Allen. Nearby is the Allenwood turf-burning power station. This is the canal's highest point above sea level, and a hotel was erected here in 1801 to accommodate 'express' canal passengers. Nowadays this building houses interesting exhibitions which form part of the Robertstown Festival, which is held in August. About 1m W of Robertstown the canal divides into two, with the main branch proceeding to Tullamore and the offshoot extending S to Rathangan and Athy to join the River Barrow.

ROCKABILL, *Cloch Dhabhiolla:*
Dabhiolla's Rock, Dublin **19 O36**
See Skerries entry.

ROCKCORRY, *Buíochar:*
Yellow Land, Monaghan **12 H61**
Numerous small loughs lie between the drumlins that are scattered over the district round this small village, and the area boasts many tiny settlements. These, and the many farms, are closely and evenly distributed. About 2½m SW is the picturesque Dartrey Estate. John R Gregg, the inventor of a well-known system of shorthand, was born at Rockcorry in 1868.

ROCKFLEET CASTLE, Mayo **9 L99**
See Newport (Mayo) entry.

ROCKINGHAM HOUSE, *Port na Carraige:*
Landing Place of the Rock, Roscommon **10 G80**
Elegant Rockingham house once stood in a lovely demesne on the banks of Lough Key. It was originally the home of Lord French, who passed it on to Lord Lorton. It was substantially altered by John Nash in the 19thc, and was burnt down twice – the last time being in 1957. The shell of the house still stands, and the demesne has been made into a public park. Interesting features of the grounds include lodges, a ruined church, gatehouses, a fishing house on the lake, and an 'eye-catcher' castle.

ROSBEG, *Ros Beag:*
Small Headland, Donegal **4 G69**
There is a good sandy beach at this Dawros Bay resort, which lies between Dawros Head and Loughros More Bay. There are magnificent sand dunes at Tramore Beach, and opportunities for bathing and surfing are good. Nearby lakes offer trout fishing. Fine views of the cliffs of Slievetooey to the S and distant Aranmore Island to the N can be enjoyed from Dawros Head, which lies about 2m WNW of the resort. Also of interest are scant remains of a church with a cross pillar, and a ruined castle at Kiltoorish Lough.

ROSCOMMON, *Ros Comáin:*
St Coman's Wood, Roscommon **16 M86**
Namesake and county seat of Co Roscommon, this community has a castle and Dominican friary that both rate as National Monuments. The castle is an imposing structure which dates from the 13thc and occupies a hillside site. It was originally built by Robert de Ufford, the Lord Justice of Ireland, and is a quadrangular-shaped building with rounded bastions at each corner.

The Dominican friary was founded in 1253 by Felim O Conor, the Lord of Roscommon. It is thought to occupy the site of an earlier foundation, created by St Coman in the 8thc, and was rebuilt in 1453. Remains of the church comprise the nave, chancel, and transept, with aisle separated from the last-mentioned by four pointed arches resting on round pillars. The 15th-c tracery in the east and west windows – which have replaced the original lancets – has largely disappeared. An original lancet is preserved in the south wall. The friary's greatest treasure is the 13th- or 14th-c effigy of Felim O Conor, which stands in a niche in the north wall near the old site of the altar. It now shares a 15th-c tomb with eight mail-clad knights, each of which occupies a niche surmounted by angels. Traces of another 15th-c tomb can be seen on the opposite wall. Also in the town are several good Georgian houses, and a courthouse designed by Sir Richard Morrison in the 18thc. Deerane Abbey lies in ruins to the NE, and about ¼m farther in the same direction is the demesne of Hollywell House. The latter is associated with the Gunning sisters, 18th-c beauties who were said to owe their fine complexions to the waters of St Brigid's Well – which rises in the grounds.

ROSCONNELL, *Ros Chonaill:*
Conall's Wood, Laois **23 S47**
Remains of Rosconnell's 13th-c nave-and-chancel church can be seen here. The structure was rebuilt in 1646, but the 13th-c east window has been preserved.

ROSCREA, *Ros Cré:*
Cré's Wood, Tipperary **23 S18**
This prosperous market town is a good centre from which to explore the Devil's Bit and Slieve Bloom Mountains, and has many sporting facilities for the visitor. The town's main interest, however, is in its rich collection of antiquarian remains. A round tower (NM) which stands on the W side of Church Street has a doorway 15ft above the ground and carries the faint representation of a ship on the inner face of a window. The top 20ft of the tower were removed to make it suitable for use as a cannon emplacement. Also in Church Street is the parish church (CI), which is dedicated to 7th-c St Cronan. The entrance to the church grounds is formed by the 12th-c west facade of the ancient monastery which once stood here. A hood moulding above the round-headed Romanesque doorway encloses the figure of a bishop or abbot – maybe St Cronan himself – and a series of blind arcades exists on each side of the door. A decorated high cross dating from the 12thc can be seen to the S of the facade.

St Cronan's Church (RC) in Abbey Street is built on the site of a friary which was founded by the O Carroll family prior to 1477. Only the east and north walls of the chancel, the bell tower, and parts of the north nave arcade exist from the old structure. Close to the west end of the modern church, which was built to designs by Dane Butler, is a pillar which displays an animal carving and may date from the 8thc. King John is credited with having built Roscrea Castle (NM), but it is thought that the structure was actually erected c1280. Its enclosure, now reached through a 19th-c gateway, was surrounded by a strong wall defended by one rectangular and two D-shaped towers. Among the remains here is a tall rectangular tower with a fine vault and a second-floor fireplace intact. Many passages lead from the upper floors to various defensive positions. Holes in the wall which faces the street indicate the place where the drawbridge was probably situated. The castle was the property of Conor O Heyne, Bishop of Killaloe, and his successors until it was granted to Edmund Butler by Edward II in 1315. The early 18th-c house in the courtyard contains a very elaborate staircase.

About 2m SE of Roscrea is Mona Incha Abbey (NM), a foundation which stands on land that was once an island in surrounding bog. The settlement is thought to have been created by St Cainnech of Aghaboe. Its nave-and-chancel church displays a finely-decorated 12th-c west doorway, and a richly-ornamented chancel arch fashioned from sandstone. A small 15th- or 16th-c sacristy exists in the northern part of the chancel. Some 2½m WNW across the Offaly border is the modern Mount Joseph Abbey, a Cistercian house which comprises a church, college, guest houses, and other domestic buildings – all set in fine grounds. A silk farm which is operated here is the only one of its kind in Ireland. The Timoney Hills, which rise 5m SE of Roscrea, feature a 100-acre site which boasts approximately 300 standing stones (NM). The Slieve Bloom range rises NE of the town. An attractive 18th-c house called Gloster stands 5m NW and features a two-storey hall. It was visited by Wesley in 1749, and was originally built for John Lloyd. It now forms the nucleus of a Salesian convent known as the Mary Immaculate House. To the SW of the town is ruined Ballinakill Castle, which was built by Piers Butler of Paulstown c1580.

ROSENALLIS, *Ros Fhionnghlaise*:
The Wood of the White Stream,
Laois **17 N 30**
Several whitewashed cottages add charm to this attractive village, which was once a Quaker settlement and a centre of the linen industry. The oldest Irish burial ground of the Society of Friends is near by, and dates from c1700. Also of interest here are the slight remains of an early monastery.

ROSGUILL PENINSULA, *Ros Goill*,
Donegal **15 C 14**
Sheep Haven and Mulroy Bay lie either side of this scenic district, which can be toured by means of the 'Atlantic Drive'

route. This road circles the head of the peninsula, near the fine sands of Tranarossan Bay, and provides magnificent views of Donegal. The panorama extends from Horn Head in the W to Melmore Head in the E, and the mountain of Muckish is prominent in the SW. One of the best times to take this route is in spring, when the sand dunes of Tranarossan Bay are covered in curious and interesting flora.

ROSS CARBERY, *Ros O gCairbre*:
The Wood of the O Cairbre Family,
Cork **27 W 23**
Caves near this popular resort, which is beautifully situated at the upper end of a narrow inlet, are known for the melancholy sound which they produce as the tide rushes through the bay. A monastery founded here by St Fachtna in the 6thc eventually became the seat of a bishopric. Slight remains of a priory can be seen at the S end of the town. Although St Fachtna's Cathedral (CI) displays some medieval work, it has a 17th-c tower and dates largely from the 19thc. The nave is divided from the choir – an unusual feature in an Irish church. The Knights Templar had an establishment 1m E at Templefaughtnan. An interesting walk along the E side of Ross Carbery Bay passes the wooded demesne of Castlefreke and continues to Galley Head, where there is a lighthouse. High on Croghan Hill, which rises near Galley Head, is the 30ft-high Carbery Cross. This was erected in memory of the 9th Baron Carbery, who died in 1918. Several old castles can be seen around Galley Head, notably at Dunnycove, Donowen, Dundeady, and Arundel. The tower of an old castle stands in the grounds of Downeen, on the W side of

Ross Carbery Bay. See also entries for Coppingers Court and Glandore.

ROSSERK FRIARY, *Mainistir Ros Eirc*:
Monastery of Earc's Headland, Mayo
9 G 22
See Killala entry.

ROSS ERRILLY FRIARY, *Ros Oirbhealagh*:
The Headland, Galway **15 M 24**
See Headford entry.

ROSSES POINT, *An Ros*:
The Headland, Sligo **10 G 64**
The fine 18-hole championship links of the Co Sligo Golf Club, considered one of the finest courses in the country, is situated at this charming resort. The West of Ireland Professional Championships take place here. A sandy, 3m bathing beach extends beneath the local cliffs, and there are magnificent views on all sides.

ROSSES, THE, *Na Rosa*:
The Headlands, Donegal **4 B 71**
An extensive coastal region of little hummocks interspersed with numerous lakes and rocky fields, this delightful district offers enough scenic variety to cater for most tastes.

ROSSLARE, *Ros Láir*:
Middle Headland, Wexford **25 T 01**
Excellent bathing can be enjoyed from this well-known seaside and golfing resort's 6m strand. Rosslare Harbour lies 3m from the town at the SE end of the strand, and to the N is a narrow tongue of land which extends into Wexford Harbour and terminates in Rosslare Point. The sea angling, particularly for bass 9m SE round Tuskar Rock, is excellent. The whole area is rich in ancient remains. Some 6½m S at Carnsore Point are a stone fort, a cross-inscribed stone, and a church and holy well dedicated to St Vogue or Veoc. This site is in an area proposed for development, but it has been suggested that the antiquities might be dismantled and reconstructed near by. In Lady's Island Lake, an inlet of the sea to the W of Carnsore Point, is Lady's Island itself. This features the remains of a granite-built Anglo-Norman castle with a leaning limestone tower, standing on the site of a stronghold built by Rudolph de Lambert. De Lambert was killed on the 3rd Crusade. Beside the castle is the site of an Augustinian priory dedicated to St Mary – still a place of pilgrimage.

ROSSLARE HARBOUR, Wexford **25 T 11**
Car-ferry services operate between Rosslare, Fishguard, and Le Havre. A long pier with a railway crosses the shallows to the embarkation point. The Tuskar Rock Lighthouse can be seen 6m out to sea. See Rosslare entry.

ROSSNOWLAGH, *Ros Neamhlach*,
Donegal **10 G 86**
One of the finest strands in Ireland can be enjoyed at this resort, which is well sited on the coast N of Ballyshannon. The 3m beach stretches along Donegal

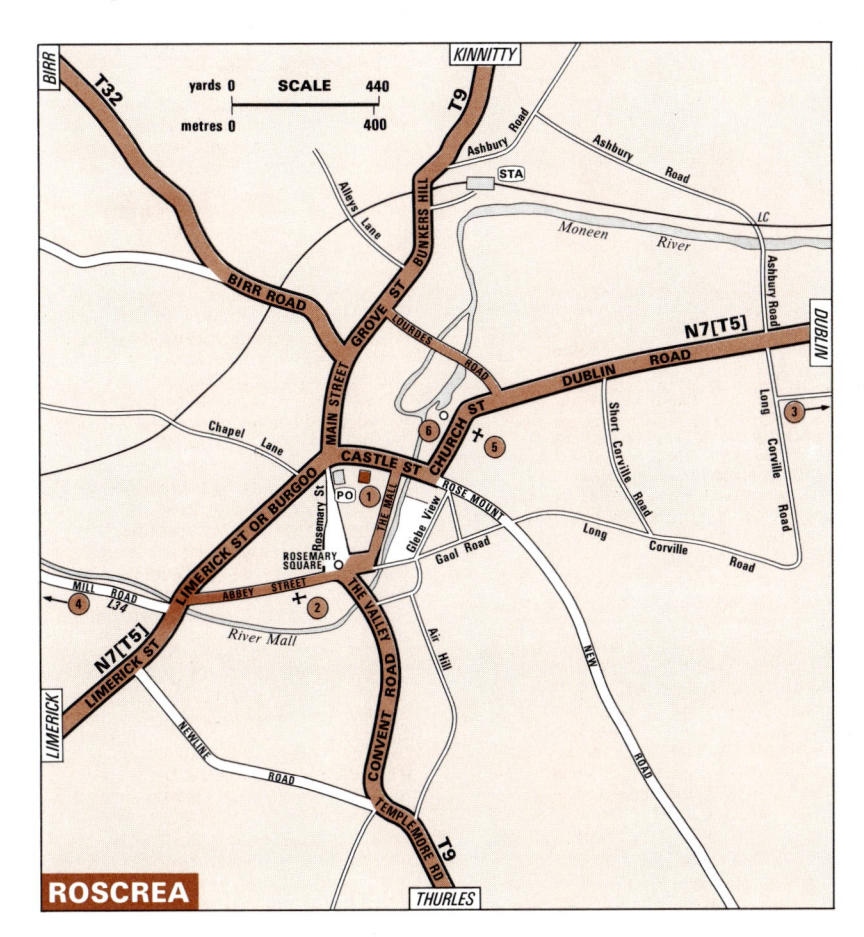

1 Castle
2 Church of St Cronan (RC)
3 Mona Incha Abbey
4 Mount St Joseph Abbey
5 Parish Church of St Cronan (CI)
6 Round Tower

Bay and is backed by fine dunes. Little hills rise inland, and there is cliff scenery to the S. Leisure facilities include a golf course, excellent fishing prospects in the River Erne, and several small trout lakes to the E. The modern Franciscan friary features a garden, shrine, and an interesting museum of local antiquities (OACT). Some 2m SW on the coast is the ruined castle of the O Sgingin family, the hereditary historians of Tir Chonnail. This family was succeeded by the O Clerys. Kilbarron Church, 1m E of the castle, dates from the 13th or 14thc and was built on the site of the original church of St Barron. The latter was founded cAD 545.

ROSTREVOR, *Ros Treabhair*:
Trevor's Wood, Down   13 J 11
This delightful resort of pleasant houses round a broad square is perfectly situated on the SW slopes of the Mourne Mountains, where they roll down to Carlingford Lough. The village is sheltered by both ancient woodland and modern forest, and because it occupies S-facing slopes it enjoys an almost tropical climate. The old natural oakwoods are fully protected as a forest nature reserve.

A delightful coast road to Kilkeel passes Killowen village, from which Lord Russell took his title. Ballyedmond Park is situated beside the lough 2½m SE of Rostrevor and includes a fine house built in the Scottish-baronial style. This now serves as a hotel, and its grounds feature the Ballyedmond single-court grave (NM).

ROUGHAUN, Clare   21 R 29
See Killinaboy entry.

ROUNDSTONE, *Cloch na Rón*:
The Stone of the Seals, Galway   14 L 74
Roundstone is a busy Connemara village situated on the W side of Bertaghboy Bay. Its well-sheltered harbour is almost landlocked, and the village itself was built in the 19thc by the Scottish engineer Alexander Nimmo. The first settlers here were Scottish fisherfolk. One of the main attractions in the area is Dog's Bay. This and Gorteen Bay are formed in the long, curving shore of a sand spit which joins a 1m-long granite island to the mainland. The two bays are set back to back, and both have sparkling white shell sand which holds many whole shells of numerous types.

On the road to Ballynahinch Lake, 2m N of Roundstone, are the slight remains of a Dominican priory which was founded by the O Flaherty family in the 15thc. The scenery here is striking.

ROUNDWOOD, *An Tóchar*:
The Causeway, Wicklow   19 O 10
Scenery and fishing are the two main attractions offered by Roundwood, a village which lies in the wooded valley of the Vartry River. To the E is the great reservoir which supplies Dublin, Bray, and Dun Laoghaire – an artificial lake that covers 400 acres and was constructed in the 19thc. A short distance W are Loughs Dan and Tay, lakes with a rare beauty which is heightened by the contrasting schist and granite masses which rise round their shores – spurs of the Wicklow Mountains. The larger of the two is Lough Dan, which lies in a hollow between the mountains of Knocknacloghole and Slieve Buckh.

The hills near Lough Dan were once a refuge for Holt, a leader of the 1798 Rebellion who evaded capture until the collapse of the rebellion. He was finally taken by English forces. Luggals, an estate on the shore of Lough Tay, has luxuriant wooded grounds that contrast pleasantly with the stark granite cliffs. The lodge by the lough-side was built for surgeon Philip Crampton, who was born in 1777, and a garden temple which once stood at Templeogue House has been erected in the grounds.

ROWALLANE, Down   13 J 45
See Saintfield entry.

ROYAL CANAL, 18 N 84 etc.
Started in 1798 and finally completed in 1817, this canal extends 100m from the environs of Dublin in the E to Richmond Harbour on the Shannon – near Cloondara in Co Longford – in the W. It is presently disused, although some parts are being restored for leisure use. The most important town on the canal's route is Mullingar, and its termination at Richmond Harbour is marked by a number of 18th-c warehouses.

RUSSBOROUGH HOUSE, Wicklow   18 N 91
Richard Cassels and Francis Rindon of Clooney in Co Clare designed this Palladian-style house for the 1st Earl of Milltown in 1741. It is considered one of the finest Georgian houses in Ireland, and comprises a central block flanked by curved colonnades. Opposite the house is the extensive Poulaphouca Reservoir.

RUTLAND ISLAND, *Inis Mhic an Doirn*:
Mac an Doirn's Island, Donegal   4 B 71
In 1785 the Duke of Rutland tried to establish a port on this island. He financed the construction of quays and stores, and for a while this was a successful competitor in the lucrative herring industry. Nowadays the ruins of these installations lie beneath the sands. Napper Tandy landed on the island with a body of French soldiers in 1798.

SAINTFIELD, *Tamhnach Naómh*:
Field of the Saints, Down   13 J 45
Set amid rolling drumlins characteristic of Co Down, this delightful village is set in a market district which also operates a linen industry. In 1798 this was the scene of an engagement between the United Irishmen under Henry Munro and the Yeomanry under Col Stapleton. Munro emerged the victor, only to be defeated at Ballynahinch. Francis Hutcheson, father of the 'Scottish School' of philosophy was born 4m NW at Drumalig in 1694. Saintfield Market House was built in 1802 by the landlord Nicholas Price. About 1m S are the Rowallane Gardens (NT) – some 50 acres of rough ground punctuated by granite outcrops which were transformed into a series of gardens in the 1920's by Mr Hugh Armytage Moore.

ST MACDARA'S ISLAND, *Oileán Mhic Dara*:
Mac Dara's Island, Galway   14 L 73
This island lies a little to the W of Carna, off the Galway coast, and features the unique Church of St Macdara (NM). The building stands on the E shore and was founded by St MacDara in the 6thc. It is a rectangular structure formed of massive slabs and features a flat-headed doorway plus a round-headed east window. A particularly-unusual feature is the fact that the antae continue up the gable and meet at the top – a form of design more usually found in wooden churches. Parts of the original stone roof are intact. To the E of the church is the Saint's Bed, near which a decorated stone finial has been found. Among the other relics of this foundation are remains of several pilgrimage stations with early-Christian decorated slabs. St MacDara was venerated by sailors, and passing ships still dip their sails as a mark of respect.

Close to the Galway shore of Mason Island is a ruined church, and the tower of ruined Ard Castle stands on the mainland.

ST MULLIN'S, *Tigh Moling*:
St Moling's House, Carlow   24 S 73
To the NW of this attractive River Barrow village is 1,694ft Brandon Hill, while the Blackstairs range culminates with 2,610ft Mount Leinster in the NE. The village itself features both early-Christian and medieval remains (NM's). The monastery was founded by 7th-c St Moling, who later became Bishop of Ferns and Glendalough, and was the royal burial place of the Kings of Leinster. Remains of St Mullin's Abbey include a medieval nave-and-chancel church with a spiral staircase. Close by are relics of a round tower, a tiny oratory, and a small granite high cross with a crucifixion scene and various ornamentations. Lower down the slope is a medieval building with a diamond-shaped east window. The 'Bath' is a small building with antae.

ST PATRICK'S ISLAND, *Inis Phádraig*:
St Patrick's Island, Dublin   19 O 26
See Skerries entry.

ST PATRICK'S PURGATORY, *Purgadóir Phadraig*:
St Patrick's Purgatory, Donegal   11 H 07
St Patrick's Purgatory is situated on flat Station Island in Lough Derg, and vies with Croagh Patrick as a place of pilgrimage. The lough measures 6 by 4m and lies a few miles N of Pettigo in the hills of S Donegal. The actual Purgatory is a deep, narrow cave which has been famous for centuries and lies in an eerie, desolate region. Local tradition relates that the island was populated with evil spirits which were a terror to the people of the district, and that St Patrick fasted in the cave for 40 days and nights until the Devil was driven from his last stronghold in Ireland. It is also said that the cave is a gateway to Hell, and that visions of that place may be had from it. Camp follower and historian Geraldus Cambensis mentions the cave in an account of his 12th-c visit to Ireland, and in 1185 Henry of Saltrey recorded an account of the pilgrimage undertaken to Lough Derg by a knight called Owen.

During the middle ages this great reputation drew pilgrims from all parts of Europe, including many high-ranking persons of state and church. In 1497 Pope Alexander VI forbade the faithful to resort to the cave, but this had little effect and the order was revoked in 1503. The pilgrims were also granted liberal indulgences, and in 1522 the legend was included in the Roman Missal. Cromwellian troops later wreaked havoc on the island, and in the 18thc an Act of Parliament was passed declaring any assembly at the cave illegal, but pilgrims continued to arrive. The cave is now sealed, but the island has lost none of its attraction and between June and August it is not unusual to find thousands of the faithful spending two nights on Station Island. An interesting building here today is William Scott's fine basilica, which features an excellent series of early 20th-c windows by Harry Clarke.

A monastery was founded by St Aed on Saint's Island, at the N end of the lough, in the 6th or 7thc. Surviving remains include a ruined medieval church which stands on the site of the original settlement.

SALRUCK, Galway **14 L76**
See Leenane entry.

SALTEE ISLANDS, *Na Sailtí:*
Salt Island, Wexford **24 X99**
These two uninhabited islands lie about 5m off the S coast of Wexford, beyond Ballyteigue Bay and Forlorn Point. Great Saltee measures over 1m in length and is the most important bird sanctuary in Ireland. Its 200ft height forms a rocky scarp which faces the full force of the SW Atlantic gales. Little Saltee is also a bird sanctuary, and both islands are breeding places for many different species. Local flora is typical of exposed marine sites. Bagenal Harvey and John Colclough, both leaders of the 1798 Rebellion, were caught on Great Saltee and later executed.

SALTERS CASTLE, Derry **6 H98**
Built by the Salters' Company of London as a Plantation stronghold c1619, the remains of this castle occupy a site on the W shore of giant Lough Neagh.

SALTHILL, *Bóthar na Trá:*
Strand Road, Galway **15 M22**
Salthill is a seaside resort which is also a suburb of Galway, situated W of the city on the shore of Galway Bay. Its attractions include good bathing and a fine promenade which affords fine views. To the S are the hills of Clare, and to the SW the Aran Islands stretch across the mouth of the bay. The RC church of Christ the King contains a wooden Crucifixion by Claire Sheridan, figures of the Sacred Heart and the Blessed Virgin by Oisin Kelly, and three altars by Michael Scott.

SANTRY, *Seantrabh:*
Old Dwelling, Dublin **19 O13**
A Swiss-style village which was created in the 19thc by Lady Domville can be seen in this Dublin suburb. Perhaps the most notable building in the village is St Pappin's Church, which occupies the site of a 6th-c foundation created by St Pappin, and a later 13th-c church. Inside is a beautiful hexagonal font of 14th-c date, and fine reredos of 1709. The John F Kennedy Athletic Stadium is situated at Santry, and the demesne of former Santry House is of note. Dublin Airport, 2m N at Collinstown, includes a modern terminal building by Desmond Fitzgerald and a mid 20th-c church by A D Devane. Some 2m NE of the suburb is a small Georgian house called Woodlands, which was erected c1720 by the Rev Jack Jackson.

SCARRIFF, *An Scairbh:*
The Shallow, Clare **22 R68**
Anglers interested in either sea or freshwater angling will be interested in this little fishing resort, which lies close to Scarriff Bay. The River Graney flows from the Slieve Aughty range and passes through Loughs Graney and O Grady before entering Lough Derg. The island of Inishcealtra (see entry) lies in Scarriff Bay.

SCARVA, *Scarbhach:*
Shallow, Down **13 J04**
Picturesquely set between two ridges, this 18th-c village is particularly noted for its July celebrations. These commemorate July 13, 1689, when Williamite forces rallied here on their advance to the S. Part of the festivities involves the decoration of a 19th-c topiary figure of William III, which is formed of hawthorn and situated by the station wall. A mock battle is fought between William of Orange and James II in front of Scarva House, an 18th-c structure with some 17th-c features. A beautiful Spanish chestnut tree here is said to have sheltered William's tent.

A 1½m length of the ancient defensive boundary known as the Danes's Cast (NM) lies SW and S of Lough Shark, in Scarva demesne. It extends between Armagh and Down and is thought to have been built by rulers of Ulster who were forced to retreat E from their great stronghold of Navan c330. The defences consist of earthern banks and ditches constructed to link natural obstacles – a good protection against cattle thieves. Numerous raths and the discovery of ancient weapons in the district seem to indicate numerous engagements. Of particular interest is the Rath of Lisnagade (NM), a trivallate structure with an associated smaller rath in the avenue leading to Lisnagade House. In plan the whole fortress is roughly pear shaped and measures 300 by 200yds. To the N of the village in Terryhoogan townland is the old church of Ballynahack. It is thought that the site may be pagan in origin, and it is chiefly remembered as the last resting place of the 17th-c highwayman Redmond O Hanlon. An ancient ecclesiastical bell found near his grave in 1725 is preserved in the Royal Irish Academy, Dublin. It carries an inscription which shows it to have been in use prior to AD 908.

SCATTERY ISLAND, *Inis Cathaigh:*
Cathach's Island, Clare **21 Q95**
See Kilrush entry.

SCHULL, *An Scoil,* Cork **27 J93**
Mount Gabriel rises to 1,339ft to the N of this remote village, which lies 15m W of Skibbereen on the shores of Schull Harbour. There is good bathing, and the surrounding district is of geological interest. A wedge-shaped gallery grave near the village is known as the 'Altar'. Ardtenant Castle stands near Schull Harbour and was once a stronghold of the O Mahonys. The village was a terminus of the Schull to Skibbereen narrow-gauge railway.

SCRABO HILL, *Screabach:*
Crusted Place, Down **13 J47**
See Newtownards entry.

SCULLOGUE GAP, *Bearna Scológ,*
Carlow; Wexford **24 S84**
Once the only access over the Blackstairs Mountains, this pass reaches a height of 600ft at its summit before winding down towards the valley of the River Barrow.

SCURLOGSTOWN CASTLE, *Baile Scorlóg:*
Scurlog's Town, Meath **18 N85**
See Trim entry.

SESS KILGREEN,
Seisíoch Chill Ghrianna:
The Seisíoch (land measure) of Grianna's Church, Tyrone **12 H65**
Two prehistoric chamber graves can be seen on this site, which lies 2m WNW of Ballygawley. Only a 4ft-high orthostat and a smaller slab survive from one of these, but the other comprises an oval chamber set in a cairn which has lost its original shape. Excavations conducted in the 19thc revealed several decorated and inscribed stones, but these are now difficult to see. In the adjacent field, however, is a stone which carries a wide variety of easily defined decorations. This ornamentation and the designs on the stones in the nearby grave link the site with a similar monument at Knockmany (see entry), and the passage-grave tradition in general.

SHANAGOLDEN, *Seanghualainn:*
Old Hill-shoulder, Limerick **21 R24**
A village situated 3m S of Foynes, Shanagolden has a Protestant church which incorporates parts of a 13th-c structure. About 2m E of the village is Monisternagalliaghduff Abbey, which is particularly noted for being recorded as one of the few nunneries in existence as early as 1298. It thrived from its foundation to the time of the Dissolution in 1541. Remains here date mainly from the 13thc, and include a church and cloister attached to a ruined Georgian house. The whole site is densely shrouded in trees and ivy. The church extends from the east face of the cloister and has a beautiful double-sided doorway, plus a piscina. The east window and north door were added in the 15thc. To the S of the church is a room called the Black Hag's Cell, where the last abbess is supposed to have dabbled in the Black Arts. A delightful little medieval pigeon house to the SW is one of the last Irish examples of its kind. Shanid Castle (see entry) lies 1½m WSW.

SHANE'S CASTLE, Antrim **7 J18**
Shane's Castle – seat of the Lord O Neill – is beautifully situated beside the N shore of Lough Neagh, midway between the towns of Antrim and Randalstown. It is the only place in Ireland where steam locomotives are in regular use for carrying passengers. A 3ft-gauge track runs for 1½m through a fine stretch of the demesne and past three stations. A 2m strip of land along the N shore of Lough Neagh is managed as a nature reserve by the RSPB in agreement with the owner, Lord O Neill. This reserve is associated with others in N Lough Neagh, and is internationally important as a wintering area for wildfowl from N Europe and Iceland. An interesting area of new woodland and plant life has appeared on ground exposed by the successive lowering of the water level in Lough Neagh. A well-planned nature trail which covers these areas extends for 1½m from the carpark to the lough shore. The Polldoo hide beside the lough is excellent for observing tufted duck and other wildfowl, while the Millburn hide – also on the lough – is especially concerned with reed buntings and sedge warblers. The trail finishes at the remains of the castle, which was destroyed by a fire thought to have been caused by a jackdaw nesting in a chimney. A colony of jackdaws still inhabits the ruins.

Edenduffcarrick (*ie Edan dubh Carrige:* 'The Brow of the Black Rock'), now known as Shane's Castle from its long association with the O Neills of Clandeboye, was first mentioned in 1470. The record appears in the *Annals of the Four Masters* and refers to a town. Earl O Neill commenced a great 19th-c castle with Italian terraces facing the lake, but this was abandoned in 1816 after the older parts were destroyed by fire. A later building on the site of the stables was burnt in 1922, but the beautiful Camellia House remains. It is said that the original square pele tower owes its survival to the presence of a remarkable human head carved on a quoin and known as 'the black head of the O Neills'. As a talisman of the family its origin is unknown, but it is thought to have been brought here by the O Neills when they conquered S Antrim in the 14thc. Two similar stones are built into the castle of Kirkiston, in the Ards Peninsula. Lord O Neill's present house was built in 1958 to a design by Arthur Jury.

SHANID CASTLE, *Seanaid:*
Hill, Limerick   **21 R24**
Although not mentioned until it was granted to Thomas Fitzmaurice in 1230, this stronghold is probably of earlier date than is implied. It was the chief castle of the Desmond family, who adopted the motto *Shanid Aboo*, meaning 'Shanid for Ever', as their war-cry. The 35ft-high motte is surrounded by a ditch and has an outer bank supporting a 35ft-high polygonal tower with a smooth, round interior.

SHANKILL, *Seanchill:*
Old Church, Dublin   **19 O22**
The situation of this village, S of Killiney Bay in the Vale of Shanganagh, affords views of 1,659ft Sugar Loaf across the Wicklow border. To the S is a dolmen, and to the W on the slopes of Carrickgolligan Hill are the ruins of the old monastery of Rathmichael (NM; see Bray entry).

SHANNONBRIDGE,
Droichead na Sionainne, Offaly   **17 M92**
A road through this village is carried across the River Shannon by a fine, sixteen-arched bridge. Immediately to the S, at the meeting-point of counties Offaly, Galway, and Roscommon, the Shannon is joined by the Suck. On the W bank of the river is a 19thc fort built at the time of the Napoleonic scares.

SHANNON HARBOUR,
Caladh na Sionainae, Offaly   **17 N01**
At one time this collection of deserted warehouses, barracks, and other buildings – including the Grand Hotel of 1806 – had a commercially important rôle. They now stare disconsolately at their reflections in the Grand Canal, whose fortunes – like their own – have foundered.

SHANNON HYDRO ELECTRIC SCHEME,
Clare   **22 R56**
See Ardnacrusha entry.

SHANNON POT, *Lag na Sionna:*
The Hollow of the Shannon, Cavan
11 H03
Although this small pool on the lower slopes of 1,949ft Tiltinbane is generally thought to be the source of the Shannon, the river's headwaters are also said to be those of the Owenmore – which rises SE on 2,188ft Cuilcagh. The Shannon itself measures 160m and is the longest river in Ireland.

SHEEP HAVEN, *Cuan na gCaorach:*
Harbour of the Sheep, Donegal   **5 C04**
See Dunfanaghy and Glen entries.

SHELTON ABBEY, *Teach na gCanónach:*
The House of the Canons, Wicklow
25 T27
See Arklow entry.

SHERKIN ISLAND, *Inis Arcáin:*
Arcán's Island, Cork   **27 W02**
See Baltimore entry.

SHILLELAGH, *Síol Ealaigh:*
Descendants of Ealach, Wicklow   **24 S96**
Tiny Shillelagh lies in the wooded valley of the Shillelagh River, below the S foothills of the Wicklow Mountains. About 1½m E is the demesne of Coolattin Park, seat of the Earl of Fitzwilliam. Remains of the once extensive Wood of Shillelagh, whose famous oaks were said to have been used by William II of England for the roofing of Westminster Hall, are of interest. It is thought that this woodland also provided the oak for roofing St Patrick's Cathedral in Dublin. There seems to be no connection between the village and the name by which the traditional Irish blackthorn is known.

SHRULE, *Sruthair:*
Stream, Mayo   **15 M25**
A bridge which spans the Black River here crosses from Galway into Mayo and was the scene of a treacherous ambush in 1641. Almost 100 clergymen and others, retreating from Castlebar under promise of safe conduct by Lord Mayo, were attacked and massacred by Edmund Burke. At the NW end of the village is an early 13th-c parish church (NM). This stands on the site of a foundation created by St Patrick and features a decorated south doorway of 15th-c date. Near by are the massive towers of a ruined, 13th-c castle.

SILENT VALLEY, Down   **13 J31**
Once known as the Happy Valley, this deep trough in the heart of the Mourne Mountains is dominated by the long and deeply-serrated ridge of 2,449ft Slieve Bignian. This mountain is known for the rare plants found in the crevices of its rocks. The Kilkeel River rises in the Silent Valley some 6m N of Kilkeel. Between 1,012ft Slievenagore and Slieve Bignian the river is dammed to form the great reservoir which supplies Belfast and N Down. Rivers that flow into the valley's N end include Mill River, which rises in Slieve Bearnagh; the Bencrom River, which rises between Slieve Meelbeg and Slieve Loughshannagh; and the Shannagh River, which flows from beautiful Lough Shannagh – 'Lake of the Foxes'. The latter is on a broad shelf at the 1,350ft contour, and is the largest lake in the Mourne Mountains. The source of the great River Bann is on the W slope of 2,198ft Slieve Muck.

SILVERMINES, *Béal Atha Gabhann:*
Ford-mouth of the Smith, Tipperary
22 R87
Lying at the foot of the Silvermines range, which culminate in 2,278ft Keeper's Hill, this little village has been a centre of mining for a period stretching back to the 14thc. The silver-bearing zinc and lead ores still yield enough to support a small working. To the NW are the Arra Mountains, and in the W are slight remains of the old O Kennedy stronghold of Dunalley Castle.

SILVERSTRAND, Wicklow   **25 T39**
See Wicklow entry.

SION MILLS, *Muileann an tSiáin:*
The Mill of the Fairy Mount, Tyrone
5 H39
This attractive model village was built to house people who worked in extensive spinning mills owned by the Herdman family. St Teresa's Church was designed in the 19th-c by Patrick Haughey.

SKELLIGS, *Na Scealaga:*
The Rock-splinters, Kerry   **26 V26**
The three Skellig islands lie 20m S of the Blaskets and 8m from the nearest coast. The usual starting point for visiting them is Knightstown on Valentia Island, and excellent views from the boat take in the fine 900ft cliffs of the Iveragh Peninsula. Of the three islands the largest is the Great Skellig, or Skellig Michael, a mass of precipitous slate rock measuring ½m long by ¼m broad. In the NE it rises to 610ft, and in the SW to 715ft. The landing-place was constructed by the Commissioners of Irish Lights, and is connected by road to the lighthouse. To reach the famous monastery ruins of Skellig Michael (NM), sited at a height of 540ft immediately above the landing-place, the road is followed almost to the lighthouse before a sharp right turn is made up a steep ascent to a small green plateau known as Christ's Saddle. A path continues the ascent to a second plateau enclosed by dry-stone walling. Here is a group of five bee-hive huts or clochans, all with corbelled roofs. Beside them stands a tiny oratory of similar construction, but with a window facing the doorway. On a lower level are a sixth hut, a second oratory, a number of crosses and cross-slabs, two wells, and the later Church of St Michael. All these buildings, except the church, are corbelled. The clochans are square in plan and have 6ft-thick walls which contain cupboards, but they have no windows. Two have corbels protruding both inside and out. The oratories resemble the famous Gallarus Oratory on the Dingle Peninsula. The largest of the cross-slabs measures 7ft high and is cut in the shape of a cross. Small areas known as The Monks' Gardens are sited on a series of terraces which cling to the cliff edge. An almost frost-free atmosphere accounts for the excellent preservation of the entire settlement and its enclosing dry-stone walling. The monastery was plundered by the Vikings early in the 9thc, but it continued until some of the monks transferred to Ballinskellig, on the mainland, in the 12thc.

SKERRIES, *Na Sceirí:*
The Reefs, Dublin   **19 O26**
Skerries is a popular seaside resort with a good sandy beach and excellent bathing and golfing facilities. It derives its name from the rock islands which lie off its coast – Red Island, now joined to the mainland; Colt Island; and Inis Patrick or St Patrick's Island, reached by foot at low tide. The latter is said to have been the scene of the saint's landing on his way from Wicklow to Ulster. During his stay of three weeks he crossed daily to Red Island, which boasts a traditional memento of his visit in the shape of his footprints cut into the solid rock. This is said to mark the spot where he stood. St Patrick's Island was chosen,

according to the 'Four Masters' for the venue of the important Synod held 22 years before the coming of the Anglo-Normans in 1148. Fifteen bishops, including Malachy and Gelasius, and 500 priests were present. The ruins of the monastery include an early nave-and-chancel church with a distinctive roof of shaped tufa-stone. This material is not found locally. The foundation dates from 1120 and is attributed to Sitric, Norse King of Dublin and founder of that city's Christ Church Cathedral.

On Shenick's Island, which lies ½m S and is connected to the mainland at low tide, is one of the martello towers erected during the Napoleonic wars. Farther out to sea is Rockabill, a double-peaked granite islet formed by the N outcrop of the great Leinster mountain fold. A lighthouse crowns one of its peaks. At the S end of the town is Holmpatrick, where the church (CI) occupies part of the site of an Augustinian priory which was transferred from St Patrick's Island. In the churchyard are tombs of 16th-c Richard de la Hayde of Loughshinny, 16th-c Elizabeth Finglas, and the last prior. There are two holy wells in the district. One is a grotto well which is dedicated to St Patrick and stands in the parish priest's garden, and the other – 1m W of Skerries – bears the name of 7th-c St Mobhi. St Mobhi's foundation exists N of Dublin at Glasnevin. A short distance W of the railway station are the remains of a fortified bivallate prehistoric site. The fine Anglo-Norman stronghold of Baldungan Castle lies 2m SSW and was erected by the de Berminghams in the 13th-c. It was battered by the guns of the parliamentary army in 1641, while the confederate Catholics were in possession, and was finally blown up by gunpowder. The remains include portions of the curtain walls' square towers. The top of one, reached by a stone staircase, affords an extensive view of the whole coast from the Mourne Mountains in the N to Killiney in the S. Scanty remains of a church (NM) can be seen close to the castle.

For 21 years Skerries was the home of Lynn Doyle (Leslie Montgomery), the Ulster humourist. About 1m NW, to the S of the road overlooking Barnageera Strand, are two prehistoric tumuli. An interesting walk leads S of the town to the little fishing village of Loughshinny, which is sited on a pretty bay where cliffs of curious texture are riddled with caves.

SKERRY, *Scire,* Antrim 7 D20
See Ballymena entry.

SKIBBEREEN, *An Sciobairín,* Cork 27 W13
This market town and fishing port is delightfully situated on the River Ilen, about 1m W of the point where it widens to form a winding estuary joined to Baltimore Bay. The surrounding infertile district was the scene of appalling suffering during the 19th-c Famine. The fine pro-Cathedral was built in the Grecian-style in 1826. There are Georgian houses around the green. To the S of the town is the small Abisdealy Lough, and beyond it are the bay and headland of Toe Head. About 1m W, on the N bank of the Ilen, are the remains of the Cistercian abbey of Abbeystrowry (see entry).

SKREEN, *An Scrín:* The Shrine, Sligo 10 G53
Skreen is situated in a pleasant coastal strip under the shelter of 573ft Red Hill, which has a large stone ringfort on its summit. The remains of an old churchyard and overgrown fragments of a medieval church mark the site of a local monastery which was once a noted religious centre. To the N are remains of the great castle of Ardnaglass, one of the chief strongholds of the O Dowds. To the NW are Aughris Quay and the viewpoint of Aughris Head, while 2m S on the lower slope of Knockachree is Lough Achree – which was formed by an earthquake in 1490.

SLADE, *An Slaod,* Wexford 24 X79
Fine castle ruins (NM) beside the pier in this village survive from the home of the Laffans, who lived here until the confiscation of their property by Cromwell. After this it became the possession of the neighbouring Loftus family, who were later to become the Marquesses of Ely. In 1641 the castle was occupied by the Catholic confederate forces. It was built in two stages, the first of which is a finely tapered, 56ft-high battlemented tower of the 15th and 16thc, with a fireplace and cupboard in a room on the third storey. The second stage was the addition of a house in the late 16th or early 17thc. Annexes (one with a corbelled roof) at the east and west ends may have been added by the builders of an 18th-c salt works which adjoins the pier. Hook Head, guarding the inlet of Waterford Harbour, lies to the SW.

SLANE, *Baile Shláine,* Meath 18 N97
Set in the lovely district of the Boyne Valley – which is famous for its salmon and trout fishing and for its proximity to many historic sites – this little town nestles beneath historic Slane Hill. Four excellent Georgian houses are built around the Square. Francis Ledwidge, the gifted poet who died in Flanders during the 1914 to 1918 war, was born at Slane.

St Patrick is said to have kindled the first Paschal Fire in Ireland N of the village on 529ft Slane Hill in AD 433 to celebrate the triumph of Christianity over paganism. On the W side of the hill is a large, univallate rath which stands 27ft high. St Erc founded a monastery here in early-Christian times, and a medieval abbey existed here. Re-building took place in 1512 with the founding of a small Franciscan friary by Sir Christopher Flemmyng. Both the church and college, founded at the same time, were confiscated at the Dissolution in 1541. In 1631 the Capuchins settled in the monastery until the arrival of Cromwell, but the foundation was abandoned in 1723. The remains (NM) of the nave-and-chancel church include a short south aisle and a tower at the west end. The east face of the tower has a window which may have come from an earlier church. The nearby college (NM) was founded by Sir Christopher Flemmyng and is for four priests, four clerks, and four choristers. It is built around an open quadrangle, with priests' quarters on the north side and a tower on the south. It has several fine windows on its south wall, which forms part of a refectory or reading room. On the north side of the river are the overgrown remains of the Hermitage of St Erc. These include a 15th-c church and earlier tower and dwelling place. Near by is a curious stone, probably a tombstone, featuring twelve carved figures said to be the apostles. Near the river is a holy well dedicated to the Blessed Virgin. This is still resorted to by pilgrims.

Magnificent Slane Castle is situated 1m W of the town, and is said to be one of the finest gothic-revival castles in Ireland. Many of the most famous names in 18th- and 19th-c architecture and design were associated with its building – James Wyatt, Francis Johnston, James Gandon, Thomas Hopper, and Capability Brown – responsible for the beautiful grounds. A mile up the river is Beauparc House, which was built in 1750. Opposite Beauparc are the beautiful and enigmatic remains of Castle Dexter. The ruins of Fennor Church and Castle are situated close to Slane Bridge.
For Brugh na Boinne and the prehistoric tombs of Dowth, Knowth, and Newgrange see inset on p176.

SLEA HEAD, *Ceann Sléibhe,* Kerry 26 V39
See Ventry entry.

SLEATY, *Graigue Shléibhte,* Laois 24 S77
To the NW of this small River Barrow hamlet are the remains of partly 12th-c Sleaty Church and two plain crosses (NM). These stand on the site of a monastery founded by St Fiach, who was

Disused buildings on the Grand Canal at Shannon Harbour – once a thriving centre of trade and commerce.

SLEATY/SLIEVEROE

Bishop of all Leinster in St Patrick's lifetime. The 7th-c Bishop Aed, one of its most famous abbots, dictated a *Life of St Patrick* and made the monastery a school for studying St Patrick's life and teachings.

SLEMISH MOUNTAIN, *Sliabh Mis:*
Mountain of Mis, Antrim **7 D20**
See Ballymena entry.

SLIDDERY, Down **13 J33**
Some 1½m SSW of Dundrum and NW of Slidderyford Bridge stands the perfect dolmen of Slidderyford (NM), a well-known landmark. This portal-grave has no recognisable chamber under its massive, 7½-ft-diameter granite capstone, which rests on a shoulder of the 6ft-high north portal. In the same field, 50 yards to the S, is a souterrain belonging to a later period. A huge 9½-ft pillar-stone is lying near by. Excavations of the sandhills to the seaward side have yielded material dating from the neolithic period.

SLIEVE BLOOM MOUNTAINS, *Sliabh Bladhma,* Offaly **17 S29**
See Kinnity entry.

SLIEVE DONARD, *Sliabh Dónairt:*
Donart's Mountain, Down **13 J32**
See Newcastle (Down) and Mourne Mountains entries.

SLIEVE GULLION, *Sliabh gCuillin:*
Mountain of the Steep Slope, Armagh
13 J02
Highest mountain in Armagh, 1,893ft Slieve Gullion is encircled by a ring of craggy hills measuring about 7m in diameter and rising to over 1,000ft. This is known as the Ring of Gullion, and it stands to the W of a similar ring-dyke on the Carlingford Peninsula. It is now designated an area of outstanding natural beauty. On the summit, which affords breathtaking views, is a cairn known as Calliagh Birra's House (NM). This is of great significance in legend and archaeology. To the N along the mountain top is a small lake which is named after the Calliagh Birra and is reputed to be bottomless.

SLIEVE LEAGUE, *Sliabh Liag:*
The Mountain of Stones, Donegal
4 G57
See Carrick entry.

SLIEVE MISH MOUNTAINS, *Sliabh Mis:*
The Mountain of Mis, Kerry **20/26 Q70**
This fine group of hills occupies part of the peninsula separating Tralee Bay from shallow and almost land-locked Castlemaine Harbour. The highest point is 2,796ft Baurtregaum. Although somewhat eclipsed by the loftier mountains to the W, these hills are nevertheless most impressive. On a spur at the W end, at an elevation of 2,713ft, is the fortress of Caherconree (NM). An ascent by road passes through Camp (see entry) and makes a good starting point for exploring these fascinating mountains.

SLIEVE NA CALLIAGH,
Sliabh na Caillí:
Hag's Mountain, Meath **18 N57**
See Oldcastle entry.

SLIEVENAMON HILL, *Sliabh na mBan:*
The Mountain of the Women, Tipperary
23 S23
See Clonmel entry.

SLIEVEROE, *Sliabh Rua:*
Red Mountain, Kilkenny **24 S61**
The RC church in this village is a

1 Abbey Remains
2 Cathedral (RC; St John's)
3 Courthouse
4 Library & Museum
5 St John's Cathedral (CI)
6 Town Hall

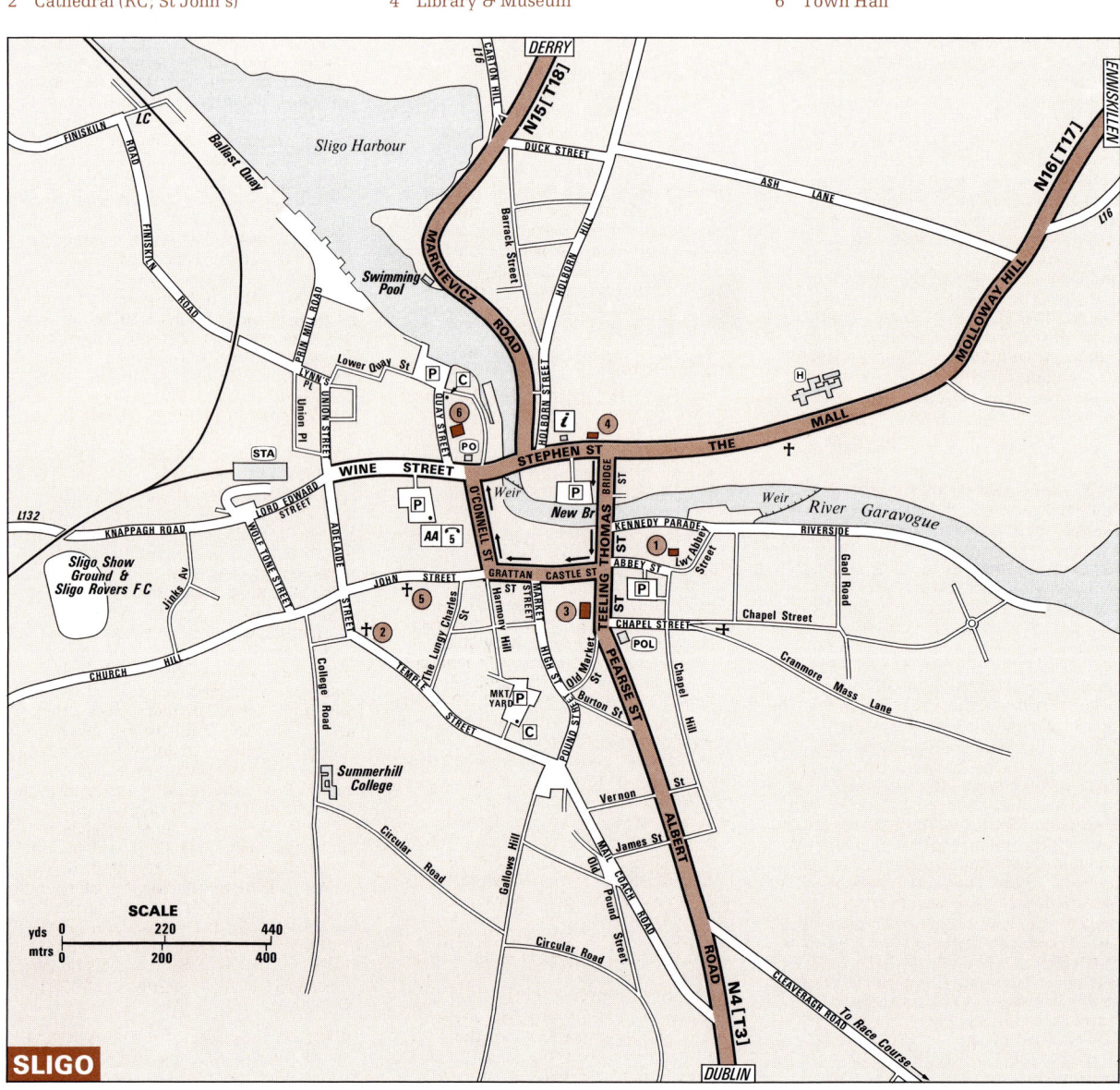

gothic-revival building by Ashlin and Coleman. Close by is ruined Kilmurray Castle, and an 18th-c cross can be seen N of the village. Near by in Nicholastown are the Three Friars pillarstones.

*SLIGO, *Sligeach:*
Shelly Place, Sligo 10 G63
This prosperous town, the second largest in Connacht, is a seaport and manufacturing and marketing centre. It is also the cathedral town of the Catholic diocese of Elphin, and of the Protestant diocese of Elphin and Ardagh. It occupies a strategic position at the ford of the River Garavogue. The river, flowing deep and broad from Lough Gill in the E, falls over ledges of rock near its estuary. The position of the ford around which this town grew is marked by the old bridge, which spans the shallower part of the river. Sligo became significant in historic times with the invasion of Connacht in 1235 by de Burgo, when the town and surrounding territories passed to Maurice Fitzgerald – Lord of Naas and Baron of Offaly. He built a castle in 1245 and founded a Dominican friary in 1253. The town and buildings suffered pillage, burnings, and destruction between 1245 and 1414. The friary (NM) – also known as Sligo Abbey – remains include a church which has a nave and side aisle and a south transept. The choir, the oldest part dating from shortly after its foundation, has eight lancet windows. The 15th-c east window replaced three of the originals. Both the altar – with its carvings of a rose and grapes – and the tower are probably of 15th-c origin. An interesting feature is the partly-reconstructed rood-screen which separated the choir from the nave. In the north wall of the nave is the O Craian tomb, which is dated 1616 and bears sculpted panels. The O Conor Sligo tomb of 1624 is also of interest. The sacristy and chapter house are both of the 13thc, but the cloister and other buildings are thought to be of the 15thc. Of particular interest is the head on the pillar in the north-west corner, and the window in the north wall of the first floor – where the reader in the refectory had his desk.

St John's Cathedral (RC) is in the 19th-c Romanesque style and was designed by George Goldie of London. The CI Cathedral of St John stands on the site of Sligo's first Protestant church, which was built in the 17thc. This was rebuilt to a design by Richard Cassells in the 18thc, and transformed into gothick style in 1812. It has low-relief effigies of 17th-c Sir Roger Jones of Banada, and of his wife Susan. The north transept boasts a tablet to Susan Mary Yeats, mother of the poet W B Yeats, and his painter brother Jack B Yeats. The reredos has a painting of the Creation by Percy Francis Gethin. Sligo's 19th-c town hall was designed in the Italian Renaissance style by William Hayne in 1865. Also of interest are the town's courthouse, museum, and library. Lough Gill (see entry) is easily approached by boat. On the E bank of the Garavogue River is 18th-c Hazelwood House, a good example of a small country mansion which was once the home of the Wynnes. It was designed by Richard Cassells. A popular excursion from Sligo is 5m W to the interesting Knocknarea passage-grave (NM; see entry).

Between Lough Gill and Knocknarea are a number of 'Giant's Graves' which are traditionally thought to be the burial sites of Queen Maeve's chieftains. They are more probably of prehistoric origin. About 4m E of Sligo is Deerpark Court Cairn (NM), one of the most famous court cairns in Ireland. The tomb has a 50ft-long oval central court from which two burial chambers open out at one end and one at the other end. In a field below is a wedge-shaped gallery grave, a fort with a souterrain, a stone circle, and other remains including a stone hut. W B Yeats was born in Sligo in 1865. The town has a number of Georgian and early 19th-c houses of distinction, and 2m WSW is the Carrowmore group of prehistoric tombs (see entry).

SMERWICK, *Ard na Caithne:*
Height of the Arbutus, Kerry 26 Q30
Smerwick village stands near the shores of a fine sandy bay, near the superb coastal scenery of Sybil Head, the Three Sisters, Ballydavid Head, and Brandon Head. Sybil Head is a splendid viewpoint which rises sheer along a sea front of 3m to the W, and can be easily visited from Ferriter's Cove. This cove was the scene of an invasion of Spaniards, accompanied by a Papal Nuncio, in 1579; they built a fort on a rocky spur projecting into Smerwick Harbour and called it *Fort-del-Oro*. It is otherwise known as *Dun-an-noir*. The following year a larger force of perhaps 600, mainly Italians, landed and entrenched there. The troops of Lord Grey stormed the fort, which was destroyed, and all but one defender was killed. Parts of the fort are still visible.

SNEEM, *An tSnaidhm:*
The Knot, Kerry 26 V66
Beautifully situated on the estuary of the Sneem River, Sneem village is a perfect base from which to explore the district on foot. The Catholic church dates from 1865 and contains the grave of Father Michael Walsh, a 19th-c parish priest who was the original 'Father O Flynn' of the song. This Italianate building was the gift of the 3rd Earl of Dunraven. The east window is a memorial to the poet Aubrey de Vere, who died in 1902. The much-altered Protestant church may date from Elizabethan times, and carries a salmon weather-cock above its tower-like exterior.

STAIGUE FORT, *Stéig:*
Rocky Ledge, Kerry 26 V66
Staigue (NM) lies 6m SW of Sneem and is one of the best known and most perfect stone forts in Ireland. Its situation is at a height of 500ft between two streams at the head of a peaceful valley, in a region of exceptional beauty. The massive circular and strongly-built dry-stone rampart reaches 18ft high and 13ft in thickness. It surrounds an area 90ft in diameter, and the interior is reached through a long passage covered with slabs. The inner face of the wall has ten flights of steps arranged cross-wise in two tiers, evidence of a more sophisticated engineering skill than is usually employed for purely defensive purposes. There are two little rooms within the thickness of the wall.

STATION ISLAND, Donegal 11 H07
See St Patrick's Purgatory entry.

STEPASIDE, Dublin 19 O12
Situated on the Dublin to Enniskerry road, this hamlet features remains of the 18th-c Church of Kilgobbin (CI) and a nearby 12th-c granite high cross (NM).

The tall cross is mounted on a square base, but the south part of the ring and arm is missing. There are simple representations of the Crucifixion on both faces. High on the SE slope of Two Rock Mountain is the Ballyedmonduff Giant's Grave (NM), a wedge-shaped megalithic tomb with a rectangular chamber divided into three unequal parts.

STEWARTSTOWN, *An Chraobh:*
The Mansion, Tyrone 12 H87
Lough Neagh lies to the E of this village, which is surrounded by hilly countryside. St Patrick's Church (CI) at nearby Donaghendry dates from the 19thc and was built on the site of an earlier foundation. The 19th-c Catholic church is a small, T-shaped gothick building. Outside the village is an attractive early 19th-c house called Annie Hill, on the road to Cookstown. Stuart Hall, the seat of Lord Castlestewart, was built by John Stewart c1760.

About 1m E is Drumcairne House, a Georgian mansion which is the seat of the Earls of Charlemont. A short distance from the shore of Lough Neagh is Mountjoy Castle (NM), which was built in 1602 as a military station by Lord Mountjoy. The Dutch engineer for Lord Mountjoy's 1602 campaign against Hugh O Neill was responsible for its star-shaped plan. The remains comprise a square stone and brick building with four projecting rectangular towers, each well supplied with loopholes. Much of the castle lies in ruins. Close to Newmills village is Roughan Castle, which was built by Sir Andrew Stewart in 1618. It is a small, square, three-storeyed castle with towers at the four corners. A crannog on Roughan Lake, about 1m NE of Newmills village, is said to be the place where Sir Phelim O Neill was captured c1653.

STILLORGAN, *Stigh Lorgan:*
Lorcan's House, Dublin 19 O22
Of particular interest in this village is Stillorgan Castle, now a hospice of the Order of St John of God. A mausoleum built by Sir Edward Lovett Pearce gives its name to Obelisk House, which he had planned to convert into a Palladian mansion. He died at Tighlorcain House, then known as The Grove, in 1733. The 2nd Viscount Allen was the victim of Swift's satire. Oriel was the birthplace of painter Sir William Orpen, who died in 1931.

STRABANE, *An Srath Bán:*
The White Holm, Tyrone 5 H39
Strabane is a large market town in an agricultural region, pleasantly situated on the banks of the Mourne River. It was once an important rail junction and is still one of the main gateways into Co Donegal. A fine bridge spans the Foyle to link with Lifford in that county. Although Strabane is associated with a middle-ages Franciscan monastery, it was little known until the 17thc. At the time of the Plantation it was granted to a Hamilton, who built a castle which fell to Sir Phelim O Neill in 1641. In 1688 the Williamites garrisoned the town, but it later passed into the hands of James II's troops. Overlooking the town is Knockavoe, the 'Hill of the Cow', where Con O Neill and his Connacht allies were utterly defeated in 1522 by O Donnell.

The view of Strabane from its approach roads is dominated by its three church spires. The Bowling Green, a square with Georgian houses along one side, is dominated by the fine 19th-c parish church of Camus-juxta-Mourne (CI). This was built as a memorial to the Rev James Smith, who was rector here from 1835 to 1860. The beautiful east window depicts the Last Supper and is a memorial to Major and Mrs Humphreys, parents of the celebrated hymn-writer Mrs Cecil Frances Alexander. Her parents once lived in Milltown House, an Elizabethan-style building which now forms the nucleus of Strabane Grammar School. It stands beside a delightful glen. Here the poetess wrote her *Hymns for Little Children*, in which appears her best-loved *All things Bright and Beautiful*, *Once in Royal David's City*, and *There is a Green Hill Far Away*. A beautiful late-Georgian house known as Camus was formerly the rectory to which the Alexanders came in 1860; it is pleasantly sited beside the River Mourne.

The town is associated with many famous men. Gray's Printing Shop (NT) has Georgian-glazed, bow-fronted windows which are a feature of the Main Street. Both John Dunlap and James Wilson served their apprenticeships here. Captain John Dunlap was the printer of the first copies of the American Declaration of Independence, and of America's first daily newspaper – the *Pennsylvania Packet* – in 1771. James Wilson married Annie Adams, an Ulsterwoman whom he met on the voyage to America, and they became the grandparents of USA President Woodrow Wilson. There are still Wilsons who live and farm the family homestead 2m ESE at Dergalt (NT), a typical Ulster farmhouse.

STRADBALLY, *An Sraidbhaile:*
Village, Laois   **18 S59**
Ireland's only steam-traction museum, together with a collection of vintage cars, is located here. Brockley Park, built in 1768 for the Earl of Roden by Davis Ducart, is a short distance to the NE. Kevin O Higgins, Ireland's first Minister for Justice, was a native of Stradbally.

STRADE, *An tSráild:*
The Street, Mayo   **9 M29**
This monastery (NM) was founded for the Franciscans in the early 13thc, but was transferred to the Dominicans in 1252 by Jordan of Exeter. The chancel has six slender side windows in the north wall and probably dates from the 13thc, but the rest of the building may be of 15th-c origin. A beautifully sculptured 15th-c tomb in the south wall is considered to be one of the finest of its kind in Ireland. Other medieval tombstones exist in the sacristy, and a memorial chapel which adjoins the abbey ruins commemorates Michael Davitt, who was born here in 1846.

STRAFFAN, *Teach Srafáin:*
Srafan's House, Kildare   **18 N93**
About 3m NW of Straffan on the River Liffey are the fragmentary remains of Rathcoffey Castle, once the residence of the Wogans. The most famous member of this family was the prominent Jacobite Sir Charles Wogan, who was born c1698 and took part in the Scottish 1715 Rising. He also served in the Dillon Regiment of the Irish Brigade in France, and rescued Princess Clementina Sobieska from Innsbruck; he brought her to Bologna to marry the Old Pretender. Lodge Park dates from the 18thc and was built for Hugh Henry. It is now the residence of R S Guinness, and features four detached pavilions.

STRANDHILL, *An Leathros:*
The Half-Headland, Sligo   **10 G63**
Facilities offered by this well-known Sligo Bay resort include sandy beaches plus golfing and fishing amenities. On the shore NW of the village is the ancient church of Killaspugbrone. Its name dates from the 5thc and is derived from one of St Patrick's disciples – Bron or Bronus – who was a friend of St Brigid's. He later became Bishop of Cassel Irra, which lies SW of Sligo.

STRANGFORD, *Baile Loch Cuan,*
Down   **13 J54**
Strangford village is beautifully situated at the narrowest part of the strait linking Strangford Lough with the sea. The Vikings, who arrived in Strangford Lough in the 9thc, established a trading settlement and a well-protected base from which to launch their merciless raids. The village occupies a site which was considered of supreme importance in the Anglo-Norman occupation of the ancient kingdom of *Ulaidh*; the approach to the coast and the pass inland are guarded by four castles. Strangford Castle (NM) is a 16th-c stronghold which stands in the village and guards the quays. Kilclief Castle (NM) lies 3m S of the village and is dated c1440, while 3m W is late 16th-c Walshestown Castle (NM). The latter is approached through the grounds of the Victorian mansion known as Myra Castle. The 15th-c stronghold of Audley's Castle (NM) stands 1m NW of Strangford in the grounds of Castle Ward (NT).

All the roads in Strangford radiate from the castle-dominated Square, which features a group of fine warehouses and a green. It is thought possible that the fine Old Quay may date from the early 17thc. It might have been built by Valentine Page, agent of the Earl of Kildare. The Watch House stands at the edge of Ferry Quarter Point and was built c1810. Ferry Quarter House is of early-Victorian origin. Other fine buildings include 19th-c Strangford Rectory; Strangford House, overlooking the village; and Old Court, guarding the N approach to Strangford. The grounds of the last-mentioned contain a two-storey defensive stone structure known as Strangford Tower. This may date from the 16thc.

STRANGFORD LOUGH, *Loch Cuan,*
Down   **13 J56**
This beautiful, almost landlocked inlet of the sea separates the Ards Peninsula from the remainder of Co Down, and is dotted with numerous islands formed by submerged drumlins. Norsemen named the lough *Strang Fiord*, ie the 'Violent Inlet', because of the fearful tide which rushes up and down the Narrows between the lake and the open sea. To the N of this turbulent water the irregularly-shaped lough extends for about 12m in length and measures up to 3m wide. Its serene landscape is dotted with gleaming white farmhouses; this, and its wonderfully rich bird and marine life, has prompted the government to designate it an area of outstanding beauty. Several nature reserves, areas of scientific interest, and the excellent Strangford Lough Wildlife Scheme (NT) operate in the designated area.

STRANORLAR, *Srath an Urláir:*
The Holm of the Floor, Donegal   **5 H19**
A many-arched bridge which spans the Finn links this valley village to neighbouring Ballybofey. Isaac Butt, father of Irish Home Rule, is buried in the Protestant churchyard. There is good salmon and trout fishing in the area. See Ballybofey.

STROKESTOWN, *Béal na mBuillí:*
Ford-mouth of the Strokes, Roscommon   **16 M98**
This market town was laid out in the 18th and early 19thc by Maurice Mahon, who was later created Baron Hartland. Its two main streets intersect at right angles. The fine 18th-c mansion of Strokestown House has some 17th-c features and can be seen at the E end. The almost unchanged kitchen illustrates the life style of the period. Nearby remains of a medieval church have been turned into a Mahon mausoleum.

STRUEL, HOLY WELLS OF, *Srúill:*
Stream, Down   **13 J54**
See Downpatrick entry.

SUGAR LOAF, GREAT, *O Cualaun:*
The Ear of Cuala, Wicklow   **19 O21**
See Kilmacanoge entry.

SUIL, LOUGH NA, *Loch na Súile:*
The Lake of the Eye, Sligo   **10 G71**
See Geevagh entry.

SUMMERHILL, *Cnoc an Línsigh:*
Lynch's Hill, Meath   **18 N84**
Considered a good example of work by an improving landlord, this village has a tree-lined mall which leads to the main avenue to Lord Longford's 18th-c mansion. This building is now in ruins. A few medieval fragments, which include the shaft of a 16th-c Lynch cross, are to be seen on the village green. A grove in the demesne of the mansion contains the remains of a 16th- or 17th-c Lynch stronghold called Knock Castle.

SUTTON CROSS, *Crois Chill Fionntain:*
The Cross of Fionntan's Church, Dublin
19 O23
Sutton Cross is situated on the narrow neck of the Howth peninsula and stands on the N shore of Dublin Bay. The artist Whistler lived here for a time in 1900. The church of St Finntan stands to the E and may date from the 9thc. See Howth entry.

SWINFORD, *Béal Atha na Muice:*
Ford-mouth of the Pig, Mayo   **9 M39**
Flat countryside surrounds this market town, which is known for its numerous souterrains. The Round Tower of Meelick (NM) rises 3m SW and features a round-headed splayed doorway. It has flat-headed and pointed windows, but the conical cap is missing. Although ruined it still stands at 70ft high, and at its foot is an old gravestone which displays interlacing ornamentation and an inscription in Irish. The tower stands on the site of an early monastery attributed to St Broccaidh.

SWORDS, *Sord:*
Pure Well, Dublin   **19 O14**
This is a very ancient village, whose foundation is associated with St Colmcille, which stands near the estuary of the Ward River. Among the ancient remains here is a 75ft round tower (NM) which stands in the Protestant churchyard. Its

doorway is now level with the ground, and both the upper storey and the conical cap were rebuilt – perhaps at the time the cross which exists here now was placed above it. Close by are remains of a 14th-c church tower. Before the Anglo-Norman invasion the village and the monastery had been transferred to the Archbishop of Dublin and Swords, and it became one of the principal archiepiscopal manors. In 1366 the prebend was held by William of Wykeham, who was Bishop of Winchester and Chancellor of England. At the N end of the main street are the ruins of the archbishop's 13th-c manorial castle (NM), a five-sided edifice which encloses a courtyard of great size. Access is by gateway, and it features a porter's room, a priest's room, and remains of 13th-c windows. The first floor is reached by a spiral staircase, and the tower at the north end of the wall was once the residence of the Constable of the castle. The town was given municipal rights by Queen Elizabeth I in 1578. About 2m W is Brackenstown House, one-time home of Robert Molesworth – the 1st Viscount Swords. It was to the latter that Swift addressed his *Drapier's Letters*. A large rath is preserved in the grounds of the house. Francis Johnston designed the village's Borough School.

TACUMSHANE, *Teach Coimsín*:
Coimsín's House, Wexford **25 T00**
A rare example of a straw-thatched Irish windmill (NM), stands in this village, which is situated some 7m SW of Rosslare. The mill was built by Nicholas Moran in 1846, was re-thatched in 1908, and reconstructed in 1952. The thatched cap could revolve, and the arms turned two mill-querns. Tacumshane Lake is a lagoon cut off from the open sea by a storm beach. To the NW of the lake is the fortified settler's residence of Bargy Castle. This is of particular interest as the former home of Bagenal Harvey, who was hanged for his part in the 1798 Insurrection. It is now a guest house.

TAGHADOE, *Teach Tua*:
St Tua's House, Kildare **18 N93**
Next to the topless, 65ft round tower (NM) here are remains of a 19th-c church.

TAGHMON, *Teach Munna*:
Munna's House, Westmeath **17 N46**
In a graveyard here, 1m E of Crookedwood, are the ruins of a 15th-c fortified church (NM) with a four-storey castle-like residential tower. In the tower are a living-room and bedroom. The church and tower room are vaulted. The church has been in almost constant use since its construction, and has been restored several times. The last restoration was in 1927.

TAGHMON, *Teach Munna*:
Munna's House, Wexford **24 S91**
The name of this market town derives from St Munna, who founded an Augustinian monastery here in the 6thc. A massive square tower is all that remains of the town's Anglo-Norman castle. The small 19th-c parish church (CI) carries a square tower, and the adjoining churchyard contains remains of an ancient granite cross of rude workmanship. H F Lyte, who wrote *Abide with me*, was curate here in 1815.

TAGOAT, *Teach Gót*, Wexford **25 T01**
This village stands halfway between

Two mill querns are turned by the arms of Tacumshane's 19th-c windmill, a rare building which was reconstructed in 1952.

Rosslare and Rosslare Harbour, and has a 19th-c church which was designed by Pugin. Greenore Point, with its sands and cliffs, lies to the E; farther S is Ballytrent House (see entry).

TAILLTEN or TELTOWN, *Tailtin*:
Teltown, Meath **18 N87**
Tailltten was once one of the most celebrated spots in Ireland. From 1420 BC until the Viking invasions the *Aonach Tailteann* – the Great Games of Ireland – were held here on the 1st of August each year. Rath Dubh, a circular earth rampart about 50 yards in diameter, was probably the centre for these games. See also Ceanannas Mor.

TALLAGHT, *Tamhlacht*:
Burial-place, Dublin **19 O02**
Situated at the foot of the Dublin Mountains, this village bears the Irish name which is said to have referred to the burial of plague victims in prehistoric times. It was the site of a famous monastery founded by St Maelruain in the 8thc. A medieval parish church was built on part of the site, but the only remnant of this is a bell tower in the churchyard of the present structure (CI). Also in the churchyard is a small cross. For many years Tallaght was on the edge of that Anglo-Norman territory known as The Pale, and for that reason was strongly fortified with castles to control the O Tooles and the O Byrnes. The latter families had their strongholds in the mountains of N Wicklow.

A fine church belonging to the Dominican Order stands in the centre of the village on ground which once belonged to the See of Dublin. The archbishops resided here in a strong castle from the 14thc to the beginning of the 19thc. All that remains of this building is a small tower in the grounds of the Dominican friary. Ruined Old Bawn House lies about ½m SE and is one of the very few examples of purely domestic 17th-c architecture surviving in Ireland. Beyond Old Bawn Bridge, across the River Dodder, stands the 18th-c house of Allenton. About 1m NE is Delaford, another 18th-c house, and 2½m NE on the road to Dublin is Spawell House. The latter marks the location of a spa which was discovered in 1732, and became fashionable with Dublin society for some years. Some 2m SE on Mount Pelier is the ruined 'Hell Fire Club' – the remains (NM) of a house built c1725 by the Rt Hon William Conolly, Speaker of the Irish House of Commons. The Club was founded in 1735 and held its revels in the then-deserted mansion. Away to the E rises 1,339ft Kilmashogue, a splendid viewpoint.

On the foothills of the Wicklow Mountains to the S are many cairns, stone circles, pillar stones, and dolmens. The largest dolmen features a 40-ton capstone and lies 4m SE at Mount Venus (NM) – beyond the River Dodder. To the S of Tallaght is the beautiful upper valley of the River Dodder, known as Glenasmole, which terminates in two reservoirs. The larger reservoir of Bohernabreena supplies water to Dublin Corporation.

TALLANSTOWN, *Baile an Tallúnaigh*:
Tallan's Homestead, Louth **12 N99**
Made up of a few buildings and a church clustered around a bridge over the River Glyde, this small village lies N of the fine Louth Hall demesne. Until recently this was the seat of Lord Louth, whose family name was Plunkett. The most notable member of the family was St Oliver, the martyred 17th-c Archbishop of Armagh. He took refuge here with his relations, and his hiding place is still pointed out. The fine 17th-c mansion has been much altered and enlarged since then. About 2m NW, opposite the gates of Thomastown House, is a series of stone-lined souterrains.

TALLOW, *Tulach an Iarainn*:
The Hill of the Iron, Waterford **12 W99**
Although once a town of some significance, Tallow lost a large proportion of its population during a 19th-c decline. It is situated in the valley of the River Bride, a tributary of the Blackwater, and was part of a territory granted by Queen Elizabeth I to Sir Walter Raleigh in 1586. Raleigh then assigned the property to Sir Richard Boyle, later Earl of Cork, who planted it with English Protestants in the early 17thc. The area was once exploited for its iron ore – hence its Irish name. Features in the town are the almshouses erected for six aged couples under the will of 19th-c John Boyce, and other almshouses erected for widows near the RC chapel c1830 under a bequest of the parish priest. The town is noted for its horse fair in early September. The 19th-c sculptor John Hogan was born in Tallow.
cont overleaf

A little to the NW of Tallow, on the N bank of the River Bride, stands Lisfinny Castle. The ruins of Mogeely Castle stand 3m W near the River Bride. This was the home of the 'Old Countess' of Desmond, who lived till she was 147. Even then she only died because she fell out of a cherry tree. Also to the W on the banks of the Bride is Conna Castle (see entry). Tallow Hill, to the E of the castle, is a good viewpoint.

TAMLAGHT, *Tamhlacht*:
Burial-place, Fermanagh **11 H24**
Some 2m S of Tamlaght is the ruined parish church (CI) of Derrybrusk (NM), which features a fine perpendicular window.

TANDRAGEE, *Tóin re Gaoith*:
Bottom to the Wind, Armagh **13 J04**
The demesne and 19th-c 'castle' of the former proprietor – the Duke of Manchester – crown a hill above this River Cusher town. The Manchester family were improving and paternalist landlords of the last century, and the town which they created became a great centre of the linen industry.

TARA, *Teamhair*:
Place With a View, Meath **18 N95**
Tara's ancient royal site, for which it is particularly famed, is described in the special gazetteer inset on page 276. About 3m S of Tara is Dunsany Castle, a structure which was built by Hugh de Lacy in the 13thc but has since been much altered and modernized. Its beautifully-wooded demesne contains the 15th-c church of St Nicholas (NM), which is divided into a nave and chancel, carries three corner turrets, and features a massive tower. The present east window was added in the 19thc. The font is worthy of note. The Hill of Skreen lies 4m E of Tara. Relics of St Columba were brought to the monastery which stood here in 875. On the summit of the hill are the remains of a church (NM) with a massive 14th- to 15th-c tower. Near by is a medieval cross. On the Drogheda road, 1m S of the hill, is St Columba's Church. Interesting carvings dating from 1571 can be seen in the churchyard.

TARBERT, *Tairbeart*:
Isthmus, Kerry **21 R04**
Built on a steep slope overlooking one of the most beautiful stretches of the River Shannon, this quiet village was once a fairly important port. It declined with the development of railways, but it has revived somewhat with the car-ferry service now operating from Killimer on the Co Clare shore of the Shannon. The local Protestant church was built in 1814. Tarbert Island is connected by causeway to a wooded headland which juts into the river from the village. On the extreme N point of the island is a lighthouse which was completed in 1835, plus a battery and barracks built to repel French invaders during the Napoleonic wars.

TEMPLE DOUGLAS, *Teampall Dúghlaise*:
The Church of the Dark Stream, Donegal **5 C01**
St Columba is reputed to have been baptised in the ancient ruined church which stands near Temple Douglas on the Glashagh River. Features of the church include an interesting 16th-c window, plus an entrance gate with curious sculptured stones. Gartan Lough lies to the NW.

TEMPLE MONACHAN, *Teampall Manacháin*:
St Manachán's Church, Kerry **26 Q40**
Remains of an oratory and well of St Monachan exist here, plus a pillar stone inscribed with ogham characters.

TEMPLEMORE, *An Teampall Mór*:
The Big Church, Tipperary **23 S17**
The nucleus round which this neat market town grew was an establishment of the Knights Templar, who had a strong castle and a monastery here. The remains of the castle and abbey church can be seen in the town's park. During the early 19thc Templemore developed rapidly through the encouragement of Sir John Craven Carden, who granted the ground on which it stands at a nominal rent and is still remembered for the erection of public buildings. He was responsible for the handsome decorated court and market house in the centre of the town. Templemore's cattle fairs were famous during the last century.

The parish church (CI) of *c*1790 has a fine spire, and the RC chapel was built on a rent-free plot in the 1820's. The old British Military Barracks on the S outskirts of the town now house a police-training depot. The writer George Borrow spent part of his youth here and described the local scenery in his book *Lavengro*.

The upper reaches of the River Suir, noted for fishing, are near the town; the 1,557ft Devil's Bit mountain rises a few miles to the NW. The name of this mountain is derived from its appearance, but it is more likely that the 'Bit' missing from its summit is due to glaciation rather than the Devil. Below the E entrance to the gap is a tower known as Carden's Folly. On the summit of the mountain – a notable viewpoint – is a 45ft-high cross erected to commemorate the Marian Year 1954. In 1790 a 12th-c, silver-plated manuscript casket was found in a cave on the mountain. It is now in Trinity College, Dublin. Some 2m SW near Barna Cross is the five-storey circular keep of Knockagh Castle. The ruins of Loughmoe Castle are $3\frac{1}{2}$m S (see entry).

TEMPLENOE, *Teampall Nua*:
New Church, Kerry **26 V86**
This small village lies 5m WSW of Kenmare on a road circuit of the Iveragh Peninsula – the famous 'Ring of Kerry'. Near the shore, about 2m W of Kenmare, are the ruins of Dunkerron Castle. This stronghold dates from 1596 and was once the chief seat of the O Sullivan-More family. The local church (CI) was erected in 1816 and fitted with teak wood from the wreck of a vessel. An interesting cromlech exists at Dreendroch. Some 4m W the River Blackwater rushes turbulently into the sea through a deep gorge, and a pathway leads down from the roadside through dense, almost tropical vegetation.

TEMPLEPATRICK, *Teampall Phádraig*:
St Patrick's Church, Antrim **7 J28**
Said to derive its name from an early preceptory of Knights Templar, this village is grouped around the stronghold of Upton Castle. Formerly known as Norton Castle, this was started in the late 16thc and incorporates some medieval remains. The oldest parts of the present building are the east wing, plus the north-east and south-west round towers – which are of 16th-c origin. The house is particularly noteworthy in being one of only two Irish examples where there are positive examples of design work by Robert Adam. Adam was commissioned in 1783 by the 1st Baron Templetown, whose family had acquired the property. In 1788 he castellated the Plantation house, and the corner and archway towers show his machicolated cornice – here reduced to a decorative scale. Adam also designed the stables, which have two courtyards and octagonal buildings at each corner. This area had one of the earliest Presbyterian settlements in Ireland.

The Rev Josiah Welsh, grandson of the Scottish reformer John Knox, was incumbent here and was buried in the cemetery of the old St Patrick's church in 1634. Lyles Hill, a famous prehistoric site that was discovered by aerial photography in 1927, is situated 2m SE of the village. The summit of this 753ft hill is ringed by a low earthwork thought to be of neolithic date. Within the enclosure is a low cairn which, on excavation, proved to be of complex composition. It held thousands of neolithic pot sherds and flints. At the centre of the cairn was a round cist containing the cremated remains of a child. Other finds in the cist put this to neolithic date. The cairn was surrounded by a ring of kerbstones, one of which – a sill jamb – was decorated. This is now in the Ulster Museum, Belfast. The site was also used in bronze-age times. A remarkably-fine cromlech exists at Cairngraine, near the road to Antrim.

TEMPO, *An tIompú Deiseal*:
The Turn to the Right, Fermanagh **11 H34**
Tempo Manor was the home of Sir John Langham, the distinguished naturalist, and stands in beautiful lake-watered grounds. The most significant of several standing stones near the village is the group known as the Grey Stones (NM), which can be seen $\frac{3}{4}$m SW at Doon. The lower of the two stones is a red sandstone boulder covered with cup marks on the top, with one bullaun on each side. The upper stone resembles a hog's back in shape, and bears a pattern of spirals dating from the bronze age. About 2m farther SW is 910ft Topped Mountain, a notable viewpoint. A large cairn (NM) at its summit was excavated in 1897 and revealed a burial cist with a bronze dagger, a small band of gold, and pieces of a richly-decorated urn. The finds were deposited in the National Museum, Dublin.

TERMONFECKIN, *Tearmann Féichín*:
St Féichín's Sanctuary Land, Louth **19 O18**
There was a church at this quiet, old village in the 6thc, and the Archbishops of Armagh had a summer residence here until the early 17thc. Their castle has now vanished, but a little way E of the valley is well-preserved, 15th-c Termonfeckin Castle (NM). This was probably a home of the Dowdall family, and has conical vaulting of corbel construction. Its fine stone spiral stairway connects the four storeys of the square tower. A high cross (NM) preserved in the local Protestant cemetery is said to mark the site of the original church. It stands more than 11ft high and probably dates from the 9thc. Also in the churchyard are the base of a small early cross and a crucifixion slab,

while an early gravestone can be seen in the church porch.

TERRYGLASS, *Tír dhá Ghlas:*
Land of Two Streams, Tipperary
16 M80
Terryglass village, near the E shore of Lough Derg, was the site of a famous 6th-c monastery which was founded by St Columba and grew to become a prominent centre of learning. The only remains are two walls of a fairly large church. These probably date from the 15thc. On the lake shore is the ruin of Terryglass Castle or Old Court (NM), a 12th- to 13th-c Butler castle of a peculiarly Irish type.

THOMASTOWN, *Baile Mhic Andáin:*
Fitzanthony's Homestead, Kilkenny
24 S54
Situated in the beautiful valley of the River Nore, this market town stood at the head of a navigable channel until the river silted up in the early 19thc. It was an early centre of trade and a military stronghold. Thomas Fitzanthony, the Anglo-Norman seneschal of Leinster, had a motte-and-bailey castle here in the 13thc. Only the motte survives. He organized the civic life of the town, built a surrounding wall with fourteen towers, and probably established a religious house. Sweetman's Castle is virtually the only survival of these medieval fortifications.

The town's main feature is its fine 13th-c parish church (NM), which was founded by Fitzanthony. Surviving remains include the nave, aisles, sacristy, west end, and south-west tower. In the churchyard there are some 16th- and 17th-c tombstones, plus the upper portion of an ancient high cross. A fine 18th-c bridge of five arches spans the Nore, and less than ½m S of Thomastown on the banks of the river stand the ruins of the Anglo-Norman fortress of Grianan (NM). This was also built by Thomas Fitzanthony. Both Grianan and Thomastown were stormed by Cromwell in March 1650. The high altar of famous Jerpoint Abbey (see entry), which lies 1½m SW, is now in Thomastown Church (RC). Ballylinch and Legan castles are of interest, the latter deriving its name from a pillar stone with an ogham inscription. The great philosopher Bishop Berkeley was born 3m SE at Dysert Castle in 1685. Near by are remains of a fortified church. About 4m W of the town is the stud farm and mansion of Mount Juliet (see entry).

THOMASTOWN, *Baile Thomáis:*
Thomas' Homestead, Tipperary **23 R93**
The main feature in this Golden Vale village is the ruin of Thomastown Castle – once a magnificent mansion of the Matthew family. The original two-storey house was built in the late 17thc. Early 18th-c additions and improvements included accommodation for 40 guests and a large formal terraced garden, traces of which remain. The proprietor, George Matthew, dispensed lavish hospitality to guests as long as they chose to remain. One of the guests was Dean Swift, who stayed for four months. When the property was inherited by Francis Matthew – 2nd Earl of Llandaff – in 1812, he commissioned Sir Richard Morrison to enlarge and alter the house in the 19th-c gothick manner. During the late 19thc the building fell into decay, and in 1938 it was bought by the historian Archbishop David Matthew – a

TERRYGLASS/TIMOLEAGUE

The façade of the RC cathedral in Thurles was modelled on that of Pisa Cathedral in Italy.

descendant of the family. The estate is now an agricultural re-afforestation centre. Celebrated Father Theobald Matthew, who converted a large portion of Ireland's population to total abstinence, was born at the castle in 1790. His statue, unveiled in 1938, stands at Thomastown Crossroads.

THOOR BALLYLEE, Galway **16 M40**
This four-storey, 16th-c tower house romantically situated by a stream 4m NE of Gort was restored as a residence by the poet W B Yeats in the 1920's. His verse of commemoration is carved on a tablet in the wall:
I, the poet William Yeats,
With old millboards and sea-green slates,
And smithy work from the Gort forge,
Restored this tower for my wife, George,
And may these characters remain,
When all is ruin once again.
The building now houses a Yeats museum.

THURLES, *Durlas:*
Strong Fort, Tipperary **23 S15**
Since the 18thc this River Suir market town has been the cathedral town of the archdiocese of Cashel and Emly (RC), one of the four into which Ireland is divided. Its strategic importance in the middle ages is evident from the numerous castles which surrounded it, seven of which were in a fair state of preservation at the beginning of the last century. Norse and Irish fought here in the 10thc, and in 1174 the Irish were led against Strongbow's Anglo-Normans by Donal O Brien and Roderick O Conor. The native forces were victorious, but the invaders eventually established a castle to command the passage across the Suir.

Two events associated with Thurles are the 19th-c National Synod of the RC church, at which the university colleges of Belfast, Cork, and Galway were condemned, and the founding of the Gaelic Athletic Association by Archbishop Croke in 1884. The RC cathedral is a fine building with a façade modelled on that of Pisa Cathedral. The bell tower is 125ft high, and the altar tabernacle – which comes from Gesú in Italy – was designed by Andre Pozzo in the 17thc. Archbishop Croke is buried in the cathedral, and a bronze statue to him has been erected in Liberty Square. St Mary's Church (CI) features a 16th-c Archer tomb. About 2m N of Thurles is Brittas Castle, an incomplete replica of Warwick Castle in England. It was never finished because the owner was killed by falling masonry during its construction. A modern residence has since been built within the confines of its foundations. Holy Cross Abbey (see entry) lies 4½m SW.

TIBBERAGHNY, *Tigh Braichne:*
Braichne's House, Tipperary **23 S42**
Reputed to have been a place of some importance from the monastic period of the 6thc, this village features slight remains of a church and foundations of an ancient town. The latter is supposed to be of Danish origin. Also of interest are remains of an Anglo-Norman fortress, and part of a well-carved cross-shaft in the local churchyard.

TIMAHOE, *Tigh Mochua:*
St Mochua's House, Laois **24 S59**
Timahoe, 5m SW of Stradbally, takes its name from the 6th-c monastery founded here by St Mochua. The only remnant of the monastery is a very well-preserved round tower (NM). This measures 96ft high and probably dates from the 12thc. It is one of the latest built in Ireland, and features a unique Romanesque doorway built of hard sandstone. To the E of the tower is a small church incorporating a 15th-c arch. This was converted into a castle in the 17thc. About ½m W of the village is a 12th-c motte-and-bailey castle known as the rath of Ballynaclogh.

TIMOLEAGUE, *Tigh Molaige:*
St Molaige's House, Cork **28 W44**
The place-name refers to a monastery founded here by St Molaig in the 6thc. Extensive ruins (NM) of a 14th-c Franciscan friary occupy the site of the old monastery, displaying substantial additions of 15th-c date. Although nominally suppressed in 1536, the monastery was still flourishing in the first half of the 17thc. The ruins are charmingly situated on the edge of the sea at the top of the W arm of Courtmacsherry Bay. When the friary was sacked by the Parliamentary army, some thousands of barrels of Spanish wine were found in the vaults. The church has chancel, nave, south transept, and a graceful 68ft-high tower at the intersection of all three. The tower was added in the 15thc. East of the transept are the remains of an oratory and fragments of the conventual buildings.
cont on page 278

TARA – ANCIENT ROYAL SITE

Tara is the setting for much that is heroic and grand in Irish folklore. Legend has it that it was here that Grainne deserted her lover Finn in favour of Diarmaid, thus starting a famous chase throughout the length and breadth of Ireland. Although the site is now a jumble of grass-grown earthworks, and although the legends may be more fantasy than fact, there is no doubt that for more than 2,000 years Tara was a place of paramount religious, and later political, importance.

Teamhair na Riogh – 'Tara of the Kings' – is situated 6m E of Navan in Co Meath, on a comparatively low hill. The 512ft hill commands an extensive view over the lush meadowland of central and eastern Ireland. Tara reached its greatest importance during the first centuries AD, when it was the seat of the High Kings of Ireland. After the introduction of Christianity it gradually declined in power, but was not finally abandoned until 1022. Its most famous king was the almost-legendary Cormac the Wise, who in the 3rdc built most of the wooden palaces and halls described in the early literature. No trace of these buildings remains above ground however. It is said that St Patrick visited Tara early in his mission in order to obtain permission from King Laoghaire to preach the gospel. The king gave his consent after St Patrick had defeated Laoghaire's druids in a contest of magic. Even after its abandonment by the High Kings Tara remained, and still remains, a symbol of Irish hope and patriotism.

Tara's history can be traced back to long before the time of the High Kings. *Dumha na nGiall* – the 'Mound of the Hostages' – is the earliest excavated monument on the site. It is a simple passage grave 17ft in length under a mound 72ft in diameter. It was constructed of stones over which a thick layer of clay had been placed. During excavations the tomb was found to contain the largest collection of artefacts known from any such Irish grave.

As well as a jumble of cremated bones the grave contained pottery, stone pendants and beads, and bone pins. The disorganized state of the burial has led archaeologists to believe that the original cremations were rather unceremoniously pushed aside to make room for some later human remains. The date given for the earliest burials is c2,000BC. During the early and middle bronze ages the clay covering of the mound was used extensively for burials, all but two of which were cremations. The burials were accompanied by a considerable number of objects, including bronze knives, daggers, and a stone battle axe. One of the inhumation burials, that of a youth, was accompanied by a necklace made of copper, jet, amber, and faience beads. The faience beads have been dated to c1,400BC. In addition to the Mound of the Hostages there are at least five other burial mounds at Tara, only one of which can be conclusively dated, and that is of iron-age origin.

The Mound of the Hostages stands inside *Rath na Riogh* – the 'Royal Enclosure' – which is an oval ringfort of iron-age date measuring 950ft long and 800ft across. Its eastern side has been very much damaged by the passage of time. The enclosing bank was strengthened on the inside by a palisade, thus confirming its defensive role, and supported by a ditch, or fosse, which is unusual in that it is on the inside of the bank. The ditch had been dug 11ft down into the underlying rock. At the centre of the Royal Enclosure are two earthworks called, respectively, *Teach Cormaic* – 'Cormac's House', and *Forradh* – the 'Royal Seat'. Both of these are bivallate earthworks, that is they have two sets of banks and ditches. Cormac's House is the larger of the two. Its earthworks extend N to include a circular mound, the purpose of which, at the present time, can only be guessed at.

The centre of Cormac's House is made up of a circular hump, possibly an iron-age burial mound, upon which stand two of the most contentious objects at Tara. The most conspicuous of these is the fairly modern statue of St Patrick, which has come in for a good deal of comment, largely uncomplimentary and much of it derisory. The other object is a 5ft granite stone called *Lia Fail*, which originally stood near the Mound of the Hostages. It was moved to its present position in 1798 to mark the graves of 37 people killed in the Insurrection of that year. It is said to have been the royal inauguration stone, and was supposed to have roared its acceptance of the rightful claimant to the throne. It is also suggested that it is the stone which Jacob used as a pillow on the night that he dreamt of a ladder rising to Heaven. Rival theories state that the real *Lia Fail* now sits under the Confessor's chair at Westminster, after having been removed to Scotland and eventually Scone by an Irish king. From Scone it was moved to its present resting place by the English.

To the S of the Royal Enclosure is Rath Laoghaire, a large, badly-preserved enclosure named after the king who ruled at Tara during the time of St Patrick. Laoghaire is said to be buried somewhere in the vicinity. He stands upright, in full armour, waiting to be joined by a vast, and by now long-ghostly army.

Almost touching the Royal Enclosure on its N side is *Rath na Seanaid* – the 'Rath of the Synods' – which is a trivallate enclosure almost totally destroyed in the 19thc by British Israelites hunting for the Ark of the Covenant. It is perhaps not very surprising that they did not find it. But exciting finds have been made at the Rath of the Sinods. In 1810 three gold-bar torcs dating from *c*1,000BC were found on the N side of the enclosure. It may be that the discovery of so much gold fostered the Ark theory. More recent excavations, conducted in a scientific manner, have shown that the rath was strongly defended with palisades and rock-cut ditches. Timber buildings which once stood inside the enclosure can be dated to the first three centuries AD by the accompanying finds of imported Roman glass and pottery. The excavations also revealed a number of cremated, as well as inhumed, burials, which experts are inclined to interpret as having a ritual significance.

Perhaps the most famous site at Tara, and certainly the one which is the scene of greatest conjecture, is *Teach Miodchuarta* – the 'House of Mead Circling' or the 'Banquet Hall'. This is situated to the N of the Rath of the Synods and appears as a 750ft-long by 75ft-wide hollow running NS. It is framed by parallel earthen banks, and is described in early Irish manuscripts as being a rectangular wooden building divided into aisles and compartments. Each grade of society and class of person had its, or his, correct place in the hall. According to the literature each grade had the cut of meat suitable to its station. There are two plans of the hall extant – one from the 15th-c *Yellow Book of Lecan*, and one from the 12th-c *Book of Leinster*. Whether these plans and descriptions can in any way be described as authentic is open to debate. It may be that the series of earthworks called the Banquet Hall were in fact a ritual entrance to the whole site. To the NW of the Banquet Hall is a series of three more earthworks. The first is Rath Grainne – named after Finn's unfaithful lover. It is a circular enclosure surrounded by a bank and ditch, and has in its centre a large mound – probably a burial mound. Partly hidden by trees on a steep slope are the two other earthworks – the *Claoin Fhearta*, or 'Sloping Trenches'. The N earthwork has been much damaged by quarrying. These two monuments are unusual in formation, and may have been purely ritualistic in function.

In the churchyard of the Church of St Patrick, which intrudes onto the E part of Tara Hill, are two standing stones. One is a low block of limestone with a rounded top. The other – Adamman's Stone – is a 5½ft sandstone block with a small human figure carved upon it. This may represent a fertility figure – *sheila-na-gig* – or it may be *Cernunnos*, the Celtic horned god. About 1mS of Tara Hill is Rath Maeve, a univallate ring-fort 750ft in diameter. Its method of construction suggests that it is contemporary with the Tara monuments.

1. Mound of the Hostages
2. Royal Enclosure
3. Royal Seat
4. Cormac's House
5. *Lia Fail*
6. Rath Laoghaire
7. Rath of the Synods
8. Banquet Hall
9. Rath Grainne
10. Sloping Trenches
11. Stones in St Patrick's churchyard

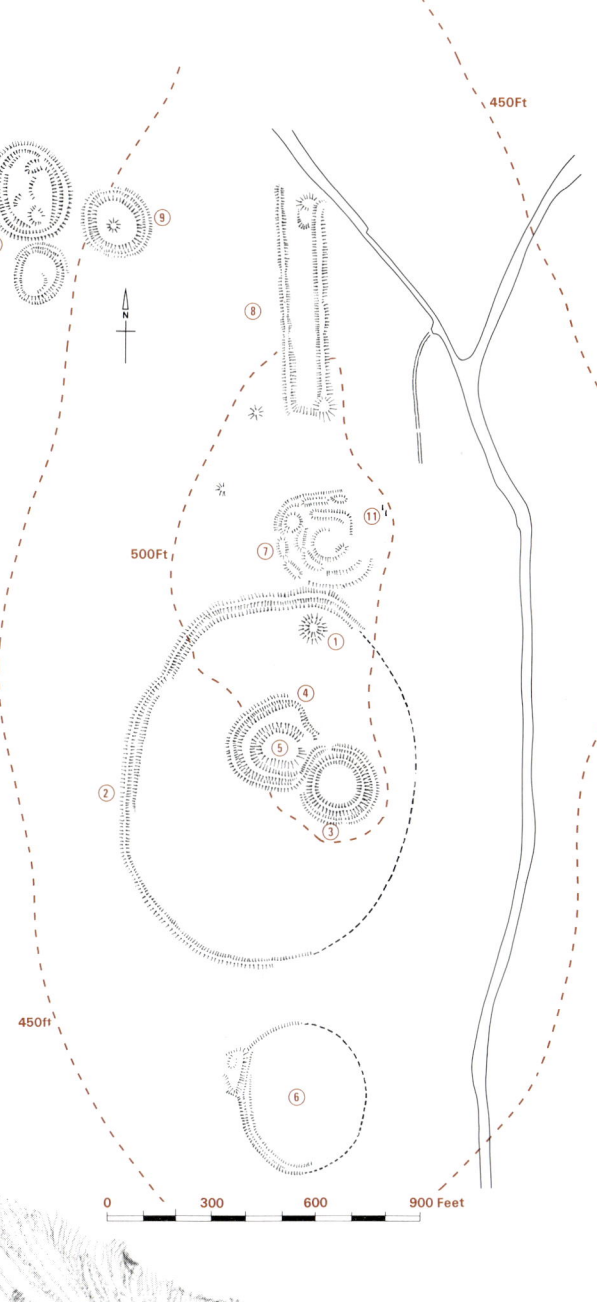

Among the most notable features is the open arcade on the south side of the nave, supported by seven arches that rest on square and cylindrical pillars without capitals. Near the transept window there is a 5½ft-long squint known as the 'Lepers' Hole', which is thought to have been used by the lepers who lived in a neighbouring retreat. This enabled them to participate in the services. The village has a Catholic church with distinguished windows by Harry Clarke. On the N outskirts of the village are the ruins of a MacCarthy Riabach castle. To the E, by the seashore at Abbeymahon, are remains of a castle and fragments of a Cistercian abbey.

TIMOLIN, *Tigh Moling:*
St Moling's Monastery, Kildare **18 S79**
A foundation was created here by St Moling of Ferns in the 7thc. In the porch of the local church (CI) is the 13th-c effigy of a recumbent Anglo-Norman knight thought to be Robert Fitzrichard. About ½m S at Moone (see entry) is an unusually slender, 9th-c high cross fashioned from granite.

TINAHELY, *Tigh na hÉille:*
House of the Thong, Wicklow **25 T07**
Situated among hills in the valley of the Derry River, this charming little town was destroyed during the Insurrection of 1798 but subsequently rebuilt. About ¼m from the town at Coolruss are slight remains of an incomplete building known as 'Black Tom's Kitchen'. To the E on the Wexford border rises 1,987ft Croghan Kinshela.

TINNAHINCH, *Tigh na hInse:*
The House of the Holm, Carlow **24 S74**
This suburb of Graiguenamagh town stands on the Carlow side of the River Barrow. Castle remains occupy a nearby rock.

TINNAHINCH HOUSE, *Tigh na hInse:*
The House of the Holm, Wicklow **19 O21**
See Enniskerry entry.

TINTERN, *Mainistir Chinn Eich:*
Monastery of Horse Head, Wexford **24 S74**
Daughter house of the Monmouthshire (Gwent) Cistercian abbey made famous by Wordsworth's poem, this abbey (NM) was founded c1200 by William le Mareschal (Earl of Pembroke) in fulfilment of a vow taken when in danger of shipwreck. It is situated on an inlet of the sea called Bannow Bay. The chancel and 15th-c tower were converted into living quarters after the Dissolution of the monasteries in the 16thc, and the nave and tower remained occupied until quite recently. The original structure is now being restored.

TIPPERARY, *Tiobraid Árann:*
Well of the River Ara, Tipperary **22 R83**
Sited on the River Ara in the Golden Vale, this market town lies S of the magnificent Galtee Mountains and was a place of some importance in medieval Ireland. John, while Lord of Ireland prior to his accession to the throne of England, built a castle here. No trace of this remains, but it became the nucleus of the town. The fact that Edward II made a three-year grant 'to the bailiffs and good men of Tipperary' in the 14thc suggests that the town was by then a well-ordered civic community. Tipperary achieved a great notoriety during the Plan of Campaign of the Land League against the payment of rent c1880. Smith Barry, the town's landlord, took a prominent part in fighting against this Plan of Campaign. As a punishment a New Tipperary was built outside his property, and such numbers of shopkeepers left the old town that it was almost deserted. The new town, however, proved a complete fiasco within a comparatively short time.

TIRRALEEN CASTLE, Galway **15 M22**
Slight remains of this 13th-c castle of the de Burgos are situated on the River Corrib, less than 1m N of Galway. The stronghold is also known as 'Terryland'.

TOBERCURRY, *Tobar an Choire:*
The Well of the Cauldron, Sligo **10 G51**
Also known as Tubbercurry, this market town is built along a single long street. In 1943 a unique example of a Saint's Belt Shrine – known as the Moylough Belt – was found near Tobercurry. This dates from the 8thc and is now in the National Museum, Dublin. Some 5m W at Banada the ruin of a 15th-c Augustinian abbey is beautifully situated beside the River Moy. About 6m E at Bunnanadan are ruins of a castle and church.

TOBERDONEY, *Tobar an Domhnaigh:*
Church Well, Antrim **7 J39**
To the NW of the village of Ballynure are remains of 13th-c Toberdoney church. Only a crumbling tower now survives, but a new church erected opposite features ark-shaped burial vaults of local families. There is also a stone-vaulted watch-house, reminiscent of the days of body-snatching.

TOBERDONEY, *Tobar an Dromhnaigh:*
Church Well, Down **13 J55**
In the local townland of Audleystown, at Temple Cormick, are the slight remains of a remarkable and little-known church. This pre-Norman, Irish structure stands in the centre of a circular churchyard surrounded by a ruinous dry-stone wall. Enough of the building survives to show that it was built without mortar or clay cement.

TOBERMORE, *An Tobar Mór:*
The Big Well, Derry **6 H89**
The Moyola River flows a little to the N of this village, which has a parish church (CI) that was rebuilt in 1816. Of interest is a fine Norman-style niche which survives from an earlier church. The local Presbyterian meeting house was built in 1728, and a nearby earthen fortification is known as William's Fort.

TOLLYMORE FOREST PARK, *Tulaigh Mhór:*
Large Hillock, Down **13 J33**
See Bryansford entry.

TOMHAGGARD, *Teach Moshagard:*
Moshagra's House, Wexford **25 T00**
Remains of a small, late 14th-c church with a characteristic east window exist in this village. The area was one of the earliest colonized by Anglo-Norman settlers, and was strongly defended by numerous castles. In this instance the settlers did not intermarry with the Irish and become 'more Irish than the Irish themselves', but retained their distinctive English dialect until the 19thc. Bargy Castle, originally built in the medieval period, has been much altered. See also Bargy and Forth.

TOOMBEOLA, *Tuaim Beola:*
Beola's Burial Mound, Galway **14 L74**
Situated at the head of an inlet of Bertraghboy Bay, this village features remains of a late 16th-c Dominican abbey-church sited on the bank of the Owenmore River.

TOOME BRIDGE, *Droichead Thuama:*
Bridge of the Burial Mound, Antrim **6 H99**
Toome Bridge is an angling centre on the River Bann. In the 19thc John Carey built a so-called 'Temple of Liberty, Learning, and Select Amusements' here. Only a few walls of this have survived, but his 'Fountain of Liberty' still stands. His former home had curious painted gateposts – several of which still stand – and his grave at local Duneane church is a remarkable piece of work which he is said to have designed himself. A 19th-c market house erected by Lord O Neill now serves as a shop and petty-sessions court. It is a pleasant gabled building of two storeys, with a roughcast exterior and Georgian-glazed windows. Church Island on nearby Lough Beg had an early monastic settlement founded by St Toide, but the ruins seen on the island today belong to a later abbey of the 13th or 14thc. The church was recorded as 'ruinous' in 1622, and in 1788 the Earl of Bristol (Bishop of Derry) added a square tower and a high octagonal spire just outside the west gable.

TOOMYVARA, *Tuaim Uí Mhéara:*
O Meara's Grave-Mound, Tipperary **23 R97**
A feature in this small village is the ruin of a 15th-c church, which contains the fragment of a tomb of the O Meara family.

TORC WATERFALL, *An Torc:*
The Wild Boar, Kerry **27 V98**
Considered one of the finest in Ireland, this fall plunges 60ft over a series of precipitous sandstone rocks.

TORR HEAD, Antrim **7 D24**
About 1½m SW of this headland is the fine passage grave of Carnamore, the best example of a type peculiar to Antrim. It displays interesting rock scribings.

TORY ISLAND, *Toraigh:*
Place of Towers, Donegal **4 B84**
Accessible by boat from Magheraroarty pier, some 3½m from Gortahork on Ballynass Bay, this 3 by 1m island lies 7m from the mainland and is a prominent feature of the Donegal coast. A person visiting this isolated place in poor weather is likely to be stranded on the island for days. St Columba is reputed to have founded a monastery here in the 6thc, but the only remains of the monastic period are a small, undecorated, T-shaped cross made of a thick mica slate, and a unique 57ft-high round tower (NM). The latter is built of rounded beach stones and rough blocks of granite, and has a round-headed doorway 8ft from the ground. Slight remains of two churches also exist. All these remains are in West Town, the principal village on Tory. The NE side of the island has very fine cliff scenery, and in contrast the SW extremity is very flat. The dangerous rocks which fringe this end have been the cause of many shipwrecks. One of the most serious was the wreck of the gun boat *Wasp* in September 1884, when all except six of the crew perished. In consolation for the barren soil the local farmer

pays no rent, no rates, and no taxes. Efforts to make him pay have been to no avail – it was in one of these efforts that the *Wasp* was lost.

TOUREEN, Tipperary 23 S02
Toureen village stands at the foot of the Galtee Mountains and is noted for the remains (NM) of an early monastic foundation created by St Peakan.

*TRALEE, *Trá Lí*:
Strand of Lí, Kerry 20 Q81
Tralee is the chief town of Co Kerry. During the 18thc it was known as a chalybeate-spa resort, and until recently it operated as a port. Small vessels came up from Blennerville Bay by the now-disused ship canal, and larger ships berthed 8m W at Fenit Pier on Tralee Bay. The town is a well-known touring centre, and has a number of fine bathing places within easy reach.

The town is closely identified with the history of the Desmonds, and at one time was the chief seat of the family. Their great castle stood at the junction of Denny Street and the Mall, but only a fragment of a wall now survives. The last episode in the drama of the downfall of the Desmonds was enacted near the town in 1583. The last earl, hard-pressed by the English forces, fled W and hid in the district SE of Tralee. He was finally captured at Glenageenty, a deep glen 8m E of the town, and after he was executed his head was sent to the Queen to be exposed to view on London Bridge. The Desmond property in Tralee, including the castle, was granted to Sir Edward Denny. In the 1640's the castle bore the brunt of a severe attack by the Catholic Confederates. Later, when Lord Inchiquin was advancing at the head of troops in the service of the English Parliament, the Irish garrison set fire to both castle and town. The forces who held the castle for James II in 1691 adopted the same tactics on the appearance of William III's troops in the neighbourhood.

The Dominican church of Holy Cross was designed by Pugin and executed under the direction of his pupil, George Ashlin. It features fine stained glass by Michael Healy. Attached to the church is a priory, which contains many sculptured stones from the old Dominican Holy Cross Abbey. The courthouse, with its Ionic portico, is flanked by Crimean and Indian mutiny memorials. Georgian houses exist in The Mall and Castle Street, and the impressive 1798 memorial in Denny Street was by Albert Power. William Mulchinock, who died in Tralee in 1864, composed the famous song *The Rose of Tralee*. His family lived in Cloghers House at nearby Ballymullen, and he is honoured by a memorial set amid roses in the town park. Also in the park is the imposing Thomas Ashe Memorial Hall. Some 3m E is 18th-c Ballyseedy House. The Dingle Peninsula, with its numerous prehistoric and Christian remains, can be visited very conveniently from the town. Ratass Church lies 1m E of Tralee and is a small, early-Irish structure built of sandstone blocks (see entry). The ruin of a medieval parish church (NM) can be seen SW of Tralee at Annagh. Inside is a 13th-c carving of an armed horseman.

TRAMORE, *Trá Mhór*:
Big Strand, Waterford 29 S50
The long, 3m strand boasted by this popular resort is washed on the S side by the open sea and on the N side by a large lagoon. The latter is connected with the sea by a narrow channel at the E end. The bay is much exposed to gales from the S, and in 1816 a troop ship homeward-bound from the Peninsular War was wrecked here with the loss of 363 lives. On the W side of the bay are the precipitous Doneraile cliffs, crowned by three towers on the summit of Great Newtown Head. One of these features a figure known as the 'Metal Man'. Two similar towers stand opposite on Brownstown Head. There is a racecourse at Tramore. Ruined Dunhill Castle lies 5m W and dates from the 17thc. It was once a fortress of the le Poer family. The coastline in the vicinity includes cliffs, caves, and the rugged Kilfarassy Strand. A few miles W is the small resort of Annestown, which has a good sandy beach. Some 5m ENE at Kilmacleague a ruined church with an ancient font and a bullaun stands on the site of a monastery.

1 Courthouse
2 Dominican Church of Holy Cross
3 Memorial to the 1798 Rising
4 *Rose of Tralee* Memorial
5 Thomas Ashe Memorial Hall

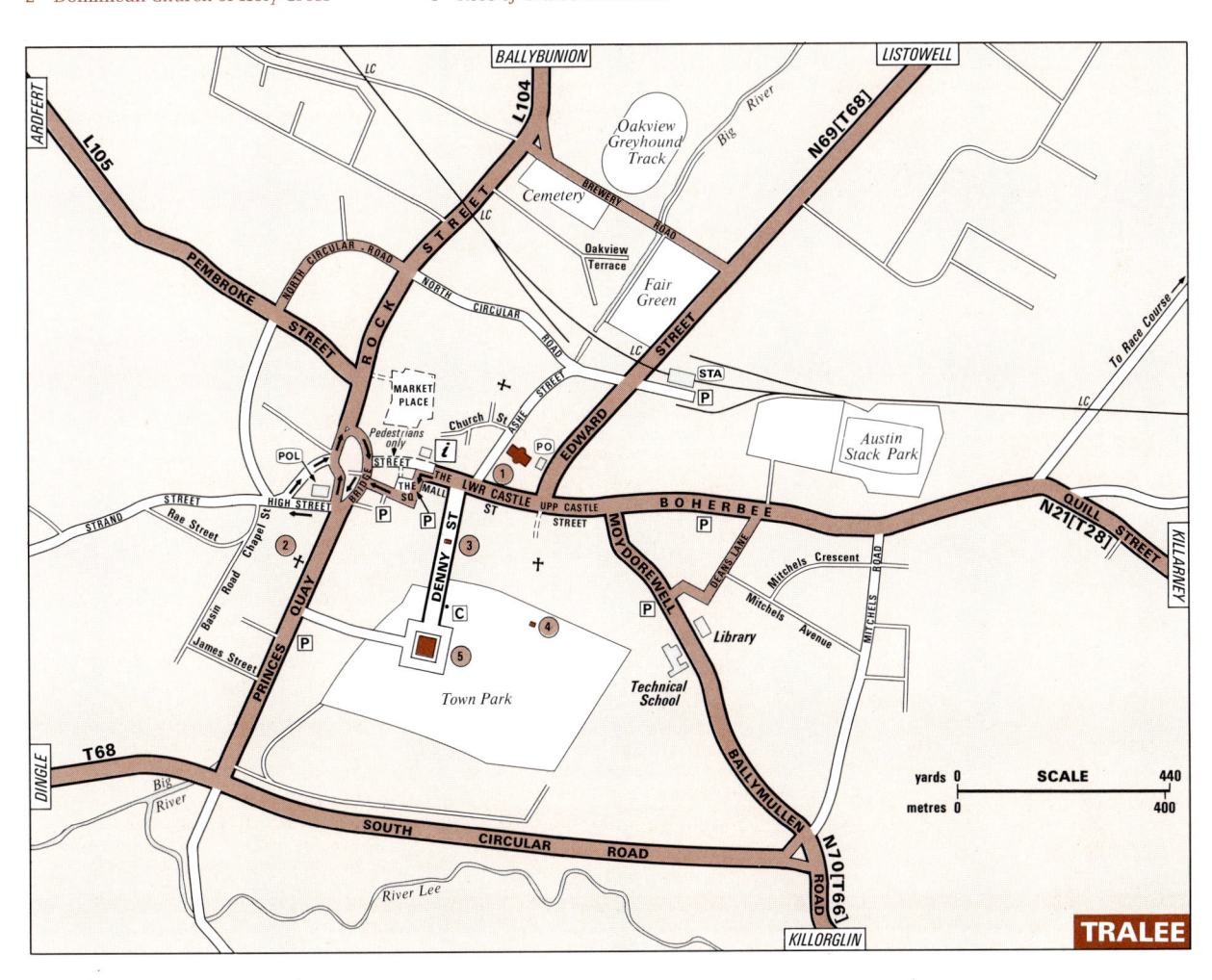

Entries marked * are the starting point of drives included in the Day Drive section of the book (pages 79 to 144).

TRILLICK, Treileac:
Three Flagstones, Tyrone 11 H35
Remains of a Plantation castle which was probably built c1630 by Lord Castlehaven exist here. The village itself stands at the base of 1,046ft Brougher Mountain on the Fermanagh border.

TRIM, Baile Átha Troim:
The Town of the Ford of the Elder Tree, Meath 18 N85
Trim – a thriving market town – is situated on a particularly-attractive part of the River Boyne in the heart of a fertile plain. It had one of the earliest and largest religious settlements in the country, and probably contains a greater concentration of significant antiquities than any other parish of the size in the country. The town grew up around an ancient ford crossing the river between the present bridges. St Patrick is said to have founded a monastery at this point. Following the Anglo-Norman invasion, the county of Meath was granted to Hugh de Lacy. He made Trim his capital and began to build a castle in 1173. This stronghold became the largest Anglo-Norman fortress built in Ireland during the 13thc, and its well-preserved ruins (NM) are of spectacular size and grandeur. The site occupies more than 3-acres, and the perimeter of the bawn wall totals 1,500ft. The most notable feature is the massive, three-storey keep – a square structure which was built c1200 and has 11ft-thick walls. The skilful design includes smaller square towers projecting from the middle of each wall, allowing 20 sides from which it could be defended. The curtain wall measures 486yds in length and has ten circular towers at regular intervals. Access is by two gateways positioned on the NW and S sides. One of these is well preserved and features a drawbridge, portcullis, and barbican. A ditch which encircled the walls could be turned into a moat by the diversion of a stream from the River Boyne. When the walls of the rook-inhabited keep became dangerous the Office of Public Works did some excavations to facilitate restoration. The results of these have led the archaeologist in charge to question whether the castle first erected at Trim was the usual motte-and-bailey type, and also whether there was any extensive occupation of the site before c1250. The strategic situation of Trim, on the edge of the Anglo-Norman Pale, meant that it was a centre of action throughout the middle ages and beyond. A future king of England – Prince Henry (afterwards Henry V) – and the youthful Humphrey, Duke of Gloucester, were imprisoned in Trim Castle by King Richard II.

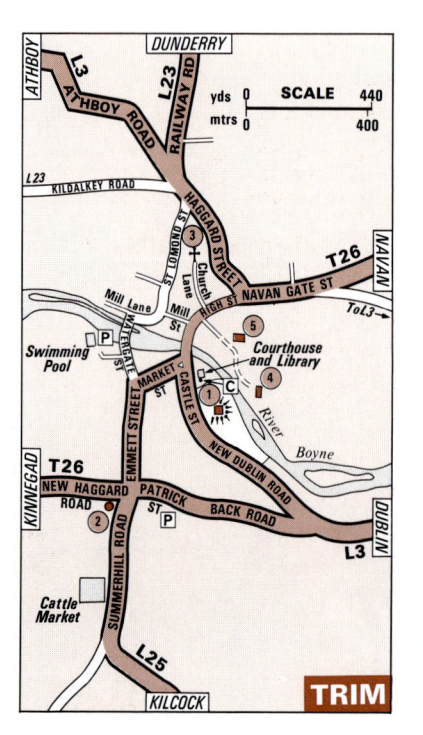

The Yellow Steeple (NM) is the most prominent ruin in the town, standing 125ft high on a ridge on the S bank of the river opposite Trim Castle. Originally part of the 13th-c Augustinian abbey of St Mary, the steeple dates from 1368. Only the east wall remains, buttressed by fragments of the south and north walls. The floor levels of the original five storeys can easily be picked out on the steeple wall. Close by the Yellow Steeple stands part of the old town walls and one of the gates, Sheep Gate (NM), with a semi-circular headed arch 15ft high. Water Gate is situated off Market Street. Talbot Castle, off the High Street, dates from 1415 and later became a school where the Duke of Wellington and Sir William Rowan Hamilton – the astronomer – were pupils. A statue in the town commemorates the Duke. Outside the walls N of the town are slight remains of a Dominican friary founded in the 13thc by Geoffrey de Geneville, who died here as a member of the Order.

The 19th-c parish Church of St Patrick (CI) was elevated to cathedral rank in 1954 and has a picturesque two-storey tower which stands 60ft high. The fine vaulted ground floor was erected in 1449 by Richard of York. There are some noteworthy monumental slabs in the churchyard. Also in the town are a number of Georgian houses and an imposing 19th-c gaol. About 1m E of Trim are the impressive remains of Newtown Trim Abbey (see entry). Along the valley of the Boyne between Trim and Navan are several typical fortified residences of the Anglo-Norman period. These are all similarly constructed – a plain massive tower with two round towers placed diagonally at the corners, eg Scurlogstown Castle, 2m E of Trim; Trubley Castle 3m E, of which the remains are scanty; and Assey Castle 6m E (see Bective entry). Near Scurlogstown Castle are a tumulus and the ruins of an old church. About 3m W stands Trimblestown Castle, the ruined 15th-c home of the Barnewalls. The Trimblestown River flows along the edge of the castle grounds, with clumps of trees scattered along the banks.

TUAM, Tuaim:
Grave-Mound, Galway 16 M45
This small market town has always been an important church centre, both in ancient and in modern times. St Jarlath founded a monastery here in the 6thc, and at present one of the four archbishops of the Roman Catholic church in Ireland lives here. At the centre of the town in the market place stands an early 12th-c high cross, partly assembled from fragments found in the churchyard. It is a ringed cross of sandstone, measuring about 14ft high, with inscriptions in memory of O Hoisin the abbot, who became archbishop in 1152 and of Turlogh O Conor, King of Connacht. The 19th-c St Mary's Cathedral (CI) has a magnificent Romanesque arch in the chancel, which dates from the 12thc and is built of red sandstone. The chancel walls and fine triple circular-leaded east windows of three lights are also portions of the ancient church, which was erected in the early 14thc with the help of King Turlogh O Conor. The rest of the cathedral is modern, having been rebuilt in harmony with the original character of the structure and consecrated in 1878. The Cathedral of the Assumption (RC) is a handsome 19th-c perpendicular-style cruciform building, with a square tower providing a prominent landmark for miles around. Beside the cathedral stands the diocesan college of St Jarlath. To the NW of the cathedral are the slight remains of Temple Jarlath, which date from c1360. Tuam is now an important centre of the beet-sugar industry and has a racecourse. Interesting local collections are housed in the town's museum. About 4½m NW stands the 16th-c de Burgo stronghold of Castlegrove.

TUAMGRANEY, Tuaim Gréine:
The Grave-Mound of, Clare 22 R68
A feature in this village is the 10th- to 11th-c church, which is still used by the parish (CI). The west doorway is supported with inclined jambs and walls of massive square-headed masonry. The remains of a castle of the O Gradys are close to the church.

TUBBERCURRY, Sligo 10 G51
See Tobercurry entry.

TULLA, An Tulach:
The Hillock, Clare 22 R47
Tulla is a little market town pleasantly situated on a hill. It is now best known as a fishing centre and has several small lakes near by. About 2m NW at Kiltanon is the strange ravine known as the Toomeens, with a good example of a subterranean stream. The course of the stream is marked by openings in its roof, which is gradually wearing away to form an open gorge. Many petrified shells are found in the limestone. On the hill of Tulla are remains of an old abbey.

TULLAHERIN, Tulach Iarainn:
Iron Hillock, Kilkenny 24 S54
Remains on this early monastic site include the ruin of a small, early-Irish church with antae and a round tower (NM).

TULLAGHOGE, Tyrone 12 H87
See Tullyhogue entry.

TULLAMORE, Tulach Mhór:
Big Hill, Offaly 17 N32
County town of Offaly, Tullamore was planned and built by the Earls of Charleville in the mid 18thc. In 1790 a huge balloon was sent up from Charleville, but it crashed on Tullamore, exploded, and flattened most of the buildings. The

1 Castle
2 Duke of Wellington Monument
3 St Patrick's Cathedral (CI)
4 Sheep Gate & Town Walls
5 Yellow Steeple (abbey remains)

Grand Canal reached here in 1798, and the town remained a terminus until 1804, when the W extension to the Shannon was completed. By then it had a hotel erected by the canal company. St Catherine's church (CI) was designed by Francis Johnston in 1818, and the market house and courthouse date from c1835. In the immediate environs are good examples of the small Elizabethan fortified residences built by settlers, such as Shrah Castle ½m to the W, built in 1588. To the SW of the town is the fine demesne of Charleville, with a mansion designed by Francis Johnston 1801.

About 5½m SE of Tullamore on the road to Mountmellick is the ancient churchyard of Killeigh. A monument here has the barely-legible inscription 'Here lyeth the body of Maximilian O Dempsey, Lord Viscount Clanmaliere who departed the 30th November 1690.' He was the last of the O Dempseys, Princes of Offaly. At Tihilly there are remains of a medieval church, an unusual high cross (NM), and an early-Christian gravestone. The pleasant village of Durrow lies 4½m N and has a very distinguished past. It marks the site of the most important monasteries of St Columcille (Columba). Many of the most famous names from early-Irish history lie here – all in unknown graves. The main feature is the fine elaborately-decorated 10th-c high cross (NM), with two fragments of other crosses and several gravestones. The present church (CI), much restored in the 18thc, may preserve parts of older churches. This was where the famous *Book of Durrow* was written c700.

TULLOW, *An Tulach:*
The Hillock, Carlow **24 S87**
Situated on the River Slaney in attractive countryside, especially around Aghadee Bridge, this market town has an Anglo-Norman castle and a 13th-c Augustinian abbey. The only remnant of the latter is a stone cross in the graveyard. The town is ringed with raths – in particular to the S and W. Castlemore, the most important, lies 1m to the W. Some 3½m E across the Wicklow border, on a lofty hill, is the ancient stone fort of Rathgall (NM), an extremely large enclosure consisting of four concentric ramparts of stone. The outer ring of this measures 1,000ft in diameter.

TULLOW (or TULLY), *An Tulach:*
The Hillock, Dublin **19 O22**
This ruined 13th-c church (NM) has a round chancel arch and two round-headed east windows, and may stand on the site of an early monastery. There are some early-Christian tomb slabs and two simple ringed crosses, one of which displays a carved female figure.

TULLYALLEN, Louth **19 O07**
This village lies 2½m NW of Drogheda near the picturesque valley called King William's Glen – where the king camped before winning the Battle of the Boyne. His victory is commemorated by an obelisk erected c1736 on a rock rising abruptly from the River Boyne.

TULLY CASTLE, *An Tulach:*
The Hillock, Fermanagh **11 H15**
There are substantial remains of a two-storey Plantation castle (NM) built here by Sir John Hume, on the SW shore of Lower Lough Erne. It was destroyed in the 1641 Rebellion.

TULLYHOGUE or TULLAGHOGE, *Tulaigh Óg:*
Hillock of Youths, Tyrone **12 H87**
Insignificant though the present village 2½m SE of Cookstown is, this was a centre of almost regal importance in Gaelic Ulster before the 16thc because it was here that the kings of Ulster were solemnly inaugurated as 'The O Neill'. On the summit of the small hill W of the village is a large circular encampment surrounded by deep fosses and earthworks on which stood the O Hagan ringfort where the inauguration took place on a large stone chair. The last to be inaugurated there was Hugh O Neill in 1595, and it was here that he retreated under pressure from Mountjoy in 1602. Mountjoy pursued him and broke to pieces the inauguration chair. The only trace of the fortress is the considerable number of unhewn blocks of limestone lying scattered around. About 1m NW of Tullyhogue is Loughry House, home of the Lindesay family and now an agricultural college. The original house was built in 1632 and rebuilt in 1671; portions of the old house with walls 3ft thick survive incorporated in the south wing of the greatly-altered and extended modern house.

TULLY HOUSE, *An Tulach:*
The Hillock, Kildare **18 N71**
See Kildare entry.

TULLYLEASE, Cork **21 R31**
Some 3m SW of Dromcolliher is this ruin of a 15th- to 16th-c nave-and-chancel church (NM), plus many fragments of tombstones.

TULSK, *Tuilsce,* Roscommon **16 M88**
This village was an incorporated market town and parliamentary borough by charter of Charles II in 1674. It features slight remains of a 15th-c Dominican abbey in a large cemetery. The ruins include a double-arch doorway divided in the centre by an elegant round pillar. There are very slight traces of the 15th-c castle of O Conor Roe, which was for long the strongest in the province of Connacht.

TURLOUGH, *Turlach:*
Dry Lake, Mayo **9 M19**
A well-preserved round tower (NM), rather lower and fatter than usual, can be seen here. The adjoining church was built in the 17th or 18thc and incorporates a 16th-c mullioned window.

TUROE STONE, Galway **16 M62**
See gazetteer inset overleaf.

TURVEY HOUSE, *Thuirbhe,* Dublin **19 O25**
This house stands NW of Donabate and was originally built in 1565 from the ruins of Grace Dieu Abbey, founded for nuns of the Order of St Augustine. At the Dissolution of the abbey the plea was made that 'in this house the women-kind of the most part of the whole Englishry of this land be brought up in virtue, learning and in the English tongue and behaviour', but the plea did not save it. An 18th-c house has been built from the remains of the earlier building.

TUSKAR ROCK, *An Tuscair,* Wexford **25 T20**
See Rosslare Harbour entry.

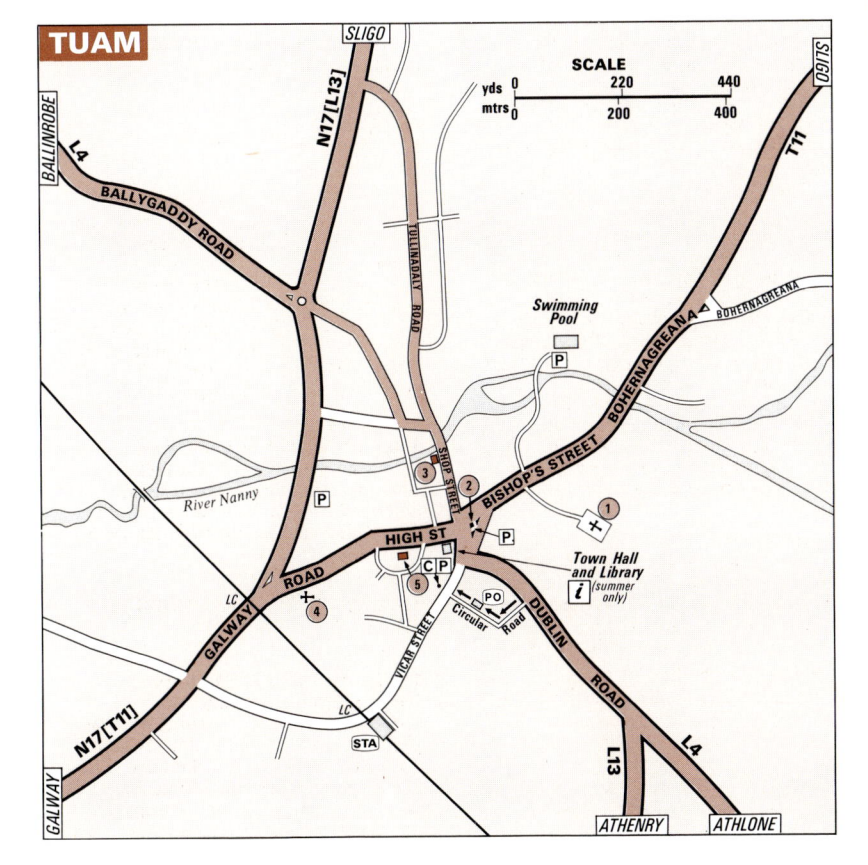

1 Cathedral of the Assumption (RC)
2 High Cross
3 Museum
4 St Mary's Cathedral
5 Temple Jarlath (remains)

TWELVE BENS (or PINS), *Na Beanna Beola:* Beola's Peaks, Galway 14 L 75
The highest of this Connemara range is 2,395ft Benbaun, which consists of a number of ridges radiating star-wise from a central point and shows numerous conical summits of quartzite. The E ridges overlook the deep trough of Lough Inagh, and rock climbing is possible in the area – notably around 1,908ft Bencorrbeg and 2,290ft Bencollaghduff. Good viewpoints include the outlying peaks of 2,220ft Derryclare, above Lough Inagh; 1,904ft Benlettery, overlooking Ballynahinch Lake; and 2,153ft Muckanaght, W of Benbaun. Splendid views of the whole group are obtained from the road which links Recess with Leenane via Clifden and Letterfrack.

TWOMILEBORRIS, *Buiríos Léith:* Borough of Liath, Tipperary 23 S 15
Situated 4½m W of Thurley, this place has the ruins of a church and an old tower retaining barbizans.

TYMON CASTLE, *Teach Motháin:* Mothán's House, Dublin 19 O 12
Only a tower remains of this castle, which was built in the 13thc by Henry de Loundres – Archbishop of Dublin. It stands on an esker ridge which is threatened with destruction by the removal of gravel.

TYNAN, *Tuíneán,* Armagh 12 H 74
Once the centre of a large and important parish belonging to the Culdees of Armagh, this village features four high crosses. One (NM), dating back perhaps to the 9thc, stands in the village street but is much defaced. Modern work has replaced some parts which were missing. The other three crosses are in the beautiful private demesne of Tynan Abbey, and consist of the 8ft Island Cross, the 8ft Well Cross, and the 11ft Terrace Cross. The last-named, possibly 12thc, is beautifully carved and stands at the end of a fine avenue of old yew trees. Tynan Abbey is a two- and three-storey house in gothick style, built originally by Rev James Stronge in 1750 but altered and reformed c1816.

TYRRELLSPASS, *Bealach an Tirialaigh:* Tyrrell's Road, Westmeath 17 N 43
This name refers to the road which runs through bogs where Richard Tyrrell ambushed and defeated an English force in 1597. The village is formally laid out round a semi-circular green, and has several houses of note. The Protestant church has a handsome monument to the Countess of Belvedere. At the W end of the village is the tower of 15th-c Tyrrell Castle. Killavally, the 17th-c birthplace of General Wade – the famous builder of roads in the Scottish Highlands – is in the neighbourhood.

ULLARD, *Ulard:* High Place, Kilkenny 24 S 74
Ullard is associated with 7th-c St Fiachra, who later lived in France and was famous for his cure of a tumour. At Ullard are the remains of a 12th-c nave-and-chancel church (NM), with granite carving on the Romanesque doorway. A 9th-c granite high cross (NM) represents the work of a local school of sculpture.

ULSTER FOLK MUSEUM (Cultra Manor, Holywood), Down 7 J 48
The museum is situated in a 136-acre park overlooking Belfast Lough, and the headquarters is in the former Kennedy family home. A display of paintings by William Conor, and various photographs of rural scenes from the Green collection can be seen inside. The museum trustees have re-erected a selection of buildings here, complete with furnishings, to reflect aspects of the social history of the province. There are now eleven outdoor exhibits open to the public, including an 18th-c cottar's house, a hip-roofed thatched cottage from Fermanagh, a Coalisland spade-mill driven by water power, a Cushendall hill farmer's cottage and another from Magilligan, a weaver's shop, and a mid 19th-c national school from Ballycastle.

THE TUROE STONE
This squat granite boulder stands 4ft high and has been shaped and carved to form a ritual object whose exact function is not yet understood. The curving complexities of the design upon the stone's surface are typically Celtic, and the object is thought to have been produced sometime between the 2ndc BC and the 1stc AD. The stone is decorated in the style called by archaeologists *La Tène* – a distinct Celtic culture noted for its complex art forms – which had its origins in Europe c500BC. Similar stones have been found both in Brittany and Germany, and another Irish example of the type can be seen in the demesne of Castle Strange, Co Roscommon. The shape of the Turoe stone can be interpreted as being phallic, and it may be that the object played a part in a fertility ritual. This does not necessarily mean that it would have acted as a sort of inanimate master of ceremonies at a Celtic orgy. The fertility of people, livestock, and crops is essential in any society, and is of especial importance in a pastoral society whose everyday life is completely dependent upon the fertility of its animals and vegetables.

Originally the stone stood outside the nearby Rath of Feerwore. On excavation the rath yielded a large quantity of finds, including glass beads and iron objects, and was shown to be a construction probably of 1stc AD built around an enclosure of probably 1stc BC date. The stone now stands in the grounds of Turoe House, near Loughrea in Co Galway.

URLANMORE CASTLE, *Urlann Mhór:* Big Forecourt, Clare 21 R 36
A small three-storeyed tower rises at one end of this building, and a lower extension contains the remains of a fine hall on the upper floor level. On the walls of a small, upper, tower room are outline paintings of animals.

URLINGFORD, Áth na nUrlainn:
The Ford of the Forecourts, Kilkenny
23 S26
This small town was a thriving woollen-manufacturing centre in the last century. Slight remains of a 16th-c castle of the Mountgarret Butlers and the ruins of an early church are of interest. There are several ruined castles in the vicinity, including the circular Balief – situated 3m E and once a home of the Shortalls; Clomantagh, with its four storeys standing 5m E and built by the Earl of Ormonde; and Tubrid, another well-preserved stronghold of the Shortall family, near Clomantagh.

USHNAGH, HILL OF, *Uisneach,*
Westmeath **17 N24**
Ireland's five ancient provinces met at the Hill of Ushnagh, 10m SW of Mullingar. A large, cleft limestone rock situated on the side of this hill is locally known as *Cat-Ushnagh*, but in ancient times it was called *Ail na Mireann* – 'The Stone of Divisions' and marked the point of meeting. Giraldus Cambrensis, remarking that this rock was at the very centre of the country, called it 'the Navel of Ireland'.

King Tuathal, who lived in the 2ndc, is said to have built a fortress-palace on the hill. He instituted a yearly meeting of the chieftains of all Ireland, which was held on the hill on May 1 and following days, and was known as the Feast of Beltane. Games and various pagan rites were celebrated, and cattle were driven between two immense fires. These fires had been lighted, with incantations, in the belief that the rite would preserve the livestock from disease. The feast seems also to have been somewhat in the nature of a fair, as articles of property were exchanged. Every chieftain who attended was required to present his horse and its trappings as a tax to the King of Connacht. The earthworks of the supposed palace remain on the E summit of the hill. They consist of an enclosure of stones and earth measuring 250ft across. Traces of buildings exist inside, and on its west side is a smaller enclosure of a similar shape. Excavation has shown that it was occupied in the 2ndc AD. Twenty Irish counties may be seen from the 690ft summit of the hill.

VALENTIA ISLAND, *Dairbhre:*
Place of Oaks, Kerry **26 V37**
This 7 by 2m island was separated from the mainland by a narrow strait ½m broad. At Portmagee village on the mainland the channel is only 120yds wide, and is now spanned by a modern bridge. The island is popular as a resort, but deep-sea fishing is available. There is an excellent harbour at Knightstown, the 'capital' of Valentia, which is named after the former proprietor the Knight of Kerry.
The surface of the island is generally bold and rocky, rising to 888ft at Jeokaun Mount. The latter, together with the Cliffs of Fogher, provide the finest scenery. The cliffs of 792ft Bray Head rise at the extreme W end of the island and open up a splendid view of the coast-line of Corcadhuibhne, or Dingle Peninsula, to the N. The Blasket Islands trail out from the peninsula, and the whole Iveragh coast extends S, with the pinnacles of the Skelligs far out to sea. Slate quarries some 2½m from Knightstown on the side of Jeokaun Mountain are worth a visit. Although now disused, they were very busy in the 19thc and there was considerable export of roofing slates and flagstones. A tunnel from which the slate has been extracted has been converted into a Lourdes Grotto.

Valentia is closely associated with the drama of the first laying of an ocean cable during the latter half of the 19thc. After several failures and partial triumphs, complete success was finally achieved in 1866. Additional cables have been laid in the intervening years. The cable station was closed early in 1966, owing to the latest developments in modern communications. There are a variety of prehistoric and early-Christian sites on the island. A delightful excursion by boat can be made from Knightstown to Church Island, E of Beginish Island, where there are the remains of an ancient oratory (NM) and some beehive huts. Ballycarbery Castle, on the mainland E of Lough Kay, can also be reached. The Skelligs are also accessible from here.

VELVET STRAND, Dublin **19 O24**
See Portmarnock.

VENTRY, *Ceann Trá:*
Strand Head, Kerry **26 Q30**
Standing at the head of a fine bay, this village is near many prehistoric remains. Between it and 1,695ft Mount Eagle, some 3m W, are almost 100 examples. The most notable are at Fahan (see entry) and the neighbouring fort of Dunbeg. Dunbeg Fort (NM) is on a headland cut off from the mainland by a massive stone rampart 1,300ft long and 15 to 25ft thick, with its entrance 3½ft high and 3ft wide inclining to 2ft at the top. There is also a subterranean entrance. The fort of Cahernamactireah (NM) lies ½m farther to the W. It is a circular stone fort 108ft in diameter with souterrains and beehive stone huts in the enclosure. Cathair Murphy (NM) is rather similar, but almost the entire enclosure is covered with buildings. Cathair an Da Dhoras (NM) is a very well-preserved triple clochan. An exceptionally picturesque corniche road, with glorious scenery, circles the coast from Ventry by way of Slea Head, Dunquin, and Clogher Head to Ferriter's Cove, near Ballyferriter. Slea Head has very fine cliff scenery. To the NW is Dunmore Head, overlooking Blasket Sound, where the Spanish Armada galleon *Santa Maria de la Rosa* was wrecked with great loss of life in 1588. Off Slea Head lie the Blasket Islands. The promontory which separates Ventry Bay from Dingle Bay is said to have been the last district in Ireland inhabited by Vikings as a separate community.

VILLIERSTOWN, *An Baile Nua:*
The New Town, Waterford **29 X19**
A remarkably-neat little village beautifully situated E of the River Blackwater, Villierstown lies S of the fine demesne of Dromana. This property of the Villiers-Stuart family features remains of an old stronghold of the Desmonds. Catherine, the second wife of the 12th Earl of Desmond, was born here and died in 1604 at the great age of 147. Some people put her age as high as 162. Her portrait is preserved at Dromana.

VIRGINIA, *Achadh an Iúir:*
The Field of the Yew, Cavan **12 N68**
This pretty little Plantation market town is beautifully situated on the wooded shore of Lake Ramor – a fine, 4m stretch of water dotted with beautifully-wooded islands. Murmod Hill rises to the N and is a good viewpoint. To the NE of the town is tiny Cuilcagh Lough. Some 5m NE of Virginia at Glebe, off the Bailieborough road, is a thatched cottage which was the home of the Sheridan family. The Sheridans emigrated to America. Their son, Phil Sheridan, was born here in 1830 and became a famous Commander-in-Chief of the American army.

WALSHESTOWN CASTLE, *Baile an Bhreatnaigh:*
Walshe's Homestead, Down **13 J54**
Walshestown (NM) is a fine example of a 16th-c four-storeyed tower house and bawn. It stands on Strangford Lough, between Downpatrick and Strangford.

WALTERSTOWN, Meath **18 N96**
Near this tiny village, 3m NE of Tara, is the fragmentary ruin of Walterstown Castle. Some 2m NE at Danestown are slight remains of a very ancient church and a circular fort measuring 12ft high by 50 yards in diameter. This stronghold is surrounded by a fosse and ramparts, and probably served as an outpost for Tara. At Ballygarvey, 2m N, is a ruined church. About 3m E at Timoole is another ruined church, with the date '1812' inscribed on the keystone of the arch. The actual building is much older.

WARD, HILL OF, *Tlachtga,*
Meath **18 N76**
See Athboy entry.

WARINGSTOWN, *Baile an Bhairínigh:*
Waring's Homestead, Down **13 J15**
As suggested by its name, this attractive village was established by William Waring in 1667. Until comparatively recently it contained something of the character of a quaint English village. Its parish church (CI) and original Waring mansion, both of the Restoration period, stand close together. Small, mainly single-storey thatched houses are set back and screened by trees along a single major thoroughfare. The parish church (CI) of 1681 was apparently a rectangular building with chancel and nave. The surviving original oak roof is a notable feature. The west tower was added c1750, and the church was enlarged in the 19thc. Waringstown House, built in 1667, was one of the first unfortified houses in Ireland. It was originally a two-storey building with attics, cellars, and rear-projecting wings. The house was much altered, enlarged, and heightened in the 18thc. The oak flooring, panelling, and staircase are probably original, but most of the interior fittings are 19thc. Near the house is a small two-storey tower with loops for defence – probably of late 17th-c date. There are two 18th-c double-storey houses E of the church.

WARRENPOINT, *An Pointe:*
The Point, Down **13 J11**
In 1780 Warrenpoint consisted of only two houses and a few fishermen's huts, but it developed as a watering place and packet station with a service to Liverpool in the early 19thc. It is now a pleasant resort, well laid out on a grid plan with a large square facing the quay

WARRENPOINT/WATERFORD

and a ½m-long, tree-lined promenade. It is rapidly developing as a port with modern harbour facilities for container traffic.

WATERFOOT, Antrim 7D22
Waterfoot, an attractive small village on the famous Antrim coast road, stands at the bridge over the Glenariff River at the N end of Red Bay. Near by is the entrance to Glenariff, often considered the most beautiful of Antrim's nine glens. Lurigethan rises to 1,154ft to dominate the landscape, while 1,304ft Crockalough and 1,817ft Trostan form the background. Fragmentary walls are all that remain of the 13th-c motte-and-bailey castle of Red Bay, described by Richard Dobbs in 1683 as 'a handsome pile, built of red freestone whereof there is good store here.' Near the bridge over the Cushenilt Burn is a totally overgrown graveyard containing slight remains of medieval Ardclinis' Church.

__WATERFORD__, *Port Láirge:*
Bank of the Haunch, Waterford 24S61
Founded by the Vikings c914, Waterford was conquered by the Anglo-Normans and grew to become a flourishing city port. Its major feature is the ¼m-long quay which extends along the S bank of the River Suir. In the late 18thc Waterford emerged as a manufacturing centre with a glass industry which was considered to be the best in Europe. This industry was destroyed in the early 19thc by the imposition of heavy duties, but was revived in 1947 and is again world famous. Famous Reginald's Tower is circular in plan and 80ft high. It stands at the angle formed by the Quay and the Mall, and was built – according to the inscription on the tablet over the main entrance – in 1003 by Reginald the Norseman. It was made into a civic museum in 1955, partly to commemorate Waterford's 750th anniversary as a chartered city.

Waterford was for centuries pre-eminent among Irish cities for its unwavering loyalty to the English crown. King Henry II landed here in October 1171 to substantiate his claim to Ireland. Prince John, while Lord of Ireland, heaped many favours upon the city and strengthened its fortifications. Richard II visited it in royal state, and confirmed and enlarged its privileges. Pretenders to the throne like Lambert Simnel and Perkin Warbeck, though supported by some of the most powerful in the land, wooed it in vain. The gates were closed in their faces – an act which won the city the royal commendation, *Urbs Intacta Manet Waterfordia*, and a Sword and Cap of Maintenance which are still preserved

1 Art Gallery & Museum
2 Chamber of Commerce
3 Christ Church Cathedral (CI)
4 City Hall
5 Clock Tower & Quay
6 Courthouse
7 Cromwell's Rock
8 Dominican Friary
9 French Church (ruins)
10 Holy Trinity Cathedral (RC)
11 Reginald's Tower (museum) & Town Walls
12 St Olaf's Church (CI)
13 St Patrick's Church (RC)
14 Waterford Glass Factory

Entries marked * are the starting point of drives included in the Day Drive section of the book (pages 79 to 144).

among the city's treasures. True to its royal attachment, it remained faithful to James II until William III was victorious at the Battle of the Boyne.

Most of the public buildings of distinction and fine Georgian streets like the Mall date from the period c1780 to 1810, when Waterford's glass industry and provision trade were exceptionally flourishing. Christ Church Cathedral (CI) is a plain Georgian building rebuilt c1770 from a design by John Roberts – a local architect – and decorated and altered in 1891. It replaced an ancient cathedral founded by Reginald the Norseman in 1050, which was levelled to the ground to make way for its successor. The ancient cathedral was enriched by the Anglo-Normans and a new chancel added. In the renovations of 1891 the architect discovered that the plan of the original cathedral corresponded very closely with the plan of the Norse cathedral of Christ Church in Dublin. Two noteworthy monuments in the cathedral are the Fitzgerald, of white Carrara marble, and the Rice, dating from 1469, which represents the body in a state of decomposition with a frog nestling in the intestines. Roberts was also responsible for many of the finest buildings and town houses in the city built before 1800. These include the City Hall of 1788 and the Chamber of Commerce c1795. He also designed Holy Trinity Cathedral (RC), built in 1796; an unusual feature here are the vestments with 14th-c Flemish workmanship which were presented by the Protestant clergy during demolition of their old cathedral c1778; these are now on loan to the National Museum. Also of interest are the museum and art gallery in O Connell Street, the 19th-c courthouse, and the 19th-c Clock Tower.

The Dominican friary, dating from 1226, is represented by a tower and belfry. The courthouse, in the Ionic style, dates from 1849. St Olaf's Church is of Norse Origin, but was reconstructed by the Normans and restored in 1734. Off the Parade are remains of the Grey Friars or 'French Church' (NM) built originally for the Franciscans in 1240 and given in 1695 to Huguenot refugees. Of the original building, finally abandoned in 1819, only the nave, chancel, north aisle, and 15th-c tower survive. There is a triple-light east window in the chancel. In 1545 the dissolved friary was converted into an almshouse and hospital and used as such for centuries, while the chancel and Lady chapel were used for the burial of famous Waterford families such as the Waddings and Powers. St Patrick's Church (RC) dates from 1727. Near it are remains of the former church. The Christian Brothers, who have their successful educational establishments in many towns in Ireland, started their first school in Waterford in 1803. Mount Sion Monastery of 1864 stands on the site of their first foundation. The 19th-c Holy Ghost Hospital in Cork Road contains some 13th- to 15th-c carvings. Luke Wadding, the historian and Philosopher, was born at Waterford in 1588 and became a member of the Franciscan Order. He was instrumental in having Rinuccini sent as Papal Nuncio to Ireland in 1642. There is a statue to him in the Mall.

A cargo steamer service connects Waterford with Fishguard in Wales.

Good views of the city and its fine harbour can be enjoyed from the ferro-concrete swing bridge erected across the Suir to replace the 18th-c wooden toll bridge built by celebrated American bridge builder Lemuel Cox. Mount Misery and Cromwell's Rock, on the N or Kilkenny bank of the river, are also good viewpoints.

There are numerous portal dolmens in the neighbourhood of the city, built c2,000 BC; the most remarkable is about 4m SW at Knockeen (NM). Some 4m WSW of the city above the River Suir stands the mid-Georgian house of Mount Congreve, with notable gardens which are shown any day by appointment. To the NW of the house are the ruins of Kilmeadon Castle, once a stronghold of the de Paors.

WATERVILLE, *An Coireán:*
The Little Whirlpool, Kerry **26 V 56**
Waterville is a resort situated on a narrow neck of land between Ballinskelligs Bay – with its lovely strand – and beautiful Lough Currane. It is in the Iveragh Peninsula, which is traversed by the famous Ring of Kerry scenic road.

Lough Currane, famous for its fishing, is fed by the River Cummeragh, which drains mountain tarns. The scenery at the upper end of the lake is very beautiful. Church Island at the N end has the ruins of an oratory (NM) attributed to 6th-c St Finian. This is circular externally, quadrangular inside, and has a primitive doorway on the north side. Also of interest is an Irish Romanesque nave-and-chancel church (NM) of the 12thc.

WATTLE BRIDGE, Fermanagh **11 H 42**
Remains of the local 18th-c parish church comprise a ruined tower and little else. A large stone circle, 100ft in diameter with some enormous stones, lies ¼m SW. This is actually the kerb of a large cairn.

*__WESTPORT,__ *Cathair na Mart:*
The Stone Fort of the Oxen, Mayo **15 L 98**
This was an important town before the advent of railways, featuring a canalized river with 18th-c bridges and quays. Lofty, deserted warehouses are witnesses to its former greatness as a distributing port which exported agricultural produce and imported timber from America and the Baltic, plus manufactured goods from Britain. Westport today is a fishing centre, beautifully situated on the banks of a small stream which flows into Clew Bay, with its galaxy of small islands. The Mall, with lime trees overlooking the river on both sides, is a charming street. Canon Hannay, who wrote novels under the pseudonym of George A Birmingham, was rector here for many years. W M Thackeray came to Westport in 1842 and described the scenery around Clew Bay as the 'most beautiful in the world'. Both the Catholic and the Protestant churches have points of interest. The modernized, early-Georgian mansion of Westport House was designed by Richard Cassels and shows additions and alterations by James Wyatt c1788. It stands at the W end of the town and shares its beautiful demesne with an attractive modern church (CI). The house and grounds are OACT, and the estate has a zoo park plus facilities for shopping, caravanning, and fishing.

*__WEXFORD,__ *Loch Garman,* Wexford **25 T 02**
Something of the atmosphere and inconveniences of a medieval walled town survive in Wexford. It is situated on the lower part of a hill close to the shore, where the estuary of the River Slaney meets Wexford Harbour – a large shallow inlet of the sea. Many acres at the S end of this inlet have been reclaimed from the sea in recent years. The town was connected at its N end with the opposite bank of the Slaney by a wooden bridge built in 1794 by the celebrated American bridge builder, Lemuel Cox, who was responsible for similar bridges at Waterford and Londonderry in the 1790's.

The town owes its foundation to the Vikings, who established a local base from which they could plunder the surrounding country. They became great traders

Beautiful Red Bay extends S of Waterfoot and features this short tunnel, which has been cut through a sandstone spur to allow access for the famous Antrim Coast Road.

Entries marked * are the starting point of drives included in the Day Drive section of the book (pages 79 to 144).

WEXFORD

when plunder ceased to pay, and Wexford developed into an important trading port. But the Vikings, formidable opponents on the sea or in open battle, proved no match for the Anglo-Normans in an organized assault or in fortification. When Robert Fitzstephen and Maurice de Prendergast landed at Bannow Bay in May 1169 they easily captured Wexford with the help of some hundred supporters of Dermot McMurrough. The town henceforth became an ordered Anglo-Norman centre with well-organized defences and religious institutions.

Little remains of Wexford's defences, the West Gate Tower near the railway station being the only survivor of the five fortified gateways. Four castles which at one time strengthened the fortifications have left no trace. There are relics of the walls from the West Gate to Georges Street, and from High Street to St Patrick's Church, but the remains of some of the religious institutions are more complete. Near the West Gate stands Selskar Abbey (NM), or the Abbey of the Holy Sepulchre, founded in the late 12thc; the square battlemented tower and the church with double nave which survive both date from c14thc. It is said that the bells of this church were taken to Liverpool by Cromwell's soldiers, and are now in the tower of a church in River Street in that city. In the E side of the town are the scanty remains of the church of St Patrick, an off-shoot of Selskar Abbey, showing four pointed arches supported by circular pillars and the central arch of the chancel. When Cromwell occupied Wexford in 1649 he gave no quarter to the garrison and wreaked havoc with the churches. The Bull Ring, the name of which is reminiscent of medieval bull-baiting, contains a well executed figure of an Irish Pikeman by Oliver Sheppard, commemorating the Wexford insurgents of 1798. The town was held by the insurgents for almost a month, when about a hundred citizens were piked on the bridge and their bodies thrown into the river. St Peter's College on Summerhill has a beautiful chapel by Pugin – the rose window is especially noteworthy. Sir Robert J McClure, the great 19th-c Arctic explorer whose outstanding achievement was the discovery of the North-West Passage in

1 Bullring
2 John Barry Statue
3 Maritime Museum
4 St Patrick's Church (ruins)
5 St Peter's College
6 Selskar Abbey or Abbey of the Holy Sepulchre
7 Theatre
8 Town Walls (remains)
9 West Gate Tower

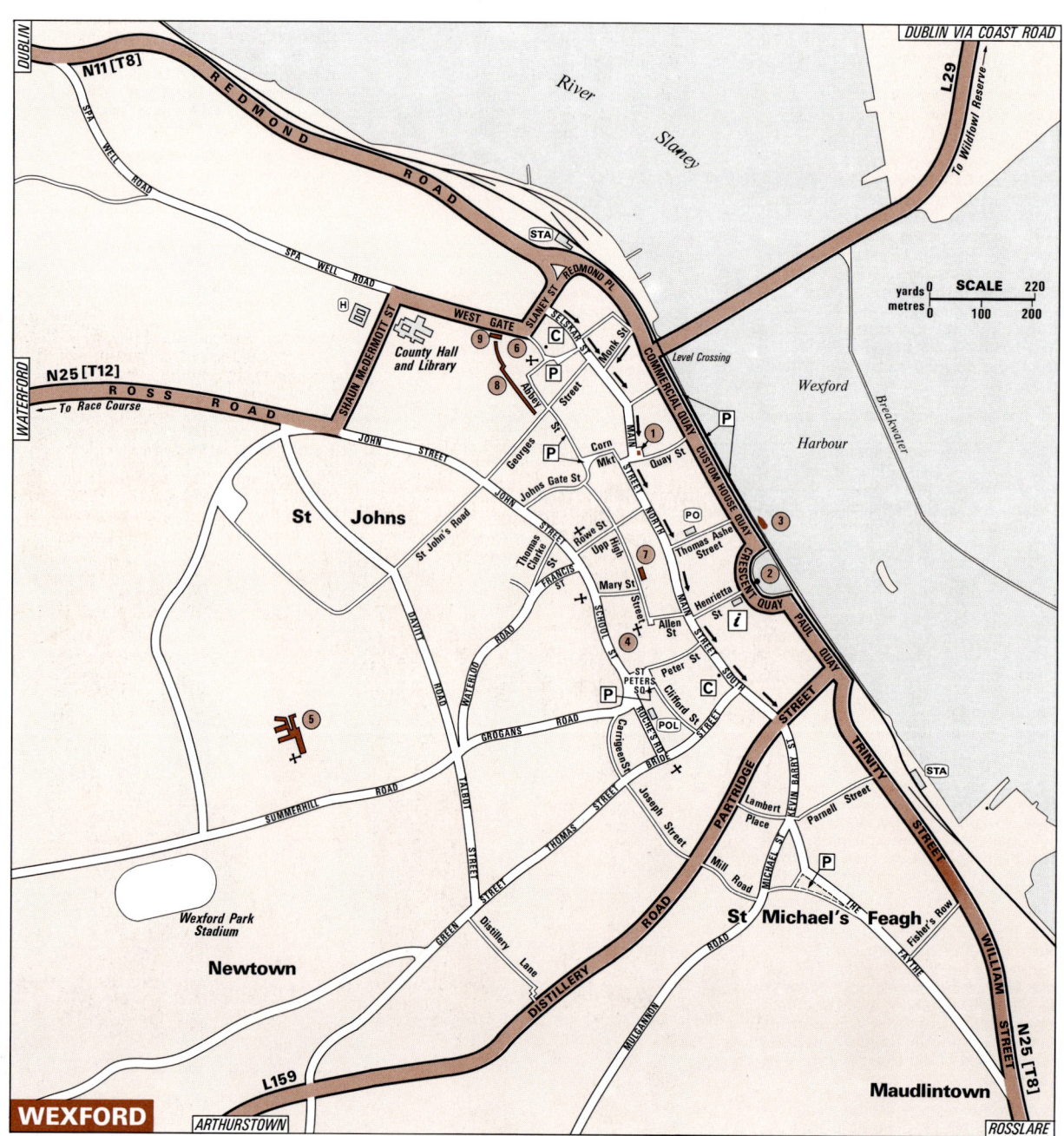

1851, was born in a house beside White's Hotel. The old rectory in Main Street was the birthplace of Lady Wilde (the patriotic 'Speranza' and mother of Oscar Wilde) in 1826. Tom Moore's mother was born in a house which still stands in Corn Market. A statue to John Barry, founder of the American Navy, stands in The Crescent. Other places of interest in the town include the Maritime Museum and a fine theatre. Wexford's business activities include the manufacture of agricultural implements and also bacon-curing. There are Georgian houses around the fishing harbour. The Wexford Festival of Art and Music takes place from the last Sunday in October to the first Sunday in November.

WHIDDY ISLAND, *Faoide,* Cork **27 V94**
This small island $1\frac{3}{4}$m W of Bantry is now famous as a major oil terminal.

WHITEABBEY, *An Mhainistir Fhionn:* The White Abbey, Antrim **7 J38**
Once a 19th-c linen-mill village on the N side of Belfast Lough, Whiteabbey is now part of Newtownabbey. On 938ft Knockagh Hill, a viewpoint $2\frac{1}{2}$m to the N, is the Co Antrim 1914 to 1918 War Memorial Obelisk. Anthony Trollope lived and wrote in the village.

WHITE ISLANDS FIGURES
The extraordinary collection of carved figures in a ruined church on White Island, taken together with the equally peculiar figures on Boa Island and the Bishop Stone at Killadeas, seems to indicate a veritable school of sculpture in the Lower Lough Erne region during early-Christian times. All these figures are executed in a similar, highly-stylized manner, and all of them seem based on a pagan sculptural tradition; indeed it may be that the Boa Island figures are wholly pagan in conception.

The church in which the White Island figures are kept dates from the 12thc and has a reconstructed Romanesque doorway in its south wall. Excavations carried out here during 1958 revealed that the church was built upon the site of an earlier wooden structure.

One of the figures is a *sheila-na-gig*, a grotesque carving with great emphasis placed upon the genital regions. It is not clear whether *sheila-na-gigs* were placed in churches as a warning against vice, or whether they are evidence of some kind of fertility cult. Two of the carvings are of heads, and one of these wears a kind of bonnet. There is one unfinished figure which was presumably abandoned when a flaw was discovered in the stone. The five remaining figures are similar in general appearance – each depicts a full length body; each has highly stylized feet; and each has a socket in the top of its head. The sockets may indicate that the figures were used as corbels supporting some kind of superstructure.

Although similar in many respects, the detailing of these figures makes each one highly individual. Three of them seem without doubt to be ecclesiastics of one sort or another, as they hold such things as croziers, bells, and in one case a book or reliquary. One of these figures was discovered built into the wall of the church during the 1958 excavations. This lent weight to the argument that at some stage (presumably when the present

WHITEHEAD, *An Cionn Bán:* The White Head, Antrim **7 J49**
Whitehead, a seaside resort on the N side of Belfast Lough, developed in the late 19thc with the coming of the railway. Slight remains of 17th-c Castle Chichester can be seen near the railway station. A walk via the cliffs to Black Head and round by the Gobbins is very fine. Some $2\frac{1}{2}$m W at Bellahill is Dalway's Bawn, a well-preserved three-towered enclosure built *c*1609.

WHITEHOUSE, Antrim **7 J38**
This mill village on the W shore of Belfast Lough was the site of the first cotton mill in Ireland, built by Nicholas Grimshaw in 1784.

WHITE ISLAND, Fermanagh **11 H16**
White Island lies on Castle Archdale Bay in Lower Lough Erne. The name is not original, but an attempt has been made to identify it with the important monastic site of *Eo-inis*. The small church (NM) near the pier has been much restored, and features a Hiberno-Romanesque doorway which belongs to the 12thc (see gazetteer inset below). On nearby Davy's Island is the ruined south wall of a small church containing a medieval doorway; this church was built) the figures were considered to be an embarrassment because of their strange style and were hidden away. The other two socketed figures are very difficult to interpret. One carries a beast (thought to be a ram) in each hand, and the other carries a sword and shield. It is not at all clear who the figures are intended to represent, or indeed if they are supposed to be

belonged to the former Augustinian Abbey of Lisgoole.

WHITE PARK BAY, Antrim **7 D04**
On top of a hillock near the centre of this bay is a stone circle measuring 36ft in diameter. Many of the basalt stones have fallen down the hill. At Templastragh, $\frac{1}{4}$m W of Portbraddan, are remains of a small 16th-c church (NM). This displays an incised cross slab in the west gable, and is built mainly with pentagonal stones of the Giant's Causeway type. See also Ballintoy entry.

WICKLOW, *Cill Mhantáin,* Wicklow **19 T39**
A quaint, attractive town situated on a stretch of elevated rugged ground, Wicklow is backed by high hills and stands at a point where the River Vartry flows into the sea. It has a shingle beach extending for several miles to the N. The creek, which is separated from the open sea by a long grassy spit of land known as the Murrow, formed an excellent harbour of refuge for the Vikings and became their *Wynkynlo* or 'Vikings Lough', one of their favourite bases on the Irish coast. After the Anglo-Norman invasion the town was granted to Maurice Fitzgerald, who started to build the Black Castle. This is now a

anybody in particular. It has been suggested that they are Celtic saints, or that some of them are figures from the life of St Patrick. It is also virtually impossible to put a date to them – all that can be said with certainty is that they were made before the 12thc AD.

picturesque ruin on the headland above the town. For centuries the castle was exposed to the frequent raids of the O Tooles and the O Byrnes until their conquest by Lord Deputy Mountjoy in 1601.

There are some remains of a 13th-c Franciscan friary near the entrance to the town from the Dublin to Wexford road. The 18th-c parish church (CI) has a fine 12th-c Romanesque carved doorway in the south porch, brought from an older building. There is also an ancient fort. Wicklow like Wexford took an active part in the 1798 Insurrection, as is evident from the statue in the Market Place to Billy Byrne, one of the leaders, and the medallions on the statue commemorating the names of other leaders. There is also a monument to Captain Halpin, commander of the Ship *Great Eastern*, which laid some of the first trans-oceanic cables in the 19thc. Favourite walks are those to Bride's Head, Wicklow Head, and the Silver Strand, which provides fine bathing. Some 6m S are the ruins of Dunganstown Castle.

WICKLOW GAP, Wicklow   **19 O00**
This pass lies in the heart of the Wicklow Mountains at a height of 1,569ft, and is traversed by a fine road which links Glendalough and Hollywood. To the N rises 2,686ft Thonelagee, which overlooks the Vale of Glendasan.

WOODENBRIDGE, *Garrán an Ghabhláin*: The Grove of the River-fork, Wicklow **25 T17**
As indicated by its name, this delightful spot is situated at the second and more charming Meeting of the Waters, where the beautiful valleys of the Aughrim, Avoca, and Gold Mine Rivers unite. Many enjoyable trips can be made in the vicinity. Croghan Kinsella rises to 1,987ft some 4½m SW of Woodenbridge, at the head of the Gold Mine Valley on the Wexford border. Gold mining was carried on here c1700. About 3m SE of Woodenbridge, off the Arklow Road and on either side of the Avoca River, are the demesnes of Glenart Castle and Shelton Abbey.

WOODTOWN, *Baile na Coille:* Homestead of the Wood, Meath **18 N88**
Near Woodtown is a well-preserved section of the Pale earthworks, consisting of a fosse and a rampart of earth.

YOUGHAL, *Eochaill:* Yew Wood, Cork **29 X17**
Youghal is a quaint market town, fishing port, and resort situated on the W side of the River Blackwater estuary. Its fine harbour opens out into the wide expanse of Youghal Bay, and is sheltered by Knockadoon Head and Ram Head. It was already a flourishing town with a well-organized civic life by the 14thc, when Roger Mortimer sailed into the harbour on Easter Sunday 1317 to challenge the Bruces and their confederates. The town walls date from the 15thc and are probably the best preserved in Ireland. Their state was declared 'deplorable' by the Earl of Ormonde, who inspected them shortly before the rebellion of Gerald, Earl of Desmond, in 1579. The rebel Earl of Desmond sacked the town in 1579, not sparing even the sacred buildings. Sir Walter Raleigh played an important part in the suppression of the Desmond rebellion, and for his services he was rewarded with 42,000 acres of the earl's forfeited estate. Although he spent little time there he was warden of the town between 1588 and 1589. He sold his estate to Sir Richard Boyle, later Earl of Cork. Cromwell made Youghal his base during a good part of his campaign in the S, and it was from here that he sailed on his return to England.

The old town lies at the foot of a long and steep hill, while the new portion stretches along the edge of the bay. The Main Street is spanned by a wide arch which carries a structure of four storeys surmounted by a clock tower. This is known as the Clock Gate and was erected in 1777. It houses a museum and tourist office. Near the Clock Gate is a much-altered 15th-c tower-house called Tynte's Castle, and opposite stands a fine 18th-c house built c1706 by Dutch architect Leuventhan. This is called the Red House. Nearby are almshouses built for Protestant widows by the Earl of Cork in 1634. At the N end of the Main Street is the site of 13th-c Dominican North Abbey, which features the west gable and lower church walls. Cromwell's Arch, also known as the Water Gate, is a 19th-c restoration. In North Main Street is the much-altered gable of St John's House, a cell (founded 1360) of the Benedictine priory of St John the Evangelist, Waterford.

1 Almshouses
2 Clock Gate (museum)
3 Cromwell's Arch or Water Gate
4 Dominican North Abbey (remains)
5 Myrtle Grove
6 Red House
7 St John's House
8 St Mary's Collegiate Church (CI)
9 Town Walls
10 Tyntes Castle (remains)

At the end of William Street is St Mary's Collegiate Church (CI) – built on an earlier foundation by Thomas, the 8th Earl of Desmond, in the second half of the 15thc. This cruciform building is the largest medieval parish church in Ireland. The choir was roofless for 300 years, but was restored in 1884. A massive square tower 63ft high with walls 8ft thick stands separated from the church and is used as a belfry. Notable features of the church are a 14th-c baptismal font, the old oak roof and arches of the nave, the massive pulpit with its canopy in carved bog oak, the six-light east window of c1468, the west doorway, and the doorway on the south side of the choir. In the south wall of the nave is a curious 17th-c wooden cradle which, when inverted, has the figure of a cross. This was used as a receptacle for the sword of the mayor when he attended divine service in state. The sword is now in the possession of the Duke of Devonshire at Lismore Castle. Many of the memorials in the church date from the 16th and 17thc. Thomas, the 8th Earl of Desmond, founded a college with a warden, eight fellows, and eight singing men at the time he built the church. The college building stood on the north side of the churchyard but was destroyed in 1579. It was rebuilt on the old foundations by the 1st Earl of Cork, and it is said that Congreve the dramatist lived in the building when his father was agent for the Earl of Cork's estate. A portion of the old town walls bounds the churchyard and carries round towers which were erected by the Earl of Cork.

To the N of the church stands Myrtle Grove, said to have been occupied by Sir Walter Raleigh when Warden of the town. The house is not open to the public, but can be seen from the precincts of St Mary's. It is an Elizabethan structure with gables, thick walls, fine fireplaces, and heavy oak panelling in some of the rooms. The mantelpiece in the drawing room is particularly fine. In later years Sir George Carew (Lord President of Munster) and the great Earl of Cork, who defended the town in the civil war of 1641, lived at Myrtle Grove. The manufacture of fine-point lace by the Presentation Sisters has been a notable feature of Youghal for about 100 years, and there is now a thriving pottery and carpet-making industry in the town. Youghal has an excellent 5m-long stretch of sandy bathing beach. Across the mouth of the harbour is Monatrea, and between Youghal and Cappoquin the river scenery in the Blackwater Valley is some of the most attractive in Ireland. The river is famous for salmon, but the best reaches are strictly preserved.

Rincrew Hill rises some 2m NW and is crowned by the dilapidated ruins of Rincrew Abbey, which was founded in the 12thc by Raymond Fitzgerald. The latter was nicknamed le Gros and is said to have been buried at Molana Abbey in 1186. About 1½m farther N is the square keep of Fitzgerald Castle; one of the round towers of the curtain wall can be seen near the old church of Temple Michael. The remains of Strancally Castle, perched on a rock overhanging the Blackwater, lie some 7m N of Youghal. A cave in the rock is locally called the Murdering Hole and is said to have been used as a prison and execution house by the Desmonds. To the S are the Broads of Clashmore, where the river becomes tidal.

Passport to the Past

Pre-Reformation churches and crosses in Ireland – an architectural heritage that can be read in the stones of ancient buildings which reflect the cultures and beliefs of their founders.

Spearheaded by the monastery founded in 563 by St Columba on the island of Iona, to the west of Scotland, Irish monks formed the northern flank of a two-pronged Christian mission which advanced on central Britain in the 6th and 7thc. The Irish clashed with the southern prong, led by Augustine of Canterbury, who had been sent from Rome by the Pope in 597 to convert the Angles. The two groups disagreed on issues which may seem somewhat abstruse to us today, *eg* how a cleric's hair should be cut and on what day Easter should be celebrated. The dispute on the latter question arose largely because each mission had its own way of computing the date of Easter. Almost predictably, each one arrived at a different answer. The Roman mission based its calculations on a 532-year cycle devised in the year 457. The Irish, however, still observed an older, 84-year cycle which had been used in the Roman church prior to the introduction of the 532-year cycle. Because they used the older of the two systems, the Irish were convinced that theirs was the correct one, and had no hesitation in telling the Pope that they were right and he was wrong. At the same time – and without any apparent sense of paradox – they admitted complete obeisance to the Chair of Peter. When matters came to a head in 664, a Synod was convoked at Whitby in Yorkshire to resolve the controversy. The decision went against the Irish, and most of them retired aggrieved and disenchanted, leaving the field to the Roman mission.

Following the introduction of Christianity into Ireland by St Patrick and others in the first half of the 5thc, the Irish church had trodden its own path in isolation, unaffected by the changes taking place in the Roman church in the meantime. The defeat of the Irish participants at the Synod of Whitby was precipitated because they had characteristically – and in their own view, rightly – adhered to older principles and revered traditions which in the eyes of others had become out-dated. This conservatism – this clinging to old, established traditions which manifested itself in the Irish churchmen at Whitby – was to characterize Irish church building right up to the 12thc.

The ecclesiastical organization of the Irish also differed from the Roman system. The place of bishoprics in the Roman church was taken in Ireland by a network of monasteries – each under the rule of its own abbot – which flourished until the 12thc. These monasteries formed one of Ireland's most valuable assets, becoming the greatest patrons of culture in the fields of literature and the visual arts which the country has ever experienced. They made Ireland, in Newman's words, 'the storehouse of the past and the birthplace of the future' by helping to preserve a great tradition of lore and learning which, through the Carolingian Empire, contributed to cultural development during the European middle ages. The monasteries flourished on a life of asceticism and hardship for the body, while the monk's mind was preoccupied with artistic and literary pursuits which reached an almost unparalleled level during the European dark ages.

Some of the 670 steps which ascend from the shore to the superb monastic site near the summit of Skellig Michael island.

PASSPORT TO THE PAST

Skellig Michael is a huge, precipitous mass of slate rock which rises to 705ft above the sea. The two groups of buildings visible in this illustration are Coastguard Stations.

If a person wishes to re-capture the spirit of this ascetic world and the conservative tradition of the early Irish church, there are few better ways of doing so than by making what can best be described as a pilgrimage to one of the most remarkable and best preserved of the old Irish monasteries. Dedicated to St Michael, it lies on an island known as the Greater Skellig, some 12m off the south-west coast of Co Kerry. En route to the island, marooned in the Atlantic a 2-hour boat trip from the mainland, the visitor passes the Smaller Skellig, alive with graceful gannets. Once ashore on the Greater Skellig he is faced with 670 antiquated and well-trodden steps which wend their way sky-wards like a Jacob's ladder. At the top, perched on a terraced ledge 550ft above the sea, is the monastery itself. The location equals, if not surpasses, those of the other two great monastic peaks of north-western Europe dedicated to the Archangel, Mont St Michel in Normandy and St Michael's Mount in Cornwall. When the visitor finally passes through the gate of the stone wall which surrounds the monastic enclosure, relief at reaching the top is coupled with a sense of spiritual rebirth as he steps back a thousand years in time. Here is a passport to the past; the sight beheld is practically unchanged from that which greeted the monks who came here to worship so long ago. The scene captures the severe monastic way of life of the early Christian Irish monks, and the deprivation which these holy men experienced in devoting their lives to God on this dizzy and almost inaccessible mountain eerie can almost be felt.

Simple, well-preserved stone buildings are outlined against the barren slopes of the island. Five stone cells which once housed the monks are laid out on a terrace, not in a monotonous line like a modern housing estate, but in such a way as to offer an unexpected surprise round every corner. These monks' huts are staggered, and each one is built on a different level. A myriad of rather small stones was used to construct the huts – placed in a circular fashion and layered on one another in an irregular patchwork – jutting ever inwards, creating buildings resembling beehives. All the huts but one are roughly square inside and round outside. The remaining structure is square inside and out. The simple doorway, with straight sides and a flat lintel, leads into a dark interior. When his eyes grow accustomed to the gloom the visitor can begin to see how ingeniously the stones have been laid to withstand the danger of collapse. One of the huts bears a cross on its outside wall. Composed of a group of white quartz stones, and sited above a solitary window high up the wall, it contrasts beautifully with the dark stones of the hut itself.

Plan of the monastic site on Skellig Michael.

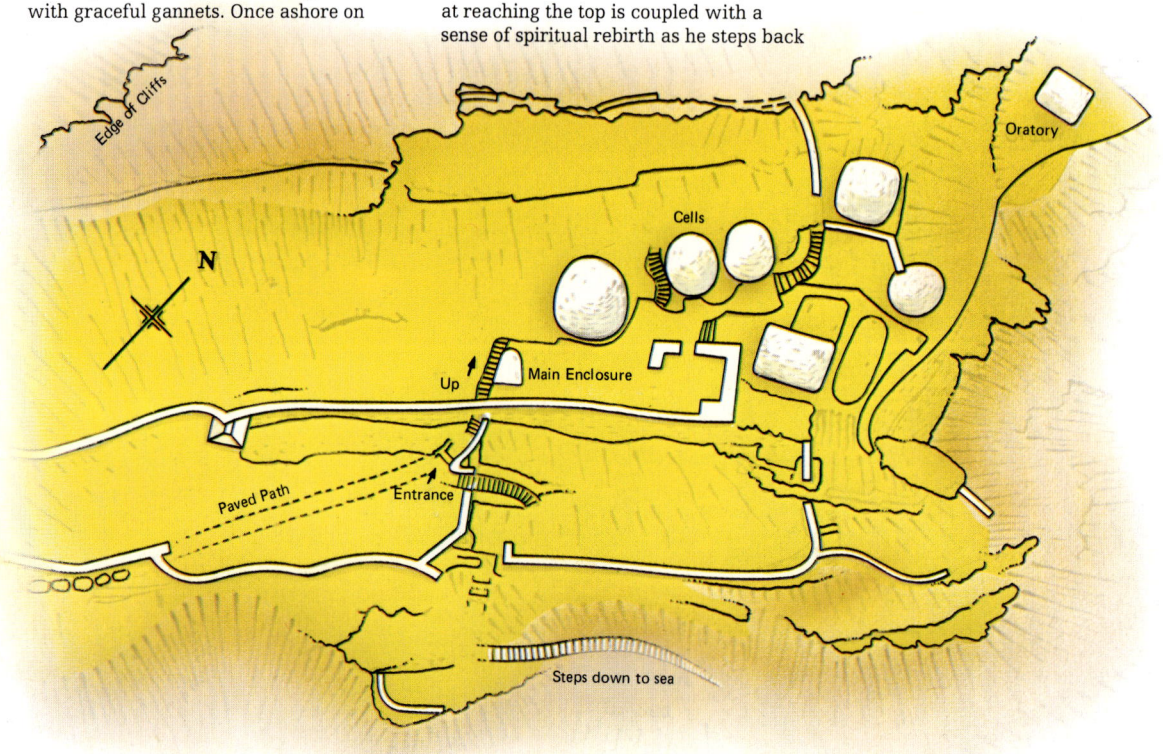

PASSPORT TO THE PAST

In front of another hut are a few steps which lead down to one of the two wells which supplied the monks with drinking water. The island supports little more than 40 botanical species – scarcely sufficient to sustain modern man! During the long winters, when the monks were cut off from the mainland, they must have supplemented their diet with a few vegetables grown on a second terrace above the huts. Fish, birds' eggs, and possibly the occasional gannet – regarded as a delicacy among some Scottish islanders today – probably provided additional nourishment.

The construction of the beehive huts described above is based on the corbel principle: horizontally laid stones which jut inwards one above the other to form what is awkwardly described as a false arch. This method of building has a venerable and widespread ancestry. It was applied $4\frac{1}{2}$ thousand years ago in the construction of burial chambers at Newgrange and Knowth in the Boyne Valley near the east coast of Ireland. Some $4\frac{1}{2}$ centuries ago it was still utilized for roofing castles in the same area – Termonfeckin in Co Louth and Dunsoghly in Co Dublin. Round huts built in this manner are also found in areas on the Continent which have a pastoral economy. In Provence and Dalmatia as well as in the heel of Italy, such huts are obviously vestiges of a very ancient form of building which was probably once widespread in the sheeplands of Europe. Huts similar to those on Ireland's Skellig Michael, but with round interiors, have been built in the south west on the nearby Dingle Peninsula during this century. These huts serve, among other things, as hen coops and outhouses. It may well be that clusters of such buildings as are found at Glenfahan, on the peninsula's tip, originally served as herdsmens' huts and were erected to act as seasonal homes for shepherds who wandered widely with their flocks. The Dingle Peninsula beehive huts belong to the most basic – and probably also to the oldest – type of corbel construction in Europe. Huts surviving on the Continent tend to possess greater structural refinements.

In Ireland these buildings are the personification in stone of the strength of native tradition on the west coast. In addition, they are valuable links with a past, most of whose other features have long since vanished. Such structures lie on the fringe of a continent which is more active at the centre than it is at the rim. They also lie on the edge of what was once the Indo-European-speaking world. Like Sanskrit, which was used at the other side of that world, the old Irish language has remained closer to the original Indo-European tongue than almost any of the languages which lie between these poles.

In some of those areas in the west of Ireland, where the age-old tradition of corbel construction is still in use, the Irish language is preserved. The great majority of Irish spoke Gaelic as late as the beginning of the last century, but the tongue is now confined to small pockets concentrated along the west coast. The people who still speak this language are, tragically, the last living links with a Celtic literary past of tremendous vitality based on a great oral tradition. Fortunately, the Irish Folklore Commission was able to tape record the stories and legends for posterity. The tales still told by the old story tellers – the *seanachies* – enliven the fertile imagination of Europe's past. A great Celtic scholar, the late and much-lamented Myles Dillon, heard the following story on the Aran Islands. It concerned a man who gouged out the sole eye of a giant and then escaped from the cave where he was being held captive by clinging to the underside of a sheep in order to avoid detection by the giant's searching hands. Perhaps the teller of this tale, or his teacher, or his teacher's teacher, had read the account of Ulysses and the Cyclops in the *Odyssey*. Perhaps, on the other hand, this was the surviving form of an old European folk-tale, one which inspired Homer nearly 3,000 years ago and which still forms part of the folk tradition in western Ireland

A beehive hut (clochan) on Skellig Michael. This type of dry-stone construction is typical of other monastic buildings on the site.

General view of the Skellig Michael site, showing a cross slab in the background and one of the two oratories on the right.

today. These old Celtic folk tales, whether heard or read, exude a sense of fantasy and a feeling for an 'otherworld', a heroic world which is rapidly disappearing in the face of international standardization. They also remind our generation of its good fortune in being able to appreciate the survival of this oral tradition.

These traditions – beehive huts and heroes' tales – have survived because they are inherently strong enough to withstand and overcome any force bent on changing or subduing them. That such traditions have survived in the west of Ireland attests to that region's resources of strength. Despite pressures from innovating influences from farther east, certain features of the past such as the beehive huts have been preserved there while elsewhere they have been swept away in the name of progress. It could be said that in its seeming timelessness, the west of Ireland has the gift of time – time to talk and time to muse and think. The farther west the visitor drives in Ireland, the more slowly his clock will advance. This area can indeed provide a fascinating window on a past which is well worth studying and yearning for.

The past of ecclesiastical building in Ireland is a fascinating subject for study. From the beginnings of Christianity, the rectangular church was presumably the common form. In the west of Ireland, the traditional mode of building round houses – the corbel technique – was adapted to the ecclesiastical. On Skellig Michael, for example, there are two small oratories which – like the beehive huts – were built without mortar. However, they are rectangular in shape both inside and out, although on the inside the corners tend to become more rounded as the building rises. To retain rigidity in these structures, the size of the openings had been reduced. The east window is little more than a horizontal slit, and the doorway is so low that it is necessary to crouch to enter the building. A more advanced variant on this structure, in which the openings are larger, is found in Gallarus oratory at the end of the Dingle Peninsula. Here traces of mortar have been found in the walls, and the stones are so well fitted together that the longer sides have not collapsed, although the north and south walls of Gallarus oratory do sag inwards slightly. Inherent in the application of the corbel principle to a rectangular structure is the danger of just such a collapse. In the other, quite numerous examples of this type, the roof has fallen.

The matter of dating these structures in the west of Ireland is a difficult one. Similar structures were being built – possibly as late as the 17thc – in the French Department of Vaucluse. The monastery of Skellig Michael was in existence in the 9thc, and it is thought to have survived until the early 13thc. Then, according to tradition, its monks moved to the mainland at nearby Ballinskelligs. Beehive huts may in fact have been built continuously, and with little change, from prehistoric times right up to the present day. It is thus difficult to say – even within a century – when the beehive cells of the Skellig monastery were constructed. They may pre-date the 9thc, although they could equally well belong to a later one. It has recently been suggested that Gallarus oratory may not date from the 8thc, as was commonly thought, but could be as late as the 12thc. The Skellig oratories need not necessarily belong to the earliest phase of the monastery. Traces of a wooden building have been found beneath a similar oratory on Church Island, Valentia, only about 15m away.

Judging by existing remains, the corbelled structures seem to form a building province all their own. Although the foundations of one beehive hut seem to exist at Glendalough in Co Wicklow, the west coast of Ireland contained a spread of such structures which appeared to be distinct from the rest of the country. In fact, this building practice on the west coast – presumably

One of two cross-shaped slabs to be seen on the island. This example resembles a slim, hooded monk when viewed from behind.

Gallarus Oratory – the most famous of some 30 early-Christian and other monuments clustered in Munster's rugged Dingle Peninsula.

deriving from traditional pre-Christian techniques – differed more from that in use in the rest of Ireland than the older churches elsewhere in the country differed from those in central Europe in the Merovingian period.

For many centuries after the coming of St Patrick, most early Irish churches were built of wood. Unlike the medieval stave churches of Norway, however, none of these has survived. Literary sources confirm their existence and the fact that they continued to be built as late as the 12thc. A commentary on the Old Irish Laws, written sometime after AD 1000, specifically mentions measurements of 15ft by 10ft for Irish wooden churches. The earliest Irish non-corbelled churches in stone, such as those at Ardagh, Co Longford or Liathmore Mochoemog in Co Tipperary, seem to conform fairly closely to the pattern of the wooden churches, reproducing quite accurately the 1.5:1 ratio. These early stone churches are simple structures. The sides of the doorway incline slightly as they rise, and are topped by a flat and usually massive lintel. The small, often round east window splays widely inwards. The stones used in the north and south walls are frequently massive on the bottom, becoming smaller as the wall rises. The majority of these stone churches share a curious feature: the *antae*, projections of the north and south sides of the church beyond the east and west walls. These *antae* are probably translations into stone of the large beams which supported the roofs of the wooden churches that served as models for their stone successors. The earliest reliable historical reference to a stone church in Ireland is in the year 788. In the succeeding centuries stone churches must have replaced the older wooden churches one by one, although the fires caused by Viking raids probably accelerated the process of replacement by demonstrating

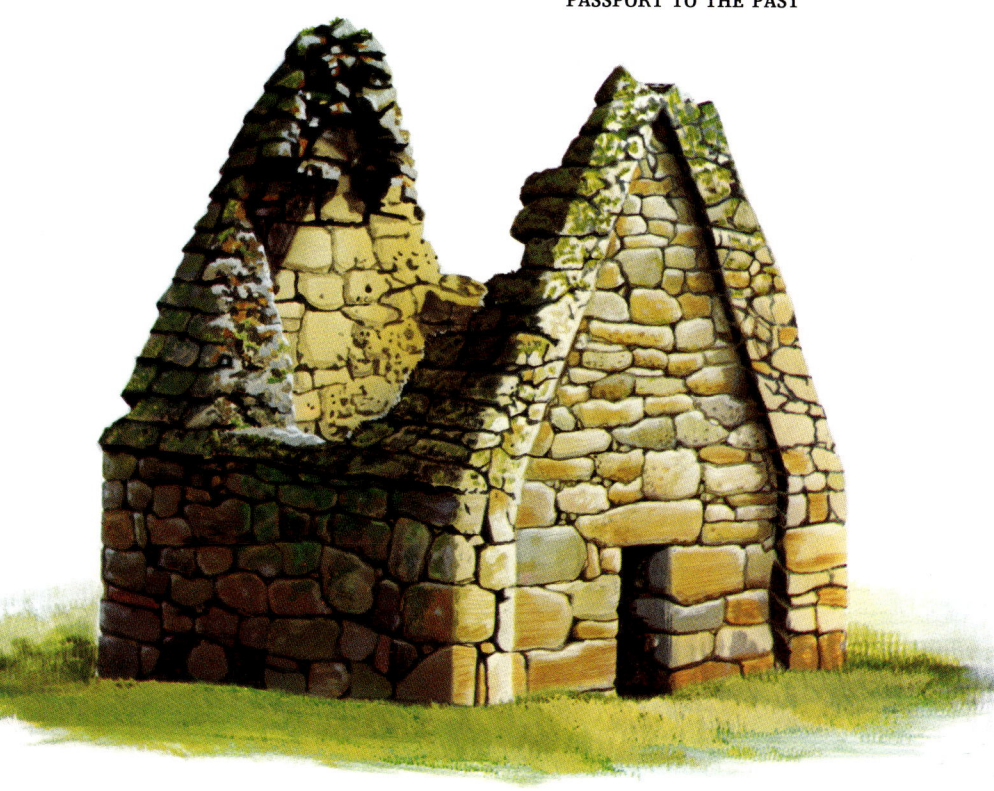

St Macdara's Island lies off the wild Connemara coast in south-western Ireland and features an interesting stone church – part of a foundation created in the 6thc.

the greater permanence of stone buildings. These simple box churches remained the norm until the 12thc, demonstrating a remarkable conservatism in the design of Irish churches throughout the whole of the early-Christian period. By contrast, vaster and much more imposing edifices had developed in the rest of Europe shortly after 800. The plan of the Swiss monastic church at St Gallen, dated c820, is a good example.

The conservatism of Ireland is well epitomized in a stone church on St Macdara's Island off the coast of Connemara. This interesting little structure, which demonstrates the imitation in stone of older wooden structures possibly as late as the 12thc, has two features of particular note. The *antae*, which in other churches are confined to the corners of the east and west walls, here climb up the gable and meet at the top; and the roof is built of stone. This in itself is not an uncommon feature in Irish churches. The corbelled oratories had stone roofs. In the 12thc, however, a number of Irish churches with upright walls used not the corbel roof but a stone roof resting on a supporting barrel vault. Cormac's Chapel at Cashel, which will be discussed later, is a good example. The Connemara church, however, lacks the barrel vault, and its roof has partially collapsed. The

A reconstruction of the monastic settlement on Church Island, off Valencia in Co Kerry, featuring beehive huts and an oratory.

PASSPORT TO THE PAST

roof of St Macdara's church is differentiated from other stone roofs by the fact that it can be seen to imitate a wooden roof. The stones of the roof have been cut carefully into rectangular shapes which overlap one another. These presumably imitate wooden slates or shingles (Irish *slinn*), which are the only materials other than rushes known to have been used in roofing Irish wooden churches. This explanation might be considered fanciful, but for one stone in the north-west corner of St Macdara's church. Too large to fit into the rectangular pattern of the other stones of the roof, it was carved by the masons into one layer overlapping the other. This procedure would appear to be pointless if the roof were not modelled on a wooden prototype. Originally, one gable of the church was topped by a stone finial – made of limestone and probably imported specially from the Aran Islands – while the rest of the church has been built of granite. The finial bears a face with high cheek-bones and ears which are placed much higher on the head than is natural – both characteristics of western Irish Romanesque decoration of the 12thc. Assuming that the finial, despite its different material, was placed on the church at the time it was built, this building can be presumed to date from the 12thc and was based on a wooden form which probably existed until replaced in stone. The wooden church was presumably based on a prototype developed around or not long after the time of St Patrick. This apparent case of longevity of tradition on the west coast fits into the picture which has already been depicted above. At the same time, it serves as a warning about the dating of Aran Island churches. Many of them are in themselves undatable and may not in all cases merit the great antiquity normally ascribed to them. This clear example in St Macdara's church of a monument in stone replacing an earlier monument of another material may possibly have some relevance in the study of early-Christian Ireland's cross-slabs and crosses.

One of the cross-shaped slabs on the Skelligs has two sets of indentations on each side, which help to stress the cross form. These also give it a remarkable if purely coincidental resemblance to a slim and hooded monk as seen from behind. One face of this upright slab has a simple cross carved in low relief on it. Variants of the cross outline can be found in two other monuments much farther north along the coast, at Fahan and Carndonagh on the Inishowen Peninsula in Co Donegal. At Fahan, the slab's upright sides are straight except for two small protruding stumps. These look as if they may have been tenons onto which projecting arms were fitted. As was the case on the Skelligs, a cross is carved in false relief. Here, however, the cross is formed of interlacing bands, and it occurs on each face. On one side two figures under the arms of the cross bear an inscription on their cloaks. At Carndonagh, a much taller monument beside the road has the full outline of a cross, with free-standing arms and a Crucifixion scene on the shaft.

In contrast, an upright rectangular stone without any arms is sited in the adjoining churchyard scarcely 20yds away. This bears a carving in false relief showing two men standing on either side of the handle of a so-called *flabellum* or fan-like object, with a Maltese cross beneath. The simple Maltese cross within a circle is the most common decoration on Irish cross-slabs. While it occasionally is found in the eastern part of Ireland, it seems to be much more of a speciality of the west coast, where its distribution partially coincides with that of the corbelled oratories. The slabs bearing the above-described motif, such as that at Reask in Co Kerry, are normally dated to about the 7th or 8thc. Not all such slabs are located in coastal areas. There is one sited somewhat inland at Ballyvourney in Co Cork, which depicts a charming little cleric with two wisps of hair parted in the middle. He is shown strutting along with his crozier on top of the encircled Maltese cross. Interestingly, this slab is located in an area where the Irish language survives today as a small enclave. Thus the pattern is the same as that in west Kerry, where the Irish

Fahan Cross, on Co Donegal's Inishowen Peninsula, is ornamented with interlacing bands carved in false relief on both sides. The projecting stumps may possibly be tenons on which larger arms might have been fitted.

Also on the Inishowen is Carndonagh Cross, an elaborately-decorated 7th-c cross slab with the proportions and something of the character of high crosses.

language, the cross-slabs, and the corbelled oratories are clustered in areas in which traditions are strongly retained.

The figures carved in false relief on the decorated stones at Fahan and Carndonagh are a feature which links these monuments with the earlier series of high crosses found largely east of the Shannon. These high crosses are among the finest and best known products of the early monasteries of Ireland. Although the most famous examples bear scenes from the Old and New Testaments, the series probably started without any scriptural sculpture at all. The ring surrounding the central part of the cross, one of the most characteristic features, may not have appeared on the first high crosses. The presence of this ring has not yet been satisfactorily explained, either as to its origin or its function. It apparently first appeared in Ireland *c*700. Although the Maltese crosses of the western-Irish slabs were surrounded by circles, the rings on the high crosses may not have been a derivation of these, but rather of smaller crosses in bronze. The early ringed high crosses in stone – 8th-c examples from such places as Ahenny in County Tipperary – were apparently copied from smaller bronze originals, as the decorative designs upon the shafts of such early crosses appear to have been modelled on those used in metalwork of a contemporary if not earlier period. It is still an open question as to whether the ring on these prototypes was a functional element to hold the arms in place and support them, or whether it had a deeper, symbolic significance. Crosses of the 8thc, such as those at Ahenny, rise from bases which are decorated with strange scenes involving human figures and animals. These decorations, like those seen on the Pictish cross-slabs of eastern Scotland, may have been derived from Northumbrian carving in ivory and other materials. One of the Ahenny figures bears a processional cross which is ringed, implying that the ringed cross could conceivably have come from Northumbria as well.

Sometime around 800, scenes from the Scriptures begin to appear on stone high crosses in the eastern half of Ireland. The scenes are taken from the *Old* and *New Testament*, and usually depict events in the life of Christ together with the Old Testament events which foreshadowed them. The series normally begins with Adam and Eve, whose original sin made necessary Christ's ultimate sacrifice on the cross. This scene in the Garden of Eden is often combined with the depiction of Cain slaying Abel, the latter being the first forerunner of Christ as the innocent victim. Other recurring themes are those of Daniel in the Lions' Den, the Sacrifice of Isaac and the Three Children in the Fiery Furnace – all examples of God coming to the aid of those in need. The same idea underlies the *New Testament* accounts of the Flight into Egypt, the Marriage Feast of Cana and the Feeding of the Five Thousand on the Mount, representations of which are also found on the crosses. These scenes lead up to that of the Crucifixion, which usually – although not always – occupies the central position on the cross at the intersection of arms and shaft. The same position on the other face of the cross brings the entire sequence to its climax with the Triumphant Christ shown on the Day of Judgement. Not all of these scenes necessarily occur on every cross, and the crosses themselves have regional differences both in their themes and in the type of stone used.

One group of crosses in south Leinster, centred around Castledermot, is carved from the local granite. It is a most difficult material with which to try to achieve a rounded finish, and yet this is the stone used in what is possibly the most appealing cross of all – that located on the site of the old monastery at Moone in Co Kildare. This cross has more slender proportions than any other in the series, and its carving possesses an irresisitible, naive charm. The Crucifixion is found on one face, and the shaft is divided into panels filled with fabulous animals which are scarcely Irish in origin. The main Gospel scenes are confined to the tall and tapering base, where the Crucifixion is again found, together with the Twelve Apostles, the Flight into Egypt, Adam and Eve, the

The 7th- or 8th-c cross-slab at Ballyvourney in Co Cork.

South Cross, one of two 8th-c high crosses to be found at Ahenny in Co Tipperary. Both are richly carved on the shafts and rings, and each stands on a pedestal decorated with figured scenes.

Sacrifice of Isaac, and the Three Children in the Fiery Furnace. The human figures have stylized, square or rectangular bodies with heads like inverted pears. A representation of the Miracle of the Loaves and Fishes is achieved in a most delightful way and with a great economy of means; instead of using human figures, the story is told simply by a symmetrical arrangement of two fat and two thin fish which form a surround for five flat loaves. Non-biblical scenes are depicted also. In one, Saints Paul and Anthony are meeting in the desert, and in another St Anthony is shown resisting the temptations which his biographer Athanasius described more than 1,500 years ago. These figures may, at first sight, seem out of place on crosses on which biblical scenes predominate. These saints are the founding fathers of the monastic life, however, so it is easy to appreciate how appropriate they were on crosses which formed one of the focal points of the early Irish monasteries. These monasteries may well have taken the place of the episcopal and parish churches in other parts of Christendom, and presumably must have served as the religious centres for the people who lived in the surrounding area. In this context, the crosses can be seen to have served not only as aids to meditation and scriptural exegesis for the monks, but also as a way of teaching the Bible to the unlettered laity of the neighbourhood.

The high crosses reach their apogee in those using a close-grained sandstone; such monuments have stood the test of time better in the middle and east of Ireland than in the north. In the midlands they are found at Clonmacnoise and Durrow in Co Offaly, and in the north at Armagh and at Arboe and Donaghmore in Co Tyrone. Some of the finest examples can be seen in the catchment area of the River Boyne at places like Kells in Co Meath and Monasterboice in Co Louth. It is unnecessary to give a detailed description of each of these crosses; suffice it to say that on almost all of them there is a flexible arrangement of biblical scenes – not all of which can be satisfactorily interpreted – in which a considerable number of figures are enclosed in a series of panels without imparting a sense of overcrowding. These figures are distinguished by a more marked naturalism than those at Moone. This must be accepted as a considerable achievement for Irish craftsmen, considering that earlier Celtic artists shied away from the human figure. When they were forced to depict it they chose a stylized representation, shunning the naturalism of classical sculpture which had been adapted, for instance, on the somewhat earlier crosses in northern England and southern Scotland. In the scriptural scenes it is possible to sense that the Irish stonemason has adopted ordered compositions from elsewhere, again possibly Northumbria, but adapted them cleverly to his own needs. Similarly, the round towers which dominate many of the old Irish monasteries were not an Irish invention, and may have been adopted as a form of campanile from Italy or elsewhere on the Continent.

The great series of sandstone crosses with scriptural scenes seems to date from the 9th and early 10thc, after which production apparently came to a virtual halt in the eastern half of the country. There is, however, one instance at Glendalough of a cross being carved in the 12thc. The Glendalough cross differs from the earlier examples in a number of respects. The scriptural scenes are no longer present, having been replaced by two large figures on the shaft and another on the base of one side of the cross which stand out in bold relief. One of the figures is Christ; the others cannot be identified with certainty. In addition, the ring is no longer present. Crosses with these features can be found in parts of north Munster and Connacht, however, at Cashel and Monaincha in

Situated in the demesne of Moone Abbey in Co Kildare, the 17½ft-high Cross of Moone is richly carved and may possibly mark the site of an early-Christian monastery. Figures on the base of the cross represent the Twelve Apostles.

Panels featured by the Cross of Moone – top, 'The Flight into Egypt'; bottom, 'The Miracle of the Loaves and the Fishes'; right, 'Adam and Eve'.

Co Tipperary, Dysert O Dea and Kilfenora in Clare, and Tuam in Co Galway. On these more westerly crosses the ring is sometimes present. It is not possible to date these to the year, although a particular kind of animal ornament of Scandinavian extraction which appears on them has a close parallel on datable metalwork of the 12thc, such as the Cross of Cong in Dublin's National Museum. This suggests that the stone crosses can be dated to the same period – that of the Romanesque – although they display very few features which could genuinely be described as Romanesque in the European sense.

When the crosses of east and west are compared, a conundrum is met. The crosses in the eastern part of the country belong largely to the 9th and 10thc. The lone appearance of a 12th-c cross which shares the characteristics of a type more common in the western part of the country is indeed a puzzle. In the west there is scarcely a high cross (as opposed to a cross-slab) which can be said to pre-date 1100, with the possible though unlikely exception of one on the Aran Islands. These facts raise many questions. What was going on in North Munster and west of the Shannon in the 9th and 10thc while the great series of scripture crosses was being carved east of the river? Were any crosses or cross-slabs being erected in the west at that time? Were wooden crosses being created which would serve as prototypes for the 12th-c stone crosses and might these wooden ones have evolved either before the ringed cross became common in the east or outside the sphere of the ringed cross? The latter suggestion might be given support by the cross in Cashel, the arms of which are supported by unusual struts that could be skeumorphs of a wooden original. Or is it possible that many of the cross-slabs found along the west coast are not as early as the 7th or 8thc, but rather are either continuing an earlier tradition in a later century, or are replacements in stone of an earlier, now vanished wooden prototype? The above suggestion may seem odd, but there have been similar translations into stone of church buildings along the west coast, possibly as late as the 12thc, as was postulated in the case of St Macdara's church. If the early-looking cross-slabs of the west were set up as gravestones, as seems quite likely, and the stone crosses or their possible wooden prototypes were erected for some other purpose, the crosses may have developed independently of the cross-slabs. In this case there is no need to expect continuity in the west between the earlier cross-slabs and the later crosses.

But for one interesting example, the extreme south of the country was excluded from the stone-cross development outlined above. This exception stands in splendid isolation at Kilnaruane near Bantry in west Cork. Only the shaft remains, and on it are carved scenes in a flat false relief remotely akin to Moone. On one side the Crucifixion scene is accompanied by a depiction of the two desert fathers, Paul and Anthony, while on the other side there is a curious representation of a boat being rowed vertically up the shaft. The boat carries four oarsmen and a helmsman with a steering oar at the stern. The bow rises in a long, lifting line, whereas the stern, topped by a cross, climbs more abruptly. Maritime historians agree that the type of boat represented is none other than a currach. This type of craft has a skeleton framework of light wooden laths over which tarred canvas is stretched. In former times the frame was covered with animal skins, including horse hide. This vessel exists in a number of variants on the west coast of Ireland today, thus providing another interesting example of the continuity of tradition on the western littoral. The presence of the currach on the Kilnaruane stone, carved at least a 1,000 years ago, is not the only known instance of its use in the early Christian period. The old Irish monks presumably crossed to the Skelligs in just such boats, and it was in a currach that the great Kerry saint, Brendan the Navigator, undertook his voyages. The description of these passages gave rise to the theory that Brendan may have discovered America many years before the Vikings and almost a millennium before Columbus. The origin of the currach must go back much further than this, but in the absence of pictorial representations and literary references it is impossible to say how much further.

While the west coast often clung doggedly to its old traditions, North Munster and Connacht showed themselves, at times, to be in the forefront of architectural development in Ireland. This occurred during the Romanesque period of the 12thc, and

The Cross of Cashel, in Co Tipperary, portrays the Crucifixion. The thin stone pillar on the right originally had a counterpart on the left and is thought to represent one of the Thieves' crosses.

Two figures – Christ at the top and an ecclesiastic with a crook beneath – adorn the 9ft Cross of Dysert O Dea, in Co Clare.

again in the gothic period. Churches built in the Romanesque style had been known on the Continent for more than a century before the Irish were first exposed to it at home. The monumentality of these Continental structures was at first not to the taste of the Irish, and only a few of Ireland's 12th-c churches can genuinely be described as Romanesque in the Continental sense. The majority were little more than continuations of older Irish churches, with the addition of decoration to their doorways, chancel arches and – only occasionally – their windows. While the ubiquitous chevron ornamentation is the most obvious adoption of Norman Romanesque styles prevailing in England, the Irish gave their own peculiar twist to the decoration by applying in a low relief the same type of Scandinavian-derived animal ornament which was used on the 12th-c crosses already discussed.

Perhaps the only – and possibly the earliest – surviving native Irish 12th-c church which can truly be termed 'architecture' rather than labelled as a decorated box is Cormac's Chapel on the Rock of Cashel in County Tipperary. Built by Bishop Cormac MacCarthy, the church stands on the site of the centre of the old MacCarthy dynasty, which handed it over to the church in 1101. Together with the 13th-c gothic cathedral, which tends to dwarf the Romanesque structure, it forms the most imposing cluster of ecclesiastical remains in the country. Cormac's Chapel has a number of unusual features. As mentioned earlier, it has a stone roof which is supported by a barrel vault, a scheme unique to Ireland. Its use at Cashel probably served as a model for churches at Kells in Co Meath, Killaloe in Co Clare, Glendalough in Co Wicklow, Louth in Co Louth, and the collapsed example on Devenish Island in Co Fermanagh. Where churches outside Ireland would have had transepts, Cormac's Chapel has two almost identical towers. The inspiration for these may well have originated with Irish monks residing in Bavaria who had come to Munster to collect alms for the construction of their own church, the *Schottenkirche* or church of St James at Ratisbon/Regensburg, which has similar towers. The Cashel chapel has three doorways – one in the north tower (now blocked up) and the other two in the north and south walls of the nave. Each of the latter doorways has a tympanum, a rare feature in Ireland. In this instance, it was probably derived from England, as doubtless the idea of the much-used chevron decoration was. The articulation of the interior and exterior walls with a number of layered arcades and panels divided by semi-engaged pilasters is another remarkable feature of Cormac's Chapel. It was copied on a reduced scale on churches at Roscrea in Co Tipperary and Ardfert in Co Kerry. The Cashel chapel also presents an element which seems to have fired the imagination of Irish stonemasons at the time, the fashion of carving individual and largely stylized human heads. These are found under the exterior eaves and on the chancel arch in Cashel, and are used on doorways, as at Dysert O Dea in Co Clare, where their radial arrangement may have been influenced by churches in the west of France.

According to the old *Irish Annals*, Cormac's Chapel was begun in 1127 and consecrated in 1134, making it by far the earliest datable church with Romanesque decoration in Ireland. The chapel must have caused quite a sensation in Ireland when it was completed, as nothing like it had been known up to that time, and its decoration seems to have inspired a number of other building projects undertaken in subsequent decades. Several of these were in Limerick, North Tipperary, and Clare; places such as Clonkeen in Co Limerick, Monaincha in Co Tipperary, and Killaloe, Inishcaltra, Dysert O Dea, and Kilfenora in Co Clare are called to mind. This vigorous building activity must be viewed in conjunction with the carving of the 12th-c high crosses in the same area – the Romanesque churches and high crosses are frequently co-located. Kerry also has its share of Romanesque churches, at Ardfert, which is mentioned above, and, on a physically smaller scale, in the Killarney area at Aghadoe and on the romantically situated island of Innisfallen. It is interesting to note that the Romanesque influence was sufficiently strong in this county to break through into areas where corbelled structures were the tradition, as at the Romanesque churches at Kilmalkedar – on the tip of

Cormac's Chapel is a major feature of the most imposing cluster of ecclesiastical remains in Ireland – the complex which crowns the Rock of Cashel in Co Tipperary. It is possible that this is the only surviving example of 12th-c Irish architecture.

Dingle Peninsula – and on Church Island in Lough Currane, near Waterville.

It was only in the middle decades of the 12thc that the Romanesque decoration of Irish churches gradually spread from Munster to more central and eastern districts of the country. Here, the use of the Scandinavian-originated interlacing of animals can be noted on such fine doorways as those of Killeshin in Co Laois and Kilmore in Co Cavan. Two fine examples in these regions can be ascribed to the 1160's or later. One is the Nuns' Church at Clonmacnoise, Co Offaly, the doorway and chancel arch of which are heavily decorated with chevrons and animal ornament. The other, the doorway of Clonfert Cathedral in Co Galway, is – together with Cormac's Chapel – the most impressive product of 12th-c stone decoration in Ireland. The arches, pillars, and capitals of the doorway are packed with a riot of ornament. A pointed gable above is filled out with an arcade inspired by Cashel as well as with sunken and protruding triangles, which are interspersed with a number of single stone heads. During this period, round towers began to have their doorways decorated with Romanesque ornament also; the best examples are Timahoe in Co Laois and Kildare in Co Kildare.

Within a decade of the consecration of Cormac's Chapel, new developments were taking place in the north-east of the country. These not only demonstrated that this area could also be in the vanguard of architectural development in Ireland, but also served to alter, with two fell strokes, the entire style of church architecture in Ireland. Both moves were masterminded by Ireland's greatest 12th-c church reformer, the saintly and forward-looking Malachy of Armagh, a friend of that other great architectural innovator Cormac MacCarthy of Cashel. According to Bernard of Clairvaux – who greatly admired St Malachy and wrote his life story – around 1140 Malachy began to build a church at Bangor in Co Down which was similar to those he had seen in other lands (presumably meaning France). Because the church has unfortunately not survived, it is only possible to surmise that it was the first attempt to introduce into Ireland the larger kind of three-aisled basilica-type church common on the Continent at the time. St Malachy could not have hoped to introduce such an innovation without the expected reactionary opposition, and the questions of one of his detractors, quoted from St Bernard's account, shed some light on the conservative and yet praiseworthily humble attitude of the early Irish church. "Good Sir," the man said to St Malachy, "why have you thought good to introduce this novelty into our regions? We are *Scotti* (Irish), not Gauls. . . . What need was there for a work so superfluous and so proud? Where will you, a poor and needy man, find the means to finish it?"

Interior of Cormac's Chapel. This view has been taken from the nave and extends down into the choir and apse.

St Malachy's other important innovation was the founding, in 1142, of Ireland's first Cistercian monastery at Mellifont in Co Louth. This marked, for all intents and purposes, the first important foundation of one of the new medieval religious orders in Ireland. The arrival of the Cistercians, later followed by the Dominicans, Benedictines, and Franciscans, not only brought new life to the flagging spirits of Irish monasticism. It also brought the beginning of the end for the old Irish monastic system, with more and more people flocking to the new order foundations – gradually deserting many of the centuries-old Irish monasteries. Those which adopted the Augustinian rule, however, had their existence prolonged for several centuries.

The new orders, such as the Cistercians, brought orderliness both into monastic life and into its buildings. These latter were centred around the square or rectangular cloister garth, with the church usually on the south side, the chapter house on the east, and the kitchen and refectory on the north, while the west side probably housed stores on the ground floor and a communal dormitory above it. The church was no longer the small nave-and-chancel affair of the native Irish monastery, although it must have been similar in concept to St Malachy's church at Bangor but most likely employing the Burgundian Cistercian church as its model. The church at Mellifont would appear to have had a greater influence

Interior decoration in Kilmalkedar Church, Co Kerry, suggests that the builders were influenced by Cormac's Chapel. Remains of the structure itself include the nave, chancel, and part of the original stone roof.

PASSPORT TO THE PAST

than the Bangor church, and in following the dictates laid down by their order, the Cistercians helped to popularize the larger sized church in Ireland, thus gradually luring the Irish away from their traditional box-shaped structures. The first church at Mellifont was badly damaged by fire more than a century after it was built, and little more than its foundations can now be traced. It was certainly built in the Romanesque style, however, and having come to fruition under the shadow of St Bernard – who had banished sculptural ornament from his churches – it must have relied for its effect on the simple and graceful lines which can be seen in better-preserved examples such as Alcobaça in Portugal.

The style of building introduced at Mellifont fanned out rapidly in Ireland. Within two decades Mellifont fostered daughter houses at Baltinglass in Co Wicklow, Jerpoint in Kilkenny, Monasternenagh in Co Limerick, and Boyle in Roscommon, to mention but a few of the better-preserved examples. The earliest surviving parts of these buildings still display a Romanesque style in their rounded arches. The geometrically-decorated capitals, however, demonstrate a slight break from the dictates of simplicity laid down by St Bernard, and also show a certain individual Irish style of their own. When the Normans came to Ireland in 1169–70 they did not at first change the building style, but kept the Romanesque which had been in use in Ireland for almost half a century before their arrival. After a decade or two, however, they had gained a sufficiently strong foothold in the country to create their own new Cistercian foundations such as Dunbrody in Wexford, and to start building Christchurch Cathedral in their capital at Dublin. The earliest parts of the Dublin Cathedral, and in particular the transepts, are built in a late Romanesque style which was heavily influenced by churches in the west of England.

The advent of the Normans, with their rapid conquest of large areas of the eastern half of the country and eventual penetration into the western half, was to ensure for the next 150 years an eastern Irish predominance in church building which had been growing since the founding of Mellifont. The Normans, and the monastic orders in their lands, brought about the introduction and later the exclusive use of gothic architecture in Ireland. The two abbeys of Inch and Grey Abbey, both in Co Down, were founded by John de Courcy in 1180 and 1193 respectively. The first two entirely gothic structures built in Ireland, they show – as Bangor did earlier – north-eastern Ireland to be the willing receiver of new ideas. The monasteries, churches, and cathedrals founded by the Normans after this period were built generally in a purely gothic style.

The Normans were engaged in constant battle with the native Irish, and thus did not have as much money at their disposal as was available in England for the building and decoration of large churches and cathedrals. The medieval parish churches rarely attained the size of their English counterparts, and the decoration of even some of the largest examples, such as St Mary's at New Ross in Co Wexford, St Multose at Kinsale in Co Cork, or St Mary's at Youghal in Co Cork, can scarcely be described as profuse. In the absence of any surviving early-gothic woodwork it is impossible to say whether the interior church furnishings may have made up for the lack of ornamental details in stone.

The doorway of 12th-c Clonfert Cathedral is a fantasy mixture of Continental Romanesque and Irish Art.

The Normans can nonetheless be credited with the building of many of Ireland's finest cathedrals. Christchurch in Dublin was completed during the 13thc, as was its near neighbour St Patrick's. Of the other Norman cathedrals, perhaps the finest is St Canice's in Kilkenny, which also dates from the 13thc. The latter lies in beautifully kept surroundings, and although less lofty than its Dublin fellows, it contains much more original work; the Dublin cathedrals were heavily restored in the last century. St Canice's also preserves what can be classed among the most decorative of Irish cathedral doorways and, like so many other Norman buildings in the east of Ireland, it displays a number of characteristics which were borrowed from the west of England, homeland of Ireland's Norman conquerors. The Norman Irish did not have as much money for building fine cathedrals as the English, but the native Irish had even less. Only the cathedral at Cashel, constructed during the reigns of at least three bishops between 1224 and 1289 and even then left unfinished, comes at all close to the Norman cathedrals in its decorative capitals with many interesting heads. The cathedral at Ardfert in

Nun's Church at Clonmacnoise was founded in 1187 to replace a wooden structure which was burnt in 1080. Illustrated is the fine doorway, which depicts snakes battling with monsters in its columns and zig-zags.

PASSPORT TO THE PAST

Founded between 1148 and 1151, Monasteraneagh Abbey in Co Limerick was completed for the Cistercian Order in 1194. Both the cloister and refectory were destroyed during 16th-c warfare, and the remains that exist today are of the church only.

Co Kerry is an example of the attempt by Irish prelates to utilize the gothic style without having the means to add much architectural decoration.

In the late 12th and early 13thc, when the Normans were already building in the gothic style and some of the native Irish were making their first attempts in that direction, some areas continued to produce minor masterpieces in the Romanesque fashion. The area of Munster, where Romanesque architecture was first practised in Ireland, and that of Connacht are prime examples. Only occasionally did they acknowledge the gothic style by using the pointed arch. The Romanesque doorway built into the south wall of Killaloe Cathedral, and the splendidly ornamental chancel arch forming the only remaining Romanesque part of Tuam Cathedral in Co Galway, are two fine examples of the continued use of Romanesque ornamentation in the west of Ireland in the late 12thc. The subtlety and variety of the shallowly-carved foliate and animal decoration of the east window at Annaghdown, also in Galway, taken together with the decoration at Killaloe and Tuam, gives some idea of the quality of the work being produced by western Irish stonemasons at the time. The Cistercian abbey at Corcomroe, at the northern end of the Burren in Co Clare, is one of the most attractive of these western structures of the period. Its grey limestone walls give it a haunting beauty in the small, green oasis created by the monks out of the seemingly barren rock. Its stone-ribbed vault with herring-bone decoration, and the menacing beasts on the exterior corners of the chancel, identify it as basically Romanesque. This despite the fact that it is scarcely earlier than 1200, and that some gothic building principles are incorporated in its architectural design.

It was in the neighbouring O'Conor kingdom, however, that the Romanesque style survived well into the first quarter of the 13thc. The nearby church at Drumacoo, over the boundary in Galway, the monastic nave-and-chancel church at Inishmaine beside Lough Mask in Co Mayo, and the Augustinian churches at Ballintubber and Cong represent the final flowering of the Romanesque style in the west. At Cong, in particular, there is a considerable variety and exuberance in the foliate decoration of the capitals. Here too are the undercut chevrons which this west of Ireland school borrowed from the west of England, probably through the influence of the Augustinian canons who had used them sometime before on the north transept doorway of Christchurch Cathedral in Dublin. Owing to the internal squabbles of the O'Conor dynasty, however, the artists and craftsmen of Connacht were banished from the province in 1228. At least one of them seems subsequently to have wandered as far afield as Regensburg in Bavaria, where there were long-standing Irish architectural connections; there he helped with the decoration of a doorway in the monastery of St Emmeram. This disastrous act of banishment sounded the death knell for Romanesque style in its last bastion in north-western Europe. Had the O'Conors acted otherwise, the Romanesque building tradition would doubtless have continued unhindered for a few more years before capitulating finally to the general use of gothic. As it was, the Norman invasion of Connacht seven years later brought one of the last remaining areas of native Ireland under Norman domination. Native building activity was laid to rest, not to revive for another two centuries. The Normans did, however, build some important gothic structures at places like Athenry and Tuam in Co Galway within the succeeding 100 years.

Towards the end of the 13thc several fine friaries and other ecclesiastical establishments were constructed, including the Dominican friary at Kilmallock in Co Limerick. The Dominicans, now joined by the Franciscans, were just beginning to get into their building stride when they were stopped in their tracks by the Bruce invasion of 1315–18, which devastated many parts of Ireland and began to sap the life-blood of Norman church-building activity in Ireland. About the same time, and subsequently, the country's coffers

Jerpoint Abbey in Co Kilkenny is a 12th-c foundation which includes 14th-c additions. The north side of the quadrangle is occupied by a three-aisled church; the other sides being taken up by the cloisters and domestic buildings.

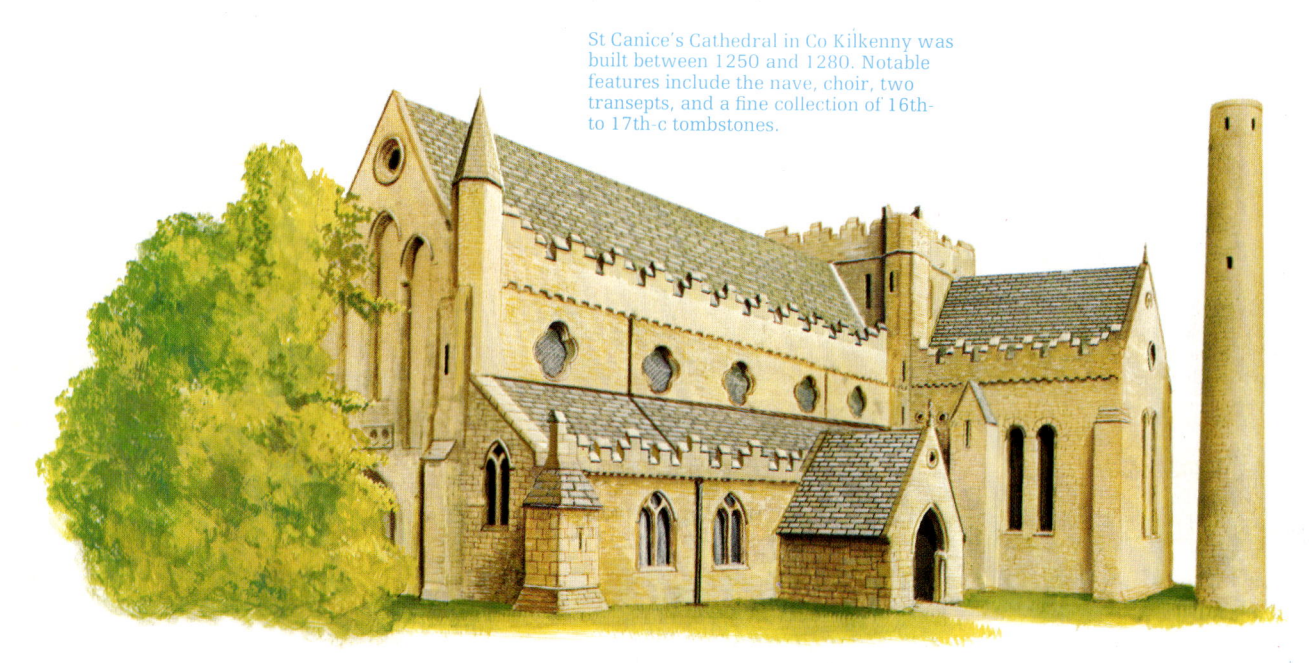

St Canice's Cathedral in Co Kilkenny was built between 1250 and 1280. Notable features include the nave, choir, two transepts, and a fine collection of 16th- to 17th-c tombstones.

were gradually being depleted by the English treasury, and the Black Death of 1348–50 administered the *coup-de-grâce*. Norman architecture in Ireland never fully recovered.

There are few buildings in Ireland which can be dated with any certainty to the second half of the 14thc, following the Black Death. The lack of precisely datable characteristics and historical documentation has kept the number so identified by architectural historians at a very conservative estimate. Shortly after 1330, Gaelic Ireland began to revive in strength, and the Anglo-Norman lords started to harbour the desire for self-determination. These tendencies led to the development of a native brand of architecture and sculpture which manifested itself, and indeed largely developed, in the west of Ireland; Franciscan friaries offer the most striking instances here. The friary at Quin, although not the earliest, best symbolizes the rebirth of native Ireland from the devastations of the Norman period. Begun *c*1433, it tramples, as it were, upon the ruins of a Norman fortress razed to the ground in 1278 by an ancestor of its Macnamara founder. The Quin friary was preceded by that at Askeaton in Co Limerick started *c*1420, and it was followed by a host of others, including Muckross near Killarney, Ross Errilly in Galway, and the two Mayo friaries of Moyne and Rosserk. These buildings can be recognised, even from a distance, by the characteristically tall and slender towers standing near the centre of a long and often narrow church, which often had a south aisle, or transept, or both. The domestic buildings are grouped around a quadrangular or rectangular cloister, and in many cases supported a floor directly above. The only cloister to bear rich figure sculpture is the Cistercian example at Jerpoint which stands in splendid isolation in the period *c*1400.

In the 15thc, the Cistercians – unlike the Franciscans – did not create any new foundations, but instead concentrated their efforts on re-furbishing their older monasteries. Their most splendid works of this period are in Co Tipperary – Holycross and Kilcooly. The former, which is now being restored to its former glory, dates from the middle of the century; it is the 12th-c church, almost entirely rebuilt. It contains some of the finest later medieval stonework in the country. Its rib-vaulted chancel is one of the most perfectly preserved in Ireland, and the carved sedilia are interesting, among other things, for being decorated with the arms of a king of England. Bective Abbey in Meath, although rebuilt in the 15thc in the Norman lands of eastern Ireland, is today but a shadow of its former self. The most characteristic

All the domestic buildings of Co Clare's Corcomroe Abbey have gone, leaving only the cruciform church to mark the site of this foundation. Each of the church's transepts has one chapel.

architectural contributions of the east of Ireland during this period are a homogeneous group of churches erected by and for the Plunket family on their lands at Dunsany, Killeen, and Rathmore in Co Meath. These have some fine window tracery with carved heads on the exterior label-stops of the windows, and small towers at two or four of the church corners. Apart from the addition of strong towers to some of the smaller parish churches of The Pale, comparatively few new fine buildings, or for that matter repairs to existing buildings, were undertaken in the 15thc anywhere near the east coast, despite the fact that the centre of power resided here. The cathedrals at Dublin were little altered – possibly because it was scarcely necessary – while that at Newtown Trim was actually reduced in size.

Few of the churches built in other areas of Ireland before the onslaught of the Black Death were left untouched by the great building activity of the 15thc. The slender, narrow lancet windows of the 13thc were often replaced by larger traceried windows which allowed in more light. Unfortunately, only minute and insignificant fragments of their stained glass panels have endured. A western cathedral like Limerick was enhanced by the addition of a number of chapels, and was further enriched with a fine set of carved choir stalls. The latter are the only major specimens of medieval Irish woodwork to survive. Except for the west gable with its splendid Romanesque doorway, almost all of the cathedral at Clonfert was re-built from the foundations in the 15thc. The largest of the western parish churches, St Nicholas in Galway, was graced with considerable additions in the course of the 15th and 16thc.

The Reformation, however, curtailed the great spate of medieval Irish monastic building. With the Suppression of the Monasteries, starting in 1536, most of the religious communities departed from their cloisters. The ensuing lack of maintenance, coupled with the effects of weathering and the ravages of Cromwell, deprived the abbeys and friaries of their

Features of Quin Abbey in Co Clare include a tower, well-preserved windows, and probably the best-preserved Franciscan cloisters in Ireland.

roofs and left them in the ruined state in which they are found today. Further decay was halted only when many of them were taken into state care within the last hundred years. It is a tragic fact that there are scarcely more than a dozen medieval churches in Ireland which are still in use today; of those, however, many continue to serve as the cathedrals of the Church of Ireland. With the end of the great monastic churches came a decline in the stature and standards of Irish ecclesiastical structures. For nearly two centuries following the Reformation, Ireland rarely rose above the level of the simple and unadorned parish church. It was only in the 18thc that a new impetus was given to ecclesiastical architecture with the introduction of churches built on classical models and decorated in an attempt to invoke and revive the grandeur of Greece and Rome. These buildings represent a new tradition, forming a break with the older Irish churches described above. As such they lie outside the framework of this discussion.

It is hoped that in this review some idea has been conveyed of the conservative nature of early Irish church building and of the clinging to old traditions along and near the west coast. These are factors

Fine cloisters and magnificent stonework survive on the site of Cong Abbey, in Co Mayo, though little remains of the church.

that played on the creation of a highly individual and sometimes retardatory building province in the early-Christian period. The combination of a chronological and a regional approach to this subject may have helped to illuminate the way in which various areas contributed to the importation of architectural innovations at different times and for different reasons. By offering something for both layman and specialist, it is hoped that this article will encourage the traveller to pose – and seek a solution to – some of the questions left unanswered here by studying the individual ecclesiastical monuments at first hand.

Christian Monuments

A selection of pre-Reformation ecclesiastical monuments in Ireland. Symbols shown in red mark the locations of places illustrated in the preceding text.

Locations shown on map:
- Carndonagh
- Fahan
- Arboe
- Donaghmore
- Devenish Island
- Grey Abbey
- Inch Abbey
- Moyne Friary
- Rosserk Friary
- Boyle Abbey
- Monasterboice
- Kells (Ceanannas Mór)
- Mellifont Abbey
- Bective Abbey
- Inishmaine Abbey
- Cong Abbey
- Tuam
- Ross Errilly Abbey
- Galway (St Nicholas)
- St Macdara's Island
- Athenry Friary
- Clonmacnoise
- Durrow
- Dublin (Christchurch)
- Clonfert
- Corcomroe Abbey
- Kilfenora
- Moone
- Glendalough
- Dysert O'Dea
- Inishcaltra
- Roscrea
- Mona Incha
- Timahoe
- Quin Abbey
- Killaloe
- Killeshin
- Liathmore
- Kilkenny (St Canice)
- Limerick (Cathedral)
- Holy Cross Abbey
- Askeaton Friary
- Jerpoint Abbey
- Monasteraneagh
- Rock of Cashel
- Ahenny
- Ardfert
- Kilmalkedar
- Gallarus
- Aghadoe
- Church Island
- Ballyvourney
- Skellig Michael

KEY TO SYMBOLS
- Abbey/friary
- Cathedral
- Cross slab
- Early church
- Early monastic site
- High cross
- Oratory
- Romanesque building
- Round tower

Glossary of Terms

Altar Tomb, an altar- or box-shaped tomb situated in a wall niche of a church. The covering slab is often ornamented with an effigy. Burial near the High Altar was an honour generally given to the church's founder or benefactors.
Anchorite, one who lives the life of a total recluse.
Anglo Norman, a name given to the mixture of Norman, English, and Welsh nationals who invaded Ireland in the 12thc. Most of these people came from south-west Britain.
Antae, extensions of the side walls at the gable-end of a church. This is an early feature.
Arcade, an architectural feature comprising a series of arches.
Ashlar, a type of masonry constructed of square-hewn stones, often used to face a rubble or brick wall.
Bailey, the space enclosed by the walls of a castle, or the enclosed space attached to a motte (see motte-and-bailey).
Barbican, a castle outwork built to defend a gate or drawbridge.
Barrel-vaulting, simple roof vaulting of semi-circular form.
Bartizan, a defensive projection generally built over an angle at the top of a castle wall.
Bastion, a projecting feature designed to command the approaches to the main wall of a fortification.
Batter, a concave slope in the wall of a building.
Battlement, a parapet pierced with gaps (embrasures) through which defenders could discharge their missiles.
Bawn, a walled enclosure forming the outworks of a fortification. Besides being an outer defence it formed a safe enclosure for cattle during times of trouble.
Beehive hut, a small stone building of circular plan, built in the shape of an old-fashioned beehive. See also clochan.
Bivallate, a concentric defensive system of two banks and their associated ditches, usually found in ringforts.
Bronze Age, the earliest metal-using period – from the end of the stone age to the beginning of the iron age. In Ireland this was c2000BC to 500BC.
Bullaun, a stone with one or more hemispherical depressions of uncertain significance. They occur chiefly on ecclesiastical sites, and may have been used as mortars.
Cáher, a stone fort.
Cairn, a mound of stones heaped over a prehistoric grave – often a chambered tomb.
Capital, an architectural term used to describe the head of a column on which a lintel or arch is supported. Many capitals display intricate decoration.
Cashel, a stone enclosure surrounding a defended habitation site.
Cellarium, the wine cellar of a monastery.
Chalybeate, term used to describe the impregnated waters of a mineral spring.
Chancel or **Choir,** the east end of a church – reserved for the clergy and choir – where the High Altar is situated.
Chantry Chapel, a church chapel founded and endowed by a particular guild or person for the saying of special masses.
Chapter House, the chamber in which the governing body of a church or monastery met.

Chevaux-de-frise, an area of ground covered with vertical stakes or rocks to form the outer defence of a fortification.
Chi-rho Monogram, a Christian symbol formed by the initials of Christ.
Cist, a box-like grave built of stone slabs to contain an inhumed or cremated burial.
Clerestory, the part of a building's wall which rises above a lean-to roof. The clerestory of a church is generally supported on the nave arcades and has windows which face over the lean-to roofs of the aisles.
Clochan, another name for the beehive hut.
Cloisters, a rectangular open space which is surrounded by a covered passage and is used to provide common access to all parts of a monastery.
Columbarium, a dovecote.
Corbel, a projecting stone usually intended to carry a beam or other structural member.
Corbelling, the construction of a dome by laying horizontal rings of stone which decrease in diameter towards the top of the structure, thus overlapping on each course. The gap left at the top of the dome is closed by a single stone.
Corinthian, the third order of Greek and Roman architecture, distinguished by the capital's acanthus-leaf ornamentation. Corinthian is a development of the Ionic order.
Court Cairn, a type of megalithic tomb which includes one or more open courts for ritual purposes as well as a covered gallery for burials.
Crannog, an artificial or stockaded island constructed in a lake or marsh to provide a dwelling place in an easily defended position.
Crenellated, relating to a parapet provided with openings through which the defenders could discharge missiles.
Croft, an apartment between the pitched outer roof and arched inner roof of a building.
Crossing, the space where the nave and transepts of a church intersect. This area is often surmounted by a tower.
Cruciform, in the shape of a cross – as in a church which consists of nave, choir, and transepts.
Culdee, from the Irish *Céle Dé*, meaning 'Spouse of God'. This is the name given to a strict monastic movement which emanated from the Tallagh Monastery during the 8th or 9thc.
Currach, a light, sea-going vessel fashioned from tarred canvas stretched over a wooden frame. Currachs have been used for thousands of years, and can still be seen on the west coast of Ireland. Early vessels used animal skins for the hull.
Curtain Wall, the high wall usually constructed around a castle and its bailey. This usually included a number of towers.
Demesne, landed property attached to a house or castle.
Dolmen, the simplest form of megalithic tomb, comprising a large capstone and three or more supporting uprights. It is thought that some dolmens may have been covered by mounds or cairns.
Donjon, the keep or main tower of a castle.
Doric, the first order of Greek and Roman architecture, distinguished by plain capital columns without bases.
Drawbridge, a bridge which spanned the fosse of a castle and could be raised or lowered as required.

Drumlin, a long, oval mound formed by glaciers during the ice age.
Dun, a fort, usually built of stone and inclusive of formidable defences.
Early English, the earliest (ie 13thc) gothic architecture of Ireland and England. This style is characterized by narrow lancet windows, high pointed arches, and the use of rib vaulting.
Embrasure, the gaps in a battlement.
Entablature, the part of an architectural order above a column, including the architrave, frieze, and cornice.
Esker, a bank or ridge of gravel and sand deposited by sub-glacial streams.
Festoons, carved chains of flowers, fruit, leaves, etc used as architectural ornamentation.
Finial, an architectural feature formed by the crossing of rafters, or the projection of the ridge at the gable of a pitched roof. Some early-Irish churches include ornamented stone finials.
Flamboyant, the latest style of French-gothic architecture, popular in the 15th and 16thc. It is named from the flame-like forms of its window tracery.
Flanker, a fortification designed to guard the vulnerable flank of a stronghold or defensive position.
Floriated, decorated with floral designs.
Folly, a non-functional building erected to 'improve' the view or perform an equally eccentric purpose.
Fosse, a defensive ditch or moat round a fortification.
Fresco, a painting executed with natural earth colours on freshly-laid plaster; a term often erroneously applied to any wall painting.
Gallaun, see Standing Stone.
Garderobe, a type of toilet found in early castles and fortified buildings.
Gothic, the pointed-arch type of architecture used – with several major variations – from the 12th to 16thc.
Gothick, a romantic, 'quirky' revival of ancient gothic style in the 18th and 19thc.
Groin-vaulting, a form of vaulting comprising intersecting, semi-cylindrical stretches of stone roofing. The sharp lines of intersection form the groins.
Harled, the roughcasting of an exterior wall with lime and small gravel. This is generally whitewashed.
Henge Monument, a circular enclosure or sanctuary, often inclusive of a stone circle.
Hillfort, a fort with defences which follow a contour round a hill to enclose and fortify the summit. These are generally assigned to the iron age.
Hipped Roof, any roof with sloped instead of vertical ends.
Hospital, a medieval almshouse or house of hospitality, with provision for spiritual as well as bodily welfare of a specific class or group of people.
Inhumation, the burial of a whole body rather than ashes from a cremation.
Ionic, the second order of Greek and Roman architecture, distinguished by tall, fluted columns of slender proportions.
Iron Age, the earliest iron-using period. In Ireland the iron age lasted from the end of the bronze age to the coming of Christianity in the 5thc.
Jamb, the side of a doorframe, window frame, fireplace, etc.
Keep, the main tower of a castle, serving as the innermost stronghold. Most keeps surviving in Ireland are of rectangular form.

305

Kitchen Midden, a prehistoric refuse heap – often rich in discarded artefacts.

Lady Chapel, a chapel – usually in the east end of the church – dedicated to the Blessed Virgin.

Lancet, a tall, narrow window ending in a pointed arch, characteristic of early-English architecture. Lancets usually appear in groups of three, five, or seven.

La Tène, a name given to the second phase of the early iron age in central and western Europe. In Ireland this started c400BC.

Lavabo, a washing room or building near the refectory of a monastery.

Lectorium, the part of a monastic refectory from which texts were read at mealtimes.

Leper Window, a low opening or 'squint' through which a person outside the church could Communicate.

Lis, the open space enclosed by a rath. This term is often used in relation to the whole structure.

Lunette, an arched aperture included in a curved ceiling to admit light, or a decorated semicircular or crescent-shaped space in a dome.

Machicolation, a projecting shelf or parapet on a castle wall. Openings in the bottom of this allowed the discharge of missiles on to the heads of attacking troops.

Megalithic Tomb, a neolithic or early bronze-age tomb constructed of large stones and intended for collective burial.

Menhir, the Continental name for a standing stone.

Meso-gothic, a term meaning middle gothic, generally applied to lettering.

Midden, see Kitchen Midden.

Misericord or Misere, a carved projection on the underside of a folding seat. When the seat was raised this gave a measure of support to the infirm during the parts of a church service through which they had to stand.

Moat, a water-filled fosse or ditch surrounding a ringfort or castle.

Motte-and-Bailey, an early type of fort erected by the Normans. The motte was a flat-topped mound surrounded by a ditch and surmounted by a keep. This was adjoined by the bailey, a refuge for cattle and their retainers, which was bounded by a ditch, bank, and pallisade. Motte-and-bailey castles were built up until the early 13thc.

Mullion, the vertical member between the lights of a window or screen.

Muniment Chest, a chest for preserving charters, leases, and other important documents.

Nave, the main body of a church, sometimes separated from the choir by a screen.

Neolithic, pertaining to the new stone age, a period which ended c2000BC in Ireland and was characterized by the practice of agriculture.

Niche, an arched recess in a wall.

Norman, an old-fashioned term for English Romanesque architecture designed after the Conquest.

Ogham, early-Irish linear writing, usually inscribed on stone. The characters are strokes positioned above, below, or across a keyline.

Oriel, a window projecting from a wall and supported by brackets or corbels.

Orthostats, stones set to stand upright.

Over-croft, see Croft.

Pale, The, a district around Dublin in which Anglo-Norman rule was effective for some four centuries after the invasion of 1169.

Passage Grave, a type of megalithic tomb comprising a burial chamber and long approach passage within a round cairn or mound.

Patera, a small, flat, circular or oval ornament used in classical architecture.

Pattern, a festival held on a day traditionally assigned to the death of a patron saint.

Pediment, a term used in classical architecture to describe the formally-treated gable end of a roof, or a gable-shaped feature.

Pele or Peel, a small refuge tower of the type built along the Anglo-Scottish border.

Perpendicular, a late-gothic style of architecture used in England from the 14th to 16thc. It is characterized by vertical lines and shallow, flat arches.

Piscina, a washing basin set into a wall niche south of a church altar, used at the Lavabo of the Mass.

Plantation Castles, defensive buildings erected in Ireland by English and Scottish settlers during the 17th-c Plantation colonization scheme.

Pointed, an alternative term for early gothic architecture, derived from the typical pointed arches of the style.

Portcullis, a heavy grating designed to quickly seal off a castle entrance by dropping along slots cut into the jambs of the gateway.

Portico, a porch consisting of a roofed colonade in front of the entrance of a building.

Quoins, dressed stone at the angles of a building.

Rath, the rampart of an earthern ringfort. This term is often used to describe the whole structure.

Refectory, the dining hall of a monastery.

Renaissance, the 15th-c revival of classical art, architecture, and literature.

Reredos, a wall or screen behind a church altar, usually panelled and ornamented.

Revetted, faced with trimmed stone or masonry.

Rib-vaulting, a method of roofing in which the weight of the superstructure is carried on slender intersecting 'ribs' or arches of stone. The spaces between the arches contained a light stone filling which served no structural purpose.

Ringfort, one or more banks and ditches enclosing a circular habitation area. This type of structure was typical of early-Christian settlements in Ireland, but examples are known from c1000BC to cAD1000. A timber palisade was sometimes built on the bank.

Rococo, the latest phase of the highly-ornate baroque style which swept Europe between c1730 and c1760.

Romanesque, the style of architecture which prevailed in Europe until the emergence of gothic in the 12thc. It is characterized by round arches and vaulting.

Round Towers, tall, circular towers of stone which taper towards the top and include a doorway which is usually situated about 12ft from the ground. Round towers were erected from the 9th to 12thc as refuges from the Viking raiders.

Rundale, a system of holding land in strips or detached portions, ensuring that all members of a community had fair shares of good and bad land alike.

Rustication, the facing of a wall with rough-faced stone blocks, or smooth blocks with the joints greatly emphasized. A form of ashlar work.

Sacristy, a church apartment where the vestments, vessels, etc are kept.

Schist, a kind of rock which shows attractive bands of different minerals, and can be split into thin, irregular plates.

Scriptorium, the writing room of a monastery.

Sedilia, seats recessed in the south wall of the chancel – near the altar – for the use of the clergy.

Sept, a ruling Irish family who could trace their descent from a common ancestor.

Sessile, term often used to describe trees or plants with leaves that attach directly without a stalk.

Sheila-na-gig, a grotesque female figure found carved in stone on the outside of some castles and churches. Its meaning is obscure, but it might be a cult symbol, fertility symbol, or a warning against lechery.

Soffit, the visible underside of an architectural feature – often ornamented.

Souterrain, artificially-made underground chambers and passages which may have served as refuges, stores, or even as dwellings. They commonly occur in ringforts and date from the bronze age to at least early-Christian times.

Splay, an acute angle in a door or window jamb.

Squint, see leper window.

Standing Stone, an upright stone set in the ground. These date from various periods and served various purposes – burial markers, boundary stones, or cult beliefs.

Stonefort, a ringfort built of drystone walling, ie without mortar.

Talus, a sloping mass of rock fragments at the foot of a cliff.

Torc, an ornament made of ribbon- or bar-gold which has been twisted like a rope and bent round to form a complete loop. Such antiquities date from the middle to the late bronze age.

Trabeate, a form of construction where beams or vaulting are used instead of arches.

Tracery, the open-work pattern formed by the stone in the upper part of a middle- or late-gothic window.

Transepts, the arms of a church extending at rightangles north and south from the junction of nave and choir.

Travelling Earthwork, one or a number of earthern ramparts with accompanying ditches, constructed in straight lengths to form a system of defence.

Trefoil, an object shaped like three symmetrically arranged leaves.

Triforium, an arcade over the arches of the nave, choir, or transept arcade of a church.

Tympanum, the space between the lintel and surmounting arch of a doorway.

Undercroft or Crypt, an apartment under the floor of a church, often used as a chapel.

Undertaker, an English or Scottish planter who was given confiscated Irish land during the 16thc. They 'undertook' various obligations designed to prevent the dispossessed owners from re-acquiring their land.

Vallum, a bank formed of material thrown up during the excavation of a ditch or fosse.

Vaulting, a roof or ceiling formed by arching over a space. The three main types were barrel vaulting, groin vaulting, and rib vaulting; many variations of these were also used.

Ward, see Bailey.

Zoomorphic, based on the forms of animals.

Touring Atlas of Ireland

The Irish National Grid

IRISH NATIONAL GRID EXPLANATION

The Irish National Grid referencing system can be applied to any sized map and is accurate within the limitations of scale. It divides Ireland into 100Km squares (as shown on the map), each of which is sub-divided into one-hundred 10Km squares. The large squares appear in the following atlas as thick blue lines and are identified by a single letter eg B etc; the small sub-divisions are shown as thin blue lines and are numbered from 0 to 9 for each major square. Numbers appearing on the top and bottom of the map are the eastings, and those at the sides the northings. Eastings are numbered from the bottom or top left-hand corner of each major square; northings are numbered from the bottom left or right-hand corner.

The grid reference comprises one letter and two numbers, and is preceded by the map page number. The diagram illustrates the position of Killarney in relation to the National Grid. The town's reference is 27V99 The map appears on page 27, the relevant major square is identified by the letter V and easting 9 bisects northing 9 to form the bottom left-hand corner of the 10Km square in which the town appears. Where a place is cut through by a line, the reference given is for the square in which most of the town appears. The Ordnance Survey are not responsible for the accuracy of the National Grid in this publication.

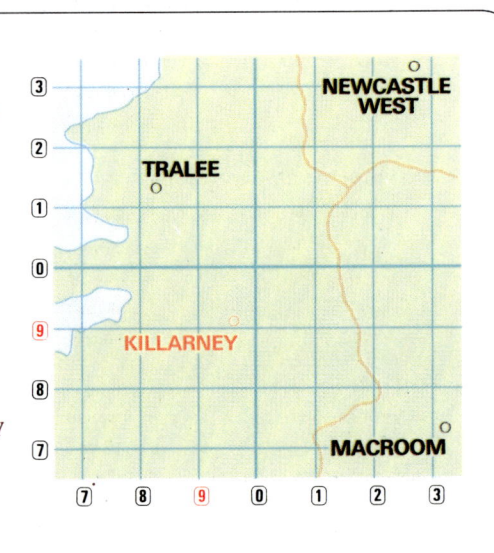

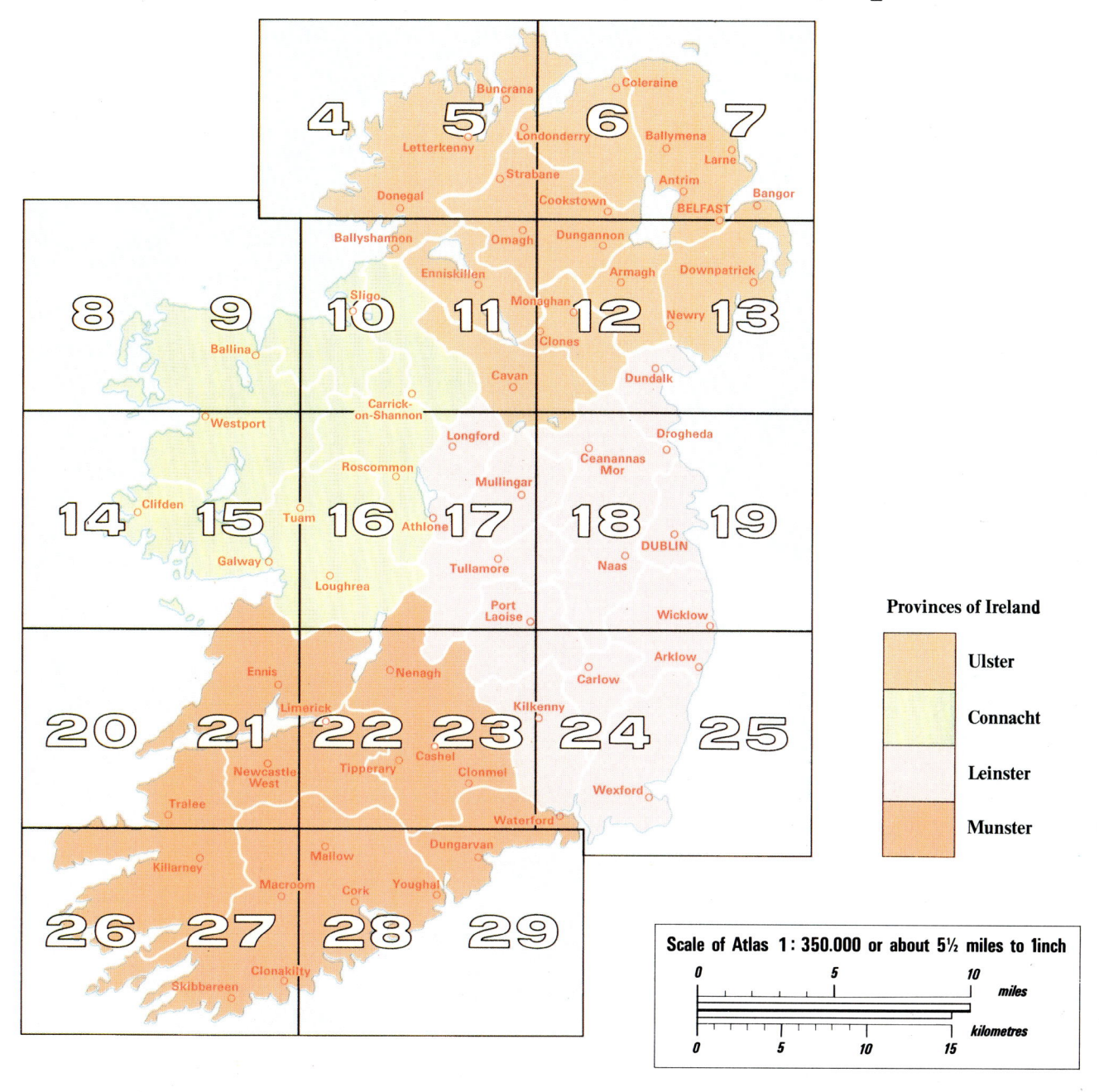

Key to Atlas

Provinces of Ireland
- Ulster
- Connacht
- Leinster
- Munster

Scale of Atlas 1:350,000 or about 5½ miles to 1 inch

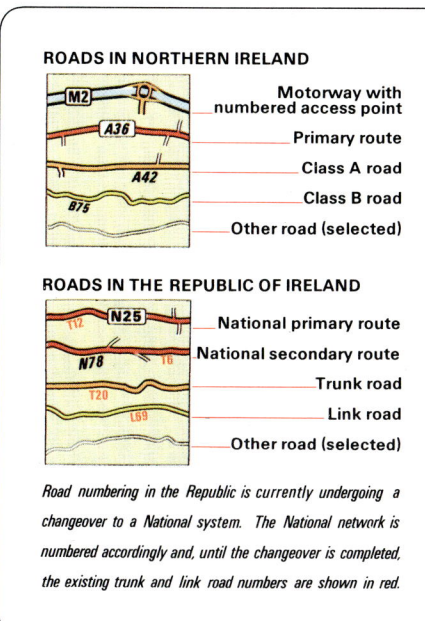

ROADS IN NORTHERN IRELAND
- Motorway with numbered access point (M2)
- Primary route (A36)
- Class A road (A42)
- Class B road (B75)
- Other road (selected)

ROADS IN THE REPUBLIC OF IRELAND
- National primary route (N25)
- National secondary route (N78)
- Trunk road (T20)
- Link road (L69)
- Other road (selected)

Road numbering in the Republic is currently undergoing a changeover to a National system. The National network is numbered accordingly and, until the changeover is completed, the existing trunk and link road numbers are shown in red.

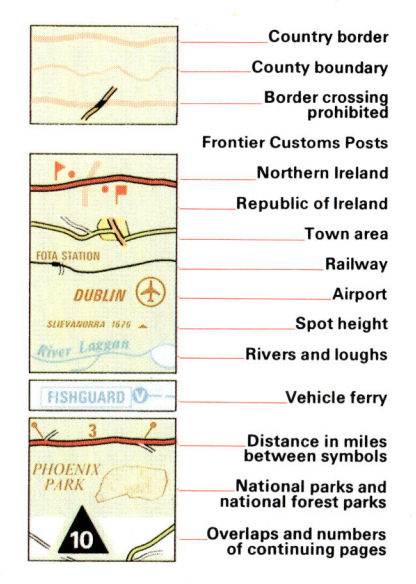

- Country border
- County boundary
- Border crossing prohibited
- Frontier Customs Posts
- Northern Ireland
- Republic of Ireland
- Town area
- Railway
- Airport
- Spot height
- Rivers and loughs
- Vehicle ferry
- Distance in miles between symbols
- National parks and national forest parks
- Overlaps and numbers of continuing pages

- AA and RAC telephones
- AA Service Centre (emergency services)
- AA Road Service Centre (normally 0900-1800 hrs)

CLARA — All places shown in red have an entry in the gazetteer
Castletown
High Island
GLINSK CASTLE

CONTOURS
FEET	METRES
1500	457
1000	305
500	152
200	61
SEA LEVEL	

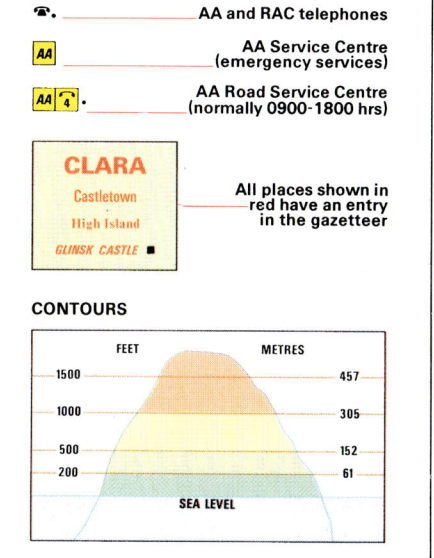

ATLANTIC OCEAN
B
G
Tory Island
West Town
Camusmore Bay
Tory Sound
Inishbeg
Inishdooey
Inishbofin
Pollaguill
Dooros Pt
Ranaghroe Pt
Bloody Foreland
Meenaclady
Ballyness Bay
Ray
Falcarragh
Gortahork
CLOGHANEELY
Inishsirrer
Inishmeane
Umfin I
Gola Island
GWEEDORE
Lagha
Tullaghobegly
Derrybeg
Middletown
Inishfree
Inishinny
Bunbeg
Owey Island
Inishfree Bay
Gweedore
Meenacung
Altan Lough
ERRIGAL 2466
Cruit Island
Torneady Pt
Rinrawros Pt
Rosses Bay
Kincaslough
Annagary
Crolly
Upper L Nacung
Dunlewy
THE ROSSES
Inishinny
Eighter I
Loughanure
Aran Island
Leabgarrow
Burtonport
Rutland I
L Anure
L Keel
Glentornan L
Poisoned Glen
DERRYVEAGH
SLIEVE SNAGHT 2240
Inishkeeragh
Inishfree Upper
Illancrone
Inishal
Dungloe
L Craghy
L Croangar
L Barra
Maghery Bay
Crohy Head
Maghery
Derrydruel
L Muck
Doochary
Gweebarra Bay
Trawenagh Bay
Dooey Pt
Roaninish
Ballynacarrick
Fintown
Lough Finn
Dunmore Hd
Inishkeel
Lettermacaward
GWEEBARRA BRIDGE
Portnoo
Narin
Clooney
Maas
AGHLA MTN 1961
Dawros Head
Rosbeg
Dawros Bay
Kiltooris
L Fad
Kilclooney
Inishbarnog
Loughros More Bay
L Aderry
Glenties
Tangaveane
Loughros Pt
Loughros Beg Bay
L Machugh
Owenea River
L Anna
Crannogeboy
Kilrean
Magrath Loughs
Tormore I
Croagh
1458 SLIEVETOOY
Ardara
Owentocher
LAVAGH MORE 2211
Croaghgorm or Blue Stack
BLUE ST 2219
Loughraherk
Laconnell
L Nalughraman
Stravally
Glen Head
Glen Bay
Glencolumbkille
Rossan Pt
Crove
L Divna
Glen River
Meentullynagarn
Tamur L
Eanybeg Water
Eanymore
Lough Eske
Malin Bay
Malin More
L Auva
L Unna
Meenavea
Namanfin
L Croagh
Croagh
Letterbarra
Rathlin O'Birne I
Malin Beg
SLIEVE LEAGUE 1972
Carrick
Teelin Bay
Frosses
Eany Water
R Eske
Inver
Mount Charles
Donegal
Teelin
Largy
Kilcar
Killybegs
Dunkineely
Tullyvoos
Bell's Isle
Laghy
Carrigan Head
Tawny Bay
Muckros Head
Shalwy Pt
Fintragh Bay
Drumanoo Hd
Mc Swynes Bay
Inver Bay
Doorin Pt
Bridgetown
Pound Pt
St Johns Pt
Rossnowlagh
Ballintra
Coolmore
N56
N15
T72
T72A
L74
L75
L82
L130
10

Inishtrahull
Inishtrahull Sound
Garvan Is
Malin Head
Hell's Hole
Ballyhillin
Glengad Head
Lag
Malin
Culdaff Bay
Dunmore Head
Culdaff
Rubonid Pt
Tremone Bay
Croaghdoo
Doagh Isle
Pollan Bay
Tullagh Pt
Trawbreaga Bay
Rockstown Harb
Dunaff Head
Fanad Head
Pollacheeny Pt
Rinmore Pt
Rinboy Pt
Arryheernabin
Shanagh
Doaghbeg
Kinny L
Leel Pt
Dunaff
Dunaff Bay
Claggan
Lenan Hd
Lenan Bay
Straid
Clonmany
Ballyliffin
Carndonagh
Balbane
Gleneely
Melmore Hd
Boyeeghter Bay
Tranarossan Bay
Mulroy Bay
Kindrum L
Atlantic Drive
Rosguill Peninsula
Doagh
Downings
Mevagh
Glinsk
Ballyheerin
L.Roy
Tamney
Rosnakill
Portsalon
Ballymastocker Bay
Dunree Hd
Magherabane
L Fad
L Naminn
Glentogher
Slieve Snaght 2019
Drumfree
INISHOWEN
Greencastle
Claggan
Cooley
Moville
L Fad
L Inn
SHEEPHAVEN
Horn Head
Horn Hd Little
Breaghy Hd
Port-na-Blagh
Rosapenna
Dunfanaghy
Ballymore
Marble Hill
Clonmass Bay
Ards Forest Park
Ards House
Carrigart
Port L
Doe Cas
Cranford
Creeslough
Cashel
Glen
Glen L
Muckish Mt 2197
Ballynashannagh
LOUGH SWILLY
Glenvar
Lehardan
Kerrykeel
Drumhallagh
Rathmullan
Ballymagan
BUNCRANA
Crana R
1309 Crockglass
Carrowkeel
Quigleys Pt
LOUGH FOYLE
Mill Bay
1377 Eskaheen Mtn
Fahan
1589 Scalp Mtn
Muff
Milford
Salt Mtn 1546
Greenan L
Agannive
Keel L
Fern L
Termon
Glenveagh
Beagh L
Inch Island
Inch
Ray
The Cul Bay
Aughinish I
Carnaghan
Mill Bay
Whale Head
Speenoge
Burnfoot
Ballyarnet
Culmore
Coolkeeragh
Eglinton
Faughan Br
Ballykelly
Limavady Junction
Ballarena
Bellarena
River Roe
Kilmacrenan
Rathmelton
Fort Stewart
Killydonnell Friary
Bridge End
Grianan of Aileach
LONDONDERRY
Londonderry (Waterside)
Drumahoe
Ardmore
Gartan L
Treantagh
Ellistrin
Church Hill
Glendowan
Temple Douglas
LETTERKENNY
River Swilly
Newtowncunningham
Gortree
Magherabeg
Manorcunningham
Dooish Mtn 841
Carrigans
R Foyle
Drumoghill
LONDONDERRY
Ervey Cross Roads
Bovevagh
Killaloo
Claudy
Dungiven
Breenagh
New Mills
LAGAN
St Johnstown
Sheskinapoll
Bready
Kingarrow
Mountcastle
Donemana
Ballyneaner
Feeny
Banagher Glen
Banagher
Park
Ballydonegan
1205 Cark Mtn
Aughkeely
Raphoe
Drumbeg
Port Hall House
Convoy
Swilly B
Ballindrait
Ballymagorry
B Dennet
L Ash
Glenelly
Cloghan
River Deele
Lifford
STRABANE
Dergalt
Moor L
Sawel 2240
Dart Mtn 2040
Meenard Mt 2061
Sperrin Mountains
Mullaghclogha 2088
Mullaghasturrakeen 1904
Mount Hamilton
Welchtown
Commeen
Altnapaste
Stranorlar
Killygordon
Castlefinn
Ballybofey
R Finn
Cross Roads
Clady
Sion Mills
Cranagh
Glenelly River
Carnanelly 1851
Meenglass
Plumbridge
L Mourne
Ardstraw
Mourne River
Glenhull
Owenkillew River
Rousky
Gortin
Barnesmore Gap
Mourne Beg River
Castlederg
Newtownstewart
Catherine L
Baronscourt
1387 Bessy Bell
Strule River
Gortin Glen Forest Park
Sheskinshule
Beaghmore
TYRONE
Killeter
Killen
Mullaghcarn 1778
Mountjoy
Gortnagarn Bridge
Mountfield
L Fingrean
Creggan
River Derg
Fairy Water
L Macrory
L Cam
L Golagh
Barderg
L Derg
Station I
Dunragh L
L Lack
Drumquin
Killyclogher
Drumnakilly
OMAGH
Carrickmore
Pomeroy
L Bradan
Cloghfin R
Camowen River
Clanabogan
Owenreagh River
Sixmilecross
Beragh
Gortaclare
L Avehy
Pettigo
Clonelly
Lack

Inishtrahull
Inishtrahull Sound
Malin Head
Garvan Is
Hell's Hole
Ballyhillin
Glengad Head
Lag
Pollan Bay
Doagh Isle
Tullagh Pt
Malin
Culdaff
Culdaff Bay
Dunmore Head
Rubonid Pt
Tremone Bay
Croaghdoo
Ballyliffin
Trawbreaga Bay
Clonmany
Dunaff Head
Dunaff
Straid
Claggan
Raghtin More 1657
Carndonagh
Culdaff
Gleneely
Balbane Hd
Inishowen Head
L Fad
L Naminn
Urris Hills
Glentogher
Magherabane
Drumfree
Slieve Snaght 2019
INISHOWEN
Greencastle
Claggan
Cooley
Moville
Magilligan Point
Lough Swilly
Ballymagan
BUNCRANA
Crana R
Crockglass
Carrowkeel
Quigleys Pt
LOUGH FOYLE
Mill Bay
Fahan
Eskaheen Mtn
Scalp Mtn
Muff
Inch Island
Inch
Carnaghan
Burnfoot
Culmore
Speenoge
Ballyarnet
Bridge End
Grianan of Aileach
Coolkeeragh
Faughan Br
Eglinton
LONDONDERRY
Newtowncunningham
Drumahoe
Gortree
Doodish Mtn 841
Carrigans
R Foyle
Ardmore
Ervey Cross Roads
Burntollet
Johnstown
Bready
Killaloo
Claudy
Mountcastle
Port Hall House
Donemana
Ballyneaner
Drumbeg
Ballymagorry
Lifford
STRABANE
Dergalt
Sion Mills
Clady
Ardstraw
Newtownstewart
Baronscourt
Bessy Bell
Mountjoy
Gortin
Gortin Glen Forest Park
Gortnagarn Bridge
Mountfield
Killyclogher
Drumquin
Fairy Water
OMAGH
Clanabogan
Drumnakilly
Carrickmore
Beragh
Sixmilecross
Gortaclare
Camowen River
Cloghfin R
Owenkillew River
Glenhull
Rousky
Sheskinshule
Beaghmore
Dunnamore
Creggan
L Fingrean
L Macrory
L Cam
Kildress
Drum Manor
COOKSTOWN
Pomeroy
L Bracken
Plumbridge
Glenelly River
Cranagh
Mount Hamilton
SPERRIN MOUNTAINS
Sawel 2240
Dart Mtn 2040
Mullaghcloga 2088
Mullaghasturrakeen 1904
Carnanelly 1851
Mullaghturk 1353
Meenard Mt 2061
Mullaghaneany 2070
Feeny
Park
Ballydonegan
Banagher
Dungiven
Bovevagh
Carn
Glenshane Pass
White Mtn 1774
Mullaghmore 1825
Moneyneany
Draperstown
Lisnamuck
Moyola R
Tobermore
Desertmartin
Magherafelt
Slieve Gallion
Lissan
Moneymore
Ballyronan
The Loup
Salters Castle
Mullan Pt
Coagh
Drumenny
Stanierds Pt
Newport Trench
Ardboe
Ardboe Pt
Farsnagh
Kiltagh Pt
Killycolpy
Ballinderry
Grange
Tullyhogue
Stewartstown
Kells Pt
Coalisland
Washing Bay
Roskeen Pt
Donaghmore
Mullygruen
Torrent
Roughan L
Magilligan
Magilligan Strand
Downhill
Mussenden Temple
Ballyaghran
Castlerock
Liffock
Articlave
Ballarena
Bellarena
Binevenagh 1260
Limavady Junction
Ballykelly
LIMAVADY
River Roe
Macosquin
COLERAINE
Mountsandel
PORTSTEWART
Portstewart Pt
PORTRUSH
Ramore Hd
The Skerries
Dhu Varren
Dunluce Cas
Portballintrae
Giants Causeway
Runkerry Pt
Benbane Head
Causeway Head
Dunseverick
Lisnagunogue
Bushmills
Ballyloughbeg
Bush River
Toberdowney
Derrykeighan
Ballyrashane
Ballybogy
Milltown
Ringsend
Aghadowey
Agivey
Drumsurn
Garvagh
Ballynameen
Kilrea
Ballylintagh
Bendooragh
Garryduff
Finvoy
Swatragh
Lislea
Upperlands
Claudy
Maghera
Gulladuff
Knockcloghrim
Bellaghy
Lough Beg
Castledawson
Coney
Brockish Bay
Traad Pt
Rasha
A2
A5
A6
A29
A54
A505
A37
A26
A42
B4
B40
B44
B47
B48
B64
B66
B69
B74
B162

NORTH CHANNEL
D
J
Rathlin Island
Lack Pt
Bull Point
Altacorry Bay
Church Bay
Arkill Bay
Cooraghy Bay
Ushet L
Doon Pt
Ushet Pt
Rue Pt
White Park Bay
Larry Bane Hd
Carrick-a-rede
Portbraddan
Ballintoy
Fair Head
Murlough Bay
Ballycastle Bay
Ballyvoy
Torr Hd
BONAMARGY FRIARY
BALLYCASTLE
Portaleen Bay
Loughan Bay
Runabay Hd
Ballinlea
Moyarget
1695 KNOCKLAYD
Loughareema
Tornamoney Pt
Armoy
Glendun
Cushendun
Knocknacarry
Drumdallagh
Kilraghts
Loughguile
SLIEVANORRA 1676
OSSIAN'S GRAVE
Cushendall
GLENS OF ANTRIM
Red Bay
Glenariff (Waterfoot)
Garron Pt
1817 TROSTAN
L Guile
Corkey
PARKMORE FOREST
ANTRIM COAST AND GLENS
Hunters Pt
Carnlough Bay
Newtown Crommelin
Clough Mills
Carnlough
Straidkilly Pt
Glenarm Bay
1426 COLLIN TOP
Glenarm
Clough
Martinstown
Drummore
Drumnagreagh Port
BLACK HILL 1259
Ballymena Water
The Sheddings
Craigs
Ballygalley
Ballygalley Head
Drains Bay
STRANRAER
Carncastle
Cullybackey
Broughshane
1437 SLEMISH
Galgorm
BALLYMENA
LARNE
Barrs Pt
Browns Bay
Skernaghan Pt
Portmuck Bay
Isle of Muck
Portmuck
Ahoghill
Harryville
Gracehill
Kilwaughter
OLDERFLEET CASTLE
Larne Lough
Mullaghboy
Moorfields
Glenwhirry
ISLAND MAGEE
Glynn
Magheramorne
Kells
Connor
Glenoe
Ballyeaston
Ballynure
Ballycarry
Black Hd
Straid
L Mourne
BALLYCLARE
WHITEHEAD
Randalstown
Doagh
Milebush
Cloghan Pt
Eden
Kilroot
Donegore
Parkgate
Woodburn
Bonnybefore
SHANE'S CASTLE
CARRICKFERGUS
Staffordstown
Farrs Bay
Antrim
Templepatrick
Dunadry
Lighthouse Island
Lighthouse Mew Island
DOUGLAS LIVERPOOL
Antrim Bay
Greenisland
Whiteabbey
Ballymacormick Pt
Groomsport
Copeland Island
Rabbit Pt
Churchtown Pt
Dunore Pt
Monkstown
NEWTOWNABBEY
Helen's Bay
Ballyholme Bay
Glengormley
Whitehouse
Crawfordsburn
Foreland Pt
Carmavy
BELLEVUE & HAZELWOOD
ULSTER FOLK MUS
BANGOR
DONAGHADEE
Ardmore Pt
BELFAST AIRPORT (ALDERGROVE)
Aldergrove
SQUIRES HILL
CAVE HILL
Greencastle
BELFAST LOUGH
HOLYWOOD
CLANDEBOY HOUSE
Conlig
Six Road Ends
LOUGH NEAGH
Legoniel
Crumlin
Dundrod
BELFAST
Sydenham
MOVILLA ABBEY
Millisle
Donaghadee
Hog Park Pt
Cochranstown
Glenavy
NEWTOWNARDS
Rams Island
Sandy Bay
Leathemstown Corner
DUNDONALD
Scrabo Hill
Ballyferis Pt
Balmoral
Cunningburn
Carrowdore
Lady Bay
Dunmurry
Newtownbreda
COMBER
MOUNTSTEWART HOUSE
STRANGFORD LOUGH
Greyabbey
Ballywalter
Portmore or L Beg
Ballinderry
Moneyreagh
Rough I
Chapel I
Ballylesson
ARDS PENINSULA
Tolan Pt
Aghalee
LISBURN
Lambeg
Drumbeg
Carryduff
Drumbo
Reagh I
South I
Biggan
Lisbane
Nuns Quarter
A2
A26
A42
A36
A8
A6
A52
A57
A24
A20
A21
A22
A23
A30
A43
A44
A48
A504
M1
M2
M22
B15
B147
B62
B64
B90
B95
B100
B170
B172
13

ATLANTIC

Stacks of Broadhaven
Benwee Head Portacloy Bay
Carrowtiege Portacloy
Erris Hd Broad Haven
Eagle I Ooghran Pt Rinroe Pt
Doonamo Pt Duveel Pt
Port Pt Corclogh Pollatomish Sruwaddacon Bay
Annagh Hd Knocknalina Knocknalower
Belmullet Moyrahan Pt Barnatra Bellan Bridge
Inishglora Cross Pt T58 L133 Carrowmore Lough
Corraun Pt Binghamstown Muings Bridge
THE MULLET Trawmore Bay Bunnahowen
Ardmore Pt 12
Carrickmoylenacurhoga Barranagh I Doolough Pt
Tiraun Pt Elly Bay Srahmore Bango
Inishkea North Ardelly Pt T58
Feorinyeeo Bay Owenmore R T71
Inishkea South Moyrahan Pt
Aghleam Doobeg Pt Dooyork Gweesalia
Blacksod Bay Tullaghan Bay Tarsaghaunmore
Roy L
Duvillaun Beg Doohooma
Duvillaun More Srahnamanragh Bridge
Owenduff River
Fahy L
Seal Caves Ridge Pt Sruhill L 20 Ballycroy
Saddle Hd Gubnahinneora Pt 2204 SLIEVEMORE Inishbiggle Castlehill Bellagarvaun Srah
Doogort Bulls Mouth T71
Achill Head CROAGHANN 2192 L141 Annagh I N59
Dooagh Keel L141 Bunacurry Mweelaun Pt
Moyteoge Hd Keem Bay MENAWN 1530 ACHILL ISLAND Salia Bay
Dooega Hd Achill Sound L141
Sraheens Glennanean Br
Dooega Corraun Peninsula Mulrany Rost
Kildownet Glassillaun Dooghbeg T71
Cloghmore L Ard Gubbaun Pt Moynish More
Bolinglanna
Achillbeg I
Island
Clare Island Ballytoohy CLEW BAY
Dromore Hd
Old Hd Lecka

O C E A N
G
SLIGO BAY
KILLALA BAY
Downpatrick Hd
Belderg Harb
Porturlin
Bunatrahir Bay
Creevagh Hd
Rathlackan
Lackan Bay
Kilcummin
Belderg
Ballycastle
Lougherglass
1247 MAUMAKEOGH
Carrowmore
Rathfran Bay
RATHFRAN FRIARY
Ross Pt
Rinnaun Pt
Bartragh I
Kincon
Killala
MOYNE ABBEY
ROSSERK FRIARY
Rathoma
Corvoley
Sheskin
1090 SLIEVE FYAGH
Glenamoy
Glenamoy R
Ballinglen R
Cloonaghmore R
Doobehy
Largan
Oweniny River
L Dahybaun
Bellacorick
Eskeragh Br
Crossmolina
Deel R
Deel Bridge
Rake Street
Castlehill
Keenagh
Letterbrick
Derreen
Lahardaun
LOUGH CONN
Knockmore
Illannaglashy
Pontoon Br
Pontoon
Glen Nephin
Levally L
L Cullin
2646 NEPHIN
2065 NEPHIN BEG
Bunaveela L
1785 CORSLIEVE
2369
2067 Corryloughaphuill
BIRREENCORRAGH 2295
1390 MT EAGLE
2343 CUSHCAMCARRAGH
Lough Feeagh
Furnace Lough
Beltra
L Beltra
Knockmoyle Bridge
Newport R
Newport
ROCKFLEET CAS
BURRISHOULE ABBEY
Newport Bay
Inishturk
Carraholly
Westport Quay
Westport Bay
Annagh I
WESTPORT
Clogher
Islandeady L
Castlebar Lough
CASTLEBAR
L Mallard
Burren
Derryhick L
Levallinree L
Clydagh R
Turlough
Bellavary
Strade
Breaghwy
Manulla
Carrowmore L
L Naminnoo
Balla
Ballycarra
Ballyhean
Buncam L
Cloonkeen
BALLINA
L Cloonagh
Rathroeen L
Rathroeen
Crockets Town
Castleconor
Garrycloonagh
L Alick
Newtown Cloghans
Ballymore L
KILDERMOT CH
Attymass
Behy Bridge
R Moy
Foxford
Muck L
Kilmore
Callow Loughs
Callow
Swinford
Moy River
Bohola
Kiltimagh
Cloonfallagh
Bruff
Cloonlee
Knock
Cullentragh
Mannin L
Kilkelly
L Roe
Urlaur L
Cloonacolly L
Cloonagh L
Errit L
L Caheer
Cloonfower
Lenadoon Pt
Carrickadda Pt
Cooanmore Pt
Rathlee Hd
Rathlee
Easky
Easky R
Kilglass
Owenbeg
Enniscrone
Culleens
Corbally
Bunnyconnellan
Dromore West
Templeboy
Skreen
Dromard
Aughris Head
Aughris
Carrowreagh
Killaspug Pt
Strand
Cone
L Easky
SLIEVE GAMPH OR THE OX MOUNTAINS
Gleneask
L Talt
Mullany's Cross
Aclare
Banada
Cloonacool
Lavagh
Tobercurry
Achonry
Cloonacleigh
Temple
Coolaney
Owengarve
Curry
Doocastle
Cloonakillina L
Roosky
Bellahy
Charlestown
Cloonmore
Carracastle
Tawnyinah
Kilmovee
Ballyglass
L Nanoge
Inishmurray
Rue Pt
Clashymore Harbour
Ballyconnell
Cloghboley
Raghly
Rossan Pt
Glencolumbkille
Malin Bay
Malin More
Malin Beg
L Auva
Meenavea
Rathlin O'Birne I
SLIEVE LEAGUE 1972
Teelin
Teelin Bay
Carrigan Head
Tawny Bay
M
N59
N57
N58
N5
N60
N17
L133
L140
L134
L136
L137
L138
L139
L150
L21
L22
L27
T40
T58
T39
T77
T11
T72A
10
15

Rossan Pt
Glencolumbkille
Malin Bay
Malin More
Malin Beg
Rathlin O'Birne I
Meenavea
Carrick
Slieve League
Teelin
Carrigan Head
Kilcar
Tawny Bay
Muckros Head
Shalwy Pt
Largy
Fintragh Bay
Drumanoo Hd
Killybegs
Mc Swynes Bay
Dunkineely
Inver Bay
Inver
Crove
Meentullynagarn
Croagh
Frosses
Letterbarra
Mount Charles
Donegal
Tullyvoos
Bell's Isle
Laghy
Doorin Pt
Pound Pt
St Johns Pt
Bridgetown
Ballintra
Rossnowlagh
Coolmore
ATLANTIC
OCEAN
DONEGAL BAY
Kildoney Pt
Tullan Strand
BALLYSHANNON
Belleek
Bundoran
Tullaghan
Mullaghmore
Bunduff Strand
Roskeeragh Pt
Trawalua Strand
Inishmurray
Rue Pt
Clashymore Harbour
Dernish I
Conors I
Streedagh Pt
Creevykeel
Cliffony
Kinlough
Askill
Inisheher
Inishmean
Inishtemple
Lough Melvin
Buckode
Garrison
Ross Pt
Largydonnell
Moneygold
Grange
Moneylahan
Dartry Mts
Truskmore
Benbulben
Glenade
Rossinver
Ballyconnell
Lissadell Ho
Cloghboley
Raghly
Carney
Drumcliff
Drumcliff Bay
Glencar L
Kiltyclogher
Saddle Hill
Manorhamilton
SLIGO BAY
Rosses Point
Cregg
Oyster I
Coney I
Killaspug Pt
Lenadoon Pt
Carrickadda Pt
Cooanmore Pt
Aughris Head
Aughris
Carrowreagh
Easky
Rathlee Hd
Rathlee
Kilglass
Strandhill
SLIGO
Knocknarea
Carrowmore
Colgagh
Killenna
Hazelwood Ho
Kilmore Cas
Church I
Cottage I
L Gill
Innisfree
Carrigeengo
Dromore West
Templeboy
Skreen
Dromard
Ballysadare Bay
Owenbeg
Enniscrone
Culleens
Creevelea Friary
Dromahair
Killarga
Ballysadare
Ballintogher
Ballygawley
Lisacoghil
Castleconor
Corbally
Collooney
Coolaney
Owenbeg R
Annaghmore
Toberscanavan
Drumkeeran
Coola
L Easky
OX MOUNTAINS
Crockets Town
Riverstown
Bunnyconnellan
Behy Bridge
SLIEVE GAMPH OR THE OX MOUNTAINS
Gleneask
Cloonacool
Lavagh
Templehouse
Ballymote
Heapstown Cairn
L Bo
Geevagh
Ballindoon Friary
L Arrow
Arigna
Ballyfarnan
Kilronan Ch
Meelagh
Keadue
L Skean
Attymass
L Talt
Mullany's Cross
Tobercurry
Achonry
Bunnanaddan
Carrowkeel Cemetery
Kesh
Ray's I
Aclare
Banada
Ballinafad
Doocastle
Owengarve
Cloonakillina L
Curry
Roosky
Cullin
Callow Loughs
Foxford
Callow
Kilmore
Cloonmore
Cloontia
Gorteen
Mullaghroe
Curlew Mts
Lough Key
Lough Key Forest Park
Cootehall
Boyle
Rockingham Ho
Bellahy
Charlestown
Swinford
Carracastle
Cloonloogh
Inch I
L Gara
Boyle River
Monasteraden
Carrick
Killukin
Jamestown
Bohola
Tawnyinah
Kilmovee
Ballaghaderreen
Ballyglass
Kingsland
Ballinameen
Ratallen
Croghan
Cavetown L
Hill Street
Rodeen
Kilkelly
Kiltimagh
L Nanoge
Old Lung Bridge
Churchstreet
Lurgan
Ardagh
Caldragh
Frenchpark
Mullen
Brackloon
Elphin
Drummullin
Cloonfallagh
Bruff
Urlaur L
Cloonacolly L
Cloonagh
Moyne
L Glinn
Bellanagare
Mantua
Mannin L
Loughglinn
Ballyglass West
Brackloon
Rathcroghan
Cloonyquin
Cloonlee
Knock
Cloonfower
SLIGO
MAYO
ROSCOMMON

Castlederg
GORTIN GLEN FOREST PARK
Sheskinshule
Killeter
Killen
Mountjoy
Gortnagarn Bridge
Mountfield
Creggan
Drumquin
OMAGH
Killyclogher
Drumnakilly
Carrickmore
L. Derg
Pettigo
Clonelly
Clanabogan
Lack
Sixmilecross
Beragh
Gortaclare
Ederny
Kesh
Dromore
Seskinore
Boa Island
LOWER LOUGH ERNE
CASTLECALDWELL
Hare I
Cruninish
Lusty I
Crevinishaughy I
White I
Inishmakill
Duross Pt
CASTLE ARCHDALE
Irvinestown
Fintona
Garvaghy
Eskragh
ERRIGAL KEERGE
Ballygawley
TULLY CAS
Killadeas
Kilskeery
Trillick
Augher
Lisdoart
Inishmacsaint
Whitehill
Ballinamallard
Coa
Clogher
FAVOUR ROYAL
Derrygonnelly
Monea
Imeroo
Clabby
Murley
Fivemiletown
FARDROSS FOREST
Carrickroe
Devenish I
Tempo
Creagh
Emyvale
COLEBROOKE HOUSE
ENNISKILLEN
CASTLECOOLE HOUSE
LISGOOLE ABBEY
Boho
Tamlaght
Lisbellaw
Brookeborough
L. Macnean Upper
Holywell
Belcoo
Letterbreen
Blacklion
Bellanaleck
Arney
Maguires Bridge
Tedavnet
Tirnane
Carry Bridge
Derryharney
Scotstown
Bellanode
Wheathill
Ballindarragh
Lisnaskea
MONAGHAN
MARBLE ARCH
FLORENCE COURT
Upper Lough Erne
Inishleague
Derrynawill
Rosslea
Kinawley
Tully
Ballagh
Cloghmore
Smithborough
Donagh
Magheraveely
Stone Bridge
Cavanagarvan
Glengavlen
Swanlinbar
Greenan's Cross Roads
Newtown Butler
CLONES
Killeevan
Anlore
Bellavally Gap
CROM CASTLE
Ballinagleragh
Derrynacreeve
Newbliss
Swan's Cross Roads
IRON MOUNTAINS
Wattle Br
Scotshouse
Rockcorry
Bawnboy
Kilconny
Drum
Ballyconnell
Drumasladdy
Belturbet
Redhills
Treehoo
Aghnamullen
Aughnasheelan
Killycluggin
Ardlougher
Milltown
Lisnageer
Cootehill
DRUMLANE
Ballinamore
Garadice L.
Butler's Bridge
Ballyhaise
Tullyvin
Kill
Newtown Gore
Foxfield
Keshcarrigan
Fenagh
Killashandra
Kilmore
CAVAN
Stradone
Garvagh
Lavey
Canningstown
Kilnagross
Carrigallen
Shannon
Crossdoney
Cloone
Aghavas
Cloone Grange
Ballinagh
Drumsna
Mohill
Arvagh
Cross Keys
Aghamore
Moyne
New Inn
Carrigan
Leggah
Killinkere
Teevurcher
Gowna
Crosserlough
Ballyjamesduff
Lisgrea
Drumod
Farnaght
Ballinamuck
Kilnaleck
Roosky
Aghnacliff
Ballyheelan
Virginia
Kilcogy
Ballymachugh
Castlerahan
Johnstonsbridge
Drumlish
Inchmore
LOUGH SHEELIN
Mount Nugent
Dring
Lisduff
Esker South
12
17
5

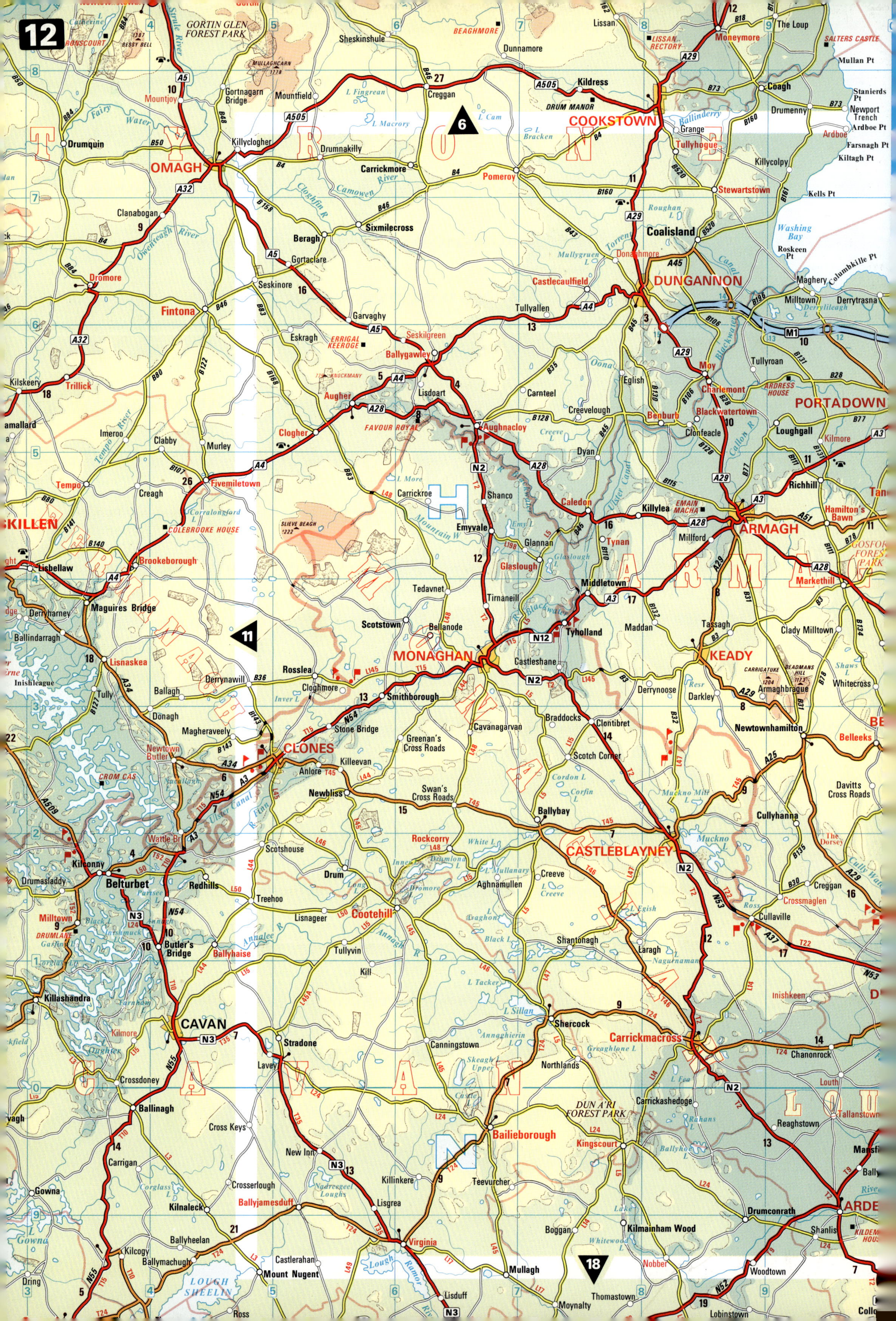
GORTIN GLEN FOREST PARK
Sheskinshule
BEAGHMORE
Dunnamore
Lissan
LISSAN RECTORY
Moneymore
The Lupp
SALTERS CASTLE
Mullan Pt
Mountjoy
Gortnagarn Bridge
Mountfield
Creggan
Kildress
DRUM MANOR
Coagh
Stanierds Pt
Newport Trench
Ardboe Pt
Drumenny
Ardboe
Farsnagh Pt
Kiltagh Pt
COOKSTOWN
Grange
Tullyhogue
Drumquin
Killyclogher
Drumnakilly
OMAGH
Carrickmore
Pomeroy
Killycolpy
Stewartstown
Kells Pt
Clanabogan
Sixmilecross
Beragh
Gortaclare
Coalisland
Washing Bay
Roskeen Pt
Columbkille Pt
Donaghmore
DUNGANNON
Maghery
Milltown
Derrytrasna
Dromore
Seskinore
Castlecaulfield
Fintona
Garvaghy
Tullyallen
Eskragh
ERRIGAL KEEROGE
Seskilgreen
Ballygawley
Moy
Tullyroan
Kilskeery
Trillick
KNOCKMANY
Augher
Lisdoart
Carnteel
Eglish
Charlemont
ARDRESS HOUSE
PORTADOWN
Creevelough
Benburb
Blackwatertown
Clogher
FAVOUR ROYAL
Aughnacloy
Clonfeacle
Loughgall
Kilmore
amallard
Imeroo
Clabby
Murley
Dyan
Tempo
Fivemiletown
Creagh
Carrickroe
Shanco
Caledon
Killylea
EMAIN MACHA
Richhill
Hamilton's Bawn
SKILLEN
COLEBROOKE HOUSE
SLIEVE BEAGH
Emyvale
Glennan
Tynan
Millford
ARMAGH
Lisbellaw
Brookeborough
Glaslough
GOSFORD FOREST PARK
Middletown
Markethill
Maguires Bridge
Tedavnet
Tirnaneill
Derryharney
Ballindarragh
Scotstown
Bellanode
Tyholland
Maddan
Tassagh
Clady Milltown
Lisnaskea
MONAGHAN
Castleshane
KEADY
Inishleague
Rosslea
Derrynawill
Cloghmore
Smithborough
Derrynoose
Darkley
Armaghbrague
Whitecross
Ballagh
Tully
Donagh
Braddocks
Clontibret
Magheraveely
Stone Bridge
Cavanagarvan
Greenan's Cross Roads
Newtownhamilton
Belleeks
Newtown Butler
CLONES
Killeevan
Scotch Corner
CROM CAS
Anlore
Newbliss
Swan's Cross Roads
Davitts Cross Roads
Ballybay
Cullyhanna
Wattle Br
Rockcorry
Muckno
CASTLEBLAYNEY
Kilconny
Belturbet
Scotshouse
Drumasladdy
Drum
Creeve
Aghnamullen
Redhills
Treehoo
Cootehill
Creggan
Crossmaglen
Milltown
Lisnageer
Cullaville
Butler's Bridge
Ballyhaise
Tullyvin
Shantonagh
Laraghi
Kill
Killashandra
Inishkeen
CAVAN
Kilmore
Stradone
Shercock
Carrickmacross
Canningstown
Lavey
Northlands
Chanonrock
Crossdoney
Louth
Ballinagh
DUN A'RI FOREST PARK
Carrickashedoge
Cross Keys
Bailieborough
Kingscourt
Reaghstown
Tallanstown
Carrigan
New Inn
Gowna
Crosserlough
Killinkere
Teevurcher
Kilnaleck
Ballyjamesduff
Lisgrea
Drumconrath
Boggan
Kilmainham Wood
Shanlis
Ballyheelan
Kilcogy
Ballymachugh
Virginia
Castlerahan
Mount Nugent
Mullagh
Woodtown
LOUGH SHEELIN
Dring
Lisduff
Moynalty
Thomastown
Lobinstown
Ross
6
11
18

BELFAST
BELFAST AIRPORT (ALDERGROVE)
NEWTOWNABBEY
BANGOR
DONAGHADEE
HOLYWOOD
NEWTOWNARDS
DUNDONALD
COMBER
LISBURN
LURGAN
CRAIGAVON
DROMORE
BANBRIDGE
Ballynahinch
DOWNPATRICK
Portaferry
Killyleagh
Saintfield
Hillsborough
NEWCASTLE
NEWRY
WARRENPOINT
KILKEEL
Rathfriland
Castlewellan
Carlingford
Cooley Peninsula
ARDS PENINSULA
STRANGFORD LOUGH
DUNDRUM BAY
DUNDALK BAY
IRISH SEA
MOURNE MOUNTAINS
TOLLYMORE FOREST PARK
DRUMKEERAGH FOREST
CASTLEWELLAN FOREST PARK
Carlingford Lough
Greencastle
Ardglass
St John's Pt
Ballagan Pt
Castlebellingham
Dunany Point
Clogher Head
Dunleek
Annagassan
Ballywalter
Ballyhalbert
Portavogie
Millisle
Greyabbey
Kircubbin
Strangford
Killough
Dundrum
Clough
Seaforde
Annalong
Gilford
Moira
Magheralin
Scarva
Loughbrickland
Poyntzpass
Jerrettspass
Camlough
Hilltown
Mayobridge
Rostrevor
Omeath
Crumlin
Glenavy
Dunmurry
Carryduff
Ballygowan
Crossgar
Kilmore
Newtownbreda
Helen's Bay
Groomsport
Copeland Island
Donard Cove
Bloody Bridge
Glasdrummon
Ballymartin
Cranfield Pt
Whites Town
Cooley Pt
Gile's Quay
Eggleston Pt
Black Rock
Dromiskin
Kilsaran
Togher
Port
Grangebellew
Clogherhead

14

CLEW BAY

Clare Island — Ballytoohy
Dromore Hd

Old Hd — Leckan
Carrickyvegraly Pt
Roonah Quay — Louisburgh — T39 — Kilsalla
Emlagh Pt — Mullagh
Formoyle
Roonah L
KILLEEN CHURCHYARD
Caher I
Inishturk — Harbour
Bunlough Pt — Killadoon — TOBERNAHALTORA TOMB — Cregganbaun
Barnabaun Pt — MURRI
Inishdalla
Glenkeen Bridge
TIEVUMMERA 2424
Allaran Pt — GLASCAME 2504
Tonakeera Pt — BENBURY 2610
Inishdegil More — MWEELREA 2688 — Doo L
Bunnamullen Bay — MWEELREA MTS
Inishbofin — Davillaun — Crump I — Delphi — BENGORM 2303
Killary Harbour
Inishark — Inishlyon — Rinvyle Pt
Inishgort — Cashleen — Renvyle — Salrock
Tully L — Gowlaun — Muck
Tully Cross
Cleggan Bay — Ballynakill Bay — Dawros — L Fee — **Leenane** — T71
High I (Ard Oilean) — Aughrus Pt — Cleggan — Ballynakill L — KYLEMORE ABBEY
Friar I — Claddaghduff — T71 — Letterfrack — 21 — Kylemore
Omey I — Moyard — N59 — MAUMTURK MO
Cruagh — Kingstown Bay — Streamstown — BENBAUN 2393
Inishturk — L Nahillion — THE TWELVE PINS 2336 — Lough Inagh
Talbot I — Clifden Bay — Owenglin River — BENCORR 2184
Clifden — T71 — Derrylea — BENGOWER
CONNEMARA — 22 — Recess
Ballinaboy — Ballynahinch L — T71 — Glendollagh L
Mannin Bay — L Fadda — Toombeola — L102
Inishdugga — L102 — Cashel
Ballyconneely — Scannive — Bunnahown — L Curr
Cromgaunt Bay — Maumeen — Derry
Slyne Head — Ballyconneely Bay — Bollard — **Roundstone**
Inishnee — Bertraghboy Bay
Doo's Bay — Gorteen Bay — Glinsk
Inishlackan — Flannery Br
Freaghillaun — Moyrus
Croaghnakeela Island — Mace Head — Carna — L Skannive — Kilkieran — Inisht
St Macdara's I — Kilkieran Bay — Lette
Mason I — Mweenish Bay — Ardmore Pt
Mweenish I — Finish I
Inishbarra — Casheen Bay
Dinish — Gor
Furnace I
Lettermullan — Isl

ATLANTIC

Golám Hd — Kiggaul Bay

OCEAN

North Soun

Brannock Islands — Onaght
Kilmurvy — Oatquarter
Oghill
Inishmore — ARAN IS — Kille
Clinew

CASTLEBAR
WESTPORT
Westport Quay
Westport Bay
Clew Bay
Inishturk
Inishlyre
Carraholly
Annagh I
Murrisk
Knappagh
Aghagower
Liscarney
Cordarragh
Owenmore Br
Carrowkennedy
Erriff Bridge
PARTRY MOUNTAINS
MAUMTRASNA
DEVILS MOTHER
KNOCKLAUR
BENWEE
Maumtrasna
Tourmakeady
Croaghrimbeg
Bohaun
Killavally
Mace
Clogher
Cloonkeen
Ballin
Islandeady
Castlebar Lough
Breaghwy
Manulla
Ballyhean
Ballycarra
Ballintober
Ballyglass
Mayo
Balla
Kiltimagh
Cloonfallagh
Bruff
Cloonlee
Knock
PLAINS OF MAYO
Ballynastangford
Barnycarroll
Ballyhaunis
Ballinlough
Claremorris
Brickeens
Knockanarra
Tulrohaun
Cloonfad
Robe River
Dalgan River
Mannin L
Island L
Cullentragh L
Derry L
Bekan L
Urlaur L
Cloonagh
MOORE HALL
Partry
Castle
Lough Carra
Tooreen
Cornanagh
Mullingar Bridge
Ballygarries
Hollymount
Ballindine
Dry Mills
Scardaun
Roundfort
Levally
Ballinrobe
Ardkill
Castleville
Milltown
Sinking R
Dunmore
Ballagh
Curragh West
Plains of Ellertrin
Foxhall
Kilmaine
Kilconly
Trean
Annagh Pt
LOUGH MASK
Inishmaine
L Nafooey
JOYCES COUNTRY
ASHFORD CASTLE
Neale
Cong
Clonbur
Plain of Moytura
Tobernadarry
Shrule
KILBENNAN TOWER
River Clare
Beagh
Clonbern
TUAM
Maam Bridge
Teernakill Bridge
Cornamona
Inishdauwee
Inishmicatreer
Inishdoorus
HEN'S CASTLE
CORCOGEMORE MTS
LECKAVREA
KINLOUGH CAS & CH
MOYNE CASTLE
ROSS ERRILLY FRIARY
KILLURSA CHURCH
Headford
Caherlistrane
Belclare
Barnaderg
Grange R
Inchagoill
LOUGH CORRIB
Inchiquin
Ballyhale
Maam Cross
Loughanillaun
Oughterard
AUGHNANURE CAS
Killarone
Carrowmoreknock
Moneen
Corrofin
BALLYGLUNIN
Abbert R
Abbeyknockmoy
Gortmore
Screeb
Kilbrickan
Rosmuck
Kinvarra
Camus Bay
Bealadangan
Rosscahill
KNOCKNALEE HILL
IAR CONNACHT
Moycullen
Lough Corrib
Annaghdown
Cloonboo
Aucloggeen
Cloghaun
Turloughmore
Carnoneen
Monivea
Clonkeenkerrill
Claregalway
Kilroghter
Menlough
Carnmore
Cashla
Athenry
Keeagh
Loughanillaunmore
Rossroe I
Carraroe
Costelloe
Rossaveel
Keeraunnagark
Cashla Bay
Greatmans Bay
Inveran
Spiddal
Barna
TIRBALEEN CAS
GALWAY
Salthill
Seaweed Pt
Oranmore
Oranmore Bay
Glennascaul
Kiltullagh
Rinville
Caheradrine
Kilcaimin
Clarinbridge
Killeeneenmore
Craughwell
Killilan Bridge
Dunkellin R
Raford River
Corrahowna Pt
Nagravin
Travore Bay
Mweeloon Bay
Kilcolgan Pt
Tawin I
Carrowmore
Dunbulcaun Bay
DRUMACOO CH
Kilcolgan
Eddy I
Killeenaran
Kiltiernan
Pollagh
Ballinderreen
Kinvarra Bay
GALWAY BAY
Parkmore
Aughinish
Newtownlynch
Finavarra
Kilchreest
Black Head
Ardrahan
Grannagh
Owenbristy
ISERTKELLY
Burren
Kinvarra
Laban
Ballyvaughan Bay
Murroogh
Cregg
CORCOMROE ABBEY
Funshin More
Cahermore
Peterswell
Fanore
Ballyvaughan
Bealaclugga
Cappaghmore
THOOR BALLYLEE CASTLE
Kiltartan
Killinny
Inishmaan
Dogs Hd
Foul Sound
Inisheer
Trawkeera Pt
Fardurris Pt
South Sound
SLIEVE ELVA
Turlough
BURREN
CLARE
Tulla
Tirneevin
Gort
Ballaba
Kilbeacanty
Bunnaglass
Ballardiggan
Toomaghera
Kilmacduagh
Caherconnell
Carran
Doolin Pt
Knockfin
Fisherstreet
Roadford
SPECTACLE BR
Lisdoonvarna
Castletown
Boston
L Bunny
LOUGHCUTRA CASTLE
L Cutra
Killafeen
Corlea Bridge
Noughaval
GLASGEIVNAGH HILL
Aughrim
Ballyeighter L
Shanaglish
Tubber
Killeen
Lough Graney
Killanena
Flagmount
Kilfenora
LEAMANEH CASTLE
Roughan
Killinaboy
Muckanagh L
Cliffs of Moher
Kilshanny
Derreen
KILMACREHY CH
Lickeen L
Inchiquin L
L George
Ballinruan
Caher
Kilclaran
Hags Head
Ennistymon
Corofin
Willbrook
L Atedaun
ANDS

Kiltimagh
Cloonfallagh
Bruff
Balla
Cloonlee
Knock
PLAINS OF MAYO
Ballynastangford
Barnycarroll
Ballyhaunis
Claremorris
Knockanarra
Brickeens
Tulrohaun
Robe River
Cloonfad
Ballindine
Dry Mills
Scardaun
Hollymount
Roundfort
Castleville
Ardkill
Milltown
Foxhall
Kilconly
Tobernadarry
KILBENNAN TOWER
Dunmore
Ballagh
Beagh
TUAM
Caherlistrane
Belclare
Headford
Moneen
Corrofin
Annaghdown
Cloonbog
Aucloggeen
Cloghaun
Claregalway
Turloughmore
Carnoneen
Kilroghter
Carnmore
Menlough
GALWAY
Glennascaul
Oranmore
Salthill
Oranmore Bay
Rinville
Caheradrine
Kilcaimin
Clarinbridge
Killeeneenmore
Carrowmore
Kilcolgan
Killeenaran
Pollagh
Ballinderreen
Kiltiernan
Parkmore
Newtownlynch
Kinvarra Bay
Kinvarra
Burren
Owenbristy
Ardrahan
Grannagh
Labane
CORCOMROE ABBEY
Funshin More
Cahermore
Cappaghmore
Killinny
Turlough
Tulla
Tirneevin
Gort
Kilmacduagh
Boston
Castletown
Aughrim
Shanaglish
Tubber
Killinaboy
Corofin
Killeen
Killafeen
Kilbeacanty
Ballardiggan
Bunnagiass
Derrybrien
SLIEVE AUGHTY MOUNTAINS
Corlea Bridge
Flagmount
Killanena
Caher
Kilclaran
Cloonusker
Lough Graney
Peterswell
Kiltartan
Ballaba
THOOR BALLYLEE CASTLE
LOUGHCUTRA CASTLE
L. Cutra
Kilchreest
ISERTKELLY
LOUGHREA
Lough Rea
Craughwell
Killilan Bridge
Athenry
Cashla
Monivea
Abbeyknockmoy
Barnaderg
Moylough
Mount Bellew
Killoscobe
Castleblakeney
Menlough
Glentane
Colmanstown
Clonkeenkerrill
Ballymacward
Gorteen
Attymon
ATTYMON JUNCTION
New Inn
Kiltullagh
TURDE STONE
Bullaun
Cappataggle
Kilreekill
Mullagh
Ballydavid
Carrowkeel
Tynagh
Garraun
Dunry
PALLAS
Killimor
Abbey
Drumkeary
Power's Cross
Woodford
Gorteeny
Coolbaun
Whitegate
Illaunmore
Lough Derg
Portumna
Portland
Lorrha
Carrigahorig
Terryglass
Ballinderry
Borrisokane
Carney
Fort William
Ballycrossaun
DERRYHIVENNY CAS
Moorfield
Eyrecourt
Kiltormer
Laurencetown
Clonfert Cross Roads
Kylemore Bridge
Oghill
Crossconnell
CLONTUSKERT ABBEY
Aughrim
Kelly's Grove
Garbally
BALLINASLOE
Kilconnell
Woodlawn
Trust
Doon
Alloon Lower
Ahascragh
Kilglass
Ballybaun
Caltra
Killaderry
Ballyvoneen
Ballinamore Bridge
Newbridge
Toomard
Kilkerrin
Clonbern
Glenamaddy
Shanbally
Gortnadeeve
Creggs
Slievemurry
Ballygar
Mount Talbot
Athleague
Knockcroghery
Lackan Cross
Four Roads
Lismoyle
Curraghboy
Ballyforan
Thomas Street
Brideswell
Killeglan
Carrowreagh
Newtown
Ballydangan
Old Town
Cloonfad
Roscommon
Fuerty
Passage
Ballymurray
Bracknagh
Emmoo
Cooltelge Cross
Four Mile House
Ballymacurly
Ballintober
Castleplunket
Carrowgarve
Gortnasillagh
Tulsk
Strokestown
Cloonyquin
Rathcroghan
Mantua
Brackloon
Elphin
Drummullin
Frenchpark
Bellanagare
Moyne
Loughglinn
Ballyglass West
Cloonfower
Castlerea
Clonkeen
Ballinlough
Trien
Ballymoe
Williamstown
Derrywode
Pollshask
Curragh West
Kilcroan
Kilsallagh
Cashel
Keeloges
Kilbegnet
Crosswell
Shrule
Kilkline
Cargin
Seaweed Pt
Tawin I
Eddy I
Mweeloon Bay
Dunbulcaun Bay
DRUMACOO CH
Rossaveel
Oughinish
Flaggy Bay
N17
N60
N63
N6
N18
N66
N65
N61
N5
N52
N67
N64

LONGFORD
Edgeworthstown
MOSTRIM (Edgeworthstown)
Granard
Abbeylara
Ballinalee
Drumlish
Roosky
Lanesborough
Killashee
Ballymahon
Virginia
Oldcastle
Mount Nugent
Finnea
Castlepollard
Delvin
Clonmellon
MULLINGAR
Multyfarnham
Ballinalack
Rathowen
Ballynacarrigy
Kinnegad
Rochfortbridge
Tyrrellspass
Kilbeggan
Moate
CLARA
Ballycumber
TULLAMORE
EDENDERRY
Daingean
Ballinagar
Geashill
Killeigh
PORTARLINGTON
Monasterevin
MOUNTMELLICK
PORT LAOISE
Stradbally
ATHY
Mountrath
BIRR
Cloghan
Ferbane
Shannon Harbour
Banagher
Kilcormac
Kinnitty
ROSCREA
THLONE
Lough Sheelin
Lough Derravaragh
Lough Owel
Lough Ennell
Lough Ree
SLIEVE BLOOM MOUNTAINS
BOG OF ALLEN
Grand Canal
Royal Canal
N4
N5
N6
N7
N8
N52
N55
N62
N80
11
18
23

Kilnaleck
Ballyjamesduff
Lisgrea
Boggan
Kilmainham Wood
Drumconrath
ARDEE
Shanlis
KILDEMOCK HOUSE
Kilcogy
Ballyheelan
Ballymachugh
Castlerahan
Mount Nugent
Virginia
Lough Ramor
Mullagh
Whitewood L.
Nobber
Woodtown
Dring
LOUGH SHEELIN
Lisduff
Moynalty
Thomastown
Lobinstown
Collon
Granard
Finnea
Kinale
Ross
Abbeylara
Ballynacree
Oldcastle
SLIEVE NA CALLIAGH 904
River Blackwater
Carnaross
Dulane
Carlanstown
Georges Cross Roads
Devlin R
ST KIERAN'S CH
Ballinlough
TOWER OF LLOYD
HEADFORT HOUSE
Wilkinstown
Lisryan
Crossakeel
Oristown
Slane
CEANANNAS MOR (Kells)
Kilberry
Knowth
Coole
Boherquill
L. Glore
Cross Keys
Kilskeer
Gibbstown
ROSNAREE
Donaghpatrick
DONAGHMORE CHURCH AND ROUND TOWER
LISCARTAN CASTLE
Street
Castlepollard
L. Bane
Killallon
Hays
Rathowen
Lough Derravaragh
L. Lene
Clonmellon
Fordstown
Bohermeen
NAVAN (An Uaimh)
Collinstown
Martinstown
Glen L
Ballinalack
Multyfarnham
Drumcree
Cloran
RATHMORE
Halltown
Kentstown
390 HILL OF WARD
Walterstown
Bunbrosna
Iron
Ballynafid
Crookedwood
Delvin
Athboy
Dunderry
Portnashangan
Taghmon
Kilbride
Garlow Cross
Robinstown
Skreen
Ballynacarrigy
Monilea
ASSEY CAS
Bective
HILL OF TARA
Tara
Lough Owel
Crazy Corner
Newtown Trim
Kilmessan
Royal Canal
Clark's Cross Roads
Brittas L
Cloghan
Tevrin
Trim
SCURLOGSTOWN CASTLE
DUNSANY CAS
KILLEEN CAS
River Deel
Shanco Bridge
Pike Corner
Rathconrath
MULLINGAR
Raharney
Ballivor
Dunshaughlin
Laracor
LAGORE HO
Killucan
Clonycavan
DANGAN CAS
Cross Keys
Drumree
The Downs
R Boyne
Rathwire
Inchamore
Rathmolyon
Gainestown
Loughanavally
Royal Canal
Cloncrave
Summerhill
Moynalvy
Kilmore
Batterstown
Coralstown
Gaybrook
Dysart
Lough Ennell
KNOCKCOSGREY HILL
Kinnegad
Clonard
Longwood
Mullagh
Garadice
Castletown Georghegan
Milltownpass
Leinster Bridge
Moyvalley
Blackwater Bridge
Baconstown
Ballynare
Ballynadrummy
Newells Bridge
Rochfortbridge
Enfield
Royal Canal
Dunboyne
Spiddaltown
Ballynagore
Templeoran
Castlejordan
Cadamstown
Johnstown
Kilcock
Maynooth
Horseleap
Tyrrellspass
River Boyne
Kilshanchoe
Torque
Kilbeggan
Brosna
CARRICK CASTLE
Carbury
Taghadoe
CASTLETOWN HOUSE
Donadea
Celbridge
Rhode
EDENDERRY
Windmill
Croghan
Grand Canal
Timahoe
Boherhole
DURROW ABBEY
Killan
Ballyfore
Corduff
Reservoir
Mainham
Straffan
LYONS HO
Derrygrogan
Killoneen
BOG OF ALLEN
R Liffey
Ardan
Daingean
Ballykilleen
Allenwood
Clane
TULLAMORE
Prosperous
ATHGOE CASTLE
Lullymore
Grand Canal
Ballinagar
Robertstown
Brackagh
Clonbullogue
Killinthomas
Sallins
Kill
Kilmeage
Carragh
Geashill
Johnstown
Furness
Allen
HILL OF ALLEN 676
Rathangan
Dunbyrne
NAAS
Coolagary
Killeigh
Rathmore
Slate R
Milltown
Gorteen Bridge
Bracknagh
Wheelam
JIGGINSTOWN HOUSE
Cushina
Annaghmore
DROICHEAD NUA (Newbridge)
Kilcavan
DROICHEAD NUA
Clonygowan
PUNCHESTOWN RACECOURSE
Blessington
PORTARLINGTON
Cherryville
Athgarvan
LEA CASTLE
KILDARE
Twomile Bridge
RUSSBOROUGH HOUSE
Clonaslee
Clarahill
PORTARLINGTON
MONASTEREVAN
TULLY HO
Brownstown
The Curragh
River Liffey
Ballymore Eustace
Rosenallis
Monasterevin
Kilcullen
Poulaphouca
Jamestown
Brannockstown
Valleymount
MOUNTAINS
MOUNTMELLICK
Ballybrittas
Suncroft
Mileytown
Owenass
Boleybeg
Hollywood
Emo
Crosskeys
Nurney
1590 CLARNAHINCH MTN
River
New Inn
Calverstown
Rossmore
Kilgowan
Ballyfin
Boley
Ballymount
Dunlavin
Knocks
Vicarstown
Fontstown
Ballydavis
PORTLAOISE
Inch
Narraghmore
REBAN CASTLE
Kilberry
Colbinstown
Ringstown
DUNAMASE
Donard
Grand Canal
PORT LAOISE
Ardscull
RATH OF MULLAGHMAST
Crookstown
Stradbally
Ballitore
INCH CAS
Mountrath
Ballintubbert
ATHY
Burtown
Timolin
River Slaney
Castletown
Moone
R Barrow
Glen of Imaal
Kilbricken
MOUNTRATH
Timahoe
Ballylynan
Kilkea
2146 KEADEEN MT
Pike of Rush Hall
Ballyroan
Luggacurren
Baltinglass
LAOIS
OFFALY
KILDARE
MEATH
WESTMEATH
WICKLOW

12
17
24

Point
Dromin
Dunleer
13
Port
Grangebellew
ATHCLARE CASTLE
Mullary
Clogher Head
GLASS PISTOL CASTLE
Clogherhead
Monasterboice
Ballymakenny
Termonfeckin
Baltray
MELLIFONT ABBEY
Tullyallen
BEAULIEU
R Boyne
Mornington
DROGHEDA
Donacarney
Dowth
BRUGH NA BOINNE
Bettystown
Donore
Laytown
Julianstown
MOSNEY (Butlin's)
Duleek
River Nanny
GORMANSTON
Gormanston
ATHCARNE CAS
Balrath
Stamullin
BALBRIGGAN
Greenanstown
Ardcath
Four Knocks
BARNAGEERA
Red I
Colt I
St Patricks I
Rockabill
Balrothery
Naul
Delvin R
SKERRIES
Shenicks I
Garristown
BALDONGAN CAS
The Five Roads
Loughshinny
Curragha
Rath
Oldtown
Ballyboghil
Lusk
RUSH
RUSH & LUSK
Ashbourne
Ratoath
Broad Meadow Water
TURVEY HO
The Nose
Lambay Island
Bishops Bay
Donaghmore
Donabate
FAIRYHOUSE RACECOURSE
Kilsallaghan
Ward River
Swords
Kilbride
MALAHIDE
Black Bull
St Margaret's
Cloghran
Kinsaley
Portmarnock
Velvet Strand
PORTMARNOCK
Ward
DUNSOGHLY CAS
DUBLIN AIRPORT
Portmarnock Pt
Ireland's Eye
Tolka R
Clonee
Mulhuddart
Santry
Kilbarrack
Baldoyle
Howth
Blanchardstown
Finglas
Killester
KILBARRACK
Sutton Cross
Nose of Howth
Clonsilla
Dunsink
Glasnevin
Drumcondra
Raheny
HARMONSTOWN
Castleknock
KNOCKMAROON HO
Clontarf
DOUGLAS (Summer Only)
Lions Head
Leixlip
PHOENIX PARK
AA
LIVERPOOL
Lucan
Palmerston
Chapelizod
(Connolly)
TARA ST (Pearse)
Kilmainham
DUBLIN
DUBLIN BAY
Ringsend
Donnybrook
Grand Canal
Clondalkin
DRIMNAGH CAS
Rathmines
Merrion
Booterstown
Milltown
Terenure
Blackrock
HOLYHEAD
Newcastle
Templeogue
Rathgar
TYMON CAS
Tallaght
Rathfarnham
DUN LAOGHAIRE
Dundrum
Stillorgan
Dalkey
Saggart
Ballyboden
Kill of the Grange
Dalkey I
Sorrento Pt
Killiney Bay
Sandyford
Cabinteely
Leopardstown
Killiney
KILGOBBIN CHURCH
Glendruid
Stepaside
TULLY CH
RATHMICHAEL CH
Golden Ball
Brittas
Kilternan
Shankill Cross
The Scalp
Glencullen
Woodbrook
BRAY (Daly)
BRAY
Kilbride
Kilmalin
Enniskerry
Bray Head
POWERSCOURT DEMESNE
KILCRONEY CH
KILRUDDERY HOUSE
TINNAHINCH HO
Glencree
2475 KIPPURE
Kilmacanogue
GREAT SUGAR LOAF 1659
KINDLESTOWN CAS
Greystones
WAR HILL 2250
Lackan
Sally Gap
2385 DJOUCE MT
Delgany
Glen of the Downs
Poulaphouca Reservoir
L. Tay
Kilpedder
Kilcoole
MULLAGHCLEEVAUN 2788
Ballynockan
Newtownmountkennedy
Newcastle
Six Mile Pt
Roundwood
Vartry Reservoir
Five Mile Pt
TONELAGEE 2686
Wicklow Gap
Ballyduff
Annamoe
Killiskey
Nahanagan
2302 TABLE MT
2296 CAMADERRY
GLENDALOUGH
Broad Lough
Ashford
Glenmalure
Laragh
Ballinalea
Newrath Bridge
MOUNT USHER GARDENS
Rathnew
REEFERT CH
WICKLOW
Brides Hd
3039 LUGNAQUILLA MT
Avonmore R
Vale of Clara
Glenealy
Wicklow Head
Silverstrand
WICKLOW MOUNTAINS
Rathdrum
25
IRISH SEA

20

ATLANTIC OCEAN

Donega
Farri
Corbally
Georges Hd
Moore Bay
Bishops Island
Fooagh Pt
Castle Pt
Goleen Bay
Fooag

Trusklieve Pt
Breaghva
Tullig Pt
Ross Bay
Cross
Carrigaholt — Carrigahoe Bay — Carrigaholt
Fodry Pt — Feeard — Kilcreda Pt
Kilbaha — Moneen — Rinevella Bay
Dunmore Hd — Kilbaha Bay — Kilcloher Pt
Loop Head

Leck Pt
Doon Pt

MOUTH OF THE SHANNON

Ballybunion Bay — Ba
Ahafone
Cashen Ri

Inshaboy Pt — Ballyduff
Ballynaskreena
Heirhill — Causeway — Grompa
Kerry Head — Oreenagh
Glenderry — Ballyheige — K E
Ballinclo
Ballyheige Bay — Akeragh
Lerrig — Baltovin
Banna — Abbeydo

The Seven Hogs or Magharee Islands
Illauntanning
Scraggane Bay — Rough Point
Fahamore — Kilshannig
Barrow Harb
Church Hill — Scrahan — Listellick
Brandon Head
Deelick Pt — Brandon Pt
BRANDON BAY — TRALEE BAY
Fehit — Spa — **TRALEE** — TRALEE (Cas
2509 MASATIOMPAN — Brandon — L Gill — Trench Bridge — Derrymore I — RATA
Ballyquin — Caher Pt — **Castlegregory** — Annagh I — N21
Cloonsharragh — Stradbally — Killiney — Derrymore — Blennerville
Ballydavid Head — 3127 BRANDON MT — Cloghane — Kilcummin — Aughacasla — Carrigagharoe Pt — Killelton — Tonevane
2766 BRANDON PK — Ballyduff — Camp — Derrymore 9
Glashabeg — 2713 BEENOSKEE — 2423 GEARHANE — 2039 SCRAGG — KNOCKAUNCORRAGH 1863
Sybil Head — Smerwick Harb — GEARHANE 2050 — D I N G L E — 2189 — GLANBRACK MT — SLIEVE MISH MOUNTAINS
Smerwick — Ballinloghig — 1814 — 26 — N70
Sybil Pt — Ballydavid — Kilmalkedar — BALLYSITTERACH — L Caum — AHERCONREE
Doon Pt — Murreagh — GALLARUS ORATORY — Connor Pass — L Adoon — 1257 KNOCKBE — Lougher — White Gate — L103
Ballyferriter — Ballynana — 2001 CROAGHSKEARDA — KNOCKANE — 11 — Aughils — L103 — Castlemain
Clogher Hd — Ballineanig — TEMPLE MONACHAN — BRICKANY 1236 — Inch — KILCOLMAN ABBEY — **Milltown**
Knockavrogeen — **Anascaul** — T68 — L103 — 6
Inishtooskert — Dunquin — Ventry — **Dingle** — Lispole — Red Cliff — Cromane Pt — CASTLEMAINE HARBOUR
BLASKET ISLANDS — Ventry Harb — Ballintaggart — 11 — Knockaunnaglashy
Coumeenoole — Dingle Harb — Acres Pt — Inch — Tullig — **Killorgin**
Great Blasket Island — Fahan — **Minard Head** — DINGLE BAY — Inch Pt — Cromane — N70 — T67
Slea Head — Reenbeg Pt — Rossbeigh
Tearaght I — Blasket Sound

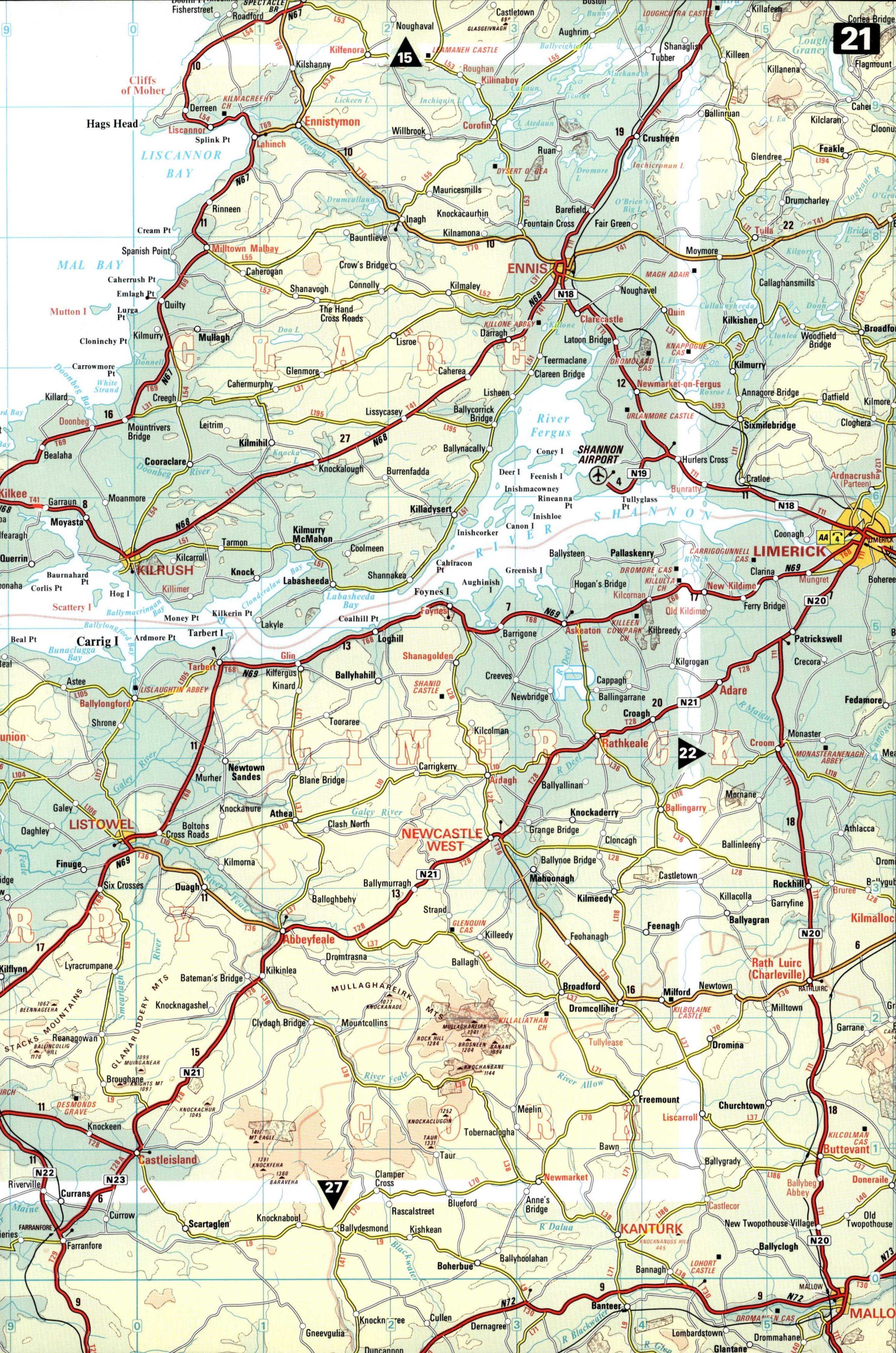
Fisherstreet
Roadford
Noughaval
Castletown
Aughrim
Killafeen
Corlea Bridge
Kilfenora
LEAMANEH CASTLE
Kilshanny
Roughan
Killinaboy
Shanaglish
Tubber
Killeen
Killanena
Lough Graney
Flagmount
Cliffs of Moher
Hags Head
Derreen
Liscannor
KILMACREEHY CH
Ennistymon
Lahinch
Splink Pt
LISCANNOR BAY
Willbrook
Corofin
Ruan
Crusheen
Ballinruan
Kilclaran
Caher
Cloonusker
Feakle
Glendree
Drumcharley
Mauricesmills
DYSERT O'DEA
Barefield
Rinneen
Inagh
Knockacaurhin
Fountain Cross
Fair Green
Tulla
Cream Pt
Bauntlieve
Kilnamona
Spanish Point
Milltown Malbay
MAL BAY
Caherogan
Crow's Bridge
ENNIS
Moymore
Caherrush Pt
Emlagh Pt
Shanavogh
Connolly
Kilmaley
MAGH ADAIR
Callaghansmills
Mutton I
Lurga Pt
Quilty
The Hand Cross Roads
Noughaval
Quin
Kilkishen
Broadford
Kilmurry
Mullagh
Doo L
Darragh
KILLONE ABBEY
Clarecastle
Cloninchy Pt
Lisroe
Latoon Bridge
Woodfield Bridge
Carrowmore Pt
CLARE
White Strand
Glenmore
Caherea
Teermaclane
Clareen Bridge
KNAPPOGUE CAS
DROMOLAND CAS
Kilmurry
Newmarket-on-Fergus
Rosroe L
Annagore Bridge
Oatfield
Kilmore
Killard
Doonbeg Bay
Cahermurphy
Creegh
Lisheen
URLANMORE CASTLE
Doonbeg
Mountrivers Bridge
Lissycasey
Ballycorrick Bridge
River Fergus
Sixmilebridge
Cloghera
Bealaha
Leitrim
Kilmihil
Ballynacally
Coney I
SHANNON AIRPORT
Hurlers Cross
Cooraclare
Doonbeg River
Knockalough
Burrenfadda
Deer I
Feenish I
Cratloe
Ardnacrusha (Parteen)
Kilkee
Moanmore
Garraun
Moyasta
Inishmacowney
Rineanna Pt
Tullyglass Pt
Bunratty
Killadysert
Inishloe
SHANNON
Canon I
Inishcorker
Querrin
Kilrush
Tarmon
Kilmurry McMahon
Coolmeen
RIVER
Ballysteen
Pallaskenry
CARRIGOGUNNELL CAS
LIMERICK
Baurnahard Pt
Kilcarroll
Corlis Pt
Knock
Labasheeda
Shannakea
Cahiracon Pt
Aughinish I
Greenish I
DROMORE CAS
Hogan's Bridge
KILLULTA CH
Clarina
Mungret
Scattery I
Killimer
Hog I
Labasheeda Bay
Foynes I
Kilcornan
New Kildimo
Old Kildimo
Ferry Bridge
Money Pt
Kilkerin Pt
Lakyle
Coalhill Pt
Foynes
Askeaton
KILLEEN COWPARK CH
Kilbreedy
Patrickswell
Beal Pt
Carrig I
Ardmore Pt
Tarbert I
Barrigone
Crecora
Bunaclugga Bay
Tarbert
Glin
Loghill
Shanagolden
Kilfergus
Kinard
Ballyhahill
Creeves
Kilgrogan
Astee
LISLAUGHTIN ABBEY
Ballylongford
SHANID CASTLE
Newbridge
Cappagh
Ballingarrane
Adare
Fedamore
Shrone
Tooraree
Croagh
Kilcolman
LIMERICK
Monaster
Rathkeale
Croom
MONASTERANENAGH ABBEY
Newtown Sandes
Murher
Blane Bridge
Carrigkerry
Ardagh
Ballyallinan
Mornane
Galey
Knockanure
Athea
Galey River
Knockaderry
Ballingarry
Athlacca
LISTOWEL
Daghley
Boltons Cross Roads
Clash North
NEWCASTLE WEST
Grange Bridge
Cloncagh
Ballinleeny
Finuge
Kilmorna
Ballynoe Bridge
Castletown
Six Crosses
Duagh
Ballymurragh
Mahoonagh
Kilmeedy
Killacolla
Rockhill
Garryfine
Bruree
Balloghbehy
Strand
Feenagh
Ballyagran
Kilmallock
GLENQUIN CAS
Killeedy
Feohanagh
Abbeyfeale
Dromtrasna
Ballagh
Rath Luirc (Charleville)
Kilflynn
Lyracrumpane
Bateman's Bridge
Kilkinlea
MULLAGHAREIRK MTS
Broadford
Dromcolliher
Milford
Newtown
Knocknagashel
KILBOLANE CASTLE
Milltown
STACKS MOUNTAINS
Clydagh Bridge
Mountcollins
KILLALIATHAN CH
Tullylease
Dromina
Garrane
Reanagowan
GLANARUDDERY MTS
River Feale
River Allow
Freemount
Broughane
DESMONDS GRAVE
Meelin
Liscarroll
Churchtown
Knockeen
Tobernacloghа
Castleisland
MT EAGLE
Taur
Bawn
Ballygrady
Buttevant
KILCOLMAN CAS
Riverville
Currans
Clamper Cross
Newmarket
Ballybeg Abbey
Doneraile
Rascalstreet
Blueford
Anne's Bridge
Castlecor
Farranfore
Currow
Scartaglen
Knocknaboul
Ballydesmond
Kishkean
R Dalua
KANTURK
New Twopothouse Village
Old Twopothouse
Ballyhoolahan
Boherbue
Bannagh
LOHORT CASTLE
Ballyclogh
Banteer
Mallow
Cullen
Dernagree
Gneevgulia
Duncannon
Lombardstown
Glantane
Drommahane
DROMANEEN CAS

22

PORT LAOISE
Mountrath
Castletown
Cromoge
Kilbricken
MOUNTRATH
Pike of Rush Hall
Shanahoe
Aghaboe
Old Town
Abbeyleix
Cuffsborough
Ballacolla
Ballinakill
Rosconnell
Rathdowney
Durrow
Attanagh
Cullahill
Lisdowney
Ballyragget
Knockmannon
Gattabaun
Johnstown
Balleen
Freshford
Clomantagh
BALLYLARKIN ABBEY
Ballylarkin
Urlingford
Tubbrid
Sart
Three Castles
Killahy
KILCOOLEY ABBEY
Boggan
SLIEVEARDAGH HILLS
Tullaroan
KILKENNY
KILKENNY (McDonagh)
Commons
Kilmanagh
Ballycallan
Grange
Ballingarry
Ballyline
Callan
Mullinahone
Kilvemnon
Mullennaglogh
Windgap
Killamery
Ahenny
Kilcash
Kilsheelan
Kilkieran
CASTLETOWN (COX) HO
CARRICK-ON-SUIR
Piltown
Tibberaghney
Fiddown
Killinaspick
Rathgormuck
Ballyquin
Mothel
Portlaw
CURRAGHMORE HOUSE
Clonea
Glennaphuca
Guilcagh
Kildermody
Newtown
Kilmacthomas
Furraleigh
Georgetown
Knockaderry Reservoir
Faha
Lemybrien
Ballylaneen
Drumlohan
Dalligan Bridge
Kill
Dunhill
Fennor
Annestown
Bunmahon
Ballygorran
Stradbally
Ballyvoyle
Dunabrattin Bay
Gt Newtown Hd
Tramore Bay
Brownstown Head
Swines Hd
Ballymacaw
Back Strand
TRAMORE
Ballymorris
Clohernagh
Dunmore East
Killea
Woodstown
Monamintra
Lisnakill Cross
Carroll's Cross Roads
Ballyduff
Kilmeadan
Mooncoin
Aglish
GRANAGH CAS
WATERFORD
WATERFORD (Plunkett)
Licketstown
Killbarry
Knockeen
Halfway House
Passage East
GENEVA
Cheekpoint
Ballyhack
Slieverue
Dunkitt
Bishopshall
Ballincrea
Priesthaggard
Rochestown
Glenmore
Mullinavat
Ballyfasy
Lukeswell
Listerlin
Harristown
KILMOGUE DOLMEN
BOOLEY HILLS
Tullaghought
Kilmaganny
Newmarket
Knocktopher
Ballyhale
Dunnamaggan
Barrettstown
KILREE
Stonyford
MOUNT JULIET HOUSE
JERPOINT ABBEY
Thomastown
Burnchurch
Bennettsbridge
Danesfort
Dungarvan
Tullaherin
Kilfane
Inistioge
The Rower
Graiguenamanagh
Tinnahinch
BRANDON HILL
St Mullin's
Ballinvarry
Glynn
Ullard
Borris
Goresbridge
Gowran
Paulstown
Flagmount
CLARA CASTLE
Castlewarren
Royal Oak
Muine Bheag (Bagenalstown)
BALLYMOON CAS
Fennagh
Leighlinbridge
Oldleighlin
Nurney
The Butts
Bilboa
Rossmore
Killeshin
Gorteen
Coolbaun
Castlecomer
Barrack Village
Mohil
Jenkinstown
DUNMORE CAVES
Clogh
Newtown
Swan
Spink
Wolfhill
Luggacurren
Timahoe
Ballyroan
Ballintubbert
Stradbally
ATHY
Ballylynan
Arless
Ballickmoyler
Levitstown Cross Roads
Maganey
Graigue
CARLOW
Sleaty
Kilkea
INCH CAS
Ardscull
RATH OF MULLAGHMAST
Burtown
Crookstown
Ballitore
Timolin
Moone
Baltinglass
Castledermot
Graney
Knocknacree
Palatine
Ballyhacket
Killerrig
Grangeford
Tullow
Rathvilly
Hacketstown
Kiltegan
Rathdangan
KEADEEN MT
Clonmore
Mullinacuff
Aghowle
Shillelagh
Ballon
CARLOW
Clonegal
HUNTINGTON CAS
Kildavin
Watch Ho Village
Myshall
Bunclody
Clohamon
MT LEINSTER
Strahart
Ballindaggan
Kiltealy
Ballymurphy
Scullogue Gap
BLACKSTAIRS MT
BLACKSTAIRS MOUNTAINS
Gowlin
Killan
Rathnure
Rathfylane
Milehouse
Clonroche
Donard
BORODALE
Bree
Chapel
The Leap
Adamstown
Galbally
Killurin
Mountgarret Bridge
NEW ROSS
Rosbercon
Old Ross
Raheen
Ballynabola
Dunganstown
Cassagh
Newbawn
Whitechurch
JOHN F KENNEDY MEMORIAL PARK
Foulkesmill
Taghmon
Gusserane
Campile
DUNBRODY ABBEY
Ballycullane
WELLINGTONBRIDGE
Wellington Bridge
Hilltown
Tullycanna
Waddingtown
Knocktown
DUNCORMICK
Duncormick
Ramsgrange
Arthurstown
Duncannon
Garrycullen
TINTERN ABBEY
Saltmills
Bannow Bay
Carrick
Newtown
Cullenstown
COOLHULL CASTLE
Bannow
Fethard
Fethard Bay
Templetown
Newtown Hd
Booley Bay
Creadan Hd
Waterford Harbour
Churchtown
Dunmore Bay
Woarwoy Bay
Patricks Bay
Slade
Hook Head
Baginbun Head
BALLYTEIGE BAY
Forlorn Point
Park
Killag
Kilmore
Saltee Islands
(Little)
(Great)

25

IRISH SEA

ST GEORGE'S CHANNEL

- Glendalough
- Laragh
- Ballinalea
- Newrath Bridge
- Ashford
- WICKLOW
- Brides Hd
- Wicklow Head
- Glenealy
- Silverstrand
- Rathdrum
- Avondale House
- Ardmore Pt
- Jacks Hole
- WICKLOW MOUNTAINS
- Aghavannagh
- Ballinaclash
- Greenan
- Kilcarney
- Meeting of the Waters
- Avondale Forest Park
- Brittas Bay
- Knockananna
- Craffield
- Mizen Head
- Askanagap
- Aughrim
- Avoca
- Moyne
- Annacurragh
- Johnstown
- Shelton Abbey
- Bridgeland
- Woodenbridge
- Tinahely
- Ferrybank
- ARKLOW
- Johnstown
- Arklow Hd
- Clonroe
- Coolgreany
- Clogga
- Coolattin
- Inch
- Scarnagh
- Kilmichael Pt
- Monaseed
- Castletown
- Hollyfort
- Craanford
- GOREY
- Ballymoney
- Clogh
- N11
- Courtown
- Camolin
- Riverchapel
- Ballycanew
- Ardamine Cove
- Roney Pt
- Killenagh
- Glascarrig Pt
- Ballygarrett
- Cahore Pt
- The Harrow
- Clonevin
- Tinnacross
- Crane
- Clondaw
- Kilnamanagh
- Oulart
- Ford
- ENNISCORTHY
- Kilmuckridge
- Kilcotty
- Ballaghkeen
- Darby's Gap
- Castleellis
- Blackwater
- Dilgate
- Screen
- N11
- Castlebridge
- Wexford Bay
- Crossabeg
- Curracloe
- Ferrycarrig
- WEXFORD (O'Hanrahan)
- WEXFORD SOUTH
- The Raven Pt
- WEXFORD HARBOUR
- Kerlogue
- Rosslare Point
- Drinagh
- Rosslare Bay
- N25
- FISHGUARD
- Rosslare
- ROSSLARE STRAND
- Killinick
- LE HAVRE
- Tagoat
- Rosslare Harbour
- Kilrane
- Greenore Pt
- Twelveacre
- Ballytrent Ho
- Tacumshane
- Tuskar Rock
- Tacumshin Lake
- Lady's Island
- Churchtown
- Carnsore Point

Rough Point
Kilshannig
Fahamore
Barrow Harb
Church Hill
Scrahan
Listellick
Brandon Head
Deelick Pt
Brandon Pt
BRANDON
TRALEE
BAY
Brandon
Ballyquin
Caher Pt
Trench Bridge
Castlegregory
Fenit
Spa
TRALEE
N21
Ballydavid Head
Cloonsharragh
Cloghane
Stradbally
Killiney
Derrymore I
Annagh I
Blennerville
Tonevane
Carrigagharoe Pt
Killelton
Derrymore
Glashabeg
Kilcummin
Aughacasla
Smerwick Harb
Ballyduff
Camp
Sybil Head
Smerwick
Ballydavid
Murreagh
Ballinloghig
Kilmalkedar
Sybil Pt
Doon Pt
Ballyferriter
GALLARUS ORATORY
Ballynana
Lougher
SLIEVE MISH MOUNTAINS
Boolteens
Clogher Hd
Ballineanig
Knockavrogeen
TEMPLE MONACHAN
KNOCKANE
Anascaul
White Gate
Aughils
Castlemaine
Inishtooskert
Dunquin
Ventry
Milltown
Dingle
Inch
KILCOLMAN ABBEY
Milltown
BLASKET ISLANDS
Ventry Harb
Dingle Harb
Ballintaggart
Lispole
Red Cliff
Cromane Pt
CASTLEMAINE HARBOUR
Great Blasket Island
Blasket Sound
Dunmore Hd
Coumeenoole
Fahan
Slea Head
Parkmore Pt
Reenbeg Pt
Bulls Head
Minard Head
Acres Pt
Inch
Knockaunnaglashy
Tullig
Killorglin
Inch Pt
Cromane
Tearaght I
Inishnabro
Inishvickillane
DINGLE BAY
Rossbeigh Creek
Illaunstookagh
Kilcoolaght
BALLYMALIS CASTLE
Rossbeigh
Knockaunroe
Caragh Br
Beaufort
Glenbeigh
Lough Caragh
Kells Bay
Glencar
Coonanna Harbour
Darby's Bridge
Kells
Canglass Pt
MACGILLYCUDDY'S REEKS
Coomasaharn
Bealalaw Bridge
KIMEGO WEST STONE FORT
Dromalonhurt Bridge
Doulus Head
Doulas Bay
Reenadrolaun Pt
Beginish
Cahirciveen
Ballaghbeama Pass
VALENTIA ISLAND
Knightstown
Reenard Cross
Beennakryraka Hd
Chapeltown
Owroe Bridge
Lissatinnig Bridge
Beenaniller Hd
Aghnagar Bridge
Killeenleagh Bridge
Bray Head
Portmagee
Doon Pt
Derriana L
Ballynahow
Gearha Bridge
Templenoe
Saliahig
Blackwater Bridge
Puffin Island
Killurly
Church Island
ST FINAN'S BAY
Waterville
L Currane
Sneem
Ballinskelligs
Tahilla
Rossmore I
Horse I
Ballybrack
STAIGUE FORT
Parknasilla
Cangarriff Pt
Ducalla Hd
BALLINSKELLIGS BAY
Rossdohan I
Bolus Hd
Coomakista Pass
Hogs Hd
Sherky I
Bunaw
Skellig Rock
Caherdaniel
DERREEN HO
Lauragh
Sheehans Pt
KENMARE RIVER
Ardgroom Harb
Abbey I
Collorus
Deenish Pt
Darrynane Bay
Cleanderry Harbour
Scariff
Deenish
Lamb's Head
Kilcatherine Pt
Ardgroom
CAHA MOUNTAINS
Inishfarnard
Reen Pt
BEARA
COULAGH BAY
Eyeries
Adrigole
ATLANTIC OCEAN
Cod's Head
SLIEVE MISKISH MOUNTAINS
Derreeny
Trafrask
Castletownbere
Curryglass
Shot Hd
Ballydonegan Bay
Allihies
BEAR HAVEN
Lonehort Pt
Garnish Pt
Keam Pt
Ballydonegan
Ballynakilla
Rerrin
Leahern's Pt
Ballynacallagh
BEAR ISLAND
Firkeel
Fair Head
Doombeg Hd
Gouladoo
BANTRY BAY
Dursey Island
Kilmichael
Cahermore
Pulleen Harb
Ahakista
Dursey Head
Crow Head
Horn Pt
White Ball Head
Black Ball Head
Dromnea
Kilcrohane
Caher
Ballyroon
Carbery I
Muntervary or Sheeps Head
DUNMANUS BAY
Dunmanus
Toormore
Toor Pt
Goleen
Three Castle Hd
Spanish Cove
Dough
Streek Hd
Crookhaven
Reen Pt
Mizen Head
Barley Cove
Brow Head

27
21
28
Clydagh Bridge
Mountcollins
Dromina
Reanagowan
Broughane
Knockeen
Castleisland
Riverville
Currans
Currow
Fieries
Farranfore
Scartaglen
Knocknaboul
Clamper Cross
Rascalstreet
Blueford
Ballydesmond
Kishkean
Boherbue
Ballyhoolahan
Meelin
Tobernacloghа
Taur
Newmarket
Anne's Bridge
Freemount
Churchtown
Liscarroll
Bawn
Ballygrady
Buttevant
Doneraile
Castlecor
New Twopothouse Village
Old Twopothouse
KANTURK
Ballyclogh
Bannagh
Banteer
MALLOW
Lombardstown
Glantane
Drommahane
Dromaneen Cas
Knocknagree
Cullen
Dernagree
Gneevgulia
Duncannon Bridge
Rathmore
Rathcool
Lyre
Millstreet
Drishane Castle
Kilcorney
Aghadoe
KILLARNEY
Innisfallen
Lough Leane
Barraduff
Muckross
Lough Guitane
Upper Lake
Galwey's Br
Torc Waterfall
Bourn Vincent Park
Garries Bridge
Poulgorm Bridge
Derrynasaggart Mountains
Boggeragh Mountains
Carrigagulla
Knockdrislagh
Ahadallane
Lyradane
Grenagh
Donoughmore
Rylane Cross
Carriganimmy
Ballynagree
Aghabullogue
Ballyvourney
Ballymakeery
Garrane
Morley's Bridge
Inchee Bridge
Kilgarvan
Kenmare
Derryfineen
MACROOM
Carrigaphooca Castle
Toon Bridge
Carrigadrohid
Coachford
Dripsey
Cloghroe
Inishcarra
Killinardrish
Mashanaglass Castle
Ovens
Kilcrea
Aherla
Crookstown
More Castle
Gougane Barra
Ballingeary
Inchigeelagh
Rossmore
Toames
Kilmichael
Teerelton
Kilmurry
Knocknahilan
Curraclogh
Templemartin
Bealnablath
Cross Barry
Commons
Coppeen
Poulnaberry Bridge
Shanacrane
Newcestown
Kilpatrick
Inishannon
Coomhola Bridge
Glengarriff
Snave Br
Kealkill
Cousane
Farnanes
Togher
Kinneigh Round Tower
Scrahane
Coolkellure
Pierson's Bridge
Ballylickey
Dunmanway
Ballineen
Enniskean
Kilcolman
BANDON
Glengarriff Harbour
Garinish Island
Whiddy I
Manch Bridge
Ballynacarriga
Ballinadee
BANTRY
Relane Pt
Tedagh
Gerahies
Drimoleague
Curraghalicky
Ballingurteen
Knocks
Knockskagh
Ballinascarty
Kilbrittain
Ballinspittle
Collamane
Durrus
Drinagh
Ardigeen Br
Bealad
Timoleague
Killeenleagh
Driminidy
Reavouler Bridge
Carrigbaun
CLONAKILTY
Courtmacsherry
Garrettstown Strand
Carrigeeny
Maulatrahane
Connonagh
Inchydoney
North Ring
Barryroe
Barry's Pt
Drishane Bridge
Rathruane
Leap
Newmills
Muckruss Hd
Duneen Pt
Butlerstown
Courtmacsherry Bay
Seven Heads Bay
Ballydehob
SKIBBEREEN
Abbeystrowry
Glandore
Ross Carbery
Unionhall
Coppinger's Court
Cregg
Rosscarbery Bay
Clonakilty Bay
Dunworly Bay
Seven Heads
Rinneen
Rahine Castle
Tralong Bay
Ringlea Pt
Glandore Harb
Dunnycove Bay
Schull
Horse I
Inishbeg
Creagh
Knockdrum Fort
Castletownshend
Blind Harb
Castle Haven
Dundeady I
Galley Head
Dunowen Hd
Roaringwater Bay
Castle I
Long I
Ringarogy I
Hare I
Calf Islands
Sandy Cove
Scullane Pt
Gokane Pt
Toe Head
Toe Head Bay
Baltimore
Baltimore Bay
Clear Island
Sherkin I
Gascanane Sound
Cape Clear

29

ATLANTIC OCEAN

Geological Map of Ireland

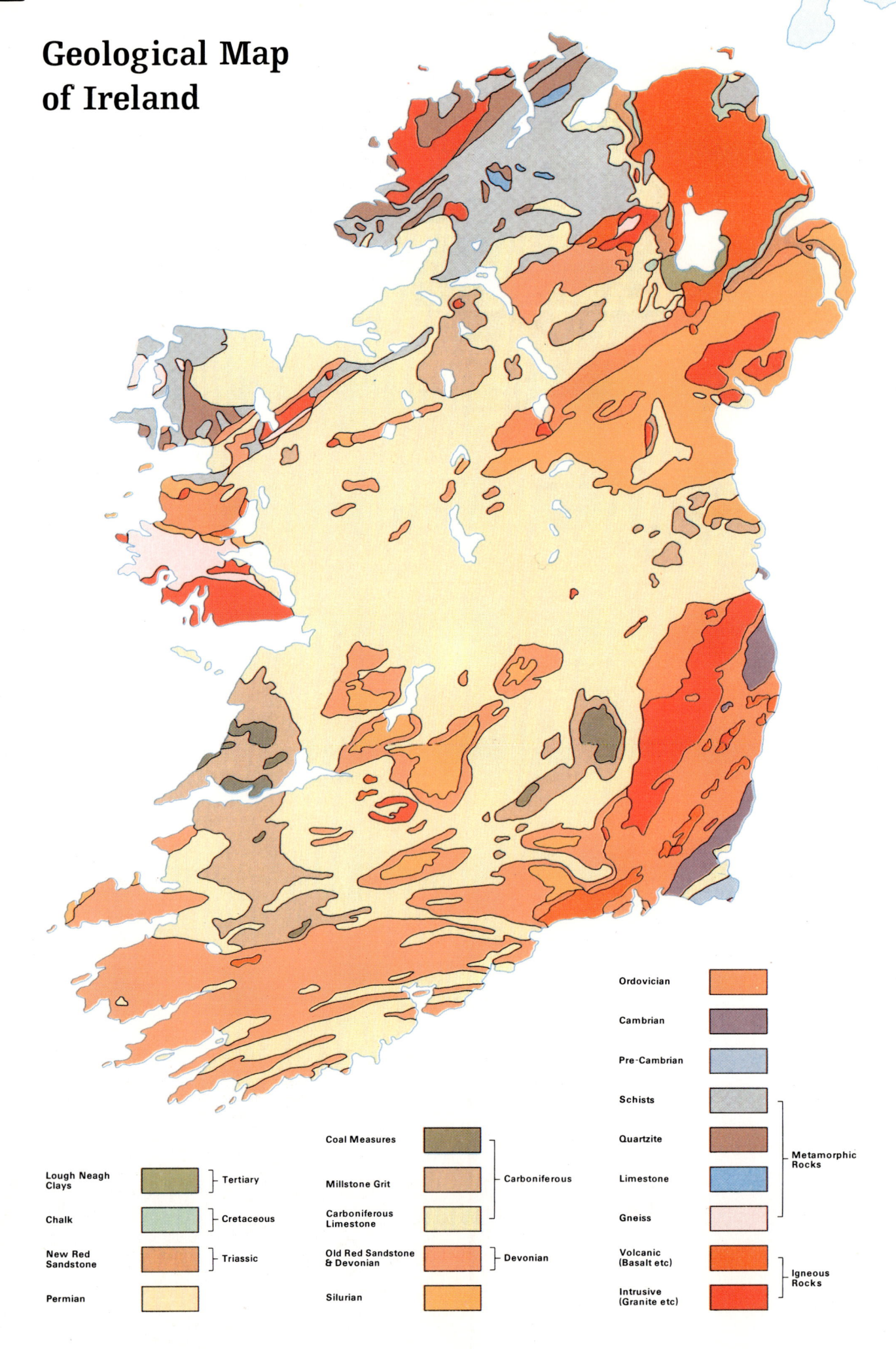

Legend		
Lough Neagh Clays	Tertiary	
Chalk	Cretaceous	
New Red Sandstone	Triassic	
Permian		
Coal Measures	Carboniferous	
Millstone Grit	Carboniferous	
Carboniferous Limestone	Carboniferous	
Old Red Sandstone & Devonian	Devonian	
Silurian		
Ordovician		
Cambrian		
Pre-Cambrian		
Schists	Metamorphic Rocks	
Quartzite	Metamorphic Rocks	
Limestone	Metamorphic Rocks	
Gneiss	Metamorphic Rocks	
Volcanic (Basalt etc)	Igneous Rocks	
Intrusive (Granite etc)	Igneous Rocks	

C O U N T Y
Summerhill & Trim Rd
Blackbull Rd
Dunboyne Rd
Kilcock
Common
Newtown
Trim Rd
Moyglare
Great Killany
Owenstown
Hamwood
Dunboyne Rd
Ash-hill
Trim Rd
Dunboyne
Saltstown
Morass
Ophaly Br.
Old Carton
Milestown
Tinard
Mause
Brangans town
Crewhill or Park of Maynooth
Moyglaady
Catherinestown
Ravensdale
Gerards
Carton Park
Quarry
Sion
Common
Meath
Laraghbryan Ca. Rs.
Ballycurraghan
Threadstown
Maynooth
Kellystown
Shaghlans Well
Moor of Mulroony Hill
Craig-heder
Roes-town
Knockpatch
LARAGHBRYAN P.
Blakestown
Sandford's Bridge
The Island
Grange
Confoy Ca.
CONFOY P
Clonsast
Laragh
Cormickstown
Grinstown
Newtown
Ballygorn
Obelisk
Mount Thunder
Collinstown
Maudshill
Bleachfield
Newtown
Ballyhegan Well
Roanstown
Monacoole
Kilmacredock
LEIXLIP
Leixlip
NORTH
SALT
By
Lyreen R.
Clonfert
Derrinstown
Donoghstown
Dowdstown
KILDRAUGHT P.
Moortown
Castletown Park
New Barn
The Castle Park
Water fall
Graiglin
Taghadoe
Tooltown
Bog
Kaalstown
Lady's Chapel
Corbally
Thornhill
Parsonstown
Balraheen
Coenstown
Bryanstown
Turnahary
Graigfin
Griffin rath
Kilwoan
Newbridge
Paper mill
Back Westown
TAGHADOE P.
Windgate Hill
Oldtown
Raheen
Smithstown
Kilmanour
Celbridge
St. Woolstans
Aderg Ch.Rs.
Graigsallagh
Roosk
Ballynakill
Donacomper
Possackstown
Springfield
Iohnanstown
Newtown Mc Cabe
KILLADOWN P.
Loughlanstown
Stacumney
Gulliers town Bridge
Terrils Ca. & Mills
Simonstown
Clonagh
Baulscot
Quarry
Ovidstown
Daybush
Barberstown
Killadown
Moneentane
Ardrass
Kommons
Hazlehatch
Peamount
Danielstown
STRAFFAN P.
Newtown
Priorstown
Dangin
Richardstown
Straffan
Castle dillon
LYONS P.
Constanstown
Irishtown
CASTLE DILLON P.
Reeves Ca.
Pt of Cloghnallis
Skeogh
Laga
Quarry
Beggars Lane
Cairnytown
Lady Castle
Tipperstown
NEWCASTLE
Ballyhays
Glasgow
CLOGHNALLIS
Lyons